EPIC COLLECTION



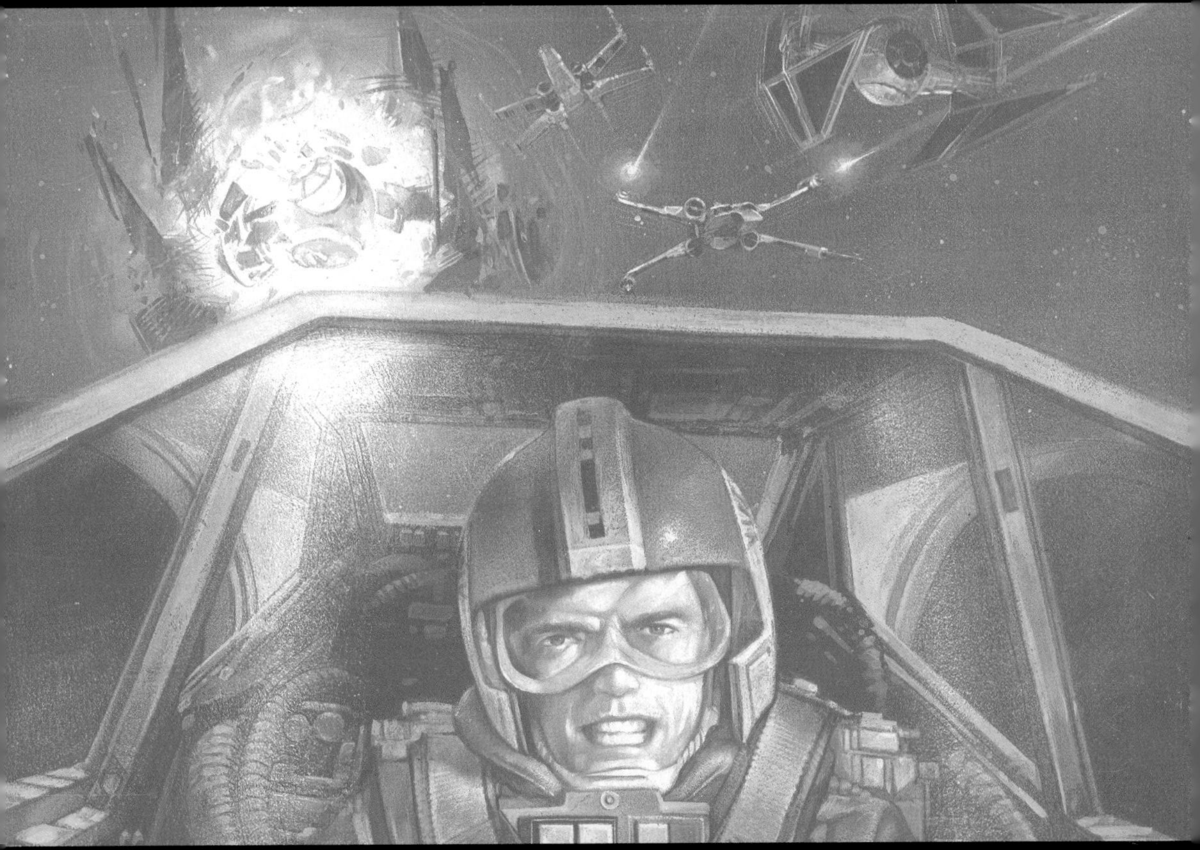

# STAR WARS®

# THE NEW REPUBLIC

**VOLUME 2**

***STAR WARS: X-WING ROGUE LEADER* #1-3 AND *STAR WARS: X-WING ROGUE SQUADRON* #1-16 & *SPECIAL* #1; AND MATERIAL FROM *STAR WARS TALES* #12 & #23**

# LEGENDS

WRITERS:

## HADEN BLACKMAN, MICHAEL A. STACKPOLE, MIKE BARON, DARKO MACAN, JAN STRNAD & SCOTT TOLSON WITH BRETT MATTHEWS, RYDER WINDHAM & ROB WILLIAMS

PENCILERS:

## TOMÁS GIORELLO, JOHN NADEAU, ALLEN NUNIS, EDVIN BIUKOVIĆ & GARY ERSKINE WITH ADRIAN SIBAR & MICHEL LACOMBE

INKERS:
**TOMÁS GIORELLO, ANDY MUSHYNSKY, EDVIN BIUKOVIĆ, JORDI ENSIGN & GARY ERSKINE** WITH **ADRIAN SIBAR, MONTY SHELDON, SERGE LAPOINTE & ANDREW PEPOY**

COLORISTS:
**MICHAEL ATIYEH, DAVE NESTELLE & PERRY MCNAMEE** WITH **GUY MAJOR, CARY PORTER & WIL GLASS**

LETTERERS:
**STEVE DUTRO, MICHAEL DAVID THOMAS, EDVIN BIUKOVIĆ, ANNIE PARKHOUSE & VICKIE WILLIAMS** WITH **MICHAEL HEISLER & DAVE COOPER**

ASSISTANT EDITORS:
**DAVE MARSHALL** WITH **PHILIP SIMON**

ASSOCIATE EDITOR:
**JEREMY BARLOW**

EDITORS:
**RANDY STRADLEY, PEET JANES & RYDER WINDHAM** WITH **DAVE LAND & JEREMY BARLOW**

FRONT COVER ARTIST:
**DAVE DORMAN**

BACK COVER ARTIST:
**MARK HARRISON**

**COLLECTION EDITOR:** MARK D. BEAZLEY
**ASSOCIATE EDITOR:** SARAH BRUNSTAD
**ASSOCIATE MANAGER, DIGITAL ASSETS:** JOE HOCHSTEIN
**ASSOCIATE MANAGING EDITOR:** ALEX STARBUCK
**EDITOR, SPECIAL PROJECTS:** JENNIFER GRÜNWALD
**VP, PRODUCTION & SPECIAL PROJECTS:** JEFF YOUNGQUIST
**RESEARCH:** MIKE HANSEN
**LAYOUT:** JEPH YORK
**PRODUCTION:** RYAN DEVALL
**BOOK DESIGNER:** RODOLFO MURAGUCHI
**SVP PRINT, SALES & MARKETING:** DAVID GABRIEL

**EDITOR IN CHIEF:** AXEL ALONSO
**CHIEF CREATIVE OFFICER:** JOE QUESADA
**PUBLISHER:** DAN BUCKLEY
**EXECUTIVE PRODUCER:** ALAN FINE

SPECIAL THANKS TO FRANK PARISI & LUCASFILM, DEIDRE HANSEN, GREGORY HECHT, STUART VANDAL & DOUG SHARK OF MYCOMICSHOP.COM

STAR WARS LEGENDS EPIC COLLECTION: THE NEW REPUBLIC VOL. 2. Contains material originally published in magazine form as STAR WARS: X-WING ROGUE LEADER #1-3; STAR WARS: X-WING ROGUE SQUADRON #1-16 and SPECIAL; and STAR WARS TALES #12 and #23. First printing 2016. ISBN# 978-0-7851-9723-2. Published by MARVEL WORLDWIDE, INC., a subsidiary of MARVEL ENTERTAINMENT, LLC. OFFICE OF PUBLICATION: 135 West 50th Street, New York, NY 10020. STAR WARS and related text and illustrations are trademarks and/or copyrights in the United States and other countries, of Lucasfilm Ltd. and/ or its affiliates. © & ™ Lucasfilm Ltd. No similarity between any of the names, characters, persons, and/or institutions in this magazine with those of any living or dead person or institution is intended, and any such similarity which may exist is purely coincidental. Marvel and its logos are TM Marvel Characters, Inc. **Printed in the U.S.A.** ALAN FINE, President, Marvel Entertainment; DAN BUCKLEY, President, TV, Publishing and Brand Management; JOE QUESADA, Chief Creative Officer; TOM BREVOORT, SVP of Publishing; DAVID BOGART, SVP of Operations & Procurement, Publishing; C.B. CEBULSKI, VP of International Development & Brand Management; DAVID GABRIEL, SVP Print, Sales & Marketing; JIM O'KEEFE, VP of Operations & Logistics; DAN CARR, Executive Director of Publishing Technology; SUSAN CRESPI, Editorial Operations Manager; ALEX MORALES, Publishing Operations Manager; STAN LEE, Chairman Emeritus. For information regarding advertising in Marvel Comics or on Marvel.com, please contact Jonathan Rheingold, VP of Custom Solutions & Ad Sales, at jrheingold@marvel.com. For Marvel subscription inquiries, please call 800-217-9158. **Manufactured between 1/29/2016 and 3/7/2016 by R.R. DONNELLEY, INC., SALEM, VA, USA.**
10 9 8 7 6 5 4 3 2 1

# THE NEW REPUBLIC — VOLUME 2

# THE NEW REPUBLIC
## VOL. 2

With the death of the evil Emperor Palpatine and the destruction of his ultimate weapon, the Death Star, the Rebel Alliance has at last ended the Empire's domination of the galaxy.

But there is chaos in the immediate aftermath of the Battle of Endor, and the Empire remains far from extinct. Legendary X-wing pilots Luke Skywalker and Wedge Antilles lead Rogue Squadron, a team of the Rebellion's best pilots, in the ensuing cleanup operations.

Despite the deaths of Palpatine and a number of his commanders, Imperial power and influence are still felt in various galactic hotspots...and much of the galaxy remains unaware of the Rebels' victory.

Now, both Luke and Wedge are questioning whether they are capable of being a part of the Rebellion's formation of a New Republic. Luke bears the burden of having to singlehandedly restore the Jedi order, while Wedge is weary from years of war....

# INCOM CORPORATION T-65 X-WING
## SPACE SUPERIORITY FIGHTER

The X-wing is the Rebellion's main single-pilot snub-fighter. The X-wing takes its name from its pair of double-layered wings, deployed into the familiar X formation for combat. During normal sublight space flight, the double-layered wings are closed, giving the fighter the appearance of having only two wings. It's known for its durability, with a reinforced titanium-alloy hull and high-powered Chempat shield generators. It is a forgiving fighter and normally can take minor hits without a serious loss of performance. It has a full ejection system, and Alliance pilots have fully sealed suits and helmets. X-wings are equipped with an Incom GBk-585 hyperdrive unit for travel to other systems. The X-wing is Rogue Squadron's fighter of choice.

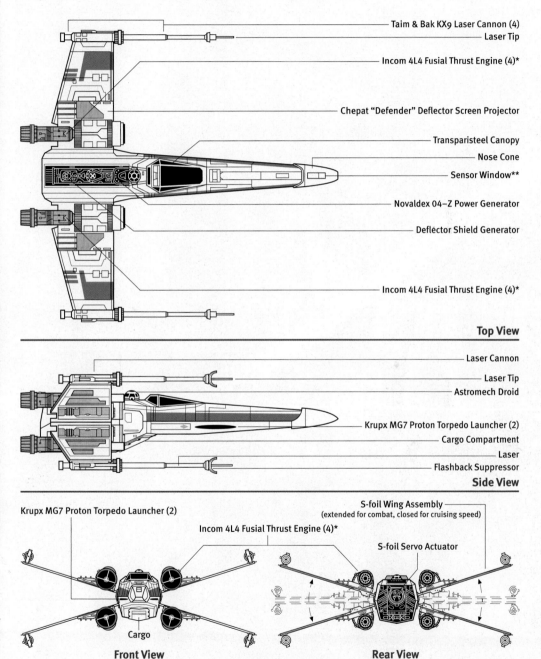

**Top View**

- Taim & Bak KX9 Laser Cannon (4)
- Laser Tip
- Incom 4L4 Fusial Thrust Engine (4)*
- Chepat "Defender" Deflector Screen Projector
- Transparisteel Canopy
- Nose Cone
- Sensor Window**
- Novaldex 04–Z Power Generator
- Deflector Shield Generator
- Incom 4L4 Fusial Thrust Engine (4)*

**Side View**

- Laser Cannon
- Laser Tip
- Astromech Droid
- Krupx MG7 Proton Torpedo Launcher (2)
- Cargo Compartment
- Laser
- Flashback Suppressor

Krupx MG7 Proton Torpedo Launcher (2)

Incom 4L4 Fusial Thrust Engine (4)*

S-foil Wing Assembly
(extended for combat, closed for cruising speed)

S-foil Servo Actuator

Cargo

**Front View**

**Rear View**

Schematic by Troy Vigil.

*Alternate Configurations May Use Incom 4J.4 Fusial Thrust Engines.

** Houses Carbanti Transceiver Package with Fabritech ANs-5d "Lock Track" Full-spectrum Transceiver, Melihat "Multi Imager" Dedicated Energy Receptor, Tana Ire Electro-photo Receptor and Fabritech Anq 3.6 Sensor Computer. Alternate Configuration Typically Combines Long Range Fabritech ANS-5d Units with Long Range PTSA #PA-9r Unit and Short Range PTAG #PG-7u Unit.

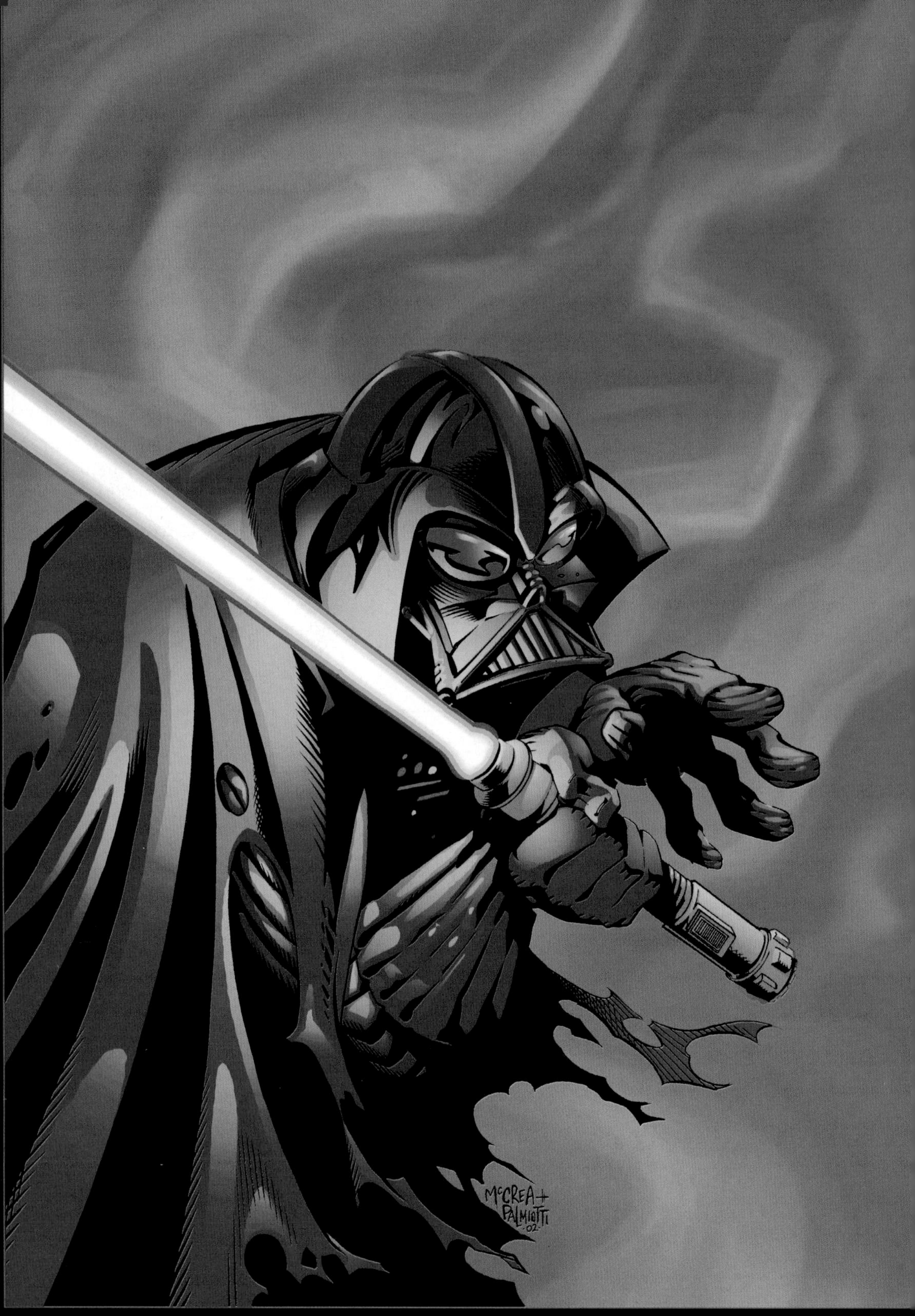
McCREA + PALMIOTTI ·02·

***STAR WARS TALES #12*** **— "A DAY IN THE LIFE"**

WRITER: BRETT MATTHEWS • ARTIST: ADRIAN SIBAR • COLORIST: GUY MAJOR • LETTERER: STEVE DUTRO
ASSISTANT EDITOR: PHILIP SIMON • EDITOR: DAVE LAND • COVER ARTISTS: JOHN MCCREA, JIMMY PALMIOTTI & DAN JACKSON

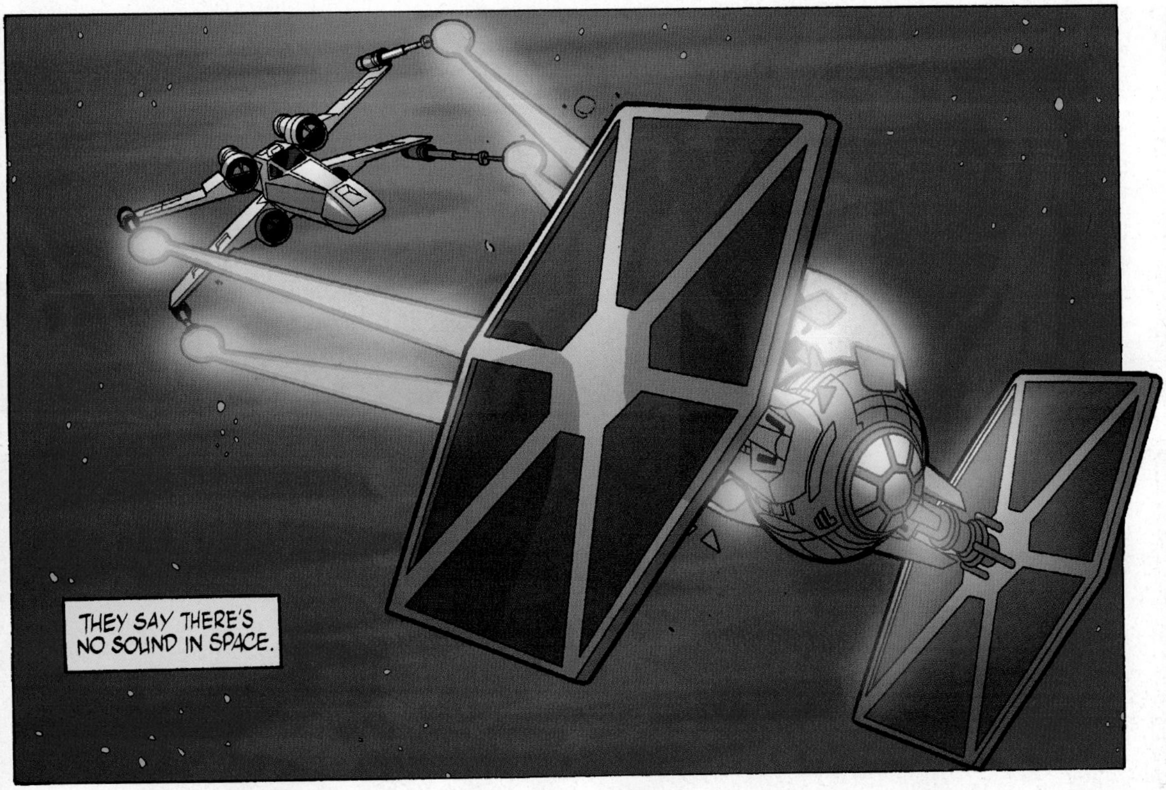
THEY SAY THERE'S NO SOUND IN SPACE.

# A Day in the Life

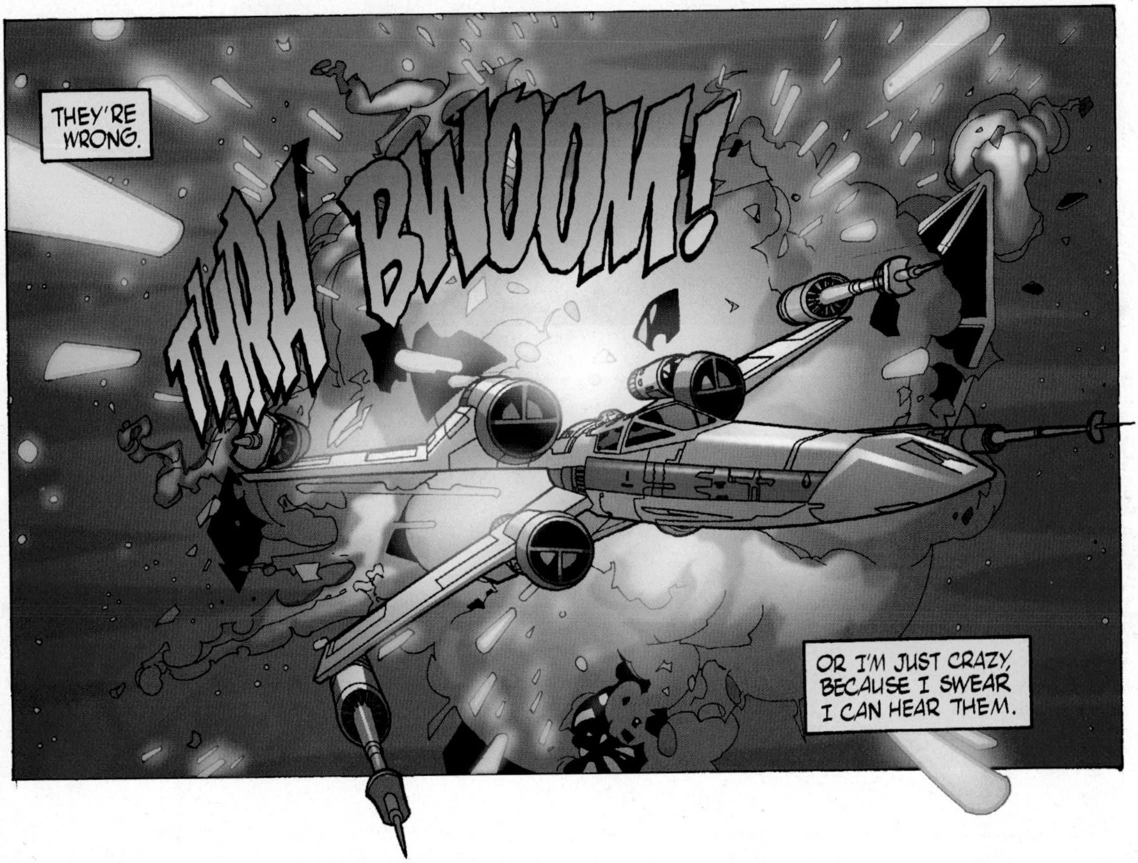
THEY'RE WRONG.
THRA BWOOM!
OR I'M JUST CRAZY, BECAUSE I SWEAR I CAN HEAR THEM.

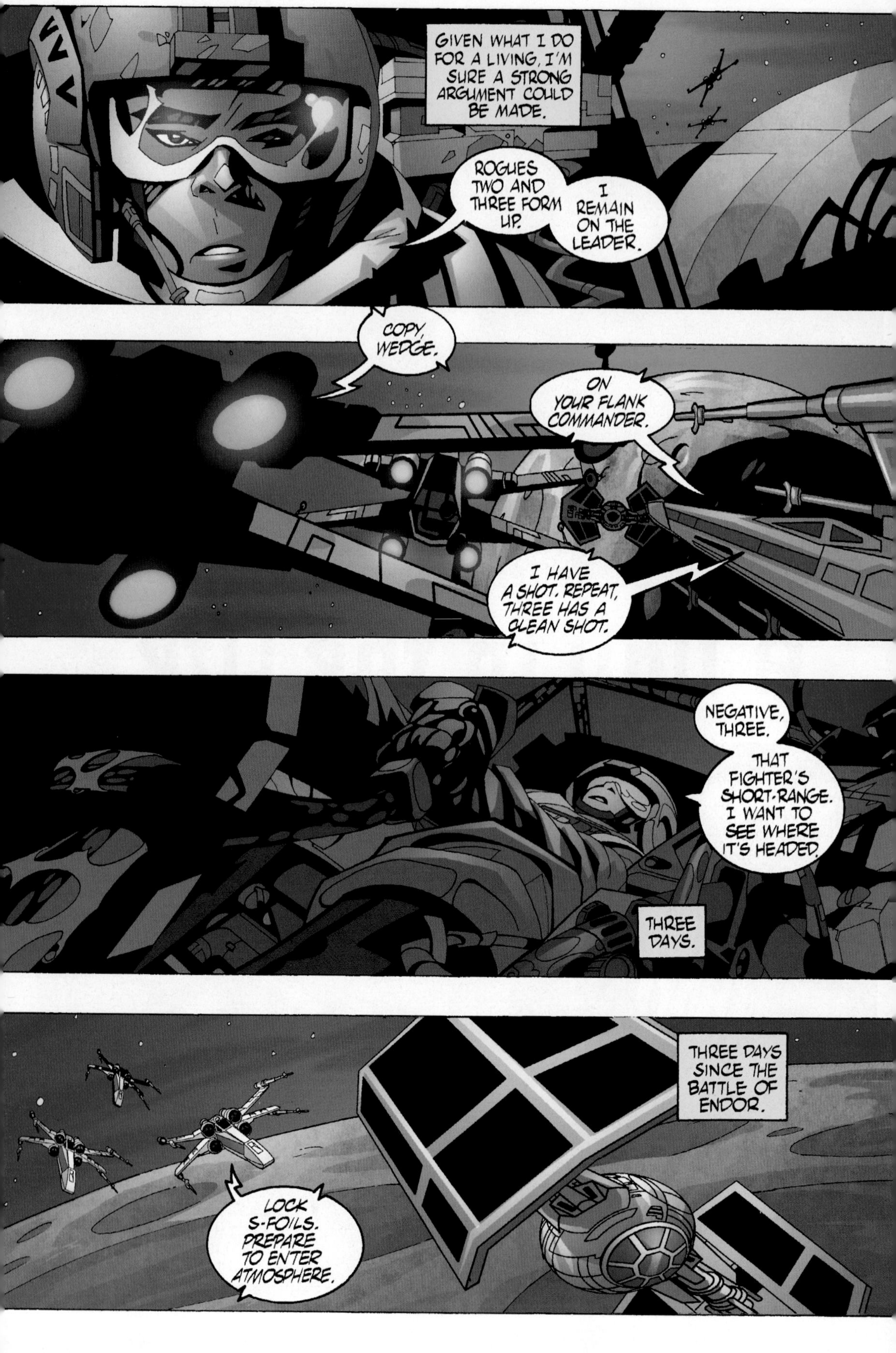
GIVEN WHAT I DO FOR A LIVING, I'M SURE A STRONG ARGUMENT COULD BE MADE.
ROGUES TWO AND THREE FORM UP.
I REMAIN ON THE LEADER.
COPY, WEDGE.
ON YOUR FLANK COMMANDER.
I HAVE A SHOT. REPEAT, THREE HAS A CLEAN SHOT.
NEGATIVE, THREE.
THAT FIGHTER'S SHORT-RANGE. I WANT TO SEE WHERE IT'S HEADED.
THREE DAYS.
THREE DAYS SINCE THE BATTLE OF ENDOR.
LOCK S-FOILS. PREPARE TO ENTER ATMOSPHERE.

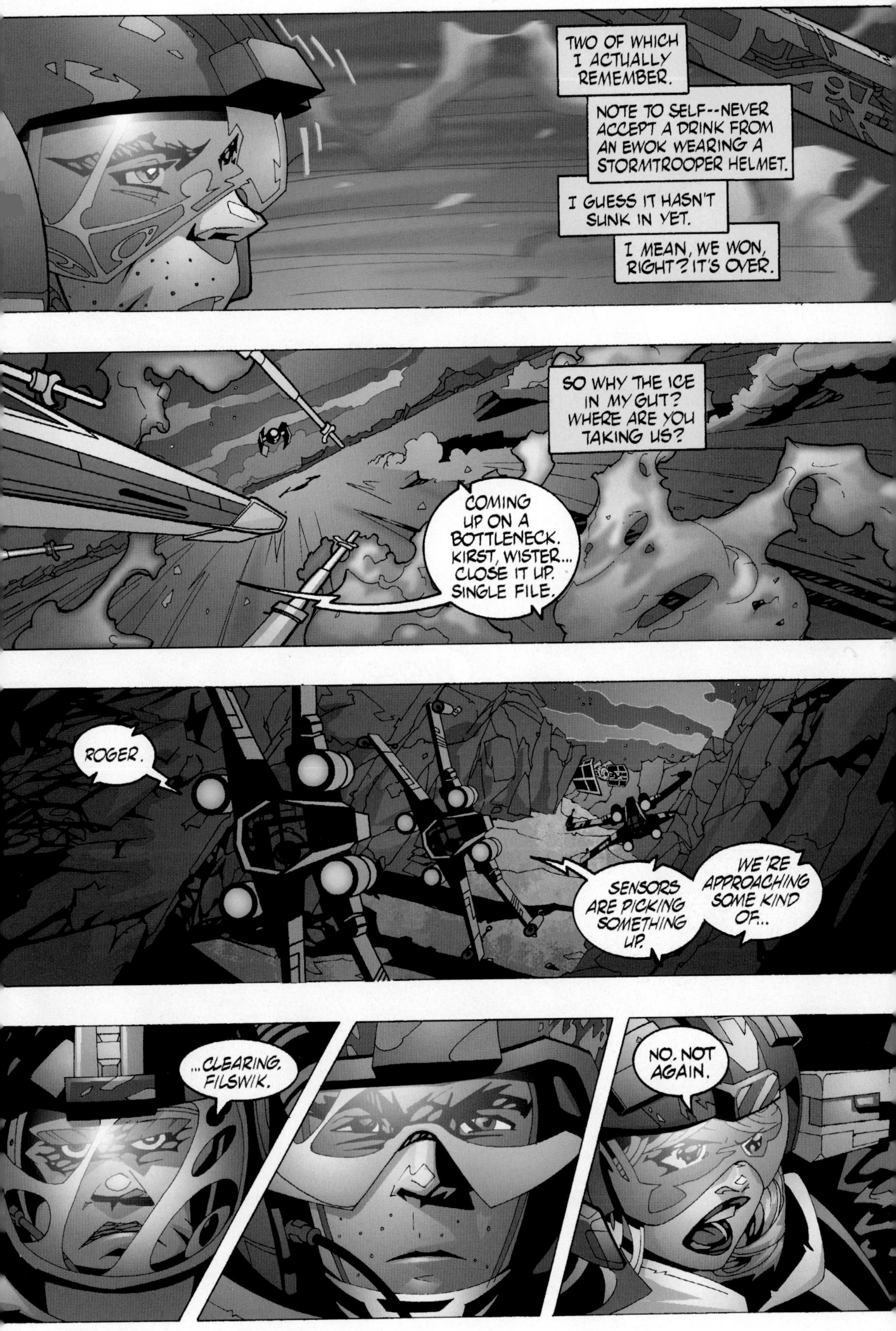
TWO OF WHICH I ACTUALLY REMEMBER.
NOTE TO SELF--NEVER ACCEPT A DRINK FROM AN EWOK WEARING A STORMTROOPER HELMET.
I GUESS IT HASN'T SUNK IN YET.
I MEAN, WE WON, RIGHT? IT'S OVER.
SO WHY THE ICE IN MY GUT? WHERE ARE YOU TAKING US?
COMING UP ON A BOTTLENECK. KIRST, WISTER... CLOSE IT UP. SINGLE FILE.
ROGER.
SENSORS ARE PICKING SOMETHING UP.
WE'RE APPROACHING SOME KIND OF...
...CLEARING, FILSWIK.
NO. NOT AGAIN.

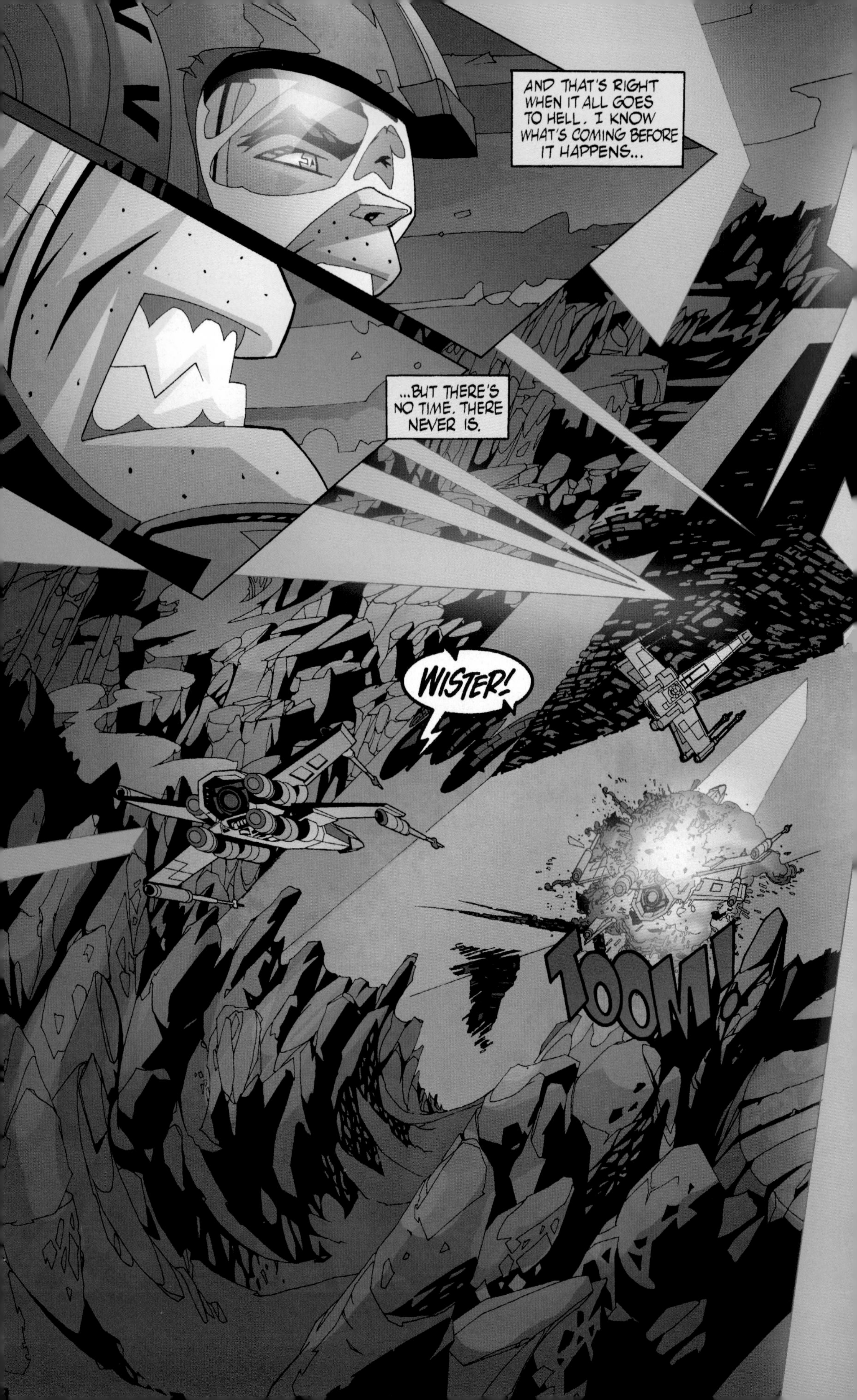
AND THAT'S RIGHT WHEN IT ALL GOES TO HELL. I KNOW WHAT'S COMING BEFORE IT HAPPENS...
...BUT THERE'S NO TIME. THERE NEVER IS.
WISTER!
TOOM!

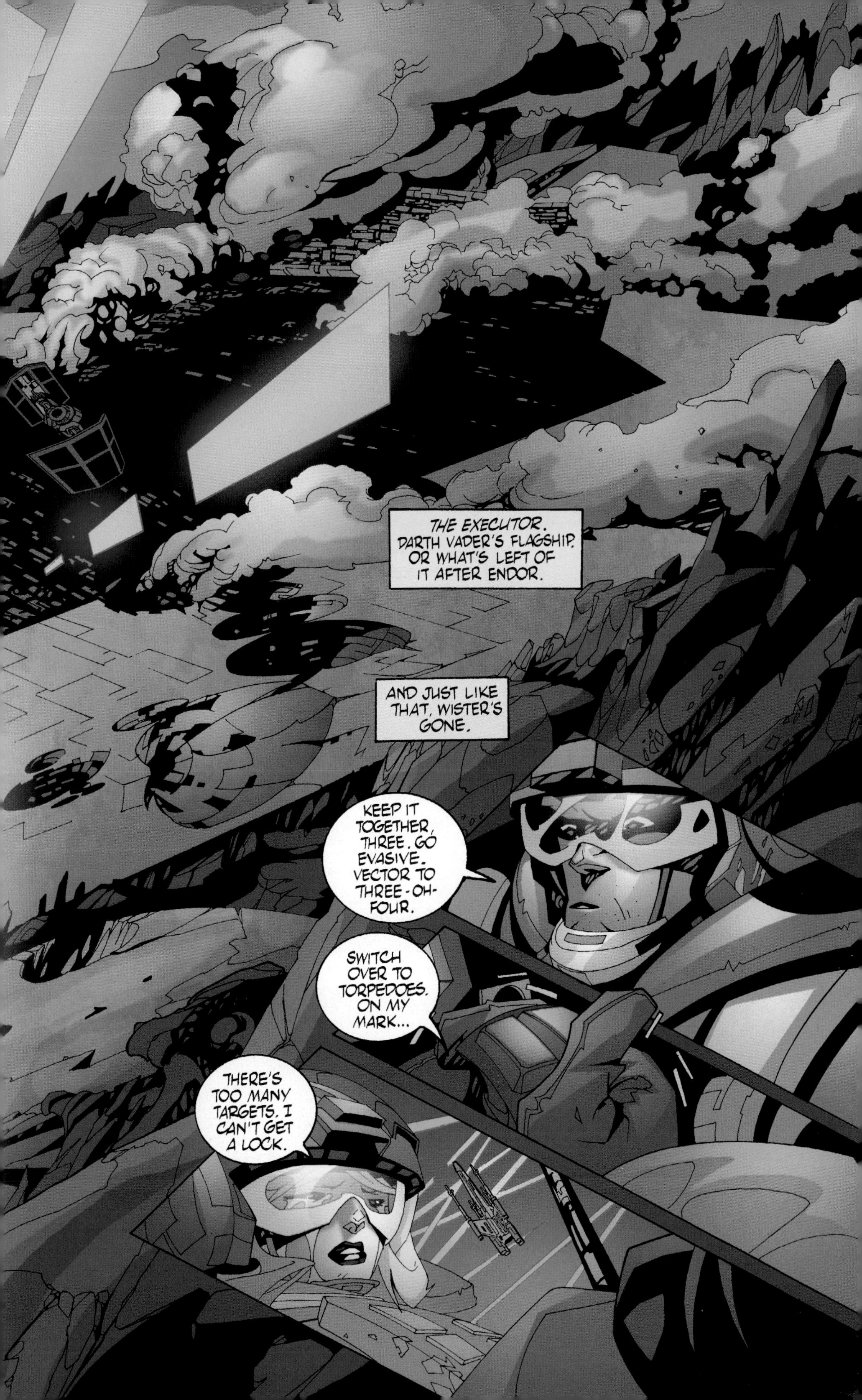

THE EXECUTOR. DARTH VADER'S FLAGSHIP. OR WHAT'S LEFT OF IT AFTER ENDOR.
AND JUST LIKE THAT, WISTER'S GONE.
KEEP IT TOGETHER, THREE. GO EVASIVE. VECTOR TO THREE-OH-FOUR.
SWITCH OVER TO TORPEDOES. ON MY MARK...
THERE'S TOO MANY TARGETS. I CAN'T GET A LOCK.

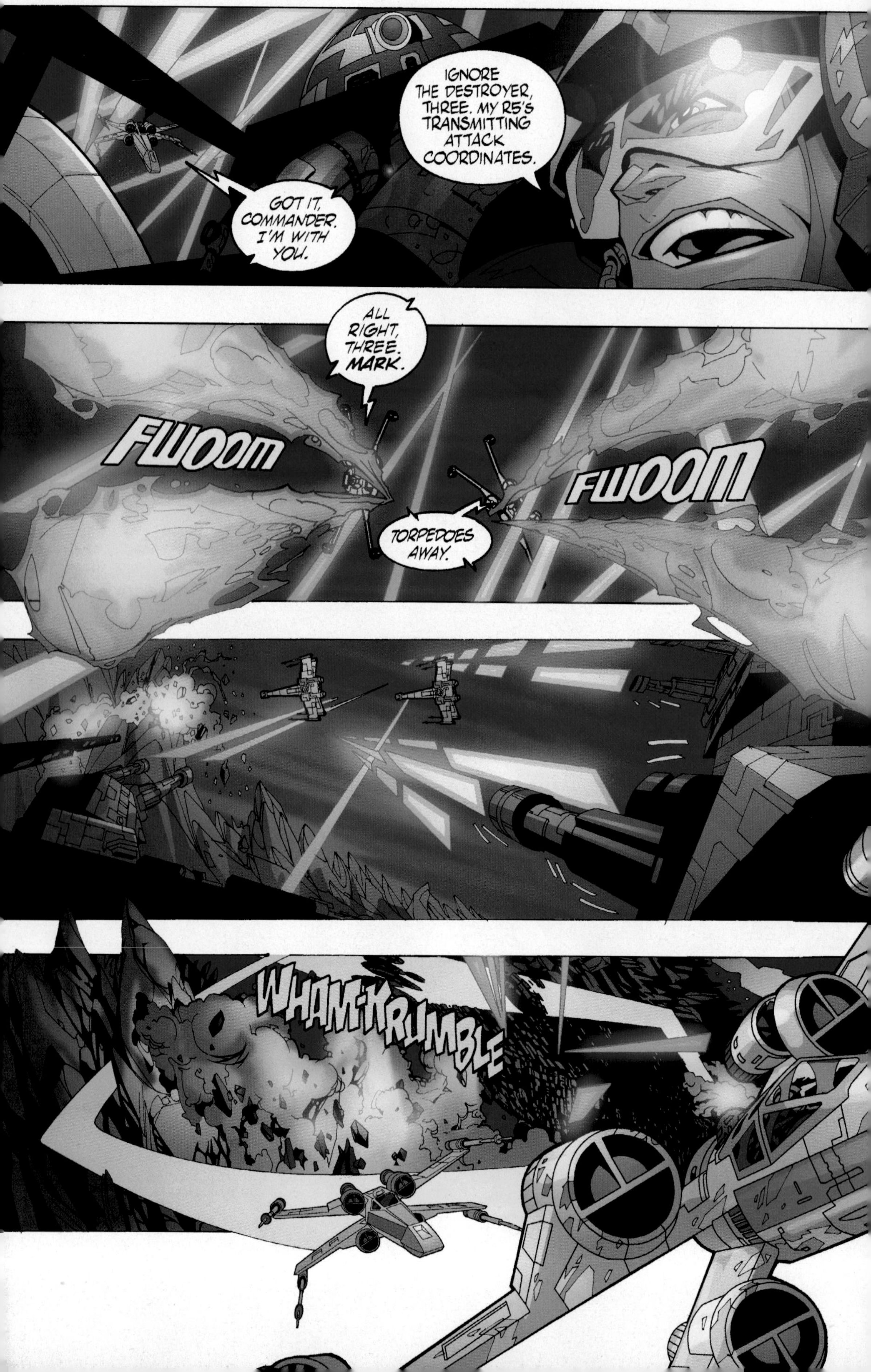
IGNORE THE DESTROYER, THREE. MY R5'S TRANSMITTING ATTACK COORDINATES.
GOT IT, COMMANDER. I'M WITH YOU.
ALL RIGHT, THREE. MARK.
FWOOM
FWOOM
TORPEDOES AWAY.
WHAM-KRUMBLE

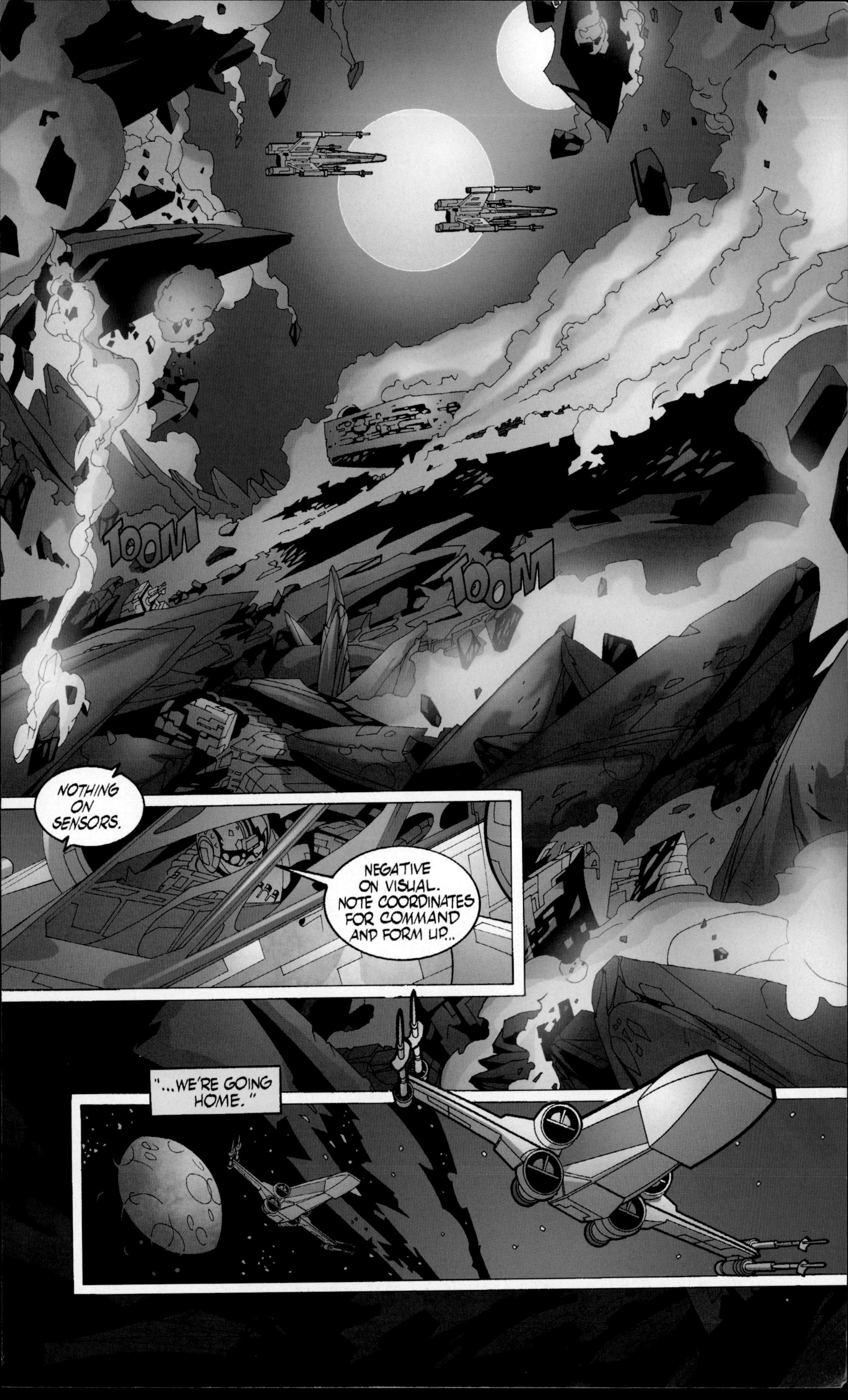
TOOM
TOOM
NOTHING ON SENSORS.
NEGATIVE ON VISUAL. NOTE COORDINATES FOR COMMAND AND FORM UP...
"...WE'RE GOING HOME."

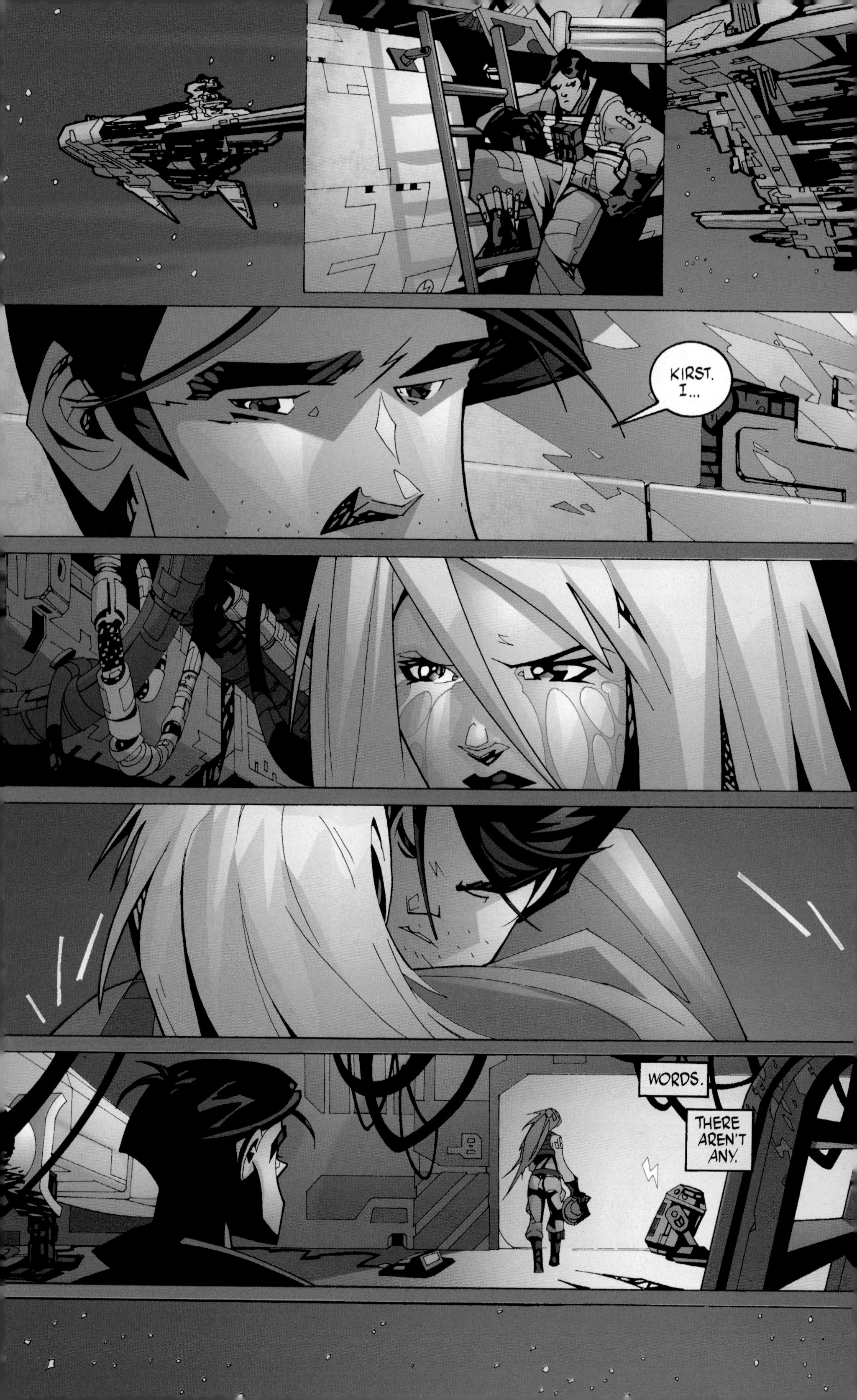
KIRST. I...
WORDS.
THERE AREN'T ANY.

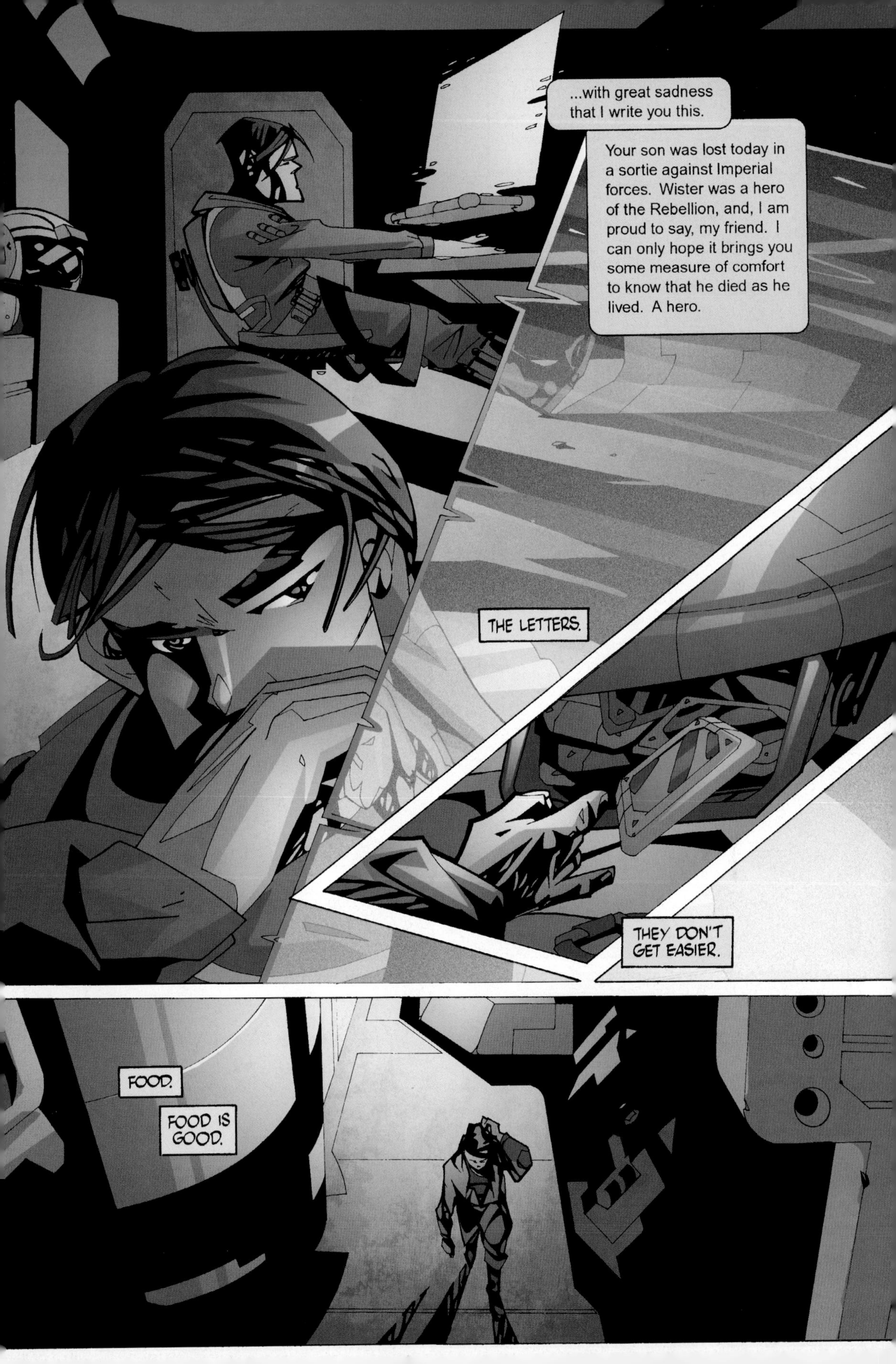

...with great sadness that I write you this.
Your son was lost today in a sortie against Imperial forces. Wister was a hero of the Rebellion, and, I am proud to say, my friend. I can only hope it brings you some measure of comfort to know that he died as he lived. A hero.
THE LETTERS.
THEY DON'T GET EASIER.
FOOD.
FOOD IS GOOD.

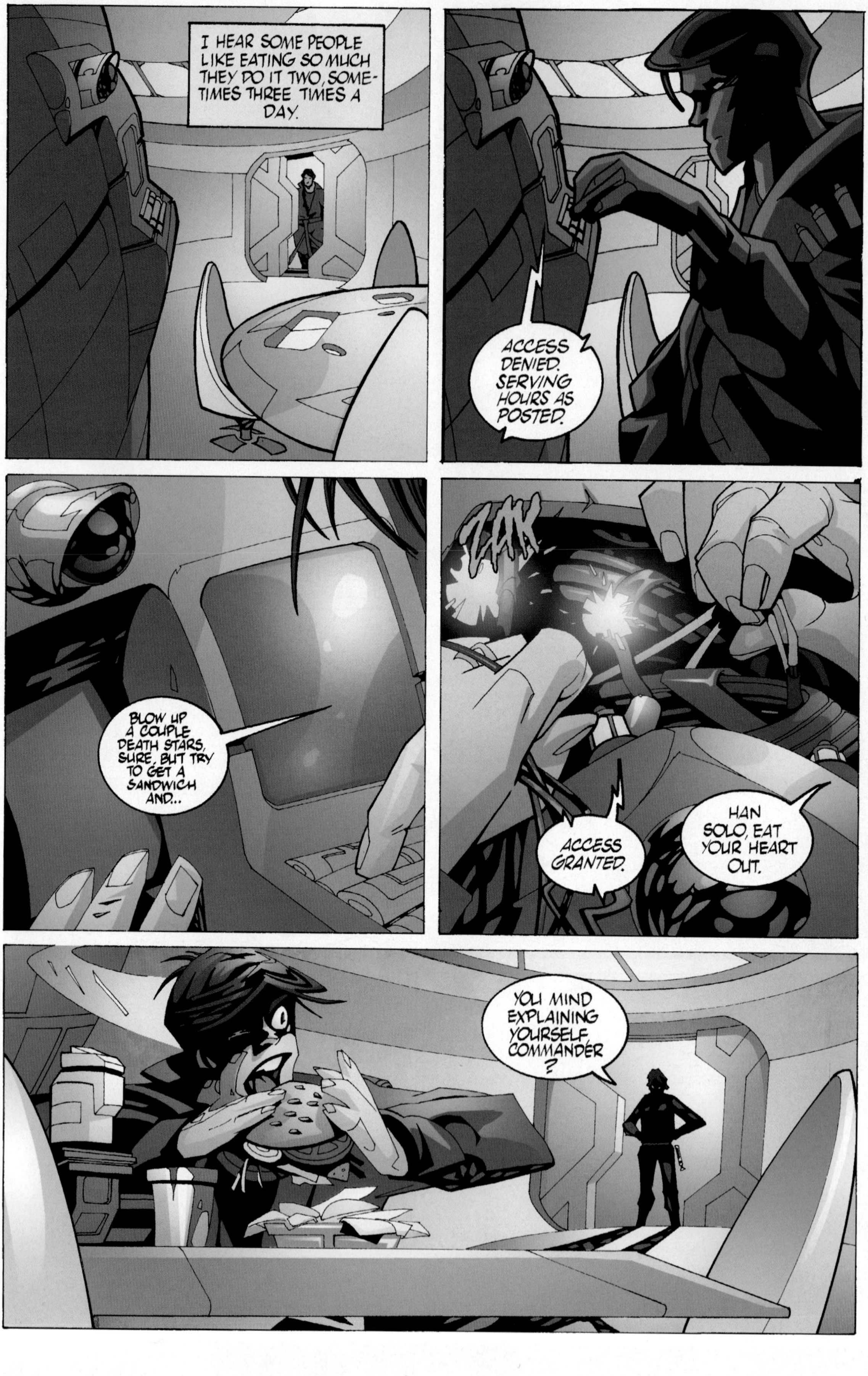
I HEAR SOME PEOPLE LIKE EATING SO MUCH THEY DO IT TWO, SOME-TIMES THREE TIMES A DAY.
ACCESS DENIED. SERVING HOURS AS POSTED.
BLOW UP A COUPLE DEATH STARS, SURE, BUT TRY TO GET A SANDWICH AND...
ZAK
ACCESS GRANTED.
HAN SOLO, EAT YOUR HEART OUT.
YOU MIND EXPLAINING YOURSELF COMMANDER ?

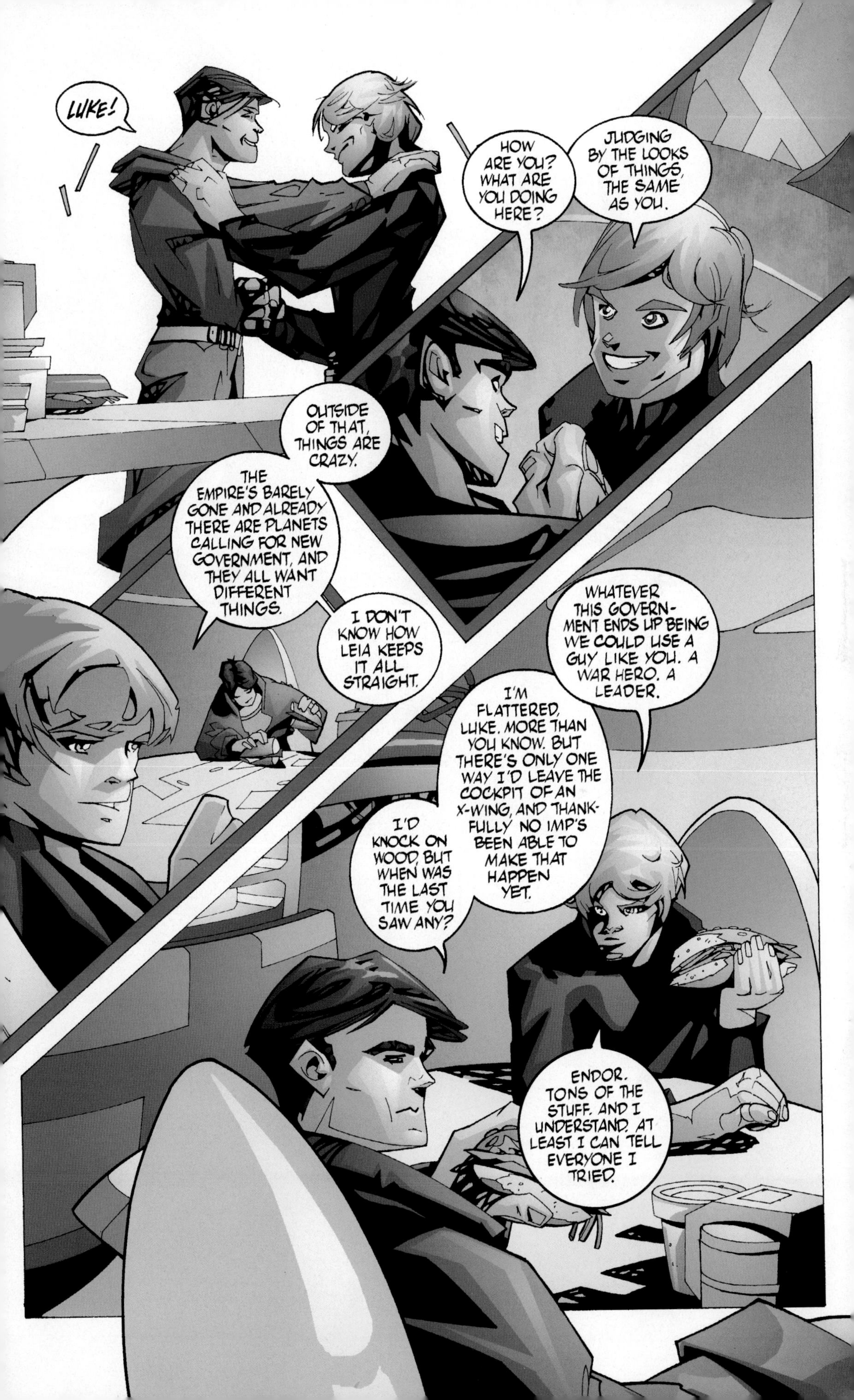
LUKE!
HOW ARE YOU? WHAT ARE YOU DOING HERE?
JUDGING BY THE LOOKS OF THINGS, THE SAME AS YOU.
OUTSIDE OF THAT, THINGS ARE CRAZY.
THE EMPIRE'S BARELY GONE AND ALREADY THERE ARE PLANETS CALLING FOR NEW GOVERNMENT, AND THEY ALL WANT DIFFERENT THINGS.
I DON'T KNOW HOW LEIA KEEPS IT ALL STRAIGHT.
WHATEVER THIS GOVERNMENT ENDS UP BEING WE COULD USE A GUY LIKE YOU. A WAR HERO. A LEADER.
I'M FLATTERED, LUKE. MORE THAN YOU KNOW. BUT THERE'S ONLY ONE WAY I'D LEAVE THE COCKPIT OF AN X-WING, AND THANKFULLY NO IMP'S BEEN ABLE TO MAKE THAT HAPPEN YET.
I'D KNOCK ON WOOD, BUT WHEN WAS THE LAST TIME YOU SAW ANY?
ENDOR. TONS OF THE STUFF. AND I UNDERSTAND. AT LEAST I CAN TELL EVERYONE I TRIED.

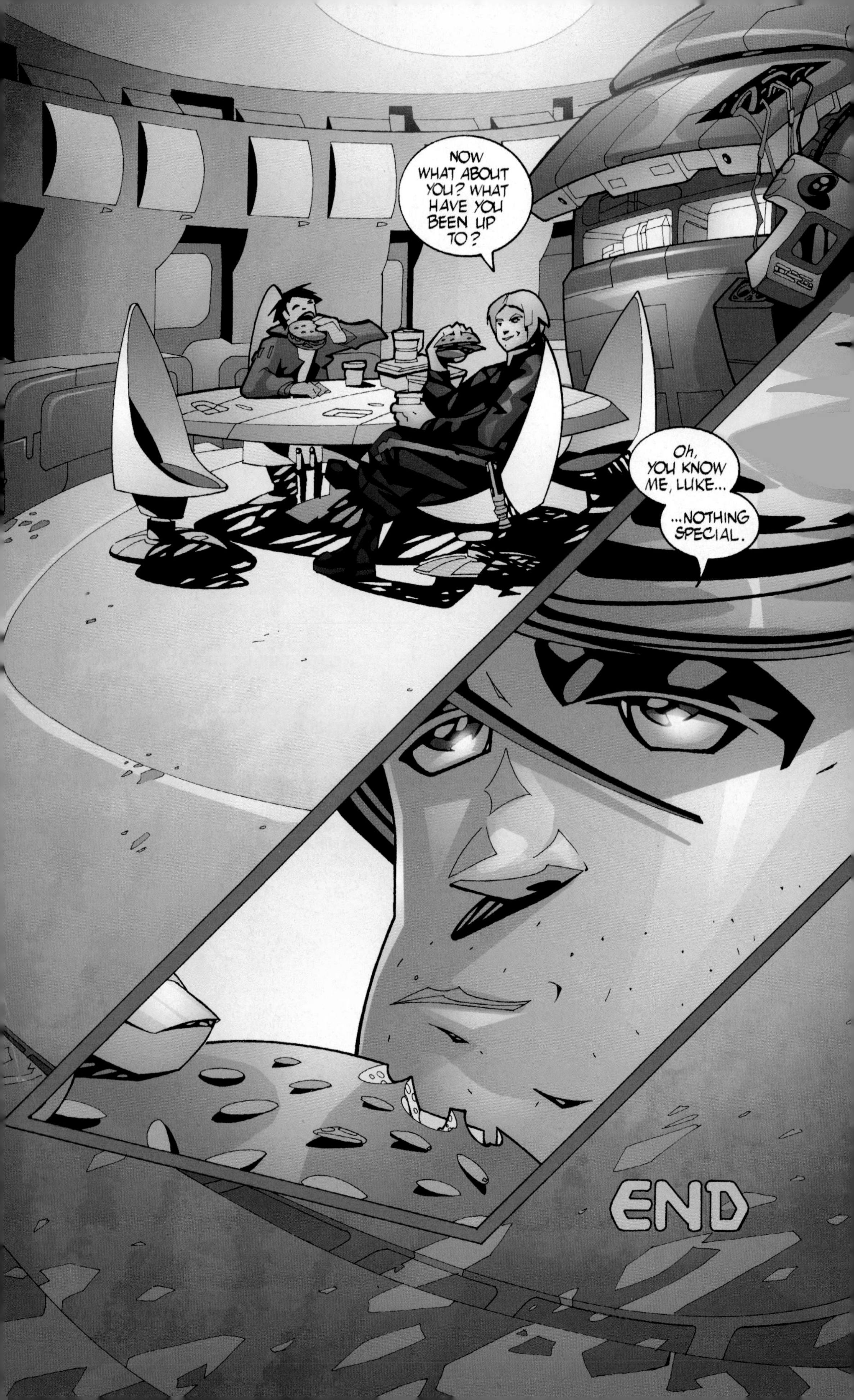
NOW WHAT ABOUT YOU? WHAT HAVE YOU BEEN UP TO?
Oh, YOU KNOW ME, LUKE...
...NOTHING SPECIAL.
END

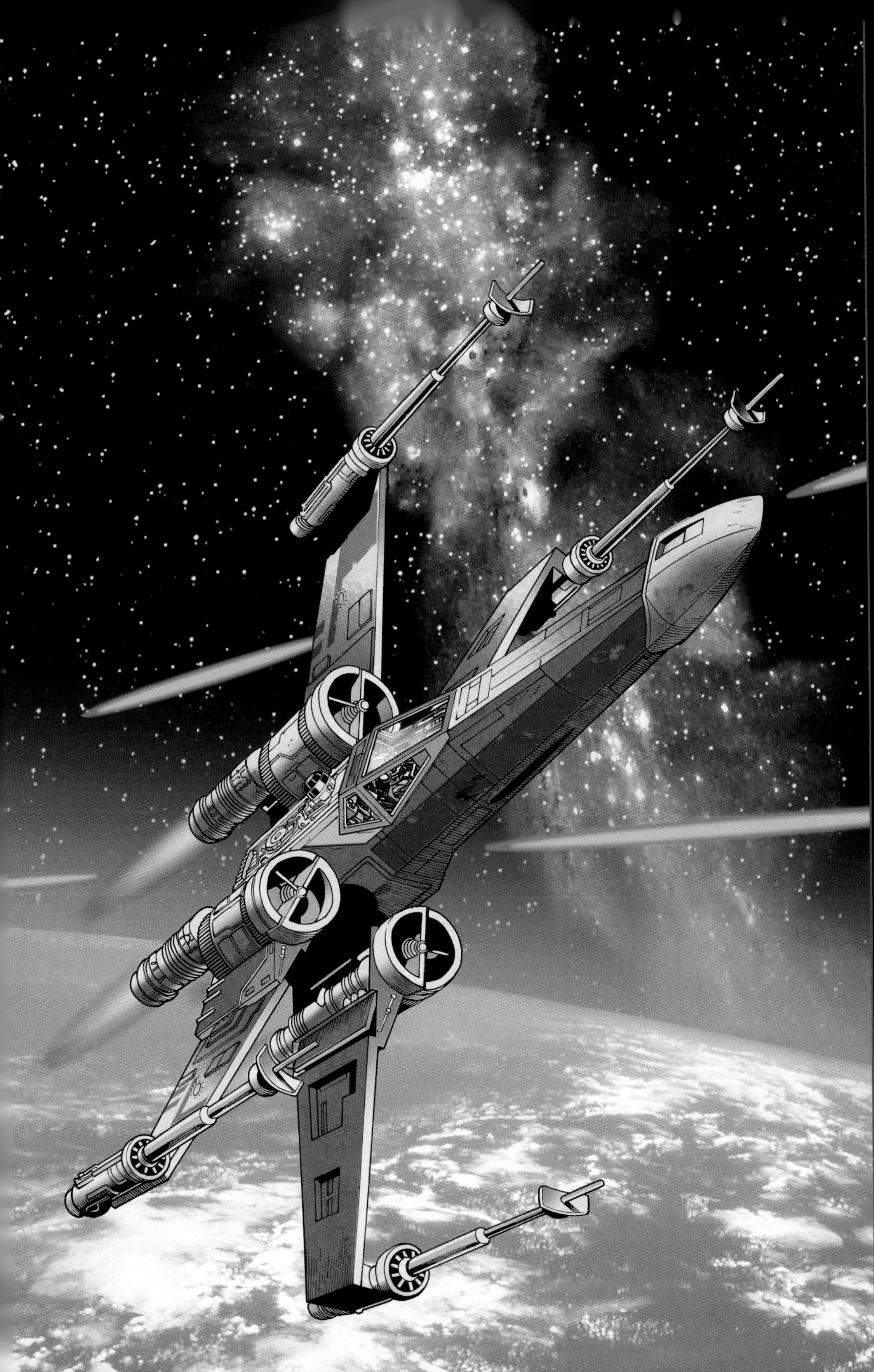

*STAR WARS: X-WING ROGUE LEADER #1*

WRITER: HADEN BLACKMAN • ARTIST: TOMÁS GIORELLO • COLORIST: MICHAEL ATIYEH • LETTERER: MICHAEL DAVID THOMAS
ASSISTANT EDITOR: DAVE MARSHALL • ASSOCIATE EDITOR: JEREMY BARLOW • EDITOR: RANDY STRADLEY • COVER ARTIST: GARY ERSKINE

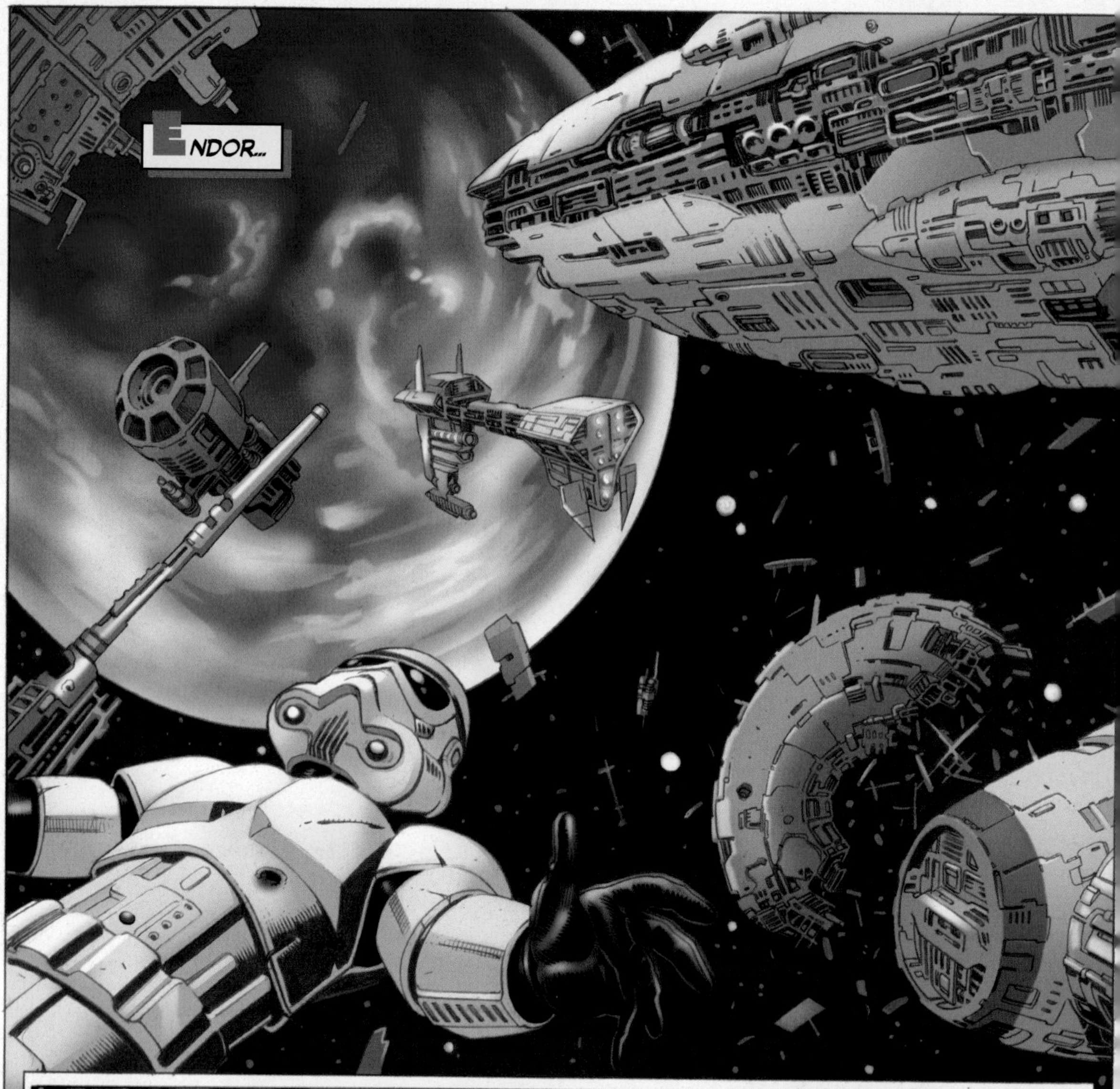
ENDOR...
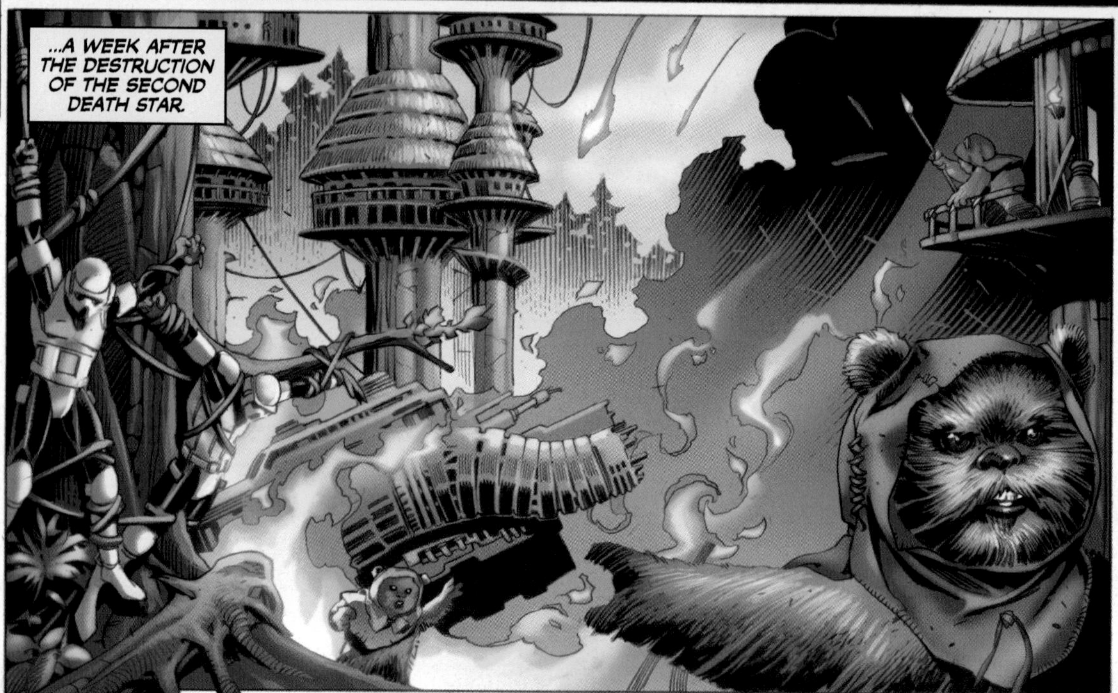
...A WEEK AFTER THE DESTRUCTION OF THE SECOND DEATH STAR.

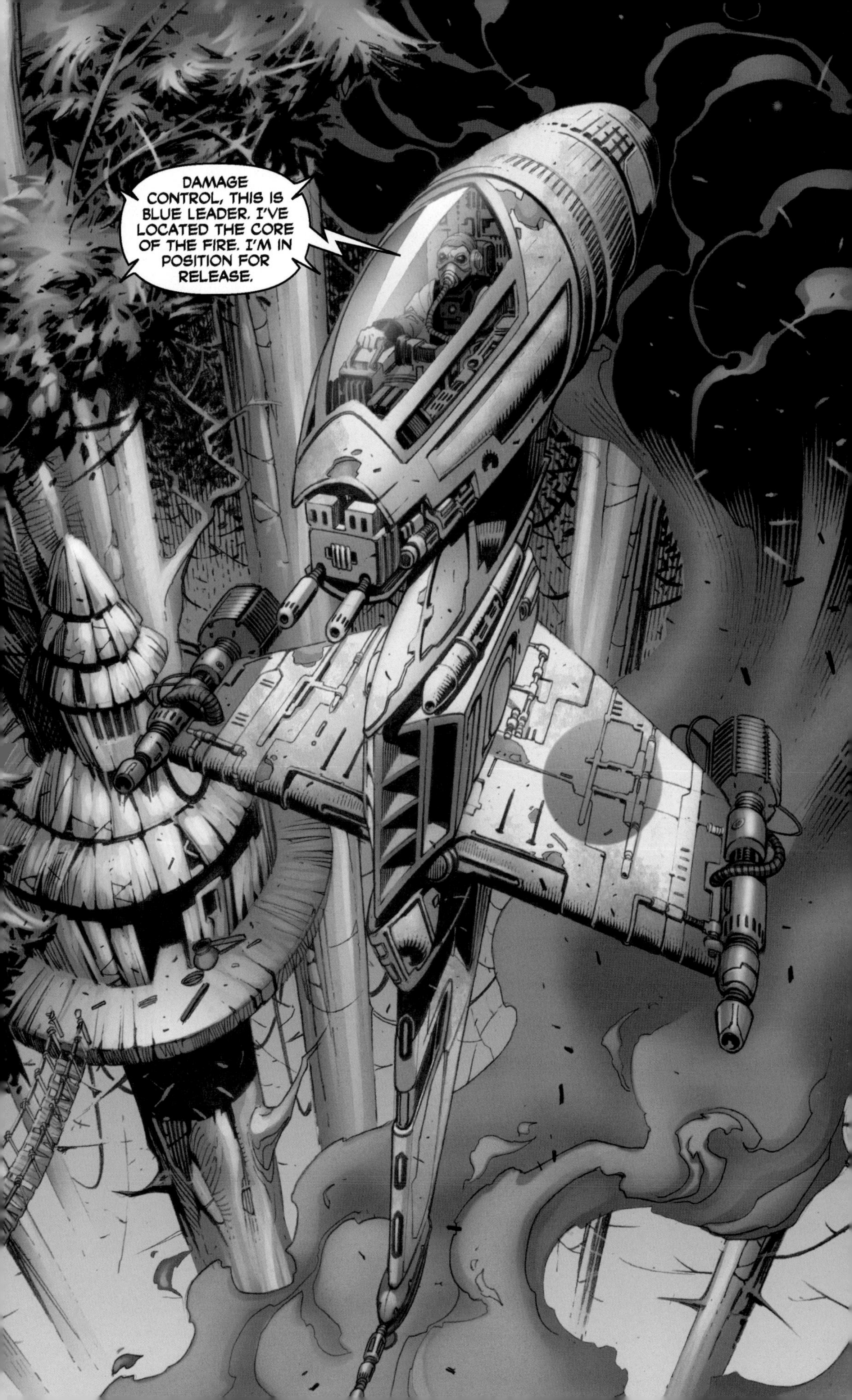
DAMAGE CONTROL, THIS IS BLUE LEADER. I'VE LOCATED THE CORE OF THE FIRE. I'M IN POSITION FOR RELEASE.

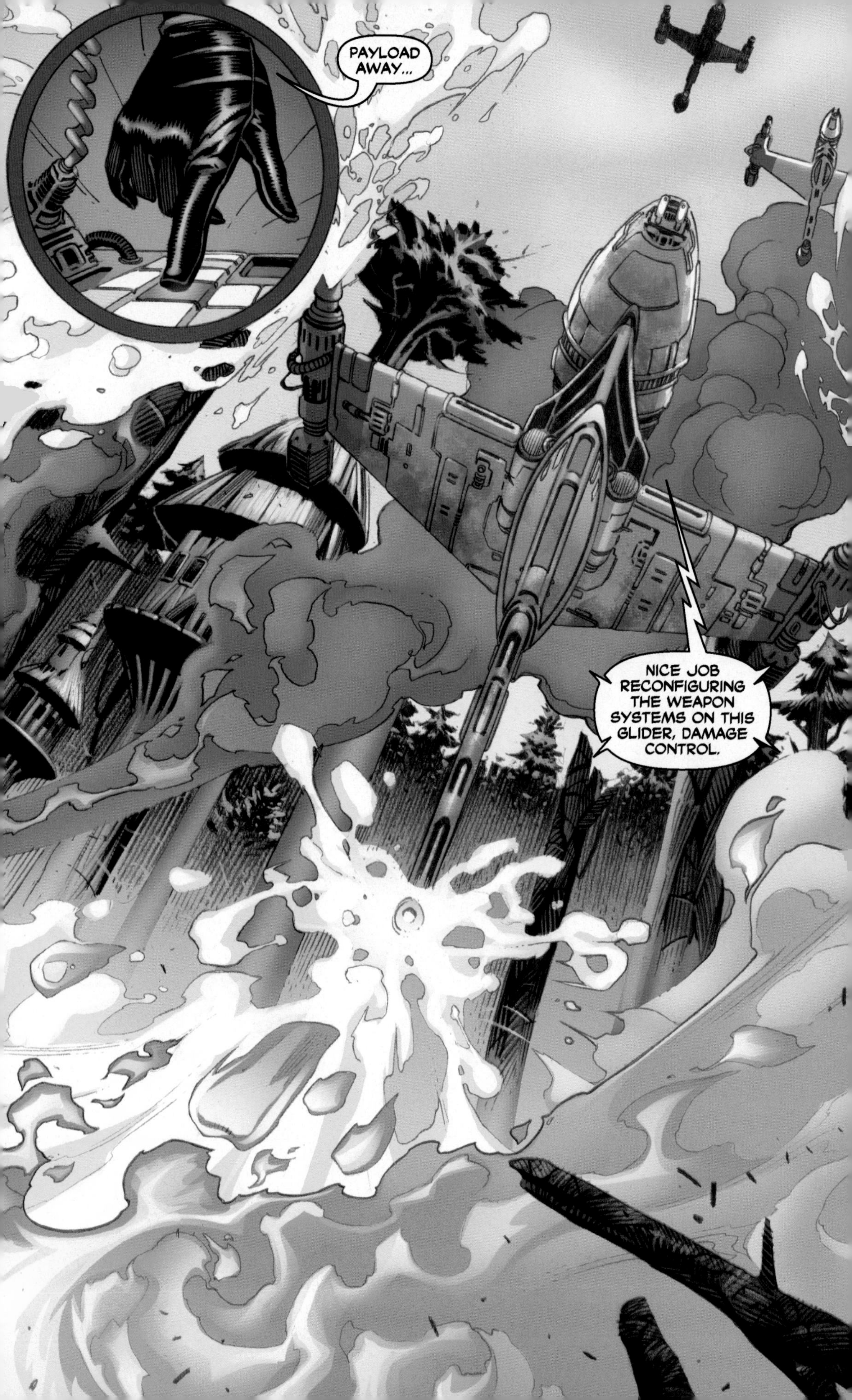
PAYLOAD AWAY...
NICE JOB RECONFIGURING THE WEAPON SYSTEMS ON THIS GLIDER, DAMAGE CONTROL.

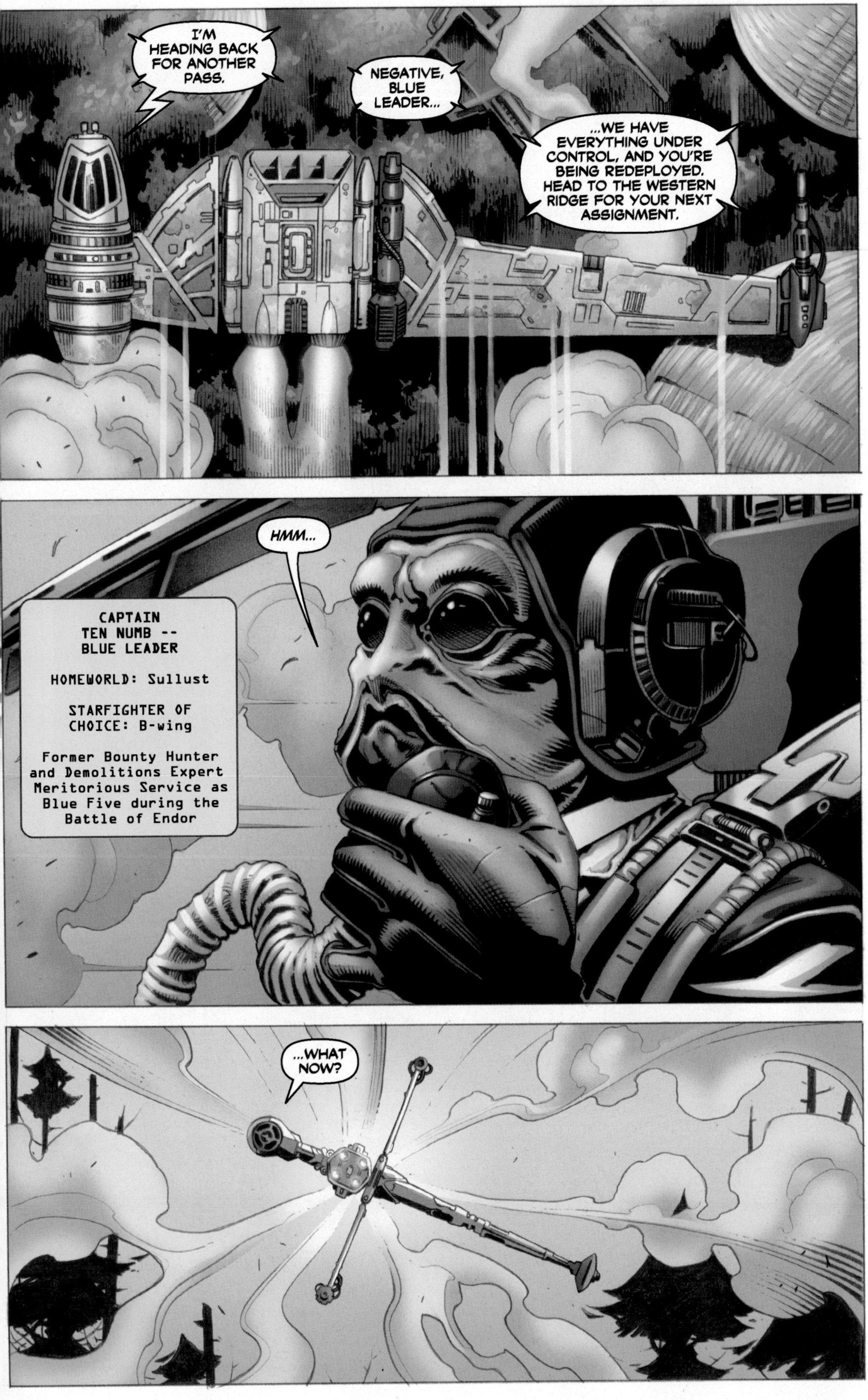
I'M HEADING BACK FOR ANOTHER PASS.
NEGATIVE, BLUE LEADER...
...WE HAVE EVERYTHING UNDER CONTROL, AND YOU'RE BEING REDEPLOYED. HEAD TO THE WESTERN RIDGE FOR YOUR NEXT ASSIGNMENT.
HMM...
CAPTAIN TEN NUMB -- BLUE LEADER
HOMEWORLD: Sullust
STARFIGHTER OF CHOICE: B-wing
Former Bounty Hunter and Demolitions Expert Meritorious Service as Blue Five during the Battle of Endor
...WHAT NOW?

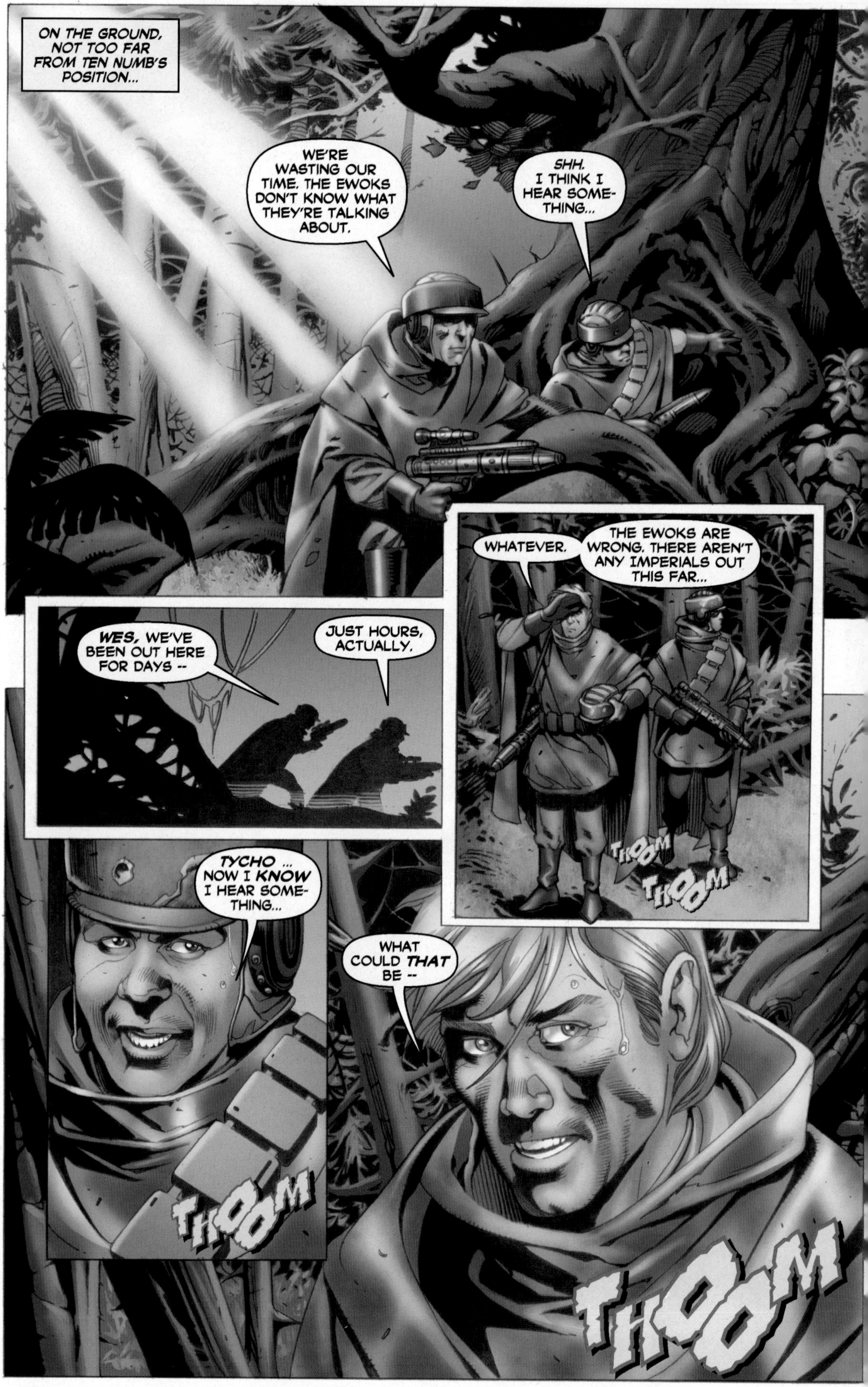

ON THE GROUND, NOT TOO FAR FROM TEN NUMB'S POSITION...
WE'RE WASTING OUR TIME. THE EWOKS DON'T KNOW WHAT THEY'RE TALKING ABOUT.
SHH. I THINK I HEAR SOMETHING...
WES, WE'VE BEEN OUT HERE FOR DAYS --
JUST HOURS, ACTUALLY.
WHATEVER.
THE EWOKS ARE WRONG. THERE AREN'T ANY IMPERIALS OUT THIS FAR...
THOOM
THOOM
TYCHO ... NOW I KNOW I HEAR SOMETHING...
WHAT COULD THAT BE --
THOOM
THOOM

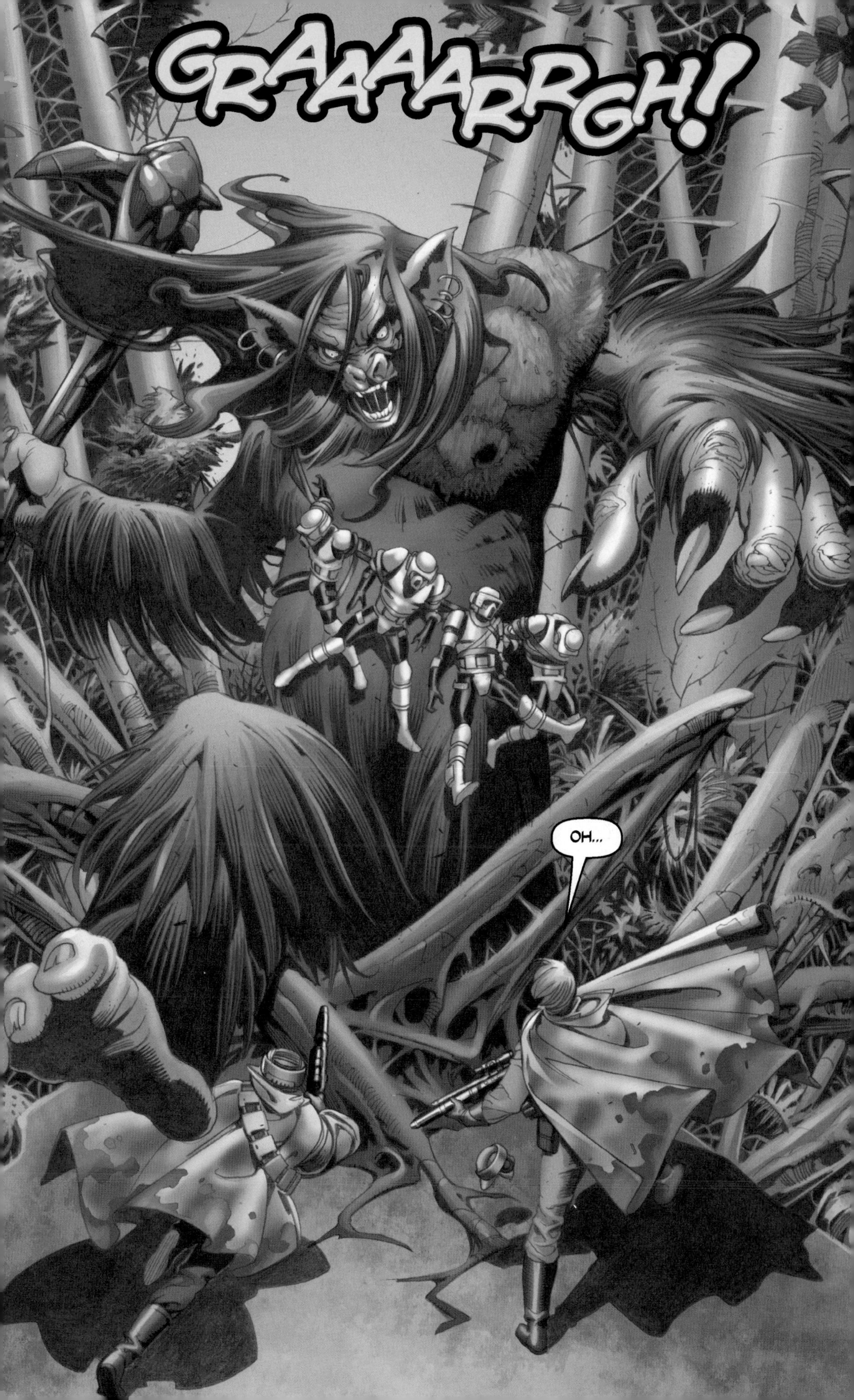
GRAAAARRGH!
OH...

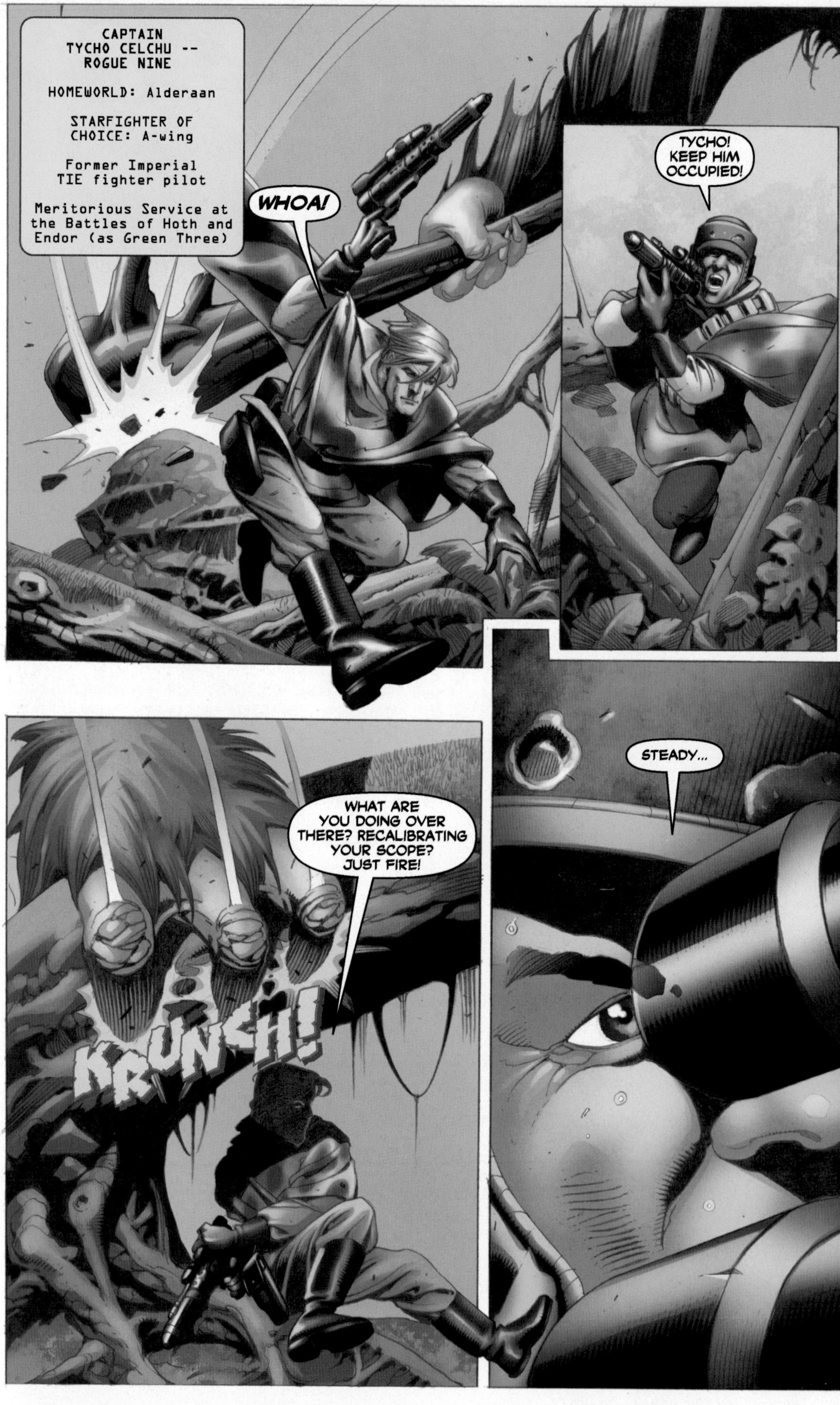
CAPTAIN TYCHO CELCHU -- ROGUE NINE
HOMEWORLD: Alderaan
STARFIGHTER OF CHOICE: A-wing
Former Imperial TIE fighter pilot
Meritorious Service at the Battles of Hoth and Endor (as Green Three)
WHOA!
TYCHO! KEEP HIM OCCUPIED!
WHAT ARE YOU DOING OVER THERE? RECALIBRATING YOUR SCOPE? JUST FIRE!
KRUNCH!
STEADY...

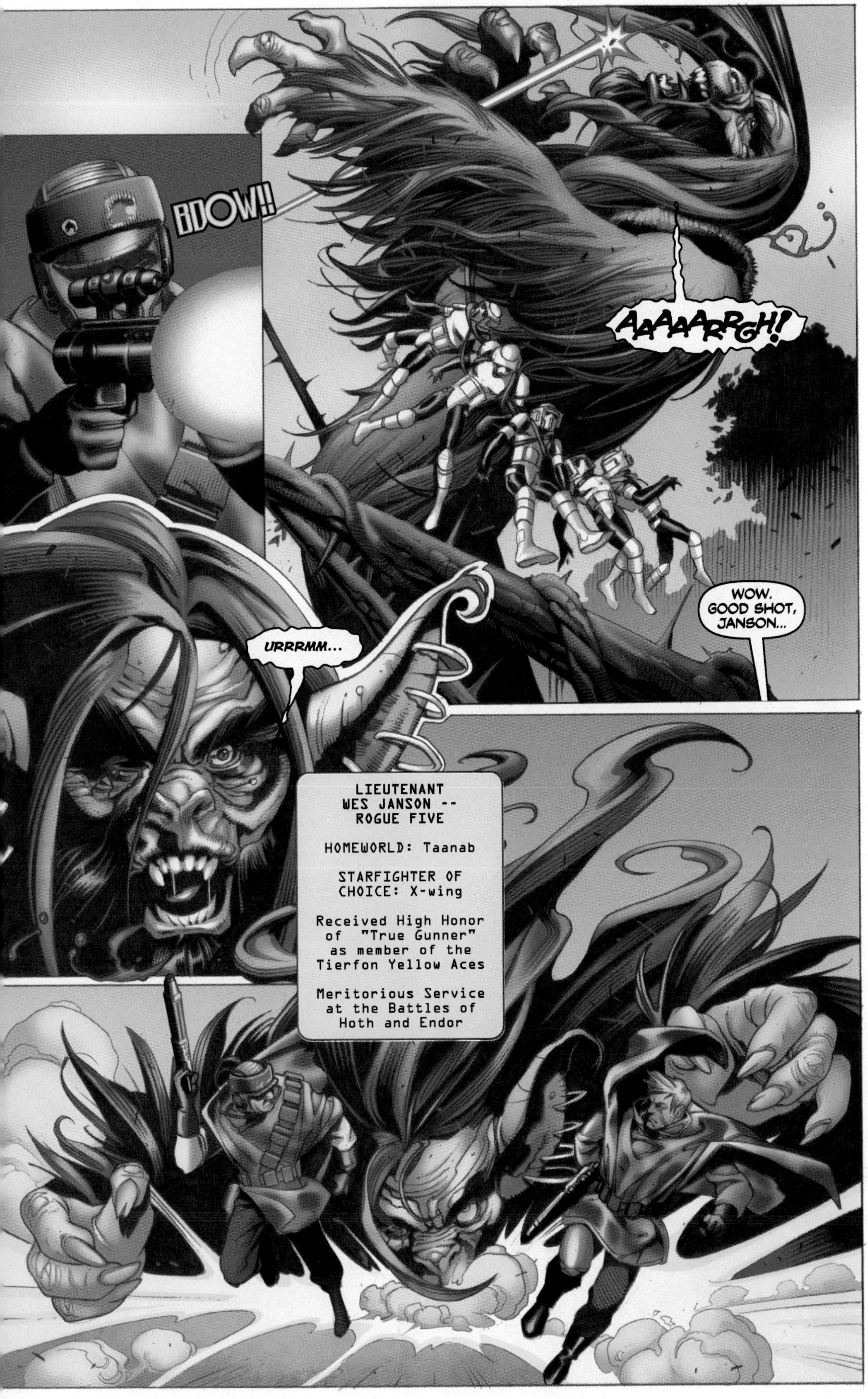
BDOW!!
AAAAARRGH!
WOW. GOOD SHOT, JANSON...
URRRMM...
LIEUTENANT WES JANSON -- ROGUE FIVE
HOMEWORLD: Taanab
STARFIGHTER OF CHOICE: X-wing
Received High Honor of "True Gunner" as member of the Tierfon Yellow Aces
Meritorious Service at the Battles of Hoth and Endor

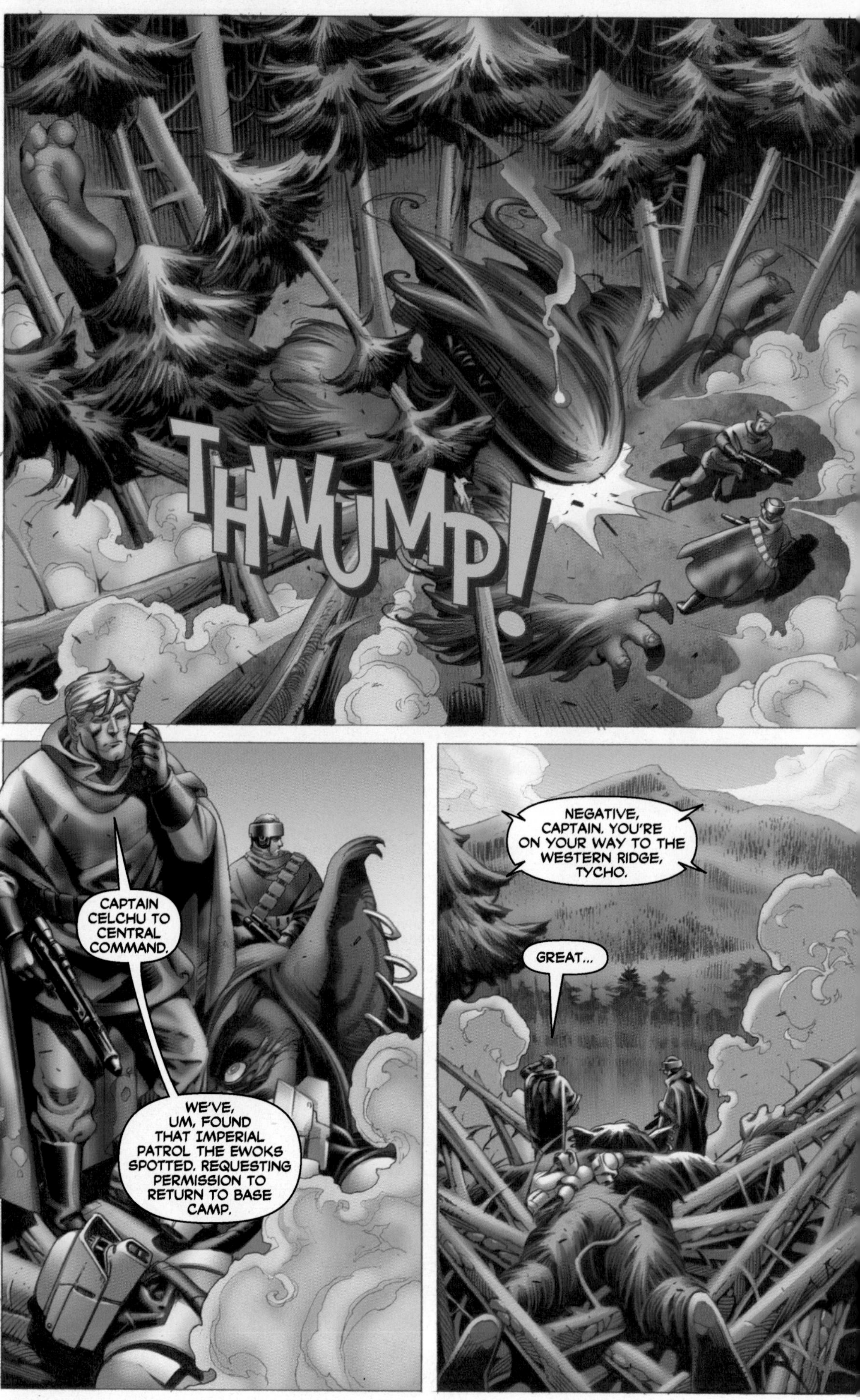
THWUMP!
CAPTAIN CELCHU TO CENTRAL COMMAND.
WE'VE, UM, FOUND THAT IMPERIAL PATROL THE EWOKS SPOTTED. REQUESTING PERMISSION TO RETURN TO BASE CAMP.
NEGATIVE, CAPTAIN. YOU'RE ON YOUR WAY TO THE WESTERN RIDGE, TYCHO.
GREAT...

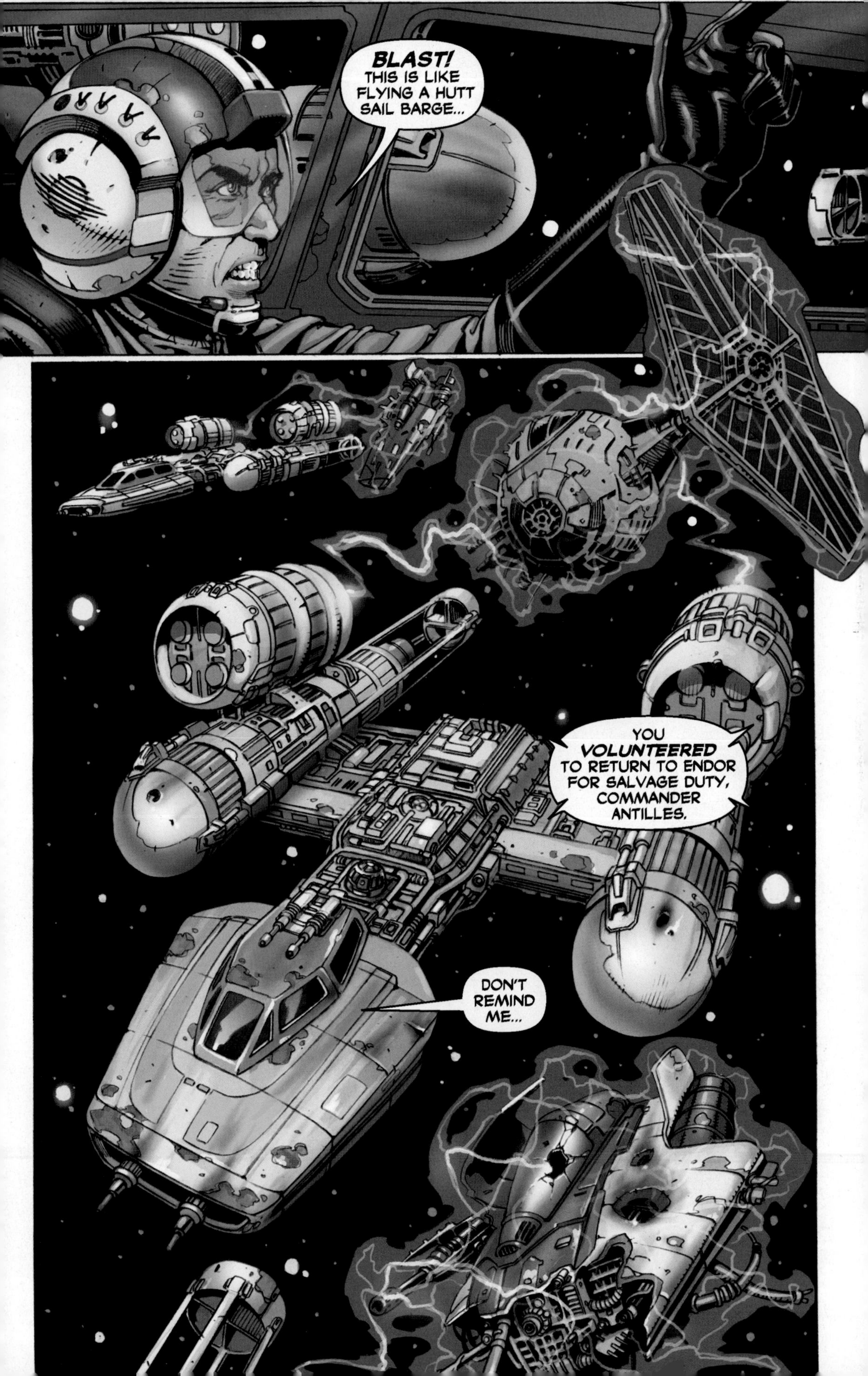
BLAST! THIS IS LIKE FLYING A HUTT SAIL BARGE...
YOU VOLUNTEERED TO RETURN TO ENDOR FOR SALVAGE DUTY, COMMANDER ANTILLES.
DON'T REMIND ME...

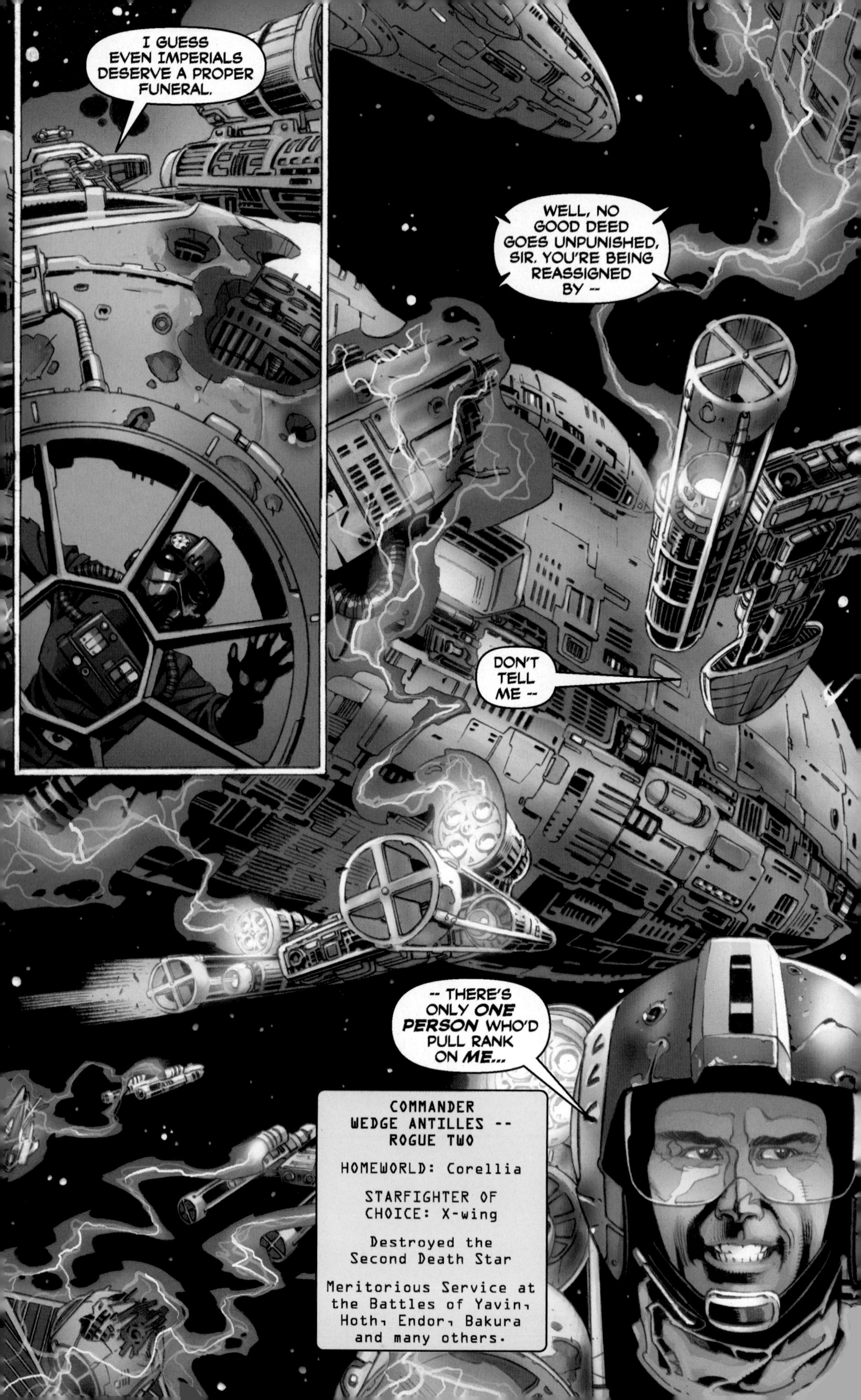
I GUESS EVEN IMPERIALS DESERVE A PROPER FUNERAL.
WELL, NO GOOD DEED GOES UNPUNISHED, SIR. YOU'RE BEING REASSIGNED BY --
DON'T TELL ME --
-- THERE'S ONLY *ONE PERSON* WHO'D PULL RANK ON *ME...*
COMMANDER WEDGE ANTILLES -- ROGUE TWO
HOMEWORLD: Corellia
STARFIGHTER OF CHOICE: X-wing
Destroyed the Second Death Star
Meritorious Service at the Battles of Yavin, Hoth, Endor, Bakura and many others.

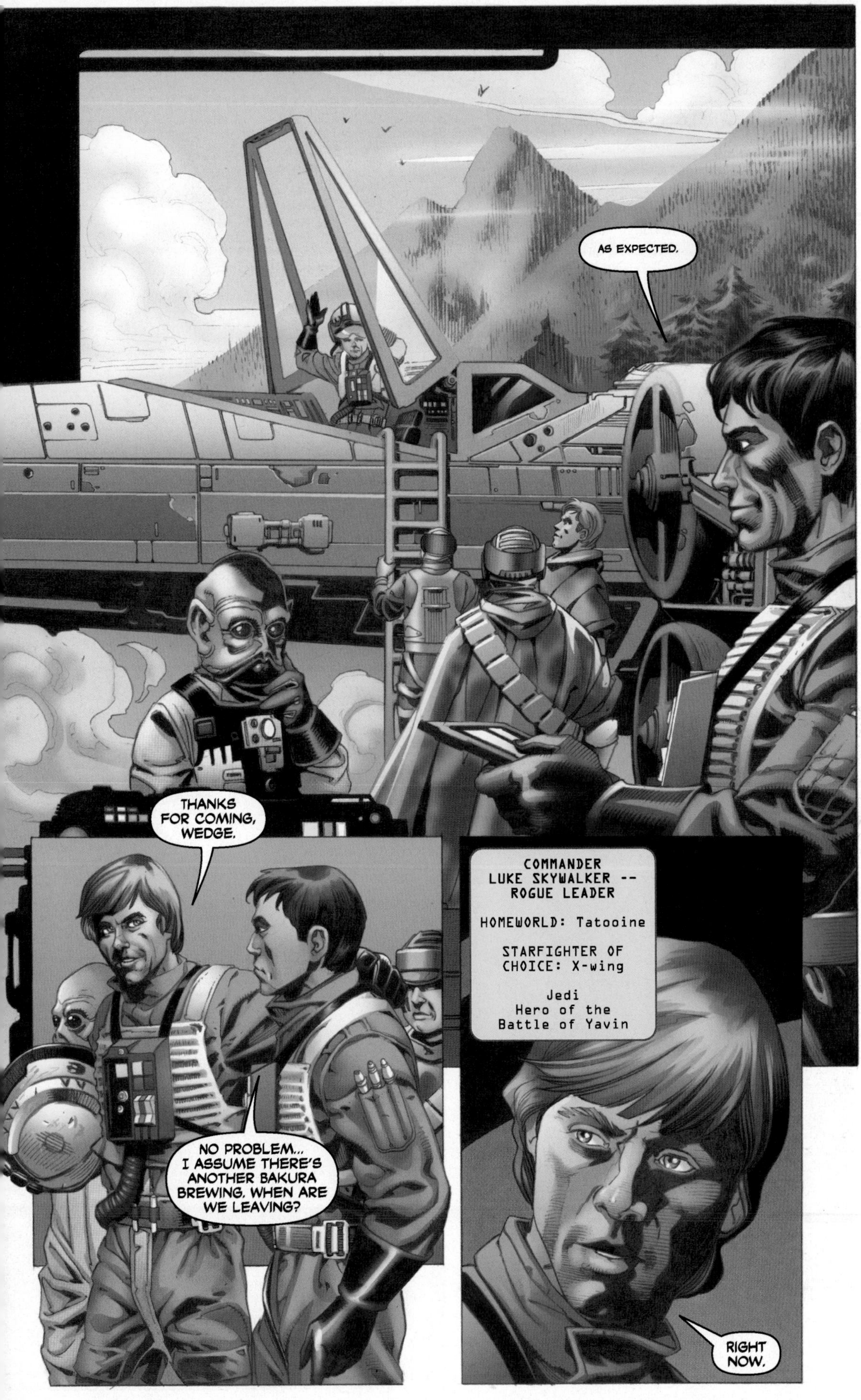
AS EXPECTED.
THANKS FOR COMING, WEDGE.
NO PROBLEM... I ASSUME THERE'S ANOTHER BAKURA BREWING. WHEN ARE WE LEAVING?
COMMANDER LUKE SKYWALKER -- ROGUE LEADER
HOMEWORLD: Tatooine
STARFIGHTER OF CHOICE: X-wing
Jedi
Hero of the Battle of Yavin
RIGHT NOW.

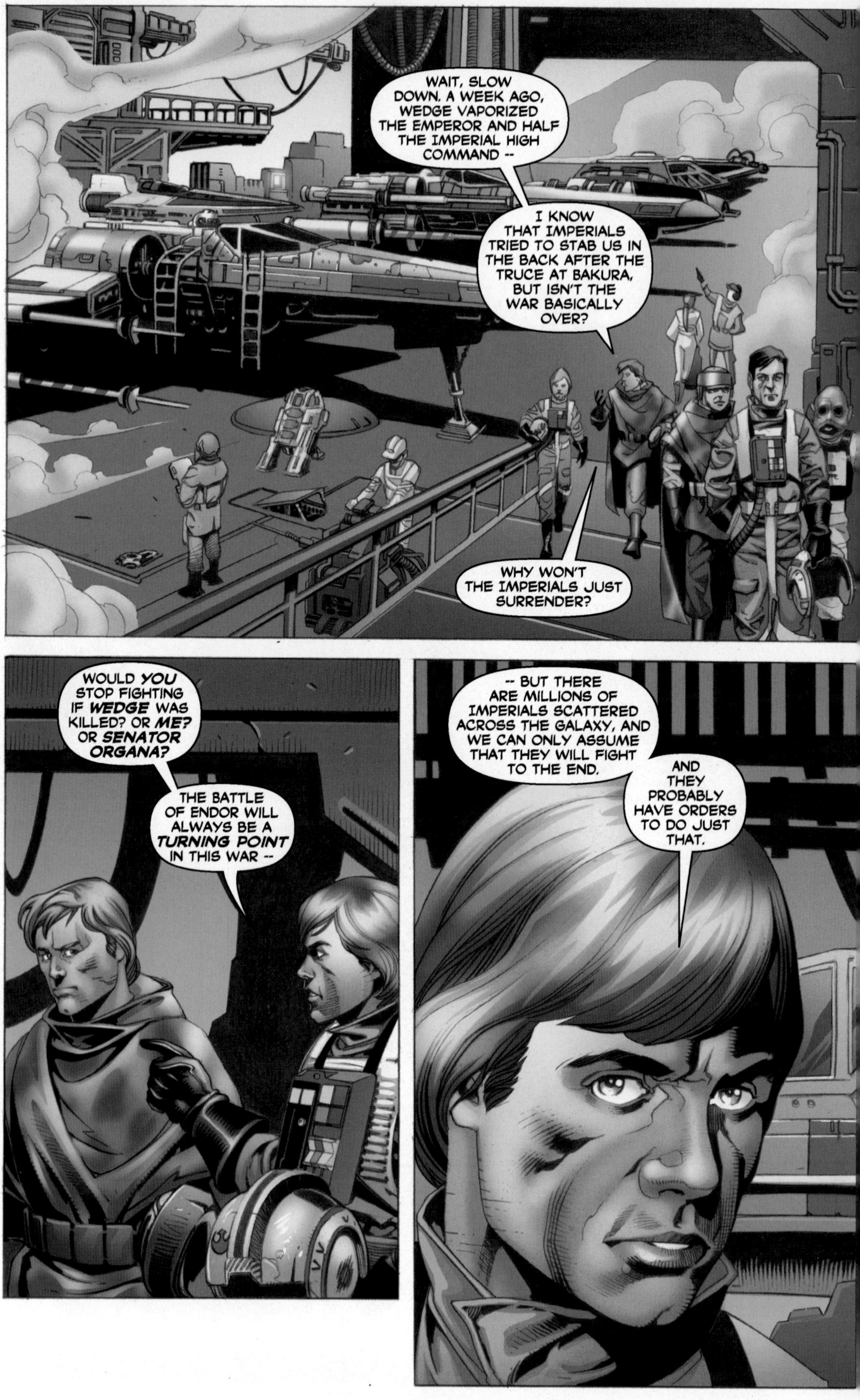
WAIT, SLOW DOWN. A WEEK AGO, WEDGE VAPORIZED THE EMPEROR AND HALF THE IMPERIAL HIGH COMMAND --
I KNOW THAT IMPERIALS TRIED TO STAB US IN THE BACK AFTER THE TRUCE AT BAKURA, BUT ISN'T THE WAR BASICALLY OVER?
WHY WON'T THE IMPERIALS JUST SURRENDER?
WOULD *YOU* STOP FIGHTING IF *WEDGE* WAS KILLED? OR *ME?* OR *SENATOR ORGANA?*
THE BATTLE OF ENDOR WILL ALWAYS BE A *TURNING POINT* IN THIS WAR --
-- BUT THERE ARE MILLIONS OF IMPERIALS SCATTERED ACROSS THE GALAXY, AND WE CAN ONLY ASSUME THAT THEY WILL FIGHT TO THE END.
AND THEY PROBABLY HAVE ORDERS TO DO JUST THAT.

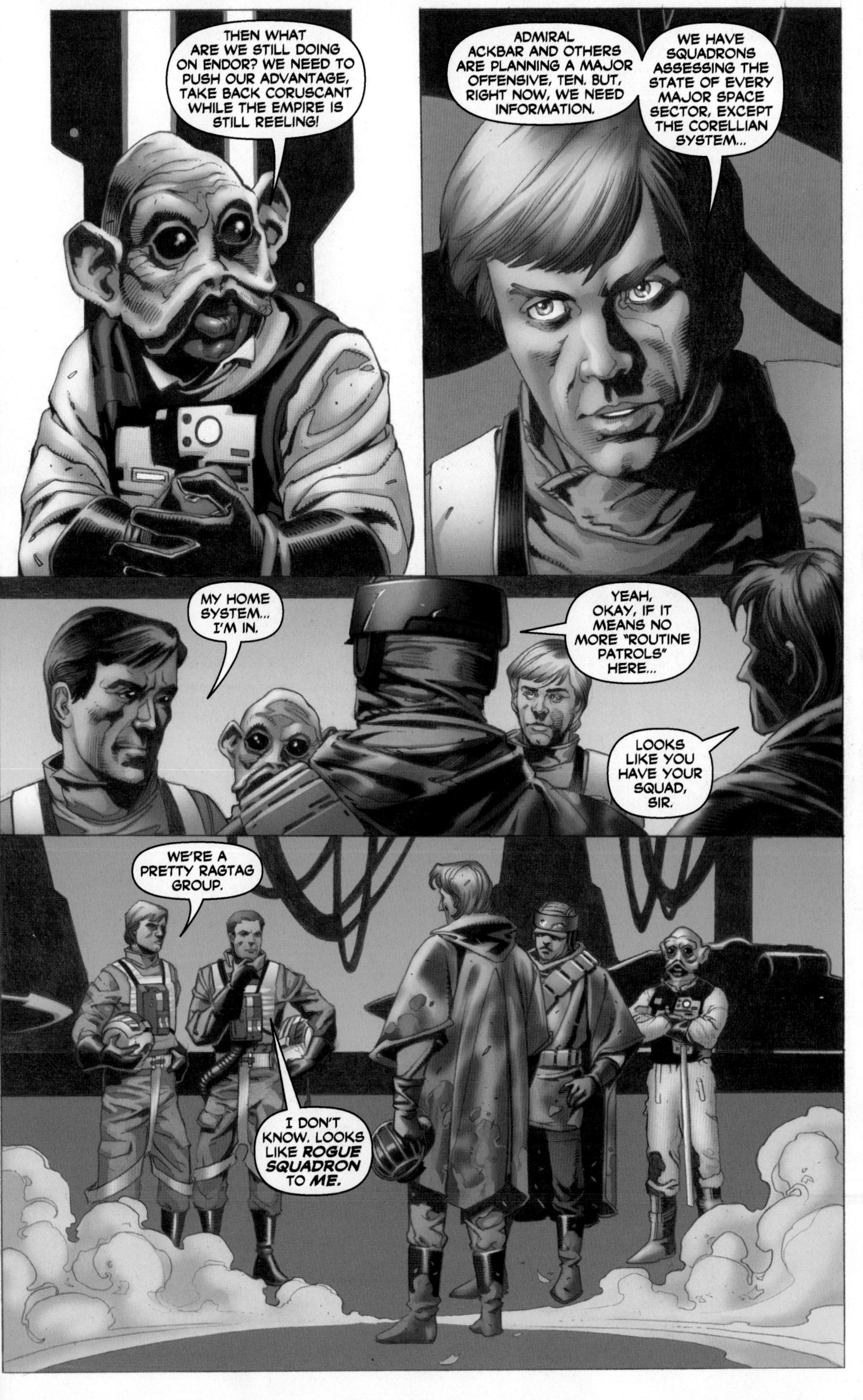
THEN WHAT ARE WE STILL DOING ON ENDOR? WE NEED TO PUSH OUR ADVANTAGE, TAKE BACK CORUSCANT WHILE THE EMPIRE IS STILL REELING!
ADMIRAL ACKBAR AND OTHERS ARE PLANNING A MAJOR OFFENSIVE, TEN. BUT, RIGHT NOW, WE NEED INFORMATION.
WE HAVE SQUADRONS ASSESSING THE STATE OF EVERY MAJOR SPACE SECTOR, EXCEPT THE CORELLIAN SYSTEM...
MY HOME SYSTEM... I'M IN.
YEAH, OKAY, IF IT MEANS NO MORE "ROUTINE PATROLS" HERE...
LOOKS LIKE YOU HAVE YOUR SQUAD, SIR.
WE'RE A PRETTY RAGTAG GROUP.
I DON'T KNOW. LOOKS LIKE ***ROGUE SQUADRON*** TO ***ME.***

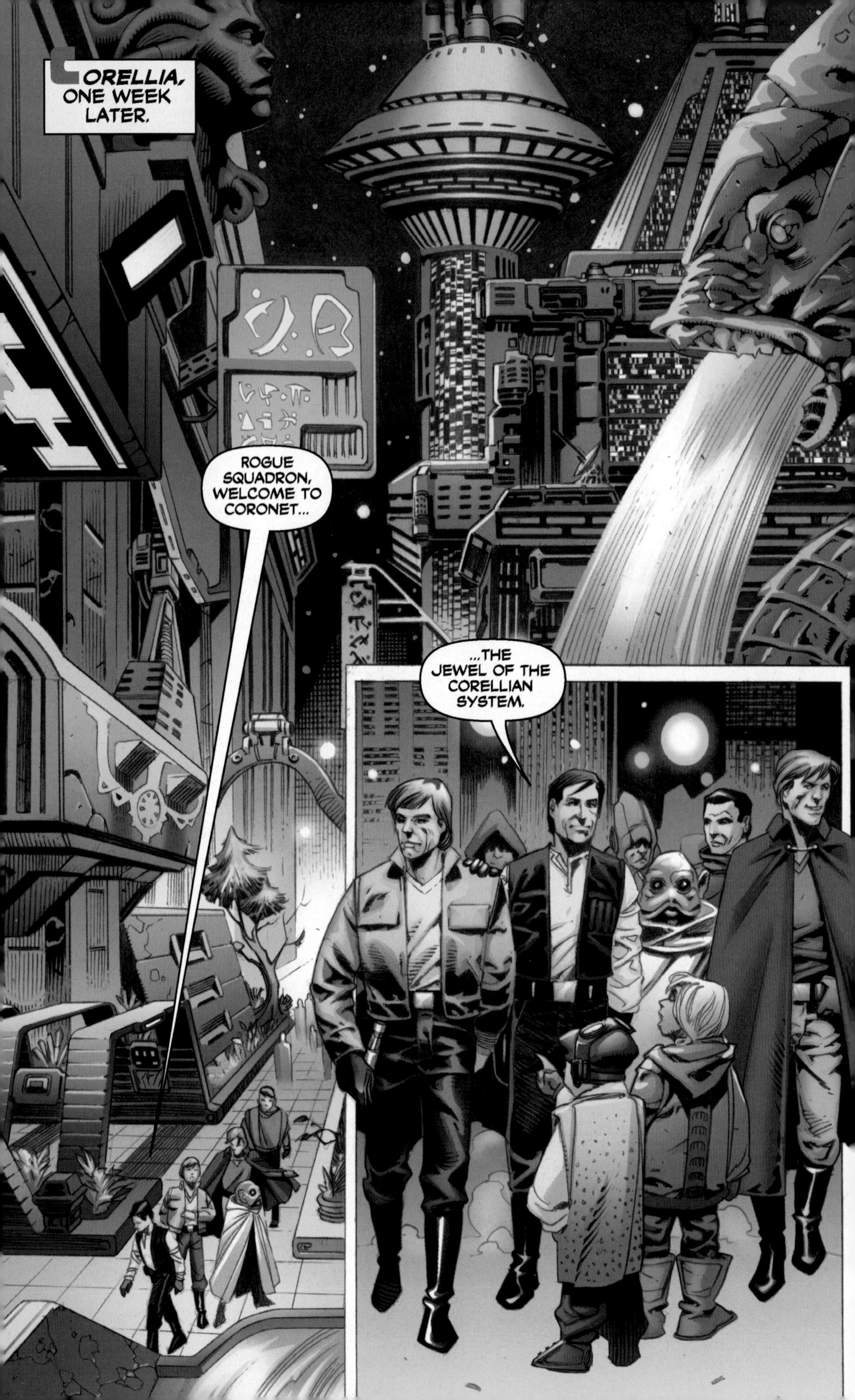
CORELLIA, ONE WEEK LATER.
ROGUE SQUADRON, WELCOME TO CORONET...
...THE JEWEL OF THE CORELLIAN SYSTEM.

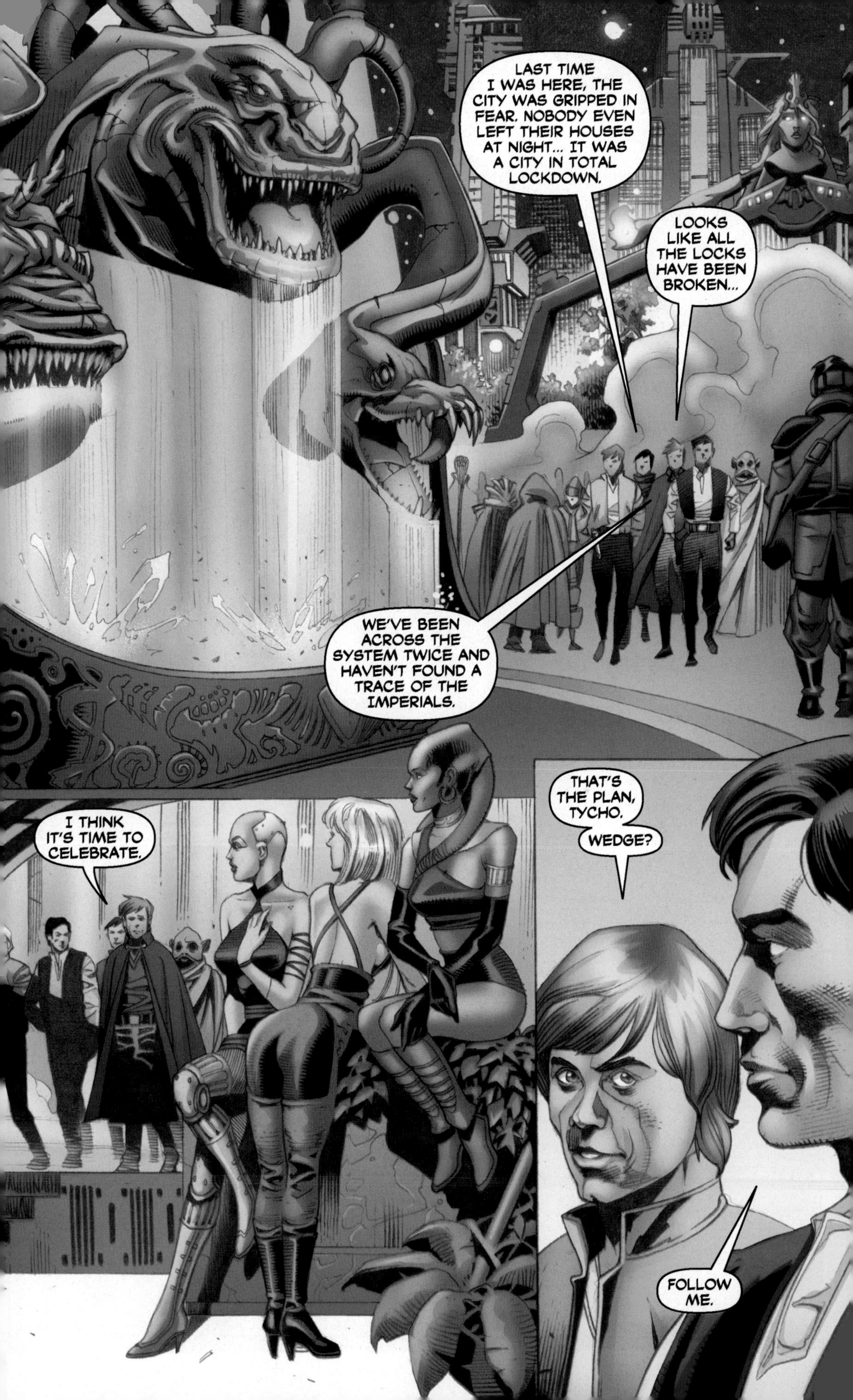
LAST TIME I WAS HERE, THE CITY WAS GRIPPED IN FEAR. NOBODY EVEN LEFT THEIR HOUSES AT NIGHT... IT WAS A CITY IN TOTAL LOCKDOWN.
LOOKS LIKE ALL THE LOCKS HAVE BEEN BROKEN...
WE'VE BEEN ACROSS THE SYSTEM TWICE AND HAVEN'T FOUND A TRACE OF THE IMPERIALS.
I THINK IT'S TIME TO CELEBRATE.
THAT'S THE PLAN, TYCHO.
WEDGE?
FOLLOW ME.

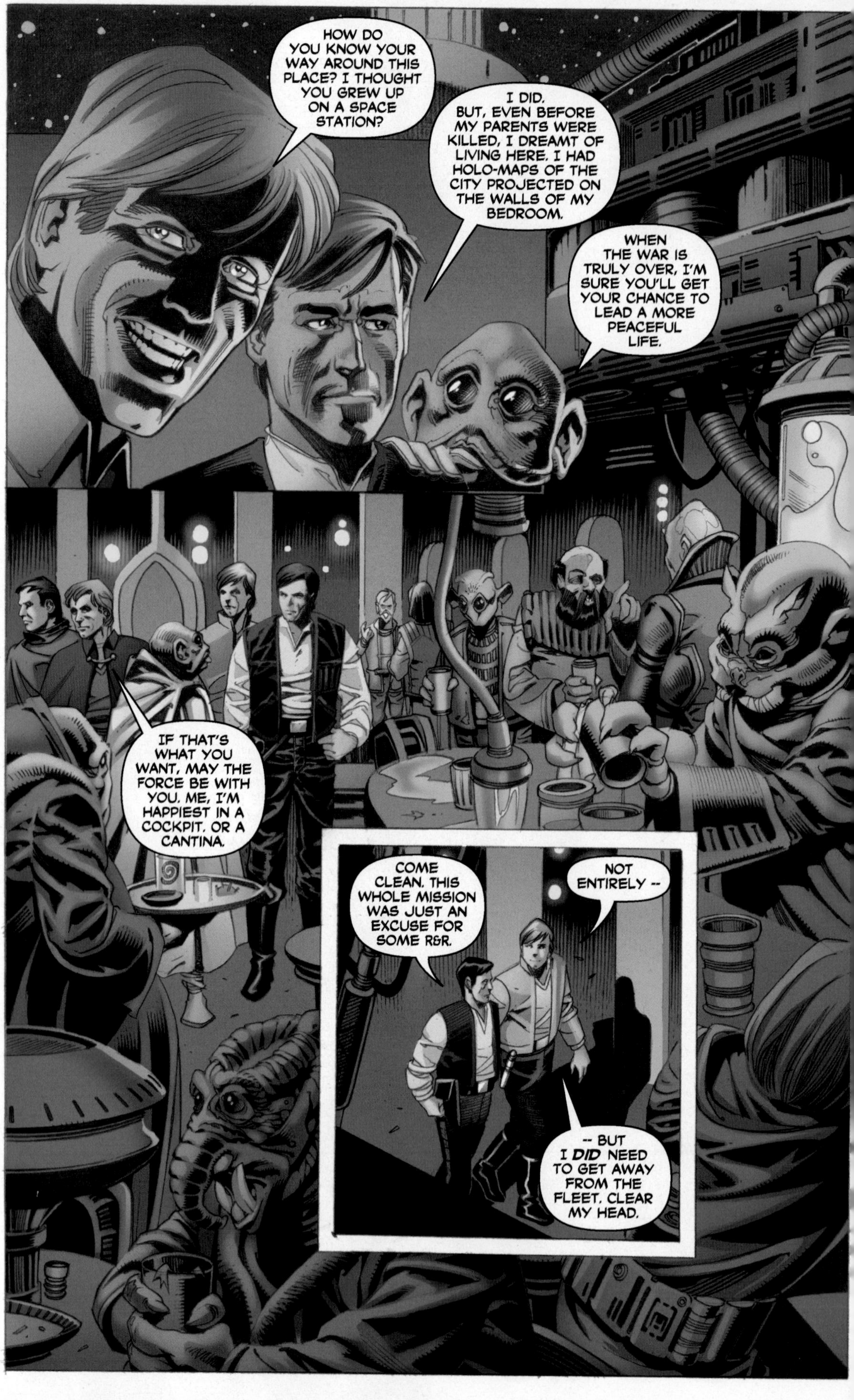
HOW DO YOU KNOW YOUR WAY AROUND THIS PLACE? I THOUGHT YOU GREW UP ON A SPACE STATION?
I DID. BUT, EVEN BEFORE MY PARENTS WERE KILLED, I DREAMT OF LIVING HERE. I HAD HOLO-MAPS OF THE CITY PROJECTED ON THE WALLS OF MY BEDROOM.
WHEN THE WAR IS TRULY OVER, I'M SURE YOU'LL GET YOUR CHANCE TO LEAD A MORE PEACEFUL LIFE.
IF THAT'S WHAT YOU WANT, MAY THE FORCE BE WITH YOU. ME, I'M HAPPIEST IN A COCKPIT. OR A CANTINA.
COME CLEAN. THIS WHOLE MISSION WAS JUST AN EXCUSE FOR SOME R&R.
NOT ENTIRELY --
-- BUT I *DID* NEED TO GET AWAY FROM THE FLEET. CLEAR MY HEAD.

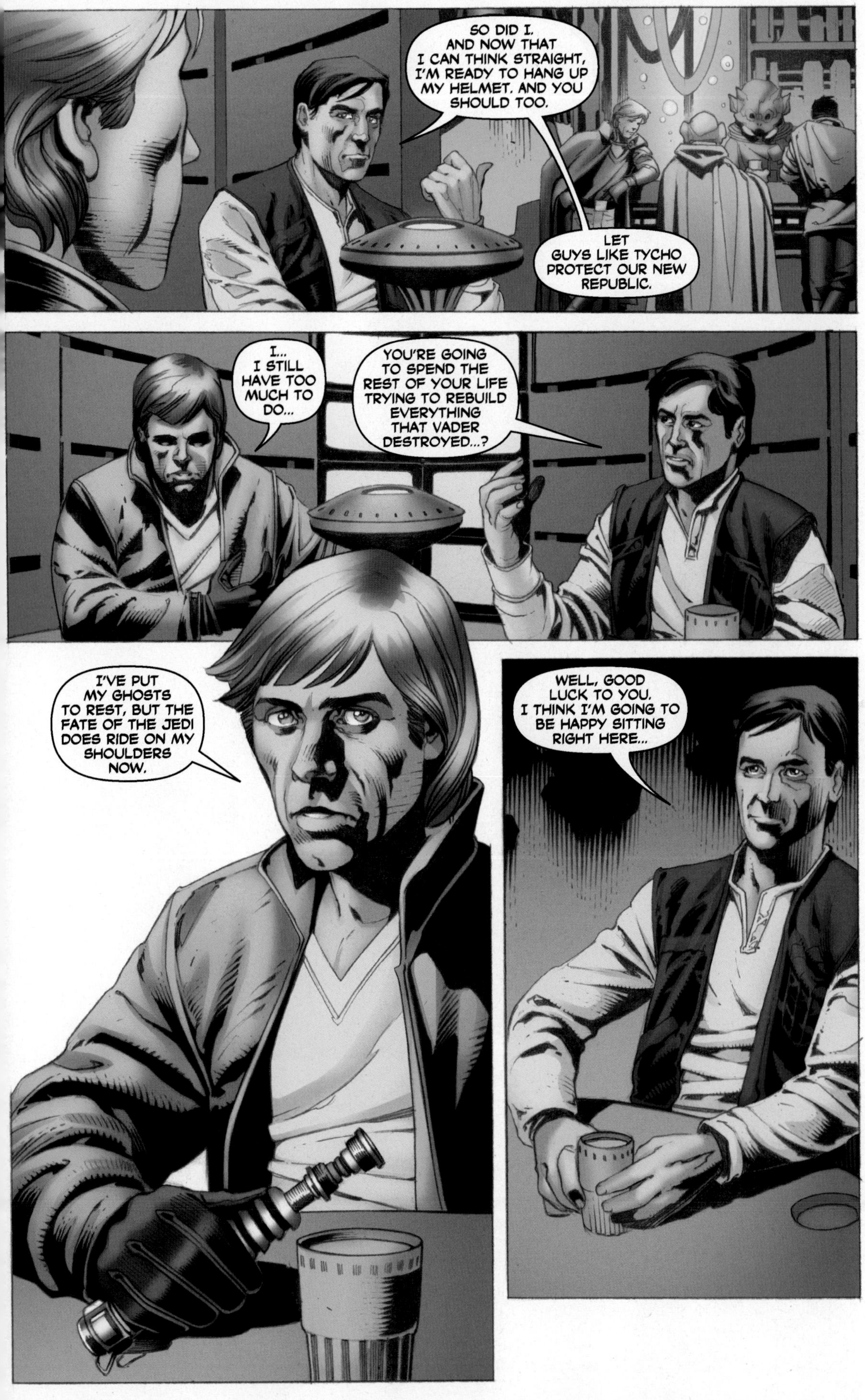
SO DID I. AND NOW THAT I CAN THINK STRAIGHT, I'M READY TO HANG UP MY HELMET. AND YOU SHOULD TOO.
LET GUYS LIKE TYCHO PROTECT OUR NEW REPUBLIC.
I... I STILL HAVE TOO MUCH TO DO...
YOU'RE GOING TO SPEND THE REST OF YOUR LIFE TRYING TO REBUILD EVERYTHING THAT VADER DESTROYED...?
I'VE PUT MY GHOSTS TO REST, BUT THE FATE OF THE JEDI DOES RIDE ON MY SHOULDERS NOW.
WELL, GOOD LUCK TO YOU. I THINK I'M GOING TO BE HAPPY SITTING RIGHT HERE...

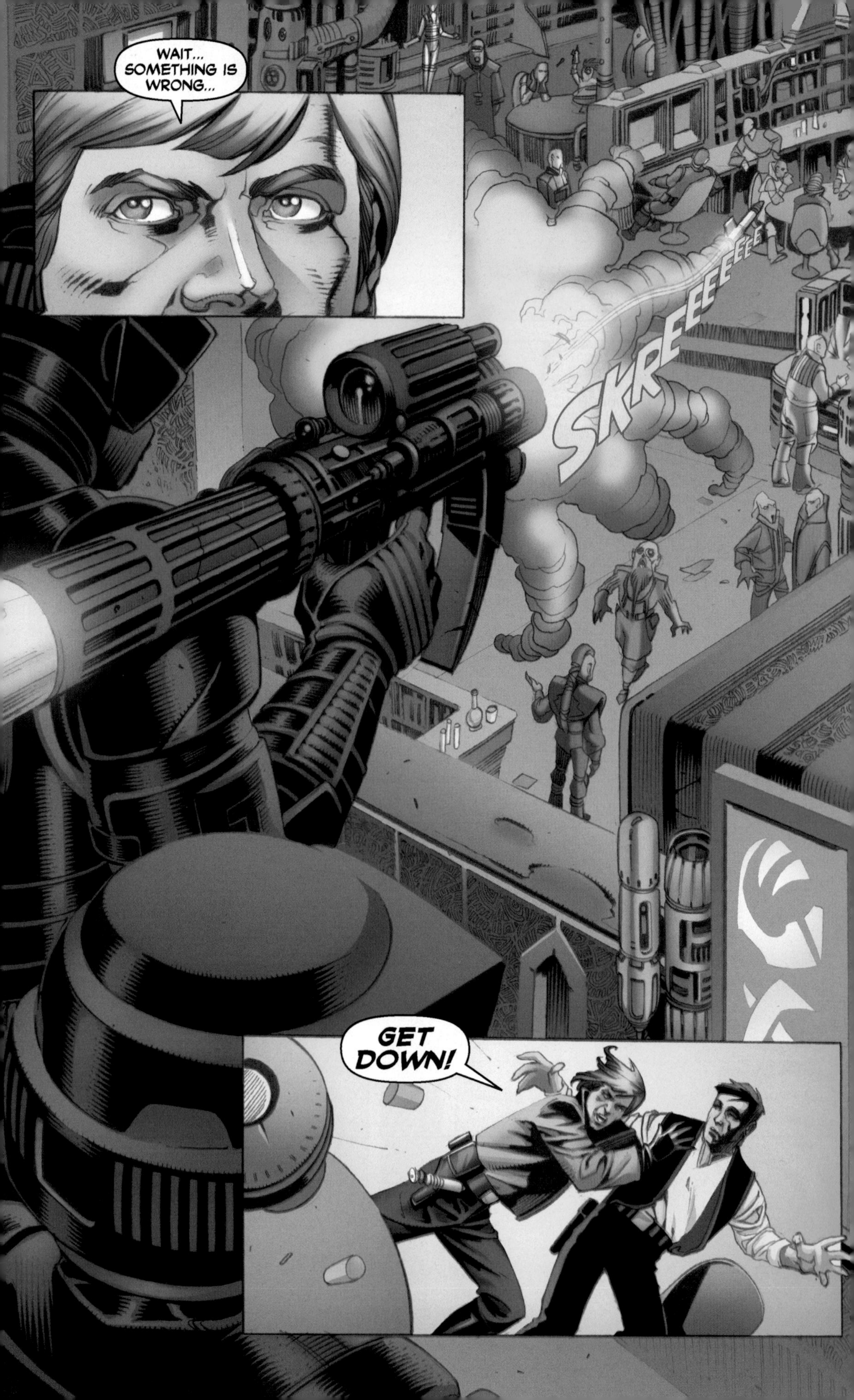
WAIT... SOMETHING IS WRONG...
SKREEEEEEE-E
GET DOWN!

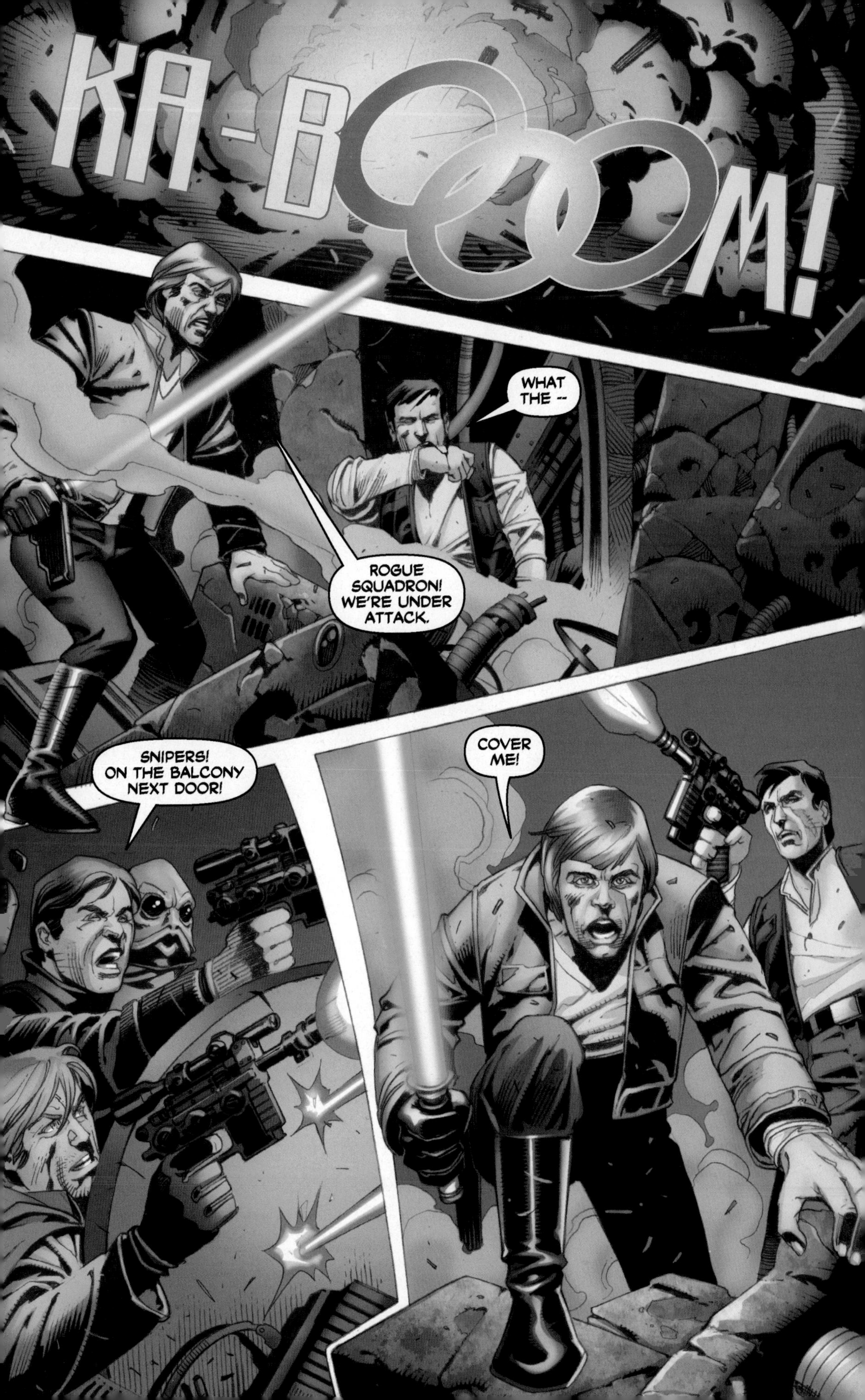
KA-BOOOM!
WHAT THE --
ROGUE SQUADRON! WE'RE UNDER ATTACK.
SNIPERS! ON THE BALCONY NEXT DOOR!
COVER ME!

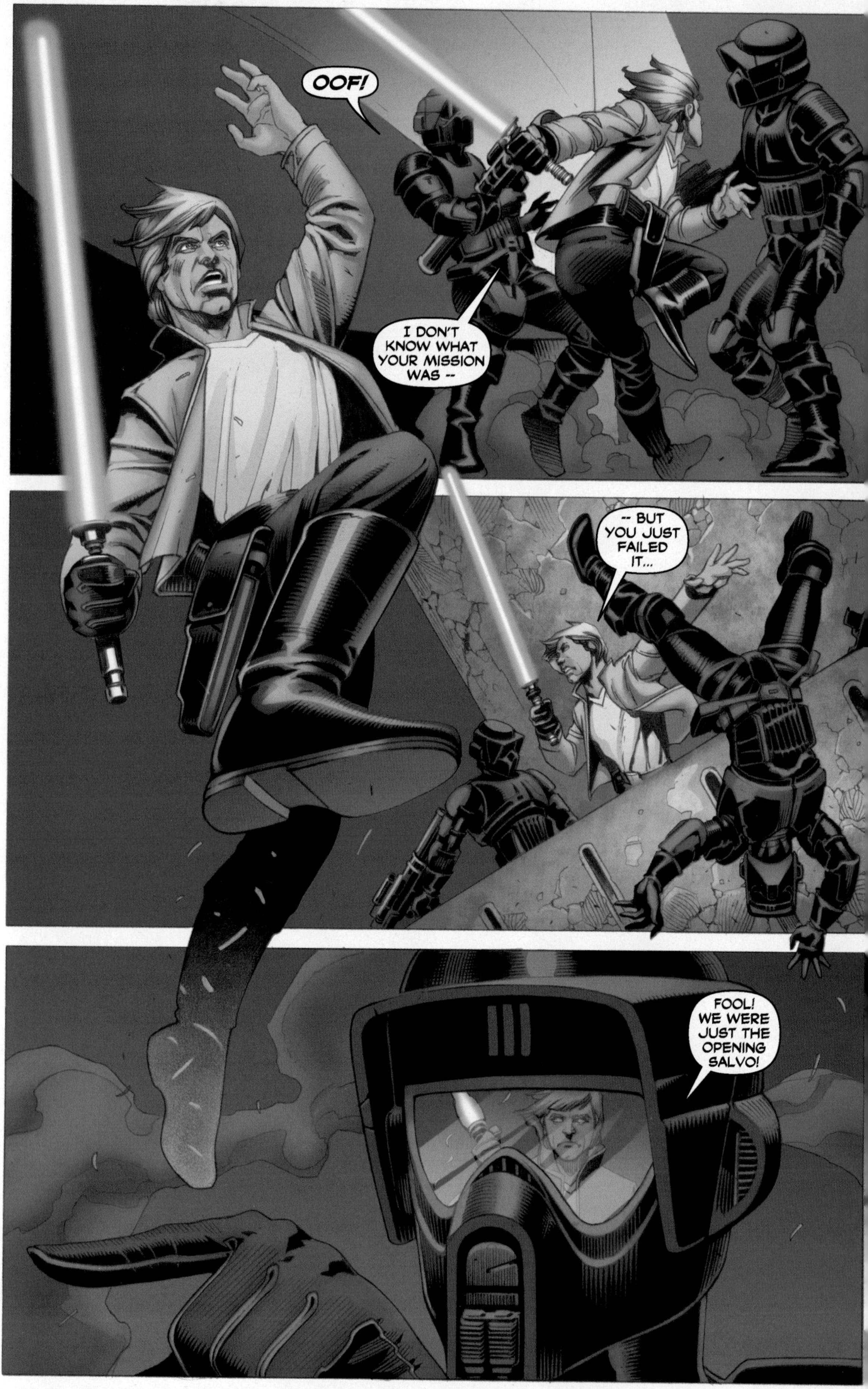
OOF!
I DON'T KNOW WHAT YOUR MISSION WAS --
-- BUT YOU JUST FAILED IT...
FOOL! WE WERE JUST THE OPENING SALVO!

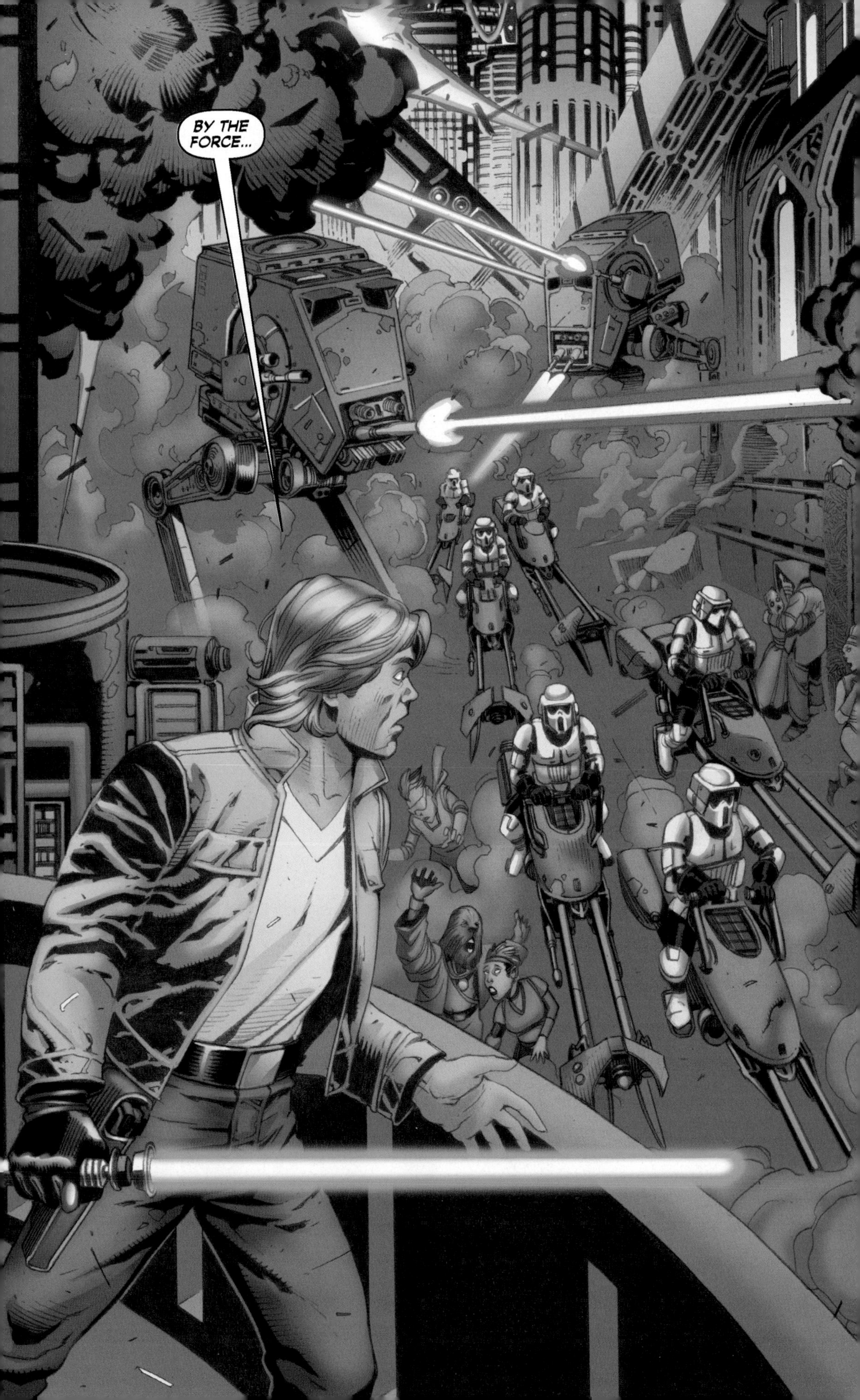
BY THE FORCE...

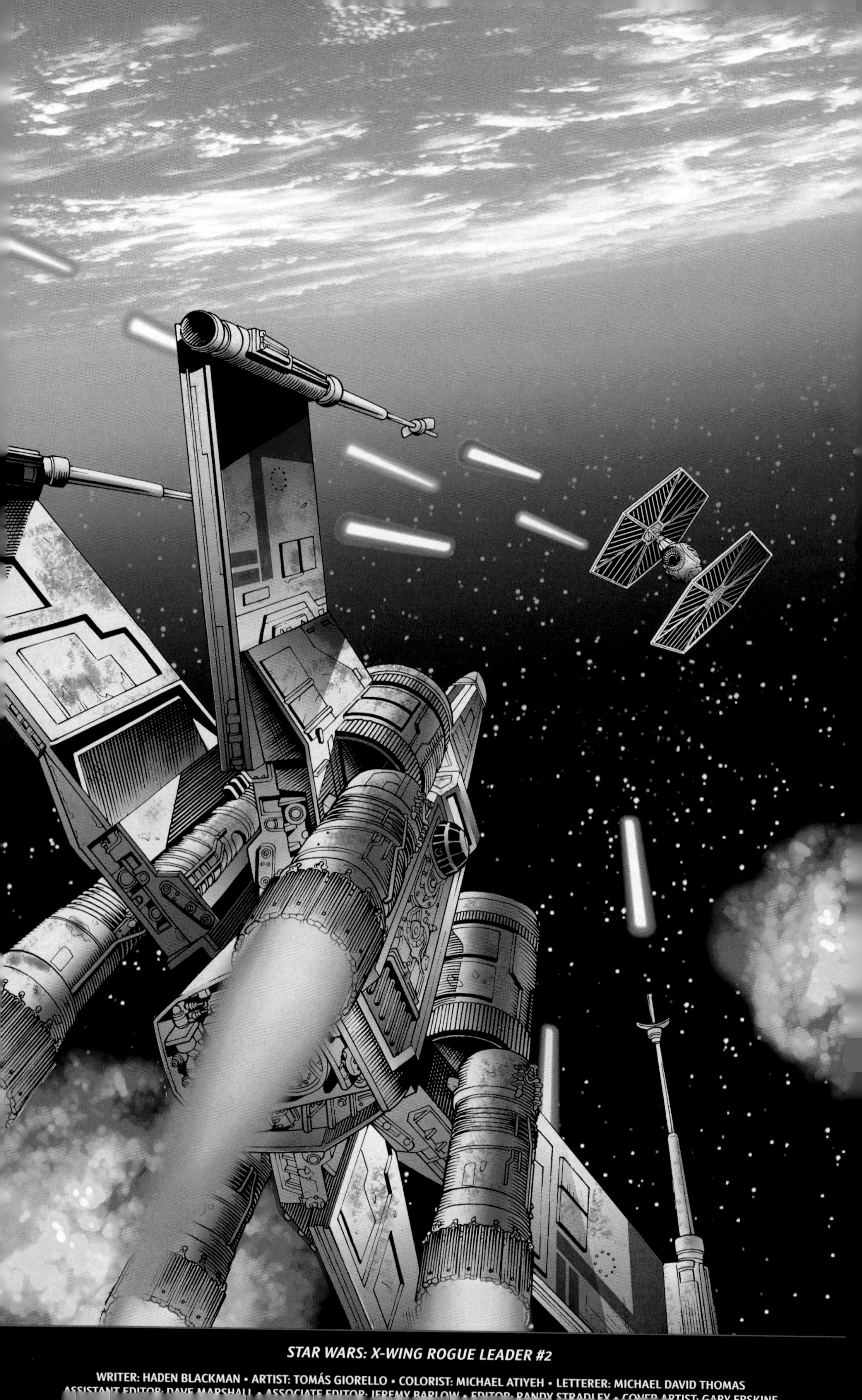

***STAR WARS: X-WING ROGUE LEADER #2***

WRITER: HADEN BLACKMAN • ARTIST: TOMÁS GIORELLO • COLORIST: MICHAEL ATIYEH • LETTERER: MICHAEL DAVID THOMAS
ASSISTANT EDITOR: DAVE MARSHALL • ASSOCIATE EDITOR: JEREMY BARLOW • EDITOR: RANDY STRADLEY • COVER ARTIST: GARY ERSKINE

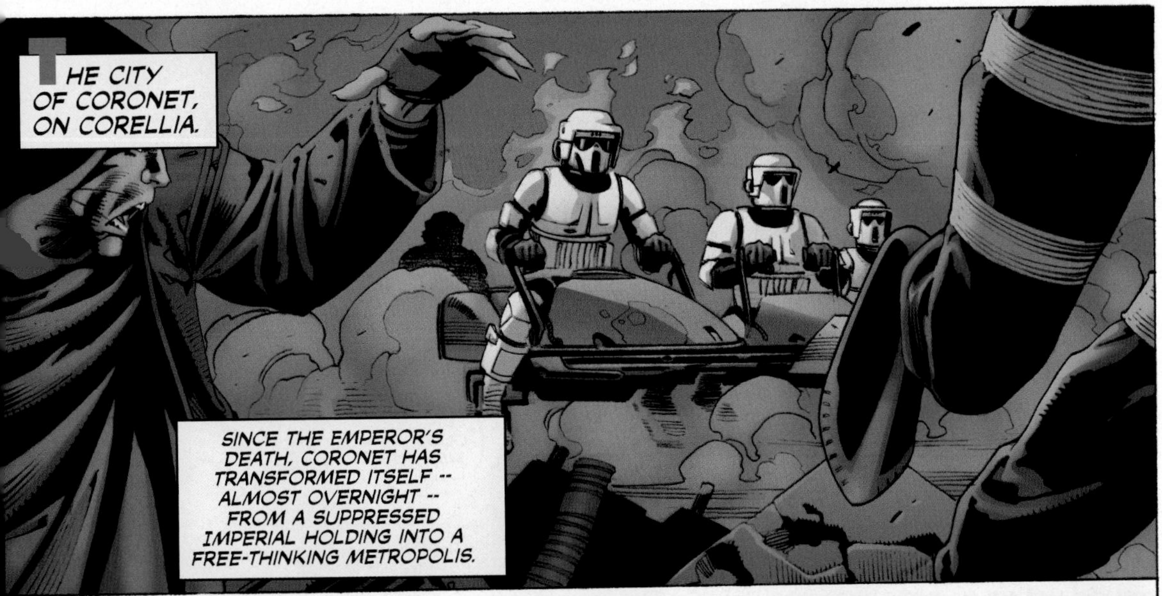
THE CITY
OF CORONET,
ON CORELLIA.
SINCE THE EMPEROR'S DEATH, CORONET HAS TRANSFORMED ITSELF -- ALMOST OVERNIGHT -- FROM A SUPPRESSED IMPERIAL HOLDING INTO A FREE-THINKING METROPOLIS.

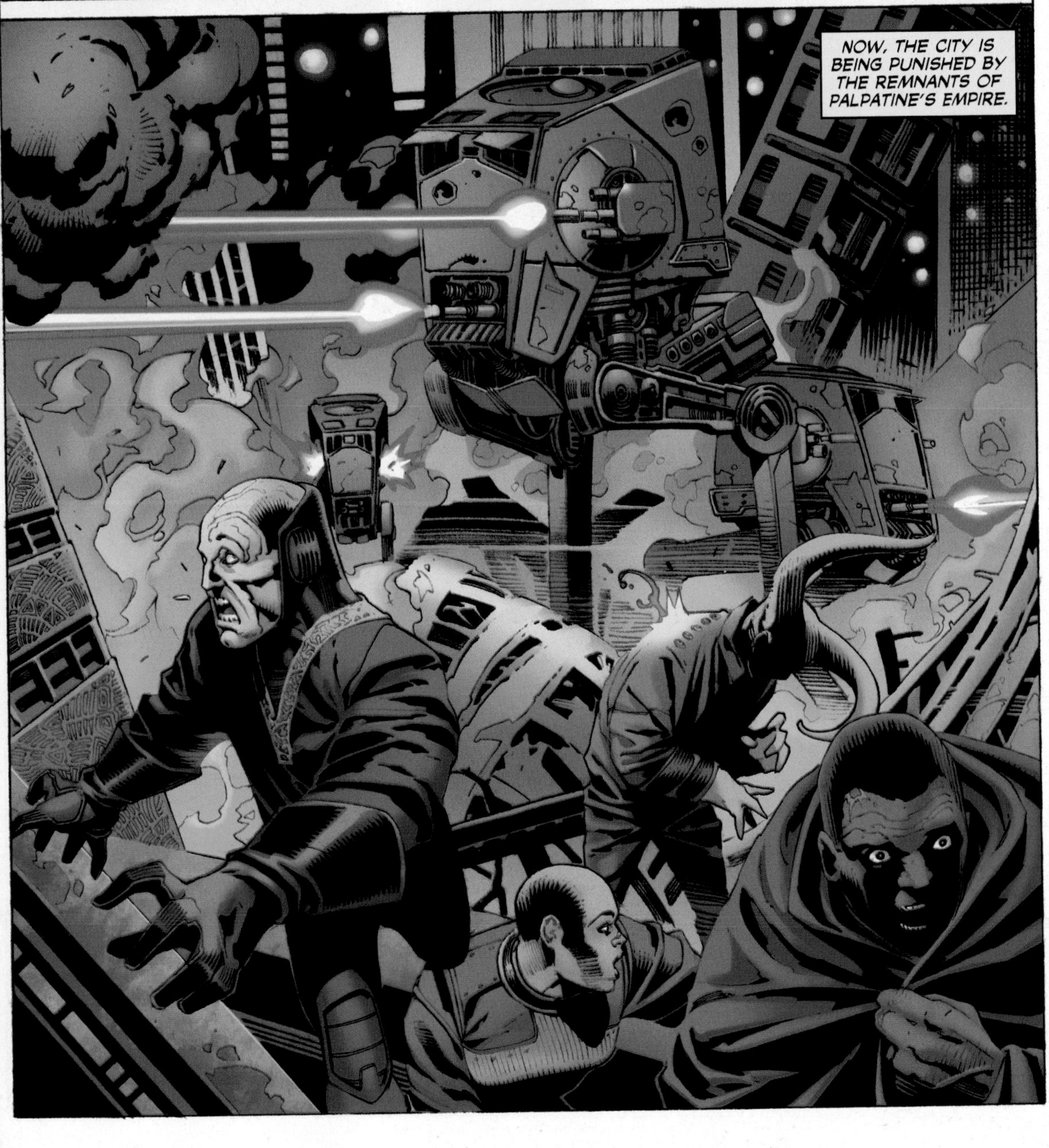
NOW, THE CITY IS BEING PUNISHED BY THE REMNANTS OF PALPATINE'S EMPIRE.

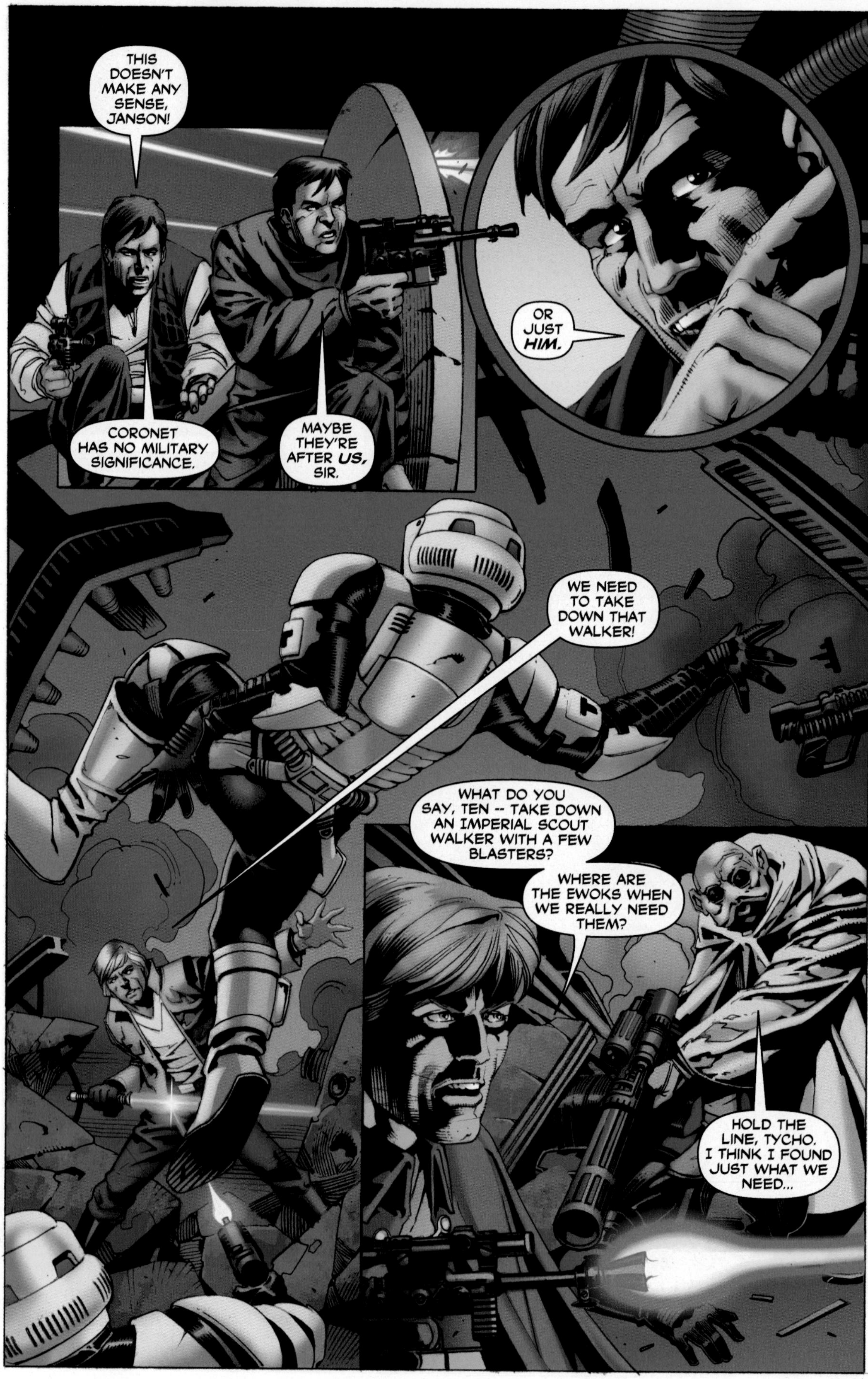
THIS DOESN'T MAKE ANY SENSE, JANSON!
CORONET HAS NO MILITARY SIGNIFICANCE.
MAYBE THEY'RE AFTER *US,* SIR.
OR JUST *HIM.*
WE NEED TO TAKE DOWN THAT WALKER!
WHAT DO YOU SAY, TEN -- TAKE DOWN AN IMPERIAL SCOUT WALKER WITH A FEW BLASTERS?
WHERE ARE THE EWOKS WHEN WE REALLY NEED THEM?
HOLD THE LINE, TYCHO. I THINK I FOUND JUST WHAT WE NEED...

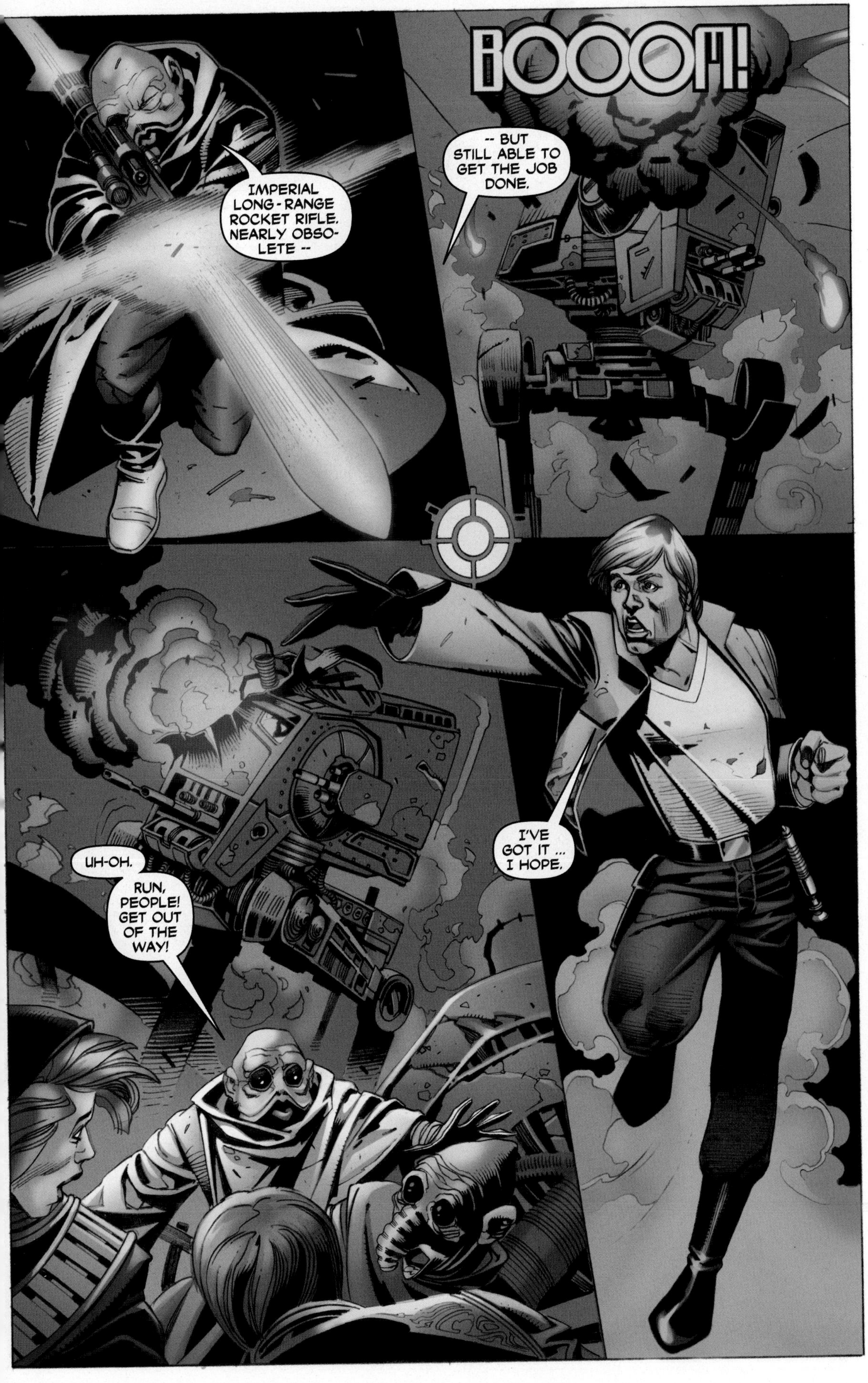
IMPERIAL LONG-RANGE ROCKET RIFLE. NEARLY OBSO-LETE --
BOOOM!
-- BUT STILL ABLE TO GET THE JOB DONE.
I'VE GOT IT ... I HOPE.
UH-OH.
RUN, PEOPLE! GET OUT OF THE WAY!

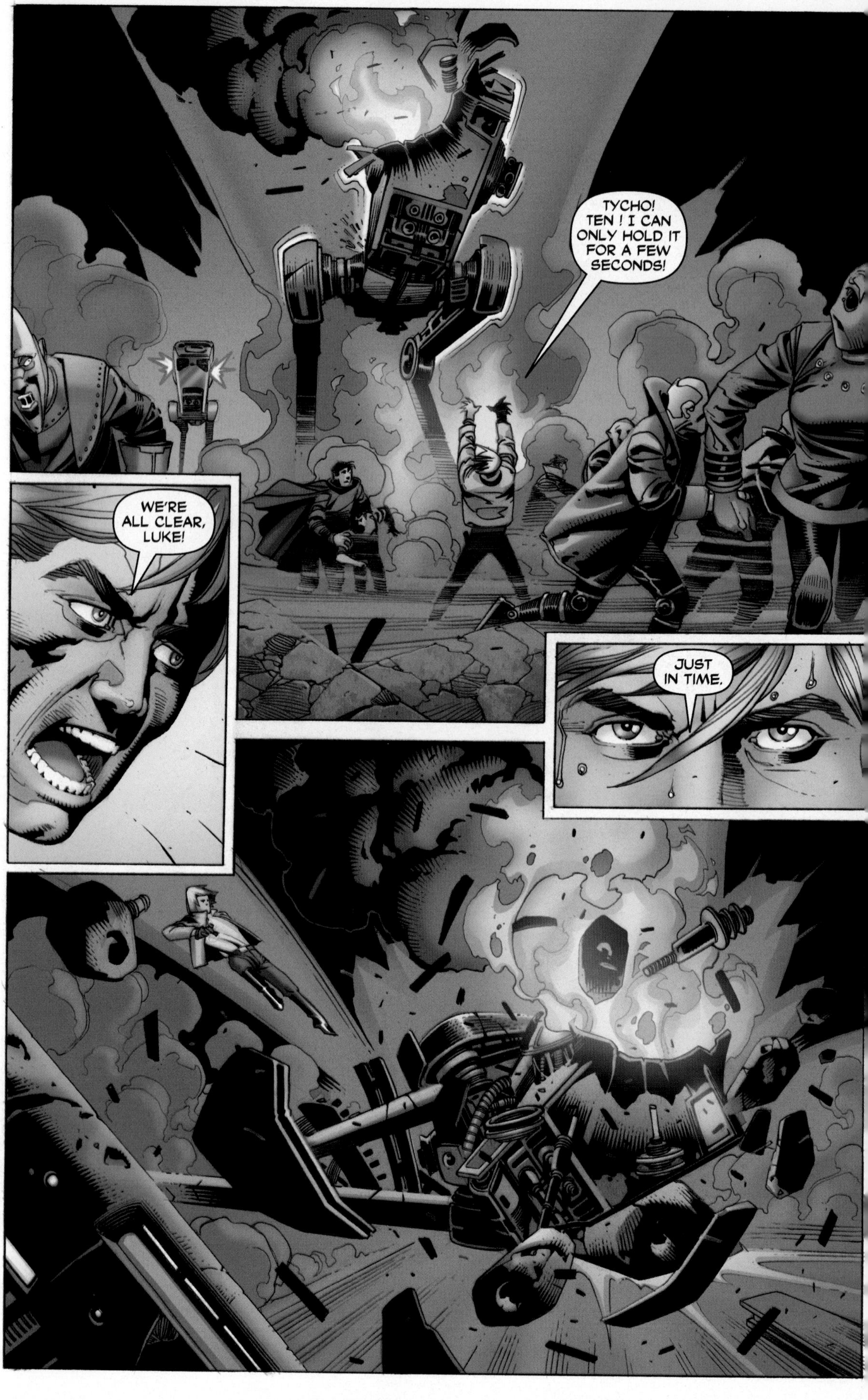
TYCHO! TEN ! I CAN ONLY HOLD IT FOR A FEW SECONDS!
WE'RE ALL CLEAR, LUKE!
JUST IN TIME.

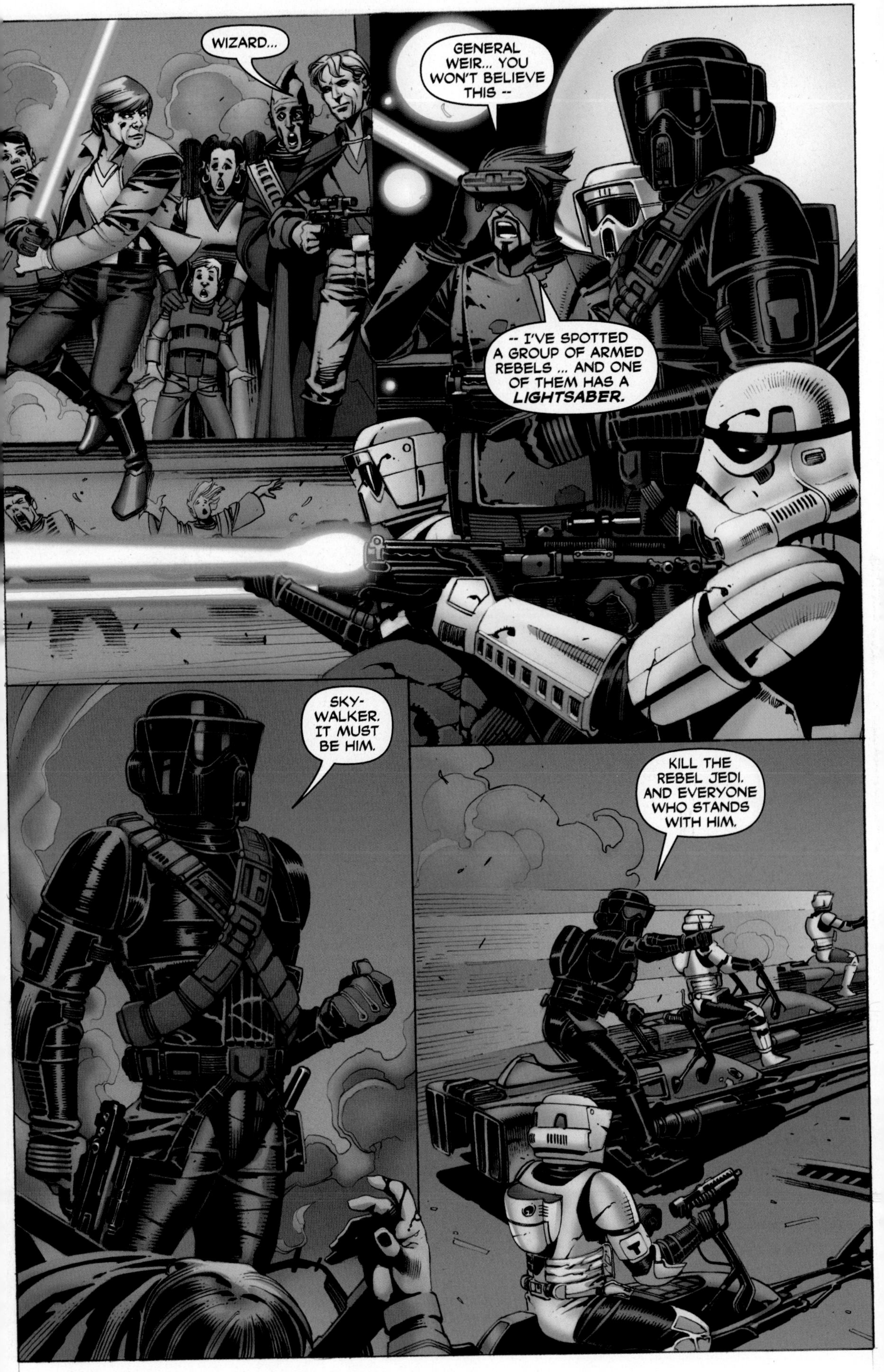
WIZARD...
GENERAL WEIR... YOU WON'T BELIEVE THIS --
-- I'VE SPOTTED A GROUP OF ARMED REBELS ... AND ONE OF THEM HAS A LIGHTSABER.
SKY-WALKER. IT MUST BE HIM.
KILL THE REBEL JEDI. AND EVERYONE WHO STANDS WITH HIM.

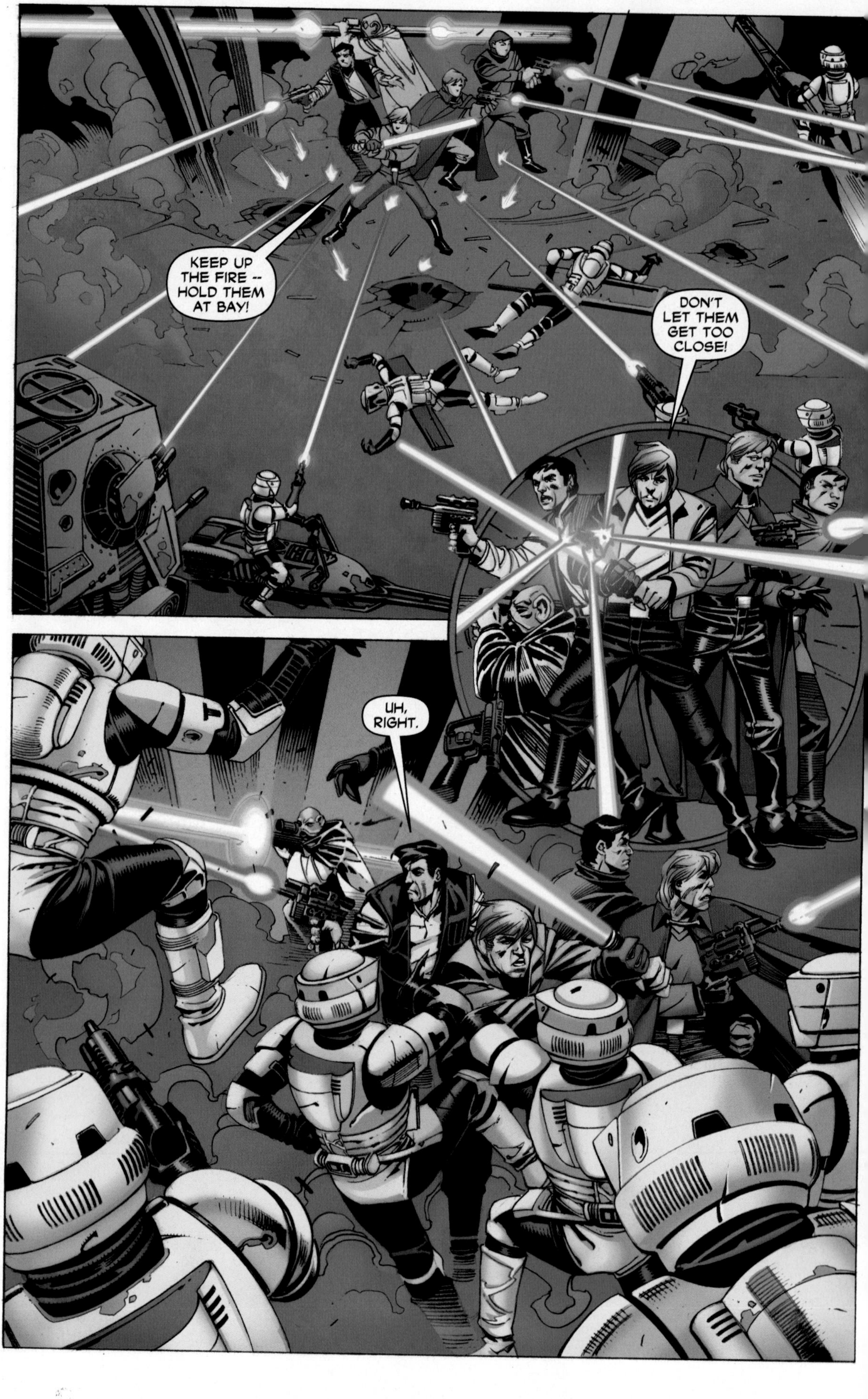
KEEP UP THE FIRE -- HOLD THEM AT BAY!
DON'T LET THEM GET TOO CLOSE!
UH, RIGHT.

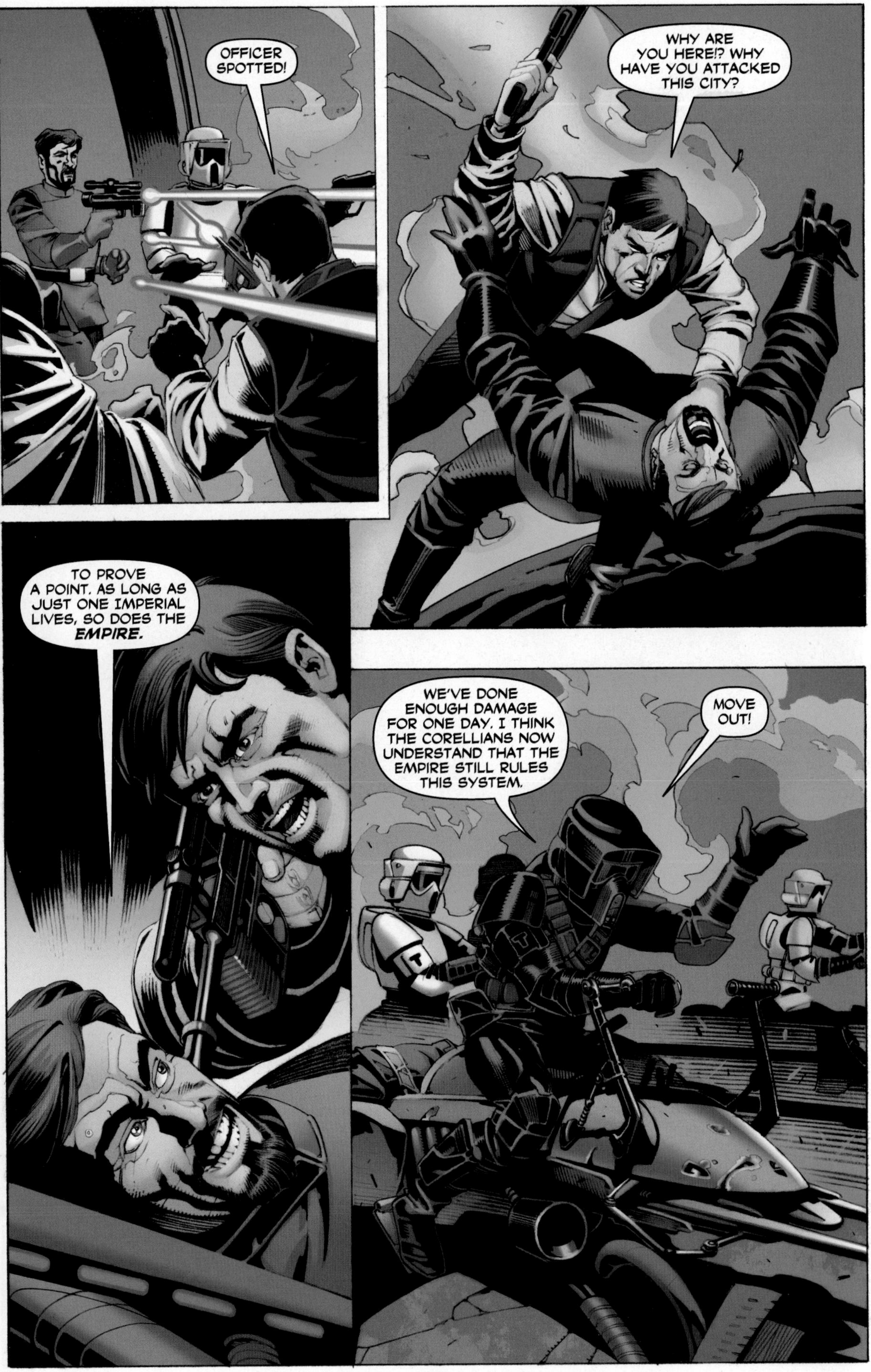
OFFICER SPOTTED!
WHY ARE YOU HERE!? WHY HAVE YOU ATTACKED THIS CITY?
TO PROVE A POINT. AS LONG AS JUST ONE IMPERIAL LIVES, SO DOES THE *EMPIRE.*
WE'VE DONE ENOUGH DAMAGE FOR ONE DAY. I THINK THE CORELLIANS NOW UNDERSTAND THAT THE EMPIRE STILL RULES THIS SYSTEM.
MOVE OUT!

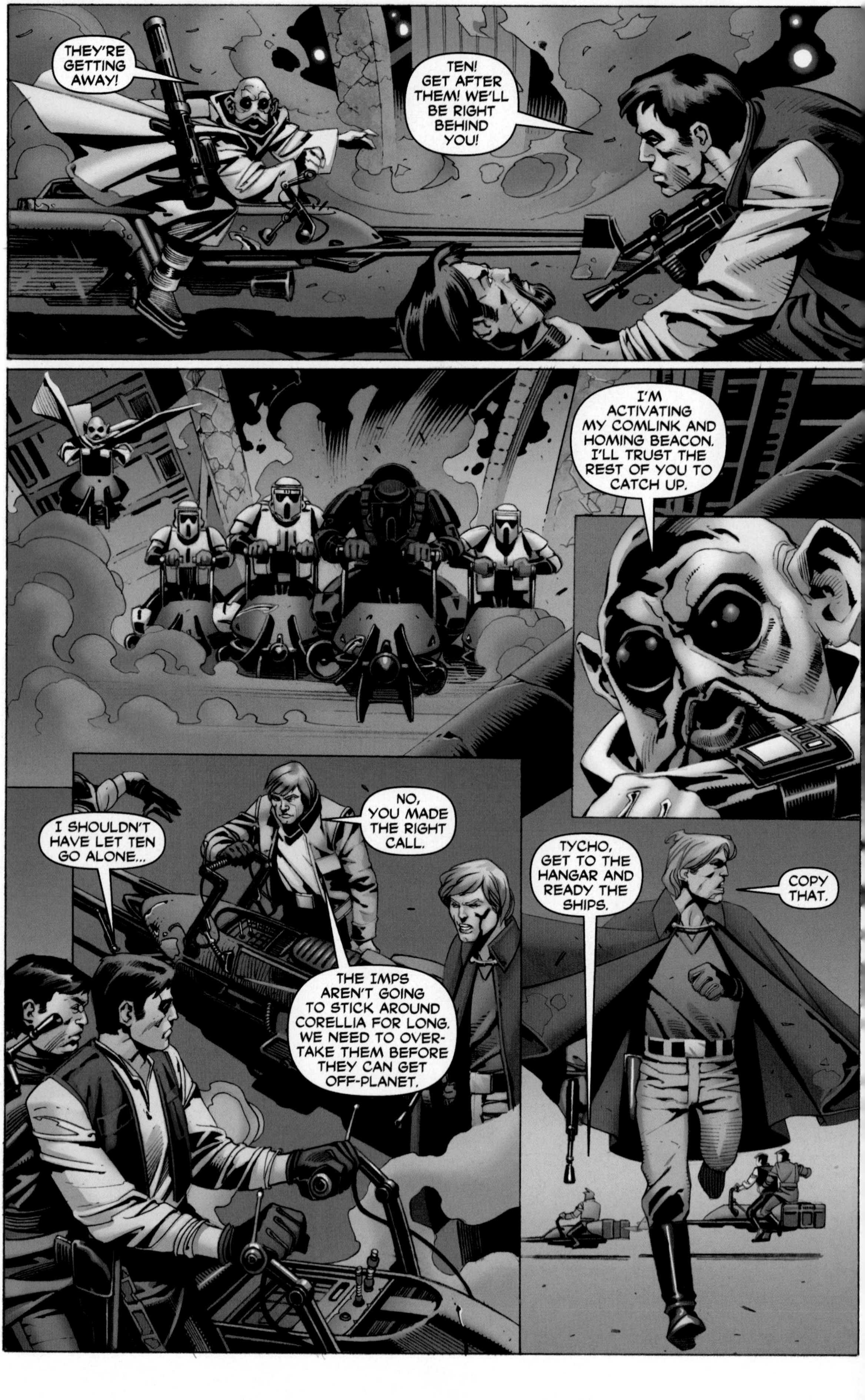
THEY'RE GETTING AWAY!
TEN! GET AFTER THEM! WE'LL BE RIGHT BEHIND YOU!
I'M ACTIVATING MY COMLINK AND HOMING BEACON. I'LL TRUST THE REST OF YOU TO CATCH UP.
I SHOULDN'T HAVE LET TEN GO ALONE...
NO, YOU MADE THE RIGHT CALL.
THE IMPS AREN'T GOING TO STICK AROUND CORELLIA FOR LONG. WE NEED TO OVER-TAKE THEM BEFORE THEY CAN GET OFF-PLANET.
TYCHO, GET TO THE HANGAR AND READY THE SHIPS.
COPY THAT.

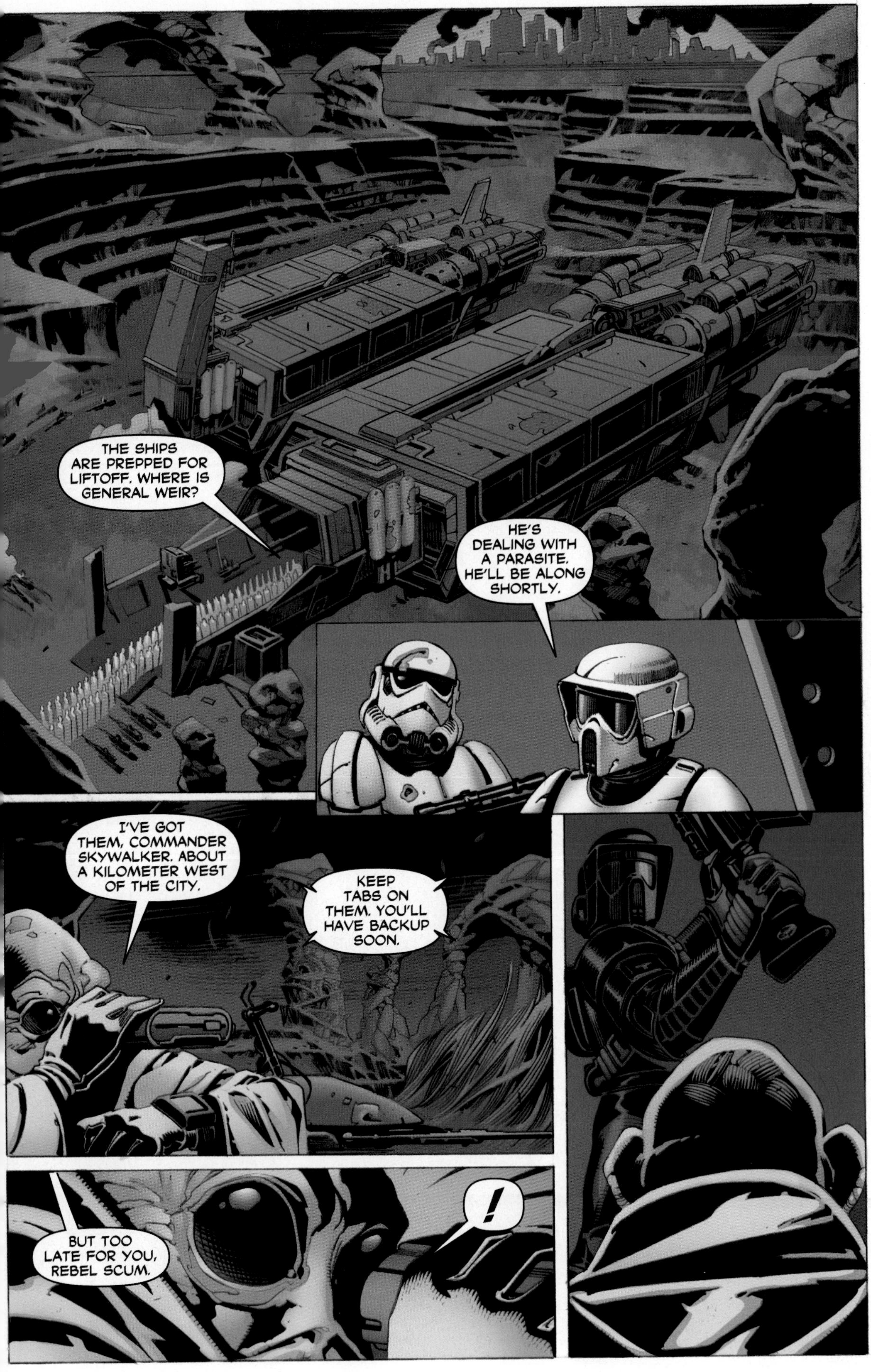
THE SHIPS ARE PREPPED FOR LIFTOFF. WHERE IS GENERAL WEIR?
HE'S DEALING WITH A PARASITE. HE'LL BE ALONG SHORTLY.
I'VE GOT THEM, COMMANDER SKYWALKER. ABOUT A KILOMETER WEST OF THE CITY.
KEEP TABS ON THEM. YOU'LL HAVE BACKUP SOON.
BUT TOO LATE FOR YOU, REBEL SCUM.
!

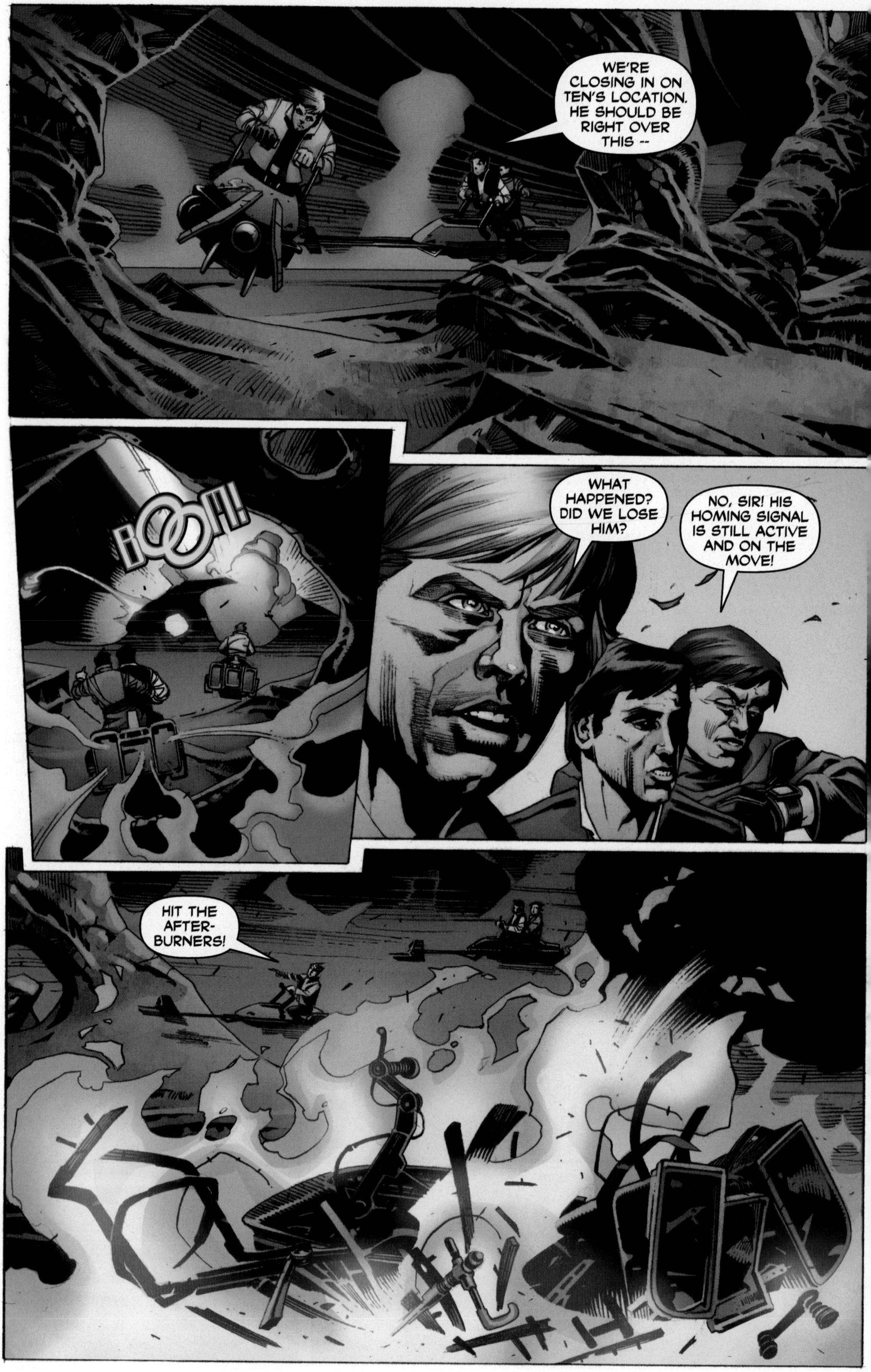
WE'RE CLOSING IN ON TEN'S LOCATION. HE SHOULD BE RIGHT OVER THIS --
BOOM!
WHAT HAPPENED? DID WE LOSE HIM?
NO, SIR! HIS HOMING SIGNAL IS STILL ACTIVE AND ON THE MOVE!
HIT THE AFTER-BURNERS!

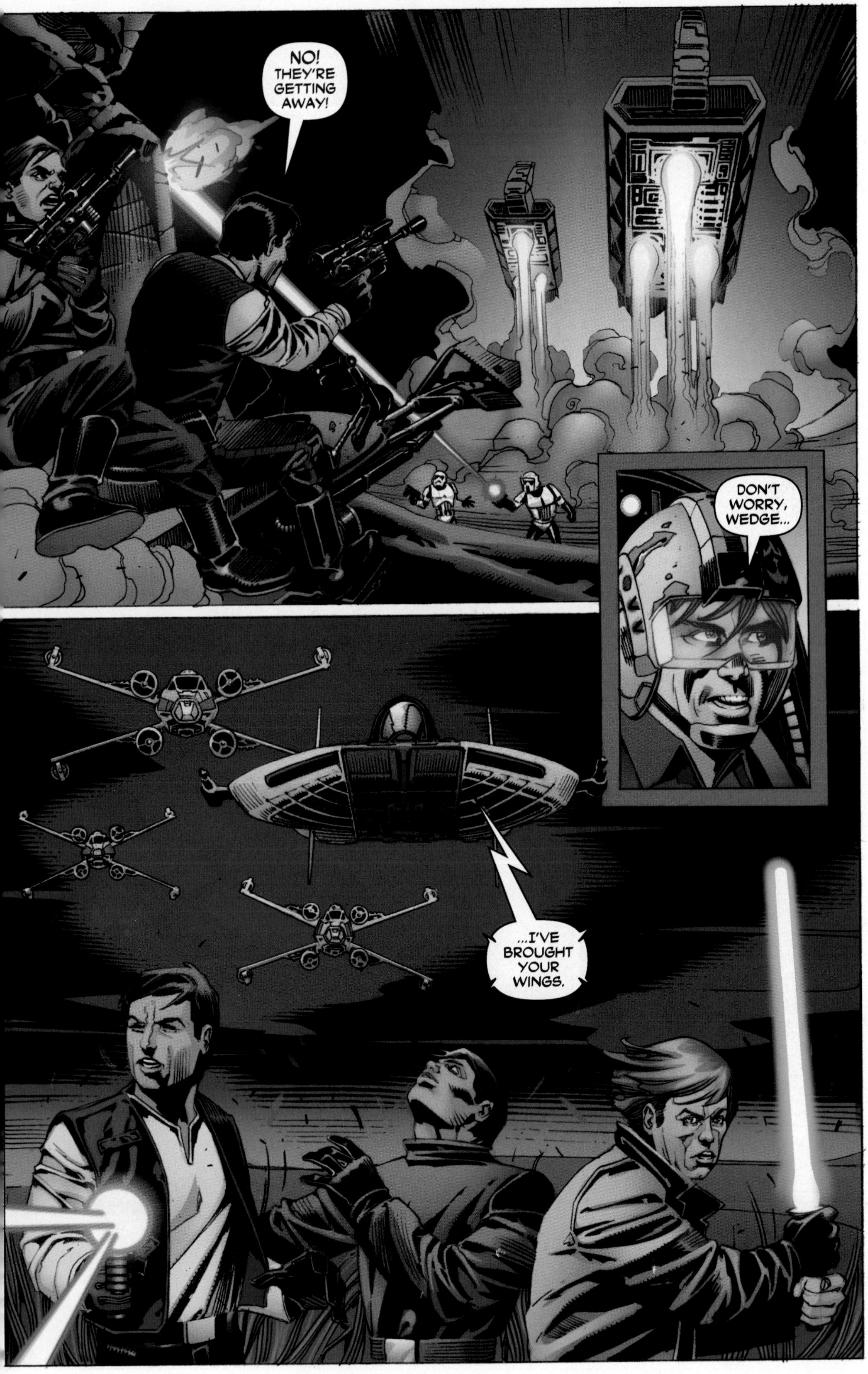
NO! THEY'RE GETTING AWAY!
DON'T WORRY, WEDGE...
...I'VE BROUGHT YOUR WINGS.

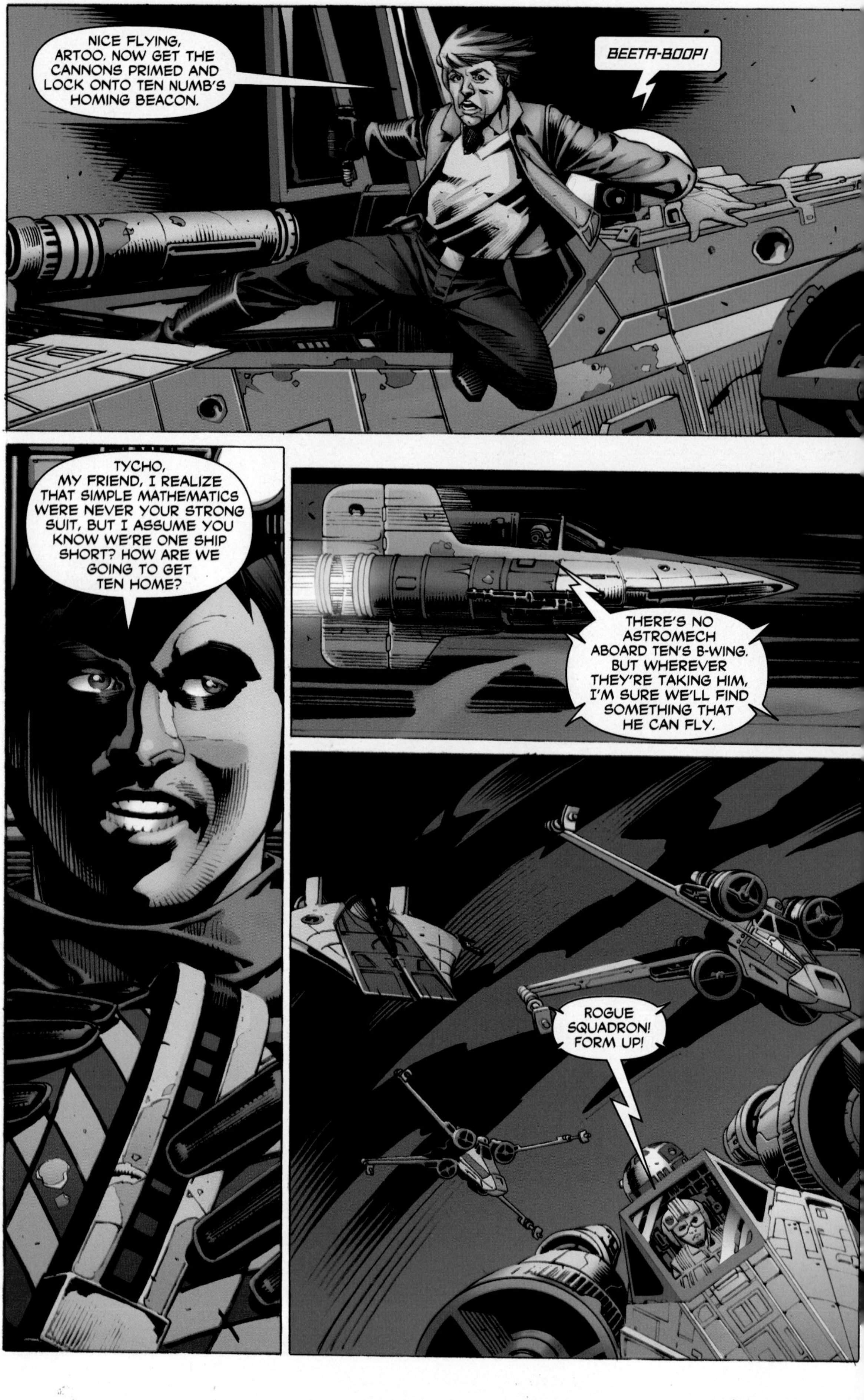
NICE FLYING, ARTOO. NOW GET THE CANNONS PRIMED AND LOCK ONTO TEN NUMB'S HOMING BEACON.
BEETA-BOOP!
TYCHO, MY FRIEND, I REALIZE THAT SIMPLE MATHEMATICS WERE NEVER YOUR STRONG SUIT, BUT I ASSUME YOU KNOW WE'RE ONE SHIP SHORT? HOW ARE WE GOING TO GET TEN HOME?
THERE'S NO ASTROMECH ABOARD TEN'S B-WING. BUT WHEREVER THEY'RE TAKING HIM, I'M SURE WE'LL FIND SOMETHING THAT HE CAN FLY.
ROGUE SQUADRON! FORM UP!

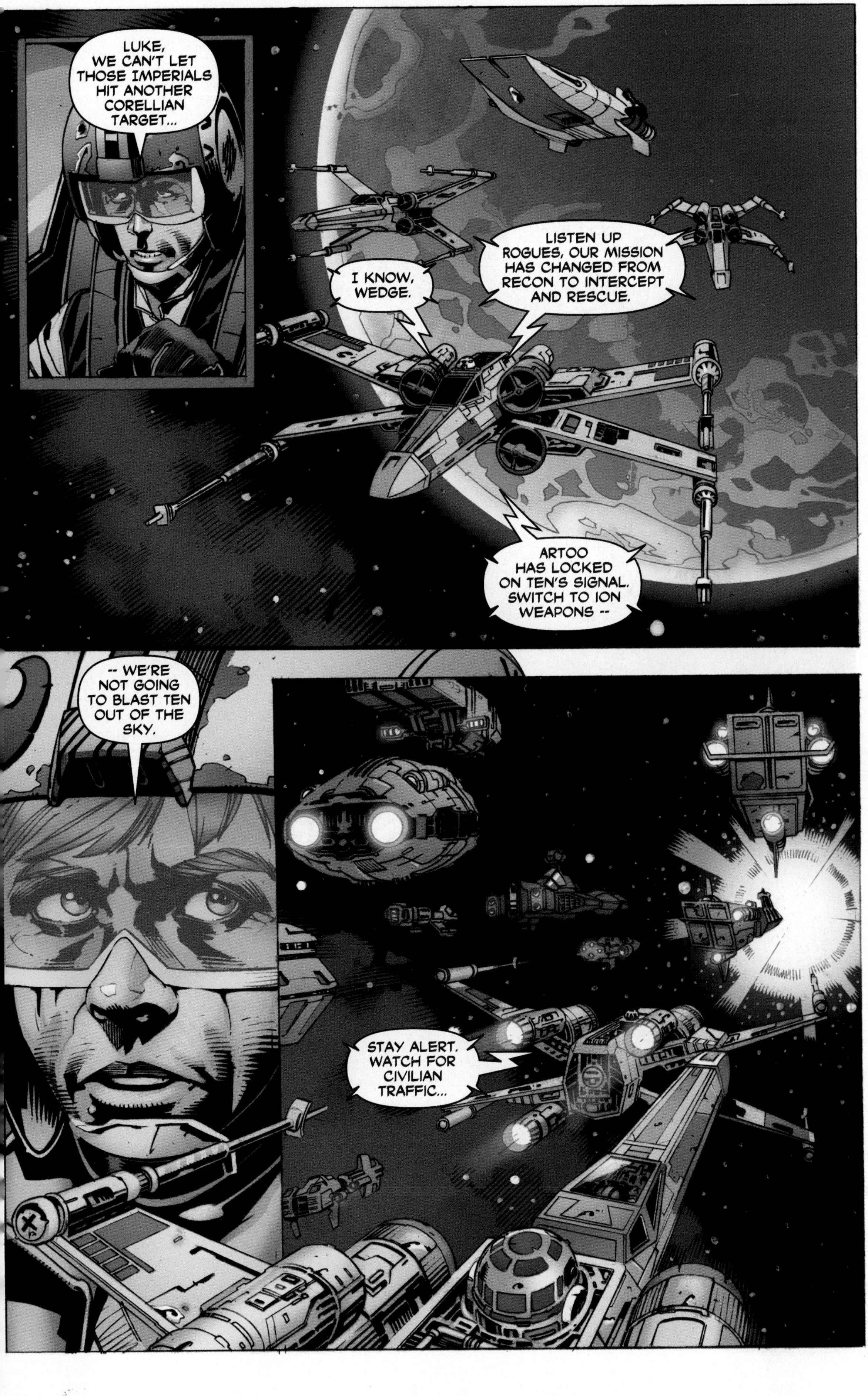
LUKE, WE CAN'T LET THOSE IMPERIALS HIT ANOTHER CORELLIAN TARGET...
I KNOW, WEDGE.
LISTEN UP ROGUES, OUR MISSION HAS CHANGED FROM RECON TO INTERCEPT AND RESCUE.
ARTOO HAS LOCKED ON TEN'S SIGNAL. SWITCH TO ION WEAPONS --
-- WE'RE NOT GOING TO BLAST TEN OUT OF THE SKY.
STAY ALERT. WATCH FOR CIVILIAN TRAFFIC...

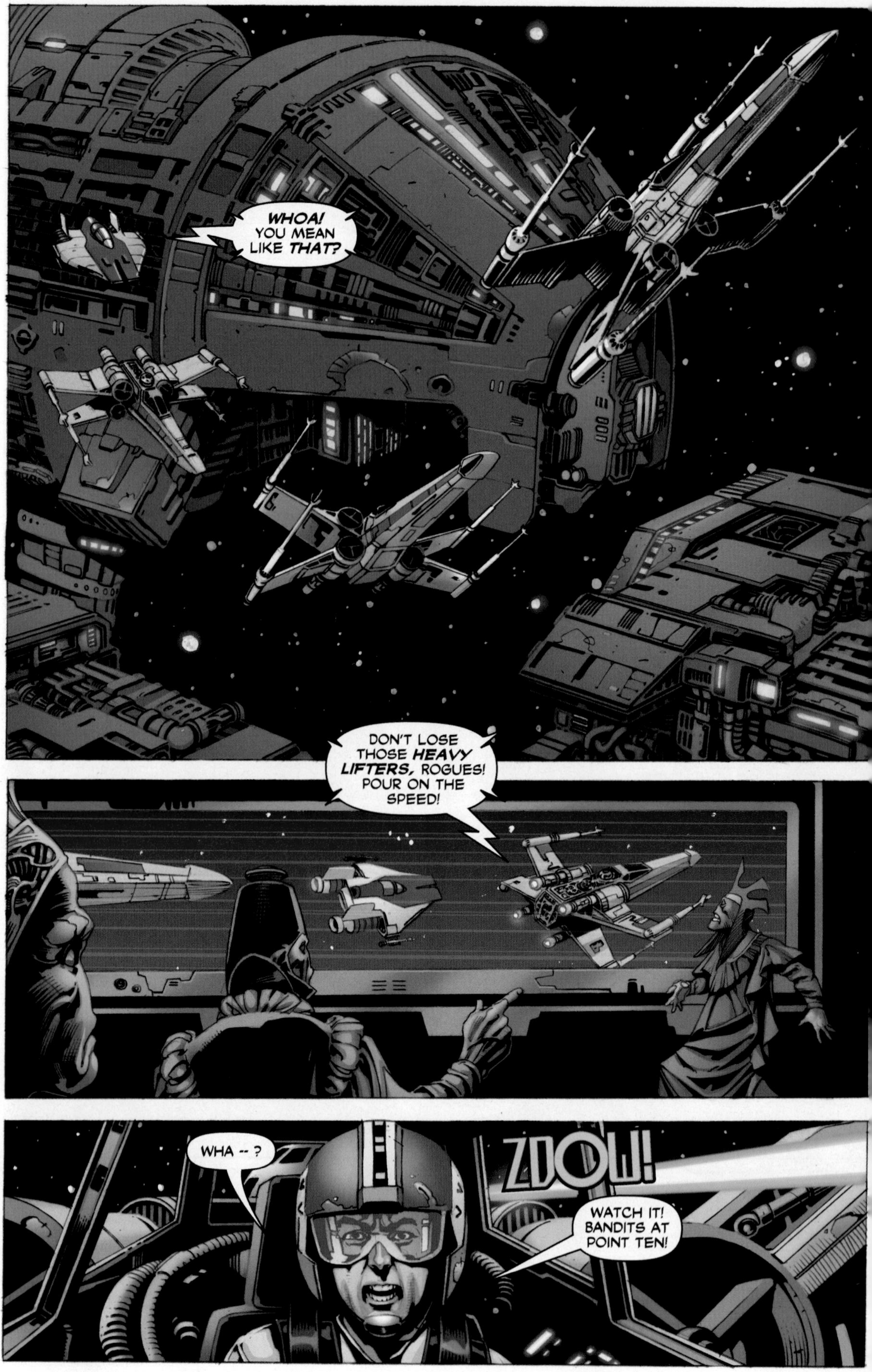
WHOA! YOU MEAN LIKE THAT?
DON'T LOSE THOSE HEAVY LIFTERS, ROGUES! POUR ON THE SPEED!
WHA -- ?
ZDOW!
WATCH IT! BANDITS AT POINT TEN!

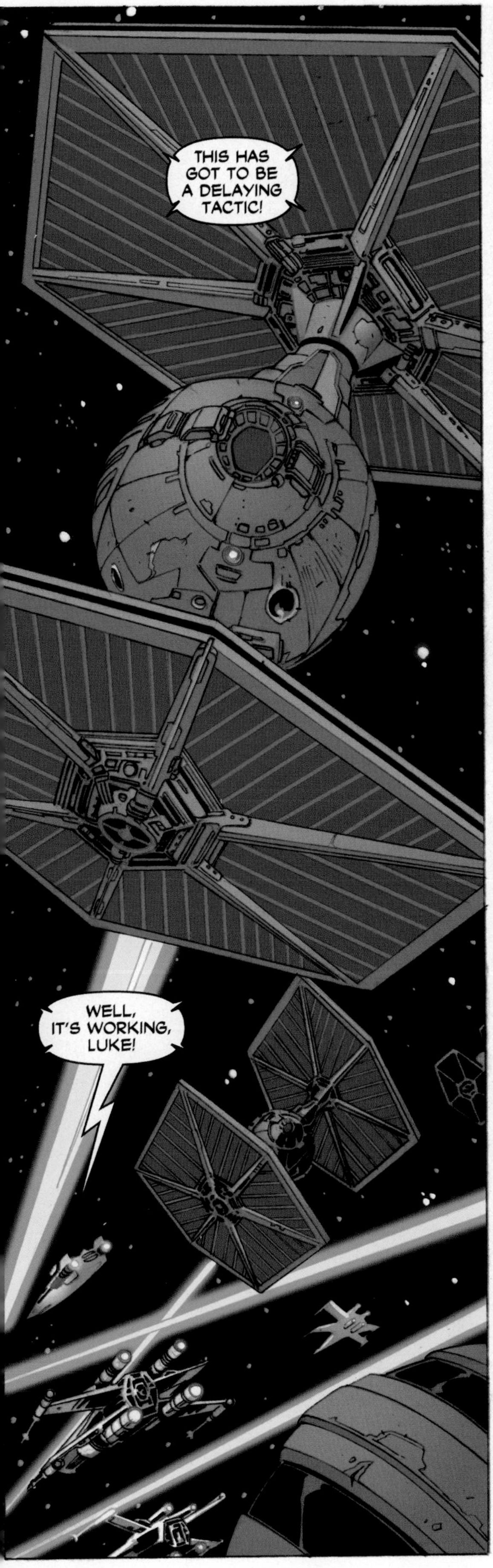
THIS HAS GOT TO BE A DELAYING TACTIC!
WELL, IT'S WORKING, LUKE!

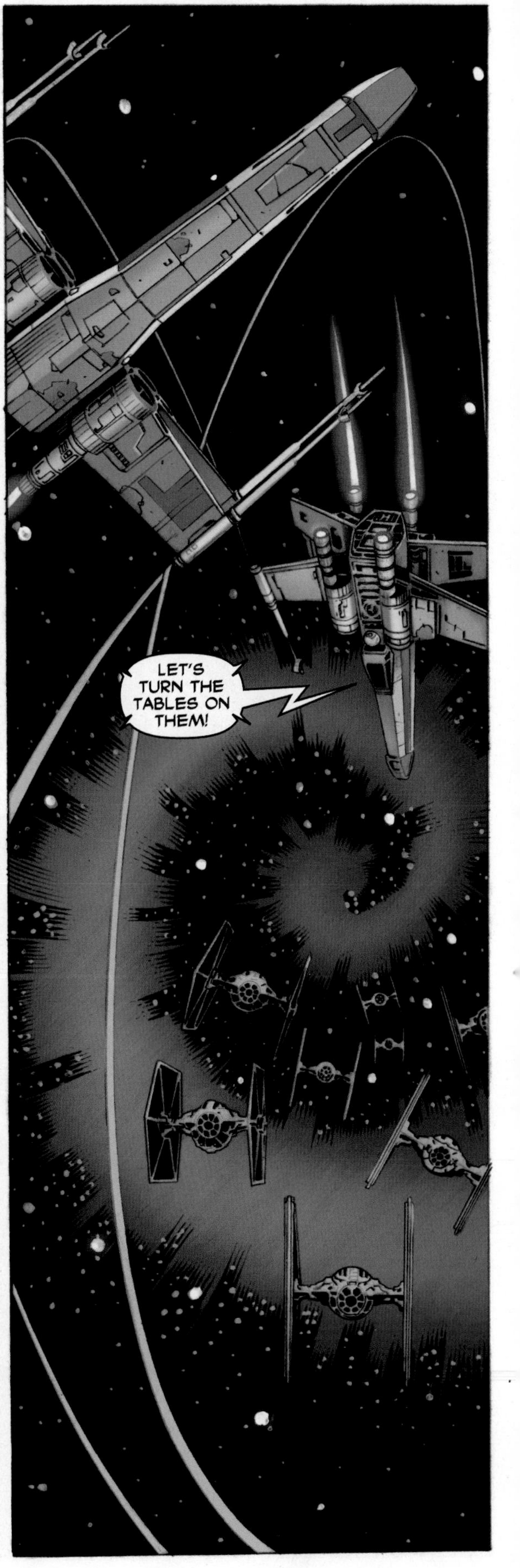
LET'S TURN THE TABLES ON THEM!

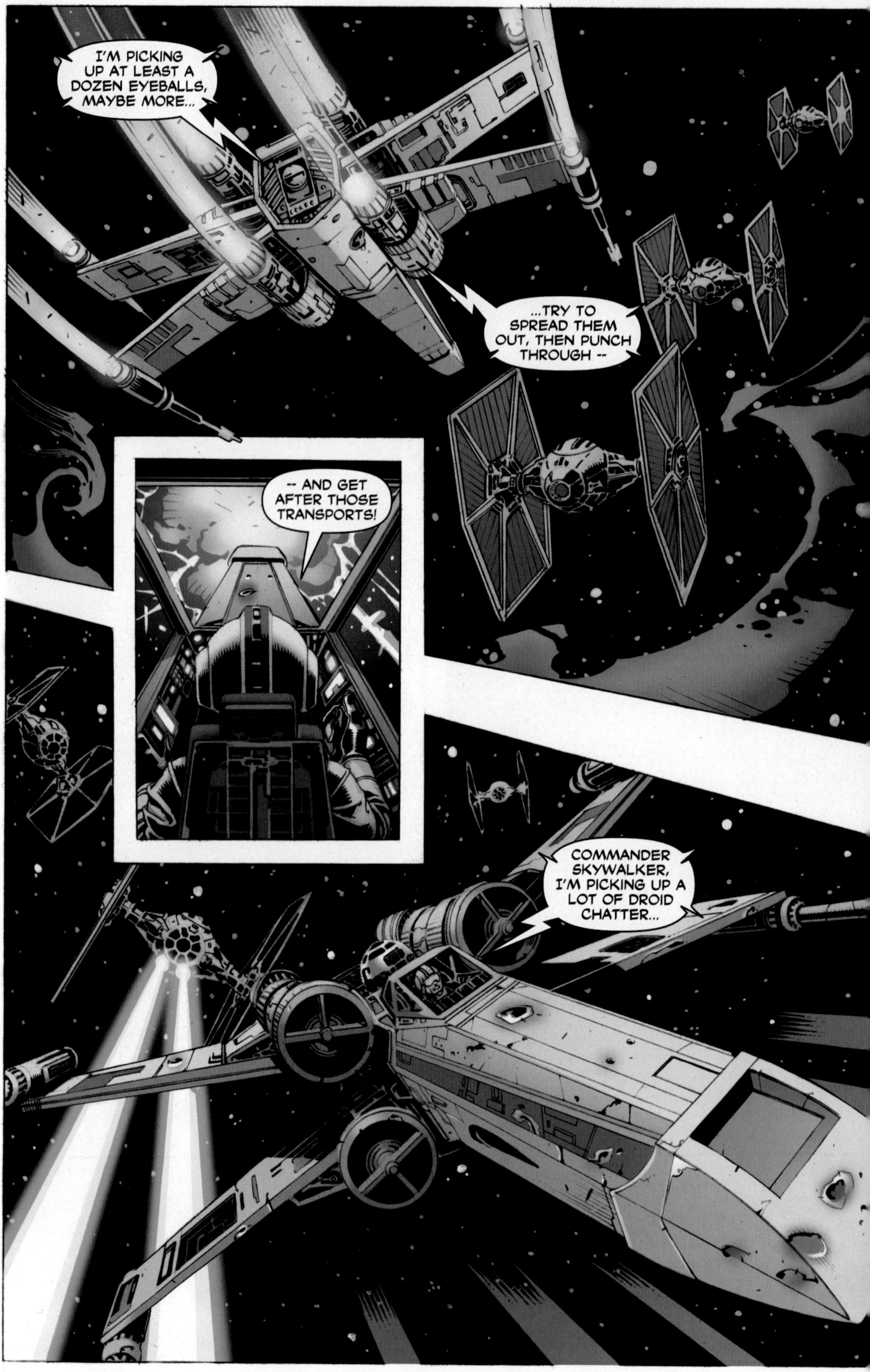
I'M PICKING UP AT LEAST A DOZEN EYEBALLS, MAYBE MORE...
...TRY TO SPREAD THEM OUT, THEN PUNCH THROUGH --
-- AND GET AFTER THOSE TRANSPORTS!
COMMANDER SKYWALKER, I'M PICKING UP A LOT OF DROID CHATTER...

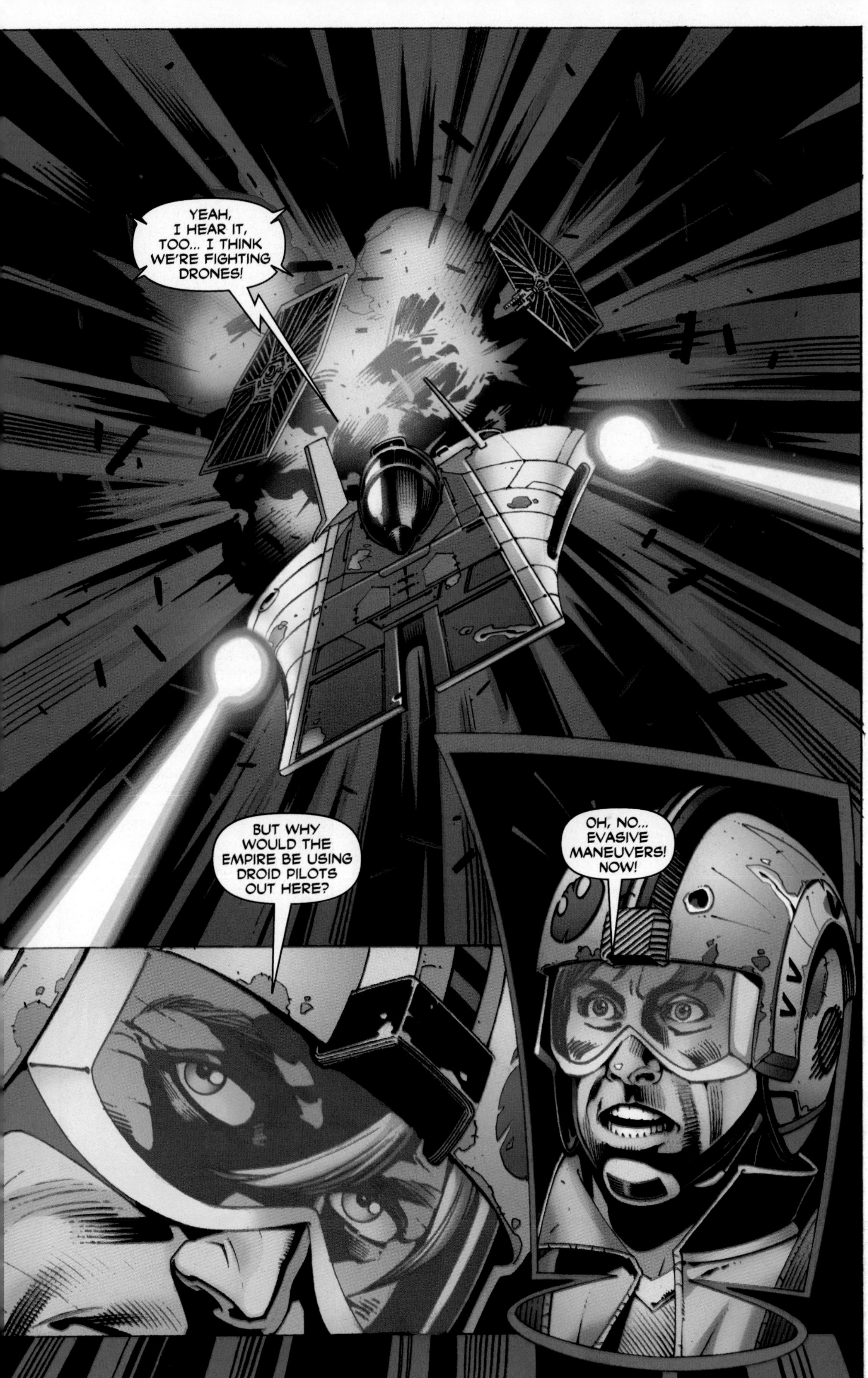
YEAH, I HEAR IT, TOO... I THINK WE'RE FIGHTING DRONES!
BUT WHY WOULD THE EMPIRE BE USING DROID PILOTS OUT HERE?
OH, NO... EVASIVE MANEUVERS! NOW!

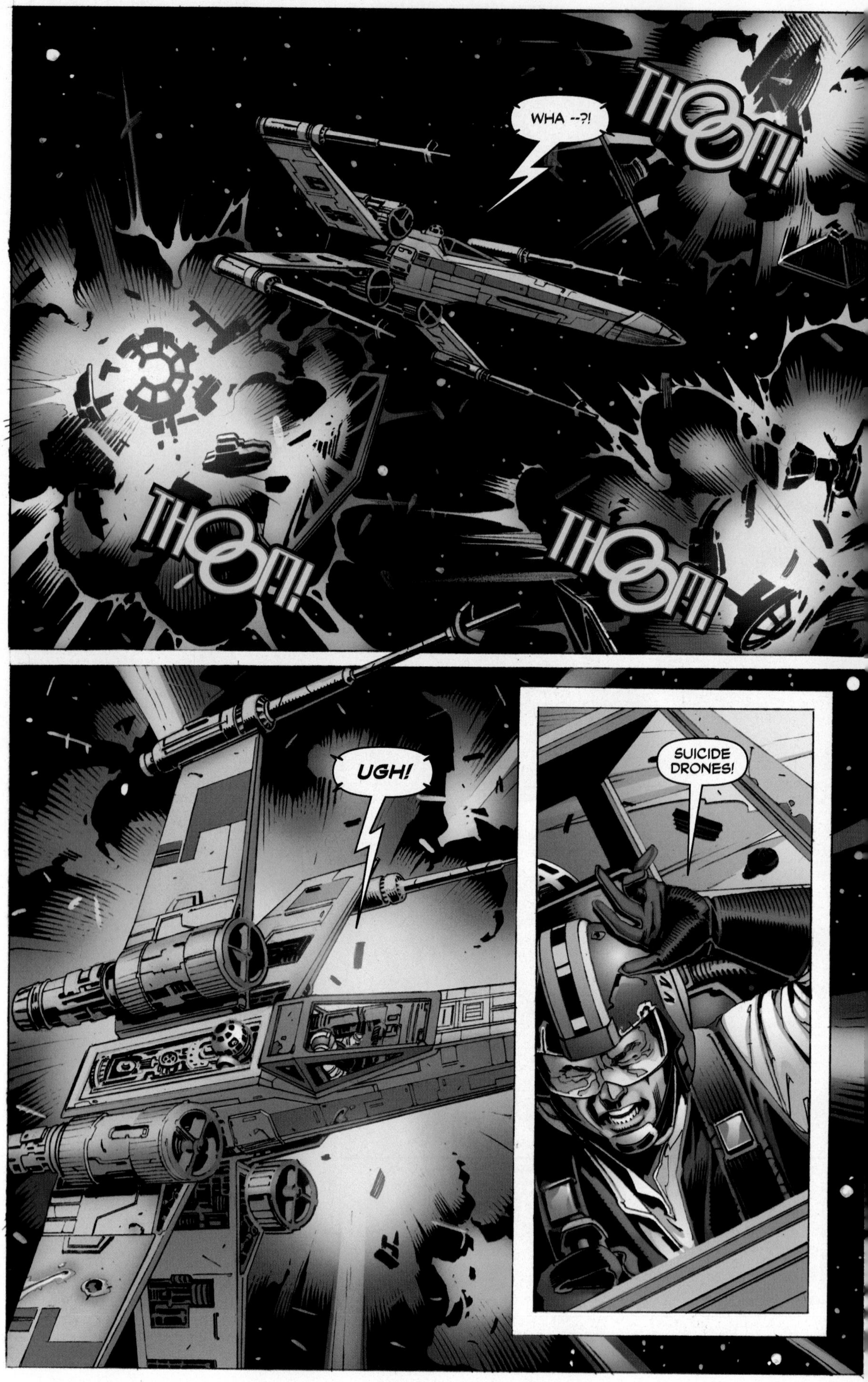
WHA --?!
THOOM!
THOOM!
THOOM!
UGH!
SUICIDE DRONES!

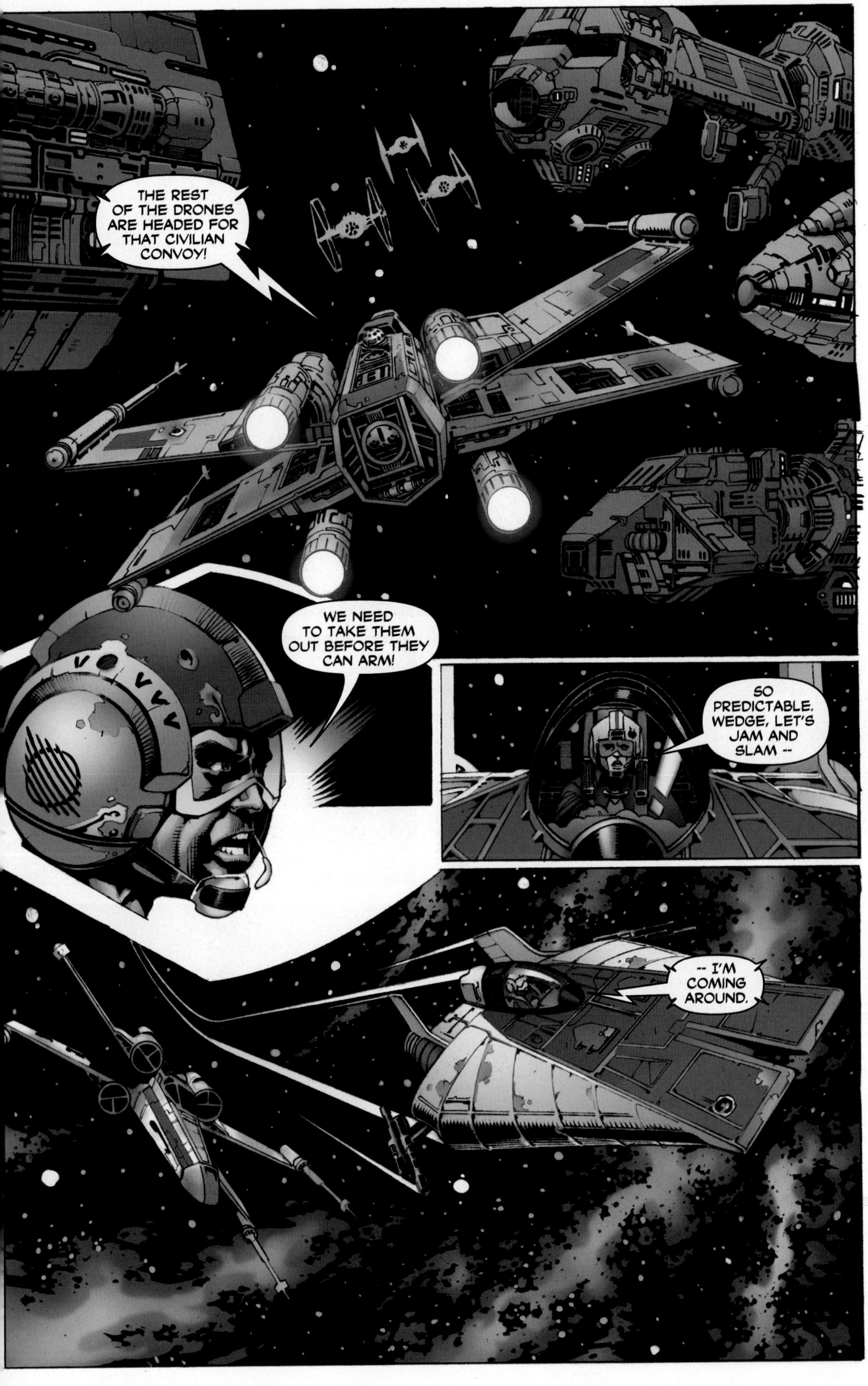
THE REST OF THE DRONES ARE HEADED FOR THAT CIVILIAN CONVOY!
WE NEED TO TAKE THEM OUT BEFORE THEY CAN ARM!
SO PREDICTABLE. WEDGE, LET'S JAM AND SLAM --
-- I'M COMING AROUND.

ONE'S HEADED BACK YOUR WAY, WEDGE!

I'M ON IT!

NICE WORK, TYCHO.

BUT THE DRONES' DISTRACTION WORKED -- WE'VE JUST LOST TEN'S HOMING BEACON.

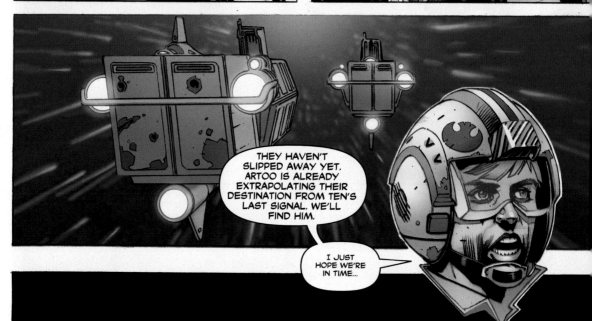

THEY HAVEN'T SLIPPED AWAY YET. ARTOO IS ALREADY EXTRAPOLATING THEIR DESTINATION FROM TEN'S LAST SIGNAL. WE'LL FIND HIM.

I JUST HOPE WE'RE IN TIME...

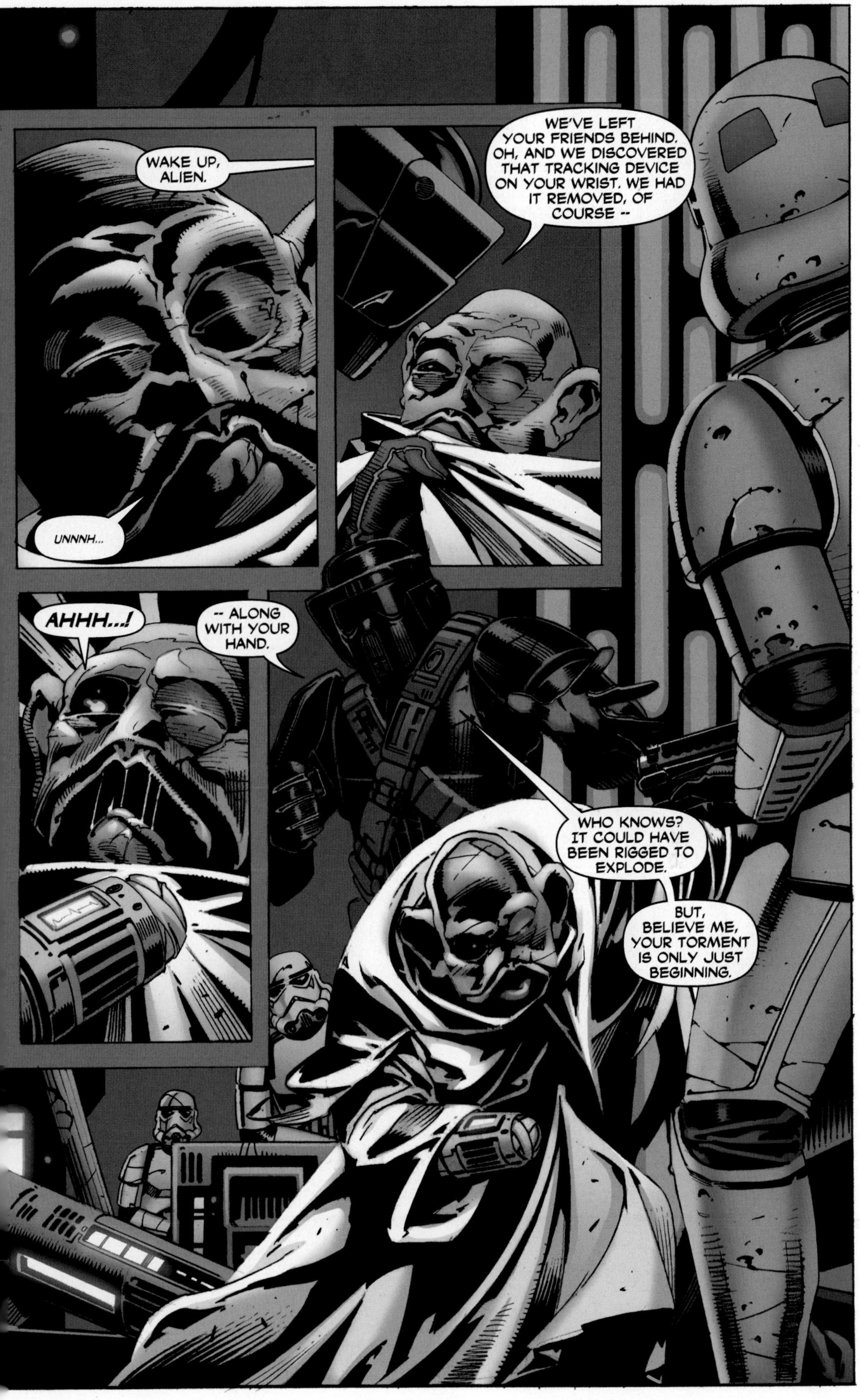
WAKE UP, ALIEN.
UNNNH...
WE'VE LEFT YOUR FRIENDS BEHIND. OH, AND WE DISCOVERED THAT TRACKING DEVICE ON YOUR WRIST. WE HAD IT REMOVED, OF COURSE --
AHHH...!
-- ALONG WITH YOUR HAND.
WHO KNOWS? IT COULD HAVE BEEN RIGGED TO EXPLODE.
BUT, BELIEVE ME, YOUR TORMENT IS ONLY JUST BEGINNING.

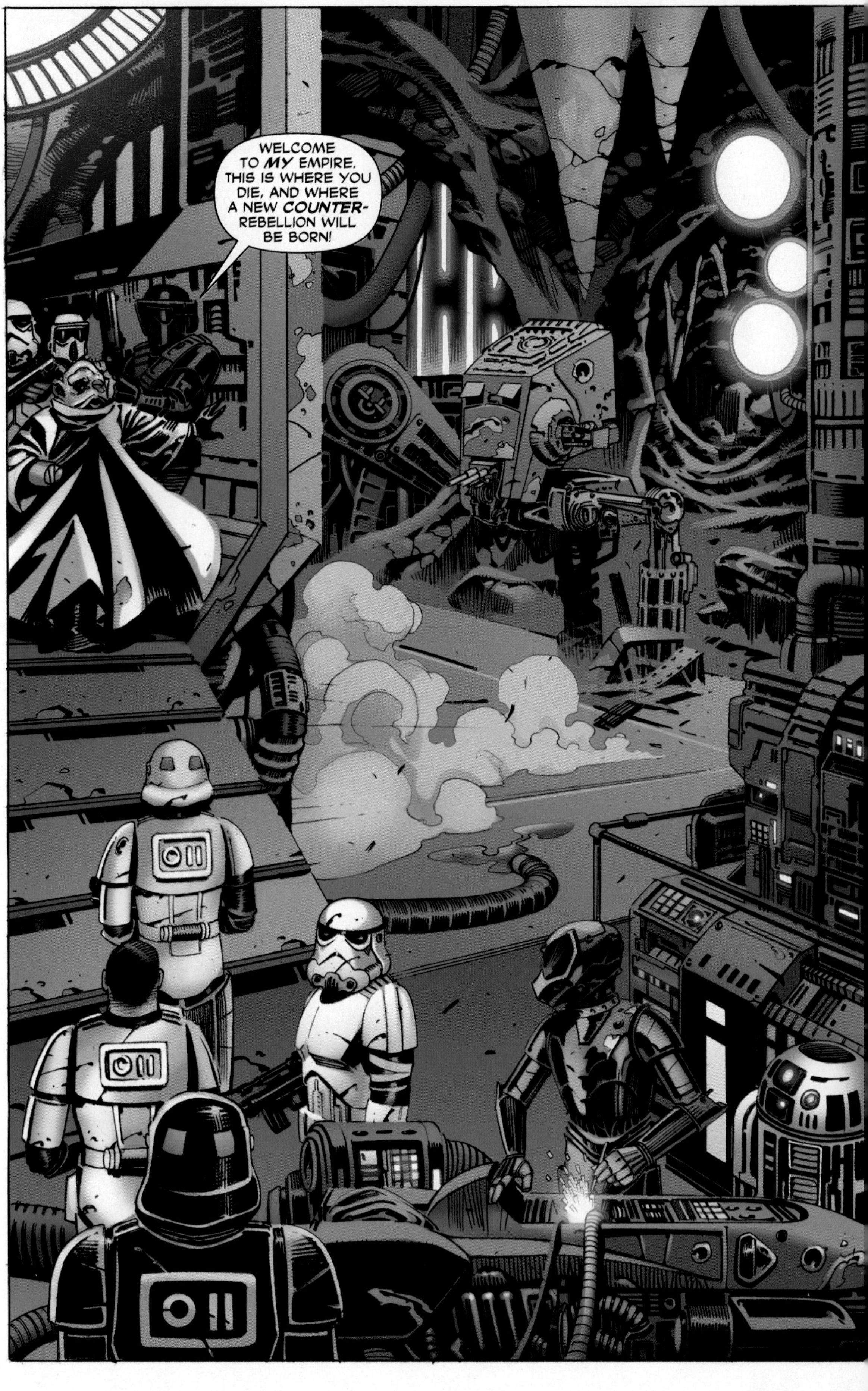
WELCOME TO *MY* EMPIRE. THIS IS WHERE YOU DIE, AND WHERE A NEW *COUNTER*-REBELLION WILL BE BORN!

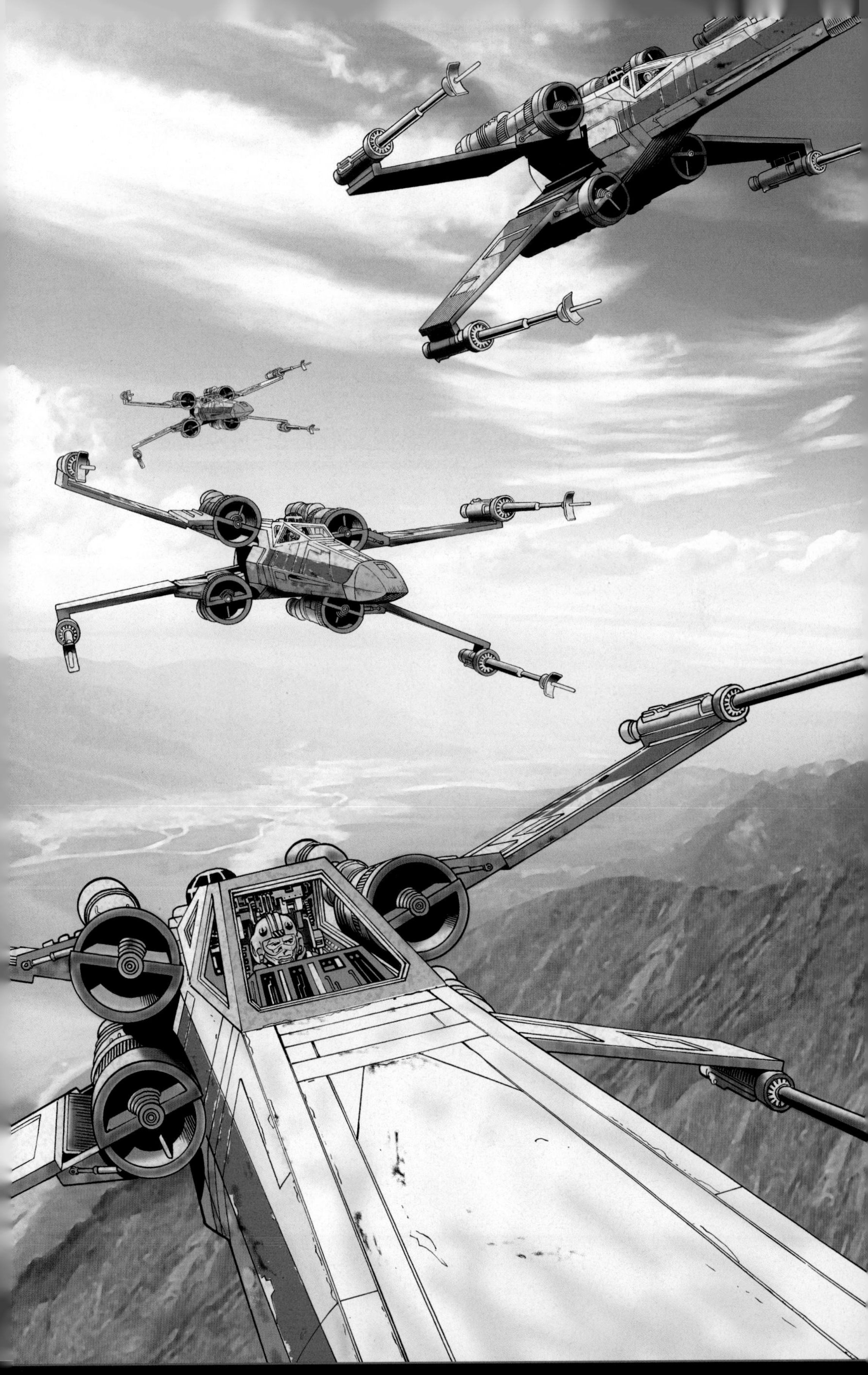

**_STAR WARS: X-WING ROGUE LEADER #3_**

WRITER: HADEN BLACKMAN • ARTIST: TOMÁS GIORELLO • COLORIST: MICHAEL ATIYEH • LETTERER: MICHAEL DAVID THOMAS
ASSISTANT EDITOR: DAVE MARSHALL • ASSOCIATE EDITOR: JEREMY BARLOW • EDITOR: RANDY STRADLEY • COVER ARTIST: GARY ERSKINE

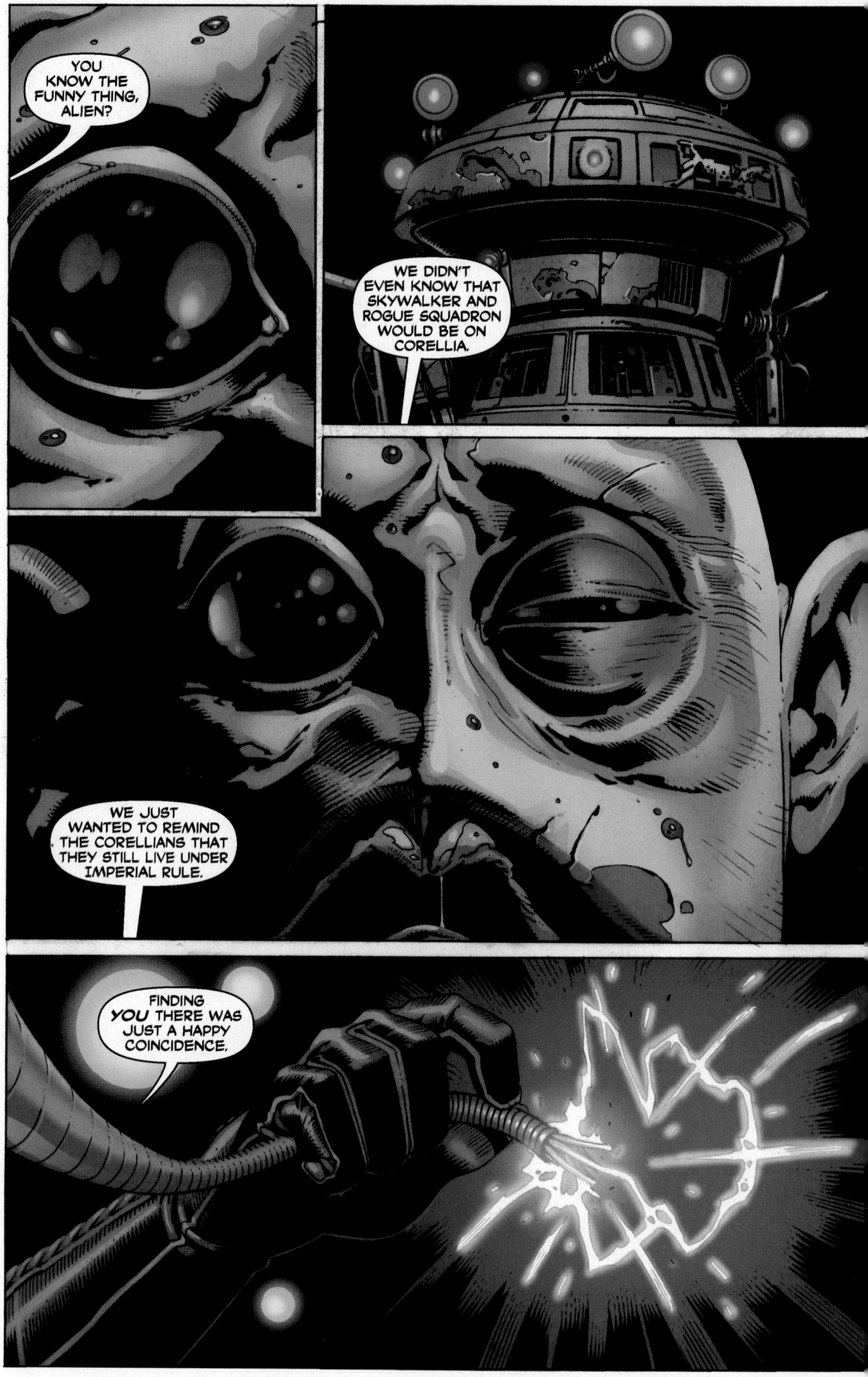
YOU KNOW THE FUNNY THING, ALIEN?
WE DIDN'T EVEN KNOW THAT SKYWALKER AND ROGUE SQUADRON WOULD BE ON CORELLIA.
WE JUST WANTED TO REMIND THE CORELLIANS THAT THEY STILL LIVE UNDER IMPERIAL RULE.
FINDING *YOU* THERE WAS JUST A HAPPY COINCIDENCE.

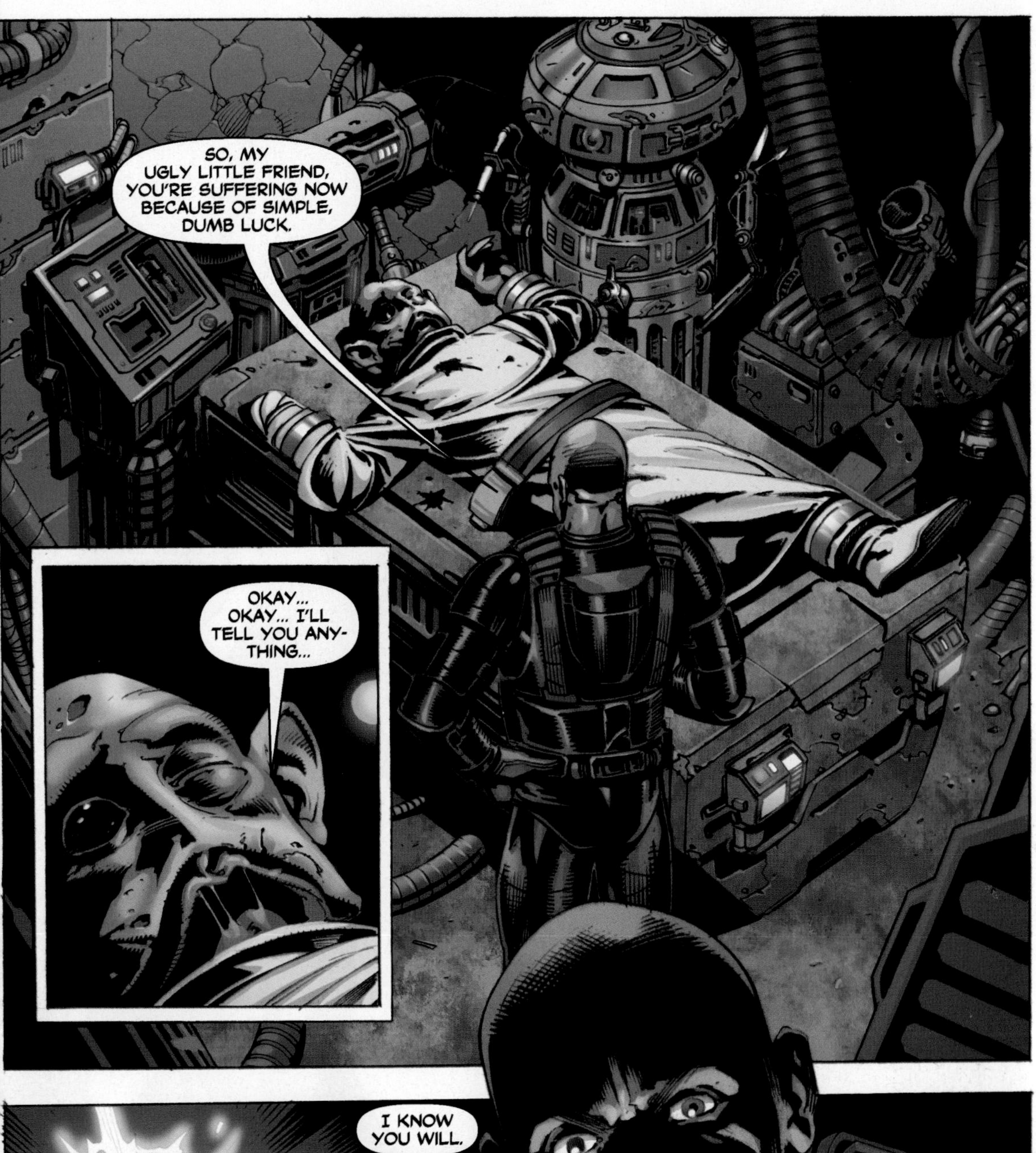
SO, MY UGLY LITTLE FRIEND, YOU'RE SUFFERING NOW BECAUSE OF SIMPLE, DUMB LUCK.
OKAY... OKAY... I'LL TELL YOU ANY-THING...
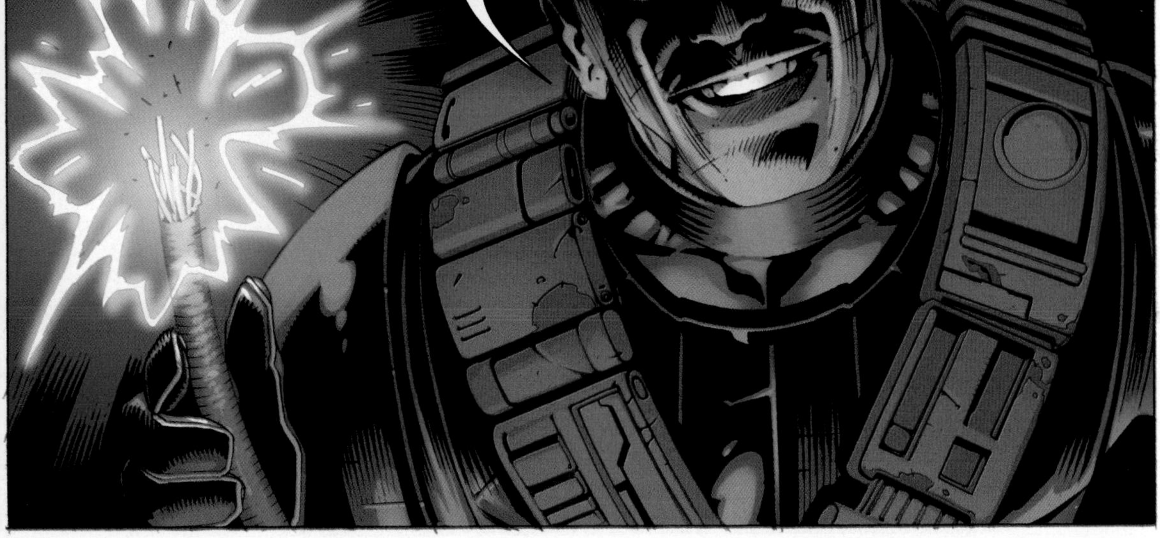
I KNOW YOU WILL.

WELCOME TO TRALUS, ROGUES...

YOU SURE WE'RE HEADED THE RIGHT WAY? DO WE EVEN KNOW WHERE WE ARE ANYMORE?

ARTOO HAS BEEN MAPPING OUR PROGRESS AND HAS OUR POSITION LOCKED, TYCHO. WE'RE NOT LOST... YET.

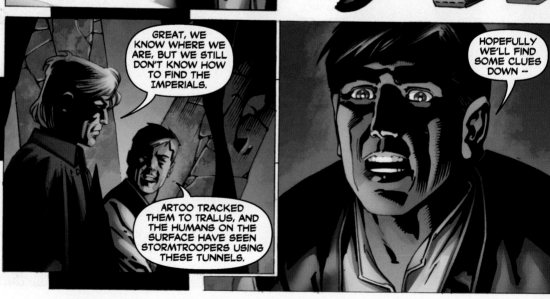

GREAT, WE KNOW WHERE WE ARE, BUT WE STILL DON'T KNOW HOW TO FIND THE IMPERIALS.

ARTOO TRACKED THEM TO TRALUS, AND THE HUMANS ON THE SURFACE HAVE SEEN STORMTROOPERS USING THESE TUNNELS.

HOPEFULLY WE'LL FIND SOME CLUES DOWN --

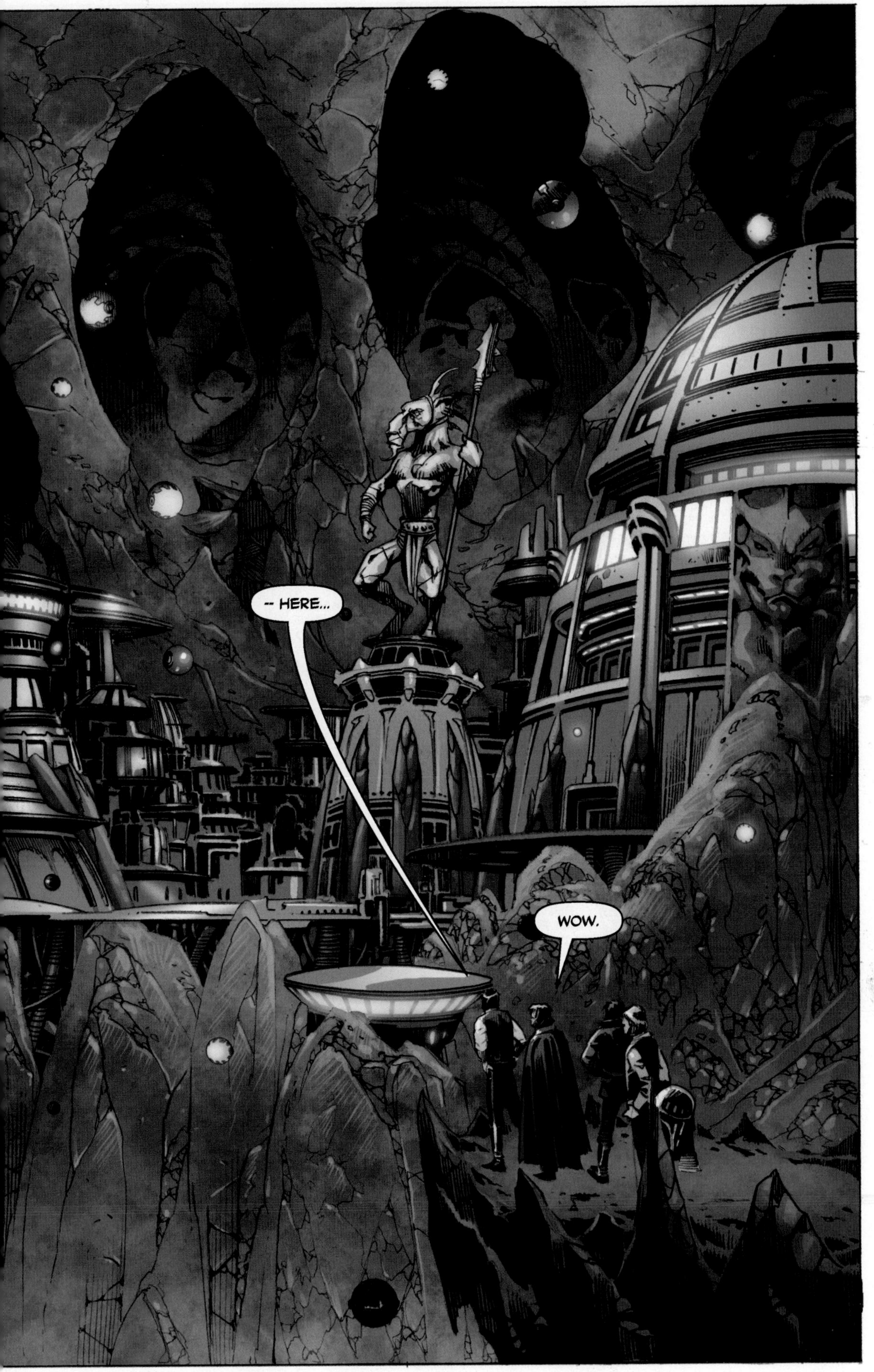
-- HERE...
WOW.

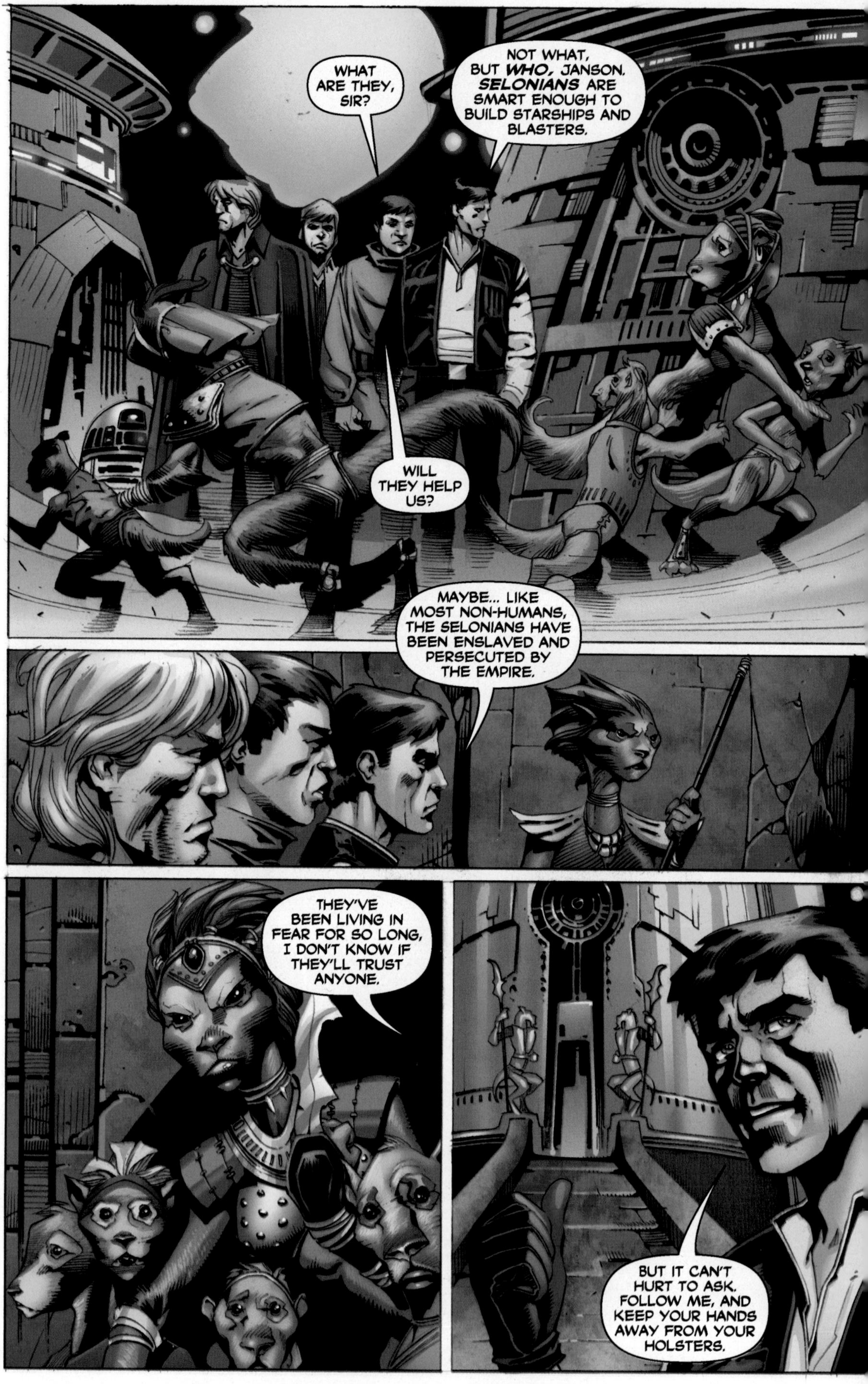
WHAT ARE THEY, SIR?
NOT WHAT, BUT WHO, JANSON. SELONIANS ARE SMART ENOUGH TO BUILD STARSHIPS AND BLASTERS.
WILL THEY HELP US?
MAYBE... LIKE MOST NON-HUMANS, THE SELONIANS HAVE BEEN ENSLAVED AND PERSECUTED BY THE EMPIRE.
THEY'VE BEEN LIVING IN FEAR FOR SO LONG, I DON'T KNOW IF THEY'LL TRUST ANYONE.
BUT IT CAN'T HURT TO ASK. FOLLOW ME, AND KEEP YOUR HANDS AWAY FROM YOUR HOLSTERS.

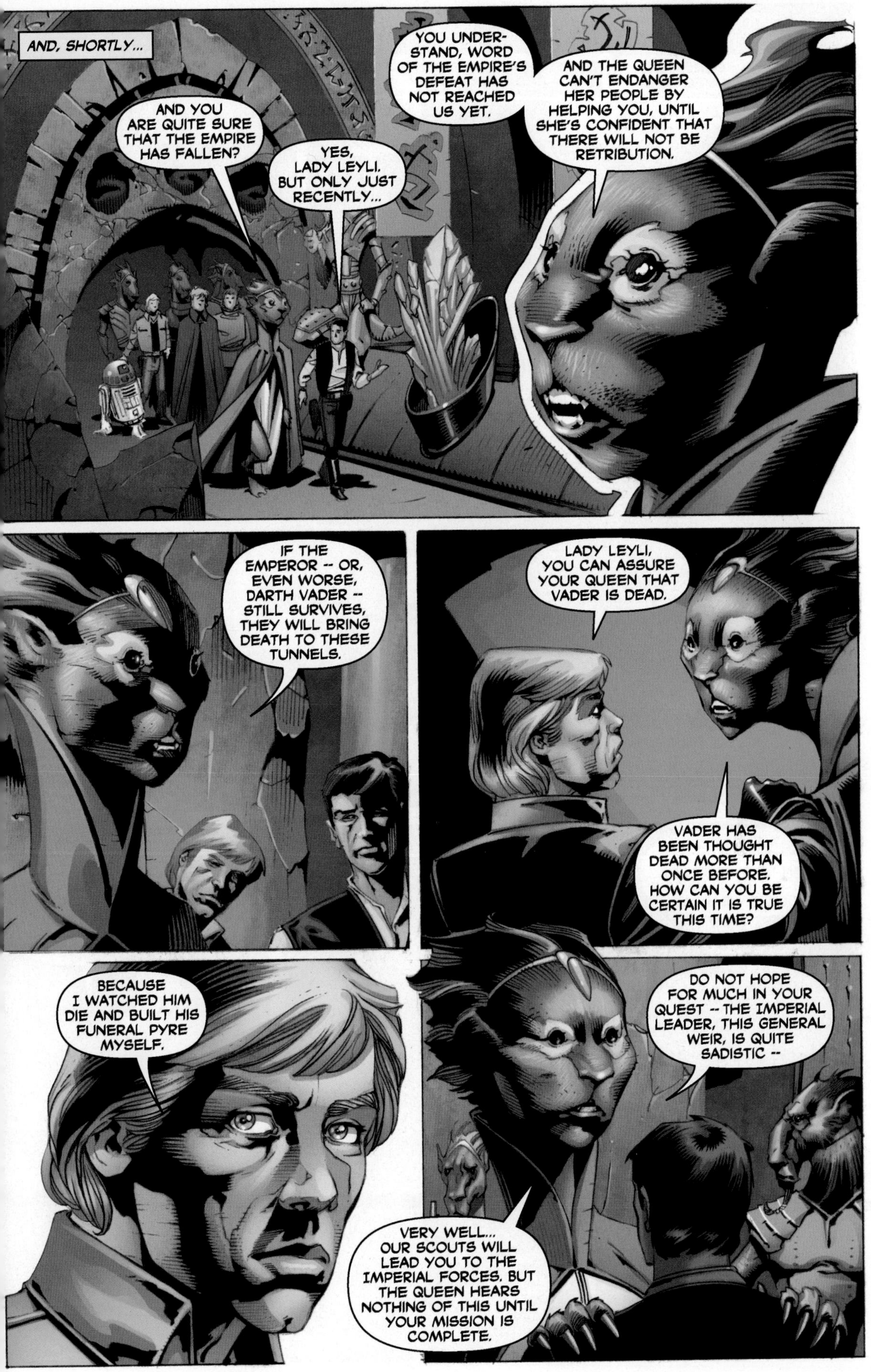
AND, SHORTLY...
AND YOU ARE QUITE SURE THAT THE EMPIRE HAS FALLEN?
YES, LADY LEYLI, BUT ONLY JUST RECENTLY...
YOU UNDER-STAND, WORD OF THE EMPIRE'S DEFEAT HAS NOT REACHED US YET.
AND THE QUEEN CAN'T ENDANGER HER PEOPLE BY HELPING YOU, UNTIL SHE'S CONFIDENT THAT THERE WILL NOT BE RETRIBUTION.
IF THE EMPEROR -- OR, EVEN WORSE, DARTH VADER -- STILL SURVIVES, THEY WILL BRING DEATH TO THESE TUNNELS.
LADY LEYLI, YOU CAN ASSURE YOUR QUEEN THAT VADER IS DEAD.
VADER HAS BEEN THOUGHT DEAD MORE THAN ONCE BEFORE. HOW CAN YOU BE CERTAIN IT IS TRUE THIS TIME?
BECAUSE I WATCHED HIM DIE AND BUILT HIS FUNERAL PYRE MYSELF.
DO NOT HOPE FOR MUCH IN YOUR QUEST -- THE IMPERIAL LEADER, THIS GENERAL WEIR, IS QUITE SADISTIC --
VERY WELL... OUR SCOUTS WILL LEAD YOU TO THE IMPERIAL FORCES. BUT THE QUEEN HEARS NOTHING OF THIS UNTIL YOUR MISSION IS COMPLETE.

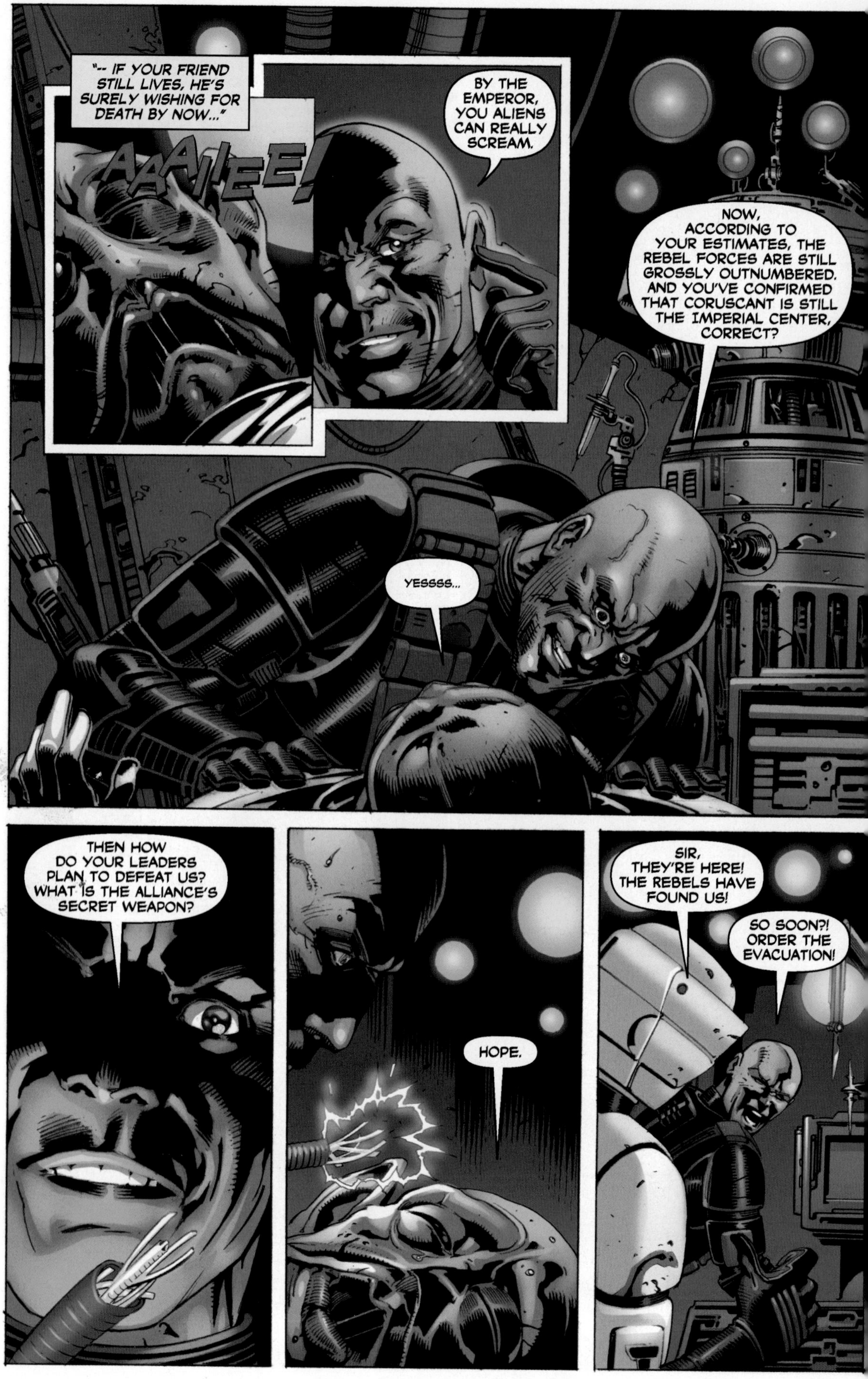

"-- IF YOUR FRIEND STILL LIVES, HE'S SURELY WISHING FOR DEATH BY NOW..."
AAAIIEEE!
BY THE EMPEROR, YOU ALIENS CAN REALLY SCREAM.
NOW, ACCORDING TO YOUR ESTIMATES, THE REBEL FORCES ARE STILL GROSSLY OUTNUMBERED. AND YOU'VE CONFIRMED THAT CORUSCANT IS STILL THE IMPERIAL CENTER, CORRECT?
YESSSS...
THEN HOW DO YOUR LEADERS PLAN TO DEFEAT US? WHAT IS THE ALLIANCE'S SECRET WEAPON?
HOPE.
SIR, THEY'RE HERE! THE REBELS HAVE FOUND US!
SO SOON?! ORDER THE EVACUATION!

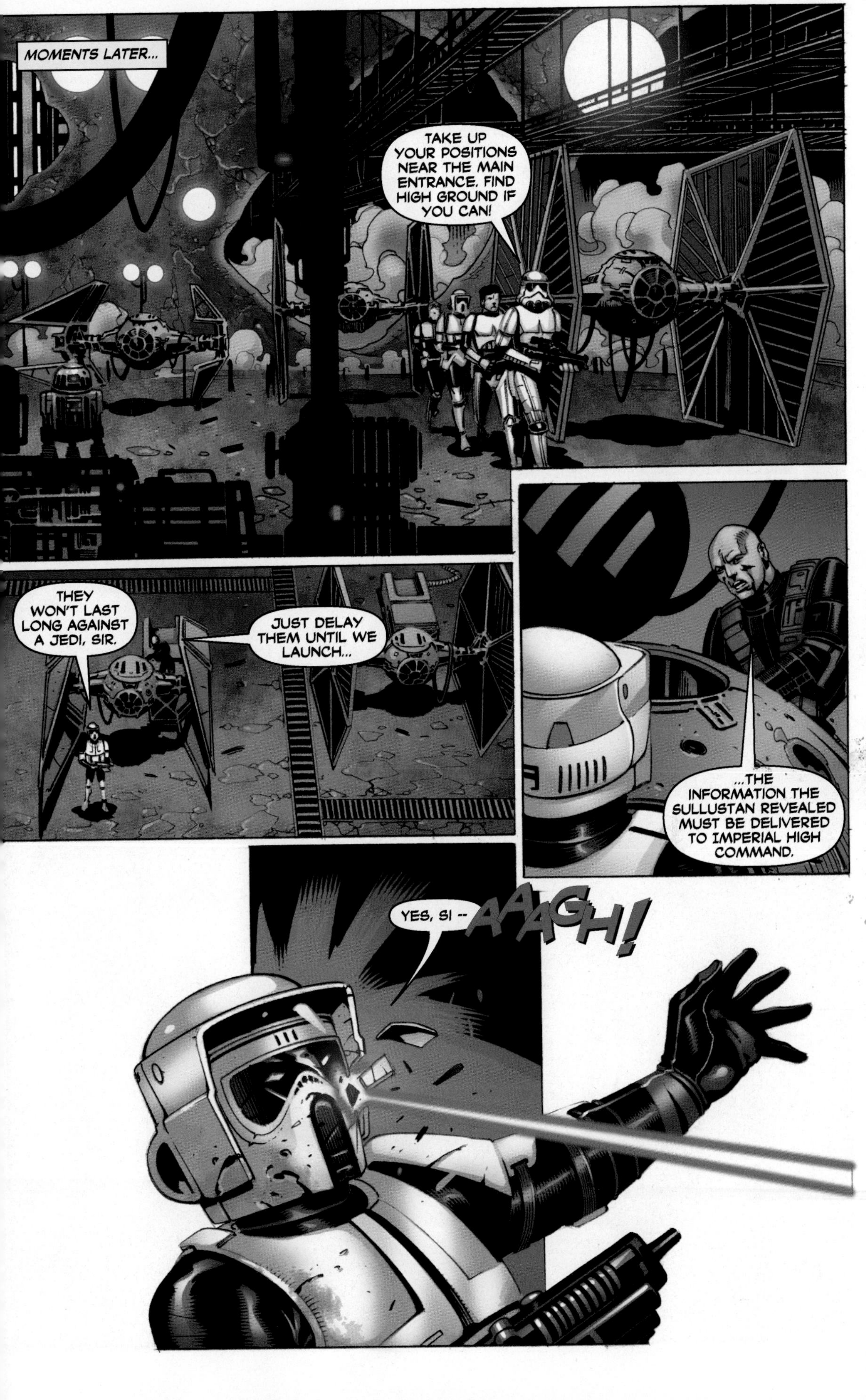
MOMENTS LATER...
TAKE UP YOUR POSITIONS NEAR THE MAIN ENTRANCE. FIND HIGH GROUND IF YOU CAN!
THEY WON'T LAST LONG AGAINST A JEDI, SIR.
JUST DELAY THEM UNTIL WE LAUNCH...
...THE INFORMATION THE SULLUSTAN REVEALED MUST BE DELIVERED TO IMPERIAL HIGH COMMAND.
YES, SI --
AAAGH!

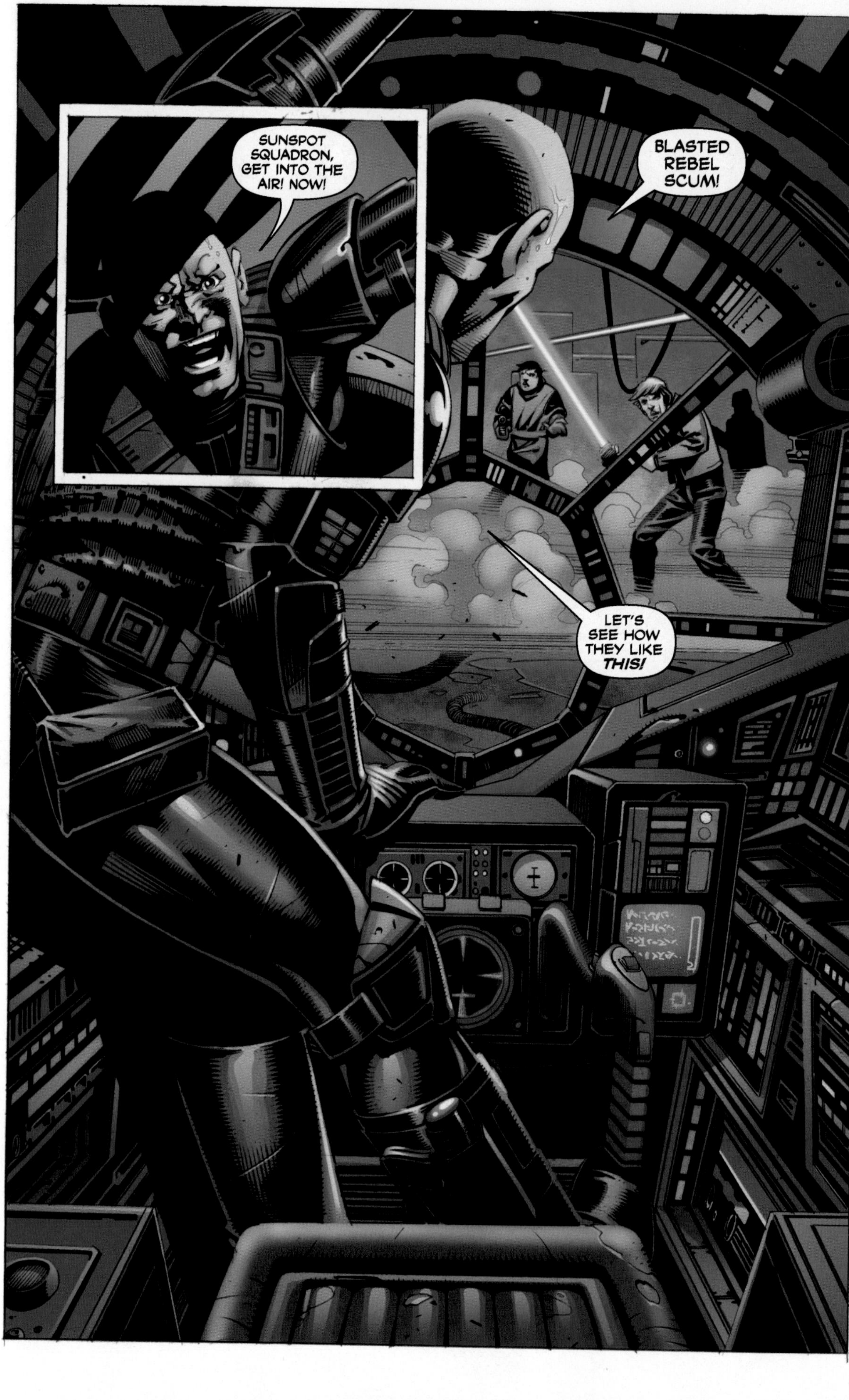
SUNSPOT SQUADRON, GET INTO THE AIR! NOW!
BLASTED REBEL SCUM!
LET'S SEE HOW THEY LIKE *THIS!*

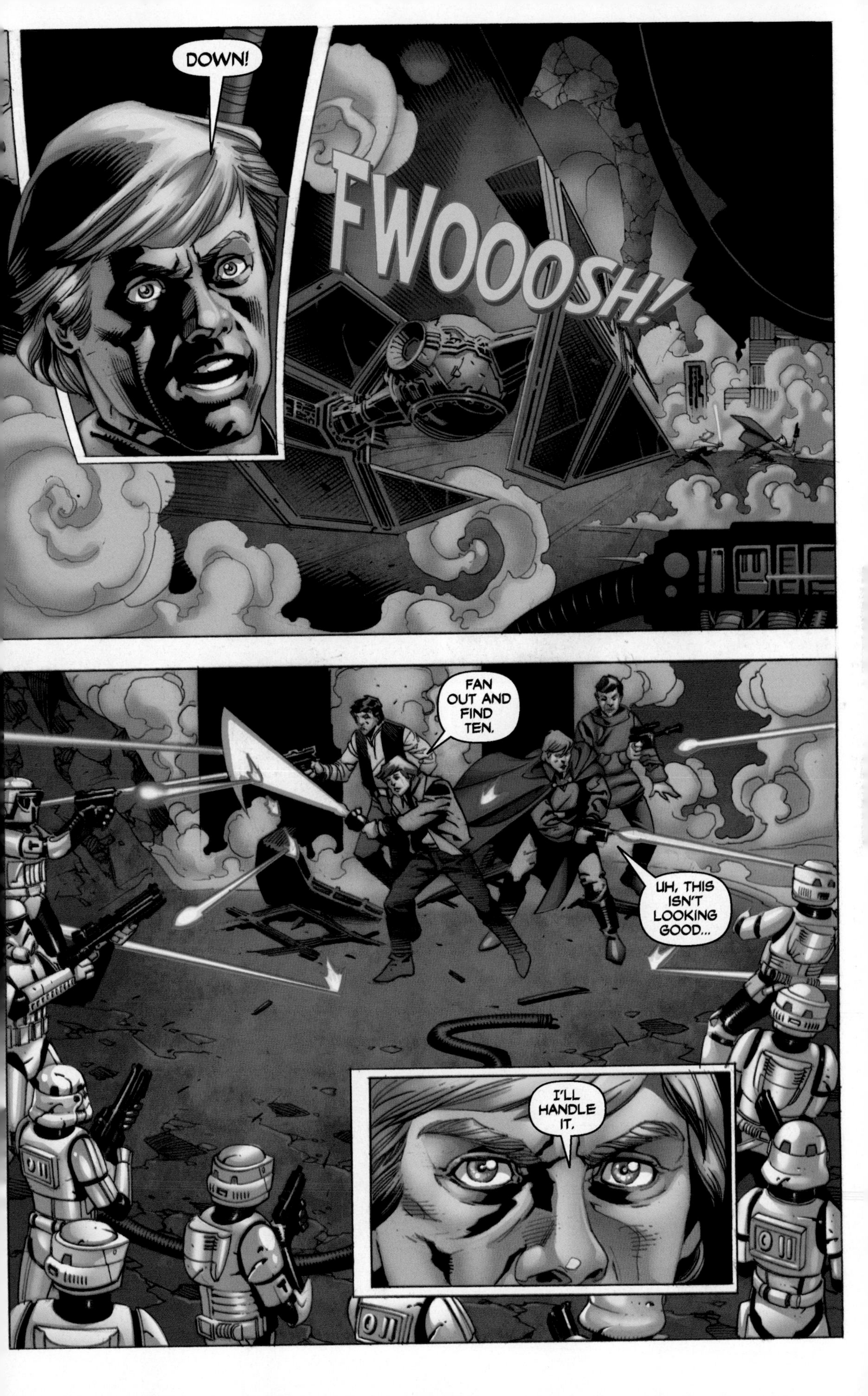
DOWN!
FWOOOSH!
FAN OUT AND FIND TEN.
UH, THIS ISN'T LOOKING GOOD...
I'LL HANDLE IT.

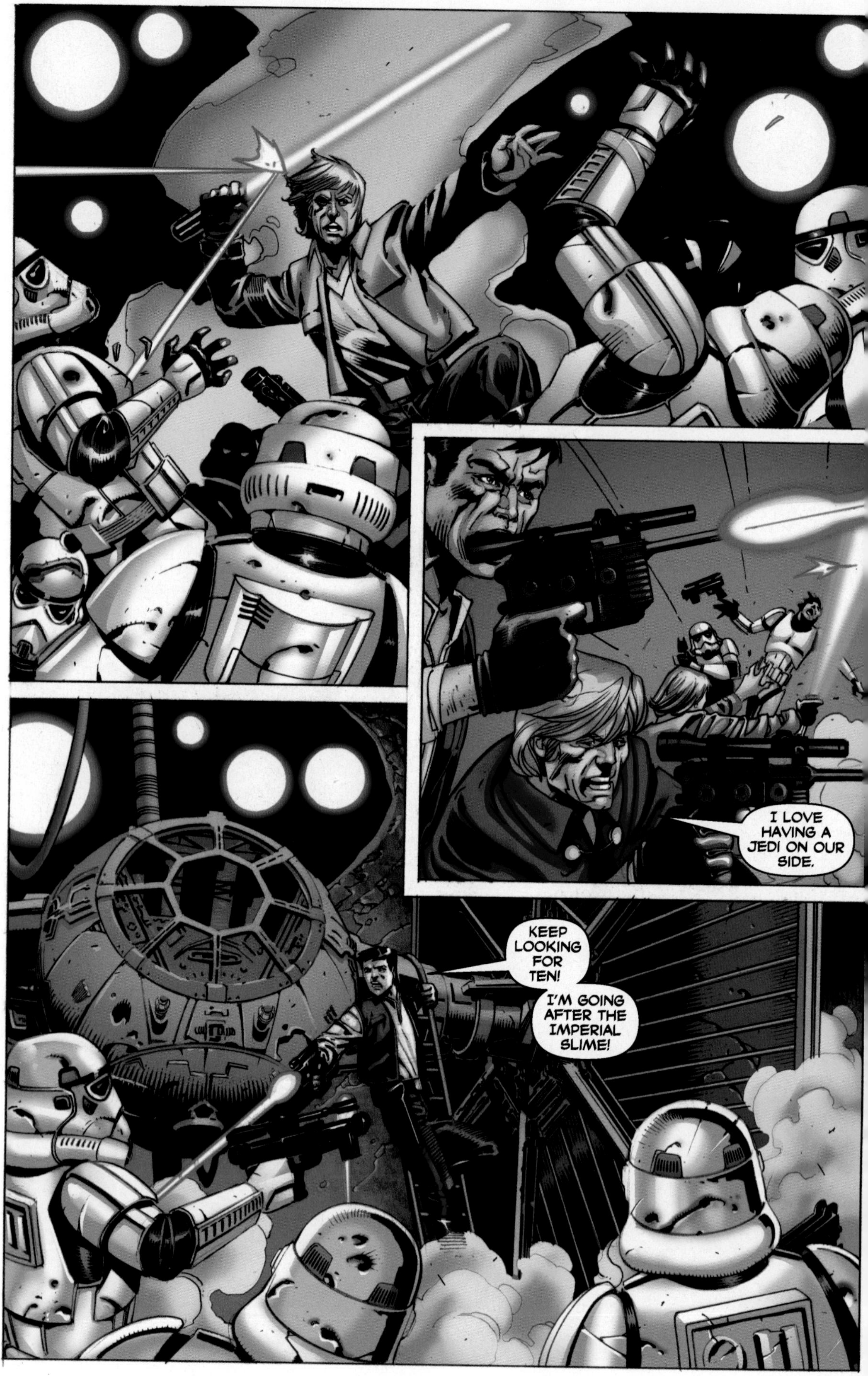
I LOVE HAVING A JEDI ON OUR SIDE.
KEEP LOOKING FOR TEN!
I'M GOING AFTER THE IMPERIAL SLIME!

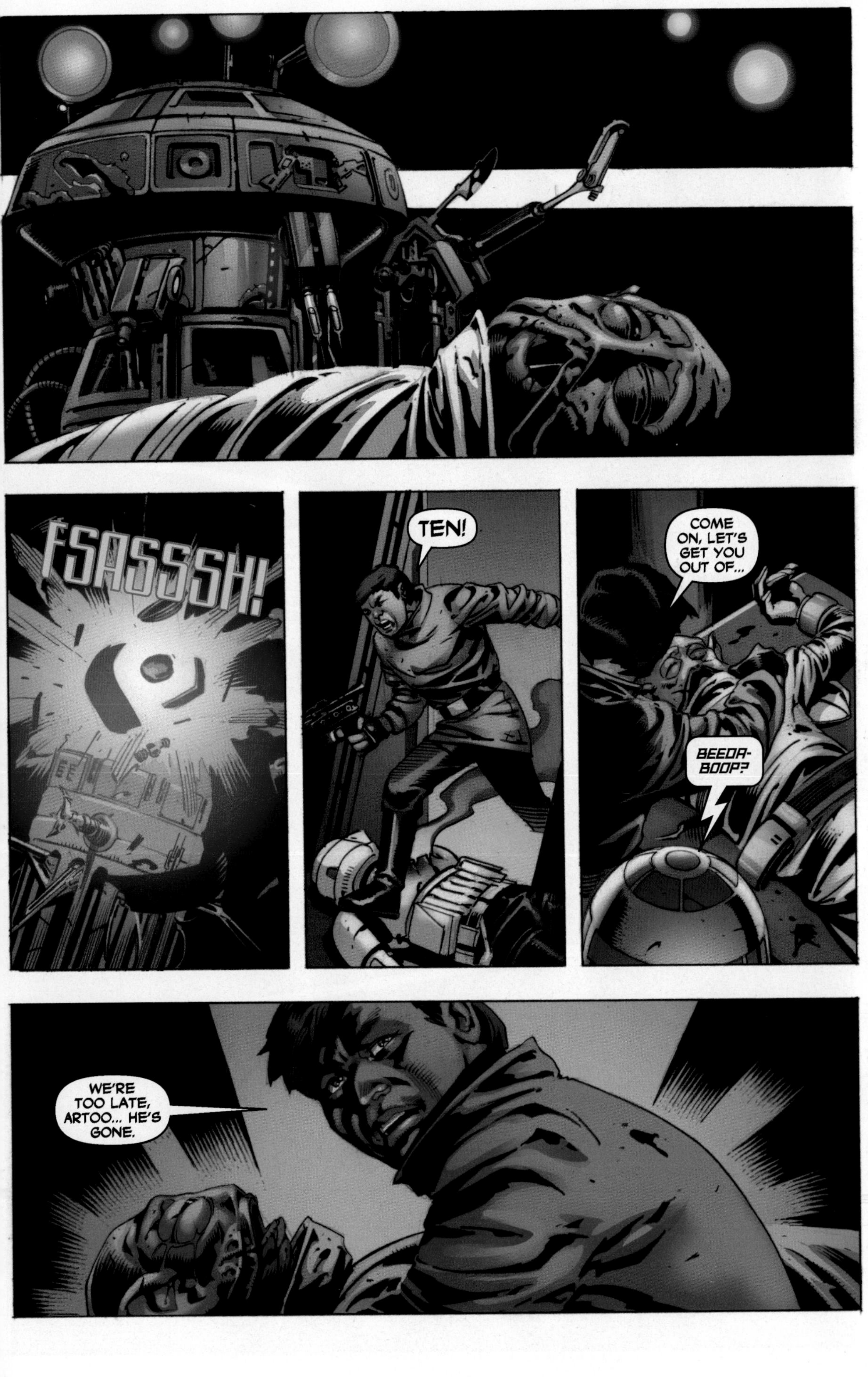
FSASSSH!
TEN!
COME ON, LET'S GET YOU OUT OF...
BEEDA-BOOP?
WE'RE TOO LATE, ARTOO... HE'S GONE.

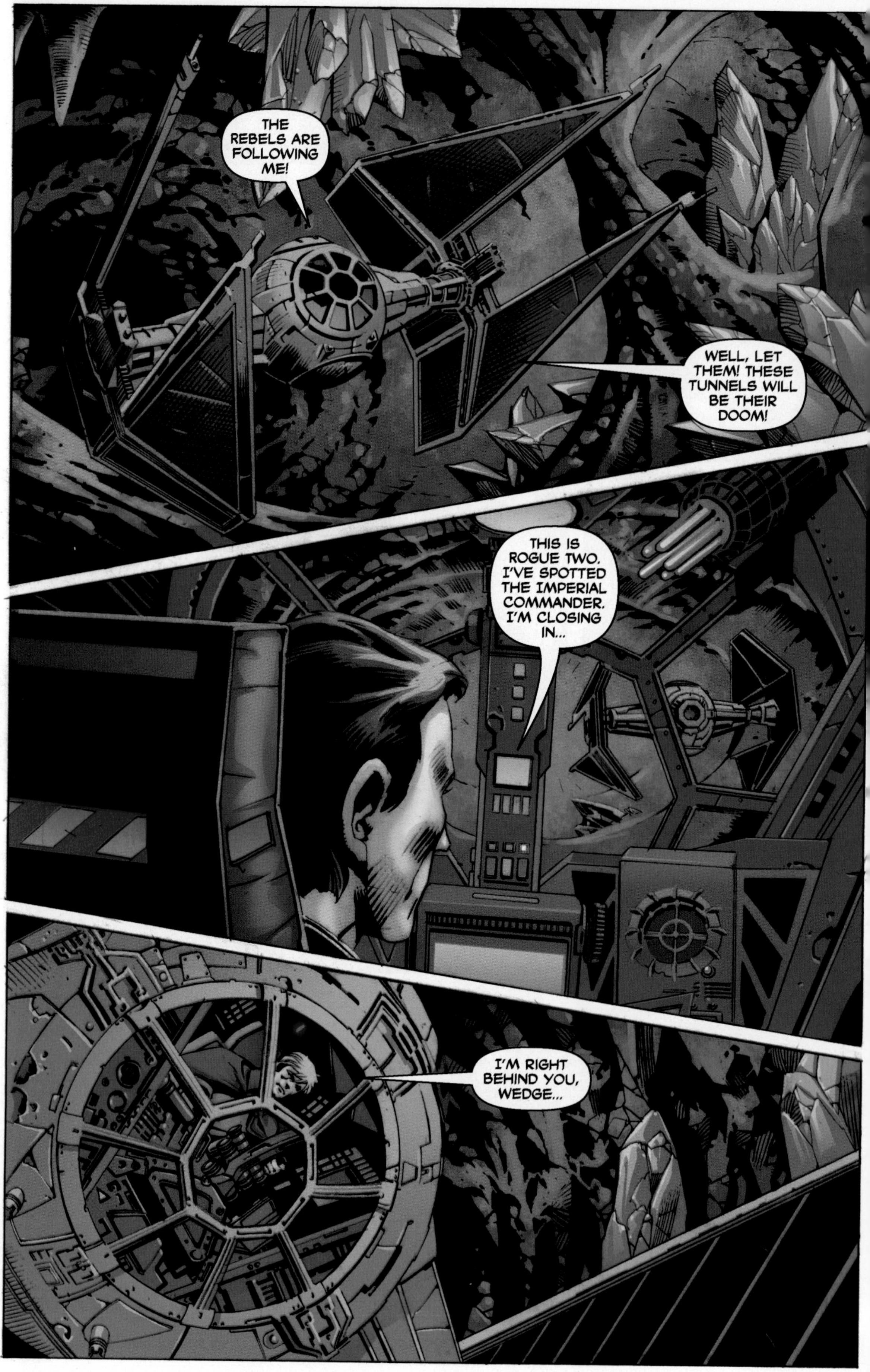
THE REBELS ARE FOLLOWING ME!
WELL, LET THEM! THESE TUNNELS WILL BE THEIR DOOM!
THIS IS ROGUE TWO. I'VE SPOTTED THE IMPERIAL COMMANDER. I'M CLOSING IN...
I'M RIGHT BEHIND YOU, WEDGE...

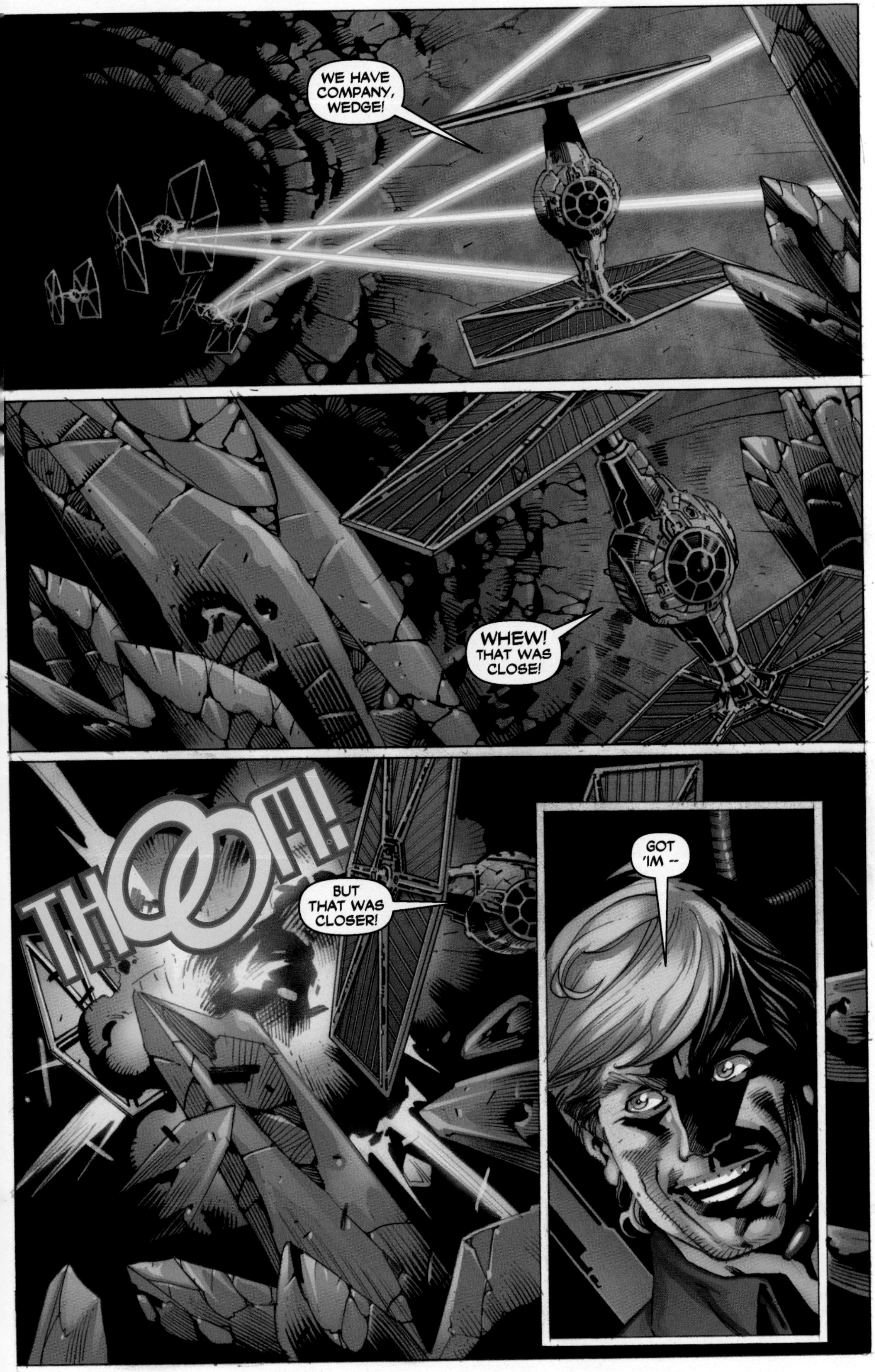
WE HAVE COMPANY, WEDGE!
WHEW! THAT WAS CLOSE!
THOOM!
BUT THAT WAS CLOSER!
GOT 'IM --

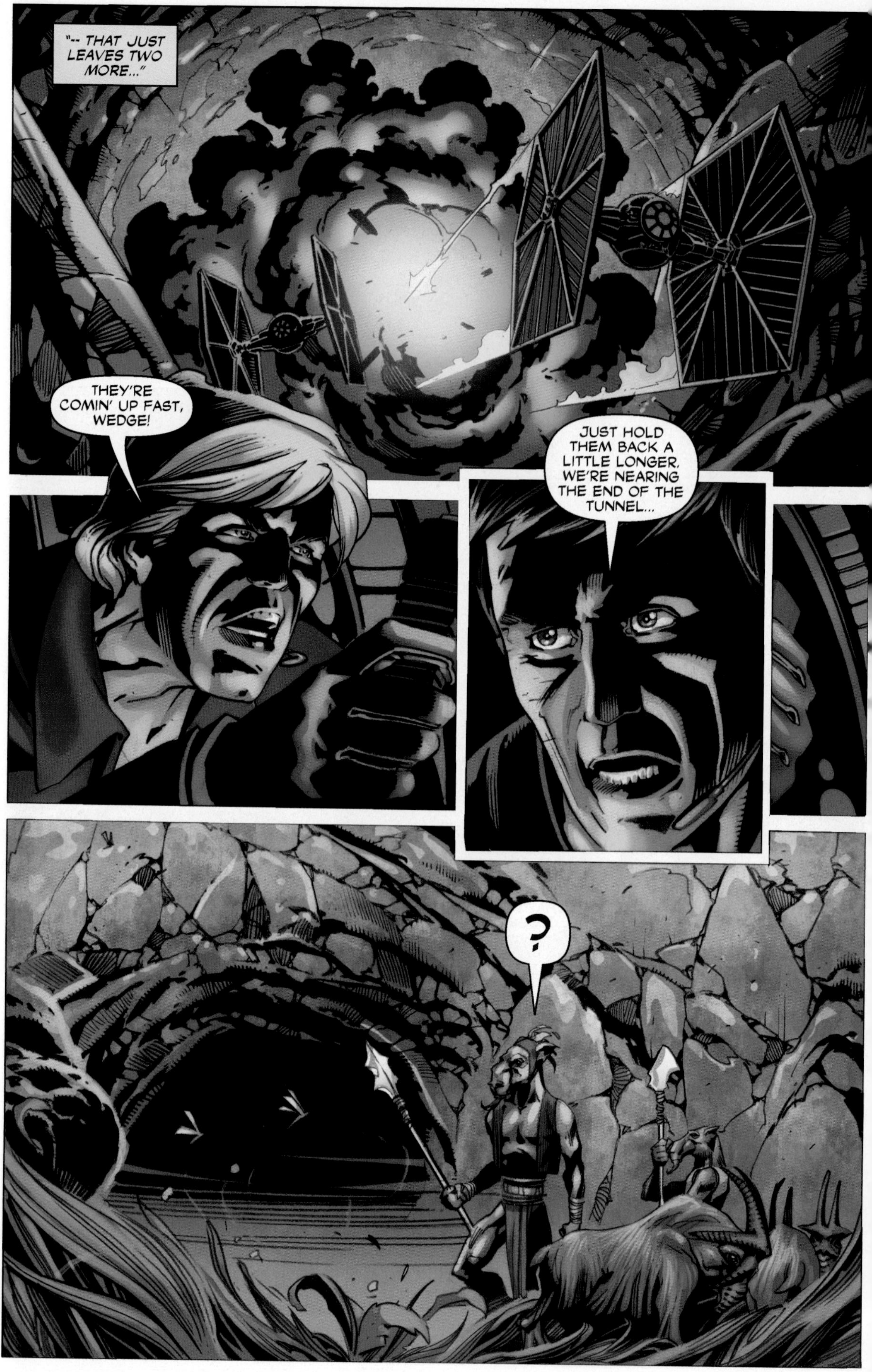
"-- THAT JUST LEAVES TWO MORE..."
THEY'RE COMIN' UP FAST, WEDGE!
JUST HOLD THEM BACK A LITTLE LONGER. WE'RE NEARING THE END OF THE TUNNEL...
?

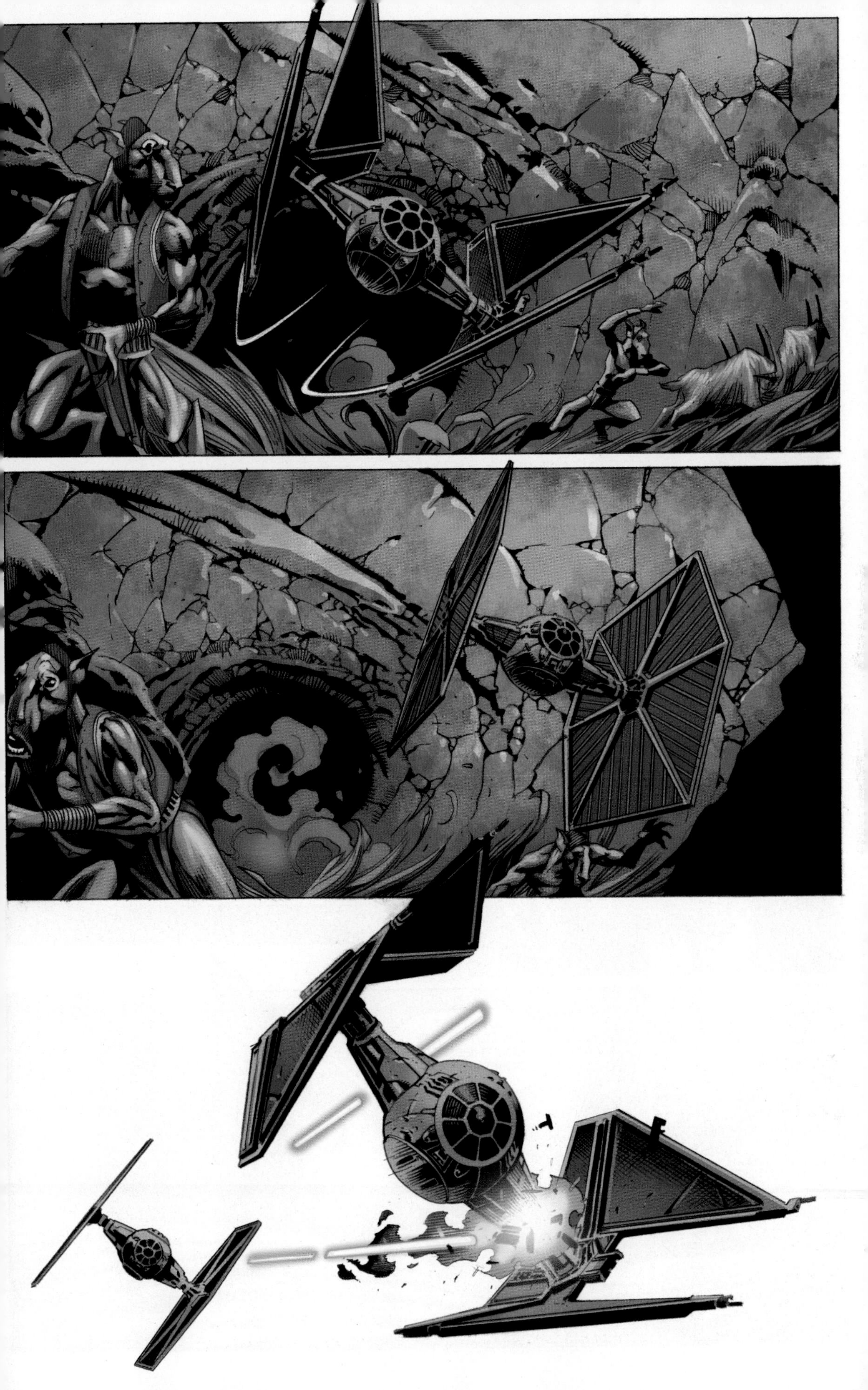

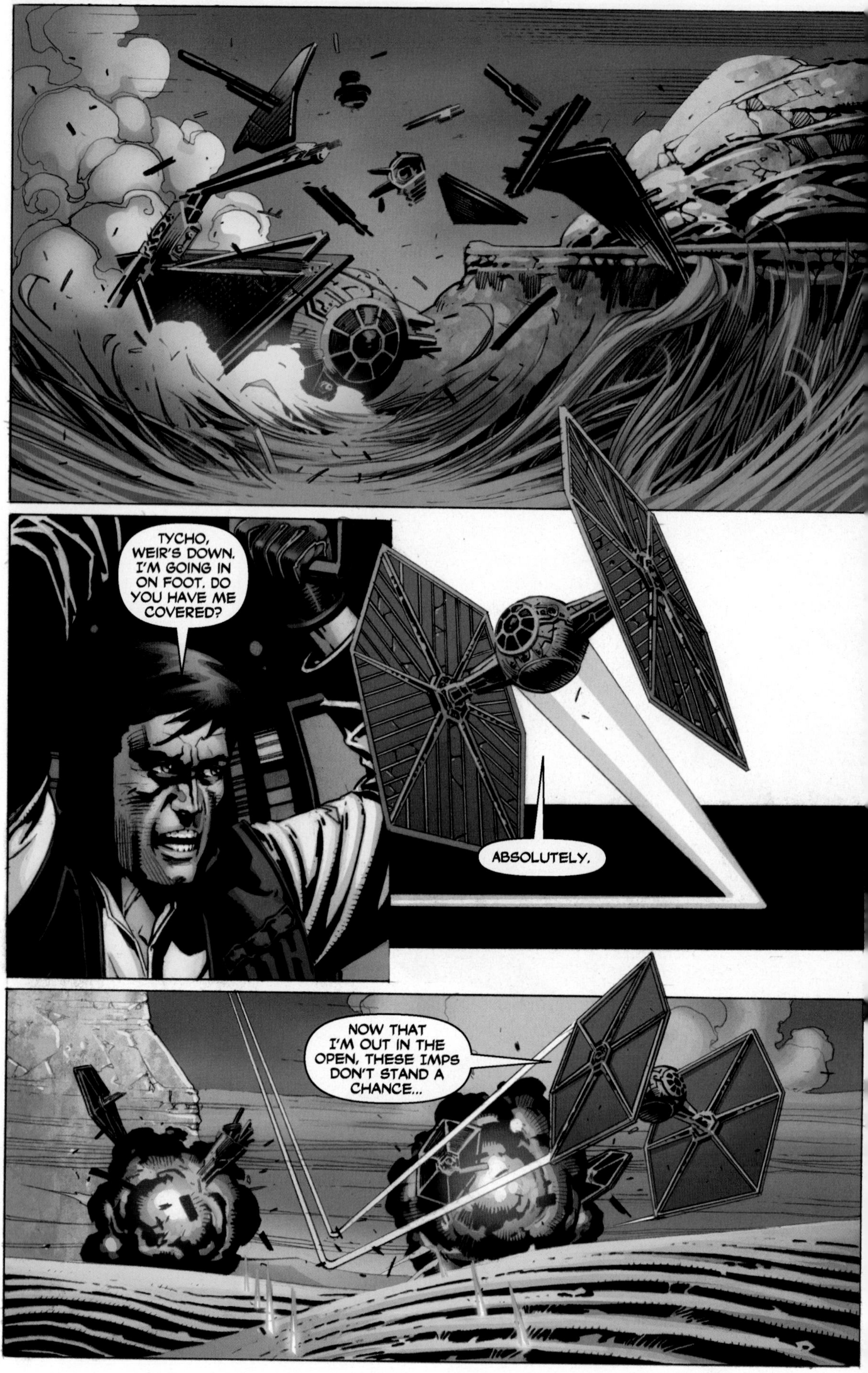
TYCHO, WEIR'S DOWN. I'M GOING IN ON FOOT. DO YOU HAVE ME COVERED?
ABSOLUTELY.
NOW THAT I'M OUT IN THE OPEN, THESE IMPS DON'T STAND A CHANCE...

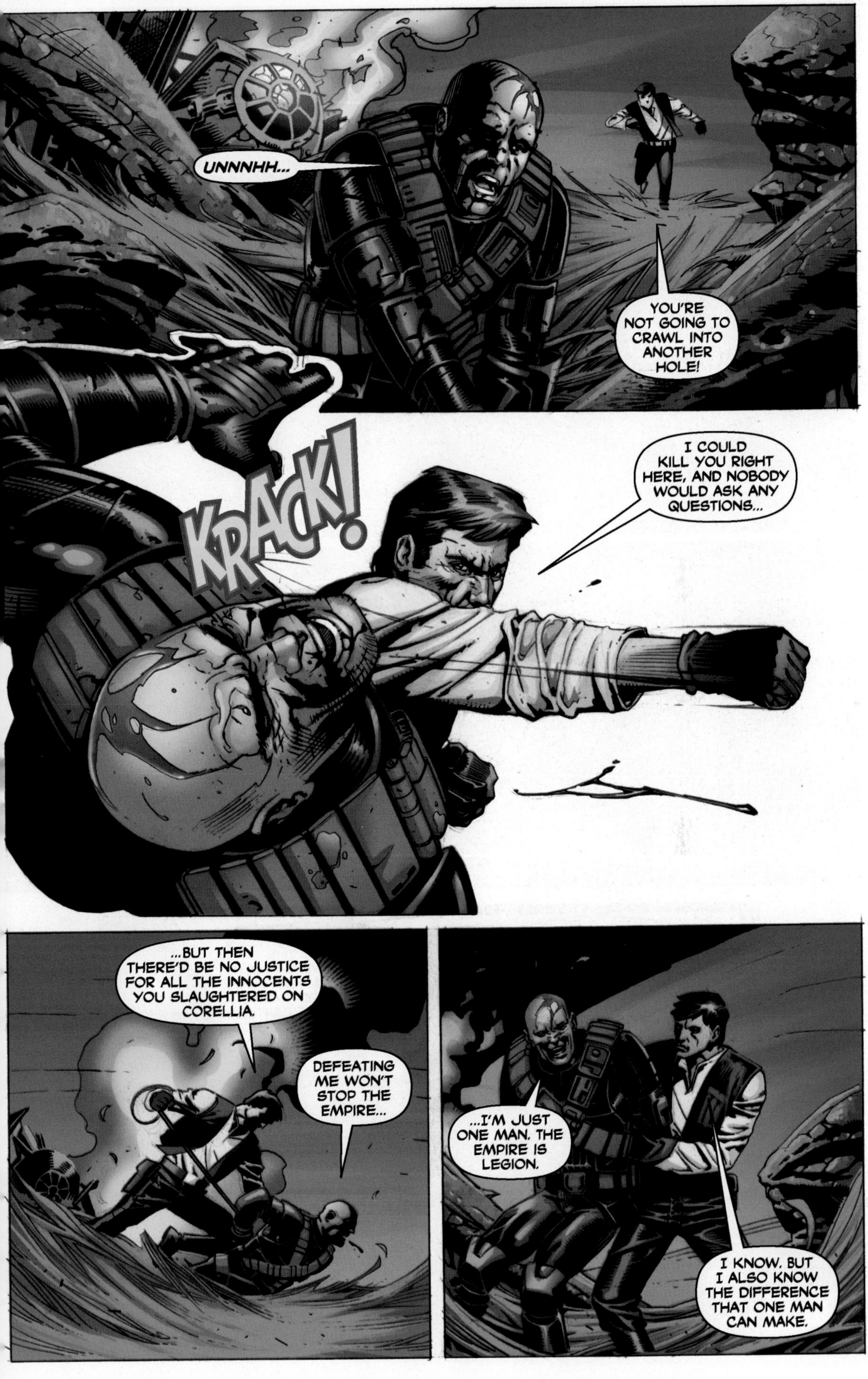
UNNNHH...
YOU'RE NOT GOING TO CRAWL INTO ANOTHER HOLE!
KRACK!
I COULD KILL YOU RIGHT HERE, AND NOBODY WOULD ASK ANY QUESTIONS...
...BUT THEN THERE'D BE NO JUSTICE FOR ALL THE INNOCENTS YOU SLAUGHTERED ON CORELLIA.
DEFEATING ME WON'T STOP THE EMPIRE...
...I'M JUST ONE MAN. THE EMPIRE IS LEGION.
I KNOW. BUT I ALSO KNOW THE DIFFERENCE THAT ONE MAN CAN MAKE.

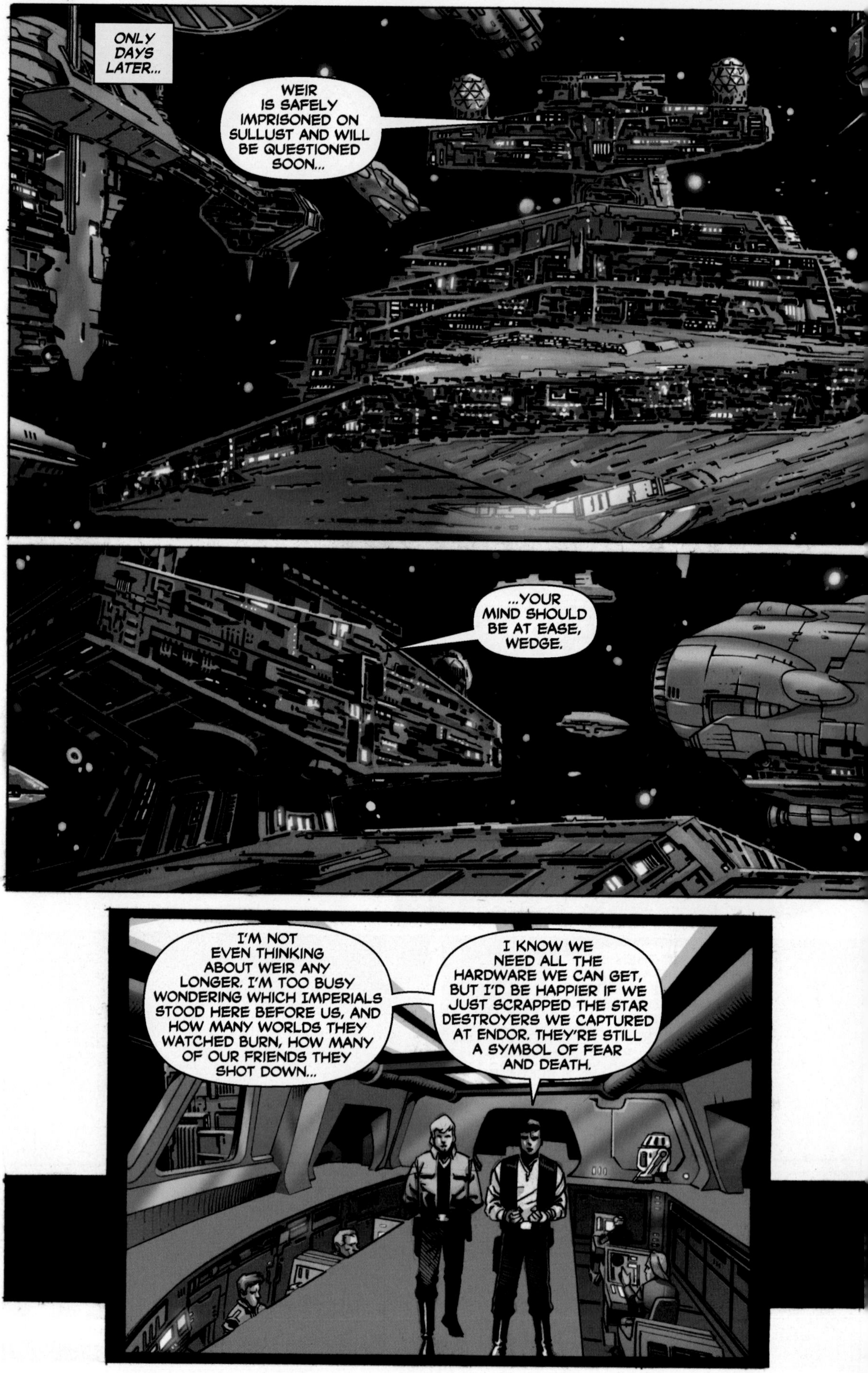
ONLY DAYS LATER...
WEIR IS SAFELY IMPRISONED ON SULLUST AND WILL BE QUESTIONED SOON...
...YOUR MIND SHOULD BE AT EASE, WEDGE.
I KNOW WE NEED ALL THE HARDWARE WE CAN GET, BUT I'D BE HAPPIER IF WE JUST SCRAPPED THE STAR DESTROYERS WE CAPTURED AT ENDOR. THEY'RE STILL A SYMBOL OF FEAR AND DEATH.
I'M NOT EVEN THINKING ABOUT WEIR ANY LONGER. I'M TOO BUSY WONDERING WHICH IMPERIALS STOOD HERE BEFORE US, AND HOW MANY WORLDS THEY WATCHED BURN, HOW MANY OF OUR FRIENDS THEY SHOT DOWN...

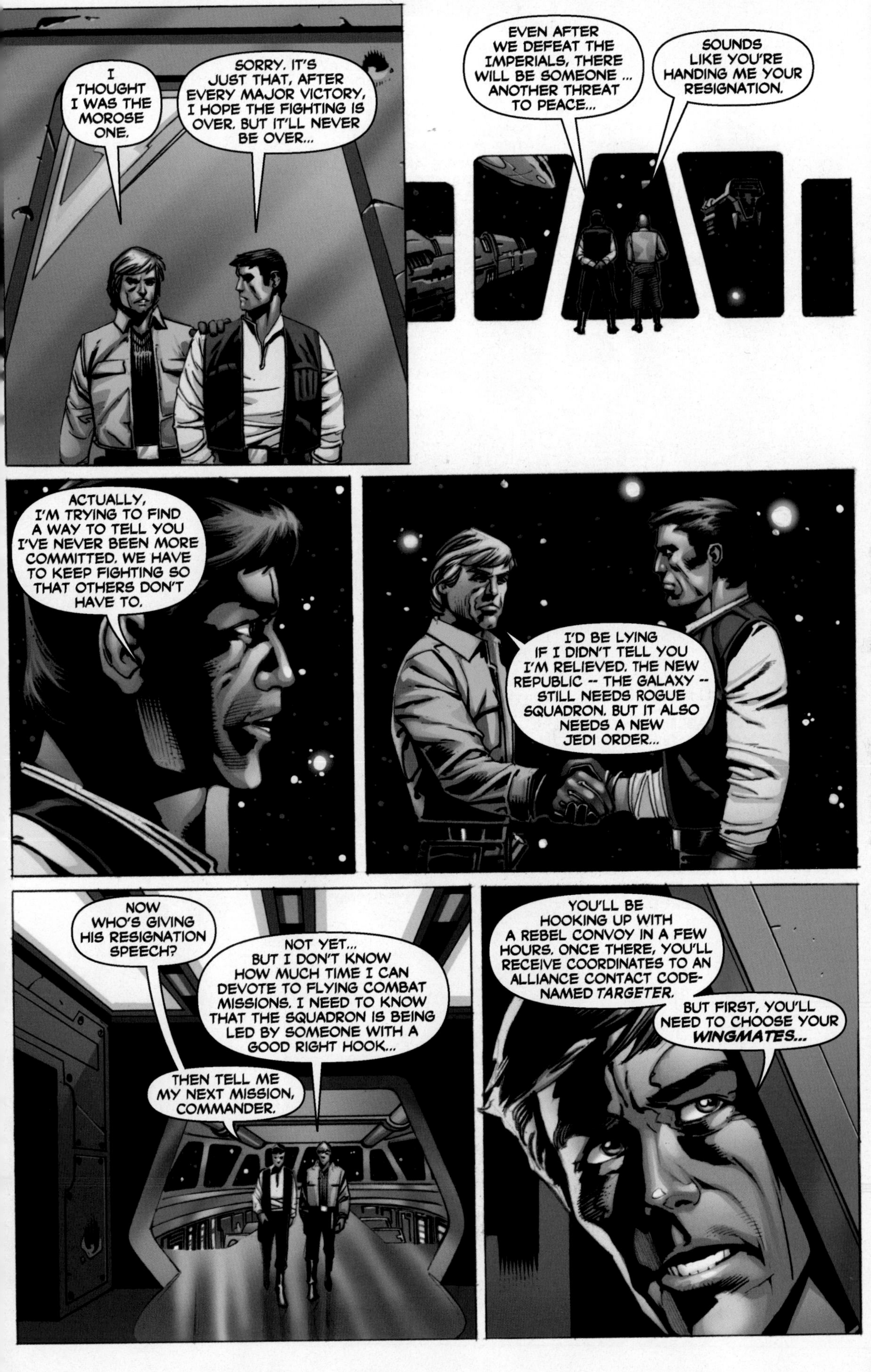
I THOUGHT I WAS THE MOROSE ONE.
SORRY. IT'S JUST THAT, AFTER EVERY MAJOR VICTORY, I HOPE THE FIGHTING IS OVER. BUT IT'LL NEVER BE OVER...
EVEN AFTER WE DEFEAT THE IMPERIALS, THERE WILL BE SOMEONE ... ANOTHER THREAT TO PEACE...
SOUNDS LIKE YOU'RE HANDING ME YOUR RESIGNATION.
ACTUALLY, I'M TRYING TO FIND A WAY TO TELL YOU I'VE NEVER BEEN MORE COMMITTED. WE HAVE TO KEEP FIGHTING SO THAT OTHERS DON'T HAVE TO.
I'D BE LYING IF I DIDN'T TELL YOU I'M RELIEVED. THE NEW REPUBLIC -- THE GALAXY -- STILL NEEDS ROGUE SQUADRON. BUT IT ALSO NEEDS A NEW JEDI ORDER...
NOW WHO'S GIVING HIS RESIGNATION SPEECH?
NOT YET... BUT I DON'T KNOW HOW MUCH TIME I CAN DEVOTE TO FLYING COMBAT MISSIONS. I NEED TO KNOW THAT THE SQUADRON IS BEING LED BY SOMEONE WITH A GOOD RIGHT HOOK...
THEN TELL ME MY NEXT MISSION, COMMANDER.
YOU'LL BE HOOKING UP WITH A REBEL CONVOY IN A FEW HOURS. ONCE THERE, YOU'LL RECEIVE COORDINATES TO AN ALLIANCE CONTACT CODE-NAMED *TARGETER*.
BUT FIRST, YOU'LL NEED TO CHOOSE YOUR ***WINGMATES...***

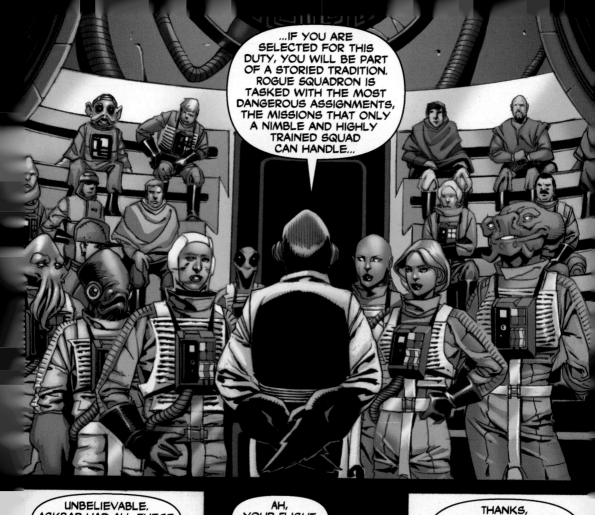

...IF YOU ARE SELECTED FOR THIS DUTY, YOU WILL BE PART OF A STORIED TRADITION. ROGUE SQUADRON IS TASKED WITH THE MOST DANGEROUS ASSIGNMENTS, THE MISSIONS THAT ONLY A NIMBLE AND HIGHLY TRAINED SQUAD CAN HANDLE...

UNBELIEVABLE. ACKBAR HAD ALL THESE PILOTS REASSIGNED TO ROGUE SQUADRON?

NO. THEY ALL VOLUNTEERED.

AH, YOUR FLIGHT LEADER IS ON DECK...

COMMANDER ANTILLES, WELCOME BACK.

THANKS, ADMIRAL. WE'LL SORT OUT WHO IS COMING WITH ME TO THE CONVOY LATER, BUT RIGHT NOW, I NEED TO STRETCH MY WINGS.

GRAB YOUR GEAR AND GET TO YOUR SHIPS...

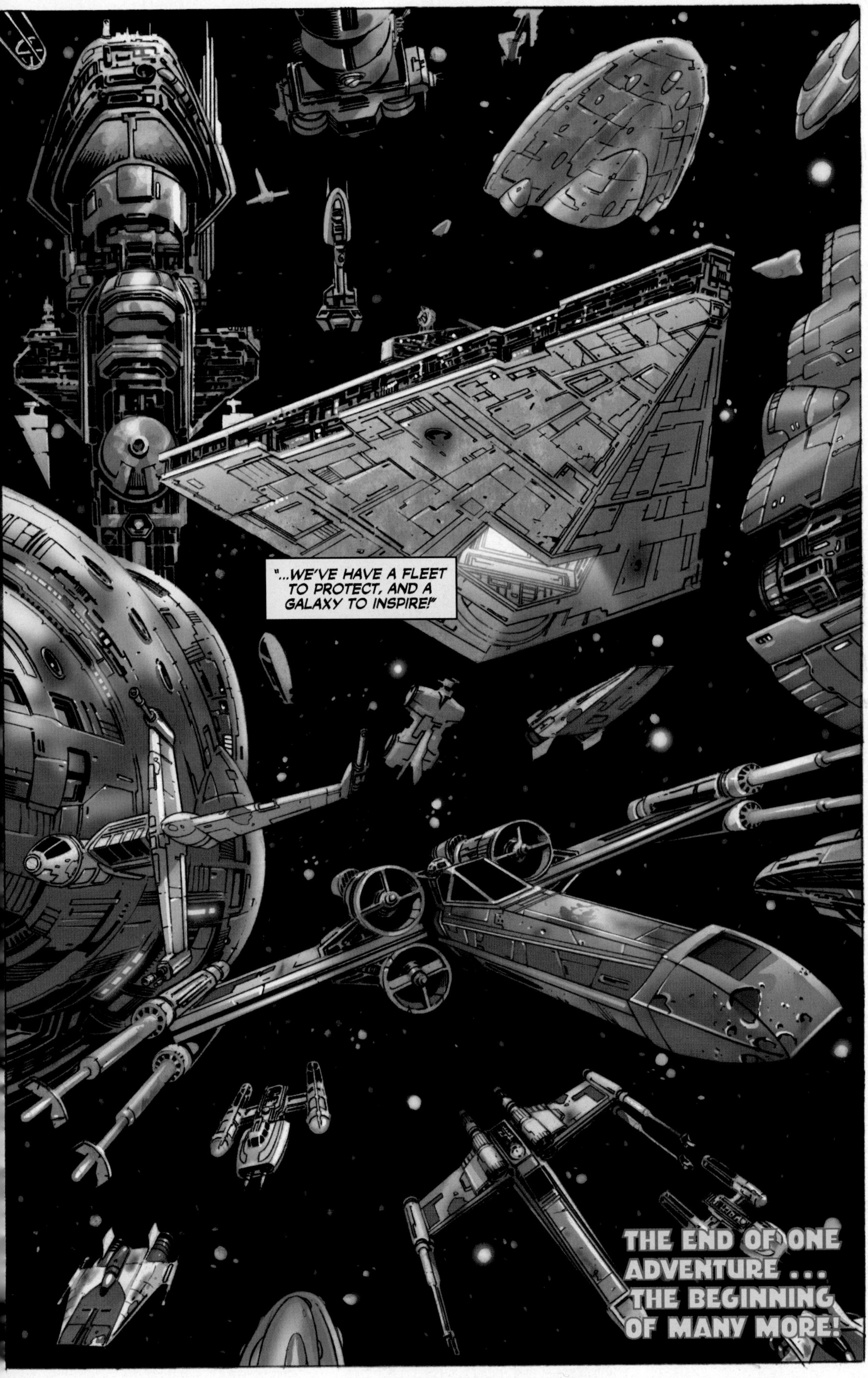
"...WE'VE HAVE A FLEET TO PROTECT, AND A GALAXY TO INSPIRE!"
THE END OF ONE ADVENTURE . . . THE BEGINNING OF MANY MORE!

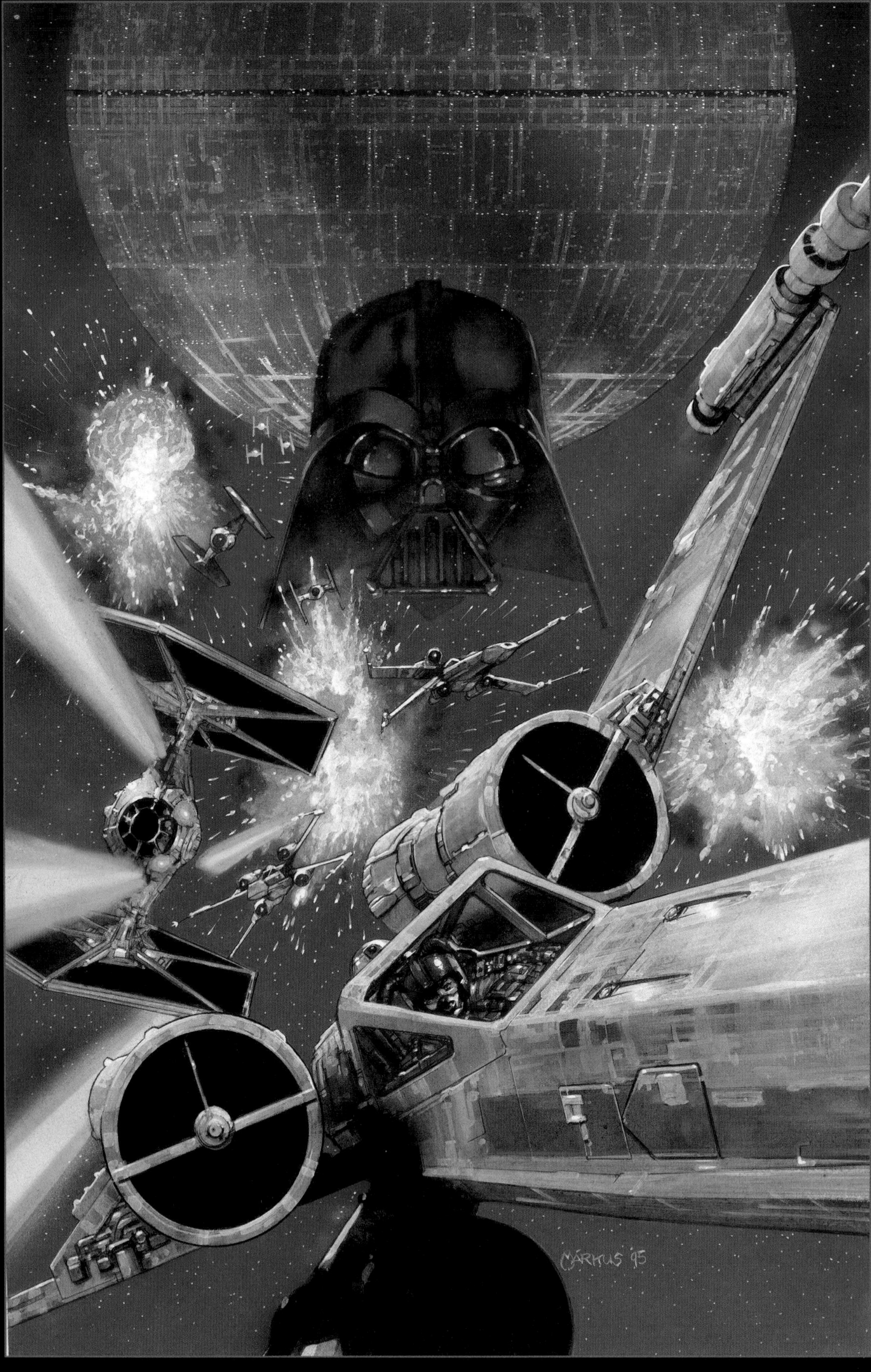

***STAR WARS: X-WING ROGUE SQUADRON SPECIAL***

WRITER: RYDER WINDHAM • PENCILER: JOHN NADEAU • INKER: MONTY SHELDON • COLORIST: CARY PORTER
LETTERER: STEVE DUTRO • EDITOR: PEET JANES • COVER ARTIST: MARK HARRISON

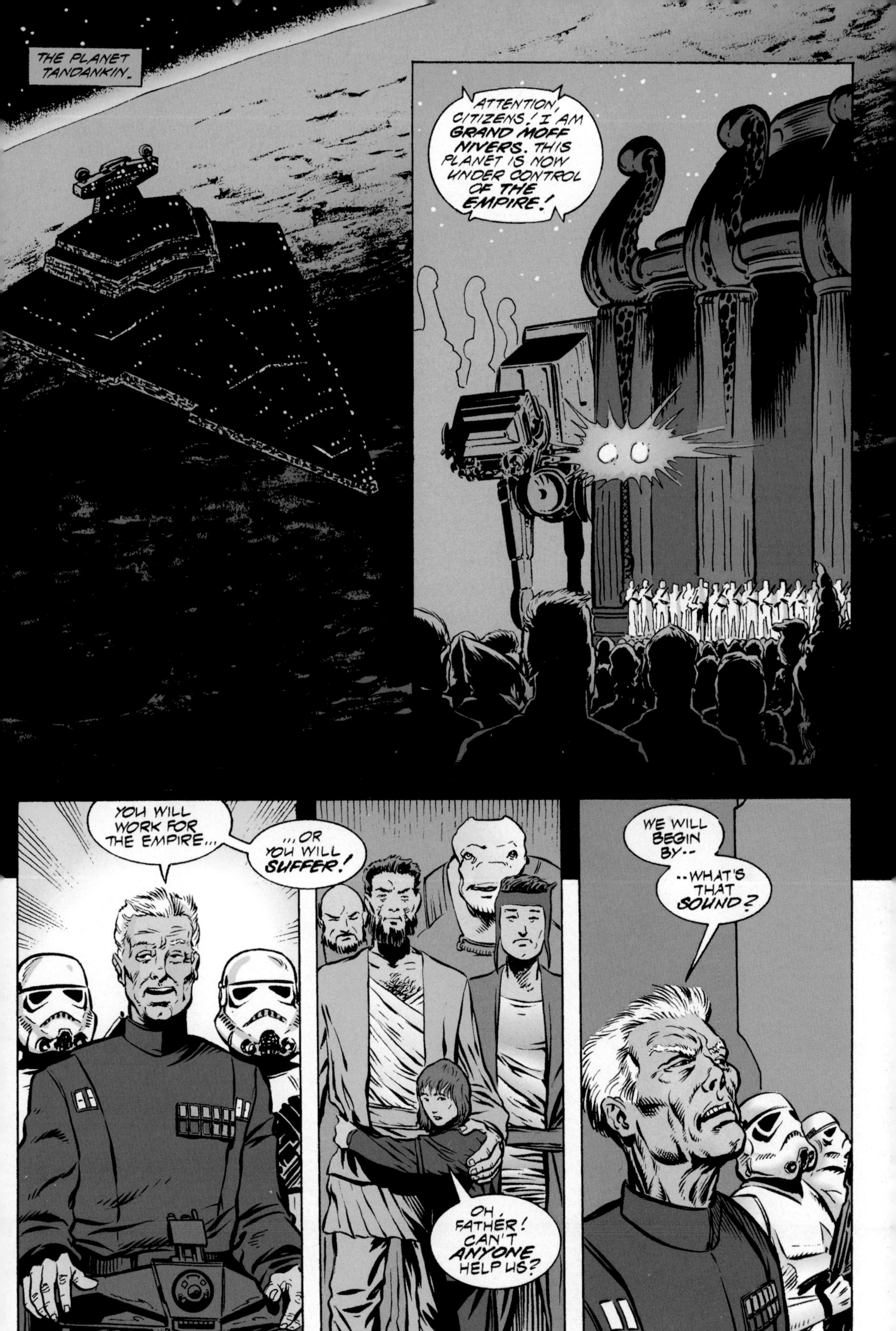
THE PLANET TANDANKIN.
ATTENTION, CITIZENS! I AM GRAND MOFF NIVERS. THIS PLANET IS NOW UNDER CONTROL OF THE EMPIRE!
YOU WILL WORK FOR THE EMPIRE...
...OR YOU WILL SUFFER!
OH, FATHER! CAN'T ANYONE HELP US?
WE WILL BEGIN BY--
--WHAT'S THAT SOUND?

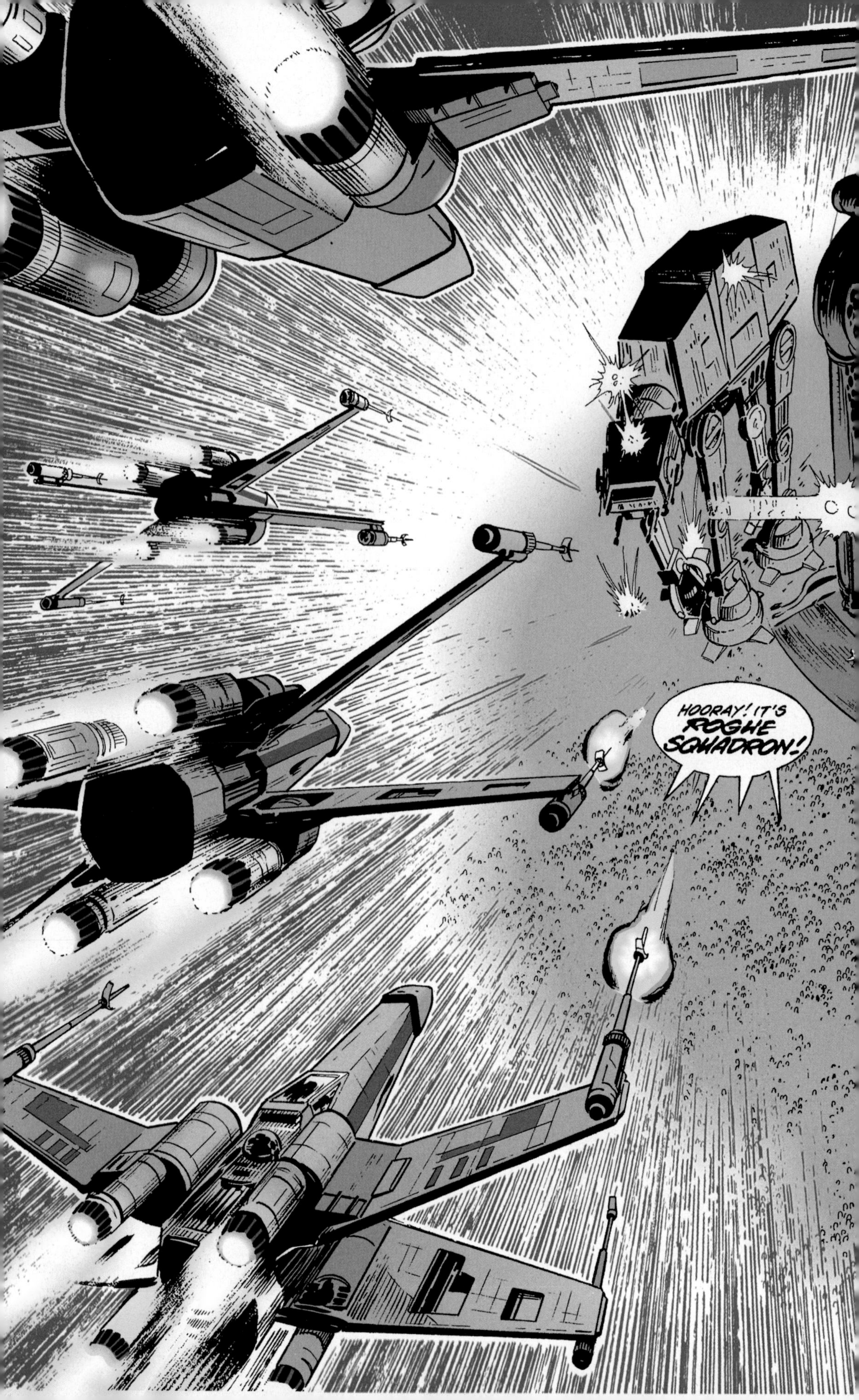
HOORAY! IT'S ROGUE SQUADRON!

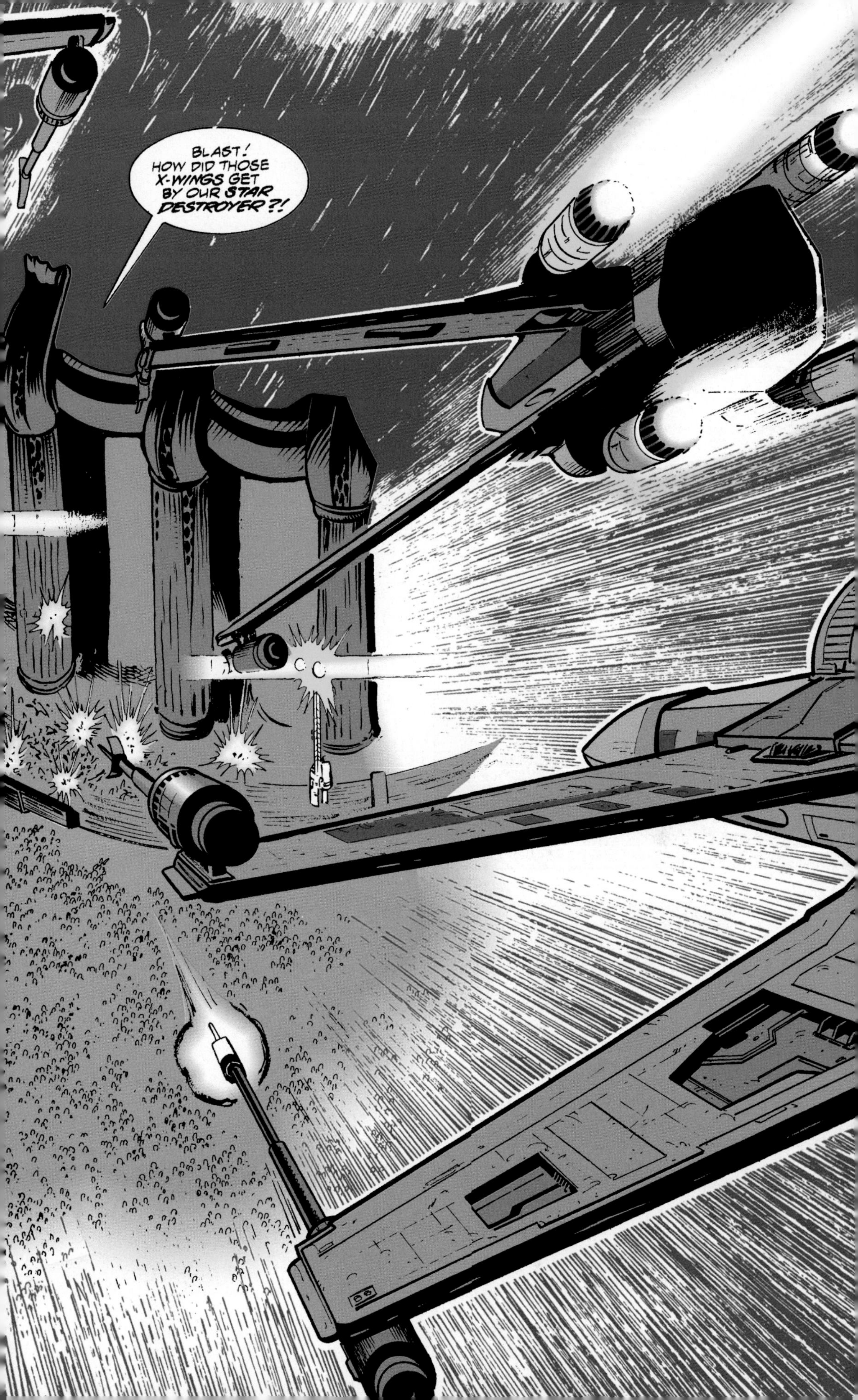
BLAST! HOW DID THOSE X-WINGS GET BY OUR STAR DESTROYER?!

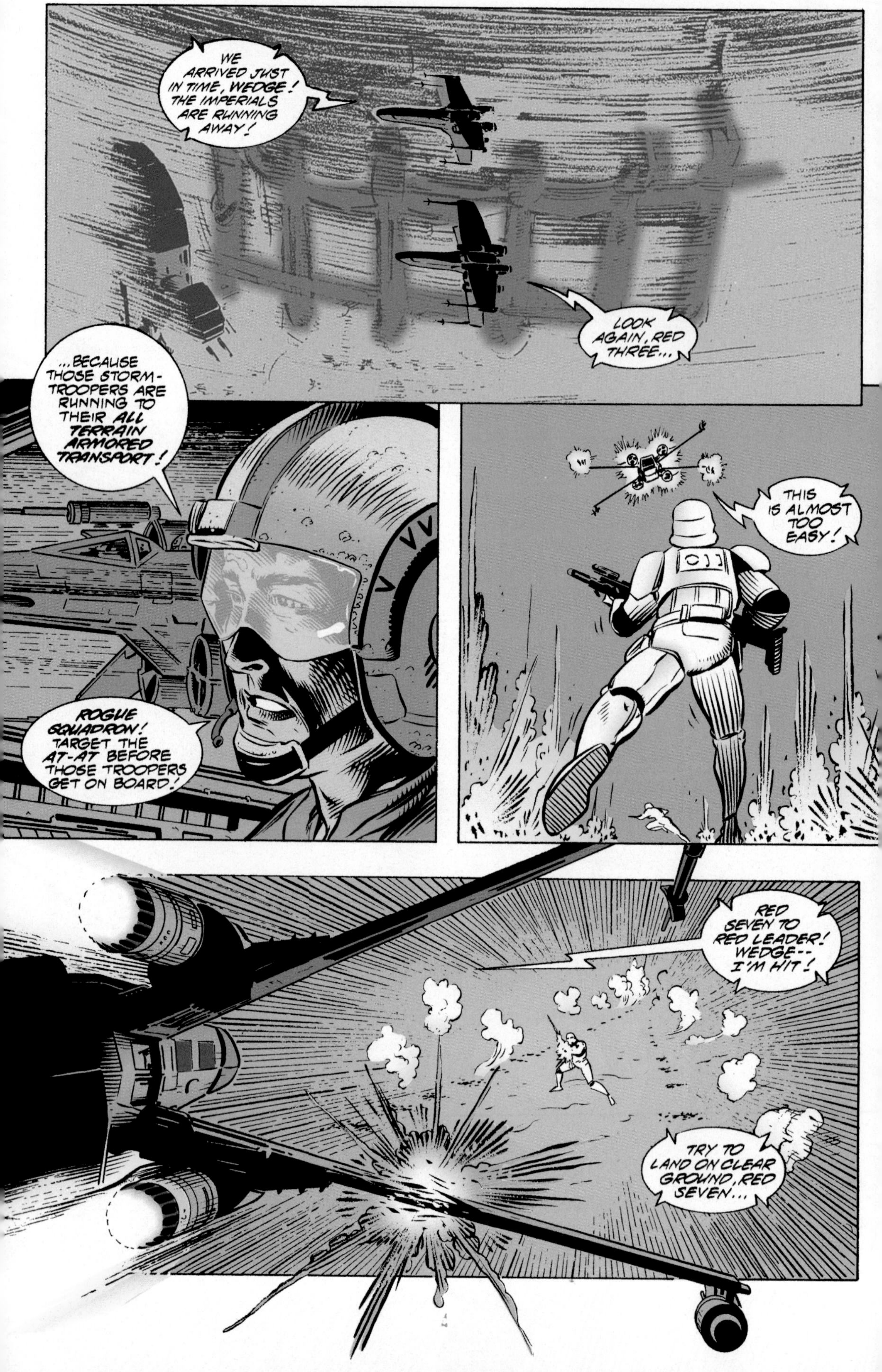
WE ARRIVED JUST IN TIME, WEDGE! THE IMPERIALS ARE RUNNING AWAY!
LOOK AGAIN, RED THREE...
...BECAUSE THOSE STORM-TROOPERS ARE RUNNING TO THEIR ALL TERRAIN ARMORED TRANSPORT!
ROGUE SQUADRON! TARGET THE AT-AT BEFORE THOSE TROOPERS GET ON BOARD!
THIS IS ALMOST TOO EASY!
RED SEVEN TO RED LEADER! WEDGE-- I'M HIT!
TRY TO LAND ON CLEAR GROUND, RED SEVEN...

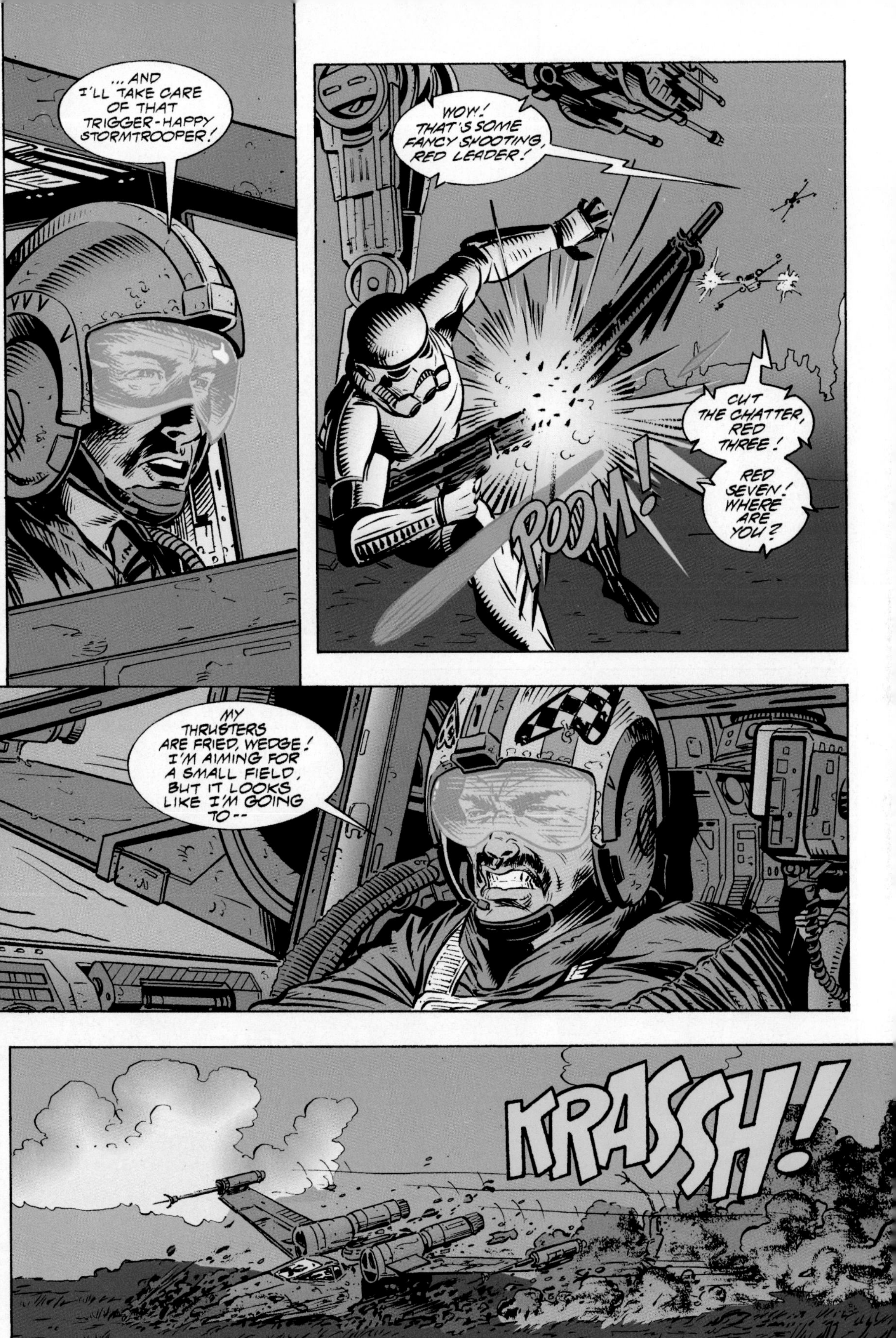
...AND I'LL TAKE CARE OF THAT TRIGGER-HAPPY STORMTROOPER!
WOW! THAT'S SOME FANCY SHOOTING, RED LEADER!
POOM!
CUT THE CHATTER, RED THREE!
RED SEVEN! WHERE ARE YOU?
MY THRUSTERS ARE FRIED, WEDGE! I'M AIMING FOR A SMALL FIELD, BUT IT LOOKS LIKE I'M GOING TO--
KRASSH!

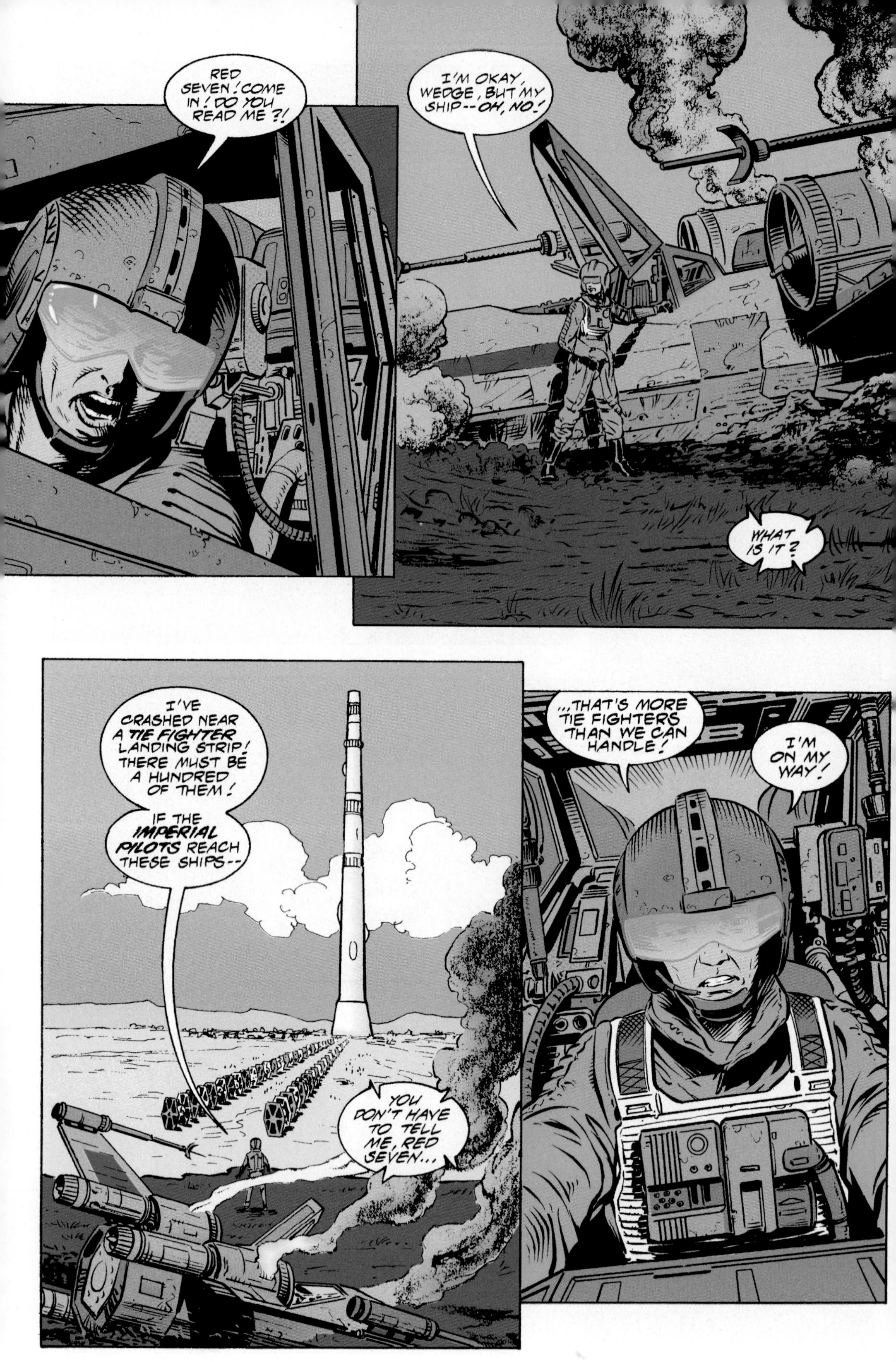
RED SEVEN! COME IN! DO YOU READ ME?!
I'M OKAY, WEDGE, BUT MY SHIP--OH, NO!
WHAT IS IT?
I'VE CRASHED NEAR A TIE FIGHTER LANDING STRIP! THERE MUST BE A HUNDRED OF THEM!
IF THE IMPERIAL PILOTS REACH THESE SHIPS--
YOU DON'T HAVE TO TELL ME, RED SEVEN...
...THAT'S MORE TIE FIGHTERS THAN WE CAN HANDLE!
I'M ON MY WAY!

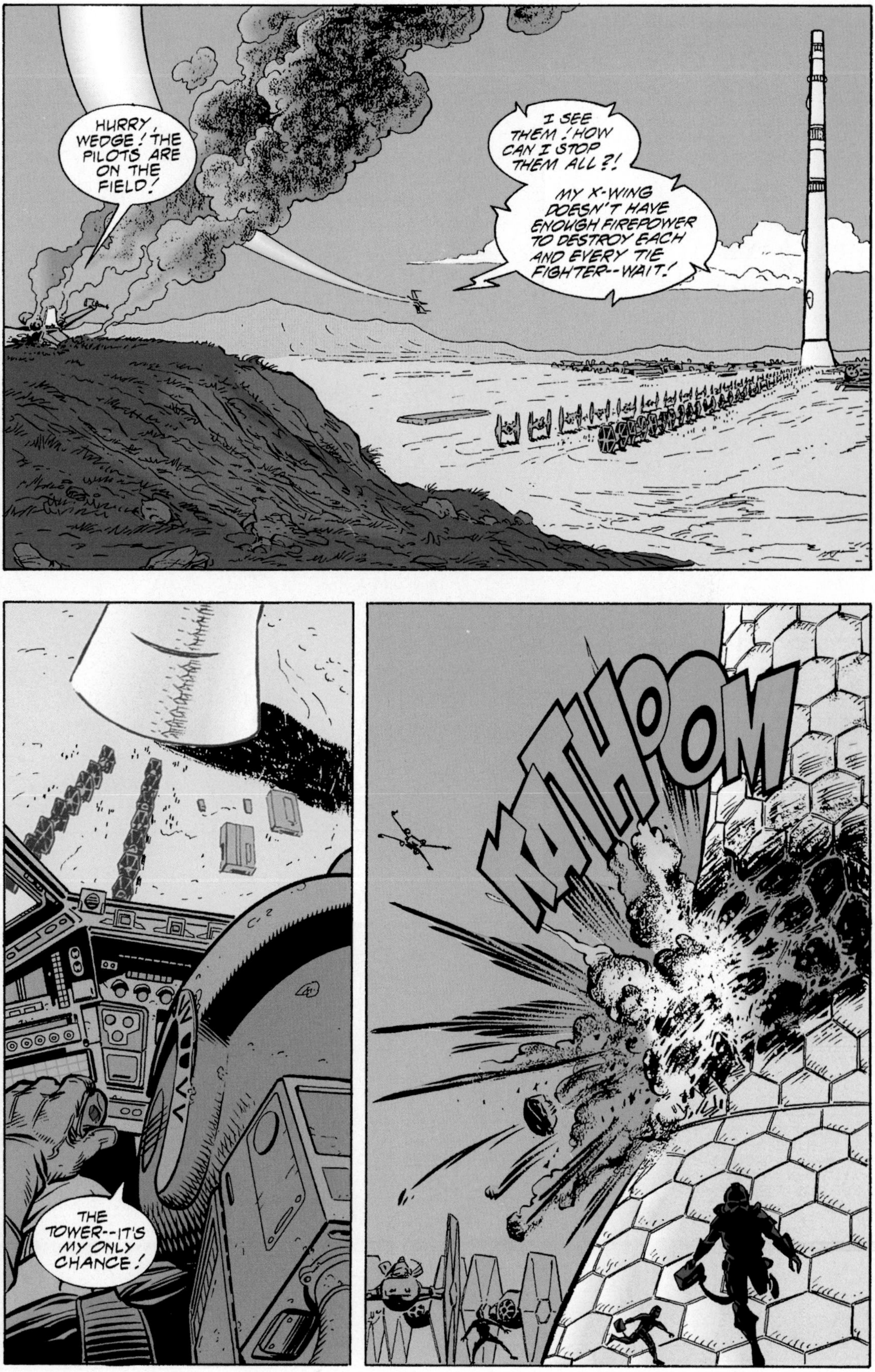
HURRY, WEDGE! THE PILOTS ARE ON THE FIELD!
I SEE THEM! HOW CAN I STOP THEM ALL?!
MY X-WING DOESN'T HAVE ENOUGH FIREPOWER TO DESTROY EACH AND EVERY TIE FIGHTER--WAIT!
THE TOWER--IT'S MY ONLY CHANCE!
KATHOOM

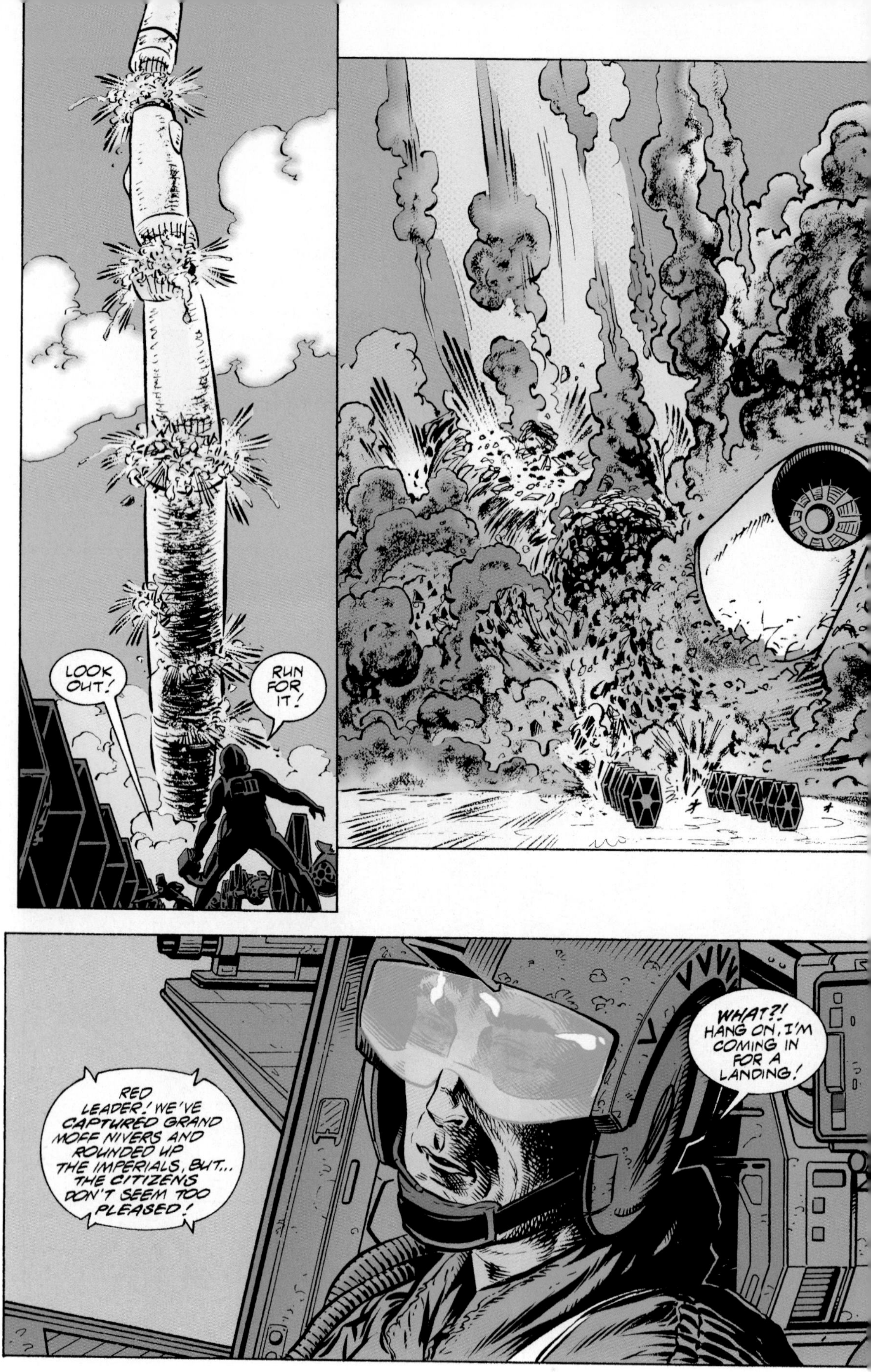
LOOK OUT!
RUN FOR IT!
RED LEADER! WE'VE CAPTURED GRAND MOFF NIVERS AND ROUNDED UP THE IMPERIALS, BUT... THE CITIZENS DON'T SEEM TOO PLEASED!
WHAT?! HANG ON, I'M COMING IN FOR A LANDING!

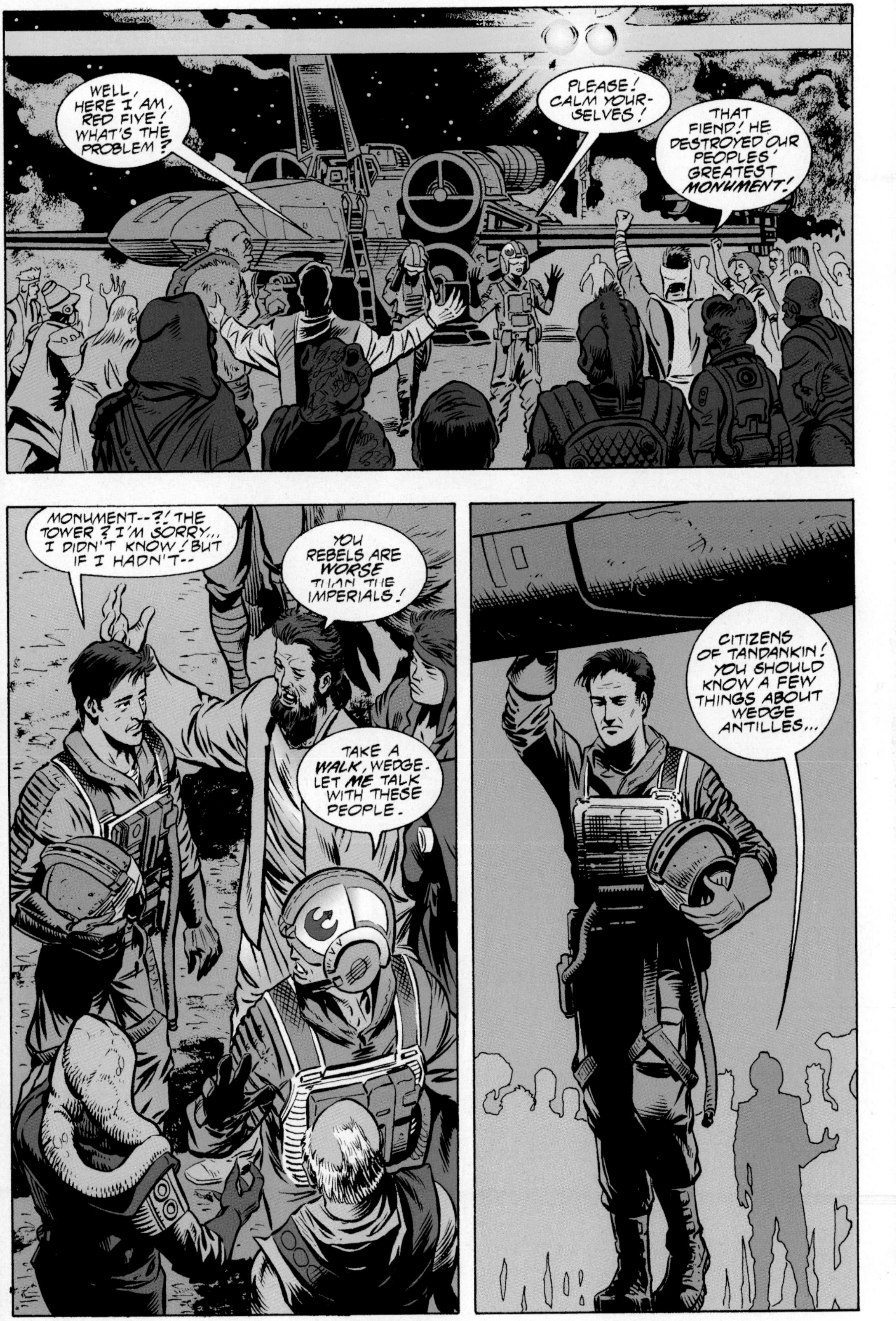
WELL, HERE I AM, RED FIVE! WHAT'S THE PROBLEM?
PLEASE! CALM YOURSELVES!
THAT FIEND! HE DESTROYED OUR PEOPLES' GREATEST MONUMENT!
MONUMENT--?! THE TOWER? I'M SORRY... I DIDN'T KNOW! BUT IF I HADN'T--
YOU REBELS ARE WORSE THAN THE IMPERIALS!
TAKE A WALK, WEDGE. LET ME TALK WITH THESE PEOPLE.
CITIZENS OF TANDANKIN! YOU SHOULD KNOW A FEW THINGS ABOUT WEDGE ANTILLES...

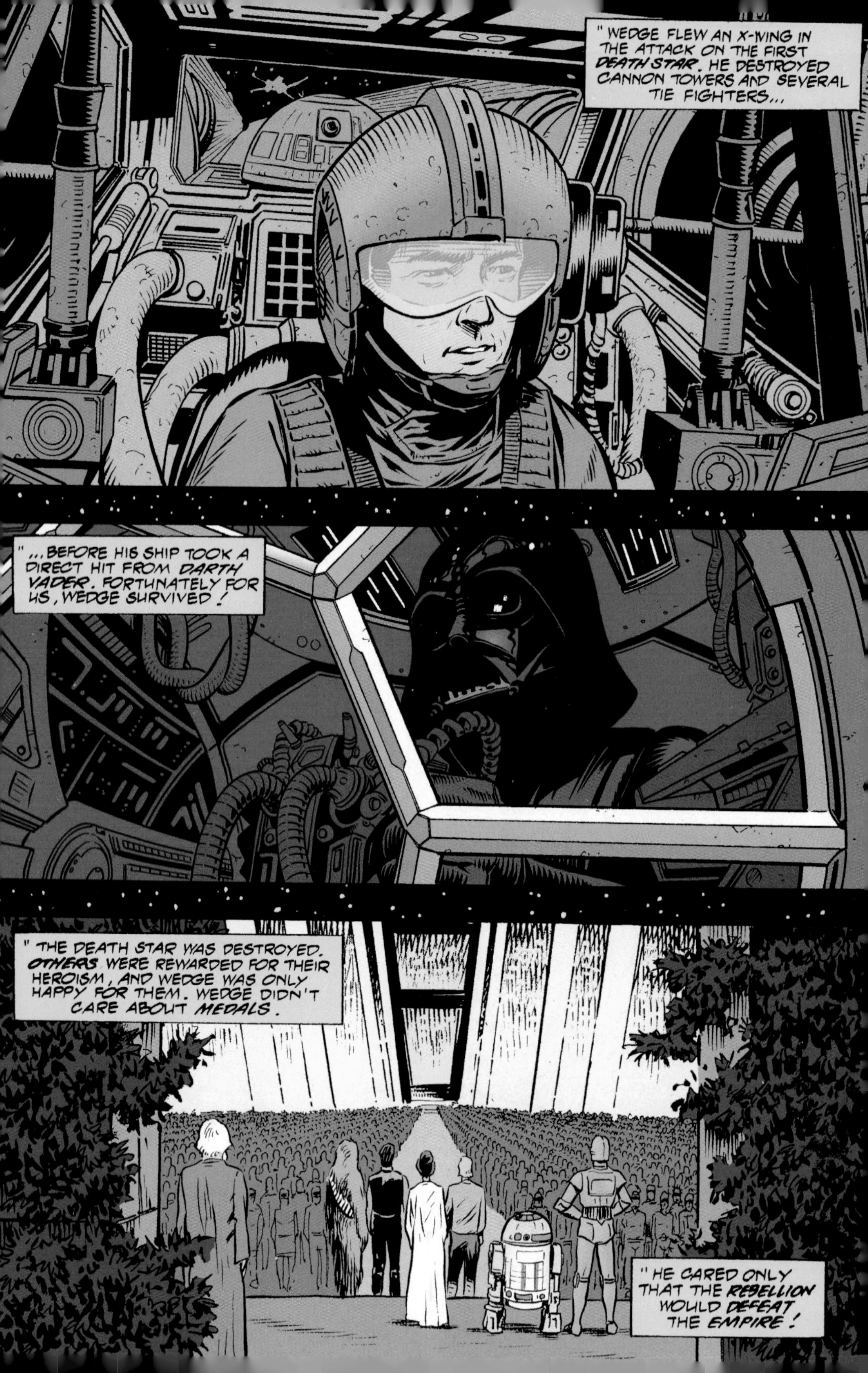
"WEDGE FLEW AN X-WING IN THE ATTACK ON THE FIRST DEATH STAR. HE DESTROYED CANNON TOWERS AND SEVERAL TIE FIGHTERS...
"...BEFORE HIS SHIP TOOK A DIRECT HIT FROM DARTH VADER. FORTUNATELY FOR US, WEDGE SURVIVED!
"THE DEATH STAR WAS DESTROYED. OTHERS WERE REWARDED FOR THEIR HEROISM, AND WEDGE WAS ONLY HAPPY FOR THEM. WEDGE DIDN'T CARE ABOUT MEDALS.
"HE CARED ONLY THAT THE REBELLION WOULD DEFEAT THE EMPIRE!

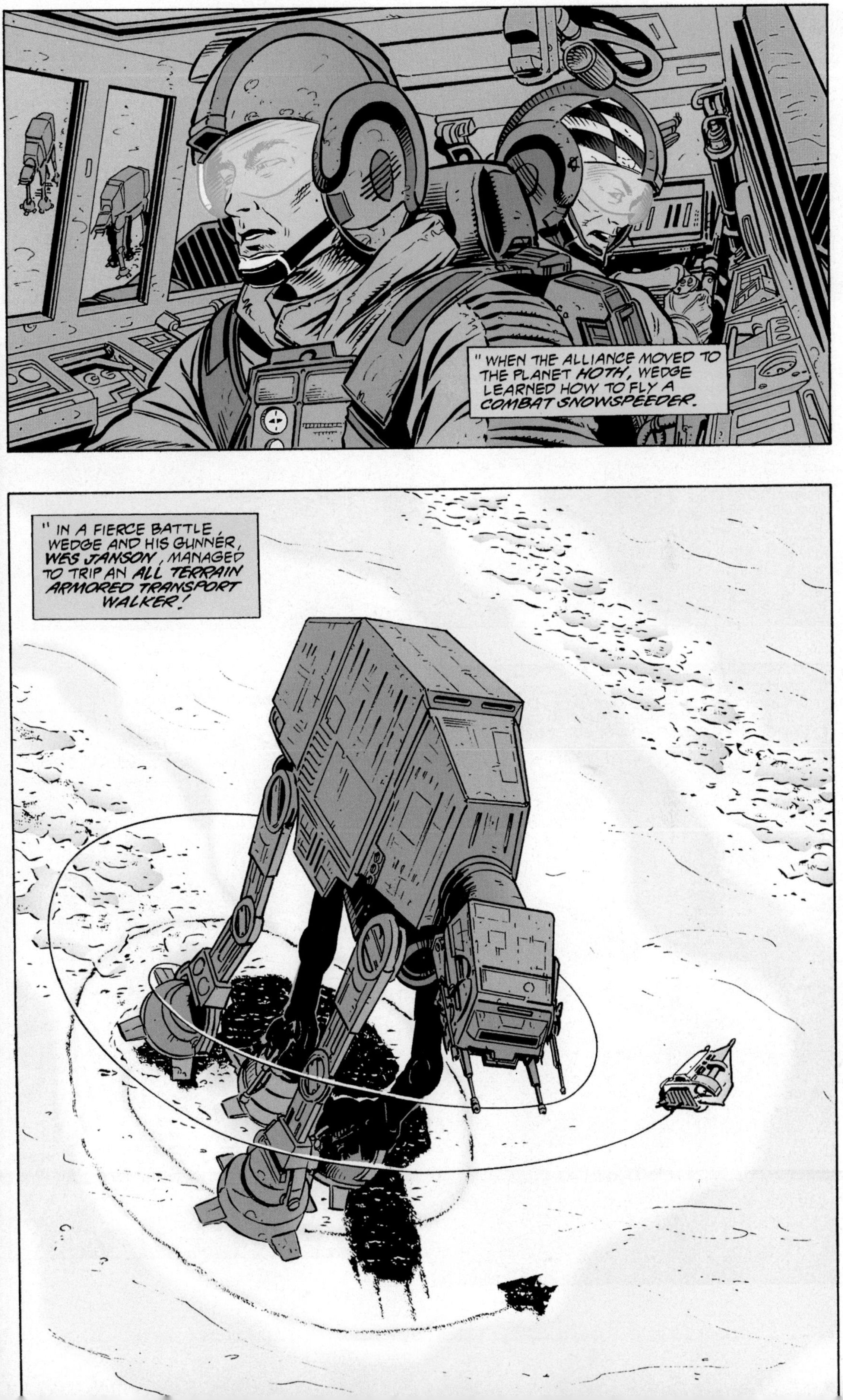
"WHEN THE ALLIANCE MOVED TO THE PLANET HOTH, WEDGE LEARNED HOW TO FLY A COMBAT SNOWSPEEDER.
"IN A FIERCE BATTLE, WEDGE AND HIS GUNNER, WES JANSON, MANAGED TO TRIP AN ALL TERRAIN ARMORED TRANSPORT WALKER!

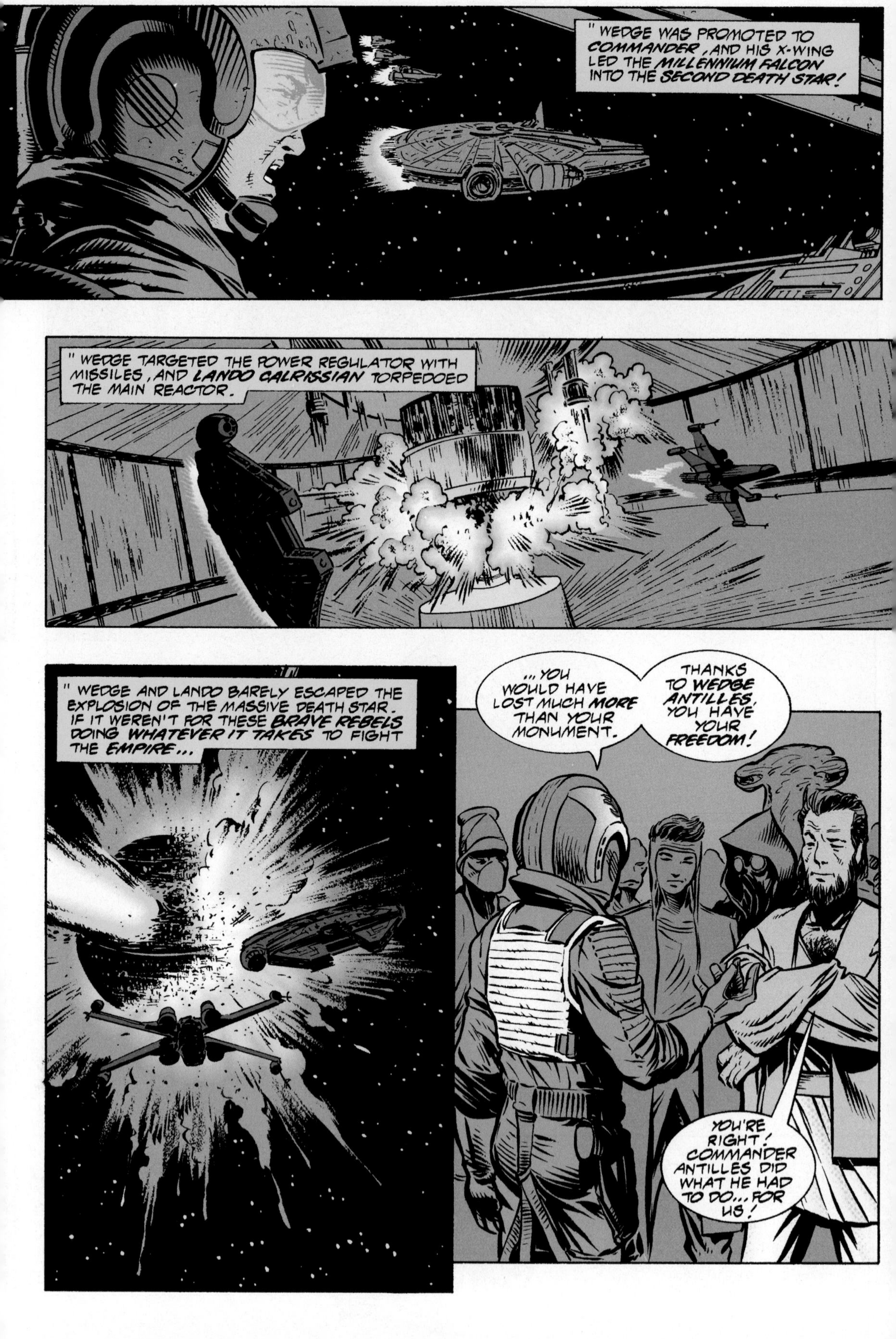
"WEDGE WAS PROMOTED TO COMMANDER, AND HIS X-WING LED THE MILLENNIUM FALCON INTO THE SECOND DEATH STAR!
"WEDGE TARGETED THE POWER REGULATOR WITH MISSILES, AND LANDO CALRISSIAN TORPEDOED THE MAIN REACTOR.
"WEDGE AND LANDO BARELY ESCAPED THE EXPLOSION OF THE MASSIVE DEATH STAR. IF IT WEREN'T FOR THESE BRAVE REBELS DOING WHATEVER IT TAKES TO FIGHT THE EMPIRE...
...YOU WOULD HAVE LOST MUCH MORE THAN YOUR MONUMENT.
THANKS TO WEDGE ANTILLES, YOU HAVE YOUR FREEDOM!
YOU'RE RIGHT! COMMANDER ANTILLES DID WHAT HE HAD TO DO... FOR US!

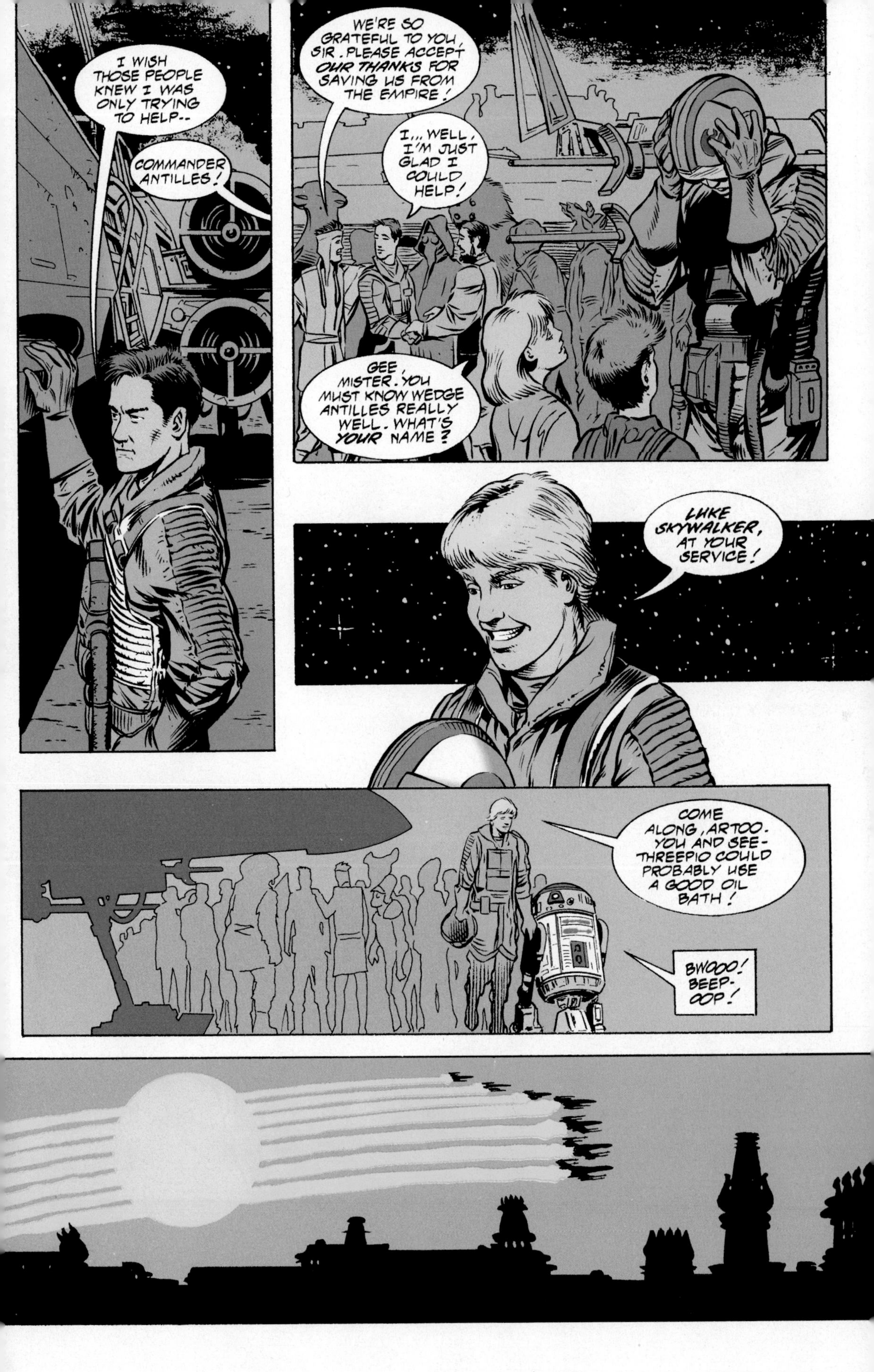
I WISH THOSE PEOPLE KNEW I WAS ONLY TRYING TO HELP--
COMMANDER ANTILLES!
WE'RE SO GRATEFUL TO YOU, SIR. PLEASE ACCEPT OUR THANKS FOR SAVING US FROM THE EMPIRE!
I... WELL, I'M JUST GLAD I COULD HELP!
GEE, MISTER. YOU MUST KNOW WEDGE ANTILLES REALLY WELL. WHAT'S YOUR NAME?
LUKE SKYWALKER, AT YOUR SERVICE!
COME ALONG, ARTOO. YOU AND SEE-THREEPIO COULD PROBABLY USE A GOOD OIL BATH!
BWOOO! BEEP-OOP!

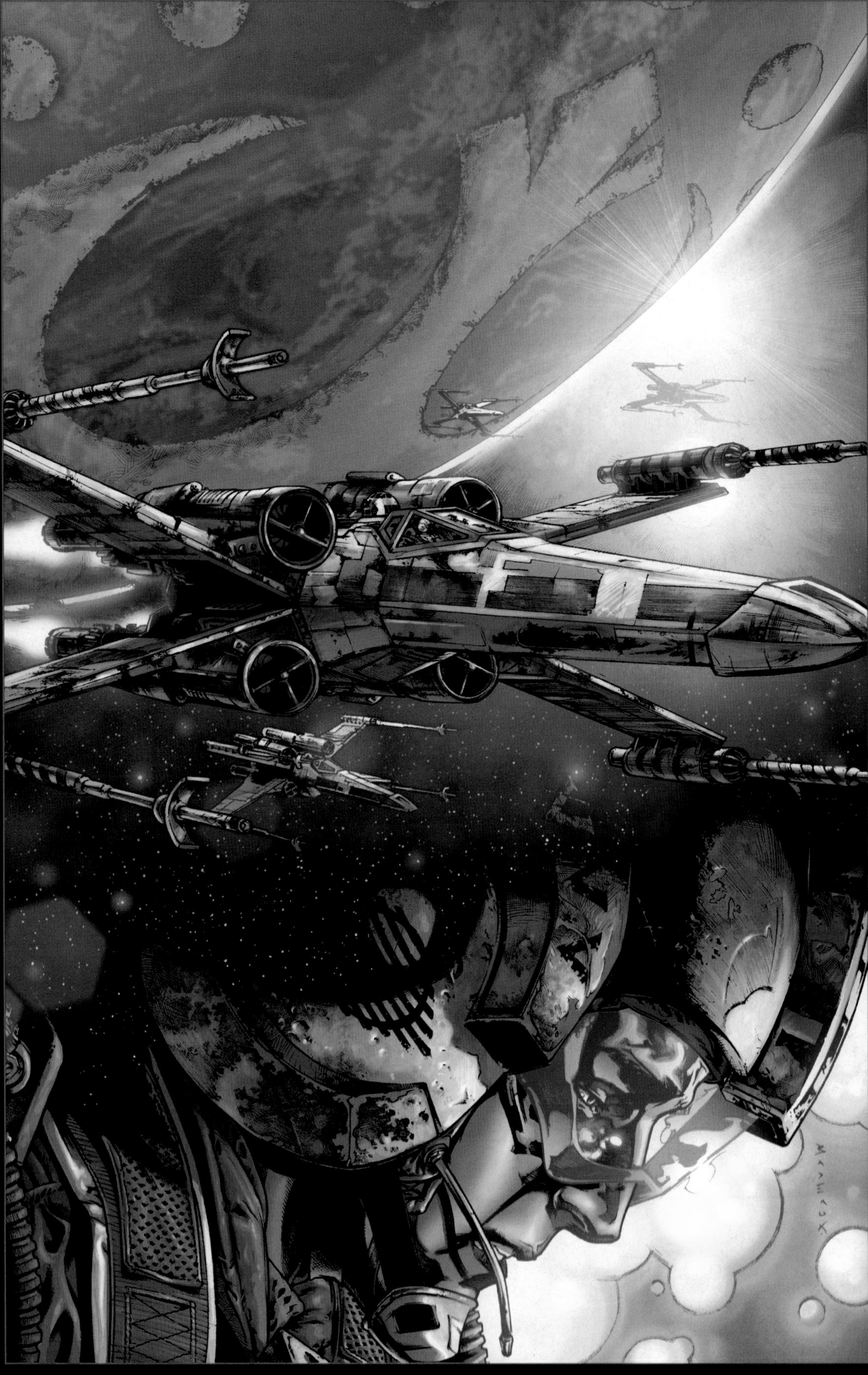

*STAR WARS TALES #23* — "LUCKY"

WRITER: ROB WILLIAMS • PENCILER: MICHEL LACOMBE • INKERS: SERGE LAPOINTE & ANDREW PEPOY • COLORIST: WIL GLASS • LETTERER: MICHAEL HEISLER
ASSISTANT EDITOR: DAVE MARSHALL • EDITOR: JEREMY BARLOW • COVER ARTISTS: BRANDON BADEAUX & BRAD ANDERSON

I AM WEDGE ANTILLES.

I SURVIVED THE BATTLE OF YAVIN.

I SURVIVED THE BATTLE OF HOTH.

HELL...JUST A COUPLE OF WEEKS AGO I BLEW UP THE DEATH STAR DURING THE BATTLE OF ENDOR.

THE REASON I'M STILL BREATHING WHEN A LOT OF OTHER GOOD REBEL PILOTS AREN'T? MAYBE IT'S BECAUSE I'M BETTER.

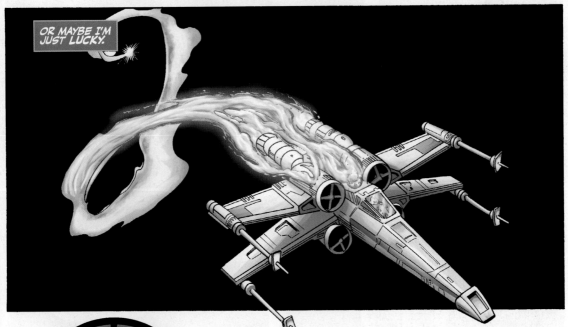

OR MAYBE I'M JUST LUCKY.

WEDGE ANTILLES IN **LUCKY**

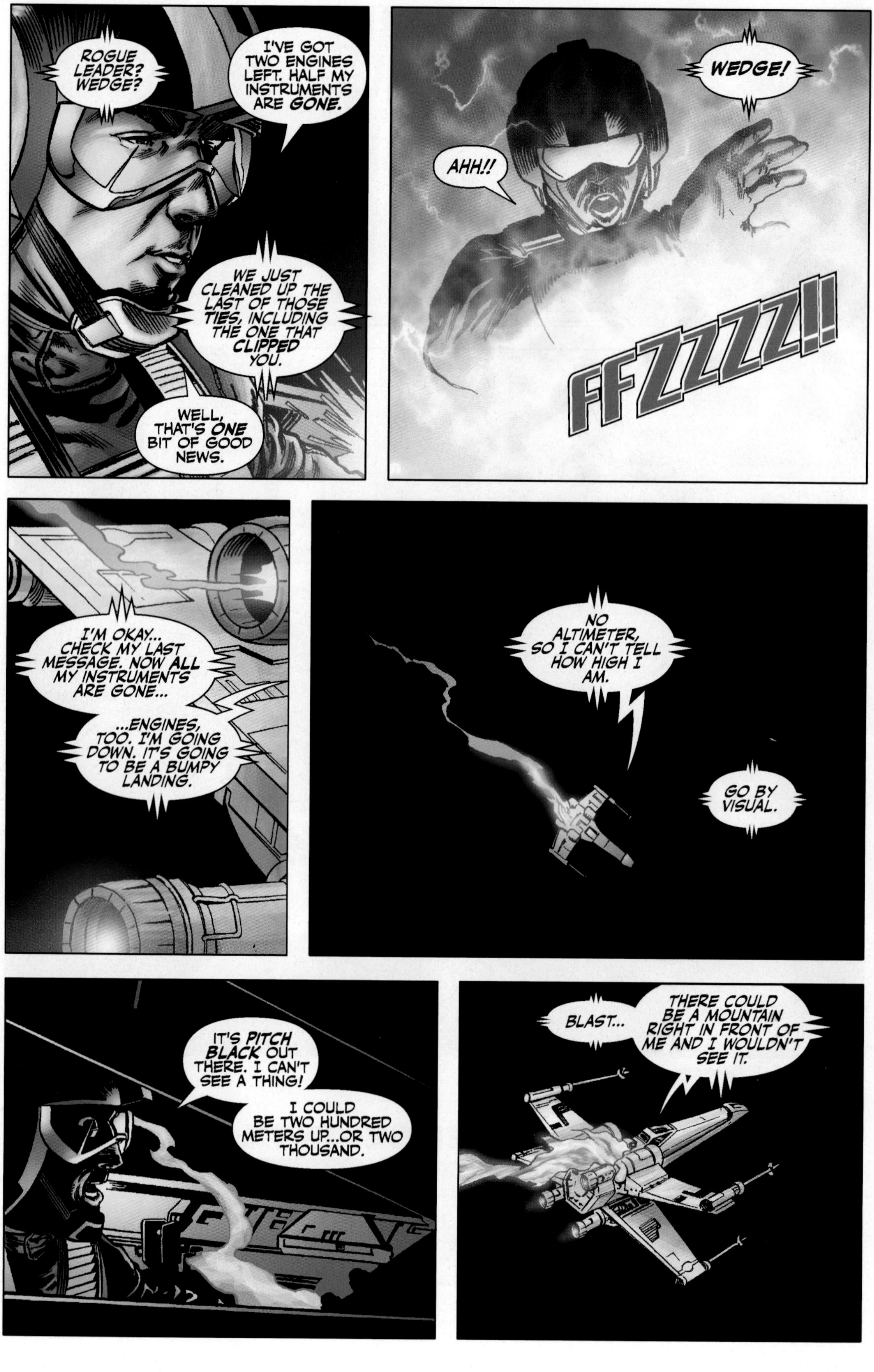
ROGUE LEADER? WEDGE?
I'VE GOT TWO ENGINES LEFT. HALF MY INSTRUMENTS ARE GONE.
WE JUST CLEANED UP THE LAST OF THOSE TIES, INCLUDING THE ONE THAT CLIPPED YOU.
WELL, THAT'S ONE BIT OF GOOD NEWS.
WEDGE!
AHH!!
FFZZZZZ!!
I'M OKAY... CHECK MY LAST MESSAGE. NOW ALL MY INSTRUMENTS ARE GONE...
...ENGINES, TOO. I'M GOING DOWN. IT'S GOING TO BE A BUMPY LANDING.
NO ALTIMETER, SO I CAN'T TELL HOW HIGH I AM.
GO BY VISUAL.
IT'S PITCH BLACK OUT THERE. I CAN'T SEE A THING!
I COULD BE TWO HUNDRED METERS UP...OR TWO THOUSAND.
BLAST...
THERE COULD BE A MOUNTAIN RIGHT IN FRONT OF ME AND I WOULDN'T SEE IT.

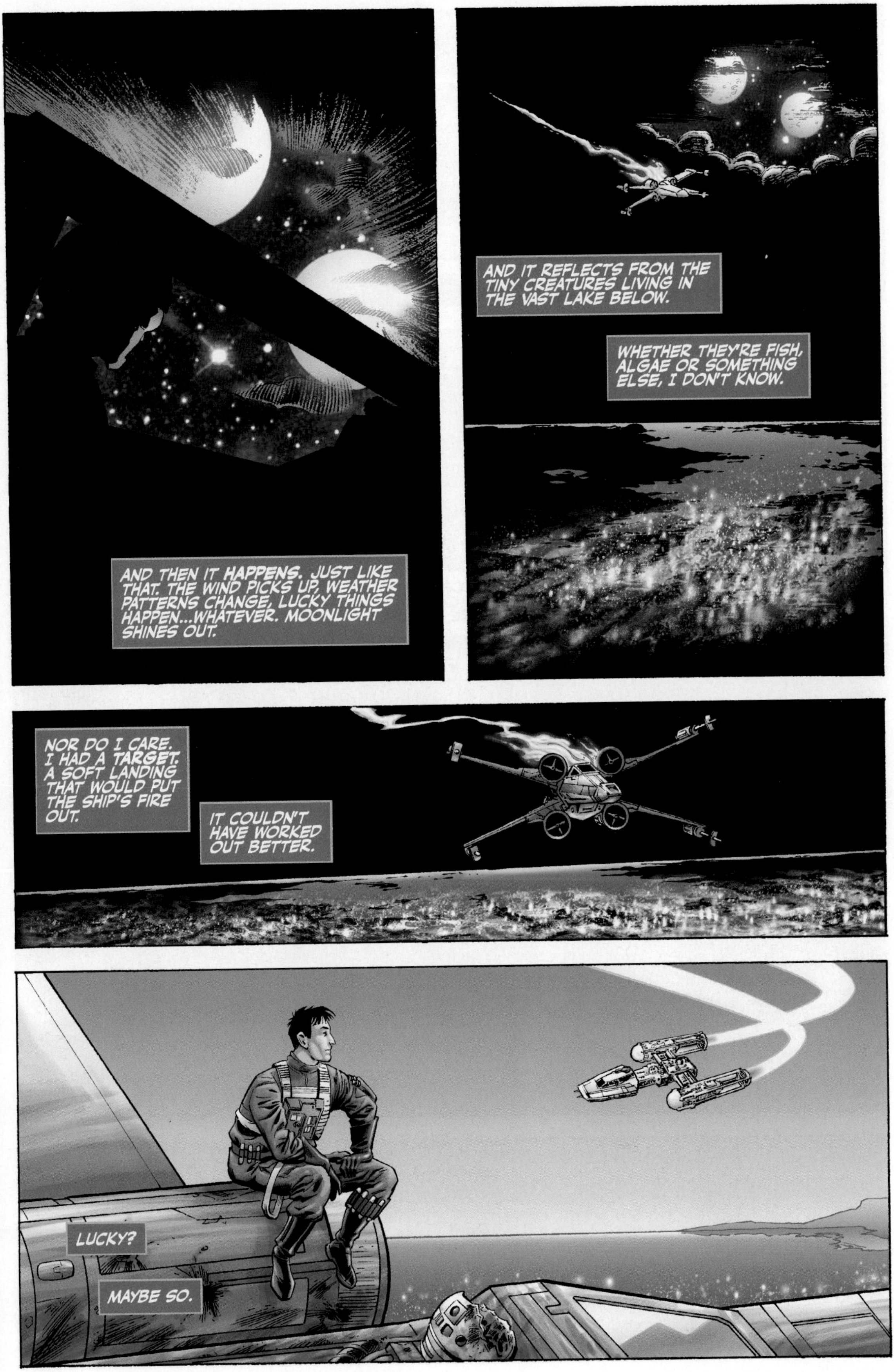
AND THEN IT HAPPENS. JUST LIKE THAT. THE WIND PICKS UP, WEATHER PATTERNS CHANGE, LUCKY THINGS HAPPEN...WHATEVER. MOONLIGHT SHINES OUT.
AND IT REFLECTS FROM THE TINY CREATURES LIVING IN THE VAST LAKE BELOW.
WHETHER THEY'RE FISH, ALGAE OR SOMETHING ELSE, I DON'T KNOW.
NOR DO I CARE. I HAD A TARGET. A SOFT LANDING THAT WOULD PUT THE SHIP'S FIRE OUT.
IT COULDN'T HAVE WORKED OUT BETTER.
LUCKY?
MAYBE SO.

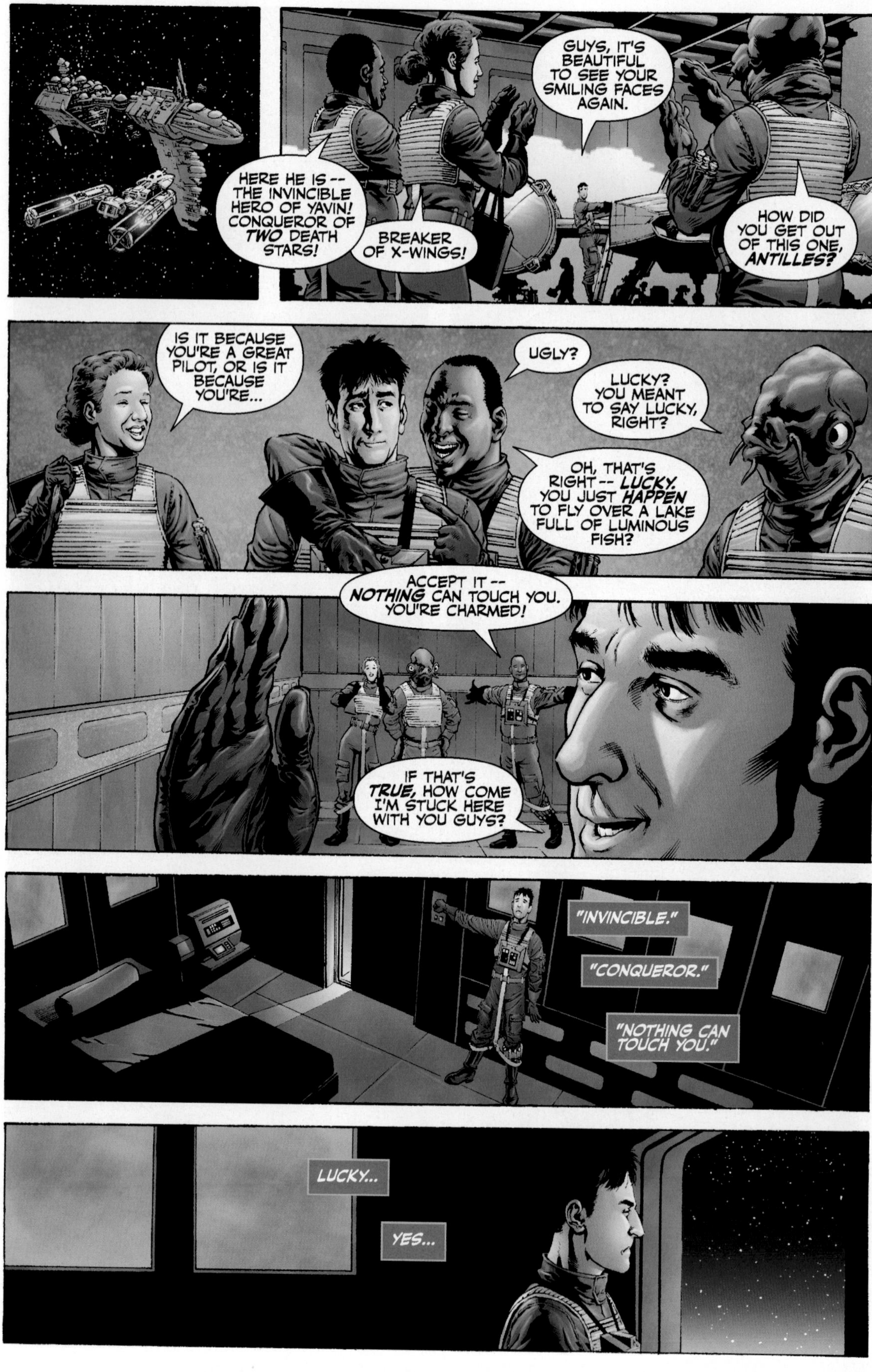
HERE HE IS -- THE INVINCIBLE HERO OF YAVIN! CONQUEROR OF *TWO* DEATH STARS!
BREAKER OF X-WINGS!
GUYS, IT'S BEAUTIFUL TO SEE YOUR SMILING FACES AGAIN.
HOW DID YOU GET OUT OF THIS ONE, *ANTILLES?*
IS IT BECAUSE YOU'RE A GREAT PILOT, OR IS IT BECAUSE YOU'RE...
UGLY?
LUCKY? YOU MEANT TO SAY LUCKY, RIGHT?
OH, THAT'S RIGHT -- *LUCKY.* YOU JUST *HAPPEN* TO FLY OVER A LAKE FULL OF LUMINOUS FISH?
ACCEPT IT -- *NOTHING* CAN TOUCH YOU. YOU'RE CHARMED!
IF THAT'S *TRUE,* HOW COME I'M STUCK HERE WITH YOU GUYS?
"INVINCIBLE."
"CONQUEROR."
"NOTHING CAN TOUCH YOU."
LUCKY...
YES...

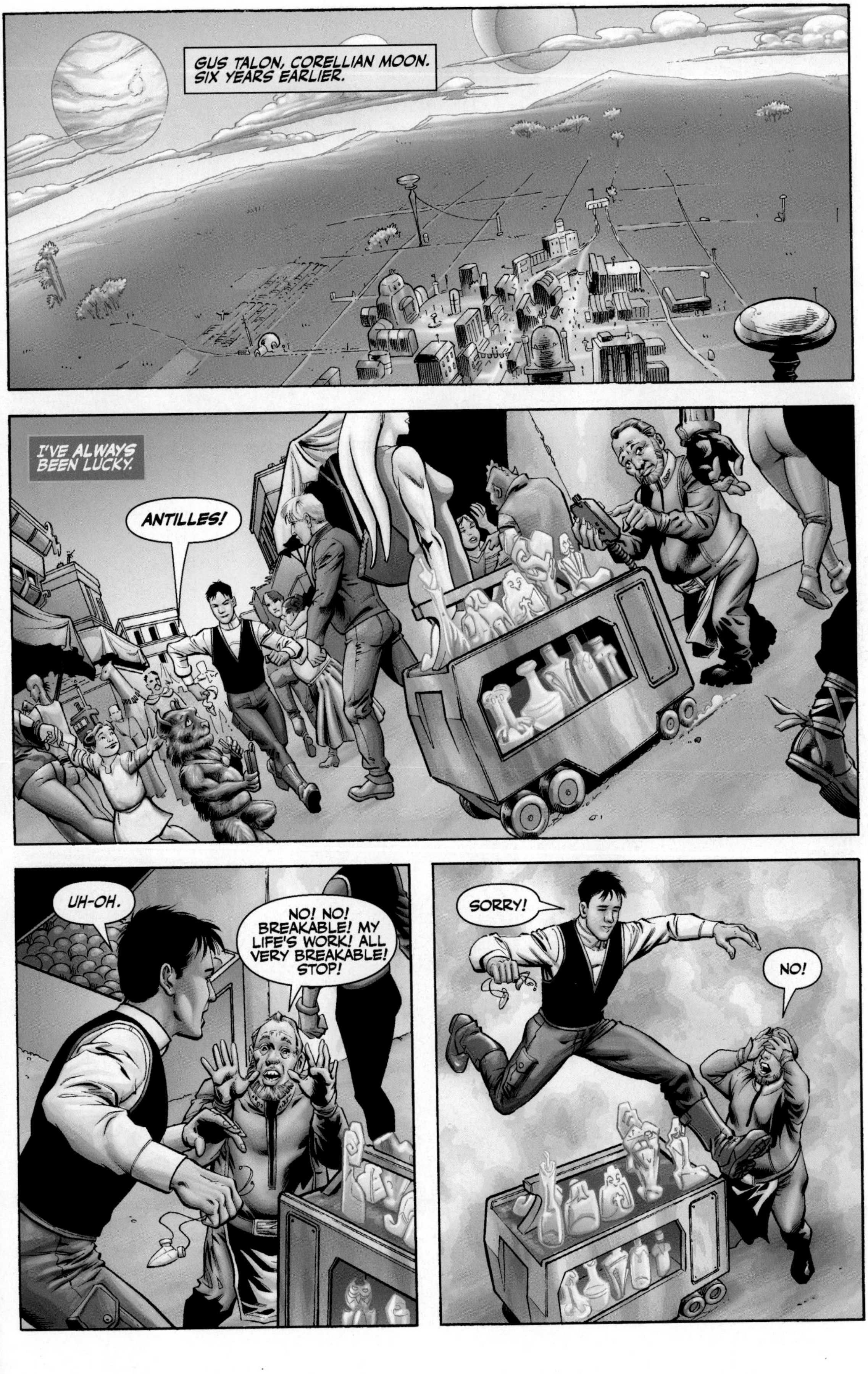

GUS TALON, CORELLIAN MOON.
SIX YEARS EARLIER.
I'VE ALWAYS BEEN LUCKY.
ANTILLES!
UH-OH.
NO! NO! BREAKABLE! MY LIFE'S WORK! ALL VERY BREAKABLE! STOP!
SORRY!
NO!

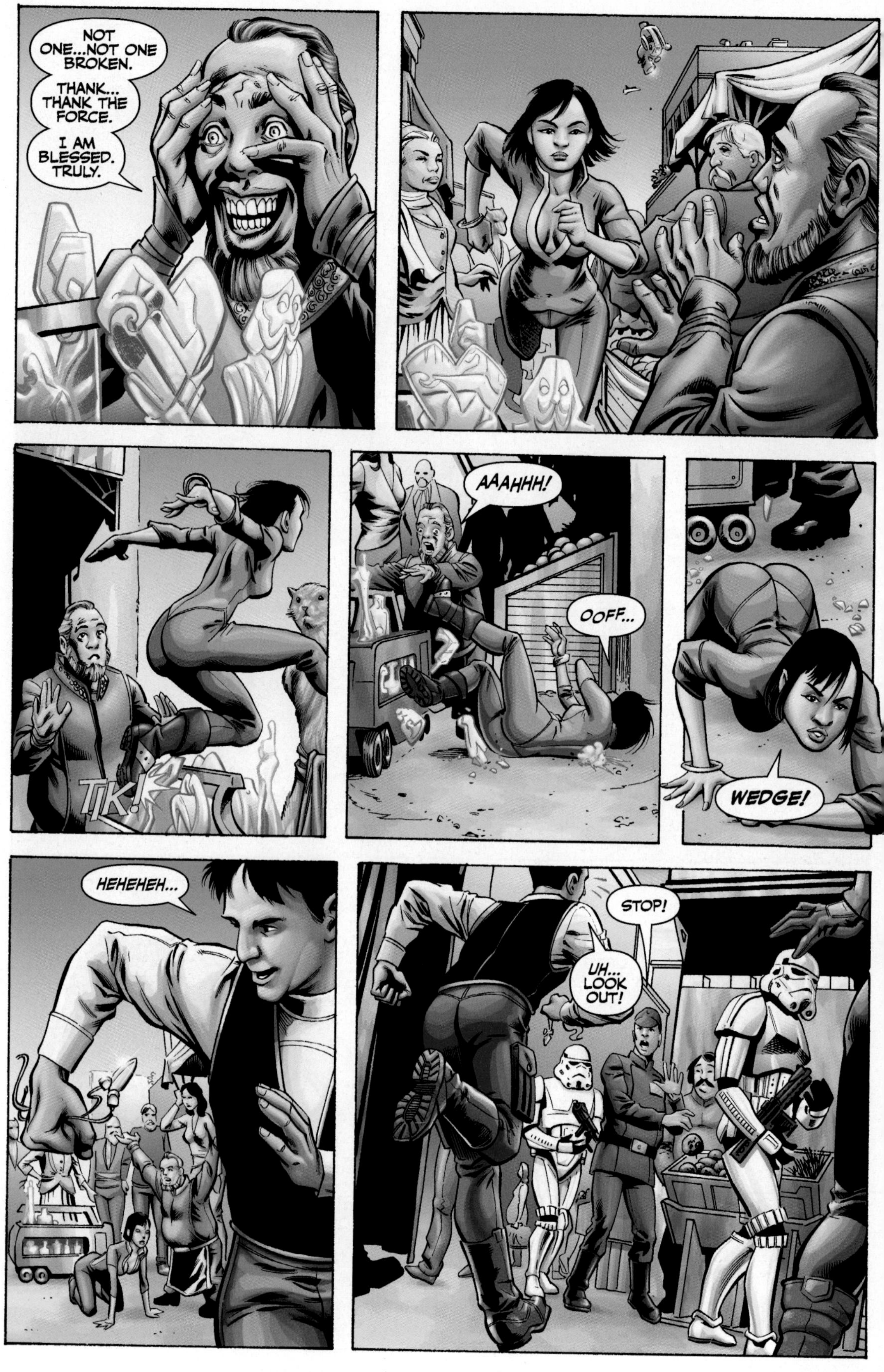

NOT ONE...NOT ONE BROKEN.
THANK... THANK THE FORCE.
I AM BLESSED. TRULY.
TIK!
AAAHHH!
OOFF...
WEDGE!
HEHEHEH...
STOP!
UH... LOOK OUT!

**GOT YOU!**

**OOFFF...**

OH, HI, **RALLO.** FANCY MEETING **YOU** HERE.

TELL THEM TO PUT THE GUNS DOWN -- HE'S JUST A BOY. HE MEANT NO HARM.

HE COULD HAVE BEEN A BOMBER, **REBEL SCUM,** ANYTHING.

AND HE LOOKS MORE LIKE A YOUNG MAN TO ME.

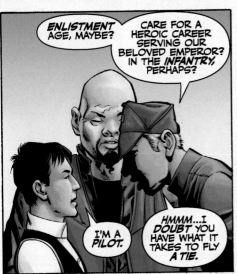

**ENLISTMENT** AGE, MAYBE?

CARE FOR A **HEROIC** CAREER SERVING OUR **BELOVED EMPEROR?** IN THE **INFANTRY,** PERHAPS?

I'M A **PILOT.**

HMMM...I **DOUBT** YOU HAVE WHAT IT TAKES TO FLY A TIE.

GET AWAY FROM HIM, **TURRANT.**

THAT'S **CAPTAIN** TURRANT.

WHEN ARE YOU AND YOUR TROOPS LEAVING?

OH, MAYBE IN A **FEW WEEKS,** MAYBE **NEVER.**

MAYBE A **PERMANENT** PRESENCE HERE IS WHAT YOU PEOPLE REALLY NEED...SOME GOOD, HEALTHY **DISCIPLINE.**

THESE ARE **DANGEROUS** TIMES. WE'VE PICKED UP INTEL ON A **REBEL CELL** OPERATING NEAR HERE. NOW...YOU WOULDN'T HAPPEN TO **KNOW** ANYTHING ABOUT THAT... **WOULD** YOU, RALLO?

I'M A **MECHANIC.** NOTHING MORE.

OF COURSE.

**WEDGE!**

I **TOLD** YOU I'D CATCH YOU. NOW, GIVE IT BACK AND KISS ME YOU **BIG CORELLIAN GUNDARK!**

I... OH... UM...HI DAD.

HELLO, **MALA.**

IT'S ONLY A MATTER OF TIME BEFORE YOUR FATHER *KILLS* ME -- YOU KNOW THAT, *RIGHT?*

HE *LIKES* YOU. WHY DO YOU THINK HE HELPS YOU WITH THE SHIP?

I GUESS... WHY DOES THE ENGINE TEMPERATURE KEEP ROCKETING?

YOU'VE GOT THE COOLANT ATTACHED TO THE MINOR VALVE INSTEAD OF THE MAJOR.

OH... THANKS.

I CAN'T *BELIEVE* I GOT THIS JOB TAKING MACHINE PARTS OFF-SYSTEM. IT'S BEEN *WEEKS* SINCE MY LAST *PAY-PACKET.*

I THOUGHT I WAS GOING TO HAVE TO SELL THE SHIP. IT COULDN'T HAVE COME AT A BETTER TIME.

LUCKY BOY.

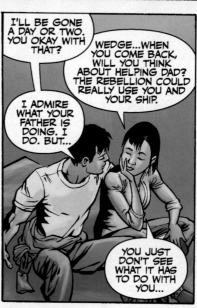

I'LL BE GONE A DAY OR TWO. YOU OKAY WITH THAT?

WEDGE...WHEN YOU COME BACK, WILL YOU THINK ABOUT HELPING DAD? THE REBELLION COULD REALLY USE YOU AND YOUR SHIP.

I ADMIRE WHAT YOUR FATHER IS DOING. I DO. BUT...

YOU JUST DON'T SEE WHAT IT HAS TO DO WITH YOU...

*EXACTLY.* I DON'T WANT THE EMPIRE HERE EITHER, BUT THEY'RE NOT *MONSTERS.*

I'M GOING TO HELP HIM, WEDGE. I NEED TO DO *SOMETHING.*

OKAY, I'LL THINK ABOUT IT... WE'LL TALK WHEN I GET BACK, OKAY?

TWO DAYS?

*TOPS.* FOR YOU, I'LL FLY LIKE THE *WIND.*

OOH. CHEESY.

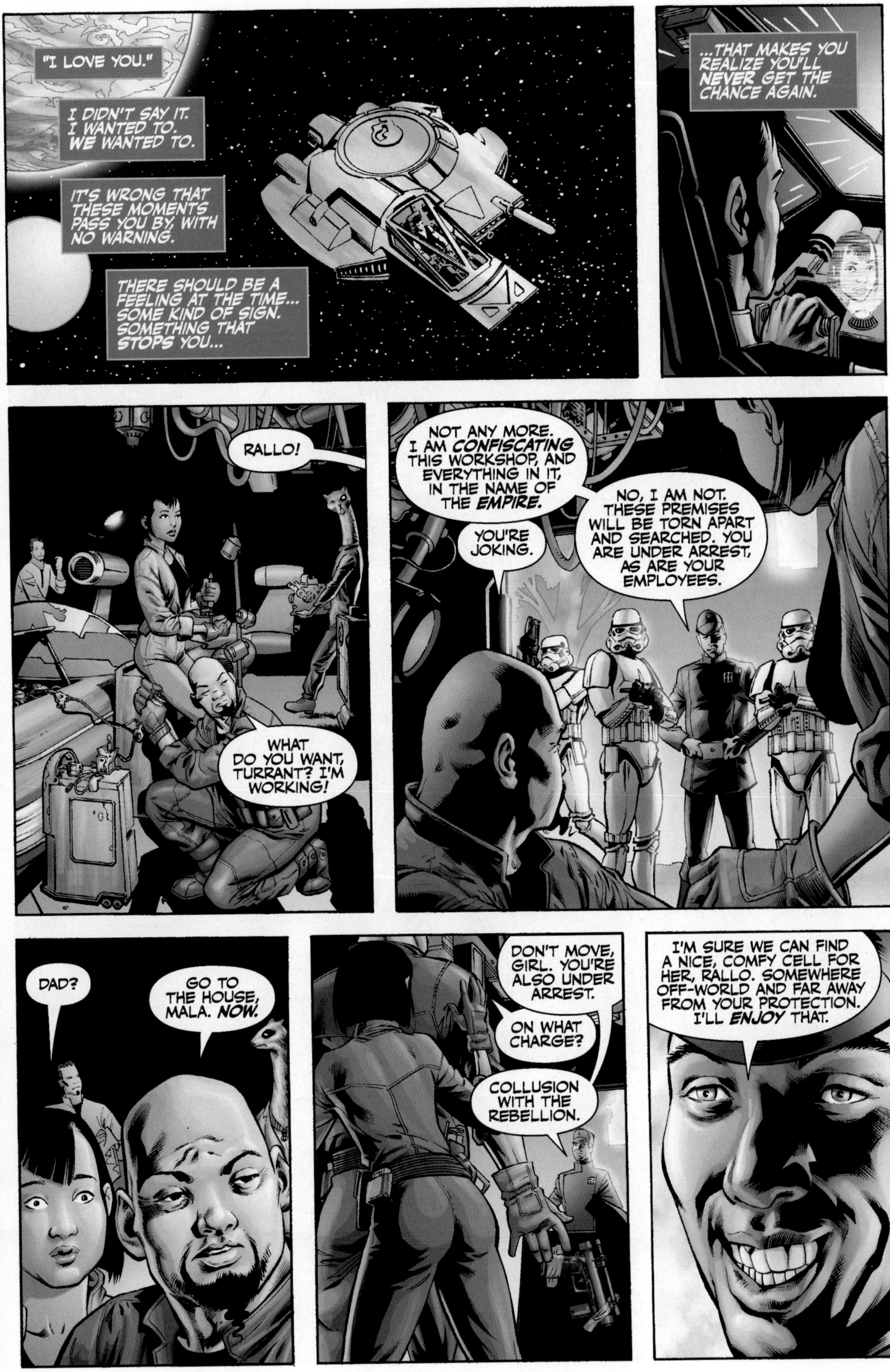
"I LOVE YOU."
I DIDN'T SAY IT. I WANTED TO. WE WANTED TO.
IT'S WRONG THAT THESE MOMENTS PASS YOU BY, WITH NO WARNING.
THERE SHOULD BE A FEELING AT THE TIME... SOME KIND OF SIGN. SOMETHING THAT STOPS YOU...
...THAT MAKES YOU REALIZE YOU'LL NEVER GET THE CHANCE AGAIN.
RALLO!
WHAT DO YOU WANT, TURRANT? I'M WORKING!
NOT ANY MORE. I AM CONFISCATING THIS WORKSHOP, AND EVERYTHING IN IT, IN THE NAME OF THE EMPIRE.
YOU'RE JOKING.
NO, I AM NOT. THESE PREMISES WILL BE TORN APART AND SEARCHED. YOU ARE UNDER ARREST, AS ARE YOUR EMPLOYEES.
DAD?
GO TO THE HOUSE, MALA. NOW.
DON'T MOVE, GIRL. YOU'RE ALSO UNDER ARREST.
ON WHAT CHARGE?
COLLUSION WITH THE REBELLION.
I'M SURE WE CAN FIND A NICE, COMFY CELL FOR HER, RALLO. SOMEWHERE OFF-WORLD AND FAR AWAY FROM YOUR PROTECTION. I'LL ENJOY THAT.

RUN, MALA!

KDEW!

KDEW!

I HEARD LATER THAT RALLO AND HIS MEN KILLED THE STORMTROOPERS...THE MEN THAT CAME TO TAKE HIS DAUGHTER AWAY.

A HEROIC STAND AGAINST AN OPPRESSIVE OCCUPYING FORCE, IT WAS SAID.

A BATTLE I'D HAVE BEEN PART OF, HAD I BEEN THERE.

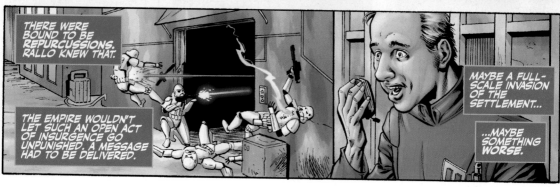

THERE WERE BOUND TO BE REPURCUSSIONS. RALLO KNEW THAT.

THE EMPIRE WOULDN'T LET SUCH AN OPEN ACT OF INSURGENCE GO UNPUNISHED. A MESSAGE HAD TO BE DELIVERED.

MAYBE A FULL-SCALE INVASION OF THE SETTLEMENT...

...MAYBE SOMETHING WORSE.

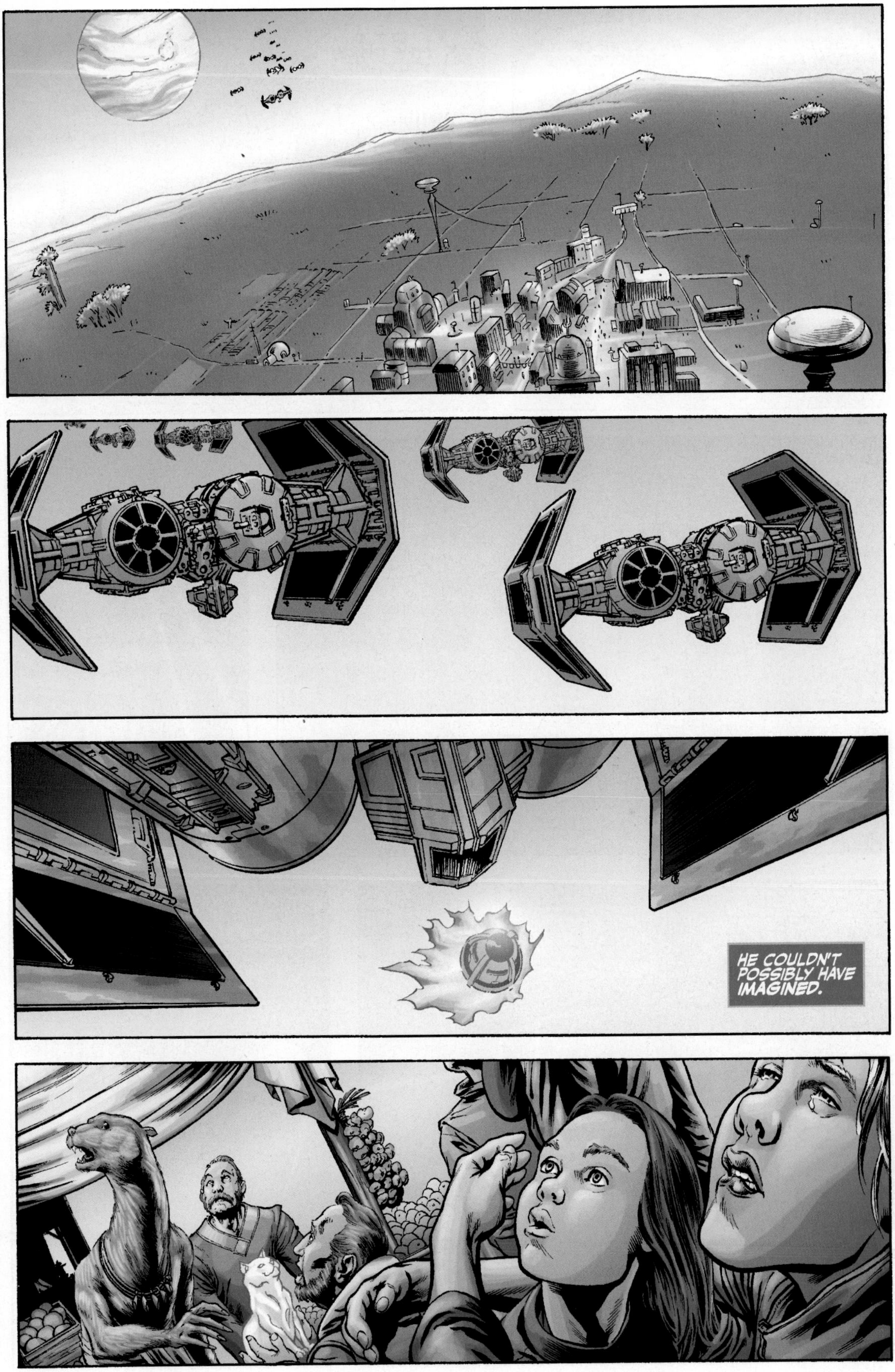
HE COULDN'T POSSIBLY HAVE IMAGINED.

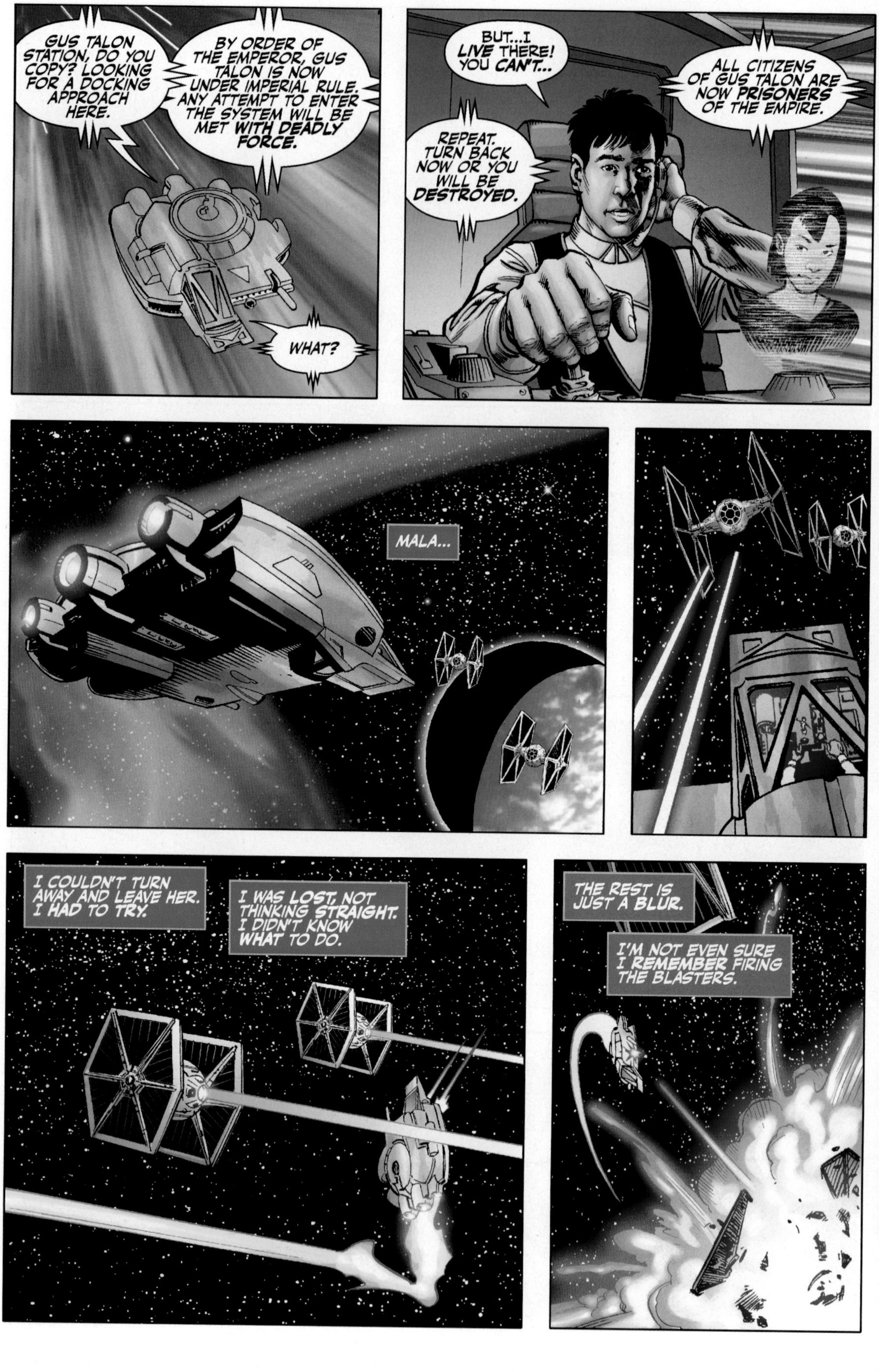
GUS TALON STATION, DO YOU COPY? LOOKING FOR A DOCKING APPROACH HERE.
BY ORDER OF THE EMPEROR, GUS TALON IS NOW UNDER IMPERIAL RULE. ANY ATTEMPT TO ENTER THE SYSTEM WILL BE MET WITH DEADLY FORCE.
WHAT?
BUT...I LIVE THERE! YOU CAN'T...
ALL CITIZENS OF GUS TALON ARE NOW PRISONERS OF THE EMPIRE.
REPEAT. TURN BACK NOW OR YOU WILL BE DESTROYED.
MALA...
I COULDN'T TURN AWAY AND LEAVE HER. I HAD TO TRY.
I WAS LOST, NOT THINKING STRAIGHT. I DIDN'T KNOW WHAT TO DO.
THE REST IS JUST A BLUR.
I'M NOT EVEN SURE I REMEMBER FIRING THE BLASTERS.

I DIDN'T WANT TO RUN, BUT THERE WERE *TOO MANY* OF THEM.

AT THAT MOMENT I WANTED TO FIGHT THE EMPIRE. THE ENTIRE EMPIRE.

I WANTED TO LAND. I WANTED TO SEARCH FOR MALA. I WANTED TO FIND HER, HOLD HER, AND TELL HER EVERYTHING WAS OKAY.

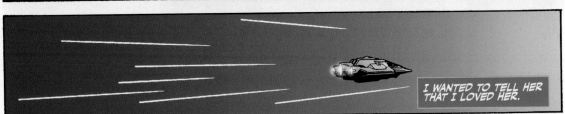

I WANTED TO TELL HER THAT I LOVED HER.

IT TOOK ME *NINE DAYS* TO GET INTO GUS TALON. SECURITY WAS TIGHT UP UNTIL THEN. DAY EIGHT WAS WHEN THE EMPIRE PULLED OUT.

YOU CAN'T BLAME THEM, AFTER ALL...

...THERE WASN'T MUCH LEFT TO GUARD. OR INVESTIGATE. OR DESTROY.

THERE WASN'T MUCH LEFT OF ANYTHING.

THE SURVIVORS TOLD ME THAT AFTER THE BOMBING, STORMTROOPERS CAME IN AND HAULED MOST PEOPLE OFF-WORLD ON PRISON SHIPS. NO ONE KNEW WHERE THEY WENT.

NO ONE KNEW IF MALA WAS WITH THEM.

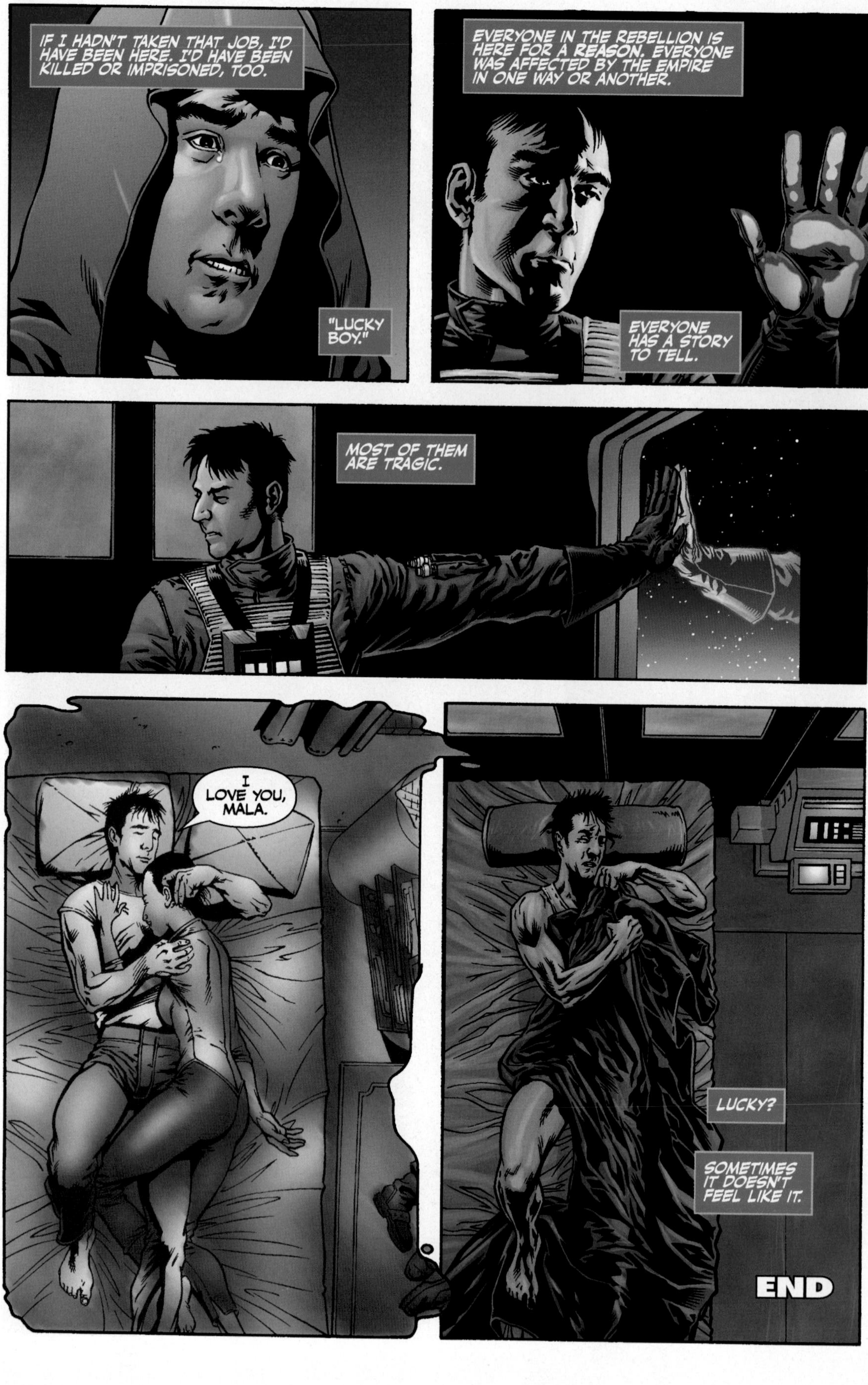
IF I HADN'T TAKEN THAT JOB, I'D HAVE BEEN HERE. I'D HAVE BEEN KILLED OR IMPRISONED, TOO.
"LUCKY BOY."
EVERYONE IN THE REBELLION IS HERE FOR A REASON. EVERYONE WAS AFFECTED BY THE EMPIRE IN ONE WAY OR ANOTHER.
EVERYONE HAS A STORY TO TELL.
MOST OF THEM ARE TRAGIC.
I LOVE YOU, MALA.
LUCKY?
SOMETIMES IT DOESN'T FEEL LIKE IT.
END

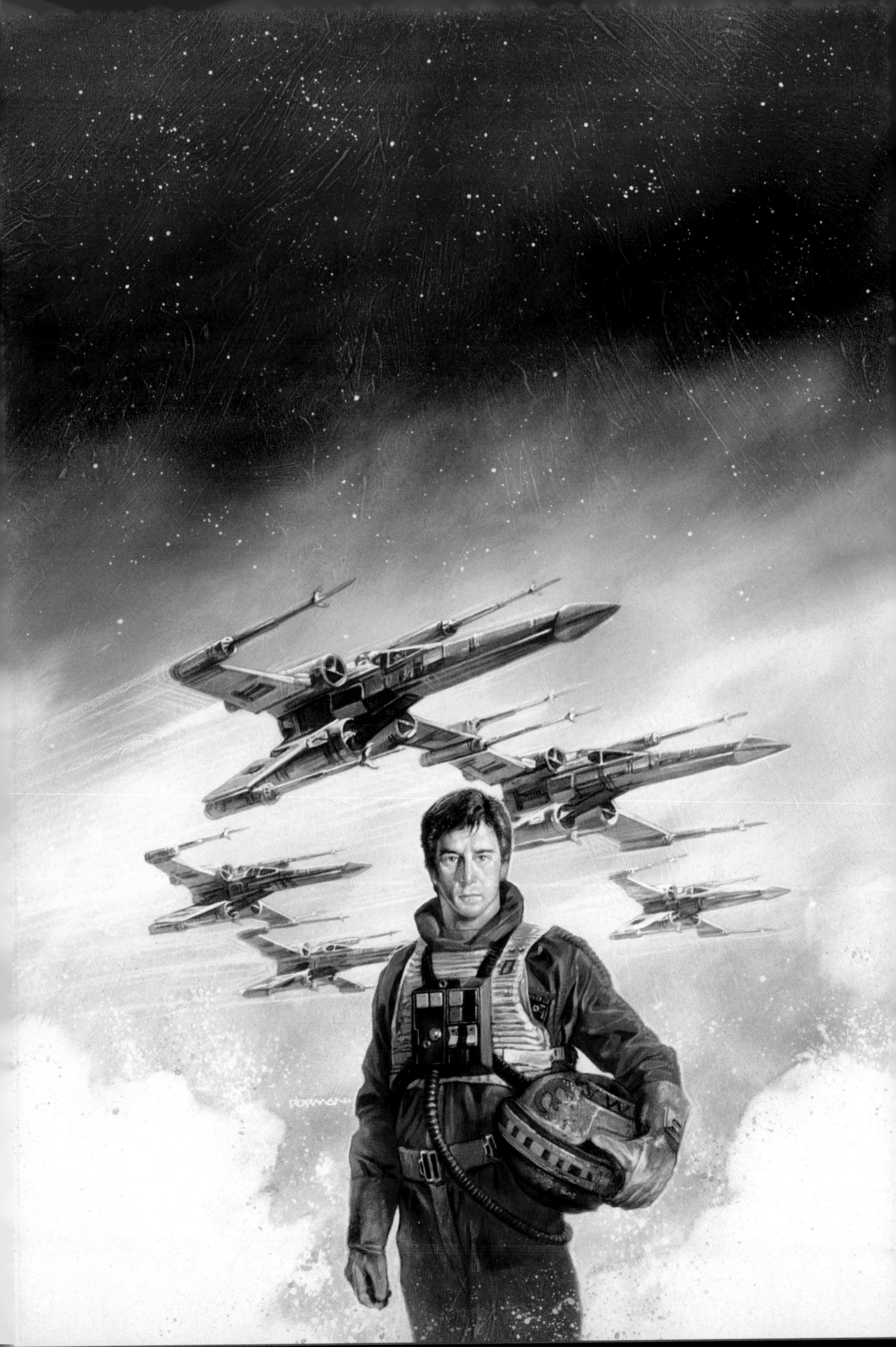

***STAR WARS: X-WING ROGUE SQUADRON #1*** **— "THE REBEL OPPOSITION, CHAPTER 1"**

PLOTTER: MICHAEL A. STACKPOLE • SCRIPTER: MIKE BARON • PENCILER: ALLEN NUNIS • INKER: ANDY MUSHYNSKY • COLORIST: DAVE NESTELLE
LETTERER: STEVE DUTRO • EDITOR: RYDER WINDHAM • COVER ARTIST: DAVE DORMAN

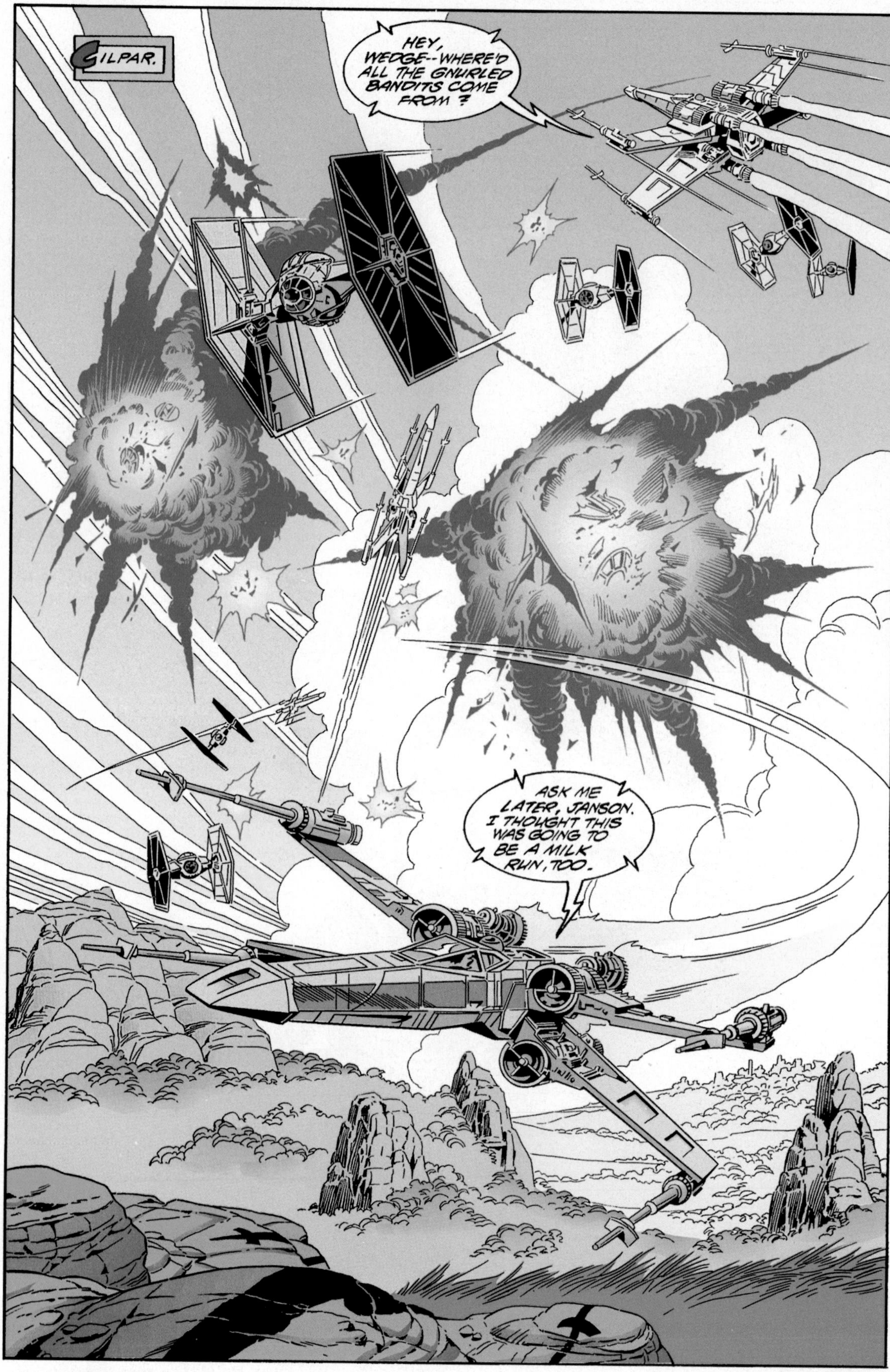
GILPAR.
HEY, WEDGE--WHERE'D ALL THE GNURLED BANDITS COME FROM?
ASK ME LATER, JANSON. I THOUGHT THIS WAS GOING TO BE A MILK RUN, TOO.

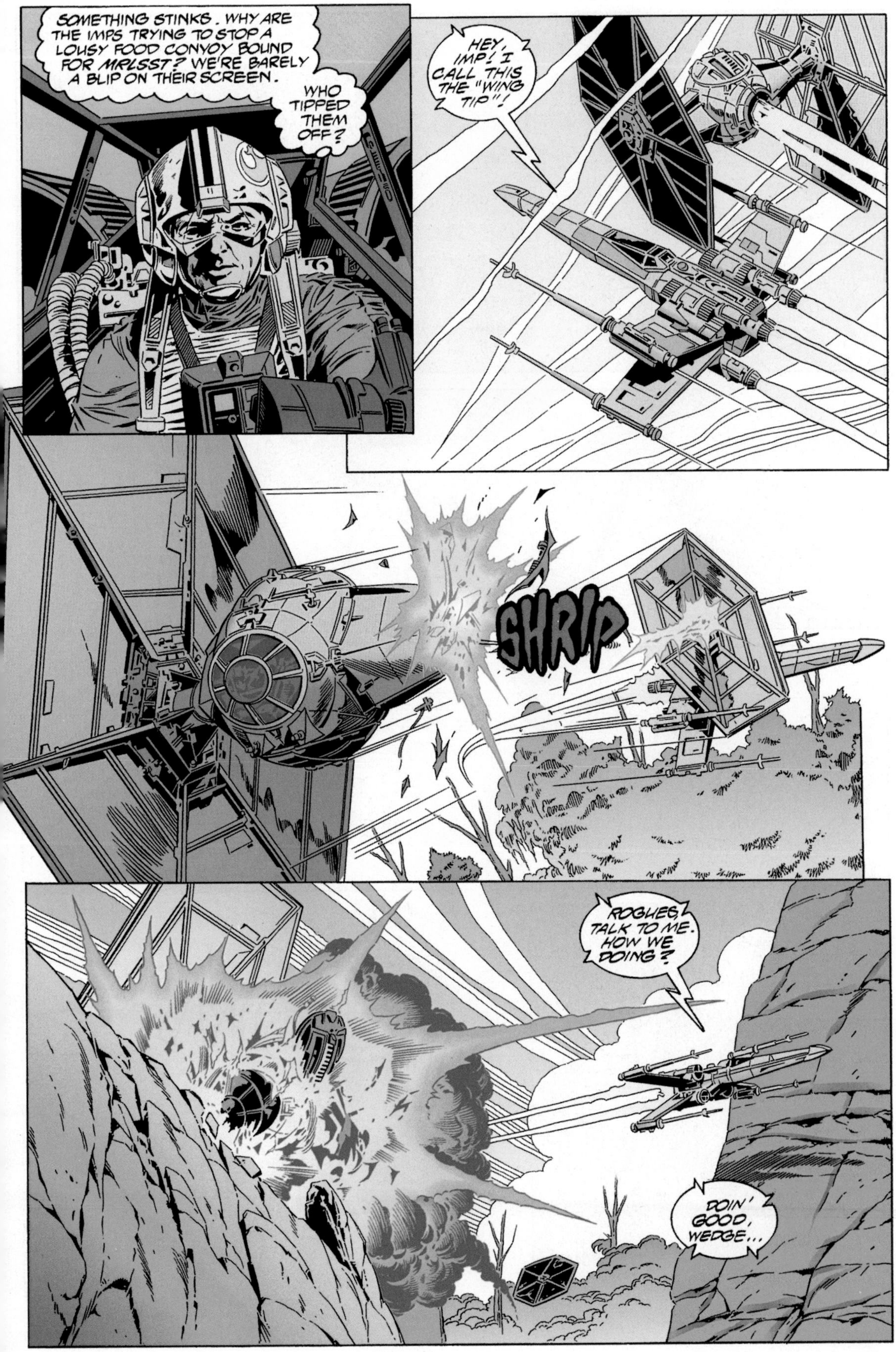
SOMETHING STINKS. WHY ARE THE IMPS TRYING TO STOP A LOUSY FOOD CONVOY BOUND FOR MRLSST? WE'RE BARELY A BLIP ON THEIR SCREEN.
WHO TIPPED THEM OFF?
HEY, IMP! I CALL THIS THE "WING TIP"!
SHRIP
ROGUES, TALK TO ME. HOW WE DOING?
DOIN' GOOD, WEDGE...

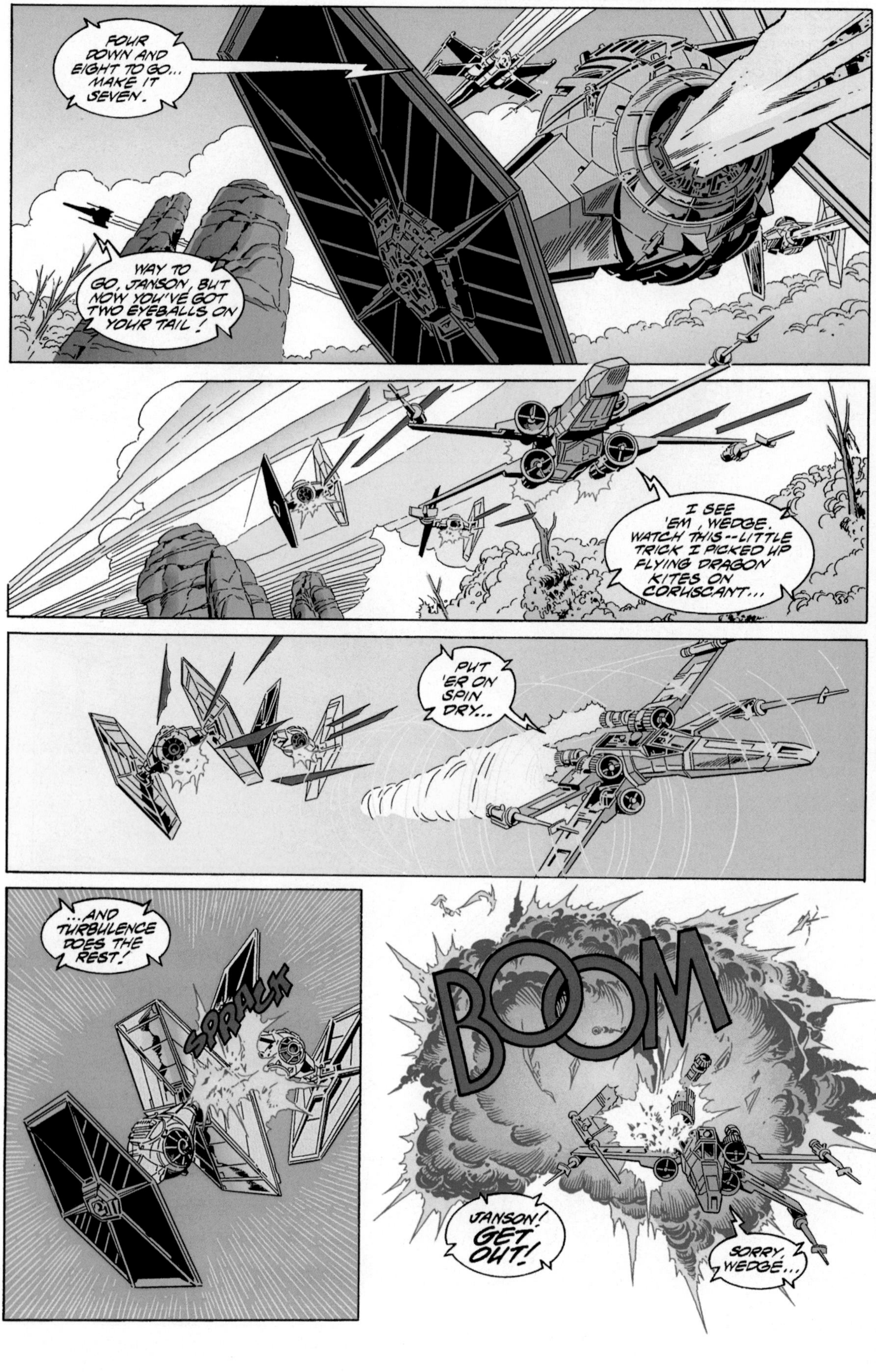
FOUR DOWN AND EIGHT TO GO... MAKE IT SEVEN.
WAY TO GO, JANSON, BUT NOW YOU'VE GOT TWO EYEBALLS ON YOUR TAIL!
I SEE 'EM, WEDGE. WATCH THIS--LITTLE TRICK I PICKED UP FLYING DRAGON KITES ON CORUSCANT...
PUT 'ER ON SPIN DRY...
...AND TURBULENCE DOES THE REST!
SPRACK
BOOM
JANSON! GET OUT!
SORRY, WEDGE...

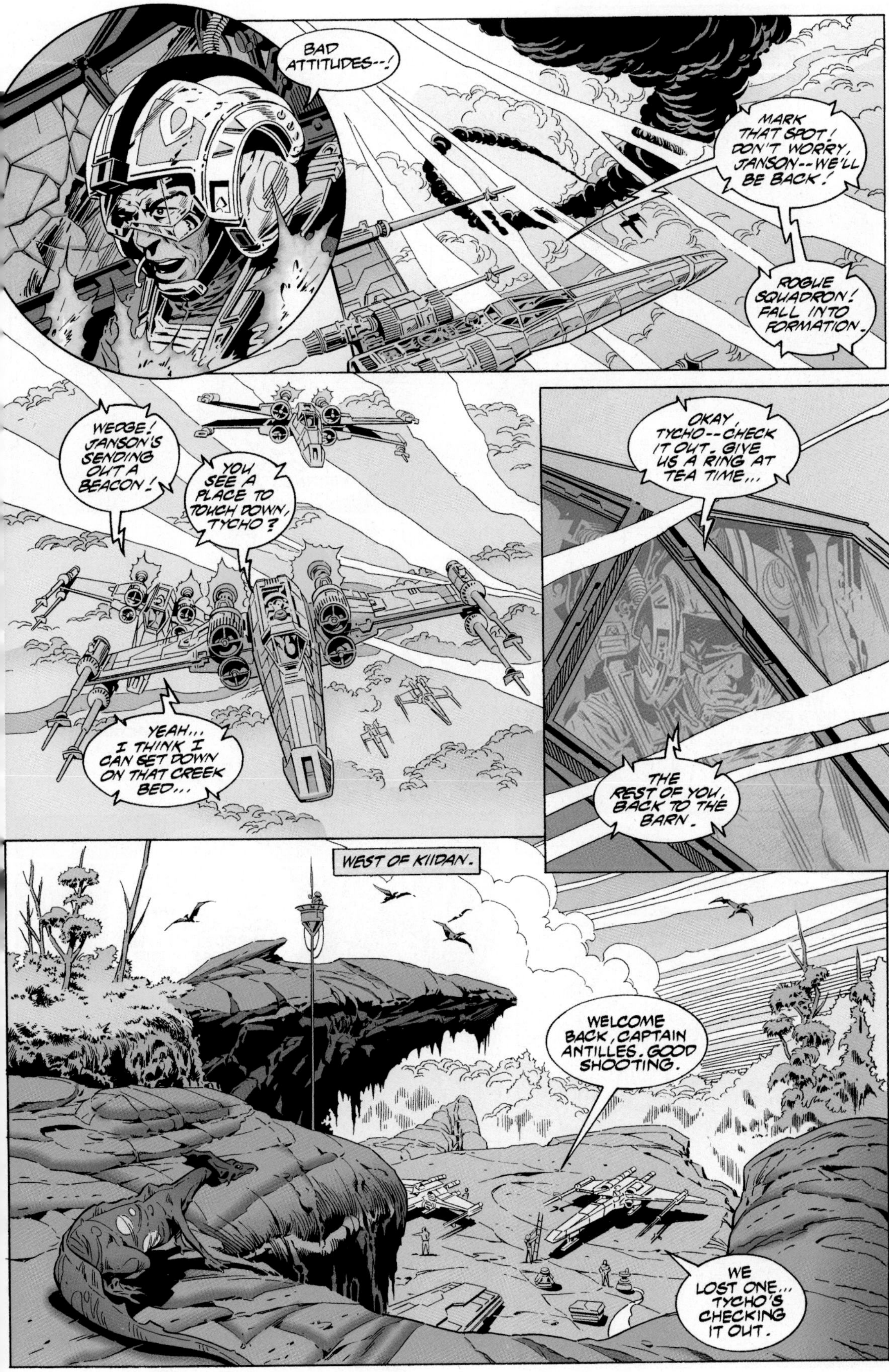
BAD ATTITUDES--!
MARK THAT SPOT! DON'T WORRY, JANSON--WE'LL BE BACK!
ROGUE SQUADRON! FALL INTO FORMATION.
WEDGE! JANSON'S SENDING OUT A BEACON!
YOU SEE A PLACE TO TOUCH DOWN, TYCHO?
YEAH... I THINK I CAN GET DOWN ON THAT CREEK BED...
OKAY, TYCHO--CHECK IT OUT. GIVE US A RING AT TEA TIME...
THE REST OF YOU, BACK TO THE BARN.
WEST OF KIIDAN.
WELCOME BACK, CAPTAIN ANTILLES. GOOD SHOOTING.
WE LOST ONE... TYCHO'S CHECKING IT OUT.

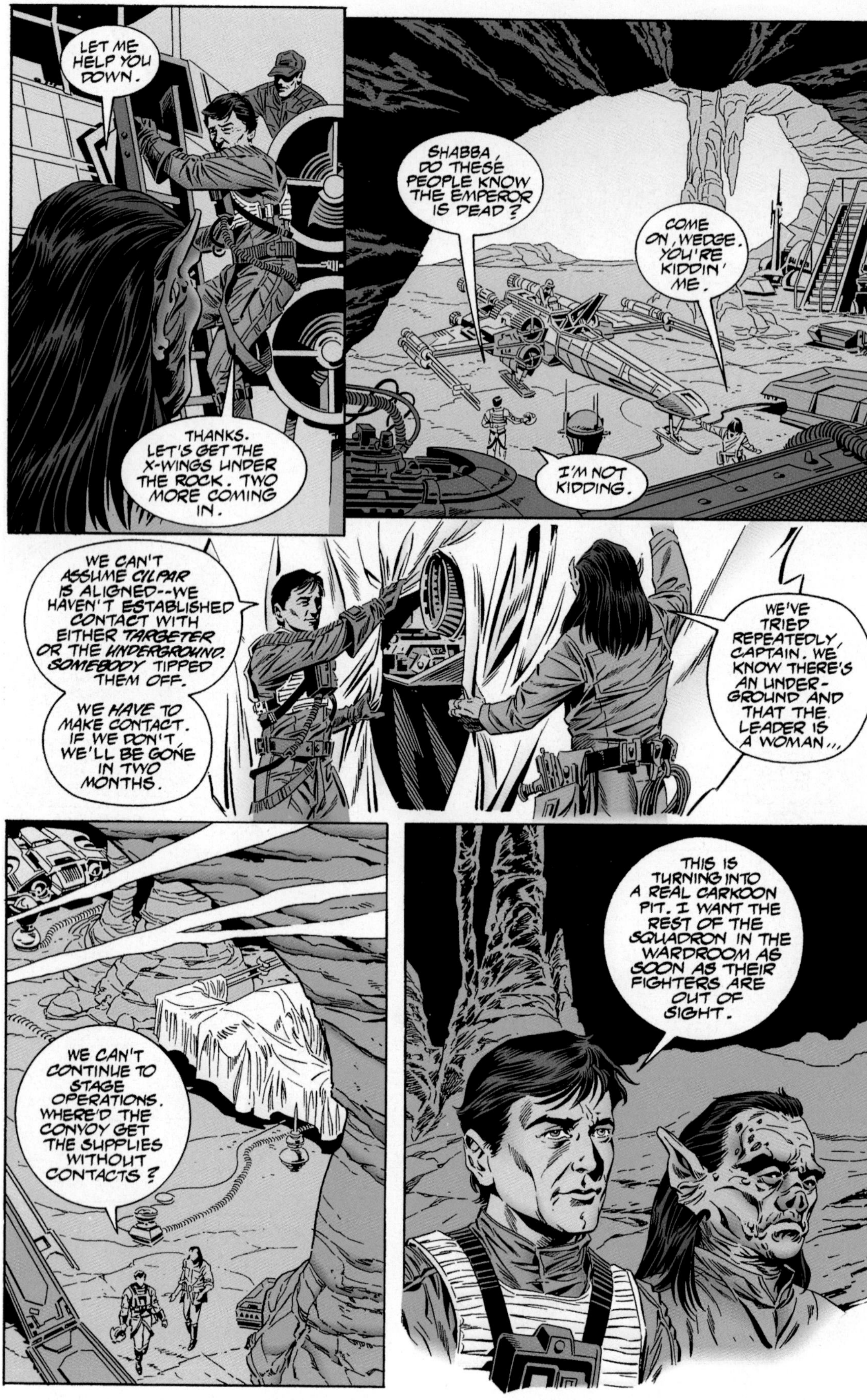
LET ME HELP YOU DOWN.
THANKS. LET'S GET THE X-WINGS UNDER THE ROCK. TWO MORE COMING IN.
SHABBA, DO THESE PEOPLE KNOW THE EMPEROR IS DEAD?
COME ON, WEDGE. YOU'RE KIDDIN' ME.
I'M NOT KIDDING.
WE CAN'T ASSUME CILPAR IS ALIGNED--WE HAVEN'T ESTABLISHED CONTACT WITH EITHER TARGETER OR THE UNDERGROUND. SOMEBODY TIPPED THEM OFF.
WE HAVE TO MAKE CONTACT. IF WE DON'T WE'LL BE GONE IN TWO MONTHS.
WE'VE TRIED REPEATEDLY, CAPTAIN. WE KNOW THERE'S AN UNDER-GROUND AND THAT THE LEADER IS A WOMAN...
WE CAN'T CONTINUE TO STAGE OPERATIONS. WHERE'D THE CONVOY GET THE SUPPLIES WITHOUT CONTACTS?
THIS IS TURNING INTO A REAL CARKOON PIT. I WANT THE REST OF THE SQUADRON IN THE WARDROOM AS SOON AS THEIR FIGHTERS ARE OUT OF SIGHT.

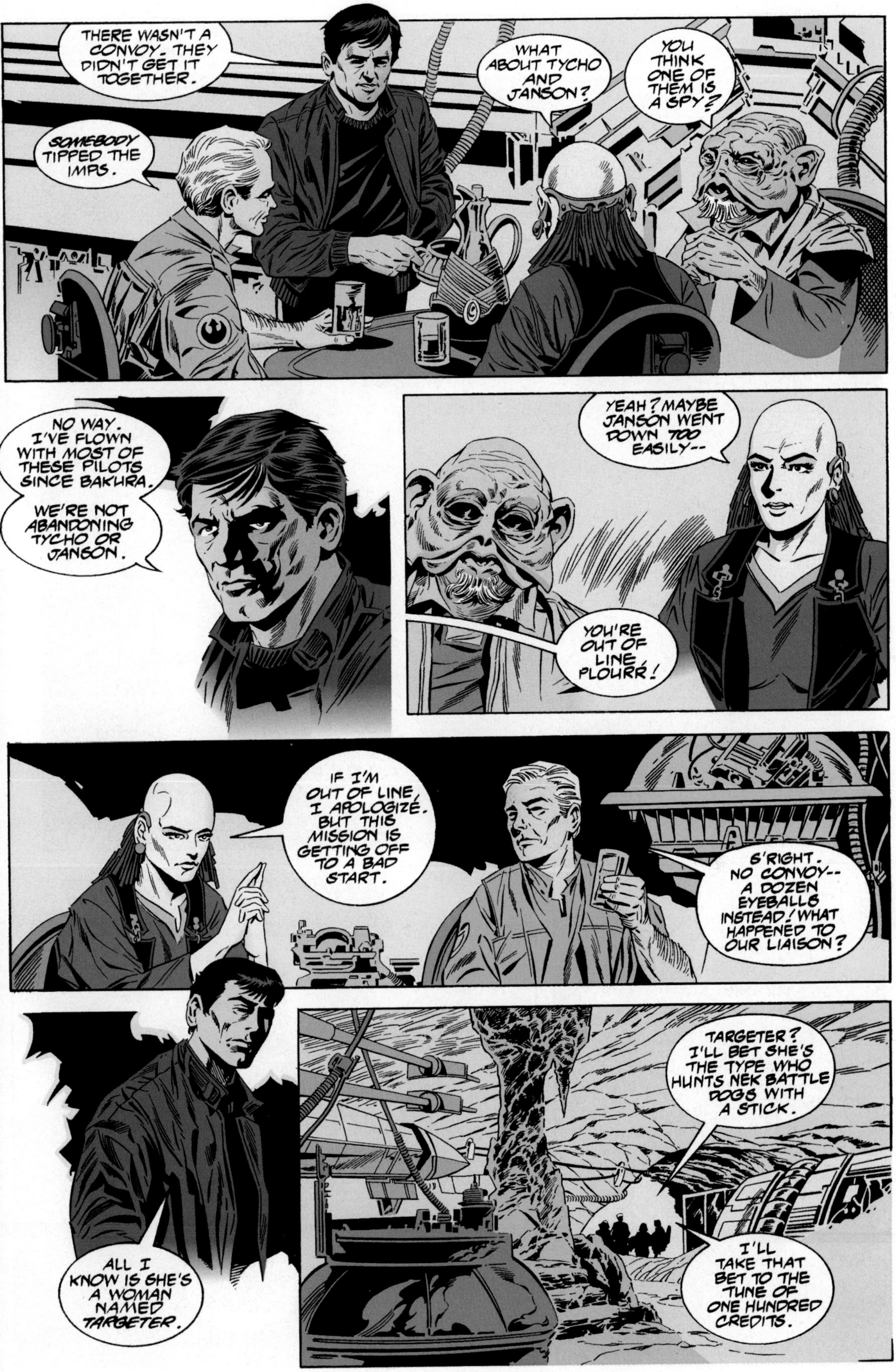
THERE WASN'T A CONVOY. THEY DIDN'T GET IT TOGETHER.
SOMEBODY TIPPED THE IMPS.
WHAT ABOUT TYCHO AND JANSON?
YOU THINK ONE OF THEM IS A SPY?
NO WAY. I'VE FLOWN WITH MOST OF THESE PILOTS SINCE BAKURA.
WE'RE NOT ABANDONING TYCHO OR JANSON.
YEAH? MAYBE JANSON WENT DOWN TOO EASILY--
YOU'RE OUT OF LINE, PLOURR!
IF I'M OUT OF LINE, I APOLOGIZE. BUT THIS MISSION IS GETTING OFF TO A BAD START.
S'RIGHT. NO CONVOY-- A DOZEN EYEBALLS INSTEAD! WHAT HAPPENED TO OUR LIAISON?
ALL I KNOW IS SHE'S A WOMAN NAMED TARGETER.
TARGETER? I'LL BET SHE'S THE TYPE WHO HUNTS NEK BATTLE DOGS WITH A STICK.
I'LL TAKE THAT BET TO THE TUNE OF ONE HUNDRED CREDITS.

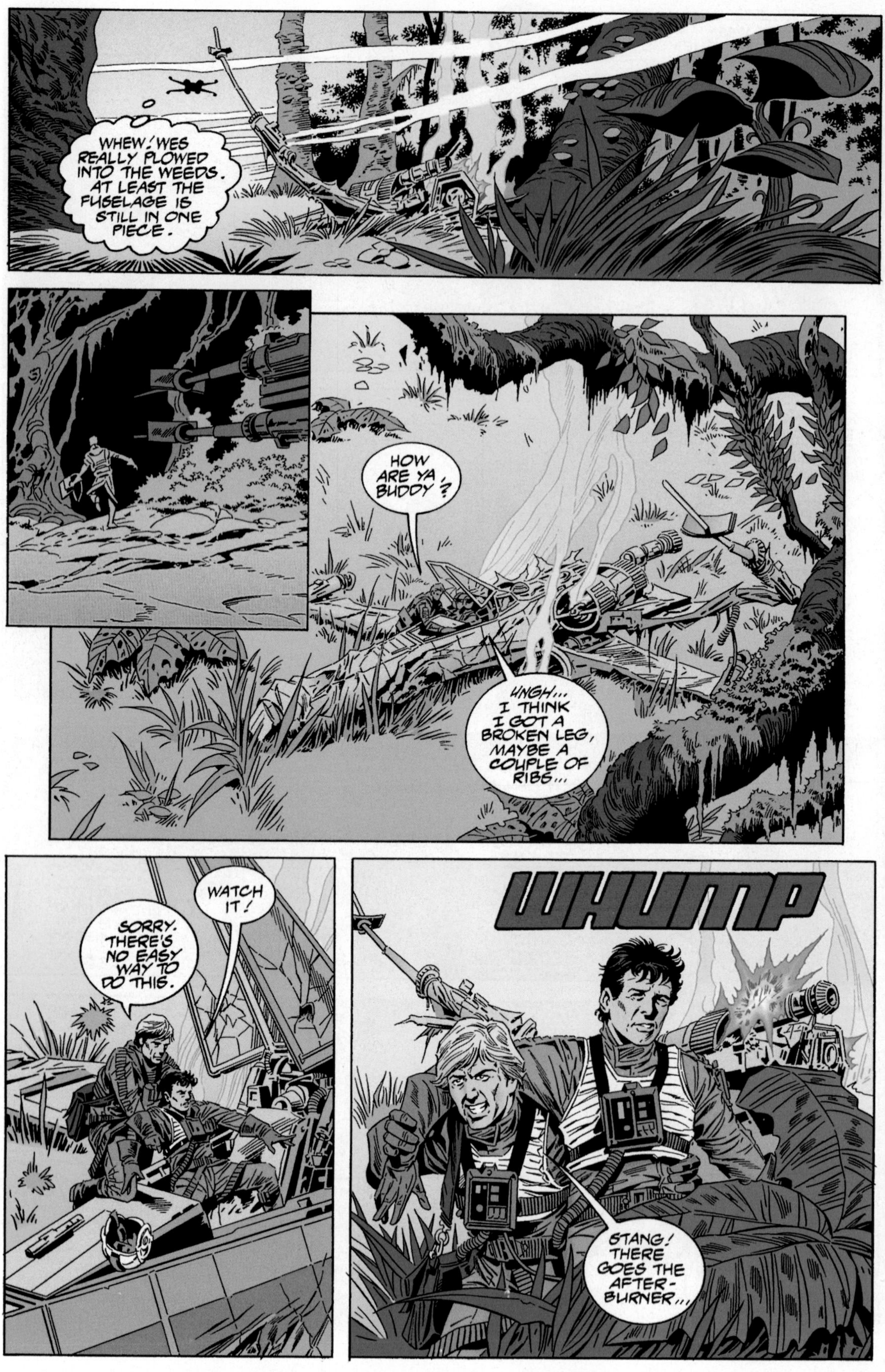
WHEW! WES REALLY PLOWED INTO THE WEEDS. AT LEAST THE FUSELAGE IS STILL IN ONE PIECE.
HOW ARE YA BUDDY?
UNGH... I THINK I GOT A BROKEN LEG, MAYBE A COUPLE OF RIBS...
WATCH IT!
SORRY. THERE'S NO EASY WAY TO DO THIS.
WHUMP
STANG! THERE GOES THE AFTER-BURNER...

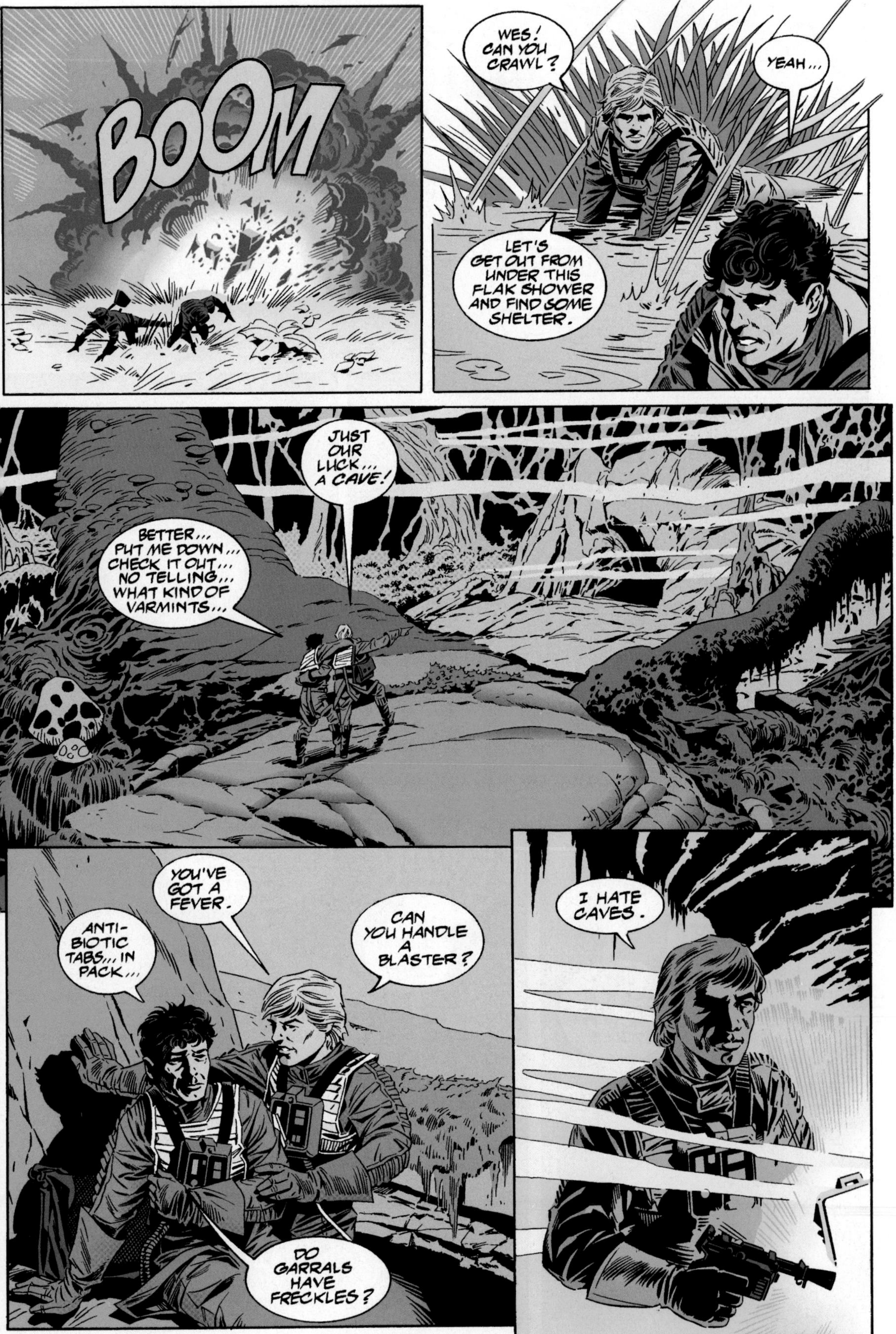
BOOM
WES! CAN YOU CRAWL?
YEAH...
LET'S GET OUT FROM UNDER THIS FLAK SHOWER AND FIND SOME SHELTER.
JUST OUR LUCK... A CAVE!
BETTER... PUT ME DOWN... CHECK IT OUT... NO TELLING... WHAT KIND OF VARMINTS...
YOU'VE GOT A FEVER.
ANTI-BIOTIC TABS... IN PACK...
CAN YOU HANDLE A BLASTER?
DO GARRALS HAVE FRECKLES?
I HATE CAVES.

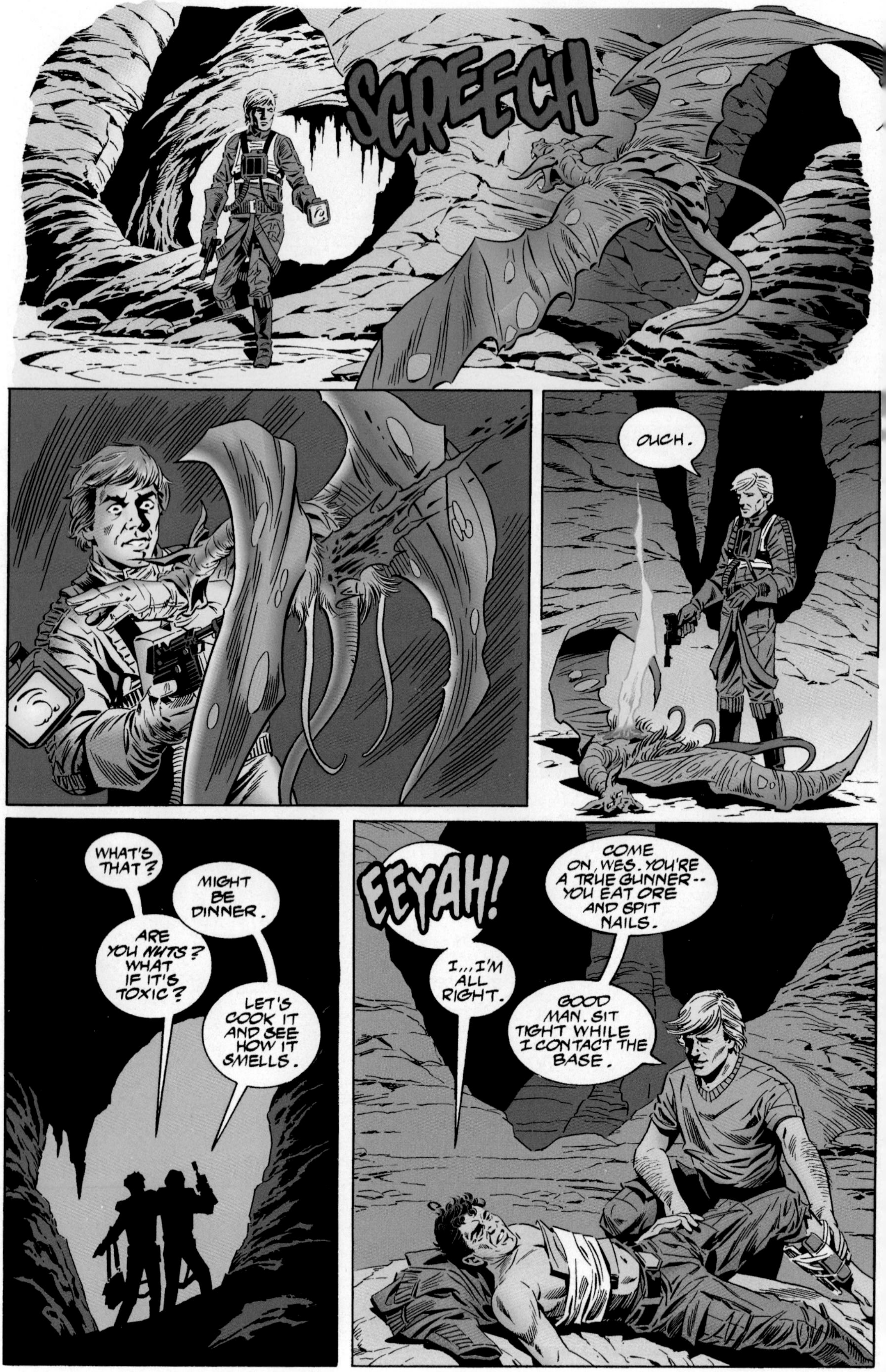
SCREECH
OUCH.
WHAT'S THAT?
MIGHT BE DINNER.
ARE YOU NUTS? WHAT IF IT'S TOXIC?
LET'S COOK IT AND SEE HOW IT SMELLS.
EEYAH!
COME ON, WES. YOU'RE A TRUE GUNNER-- YOU EAT ORE AND SPIT NAILS.
I... I'M ALL RIGHT.
GOOD MAN. SIT TIGHT WHILE I CONTACT THE BASE.

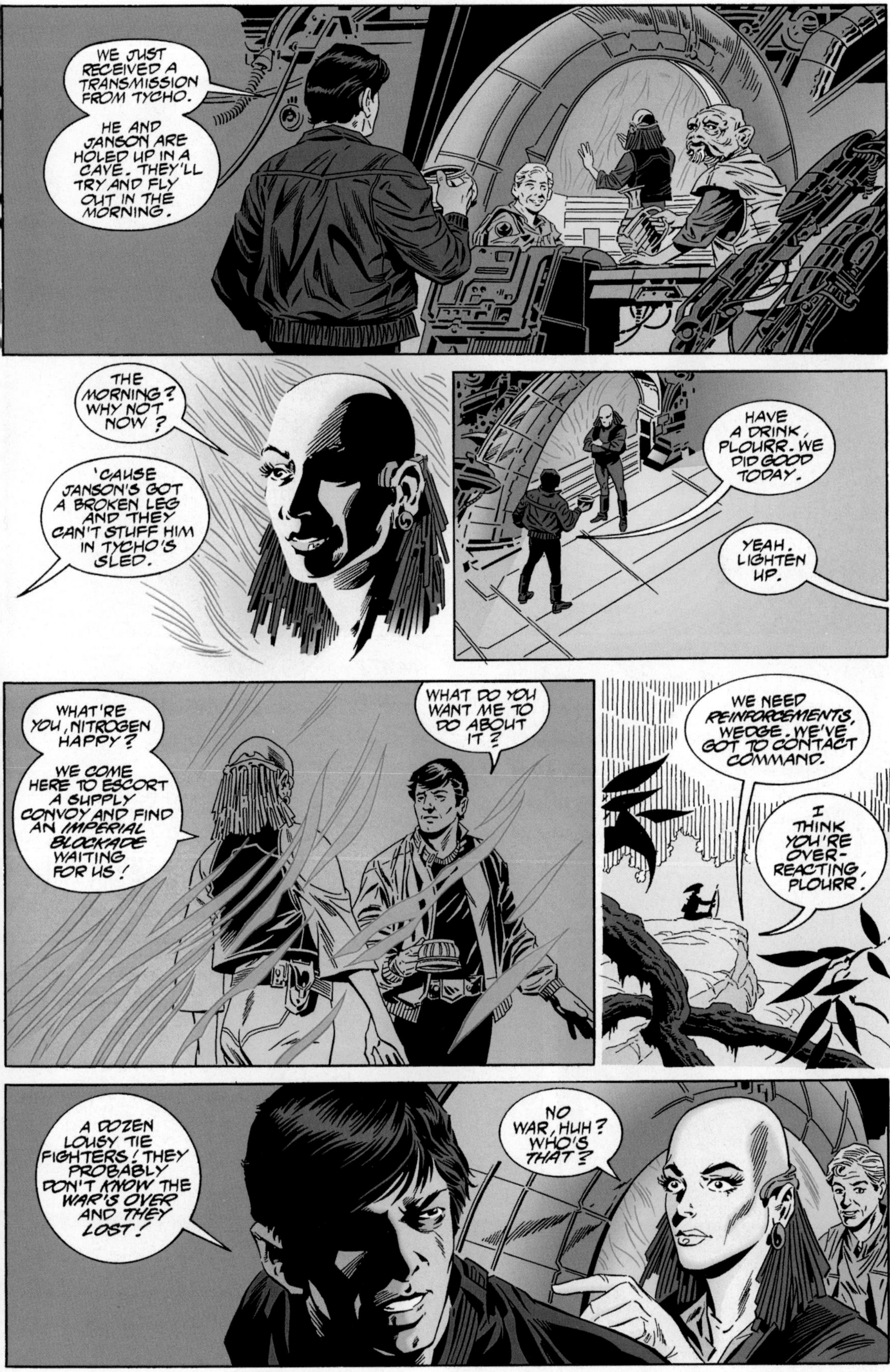
WE JUST RECEIVED A TRANSMISSION FROM TYCHO.
HE AND JANSON ARE HOLED UP IN A CAVE. THEY'LL TRY AND FLY OUT IN THE MORNING.
THE MORNING? WHY NOT NOW?
'CAUSE JANSON'S GOT A BROKEN LEG AND THEY CAN'T STUFF HIM IN TYCHO'S SLED.
HAVE A DRINK, PLOURR. WE DID GOOD TODAY.
YEAH. LIGHTEN UP.
WHAT'RE YOU, NITROGEN HAPPY?
WE COME HERE TO ESCORT A SUPPLY CONVOY AND FIND AN IMPERIAL BLOCKADE WAITING FOR US!
WHAT DO YOU WANT ME TO DO ABOUT IT?
WE NEED REINFORCEMENTS, WEDGE. WE'VE GOT TO CONTACT COMMAND.
I THINK YOU'RE OVER-REACTING, PLOURR.
A DOZEN LOUSY TIE FIGHTERS! THEY PROBABLY DON'T KNOW THE WAR'S OVER AND THEY LOST!
NO WAR, HUH? WHO'S THAT?

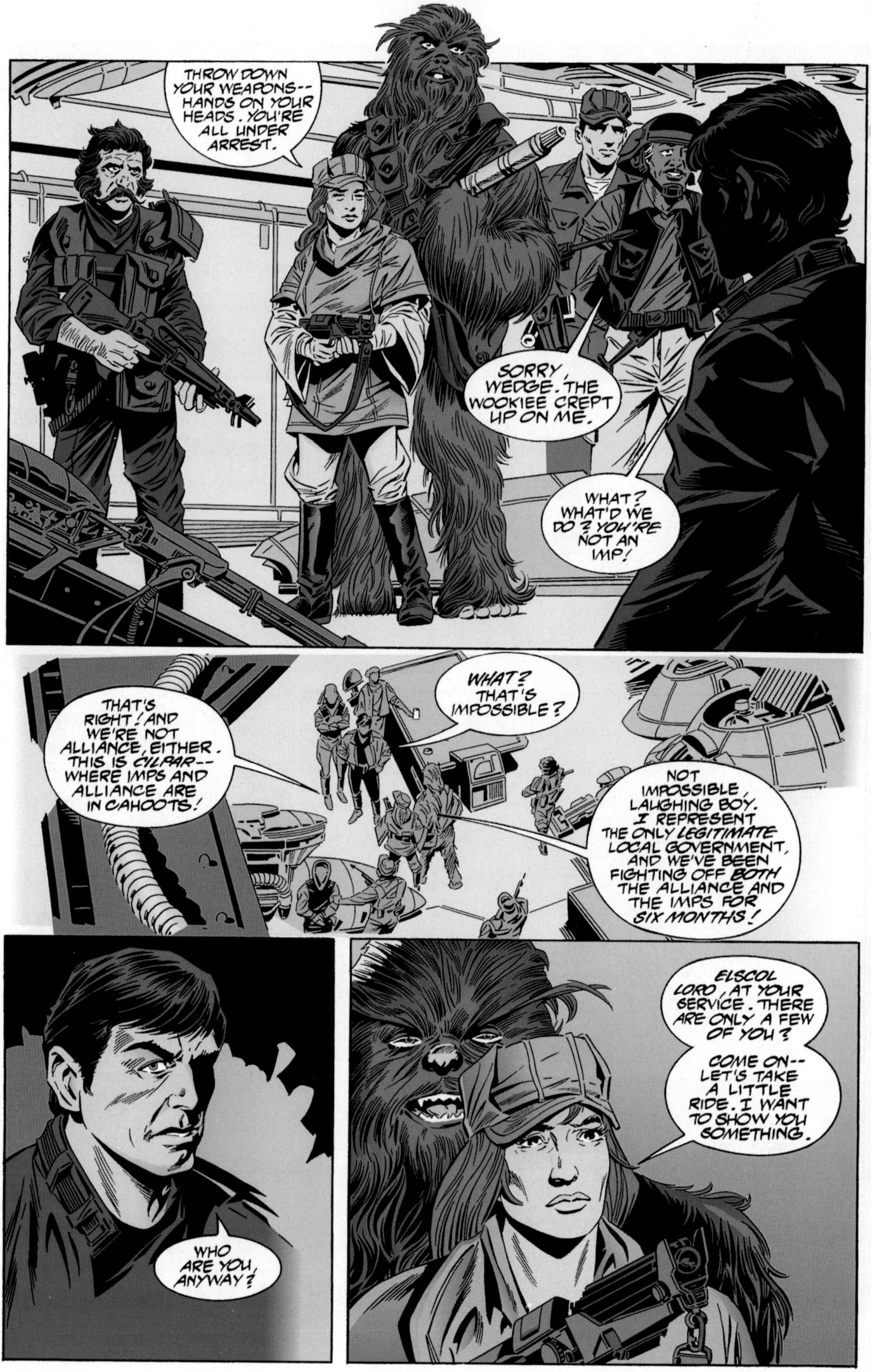
THROW DOWN YOUR WEAPONS-- HANDS ON YOUR HEADS. YOU'RE ALL UNDER ARREST.
SORRY, WEDGE. THE WOOKIEE CREPT UP ON ME.
WHAT? WHAT'D WE DO? YOU'RE NOT AN IMP!
WHAT? THAT'S IMPOSSIBLE?
THAT'S RIGHT! AND WE'RE NOT ALLIANCE, EITHER. THIS IS CILPAR-- WHERE IMPS AND ALLIANCE ARE IN CAHOOTS!
NOT IMPOSSIBLE, LAUGHING BOY. I REPRESENT THE ONLY LEGITIMATE LOCAL GOVERNMENT, AND WE'VE BEEN FIGHTING OFF BOTH THE ALLIANCE AND THE IMPS FOR SIX MONTHS!
WHO ARE YOU, ANYWAY?
ELSCOL LORO, AT YOUR SERVICE. THERE ARE ONLY A FEW OF YOU?
COME ON-- LET'S TAKE A LITTLE RIDE. I WANT TO SHOW YOU SOMETHING.

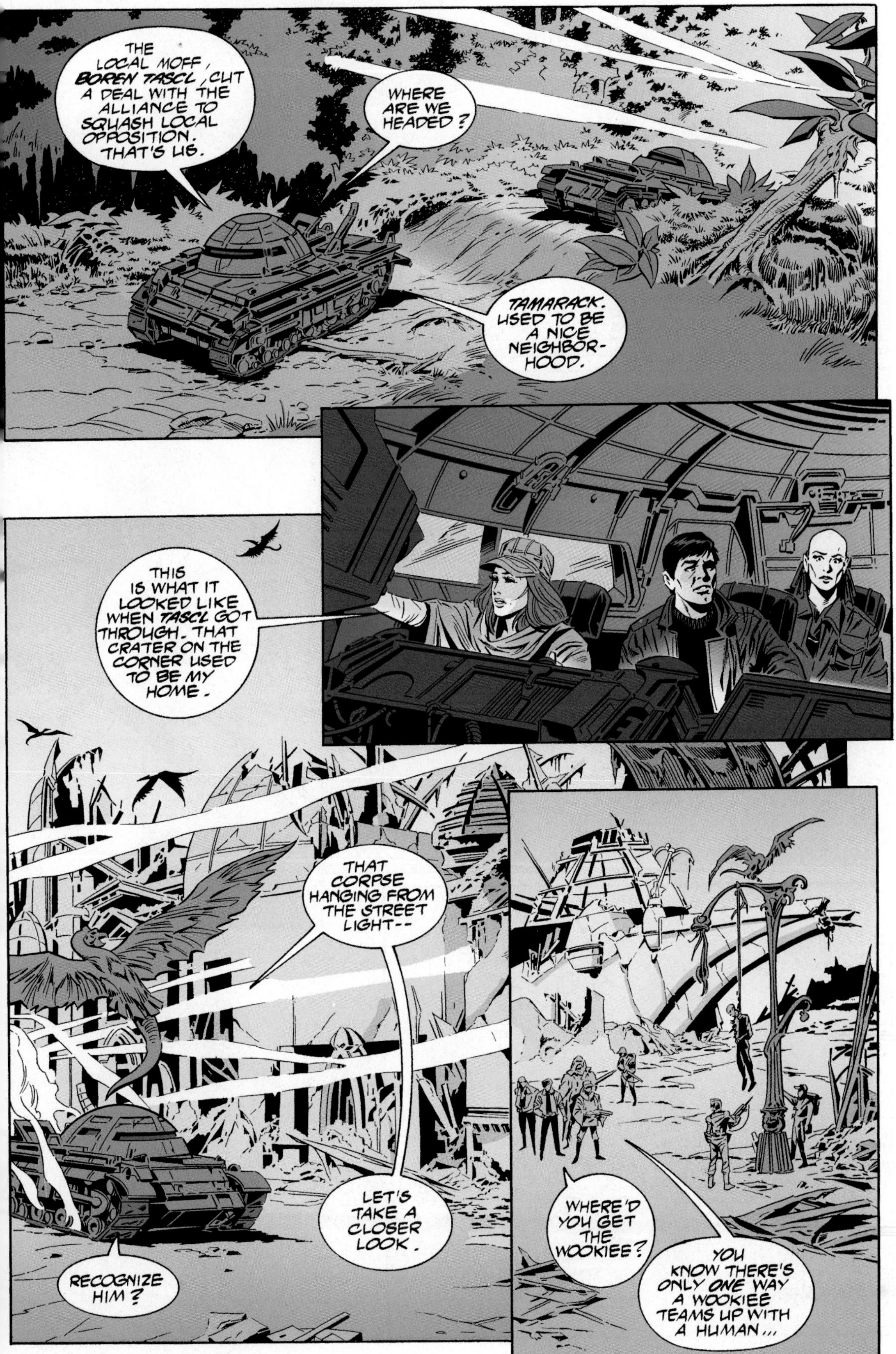
THE LOCAL MOFF, BOREN TASCL, CUT A DEAL WITH THE ALLIANCE TO SQUASH LOCAL OPPOSITION. THAT'S US.
WHERE ARE WE HEADED?
TAMARACK. USED TO BE A NICE NEIGHBORHOOD.
THIS IS WHAT IT LOOKED LIKE WHEN TASCL GOT THROUGH. THAT CRATER ON THE CORNER USED TO BE MY HOME.
THAT CORPSE HANGING FROM THE STREET LIGHT--
RECOGNIZE HIM?
LET'S TAKE A CLOSER LOOK.
WHERE'D YOU GET THE WOOKIEE?
YOU KNOW THERE'S ONLY ONE WAY A WOOKIEE TEAMS UP WITH A HUMAN...

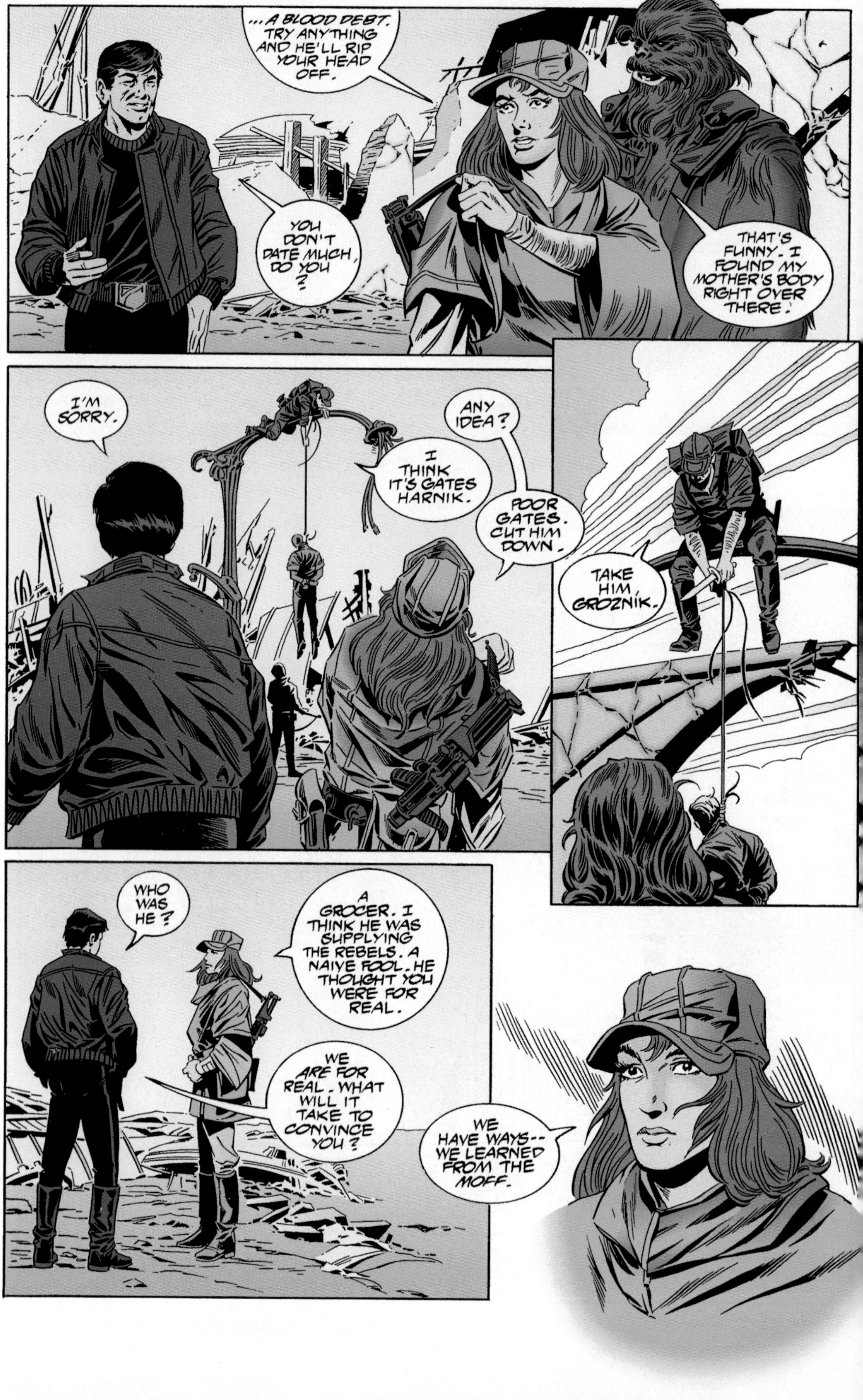
...A BLOOD DEBT. TRY ANYTHING AND HE'LL RIP YOUR HEAD OFF.
YOU DON'T DATE MUCH, DO YOU?
THAT'S FUNNY. I FOUND MY MOTHER'S BODY RIGHT OVER THERE.
I'M SORRY.
ANY IDEA?
I THINK IT'S GATES HARNIK.
POOR GATES. CUT HIM DOWN.
TAKE HIM, GROZNIK.
WHO WAS HE?
A GROCER. I THINK HE WAS SUPPLYING THE REBELS. A NAIVE FOOL. HE THOUGHT YOU WERE FOR REAL.
WE ARE FOR REAL. WHAT WILL IT TAKE TO CONVINCE YOU?
WE HAVE WAYS-- WE LEARNED FROM THE MOFF.

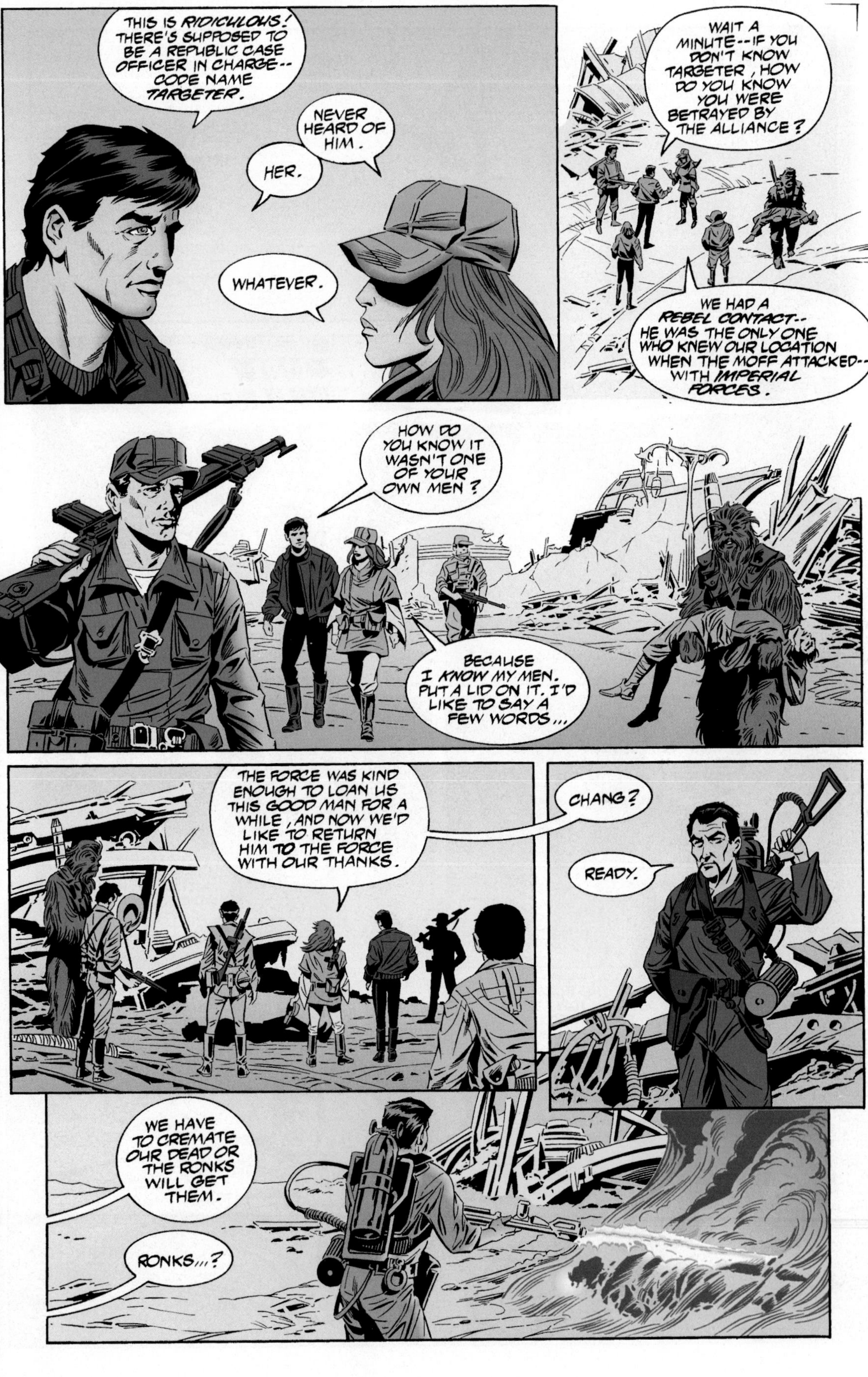
THIS IS RIDICULOUS! THERE'S SUPPOSED TO BE A REPUBLIC CASE OFFICER IN CHARGE-- CODE NAME TARGETER.
NEVER HEARD OF HIM.
HER.
WHATEVER.
WAIT A MINUTE--IF YOU DON'T KNOW TARGETER, HOW DO YOU KNOW YOU WERE BETRAYED BY THE ALLIANCE?
WE HAD A REBEL CONTACT-- HE WAS THE ONLY ONE WHO KNEW OUR LOCATION WHEN THE MOFF ATTACKED-- WITH IMPERIAL FORCES.
HOW DO YOU KNOW IT WASN'T ONE OF YOUR OWN MEN?
BECAUSE I KNOW MY MEN. PUT A LID ON IT. I'D LIKE TO SAY A FEW WORDS...
THE FORCE WAS KIND ENOUGH TO LOAN US THIS GOOD MAN FOR A WHILE, AND NOW WE'D LIKE TO RETURN HIM TO THE FORCE WITH OUR THANKS.
CHANG?
READY.
WE HAVE TO CREMATE OUR DEAD OR THE RONKS WILL GET THEM.
RONKS...?

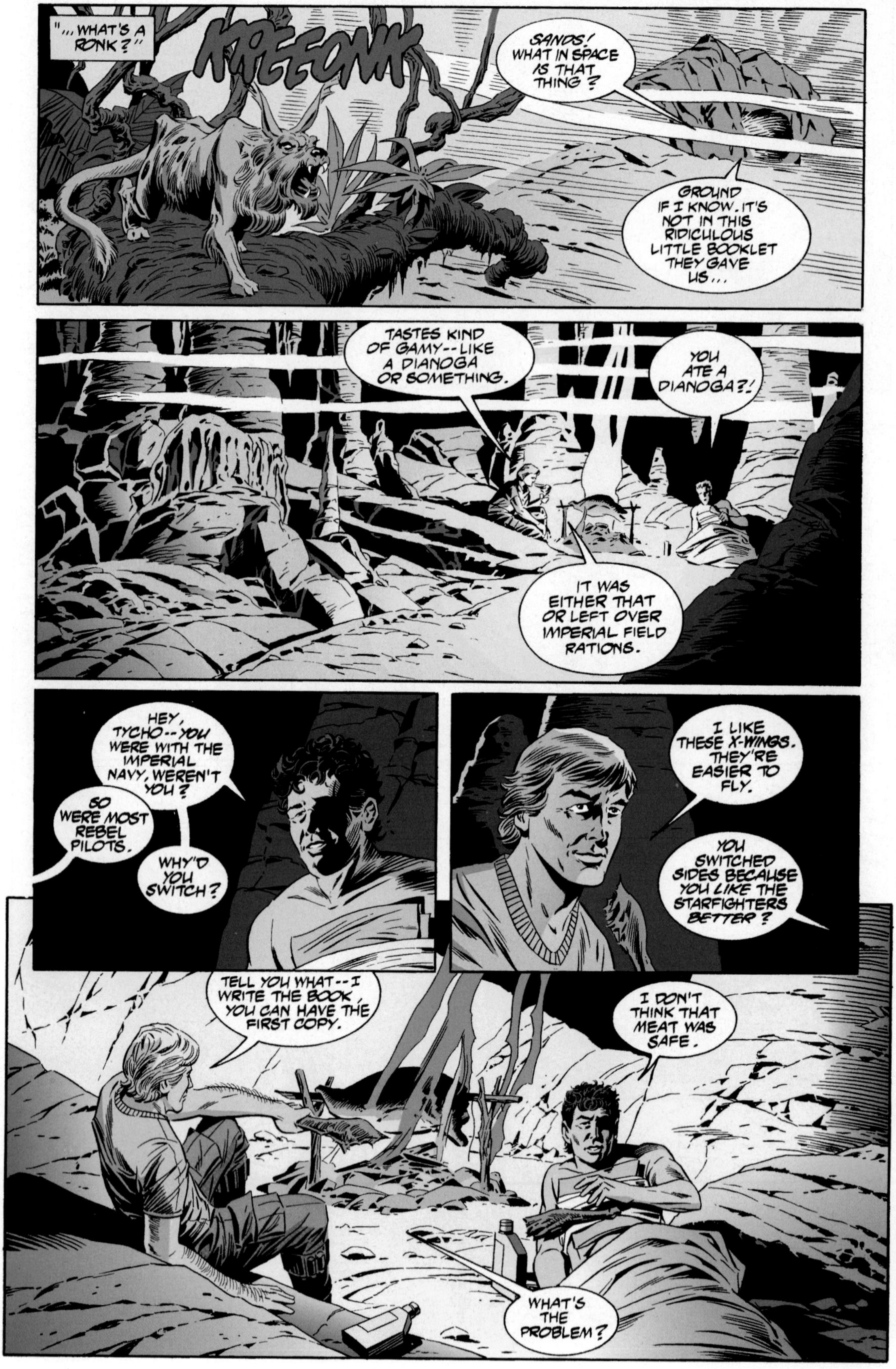
"... WHAT'S A RONK?"
KREEONK
SANDS! WHAT IN SPACE IS THAT THING?
GROUND IF I KNOW. IT'S NOT IN THIS RIDICULOUS LITTLE BOOKLET THEY GAVE US...
TASTES KIND OF GAMY--LIKE A DIANOGA OR SOMETHING.
YOU ATE A DIANOGA?!
IT WAS EITHER THAT OR LEFT OVER IMPERIAL FIELD RATIONS.
HEY, TYCHO--YOU WERE WITH THE IMPERIAL NAVY, WEREN'T YOU?
SO WERE MOST REBEL PILOTS.
WHY'D YOU SWITCH?
I LIKE THESE X-WINGS. THEY'RE EASIER TO FLY.
YOU SWITCHED SIDES BECAUSE YOU LIKE THE STARFIGHTERS BETTER?
TELL YOU WHAT--I WRITE THE BOOK, YOU CAN HAVE THE FIRST COPY.
I DON'T THINK THAT MEAT WAS SAFE.
WHAT'S THE PROBLEM?

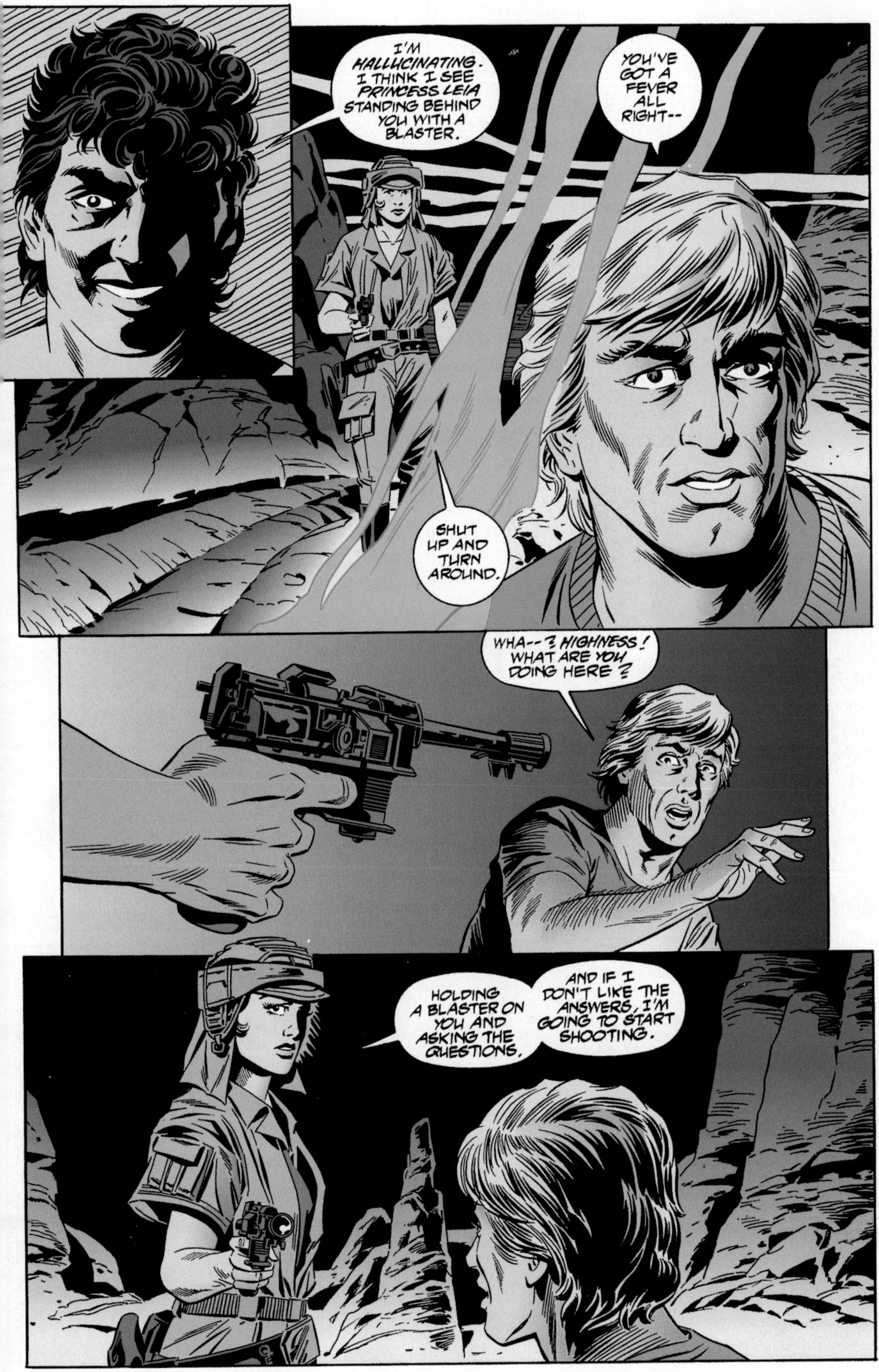
I'M HALLUCINATING. I THINK I SEE PRINCESS LEIA STANDING BEHIND YOU WITH A BLASTER.
YOU'VE GOT A FEVER ALL RIGHT--
SHUT UP AND TURN AROUND.
WHA--? HIGHNESS! WHAT ARE YOU DOING HERE?
HOLDING A BLASTER ON YOU AND ASKING THE QUESTIONS.
AND IF I DON'T LIKE THE ANSWERS, I'M GOING TO START SHOOTING.

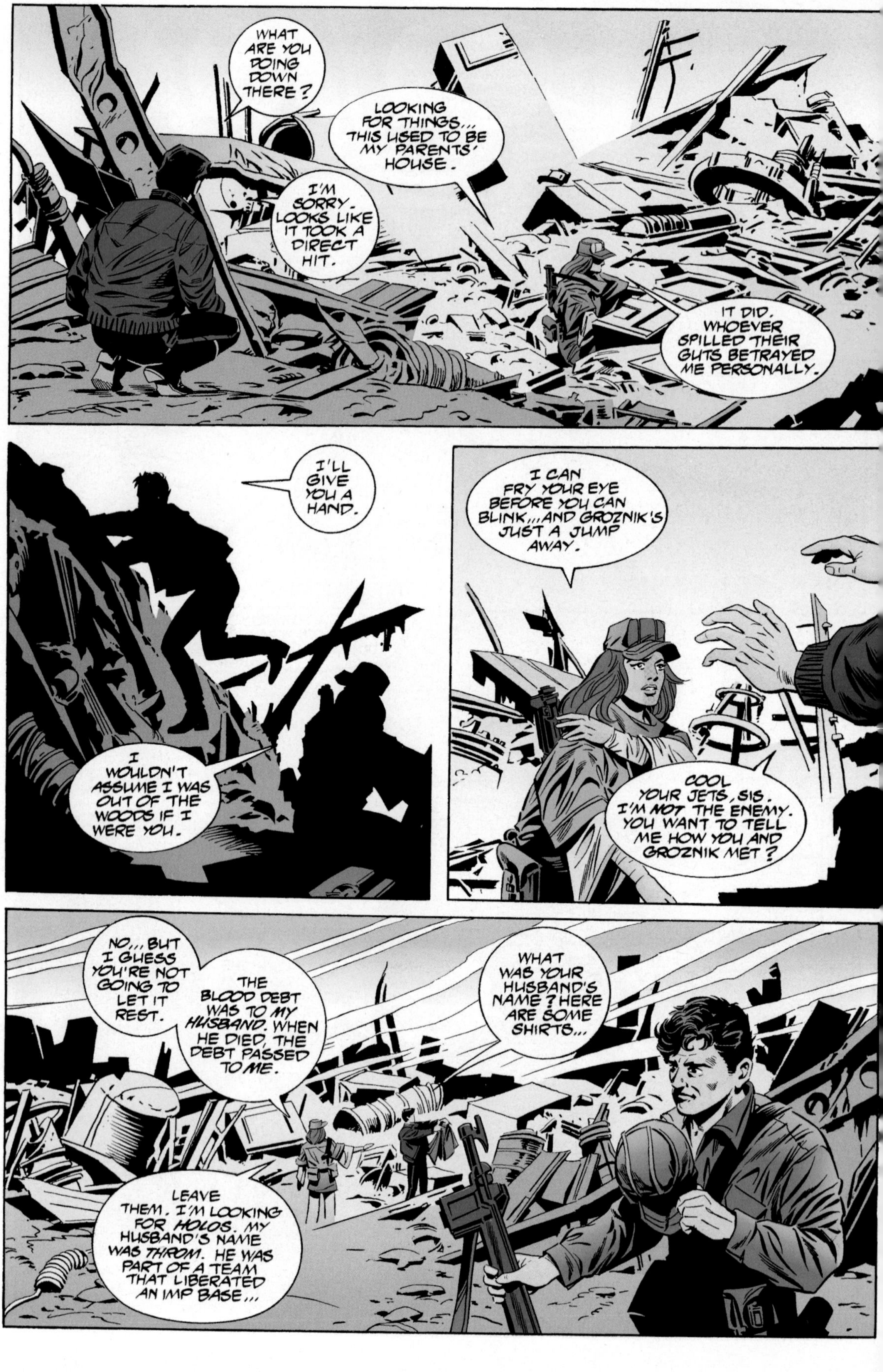
WHAT ARE YOU DOING DOWN THERE?
LOOKING FOR THINGS... THIS USED TO BE MY PARENTS' HOUSE.
I'M SORRY. LOOKS LIKE IT TOOK A DIRECT HIT.
IT DID. WHOEVER SPILLED THEIR GUTS BETRAYED ME PERSONALLY.
I'LL GIVE YOU A HAND.
I WOULDN'T ASSUME I WAS OUT OF THE WOODS IF I WERE YOU.
I CAN FRY YOUR EYE BEFORE YOU CAN BLINK... AND GROZNIK'S JUST A JUMP AWAY.
COOL YOUR JETS, SIS. I'M NOT THE ENEMY. YOU WANT TO TELL ME HOW YOU AND GROZNIK MET?
NO... BUT I GUESS YOU'RE NOT GOING TO LET IT REST.
THE BLOOD DEBT WAS TO MY HUSBAND. WHEN HE DIED, THE DEBT PASSED TO ME.
WHAT WAS YOUR HUSBAND'S NAME? HERE ARE SOME SHIRTS...
LEAVE THEM. I'M LOOKING FOR HOLOS. MY HUSBAND'S NAME WAS THROM. HE WAS PART OF A TEAM THAT LIBERATED AN IMP BASE...

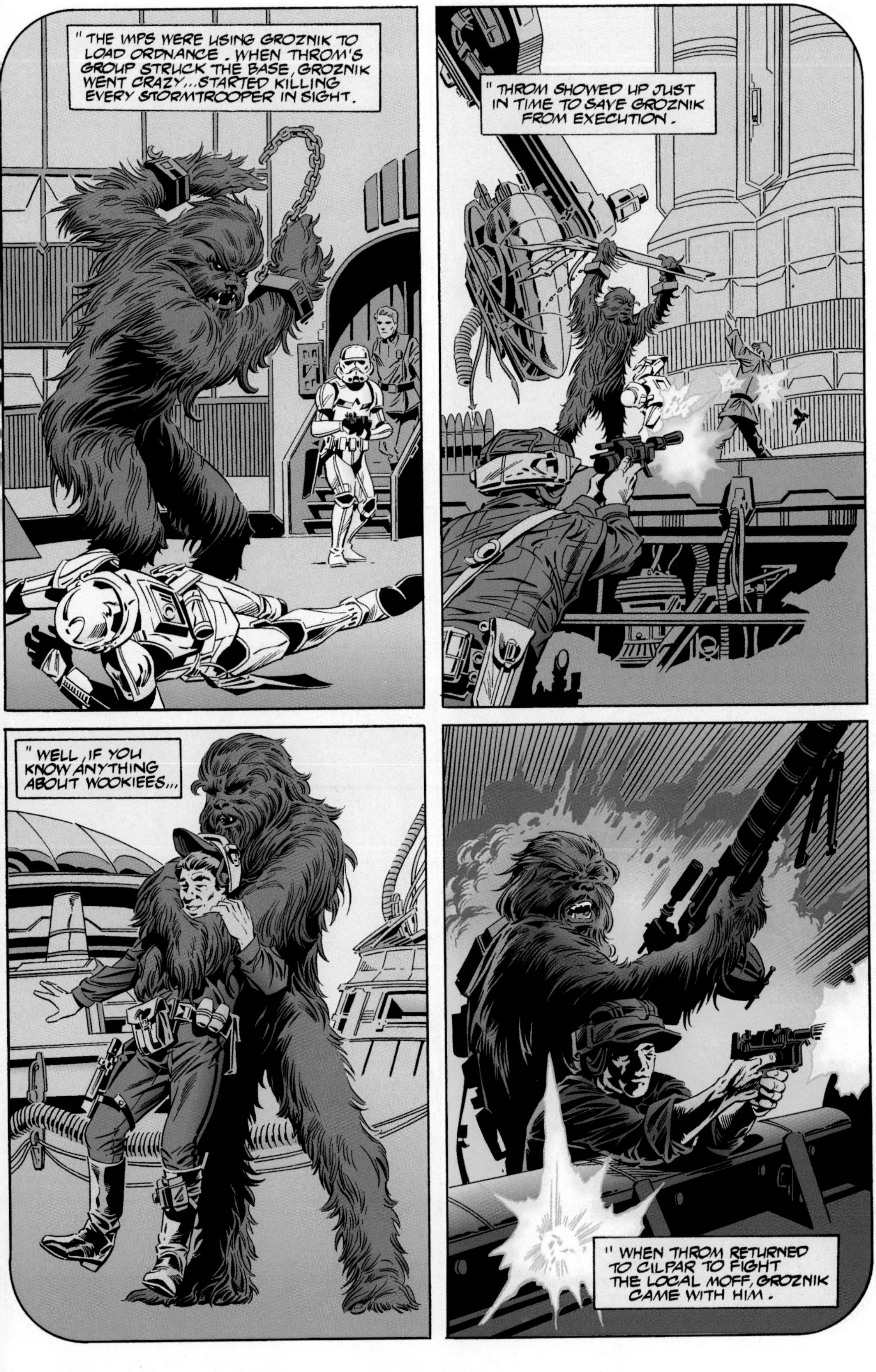
"THE IMPS WERE USING GROZNIK TO LOAD ORDNANCE. WHEN THROM'S GROUP STRUCK THE BASE, GROZNIK WENT CRAZY... STARTED KILLING EVERY STORMTROOPER IN SIGHT.
"THROM SHOWED UP JUST IN TIME TO SAVE GROZNIK FROM EXECUTION.
"WELL, IF YOU KNOW ANYTHING ABOUT WOOKIEES...
"WHEN THROM RETURNED TO CILPAR TO FIGHT THE LOCAL MOFF, GROZNIK CAME WITH HIM.

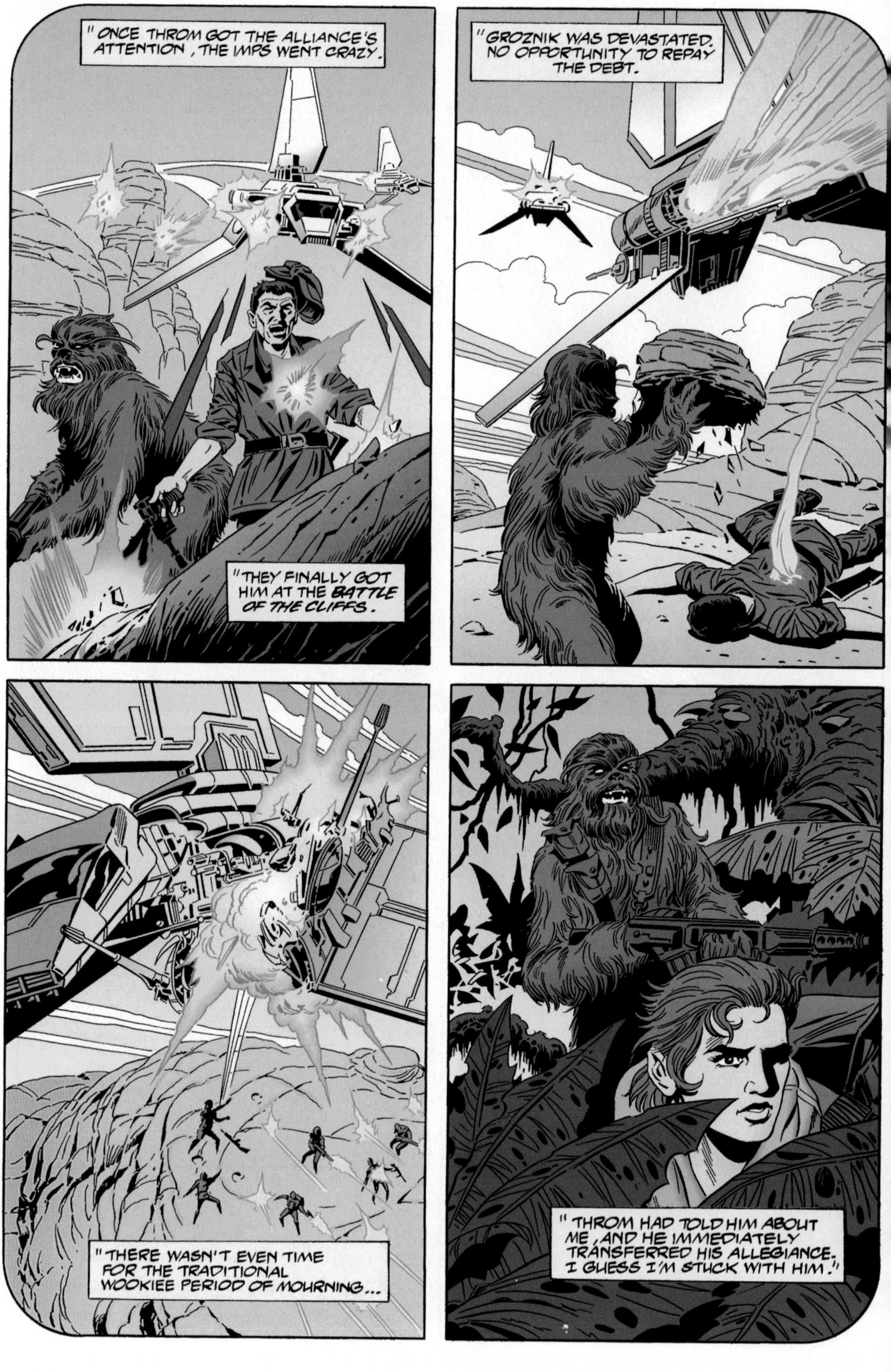
"ONCE THROM GOT THE ALLIANCE'S ATTENTION, THE IMPS WENT CRAZY.
"THEY FINALLY GOT HIM AT THE BATTLE OF THE CLIFFS.
"GROZNIK WAS DEVASTATED. NO OPPORTUNITY TO REPAY THE DEBT.
"THERE WASN'T EVEN TIME FOR THE TRADITIONAL WOOKIEE PERIOD OF MOURNING...
"THROM HAD TOLD HIM ABOUT ME, AND HE IMMEDIATELY TRANSFERRED HIS ALLEGIANCE. I GUESS I'M STUCK WITH HIM."

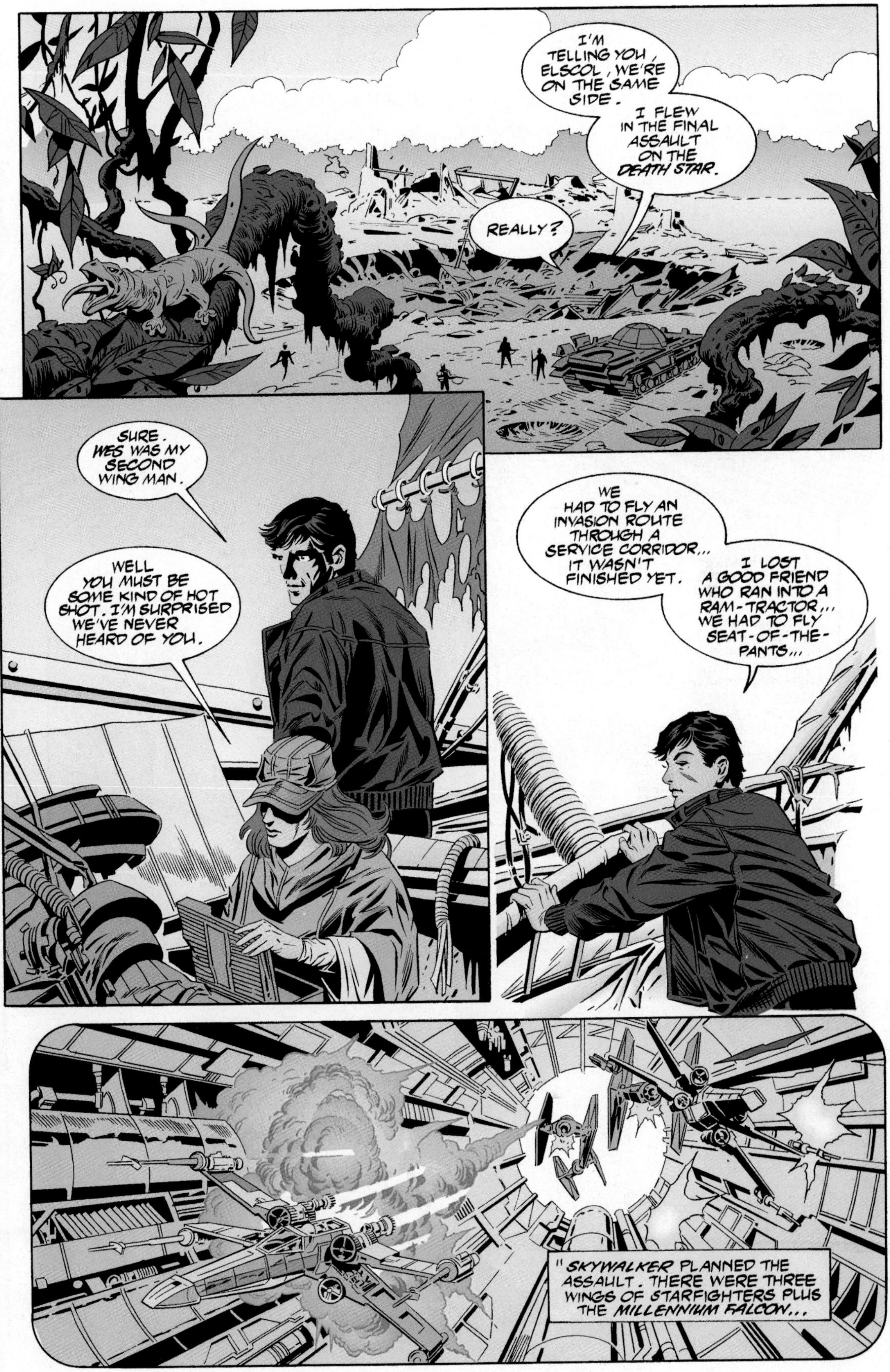
I'M TELLING YOU, ELSCOL, WE'RE ON THE SAME SIDE.
I FLEW IN THE FINAL ASSAULT ON THE DEATH STAR.
REALLY?
SURE. WES WAS MY SECOND WING MAN.
WELL YOU MUST BE SOME KIND OF HOT SHOT. I'M SURPRISED WE'VE NEVER HEARD OF YOU.
WE HAD TO FLY AN INVASION ROUTE THROUGH A SERVICE CORRIDOR... IT WASN'T FINISHED YET.
I LOST A GOOD FRIEND WHO RAN INTO A RAM-TRACTOR... WE HAD TO FLY SEAT-OF-THE-PANTS...
"SKYWALKER PLANNED THE ASSAULT. THERE WERE THREE WINGS OF STARFIGHTERS PLUS THE MILLENNIUM FALCON...

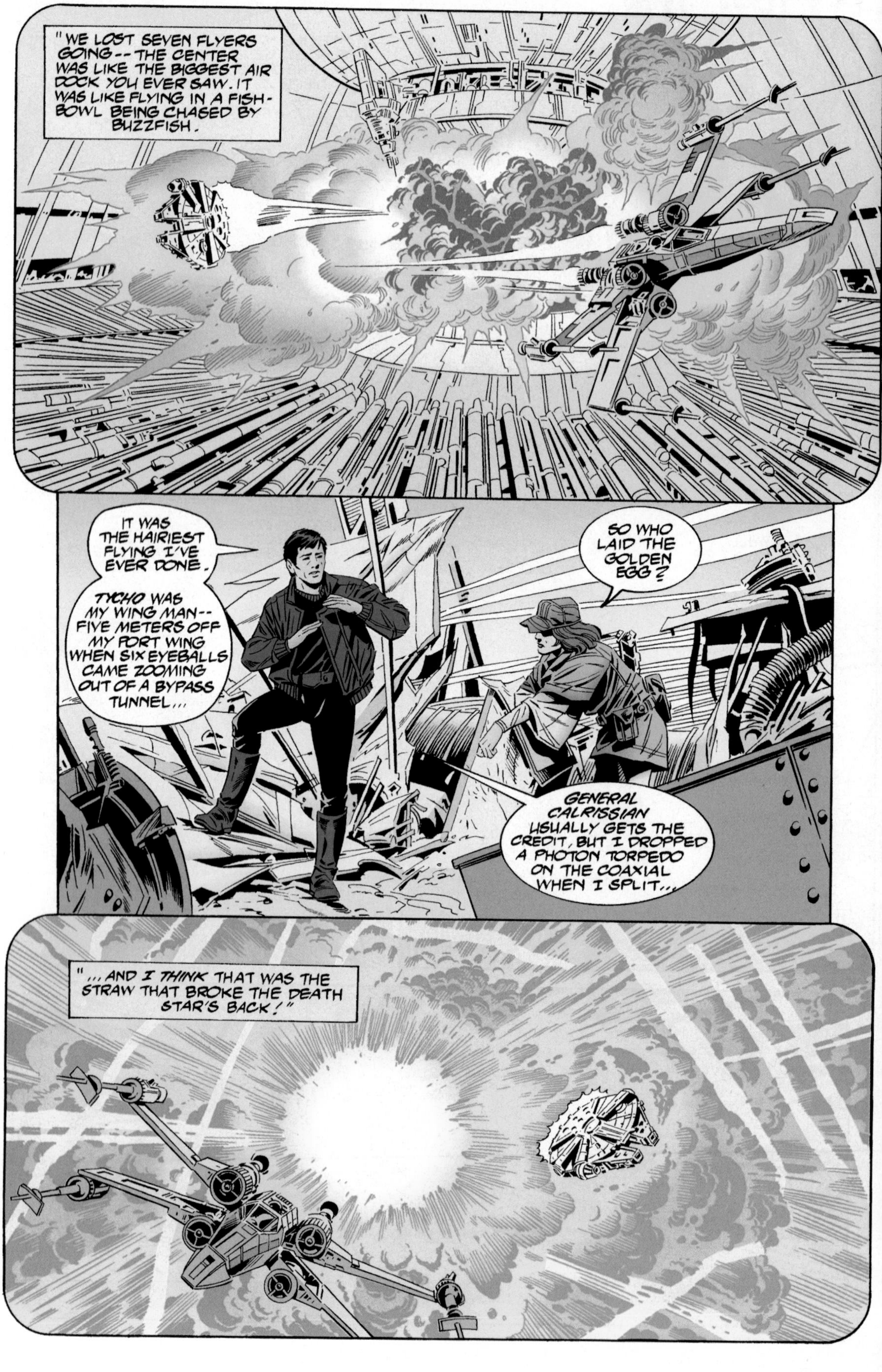
"WE LOST SEVEN FLYERS GOING-- THE CENTER WAS LIKE THE BIGGEST AIR DOCK YOU EVER SAW. IT WAS LIKE FLYING IN A FISH-BOWL BEING CHASED BY BUZZFISH.
IT WAS THE HAIRIEST FLYING I'VE EVER DONE.
TYCHO WAS MY WING MAN-- FIVE METERS OFF MY PORT WING WHEN SIX EYEBALLS CAME ZOOMING OUT OF A BYPASS TUNNEL...
SO WHO LAID THE GOLDEN EGG?
GENERAL CALRISSIAN USUALLY GETS THE CREDIT, BUT I DROPPED A PHOTON TORPEDO ON THE COAXIAL WHEN I SPLIT...
"...AND I THINK THAT WAS THE STRAW THAT BROKE THE DEATH STAR'S BACK!"

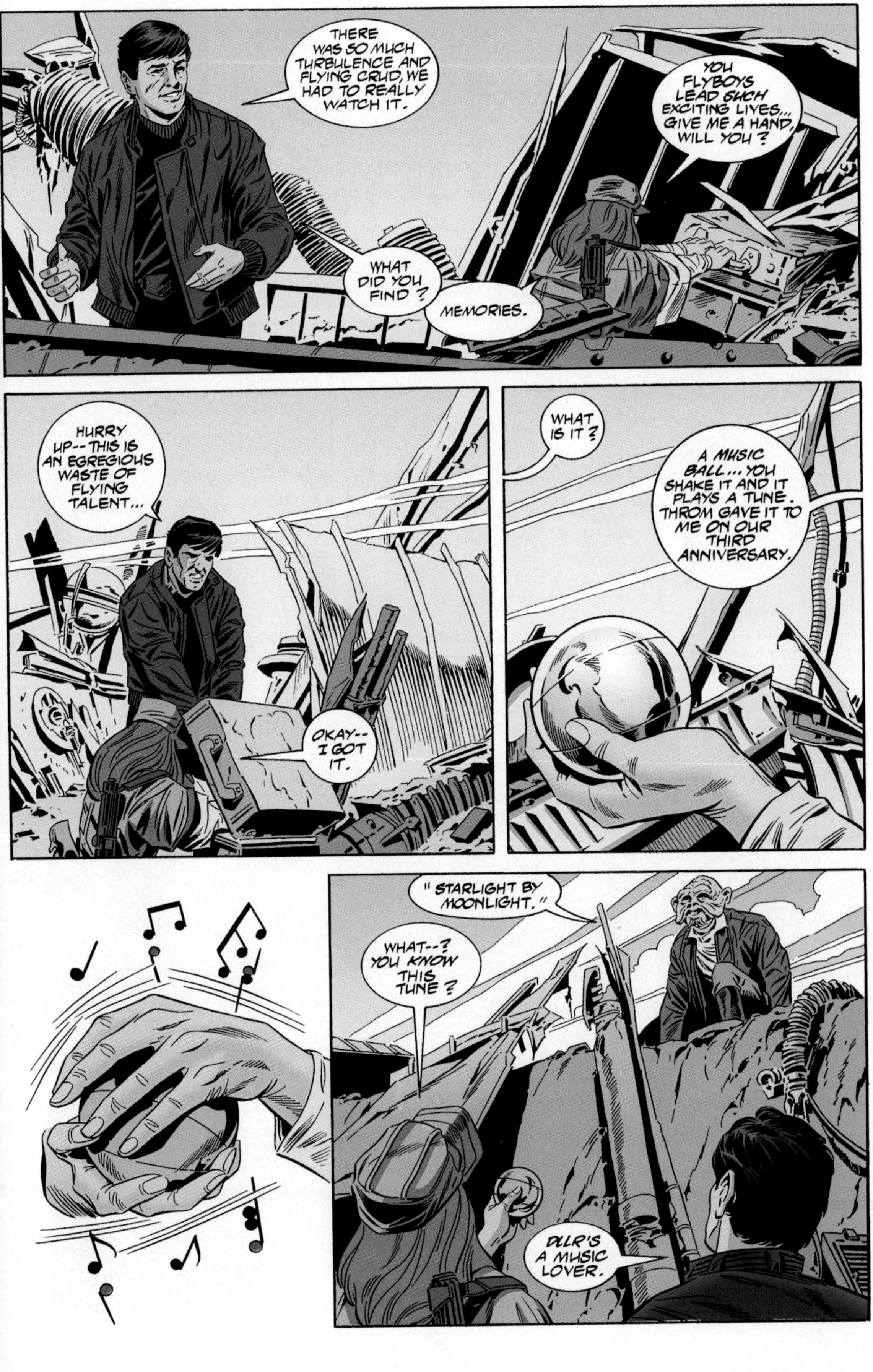
THERE WAS SO MUCH TURBULENCE AND FLYING CRUD, WE HAD TO REALLY WATCH IT.
YOU FLYBOYS LEAD SUCH EXCITING LIVES... GIVE ME A HAND, WILL YOU?
WHAT DID YOU FIND?
MEMORIES.
HURRY UP-- THIS IS AN EGREGIOUS WASTE OF FLYING TALENT...
OKAY-- I GOT IT.
WHAT IS IT?
A MUSIC BALL... YOU SHAKE IT AND IT PLAYS A TUNE. THROM GAVE IT TO ME ON OUR THIRD ANNIVERSARY.
"STARLIGHT BY MOONLIGHT."
WHAT--? YOU KNOW THIS TUNE?
DLLR'S A MUSIC LOVER.

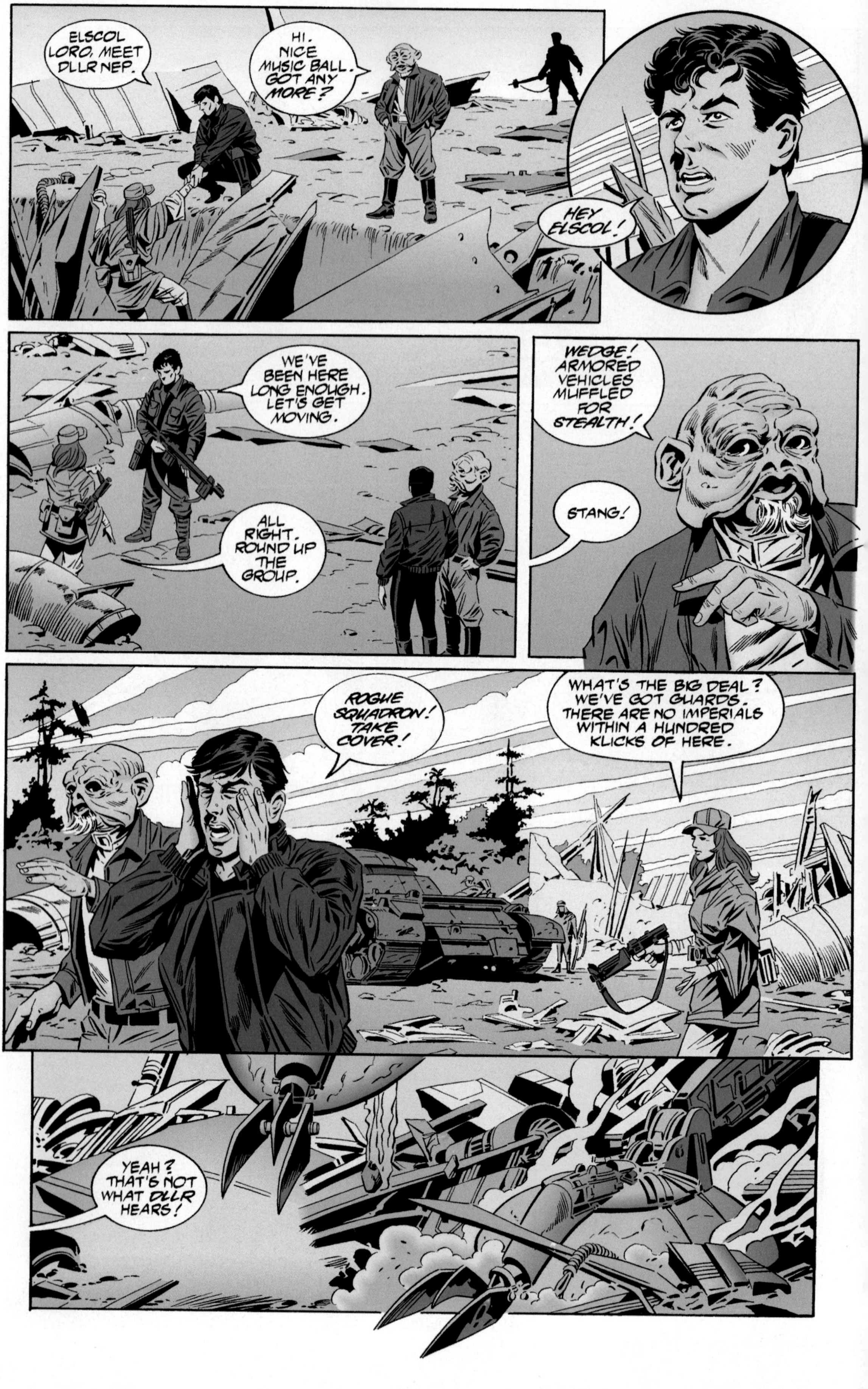
ELSCOL LORO, MEET DLLR NEP.
HI. NICE MUSIC BALL. GOT ANY MORE?
HEY ELSCOL!
WE'VE BEEN HERE LONG ENOUGH. LET'S GET MOVING.
ALL RIGHT. ROUND UP THE GROUP.
WEDGE! ARMORED VEHICLES MUFFLED FOR STEALTH!
STANG!
ROGUE SQUADRON! TAKE COVER!
WHAT'S THE BIG DEAL? WE'VE GOT GUARDS. THERE ARE NO IMPERIALS WITHIN A HUNDRED KLICKS OF HERE.
YEAH? THAT'S NOT WHAT DLLR HEARS!

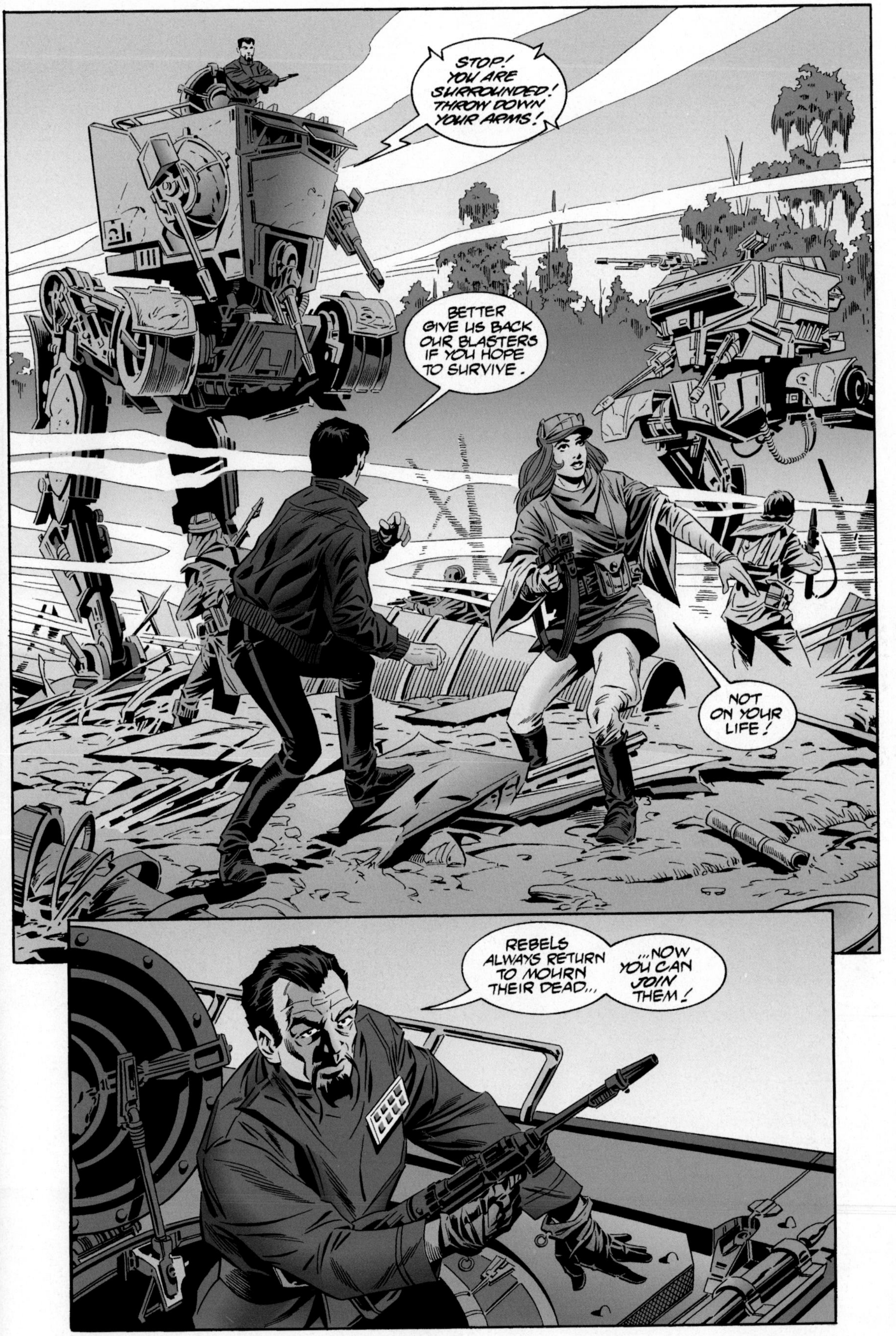
STOP! YOU ARE SURROUNDED! THROW DOWN YOUR ARMS!
BETTER GIVE US BACK OUR BLASTERS IF YOU HOPE TO SURVIVE.
NOT ON YOUR LIFE!
REBELS ALWAYS RETURN TO MOURN THEIR DEAD...
...NOW YOU CAN JOIN THEM!

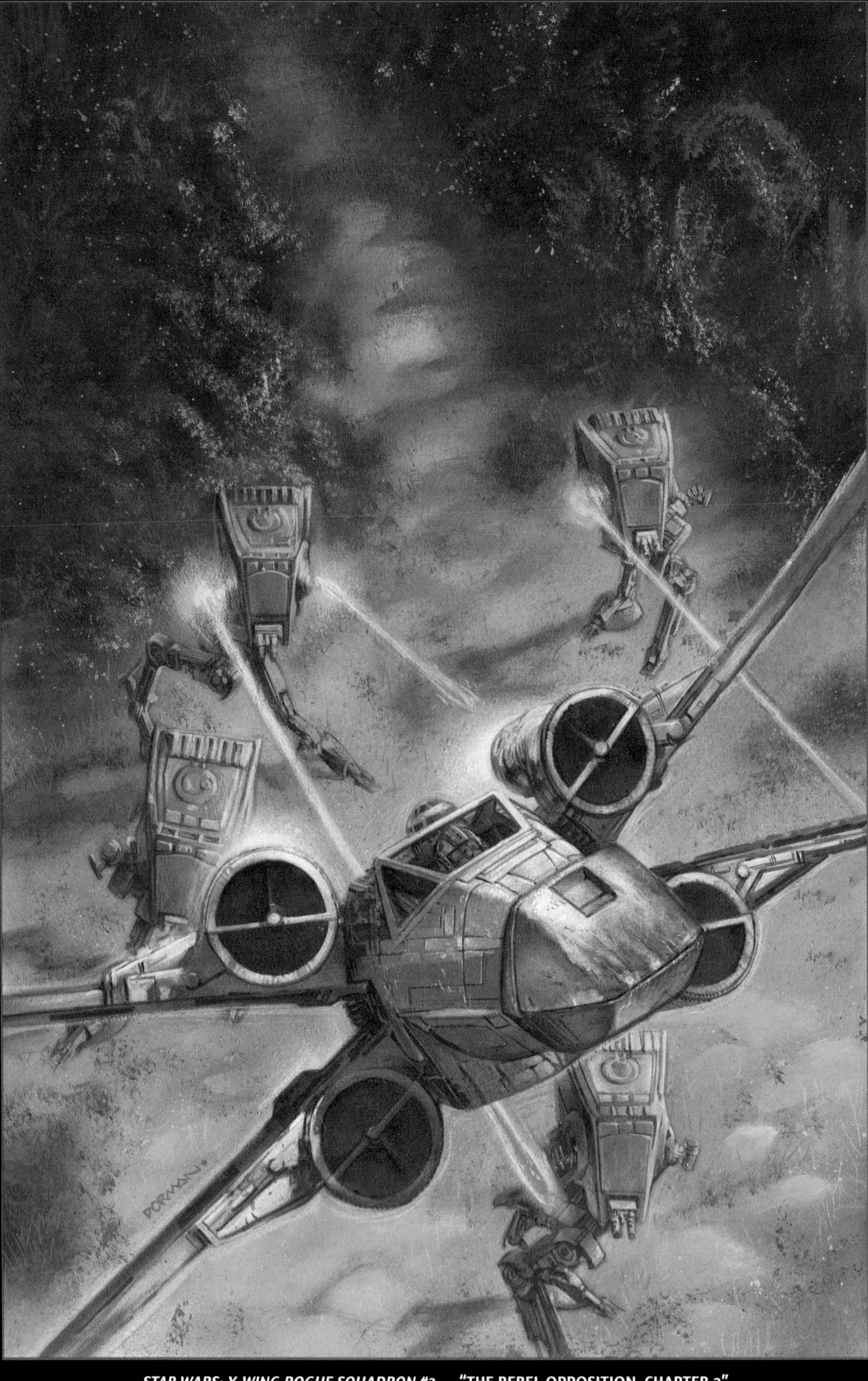
DORMAN

*STAR WARS: X-WING ROGUE SQUADRON #2* — "THE REBEL OPPOSITION, CHAPTER 2"

PLOTTER: MICHAEL A. STACKPOLE • SCRIPTER: MIKE BARON • PENCILER: ALLEN NUNIS • INKER: ANDY MUSHYNSKY • COLORIST: DAVE NESTELLE
LETTERER: STEVE DUTRO • EDITOR: RYDER WINDHAM • COVER ARTIST: DAVE DORMAN

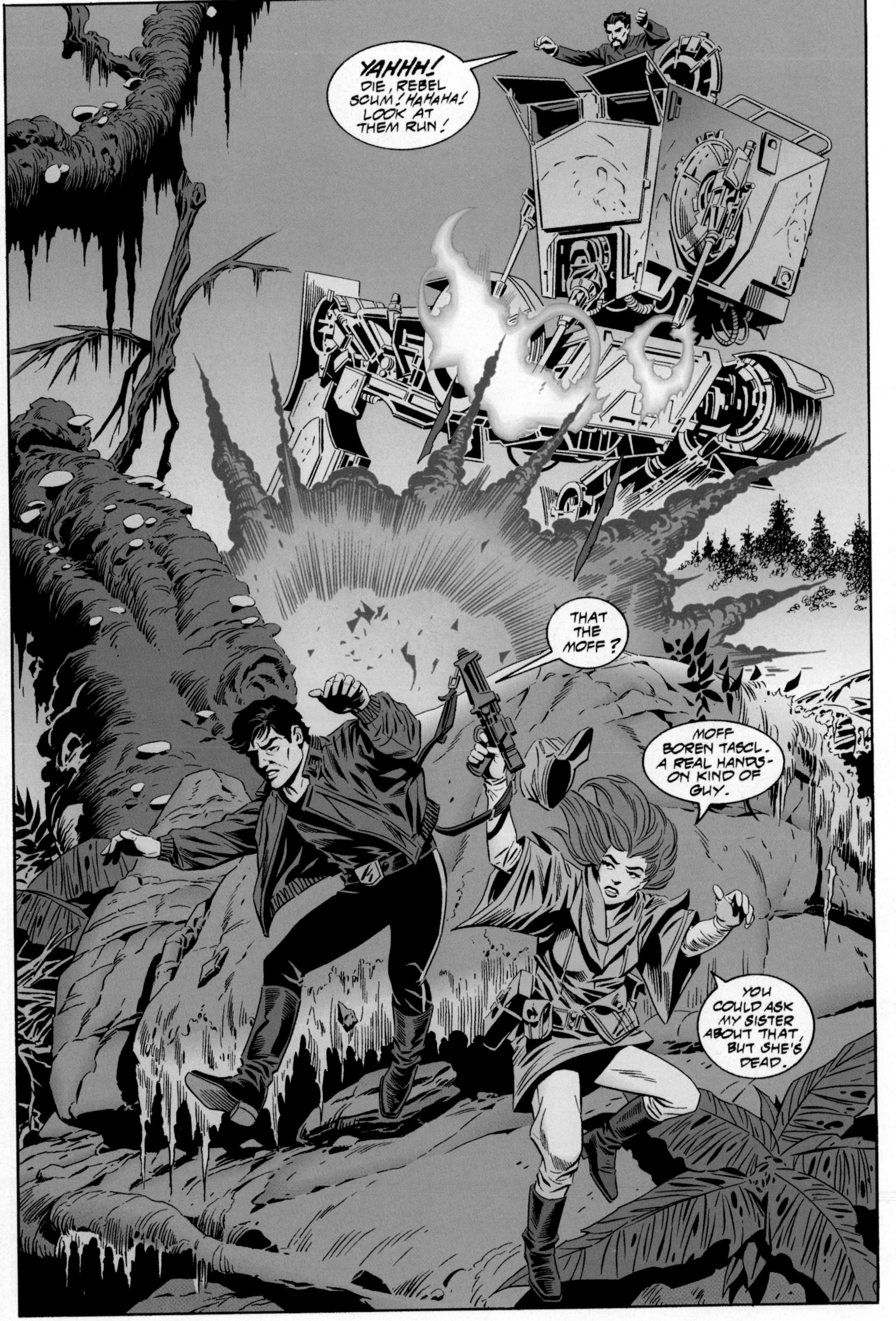

YAHHH! DIE, REBEL SCUM! HAHAHA! LOOK AT THEM RUN!
THAT THE MOFF?
MOFF BOREN TASCL. A REAL HANDS-ON KIND OF GUY.
YOU COULD ASK MY SISTER ABOUT THAT, BUT SHE'S DEAD.

WHAT IS THIS PLACE?

WE DON'T KNOW--IT PREDATES THE SETTLEMENT. OBVIOUSLY SOME KIND OF TEMPLE...

ELSCOL-- WE MUST HAVE TRIPPED AN ALARM.

WHAT'S TO STOP THEM FROM BRINGING THIS TEMPLE DOWN ON OUR HEADS?

THE ROCK. WE TRIED TO DISMANTLE THIS THING A COUPLE YEARS AGO.

DISMANTLE A NATIVE TEMPLE?

THAT'S RIGHT. WE NEEDED MONEY.--WE HAD A DEAL TO SELL THE WORKS TO TALON KARRDE...BUT WE COULDN'T PUT A CHIP IN THE STANG THING.

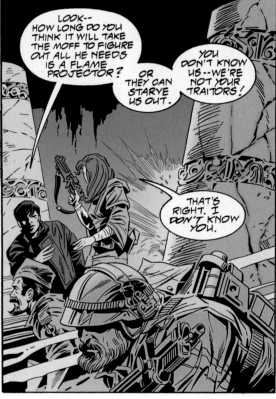

LOOK-- HOW LONG DO YOU THINK IT WILL TAKE THE MOFF TO FIGURE OUT ALL HE NEEDS IS A FLAME PROJECTOR?

OR THEY CAN STARVE US OUT.

YOU DON'T KNOW US--WE'RE NOT YOUR TRAITORS!

THAT'S RIGHT. I DON'T KNOW YOU.

GIVE US BACK OUR WEAPONS.

FORGET IT.

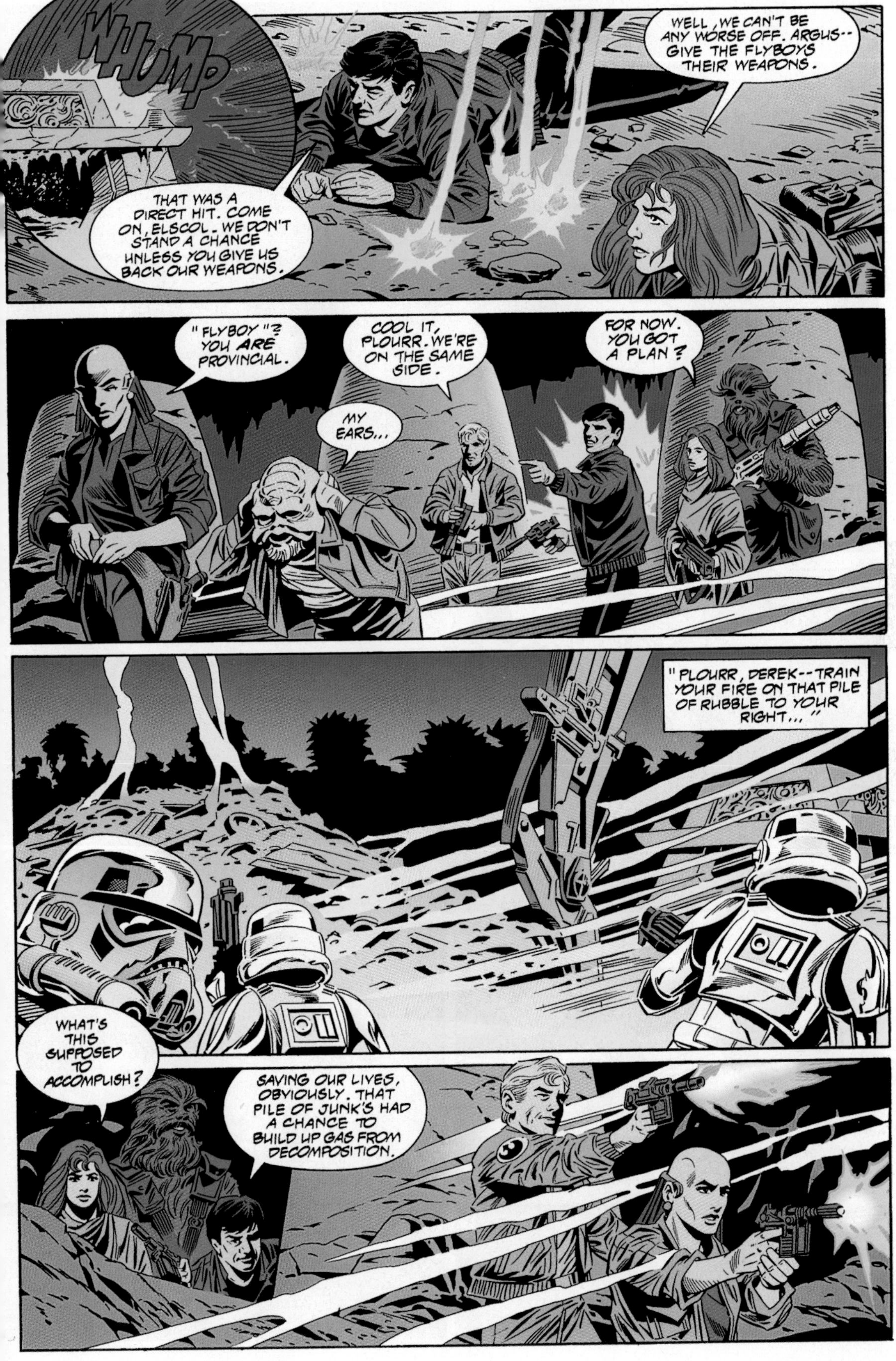
WHUMP
WELL, WE CAN'T BE ANY WORSE OFF. ARGUS-- GIVE THE FLYBOYS THEIR WEAPONS.
THAT WAS A DIRECT HIT. COME ON, ELSCOL. WE DON'T STAND A CHANCE UNLESS YOU GIVE US BACK OUR WEAPONS.
"FLYBOY"? YOU ARE PROVINCIAL.
COOL IT, PLOURR. WE'RE ON THE SAME SIDE.
FOR NOW. YOU GOT A PLAN?
MY EARS...
"PLOURR, DEREK--TRAIN YOUR FIRE ON THAT PILE OF RUBBLE TO YOUR RIGHT..."
WHAT'S THIS SUPPOSED TO ACCOMPLISH?
SAVING OUR LIVES, OBVIOUSLY. THAT PILE OF JUNK'S HAD A CHANCE TO BUILD UP GAS FROM DECOMPOSITION.

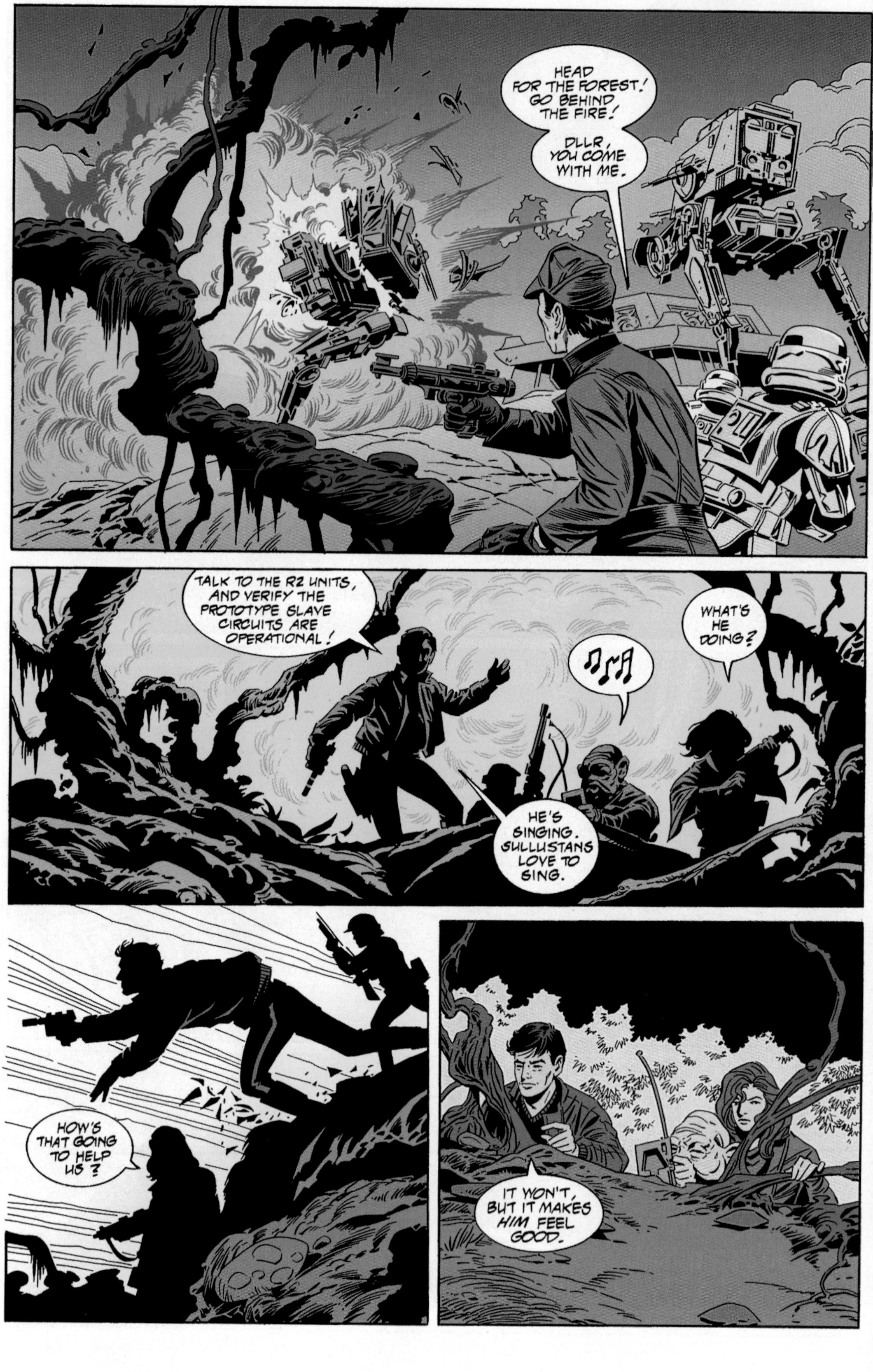

HEAD FOR THE FOREST! GO BEHIND THE FIRE!
DLLR, YOU COME WITH ME.
TALK TO THE R2 UNITS, AND VERIFY THE PROTOTYPE SLAVE CIRCUITS ARE OPERATIONAL!
WHAT'S HE DOING?
HE'S SINGING. SULLUSTANS LOVE TO SING.
HOW'S THAT GOING TO HELP US?
IT WON'T, BUT IT MAKES HIM FEEL GOOD.

TYCHO CELCHU, LIEUTENANT, REPUBLIC SPACE FORCE, SERIAL NUMBER 6B970024.

COME ON, TYCHO--IT'S PRINCESS LEIA! WHAT'S WITH THE P.O.W. ACT?

THAT'S RIGHT. IT SO HAPPENS, I'M *NOT* PRINCESS LEIA ORGANA. DAME WINTER, AT YOUR SERVICE.

YOU KNOW WHAT THEY CAN DO WITH PLASTIFORMS, WES. SHE COULD BE ANYBODY.

ALL RIGHT, TYCHO. JUST WHAT *ARE* YOU CROSS JOCKEYS DOING OUT HERE?

DAME WINTER, THERE'S SOME KIND OF CARNIVORE CREEPING UP BEHIND YOU. WE HAD SOME TROUBLE WITH THEM EARLIER--

OH, REALLY, LIEUTENANT...

...DO YOU EXPECT ME TO FALL FOR THAT?

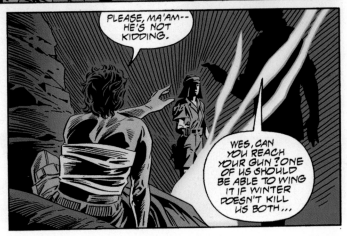

PLEASE, MA'AM-- HE'S NOT KIDDING.

WES, CAN YOU REACH YOUR GUN? ONE OF US SHOULD BE ABLE TO WING IT IF WINTER DOESN'T KILL US BOTH...

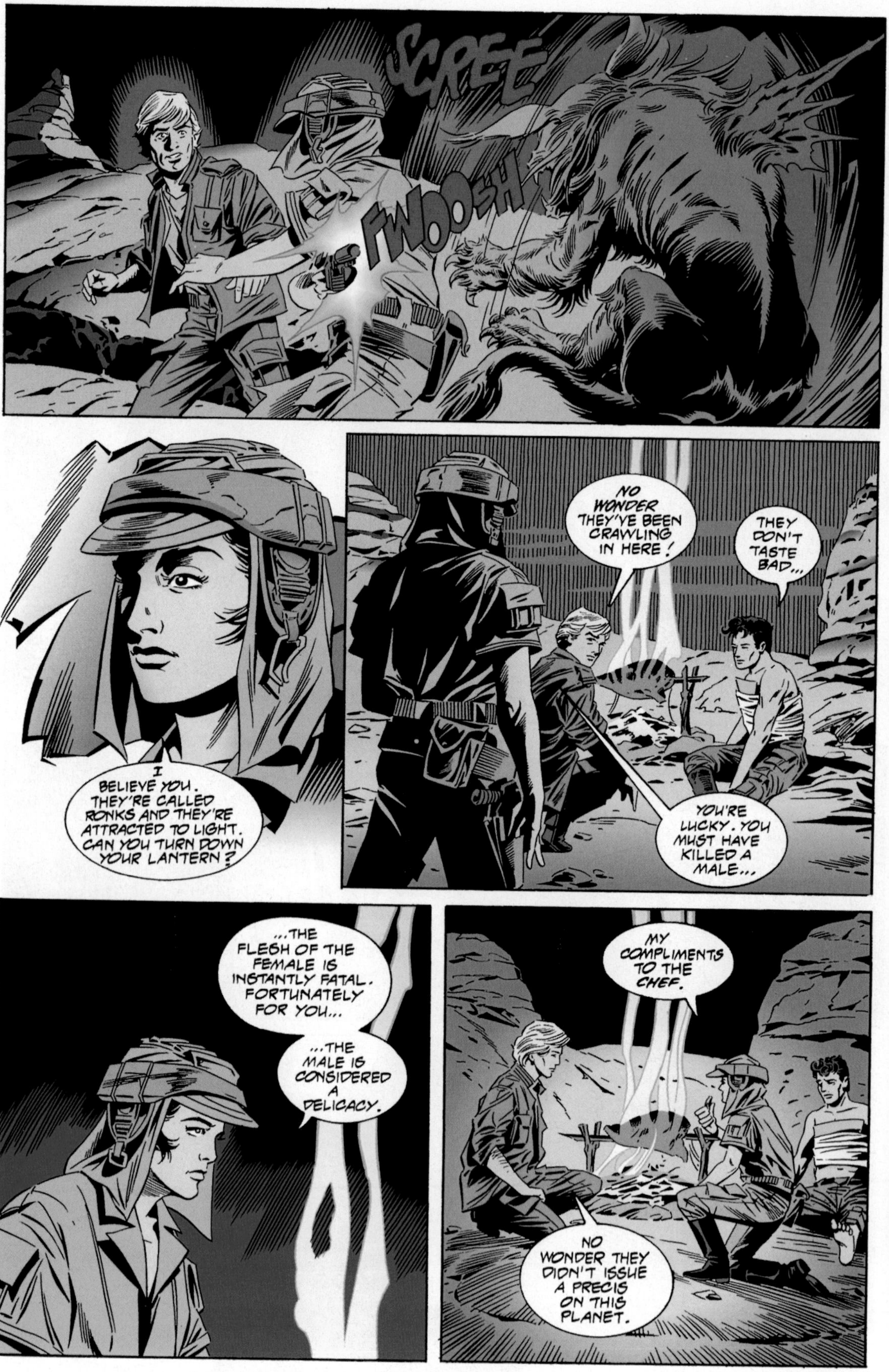
SCREE
FWOOSH
I BELIEVE YOU. THEY'RE CALLED RONKS AND THEY'RE ATTRACTED TO LIGHT. CAN YOU TURN DOWN YOUR LANTERN?
NO WONDER THEY'VE BEEN CRAWLING IN HERE!
THEY DON'T TASTE BAD...
YOU'RE LUCKY. YOU MUST HAVE KILLED A MALE...
...THE FLESH OF THE FEMALE IS INSTANTLY FATAL. FORTUNATELY FOR YOU...
...THE MALE IS CONSIDERED A DELICACY.
MY COMPLIMENTS TO THE CHEF.
NO WONDER THEY DIDN'T ISSUE A PRECIS ON THIS PLANET.

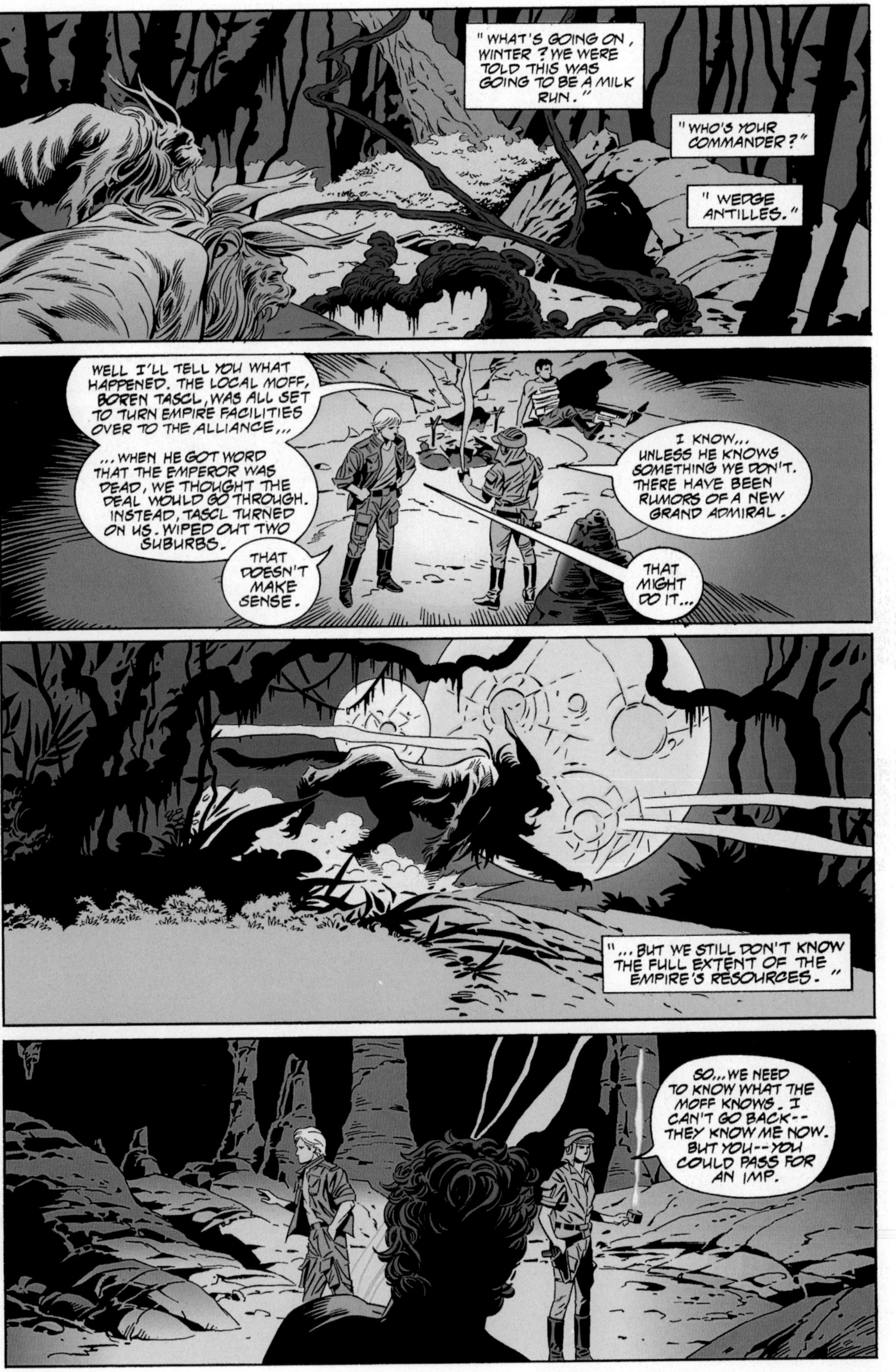
"WHAT'S GOING ON, WINTER? WE WERE TOLD THIS WAS GOING TO BE A MILK RUN."
"WHO'S YOUR COMMANDER?"
"WEDGE ANTILLES."
WELL I'LL TELL YOU WHAT HAPPENED. THE LOCAL MOFF, BOREN TASCL, WAS ALL SET TO TURN EMPIRE FACILITIES OVER TO THE ALLIANCE,...
...WHEN HE GOT WORD THAT THE EMPEROR WAS DEAD, WE THOUGHT THE DEAL WOULD GO THROUGH. INSTEAD, TASCL TURNED ON US. WIPED OUT TWO SUBURBS.
THAT DOESN'T MAKE SENSE.
I KNOW... UNLESS HE KNOWS SOMETHING WE DON'T. THERE HAVE BEEN RUMORS OF A NEW GRAND ADMIRAL.
THAT MIGHT DO IT...
"...BUT WE STILL DON'T KNOW THE FULL EXTENT OF THE EMPIRE'S RESOURCES."
SO...WE NEED TO KNOW WHAT THE MOFF KNOWS. I CAN'T GO BACK-- THEY KNOW ME NOW. BUT YOU--YOU COULD PASS FOR AN IMP.

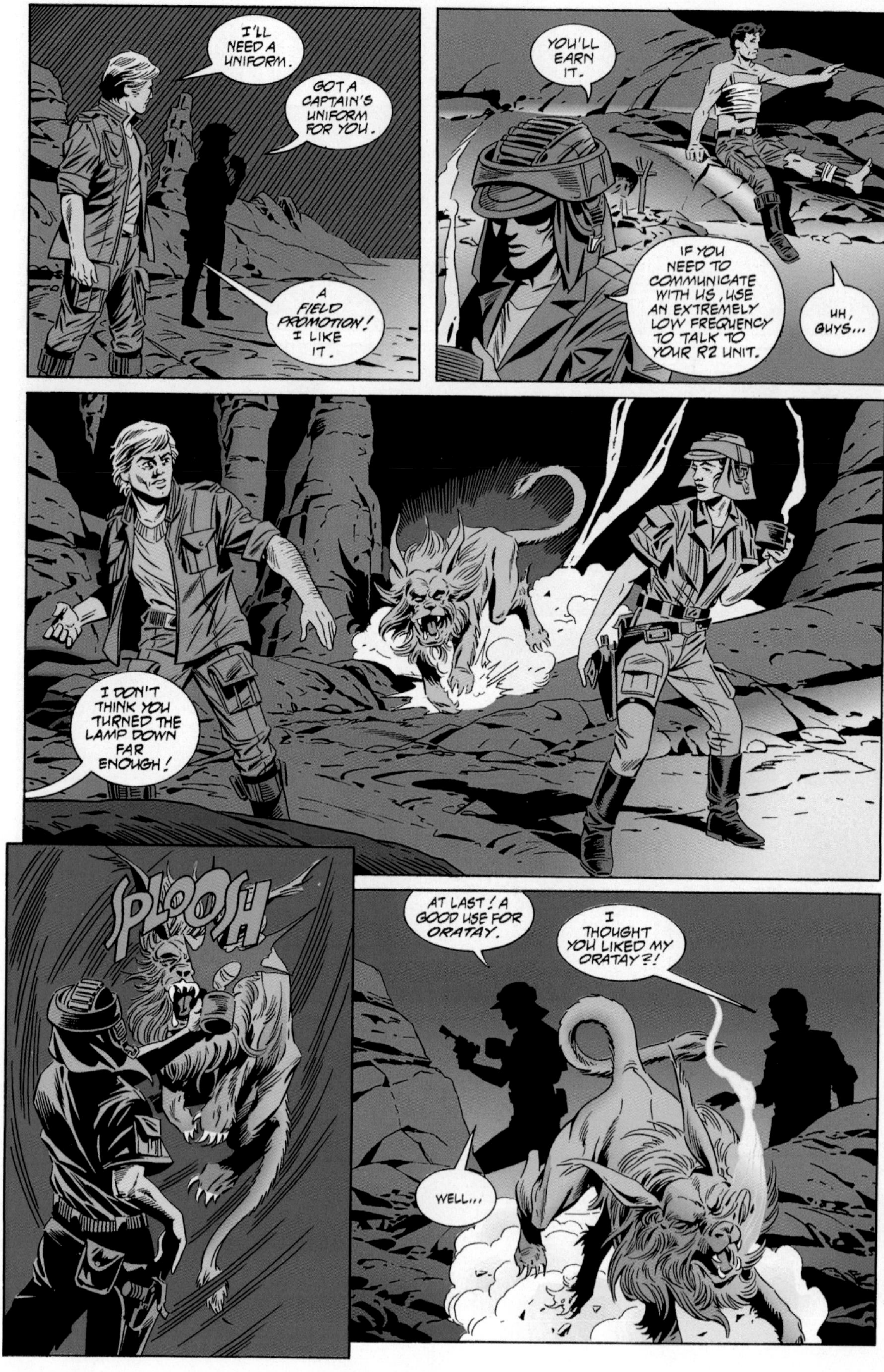
I'LL NEED A UNIFORM.
GOT A CAPTAIN'S UNIFORM FOR YOU.
A FIELD PROMOTION! I LIKE IT.
YOU'LL EARN IT.
IF YOU NEED TO COMMUNICATE WITH US, USE AN EXTREMELY LOW FREQUENCY TO TALK TO YOUR R2 UNIT.
UH, GUYS...
I DON'T THINK YOU TURNED THE LAMP DOWN FAR ENOUGH!
SPLOOSH
AT LAST! A GOOD USE FOR ORATAY.
I THOUGHT YOU LIKED MY ORATAY?!
WELL...

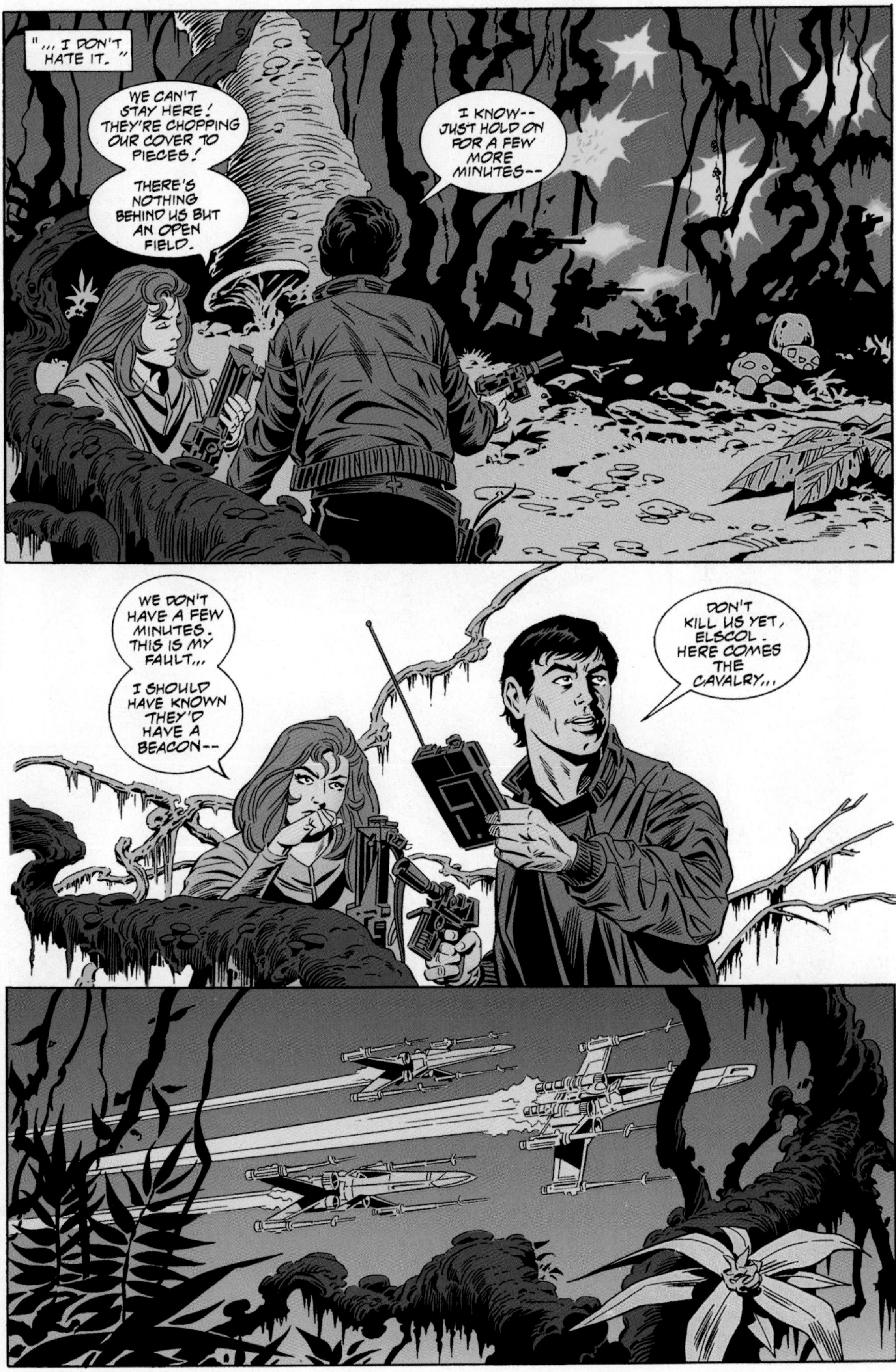
"... I DON'T HATE IT."
WE CAN'T STAY HERE! THEY'RE CHOPPING OUR COVER TO PIECES!
THERE'S NOTHING BEHIND US BUT AN OPEN FIELD.
I KNOW-- JUST HOLD ON FOR A FEW MORE MINUTES--
WE DON'T HAVE A FEW MINUTES. THIS IS MY FAULT...
I SHOULD HAVE KNOWN THEY'D HAVE A BEACON--
DON'T KILL US YET, ELSCOL. HERE COMES THE CAVALRY...

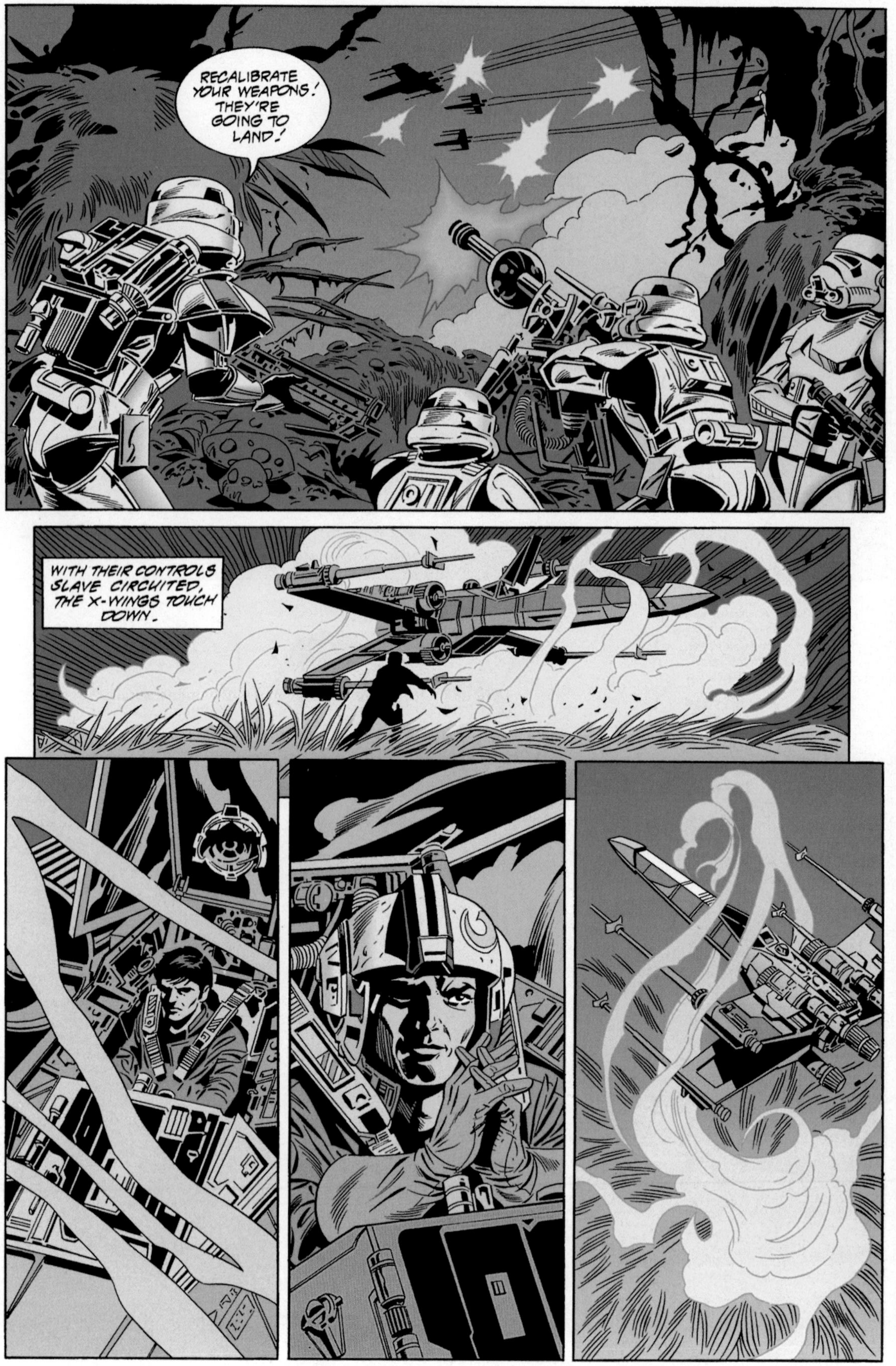
RECALIBRATE YOUR WEAPONS! THEY'RE GOING TO LAND!
WITH THEIR CONTROLS SLAVE CIRCUITED, THE X-WINGS TOUCH DOWN.

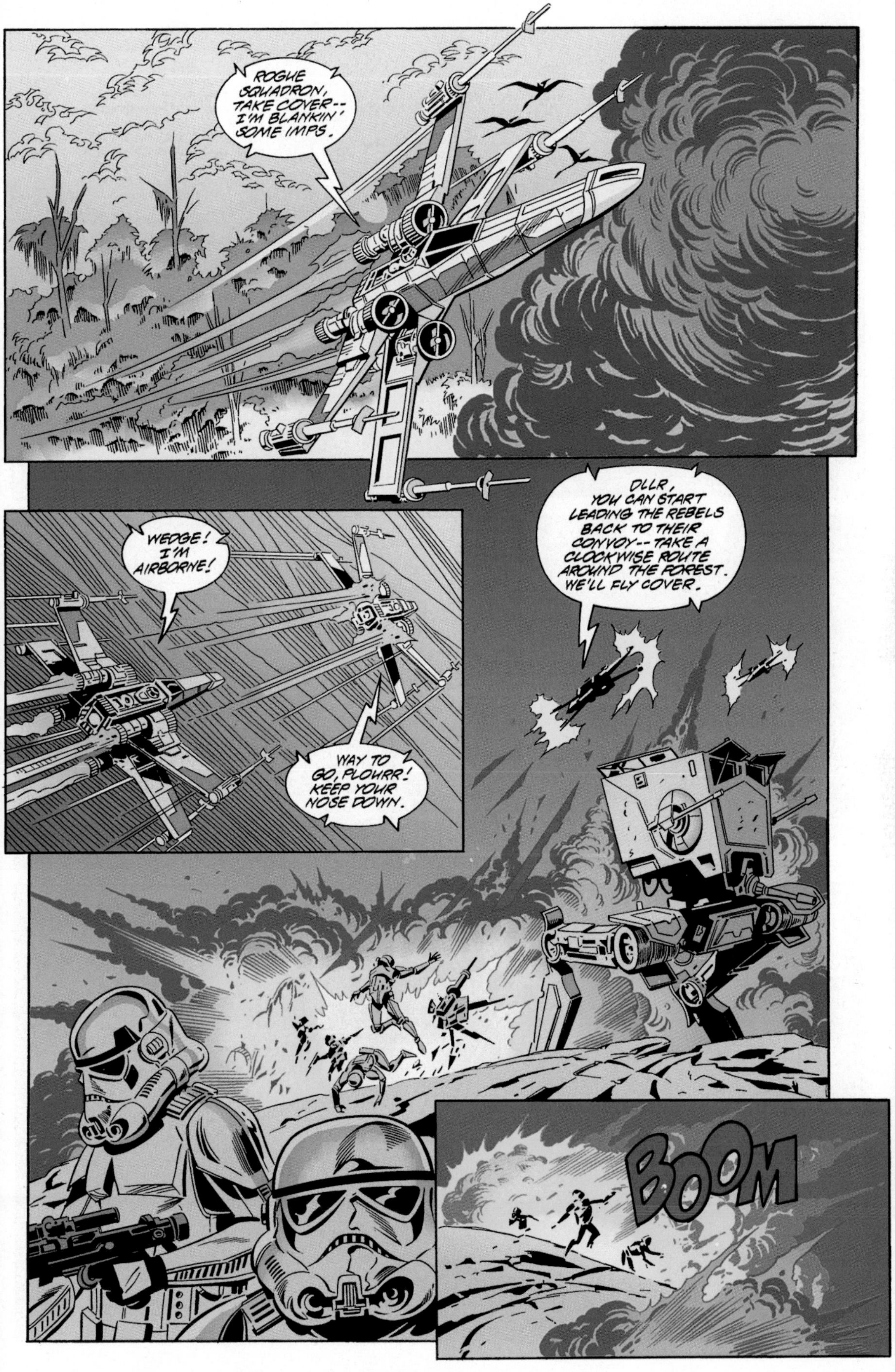
ROGUE SQUADRON, TAKE COVER-- I'M BLANKIN' SOME IMPS.
WEDGE! I'M AIRBORNE!
WAY TO GO, PLOURR! KEEP YOUR NOSE DOWN.
DLLR, YOU CAN START LEADING THE REBELS BACK TO THEIR CONVOY-- TAKE A CLOCKWISE ROUTE AROUND THE FOREST. WE'LL FLY COVER.
BOOM

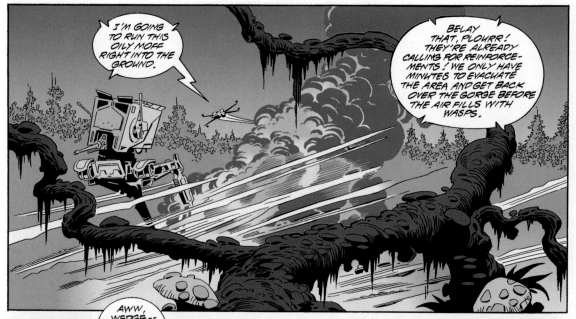

I'M GOING TO RUN THIS OILY MOFF RIGHT INTO THE GROUND.

BELAY THAT, PLOURR! THEY'RE ALREADY CALLING FOR REINFORCEMENTS! WE ONLY HAVE MINUTES TO EVACUATE THE AREA AND GET BACK OVER THE GORGE BEFORE THE AIR FILLS WITH WASPS.

AWW, WEDGE -- YOU'RE SPOILING MY FUN!

WE'LL HAVE FUN LATER. NOW GET BACK TO BASE!

WITH ROGUE SQUADRON FLYING ESCORT, THE REBELS RETREAT TOWARD THE MOUNTAINS, AND THE SQUADRON'S HIDDEN BASE.

WHAT'S WITH GROZNIK?

HE CAN MOVE FASTER AND SENSE MORE OUTSIDE THE CARRIER. IF SOMEBODY'S SET A TRAP, GROZNIK WILL TAKE THEM OUT.

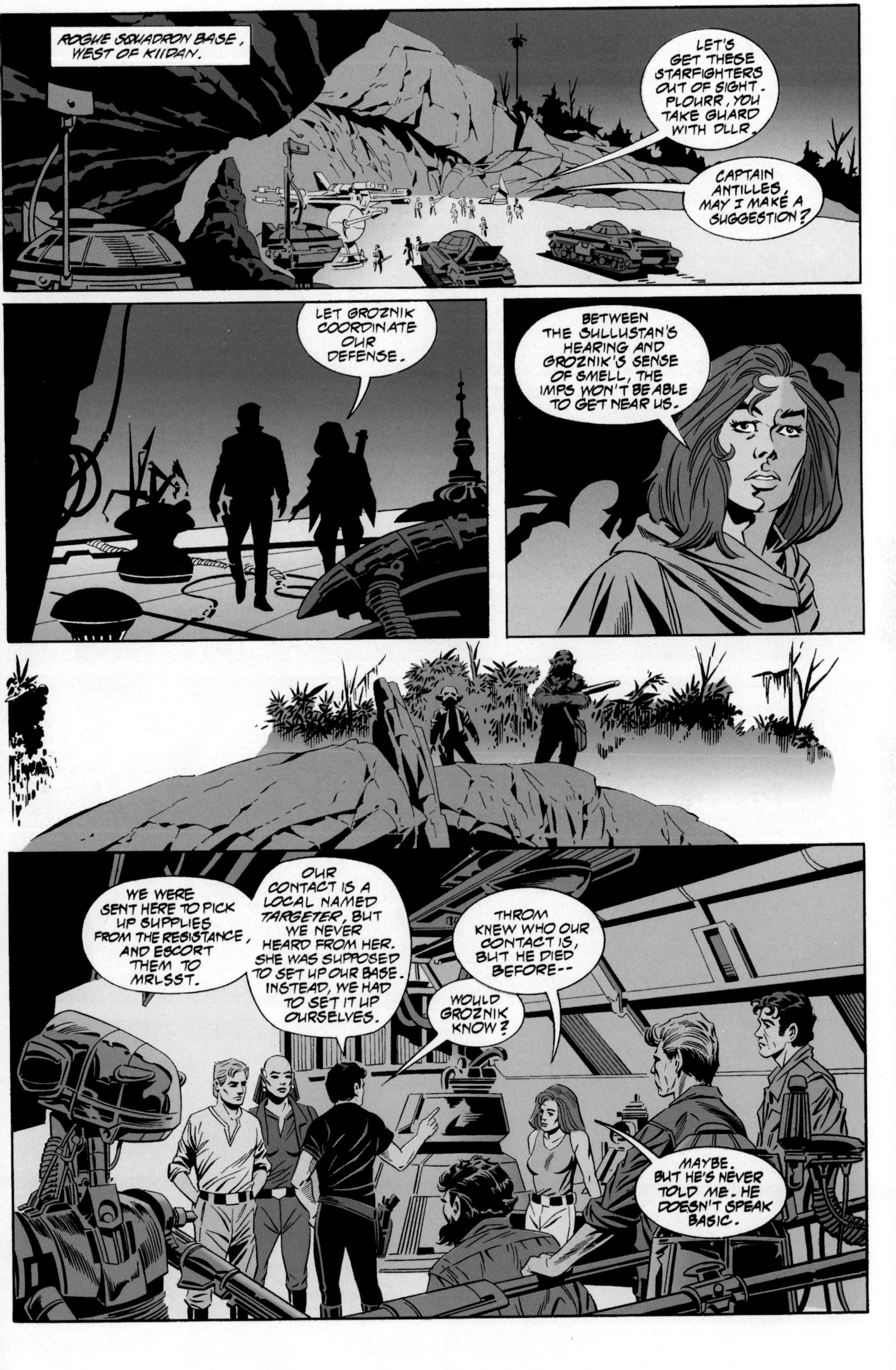
ROGUE SQUADRON BASE, WEST OF KIIDAN.
LET'S GET THESE STARFIGHTERS OUT OF SIGHT. PLOURR, YOU TAKE GUARD WITH DLLR.
CAPTAIN ANTILLES, MAY I MAKE A SUGGESTION?
LET GROZNIK COORDINATE OUR DEFENSE.
BETWEEN THE SULLUSTAN'S HEARING AND GROZNIK'S SENSE OF SMELL, THE IMPS WON'T BE ABLE TO GET NEAR US.
WE WERE SENT HERE TO PICK UP SUPPLIES FROM THE RESISTANCE, AND ESCORT THEM TO MRLSST.
OUR CONTACT IS A LOCAL NAMED TARGETER, BUT WE NEVER HEARD FROM HER. SHE WAS SUPPOSED TO SET UP OUR BASE. INSTEAD, WE HAD TO SET IT UP OURSELVES.
THROM KNEW WHO OUR CONTACT IS, BUT HE DIED BEFORE--
WOULD GROZNIK KNOW?
MAYBE. BUT HE'S NEVER TOLD ME. HE DOESN'T SPEAK BASIC.

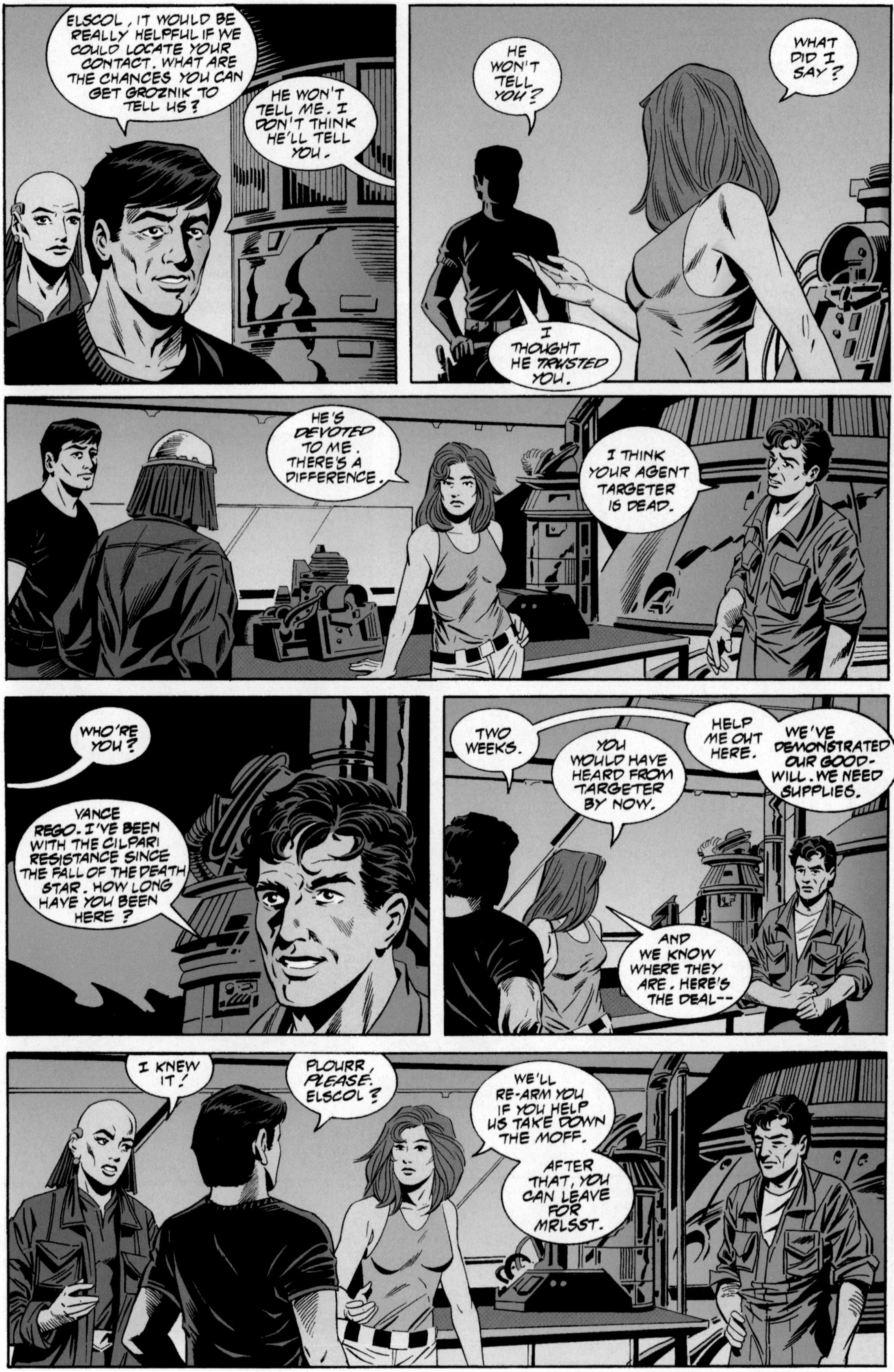
ELSCOL, IT WOULD BE REALLY HELPFUL IF WE COULD LOCATE YOUR CONTACT. WHAT ARE THE CHANCES YOU CAN GET GROZNIK TO TELL US?
HE WON'T TELL ME. I DON'T THINK HE'LL TELL YOU.
HE WON'T TELL YOU?
WHAT DID I SAY?
I THOUGHT HE TRUSTED YOU.
HE'S DEVOTED TO ME. THERE'S A DIFFERENCE.
I THINK YOUR AGENT TARGETER IS DEAD.
WHO'RE YOU?
VANCE REGO. I'VE BEEN WITH THE CILPARI RESISTANCE SINCE THE FALL OF THE DEATH STAR. HOW LONG HAVE YOU BEEN HERE?
TWO WEEKS.
YOU WOULD HAVE HEARD FROM TARGETER BY NOW.
HELP ME OUT HERE.
WE'VE DEMONSTRATED OUR GOOD-WILL. WE NEED SUPPLIES.
AND WE KNOW WHERE THEY ARE. HERE'S THE DEAL--
I KNEW IT!
PLOURR, PLEASE. ELSCOL?
WE'LL RE-ARM YOU IF YOU HELP US TAKE DOWN THE MOFF.
AFTER THAT, YOU CAN LEAVE FOR MRLSST.

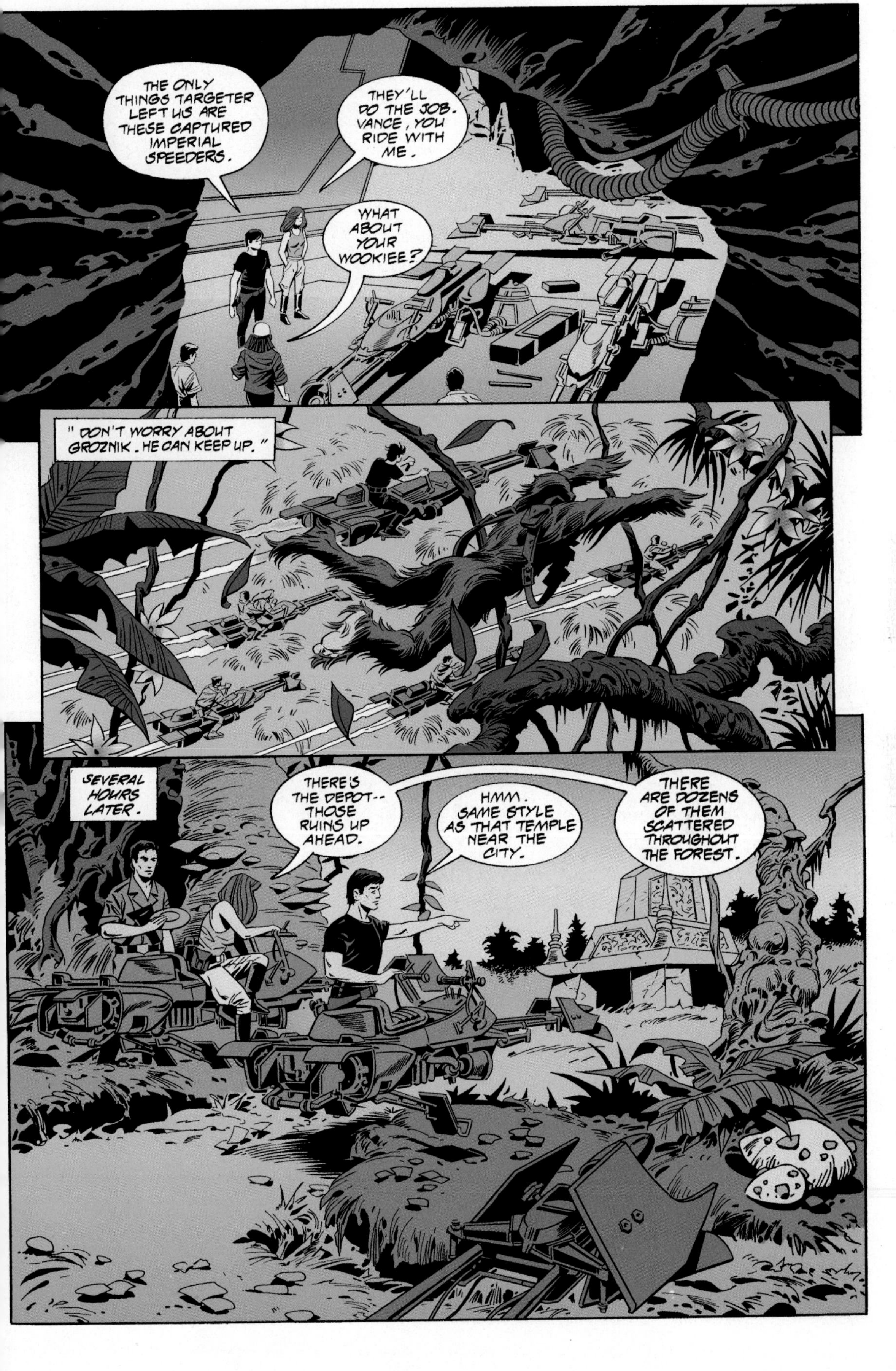
THE ONLY THINGS TARGETER LEFT US ARE THESE CAPTURED IMPERIAL SPEEDERS.
THEY'LL DO THE JOB. VANCE, YOU RIDE WITH ME.
WHAT ABOUT YOUR WOOKIEE?
"DON'T WORRY ABOUT GROZNIK. HE CAN KEEP UP."
SEVERAL HOURS LATER.
THERE'S THE DEPOT-- THOSE RUINS UP AHEAD.
HMM. SAME STYLE AS THAT TEMPLE NEAR THE CITY.
THERE ARE DOZENS OF THEM SCATTERED THROUGHOUT THE FOREST.

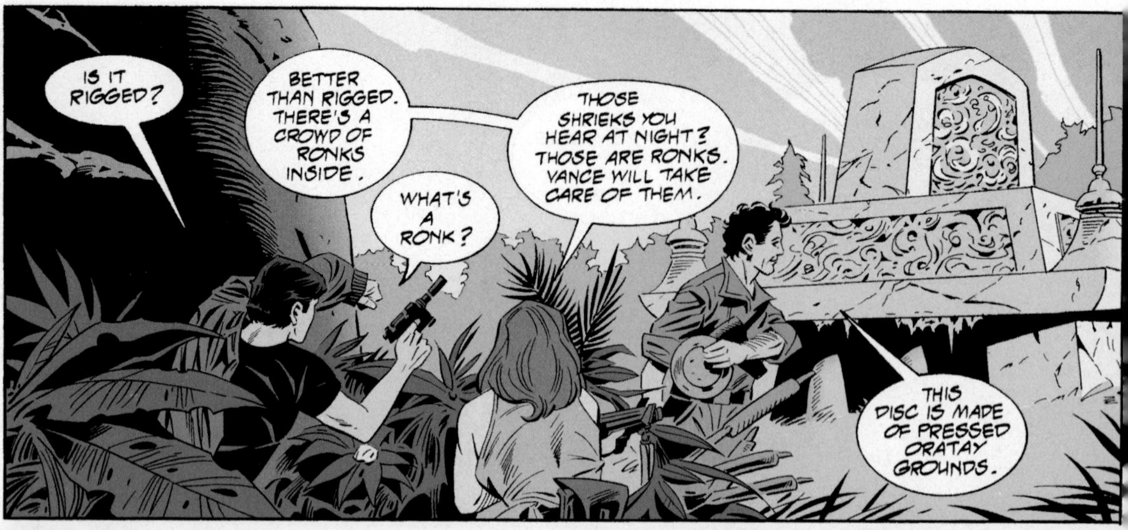
IS IT RIGGED?
BETTER THAN RIGGED. THERE'S A CROWD OF RONKS INSIDE.
THOSE SHRIEKS YOU HEAR AT NIGHT? THOSE ARE RONKS. VANCE WILL TAKE CARE OF THEM.
WHAT'S A RONK?
THIS DISC IS MADE OF PRESSED ORATAY GROUNDS.

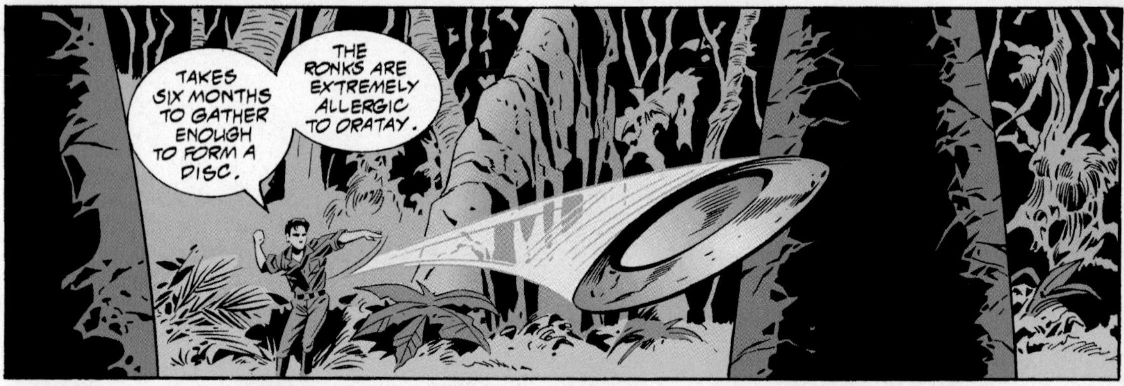
TAKES SIX MONTHS TO GATHER ENOUGH TO FORM A DISC.
THE RONKS ARE EXTREMELY ALLERGIC TO ORATAY.

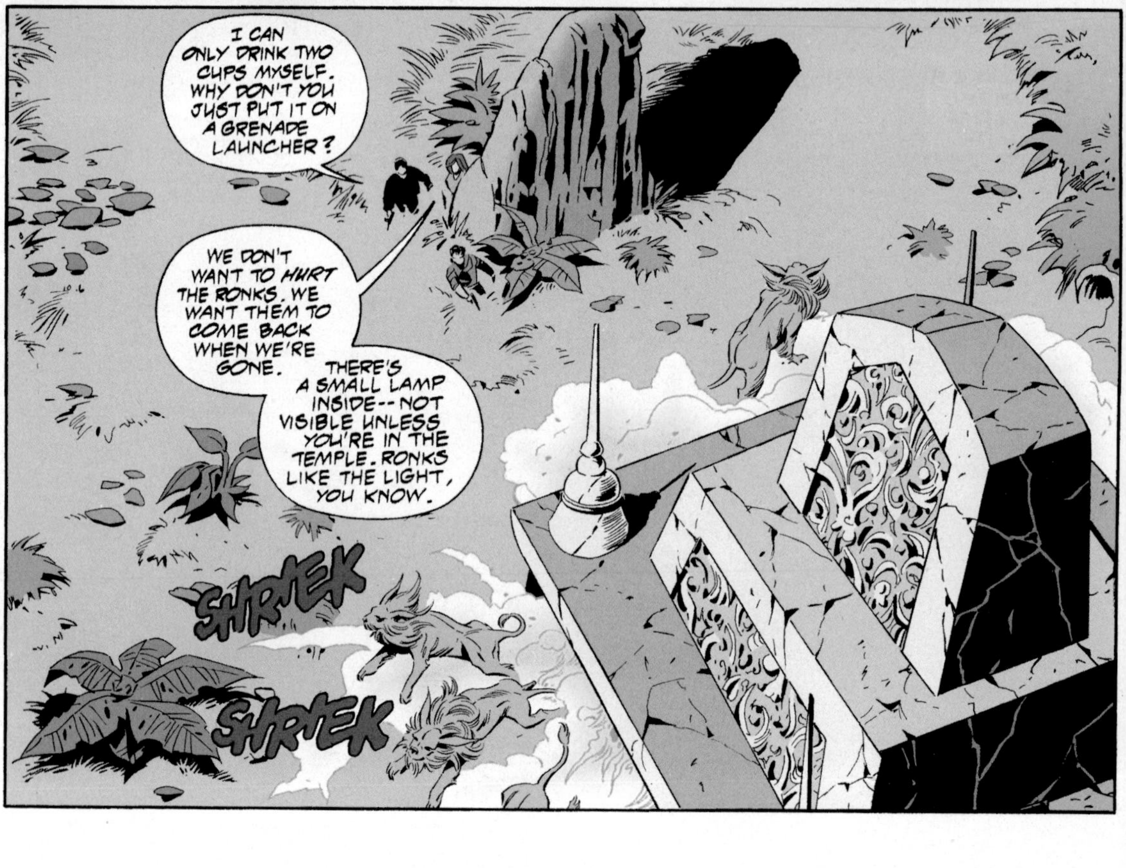
I CAN ONLY DRINK TWO CUPS MYSELF. WHY DON'T YOU JUST PUT IT ON A GRENADE LAUNCHER?
WE DON'T WANT TO HURT THE RONKS. WE WANT THEM TO COME BACK WHEN WE'RE GONE.
THERE'S A SMALL LAMP INSIDE--NOT VISIBLE UNLESS YOU'RE IN THE TEMPLE. RONKS LIKE THE LIGHT, YOU KNOW.
SHRIEK
SHRIEK

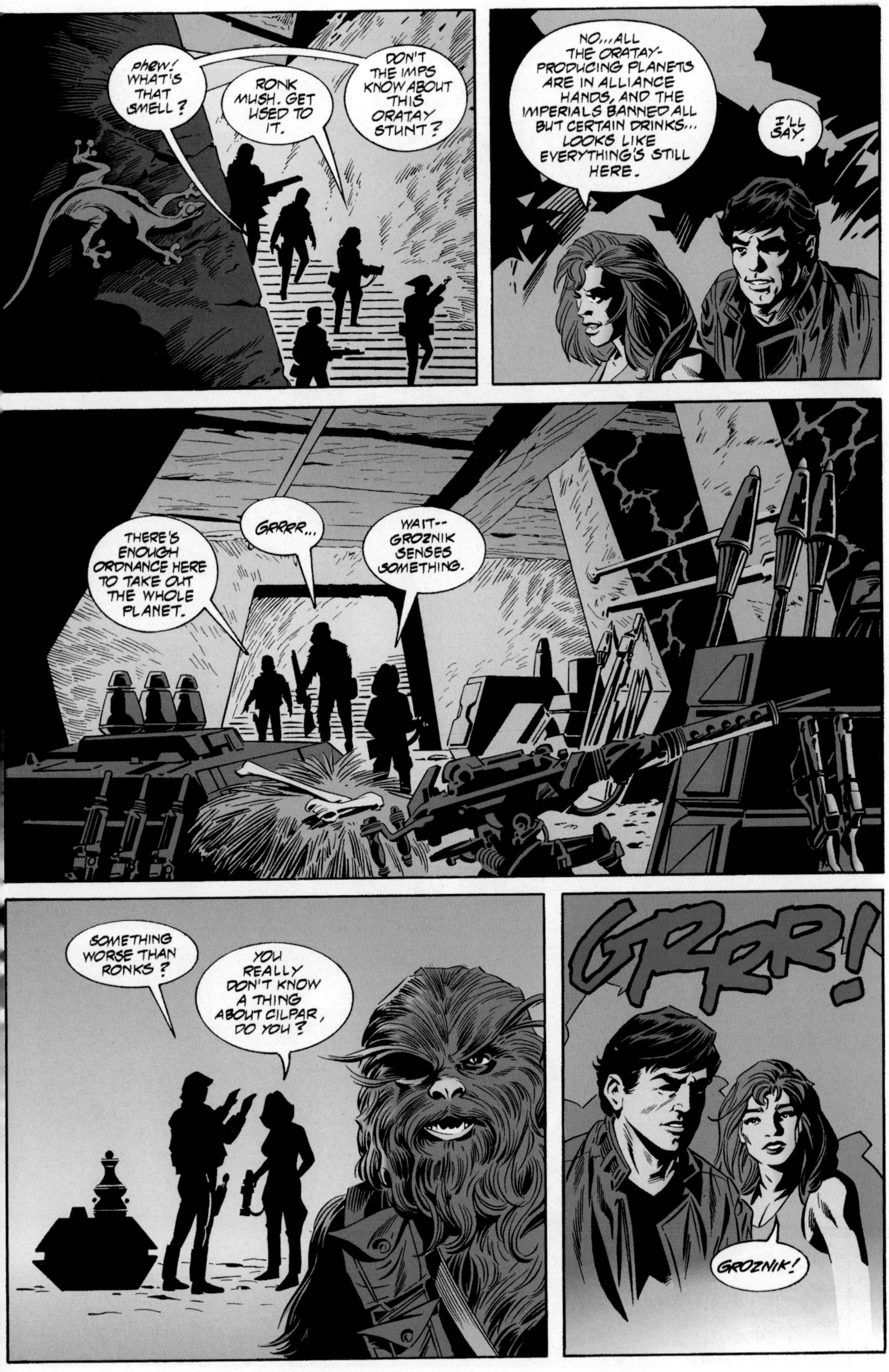
phew! WHAT'S THAT SMELL?
RONK MUSH. GET USED TO IT.
DON'T THE IMPS KNOW ABOUT THIS ORATAY STUNT?
NO...ALL THE ORATAY-PRODUCING PLANETS ARE IN ALLIANCE HANDS, AND THE IMPERIALS BANNED ALL BUT CERTAIN DRINKS... LOOKS LIKE EVERYTHING'S STILL HERE.
I'LL SAY.
THERE'S ENOUGH ORDNANCE HERE TO TAKE OUT THE WHOLE PLANET.
GRRRR...
WAIT-- GROZNIK SENSES SOMETHING.
SOMETHING WORSE THAN RONKS?
YOU REALLY DON'T KNOW A THING ABOUT CILPAR, DO YOU?
GRRR!
GROZNIK!

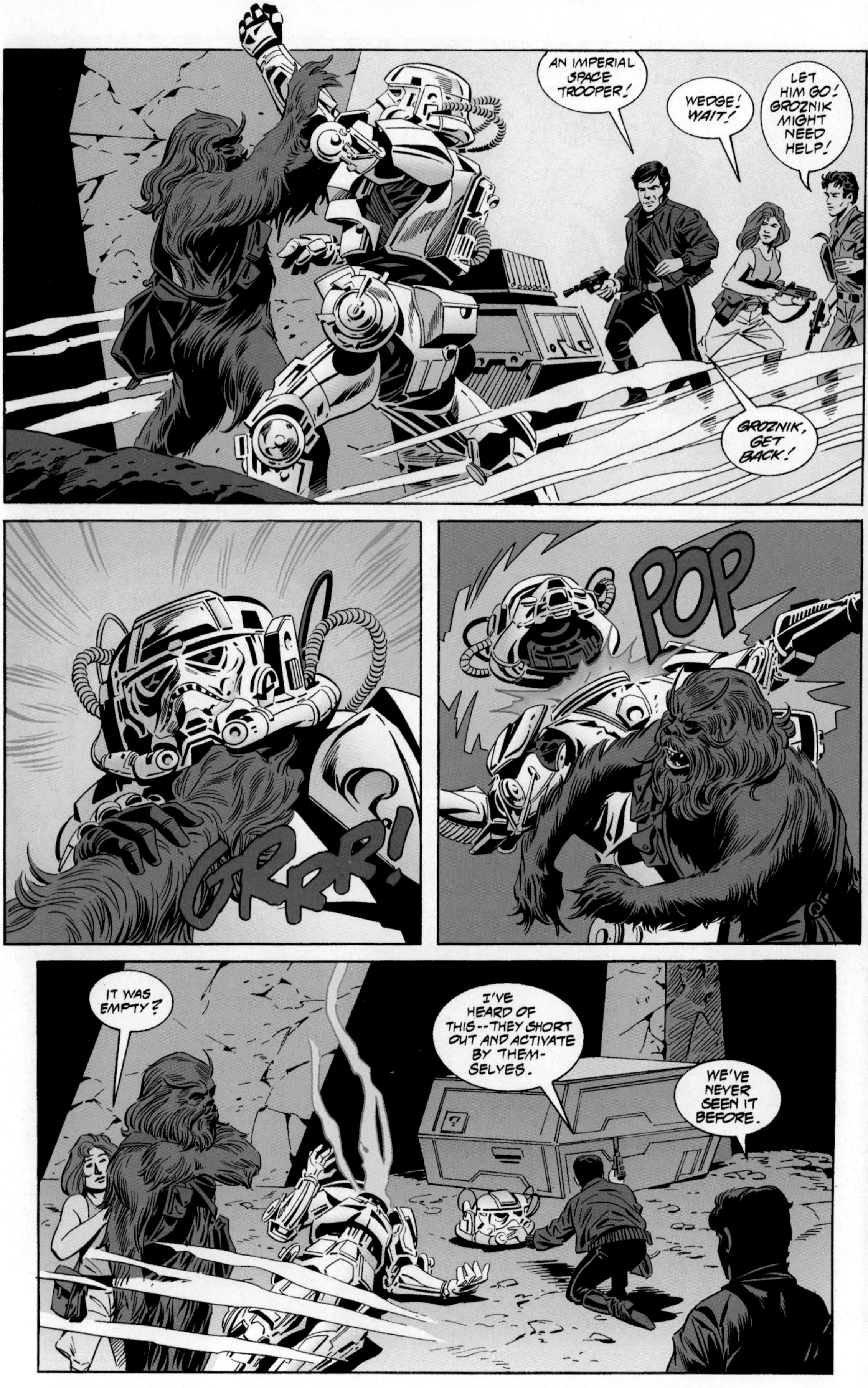
AN IMPERIAL SPACE TROOPER!
WEDGE! WAIT!
LET HIM GO! GROZNIK MIGHT NEED HELP!
GROZNIK, GET BACK!
GRRR!
POP
IT WAS EMPTY?
I'VE HEARD OF THIS--THEY SHORT OUT AND ACTIVATE BY THEM-SELVES.
WE'VE NEVER SEEN IT BEFORE.

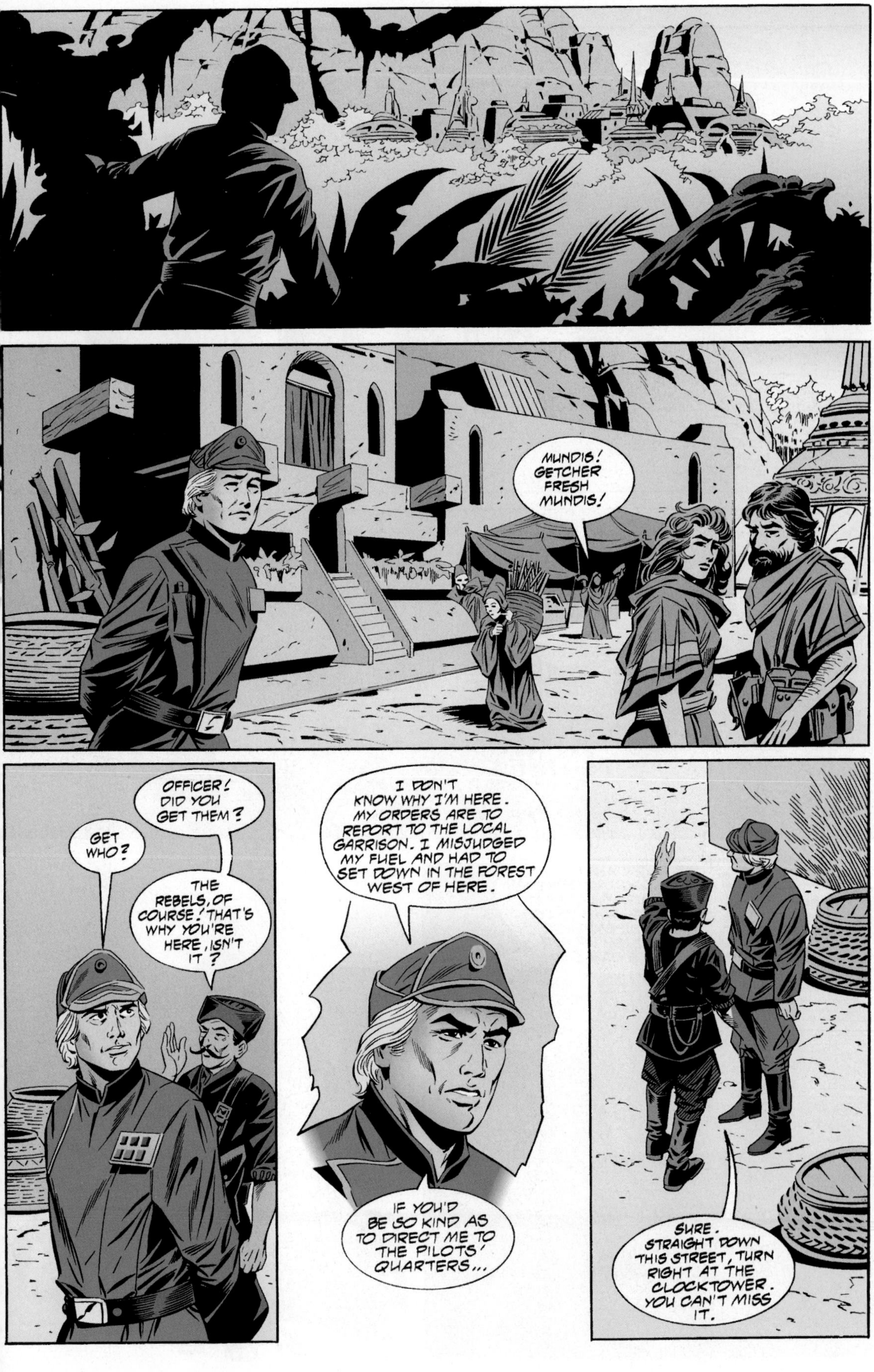
MUNDIS! GETCHER FRESH MUNDIS!
OFFICER! DID YOU GET THEM?
GET WHO?
THE REBELS, OF COURSE! THAT'S WHY YOU'RE HERE, ISN'T IT?
I DON'T KNOW WHY I'M HERE. MY ORDERS ARE TO REPORT TO THE LOCAL GARRISON. I MISJUDGED MY FUEL AND HAD TO SET DOWN IN THE FOREST WEST OF HERE.
IF YOU'D BE SO KIND AS TO DIRECT ME TO THE PILOTS' QUARTERS...
SURE. STRAIGHT DOWN THIS STREET, TURN RIGHT AT THE CLOCKTOWER. YOU CAN'T MISS IT.

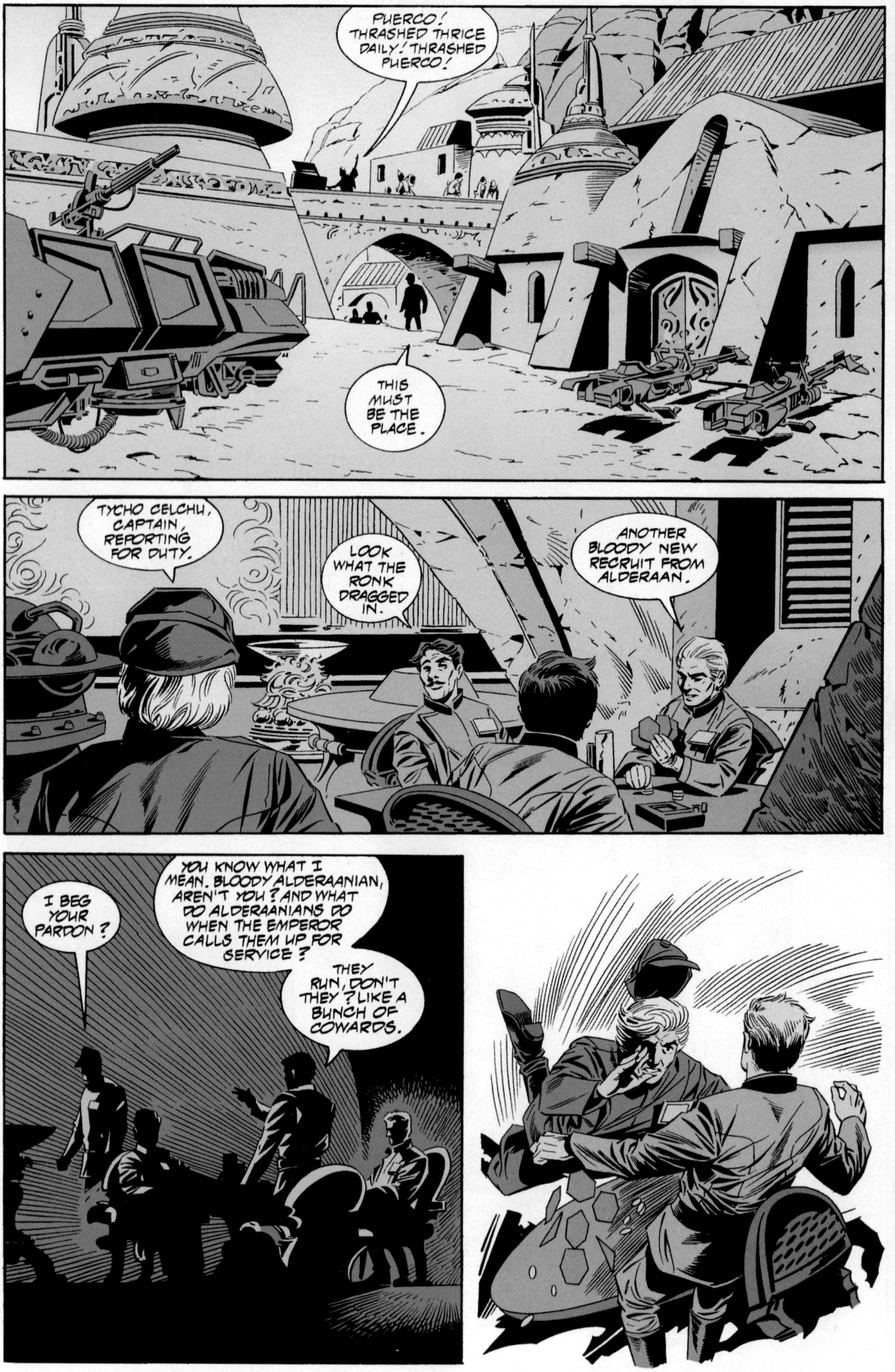
PUERCO! THRASHED THRICE DAILY! THRASHED PUERCO!
THIS MUST BE THE PLACE.
TYCHO CELCHU, CAPTAIN, REPORTING FOR DUTY.
LOOK WHAT THE RONK DRAGGED IN.
ANOTHER BLOODY NEW RECRUIT FROM ALDERAAN.
I BEG YOUR PARDON?
YOU KNOW WHAT I MEAN. BLOODY ALDERAANIAN, AREN'T YOU? AND WHAT DO ALDERAANIANS DO WHEN THE EMPEROR CALLS THEM UP FOR SERVICE?
THEY RUN, DON'T THEY? LIKE A BUNCH OF COWARDS.

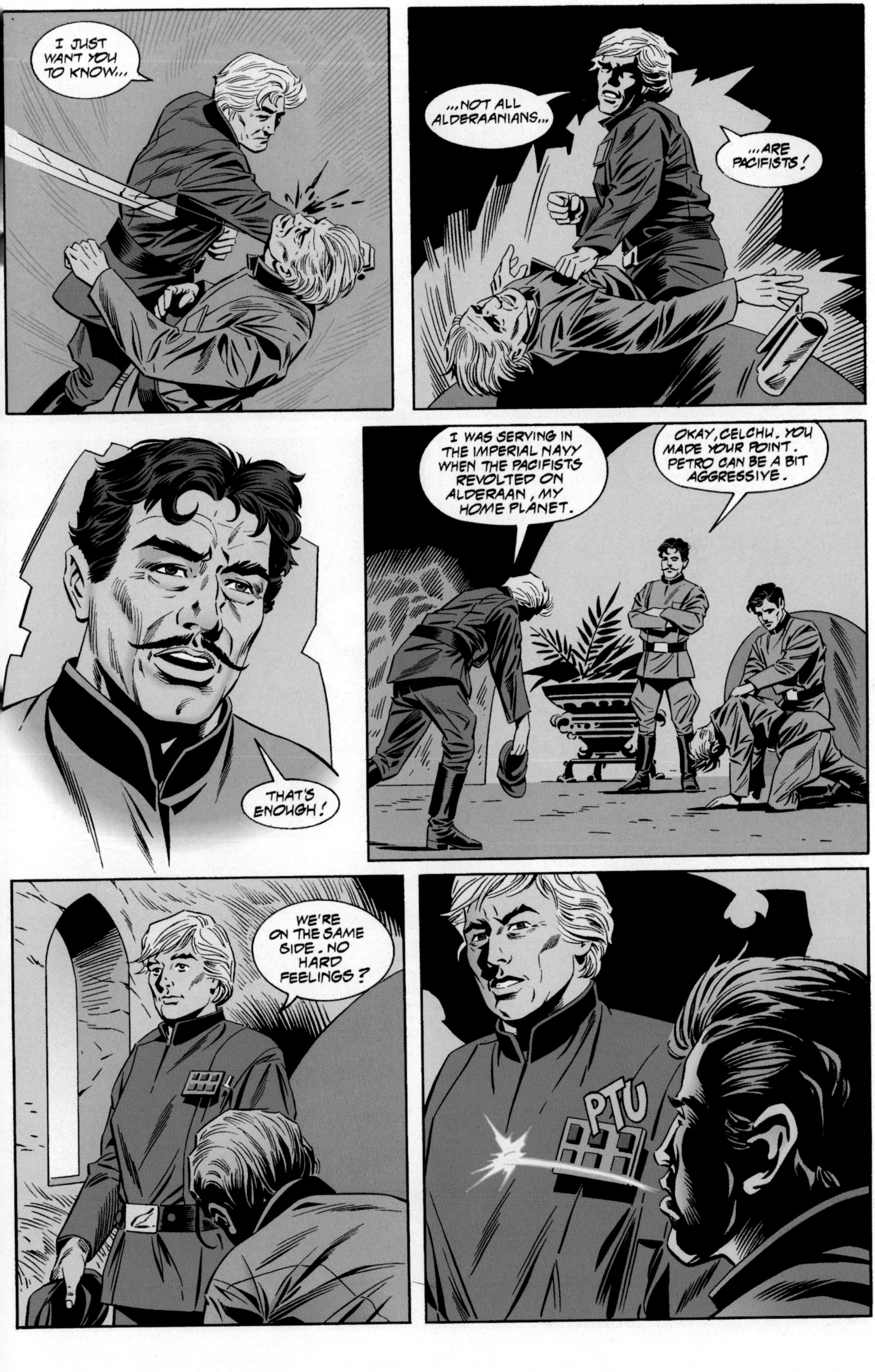

I JUST WANT YOU TO KNOW...
...NOT ALL ALDERAANIANS...
...ARE PACIFISTS!
THAT'S ENOUGH!
I WAS SERVING IN THE IMPERIAL NAVY WHEN THE PACIFISTS REVOLTED ON ALDERAAN, MY HOME PLANET.
OKAY, CELCHU. YOU MADE YOUR POINT. PETRO CAN BE A BIT AGGRESSIVE.
WE'RE ON THE SAME SIDE. NO HARD FEELINGS?
PTU

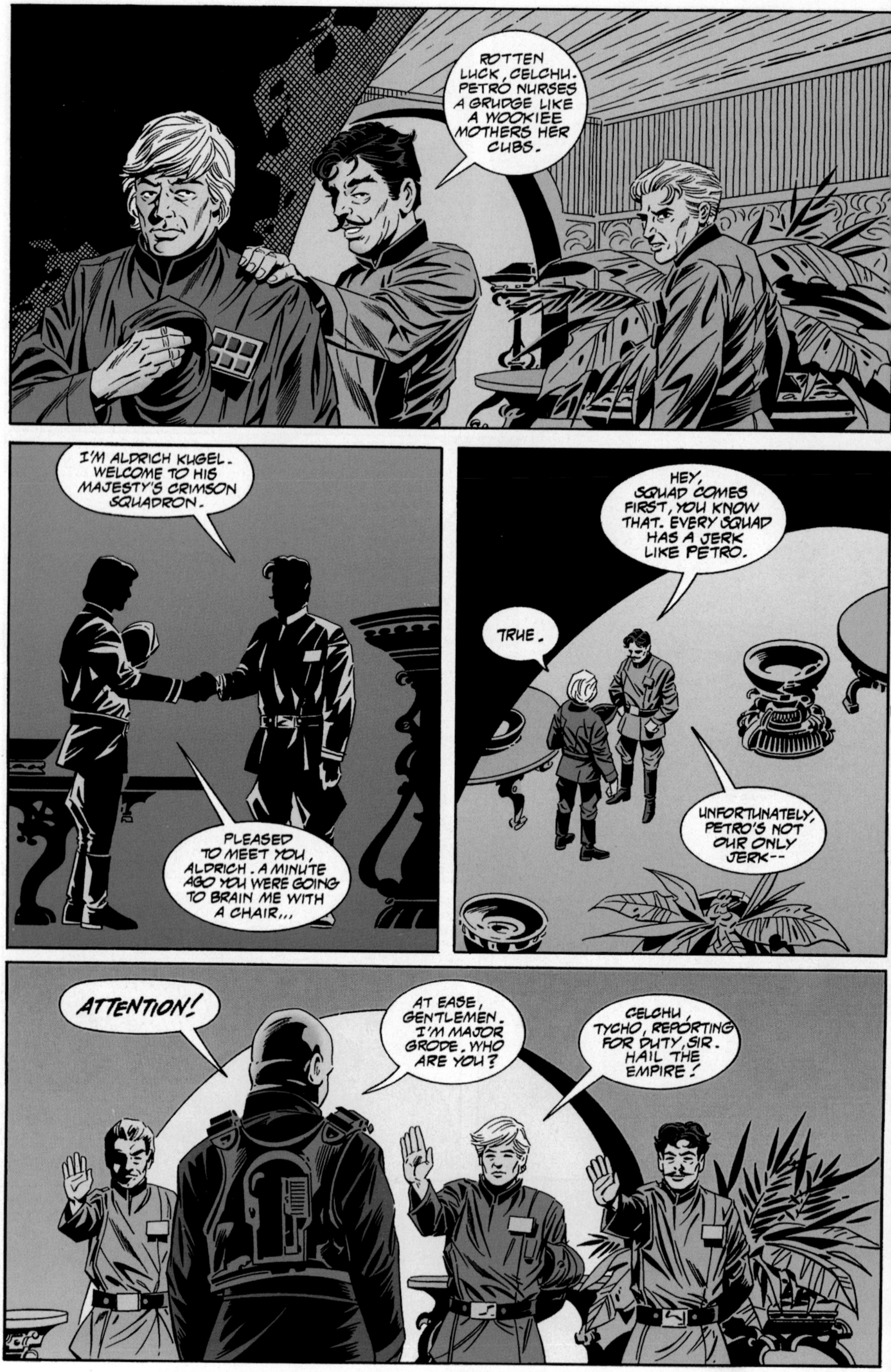
ROTTEN LUCK, CELCHU. PETRO NURSES A GRUDGE LIKE A WOOKIEE MOTHERS HER CUBS.
I'M ALDRICH KUGEL. WELCOME TO HIS MAJESTY'S CRIMSON SQUADRON.
PLEASED TO MEET YOU, ALDRICH. A MINUTE AGO YOU WERE GOING TO BRAIN ME WITH A CHAIR...
HEY, SQUAD COMES FIRST, YOU KNOW THAT. EVERY SQUAD HAS A JERK LIKE PETRO.
TRUE.
UNFORTUNATELY, PETRO'S NOT OUR ONLY JERK--
ATTENTION!
AT EASE, GENTLEMEN. I'M MAJOR GRODE. WHO ARE YOU?
CELCHU, TYCHO, REPORTING FOR DUTY, SIR. HAIL THE EMPIRE!

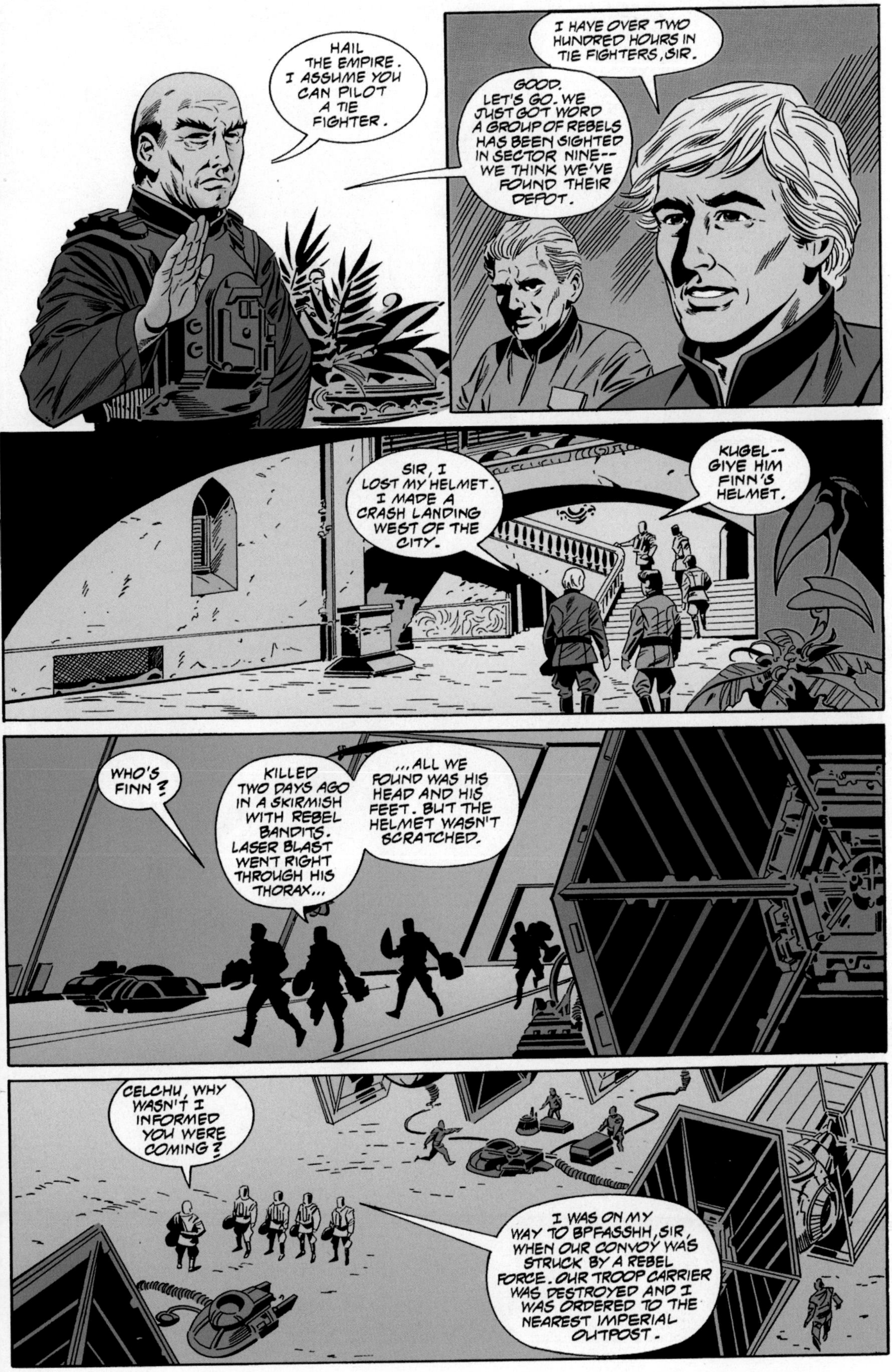
HAIL THE EMPIRE. I ASSUME YOU CAN PILOT A TIE FIGHTER.
I HAVE OVER TWO HUNDRED HOURS IN TIE FIGHTERS, SIR.
GOOD. LET'S GO. WE JUST GOT WORD A GROUP OF REBELS HAS BEEN SIGHTED IN SECTOR NINE-- WE THINK WE'VE FOUND THEIR DEPOT.
SIR, I LOST MY HELMET. I MADE A CRASH LANDING WEST OF THE CITY.
KUGEL-- GIVE HIM FINN'S HELMET.
WHO'S FINN?
KILLED TWO DAYS AGO IN A SKIRMISH WITH REBEL BANDITS. LASER BLAST WENT RIGHT THROUGH HIS THORAX...
...ALL WE FOUND WAS HIS HEAD AND HIS FEET. BUT THE HELMET WASN'T SCRATCHED.
CELCHU, WHY WASN'T I INFORMED YOU WERE COMING?
I WAS ON MY WAY TO BPFASSHH, SIR, WHEN OUR CONVOY WAS STRUCK BY A REBEL FORCE. OUR TROOP CARRIER WAS DESTROYED AND I WAS ORDERED TO THE NEAREST IMPERIAL OUTPOST.

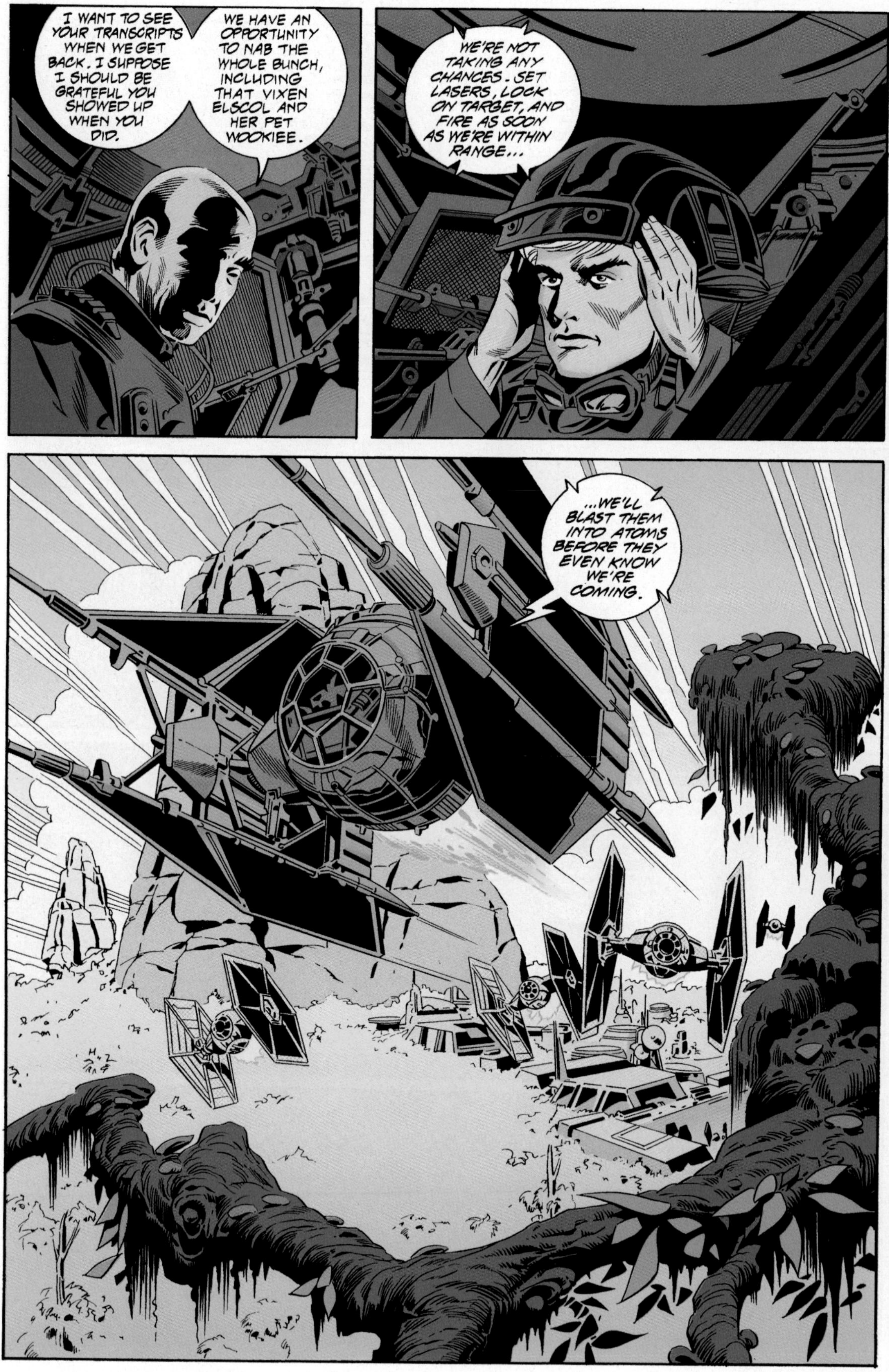
I WANT TO SEE YOUR TRANSCRIPTS WHEN WE GET BACK. I SUPPOSE I SHOULD BE GRATEFUL YOU SHOWED UP WHEN YOU DID.
WE HAVE AN OPPORTUNITY TO NAB THE WHOLE BUNCH, INCLUDING THAT VIXEN ELSCOL AND HER PET WOOKIEE.
WE'RE NOT TAKING ANY CHANCES. SET LASERS, LOCK ON TARGET, AND FIRE AS SOON AS WE'RE WITHIN RANGE...
...WE'LL BLAST THEM INTO ATOMS BEFORE THEY EVEN KNOW WE'RE COMING.

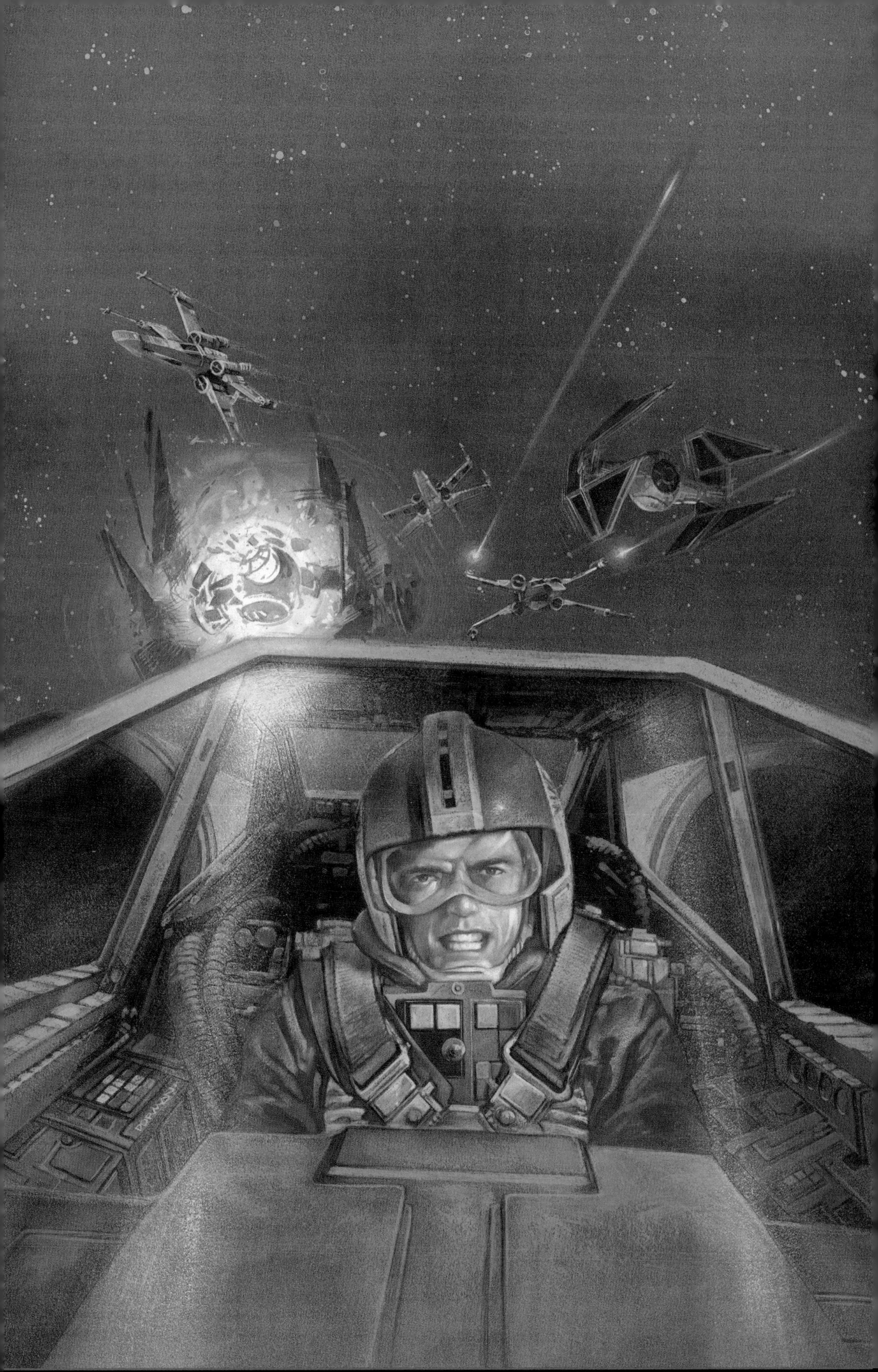

*STAR WARS: X-WING ROGUE SQUADRON #3* — "THE REBEL OPPOSITION, CHAPTER 3"

PLOTTER: MICHAEL A. STACKPOLE • SCRIPTER: MIKE BARON • PENCILER: ALLEN NUNIS • INKER: ANDY MUSHYNSKY • COLORIST: DAVE NESTELLE
LETTERER: STEVE DUTRO • EDITOR: RYDER WINDHAM • COVER ARTIST: DAVE DORMAN

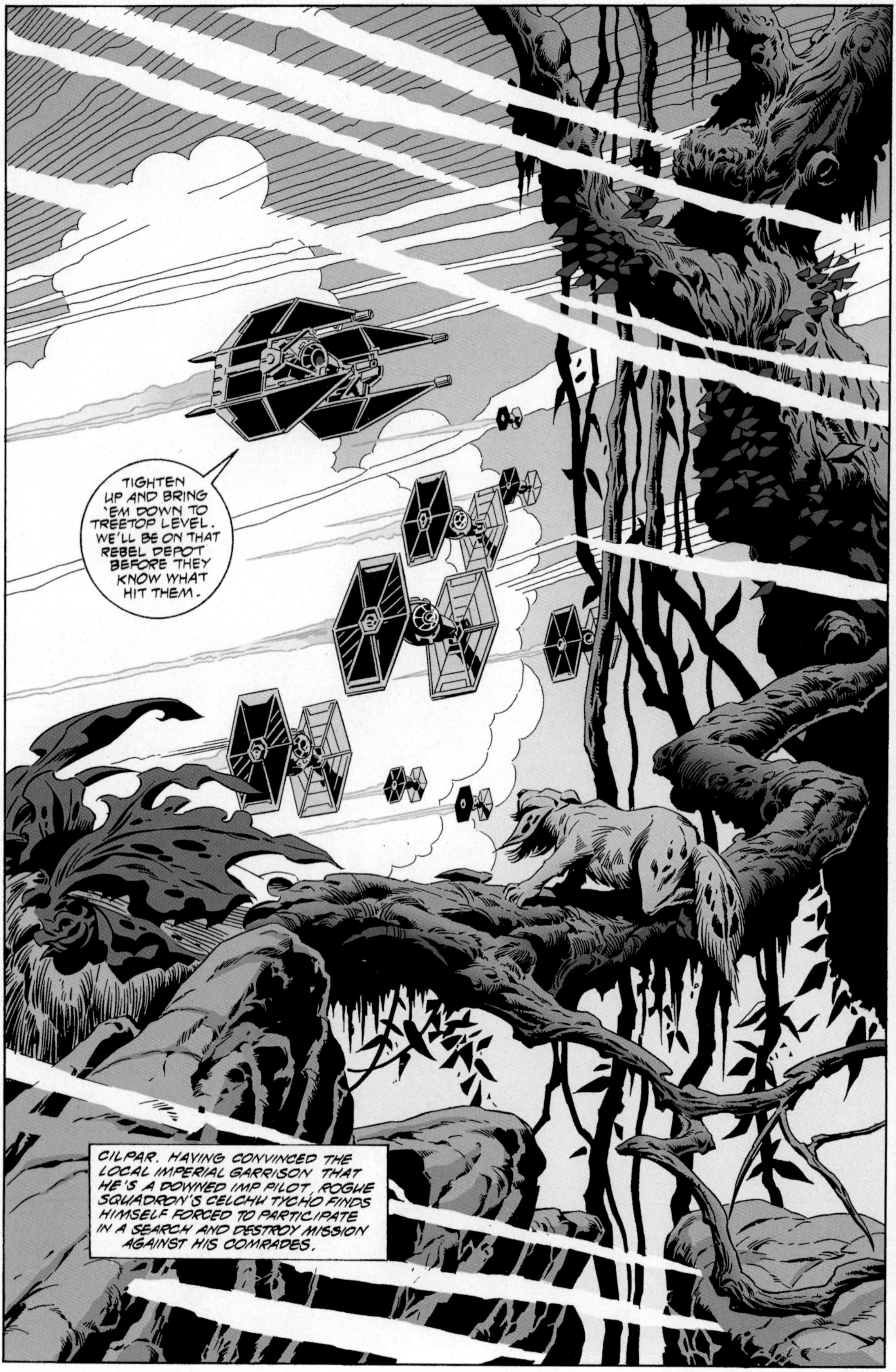
TIGHTEN UP AND BRING 'EM DOWN TO TREETOP LEVEL. WE'LL BE ON THAT REBEL DEPOT BEFORE THEY KNOW WHAT HIT THEM.
CILPAR. HAVING CONVINCED THE LOCAL IMPERIAL GARRISON THAT HE'S A DOWNED IMP PILOT, ROGUE SQUADRON'S CELCHU TYCHO FINDS HIMSELF FORCED TO PARTICIPATE IN A SEARCH AND DESTROY MISSION AGAINST HIS COMRADES.

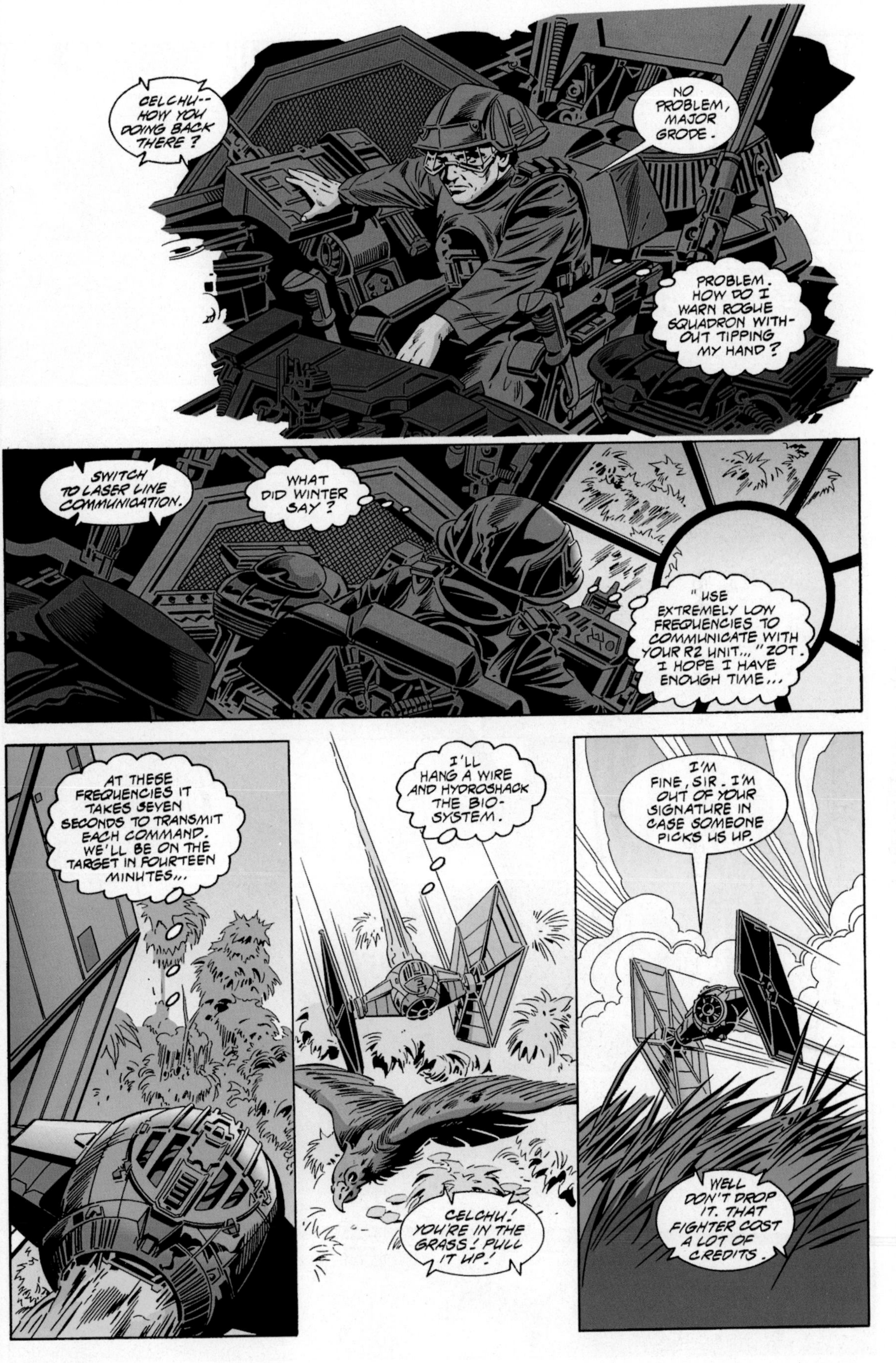
CELCHU-- HOW YOU DOING BACK THERE?
NO PROBLEM, MAJOR GRODE.
PROBLEM. HOW DO I WARN ROGUE SQUADRON WITHOUT TIPPING MY HAND?
SWITCH TO LASER LINE COMMUNICATION.
WHAT DID WINTER SAY?
"USE EXTREMELY LOW FREQUENCIES TO COMMUNICATE WITH YOUR R2 UNIT...," ZOT. I HOPE I HAVE ENOUGH TIME...
AT THESE FREQUENCIES IT TAKES SEVEN SECONDS TO TRANSMIT EACH COMMAND. WE'LL BE ON THE TARGET IN FOURTEEN MINUTES...
I'LL HANG A WIRE AND HYDROSHACK THE BIO-SYSTEM.
CELCHU! YOU'RE IN THE GRASS! PULL IT UP!
I'M FINE, SIR. I'M OUT OF YOUR SIGNATURE IN CASE SOMEONE PICKS US UP.
WELL DON'T DROP IT. THAT FIGHTER COST A LOT OF CREDITS.

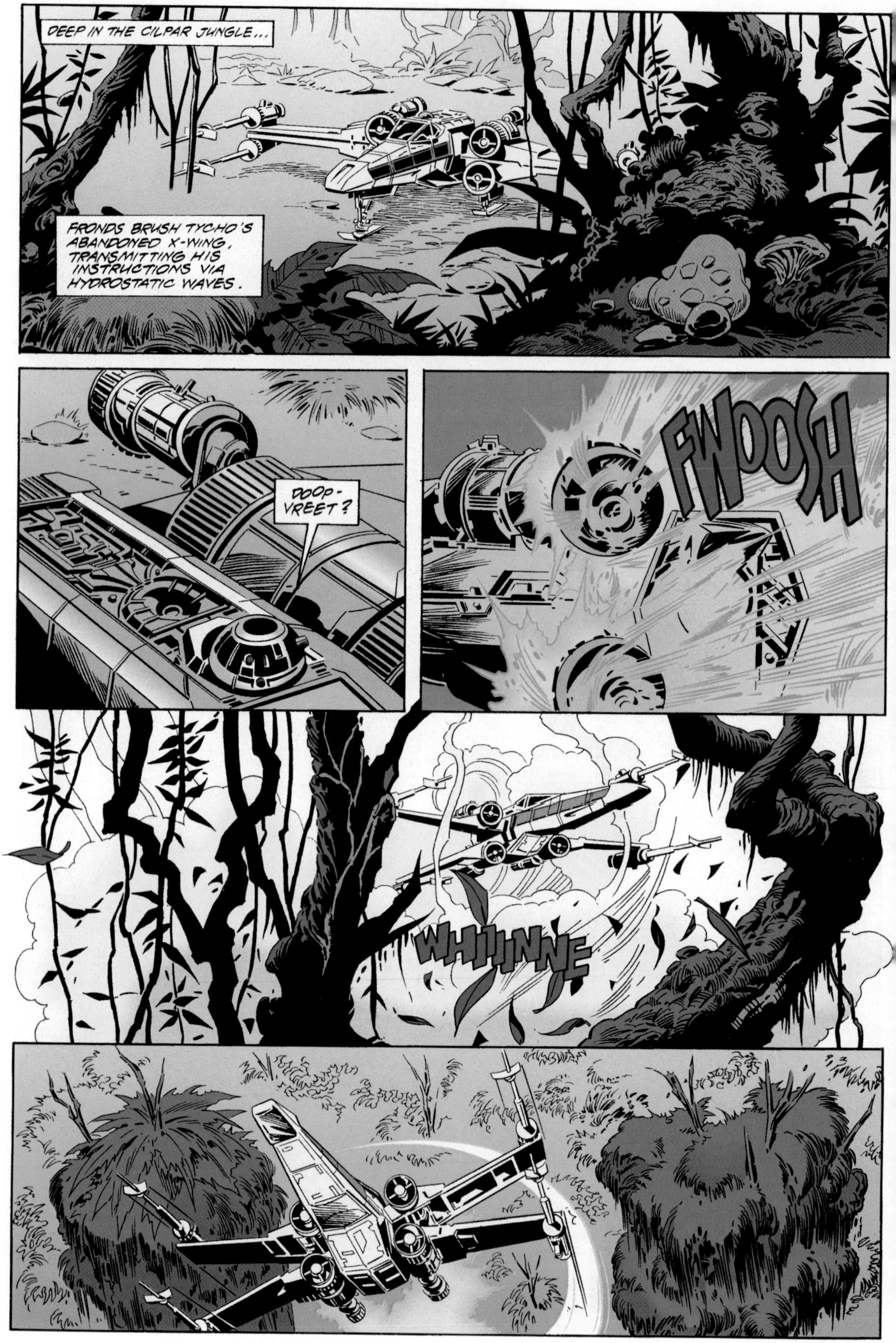
DEEP IN THE CILPAR JUNGLE...
FRONDS BRUSH TYCHO'S ABANDONED X-WING, TRANSMITTING HIS INSTRUCTIONS VIA HYDROSTATIC WAVES.
DOOP-VREET?
FWOOSH
WHIIIINNE

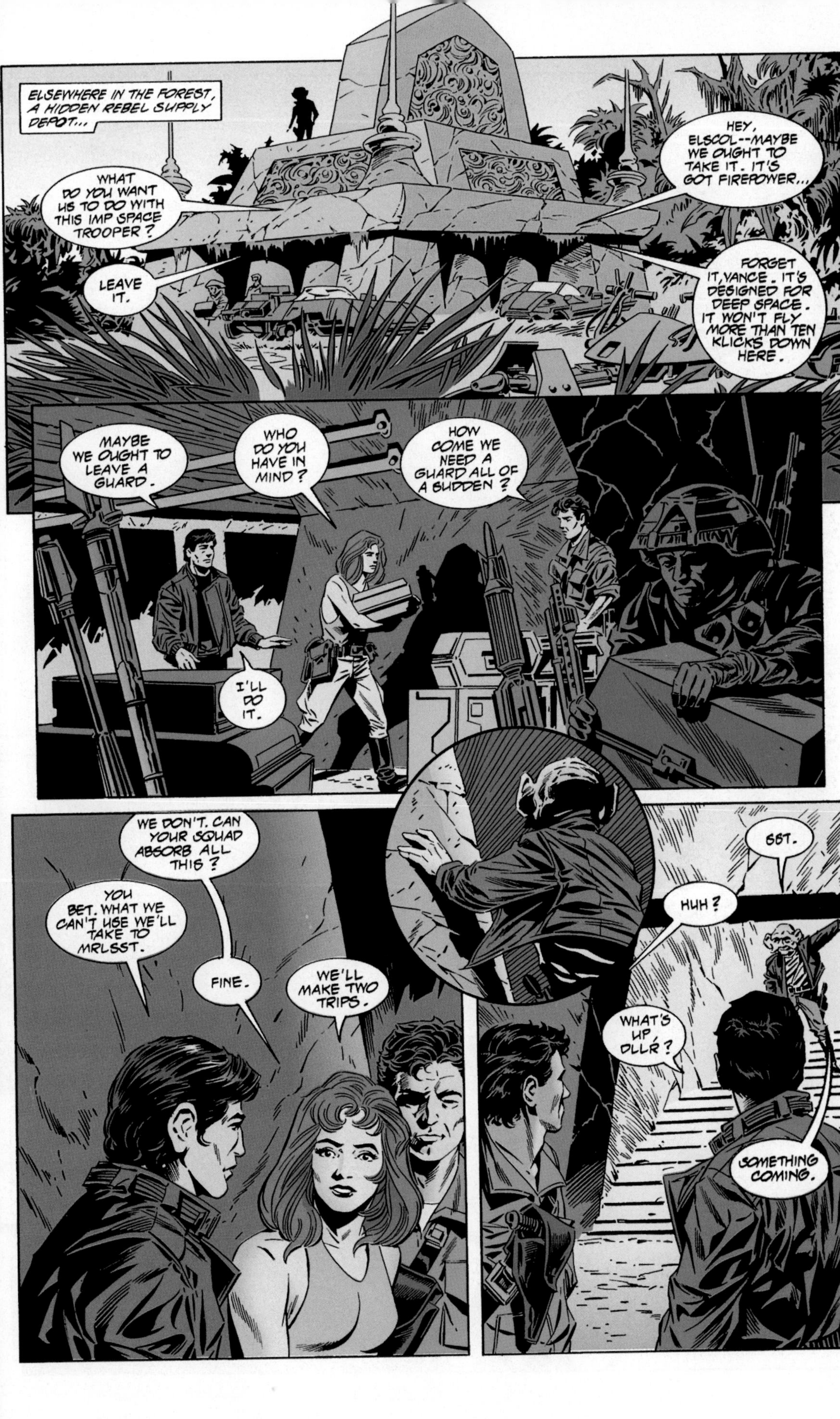
ELSEWHERE IN THE FOREST, A HIDDEN REBEL SUPPLY DEPOT...
WHAT DO YOU WANT US TO DO WITH THIS IMP SPACE TROOPER?
HEY, ELSCOL--MAYBE WE OUGHT TO TAKE IT. IT'S GOT FIREPOWER...
LEAVE IT.
FORGET IT, VANCE. IT'S DESIGNED FOR DEEP SPACE. IT WON'T FLY MORE THAN TEN KLICKS DOWN HERE.
MAYBE WE OUGHT TO LEAVE A GUARD.
WHO DO YOU HAVE IN MIND?
HOW COME WE NEED A GUARD ALL OF A SUDDEN?
I'LL DO IT.
WE DON'T. CAN YOUR SQUAD ABSORB ALL THIS?
YOU BET. WHAT WE CAN'T USE WE'LL TAKE TO MRLSST.
FINE.
WE'LL MAKE TWO TRIPS.
SST.
HUH?
WHAT'S UP, DLLR?
SOMETHING COMING.

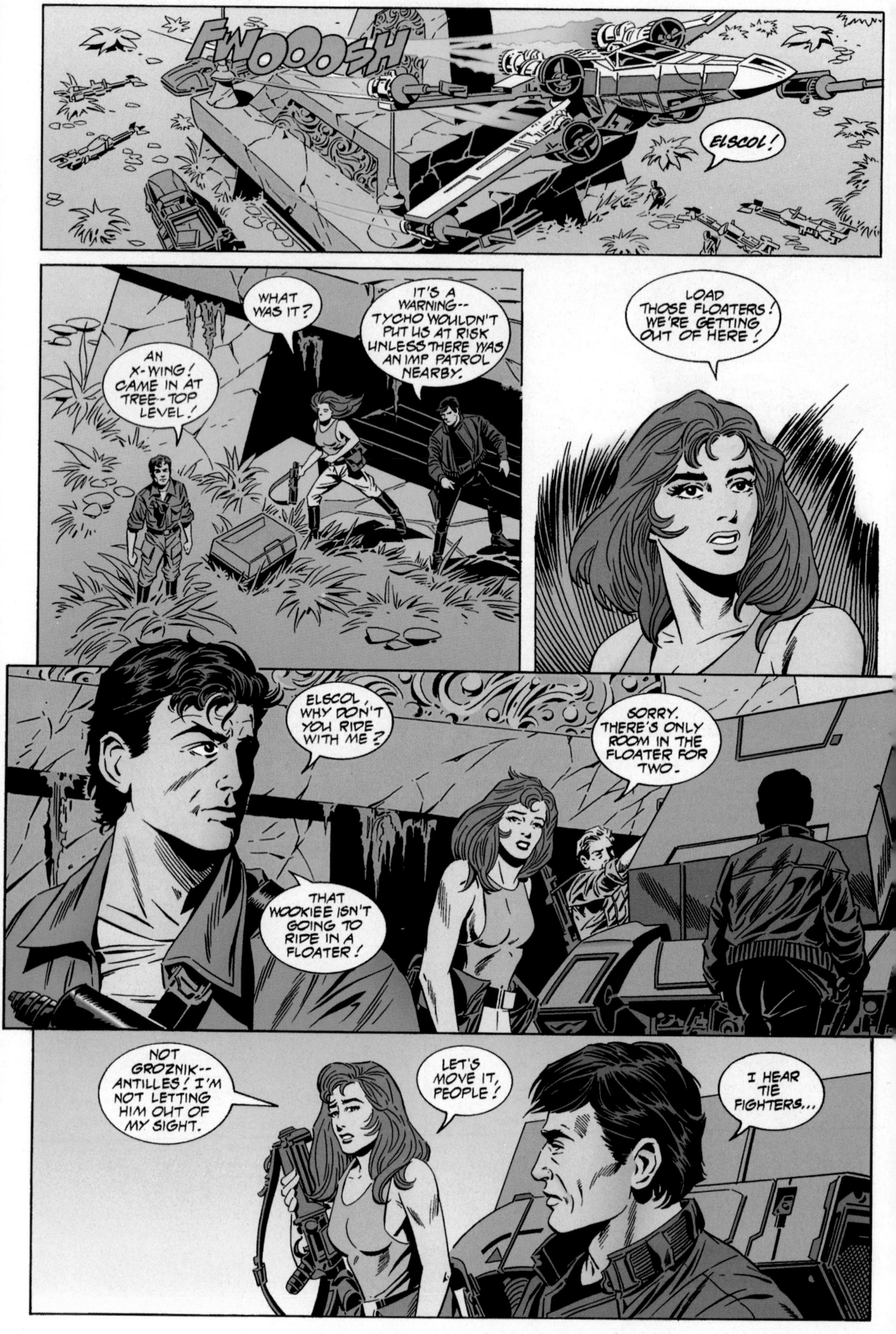
FWOOOOSH
ELSCOL!
AN X-WING! CAME IN AT TREE--TOP LEVEL!
WHAT WAS IT?
IT'S A WARNING-- TYCHO WOULDN'T PUT US AT RISK UNLESS THERE WAS AN IMP PATROL NEARBY.
LOAD THOSE FLOATERS! WE'RE GETTING OUT OF HERE!
ELSCOL, WHY DON'T YOU RIDE WITH ME?
SORRY. THERE'S ONLY ROOM IN THE FLOATER FOR TWO.
THAT WOOKIEE ISN'T GOING TO RIDE IN A FLOATER!
NOT GROZNIK-- ANTILLES! I'M NOT LETTING HIM OUT OF MY SIGHT.
LET'S MOVE IT, PEOPLE!
I HEAR TIE FIGHTERS...

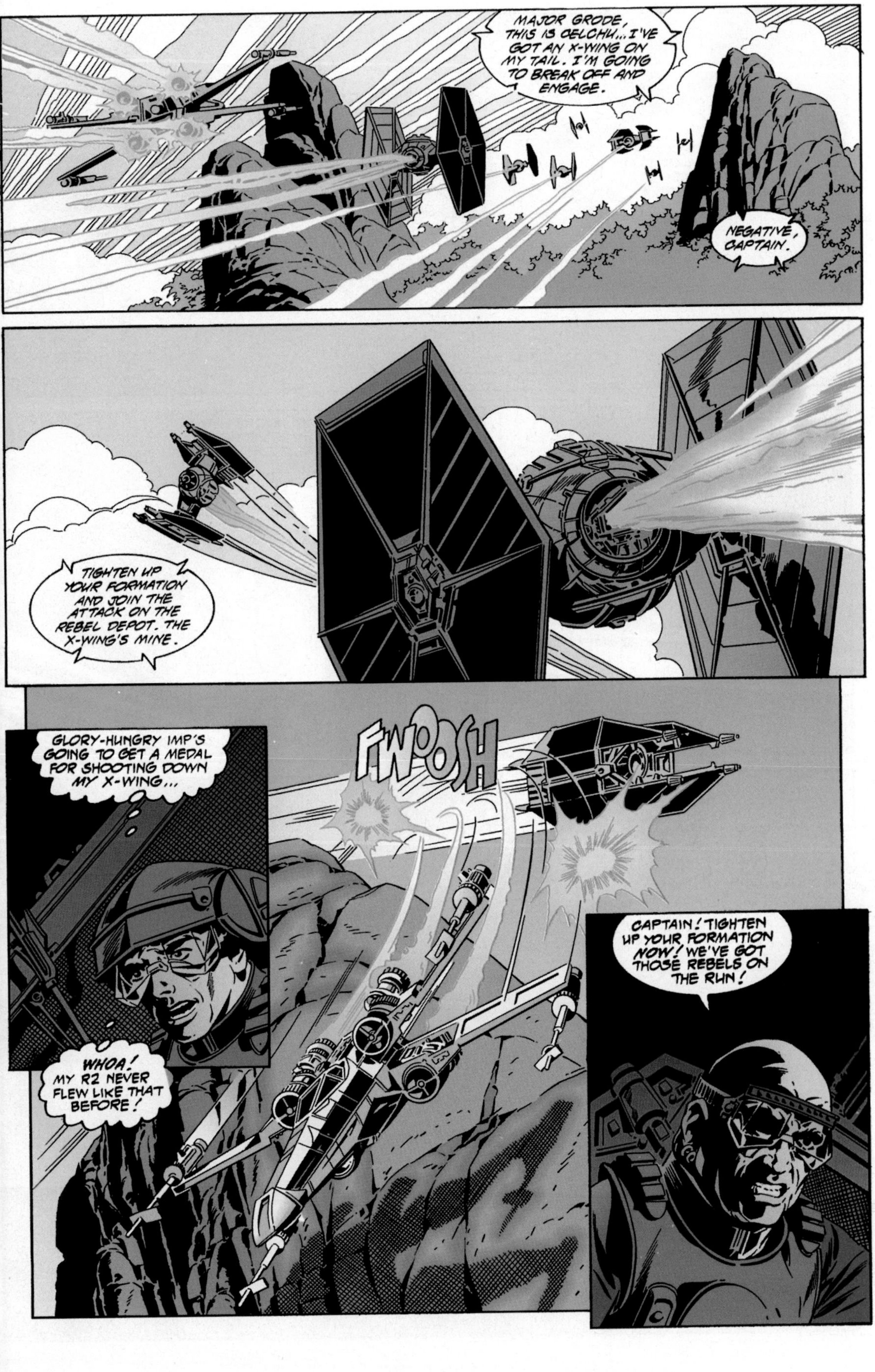
MAJOR GRODE, THIS IS OELCHU... I'VE GOT AN X-WING ON MY TAIL. I'M GOING TO BREAK OFF AND ENGAGE.
NEGATIVE, CAPTAIN.
TIGHTEN UP YOUR FORMATION AND JOIN THE ATTACK ON THE REBEL DEPOT. THE X-WING'S MINE.
GLORY-HUNGRY IMP'S GOING TO GET A MEDAL FOR SHOOTING DOWN MY X-WING...
FWOOSH
WHOA! MY R2 NEVER FLEW LIKE THAT BEFORE!
CAPTAIN! TIGHTEN UP YOUR FORMATION NOW! WE'VE GOT THOSE REBELS ON THE RUN!

THE CONTROLS ARE SIMILAR TO MY X-WING -- LET ME DRIVE.

FORGET IT!

ELSCOL, I'M A VETERAN WITH OVER THIRTY KILLS. LET ME DRIVE!

ARROGANT ROCKET JOCKEY... MY SPEEDER, MY WORLD, I DRIVE!

OKAY! OKAY!

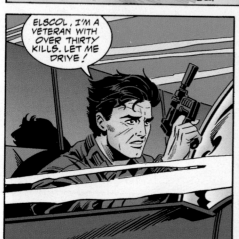

GRR....

THWACK

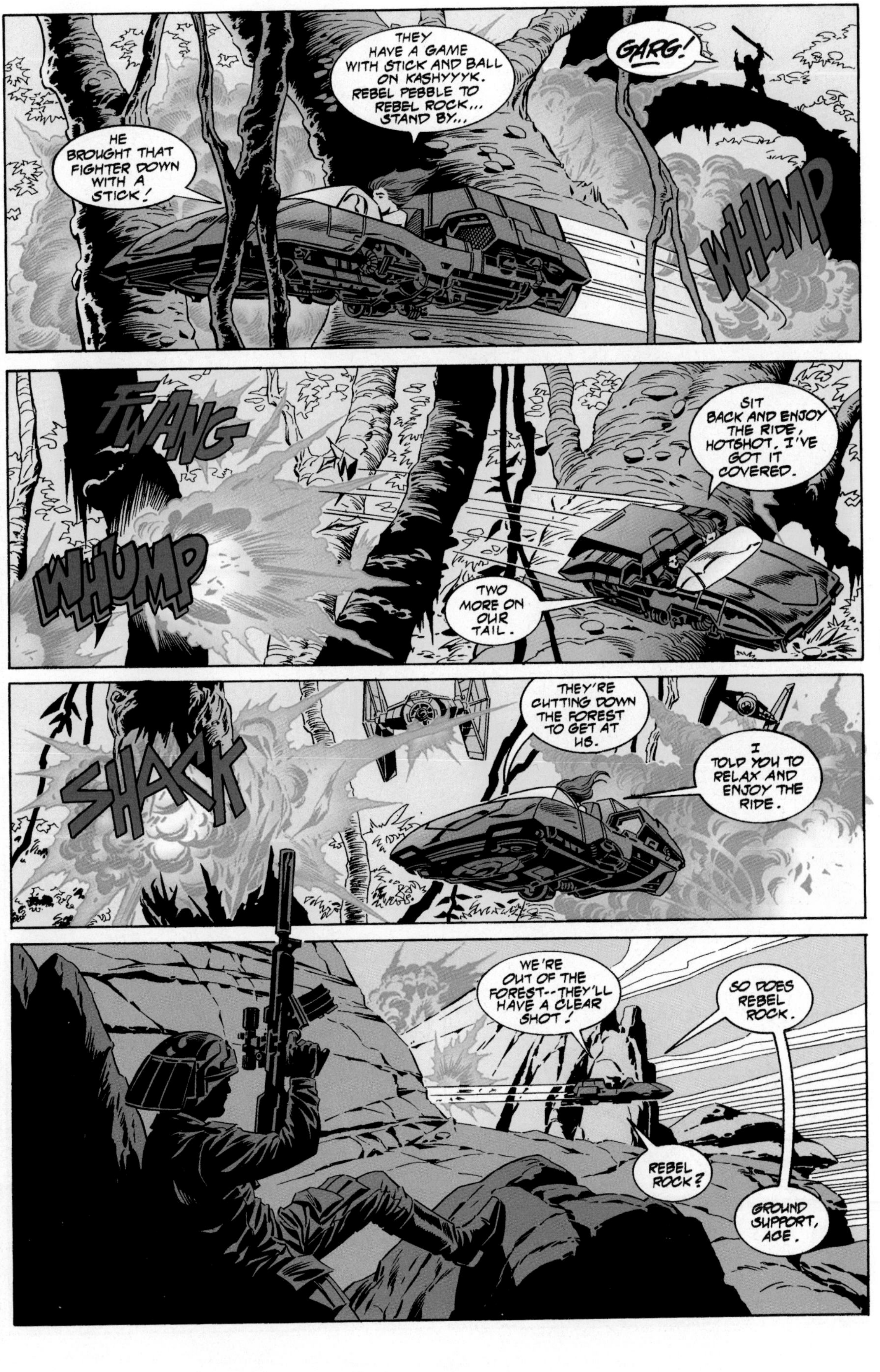
HE BROUGHT THAT FIGHTER DOWN WITH A STICK!
THEY HAVE A GAME WITH STICK AND BALL ON KASHYYYK. REBEL PEBBLE TO REBEL ROCK... STAND BY...
GARG!
WHUMP
FWANG
WHUMP
SIT BACK AND ENJOY THE RIDE, HOTSHOT. I'VE GOT IT COVERED.
TWO MORE ON OUR TAIL.
SHACK
THEY'RE CUTTING DOWN THE FOREST TO GET AT US.
I TOLD YOU TO RELAX AND ENJOY THE RIDE.
WE'RE OUT OF THE FOREST--THEY'LL HAVE A CLEAR SHOT!
SO DOES REBEL ROCK.
REBEL ROCK?
GROUND SUPPORT, ACE.

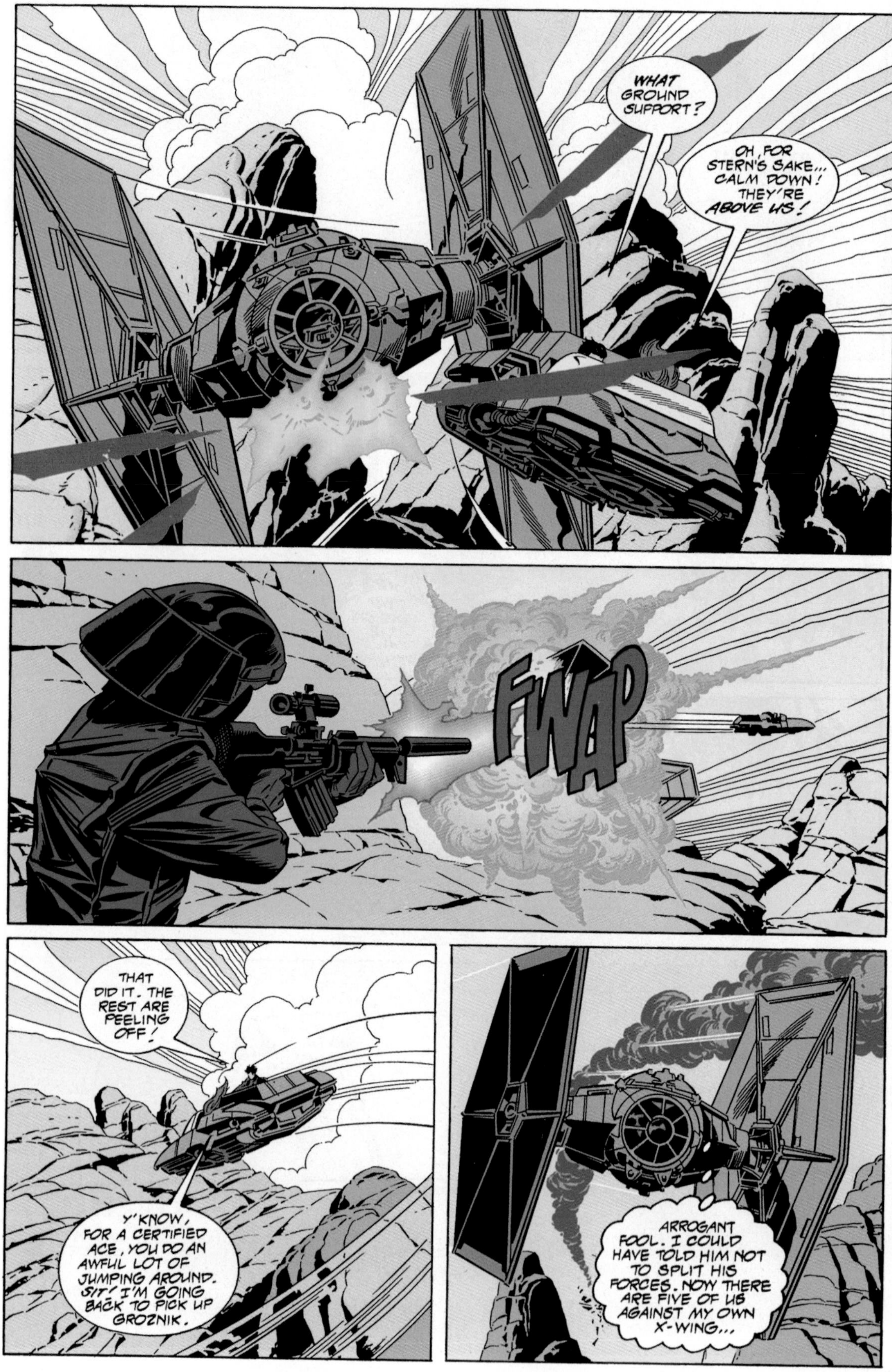
WHAT GROUND SUPPORT?
OH, FOR STERN'S SAKE... CALM DOWN! THEY'RE ABOVE US!
FWAP
THAT DID IT. THE REST ARE PEELING OFF!
Y'KNOW, FOR A CERTIFIED ACE, YOU DO AN AWFUL LOT OF JUMPING AROUND. SIT! I'M GOING BACK TO PICK UP GROZNIK.
ARROGANT FOOL. I COULD HAVE TOLD HIM NOT TO SPLIT HIS FORCES. NOW THERE ARE FIVE OF US AGAINST MY OWN X-WING...

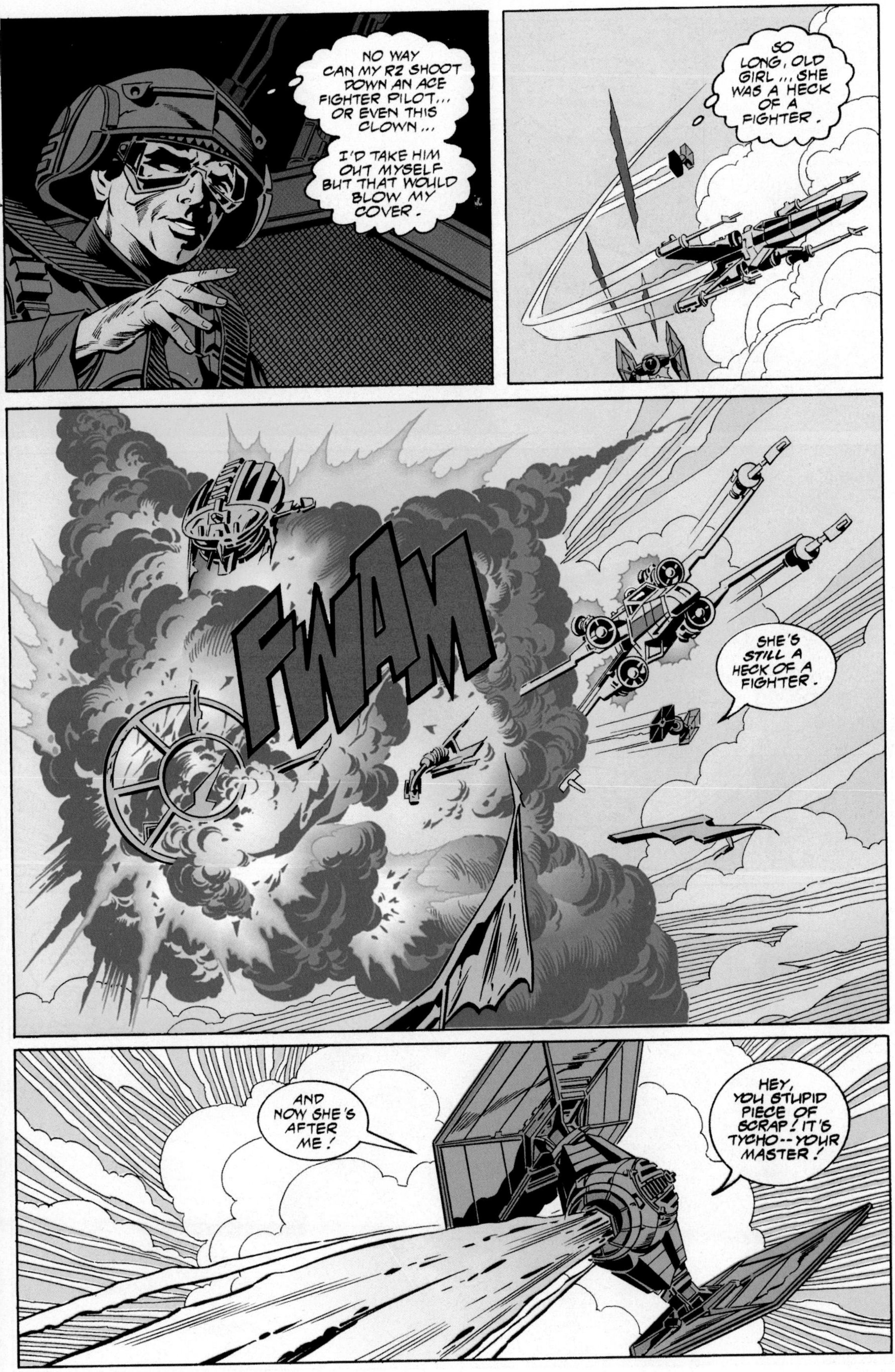
NO WAY CAN MY R2 SHOOT DOWN AN ACE FIGHTER PILOT... OR EVEN THIS CLOWN...
I'D TAKE HIM OUT MYSELF BUT THAT WOULD BLOW MY COVER.
SO LONG, OLD GIRL... SHE WAS A HECK OF A FIGHTER.
FWAM
SHE'S STILL A HECK OF A FIGHTER.
AND NOW SHE'S AFTER ME!
HEY, YOU STUPID PIECE OF SCRAP! IT'S TYCHO--YOUR MASTER!

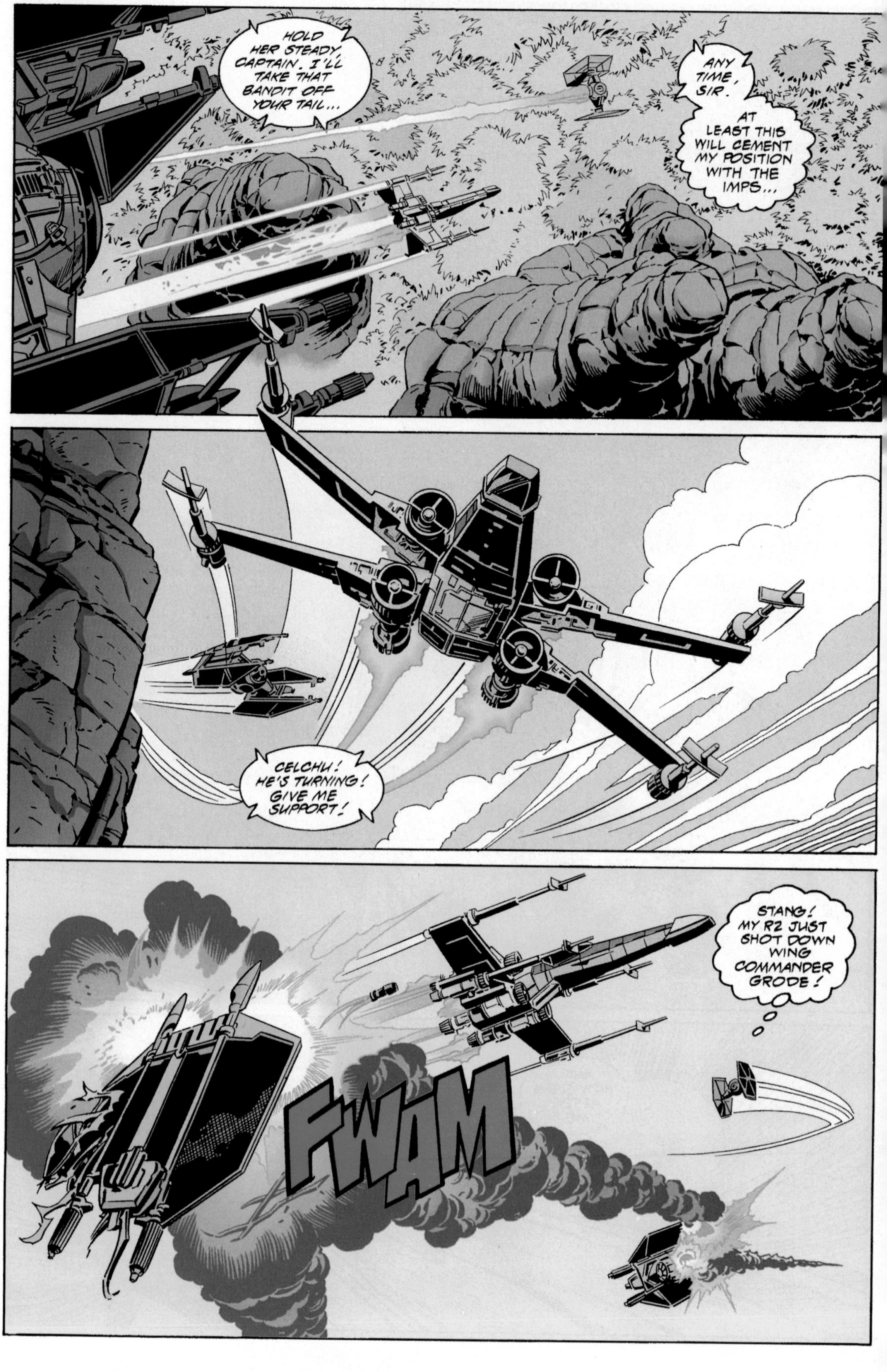
HOLD HER STEADY, CAPTAIN. I'LL TAKE THAT BANDIT OFF YOUR TAIL...
ANY TIME, SIR.
AT LEAST THIS WILL CEMENT MY POSITION WITH THE IMPS...
CELCHU! HE'S TURNING! GIVE ME SUPPORT!
STANG! MY R2 JUST SHOT DOWN WING COMMANDER GRODE!
FWAM

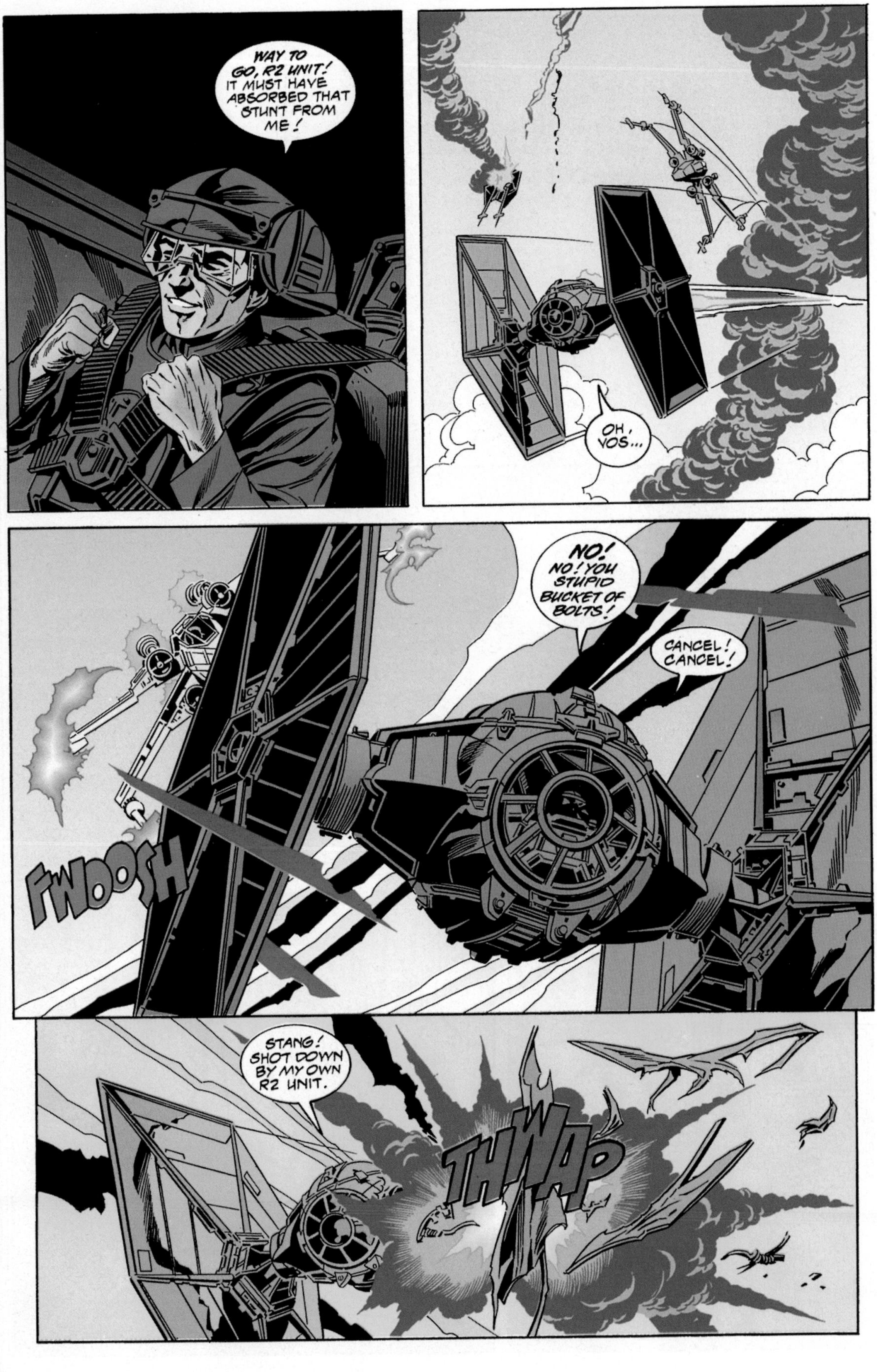
WAY TO GO, R2 UNIT! IT MUST HAVE ABSORBED THAT STUNT FROM ME!
OH, VOS...
NO! NO! YOU STUPID BUCKET OF BOLTS!
CANCEL! CANCEL!
FWOOSH
STANG! SHOT DOWN BY MY OWN R2 UNIT.
THWAP

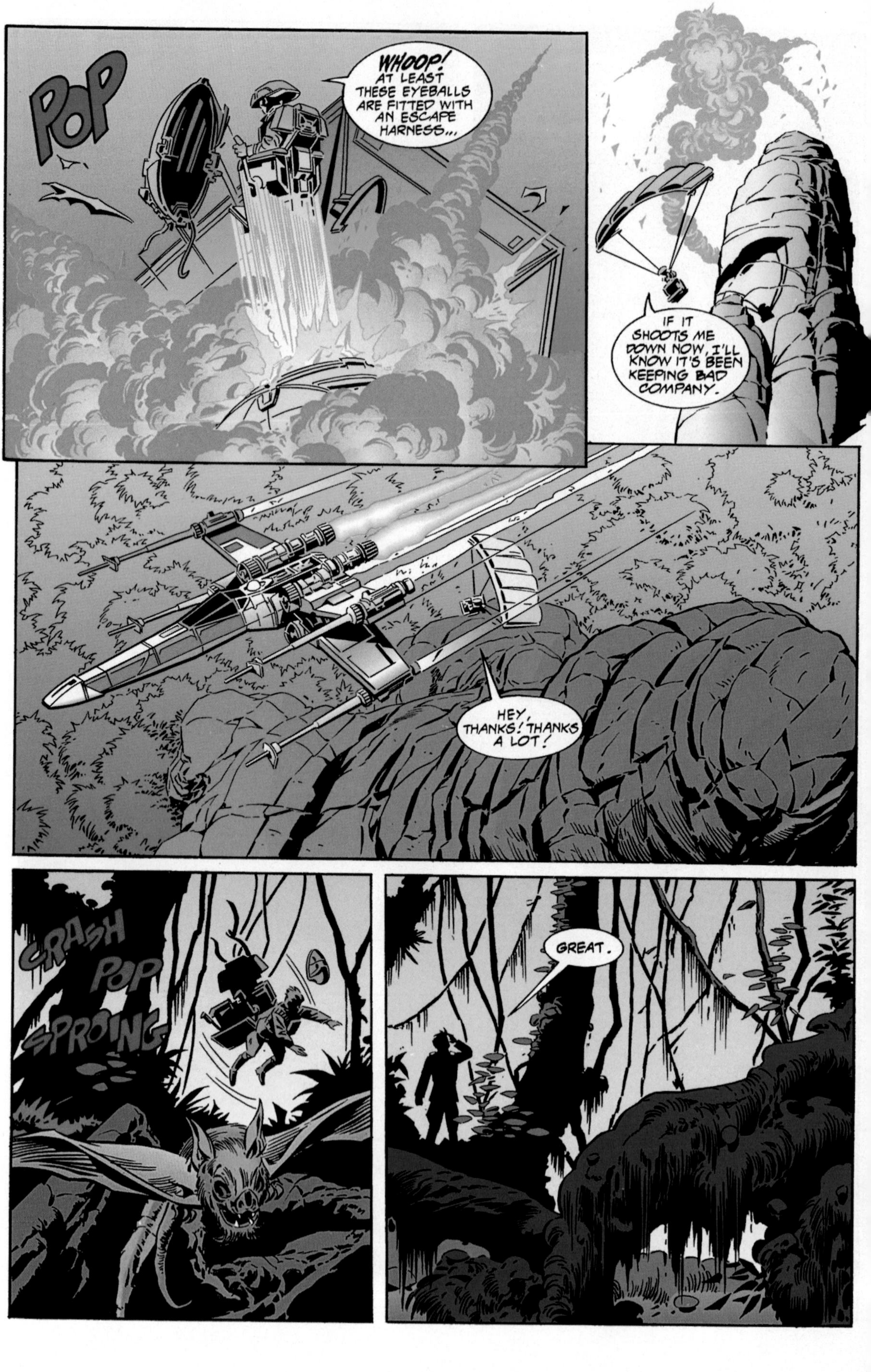
POP
WHOOP! AT LEAST THESE EYEBALLS ARE FITTED WITH AN ESCAPE HARNESS...
IF IT SHOOTS ME DOWN NOW, I'LL KNOW IT'S BEEN KEEPING BAD COMPANY.
HEY, THANKS! THANKS A LOT!
CRASH
POP
SPROING
GREAT.

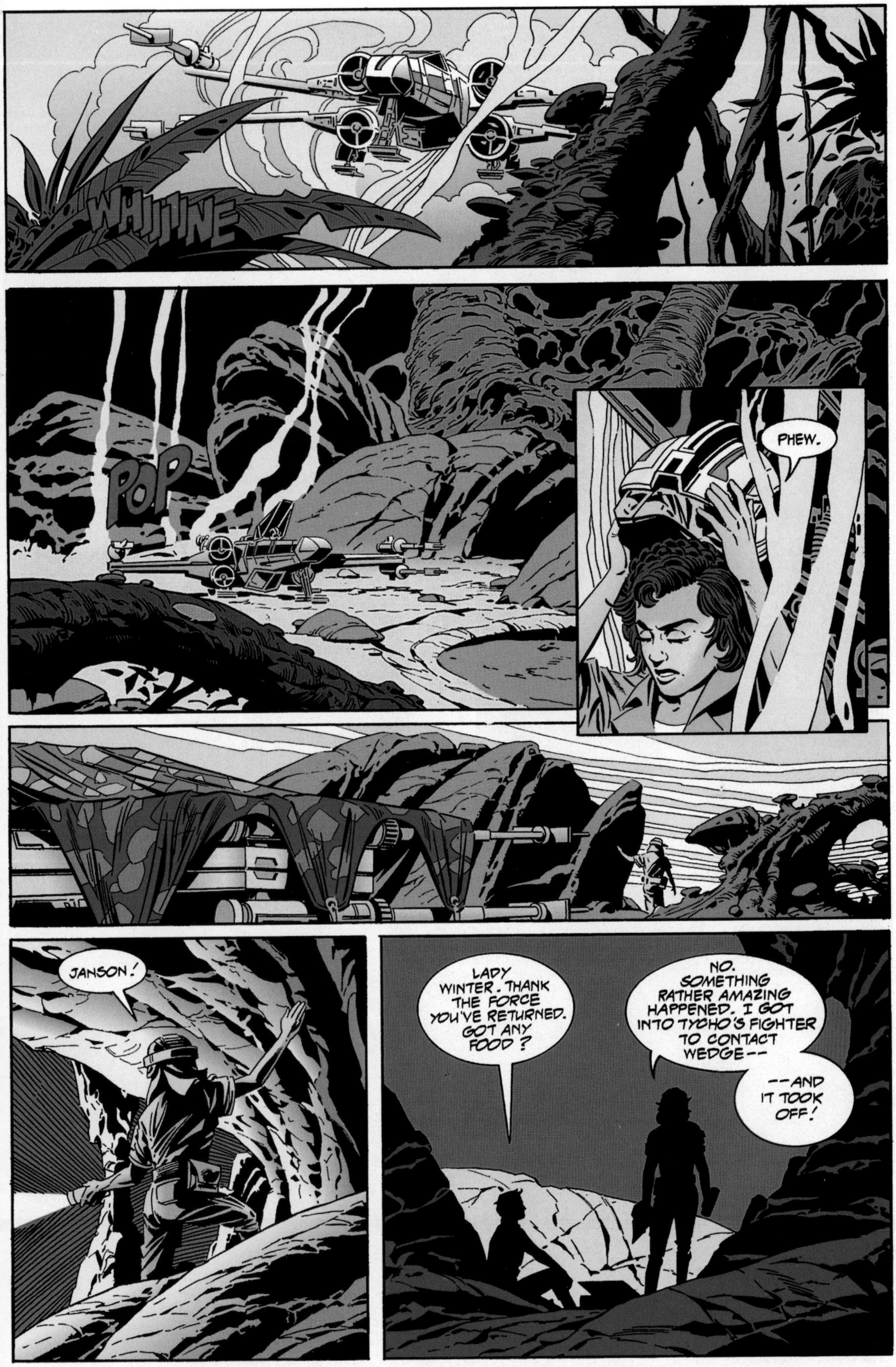
WHIIIINE
POP
PHEW.
JANSON!
LADY WINTER. THANK THE FORCE YOU'VE RETURNED. GOT ANY FOOD?
NO. SOMETHING RATHER AMAZING HAPPENED. I GOT INTO TYCHO'S FIGHTER TO CONTACT WEDGE--
--AND IT TOOK OFF!

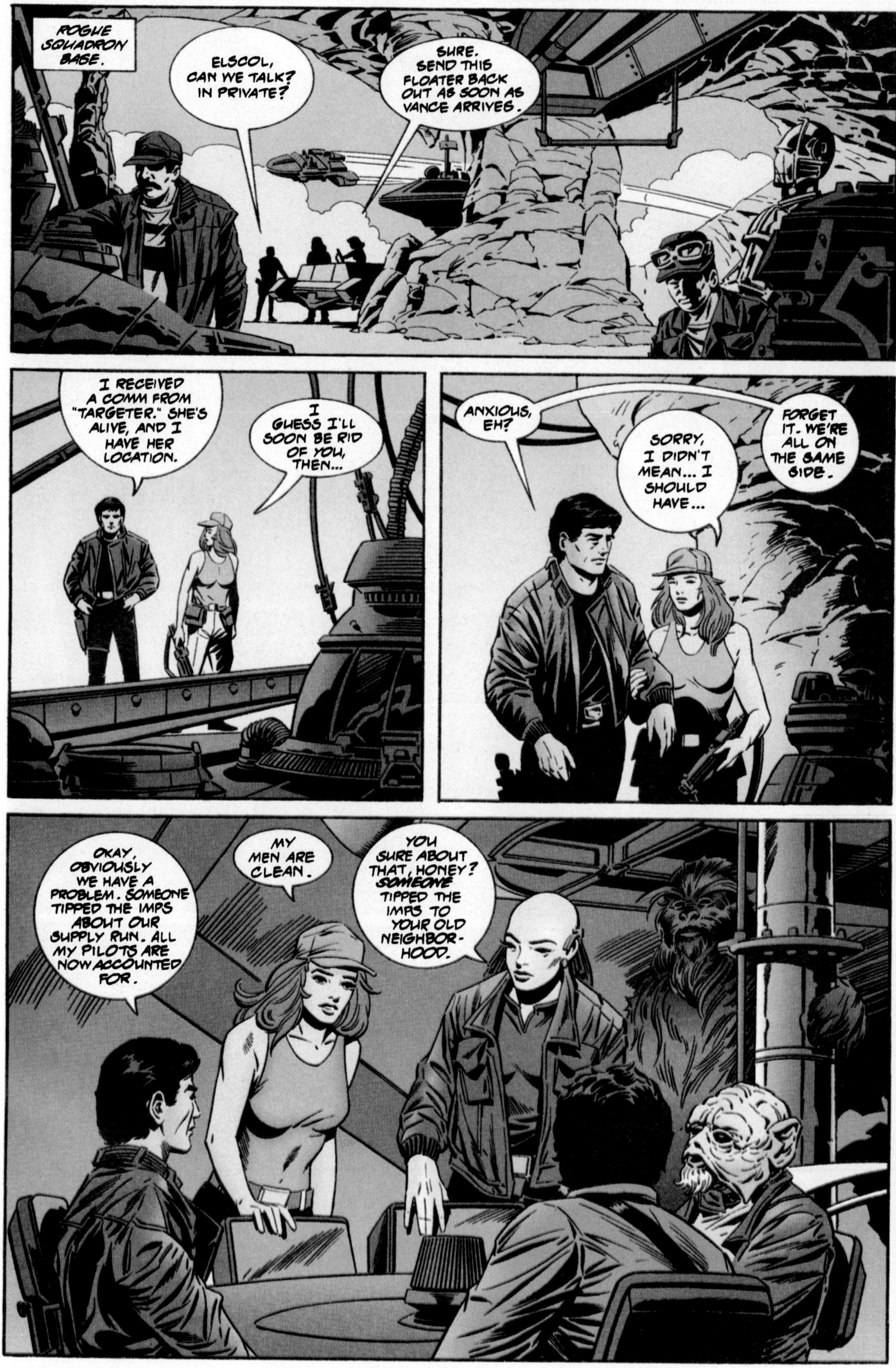
ROGUE SQUADRON BASE.
ELSCOL, CAN WE TALK? IN PRIVATE?
SURE. SEND THIS FLOATER BACK OUT AS SOON AS VANCE ARRIVES.
I RECEIVED A COMM FROM "TARGETER." SHE'S ALIVE, AND I HAVE HER LOCATION.
I GUESS I'LL SOON BE RID OF YOU, THEN...
ANXIOUS, EH?
SORRY, I DIDN'T MEAN... I SHOULD HAVE...
FORGET IT. WE'RE ALL ON THE SAME SIDE.
OKAY, OBVIOUSLY WE HAVE A PROBLEM. SOMEONE TIPPED THE IMPS ABOUT OUR SUPPLY RUN. ALL MY PILOTS ARE NOW ACCOUNTED FOR.
MY MEN ARE CLEAN.
YOU SURE ABOUT THAT, HONEY? SOMEONE TIPPED THE IMPS TO YOUR OLD NEIGHBOR-HOOD.

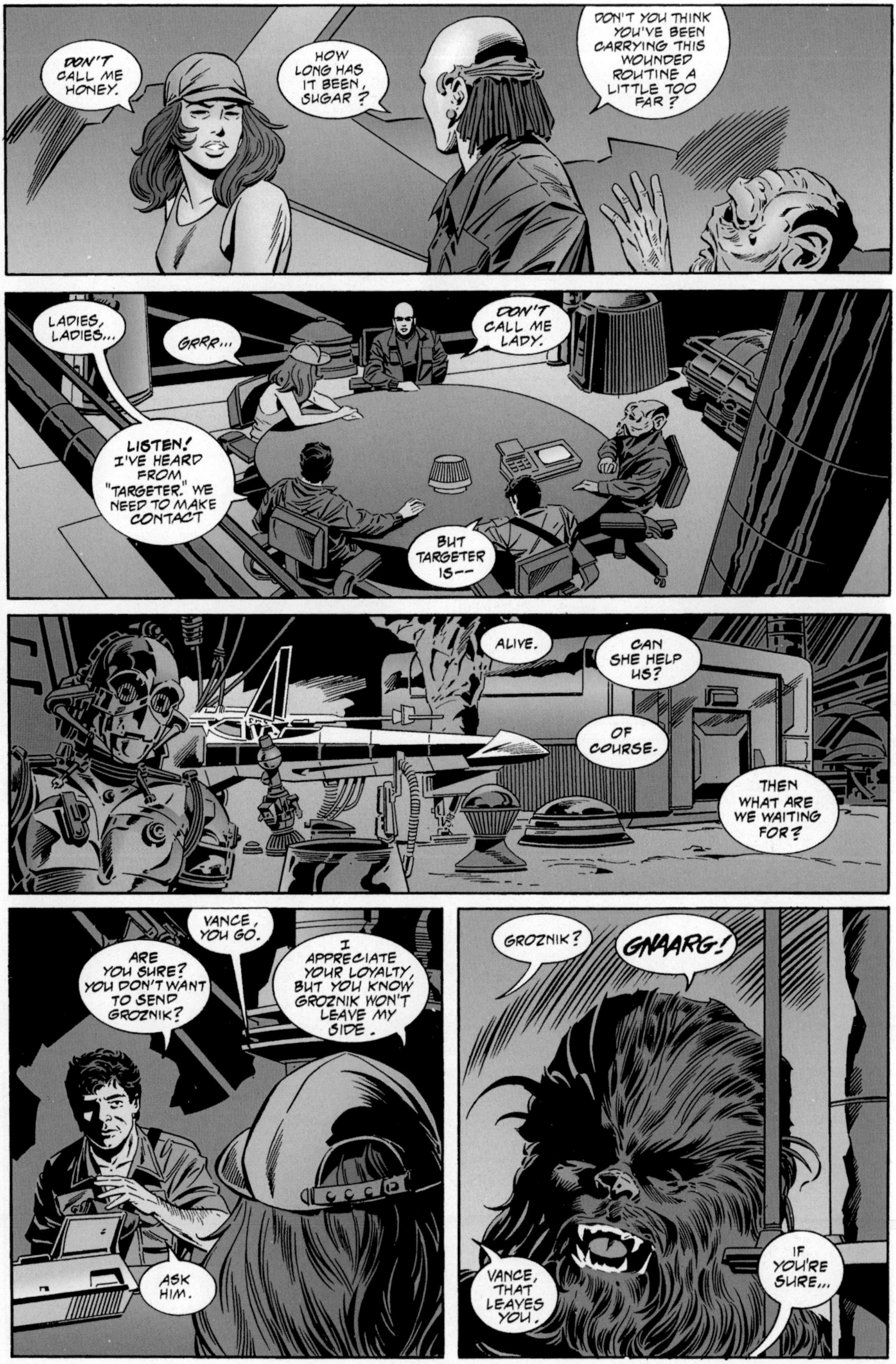
DON'T CALL ME HONEY.
HOW LONG HAS IT BEEN, SUGAR?
DON'T YOU THINK YOU'VE BEEN CARRYING THIS WOUNDED ROUTINE A LITTLE TOO FAR?
LADIES, LADIES...
GRRR...
DON'T CALL ME LADY.
LISTEN! I'VE HEARD FROM "TARGETER." WE NEED TO MAKE CONTACT
BUT TARGETER IS--
ALIVE.
CAN SHE HELP US?
OF COURSE.
THEN WHAT ARE WE WAITING FOR?
VANCE, YOU GO.
ARE YOU SURE? YOU DON'T WANT TO SEND GROZNIK?
I APPRECIATE YOUR LOYALTY, BUT YOU KNOW GROZNIK WON'T LEAVE MY SIDE.
ASK HIM.
GROZNIK?
GNAARG!
VANCE, THAT LEAVES YOU.
IF YOU'RE SURE...

PLEASE, VANCE. YOU'RE THE ONLY ONE I CAN TRUST.

ALL RIGHT.

THANKS, VANCE. BRING HER BACK HERE.

I KNOW THE ROUTINE.

HAPPY, HAPPY!

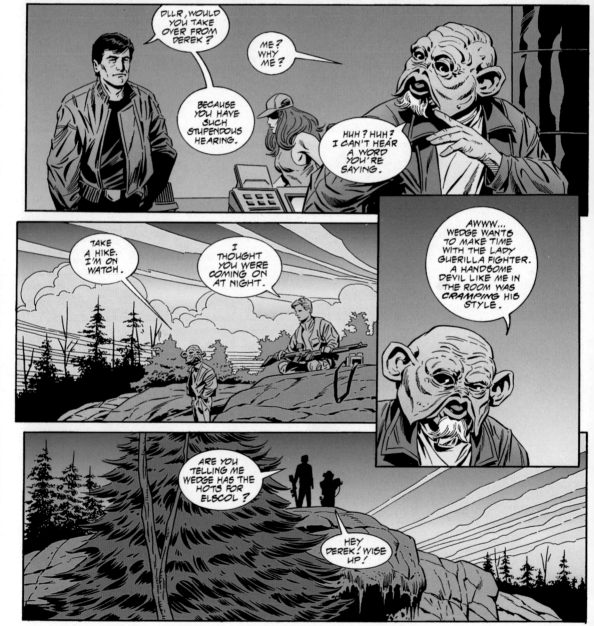

DLLR, WOULD YOU TAKE OVER FROM DEREK?

ME? WHY ME?

BECAUSE YOU HAVE SUCH STUPENDOUS HEARING.

HUH? HUH? I CAN'T HEAR A WORD YOU'RE SAYING.

TAKE A HIKE. I'M ON WATCH.

I THOUGHT YOU WERE COMING ON AT NIGHT.

AWWW... WEDGE WANTS TO MAKE TIME WITH THE LADY GUERILLA FIGHTER. A HANDSOME DEVIL LIKE ME IN THE ROOM WAS CRAMPING HIS STYLE.

ARE YOU TELLING ME WEDGE HAS THE HOTS FOR ELSCOL?

HEY DEREK! WISE UP!

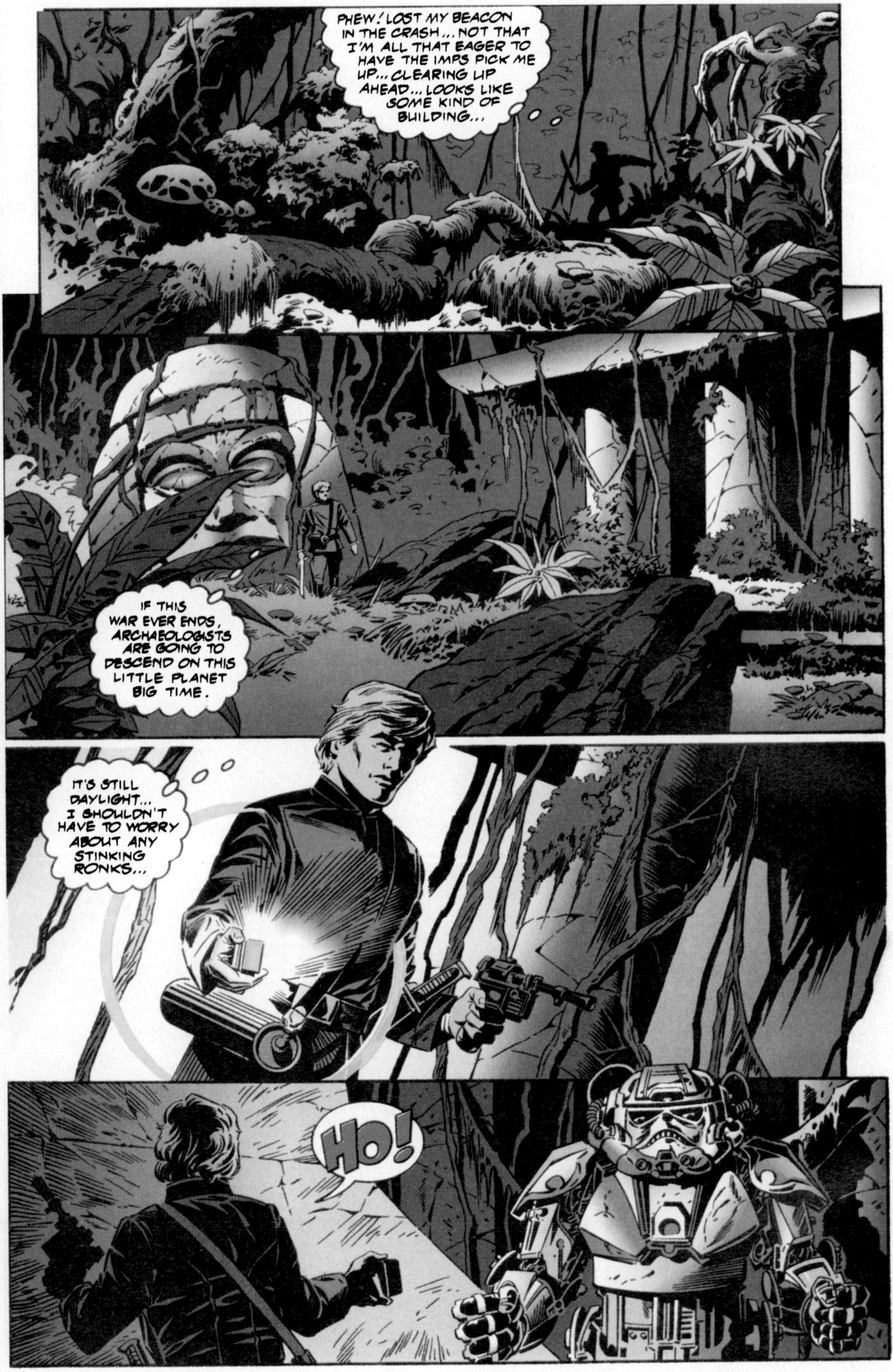
PHEW! LOST MY BEACON IN THE CRASH... NOT THAT I'M ALL THAT EAGER TO HAVE THE IMPS PICK ME UP... CLEARING UP AHEAD... LOOKS LIKE SOME KIND OF BUILDING...
IF THIS WAR EVER ENDS, ARCHAEOLOGISTS ARE GOING TO DESCEND ON THIS LITTLE PLANET BIG TIME.
IT'S STILL DAYLIGHT... I SHOULDN'T HAVE TO WORRY ABOUT ANY STINKING RONKS...
HO!

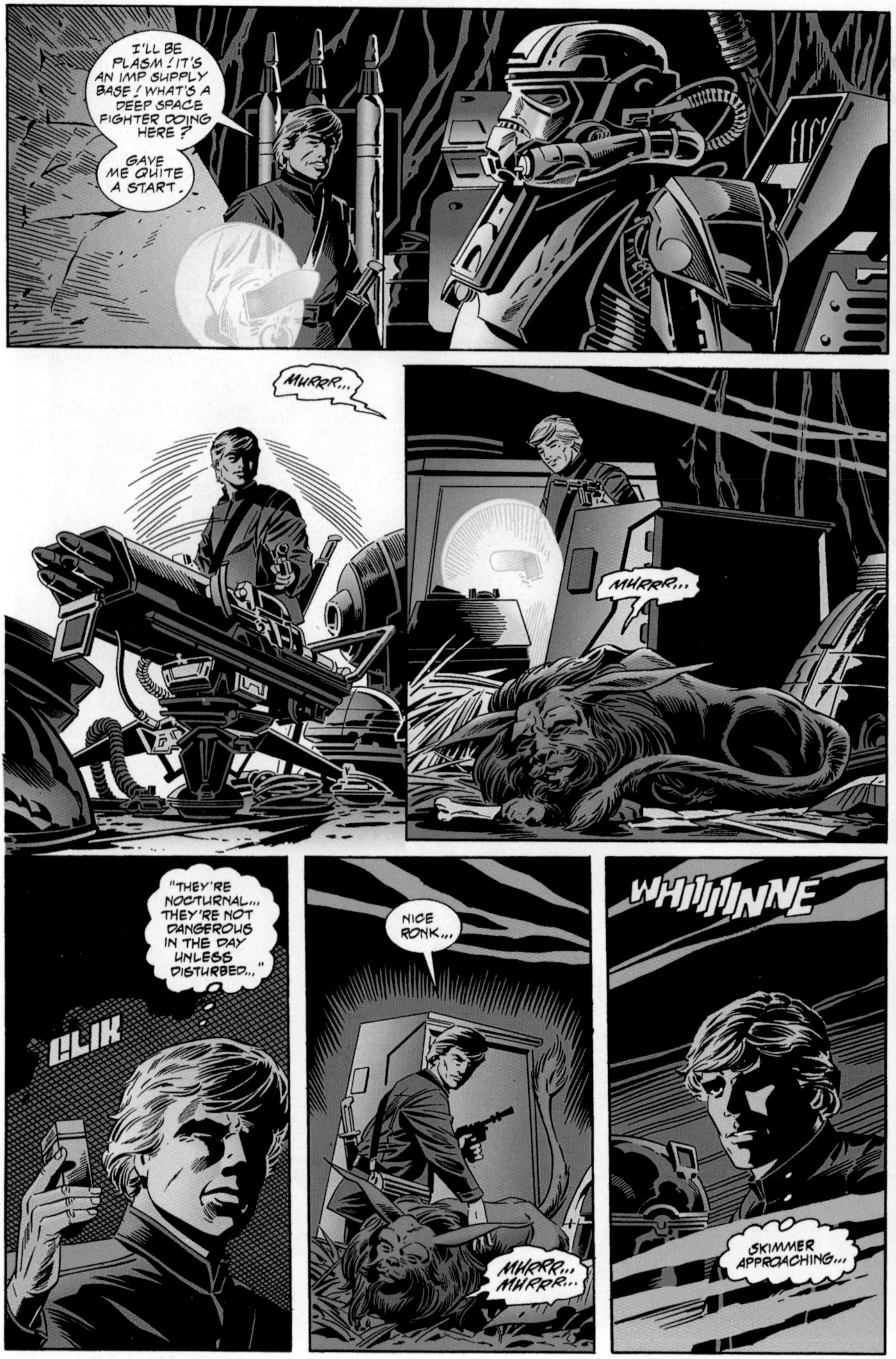
I'LL BE PLASM! IT'S AN IMP SUPPLY BASE! WHAT'S A DEEP SPACE FIGHTER DOING HERE?
GAVE ME QUITE A START.
MURRR...
MURRR...
"THEY'RE NOCTURNAL... THEY'RE NOT DANGEROUS IN THE DAY UNLESS DISTURBED..."
CLIK
NICE RONK...
MURRR... MURRR...
WHIIIIINNE
SKIMMER APPROACHING...

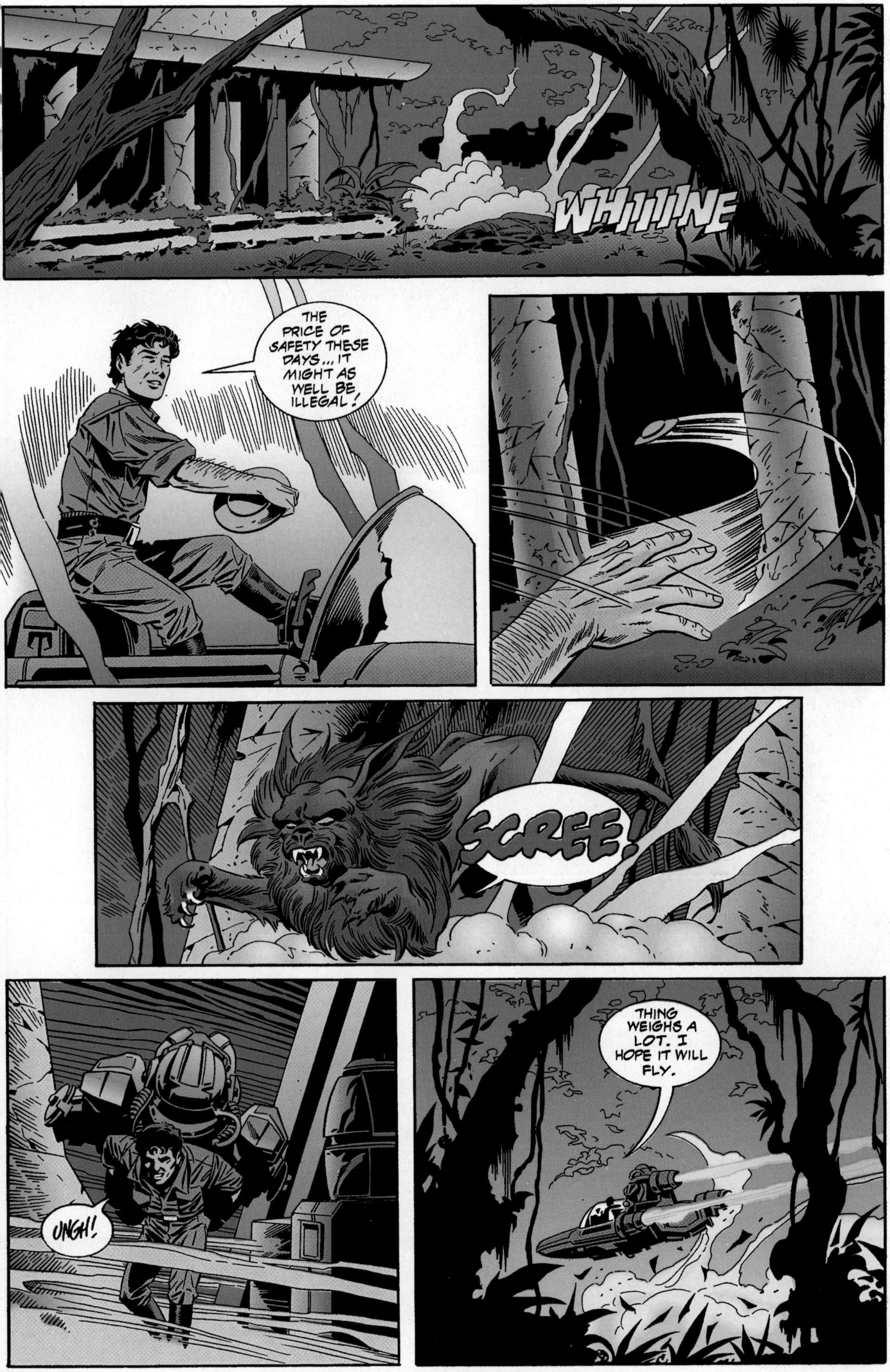
WHIIIIINE
THE PRICE OF SAFETY THESE DAYS... IT MIGHT AS WELL BE ILLEGAL!
SCREE!
UNGH!
THING WEIGHS A LOT. I HOPE IT WILL FLY.

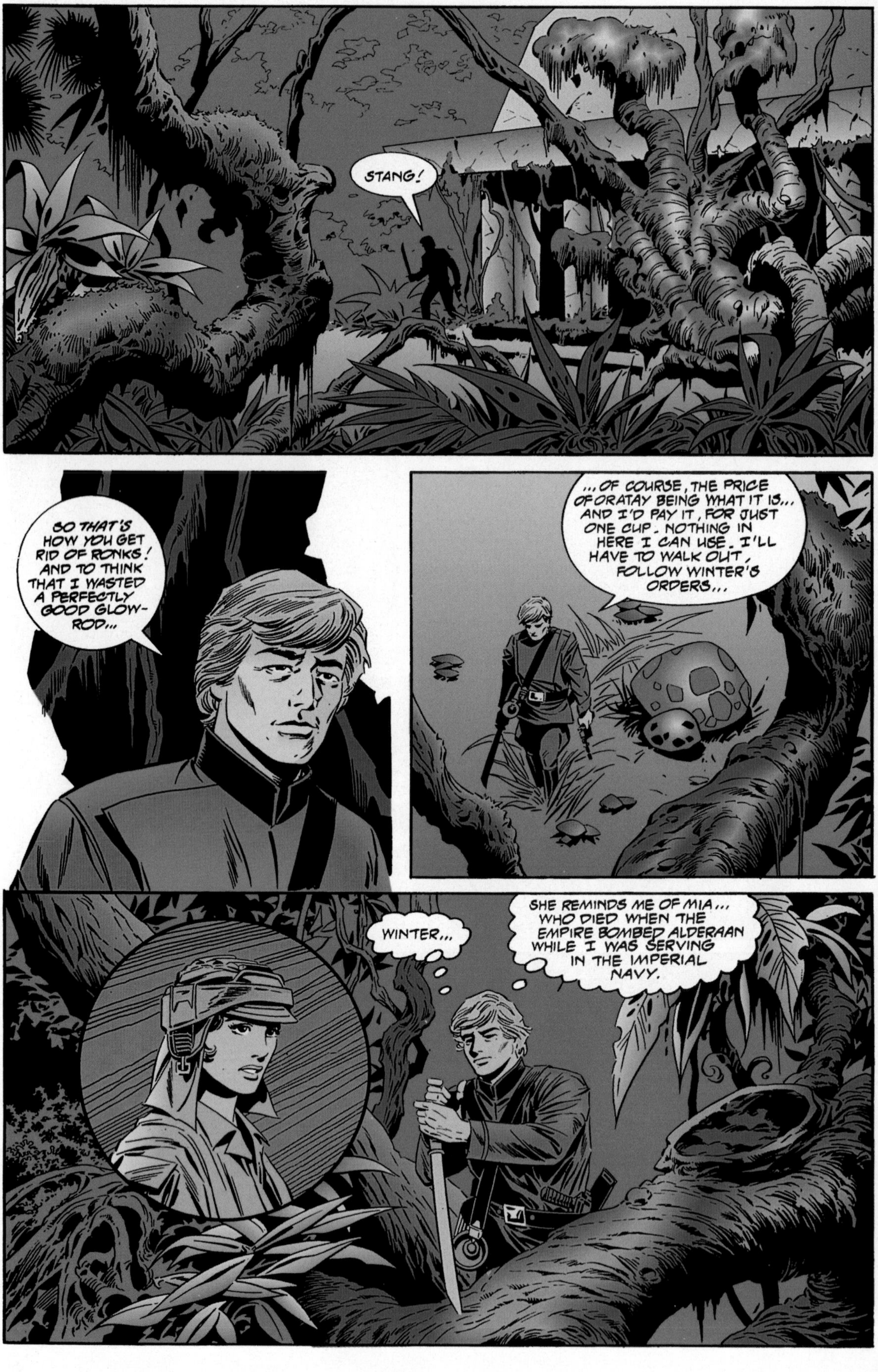
STANG!
SO THAT'S HOW YOU GET RID OF RONKS! AND TO THINK THAT I WASTED A PERFECTLY GOOD GLOW-ROD...
...OF COURSE, THE PRICE OF ORATAY BEING WHAT IT IS... AND I'D PAY IT, FOR JUST ONE CUP. NOTHING IN HERE I CAN USE. I'LL HAVE TO WALK OUT, FOLLOW WINTER'S ORDERS...
WINTER...
SHE REMINDS ME OF MIA... WHO DIED WHEN THE EMPIRE BOMBED ALDERAAN WHILE I WAS SERVING IN THE IMPERIAL NAVY.

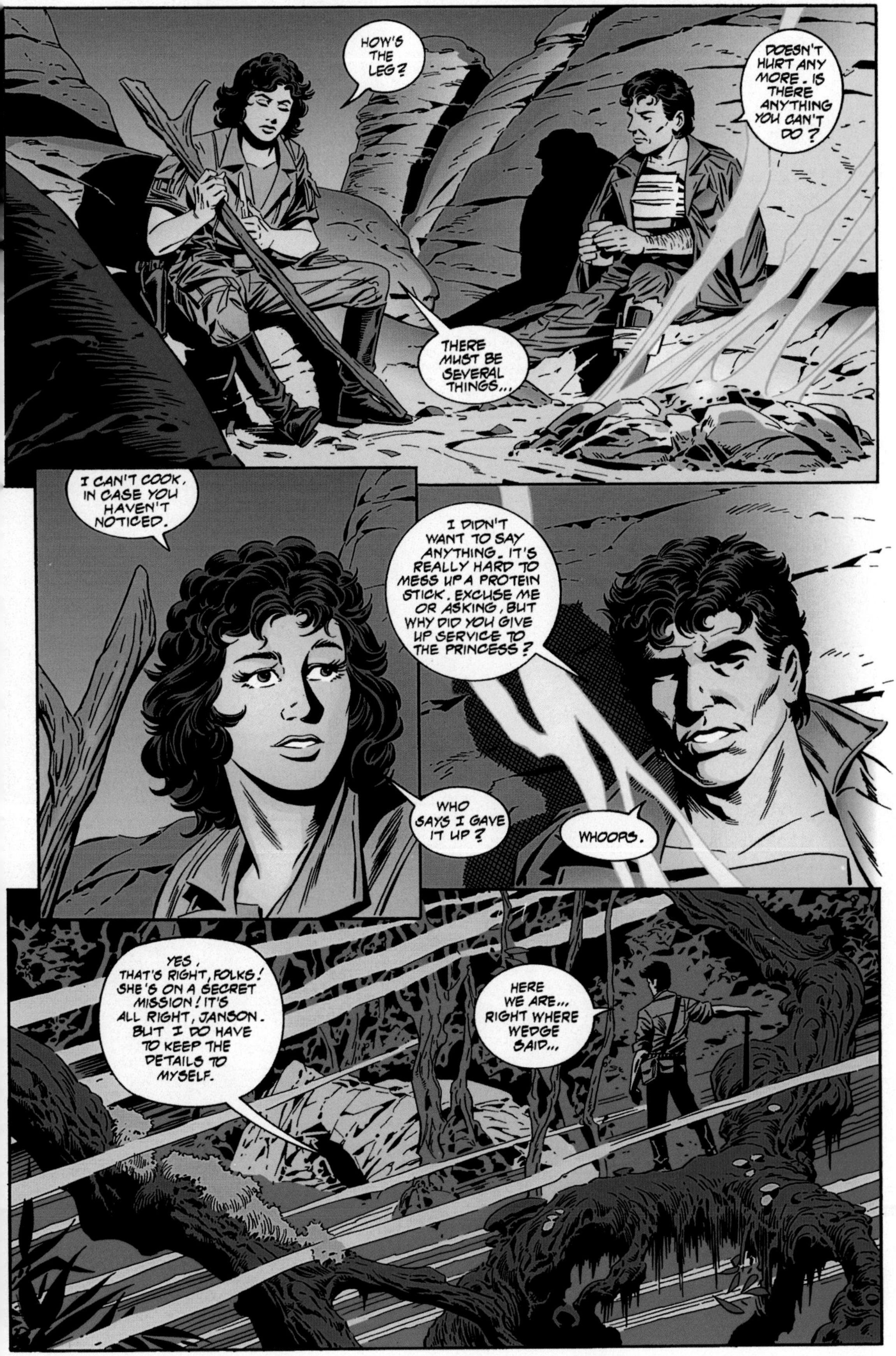
HOW'S THE LEG?
DOESN'T HURT ANY MORE. IS THERE ANYTHING YOU CAN'T DO?
THERE MUST BE SEVERAL THINGS...
I CAN'T COOK, IN CASE YOU HAVEN'T NOTICED.
I DIDN'T WANT TO SAY ANYTHING. IT'S REALLY HARD TO MESS UP A PROTEIN STICK. EXCUSE ME OR ASKING, BUT WHY DID YOU GIVE UP SERVICE TO THE PRINCESS?
WHO SAYS I GAVE IT UP?
WHOOPS.
YES, THAT'S RIGHT, FOLKS! SHE'S ON A SECRET MISSION! IT'S ALL RIGHT, JANSON. BUT I DO HAVE TO KEEP THE DETAILS TO MYSELF.
HERE WE ARE... RIGHT WHERE WEDGE SAID...

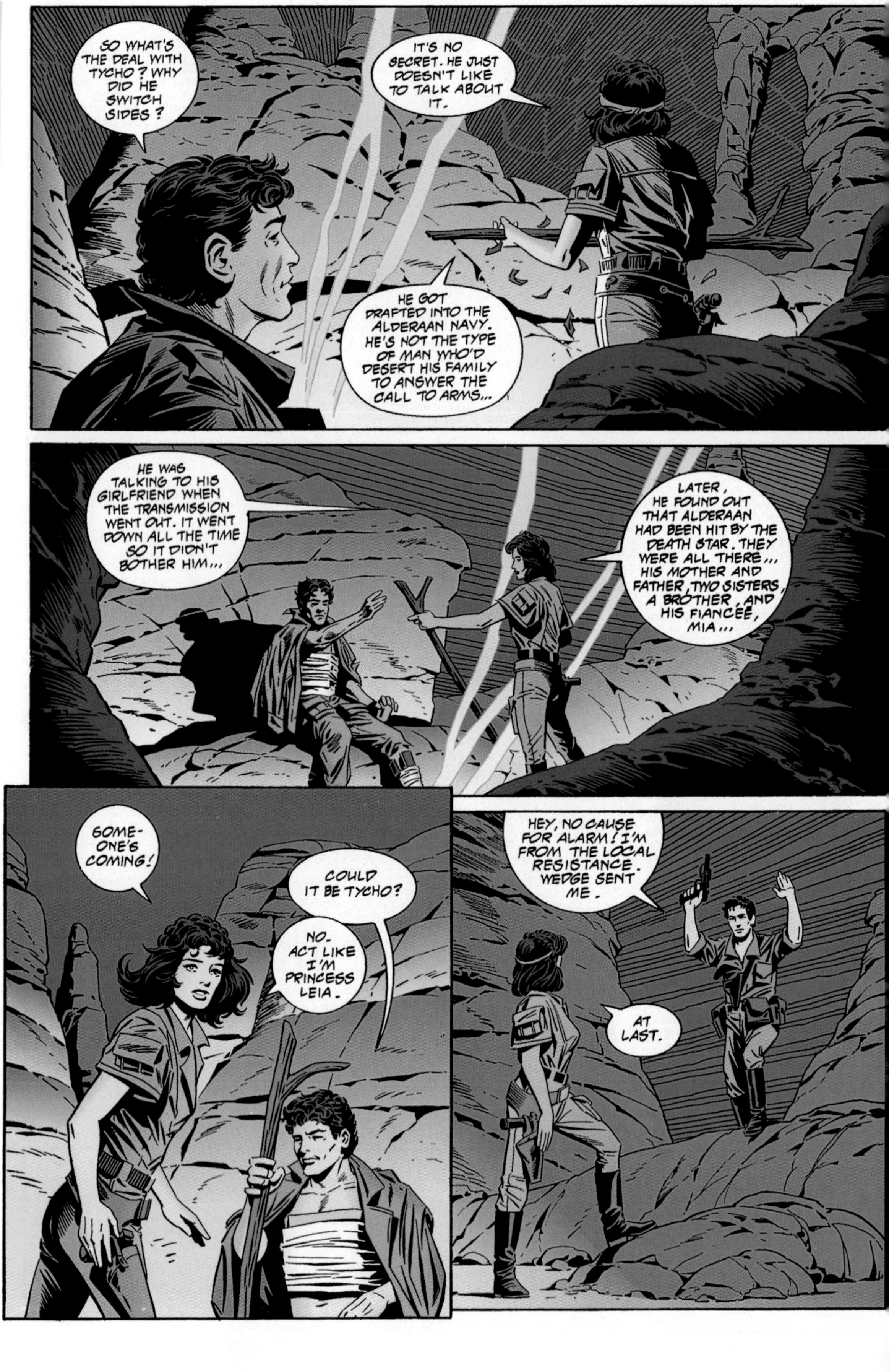
SO WHAT'S THE DEAL WITH TYCHO? WHY DID HE SWITCH SIDES?
IT'S NO SECRET. HE JUST DOESN'T LIKE TO TALK ABOUT IT.
HE GOT DRAFTED INTO THE ALDERAAN NAVY. HE'S NOT THE TYPE OF MAN WHO'D DESERT HIS FAMILY TO ANSWER THE CALL TO ARMS...
HE WAS TALKING TO HIS GIRLFRIEND WHEN THE TRANSMISSION WENT OUT. IT WENT DOWN ALL THE TIME SO IT DIDN'T BOTHER HIM...
LATER, HE FOUND OUT THAT ALDERAAN HAD BEEN HIT BY THE DEATH STAR. THEY WERE ALL THERE... HIS MOTHER AND FATHER, TWO SISTERS, A BROTHER, AND HIS FIANCÉE, MIA...
SOME-ONE'S COMING!
COULD IT BE TYCHO?
NO. ACT LIKE I'M PRINCESS LEIA.
HEY, NO CAUSE FOR ALARM! I'M FROM THE LOCAL RESISTANCE. WEDGE SENT ME.
AT LAST.

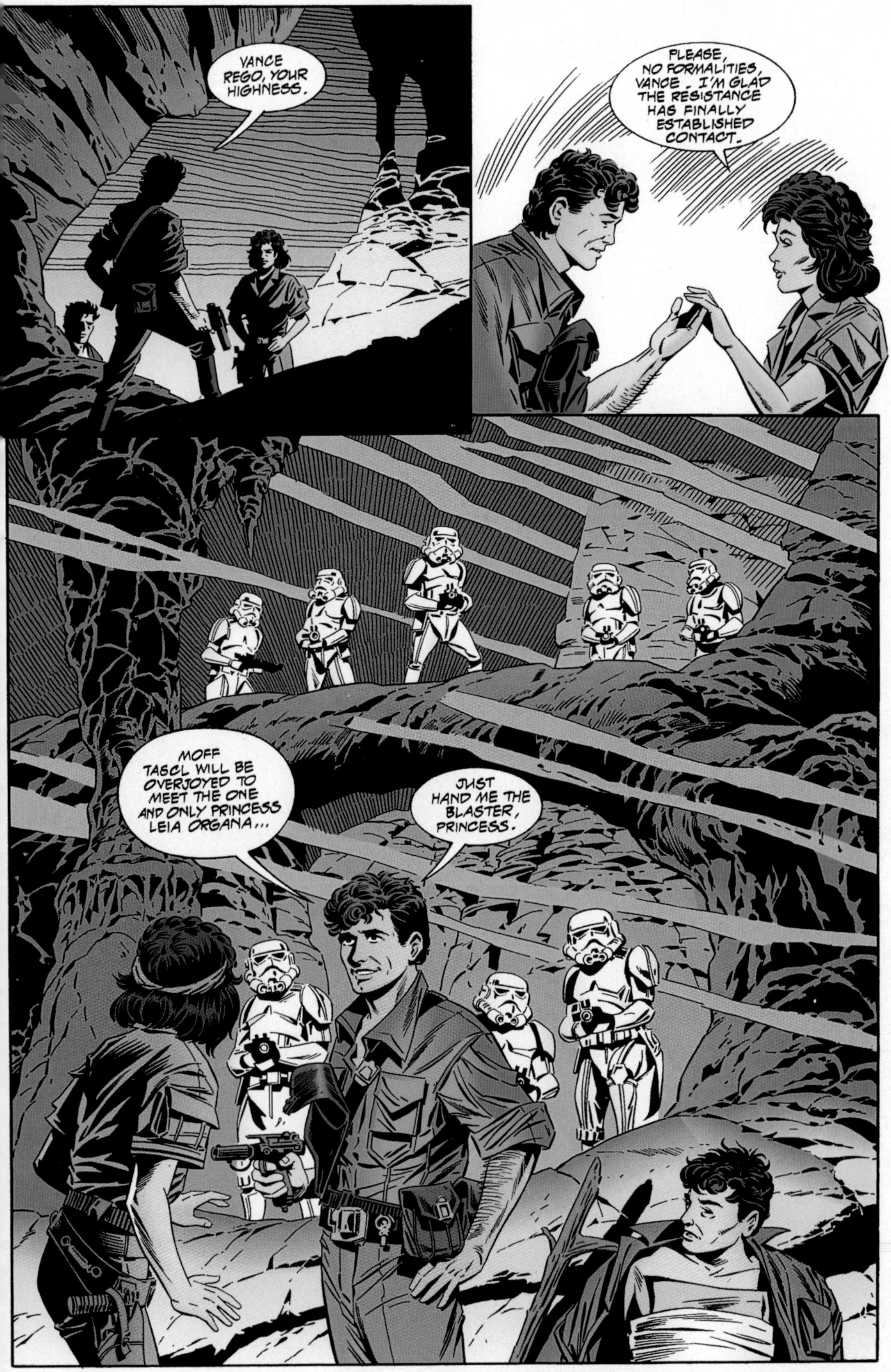
VANCE REGO, YOUR HIGHNESS.
PLEASE, NO FORMALITIES, VANCE. I'M GLAD THE RESISTANCE HAS FINALLY ESTABLISHED CONTACT.
MOFF TASCL WILL BE OVERJOYED TO MEET THE ONE AND ONLY PRINCESS LEIA ORGANA...
JUST HAND ME THE BLASTER, PRINCESS.

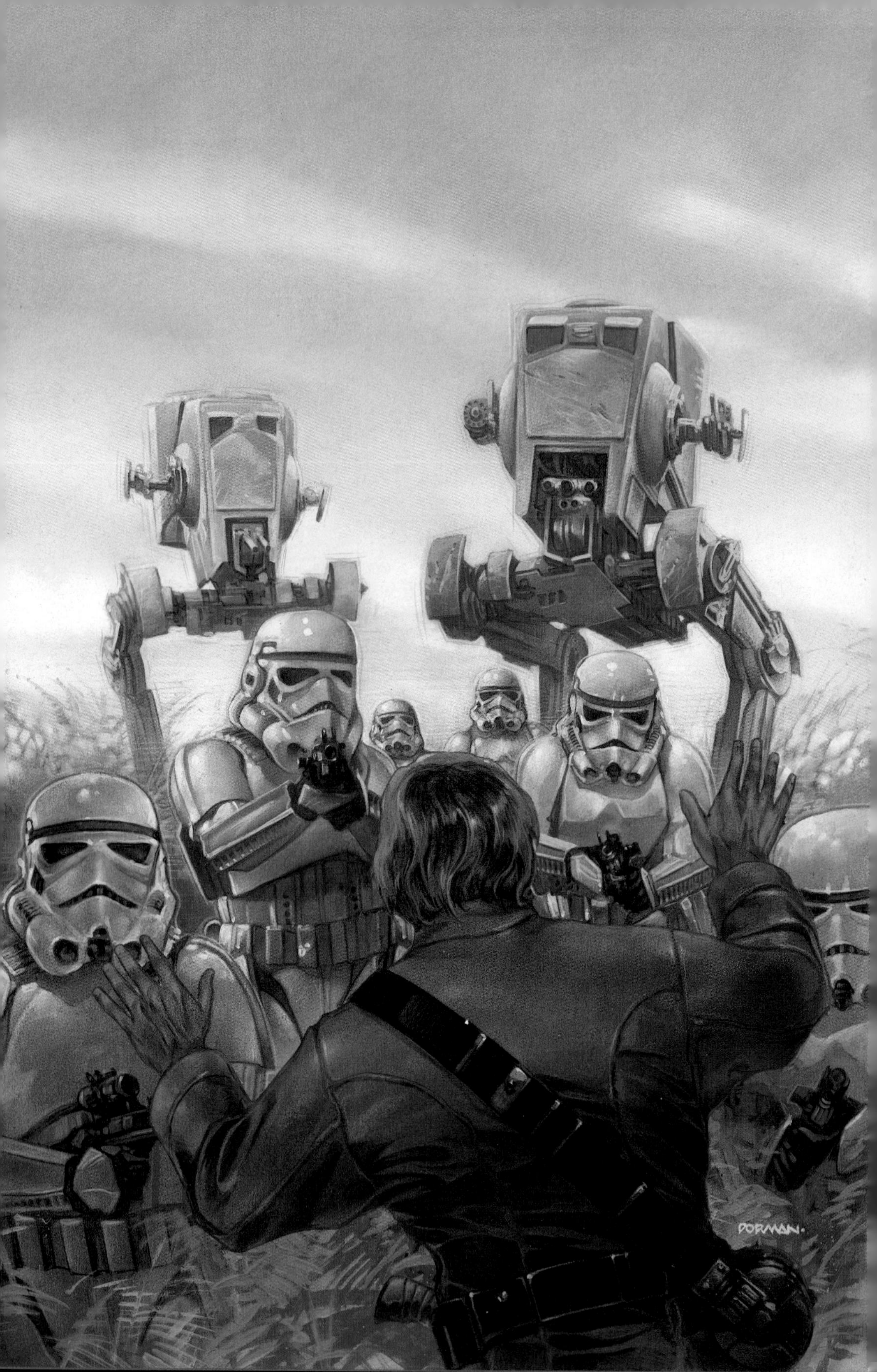
DORMAN.

***STAR WARS: X-WING ROGUE SQUADRON* #4 — "THE REBEL OPPOSITION, CHAPTER 4"**

PLOTTER: MICHAEL A. STACKPOLE • SCRIPTER: MIKE BARON • PENCILER: ALLEN NUNIS • INKER: ANDY MUSHYNSKY • COLORIST: DAVE NESTELLE
LETTERER: STEVE DUTRO • EDITORS: RYDER WINDHAM & PEET JANES • COVER ARTIST: DAVE DORMAN

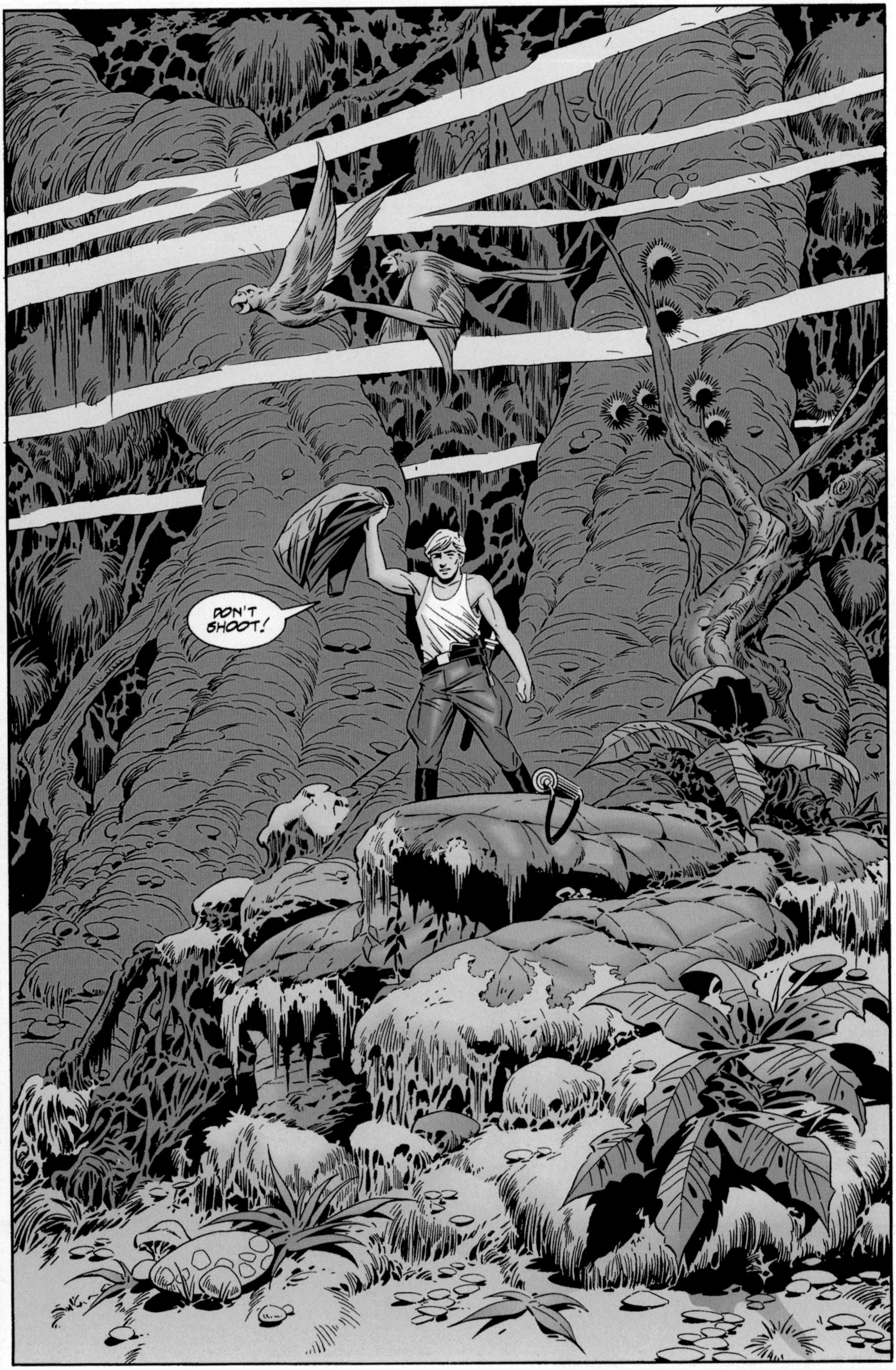
DON'T SHOOT!

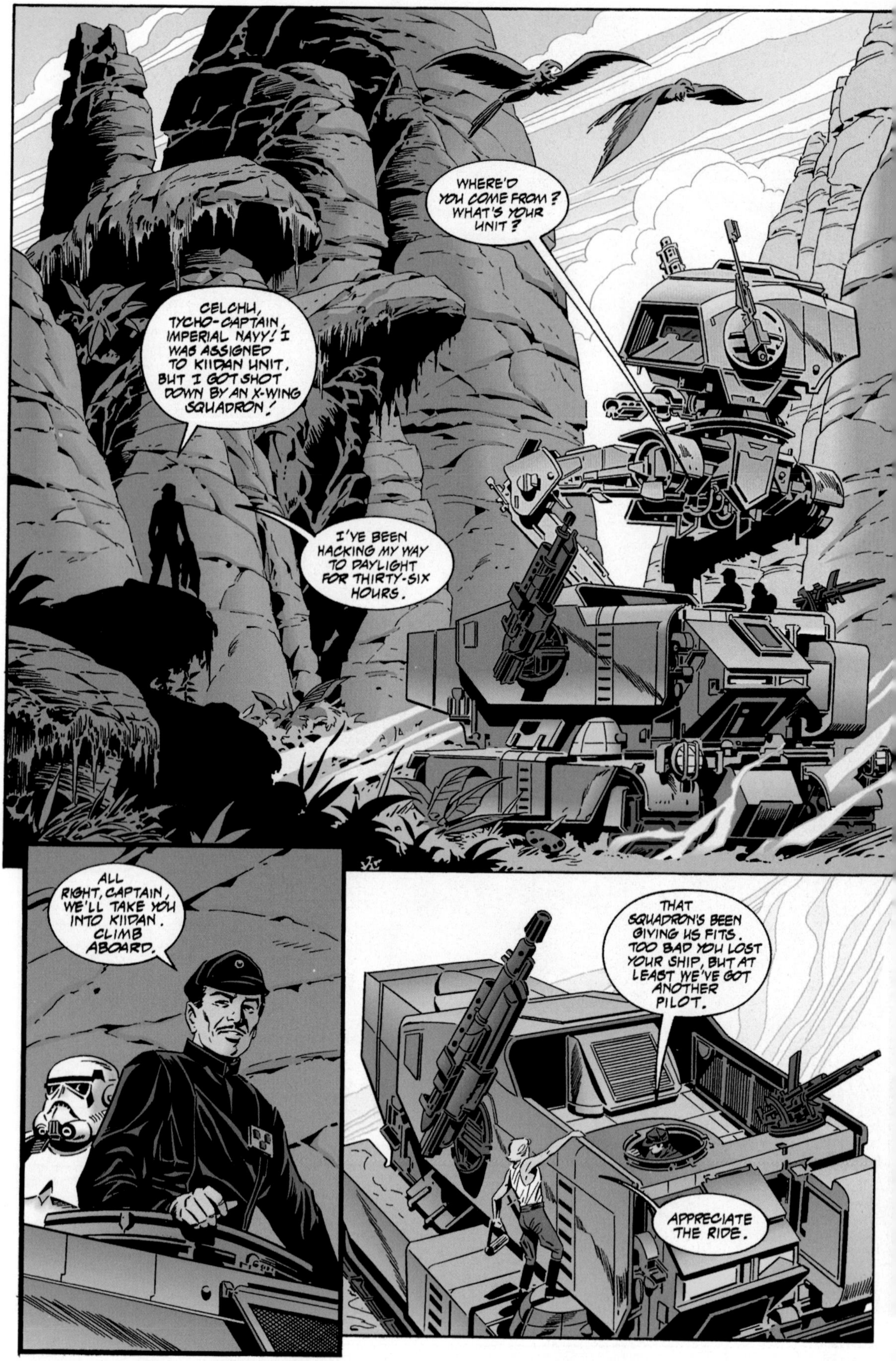
WHERE'D YOU COME FROM? WHAT'S YOUR UNIT?
CELCHU, TYCHO-CAPTAIN, IMPERIAL NAVY! I WAS ASSIGNED TO KIIDAN UNIT, BUT I GOT SHOT DOWN BY AN X-WING SQUADRON!
I'VE BEEN HACKING MY WAY TO DAYLIGHT FOR THIRTY-SIX HOURS.
ALL RIGHT, CAPTAIN, WE'LL TAKE YOU INTO KIIDAN. CLIMB ABOARD.
THAT SQUADRON'S BEEN GIVING US FITS. TOO BAD YOU LOST YOUR SHIP, BUT AT LEAST WE'VE GOT ANOTHER PILOT.
APPRECIATE THE RIDE.

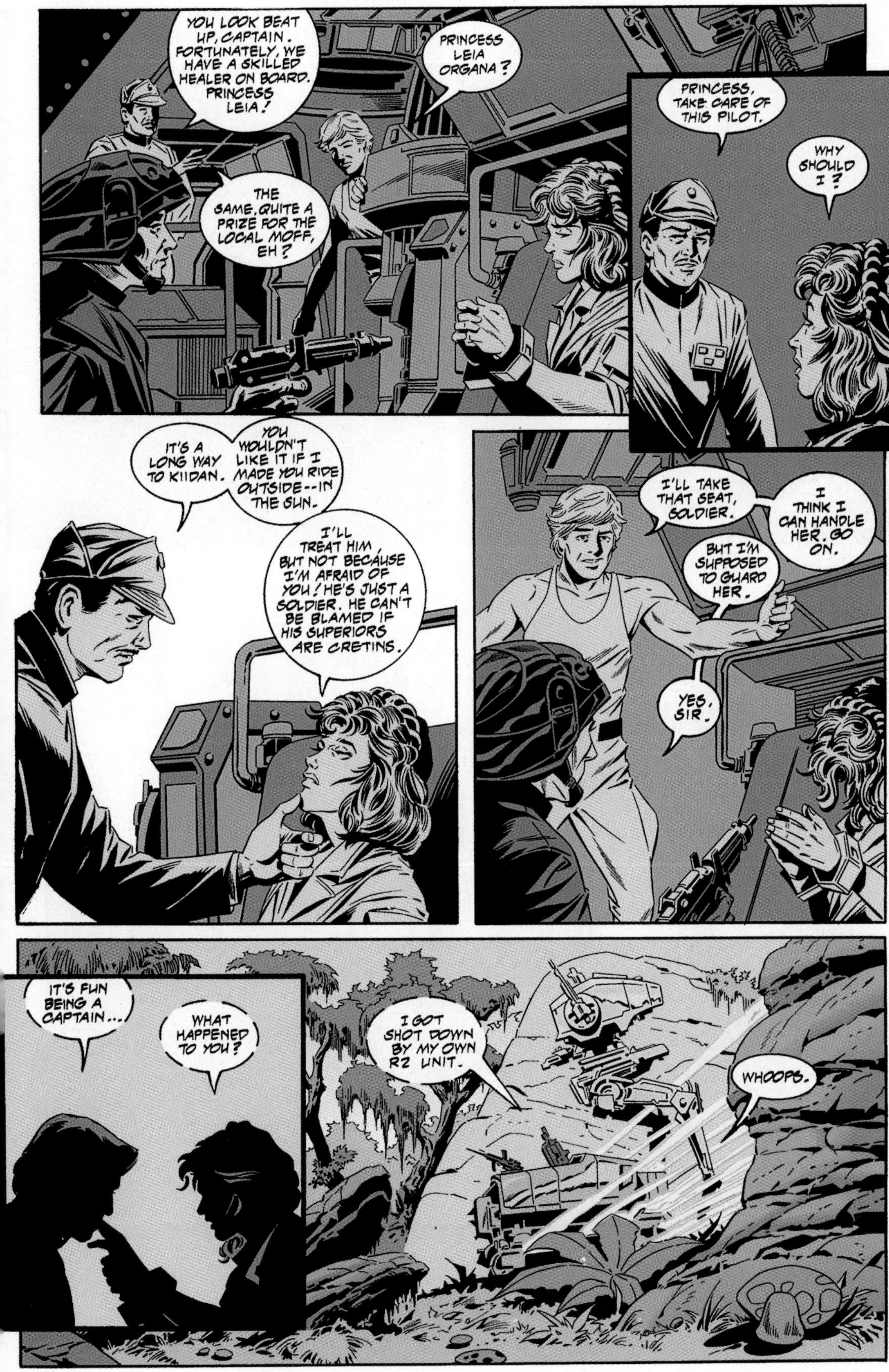
YOU LOOK BEAT UP, CAPTAIN. FORTUNATELY, WE HAVE A SKILLED HEALER ON BOARD. PRINCESS LEIA!
PRINCESS LEIA ORGANA?
THE SAME. QUITE A PRIZE FOR THE LOCAL MOFF, EH?
PRINCESS, TAKE CARE OF THIS PILOT.
WHY SHOULD I?
IT'S A LONG WAY TO KIIDAN.
YOU WOULDN'T LIKE IT IF I MADE YOU RIDE OUTSIDE--IN THE SUN.
I'LL TREAT HIM, BUT NOT BECAUSE I'M AFRAID OF YOU! HE'S JUST A SOLDIER. HE CAN'T BE BLAMED IF HIS SUPERIORS ARE CRETINS.
I'LL TAKE THAT SEAT, SOLDIER.
BUT I'M SUPPOSED TO GUARD HER.
I THINK I CAN HANDLE HER. GO ON.
YES, SIR.
IT'S FUN BEING A CAPTAIN...
WHAT HAPPENED TO YOU?
I GOT SHOT DOWN BY MY OWN R2 UNIT.
WHOOPS.

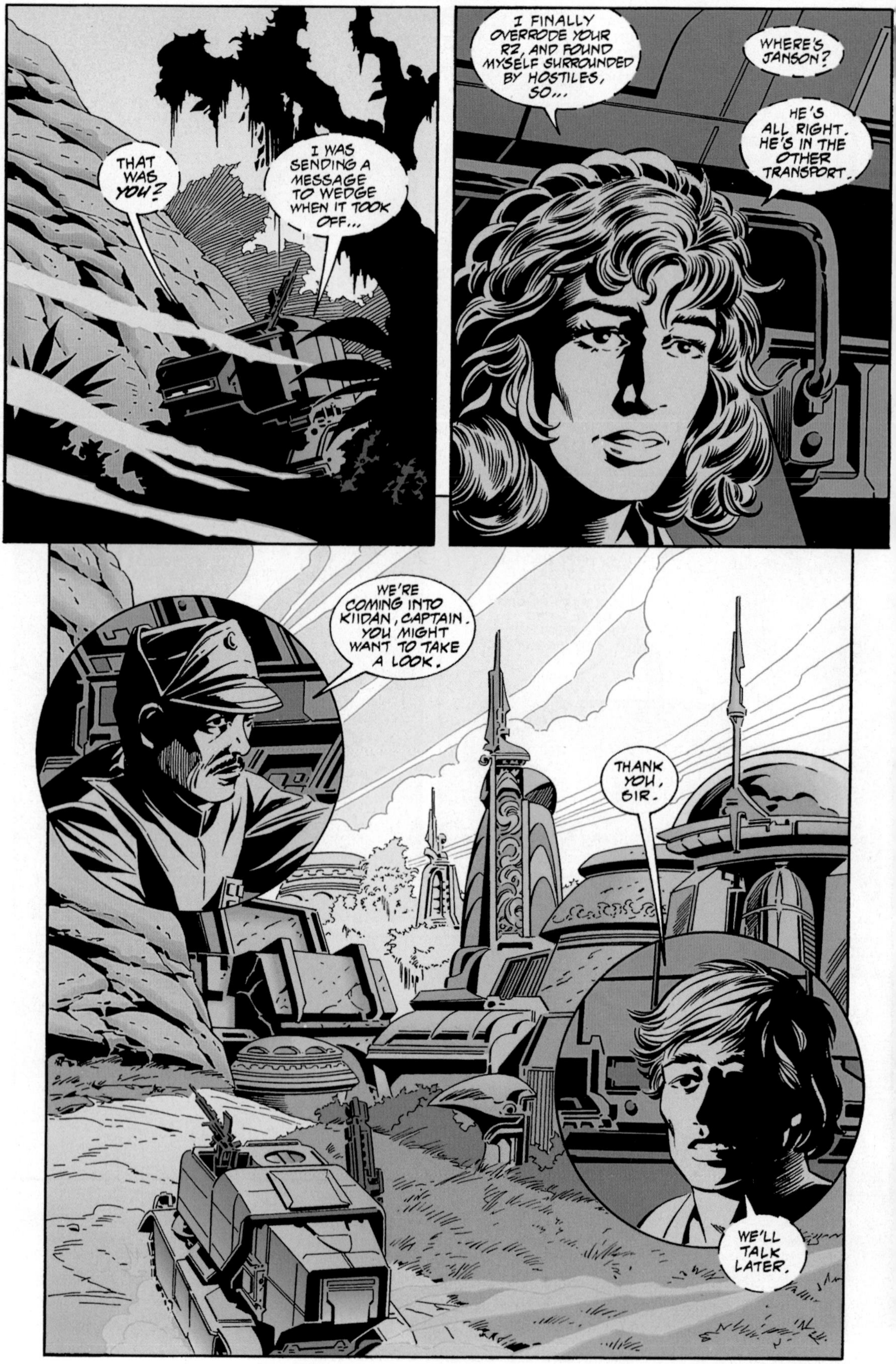
THAT WAS YOU?
I WAS SENDING A MESSAGE TO WEDGE WHEN IT TOOK OFF...
I FINALLY OVERRODE YOUR R2, AND FOUND MYSELF SURROUNDED BY HOSTILES, SO...
WHERE'S JANSON?
HE'S ALL RIGHT. HE'S IN THE OTHER TRANSPORT.
WE'RE COMING INTO KIIDAN, CAPTAIN. YOU MIGHT WANT TO TAKE A LOOK.
THANK YOU, SIR.
WE'LL TALK LATER.

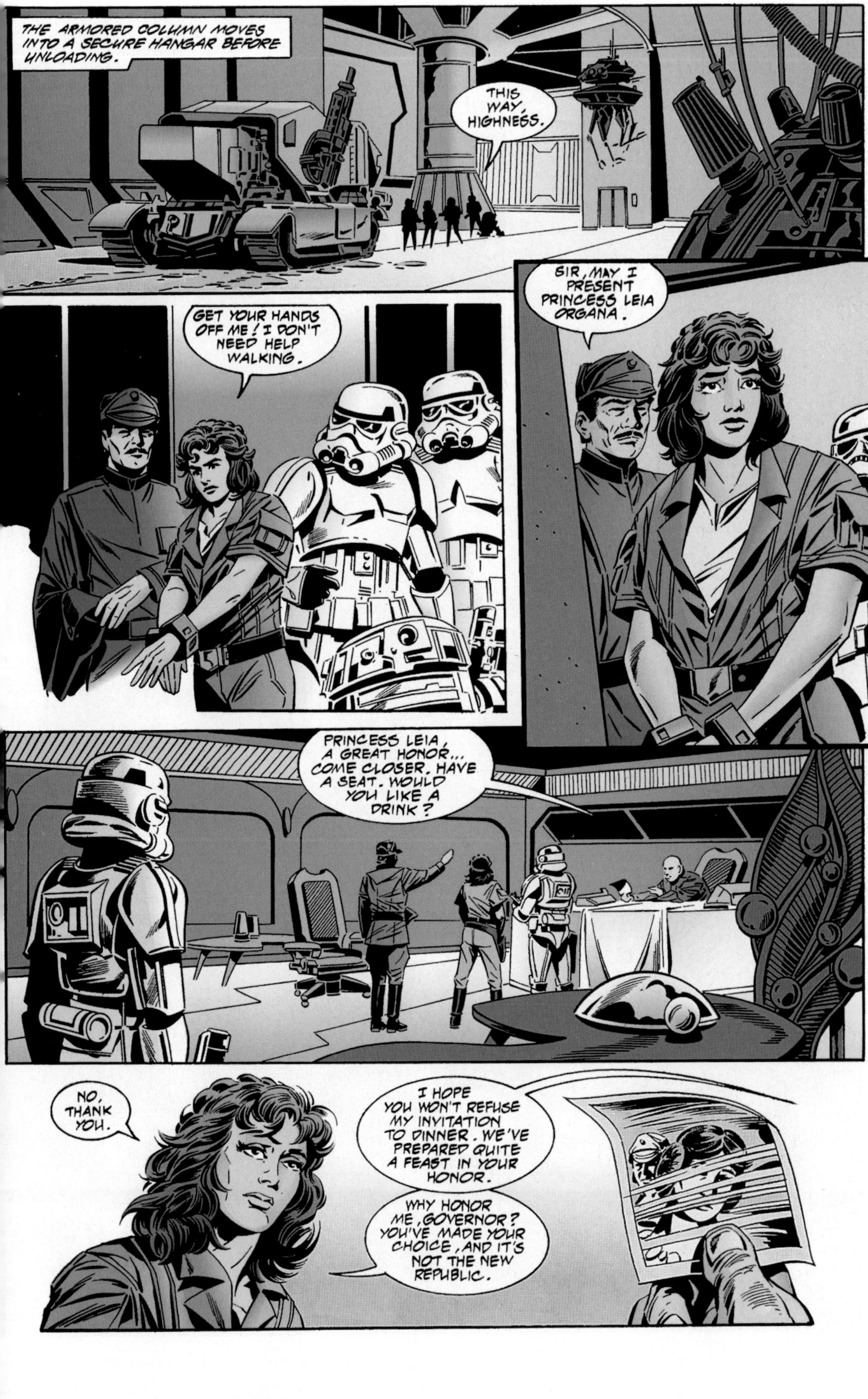
THE ARMORED COLUMN MOVES INTO A SECURE HANGAR BEFORE UNLOADING.
THIS WAY, HIGHNESS.
GET YOUR HANDS OFF ME! I DON'T NEED HELP WALKING.
SIR, MAY I PRESENT PRINCESS LEIA ORGANA.
PRINCESS LEIA, A GREAT HONOR... COME CLOSER. HAVE A SEAT. WOULD YOU LIKE A DRINK?
NO, THANK YOU.
I HOPE YOU WON'T REFUSE MY INVITATION TO DINNER. WE'VE PREPARED QUITE A FEAST IN YOUR HONOR.
WHY HONOR ME, GOVERNOR? YOU'VE MADE YOUR CHOICE, AND IT'S NOT THE NEW REPUBLIC.

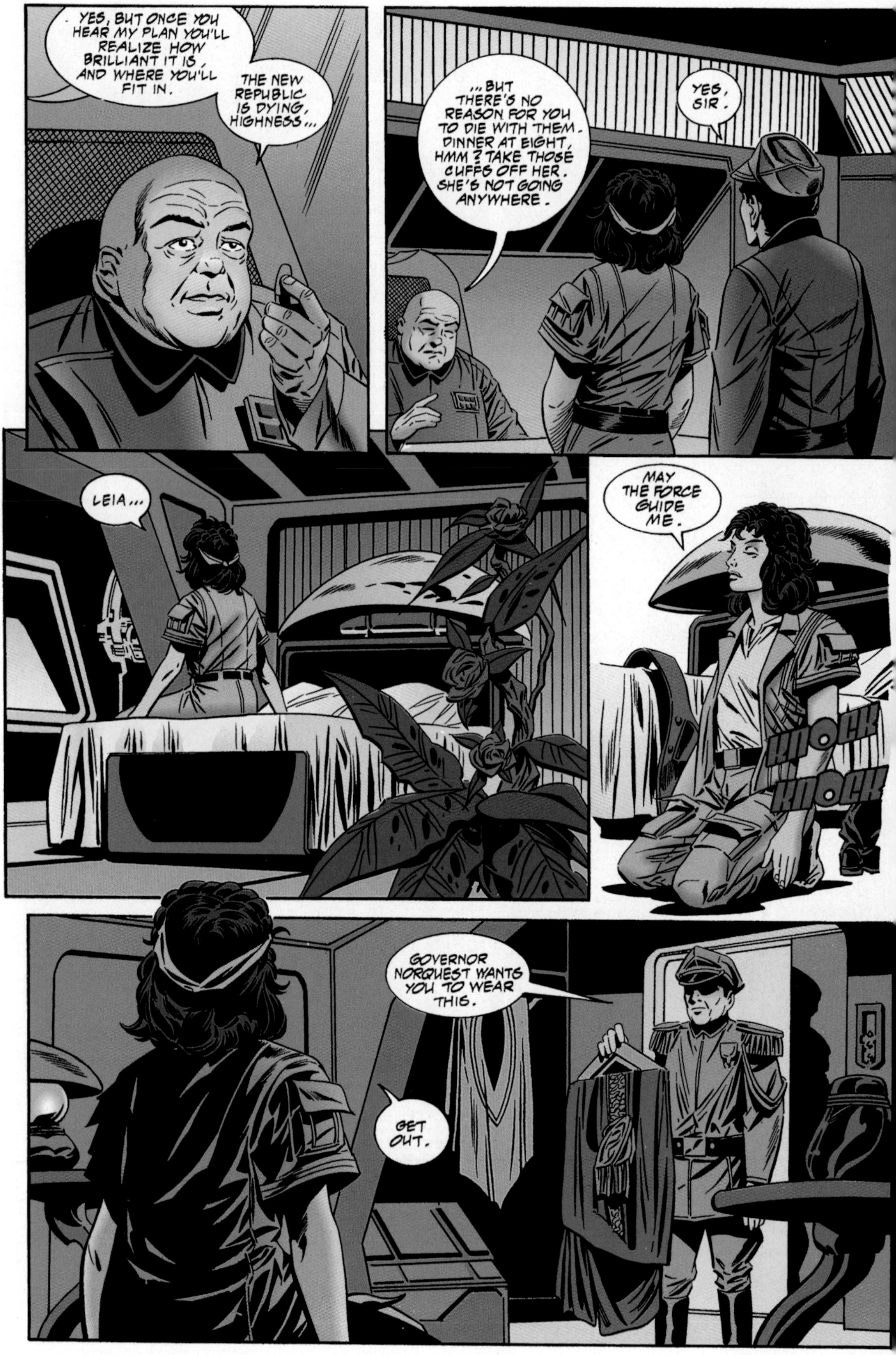
YES, BUT ONCE YOU HEAR MY PLAN YOU'LL REALIZE HOW BRILLIANT IT IS, AND WHERE YOU'LL FIT IN.
THE NEW REPUBLIC IS DYING, HIGHNESS...
...BUT THERE'S NO REASON FOR YOU TO DIE WITH THEM. DINNER AT EIGHT, HMM? TAKE THOSE CUFFS OFF HER. SHE'S NOT GOING ANYWHERE.
YES, SIR.
LEIA...
MAY THE FORCE GUIDE ME.
KNOCK
KNOCK
GOVERNOR NORQUEST WANTS YOU TO WEAR THIS.
GET OUT.

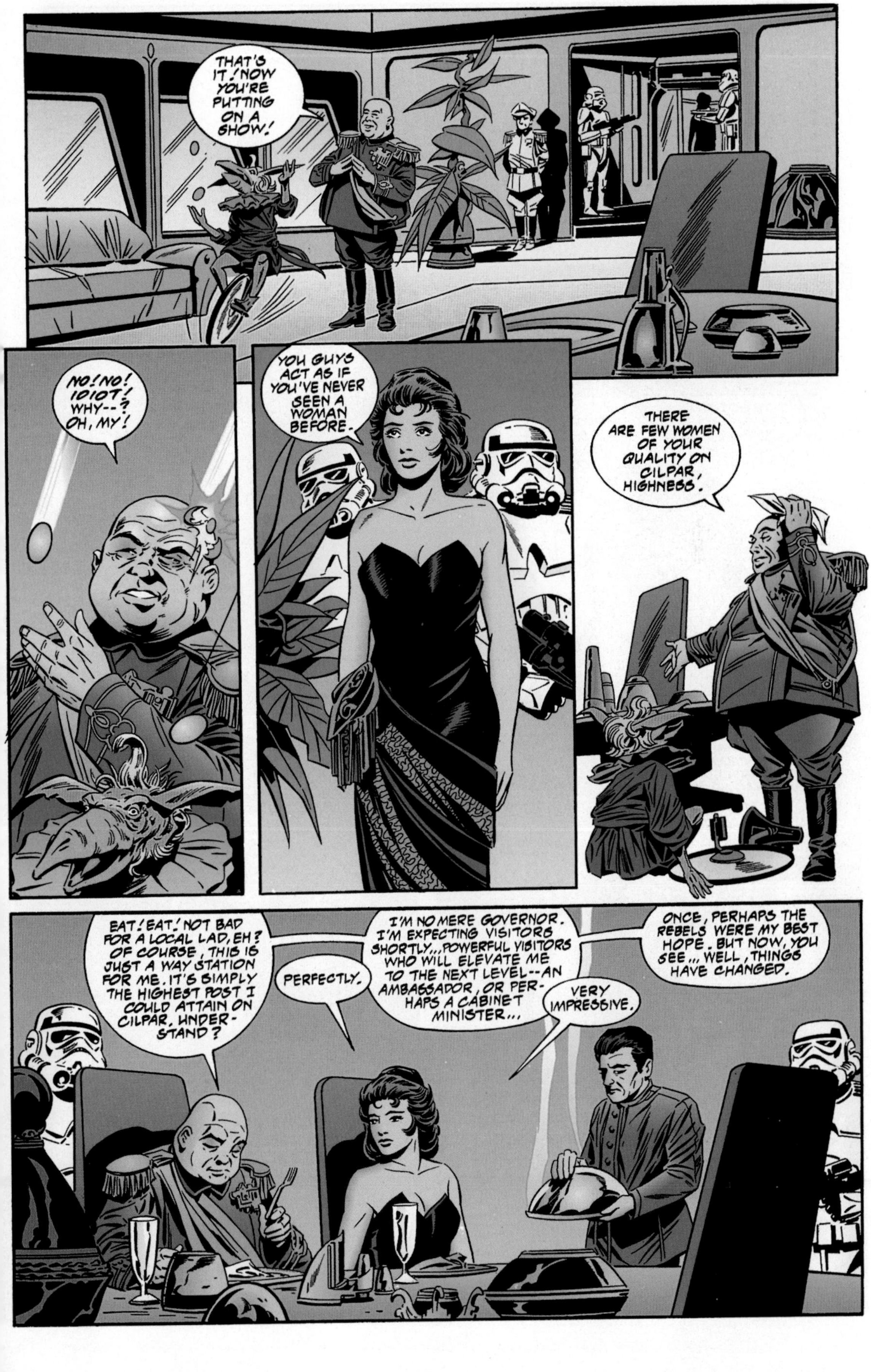
THAT'S IT! NOW YOU'RE PUTTING ON A SHOW!
NO! NO! IDIOT! WHY--? OH, MY!
YOU GUYS ACT AS IF YOU'VE NEVER SEEN A WOMAN BEFORE.
THERE ARE FEW WOMEN OF YOUR QUALITY ON CILPAR, HIGHNESS.
EAT! EAT! NOT BAD FOR A LOCAL LAD, EH? OF COURSE, THIS IS JUST A WAY STATION FOR ME. IT'S SIMPLY THE HIGHEST POST I COULD ATTAIN ON CILPAR, UNDERSTAND?
PERFECTLY.
I'M NO MERE GOVERNOR. I'M EXPECTING VISITORS SHORTLY... POWERFUL VISITORS WHO WILL ELEVATE ME TO THE NEXT LEVEL--AN AMBASSADOR, OR PERHAPS A CABINET MINISTER...
VERY IMPRESSIVE.
ONCE, PERHAPS THE REBELS WERE MY BEST HOPE. BUT NOW, YOU SEE... WELL, THINGS HAVE CHANGED.

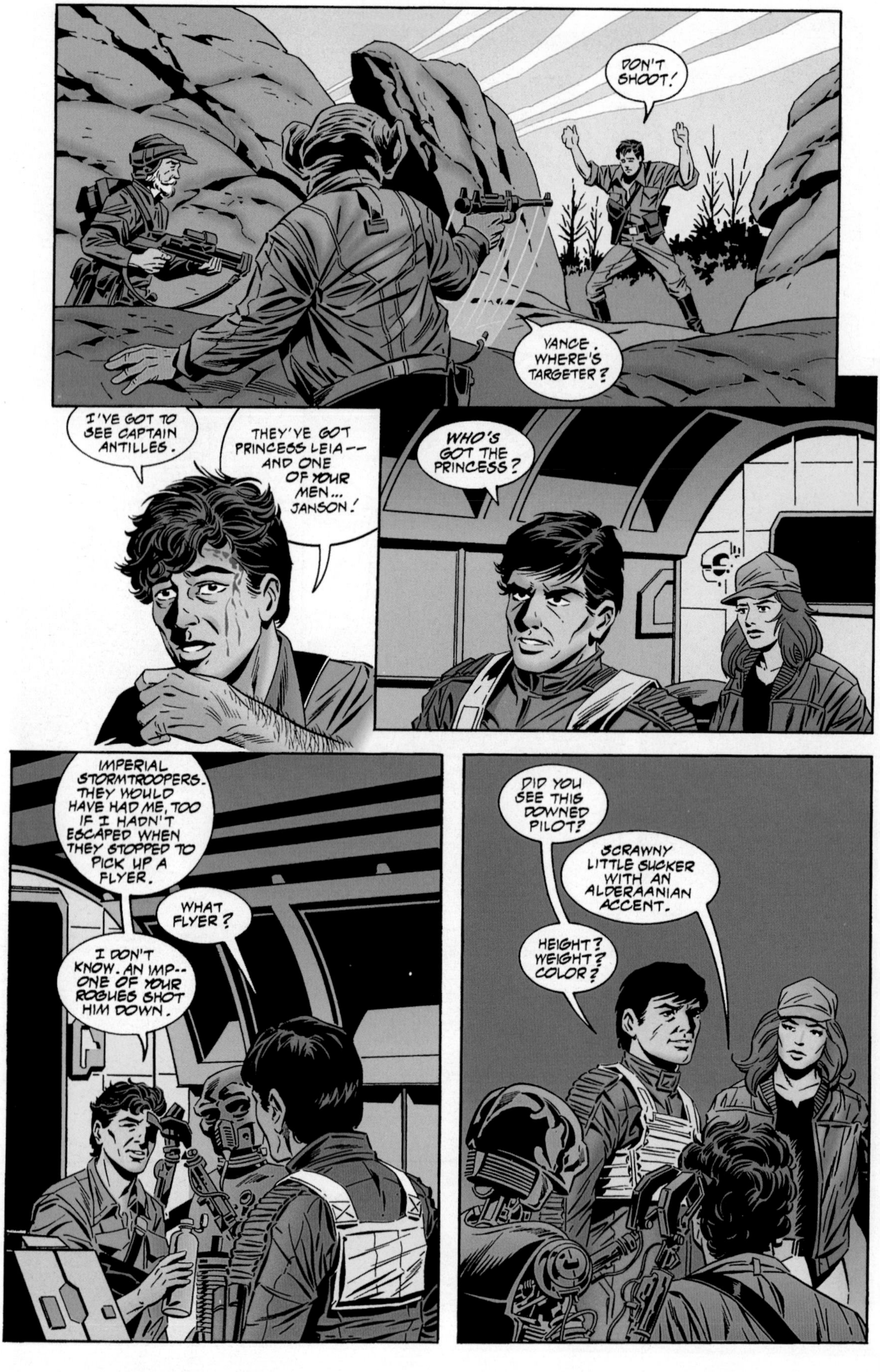
DON'T SHOOT!
YANCE. WHERE'S TARGETER?
I'VE GOT TO SEE CAPTAIN ANTILLES.
THEY'VE GOT PRINCESS LEIA-- AND ONE OF YOUR MEN... JANSON!
WHO'S GOT THE PRINCESS?
IMPERIAL STORMTROOPERS. THEY WOULD HAVE HAD ME, TOO IF I HADN'T ESCAPED WHEN THEY STOPPED TO PICK UP A FLYER.
WHAT FLYER?
I DON'T KNOW. AN IMP-- ONE OF YOUR ROGUES SHOT HIM DOWN.
DID YOU SEE THIS DOWNED PILOT?
SCRAWNY LITTLE SUCKER WITH AN ALDERAANIAN ACCENT.
HEIGHT? WEIGHT? COLOR?

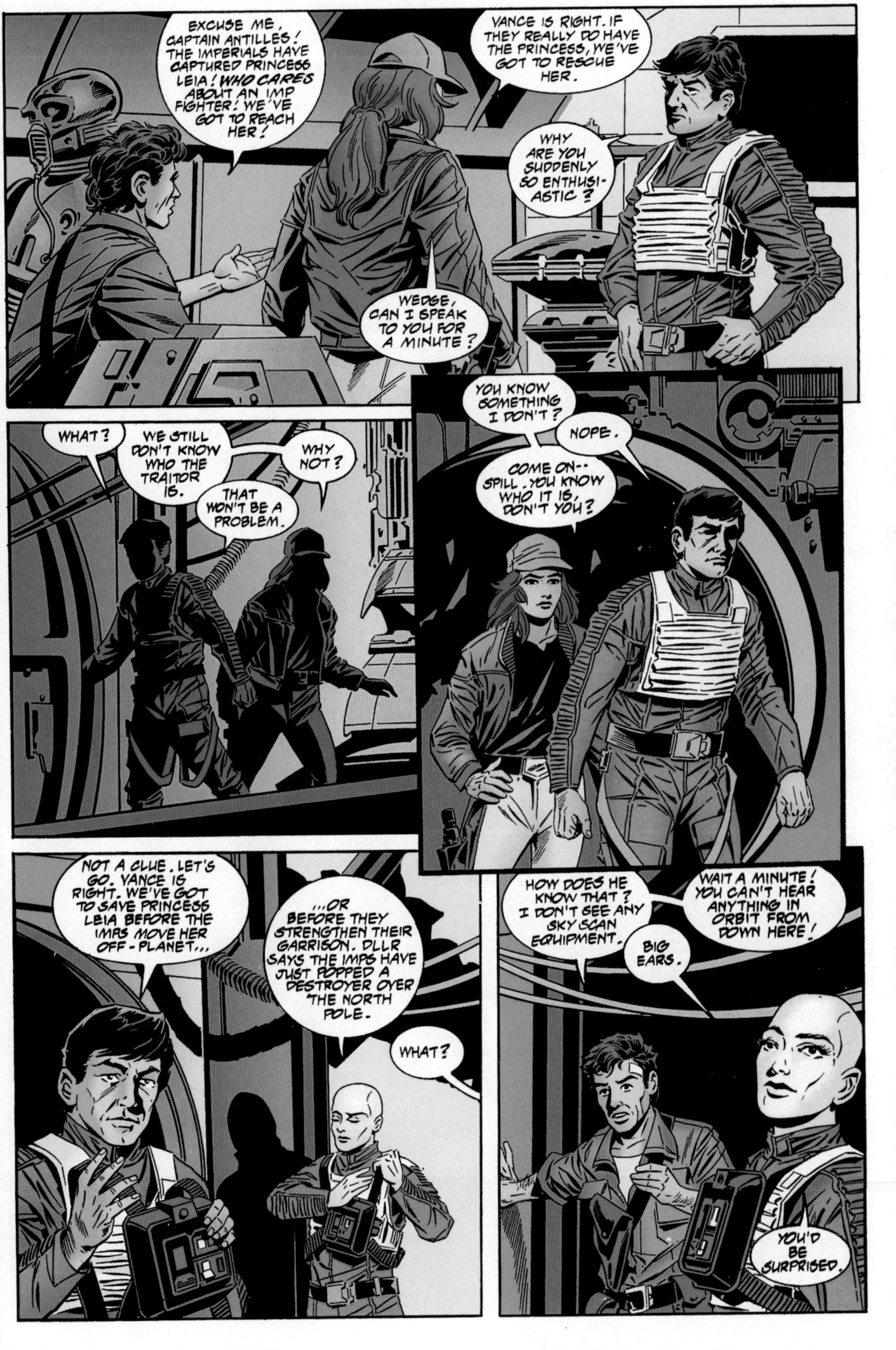
EXCUSE ME, CAPTAIN ANTILLES! THE IMPERIALS HAVE CAPTURED PRINCESS LEIA! WHO CARES ABOUT AN IMP FIGHTER! WE'VE GOT TO REACH HER!
VANCE IS RIGHT. IF THEY REALLY DO HAVE THE PRINCESS, WE'VE GOT TO RESCUE HER.
WHY ARE YOU SUDDENLY SO ENTHUSIASTIC?
WEDGE, CAN I SPEAK TO YOU FOR A MINUTE?
WHAT?
WE STILL DON'T KNOW WHO THE TRAITOR IS.
WHY NOT?
THAT WON'T BE A PROBLEM.
YOU KNOW SOMETHING I DON'T?
NOPE.
COME ON-- SPILL. YOU KNOW WHO IT IS, DON'T YOU?
NOT A CLUE. LET'S GO. VANCE IS RIGHT. WE'VE GOT TO SAVE PRINCESS LEIA BEFORE THE IMPS MOVE HER OFF-PLANET...
...OR BEFORE THEY STRENGTHEN THEIR GARRISON. DLLR SAYS THE IMPS HAVE JUST POPPED A DESTROYER OVER THE NORTH POLE.
WHAT?
HOW DOES HE KNOW THAT? I DON'T SEE ANY SKY SCAN EQUIPMENT.
BIG EARS.
WAIT A MINUTE! YOU CAN'T HEAR ANYTHING IN ORBIT FROM DOWN HERE!
YOU'D BE SURPRISED.

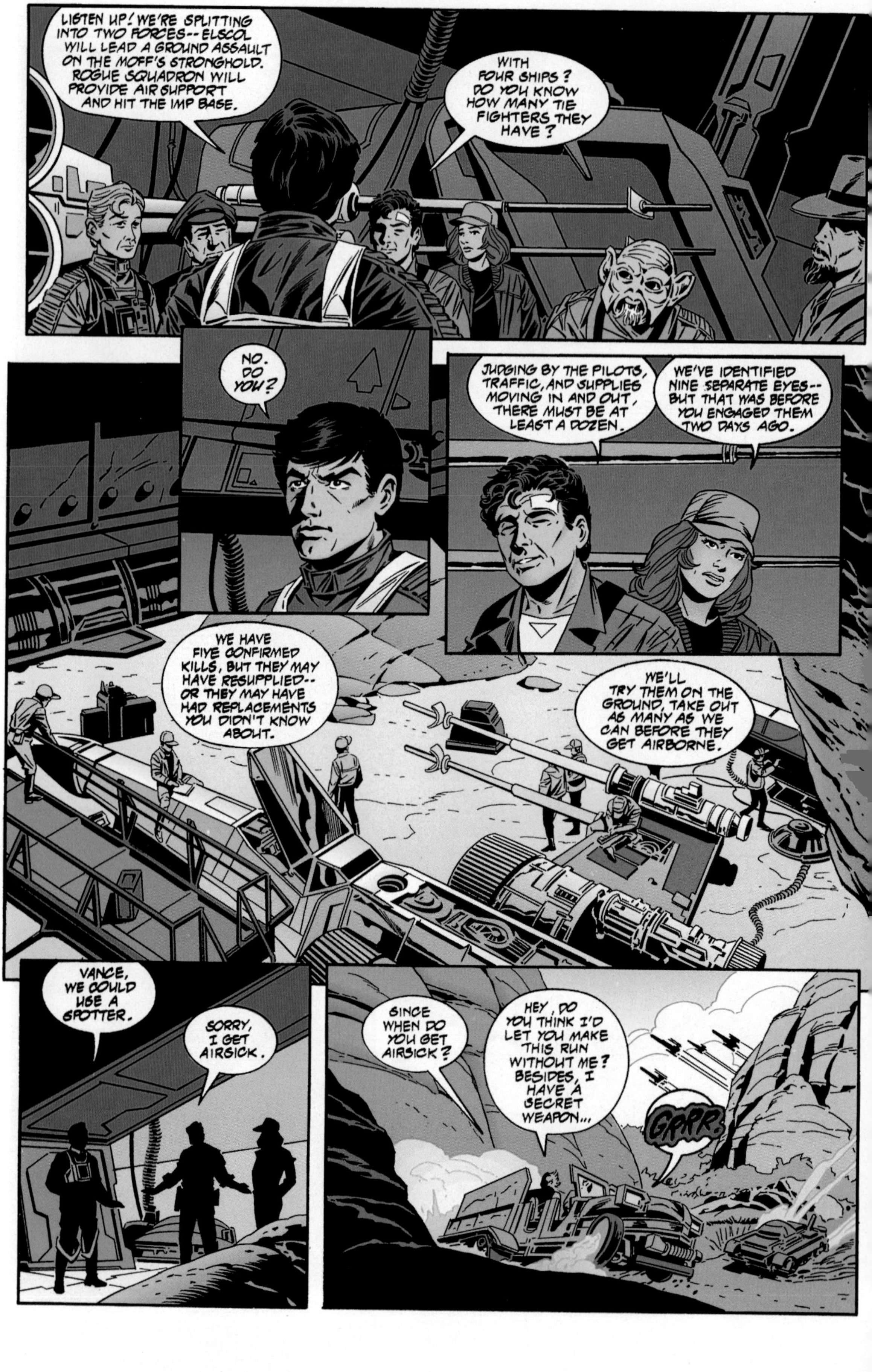
LISTEN UP! WE'RE SPLITTING INTO TWO FORCES-- ELSCOL WILL LEAD A GROUND ASSAULT ON THE MOFF'S STRONGHOLD. ROGUE SQUADRON WILL PROVIDE AIR SUPPORT AND HIT THE IMP BASE.
WITH FOUR SHIPS? DO YOU KNOW HOW MANY TIE FIGHTERS THEY HAVE?
NO. DO YOU?
JUDGING BY THE PILOTS, TRAFFIC, AND SUPPLIES MOVING IN AND OUT, THERE MUST BE AT LEAST A DOZEN.
WE'VE IDENTIFIED NINE SEPARATE EYES-- BUT THAT WAS BEFORE YOU ENGAGED THEM TWO DAYS AGO.
WE HAVE FIVE CONFIRMED KILLS, BUT THEY MAY HAVE RESUPPLIED-- OR THEY MAY HAVE HAD REPLACEMENTS YOU DIDN'T KNOW ABOUT.
WE'LL TRY THEM ON THE GROUND, TAKE OUT AS MANY AS WE CAN BEFORE THEY GET AIRBORNE.
VANCE, WE COULD USE A SPOTTER.
SORRY, I GET AIRSICK.
SINCE WHEN DO YOU GET AIRSICK?
HEY, DO YOU THINK I'D LET YOU MAKE THIS RUN WITHOUT ME? BESIDES, I HAVE A SECRET WEAPON...
GRRR.

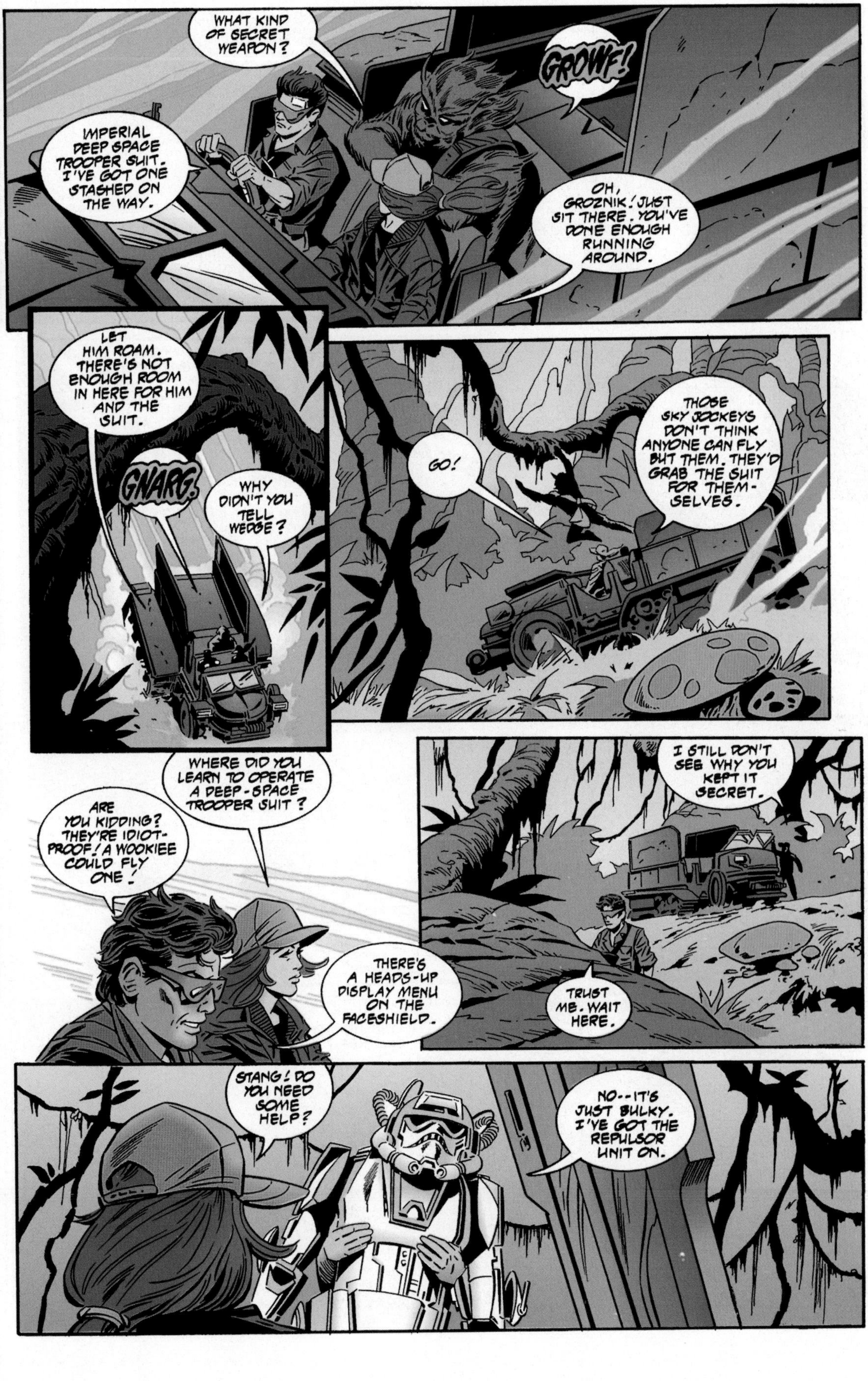
WHAT KIND OF SECRET WEAPON?
GROWF!
IMPERIAL DEEP SPACE TROOPER SUIT. I'VE GOT ONE STASHED ON THE WAY.
OH, GROZNIK! JUST SIT THERE. YOU'VE DONE ENOUGH RUNNING AROUND.
LET HIM ROAM. THERE'S NOT ENOUGH ROOM IN HERE FOR HIM AND THE SUIT.
GNARG.
WHY DIDN'T YOU TELL WEDGE?
GO!
THOSE SKY JOCKEYS DON'T THINK ANYONE CAN FLY BUT THEM. THEY'D GRAB THE SUIT FOR THEM-SELVES.
I STILL DON'T SEE WHY YOU KEPT IT SECRET.
TRUST ME. WAIT HERE.
WHERE DID YOU LEARN TO OPERATE A DEEP-SPACE TROOPER SUIT?
ARE YOU KIDDING? THEY'RE IDIOT-PROOF! A WOOKIEE COULD FLY ONE!
THERE'S A HEADS-UP DISPLAY MENU ON THE FACESHIELD.
STANG! DO YOU NEED SOME HELP?
NO--IT'S JUST BULKY. I'VE GOT THE REPULSOR UNIT ON.

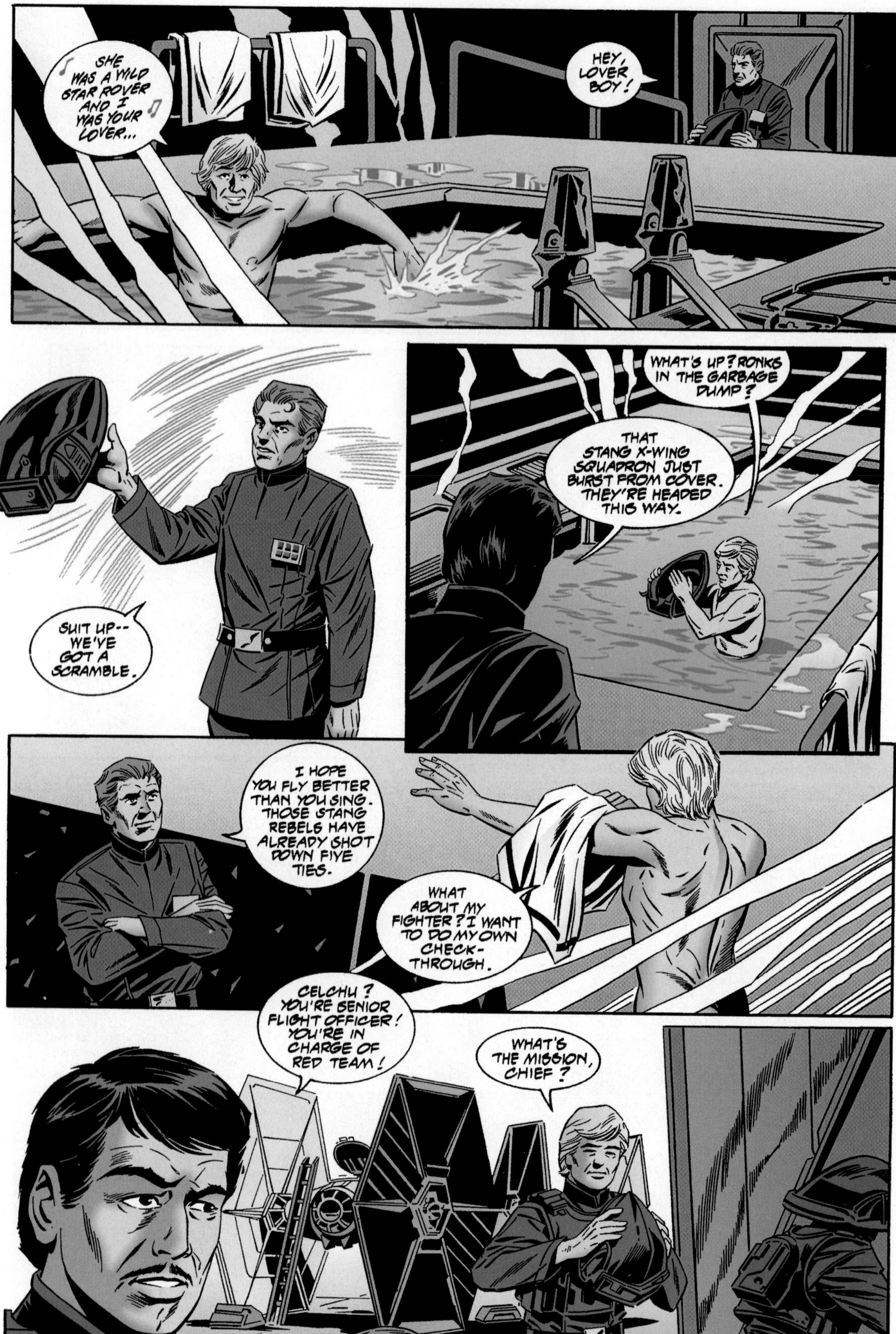
SHE WAS A WILD STAR ROVER AND I WAS YOUR LOVER...
HEY, LOVER BOY!
WHAT'S UP? RONKS IN THE GARBAGE DUMP?
THAT STANG X-WING SQUADRON JUST BURST FROM COVER. THEY'RE HEADED THIS WAY.
SUIT UP-- WE'VE GOT A SCRAMBLE.
I HOPE YOU FLY BETTER THAN YOU SING. THOSE STANG REBELS HAVE ALREADY SHOT DOWN FIVE TIES.
WHAT ABOUT MY FIGHTER? I WANT TO DO MY OWN CHECK-THROUGH.
CELCHU? YOU'RE SENIOR FLIGHT OFFICER! YOU'RE IN CHARGE OF RED TEAM!
WHAT'S THE MISSION, CHIEF?

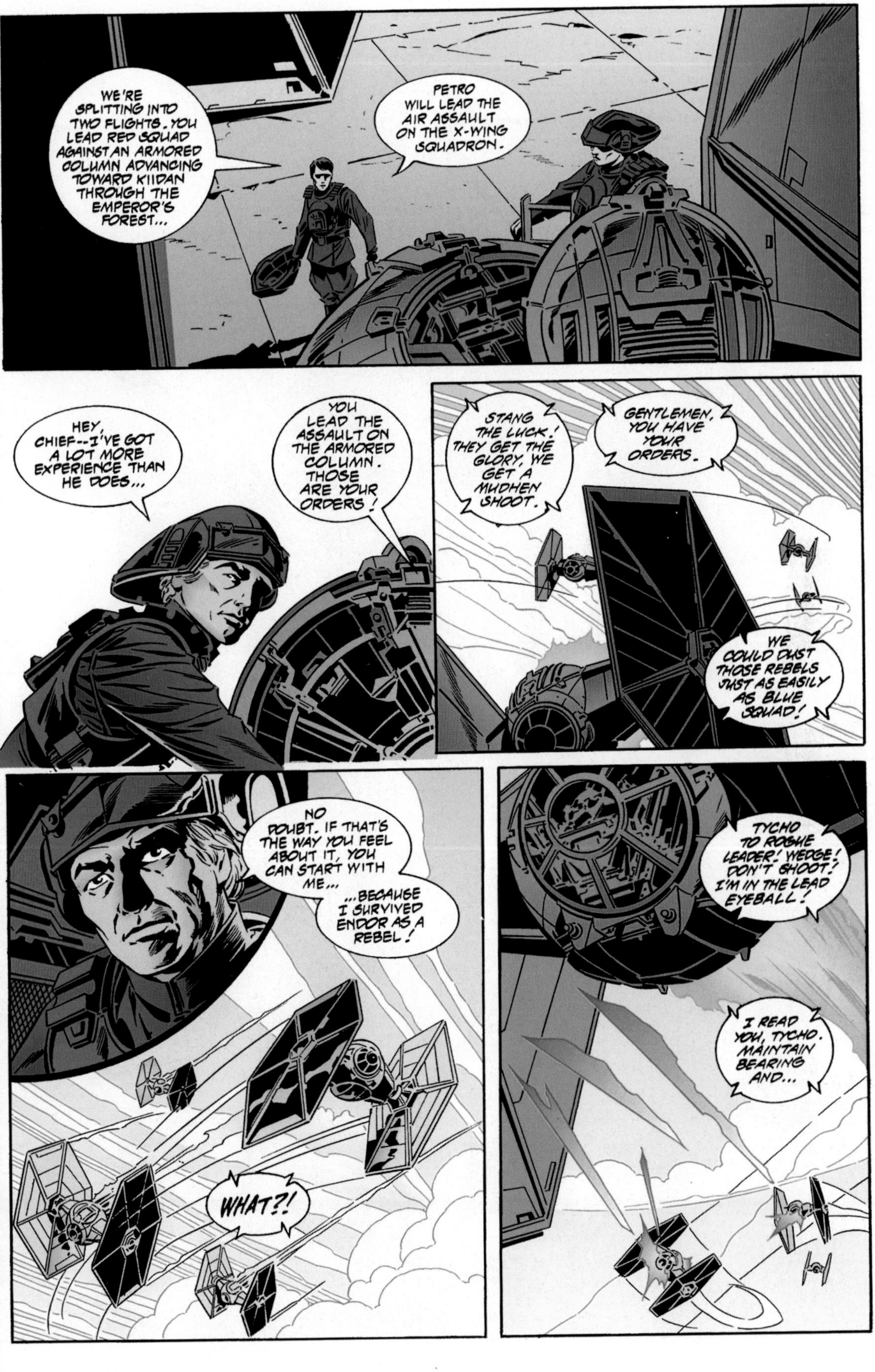
WE'RE SPLITTING INTO TWO FLIGHTS. YOU LEAD RED SQUAD AGAINST AN ARMORED COLUMN ADVANCING TOWARD KIIDAN THROUGH THE EMPEROR'S FOREST...
PETRO WILL LEAD THE AIR ASSAULT ON THE X-WING SQUADRON.
HEY, CHIEF--I'VE GOT A LOT MORE EXPERIENCE THAN HE DOES...
YOU LEAD THE ASSAULT ON THE ARMORED COLUMN. THOSE ARE YOUR ORDERS!
STANG THE LUCK! THEY GET THE GLORY, WE GET A MUDHEN SHOOT.
GENTLEMEN, YOU HAVE YOUR ORDERS.
WE COULD DUST THOSE REBELS JUST AS EASILY AS BLUE SQUAD!
NO DOUBT. IF THAT'S THE WAY YOU FEEL ABOUT IT, YOU CAN START WITH ME...
...BECAUSE I SURVIVED ENDOR AS A REBEL!
WHAT?!
TYCHO TO ROGUE LEADER! WEDGE! DON'T SHOOT! I'M IN THE LEAD EYEBALL!
I READ YOU, TYCHO. MAINTAIN BEARING AND...

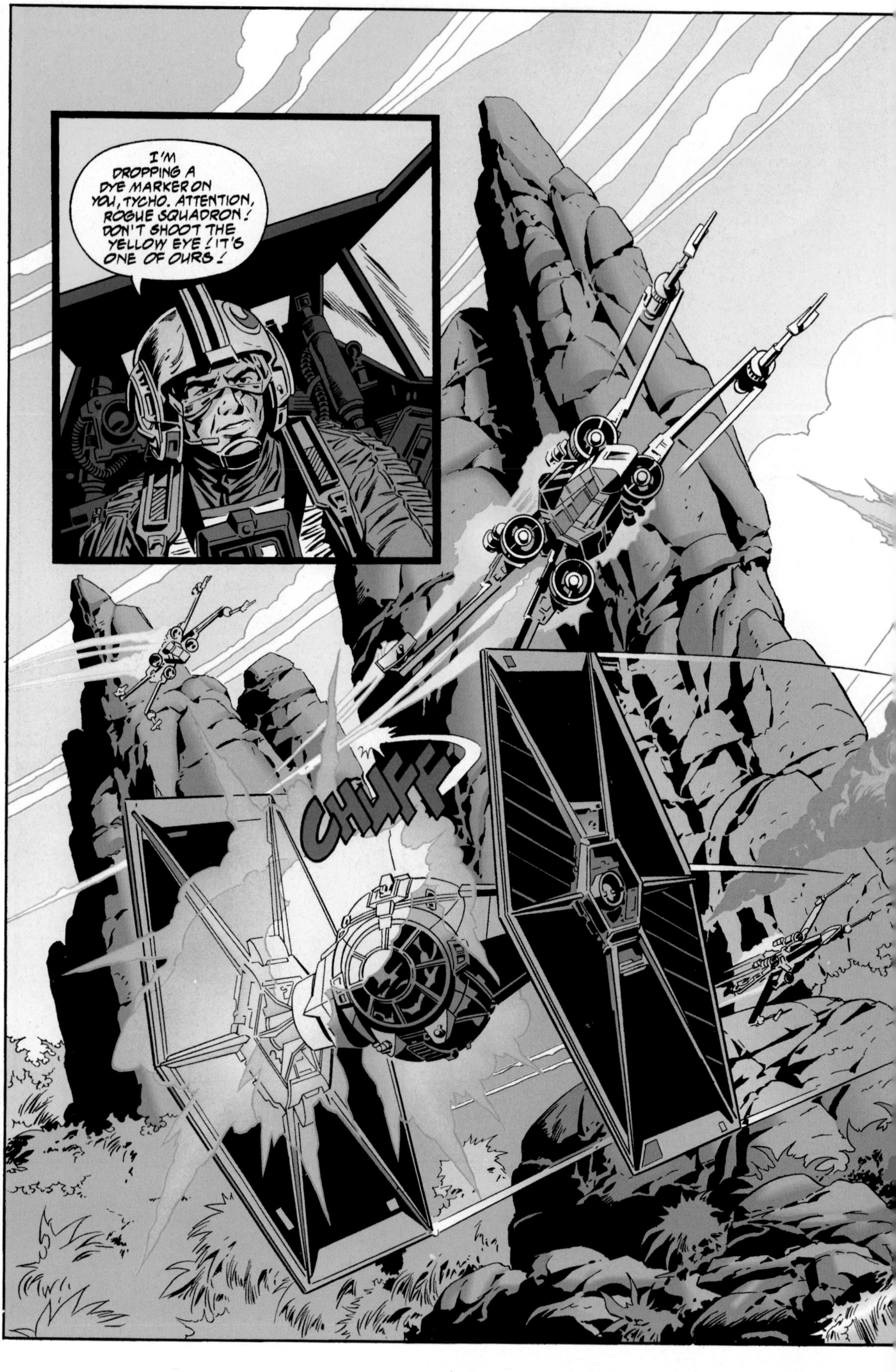
I'M DROPPING A DYE MARKER ON YOU, TYCHO. ATTENTION, ROGUE SQUADRON! DON'T SHOOT THE YELLOW EYE! IT'S ONE OF OURS!
CHUFF

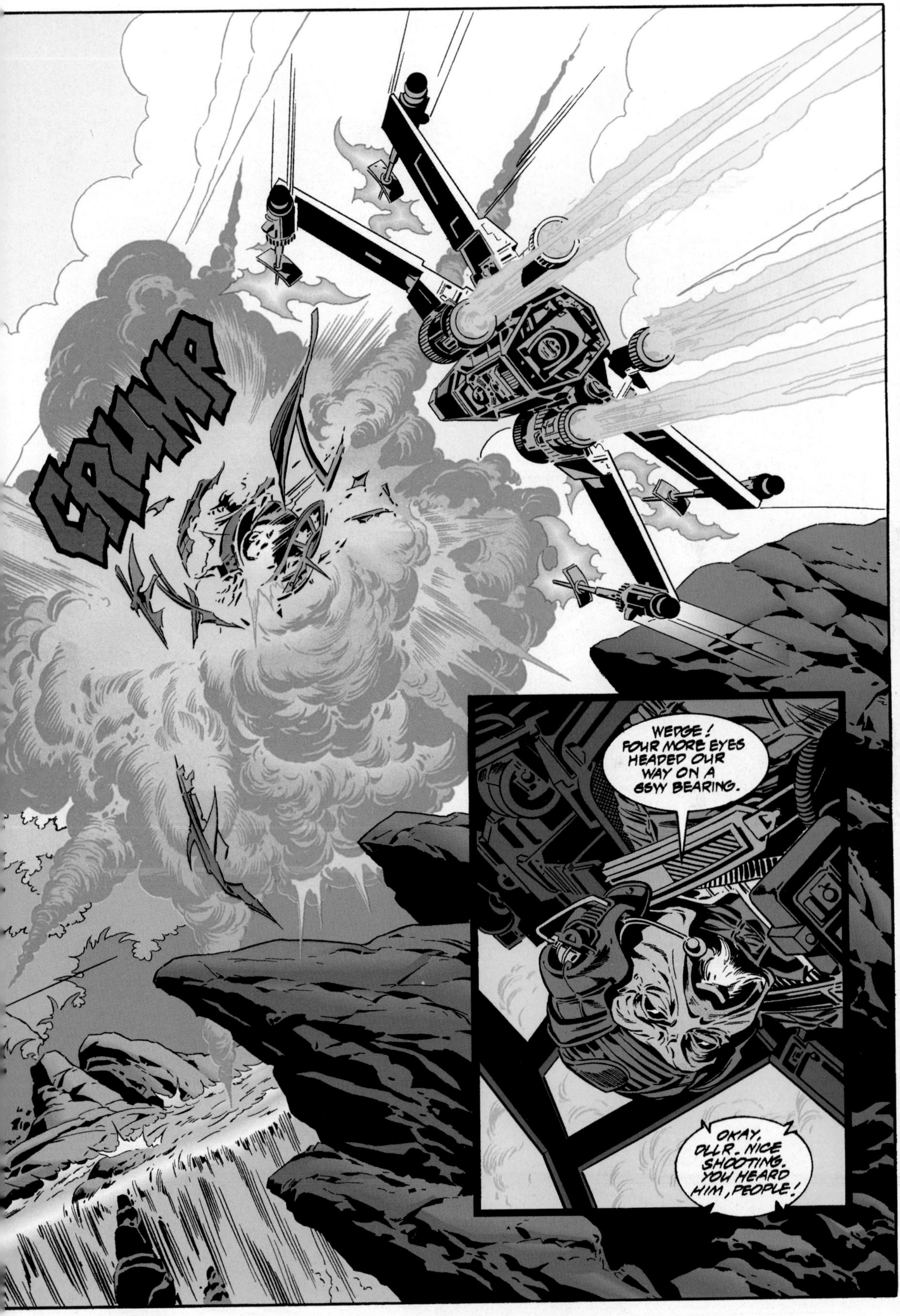
CRUMP
WEDGE! FOUR MORE EYES HEADED OUR WAY ON A 6SYY BEARING.
OKAY, OLLR. NICE SHOOTING. YOU HEARD HIM, PEOPLE!

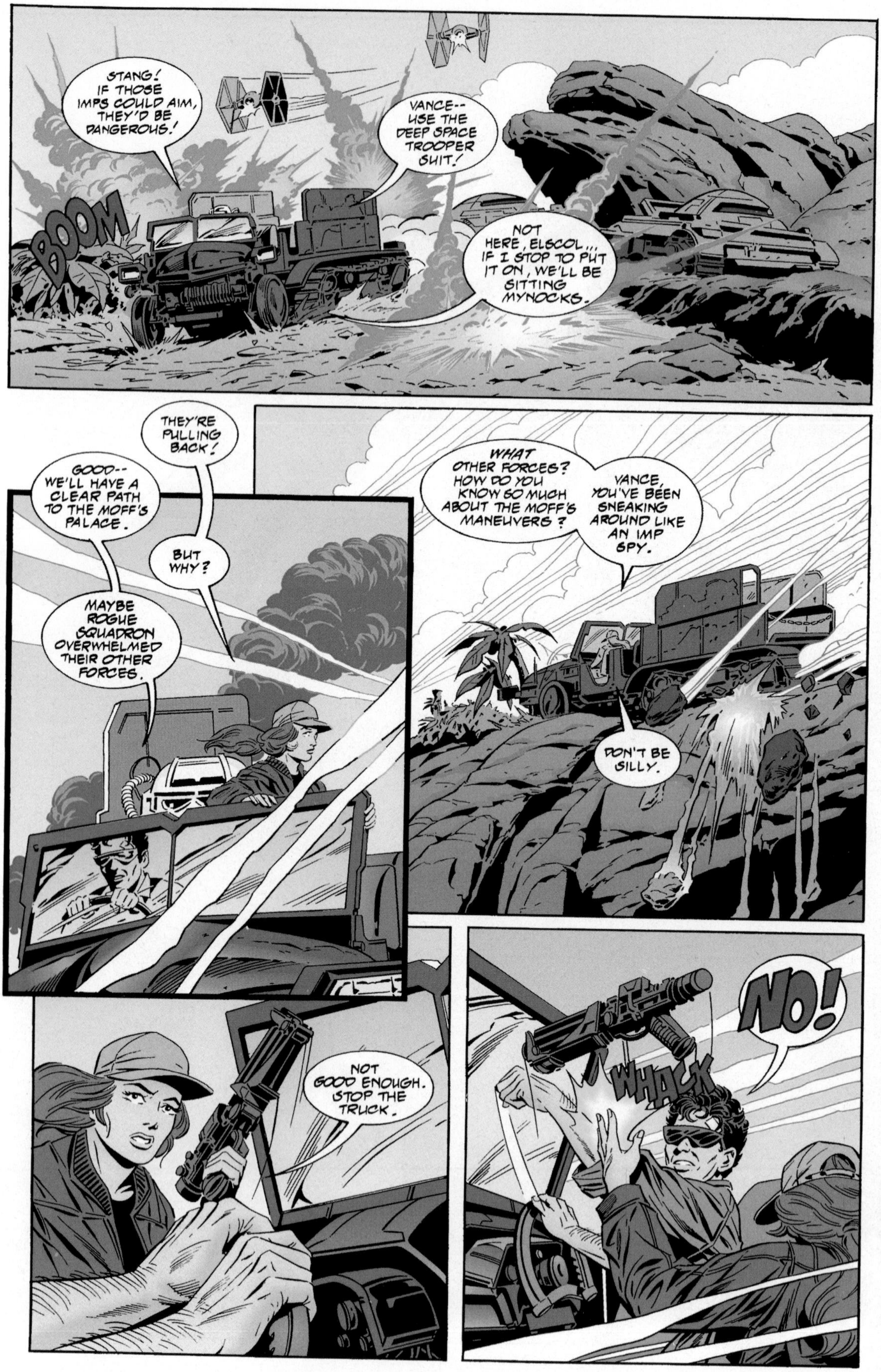
STANG! IF THOSE IMPS COULD AIM, THEY'D BE DANGEROUS!
VANCE-- USE THE DEEP SPACE TROOPER SUIT!
BOOM
NOT HERE, ELSCOL... IF I STOP TO PUT IT ON, WE'LL BE SITTING MYNOCKS.
THEY'RE PULLING BACK!
GOOD-- WE'LL HAVE A CLEAR PATH TO THE MOFF'S PALACE.
BUT WHY?
MAYBE ROGUE SQUADRON OVERWHELMED THEIR OTHER FORCES.
WHAT OTHER FORCES? HOW DO YOU KNOW SO MUCH ABOUT THE MOFF'S MANEUVERS?
VANCE, YOU'VE BEEN SNEAKING AROUND LIKE AN IMP SPY.
DON'T BE SILLY.
NOT GOOD ENOUGH. STOP THE TRUCK.
NO!
WHACK

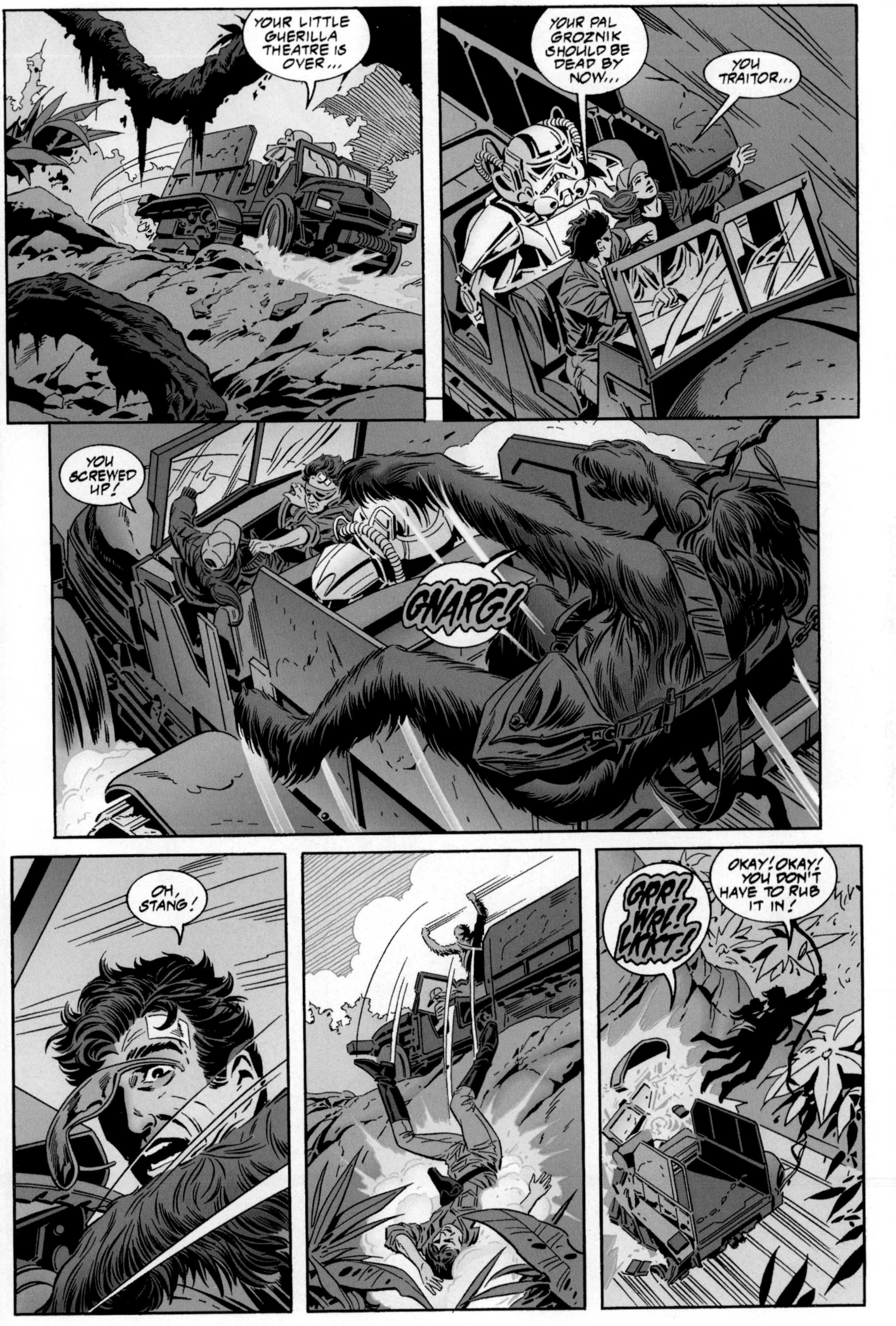
YOUR LITTLE GUERILLA THEATRE IS OVER...
YOUR PAL GROZNIK SHOULD BE DEAD BY NOW...
YOU TRAITOR...
YOU SCREWED UP!
GNARG!
OH, STANG!
GRR! WRL! LKKT!
OKAY! OKAY! YOU DON'T HAVE TO RUB IT IN!

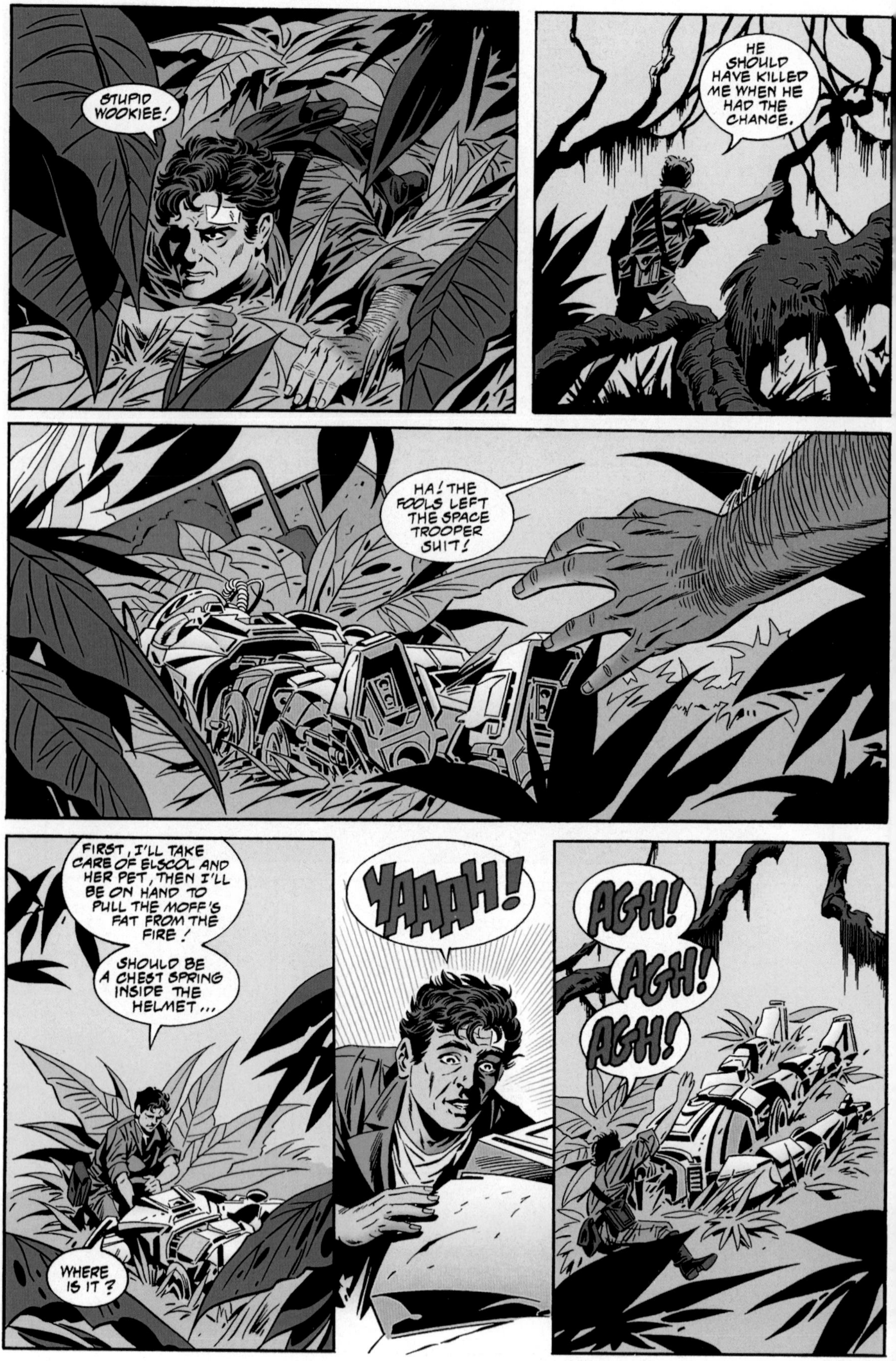
STUPID WOOKIEE!
HE SHOULD HAVE KILLED ME WHEN HE HAD THE CHANCE.
HA! THE FOOLS LEFT THE SPACE TROOPER SUIT!
FIRST, I'LL TAKE CARE OF ELSCOL AND HER PET, THEN I'LL BE ON HAND TO PULL THE MOFF'S FAT FROM THE FIRE!
SHOULD BE A CHEST SPRING INSIDE THE HELMET...
WHERE IS IT?
YAAAH!
AGH!
AGH!
AGH!

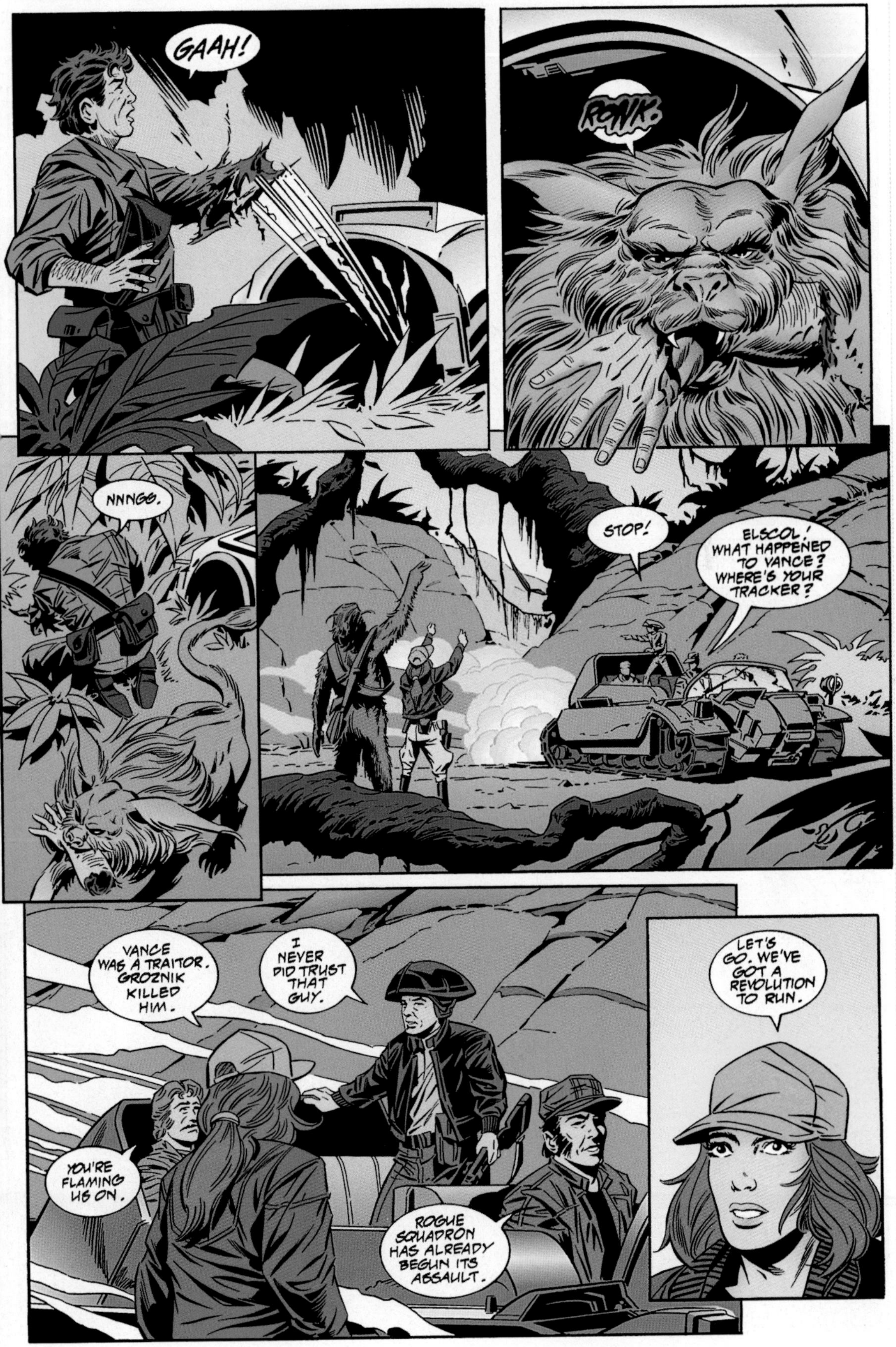
GAAH!
RONK.
NNNGG.
STOP!
ELSCOL! WHAT HAPPENED TO VANCE? WHERE'S YOUR TRACKER?
VANCE WAS A TRAITOR. GROZNIK KILLED HIM.
I NEVER DID TRUST THAT GUY.
YOU'RE FLAMING US ON.
ROGUE SQUADRON HAS ALREADY BEGUN ITS ASSAULT.
LET'S GO. WE'VE GOT A REVOLUTION TO RUN.

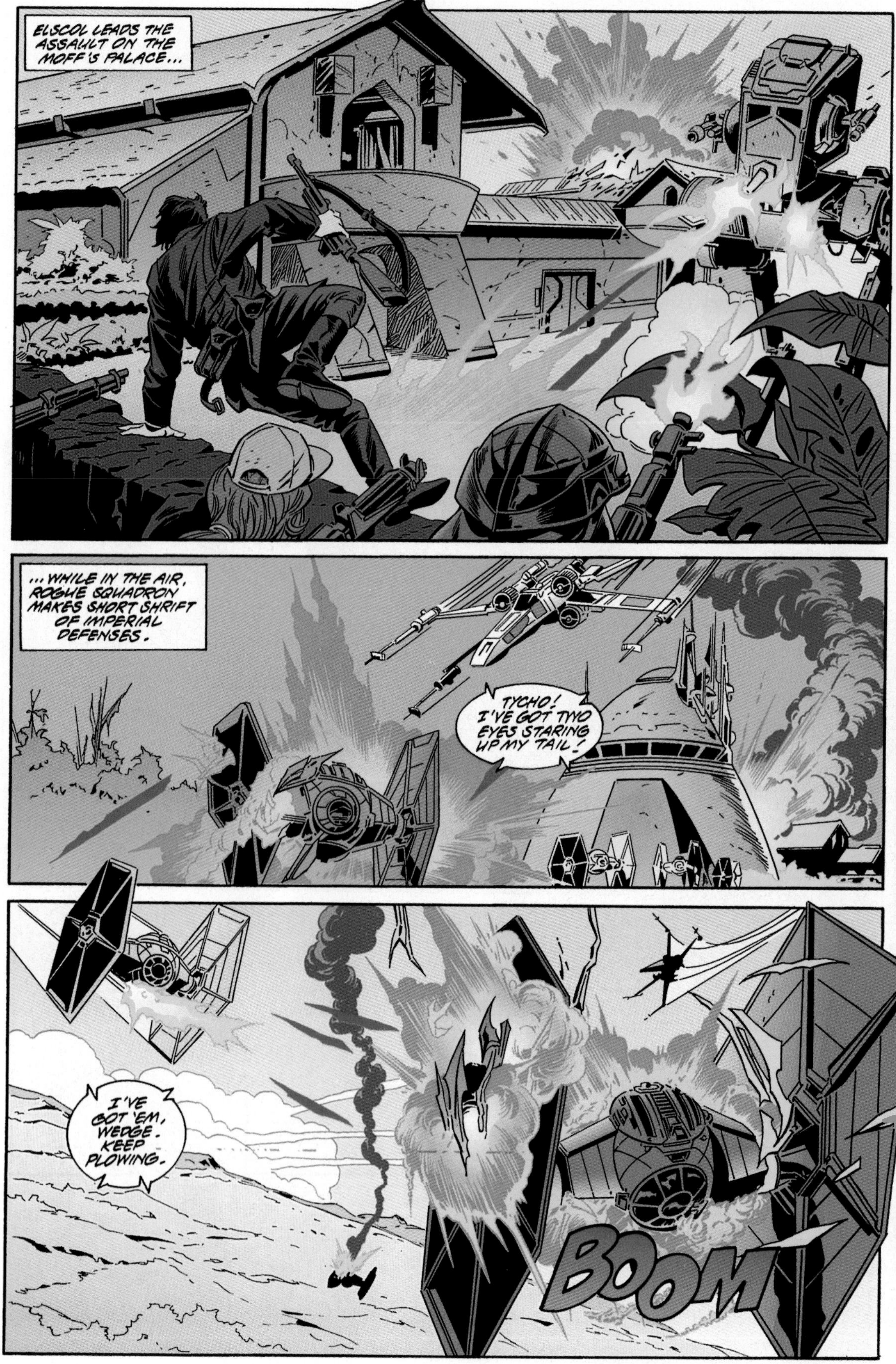
ELSCOL LEADS THE ASSAULT ON THE MOFF'S PALACE...
...WHILE IN THE AIR, ROGUE SQUADRON MAKES SHORT SHRIFT OF IMPERIAL DEFENSES.
TYCHO! I'VE GOT TWO EYES STARING UP MY TAIL!
I'VE GOT 'EM, WEDGE. KEEP PLOWING.
BOOM

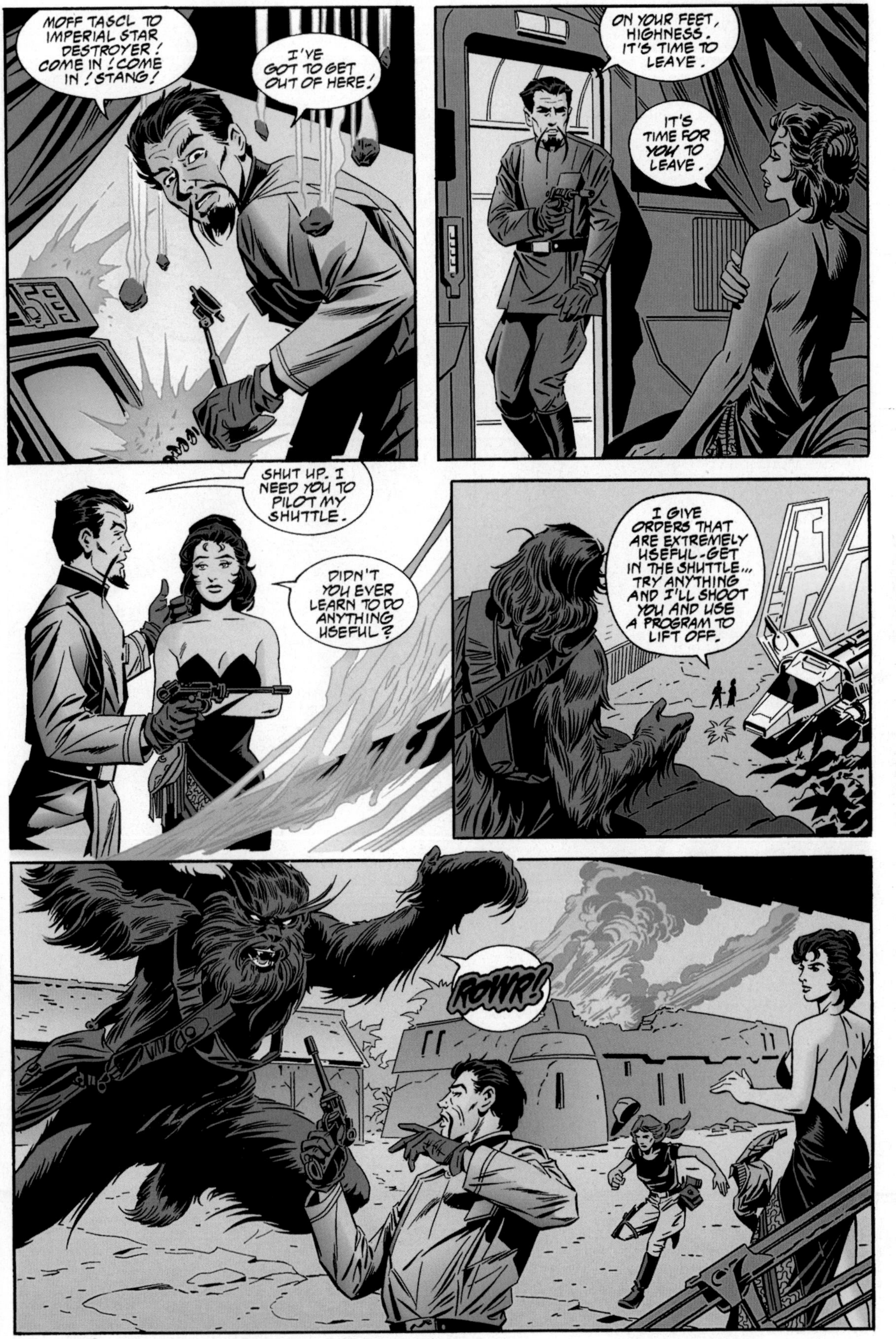
MOFF TASCL TO IMPERIAL STAR DESTROYER! COME IN! COME IN! STANG!
I'VE GOT TO GET OUT OF HERE!
ON YOUR FEET, HIGHNESS. IT'S TIME TO LEAVE.
IT'S TIME FOR YOU TO LEAVE.
SHUT UP. I NEED YOU TO PILOT MY SHUTTLE.
DIDN'T YOU EVER LEARN TO DO ANYTHING USEFUL?
I GIVE ORDERS THAT ARE EXTREMELY USEFUL-GET IN THE SHUTTLE... TRY ANYTHING AND I'LL SHOOT YOU AND USE A PROGRAM TO LIFT OFF.
ROWR!

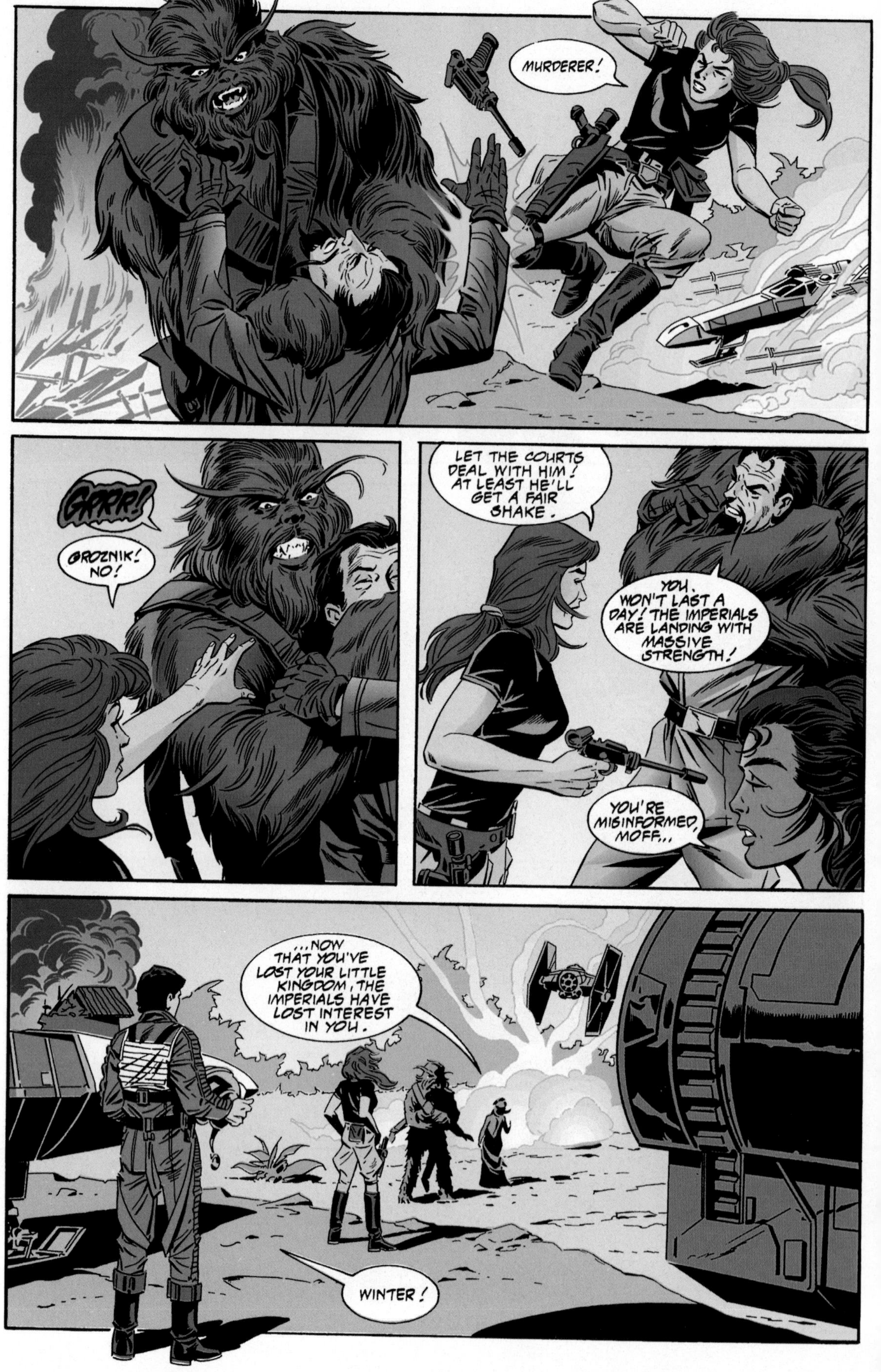
MURDERER!
GRRR!
GROZNIK! NO!
LET THE COURTS DEAL WITH HIM! AT LEAST HE'LL GET A FAIR SHAKE.
YOU. WON'T LAST A DAY! THE IMPERIALS ARE LANDING WITH MASSIVE STRENGTH!
YOU'RE MISINFORMED, MOFF...
...NOW THAT YOU'VE LOST YOUR LITTLE KINGDOM, THE IMPERIALS HAVE LOST INTEREST IN YOU.
WINTER!

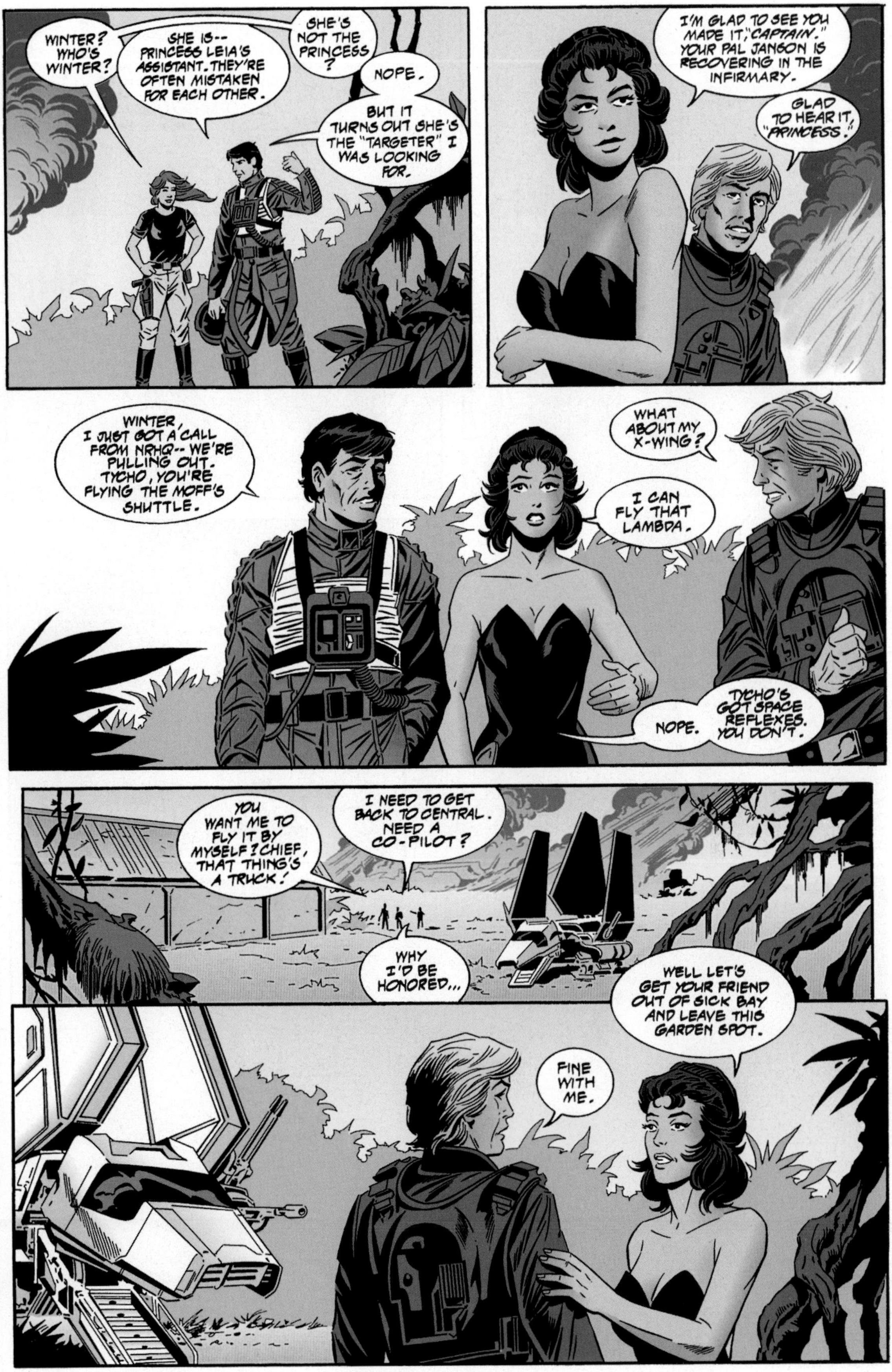

WINTER? WHO'S WINTER?
SHE IS-- PRINCESS LEIA'S ASSISTANT. THEY'RE OFTEN MISTAKEN FOR EACH OTHER.
SHE'S NOT THE PRINCESS?
NOPE.
BUT IT TURNS OUT SHE'S THE "TARGETER" I WAS LOOKING FOR.
I'M GLAD TO SEE YOU MADE IT, "CAPTAIN." YOUR PAL JANSON IS RECOVERING IN THE INFIRMARY.
GLAD TO HEAR IT, "PRINCESS."
WINTER, I JUST GOT A CALL FROM NRHQ-- WE'RE PULLING OUT. TYCHO, YOU'RE FLYING THE MOFF'S SHUTTLE.
WHAT ABOUT MY X-WING?
I CAN FLY THAT LAMBDA.
NOPE.
TYCHO'S GOT SPACE REFLEXES. YOU DON'T.
YOU WANT ME TO FLY IT BY MYSELF? CHIEF, THAT THING'S A TRUCK!
I NEED TO GET BACK TO CENTRAL. NEED A CO-PILOT?
WHY I'D BE HONORED...
WELL LET'S GET YOUR FRIEND OUT OF SICK BAY AND LEAVE THIS GARDEN SPOT.
FINE WITH ME.

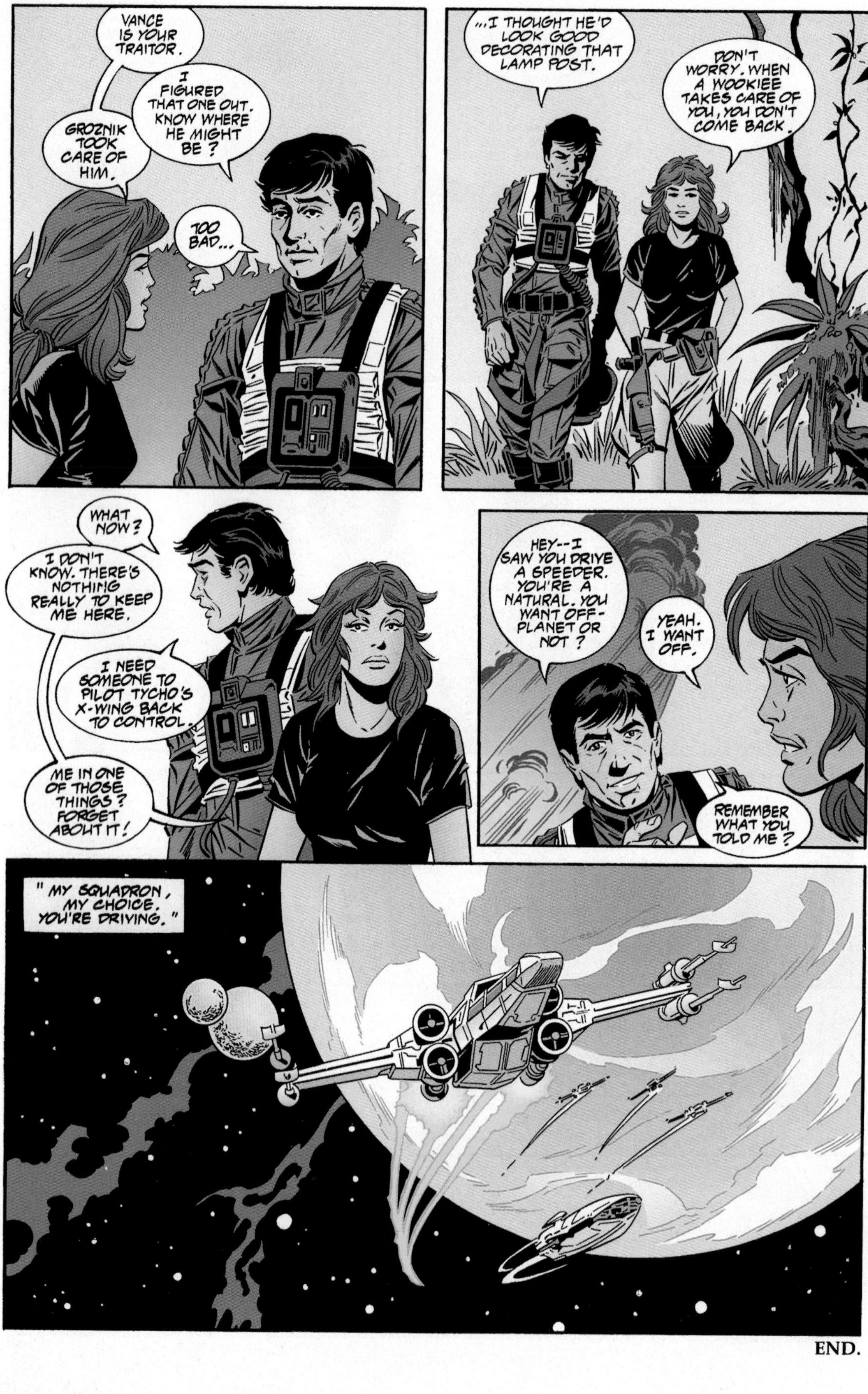
VANCE IS YOUR TRAITOR.
GROZNIK TOOK CARE OF HIM.
I FIGURED THAT ONE OUT. KNOW WHERE HE MIGHT BE?
TOO BAD...
...I THOUGHT HE'D LOOK GOOD DECORATING THAT LAMP POST.
DON'T WORRY. WHEN A WOOKIEE TAKES CARE OF YOU, YOU DON'T COME BACK.
WHAT NOW?
I DON'T KNOW. THERE'S NOTHING REALLY TO KEEP ME HERE.
I NEED SOMEONE TO PILOT TYCHO'S X-WING BACK TO CONTROL.
ME IN ONE OF THOSE THINGS? FORGET ABOUT IT!
HEY--I SAW YOU DRIVE A SPEEDER. YOU'RE A NATURAL. YOU WANT OFF-PLANET OR NOT?
YEAH. I WANT OFF.
REMEMBER WHAT YOU TOLD ME?
"MY SQUADRON, MY CHOICE. YOU'RE DRIVING."

END.

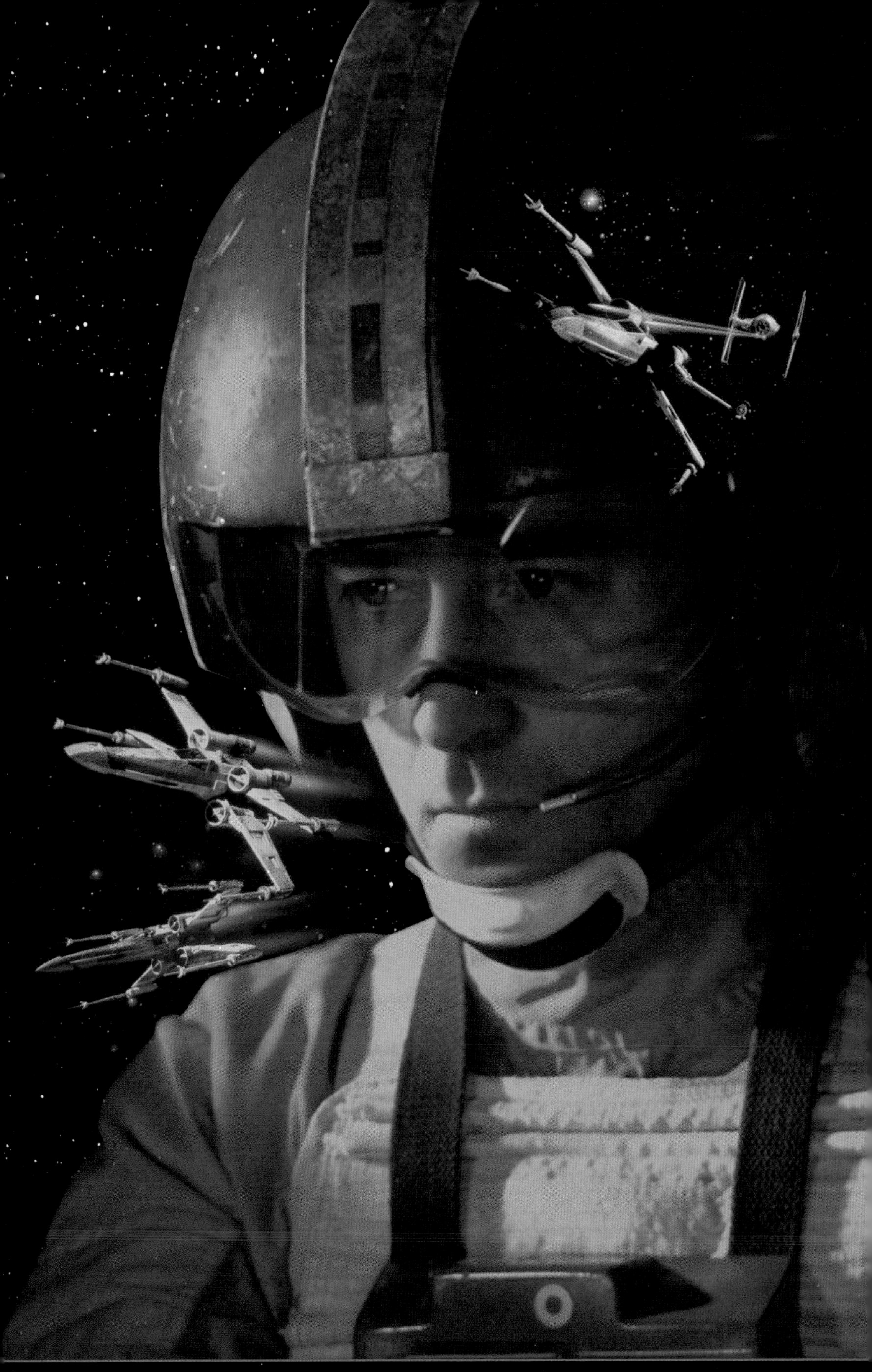

*STAR WARS TALES #23* VARIANT PHOTO COVER BY RICHARD E. JONES

**STAR WARS: X-WING ROGUE SQUADRON #5 — "THE PHANTOM AFFAIR, CHAPTER 1"**

PLOTTER: MICHAEL A. STACKPOLE • SCRIPTER: DARKO MACAN • ARTIST & LETTERER: EDVIN BIUKOVIĆ
COLORIST: DAVE NESTELLE • EDITOR: PEET JANES • COVER ARTIST: MATHIEU LAUFFRAY

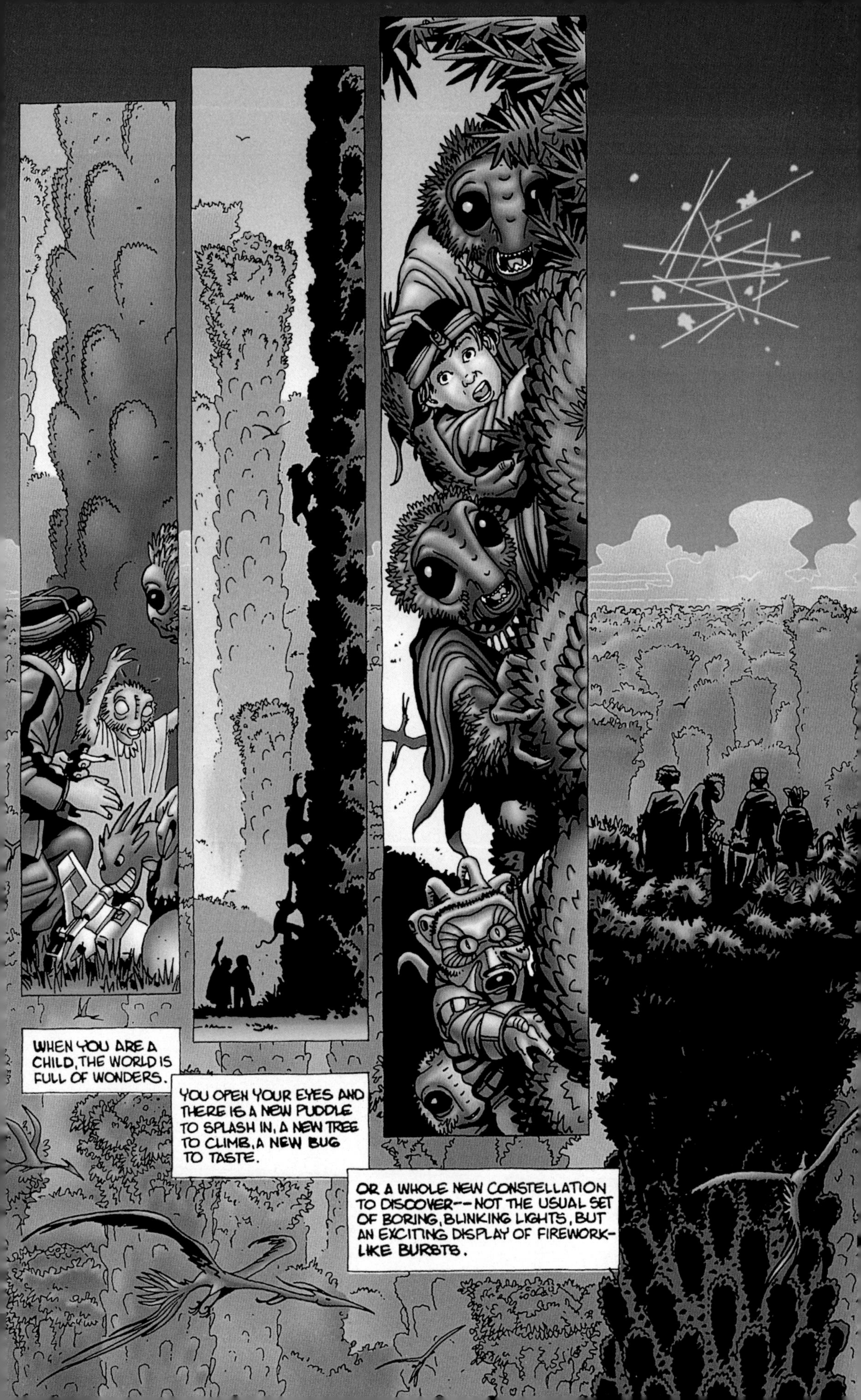
WHEN YOU ARE A CHILD, THE WORLD IS FULL OF WONDERS.
YOU OPEN YOUR EYES AND THERE IS A NEW PUDDLE TO SPLASH IN, A NEW TREE TO CLIMB, A NEW BUG TO TASTE.
OR A WHOLE NEW CONSTELLATION TO DISCOVER--NOT THE USUAL SET OF BORING, BLINKING LIGHTS, BUT AN EXCITING DISPLAY OF FIREWORK-LIKE BURSTS.

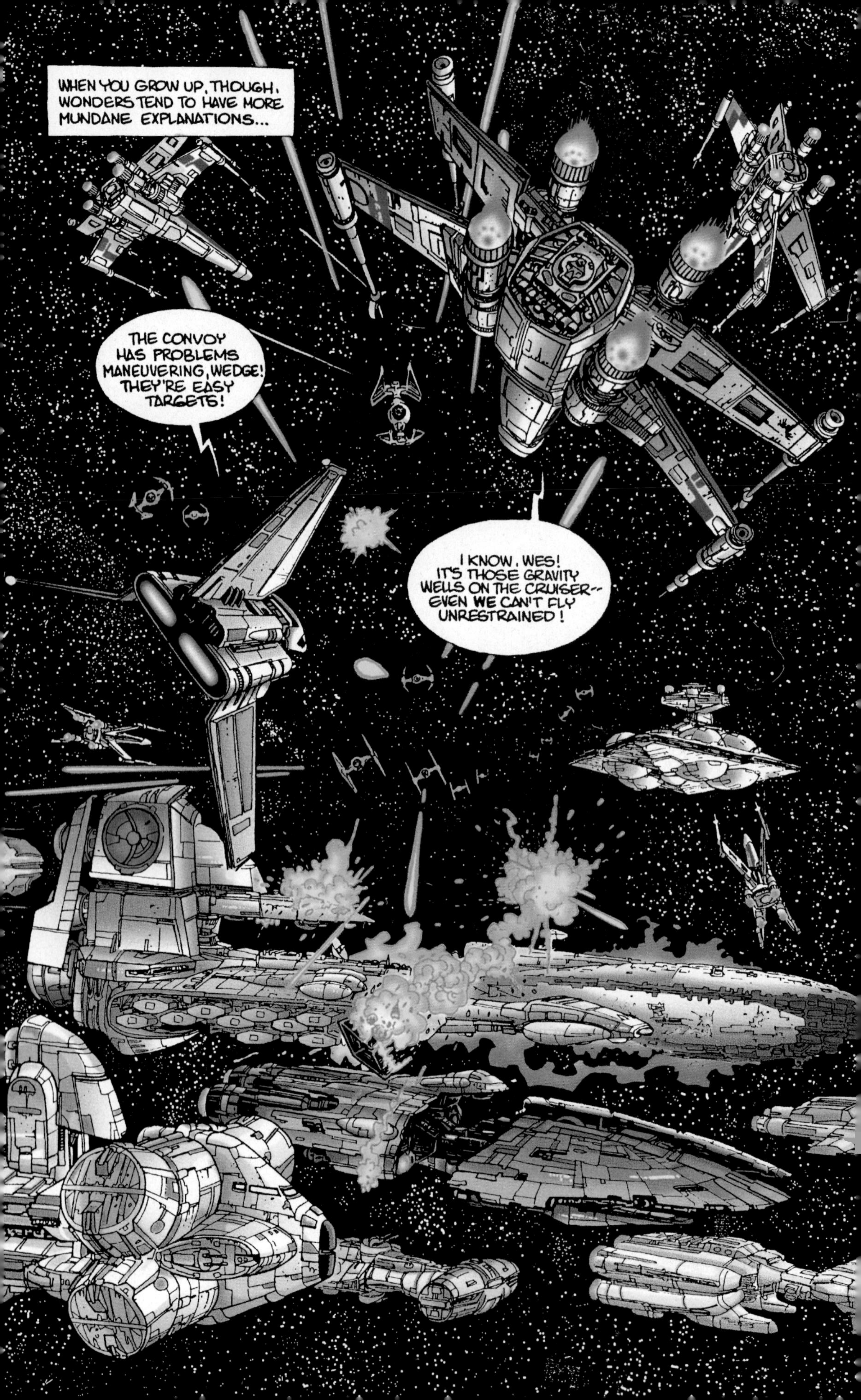
WHEN YOU GROW UP, THOUGH, WONDERS TEND TO HAVE MORE MUNDANE EXPLANATIONS...
THE CONVOY HAS PROBLEMS MANEUVERING, WEDGE! THEY'RE EASY TARGETS!
I KNOW, WES! IT'S THOSE GRAVITY WELLS ON THE CRUISER-- EVEN WE CAN'T FLY UNRESTRAINED!

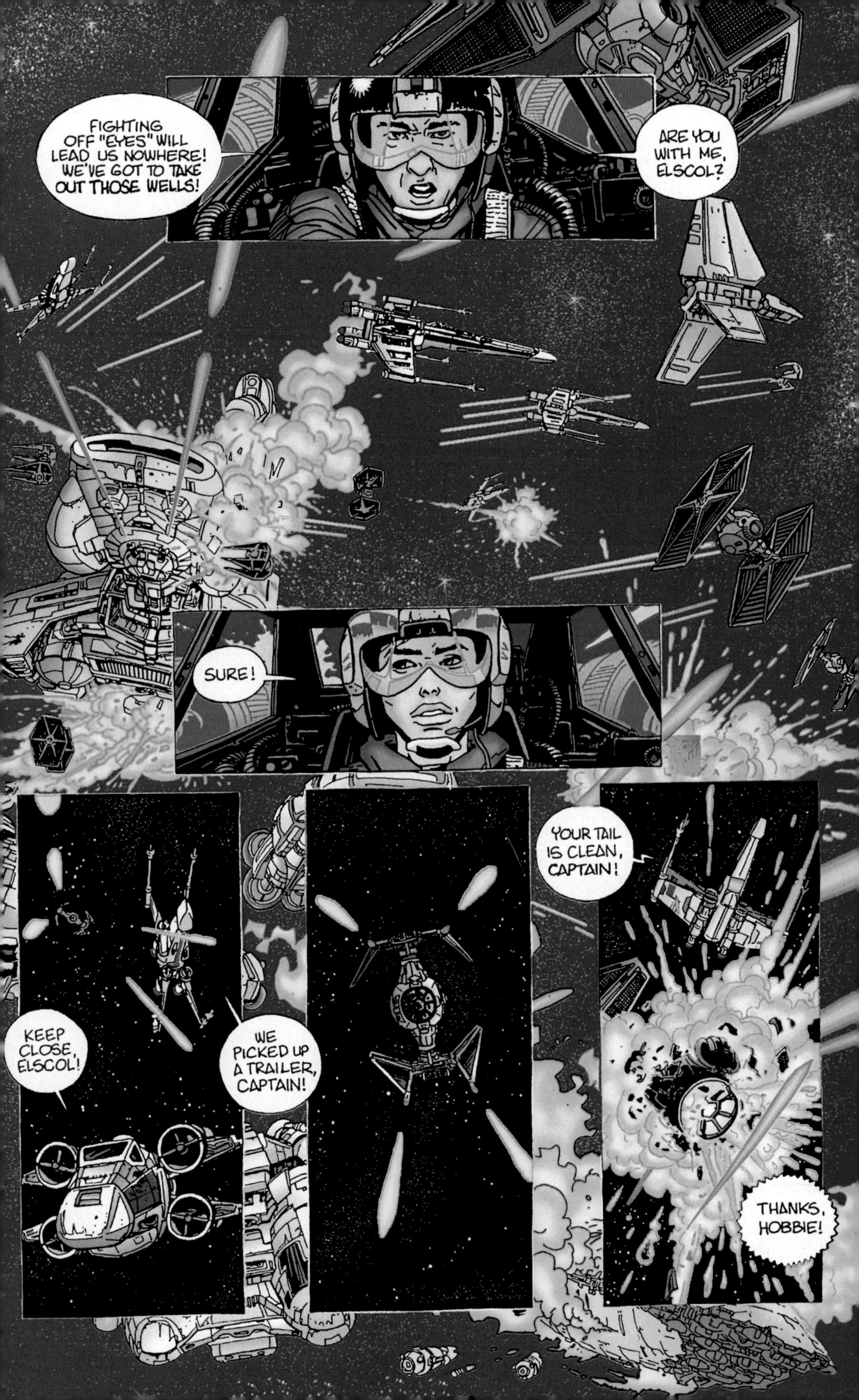
FIGHTING OFF "EYES" WILL LEAD US NOWHERE! WE'VE GOT TO TAKE OUT THOSE WELLS!
ARE YOU WITH ME, ELSCOL?
SURE!
KEEP CLOSE, ELSCOL!
WE PICKED UP A TRAILER, CAPTAIN!
YOUR TAIL IS CLEAN, CAPTAIN!
THANKS, HOBBIE!

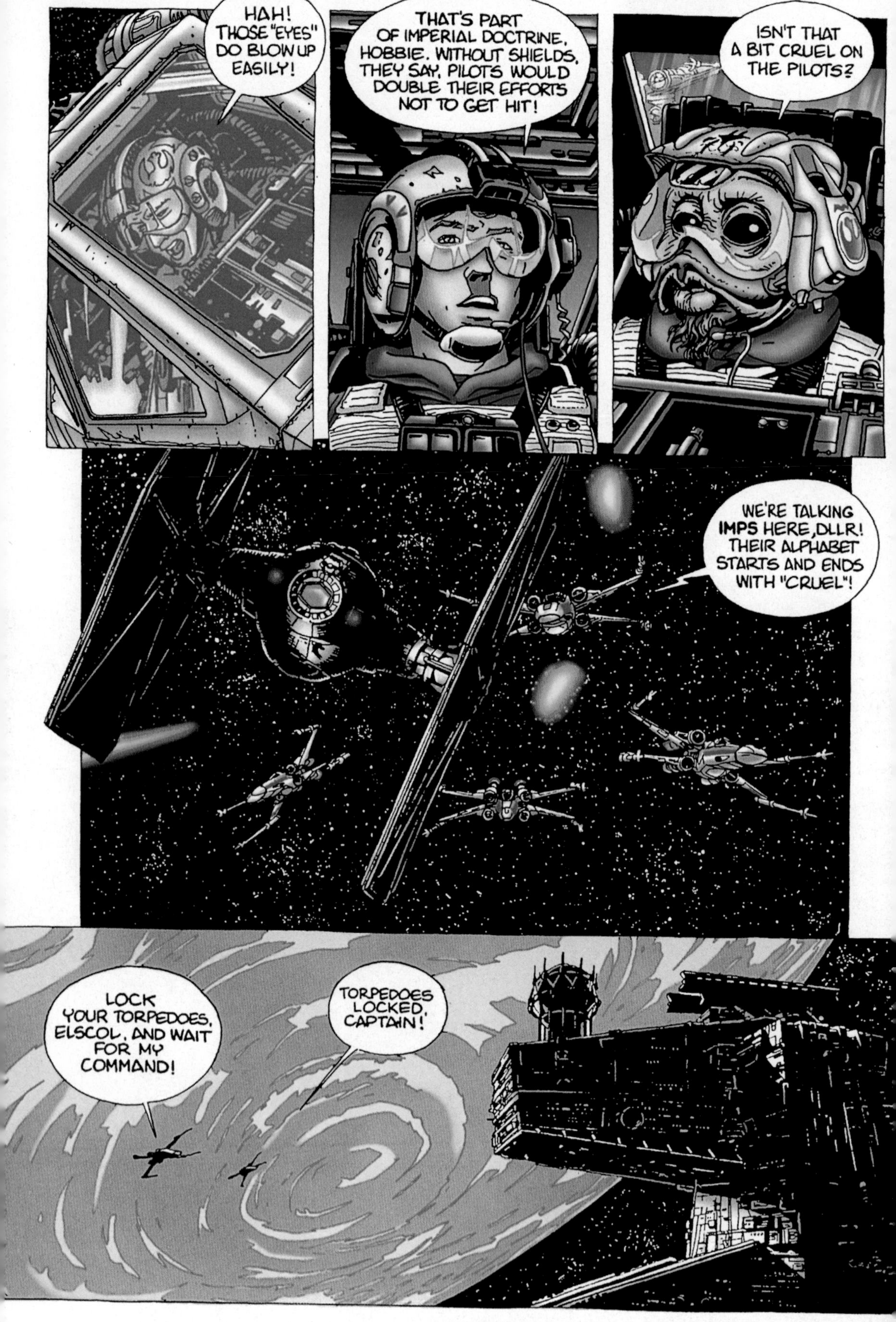
HAH! THOSE "EYES" DO BLOW UP EASILY!
THAT'S PART OF IMPERIAL DOCTRINE, HOBBIE. WITHOUT SHIELDS, THEY SAY, PILOTS WOULD DOUBLE THEIR EFFORTS NOT TO GET HIT!
ISN'T THAT A BIT CRUEL ON THE PILOTS?
WE'RE TALKING **IMPS** HERE, DLLR! THEIR ALPHABET STARTS AND ENDS WITH "CRUEL"!
LOCK YOUR TORPEDOES, ELSCOL, AND WAIT FOR MY COMMAND!
TORPEDOES LOCKED, CAPTAIN!

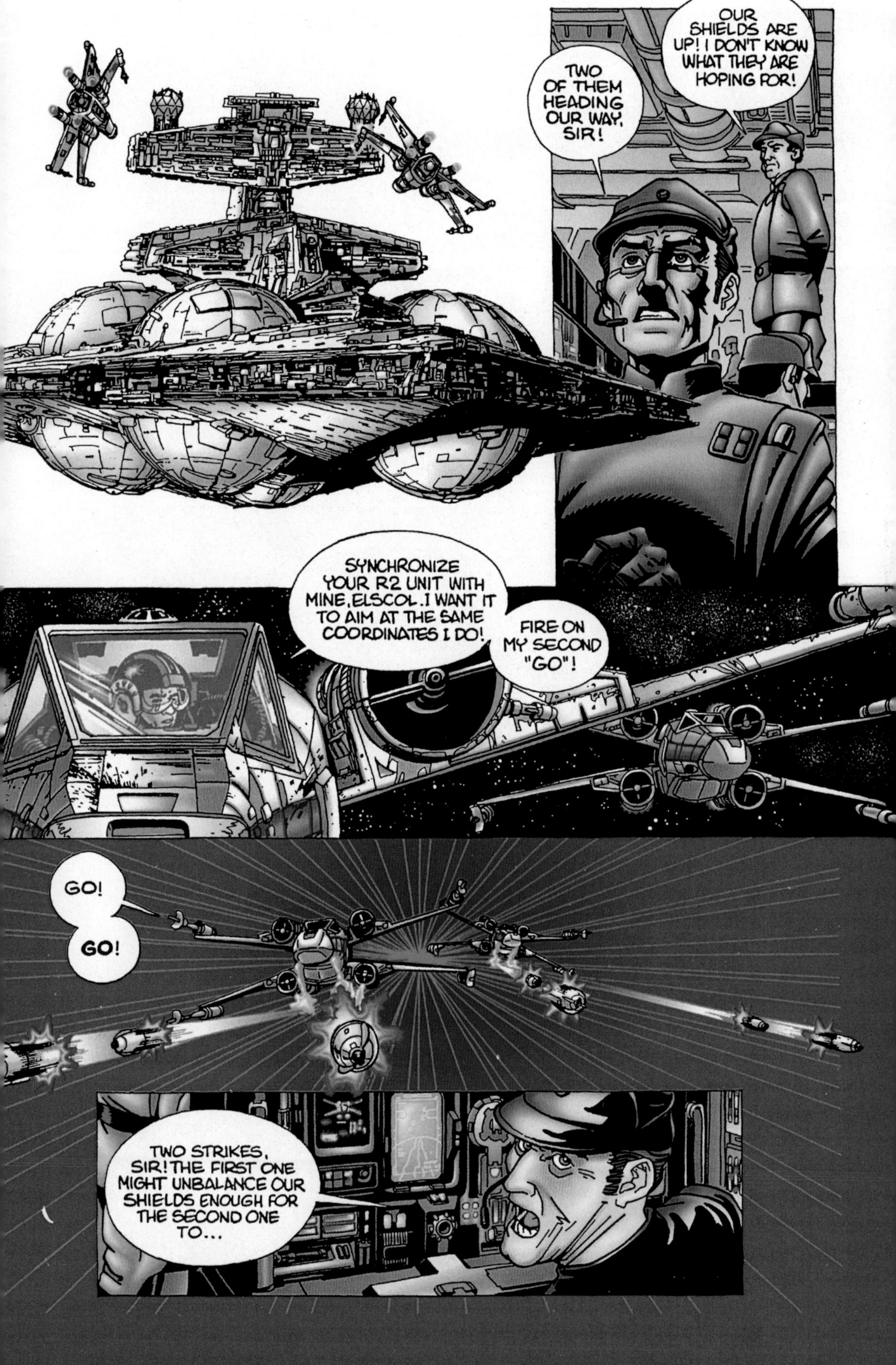
TWO OF THEM HEADING OUR WAY, SIR!
OUR SHIELDS ARE UP! I DON'T KNOW WHAT THEY ARE HOPING FOR!
SYNCHRONIZE YOUR R2 UNIT WITH MINE, ELSCOL. I WANT IT TO AIM AT THE SAME COORDINATES I DO!
FIRE ON MY SECOND "GO"!
GO!
GO!
TWO STRIKES, SIR! THE FIRST ONE MIGHT UNBALANCE OUR SHIELDS ENOUGH FOR THE SECOND ONE TO...

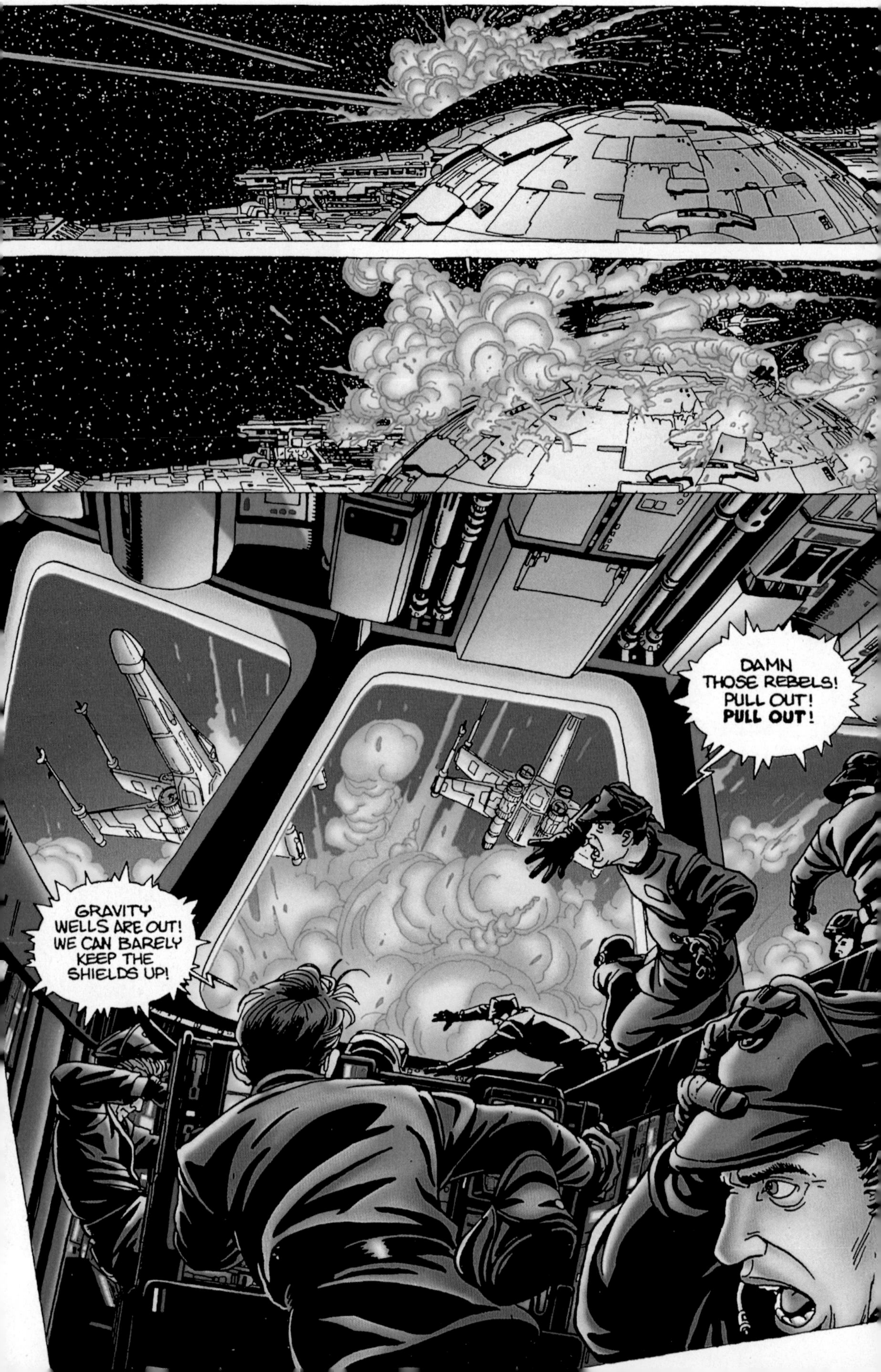
DAMN THOSE REBELS! PULL OUT! **PULL OUT**!
GRAVITY WELLS ARE OUT! WE CAN BARELY KEEP THE SHIELDS UP!

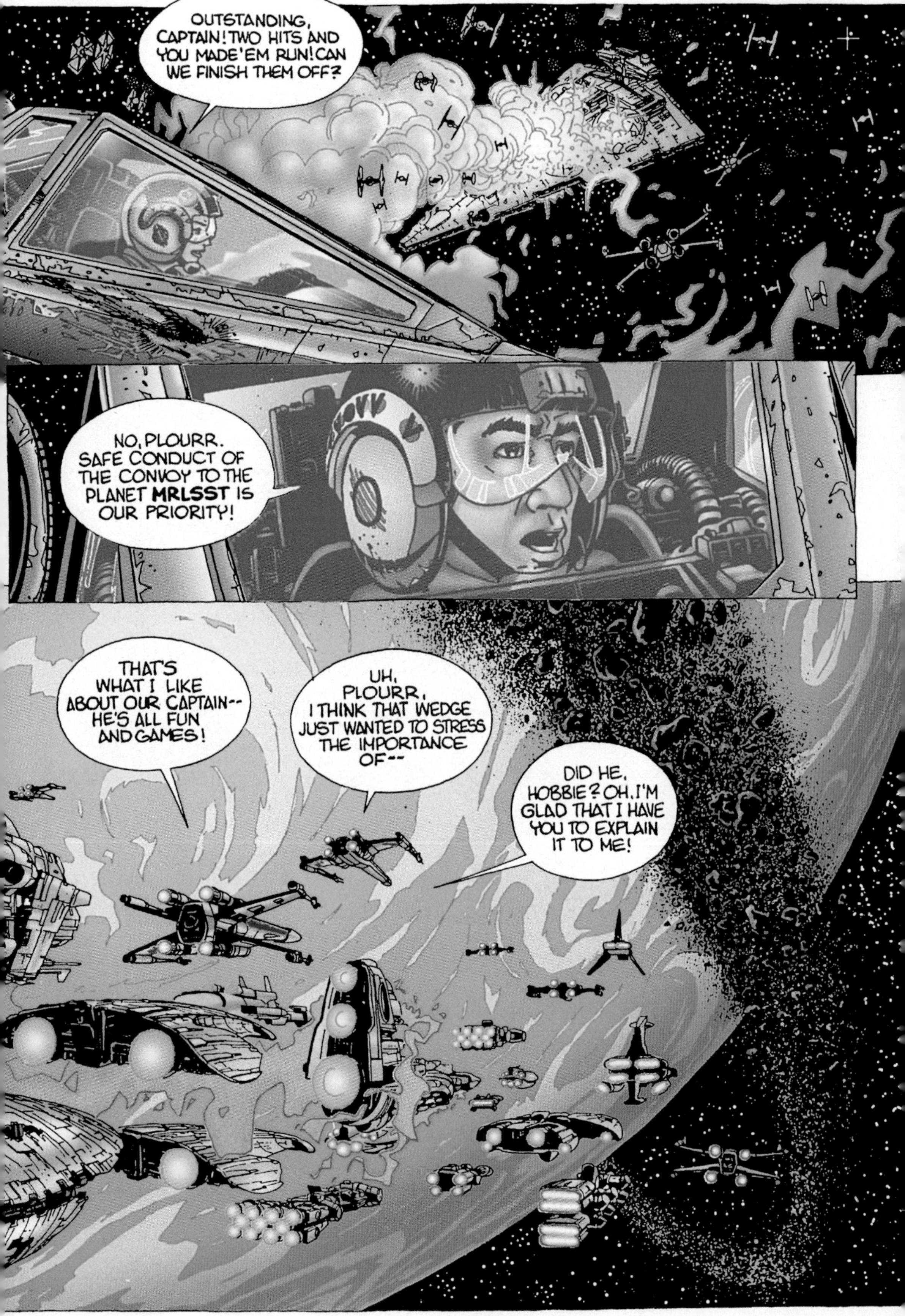
OUTSTANDING, CAPTAIN! TWO HITS AND YOU MADE'EM RUN! CAN WE FINISH THEM OFF?
NO, PLOURR. SAFE CONDUCT OF THE CONVOY TO THE PLANET **MRLSST** IS OUR PRIORITY!
THAT'S WHAT I LIKE ABOUT OUR CAPTAIN-- HE'S ALL FUN AND GAMES!
UH, PLOURR, I THINK THAT WEDGE JUST WANTED TO STRESS THE IMPORTANCE OF--
DID HE, HOBBIE? OH, I'M GLAD THAT I HAVE YOU TO EXPLAIN IT TO ME!

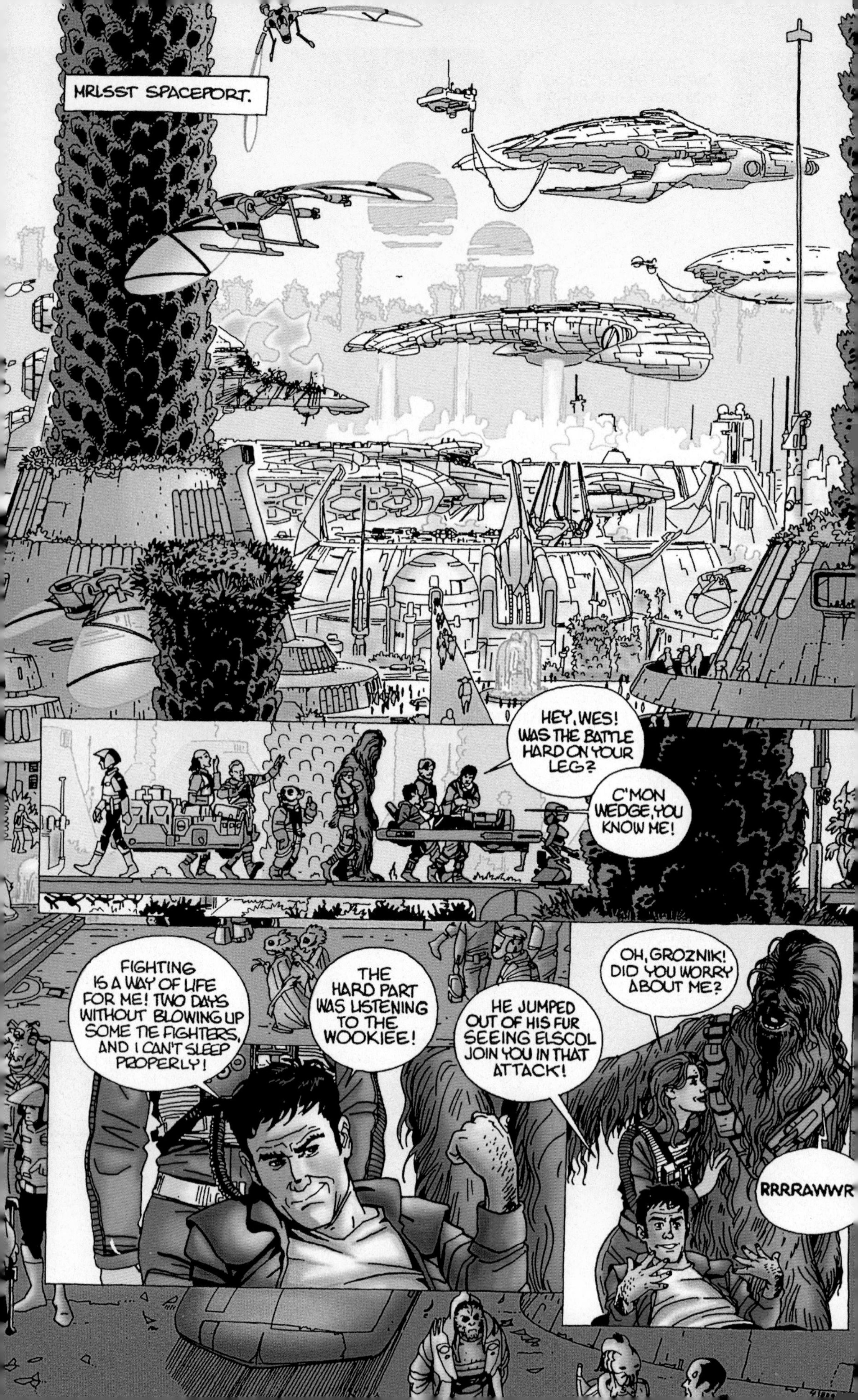
MRLSST SPACEPORT.
HEY, WES! WAS THE BATTLE HARD ON YOUR LEG?
C'MON WEDGE, YOU KNOW ME!
FIGHTING IS A WAY OF LIFE FOR ME! TWO DAYS WITHOUT BLOWING UP SOME TIE FIGHTERS, AND I CAN'T SLEEP PROPERLY!
THE HARD PART WAS LISTENING TO THE WOOKIEE!
HE JUMPED OUT OF HIS FUR SEEING ELSCOL JOIN YOU IN THAT ATTACK!
OH, GROZNIK! DID YOU WORRY ABOUT ME?
RRRRAWWR

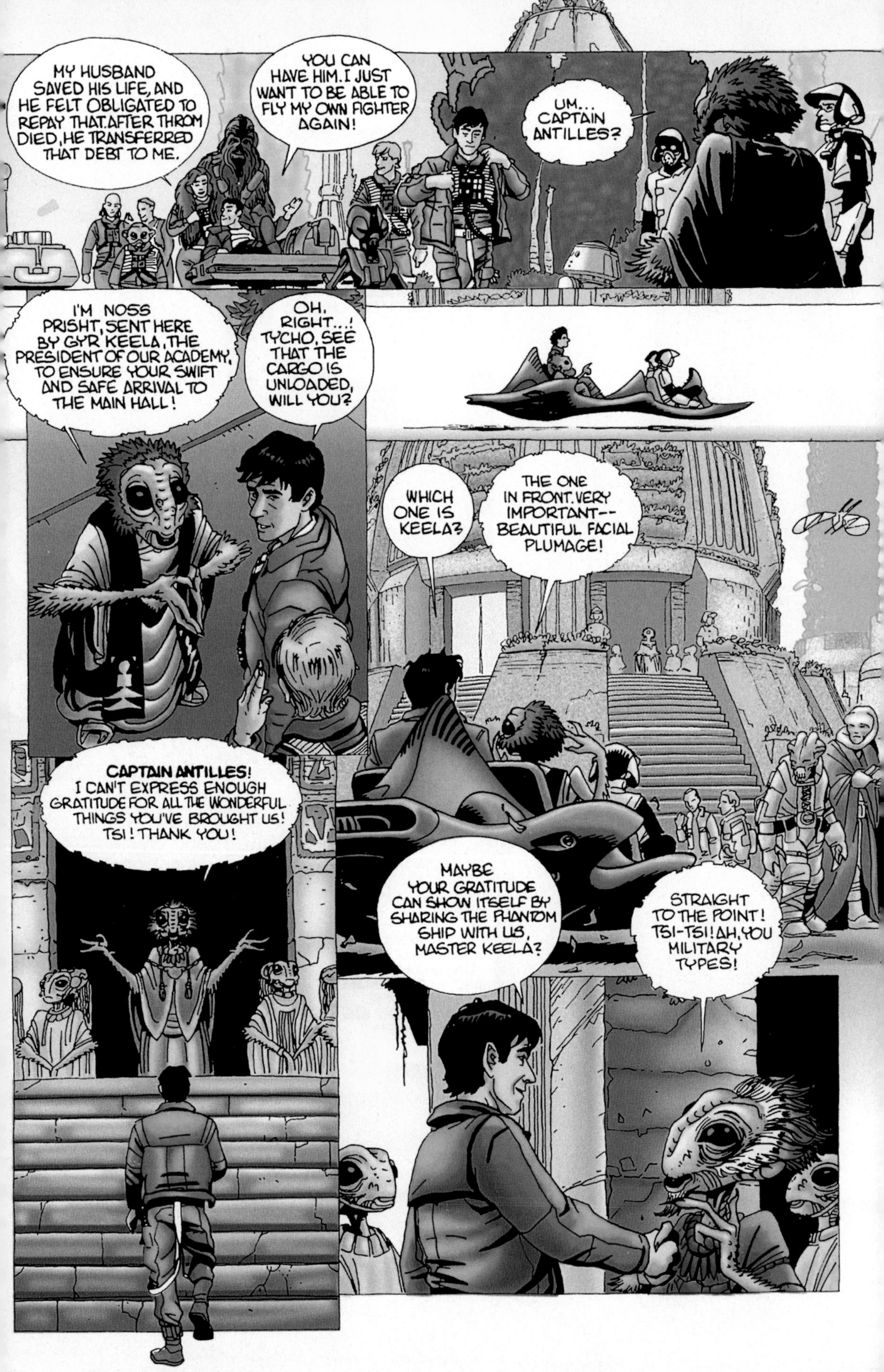
MY HUSBAND SAVED HIS LIFE, AND HE FELT OBLIGATED TO REPAY THAT. AFTER THROM DIED, HE TRANSFERRED THAT DEBT TO ME.
YOU CAN HAVE HIM. I JUST WANT TO BE ABLE TO FLY MY OWN FIGHTER AGAIN!
UM... CAPTAIN ANTILLES?
I'M NOSS PRISHT, SENT HERE BY GY'R KEELA, THE PRESIDENT OF OUR ACADEMY, TO ENSURE YOUR SWIFT AND SAFE ARRIVAL TO THE MAIN HALL!
OH. RIGHT...! TYCHO, SEE THAT THE CARGO IS UNLOADED, WILL YOU?
WHICH ONE IS KEELA?
THE ONE IN FRONT. VERY IMPORTANT-- BEAUTIFUL FACIAL PLUMAGE!
CAPTAIN ANTILLES! I CAN'T EXPRESS ENOUGH GRATITUDE FOR ALL THE WONDERFUL THINGS YOU'VE BROUGHT US! TSI! THANK YOU!
MAYBE YOUR GRATITUDE CAN SHOW ITSELF BY SHARING THE PHANTOM SHIP WITH US, MASTER KEELA?
STRAIGHT TO THE POINT! TSI-TSI! AH, YOU MILITARY TYPES!

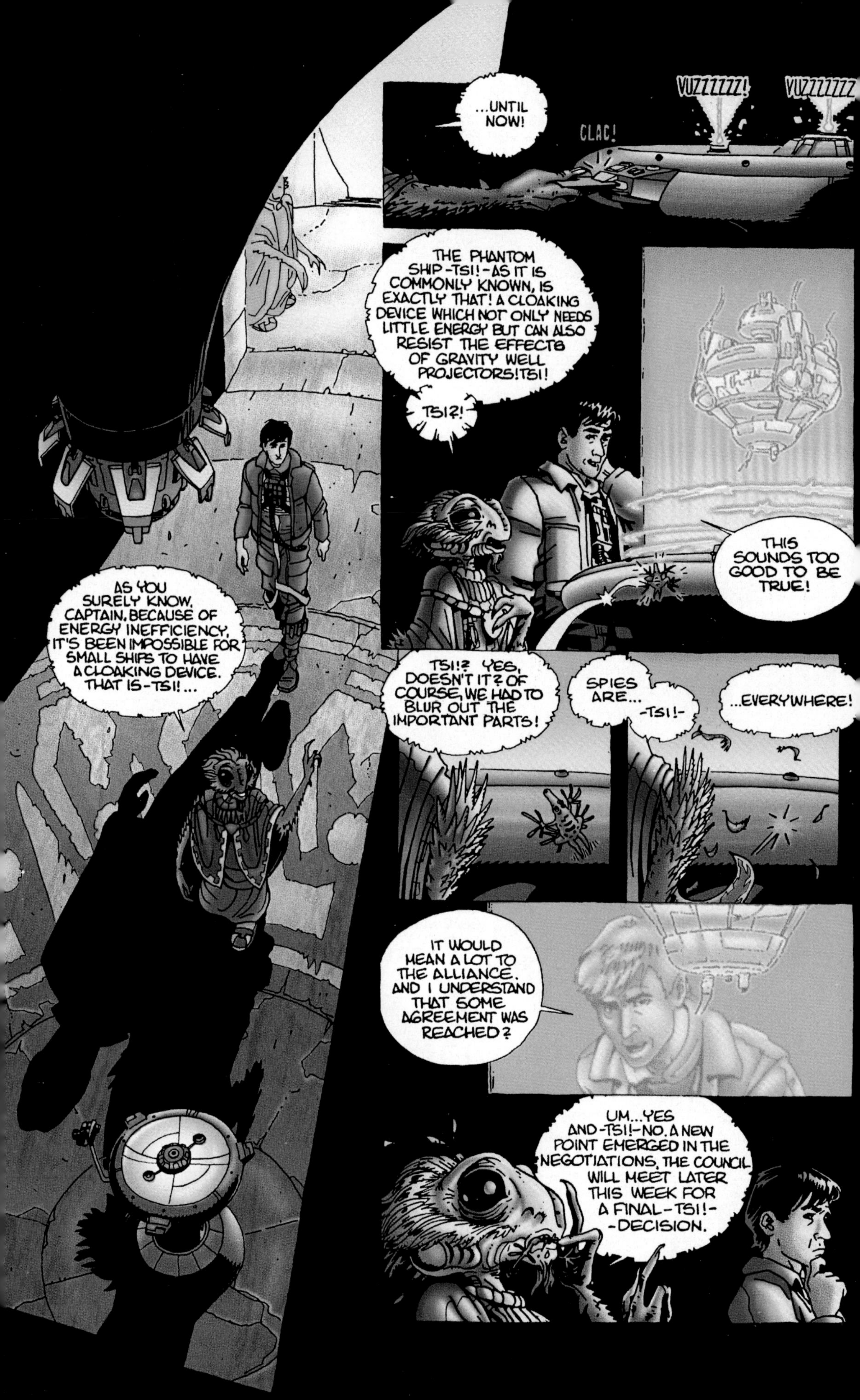
...UNTIL NOW!
CLAC!
VUZZZZZZ!
VUZZZZZZZ
AS YOU SURELY KNOW, CAPTAIN, BECAUSE OF ENERGY INEFFICIENCY, IT'S BEEN IMPOSSIBLE FOR SMALL SHIPS TO HAVE A CLOAKING DEVICE. THAT IS-TSI!...
THE PHANTOM SHIP-TSI!-AS IT IS COMMONLY KNOWN, IS EXACTLY THAT! A CLOAKING DEVICE WHICH NOT ONLY NEEDS LITTLE ENERGY BUT CAN ALSO RESIST THE EFFECTS OF GRAVITY WELL PROJECTORS! TSI!
TSI?!
THIS SOUNDS TOO GOOD TO BE TRUE!
TSI!? YES, DOESN'T IT? OF COURSE, WE HAD TO BLUR OUT THE IMPORTANT PARTS!
SPIES ARE... -TSI!-
...EVERYWHERE!
IT WOULD MEAN A LOT TO THE ALLIANCE. AND I UNDERSTAND THAT SOME AGREEMENT WAS REACHED?
UM...YES AND-TSI!-NO. A NEW POINT EMERGED IN THE NEGOTIATIONS, THE COUNCIL WILL MEET LATER THIS WEEK FOR A FINAL-TSI!- -DECISION.

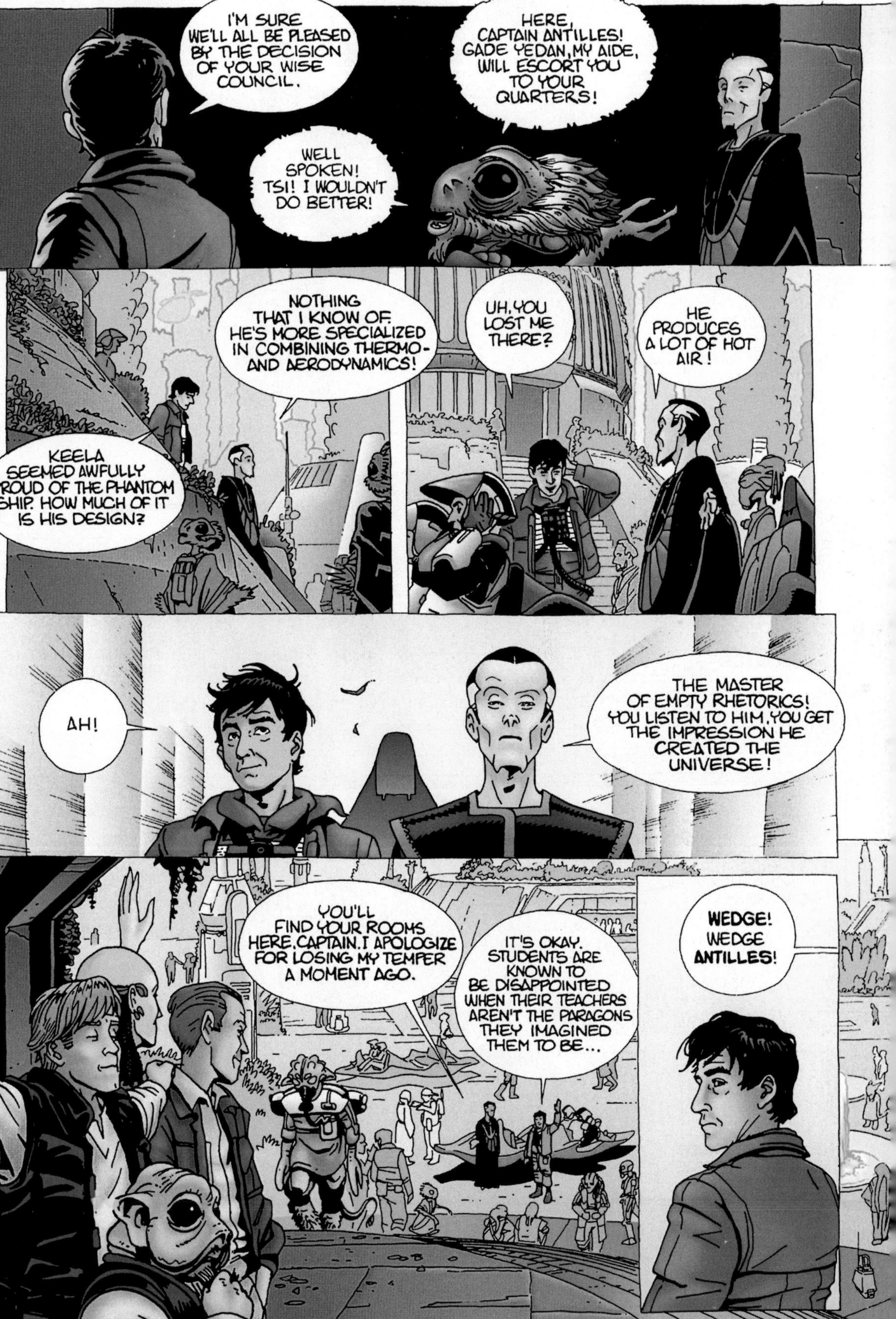
I'M SURE WE'LL ALL BE PLEASED BY THE DECISION OF YOUR WISE COUNCIL.
HERE, CAPTAIN ANTILLES! GADE YEDAN, MY AIDE, WILL ESCORT YOU TO YOUR QUARTERS!
WELL SPOKEN! TSI! I WOULDN'T DO BETTER!
KEELA SEEMED AWFULLY PROUD OF THE PHANTOM SHIP. HOW MUCH OF IT IS HIS DESIGN?
NOTHING THAT I KNOW OF. HE'S MORE SPECIALIZED IN COMBINING THERMO- AND AERODYNAMICS!
UH, YOU LOST ME THERE?
HE PRODUCES A LOT OF HOT AIR!
AH!
THE MASTER OF EMPTY RHETORICS! YOU LISTEN TO HIM, YOU GET THE IMPRESSION HE CREATED THE UNIVERSE!
YOU'LL FIND YOUR ROOMS HERE, CAPTAIN. I APOLOGIZE FOR LOSING MY TEMPER A MOMENT AGO.
IT'S OKAY. STUDENTS ARE KNOWN TO BE DISAPPOINTED WHEN THEIR TEACHERS AREN'T THE PARAGONS THEY IMAGINED THEM TO BE...
WEDGE! WEDGE ANTILLES!

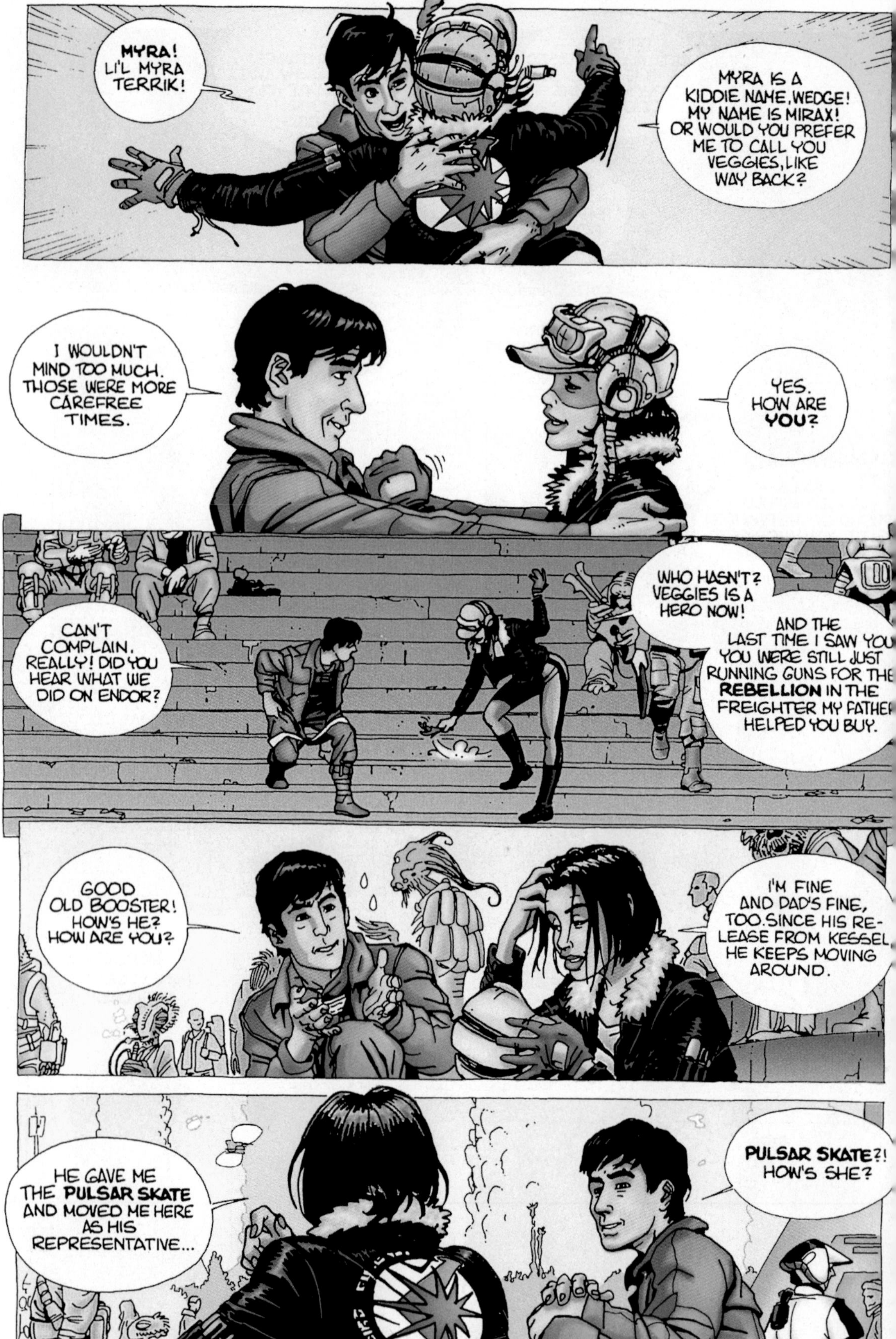
MYRA! LI'L MYRA TERRIK!
MYRA IS A KIDDIE NAME, WEDGE! MY NAME IS MIRAX! OR WOULD YOU PREFER ME TO CALL YOU VEGGIES, LIKE WAY BACK?
I WOULDN'T MIND TOO MUCH. THOSE WERE MORE CAREFREE TIMES.
YES. HOW ARE YOU?
CAN'T COMPLAIN. REALLY! DID YOU HEAR WHAT WE DID ON ENDOR?
WHO HASN'T? VEGGIES IS A HERO NOW!
AND THE LAST TIME I SAW YOU YOU WERE STILL JUST RUNNING GUNS FOR THE REBELLION IN THE FREIGHTER MY FATHER HELPED YOU BUY.
GOOD OLD BOOSTER! HOW'S HE? HOW ARE YOU?
I'M FINE AND DAD'S FINE, TOO. SINCE HIS RELEASE FROM KESSEL HE KEEPS MOVING AROUND.
HE GAVE ME THE PULSAR SKATE AND MOVED ME HERE AS HIS REPRESENTATIVE...
PULSAR SKATE?! HOW'S SHE?

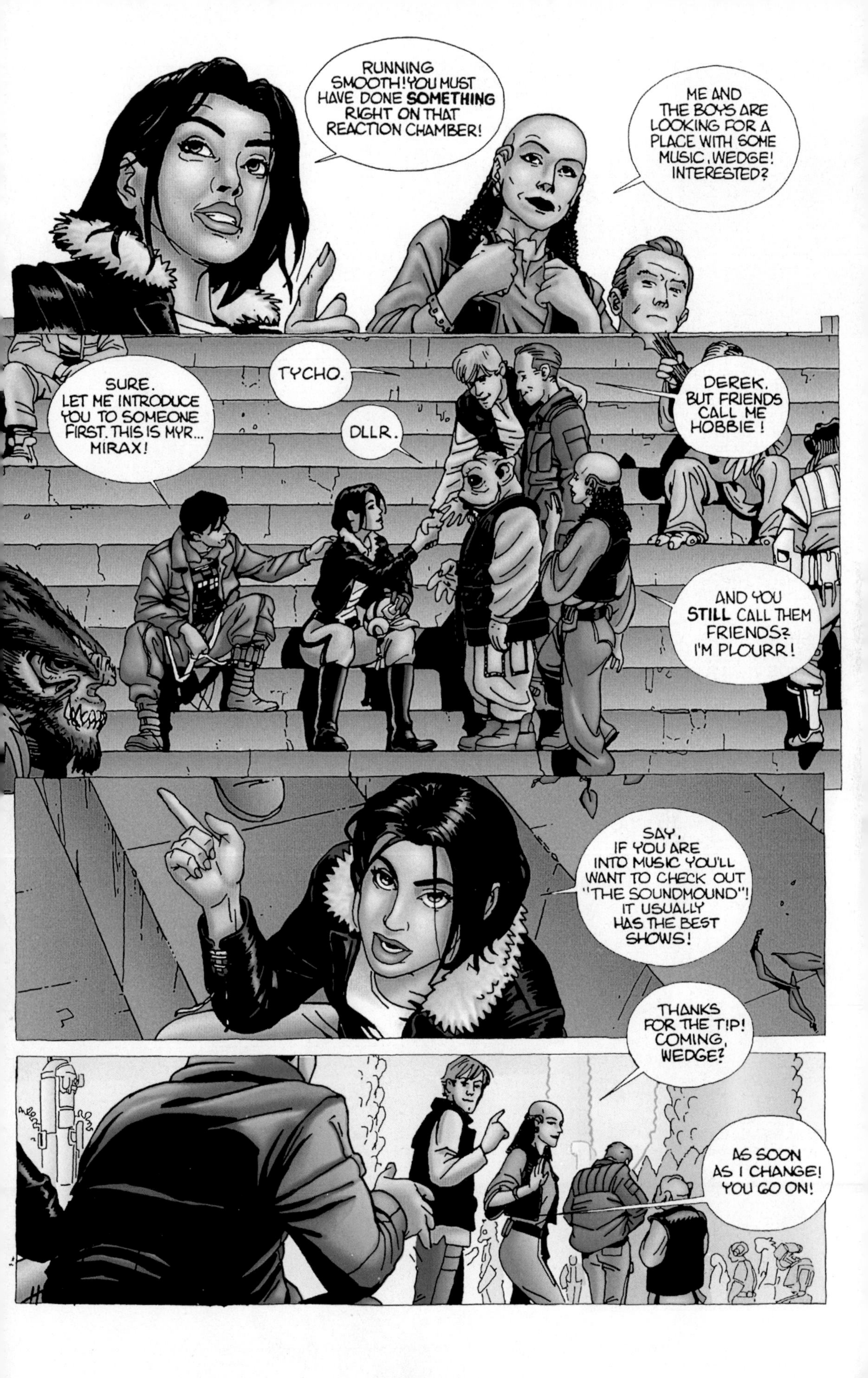
RUNNING SMOOTH! YOU MUST HAVE DONE **SOMETHING** RIGHT ON THAT REACTION CHAMBER!
ME AND THE BOYS ARE LOOKING FOR A PLACE WITH SOME MUSIC, WEDGE! INTERESTED?
SURE. LET ME INTRODUCE YOU TO SOMEONE FIRST. THIS IS MYR... MIRAX!
TYCHO.
DLLR.
DEREK. BUT FRIENDS CALL ME HOBBIE!
AND YOU **STILL** CALL THEM FRIENDS? I'M PLOURR!
SAY, IF YOU ARE INTO MUSIC YOU'LL WANT TO CHECK OUT "THE SOUNDMOUND"! IT USUALLY HAS THE BEST SHOWS!
THANKS FOR THE TIP! COMING, WEDGE?
AS SOON AS I CHANGE! YOU GO ON!

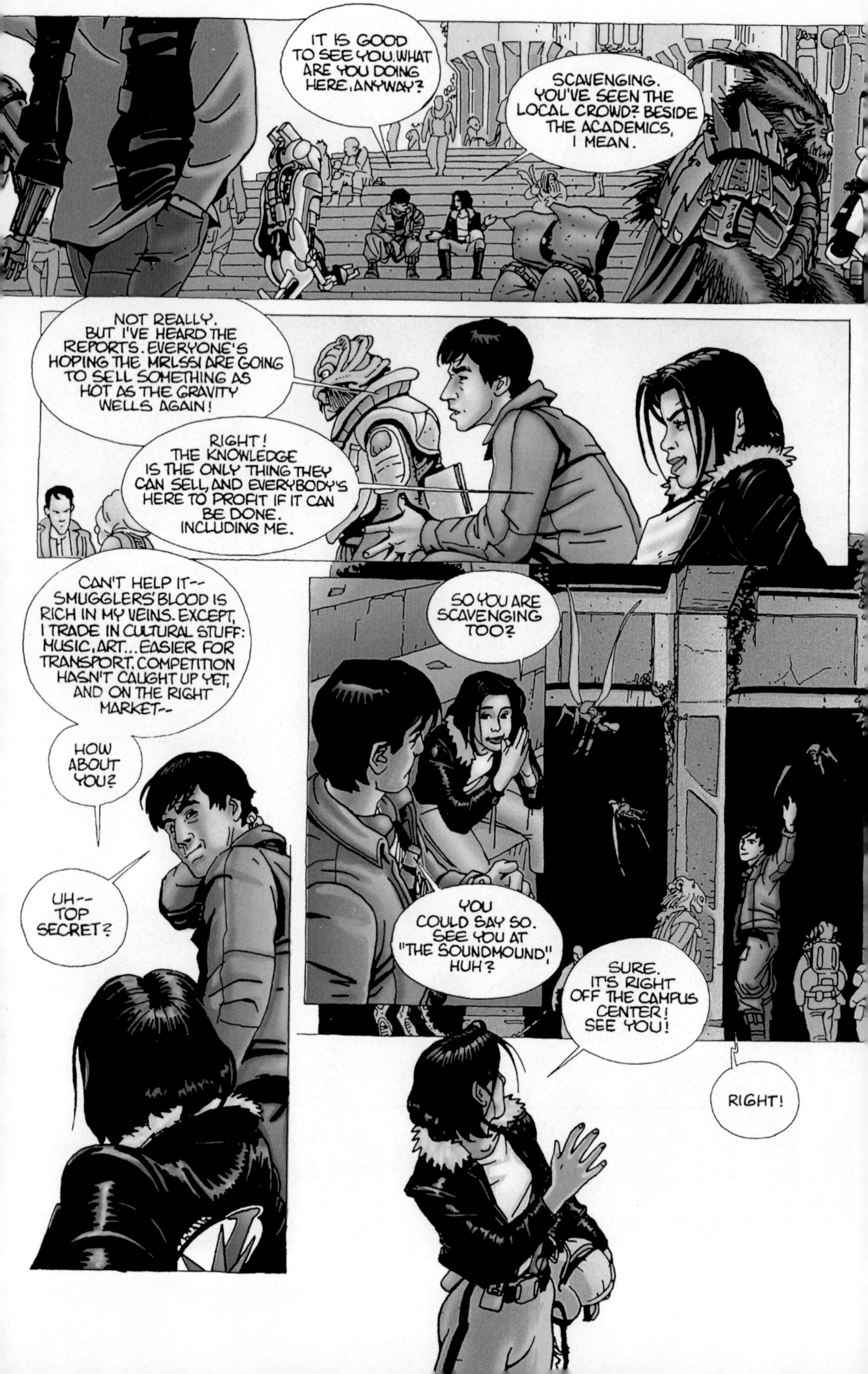

IT IS GOOD TO SEE YOU. WHAT ARE YOU DOING HERE, ANYWAY?
SCAVENGING. YOU'VE SEEN THE LOCAL CROWD? BESIDE THE ACADEMICS, I MEAN.
NOT REALLY. BUT I'VE HEARD THE REPORTS. EVERYONE'S HOPING THE MRLSSI ARE GOING TO SELL SOMETHING AS HOT AS THE GRAVITY WELLS AGAIN!
RIGHT! THE KNOWLEDGE IS THE ONLY THING THEY CAN SELL, AND EVERYBODY'S HERE TO PROFIT IF IT CAN BE DONE. INCLUDING ME.
CAN'T HELP IT-- SMUGGLERS' BLOOD IS RICH IN MY VEINS. EXCEPT, I TRADE IN CULTURAL STUFF: MUSIC, ART... EASIER FOR TRANSPORT, COMPETITION HASN'T CAUGHT UP YET, AND ON THE RIGHT MARKET--
HOW ABOUT YOU?
UH-- TOP SECRET?
SO YOU ARE SCAVENGING TOO?
YOU COULD SAY SO. SEE YOU AT "THE SOUNDMOUND", HUH?
SURE. IT'S RIGHT OFF THE CAMPUS CENTER! SEE YOU!
RIGHT!

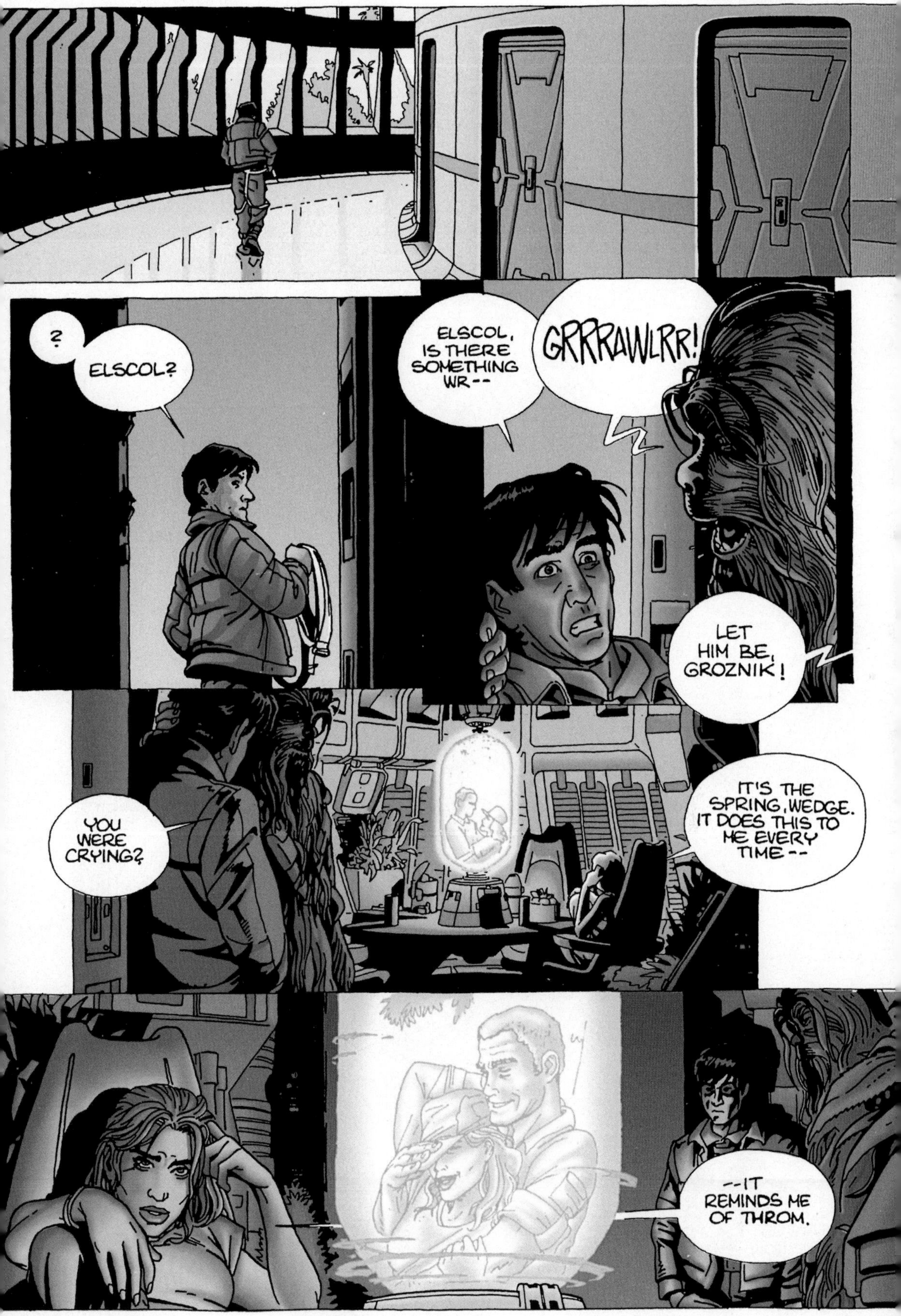
?
ELSCOL?
ELSCOL, IS THERE SOMETHING WR--
GRRRAWLRR!
LET HIM BE, GROZNIK!
YOU WERE CRYING?
IT'S THE SPRING, WEDGE. IT DOES THIS TO ME EVERY TIME--
--IT REMINDS ME OF THROM.

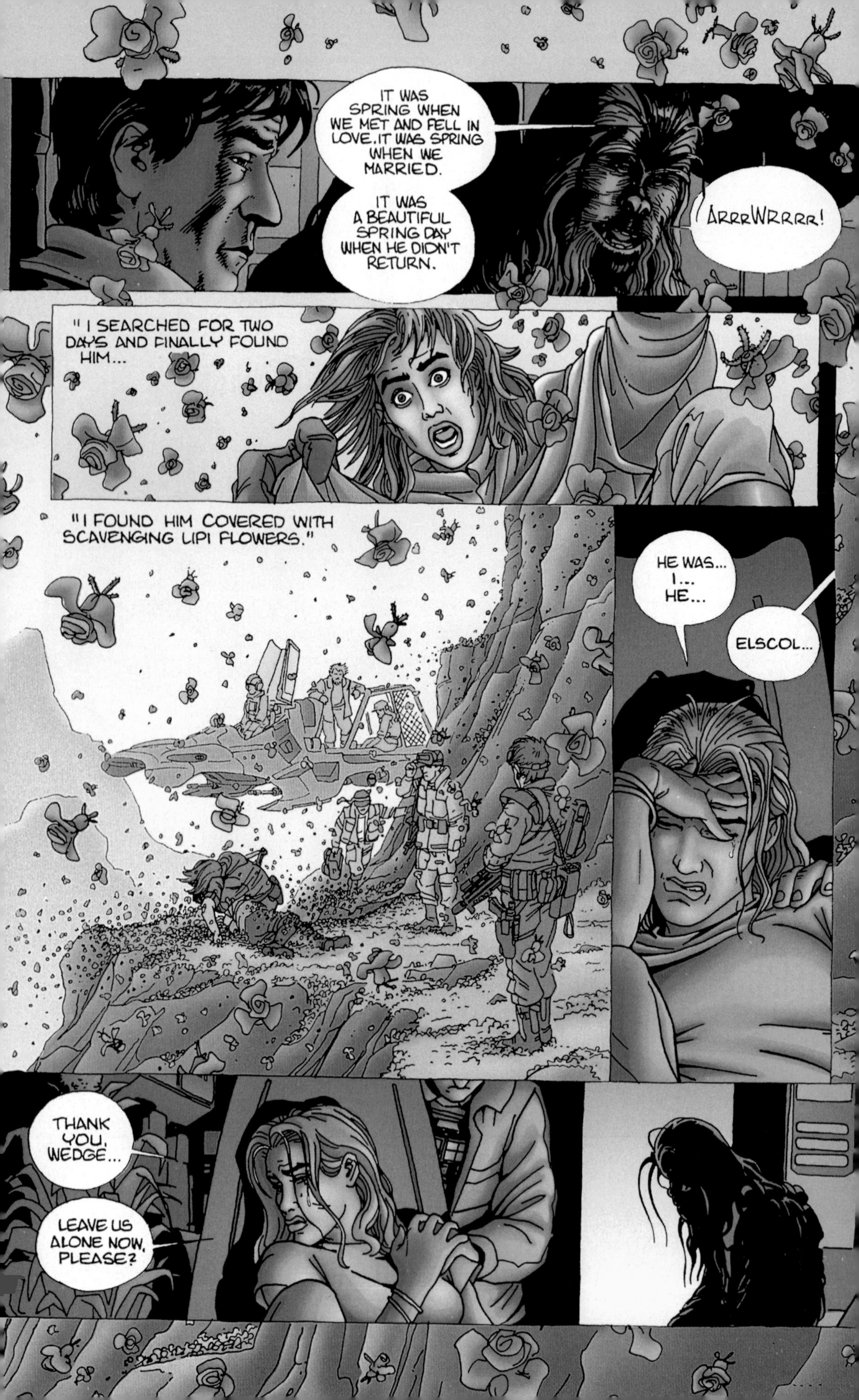
IT WAS SPRING WHEN WE MET AND FELL IN LOVE. IT WAS SPRING WHEN WE MARRIED.
IT WAS A BEAUTIFUL SPRING DAY WHEN HE DIDN'T RETURN.
ArrrWrrrr!
"I SEARCHED FOR TWO DAYS AND FINALLY FOUND HIM...
"I FOUND HIM COVERED WITH SCAVENGING LIPI FLOWERS."
HE WAS... I... HE...
ELSCOL...
THANK YOU, WEDGE...
LEAVE US ALONE NOW, PLEASE?

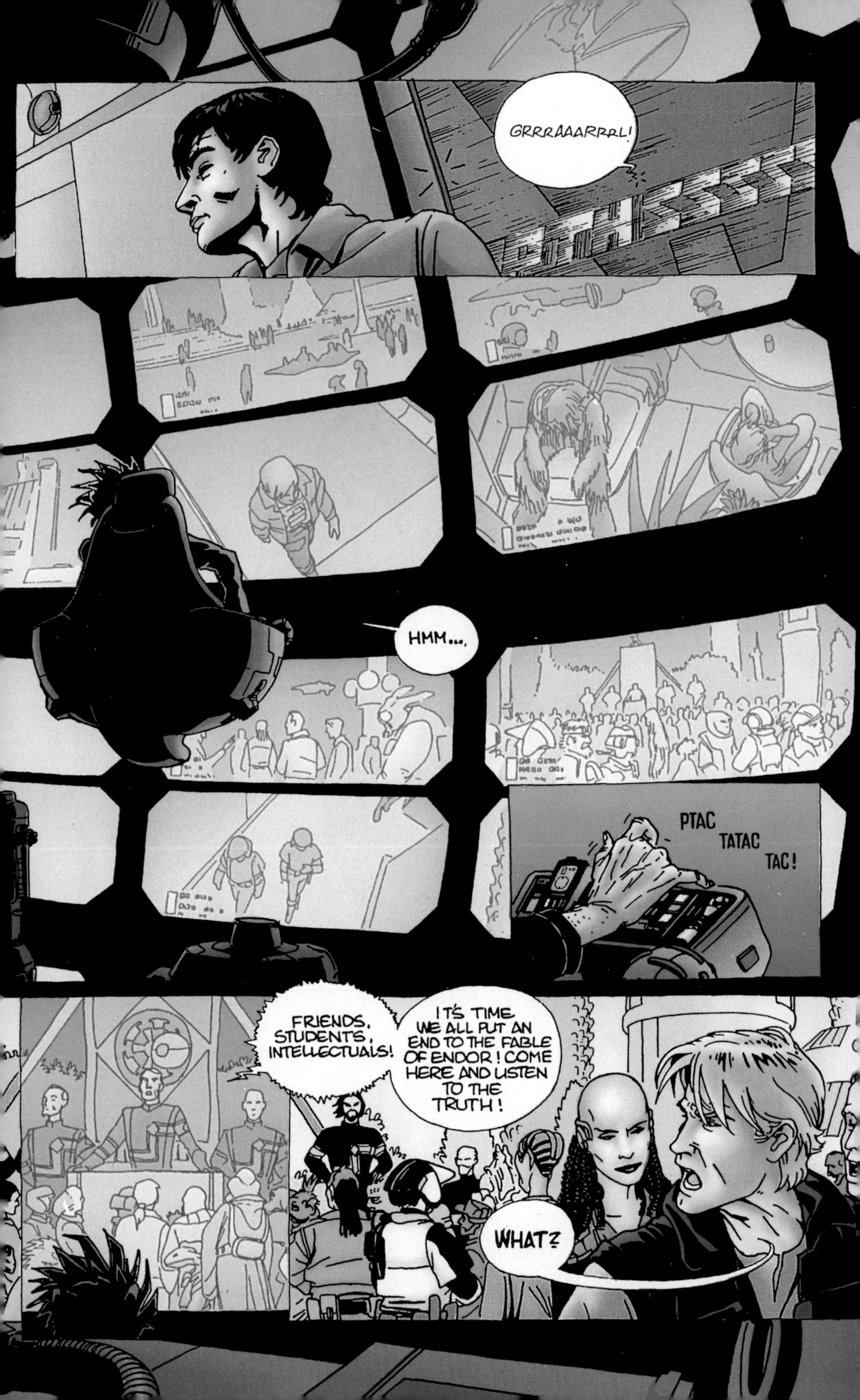
GRRRAAARRRL!
HMM...
PTAC
TATAC
TAC!
FRIENDS, STUDENTS, INTELLECTUALS!
IT'S TIME WE ALL PUT AN END TO THE FABLE OF ENDOR! COME HERE AND LISTEN TO THE TRUTH!
WHAT?

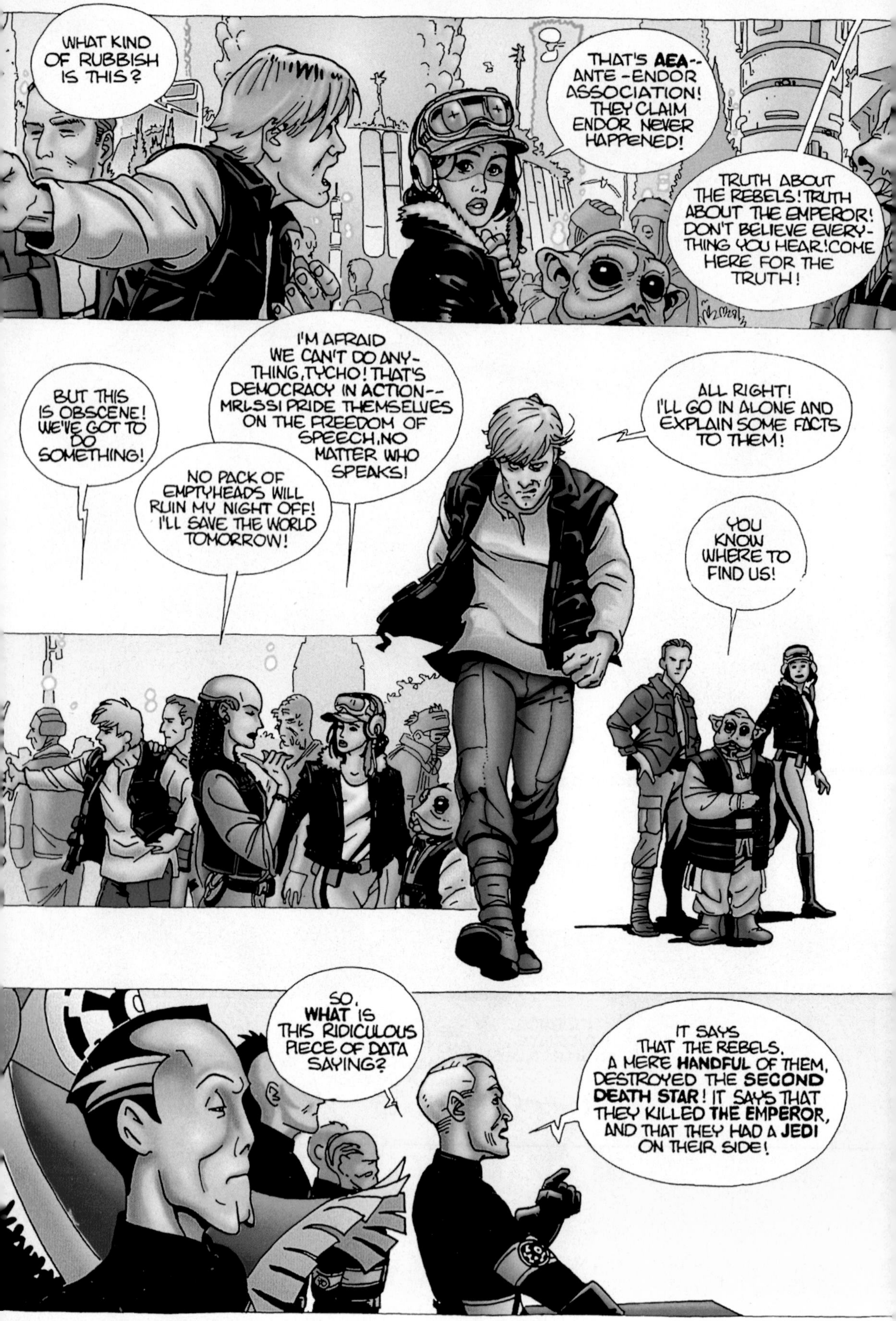
WHAT KIND OF RUBBISH IS THIS?
THAT'S **AEA**-- ANTE-ENDOR ASSOCIATION! THEY CLAIM ENDOR NEVER HAPPENED!
TRUTH ABOUT THE REBELS! TRUTH ABOUT THE EMPEROR! DON'T BELIEVE EVERYTHING YOU HEAR! COME HERE FOR THE TRUTH!
BUT THIS IS OBSCENE! WE'VE GOT TO DO SOMETHING!
I'M AFRAID WE CAN'T DO ANYTHING, TYCHO! THAT'S DEMOCRACY IN **ACTION**-- MRLSSI PRIDE THEMSELVES ON THE FREEDOM OF SPEECH, NO MATTER WHO SPEAKS!
NO PACK OF EMPTYHEADS WILL RUIN MY NIGHT OFF! I'LL SAVE THE WORLD TOMORROW!
ALL RIGHT! I'LL GO IN ALONE AND EXPLAIN SOME FACTS TO THEM!
YOU KNOW WHERE TO FIND US!
SO, **WHAT** IS THIS RIDICULOUS PIECE OF DATA SAYING?
IT SAYS THAT THE REBELS, A MERE **HANDFUL** OF THEM, DESTROYED THE **SECOND DEATH STAR**! IT SAYS THAT THEY KILLED **THE EMPEROR**, AND THAT THEY HAD A **JEDI** ON THEIR SIDE!

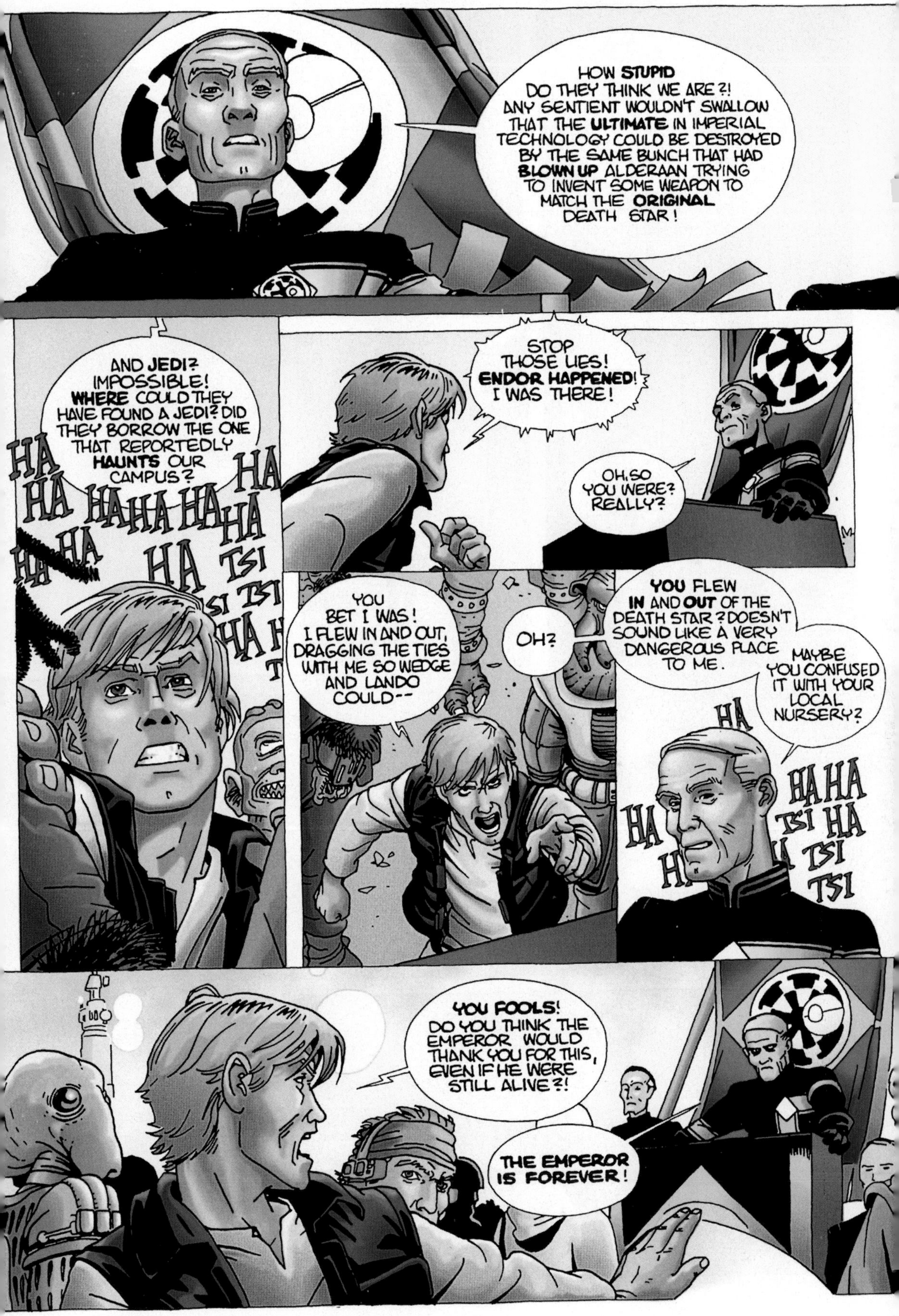
HOW STUPID DO THEY THINK WE ARE?! ANY SENTIENT WOULDN'T SWALLOW THAT THE ULTIMATE IN IMPERIAL TECHNOLOGY COULD BE DESTROYED BY THE SAME BUNCH THAT HAD BLOWN UP ALDERAAN TRYING TO INVENT SOME WEAPON TO MATCH THE ORIGINAL DEATH STAR!
AND JEDI? IMPOSSIBLE! WHERE COULD THEY HAVE FOUND A JEDI? DID THEY BORROW THE ONE THAT REPORTEDLY HAUNTS OUR CAMPUS?
HA HA HA HA HA HA HA HA HA HA TSI TSI
STOP THOSE LIES! ENDOR HAPPENED! I WAS THERE!
OH, SO YOU WERE? REALLY?
YOU BET I WAS! I FLEW IN AND OUT, DRAGGING THE TIES WITH ME SO WEDGE AND LANDO COULD--
OH?
YOU FLEW IN AND OUT OF THE DEATH STAR? DOESN'T SOUND LIKE A VERY DANGEROUS PLACE TO ME.
MAYBE YOU CONFUSED IT WITH YOUR LOCAL NURSERY?
HA HA HA HA HA TSI TSI TSI
YOU FOOLS! DO YOU THINK THE EMPEROR WOULD THANK YOU FOR THIS, EVEN IF HE WERE STILL ALIVE?!
THE EMPEROR IS FOREVER!

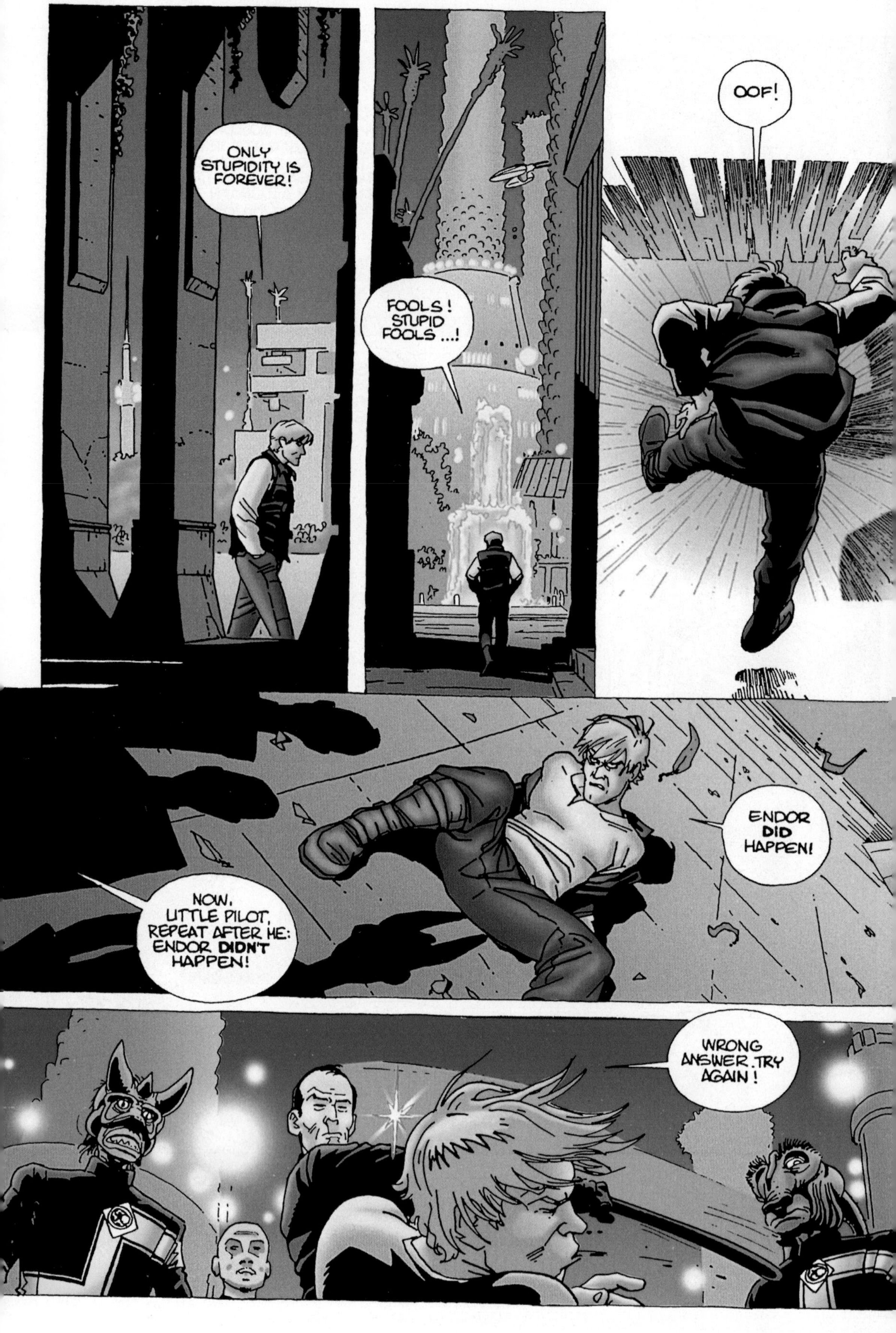
ONLY STUPIDITY IS FOREVER!
FOOLS! STUPID FOOLS...!
OOF!
WHAKK!
NOW, LITTLE PILOT, REPEAT AFTER ME: ENDOR **DIDN'T** HAPPEN!
ENDOR **DID** HAPPEN!
WRONG ANSWER. TRY AGAIN!

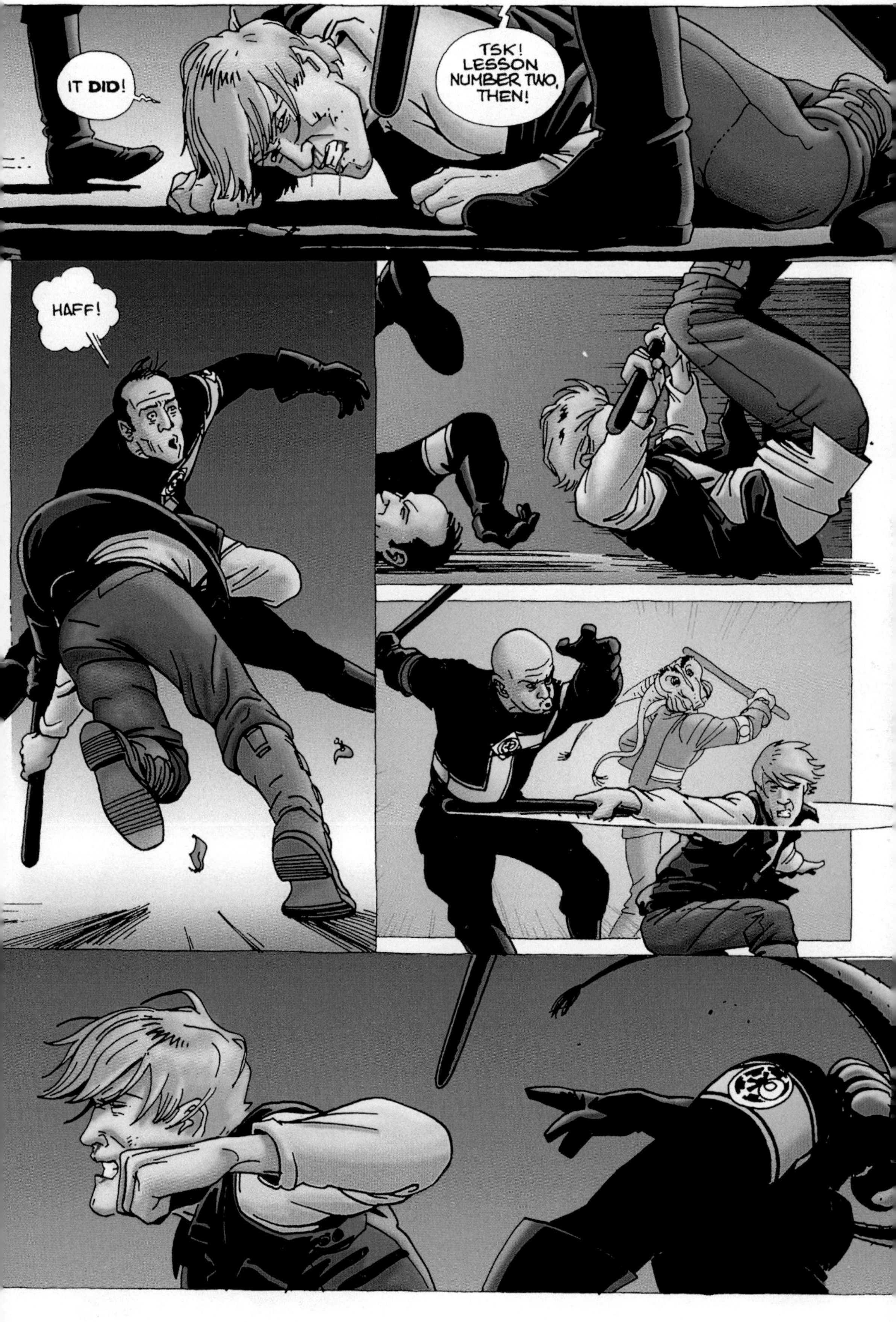
IT DID!
TSK! LESSON NUMBER TWO, THEN!
HAFF!

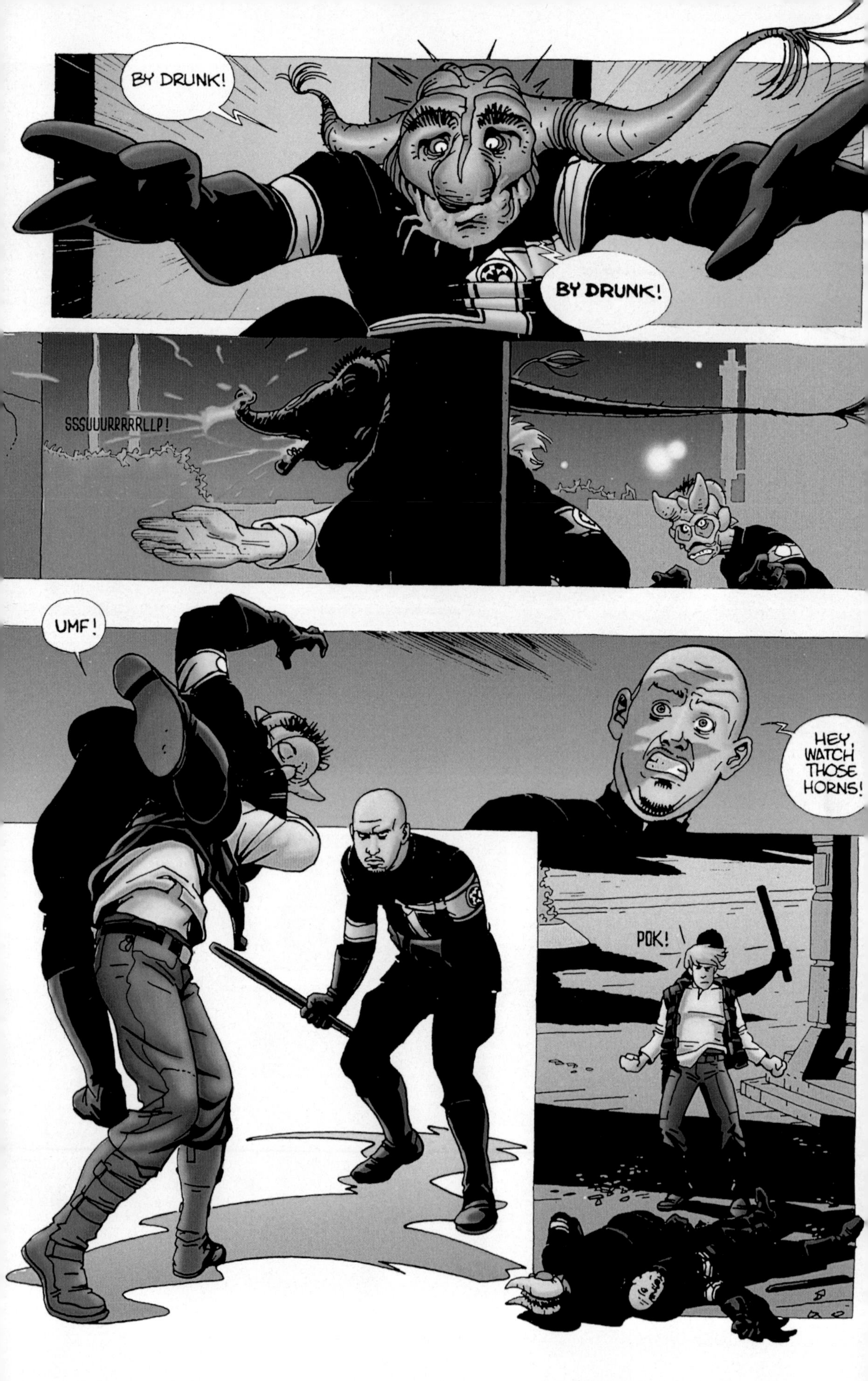
BY DRUNK!
BY DRUNK!
SSSUUURRRRRLLP!
UMF!
HEY, WATCH THOSE HORNS!
POK!

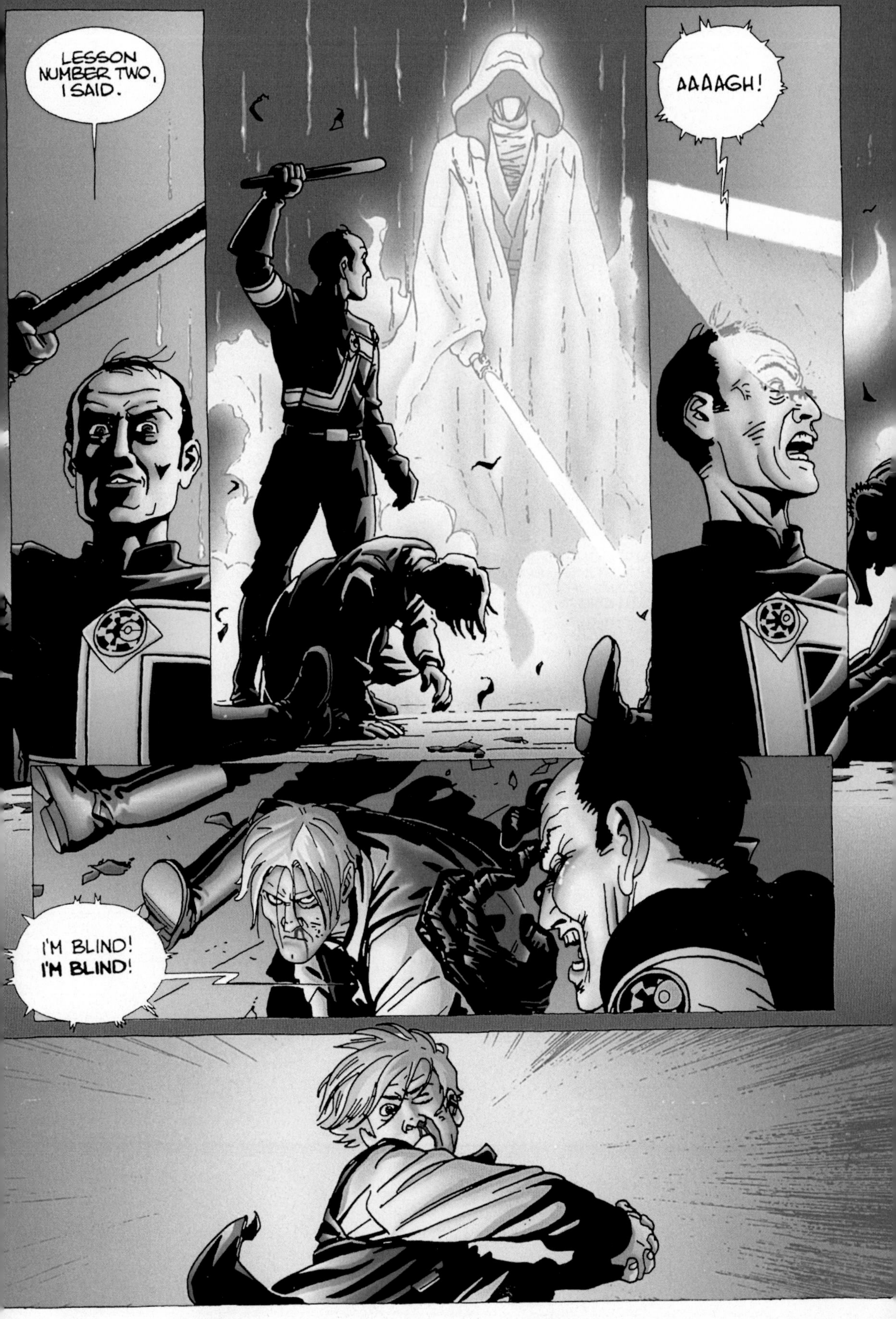
LESSON NUMBER TWO, I SAID.
AAAAGH!
I'M BLIND! I'M BLIND!

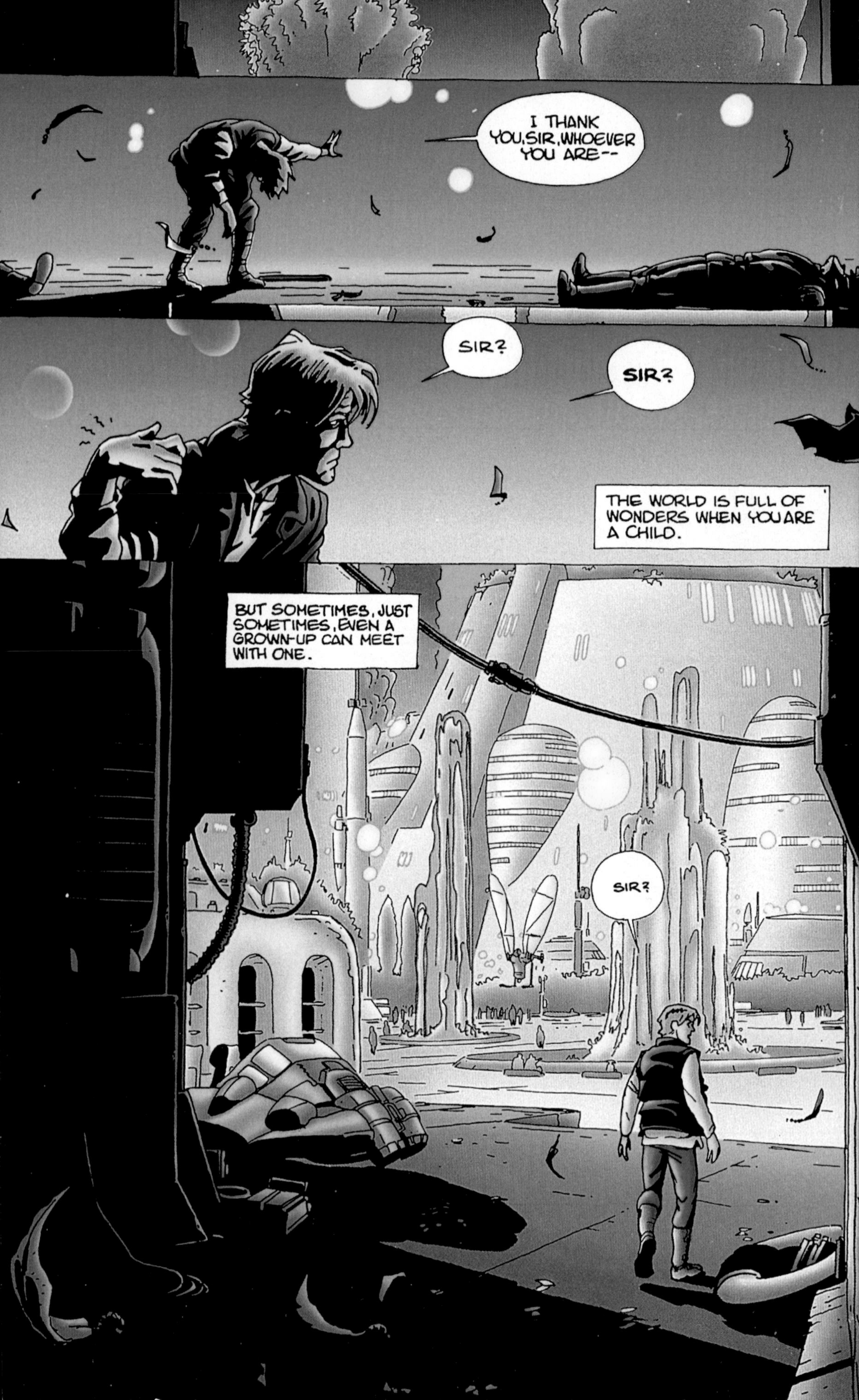
I THANK YOU,SIR,WHOEVER YOU ARE--
SIR?
SIR?
THE WORLD IS FULL OF WONDERS WHEN YOU ARE A CHILD.
BUT SOMETIMES, JUST SOMETIMES, EVEN A GROWN-UP CAN MEET WITH ONE.
SIR?

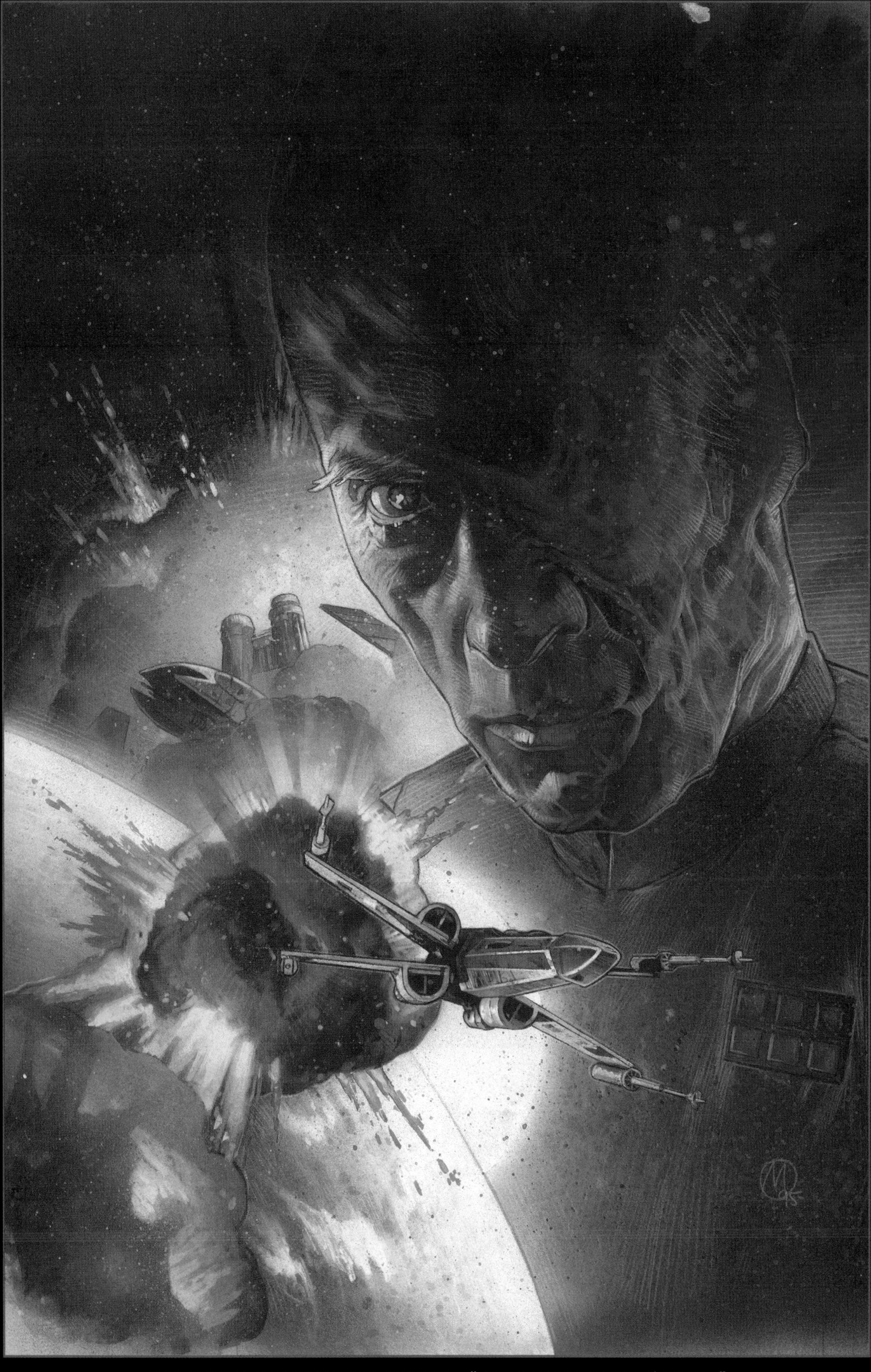

*STAR WARS: X-WING ROGUE SQUADRON #6* — "THE PHANTOM AFFAIR, CHAPTER 2"

PLOTTER: MICHAEL A. STACKPOLE • SCRIPTER: DARKO MACAN • ARTIST & LETTERER: EDVIN BIUKOVIĆ • COLORIST: DAVE NESTELLE
EDITOR: PEET JANES • COVER ARTIST: MATHIEU LAUFFRAY

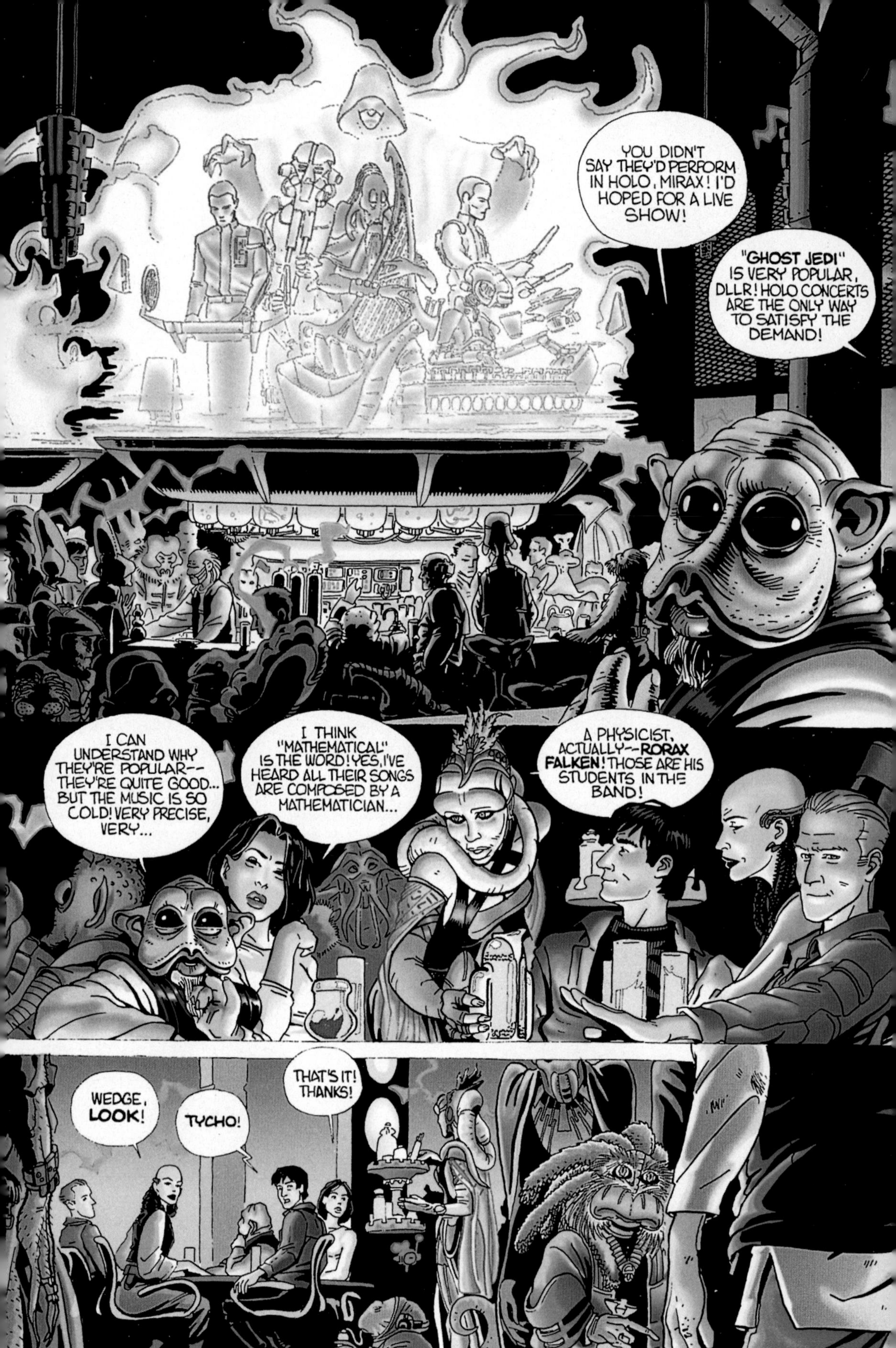
YOU DIDN'T SAY THEY'D PERFORM IN HOLO, MIRAX! I'D HOPED FOR A LIVE SHOW!
"GHOST JEDI" IS VERY POPULAR, DLLR! HOLO CONCERTS ARE THE ONLY WAY TO SATISFY THE DEMAND!
I CAN UNDERSTAND WHY THEY'RE POPULAR-- THEY'RE QUITE GOOD... BUT THE MUSIC IS SO COLD! VERY PRECISE, VERY...
I THINK "MATHEMATICAL" IS THE WORD! YES, I'VE HEARD ALL THEIR SONGS ARE COMPOSED BY A MATHEMATICIAN...
A PHYSICIST, ACTUALLY--RORAX FALKEN! THOSE ARE HIS STUDENTS IN THE BAND!
WEDGE, LOOK!
TYCHO!
THAT'S IT! THANKS!

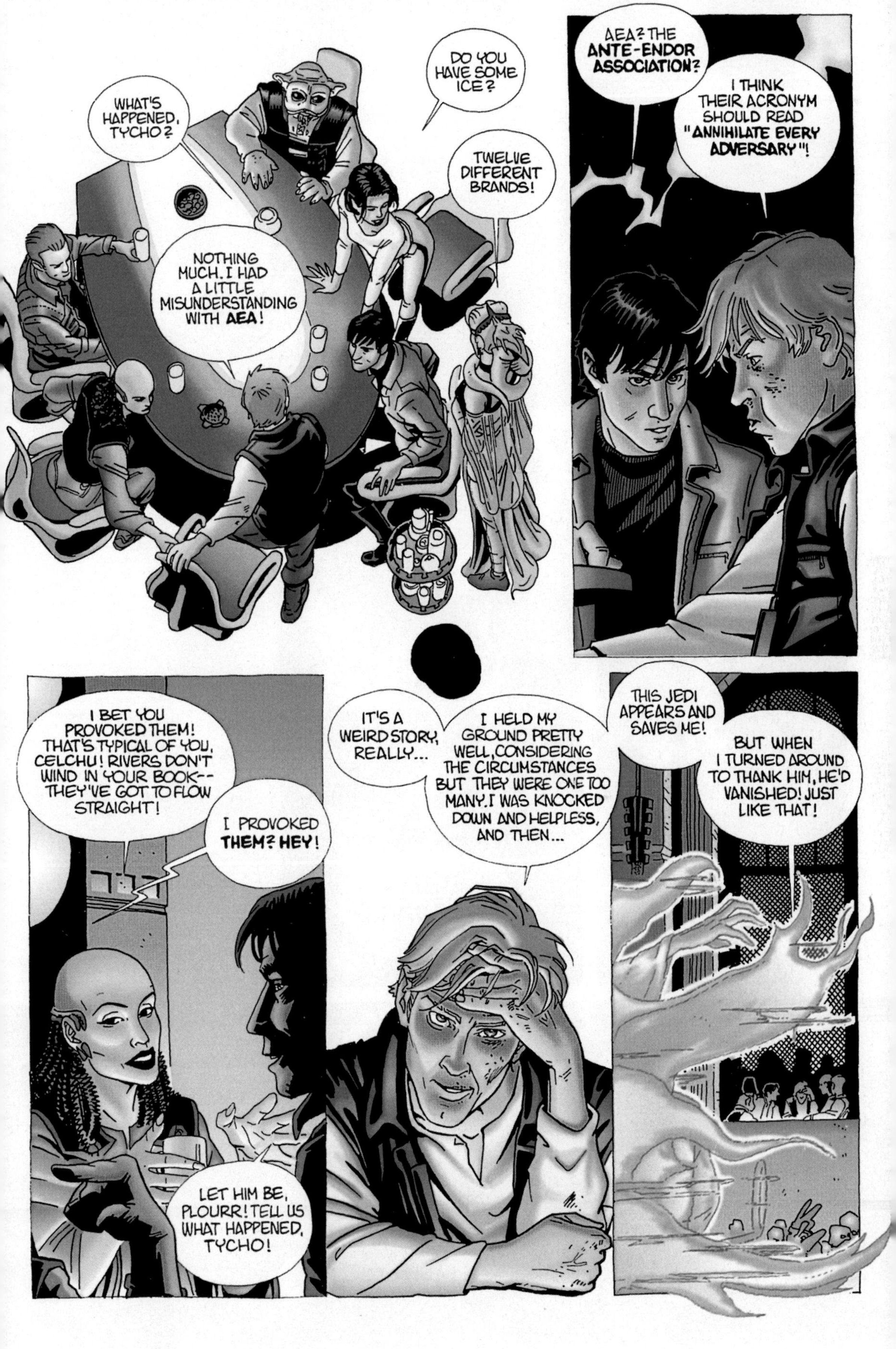
WHAT'S HAPPENED, TYCHO?
DO YOU HAVE SOME ICE?
TWELVE DIFFERENT BRANDS!
NOTHING MUCH. I HAD A LITTLE MISUNDERSTANDING WITH AEA!
AEA? THE ANTE-ENDOR ASSOCIATION?
I THINK THEIR ACRONYM SHOULD READ "ANNIHILATE EVERY ADVERSARY"!
I BET YOU PROVOKED THEM! THAT'S TYPICAL OF YOU, CELCHU! RIVERS DON'T WIND IN YOUR BOOK-- THEY'VE GOT TO FLOW STRAIGHT!
I PROVOKED THEM? HEY!
LET HIM BE, PLOURR! TELL US WHAT HAPPENED, TYCHO!
IT'S A WEIRD STORY, REALLY...
I HELD MY GROUND PRETTY WELL, CONSIDERING THE CIRCUMSTANCES BUT THEY WERE ONE TOO MANY. I WAS KNOCKED DOWN AND HELPLESS, AND THEN...
THIS JEDI APPEARS AND SAVES ME!
BUT WHEN I TURNED AROUND TO THANK HIM, HE'D VANISHED! JUST LIKE THAT!

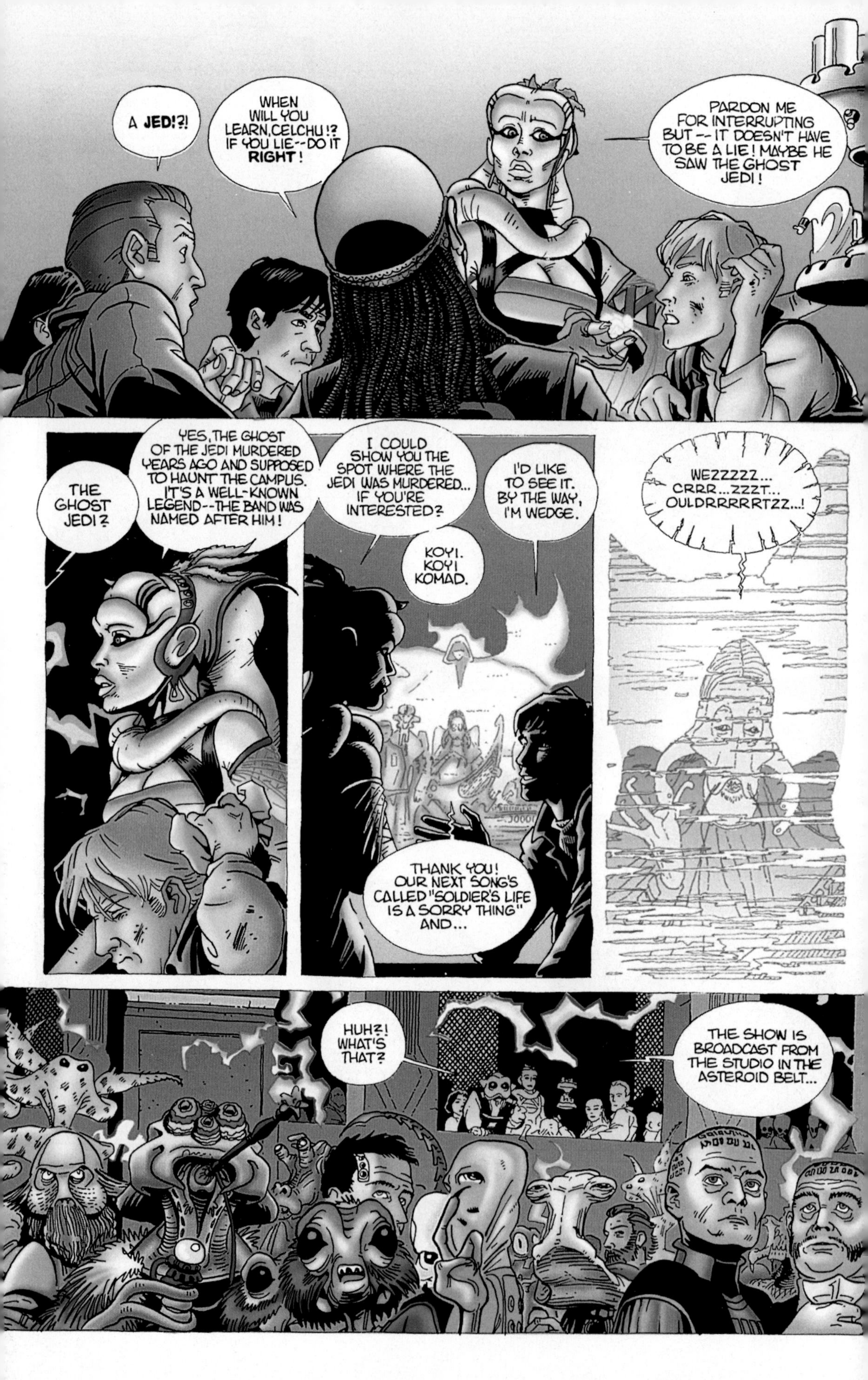
A JEDI?!
WHEN WILL YOU LEARN, CELCHU!? IF YOU LIE--DO IT RIGHT!
PARDON ME FOR INTERRUPTING BUT -- IT DOESN'T HAVE TO BE A LIE! MAYBE HE SAW THE GHOST JEDI!
THE GHOST JEDI?
YES, THE GHOST OF THE JEDI MURDERED YEARS AGO AND SUPPOSED TO HAUNT THE CAMPUS. IT'S A WELL-KNOWN LEGEND--THE BAND WAS NAMED AFTER HIM!
I COULD SHOW YOU THE SPOT WHERE THE JEDI WAS MURDERED... IF YOU'RE INTERESTED?
I'D LIKE TO SEE IT. BY THE WAY, I'M WEDGE.
KOYI. KOYI KOMAD.
THANK YOU! OUR NEXT SONG'S CALLED "SOLDIER'S LIFE IS A SORRY THING" AND...
WEZZZZZ... CRRR...ZZZT... OULDRRRRRTZZ...!
HUH?! WHAT'S THAT?
THE SHOW IS BROADCAST FROM THE STUDIO IN THE ASTEROID BELT...

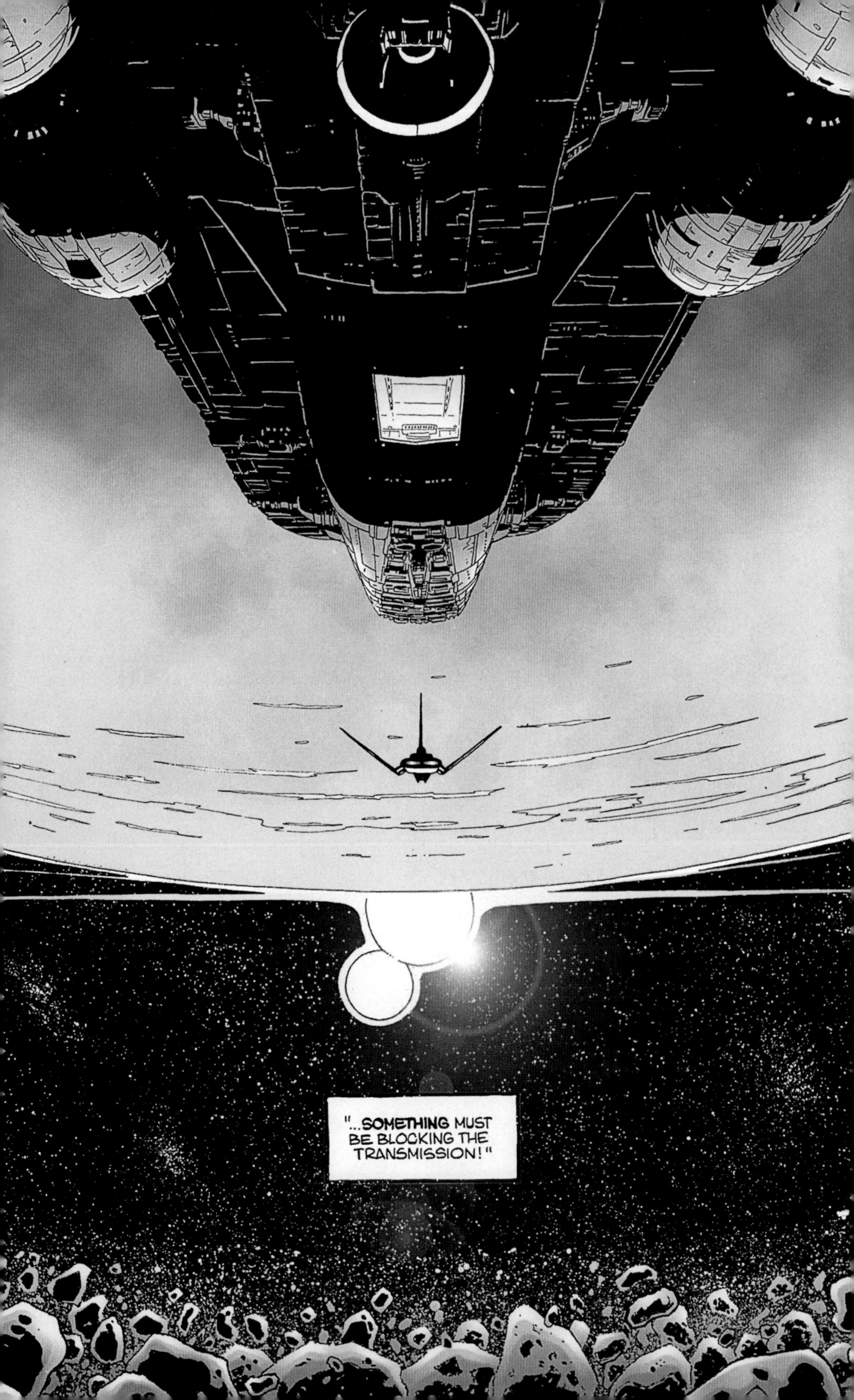
"...SOMETHING MUST BE BLOCKING THE TRANSMISSION!"

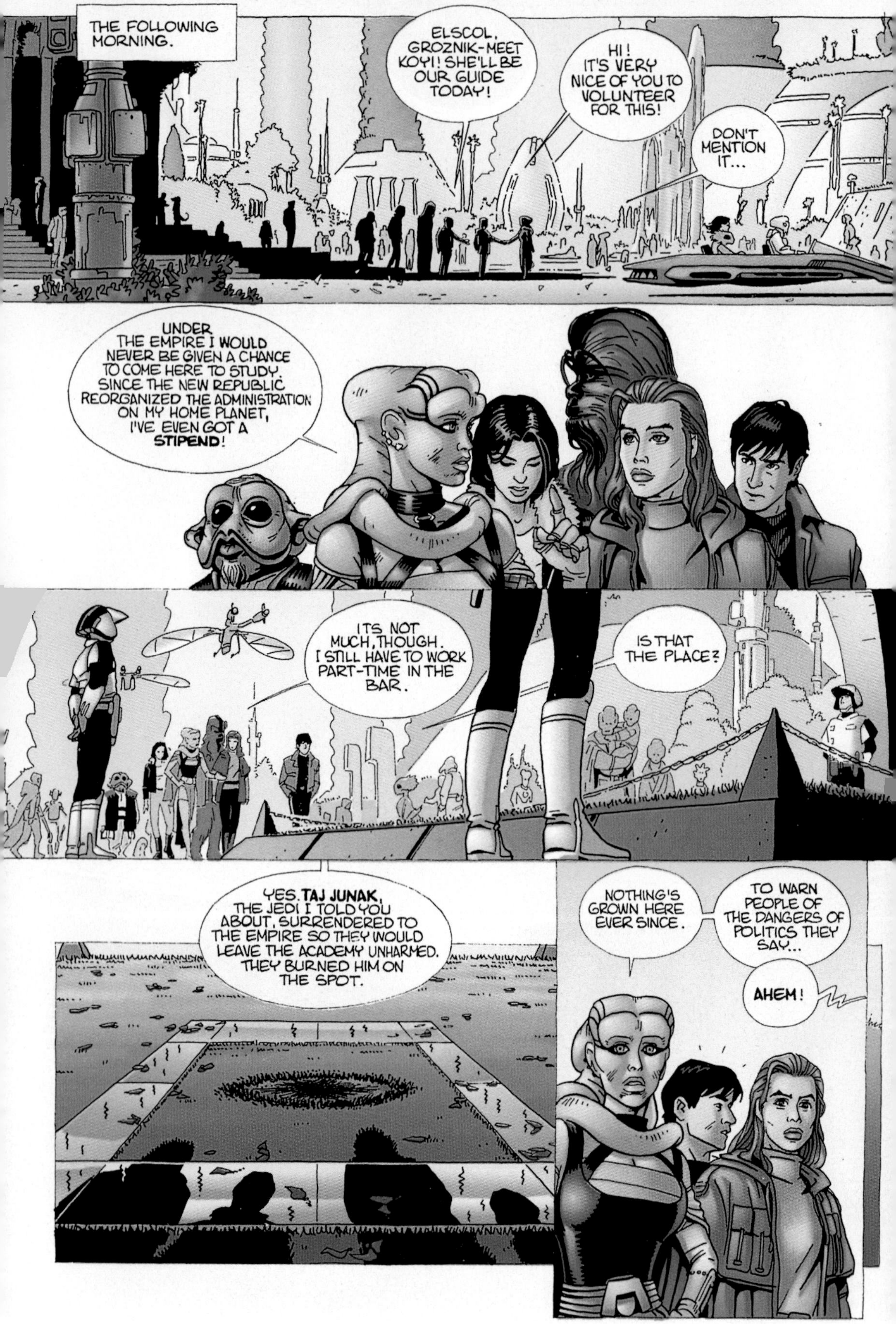

THE FOLLOWING MORNING.
ELSCOL, GROZNIK-MEET KOYI! SHE'LL BE OUR GUIDE TODAY!
HI! IT'S VERY NICE OF YOU TO VOLUNTEER FOR THIS!
DON'T MENTION IT...
UNDER THE EMPIRE I WOULD NEVER BE GIVEN A CHANCE TO COME HERE TO STUDY. SINCE THE NEW REPUBLIC REORGANIZED THE ADMINISTRATION ON MY HOME PLANET, I'VE EVEN GOT A **STIPEND**!
ITS NOT MUCH, THOUGH. I STILL HAVE TO WORK PART-TIME IN THE BAR.
IS THAT THE PLACE?
YES. **TAJ JUNAK**, THE JEDI I TOLD YOU ABOUT, SURRENDERED TO THE EMPIRE SO THEY WOULD LEAVE THE ACADEMY UNHARMED. THEY BURNED HIM ON THE SPOT.
NOTHING'S GROWN HERE EVER SINCE.
TO WARN PEOPLE OF THE DANGERS OF POLITICS THEY SAY...
**AHEM**!

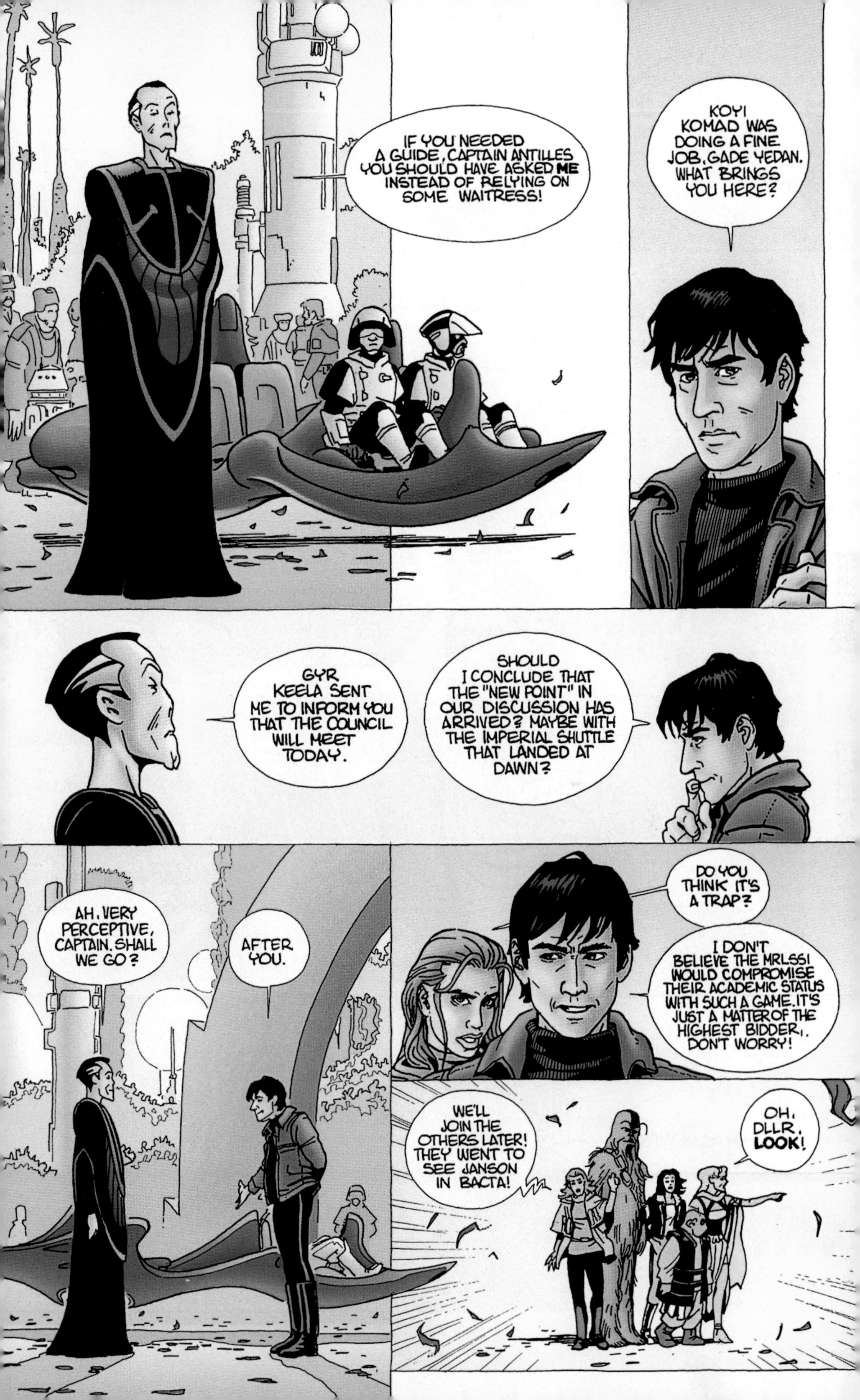
IF YOU NEEDED A GUIDE, CAPTAIN ANTILLES YOU SHOULD HAVE ASKED **ME** INSTEAD OF RELYING ON SOME WAITRESS!
KOYI KOMAD WAS DOING A FINE JOB, GADE YEDAN. WHAT BRINGS YOU HERE?
GYR KEELA SENT ME TO INFORM YOU THAT THE COUNCIL WILL MEET TODAY.
SHOULD I CONCLUDE THAT THE "NEW POINT" IN OUR DISCUSSION HAS ARRIVED? MAYBE WITH THE IMPERIAL SHUTTLE THAT LANDED AT DAWN?
AH, VERY PERCEPTIVE, CAPTAIN. SHALL WE GO?
AFTER YOU.
DO YOU THINK IT'S A TRAP?
I DON'T BELIEVE THE MRLSSI WOULD COMPROMISE THEIR ACADEMIC STATUS WITH SUCH A GAME. IT'S JUST A MATTER OF THE HIGHEST BIDDER.. DON'T WORRY!
WE'LL JOIN THE OTHERS LATER! THEY WENT TO SEE JANSON IN BACTA!
OH, DLLR, **LOOK**!

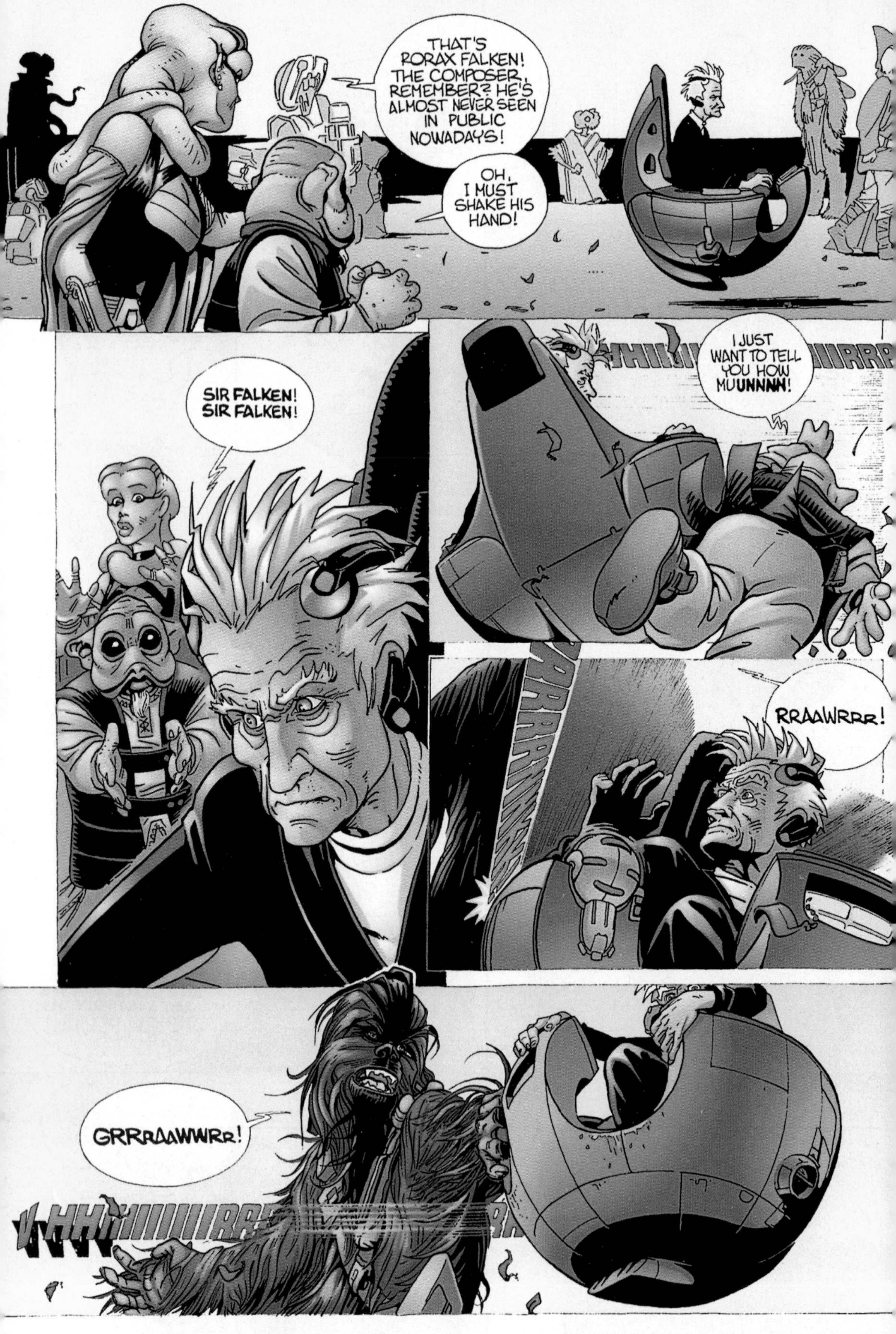
THAT'S RORAX FALKEN! THE COMPOSER, REMEMBER? HE'S ALMOST NEVER SEEN IN PUBLIC NOWADAYS!
OH, I MUST SHAKE HIS HAND!
SIR FALKEN! SIR FALKEN!
I JUST WANT TO TELL YOU HOW MUUNNNN!
RRAAWRRR!
GRRRAAWWRR!

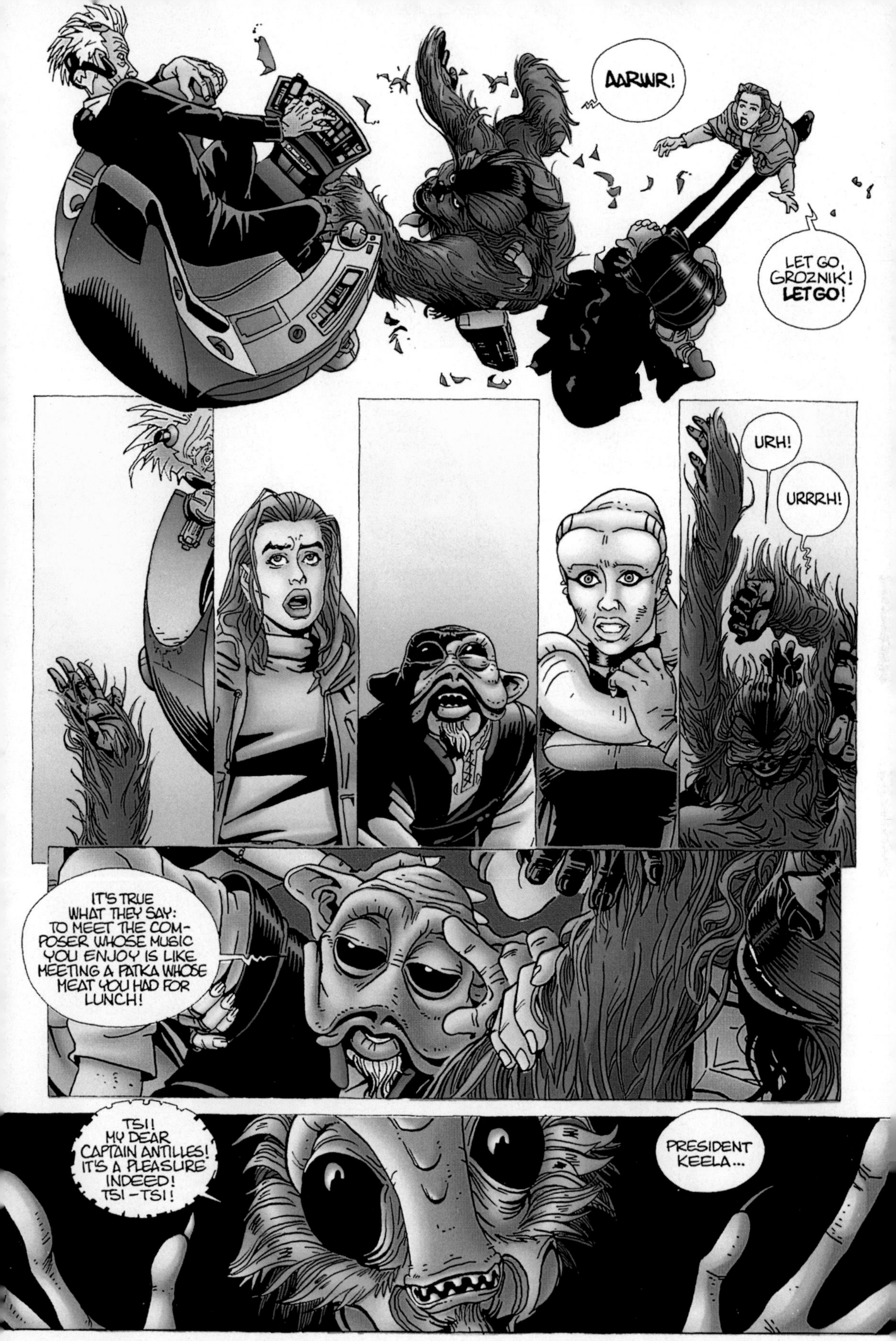
AARWR!
LET GO, GROZNIK! LET GO!
URH!
URRRH!
IT'S TRUE WHAT THEY SAY: TO MEET THE COMPOSER WHOSE MUSIC YOU ENJOY IS LIKE MEETING A PATKA WHOSE MEAT YOU HAD FOR LUNCH!
TSI! MY DEAR CAPTAIN ANTILLES! IT'S A PLEASURE INDEED! TSI-TSI!
PRESIDENT KEELA...

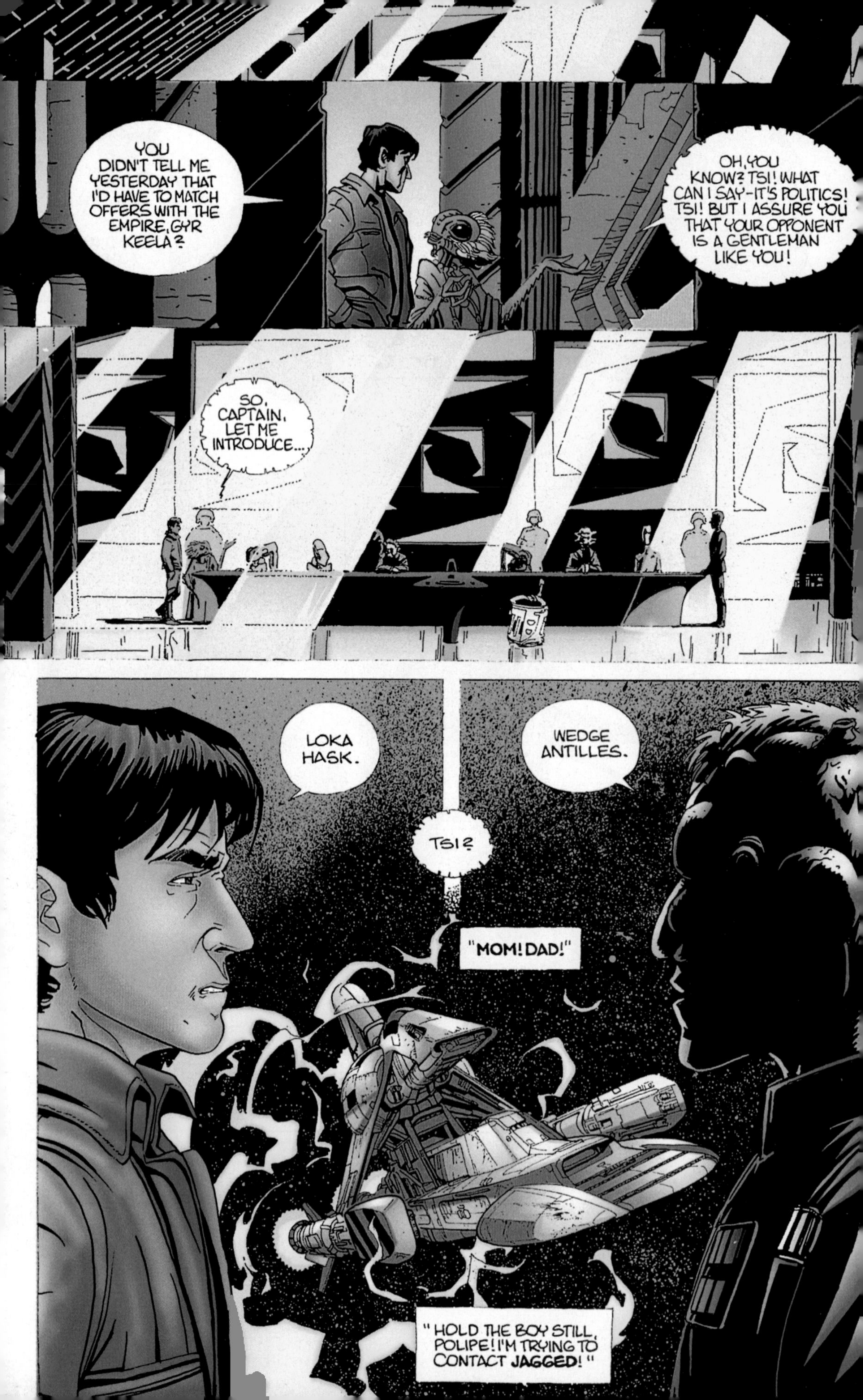
YOU DIDN'T TELL ME YESTERDAY THAT I'D HAVE TO MATCH OFFERS WITH THE EMPIRE, GYR KEELA?
OH, YOU KNOW? TSI! WHAT CAN I SAY-IT'S POLITICS! TSI! BUT I ASSURE YOU THAT YOUR OPPONENT IS A GENTLEMAN LIKE YOU!
SO, CAPTAIN, LET ME INTRODUCE...
LOKA HASK.
WEDGE ANTILLES.
TSI?
"MOM! DAD!"
"HOLD THE BOY STILL, POLIPE! I'M TRYING TO CONTACT JAGGED!"

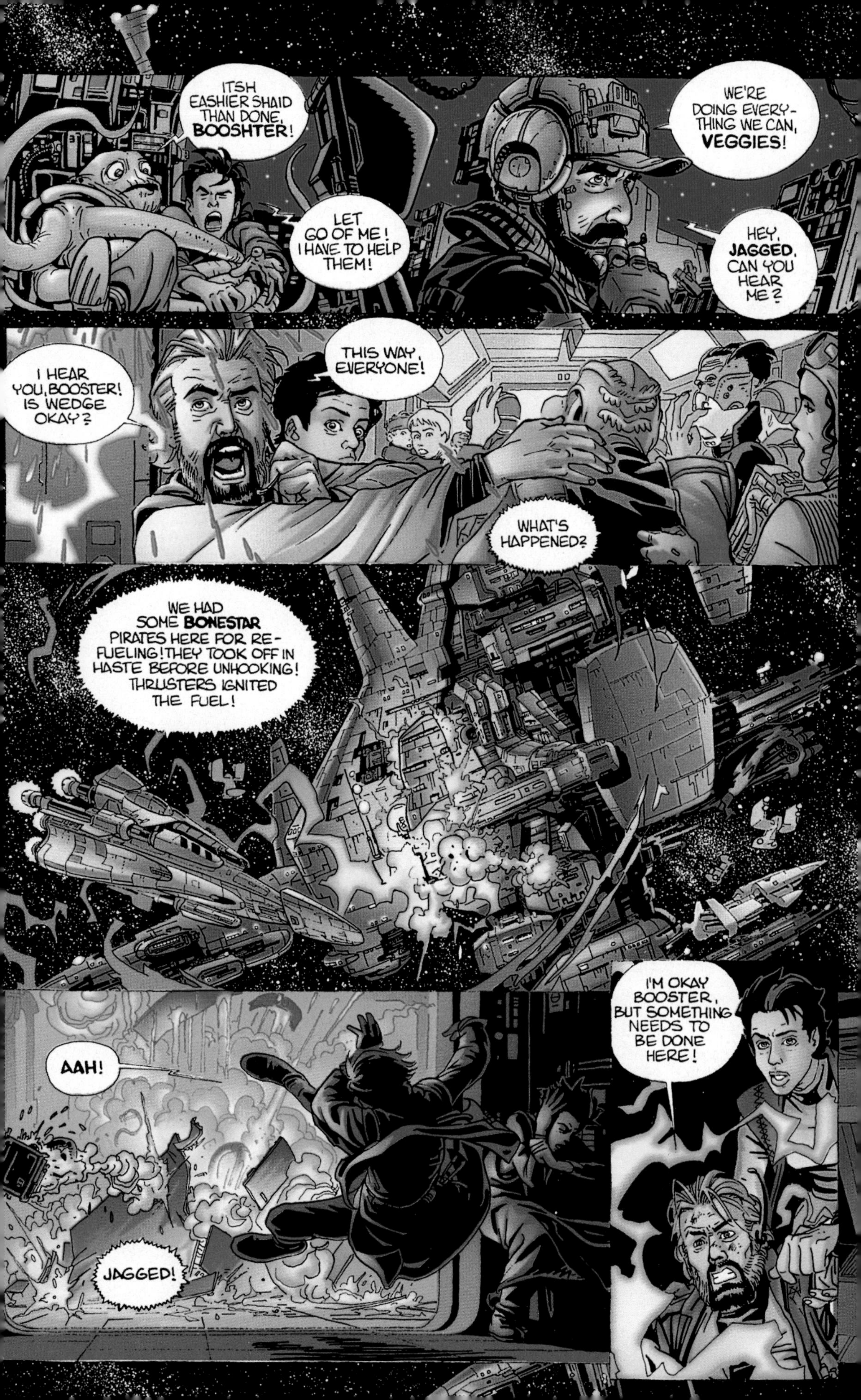
ITSH EASHIER SHAID THAN DONE, BOOSHTER!
LET GO OF ME! I HAVE TO HELP THEM!
WE'RE DOING EVERY-THING WE CAN, VEGGIES!
HEY, JAGGED, CAN YOU HEAR ME?
I HEAR YOU, BOOSTER! IS WEDGE OKAY?
THIS WAY, EVERYONE!
WHAT'S HAPPENED?
WE HAD SOME BONESTAR PIRATES HERE FOR RE-FUELING! THEY TOOK OFF IN HASTE BEFORE UNHOOKING! THRUSTERS IGNITED THE FUEL!
AAH!
JAGGED!
I'M OKAY BOOSTER, BUT SOMETHING NEEDS TO BE DONE HERE!

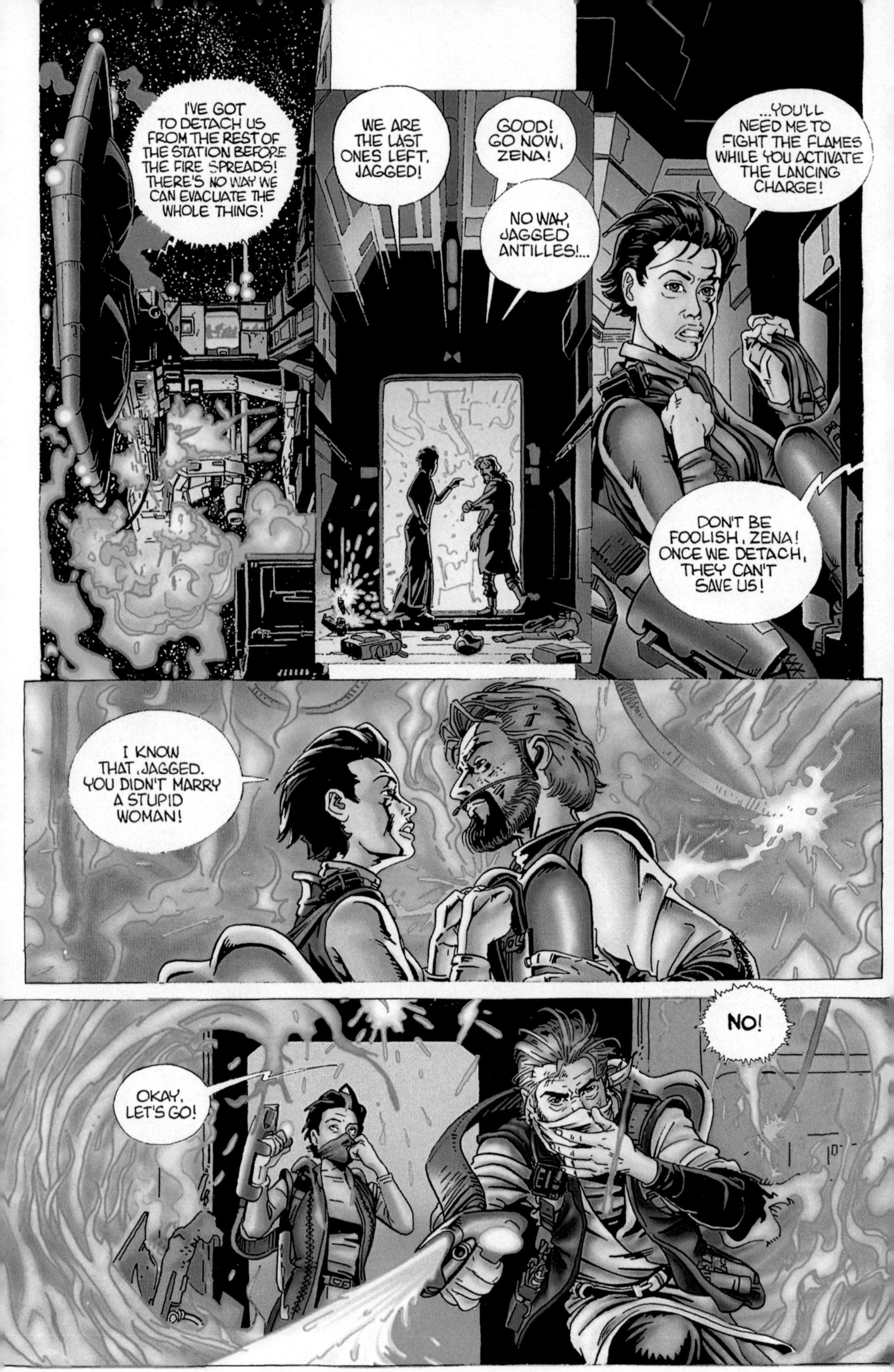
I'VE GOT TO DETACH US FROM THE REST OF THE STATION BEFORE THE FIRE SPREADS! THERE'S NO WAY WE CAN EVACUATE THE WHOLE THING!
WE ARE THE LAST ONES LEFT, JAGGED!
GOOD! GO NOW, ZENA!
NO WAY, JAGGED ANTILLES!...
...YOU'LL NEED ME TO FIGHT THE FLAMES WHILE YOU ACTIVATE THE LANCING CHARGE!
DON'T BE FOOLISH, ZENA! ONCE WE DETACH, THEY CAN'T SAVE US!
I KNOW THAT, JAGGED. YOU DIDN'T MARRY A STUPID WOMAN!
NO!
OKAY, LET'S GO!

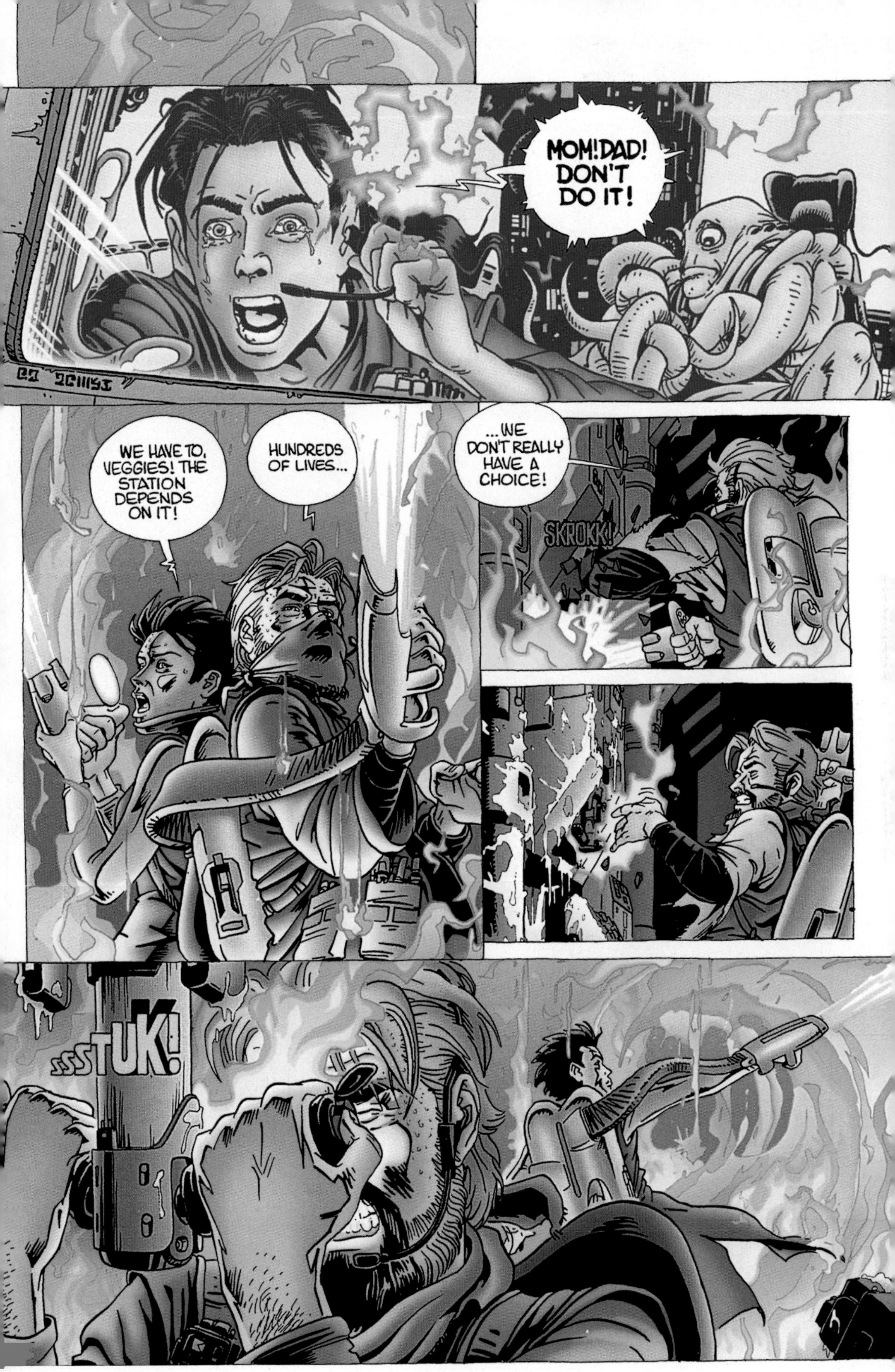
MOM! DAD! DON'T DO IT!
WE HAVE TO, VEGGIES! THE STATION DEPENDS ON IT!
HUNDREDS OF LIVES...
...WE DON'T REALLY HAVE A CHOICE!
SKROKK!
SSSTUK!

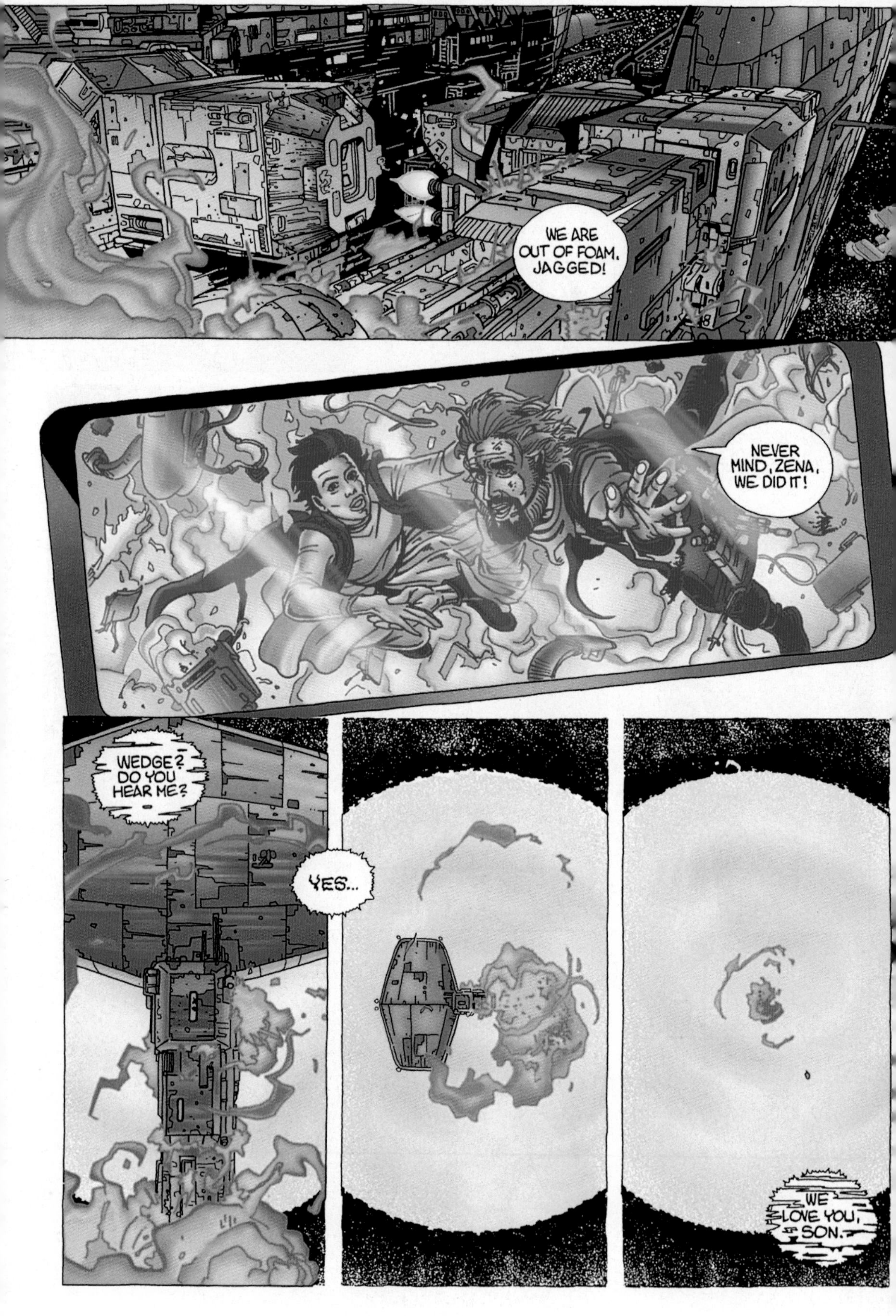
WE ARE OUT OF FOAM, JAGGED!
NEVER MIND, ZENA, WE DID IT!
WEDGE? DO YOU HEAR ME?
YES...
WE LOVE YOU, SON.

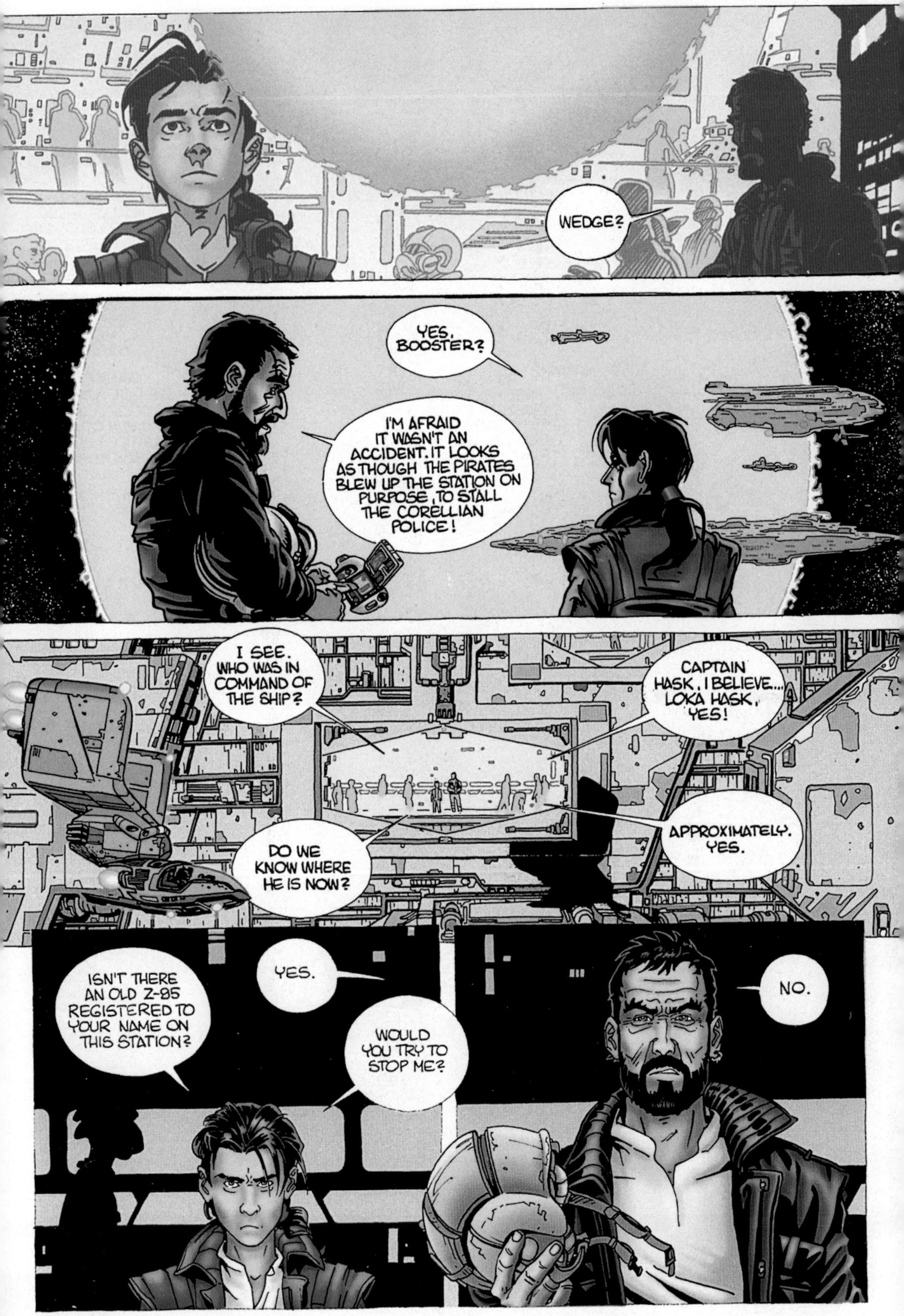
WEDGE?
YES. BOOSTER?
I'M AFRAID IT WASN'T AN ACCIDENT. IT LOOKS AS THOUGH THE PIRATES BLEW UP THE STATION ON PURPOSE, TO STALL THE CORELLIAN POLICE!
I SEE. WHO WAS IN COMMAND OF THE SHIP?
CAPTAIN HASK, I BELIEVE... LOKA HASK, YES!
DO WE KNOW WHERE HE IS NOW?
APPROXIMATELY. YES.
ISN'T THERE AN OLD Z-95 REGISTERED TO YOUR NAME ON THIS STATION?
YES.
WOULD YOU TRY TO STOP ME?
NO.

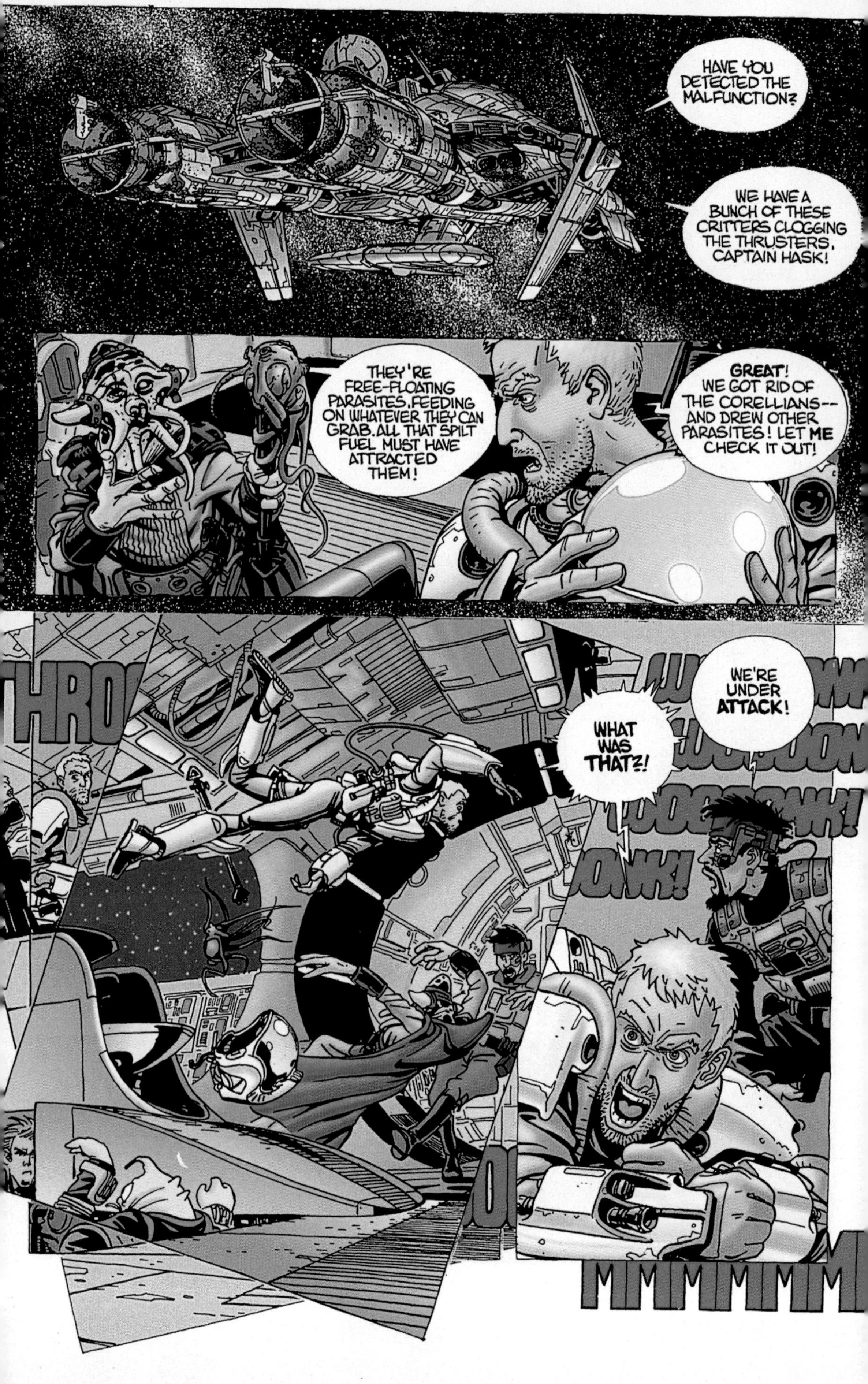
HAVE YOU DETECTED THE MALFUNCTION?
WE HAVE A BUNCH OF THESE CRITTERS CLOGGING THE THRUSTERS, CAPTAIN HASK!
THEY'RE FREE-FLOATING PARASITES, FEEDING ON WHATEVER THEY CAN GRAB. ALL THAT SPILT FUEL MUST HAVE ATTRACTED THEM!
GREAT! WE GOT RID OF THE CORELLIANS-- AND DREW OTHER PARASITES! LET ME CHECK IT OUT!
WE'RE UNDER ATTACK!
WHAT WAS THAT?!
MMMMMMM

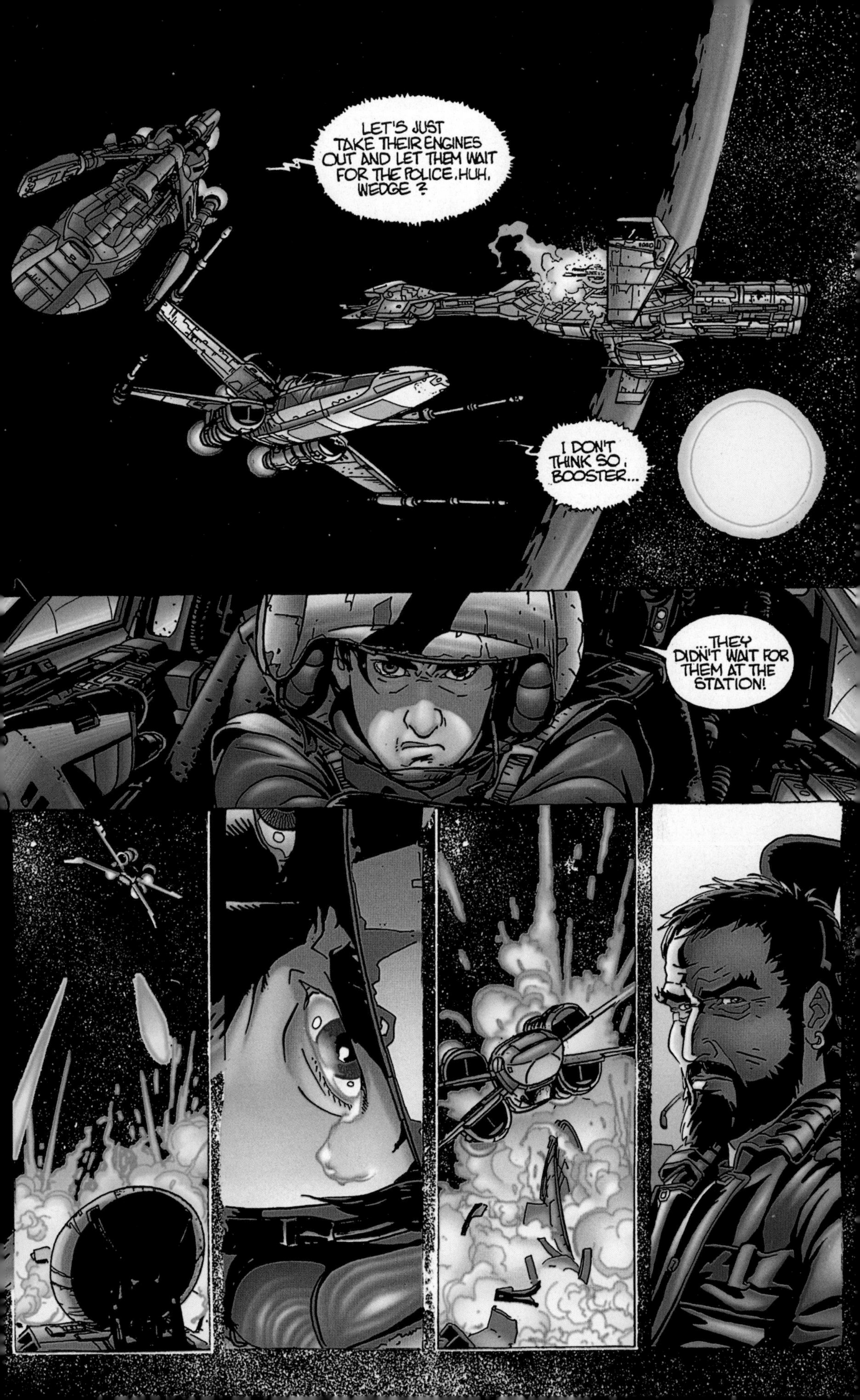
LET'S JUST TAKE THEIR ENGINES OUT AND LET THEM WAIT FOR THE POLICE. HUH, WEDGE ?
I DON'T THINK SO, BOOSTER...
...THEY DIDN'T WAIT FOR THEM AT THE STATION!

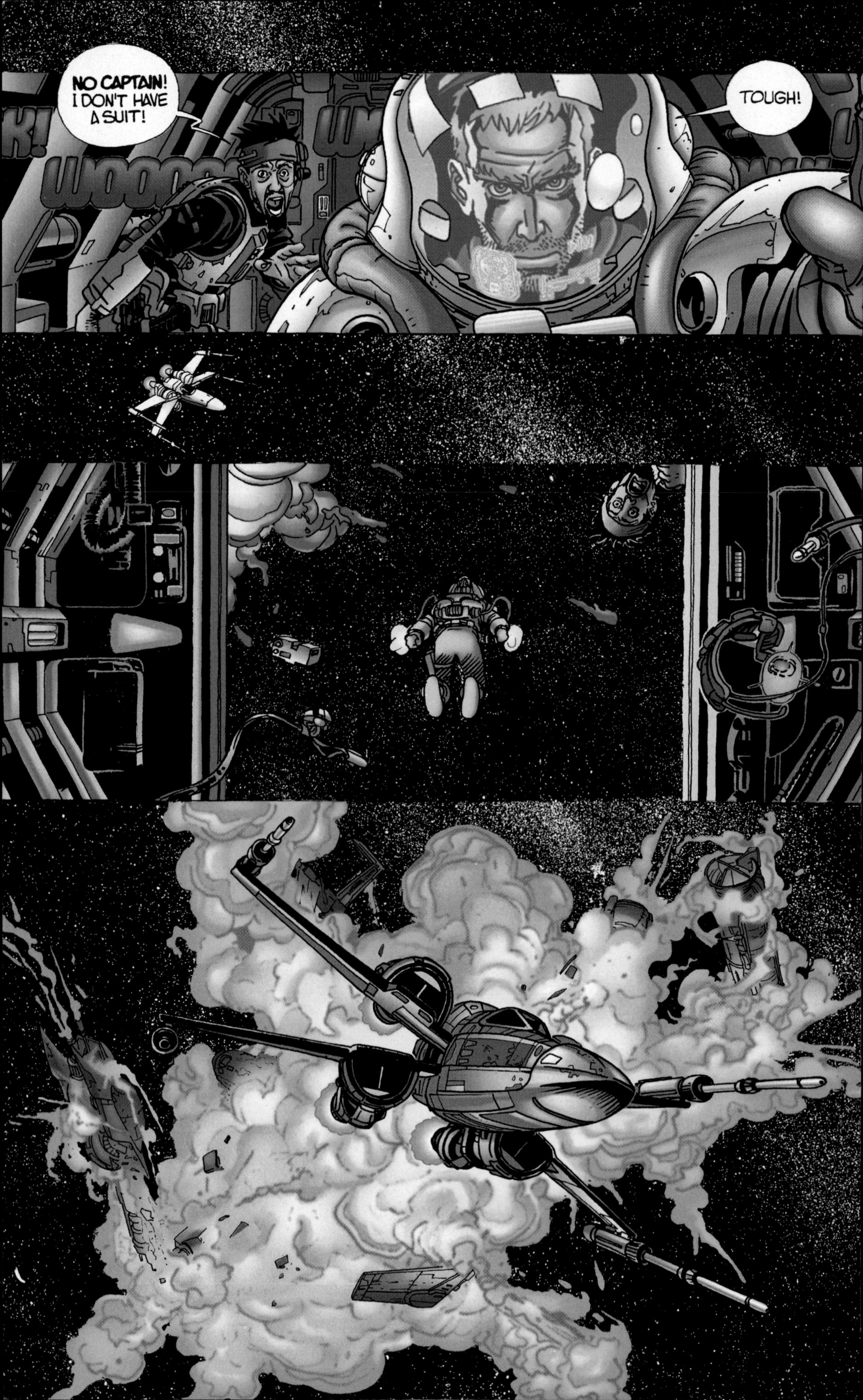
NO CAPTAIN! I DON'T HAVE A SUIT!
TOUGH!

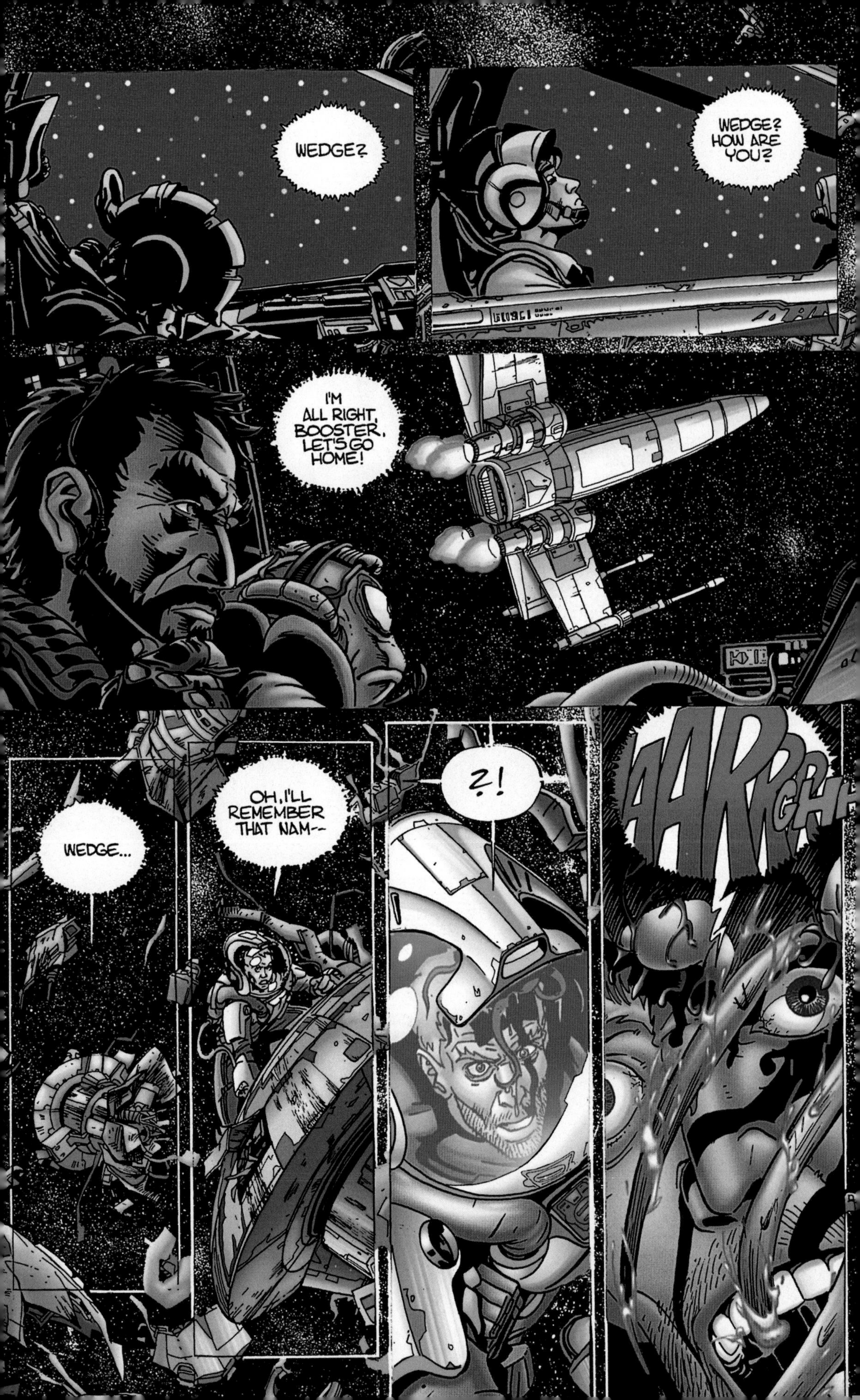
WEDGE?
WEDGE? HOW ARE YOU?
I'M ALL RIGHT, BOOSTER. LET'S GO HOME!
WEDGE...
OH, I'LL REMEMBER THAT NAM--
?!
AARRGHH

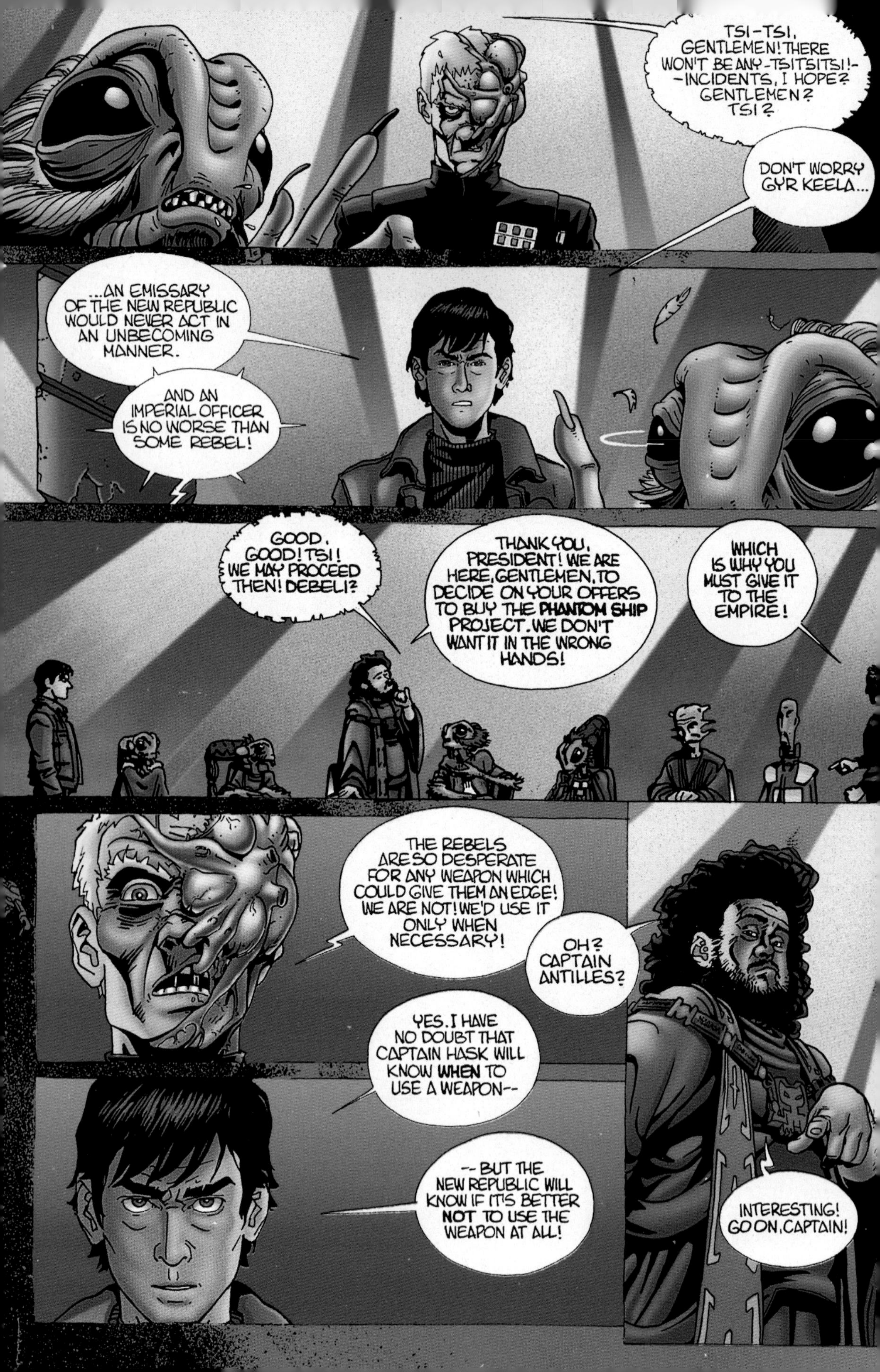
TSI-TSI, GENTLEMEN! THERE WON'T BE ANY-TSITSITSI!- -INCIDENTS, I HOPE? GENTLEMEN? TSI?
DON'T WORRY GYR KEELA...
...AN EMISSARY OF THE NEW REPUBLIC WOULD NEVER ACT IN AN UNBECOMING MANNER.
AND AN IMPERIAL OFFICER IS NO WORSE THAN SOME REBEL!
GOOD, GOOD! TSI! WE MAY PROCEED THEN! DEBELI?
THANK YOU, PRESIDENT! WE ARE HERE, GENTLEMEN, TO DECIDE ON YOUR OFFERS TO BUY THE PHANTOM SHIP PROJECT. WE DON'T WANT IT IN THE WRONG HANDS!
WHICH IS WHY YOU MUST GIVE IT TO THE EMPIRE!
THE REBELS ARE SO DESPERATE FOR ANY WEAPON WHICH COULD GIVE THEM AN EDGE! WE ARE NOT! WE'D USE IT ONLY WHEN NECESSARY!
OH? CAPTAIN ANTILLES?
YES. I HAVE NO DOUBT THAT CAPTAIN HASK WILL KNOW WHEN TO USE A WEAPON--
--BUT THE NEW REPUBLIC WILL KNOW IF IT'S BETTER NOT TO USE THE WEAPON AT ALL!
INTERESTING! GO ON, CAPTAIN!

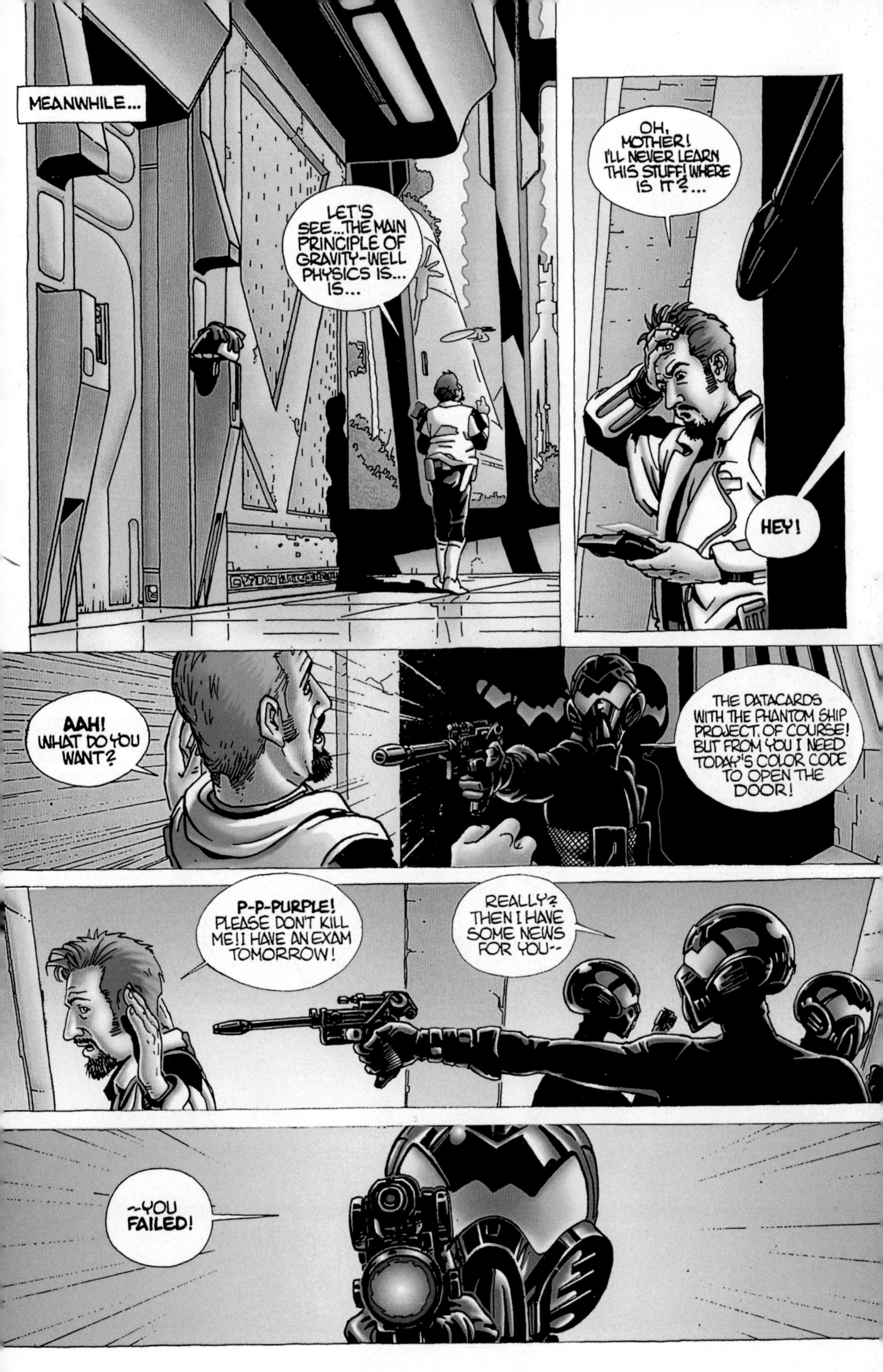
MEANWHILE...
LET'S SEE...THE MAIN PRINCIPLE OF GRAVITY-WELL PHYSICS IS... IS...
OH, MOTHER! I'LL NEVER LEARN THIS STUFF! WHERE IS IT?...
HEY!
AAH! WHAT DO YOU WANT?
THE DATACARDS WITH THE PHANTOM SHIP PROJECT, OF COURSE! BUT FROM YOU I NEED TODAY'S COLOR CODE TO OPEN THE DOOR!
P-P-PURPLE! PLEASE DON'T KILL ME!! I HAVE AN EXAM TOMORROW!
REALLY? THEN I HAVE SOME NEWS FOR YOU--
--YOU FAILED!

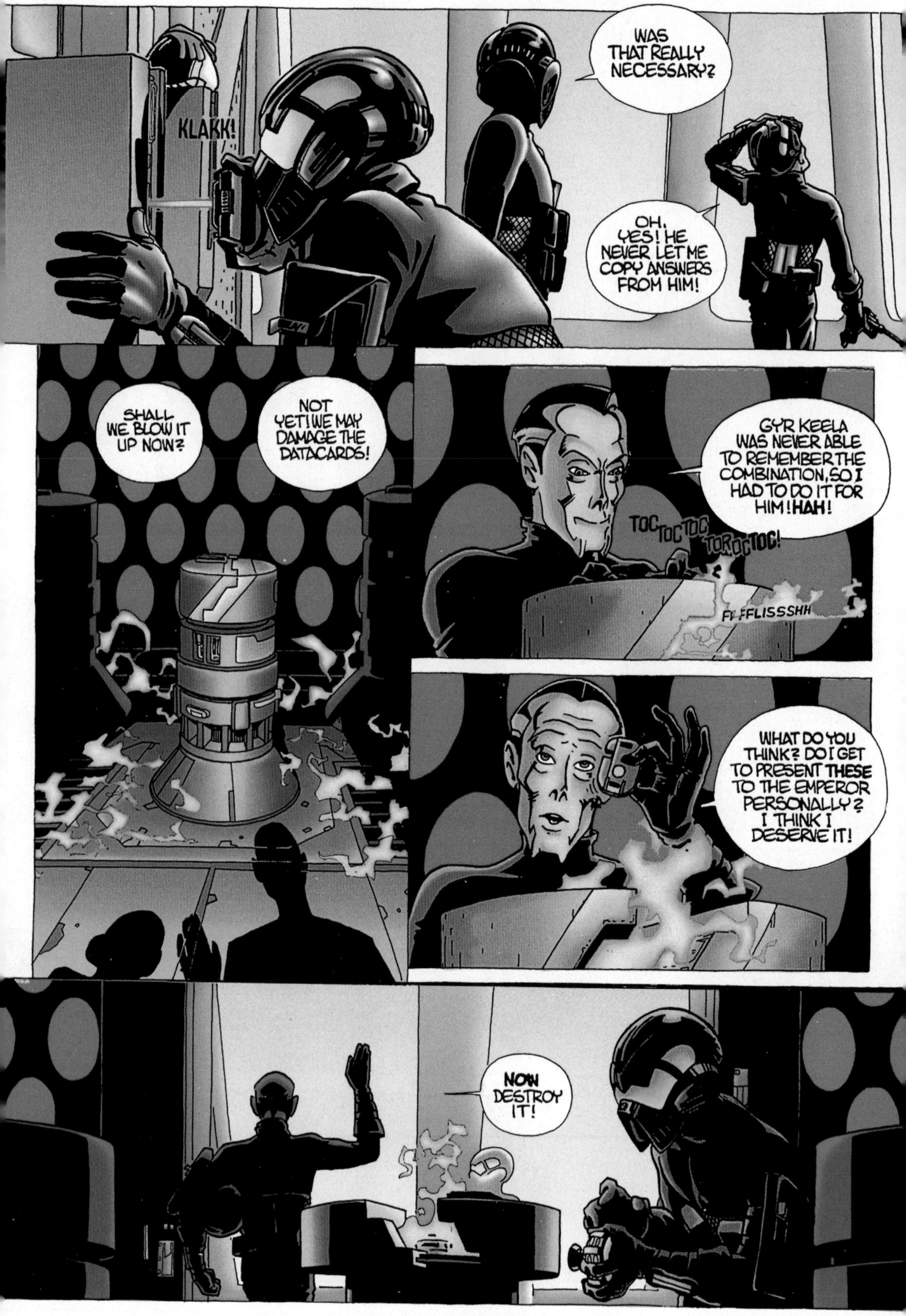
KLAKK!
WAS THAT REALLY NECESSARY?
OH, YES! HE NEVER LET ME COPY ANSWERS FROM HIM!
SHALL WE BLOW IT UP NOW?
NOT YET! WE MAY DAMAGE THE DATACARDS!
GYR KEELA WAS NEVER ABLE TO REMEMBER THE COMBINATION, SO I HAD TO DO IT FOR HIM! HAH!
TOC TOC TOC TOROC TOC!
FFFFLISSSHH
WHAT DO YOU THINK? DO I GET TO PRESENT THESE TO THE EMPEROR PERSONALLY? I THINK I DESERVE IT!
NOW DESTROY IT!

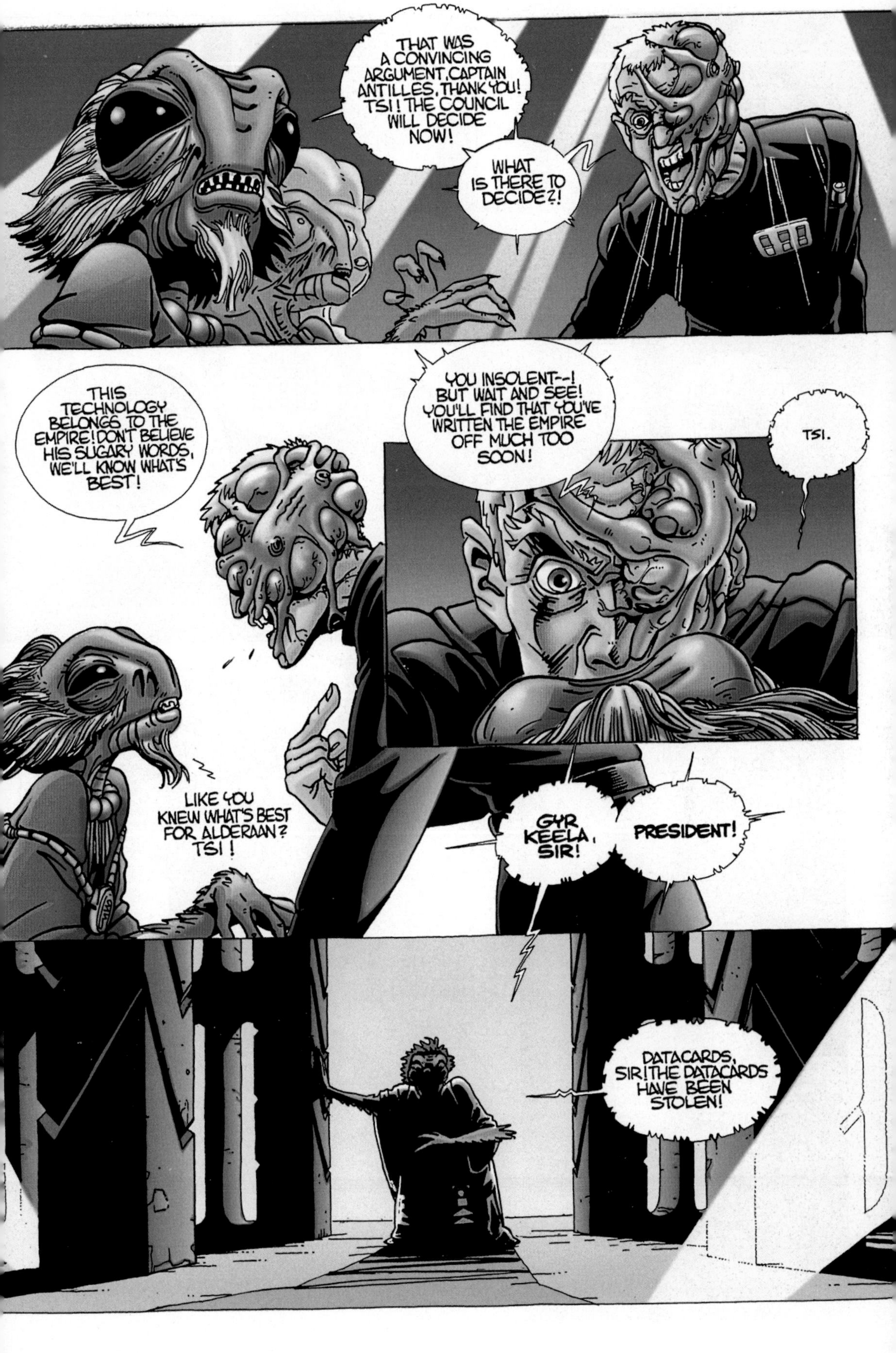
THAT WAS A CONVINCING ARGUMENT, CAPTAIN ANTILLES, THANK YOU! TSI! THE COUNCIL WILL DECIDE NOW!
WHAT IS THERE TO DECIDE?!
THIS TECHNOLOGY BELONGS TO THE EMPIRE! DON'T BELIEVE HIS SUGARY WORDS, WE'LL KNOW WHAT'S BEST!
YOU INSOLENT--! BUT WAIT AND SEE! YOU'LL FIND THAT YOU'VE WRITTEN THE EMPIRE OFF MUCH TOO SOON!
TSI.
LIKE YOU KNEW WHAT'S BEST FOR ALDERAAN? TSI!
GYR KEELA, SIR!
PRESIDENT!
DATACARDS, SIR! THE DATACARDS HAVE BEEN STOLEN!

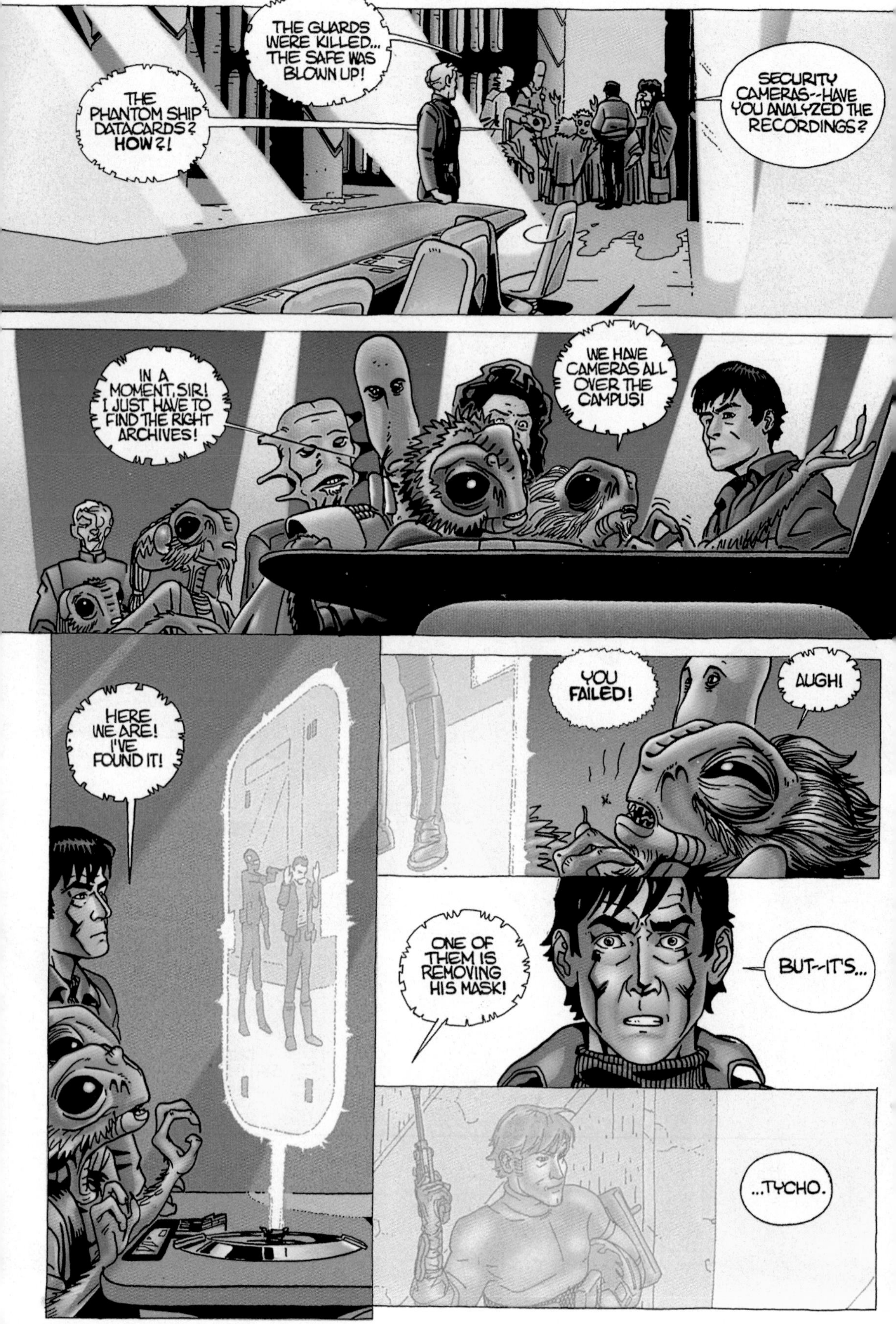
THE PHANTOM SHIP DATACARDS? HOW?!
THE GUARDS WERE KILLED... THE SAFE WAS BLOWN UP!
SECURITY CAMERAS--HAVE YOU ANALYZED THE RECORDINGS?
IN A MOMENT, SIR! I JUST HAVE TO FIND THE RIGHT ARCHIVES!
WE HAVE CAMERAS ALL OVER THE CAMPUS!
HERE WE ARE! I'VE FOUND IT!
YOU FAILED!
AUGH!
ONE OF THEM IS REMOVING HIS MASK!
BUT--IT'S...
...TYCHO.

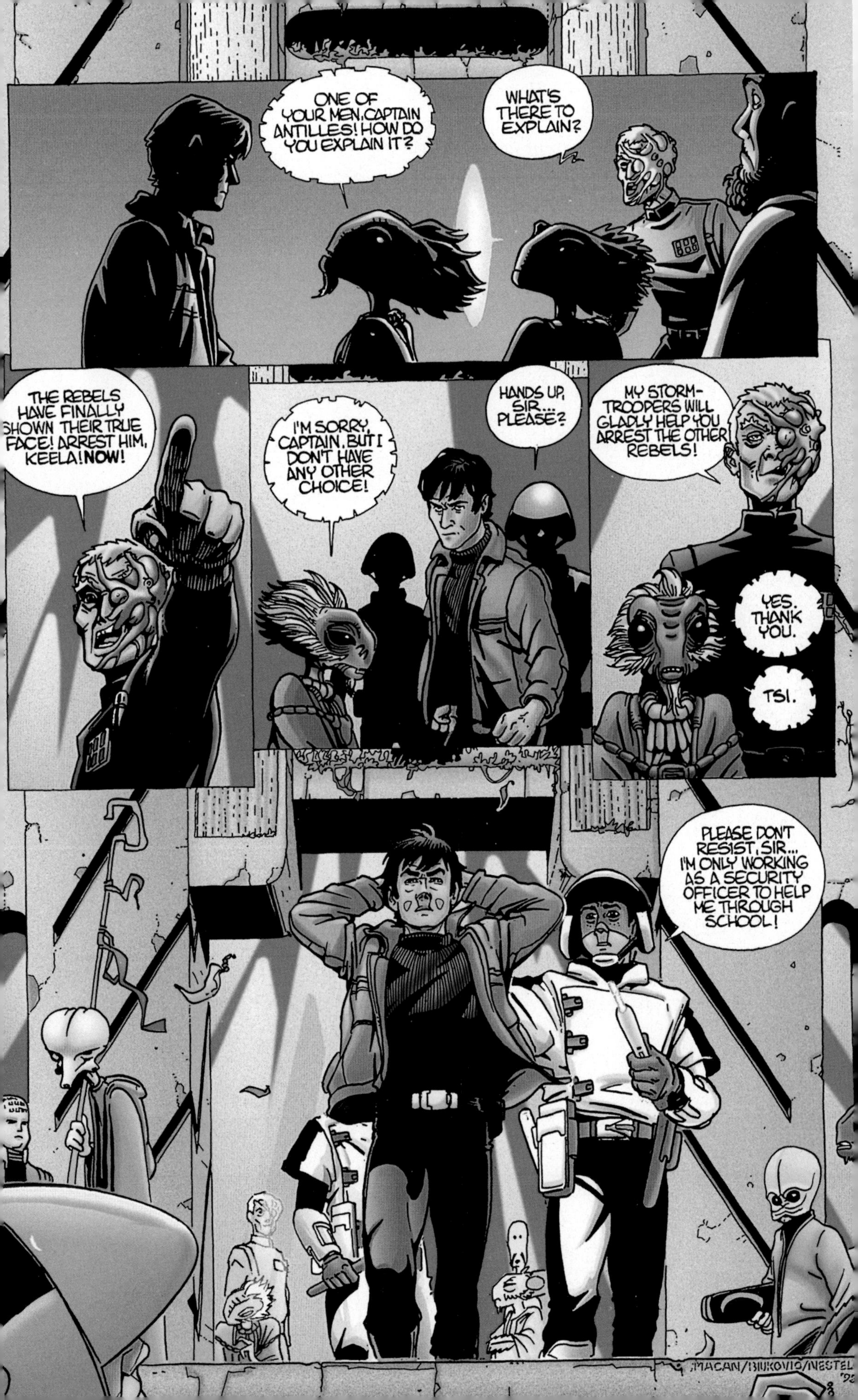
ONE OF YOUR MEN, CAPTAIN ANTILLES! HOW DO YOU EXPLAIN IT?
WHAT'S THERE TO EXPLAIN?
THE REBELS HAVE FINALLY SHOWN THEIR TRUE FACE! ARREST HIM, KEELA! NOW!
I'M SORRY, CAPTAIN, BUT I DON'T HAVE ANY OTHER CHOICE!
HANDS UP, SIR... PLEASE?
MY STORM-TROOPERS WILL GLADLY HELP YOU ARREST THE OTHER REBELS!
YES. THANK YOU.
TSI.
PLEASE DON'T RESIST, SIR... I'M ONLY WORKING AS A SECURITY OFFICER TO HELP ME THROUGH SCHOOL!
MACAN/BIUKOVIC/NESTEL

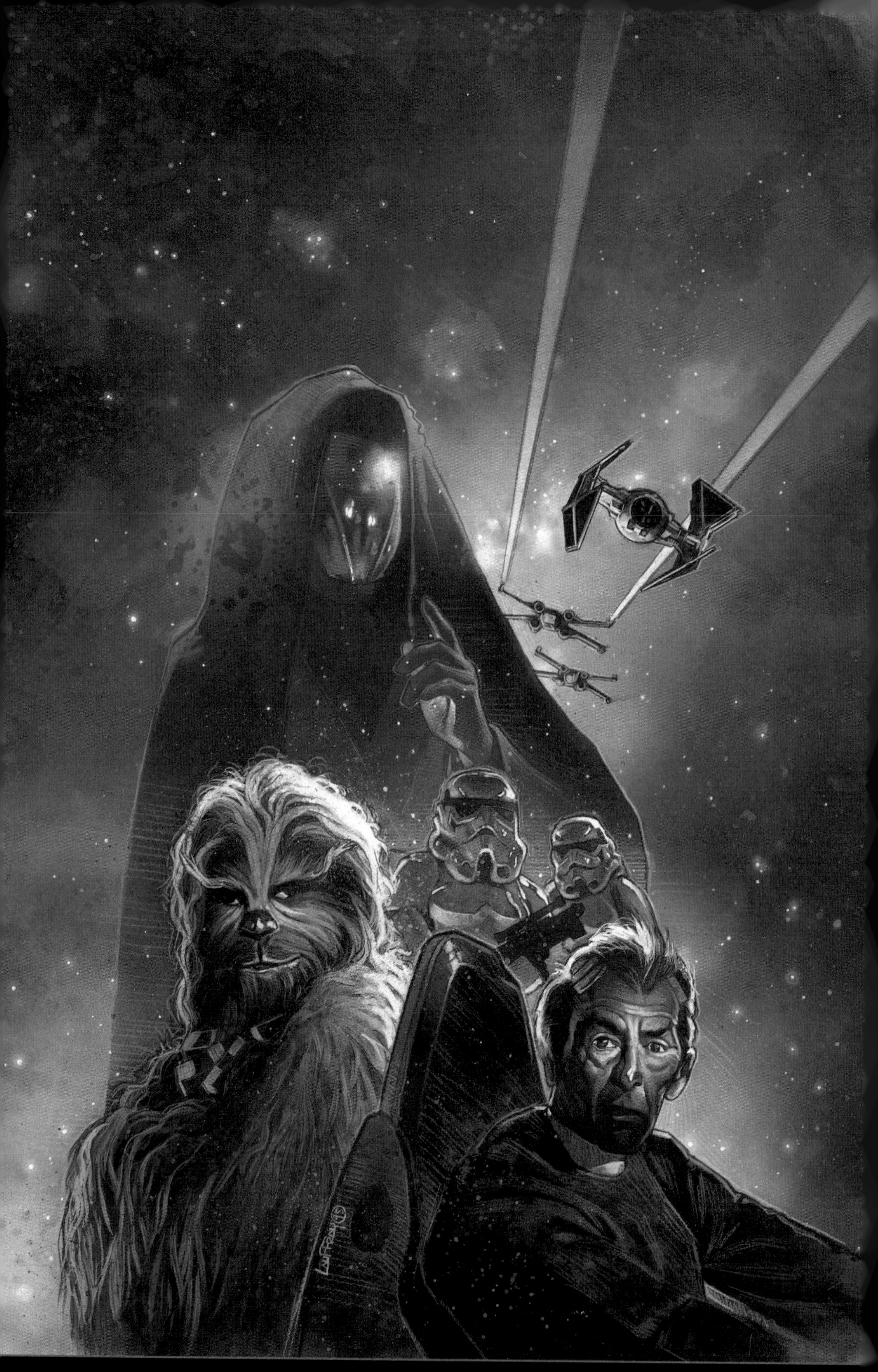

***STAR WARS: X-WING ROGUE SQUADRON #7* — "THE PHANTOM AFFAIR, CHAPTER 3"**

PLOTTER: MICHAEL A. STACKPOLE • SCRIPTER: DARKO MACAN • ARTIST & LETTERER (PAGES 1-20): EDVIN BIUKOVIĆ • PENCILER (PAGES 21-24): JOHN NADEAU
INKER (PAGES 21-24): JORDI ENSIGN • COLORIST: DAVE NESTELLE • LETTERER (PAGES 21-24): DAVE COOPER • EDITOR: PEET JANES • COVER ARTIST: MATHIEU LAUFFRAY

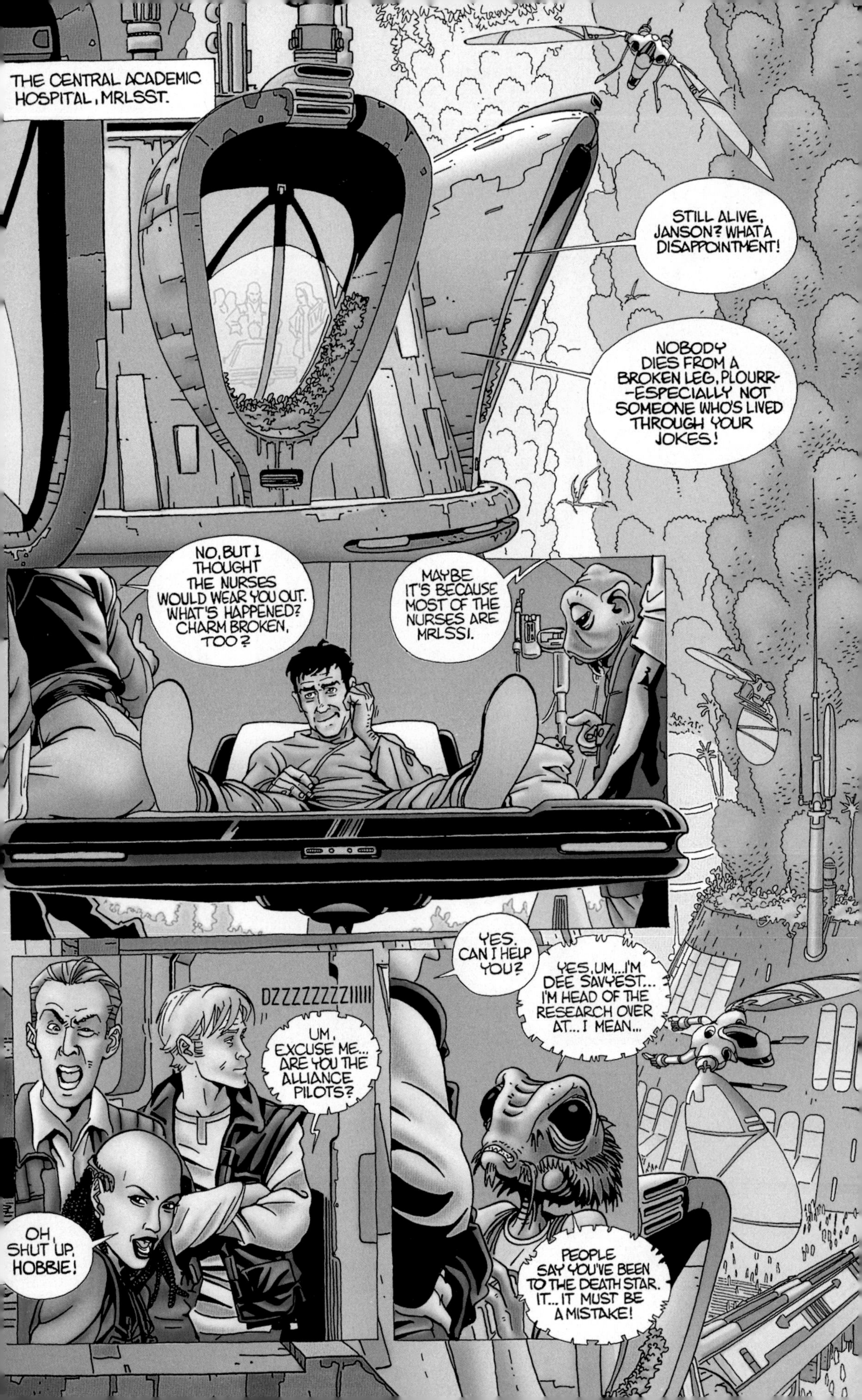
THE CENTRAL ACADEMIC HOSPITAL, MRLSST.
STILL ALIVE, JANSON? WHAT A DISAPPOINTMENT!
NOBODY DIES FROM A BROKEN LEG, PLOURR--ESPECIALLY NOT SOMEONE WHO'S LIVED THROUGH YOUR JOKES!
NO, BUT I THOUGHT THE NURSES WOULD WEAR YOU OUT. WHAT'S HAPPENED? CHARM BROKEN, TOO?
MAYBE IT'S BECAUSE MOST OF THE NURSES ARE MRLSSI.
DZZZZZZZZ!!!!!
UM, EXCUSE ME... ARE YOU THE ALLIANCE PILOTS?
OH, SHUT UP, HOBBIE!
YES. CAN I HELP YOU?
YES, UM...I'M DEE SAVYEST... I'M HEAD OF THE RESEARCH OVER AT... I MEAN...
PEOPLE SAY YOU'VE BEEN TO THE DEATH STAR. IT... IT MUST BE A MISTAKE!

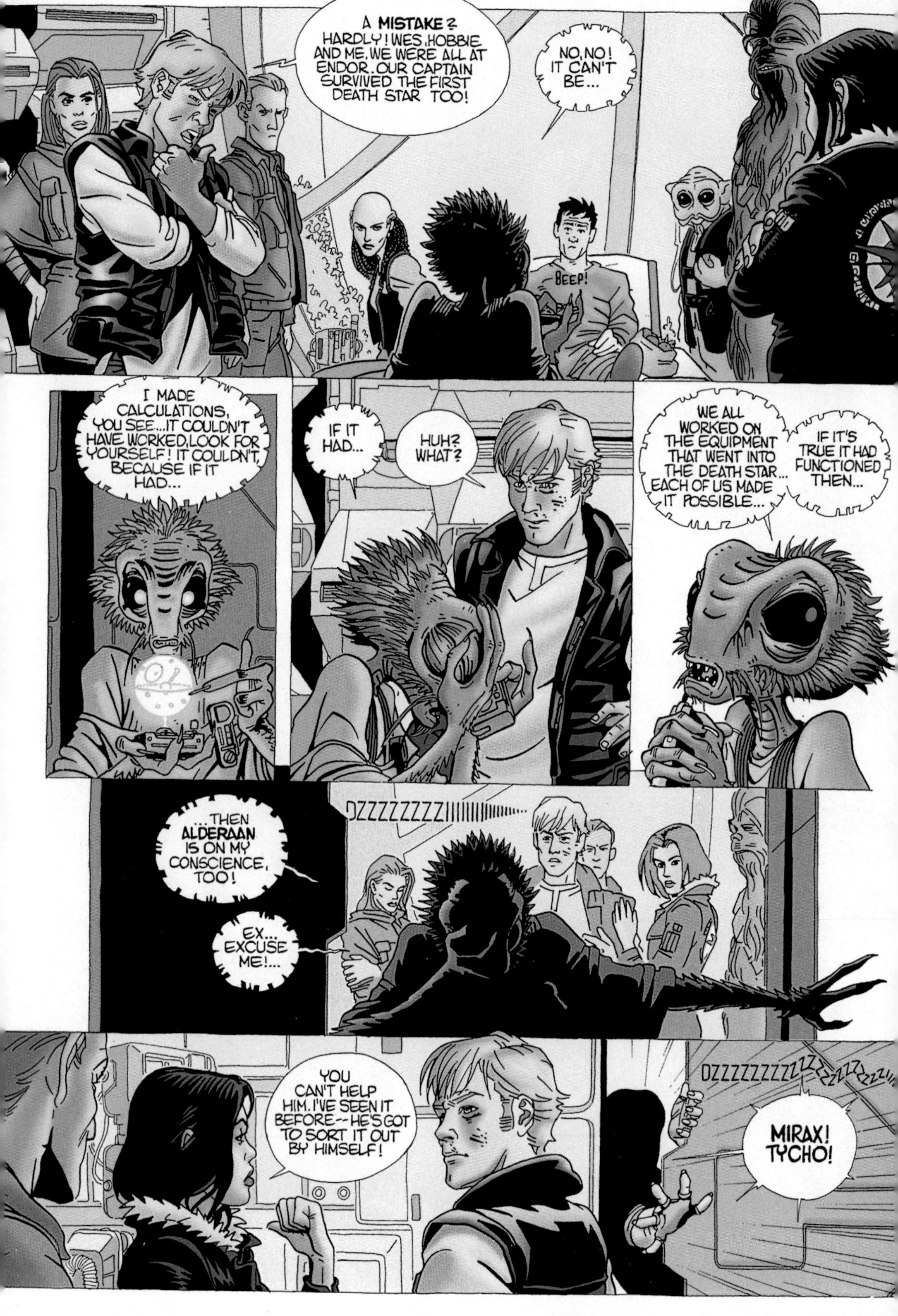
A MISTAKE? HARDLY! WES, HOBBIE AND ME, WE WERE ALL AT ENDOR. OUR CAPTAIN SURVIVED THE FIRST DEATH STAR TOO!
NO, NO! IT CAN'T BE...
BEEP!
I MADE CALCULATIONS, YOU SEE... IT COULDN'T HAVE WORKED, LOOK FOR YOURSELF! IT COULDN'T, BECAUSE IF IT HAD...
IF IT HAD...
HUH? WHAT?
WE ALL WORKED ON THE EQUIPMENT THAT WENT INTO THE DEATH STAR... EACH OF US MADE IT POSSIBLE...
IF IT'S TRUE IT HAD FUNCTIONED THEN...
...THEN ALDERAAN IS ON MY CONSCIENCE, TOO!
EX... EXCUSE ME!...
DZZZZZZZZ
YOU CAN'T HELP HIM. I'VE SEEN IT BEFORE--HE'S GOT TO SORT IT OUT BY HIMSELF!
DZZZZZZZZZZZZZZZZZ
MIRAX! TYCHO!

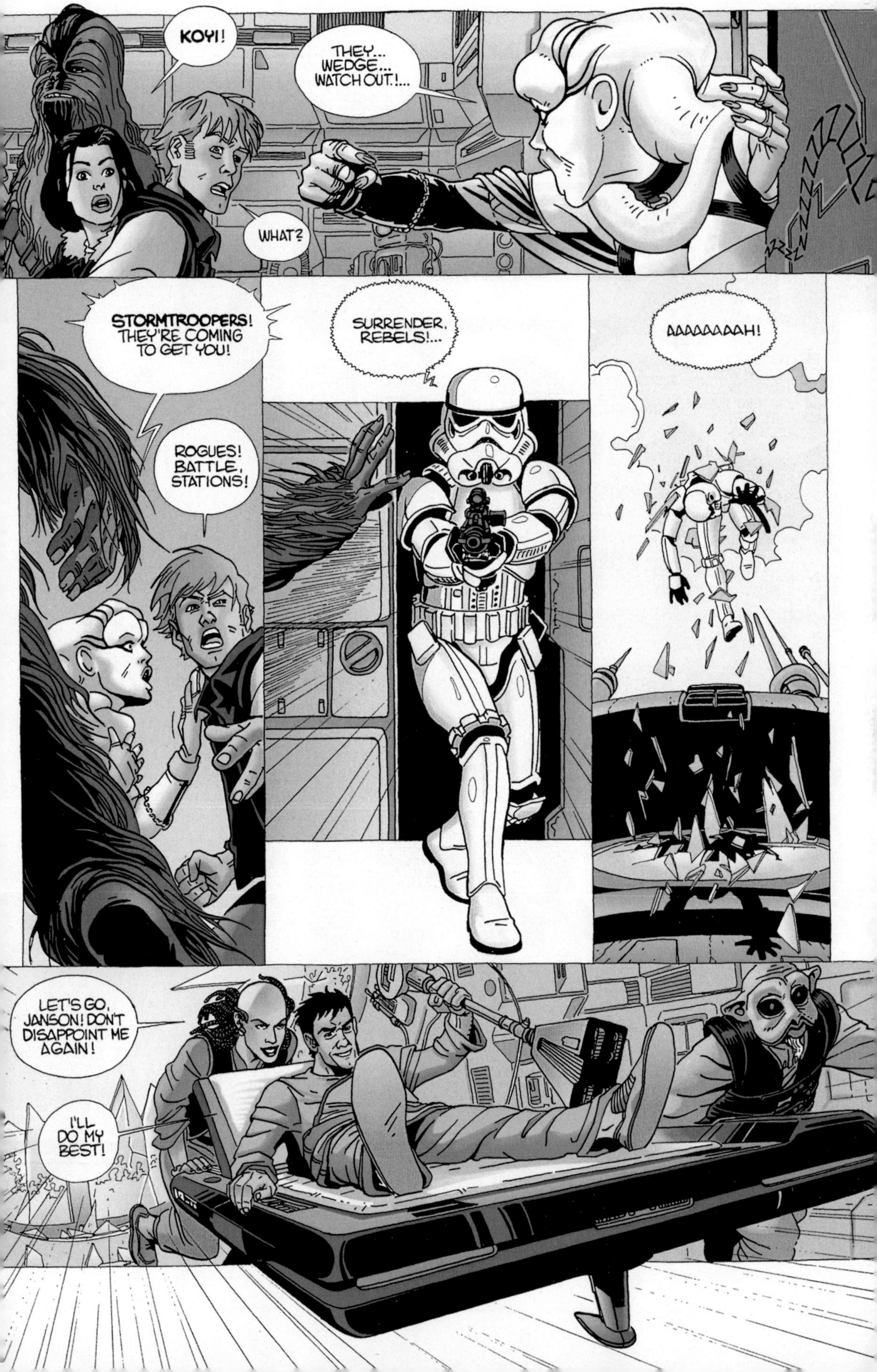
KOYI!
THEY... WEDGE... WATCH OUT!...
WHAT?
STORMTROOPERS! THEY'RE COMING TO GET YOU!
ROGUES! BATTLE STATIONS!
SURRENDER, REBELS!...
AAAAAAAAH!
LET'S GO, JANSON! DON'T DISAPPOINT ME AGAIN!
I'LL DO MY BEST!

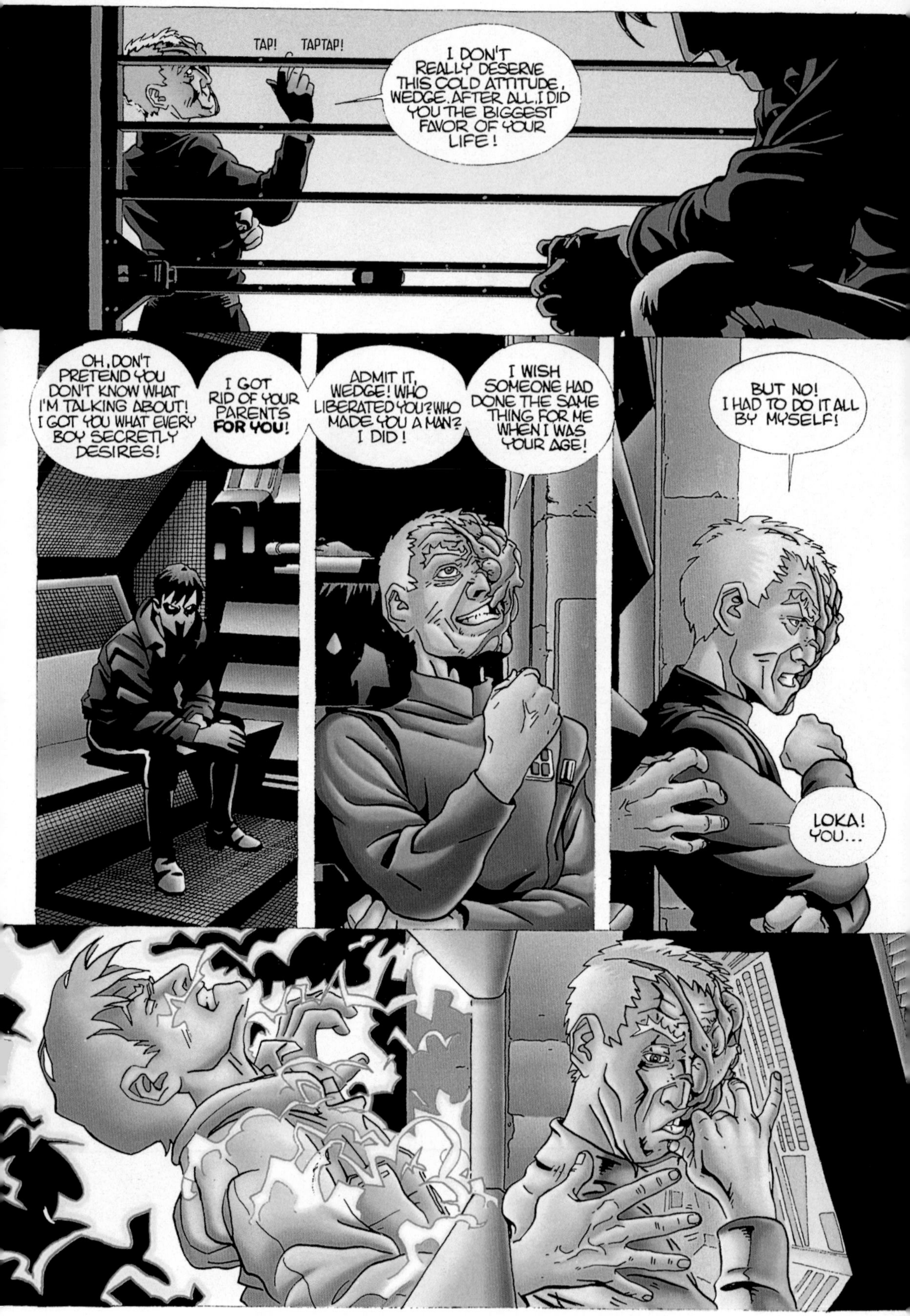
TAP! TAPTAP!
I DON'T REALLY DESERVE THIS COLD ATTITUDE, WEDGE. AFTER ALL, I DID YOU THE BIGGEST FAVOR OF YOUR LIFE!
OH, DON'T PRETEND YOU DON'T KNOW WHAT I'M TALKING ABOUT! I GOT YOU WHAT EVERY BOY SECRETLY DESIRES!
I GOT RID OF YOUR PARENTS **FOR YOU**!
ADMIT IT, WEDGE! WHO LIBERATED YOU? WHO MADE YOU A MAN? I DID!
I WISH SOMEONE HAD DONE THE SAME THING FOR ME WHEN I WAS YOUR AGE!
BUT NO! I HAD TO DO IT ALL BY MYSELF!
LOKA! YOU...

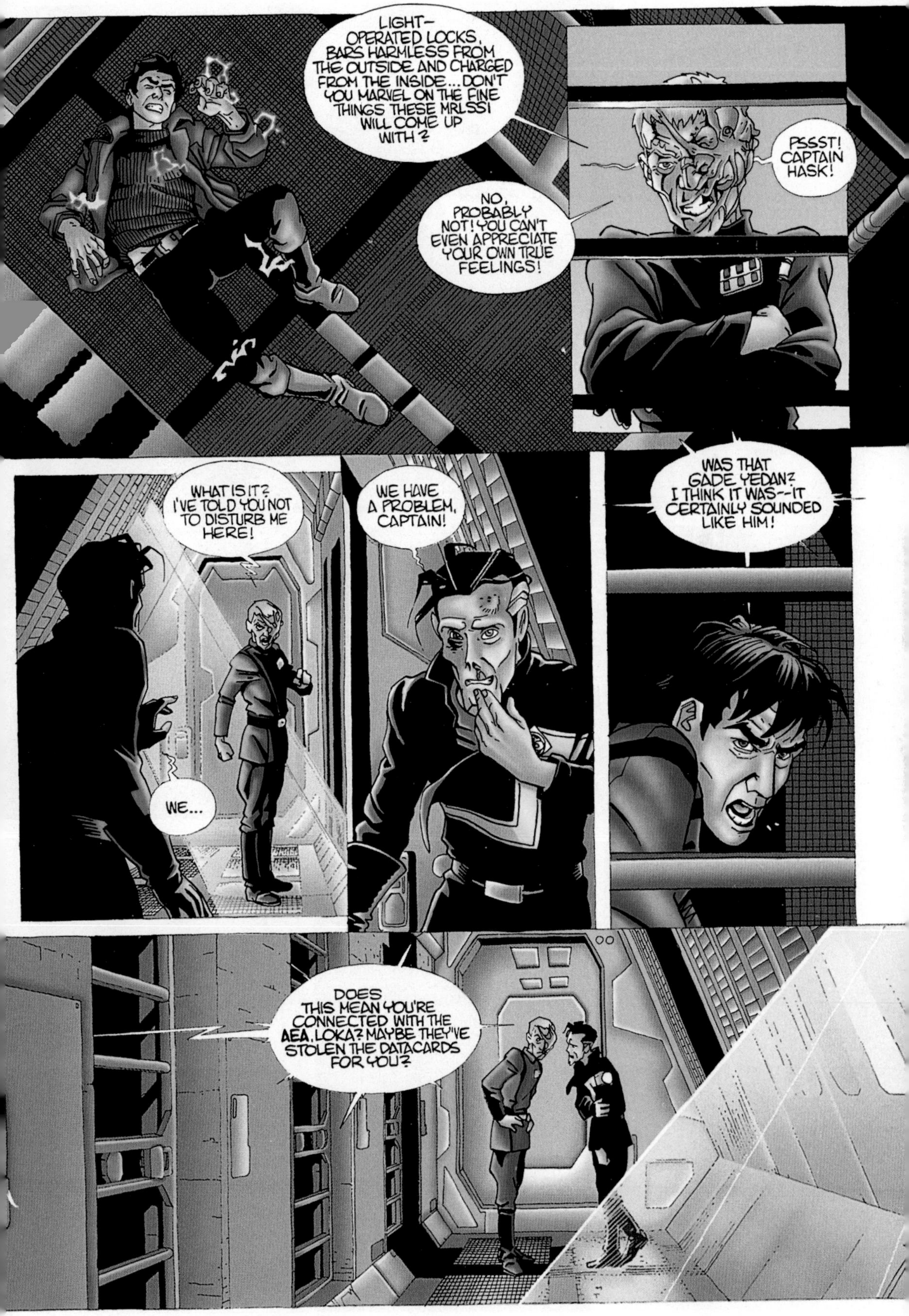
LIGHT-OPERATED LOCKS, BARS HARMLESS FROM THE OUTSIDE AND CHARGED FROM THE INSIDE... DON'T YOU MARVEL ON THE FINE THINGS THESE MRLSSI WILL COME UP WITH?
PSSST! CAPTAIN HASK!
NO, PROBABLY NOT! YOU CAN'T EVEN APPRECIATE YOUR OWN TRUE FEELINGS!
WHAT IS IT? I'VE TOLD YOU NOT TO DISTURB ME HERE!
WE...
WE HAVE A PROBLEM, CAPTAIN!
WAS THAT GADE YEDAN? I THINK IT WAS--IT CERTAINLY SOUNDED LIKE HIM!
DOES THIS MEAN YOU'RE CONNECTED WITH THE AEA, LOKA? MAYBE THEY'VE STOLEN THE DATACARDS FOR YOU?

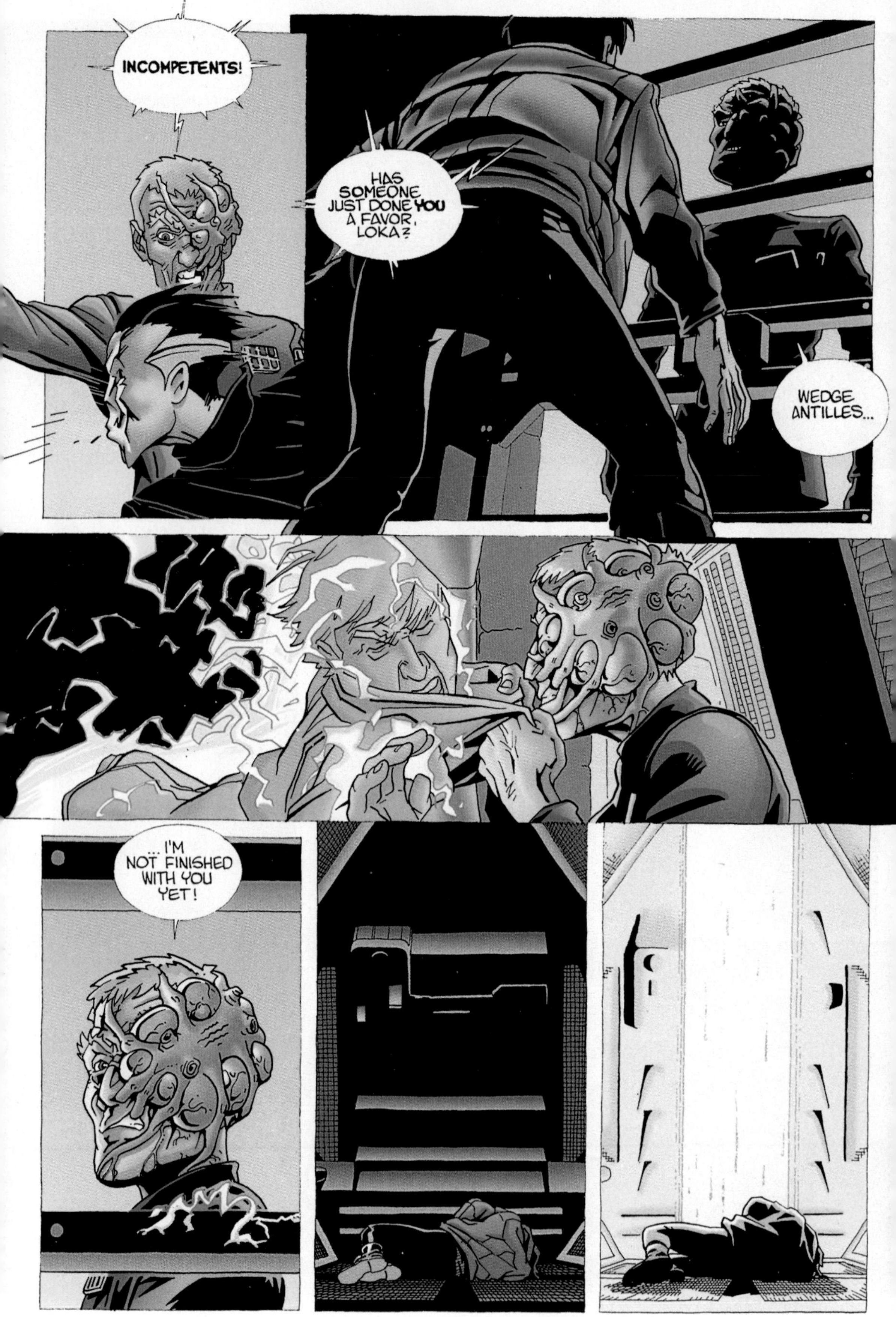
INCOMPETENTS!
HAS SOMEONE JUST DONE YOU A FAVOR, LOKA?
WEDGE ANTILLES...
...I'M NOT FINISHED WITH YOU YET!

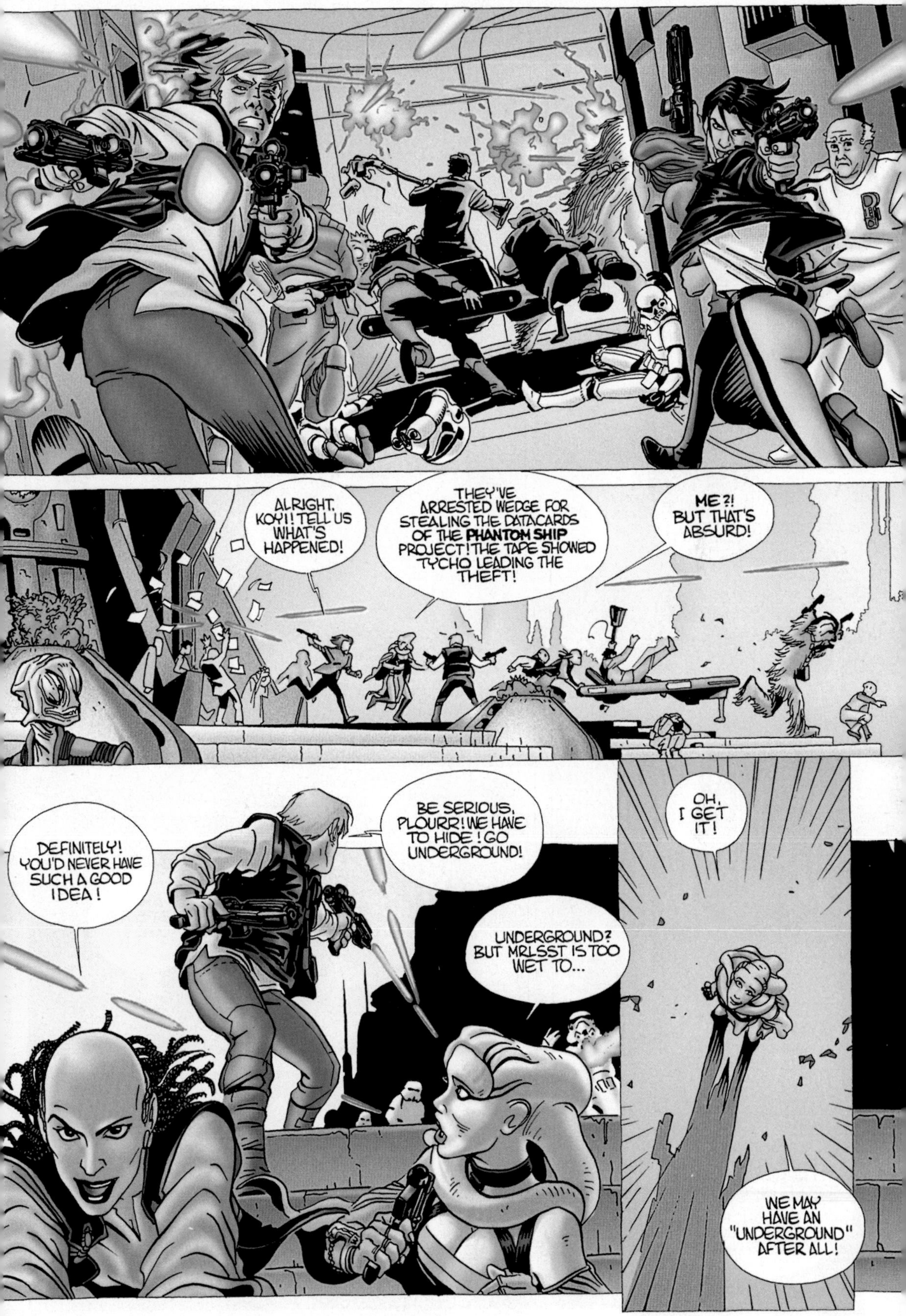
ALRIGHT, KOYI! TELL US WHAT'S HAPPENED!
THEY'VE ARRESTED WEDGE FOR STEALING THE DATACARDS OF THE PHANTOM SHIP PROJECT! THE TAPE SHOWED TYCHO LEADING THE THEFT!
ME?! BUT THAT'S ABSURD!
DEFINITELY! YOU'D NEVER HAVE SUCH A GOOD IDEA!
BE SERIOUS, PLOURR! WE HAVE TO HIDE! GO UNDERGROUND!
UNDERGROUND? BUT MRLSST IS TOO WET TO...
OH, I GET IT!
WE MAY HAVE AN "UNDERGROUND" AFTER ALL!

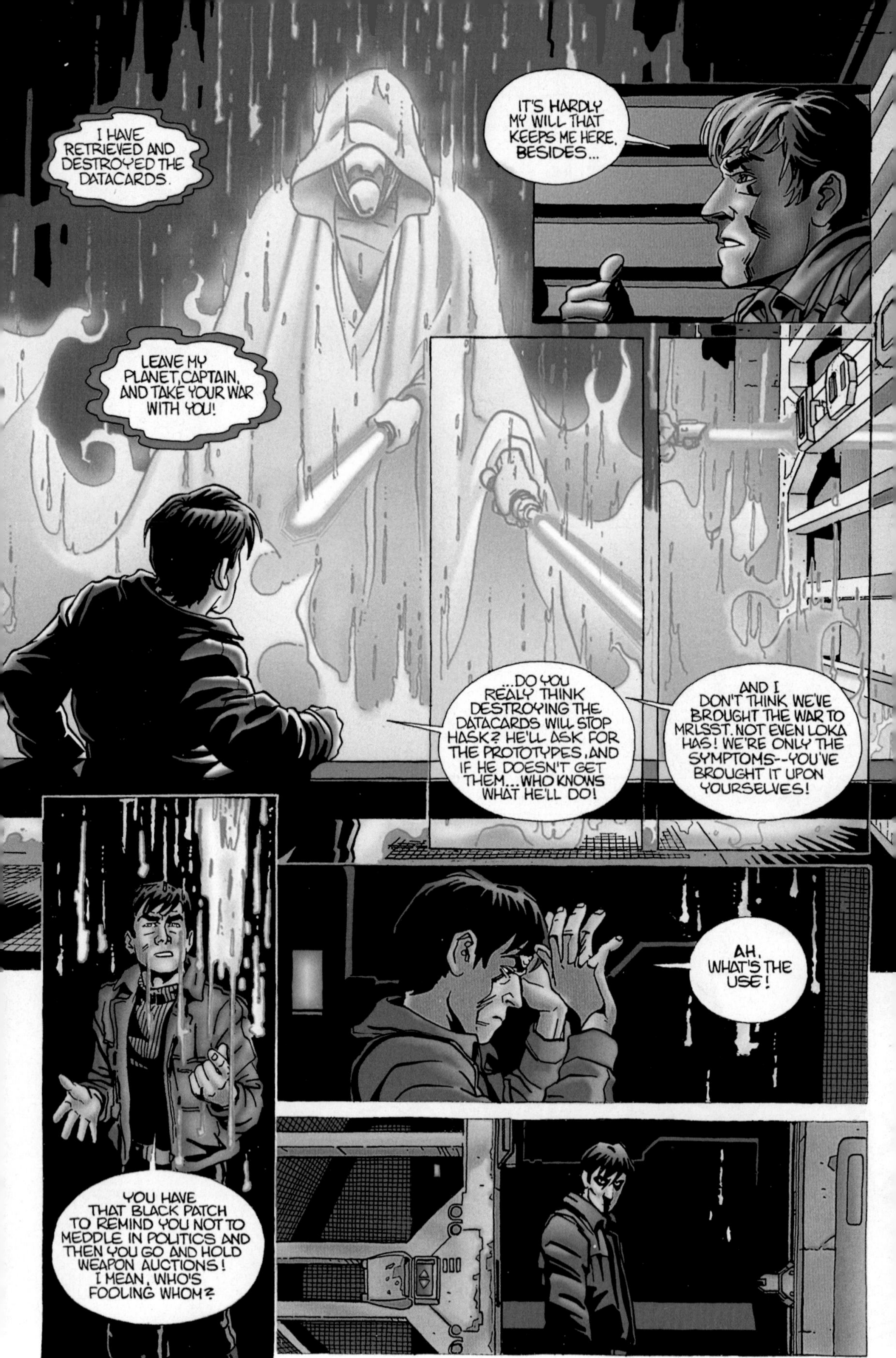
I HAVE RETRIEVED AND DESTROYED THE DATACARDS.
IT'S HARDLY MY WILL THAT KEEPS ME HERE. BESIDES...
LEAVE MY PLANET, CAPTAIN, AND TAKE YOUR WAR WITH YOU!
...DO YOU REALY THINK DESTROYING THE DATACARDS WILL STOP HASK? HE'LL ASK FOR THE PROTOTYPES, AND IF HE DOESN'T GET THEM... WHO KNOWS WHAT HE'LL DO!
AND I DON'T THINK WE'VE BROUGHT THE WAR TO MRLSST. NOT EVEN LOKA HAS! WE'RE ONLY THE SYMPTOMS--YOU'VE BROUGHT IT UPON YOURSELVES!
YOU HAVE THAT BLACK PATCH TO REMIND YOU NOT TO MEDDLE IN POLITICS AND THEN YOU GO AND HOLD WEAPON AUCTIONS! I MEAN, WHO'S FOOLING WHOM?
AH, WHAT'S THE USE!

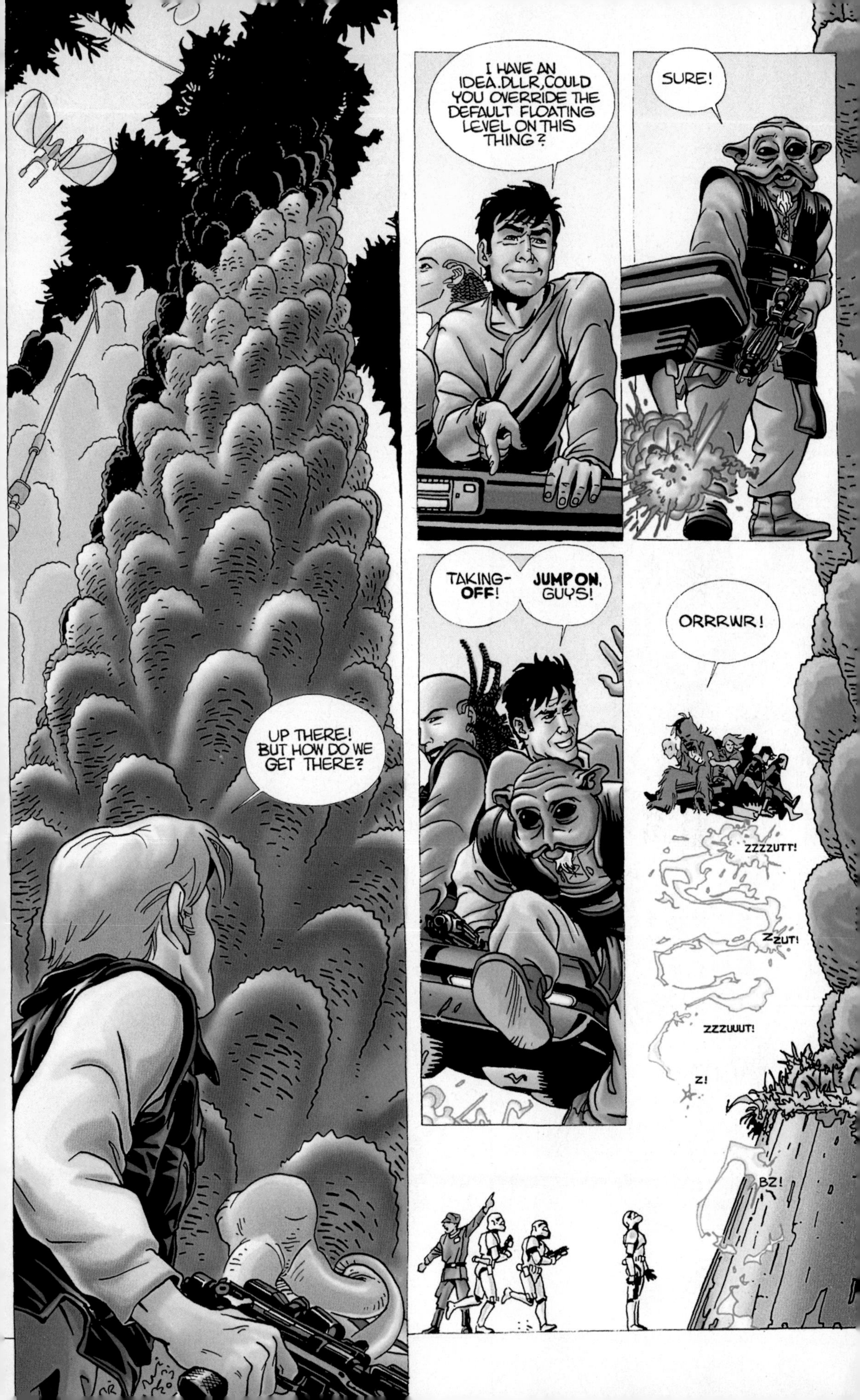
UP THERE! BUT HOW DO WE GET THERE?
I HAVE AN IDEA. DLLR, COULD YOU OVERRIDE THE DEFAULT FLOATING LEVEL ON THIS THING?
SURE!
TAKING-OFF!
JUMP ON, GUYS!
ORRRWR!
ZZZZUTT!
ZZUT!
ZZZUUUT!
Z!
BZ!

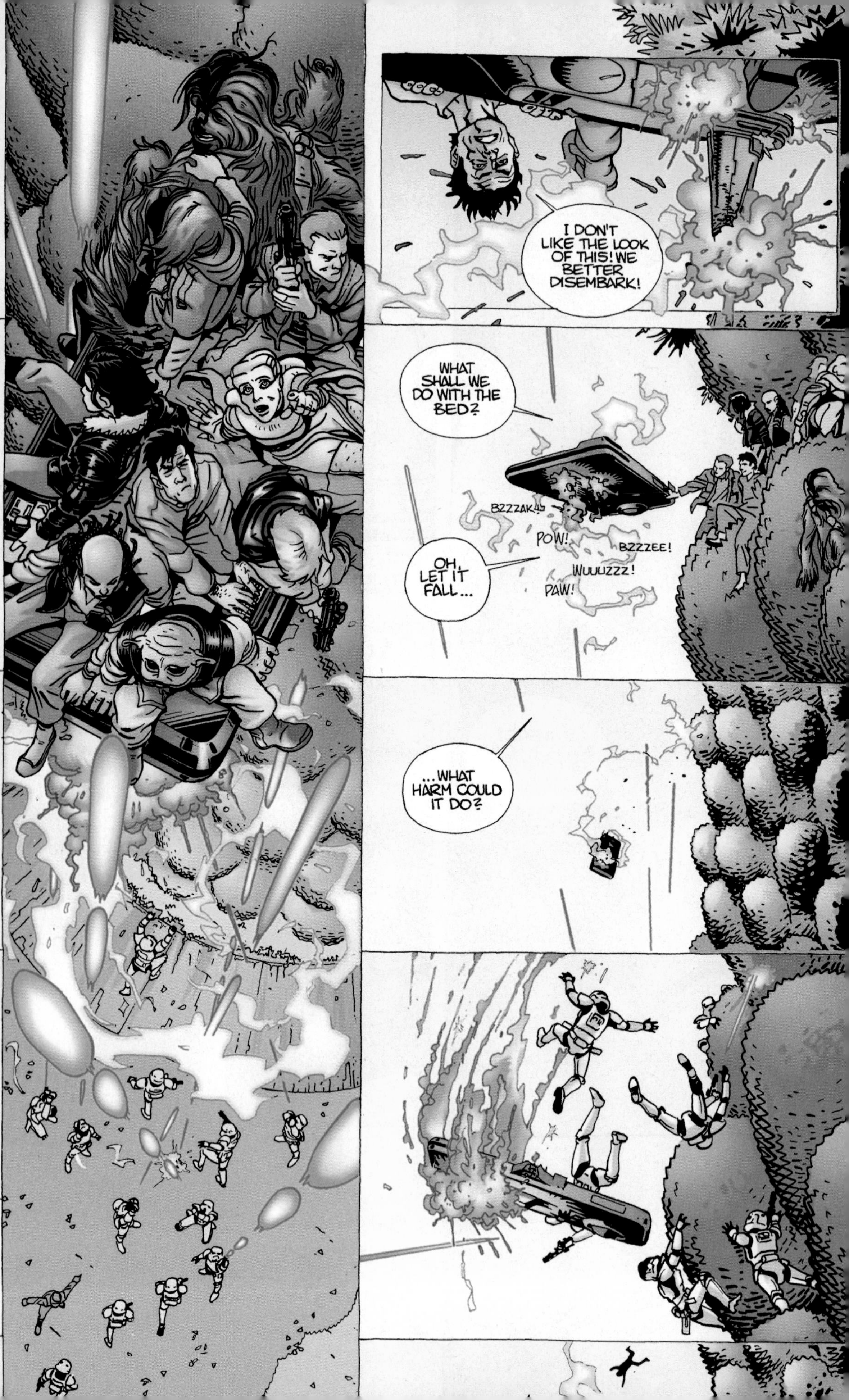
I DON'T LIKE THE LOOK OF THIS! WE BETTER DISEMBARK!
WHAT SHALL WE DO WITH THE BED?
BZZZAK!
POW!
BZZZEE!
OH, LET IT FALL...
WUUUZZZ!
PAW!
...WHAT HARM COULD IT DO?

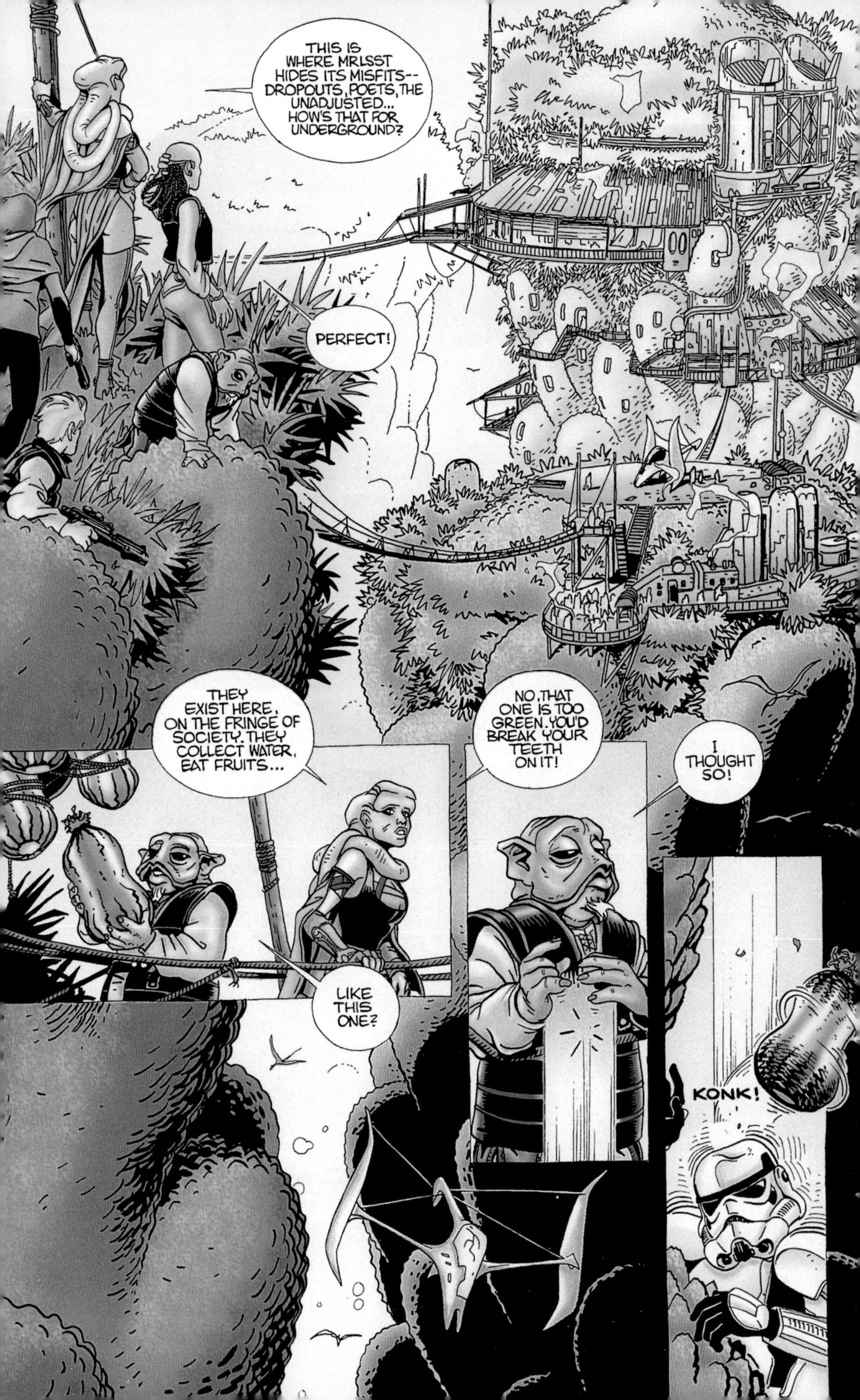
THIS IS WHERE MRLSST HIDES ITS MISFITS-- DROPOUTS, POETS, THE UNADJUSTED... HOW'S THAT FOR UNDERGROUND?
PERFECT!
THEY EXIST HERE, ON THE FRINGE OF SOCIETY. THEY COLLECT WATER, EAT FRUITS...
LIKE THIS ONE?
NO, THAT ONE IS TOO GREEN. YOU'D BREAK YOUR TEETH ON IT!
I THOUGHT SO!
KONK!

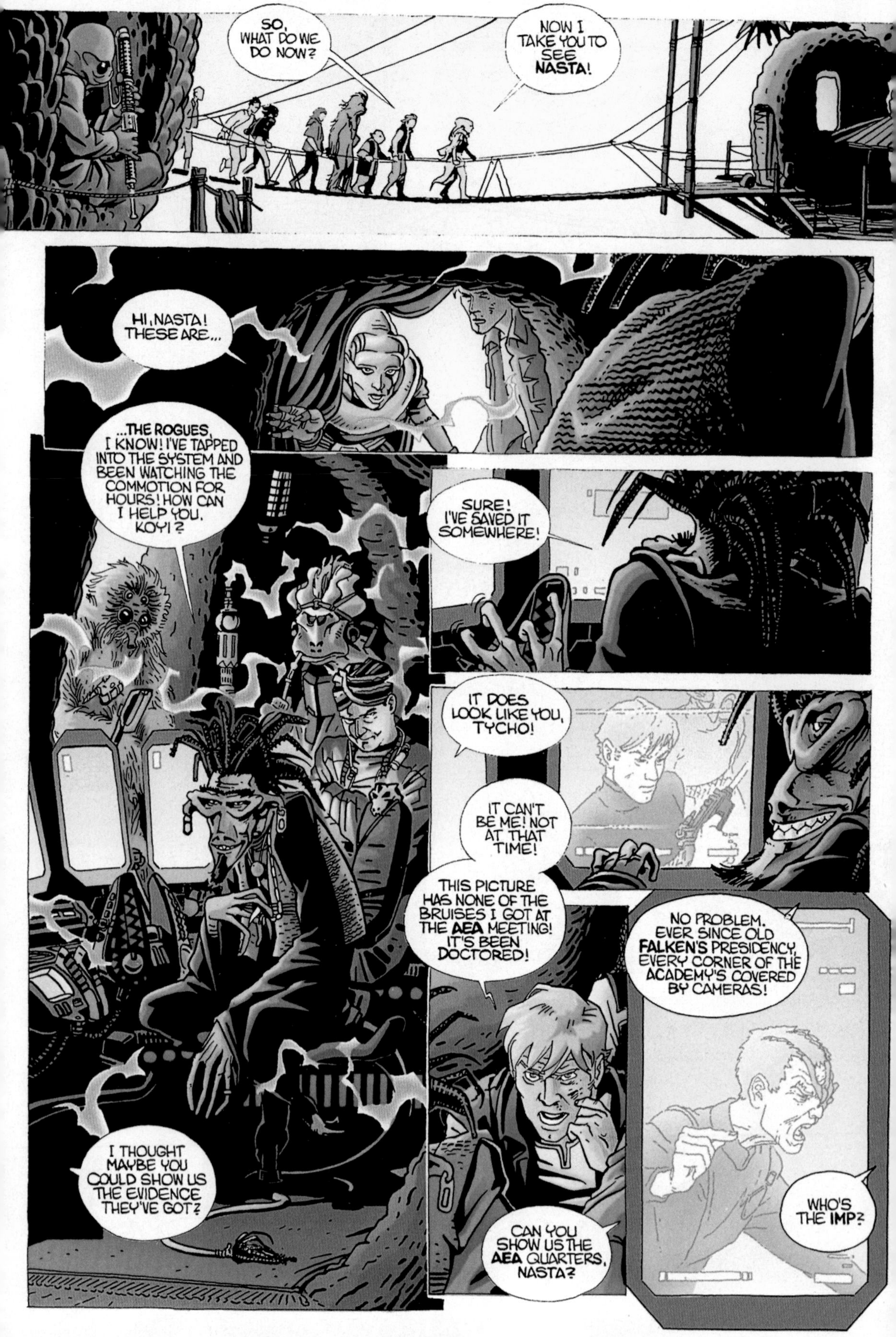

SO, WHAT DO WE DO NOW?
NOW I TAKE YOU TO SEE NASTA!
HI, NASTA! THESE ARE...
...THE ROGUES, I KNOW! I'VE TAPPED INTO THE SYSTEM AND BEEN WATCHING THE COMMOTION FOR HOURS! HOW CAN I HELP YOU, KOYI?
I THOUGHT MAYBE YOU COULD SHOW US THE EVIDENCE THEY'VE GOT?
SURE! I'VE SAVED IT SOMEWHERE!
IT DOES LOOK LIKE YOU, TYCHO!
IT CAN'T BE ME! NOT AT THAT TIME!
THIS PICTURE HAS NONE OF THE BRUISES I GOT AT THE AEA MEETING! IT'S BEEN DOCTORED!
CAN YOU SHOW US THE AEA QUARTERS, NASTA?
NO PROBLEM. EVER SINCE OLD FALKEN'S PRESIDENCY, EVERY CORNER OF THE ACADEMY'S COVERED BY CAMERAS!
WHO'S THE IMP?

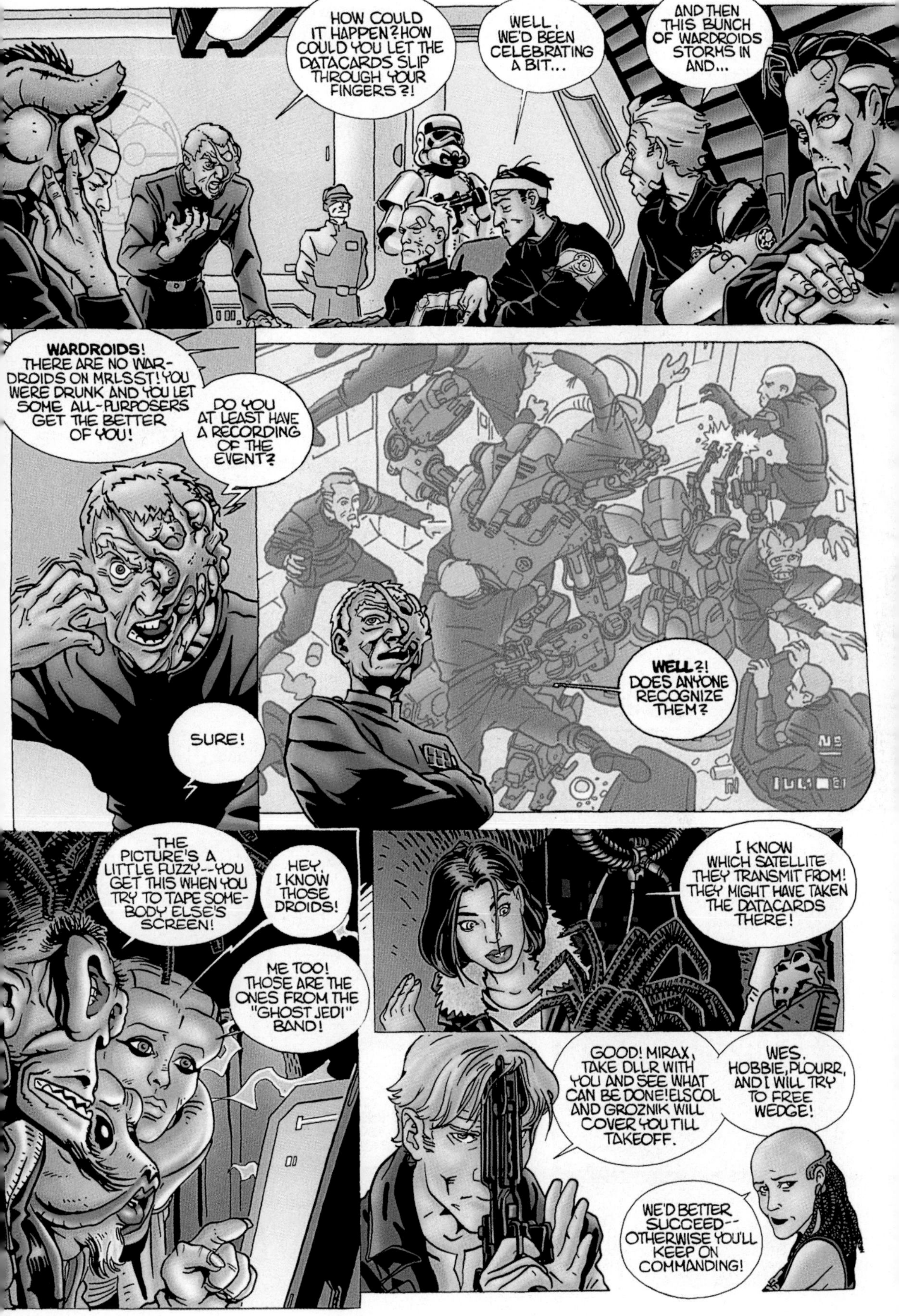
HOW COULD IT HAPPEN? HOW COULD YOU LET THE DATACARDS SLIP THROUGH YOUR FINGERS?!
WELL, WE'D BEEN CELEBRATING A BIT...
AND THEN THIS BUNCH OF WARDROIDS STORMS IN AND...
WARDROIDS! THERE ARE NO WAR-DROIDS ON MRLSST! YOU WERE DRUNK AND YOU LET SOME ALL-PURPOSERS GET THE BETTER OF YOU!
DO YOU AT LEAST HAVE A RECORDING OF THE EVENT?
SURE!
WELL?! DOES ANYONE RECOGNIZE THEM?
THE PICTURE'S A LITTLE FUZZY--YOU GET THIS WHEN YOU TRY TO TAPE SOME-BODY ELSE'S SCREEN!
HEY, I KNOW THOSE DROIDS!
ME TOO! THOSE ARE THE ONES FROM THE "GHOST JEDI" BAND!
I KNOW WHICH SATELLITE THEY TRANSMIT FROM! THEY MIGHT HAVE TAKEN THE DATACARDS THERE!
GOOD! MIRAX, TAKE DLLR WITH YOU AND SEE WHAT CAN BE DONE! ELSCOL AND GROZNIK WILL COVER YOU TILL TAKEOFF.
WES, HOBBIE, PLOURR, AND I WILL TRY TO FREE WEDGE!
WE'D BETTER SUCCEED--OTHERWISE YOU'LL KEEP ON COMMANDING!

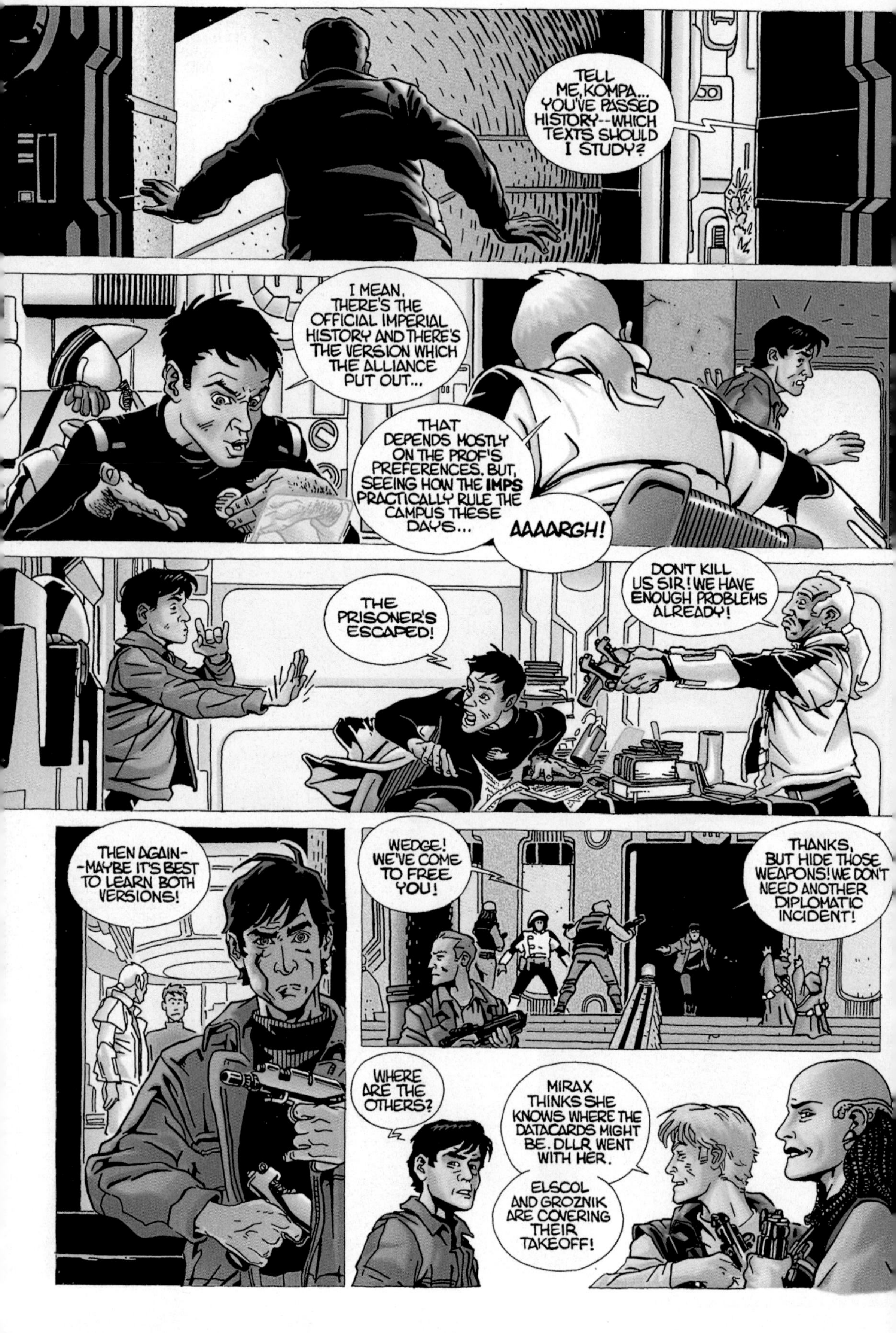
TELL ME, KOMPA... YOU'VE PASSED HISTORY--WHICH TEXTS SHOULD I STUDY?
I MEAN, THERE'S THE OFFICIAL IMPERIAL HISTORY AND THERE'S THE VERSION WHICH THE ALLIANCE PUT OUT...
THAT DEPENDS MOSTLY ON THE PROF'S PREFERENCES. BUT, SEEING HOW THE IMPS PRACTICALLY RULE THE CAMPUS THESE DAYS...
AAAARGH!
THE PRISONER'S ESCAPED!
DON'T KILL US SIR! WE HAVE ENOUGH PROBLEMS ALREADY!
THEN AGAIN--MAYBE IT'S BEST TO LEARN BOTH VERSIONS!
WEDGE! WE'VE COME TO FREE YOU!
THANKS, BUT HIDE THOSE WEAPONS! WE DON'T NEED ANOTHER DIPLOMATIC INCIDENT!
WHERE ARE THE OTHERS?
MIRAX THINKS SHE KNOWS WHERE THE DATACARDS MIGHT BE. DLLR WENT WITH HER.
ELSCOL AND GROZNIK ARE COVERING THEIR TAKEOFF!

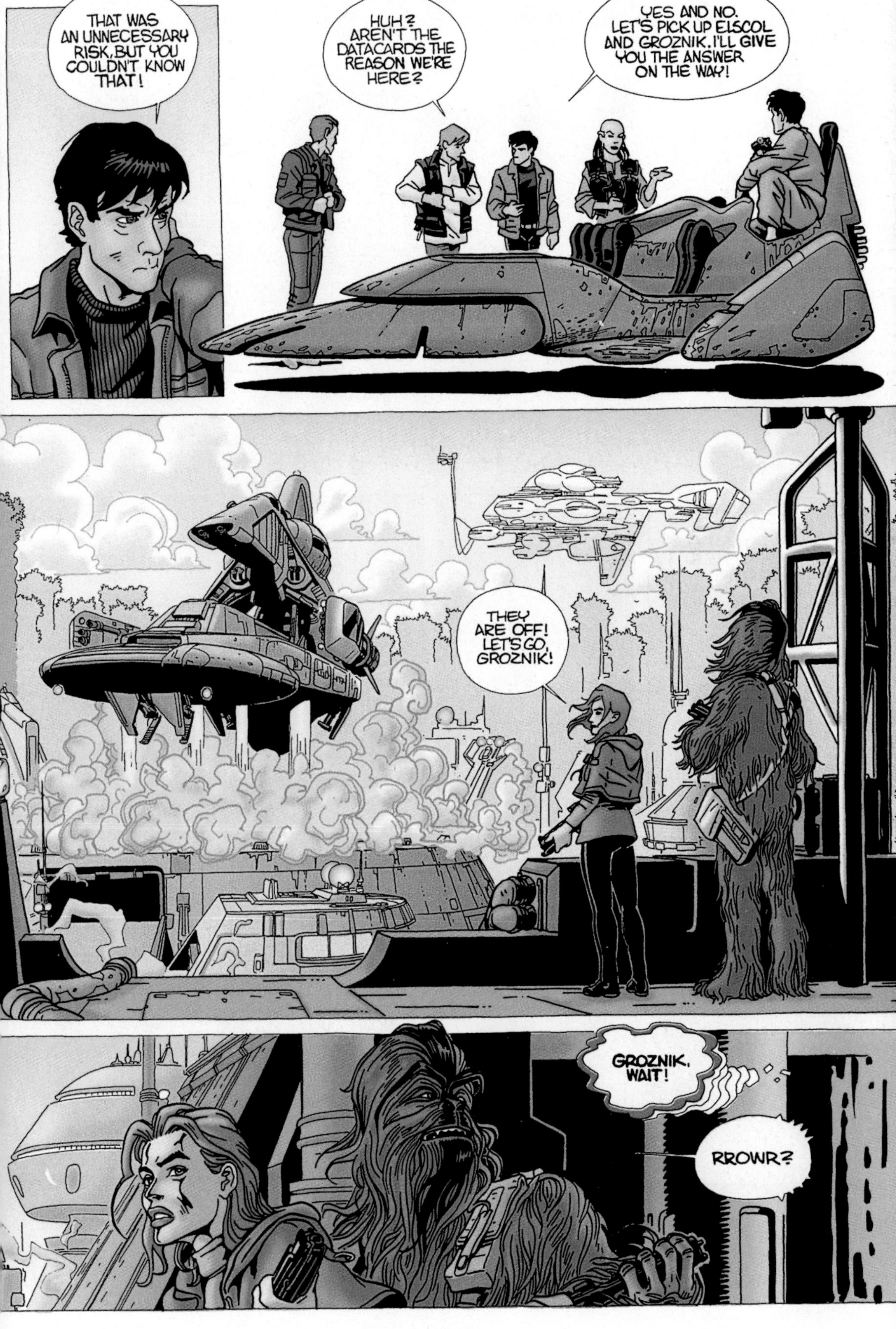
THAT WAS AN UNNECESSARY RISK, BUT YOU COULDN'T KNOW THAT!
HUH? AREN'T THE DATACARDS THE REASON WE'RE HERE?
YES AND NO. LET'S PICK UP ELSCOL AND GROZNIK. I'LL GIVE YOU THE ANSWER ON THE WAY!
THEY ARE OFF! LET'S GO, GROZNIK!
GROZNIK, WAIT!
RROWR?

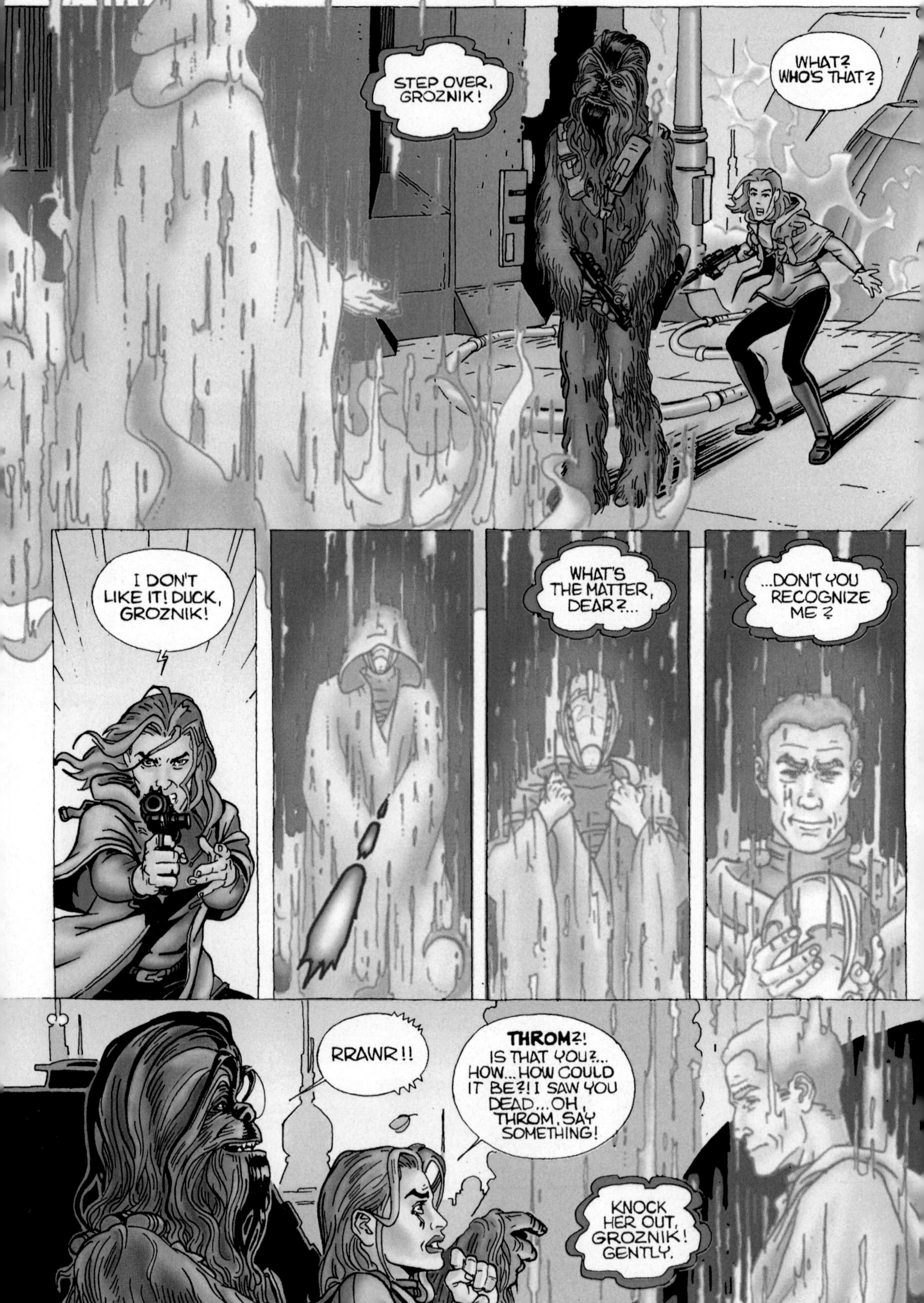
STEP OVER, GROZNIK!
WHAT? WHO'S THAT?
I DON'T LIKE IT! DUCK, GROZNIK!
WHAT'S THE MATTER, DEAR?...
...DON'T YOU RECOGNIZE ME?
RRAWR!!
THROM?! IS THAT YOU?... HOW... HOW COULD IT BE?! I SAW YOU DEAD... OH, THROM, SAY SOMETHING!
KNOCK HER OUT, GROZNIK! GENTLY.

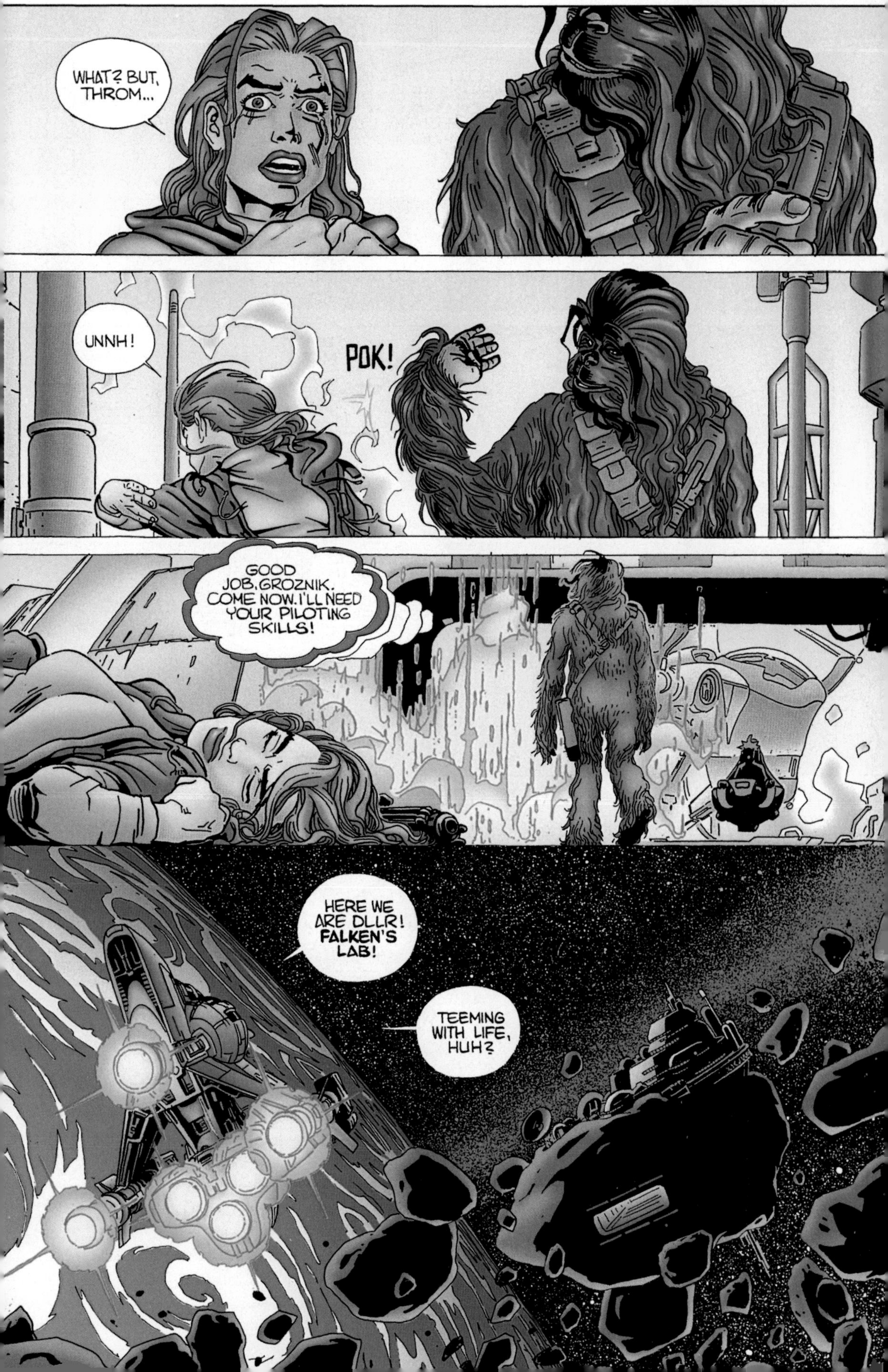
WHAT? BUT, THROM...
UNNH!
POK!
GOOD JOB, GROZNIK. COME NOW. I'LL NEED YOUR PILOTING SKILLS!
HERE WE ARE DLLR! FALKEN'S LAB!
TEEMING WITH LIFE, HUH?

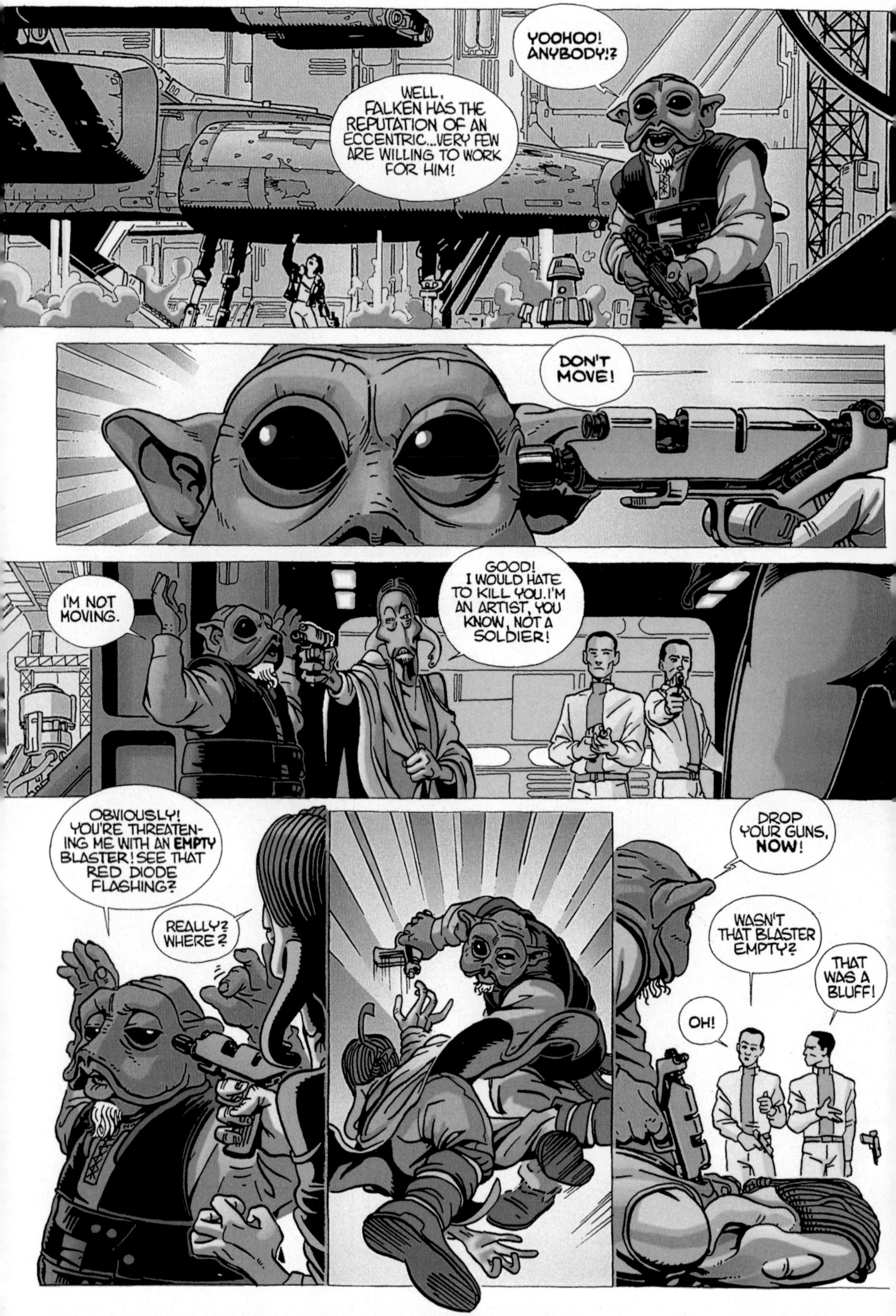
WELL, FALKEN HAS THE REPUTATION OF AN ECCENTRIC...VERY FEW ARE WILLING TO WORK FOR HIM!
YOOHOO! ANYBODY!?
DON'T MOVE!
I'M NOT MOVING.
GOOD! I WOULD HATE TO KILL YOU. I'M AN ARTIST, YOU KNOW, NOT A SOLDIER!
OBVIOUSLY! YOU'RE THREATEN-ING ME WITH AN EMPTY BLASTER! SEE THAT RED DIODE FLASHING?
REALLY? WHERE?
DROP YOUR GUNS, NOW!
WASN'T THAT BLASTER EMPTY?
OH!
THAT WAS A BLUFF!

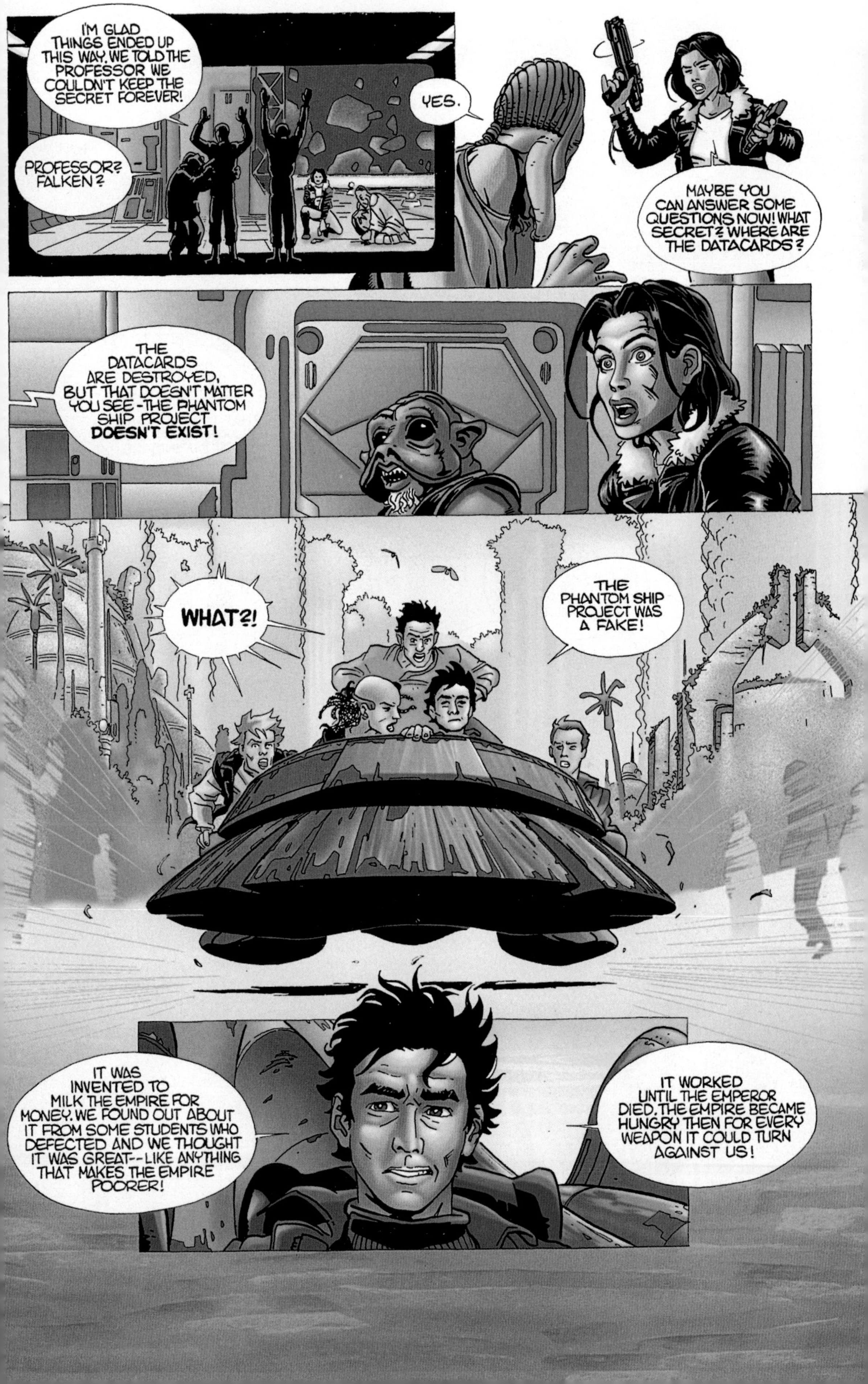

I'M GLAD THINGS ENDED UP THIS WAY. WE TOLD THE PROFESSOR WE COULDN'T KEEP THE SECRET FOREVER!
YES.
PROFESSOR? FALKEN?
MAYBE YOU CAN ANSWER SOME QUESTIONS NOW! WHAT SECRET? WHERE ARE THE DATACARDS?
THE DATACARDS ARE DESTROYED, BUT THAT DOESN'T MATTER YOU SEE--THE PHANTOM SHIP PROJECT **DOESN'T EXIST!**
WHAT?!
THE PHANTOM SHIP PROJECT WAS A FAKE!
IT WAS INVENTED TO MILK THE EMPIRE FOR MONEY. WE FOUND OUT ABOUT IT FROM SOME STUDENTS WHO DEFECTED AND WE THOUGHT IT WAS GREAT--LIKE ANYTHING THAT MAKES THE EMPIRE POORER!
IT WORKED UNTIL THE EMPEROR DIED. THE EMPIRE BECAME HUNGRY THEN FOR EVERY WEAPON IT COULD TURN AGAINST US!

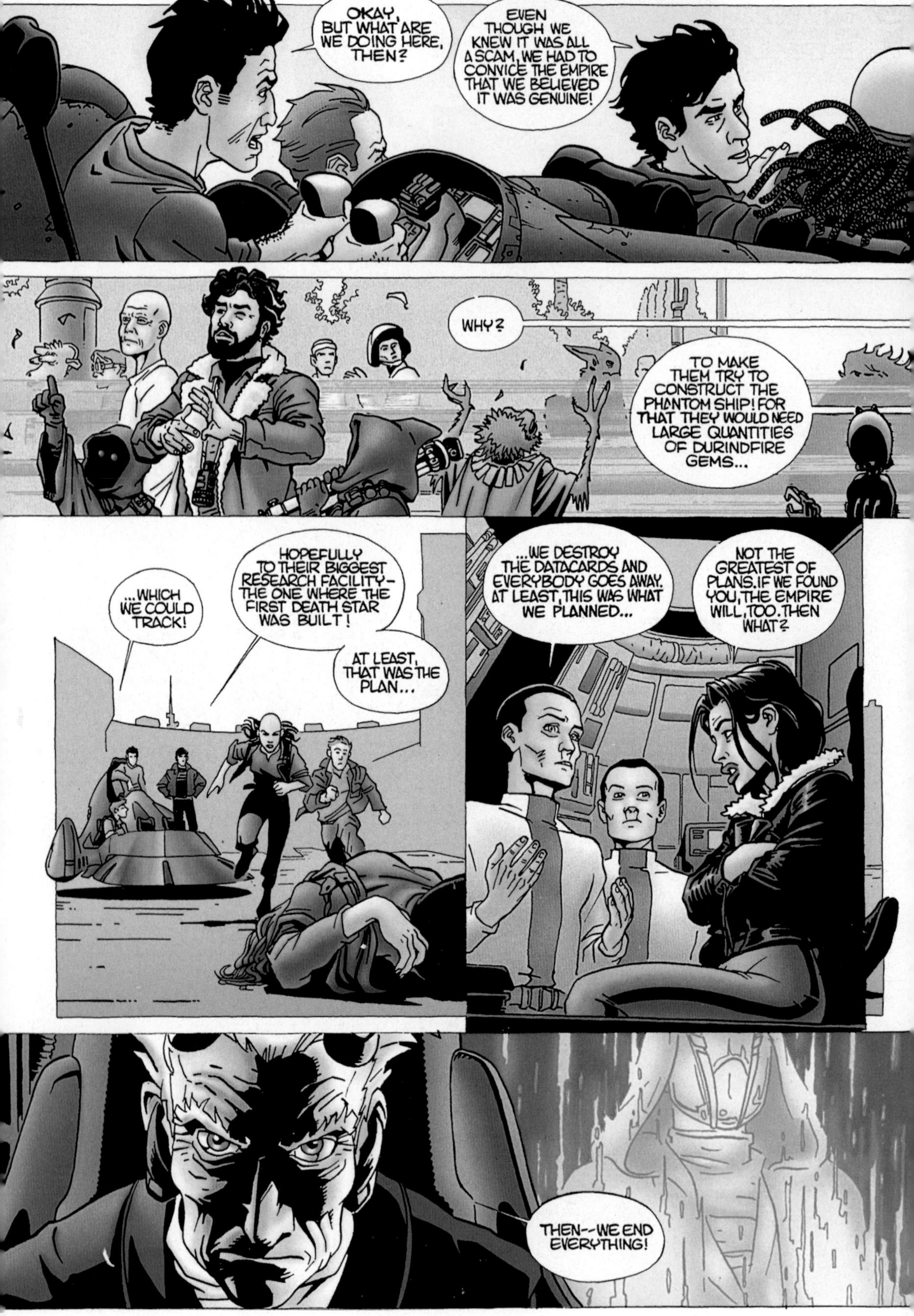
OKAY, BUT WHAT ARE WE DOING HERE, THEN?
EVEN THOUGH WE KNEW IT WAS ALL A SCAM, WE HAD TO CONVICE THE EMPIRE THAT WE BELIEVED IT WAS GENUINE!
WHY?
TO MAKE THEM TRY TO CONSTRUCT THE PHANTOM SHIP! FOR THAT THEY WOULD NEED LARGE QUANTITIES OF DURINDFIRE GEMS...
...WHICH WE COULD TRACK!
HOPEFULLY TO THEIR BIGGEST RESEARCH FACILITY-- THE ONE WHERE THE FIRST DEATH STAR WAS BUILT!
AT LEAST, THAT WAS THE PLAN...
...WE DESTROY THE DATACARDS AND EVERYBODY GOES AWAY. AT LEAST, THIS WAS WHAT WE PLANNED...
NOT THE GREATEST OF PLANS. IF WE FOUND YOU, THE EMPIRE WILL, TOO. THEN WHAT?
THEN--WE END EVERYTHING!

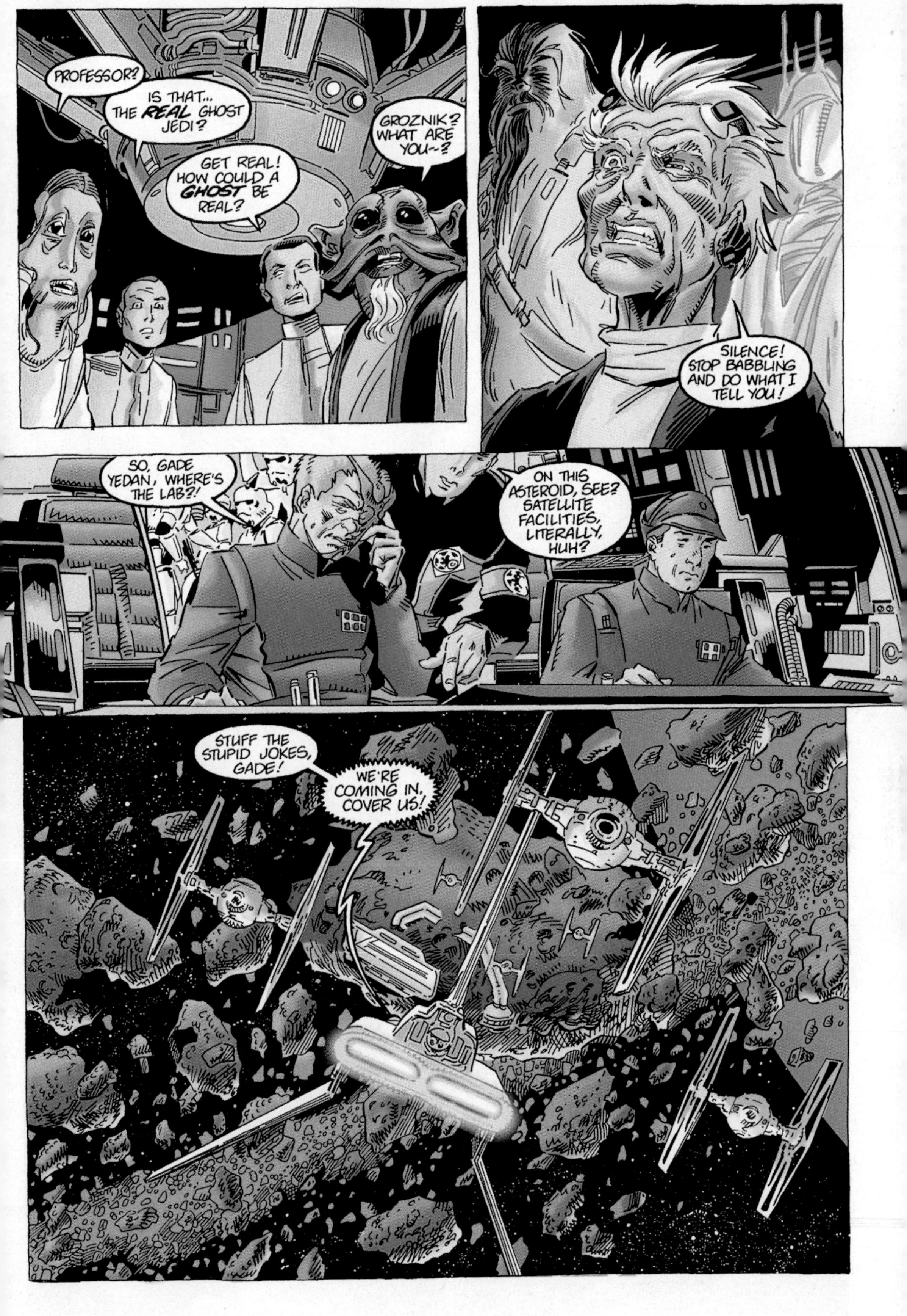
PROFESSOR?
IS THAT... THE REAL GHOST JEDI?
GET REAL! HOW COULD A GHOST BE REAL?
GROZNIK? WHAT ARE YOU--?
SILENCE! STOP BABBLING AND DO WHAT I TELL YOU!
SO, GADE YEDAN, WHERE'S THE LAB?!
ON THIS ASTEROID, SEE? SATELLITE FACILITIES, LITERALLY, HUH?
STUFF THE STUPID JOKES, GADE!
WE'RE COMING IN, COVER US!

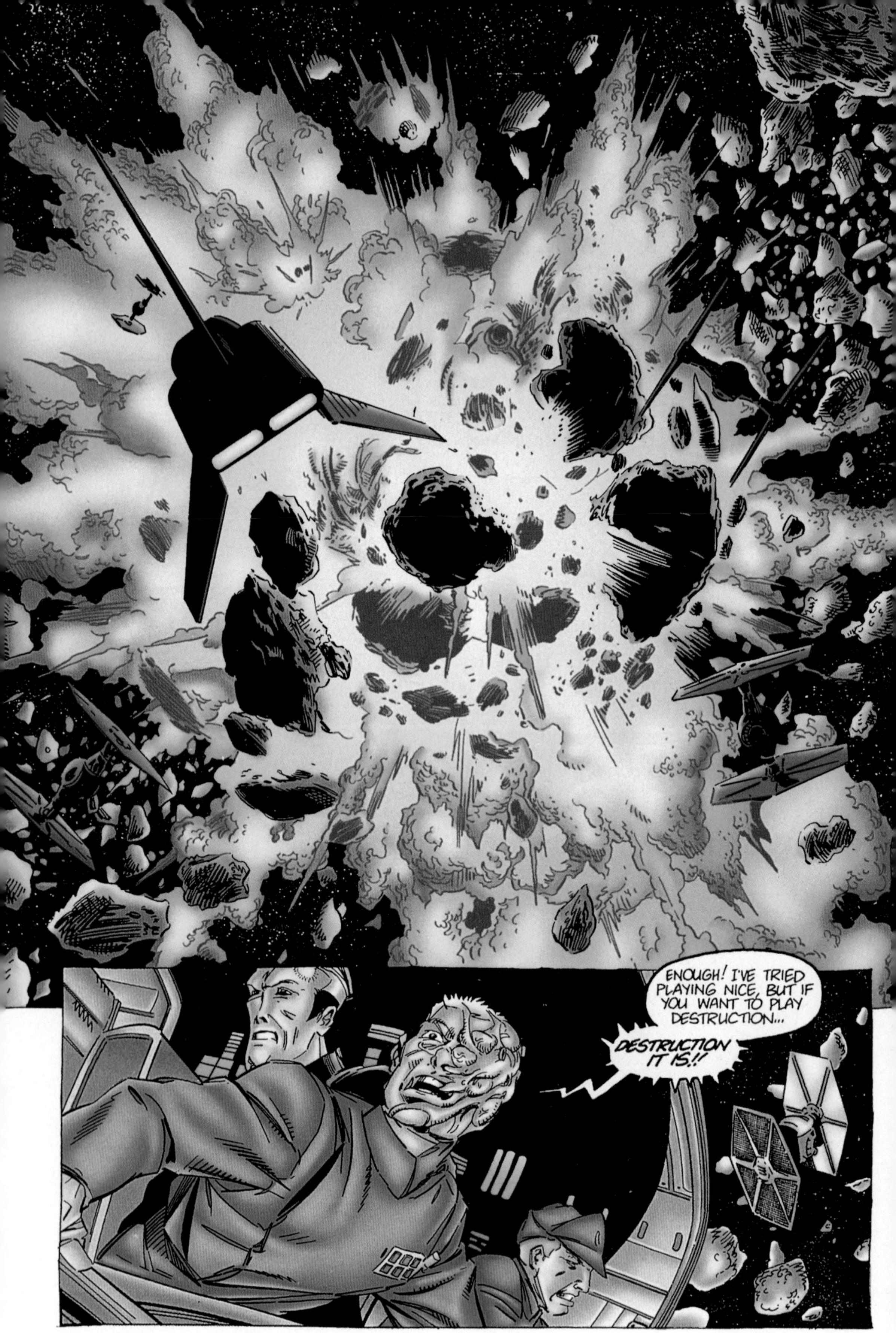
ENOUGH! I'VE TRIED PLAYING NICE, BUT IF YOU WANT TO PLAY DESTRUCTION...
DESTRUCTION IT IS!!

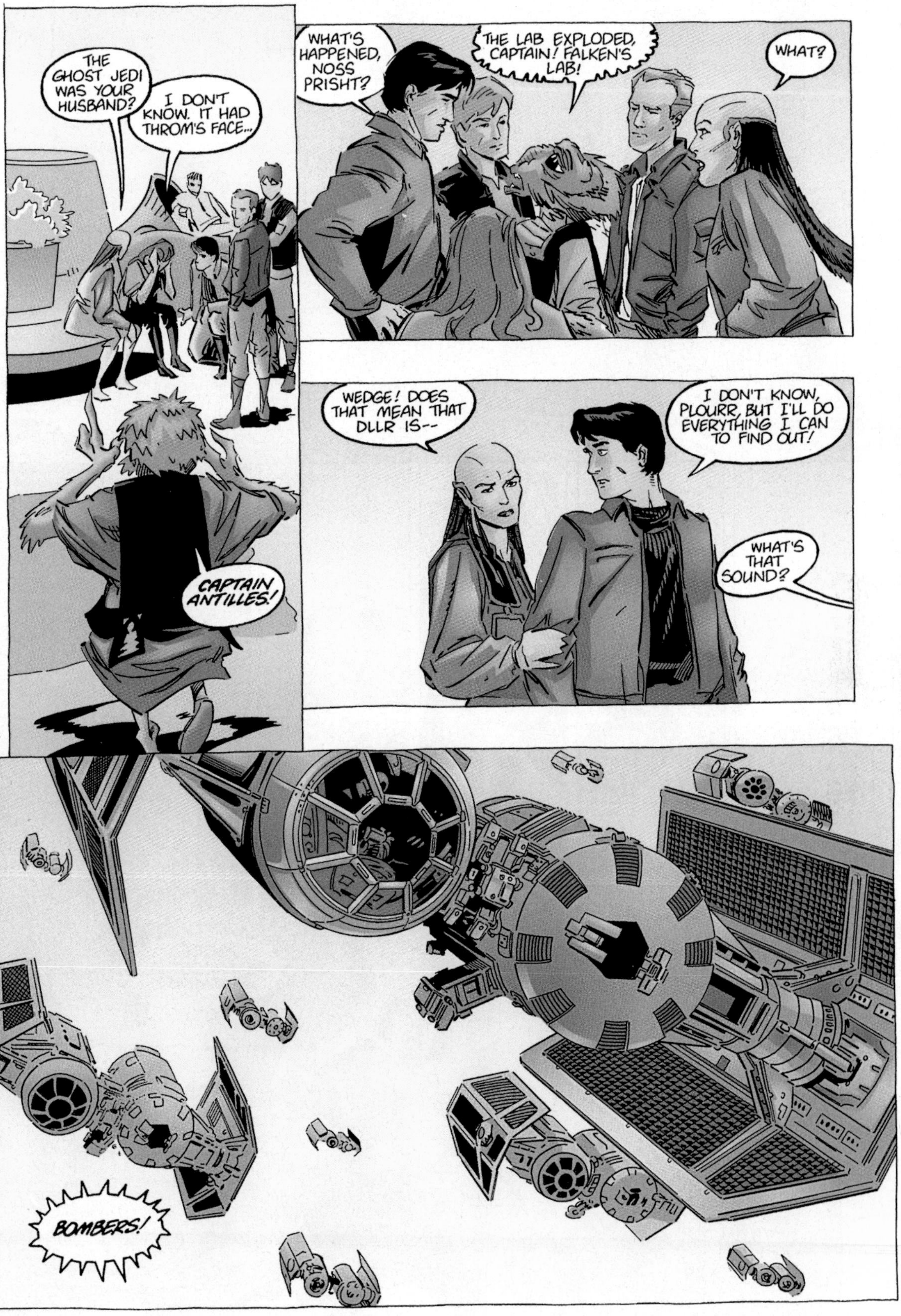
THE GHOST JEDI WAS YOUR HUSBAND?
I DON'T KNOW. IT HAD THROM'S FACE...
CAPTAIN ANTILLES!
WHAT'S HAPPENED, NOSS PRISHT?
THE LAB EXPLODED, CAPTAIN! FALKEN'S LAB!
WHAT?
WEDGE! DOES THAT MEAN THAT DLLR IS--
I DON'T KNOW, PLOURR, BUT I'LL DO EVERYTHING I CAN TO FIND OUT!
WHAT'S THAT SOUND?
BOMBERS!

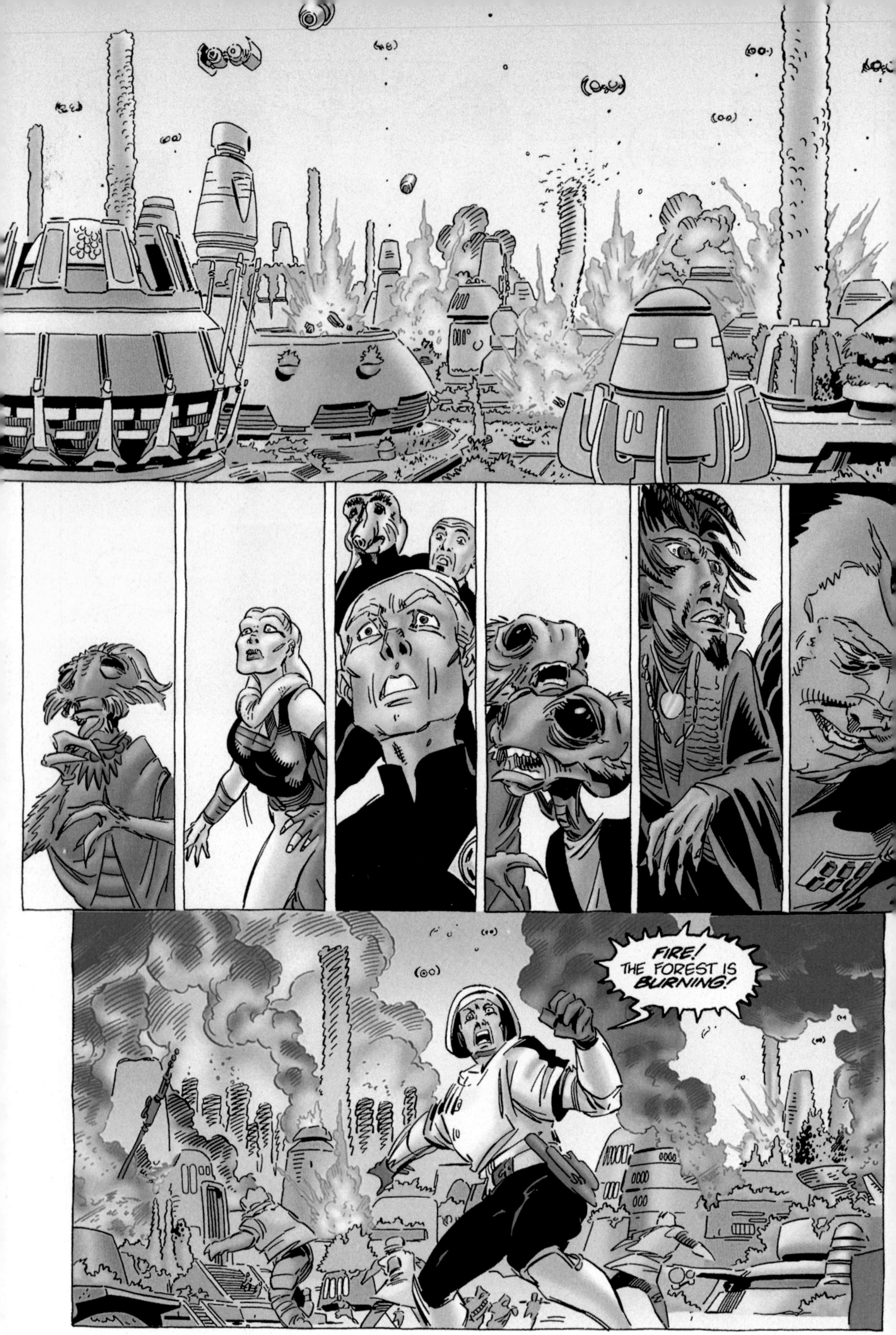
FIRE! THE FOREST IS BURNING!

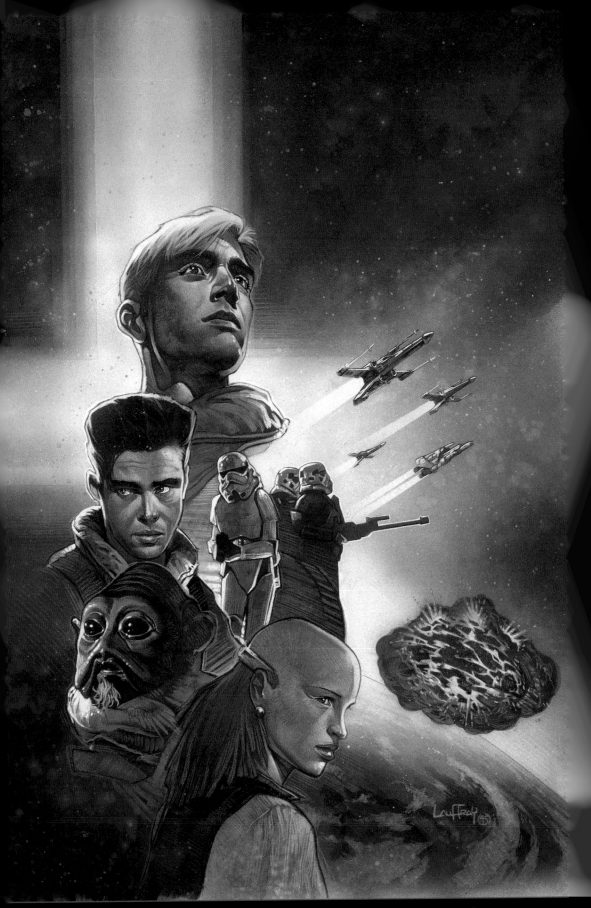

*STAR WARS: X-WING ROGUE SQUADRON #8 — "THE PHANTOM AFFAIR, CHAPTER 4"*

**PLOTTER: MICHAEL A. STACKPOLE • SCRIPTER: DARKO MACAN • ARTIST: GARY ERSKINE • COLORIST: DAVE NESTELLE**

**LETTERER: ANNIE PARKHOUSE • EDITOR: PEET JANES • COVER ARTIST: MATHIEU LAUFFRAY**

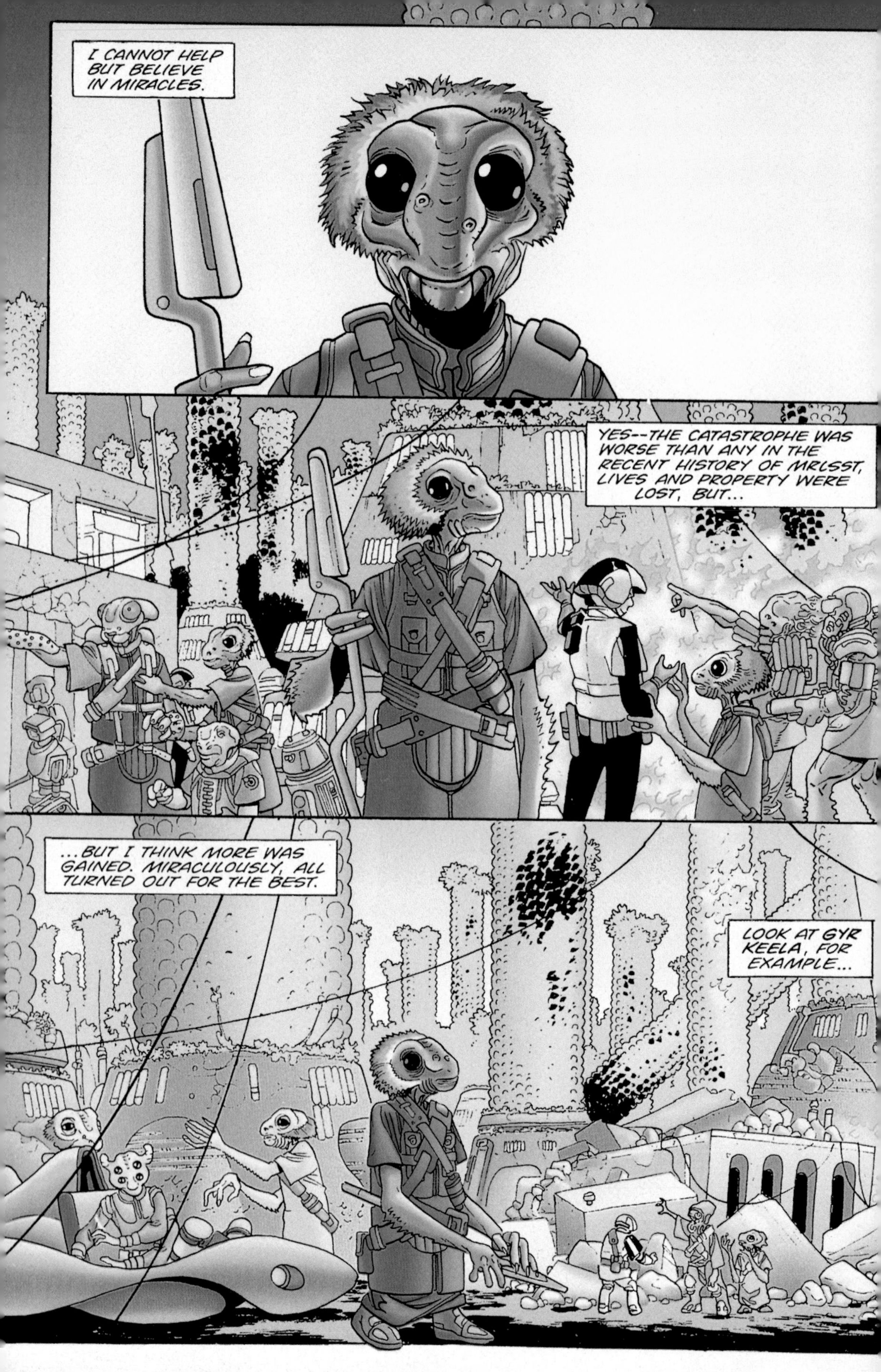
I CANNOT HELP BUT BELIEVE IN MIRACLES.
YES--THE CATASTROPHE WAS WORSE THAN ANY IN THE RECENT HISTORY OF MRLSST, LIVES AND PROPERTY WERE LOST, BUT...
...BUT I THINK MORE WAS GAINED. MIRACULOUSLY, ALL TURNED OUT FOR THE BEST.
LOOK AT GYR KEELA, FOR EXAMPLE...

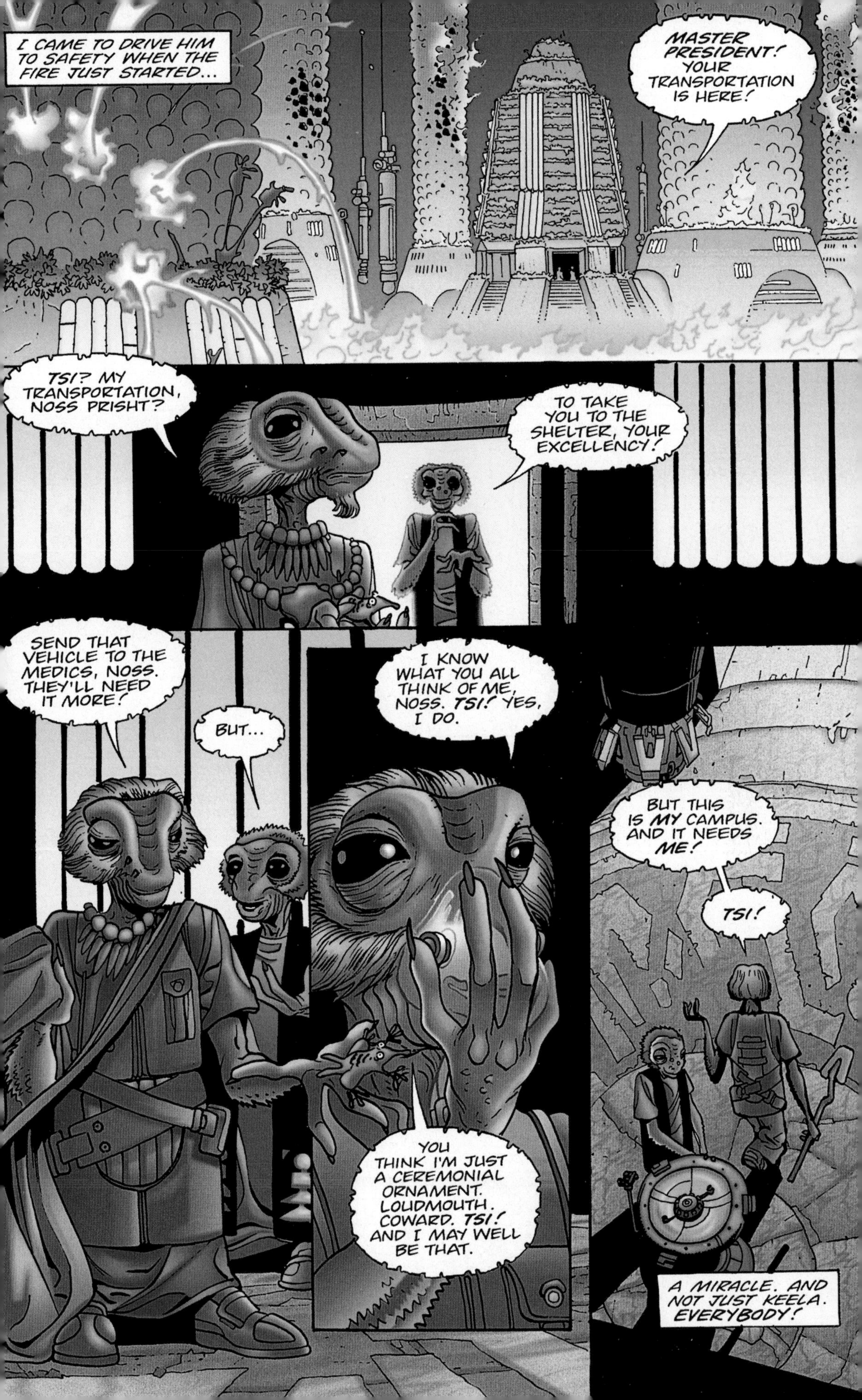

I CAME TO DRIVE HIM TO SAFETY WHEN THE FIRE JUST STARTED...
MASTER PRESIDENT! YOUR TRANSPORTATION IS HERE!
TSI? MY TRANSPORTATION, NOSS PRISHT?
TO TAKE YOU TO THE SHELTER, YOUR EXCELLENCY!
SEND THAT VEHICLE TO THE MEDICS, NOSS. THEY'LL NEED IT MORE!
BUT...
I KNOW WHAT YOU ALL THINK OF ME, NOSS. TSI! YES, I DO.
YOU THINK I'M JUST A CEREMONIAL ORNAMENT. LOUDMOUTH. COWARD. TSI! AND I MAY WELL BE THAT.
BUT THIS IS MY CAMPUS. AND IT NEEDS ME!
TSI!
A MIRACLE. AND NOT JUST KEELA. EVERYBODY!

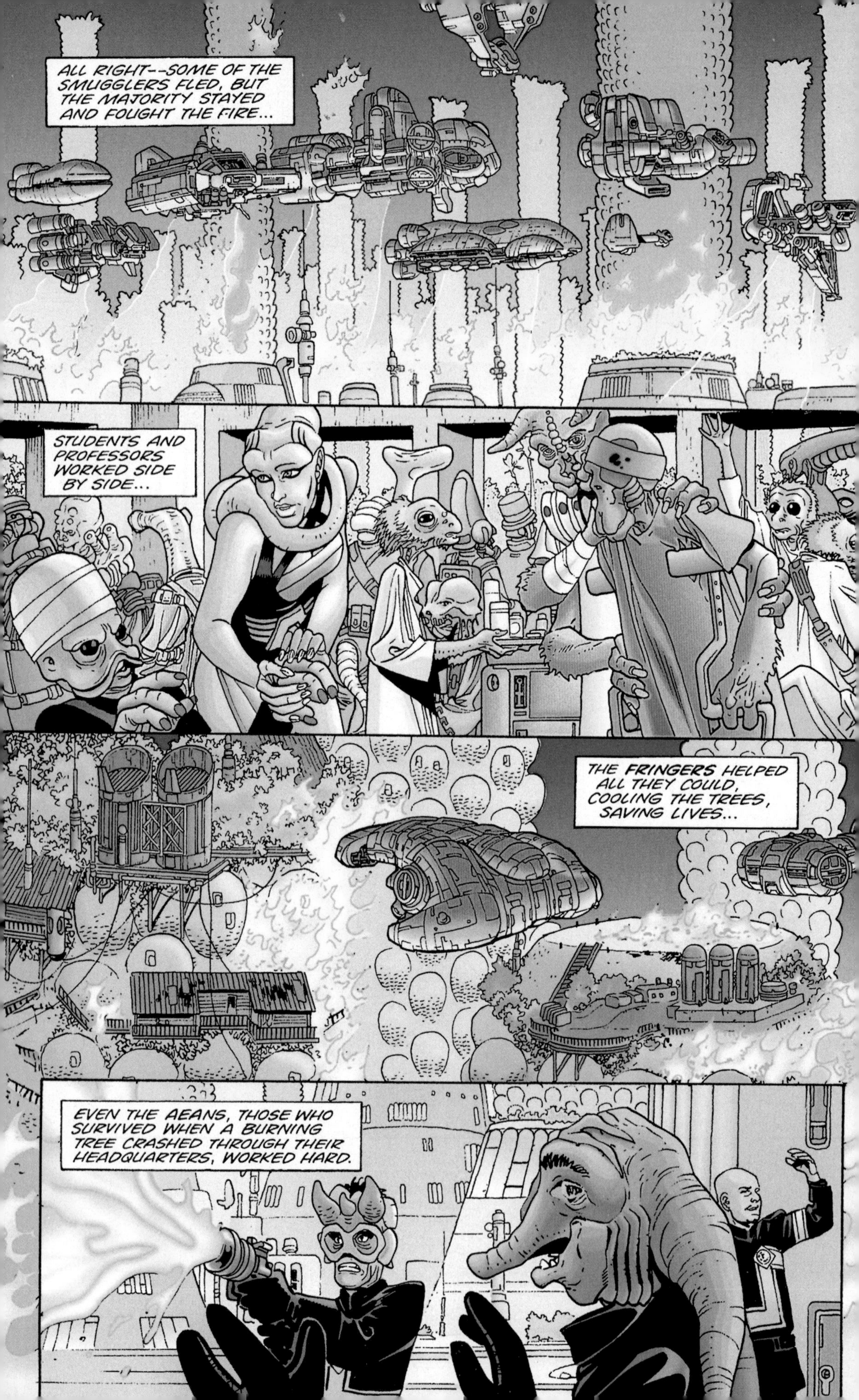
ALL RIGHT--SOME OF THE SMUGGLERS FLED, BUT THE MAJORITY STAYED AND FOUGHT THE FIRE...
STUDENTS AND PROFESSORS WORKED SIDE BY SIDE...
THE FRINGERS HELPED ALL THEY COULD, COOLING THE TREES, SAVING LIVES...
EVEN THE AEANS, THOSE WHO SURVIVED WHEN A BURNING TREE CRASHED THROUGH THEIR HEADQUARTERS, WORKED HARD.

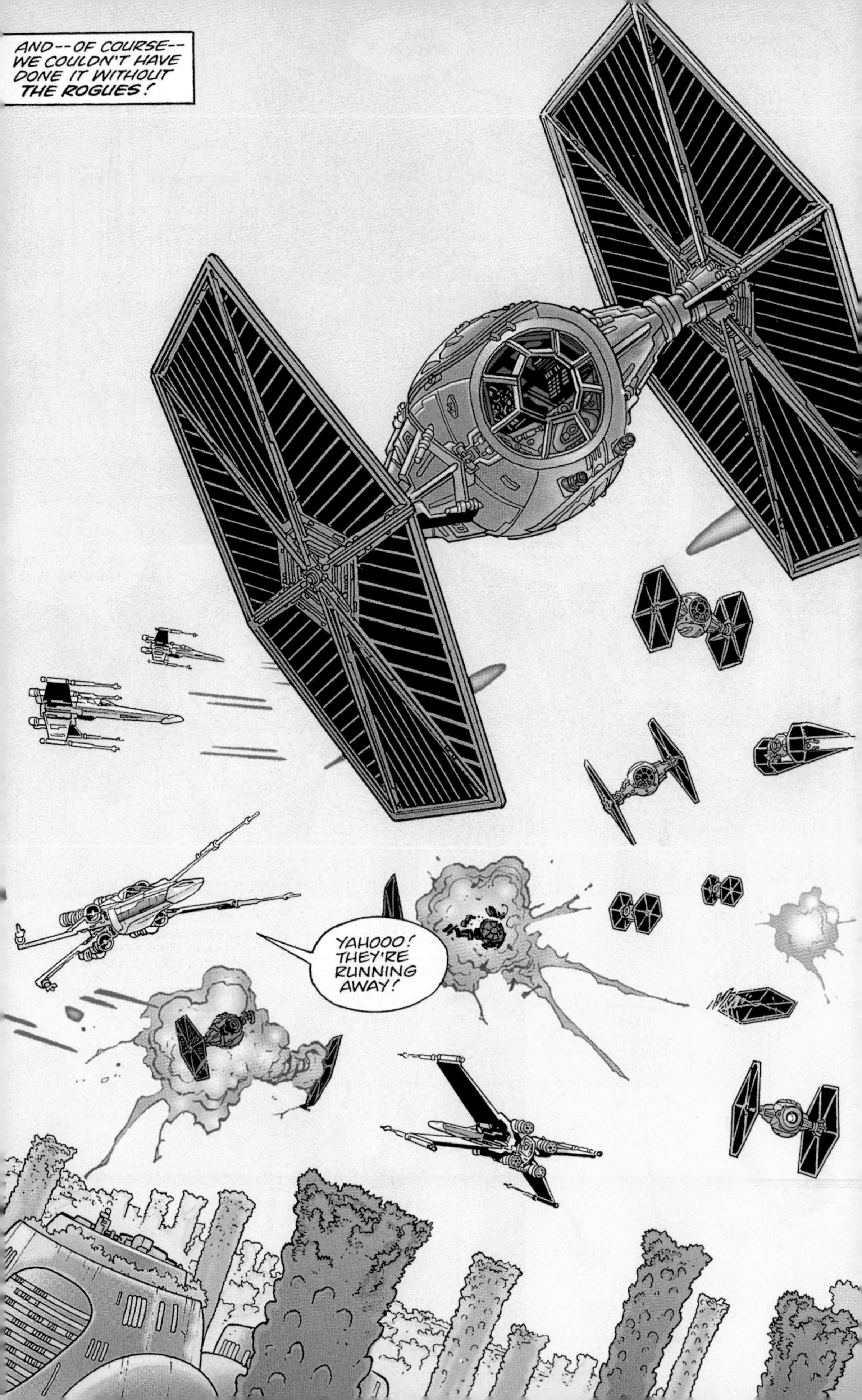
AND--OF COURSE--
WE COULDN'T HAVE
DONE IT WITHOUT
THE ROGUES!
YAHOOO!
THEY'RE
RUNNING
AWAY!

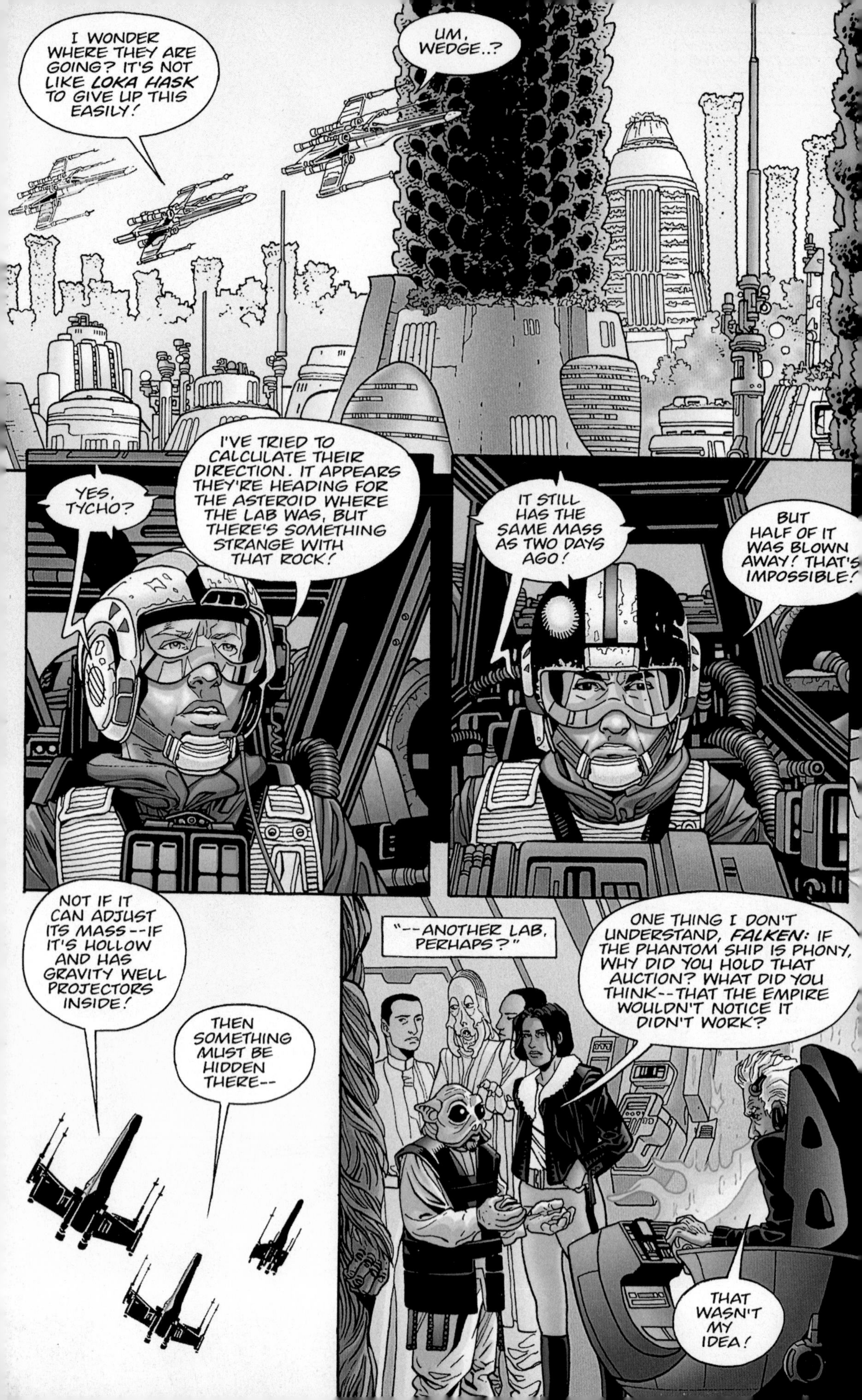
I WONDER WHERE THEY ARE GOING? IT'S NOT LIKE LOKA HASK TO GIVE UP THIS EASILY!
UM, WEDGE..?
YES, TYCHO?
I'VE TRIED TO CALCULATE THEIR DIRECTION. IT APPEARS THEY'RE HEADING FOR THE ASTEROID WHERE THE LAB WAS, BUT THERE'S SOMETHING STRANGE WITH THAT ROCK!
IT STILL HAS THE SAME MASS AS TWO DAYS AGO!
BUT HALF OF IT WAS BLOWN AWAY! THAT'S IMPOSSIBLE!
NOT IF IT CAN ADJUST ITS MASS--IF IT'S HOLLOW AND HAS GRAVITY WELL PROJECTORS INSIDE!
THEN SOMETHING MUST BE HIDDEN THERE--
"--ANOTHER LAB, PERHAPS?"
ONE THING I DON'T UNDERSTAND, FALKEN: IF THE PHANTOM SHIP IS PHONY, WHY DID YOU HOLD THAT AUCTION? WHAT DID YOU THINK--THAT THE EMPIRE WOULDN'T NOTICE IT DIDN'T WORK?
THAT WASN'T MY IDEA!

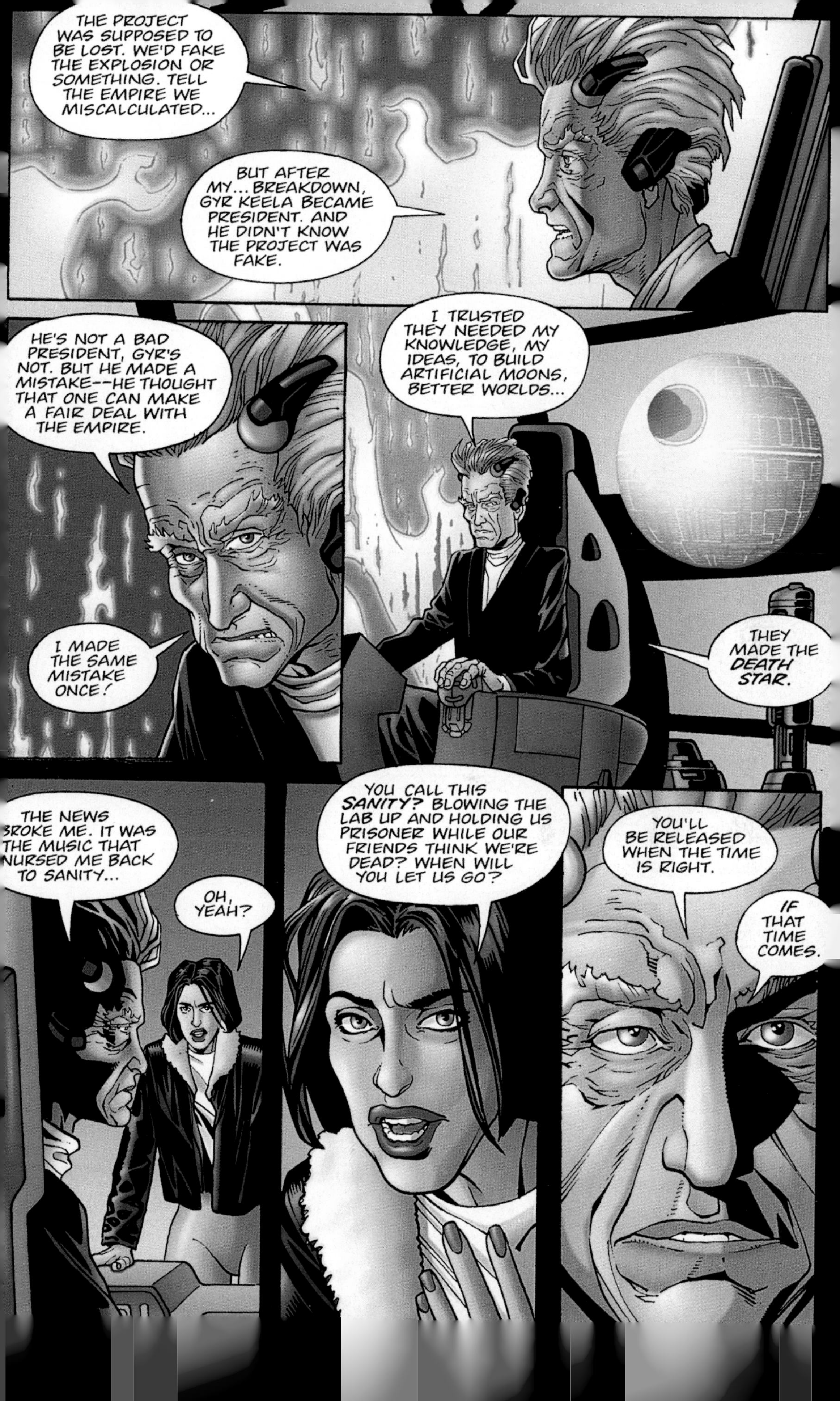
THE PROJECT WAS SUPPOSED TO BE LOST. WE'D FAKE THE EXPLOSION OR SOMETHING. TELL THE EMPIRE WE MISCALCULATED...
BUT AFTER MY... BREAKDOWN, GYR KEELA BECAME PRESIDENT. AND HE DIDN'T KNOW THE PROJECT WAS FAKE.
HE'S NOT A BAD PRESIDENT, GYR'S NOT. BUT HE MADE A MISTAKE--HE THOUGHT THAT ONE CAN MAKE A FAIR DEAL WITH THE EMPIRE.
I MADE THE SAME MISTAKE ONCE!
I TRUSTED THEY NEEDED MY KNOWLEDGE, MY IDEAS, TO BUILD ARTIFICIAL MOONS, BETTER WORLDS...
THEY MADE THE DEATH STAR.
THE NEWS BROKE ME. IT WAS THE MUSIC THAT NURSED ME BACK TO SANITY...
OH, YEAH?
YOU CALL THIS SANITY? BLOWING THE LAB UP AND HOLDING US PRISONER WHILE OUR FRIENDS THINK WE'RE DEAD? WHEN WILL YOU LET US GO?
YOU'LL BE RELEASED WHEN THE TIME IS RIGHT.
IF THAT TIME COMES.

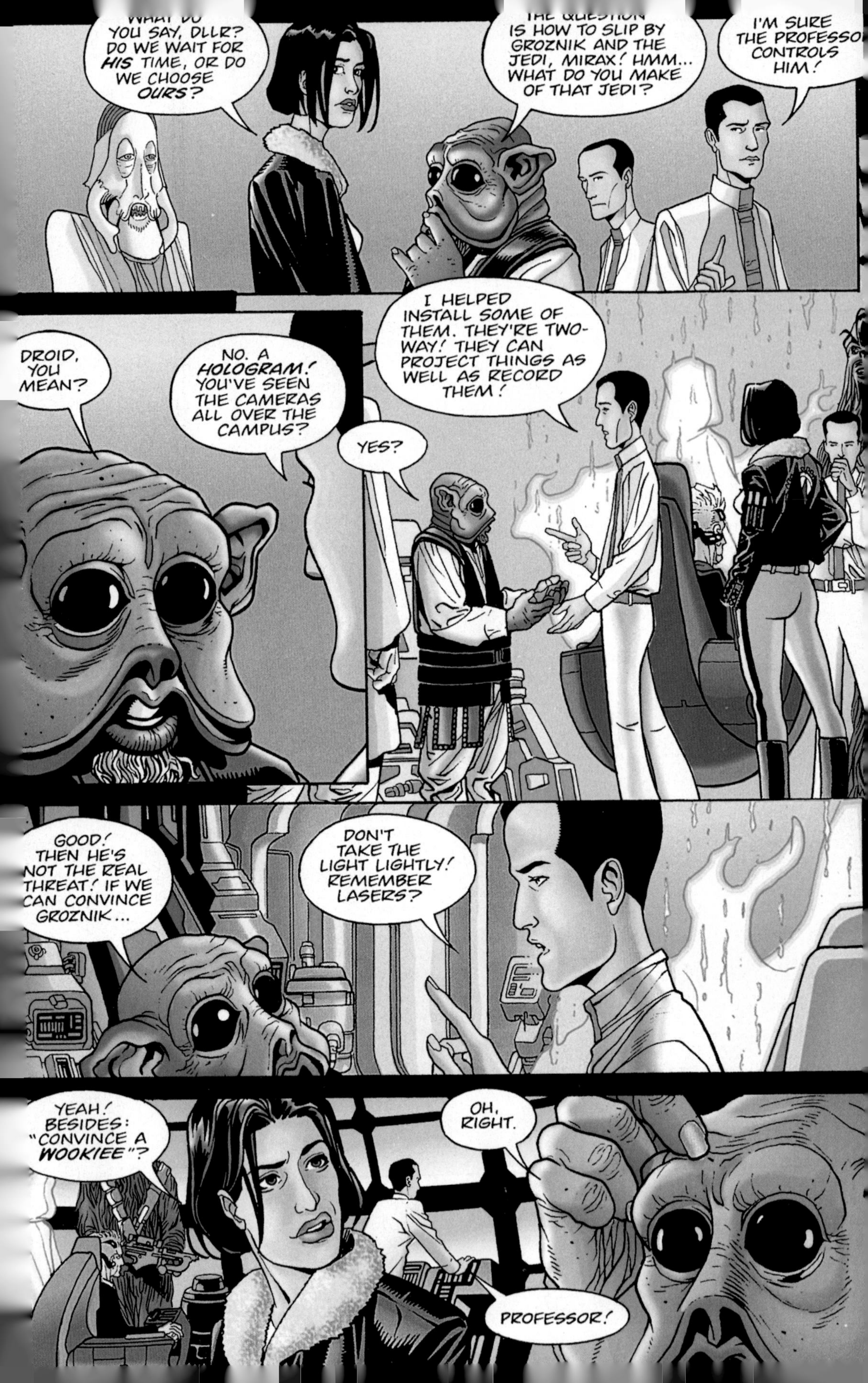

WHAT DO YOU SAY, DLLR? DO WE WAIT FOR HIS TIME, OR DO WE CHOOSE OURS?
THE QUESTION IS HOW TO SLIP BY GROZNIK AND THE JEDI, MIRAX! HMM... WHAT DO YOU MAKE OF THAT JEDI?
I'M SURE THE PROFESSO CONTROLS HIM!
DROID, YOU MEAN?
NO. A HOLOGRAM! YOU'VE SEEN THE CAMERAS ALL OVER THE CAMPUS?
YES?
I HELPED INSTALL SOME OF THEM. THEY'RE TWO-WAY! THEY CAN PROJECT THINGS AS WELL AS RECORD THEM!
GOOD! THEN HE'S NOT THE REAL THREAT! IF WE CAN CONVINCE GROZNIK...
DON'T TAKE THE LIGHT LIGHTLY! REMEMBER LASERS?
YEAH! BESIDES: "CONVINCE A WOOKIEE"?
OH, RIGHT.
PROFESSOR!

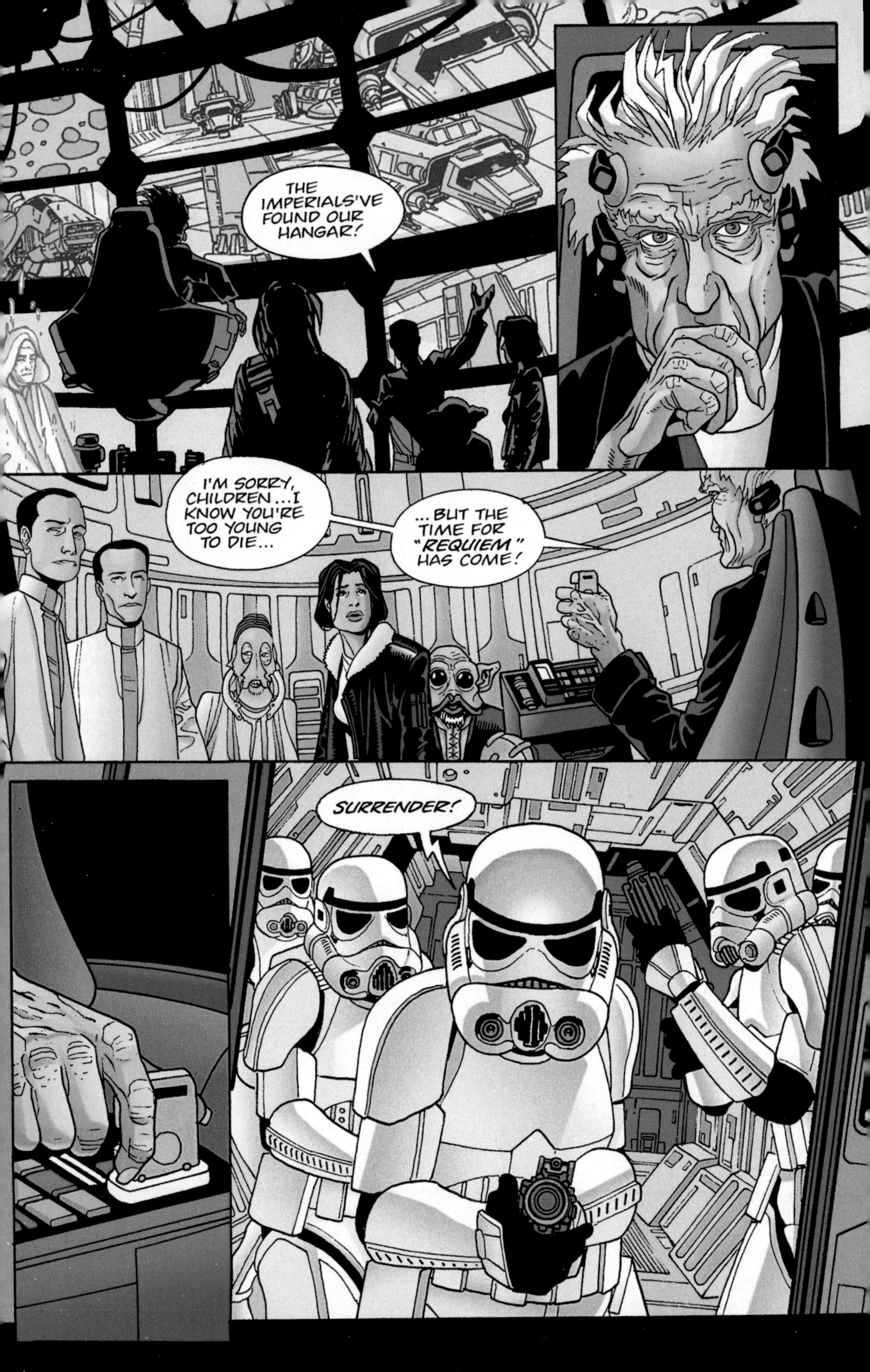
THE IMPERIALS'VE FOUND OUR HANGAR!
I'M SORRY, CHILDREN...I KNOW YOU'RE TOO YOUNG TO DIE...
...BUT THE TIME FOR "REQUIEM" HAS COME!
SURRENDER!

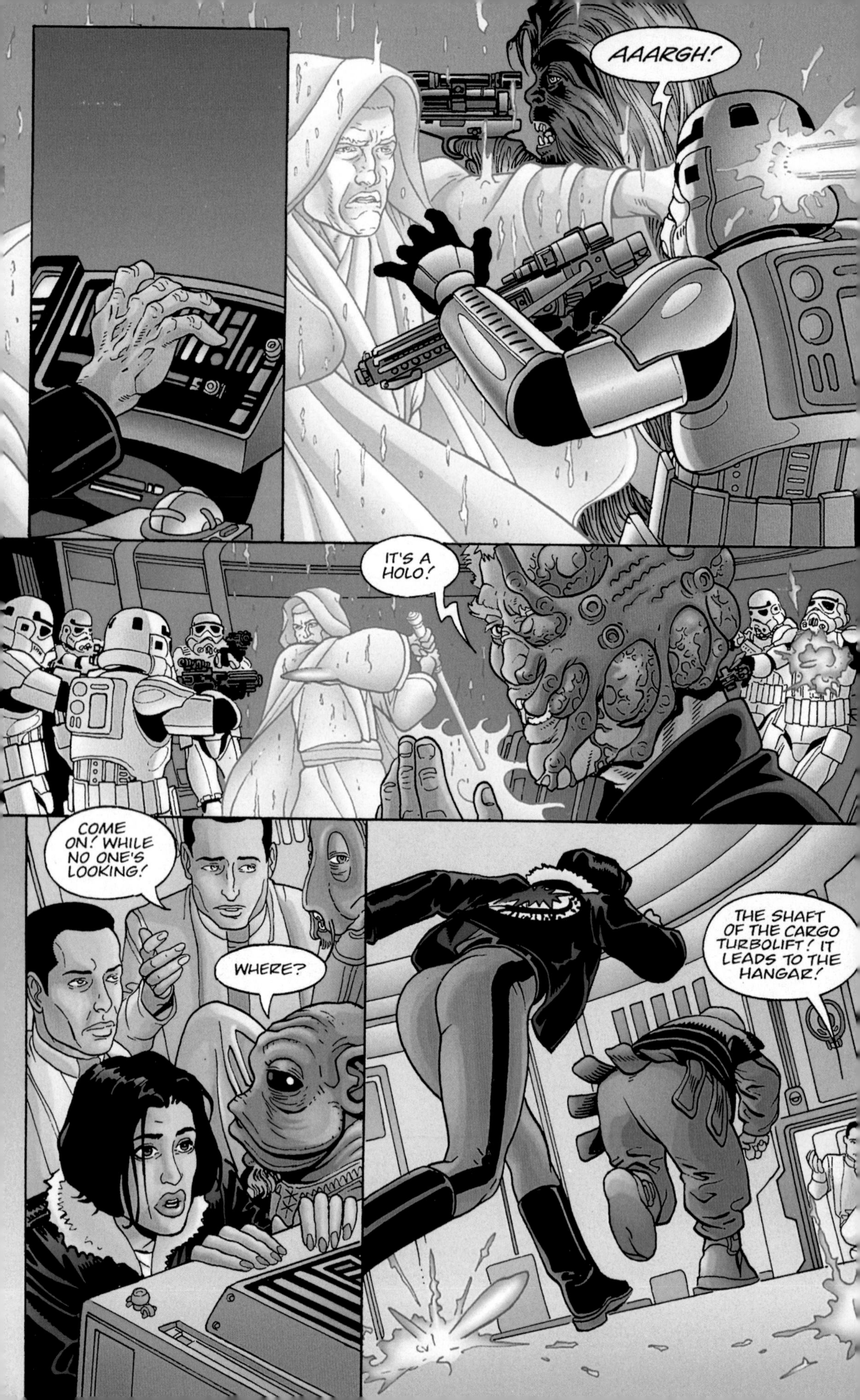
AAARGH!
IT'S A HOLO!
COME ON! WHILE NO ONE'S LOOKING!
WHERE?
THE SHAFT OF THE CARGO TURBOLIFT! IT LEADS TO THE HANGAR!

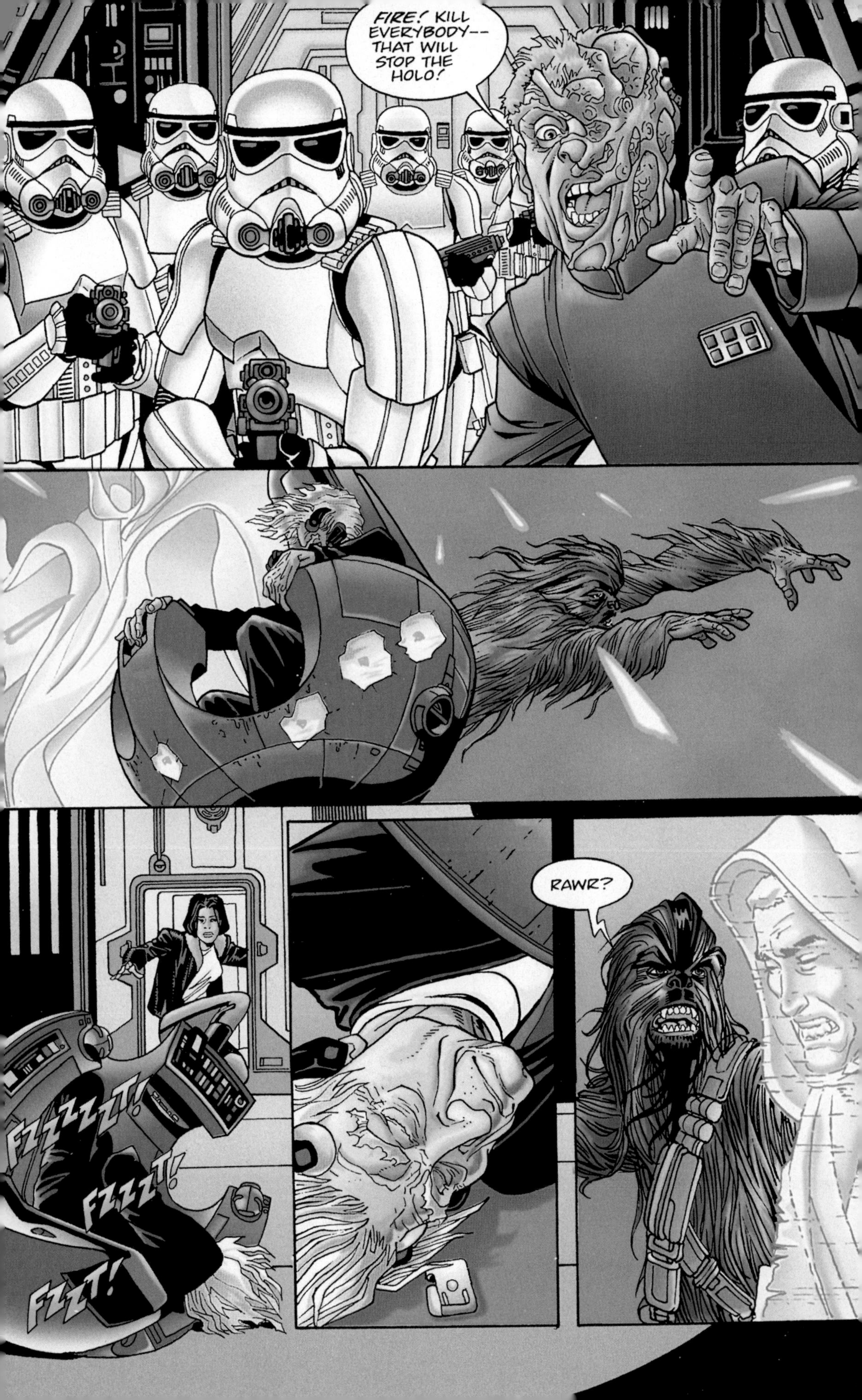
FIRE! KILL EVERYBODY-- THAT WILL STOP THE HOLO!
FZZZZZZT!
FZZZZT!
FZZT!
RAWR?

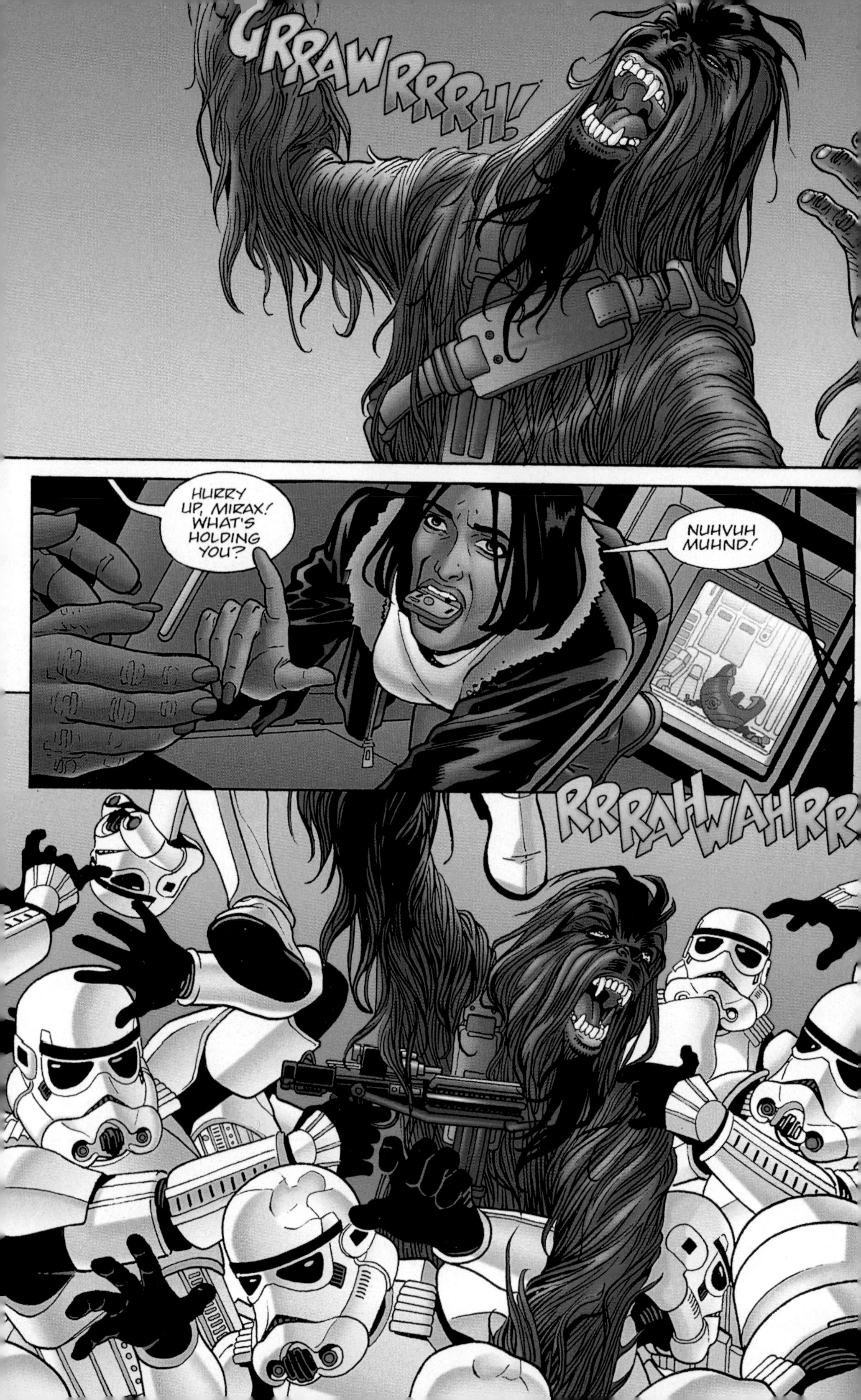
GRRAWRRRH!
HURRY UP, MIRAX! WHAT'S HOLDING YOU?
NUHVUH MUHND!
RRRAHWAHRR

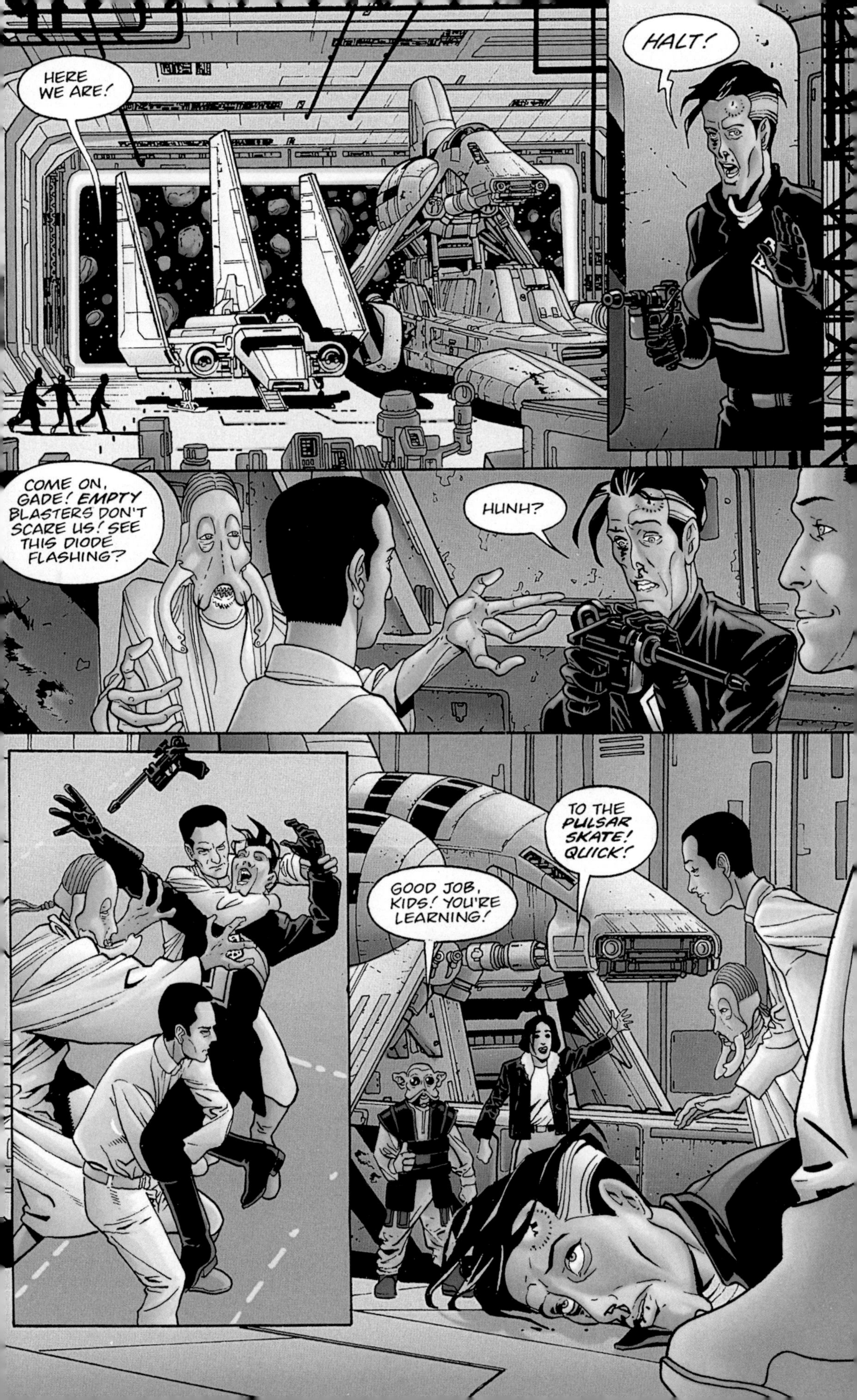
HERE WE ARE!
HALT!
COME ON, GADE! EMPTY BLASTERS DON'T SCARE US! SEE THIS DIODE FLASHING?
HUNH?
TO THE PULSAR SKATE! QUICK!
GOOD JOB, KIDS! YOU'RE LEARNING!

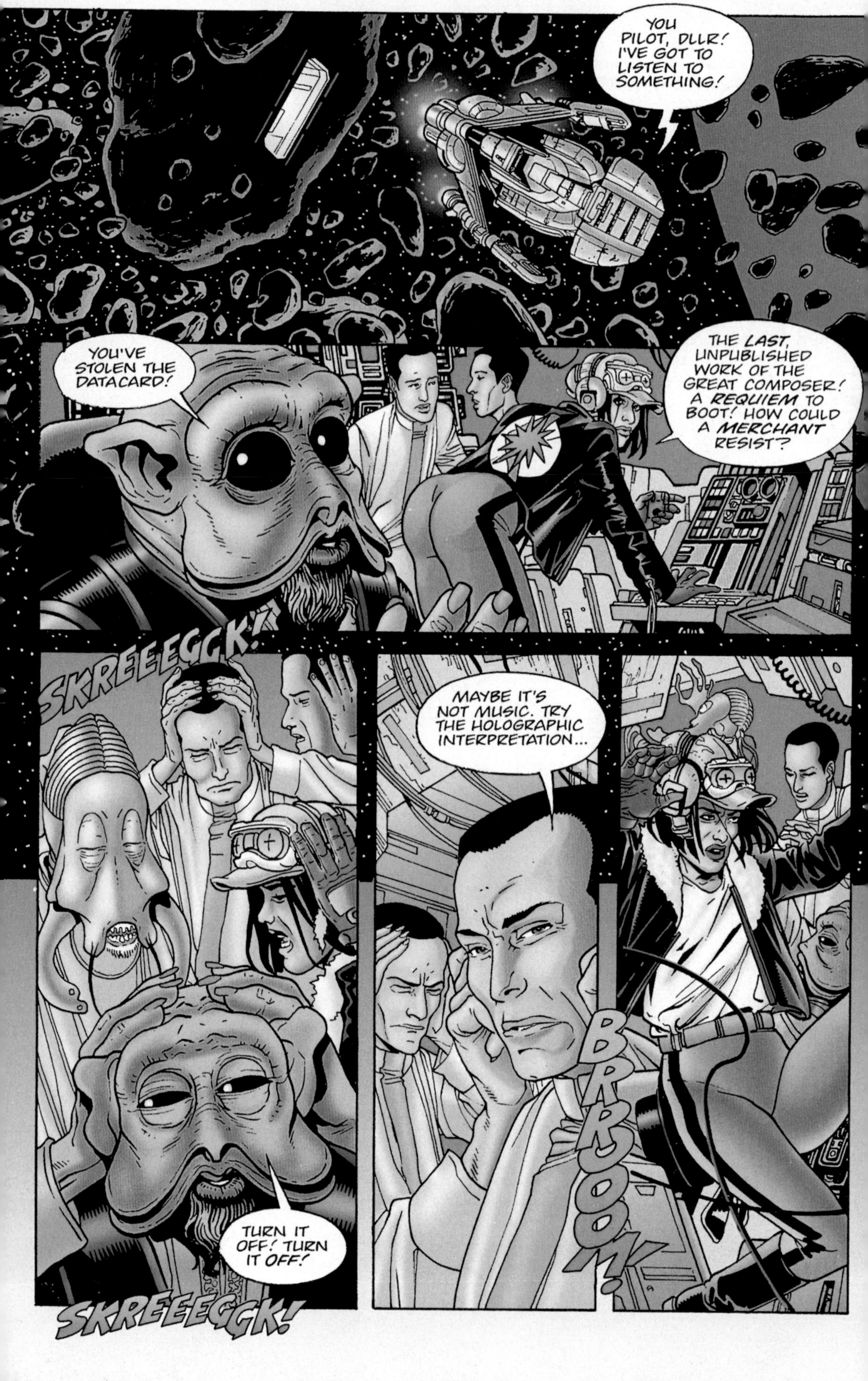
YOU PILOT, DLLR! I'VE GOT TO LISTEN TO SOMETHING!
YOU'VE STOLEN THE DATACARD!
THE LAST, UNPUBLISHED WORK OF THE GREAT COMPOSER! A REQUIEM TO BOOT! HOW COULD A MERCHANT RESIST?
SKREEEGGK!
TURN IT OFF! TURN IT OFF!
SKREEEGGK!
MAYBE IT'S NOT MUSIC. TRY THE HOLOGRAPHIC INTERPRETATION...
BRRROOOM!

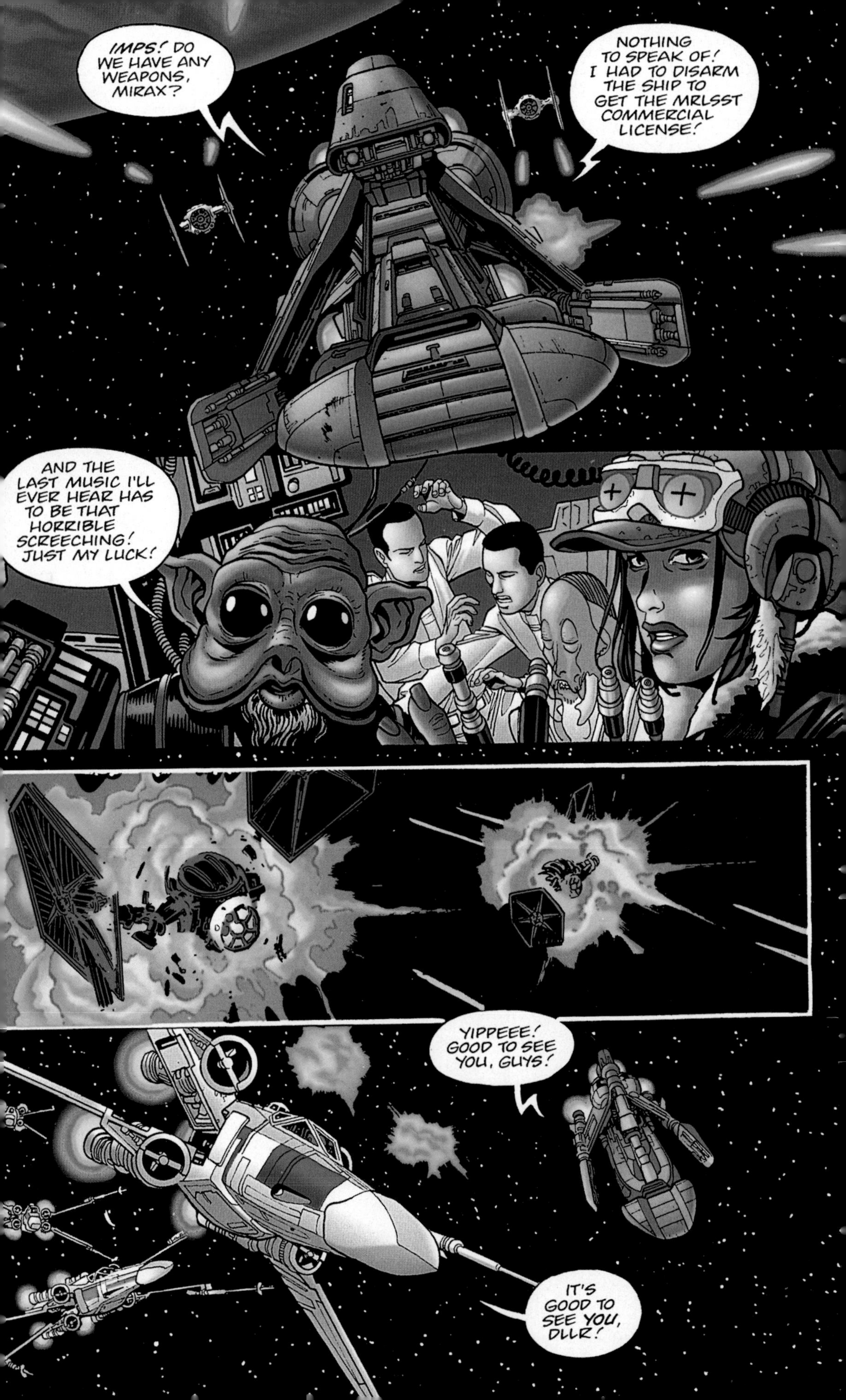
IMPS! DO WE HAVE ANY WEAPONS, MIRAX?
NOTHING TO SPEAK OF! I HAD TO DISARM THE SHIP TO GET THE MRLSST COMMERCIAL LICENSE!
AND THE LAST MUSIC I'LL EVER HEAR HAS TO BE THAT HORRIBLE SCREECHING! JUST MY LUCK!
YIPPEEE! GOOD TO SEE YOU, GUYS!
IT'S GOOD TO SEE YOU, DLLR!

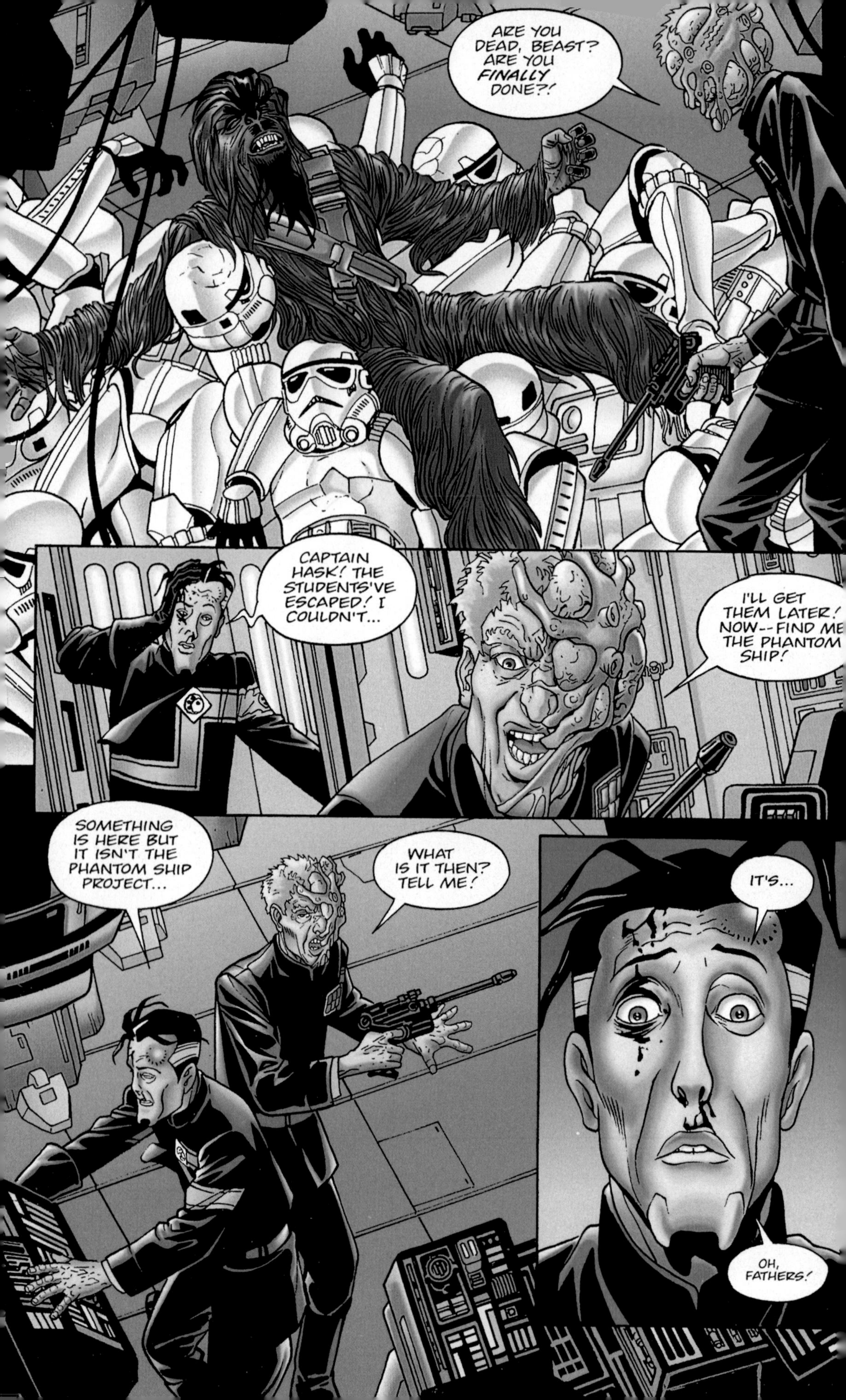
ARE YOU DEAD, BEAST? ARE YOU FINALLY DONE?!
CAPTAIN HASK! THE STUDENTS'VE ESCAPED! I COULDN'T...
I'LL GET THEM LATER! NOW--FIND ME THE PHANTOM SHIP!
SOMETHING IS HERE BUT IT ISN'T THE PHANTOM SHIP PROJECT...
WHAT IS IT THEN? TELL ME!
IT'S...
OH, FATHERS!

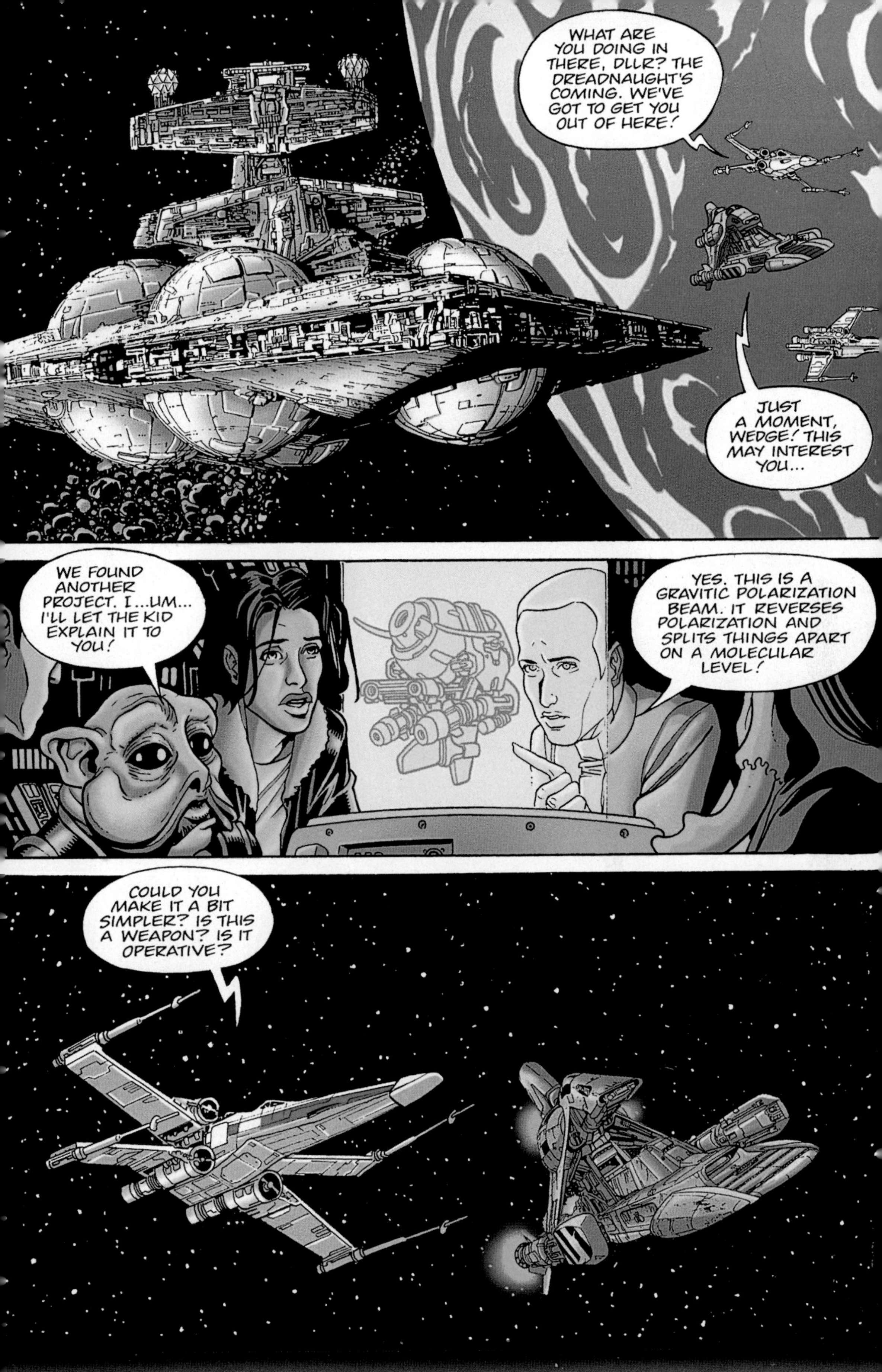
WHAT ARE YOU DOING IN THERE, DLLR? THE DREADNAUGHT'S COMING. WE'VE GOT TO GET YOU OUT OF HERE!
JUST A MOMENT, WEDGE! THIS MAY INTEREST YOU...
WE FOUND ANOTHER PROJECT. I...UM... I'LL LET THE KID EXPLAIN IT TO YOU!
YES. THIS IS A GRAVITIC POLARIZATION BEAM. IT REVERSES POLARIZATION AND SPLITS THINGS APART ON A MOLECULAR LEVEL!
COULD YOU MAKE IT A BIT SIMPLER? IS THIS A WEAPON? IS IT OPERATIVE?

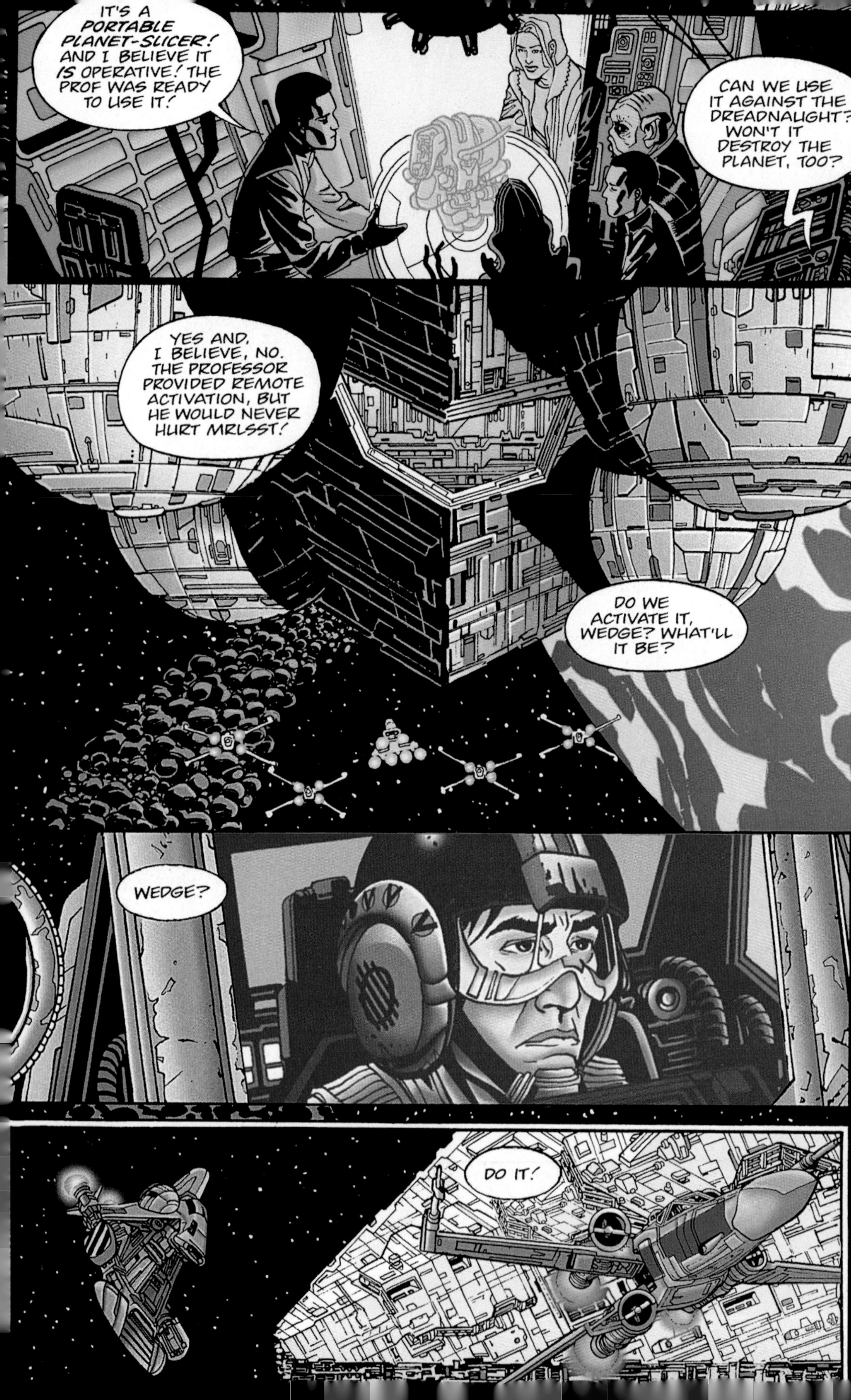
IT'S A PORTABLE PLANET-SLICER! AND I BELIEVE IT IS OPERATIVE! THE PROF WAS READY TO USE IT!
CAN WE USE IT AGAINST THE DREADNAUGHT? WON'T IT DESTROY THE PLANET, TOO?
YES AND, I BELIEVE, NO. THE PROFESSOR PROVIDED REMOTE ACTIVATION, BUT HE WOULD NEVER HURT MRLSST!
DO WE ACTIVATE IT, WEDGE? WHAT'LL IT BE?
WEDGE?
DO IT!

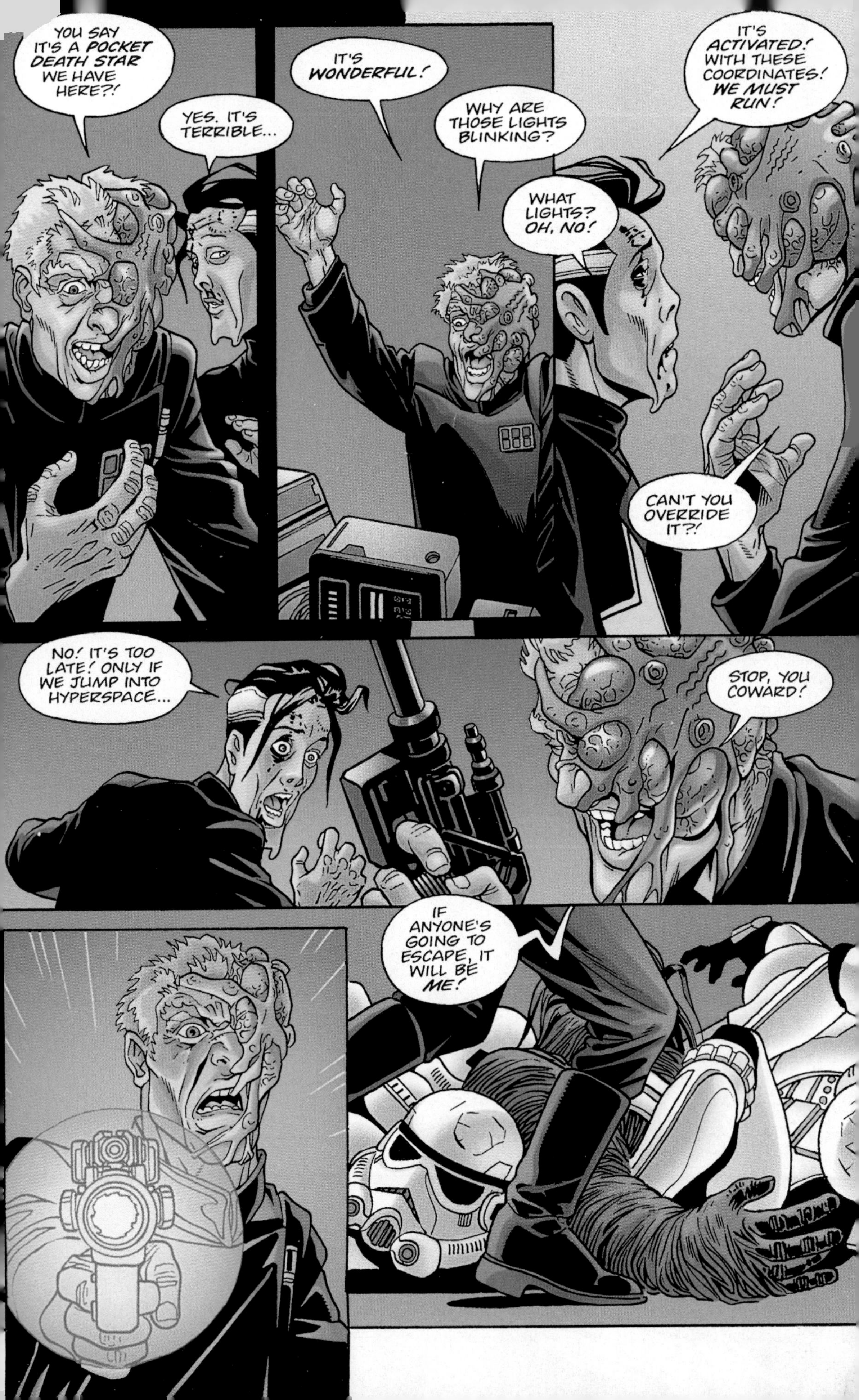
YOU SAY IT'S A POCKET DEATH STAR WE HAVE HERE?!
YES. IT'S TERRIBLE...
IT'S WONDERFUL!
WHY ARE THOSE LIGHTS BLINKING?
WHAT LIGHTS? OH, NO!
IT'S ACTIVATED! WITH THESE COORDINATES! WE MUST RUN!
CAN'T YOU OVERRIDE IT?!
NO! IT'S TOO LATE! ONLY IF WE JUMP INTO HYPERSPACE...
STOP, YOU COWARD!
IF ANYONE'S GOING TO ESCAPE, IT WILL BE ME!

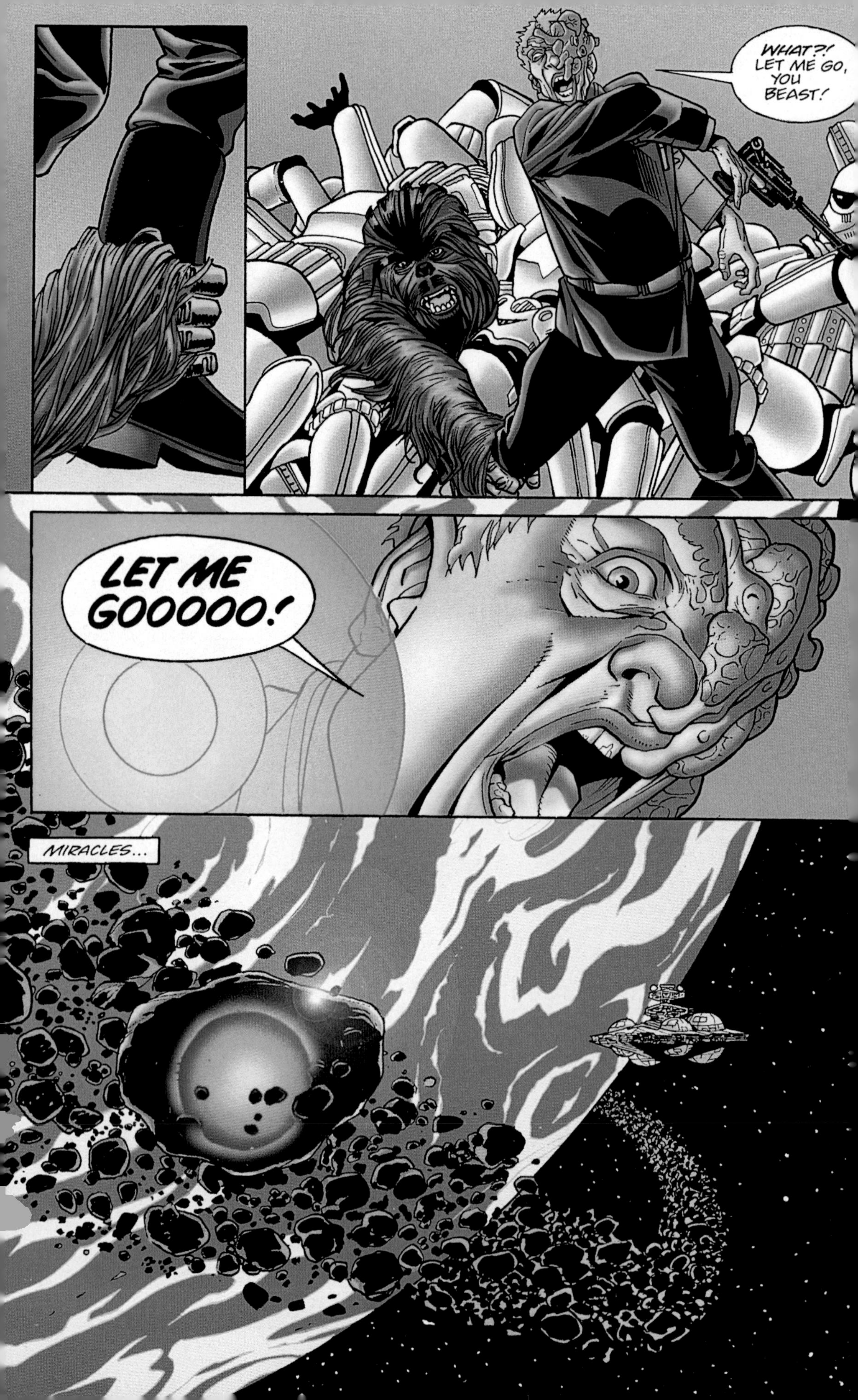
WHAT?! LET ME GO, YOU BEAST!
LET ME GOOOOO!
MIRACLES...

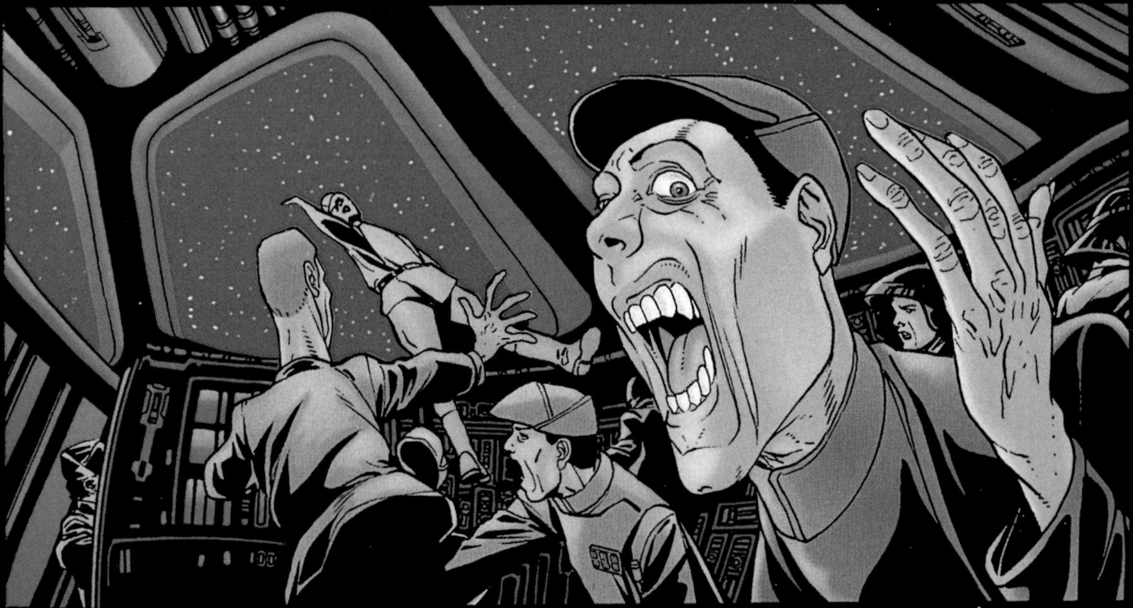

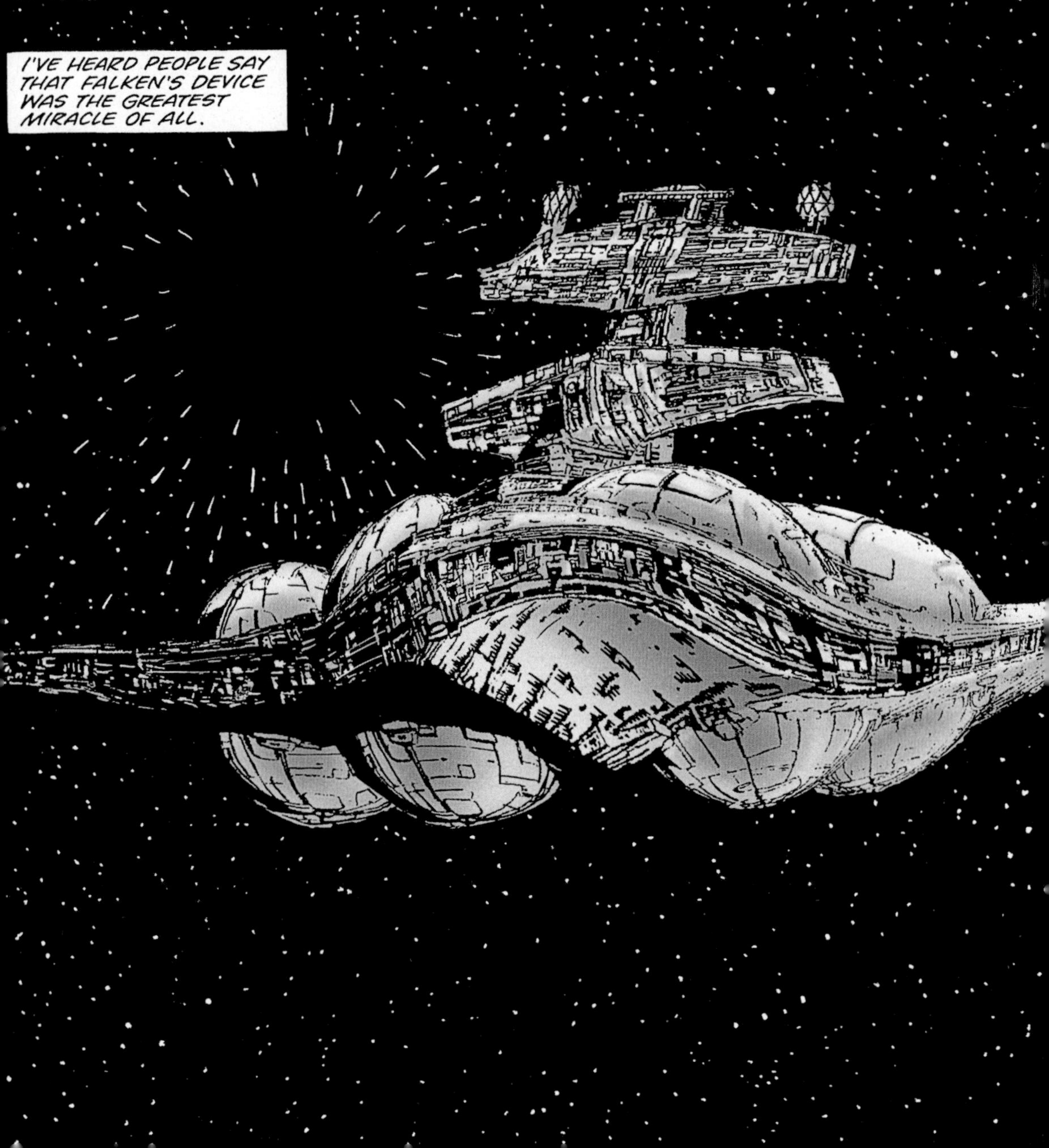
I'VE HEARD PEOPLE SAY THAT FALKEN'S DEVICE WAS THE GREATEST MIRACLE OF ALL.

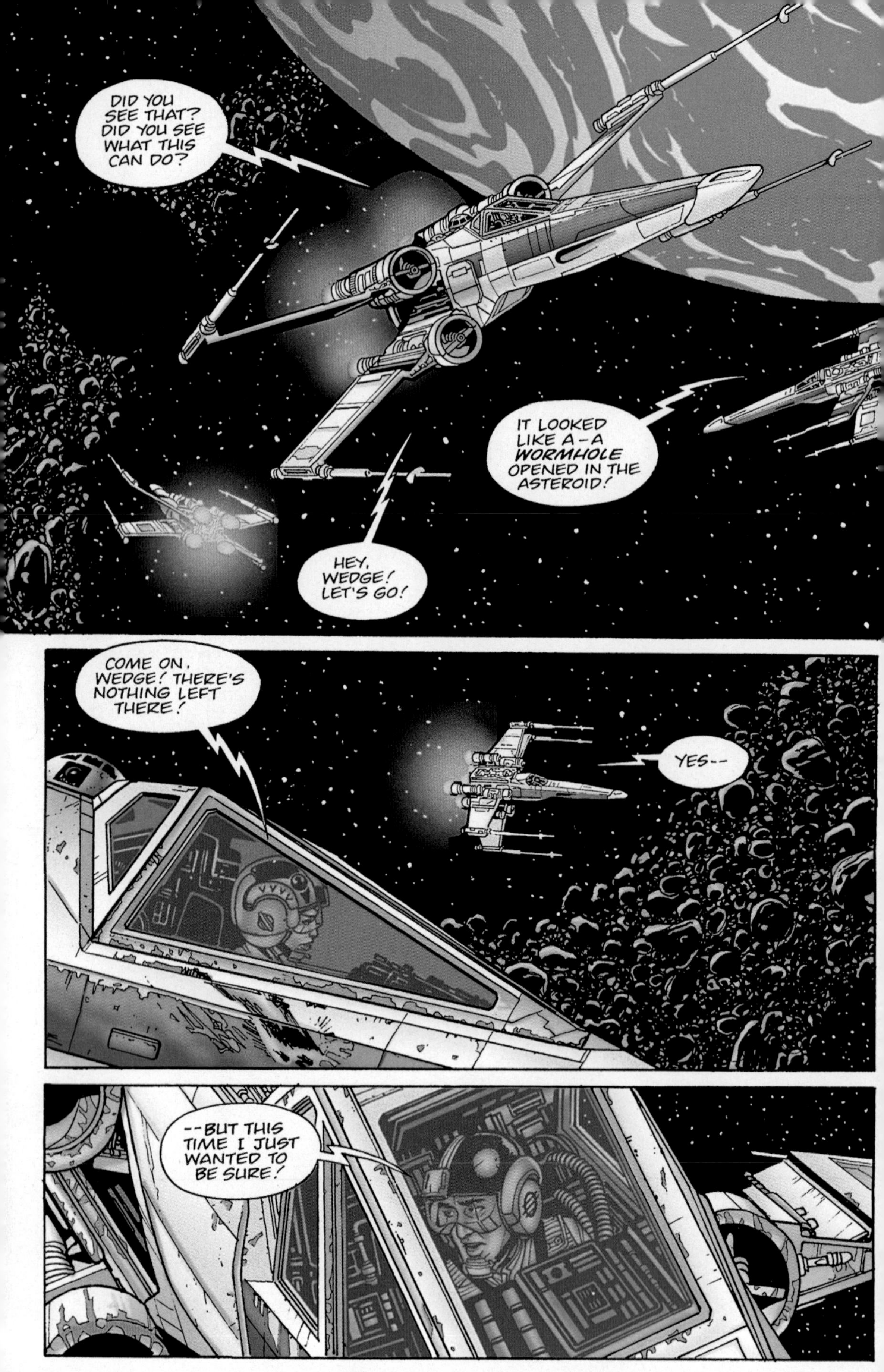
DID YOU SEE THAT? DID YOU SEE WHAT THIS CAN DO?
IT LOOKED LIKE A--A WORMHOLE OPENED IN THE ASTEROID!
HEY, WEDGE! LET'S GO!
COME ON, WEDGE! THERE'S NOTHING LEFT THERE!
YES--
--BUT THIS TIME I JUST WANTED TO BE SURE!

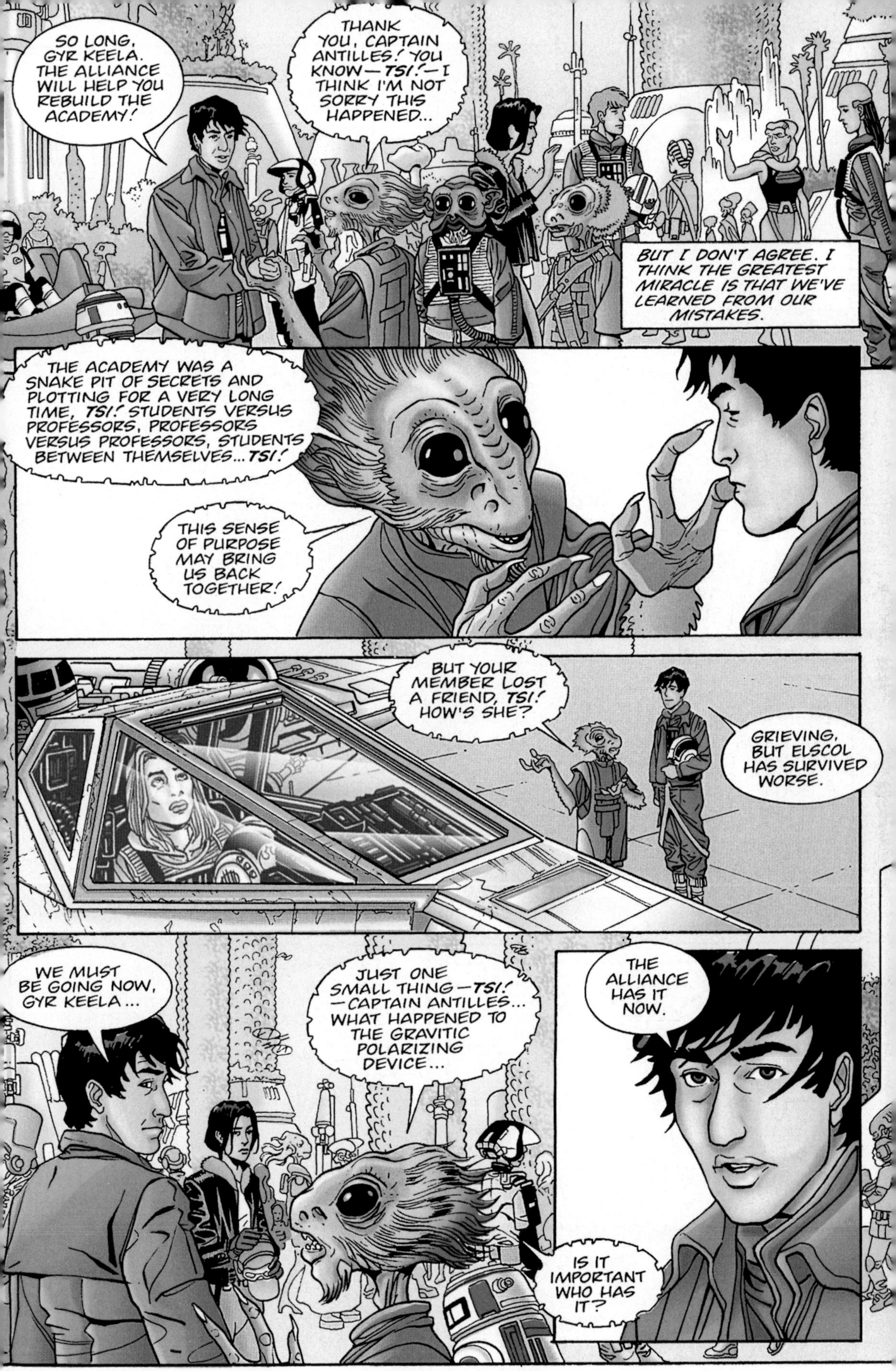
SO LONG, GYR KEELA. THE ALLIANCE WILL HELP YOU REBUILD THE ACADEMY!
THANK YOU, CAPTAIN ANTILLES! YOU KNOW—TSI!—I THINK I'M NOT SORRY THIS HAPPENED...
BUT I DON'T AGREE. I THINK THE GREATEST MIRACLE IS THAT WE'VE LEARNED FROM OUR MISTAKES.
THE ACADEMY WAS A SNAKE PIT OF SECRETS AND PLOTTING FOR A VERY LONG TIME, TSI! STUDENTS VERSUS PROFESSORS, PROFESSORS VERSUS PROFESSORS, STUDENTS BETWEEN THEMSELVES...TSI!
THIS SENSE OF PURPOSE MAY BRING US BACK TOGETHER!
BUT YOUR MEMBER LOST A FRIEND, TSI! HOW'S SHE?
GRIEVING, BUT ELSCOL HAS SURVIVED WORSE.
WE MUST BE GOING NOW, GYR KEELA...
JUST ONE SMALL THING—TSI! —CAPTAIN ANTILLES... WHAT HAPPENED TO THE GRAVITIC POLARIZING DEVICE...
THE ALLIANCE HAS IT NOW.
IS IT IMPORTANT WHO HAS IT?

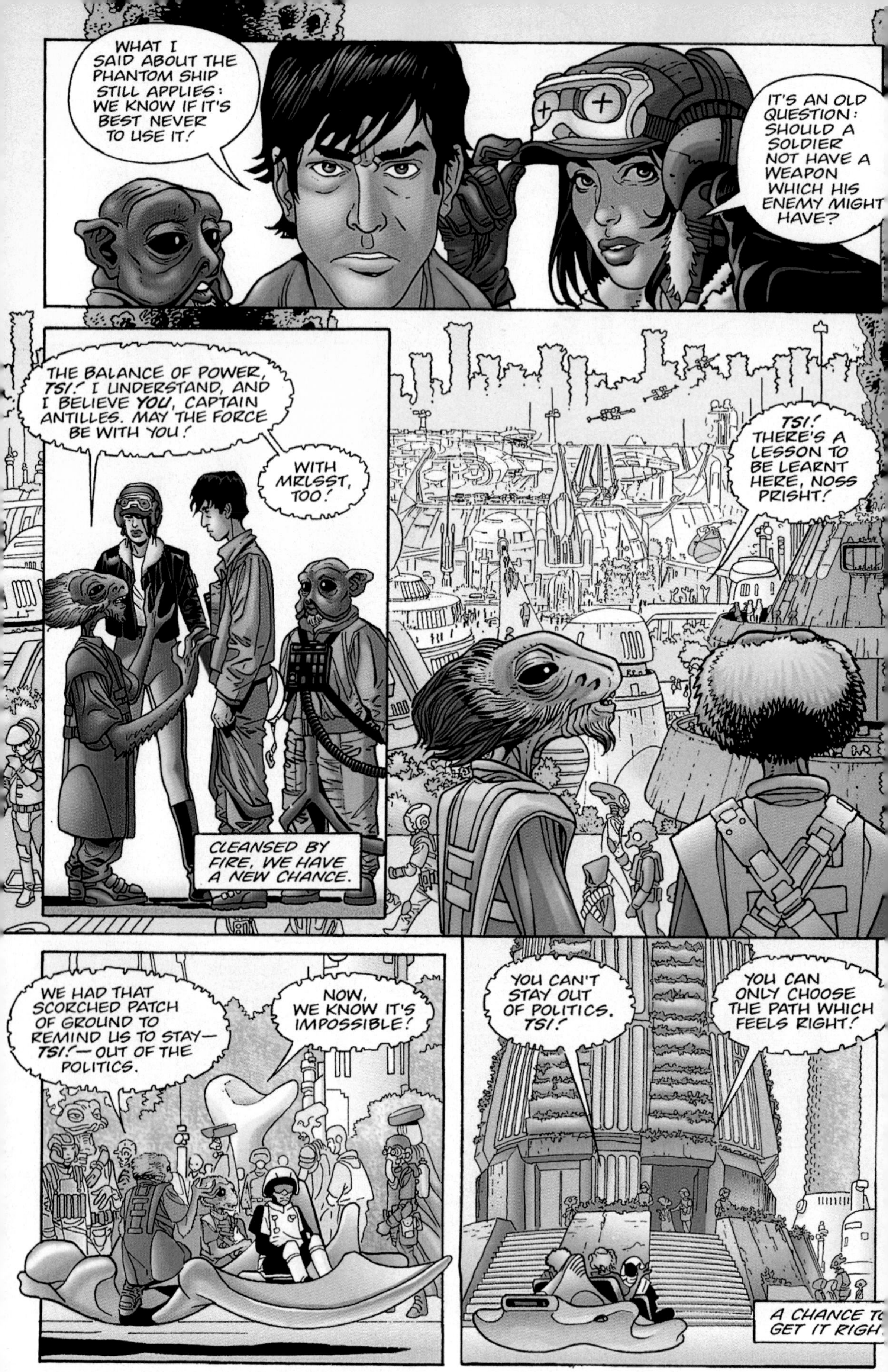

WHAT I SAID ABOUT THE PHANTOM SHIP STILL APPLIES: WE KNOW IF IT'S BEST NEVER TO USE IT!
IT'S AN OLD QUESTION: SHOULD A SOLDIER NOT HAVE A WEAPON WHICH HIS ENEMY MIGHT HAVE?
THE BALANCE OF POWER, TSI! I UNDERSTAND, AND I BELIEVE YOU, CAPTAIN ANTILLES. MAY THE FORCE BE WITH YOU!
WITH MRLSST, TOO!
CLEANSED BY FIRE, WE HAVE A NEW CHANCE.
TSI! THERE'S A LESSON TO BE LEARNT HERE, NOSS PRISHT!
WE HAD THAT SCORCHED PATCH OF GROUND TO REMIND US TO STAY— TSI!— OUT OF THE POLITICS.
NOW, WE KNOW IT'S IMPOSSIBLE!
YOU CAN'T STAY OUT OF POLITICS. TSI!
YOU CAN ONLY CHOOSE THE PATH WHICH FEELS RIGHT!
A CHANCE TO GET IT RIGH

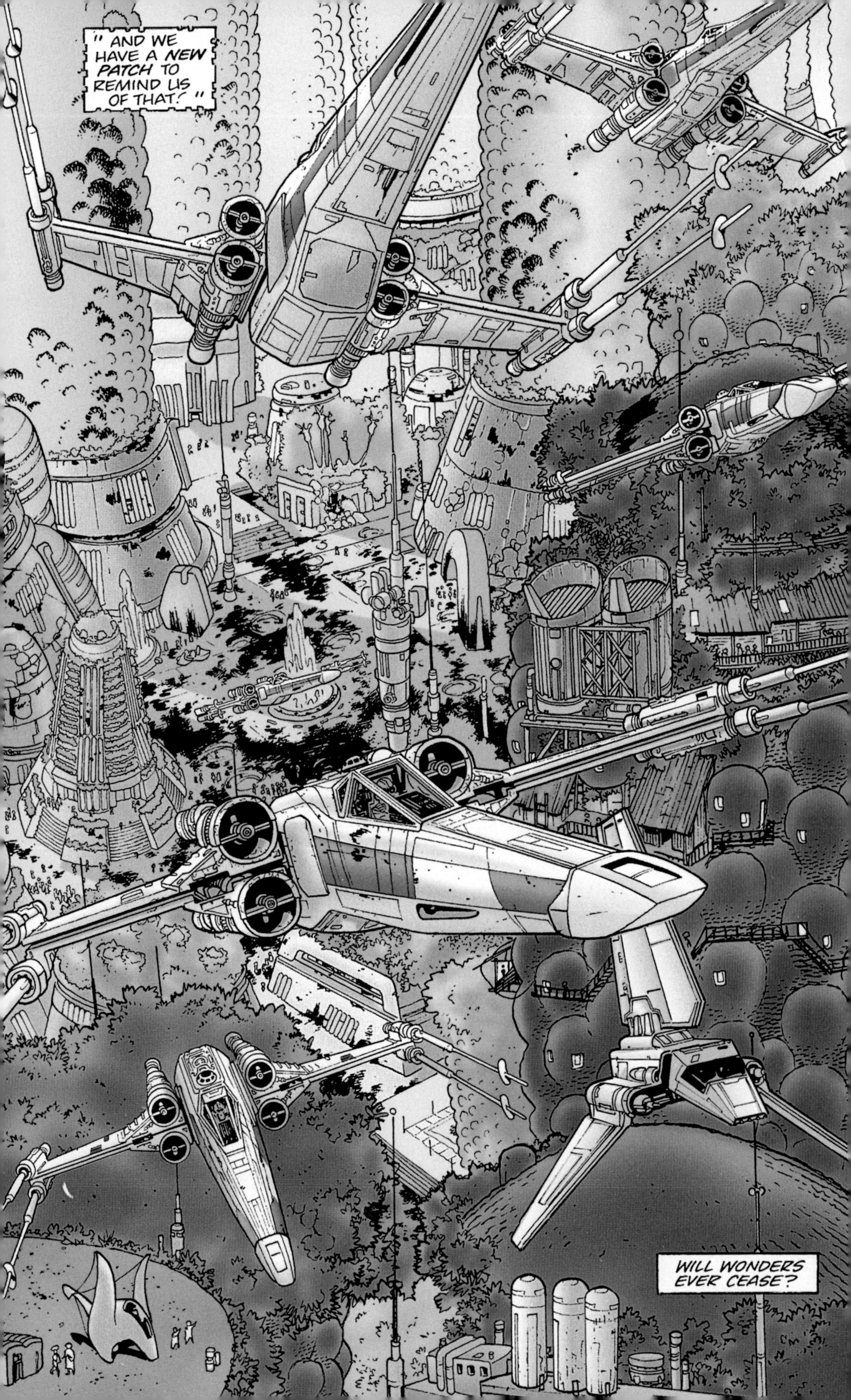
"AND WE HAVE A *NEW PATCH* TO REMIND US OF THAT."
WILL WONDERS EVER CEASE?

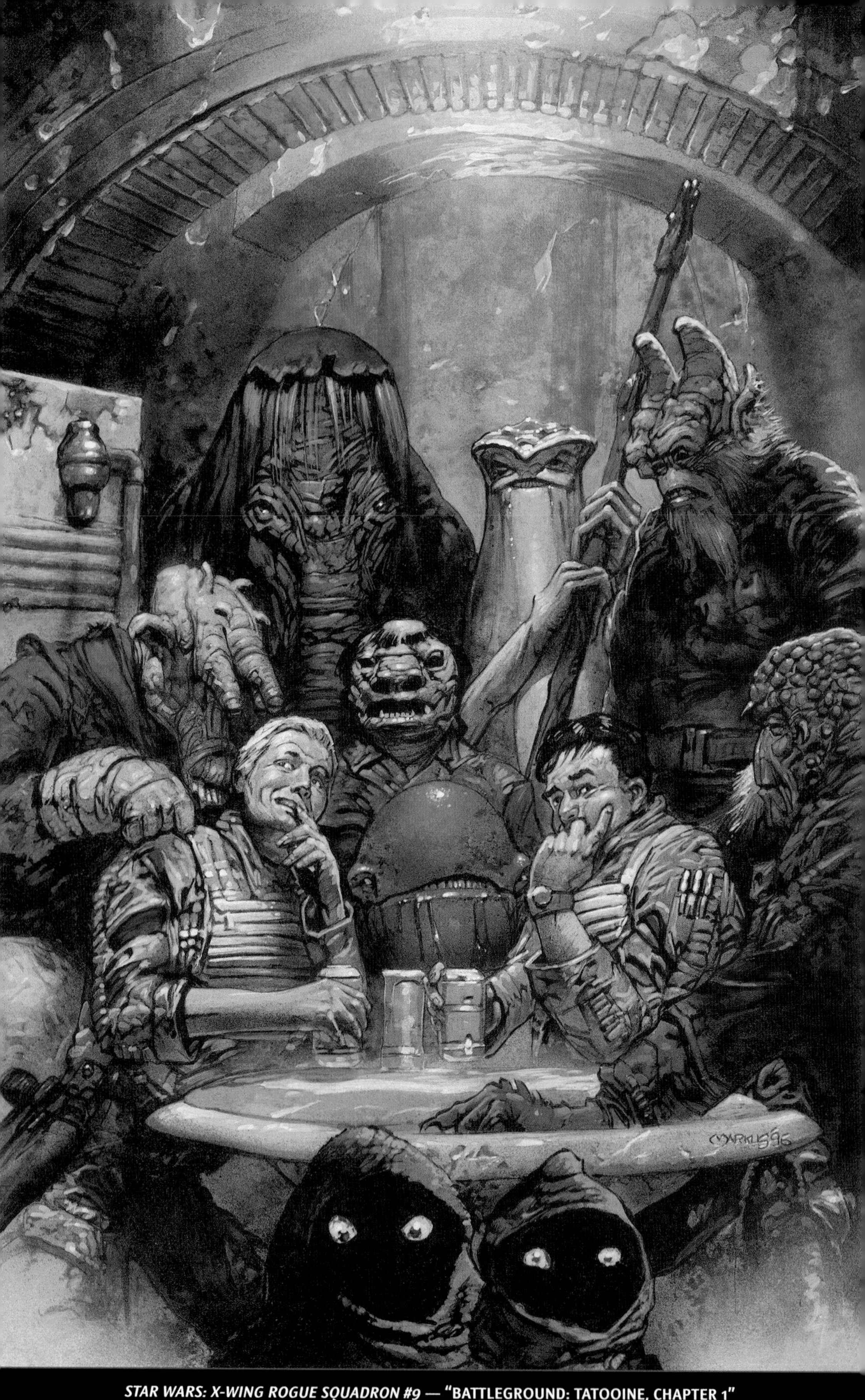

***STAR WARS: X-WING ROGUE SQUADRON #9* — "BATTLEGROUND: TATOOINE, CHAPTER 1"**

PLOTTER: MICHAEL A. STACKPOLE • SCRIPTER: JAN STRNAD • PENCILER: JOHN NADEAU • INKER: JORDI ENSIGN
COLORIST: PERRY MCNAMEE • LETTERER: VICKIE WILLIAMS • EDITOR: PEET JANES • COVER ARTIST: MARK HARRISON

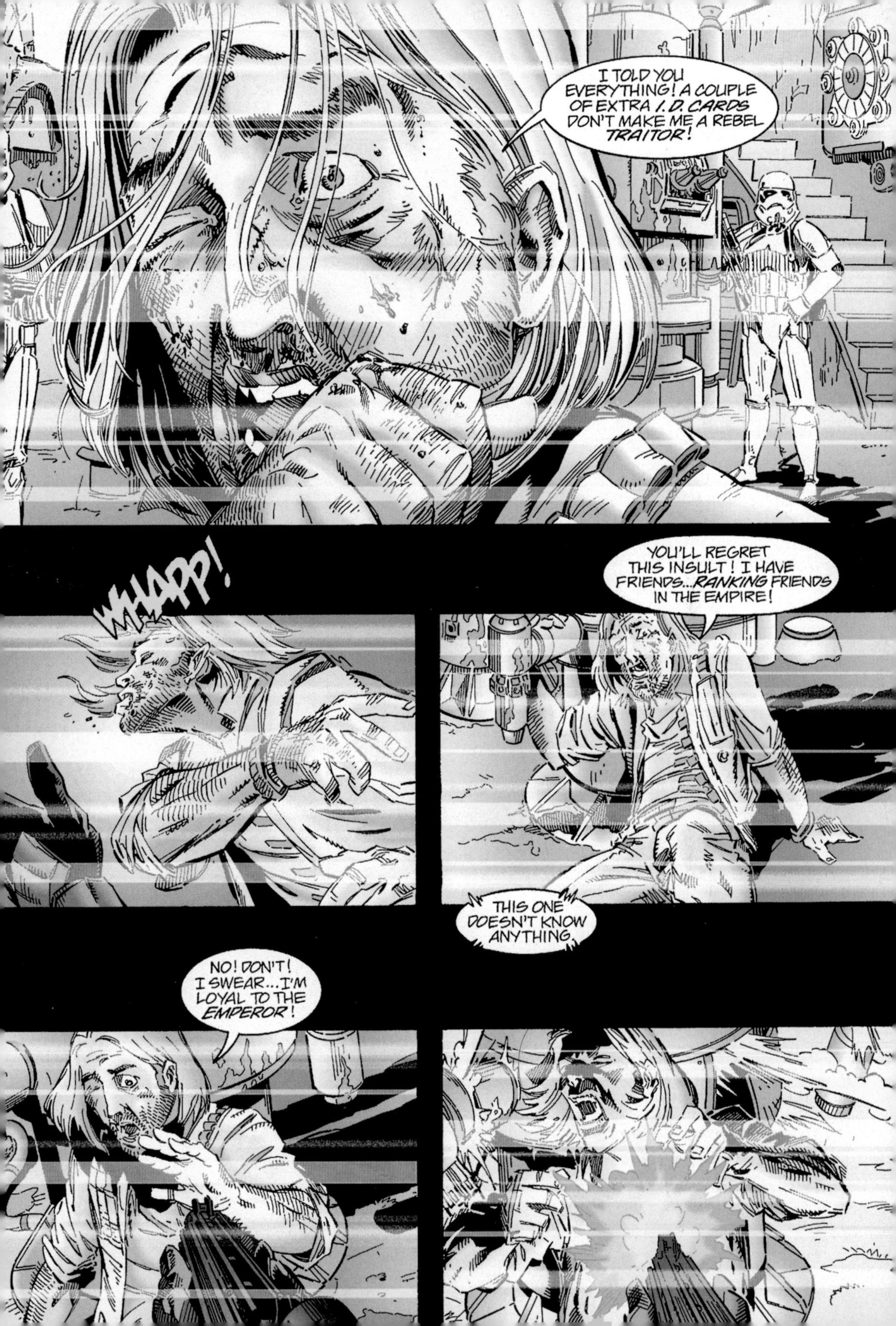
I TOLD YOU EVERYTHING! A COUPLE OF EXTRA I.D. CARDS DON'T MAKE ME A REBEL TRAITOR!
WHAPP!
YOU'LL REGRET THIS INSULT! I HAVE FRIENDS...RANKING FRIENDS IN THE EMPIRE!
THIS ONE DOESN'T KNOW ANYTHING.
NO! DON'T! I SWEAR...I'M LOYAL TO THE EMPEROR!

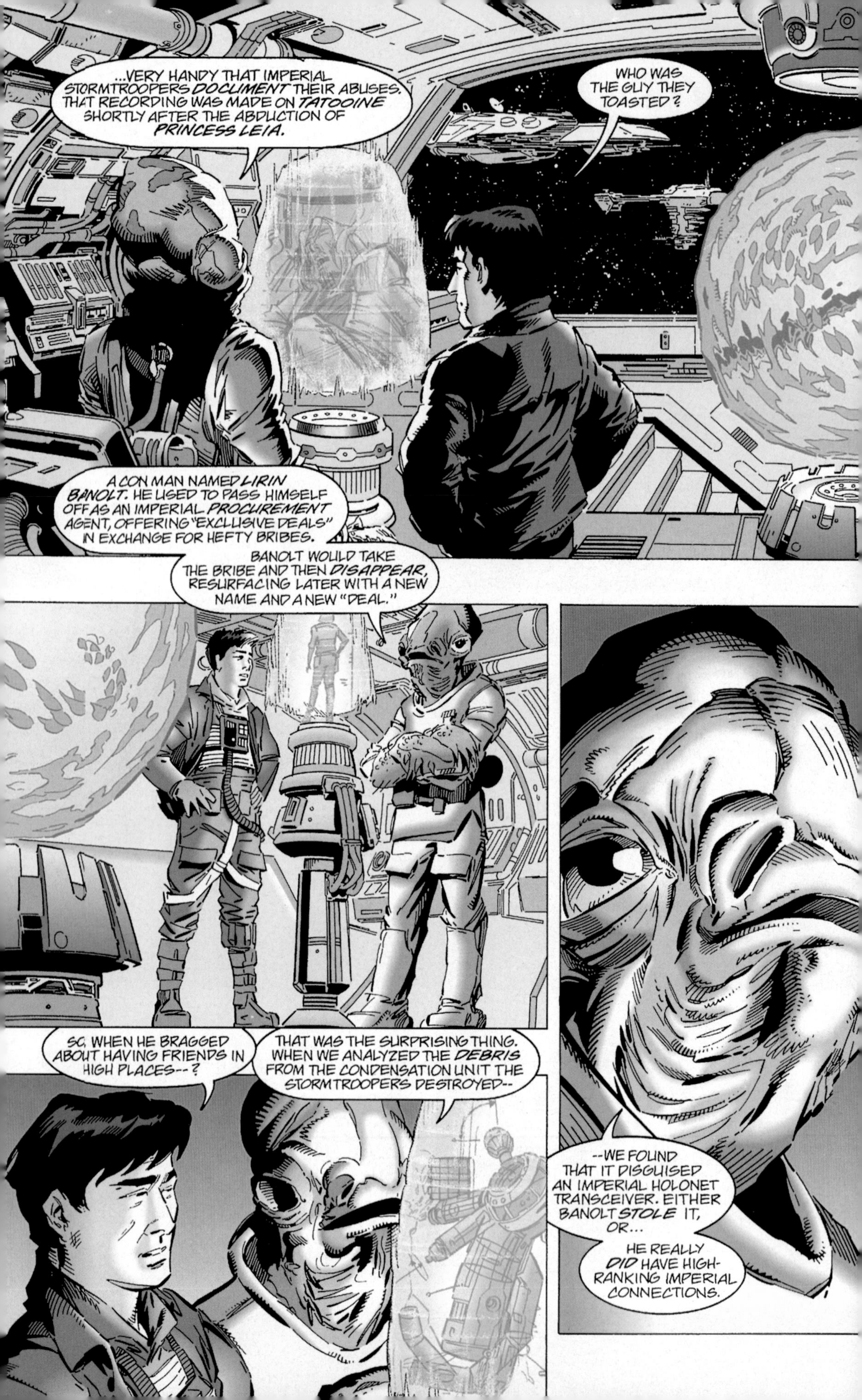
...VERY HANDY THAT IMPERIAL STORMTROOPERS DOCUMENT THEIR ABUSES. THAT RECORDING WAS MADE ON TATOOINE SHORTLY AFTER THE ABDUCTION OF PRINCESS LEIA.
WHO WAS THE GUY THEY TOASTED?
A CON MAN NAMED LIRIN BANOLT. HE USED TO PASS HIMSELF OFF AS AN IMPERIAL PROCUREMENT AGENT, OFFERING "EXCLUSIVE DEALS" IN EXCHANGE FOR HEFTY BRIBES.
BANOLT WOULD TAKE THE BRIBE AND THEN DISAPPEAR, RESURFACING LATER WITH A NEW NAME AND A NEW "DEAL."
SO, WHEN HE BRAGGED ABOUT HAVING FRIENDS IN HIGH PLACES--?
THAT WAS THE SURPRISING THING. WHEN WE ANALYZED THE DEBRIS FROM THE CONDENSATION UNIT THE STORMTROOPERS DESTROYED--
--WE FOUND THAT IT DISGUISED AN IMPERIAL HOLONET TRANSCEIVER. EITHER BANOLT STOLE IT, OR...
HE REALLY DID HAVE HIGH-RANKING IMPERIAL CONNECTIONS.

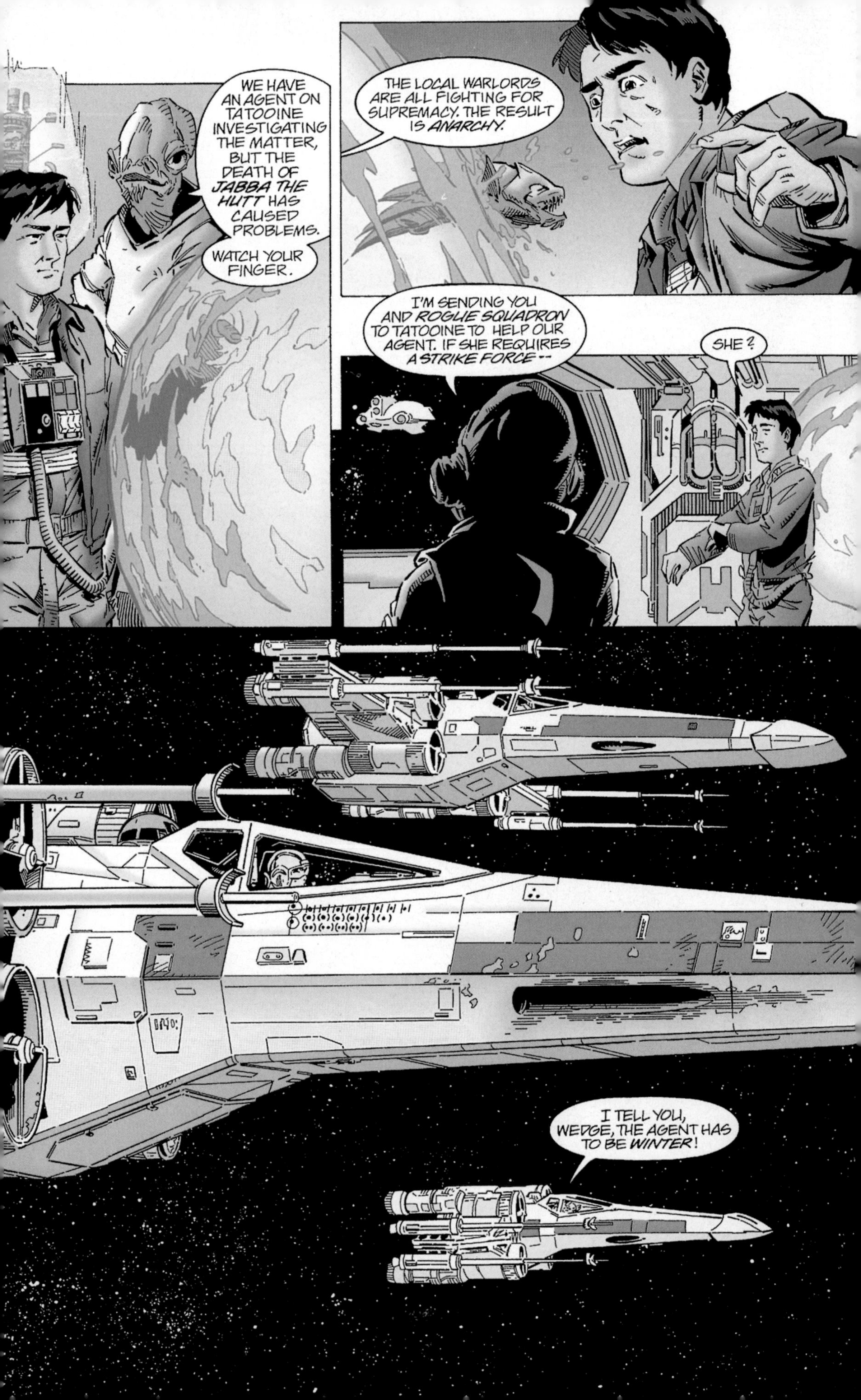
WE HAVE AN AGENT ON TATOOINE INVESTIGATING THE MATTER, BUT THE DEATH OF JABBA THE HUTT HAS CAUSED PROBLEMS.
WATCH YOUR FINGER.
THE LOCAL WARLORDS ARE ALL FIGHTING FOR SUPREMACY. THE RESULT IS ANARCHY.
I'M SENDING YOU AND ROGUE SQUADRON TO TATOOINE TO HELP OUR AGENT. IF SHE REQUIRES A STRIKE FORCE --
SHE?
I TELL YOU, WEDGE, THE AGENT HAS TO BE WINTER!

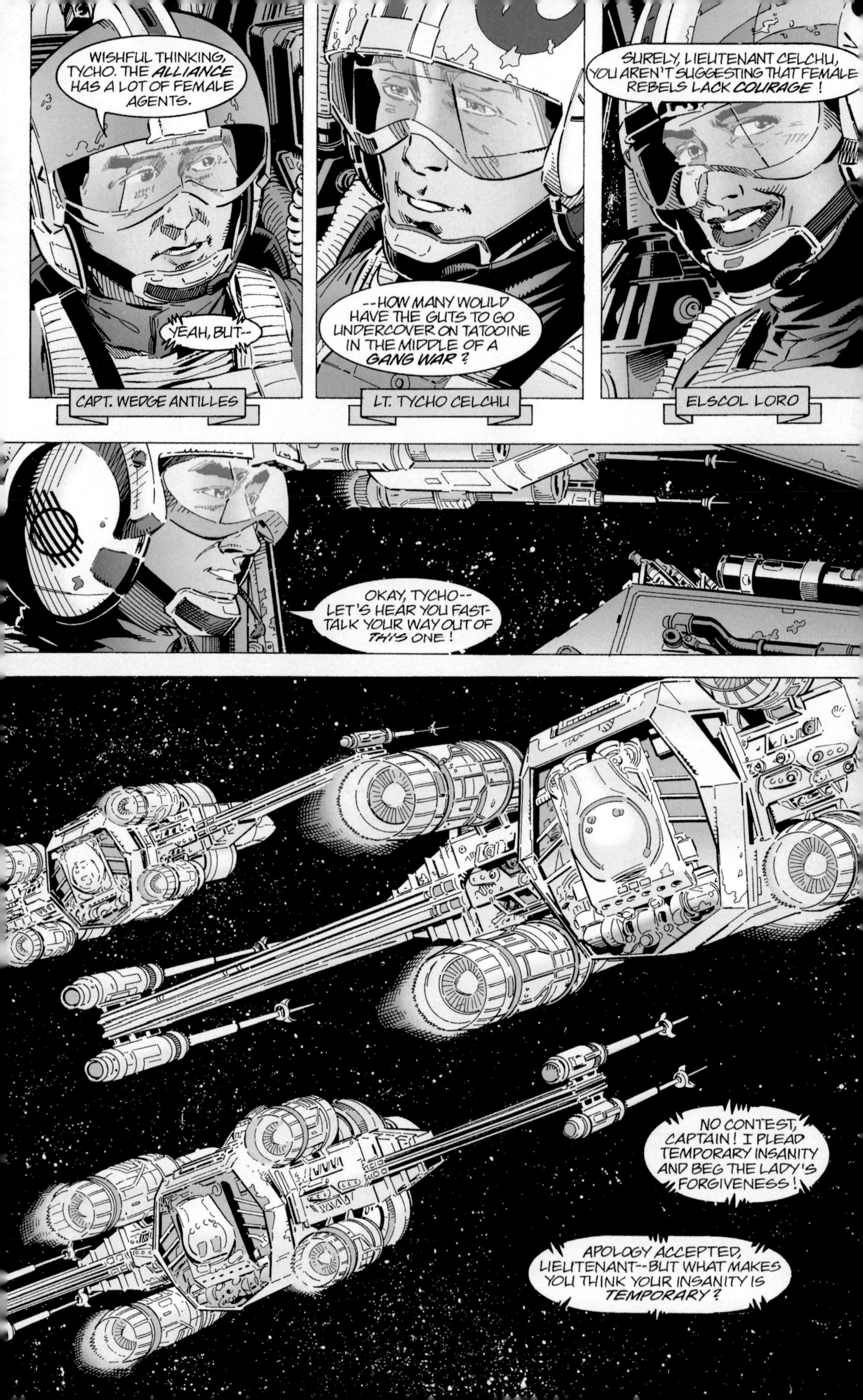
WISHFUL THINKING, TYCHO. THE ALLIANCE HAS A LOT OF FEMALE AGENTS.
YEAH, BUT--
CAPT. WEDGE ANTILLES
--HOW MANY WOULD HAVE THE GUTS TO GO UNDERCOVER ON TATOOINE IN THE MIDDLE OF A GANG WAR?
LT. TYCHO CELCHU
SURELY, LIEUTENANT CELCHU, YOU AREN'T SUGGESTING THAT FEMALE REBELS LACK COURAGE!
ELSCOL LORO
OKAY, TYCHO-- LET'S HEAR YOU FAST-TALK YOUR WAY OUT OF THIS ONE!
NO CONTEST, CAPTAIN! I PLEAD TEMPORARY INSANITY AND BEG THE LADY'S FORGIVENESS!
APOLOGY ACCEPTED, LIEUTENANT--BUT WHAT MAKES YOU THINK YOUR INSANITY IS TEMPORARY?

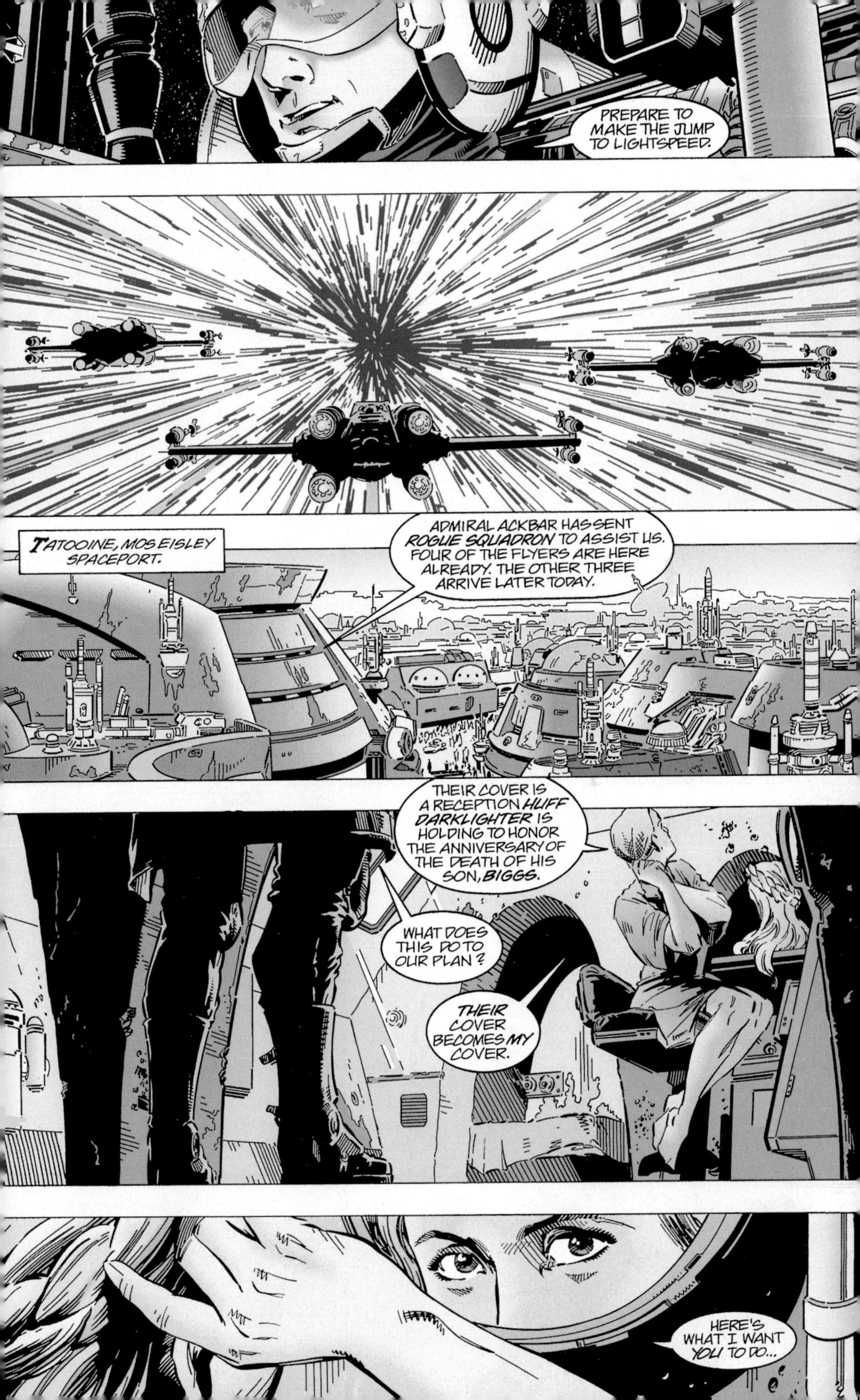
PREPARE TO MAKE THE JUMP TO LIGHTSPEED.
TATOOINE, MOS EISLEY SPACEPORT.
ADMIRAL ACKBAR HAS SENT ROGUE SQUADRON TO ASSIST US. FOUR OF THE FLYERS ARE HERE ALREADY. THE OTHER THREE ARRIVE LATER TODAY.
THEIR COVER IS A RECEPTION HUFF DARKLIGHTER IS HOLDING TO HONOR THE ANNIVERSARY OF THE DEATH OF HIS SON, BIGGS.
WHAT DOES THIS DO TO OUR PLAN?
THEIR COVER BECOMES MY COVER.
HERE'S WHAT I WANT YOU TO DO...

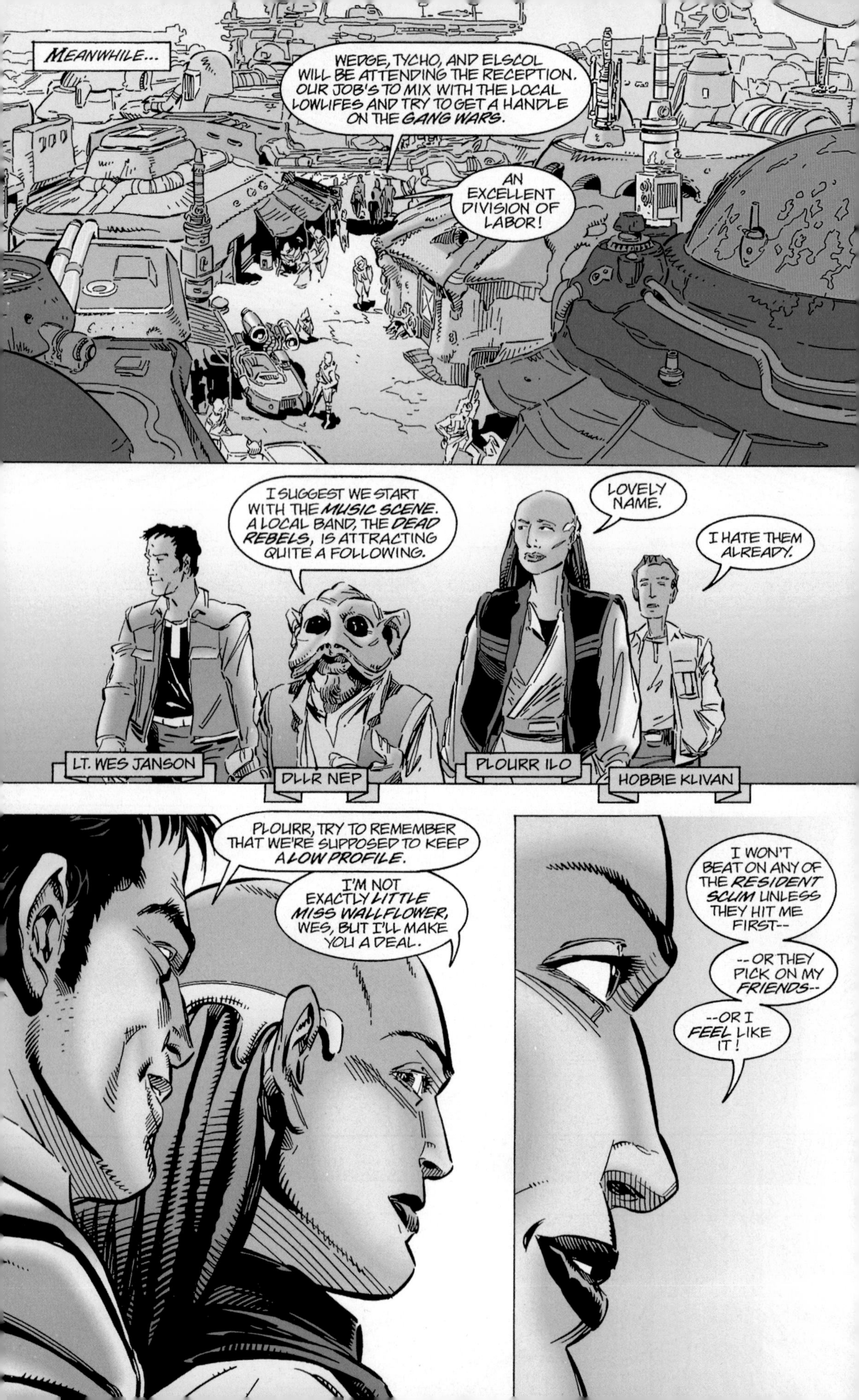
MEANWHILE...
WEDGE, TYCHO, AND ELSCOL WILL BE ATTENDING THE RECEPTION. OUR JOB'S TO MIX WITH THE LOCAL LOWLIFES AND TRY TO GET A HANDLE ON THE GANG WARS.
AN EXCELLENT DIVISION OF LABOR!
I SUGGEST WE START WITH THE MUSIC SCENE. A LOCAL BAND, THE DEAD REBELS, IS ATTRACTING QUITE A FOLLOWING.
LOVELY NAME.
I HATE THEM ALREADY.
LT. WES JANSON
DLLR NEP
PLOURR ILO
HOBBIE KLIVAN
PLOURR, TRY TO REMEMBER THAT WE'RE SUPPOSED TO KEEP A LOW PROFILE.
I'M NOT EXACTLY LITTLE MISS WALLFLOWER, WES, BUT I'LL MAKE YOU A DEAL.
I WON'T BEAT ON ANY OF THE RESIDENT SCUM UNLESS THEY HIT ME FIRST--
--OR THEY PICK ON MY FRIENDS--
--OR I FEEL LIKE IT!

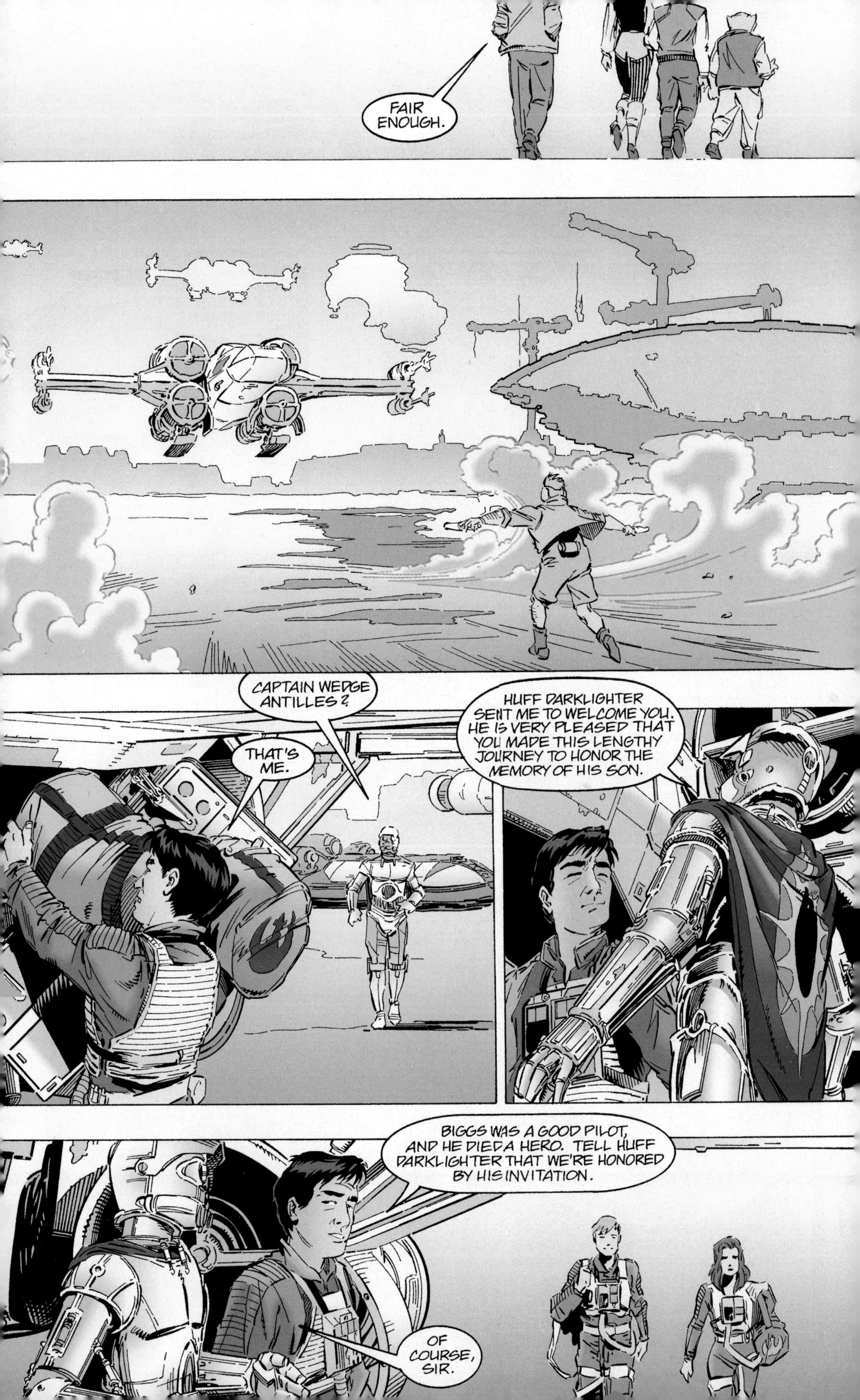
FAIR ENOUGH.
CAPTAIN WEDGE ANTILLES?
THAT'S ME.
HUFF DARKLIGHTER SENT ME TO WELCOME YOU. HE IS VERY PLEASED THAT YOU MADE THIS LENGTHY JOURNEY TO HONOR THE MEMORY OF HIS SON.
BIGGS WAS A GOOD PILOT, AND HE DIED A HERO. TELL HUFF DARKLIGHTER THAT WE'RE HONORED BY HIS INVITATION.
OF COURSE, SIR.

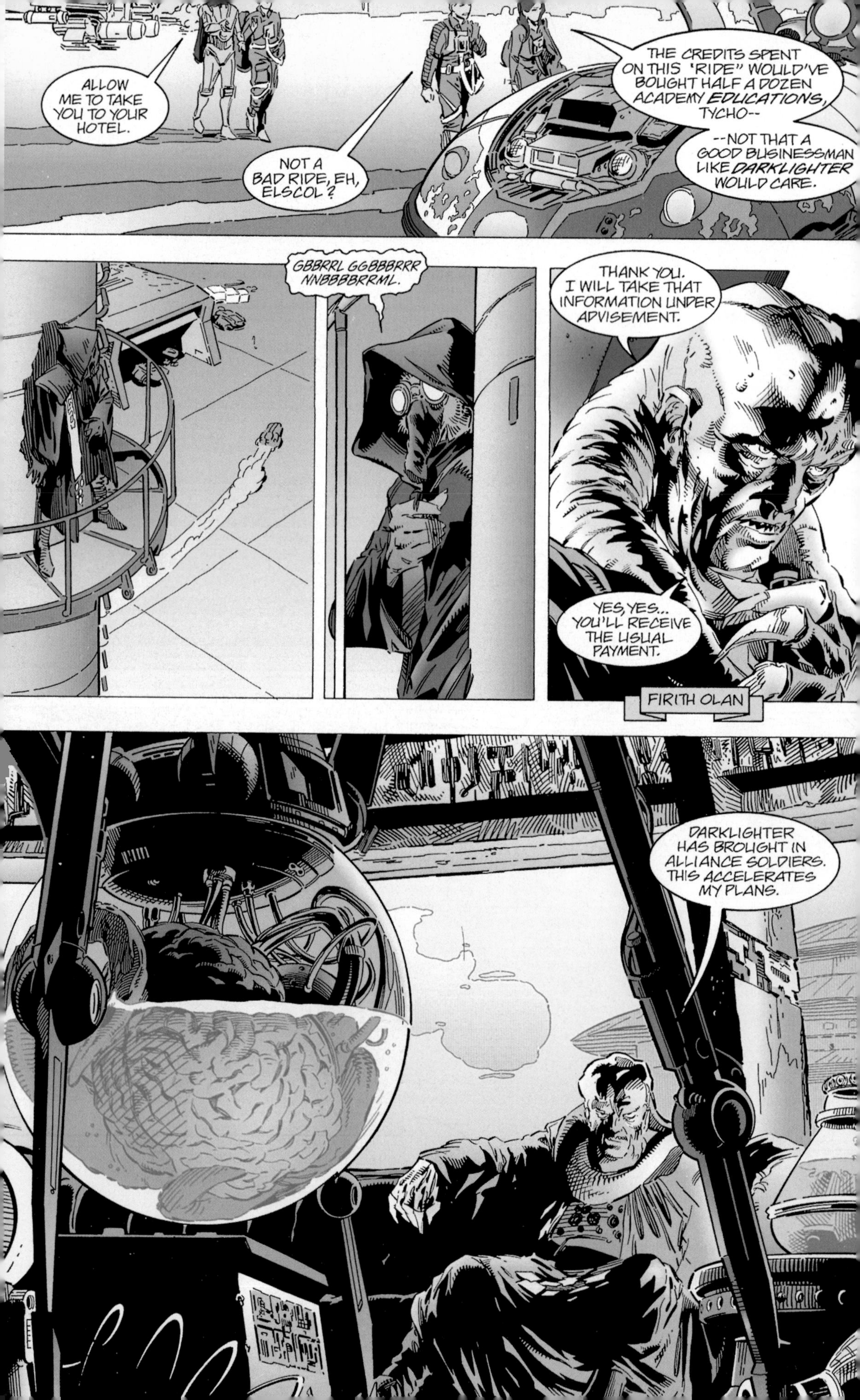
ALLOW ME TO TAKE YOU TO YOUR HOTEL.
NOT A BAD RIDE, EH, ELSCOL?
THE CREDITS SPENT ON THIS "RIDE" WOULD'VE BOUGHT HALF A DOZEN ACADEMY EDUCATIONS, TYCHO--
--NOT THAT A GOOD BUSINESSMAN LIKE DARKLIGHTER WOULD CARE.
GBBRRL GGBBBRRR NNBBBBRRML.
THANK YOU. I WILL TAKE THAT INFORMATION UNDER ADVISEMENT.
YES, YES... YOU'LL RECEIVE THE USUAL PAYMENT.
FIRITH OLAN
DARKLIGHTER HAS BROUGHT IN ALLIANCE SOLDIERS. THIS ACCELERATES MY PLANS.

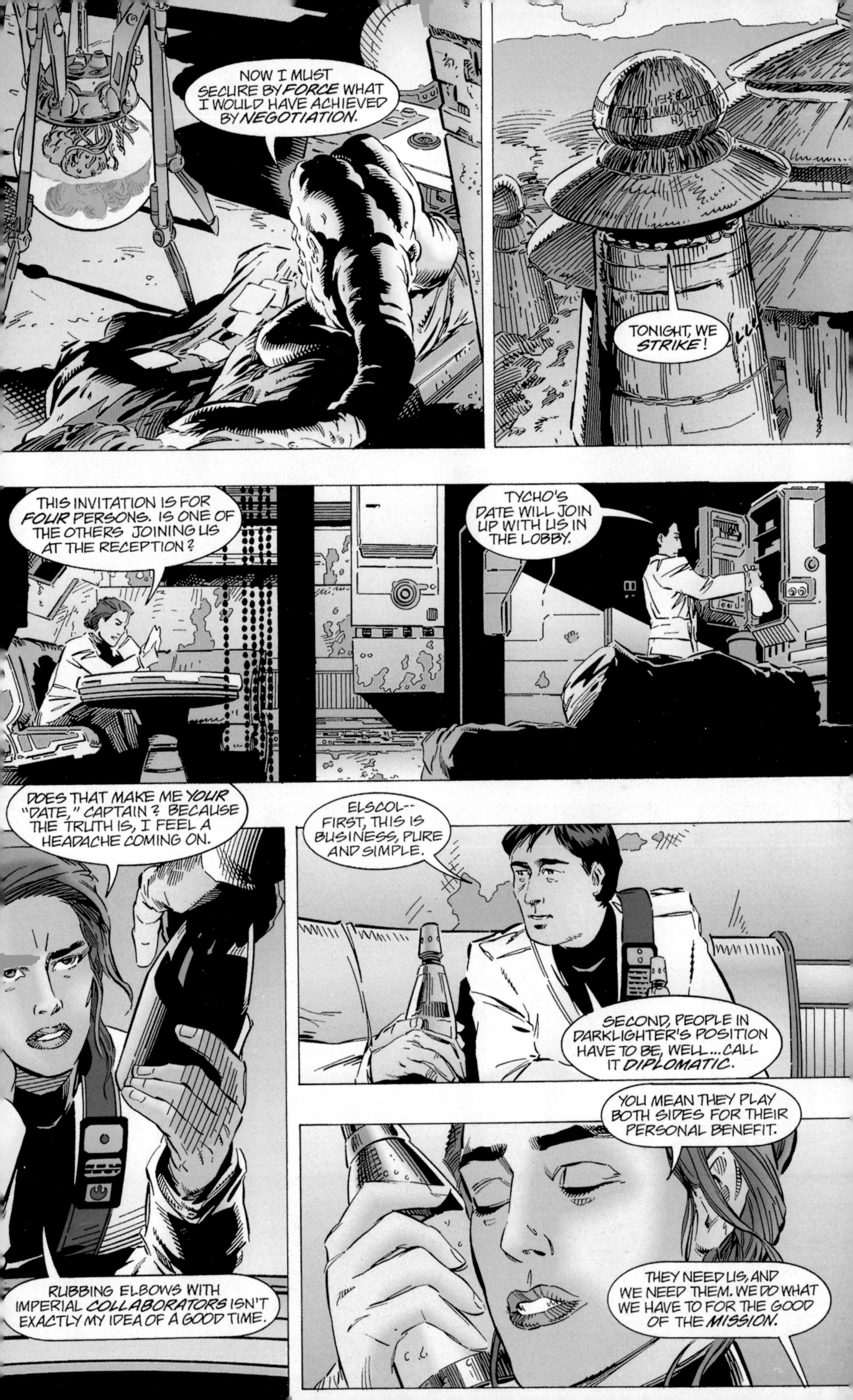
NOW I MUST SECURE BY FORCE WHAT I WOULD HAVE ACHIEVED BY NEGOTIATION.
TONIGHT, WE STRIKE!
THIS INVITATION IS FOR FOUR PERSONS. IS ONE OF THE OTHERS JOINING US AT THE RECEPTION?
TYCHO'S DATE WILL JOIN UP WITH US IN THE LOBBY.
DOES THAT MAKE ME YOUR "DATE," CAPTAIN? BECAUSE THE TRUTH IS, I FEEL A HEADACHE COMING ON.
RUBBING ELBOWS WITH IMPERIAL COLLABORATORS ISN'T EXACTLY MY IDEA OF A GOOD TIME.
ELSCOL-- FIRST, THIS IS BUSINESS, PURE AND SIMPLE.
SECOND, PEOPLE IN DARKLIGHTER'S POSITION HAVE TO BE, WELL... CALL IT DIPLOMATIC.
YOU MEAN THEY PLAY BOTH SIDES FOR THEIR PERSONAL BENEFIT.
THEY NEED US, AND WE NEED THEM. WE DO WHAT WE HAVE TO FOR THE GOOD OF THE MISSION.

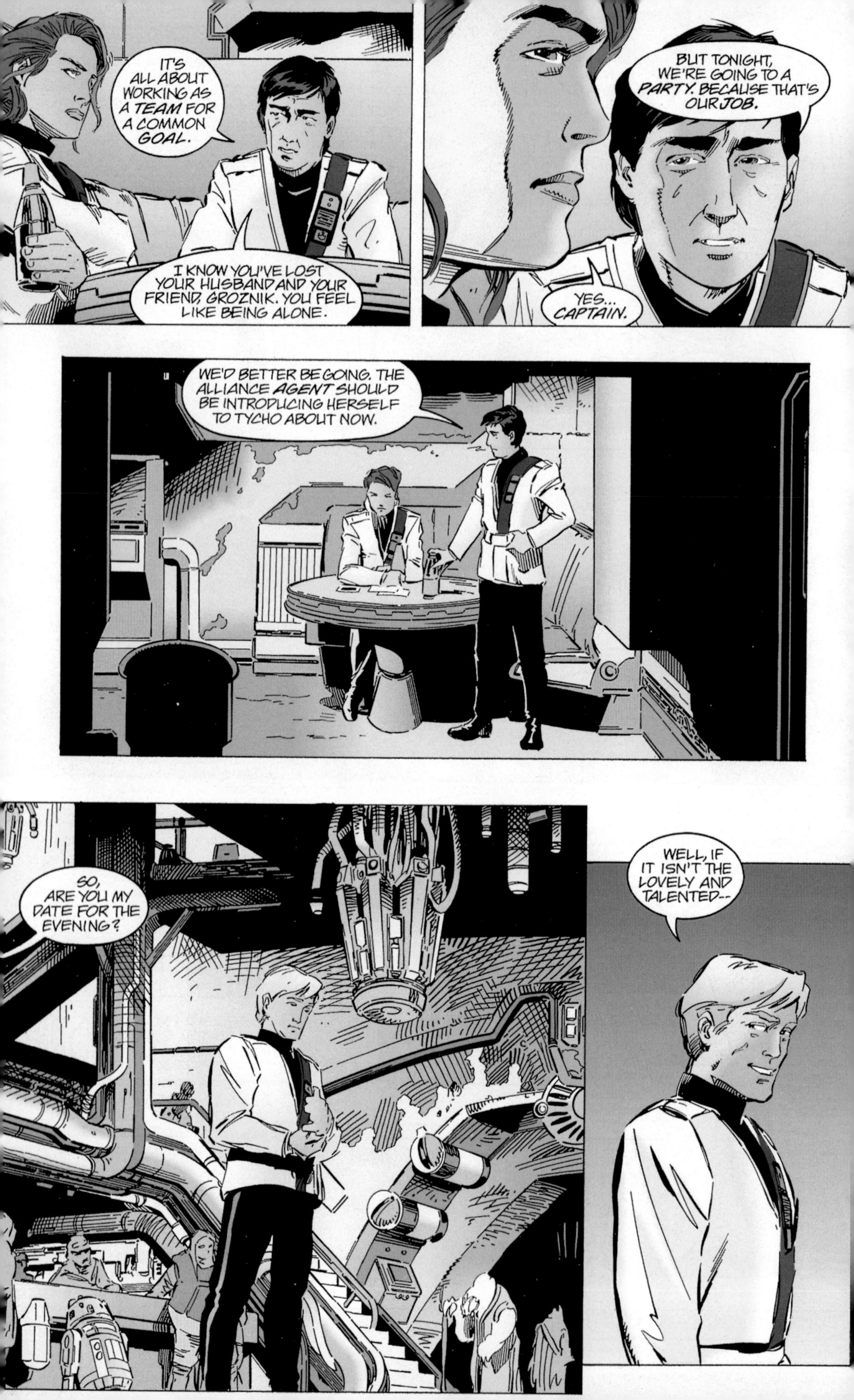
IT'S ALL ABOUT WORKING AS A TEAM FOR A COMMON GOAL.
I KNOW YOU'VE LOST YOUR HUSBAND AND YOUR FRIEND, GROZNIK. YOU FEEL LIKE BEING ALONE.
BUT TONIGHT, WE'RE GOING TO A PARTY. BECAUSE THAT'S OUR JOB.
YES... CAPTAIN.
WE'D BETTER BE GOING. THE ALLIANCE AGENT SHOULD BE INTRODUCING HERSELF TO TYCHO ABOUT NOW.
SO, ARE YOU MY DATE FOR THE EVENING?
WELL, IF IT ISN'T THE LOVELY AND TALENTED--

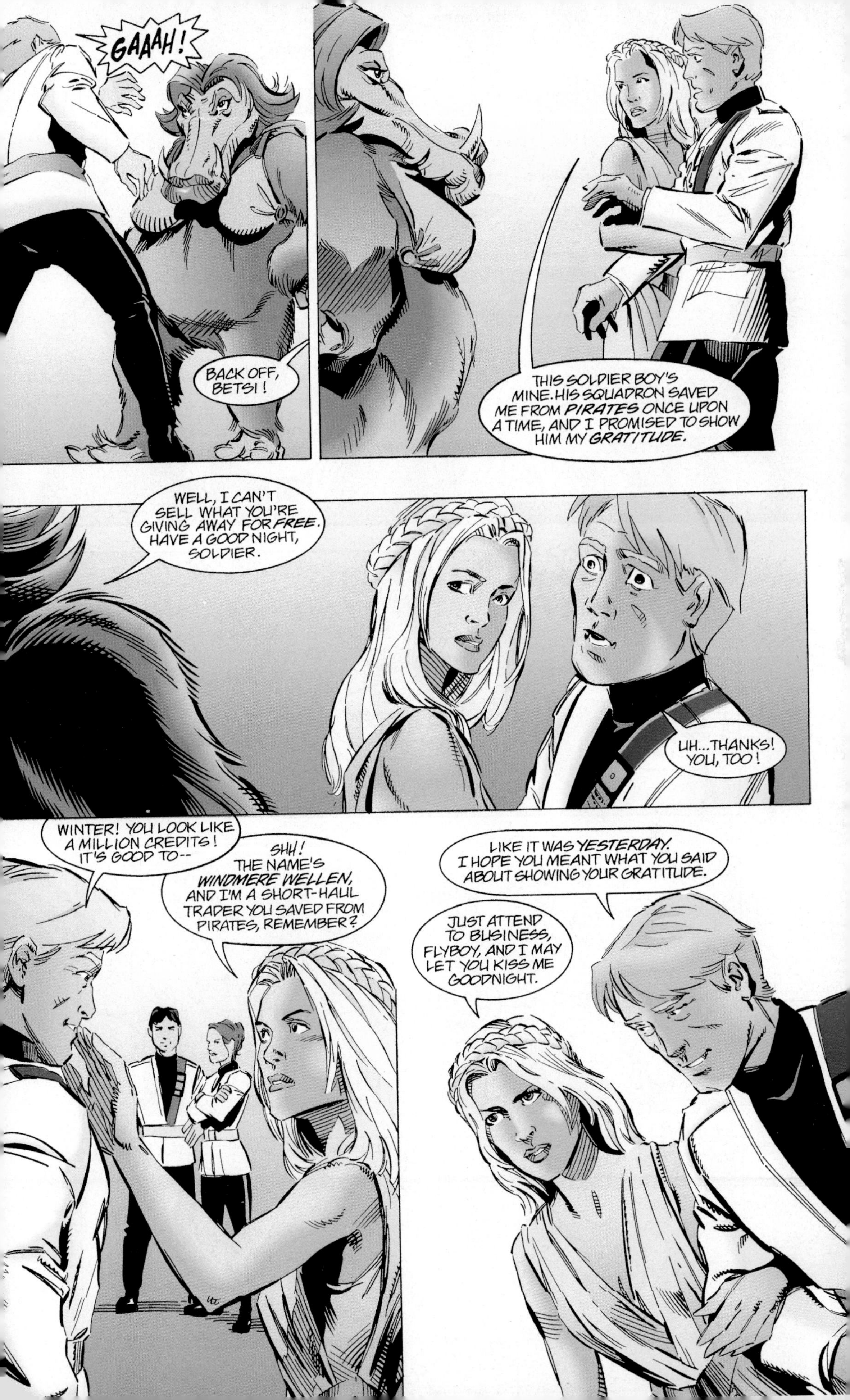
GAAAH!
BACK OFF, BETSI!
THIS SOLDIER BOY'S MINE. HIS SQUADRON SAVED ME FROM PIRATES ONCE UPON A TIME, AND I PROMISED TO SHOW HIM MY GRATITUDE.
WELL, I CAN'T SELL WHAT YOU'RE GIVING AWAY FOR FREE. HAVE A GOOD NIGHT, SOLDIER.
UH...THANKS! YOU, TOO!
WINTER! YOU LOOK LIKE A MILLION CREDITS! IT'S GOOD TO--
SHH! THE NAME'S WINDMERE WELLEN, AND I'M A SHORT-HAUL TRADER YOU SAVED FROM PIRATES, REMEMBER?
LIKE IT WAS YESTERDAY. I HOPE YOU MEANT WHAT YOU SAID ABOUT SHOWING YOUR GRATITUDE.
JUST ATTEND TO BUSINESS, FLYBOY, AND I MAY LET YOU KISS ME GOODNIGHT.

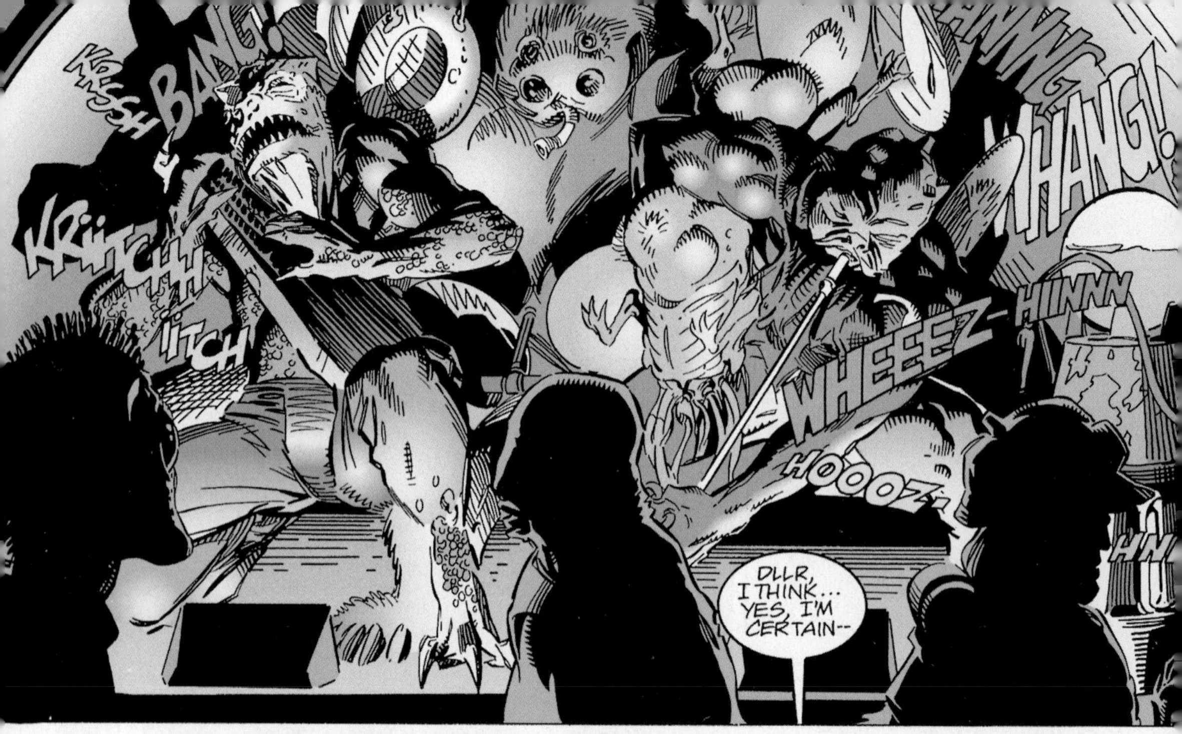
KRSSH
BANG!
KRIITCHHH
ITCH
WHANG!
WHEEEZ
HIINNN
HOOOZ
DLLR, I THINK... YES, I'M CERTAIN--

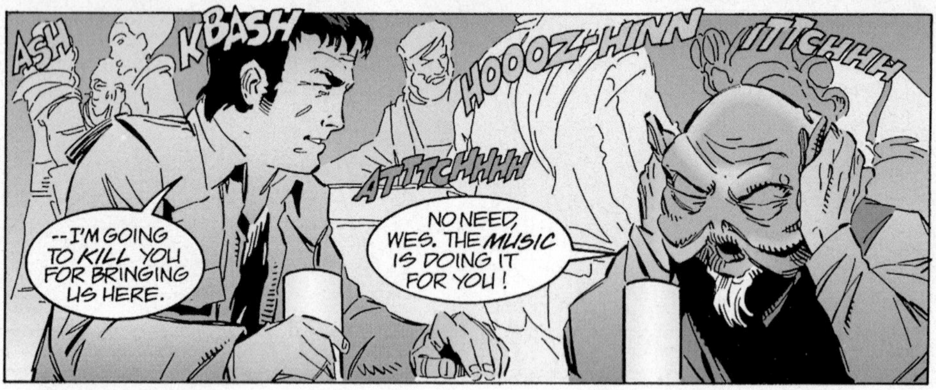
ASH
KBASH
HOOOZ-HINN
ITTCHHH
ATTTCHHHH
--I'M GOING TO KILL YOU FOR BRINGING US HERE.
NO NEED, WES. THE MUSIC IS DOING IT FOR YOU!

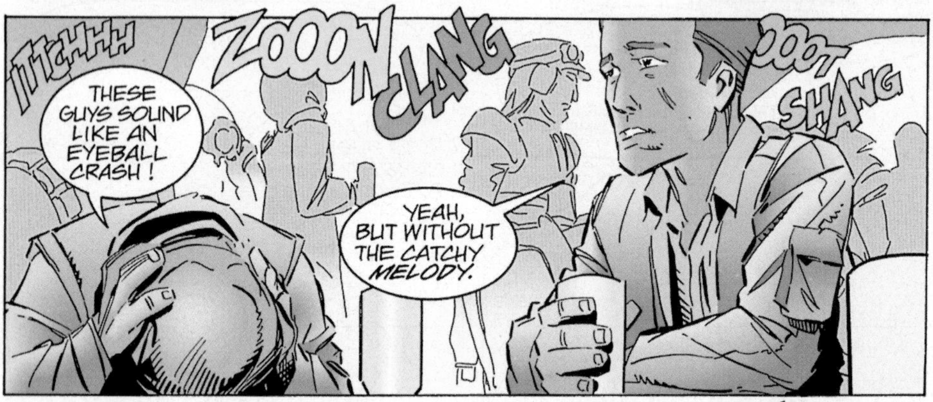
ITTCHHH
ZOOON
CLANG
SHANG
THESE GUYS SOUND LIKE AN EYEBALL CRASH!
YEAH, BUT WITHOUT THE CATCHY MELODY.

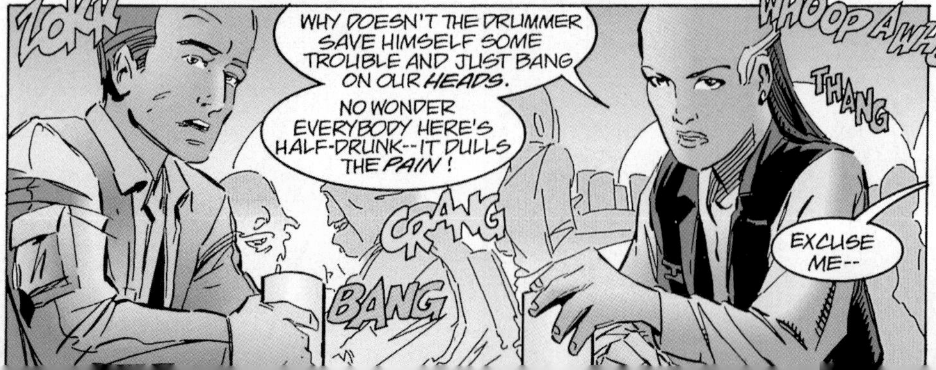
ZOKK
WHY DOESN'T THE DRUMMER SAVE HIMSELF SOME TROUBLE AND JUST BANG ON OUR HEADS.
NO WONDER EVERYBODY HERE'S HALF-DRUNK--IT DULLS THE PAIN!
WHOOP AWHOO
THANG
CRANG
BANG
EXCUSE ME--

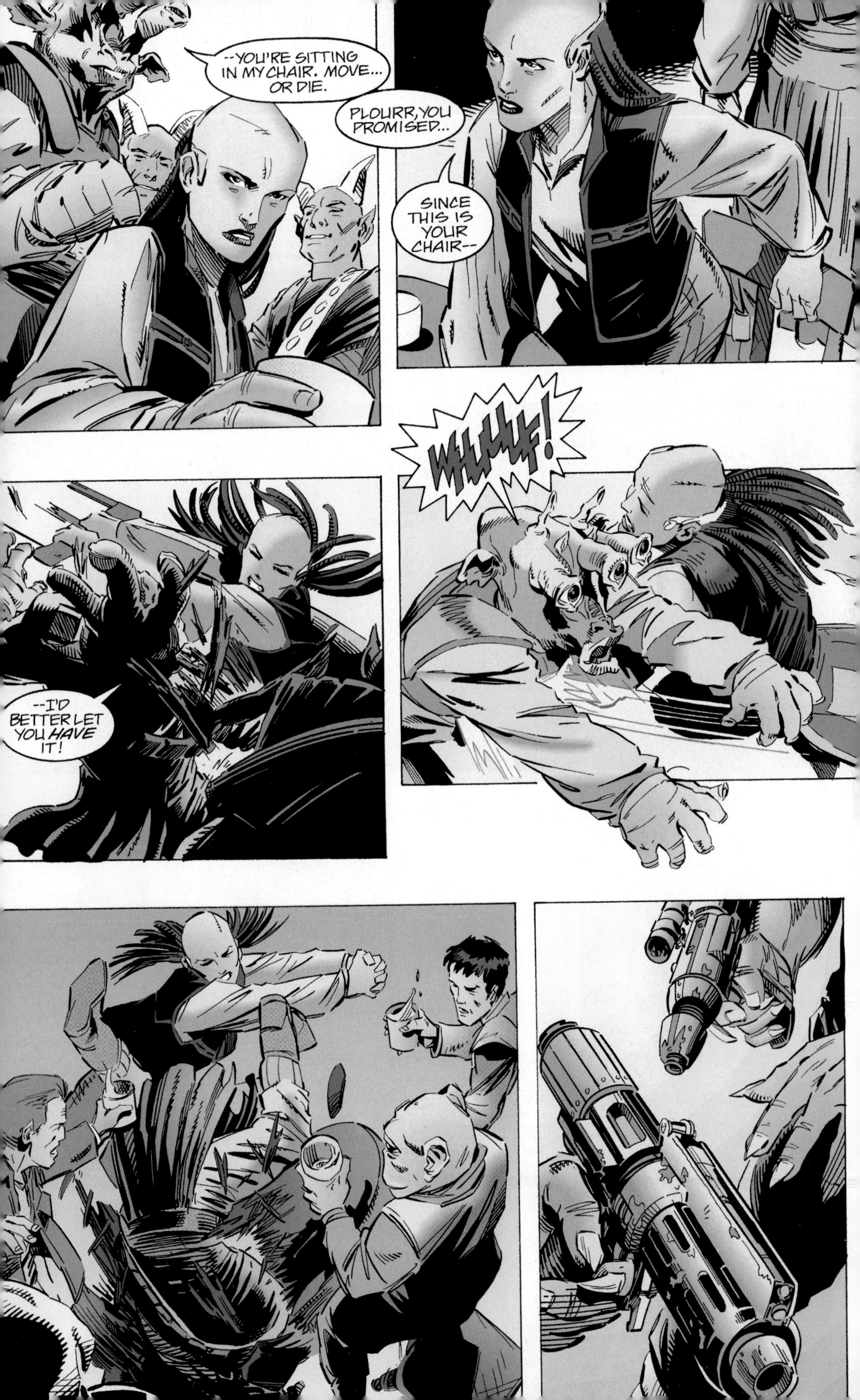
--YOU'RE SITTING IN MY CHAIR. MOVE... OR DIE.
PLOURR, YOU PROMISED...
SINCE THIS IS YOUR CHAIR--
--I'D BETTER LET YOU *HAVE* IT!
WHUUF!

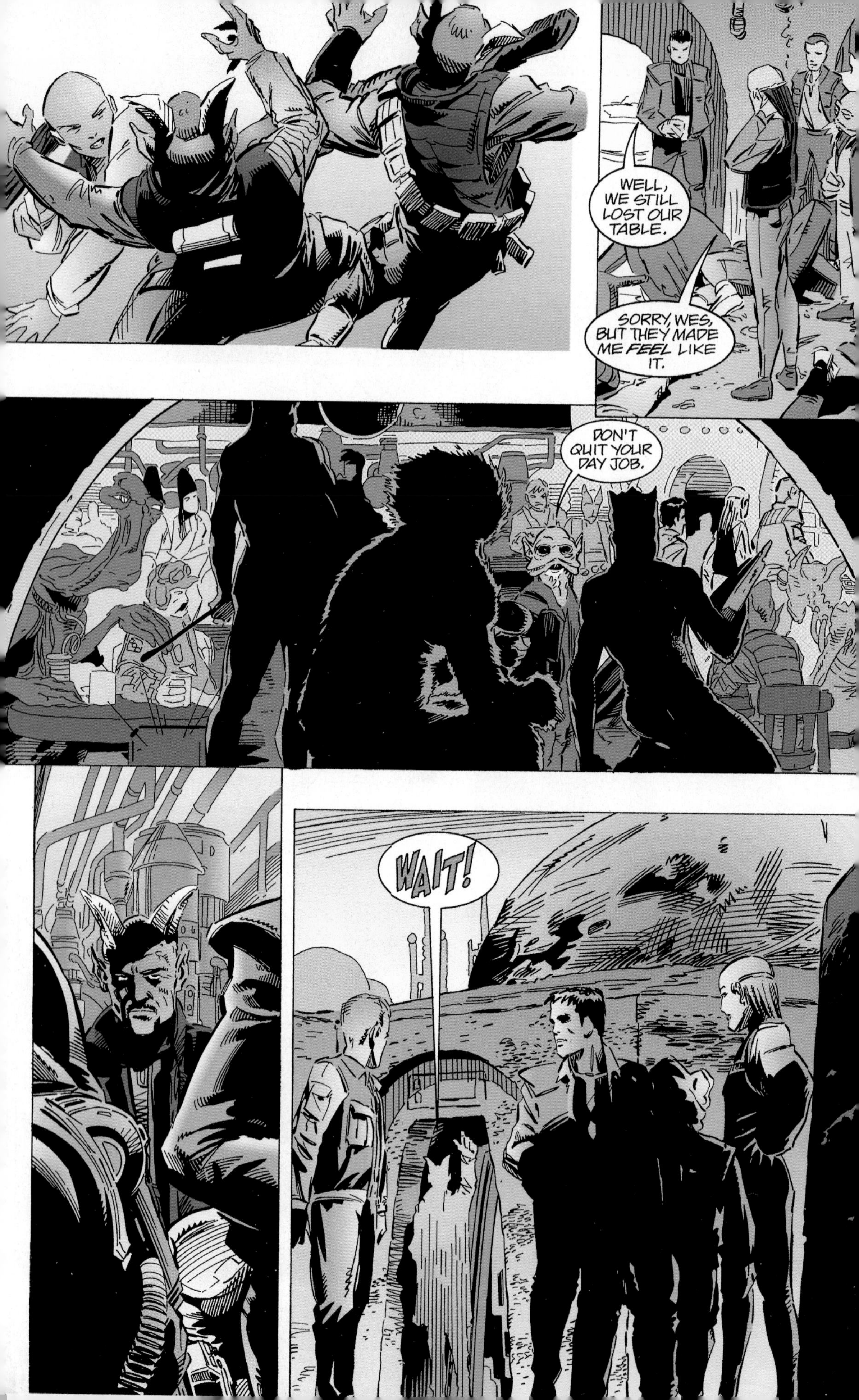

WELL, WE STILL LOST OUR TABLE.
SORRY, WES, BUT THEY MADE ME *FEEL* LIKE IT.
DON'T QUIT YOUR DAY JOB.
WAIT!

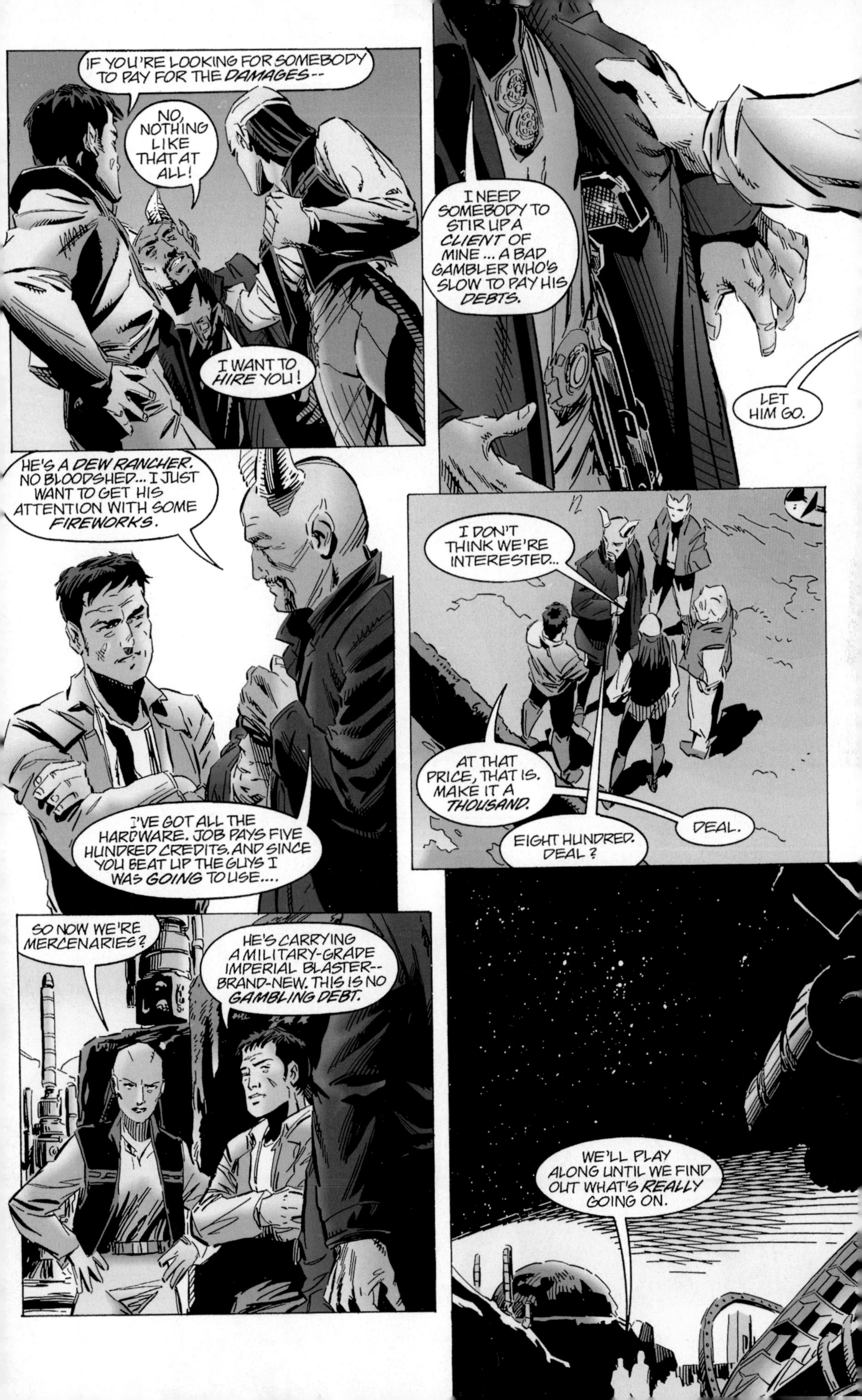
IF YOU'RE LOOKING FOR SOMEBODY TO PAY FOR THE DAMAGES--
NO, NOTHING LIKE THAT AT ALL!
I WANT TO HIRE YOU!
I NEED SOMEBODY TO STIR UP A CLIENT OF MINE ... A BAD GAMBLER WHO'S SLOW TO PAY HIS DEBTS.
LET HIM GO.
HE'S A DEW RANCHER. NO BLOODSHED... I JUST WANT TO GET HIS ATTENTION WITH SOME FIREWORKS.
I'VE GOT ALL THE HARDWARE. JOB PAYS FIVE HUNDRED CREDITS. AND SINCE YOU BEAT UP THE GUYS I WAS GOING TO USE....
I DON'T THINK WE'RE INTERESTED...
AT THAT PRICE, THAT IS. MAKE IT A THOUSAND.
EIGHT HUNDRED. DEAL?
DEAL.
SO NOW WE'RE MERCENARIES?
HE'S CARRYING A MILITARY-GRADE IMPERIAL BLASTER-- BRAND-NEW. THIS IS NO GAMBLING DEBT.
WE'LL PLAY ALONG UNTIL WE FIND OUT WHAT'S REALLY GOING ON.

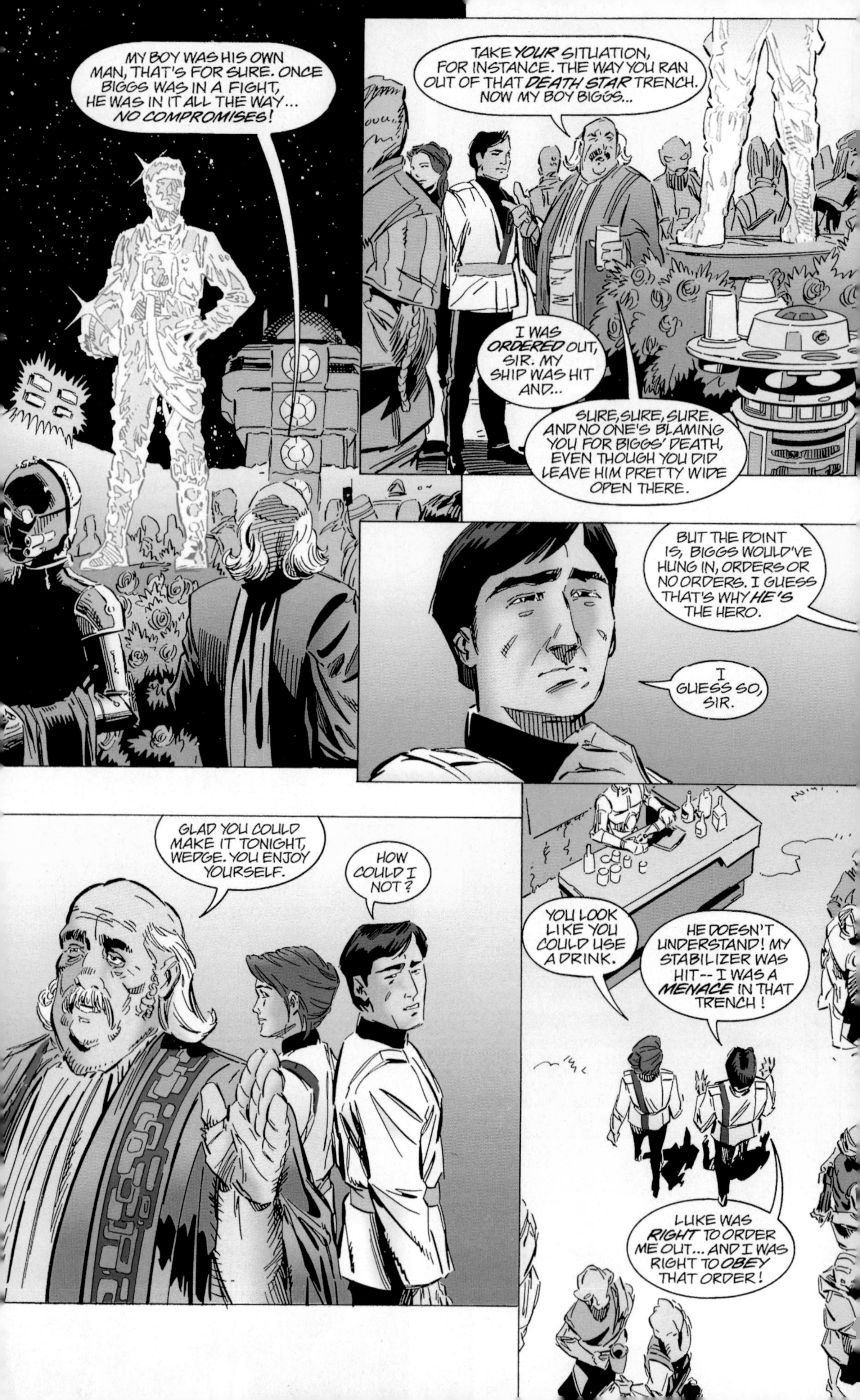
MY BOY WAS HIS OWN MAN, THAT'S FOR SURE. ONCE BIGGS WAS IN A FIGHT, HE WAS IN IT ALL THE WAY... NO COMPROMISES!
TAKE YOUR SITUATION, FOR INSTANCE. THE WAY YOU RAN OUT OF THAT DEATH STAR TRENCH. NOW MY BOY BIGGS...
I WAS ORDERED OUT, SIR. MY SHIP WAS HIT AND...
SURE, SURE, SURE. AND NO ONE'S BLAMING YOU FOR BIGGS' DEATH, EVEN THOUGH YOU DID LEAVE HIM PRETTY WIDE OPEN THERE.
BUT THE POINT IS, BIGGS WOULD'VE HUNG IN, ORDERS OR NO ORDERS. I GUESS THAT'S WHY HE'S THE HERO.
I GUESS SO, SIR.
GLAD YOU COULD MAKE IT TONIGHT, WEDGE. YOU ENJOY YOURSELF.
HOW COULD I NOT?
YOU LOOK LIKE YOU COULD USE A DRINK.
HE DOESN'T UNDERSTAND! MY STABILIZER WAS HIT-- I WAS A MENACE IN THAT TRENCH!
LUKE WAS RIGHT TO ORDER ME OUT... AND I WAS RIGHT TO OBEY THAT ORDER!

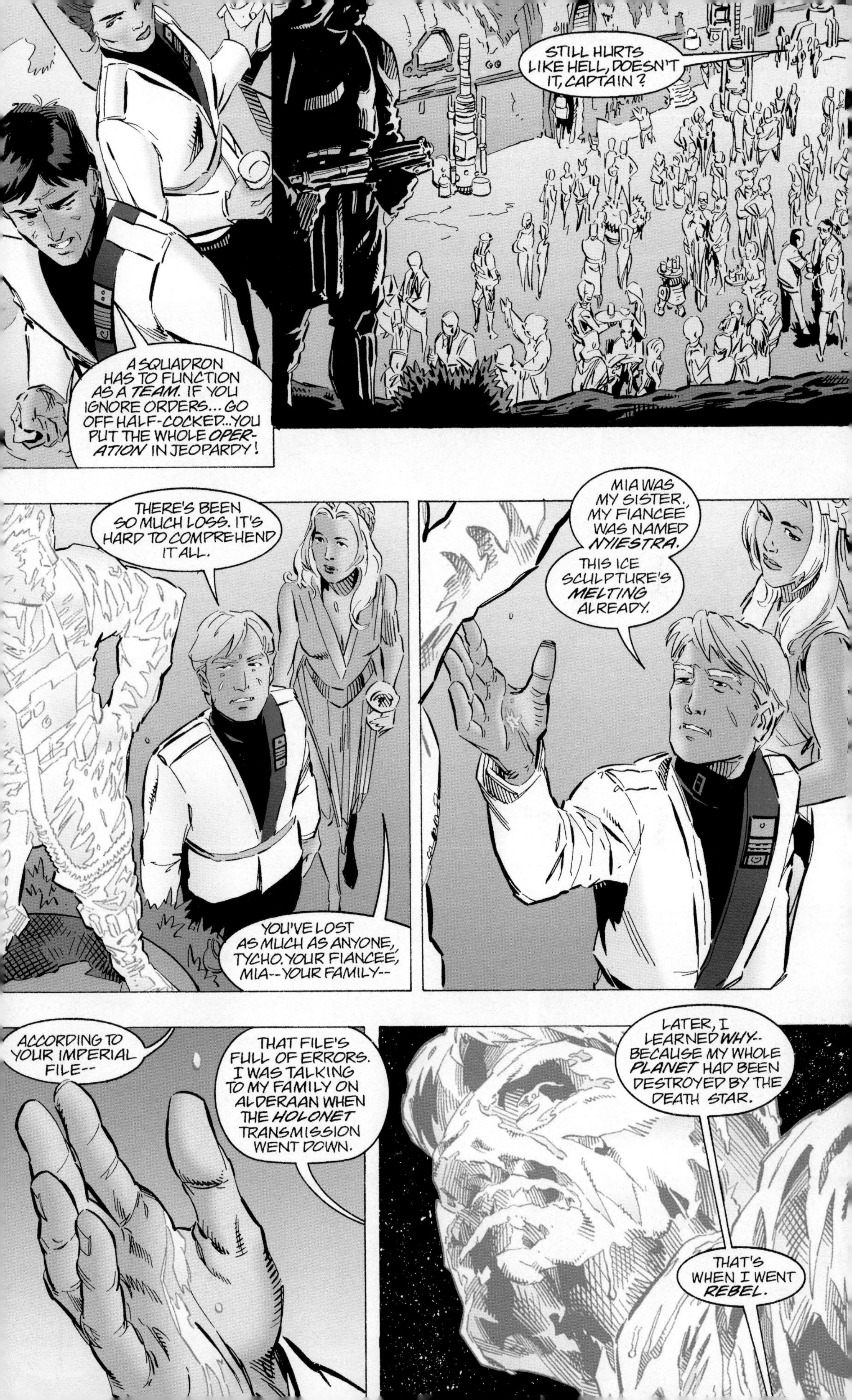
A SQUADRON HAS TO FUNCTION AS A TEAM. IF YOU IGNORE ORDERS... GO OFF HALF-COCKED...YOU PUT THE WHOLE OPERATION IN JEOPARDY!
STILL HURTS LIKE HELL, DOESN'T IT, CAPTAIN?
THERE'S BEEN SO MUCH LOSS. IT'S HARD TO COMPREHEND IT ALL.
YOU'VE LOST AS MUCH AS ANYONE, TYCHO. YOUR FIANCEE, MIA--YOUR FAMILY--
MIA WAS MY SISTER. MY FIANCEE WAS NAMED NYIESTRA.
THIS ICE SCULPTURE'S MELTING ALREADY.
ACCORDING TO YOUR IMPERIAL FILE--
THAT FILE'S FULL OF ERRORS. I WAS TALKING TO MY FAMILY ON ALDERAAN WHEN THE HOLONET TRANSMISSION WENT DOWN.
LATER, I LEARNED WHY--BECAUSE MY WHOLE PLANET HAD BEEN DESTROYED BY THE DEATH STAR.
THAT'S WHEN I WENT REBEL.

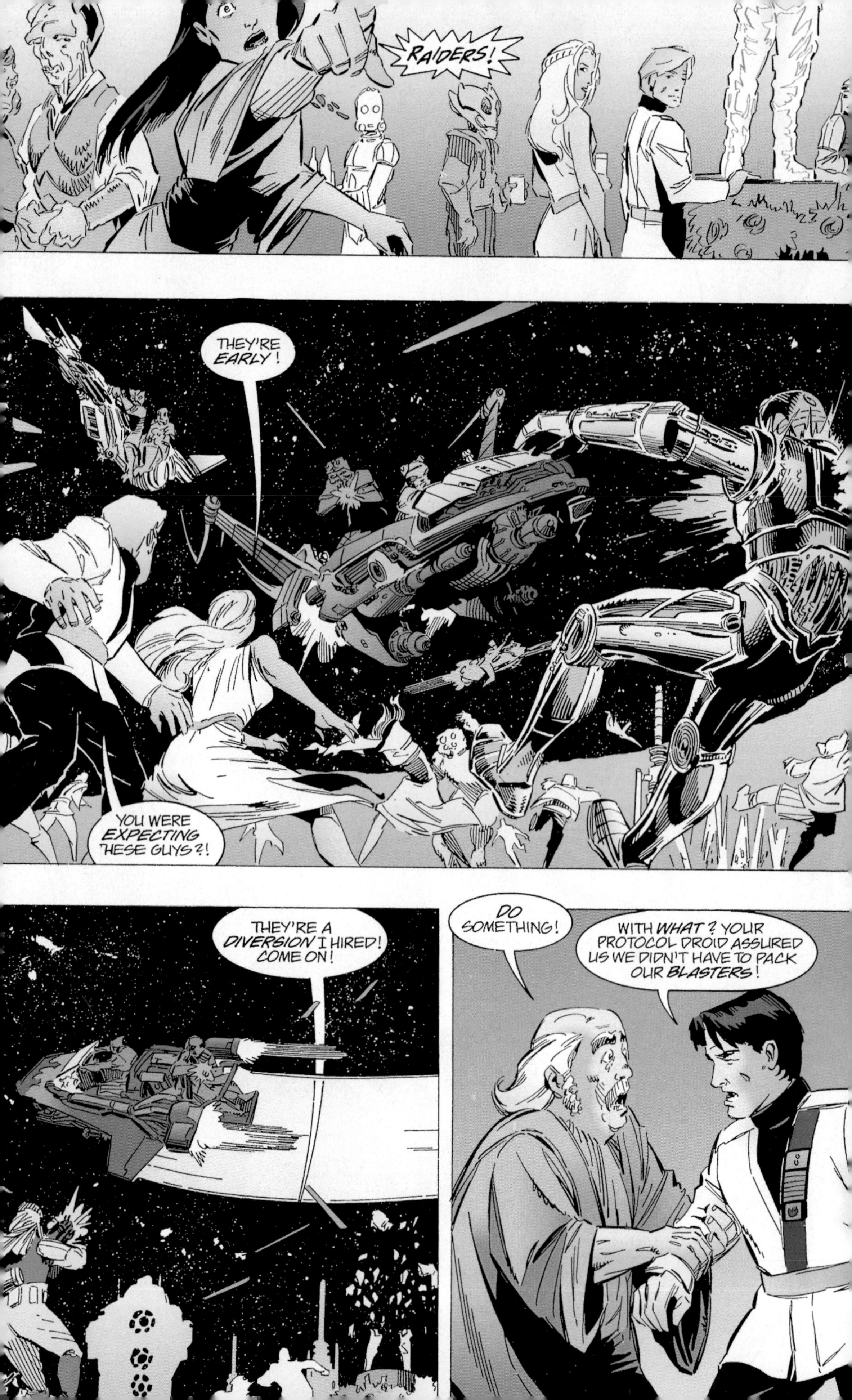
RAIDERS!
THEY'RE EARLY!
YOU WERE EXPECTING THESE GUYS?!
THEY'RE A DIVERSION I HIRED! COME ON!
DO SOMETHING!
WITH WHAT? YOUR PROTOCOL DROID ASSURED US WE DIDN'T HAVE TO PACK OUR BLASTERS!

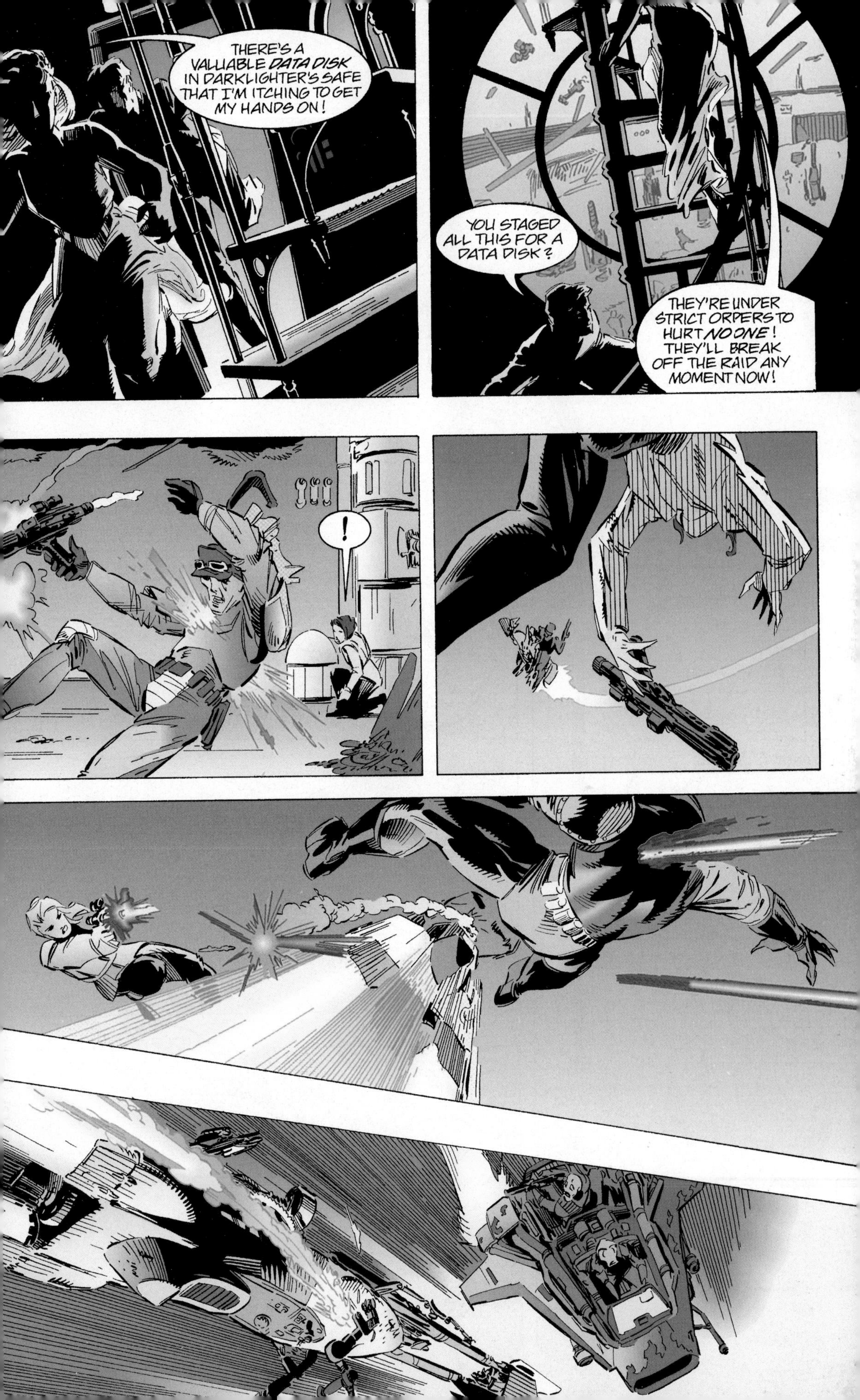
THERE'S A VALUABLE *DATA DISK* IN DARKLIGHTER'S SAFE THAT I'M ITCHING TO GET MY HANDS ON!
YOU STAGED ALL THIS FOR A DATA DISK?
THEY'RE UNDER STRICT ORDERS TO HURT *NO ONE*! THEY'LL BREAK OFF THE RAID ANY MOMENT NOW!
!

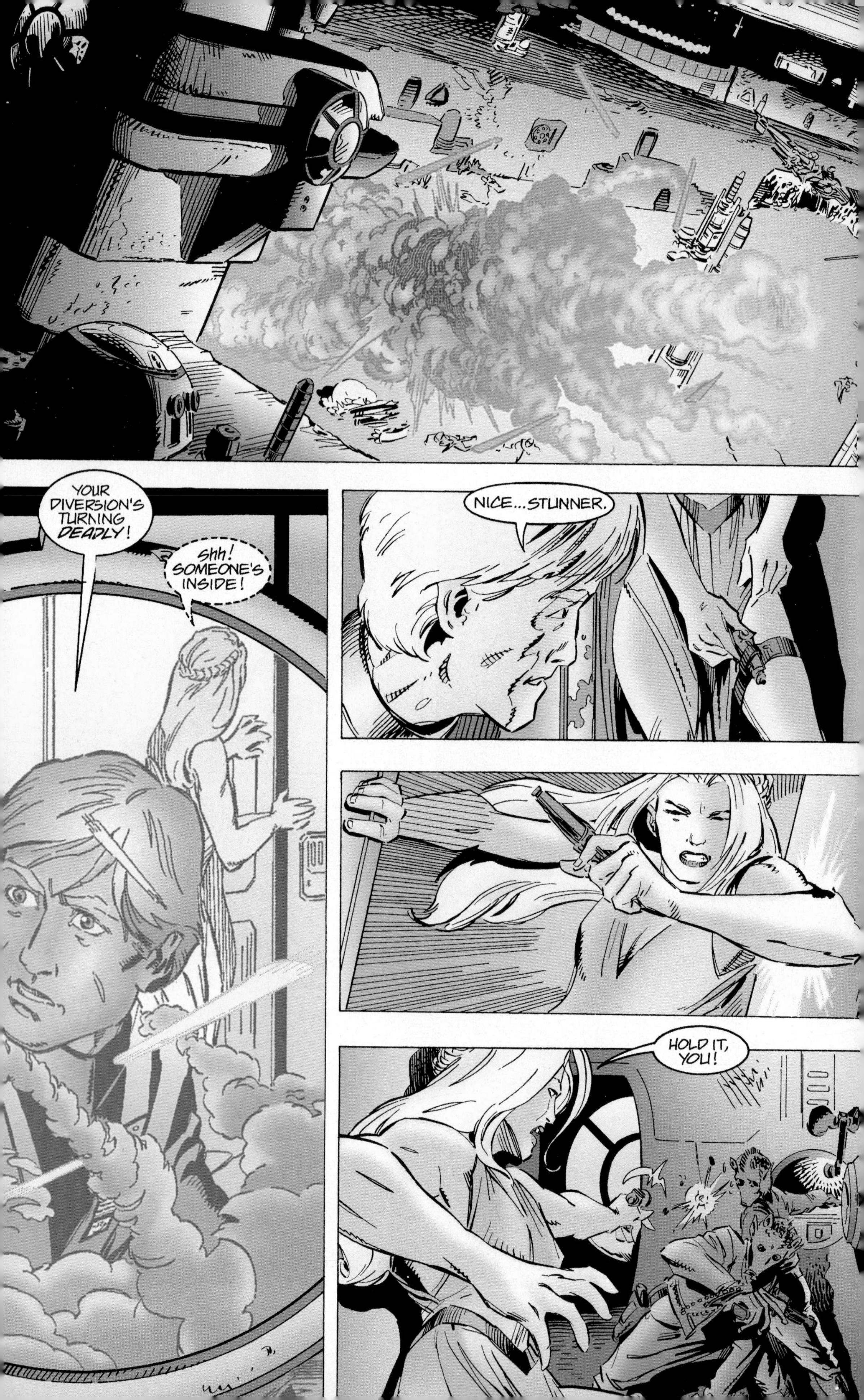
YOUR DIVERSION'S TURNING *DEADLY*!
Shh! SOMEONE'S INSIDE!
NICE...STUNNER.
HOLD IT, YOU!

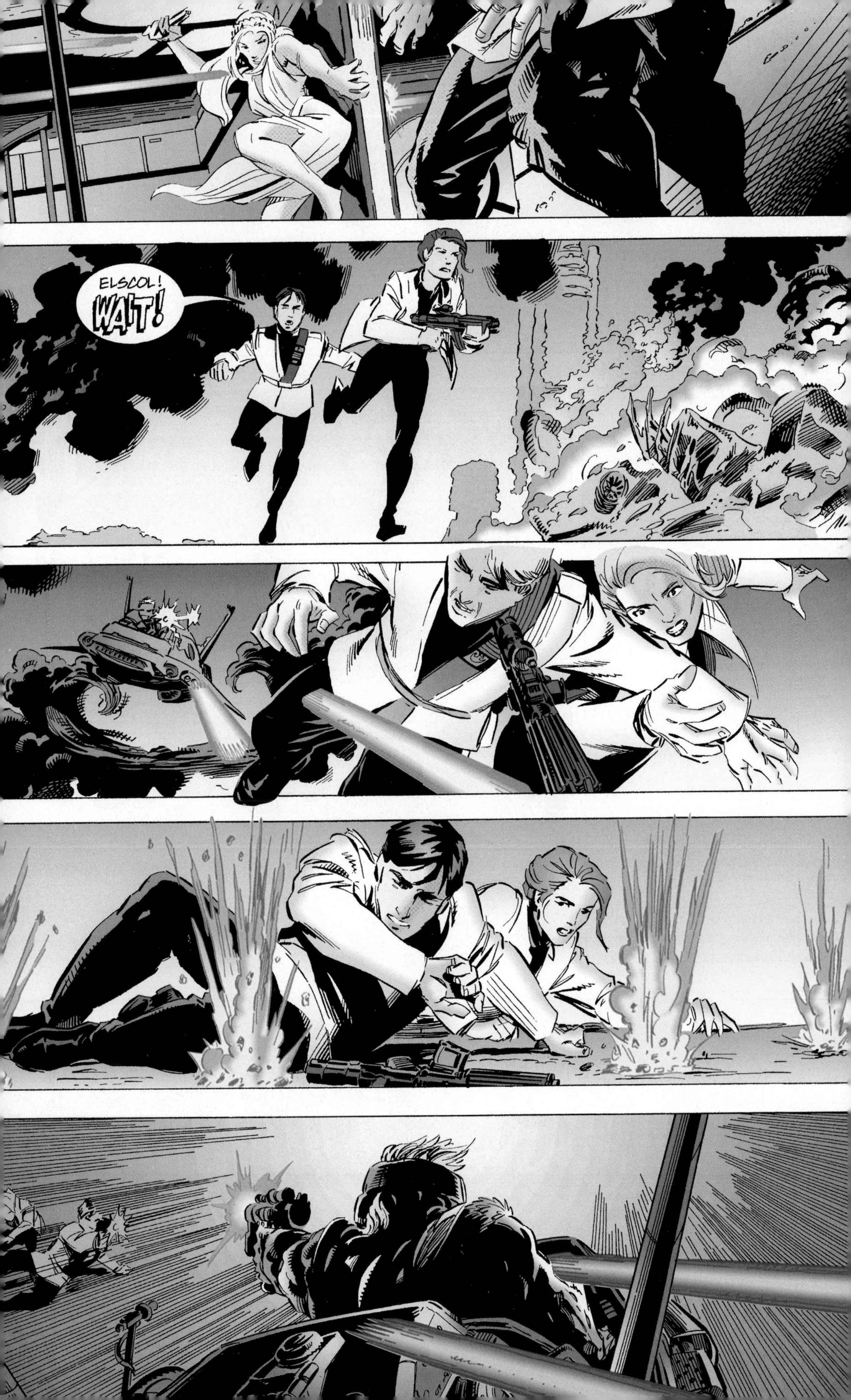
ELSCOL! WAIT!

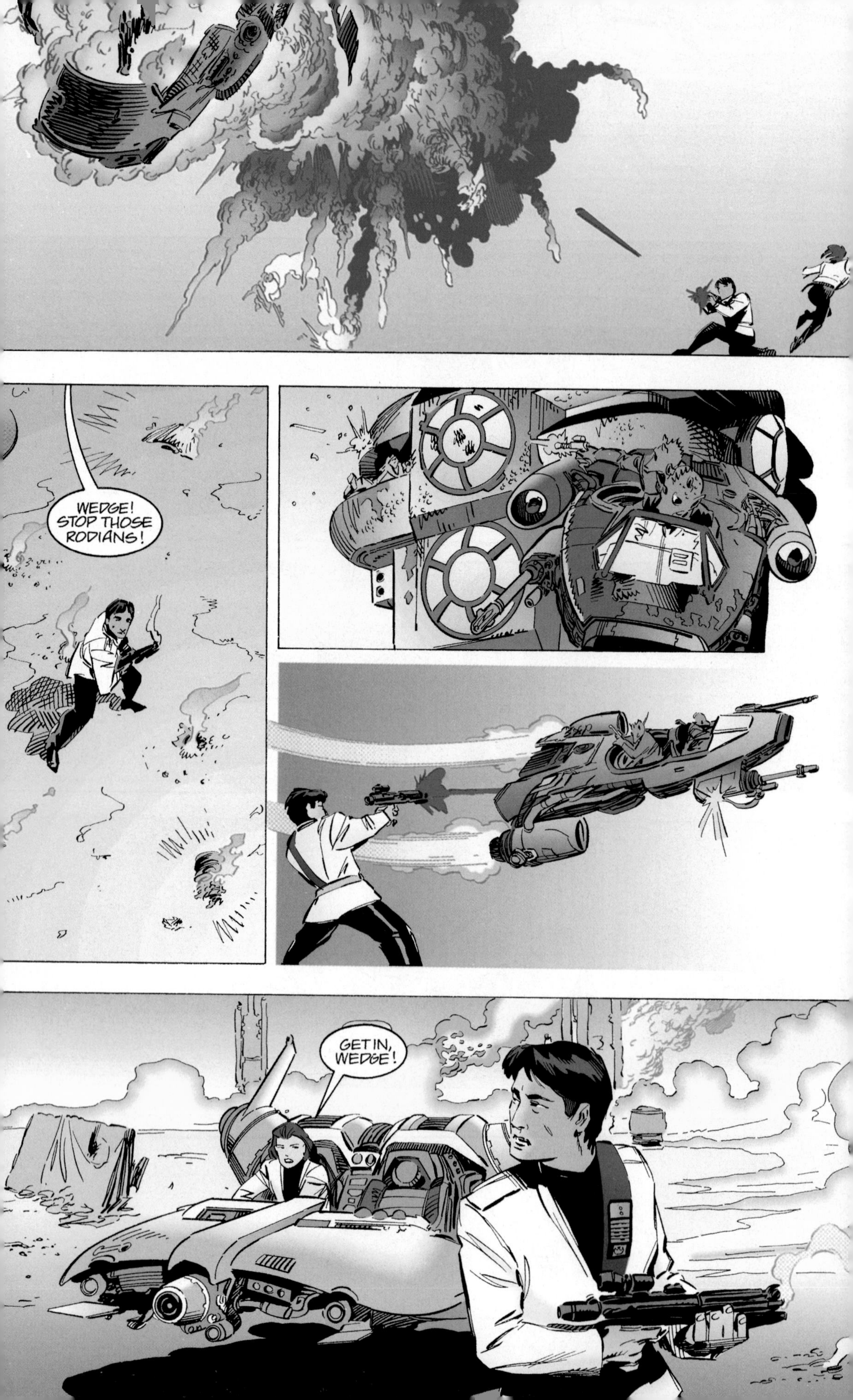
WEDGE! STOP THOSE RODIANS!
GET IN, WEDGE!

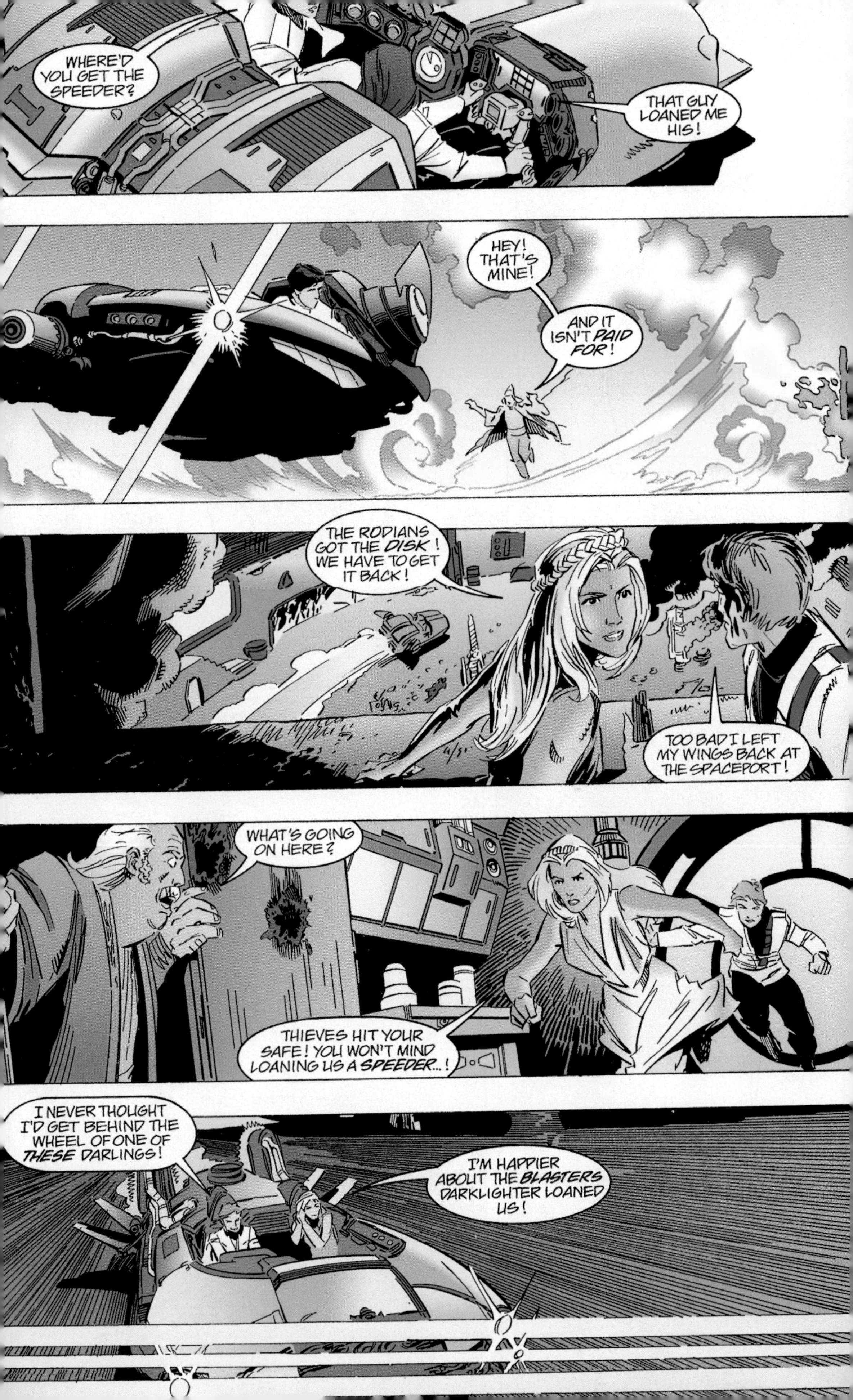
WHERE'D YOU GET THE SPEEDER?
THAT GUY LOANED ME HIS!
HEY! THAT'S MINE!
AND IT ISN'T PAID FOR!
THE RODIANS GOT THE DISK! WE HAVE TO GET IT BACK!
TOO BAD I LEFT MY WINGS BACK AT THE SPACEPORT!
WHAT'S GOING ON HERE?
THIEVES HIT YOUR SAFE! YOU WON'T MIND LOANING US A SPEEDER...!
I NEVER THOUGHT I'D GET BEHIND THE WHEEL OF ONE OF THESE DARLINGS!
I'M HAPPIER ABOUT THE BLASTERS DARKLIGHTER LOANED US!

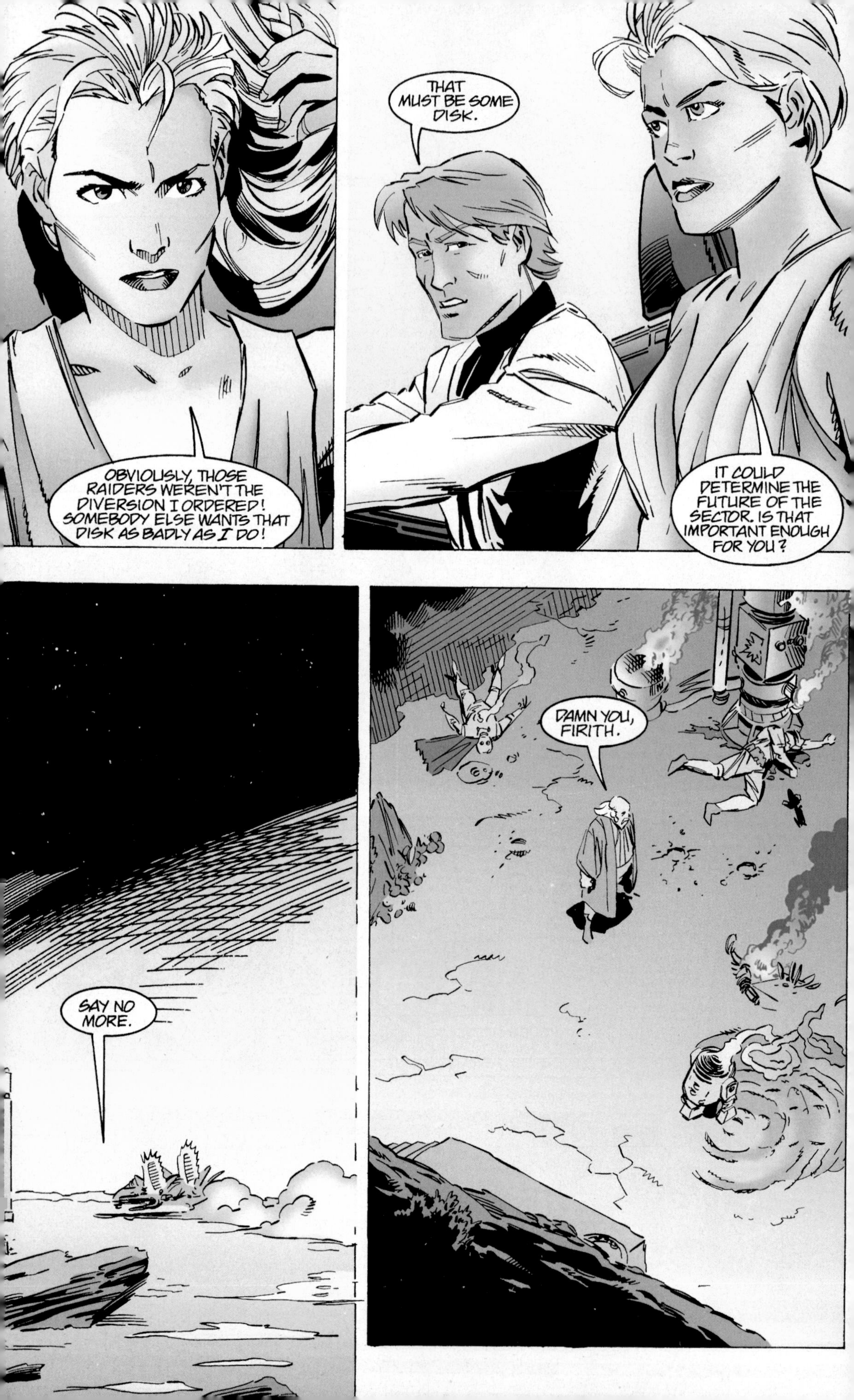
OBVIOUSLY, THOSE RAIDERS WEREN'T THE DIVERSION I ORDERED! SOMEBODY ELSE WANTS THAT DISK AS BADLY AS I DO!
THAT MUST BE SOME DISK.
IT COULD DETERMINE THE FUTURE OF THE SECTOR. IS THAT IMPORTANT ENOUGH FOR YOU?
SAY NO MORE.
DAMN YOU, FIRITH.

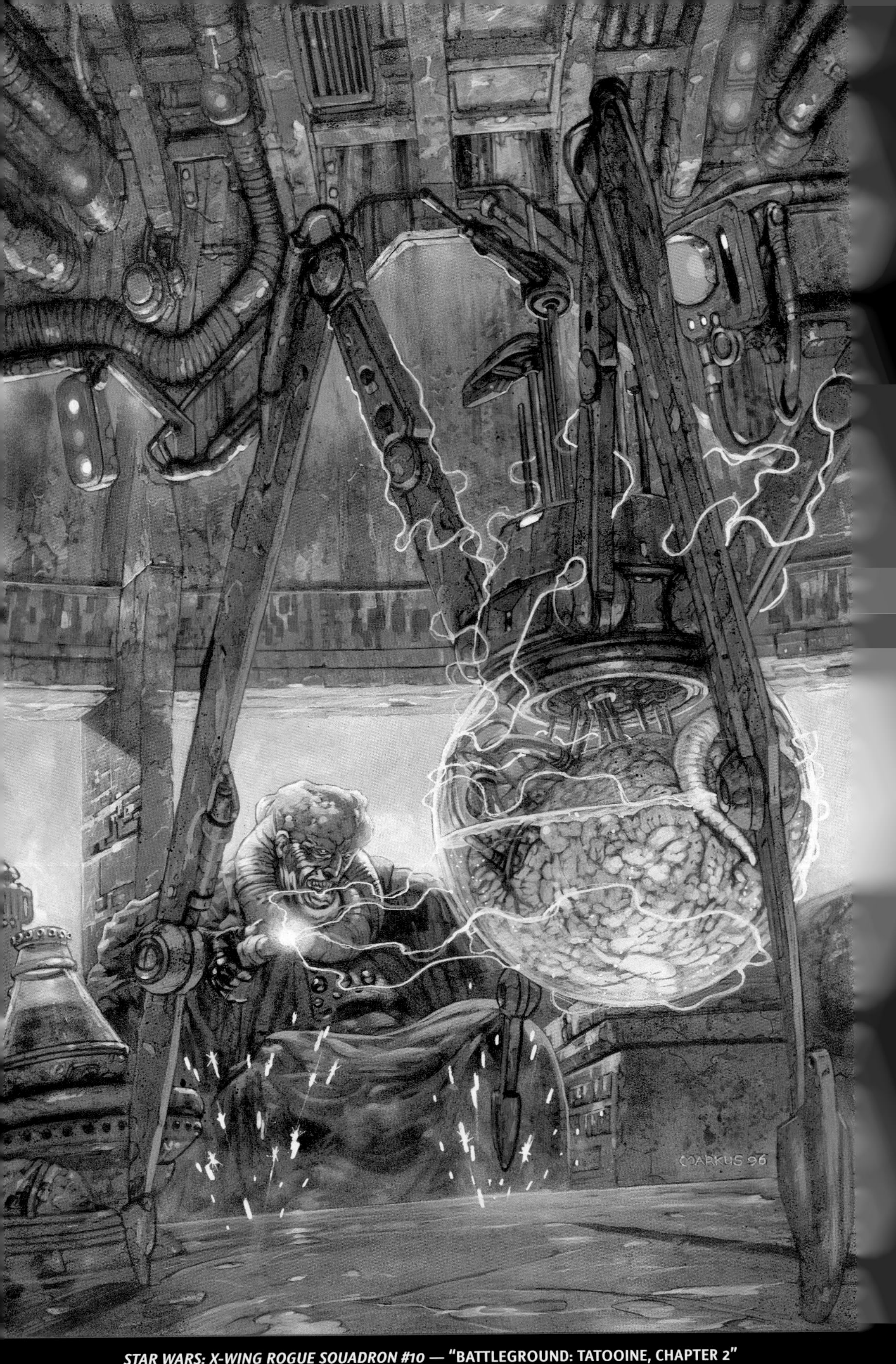
MARKUS 96

*STAR WARS: X-WING ROGUE SQUADRON #10* — "BATTLEGROUND: TATOOINE, CHAPTER 2"

PLOTTER: MICHAEL A. STACKPOLE • SCRIPTER: JAN STRNAD • PENCILER: JOHN NADEAU • INKER: JORDI ENSIGN

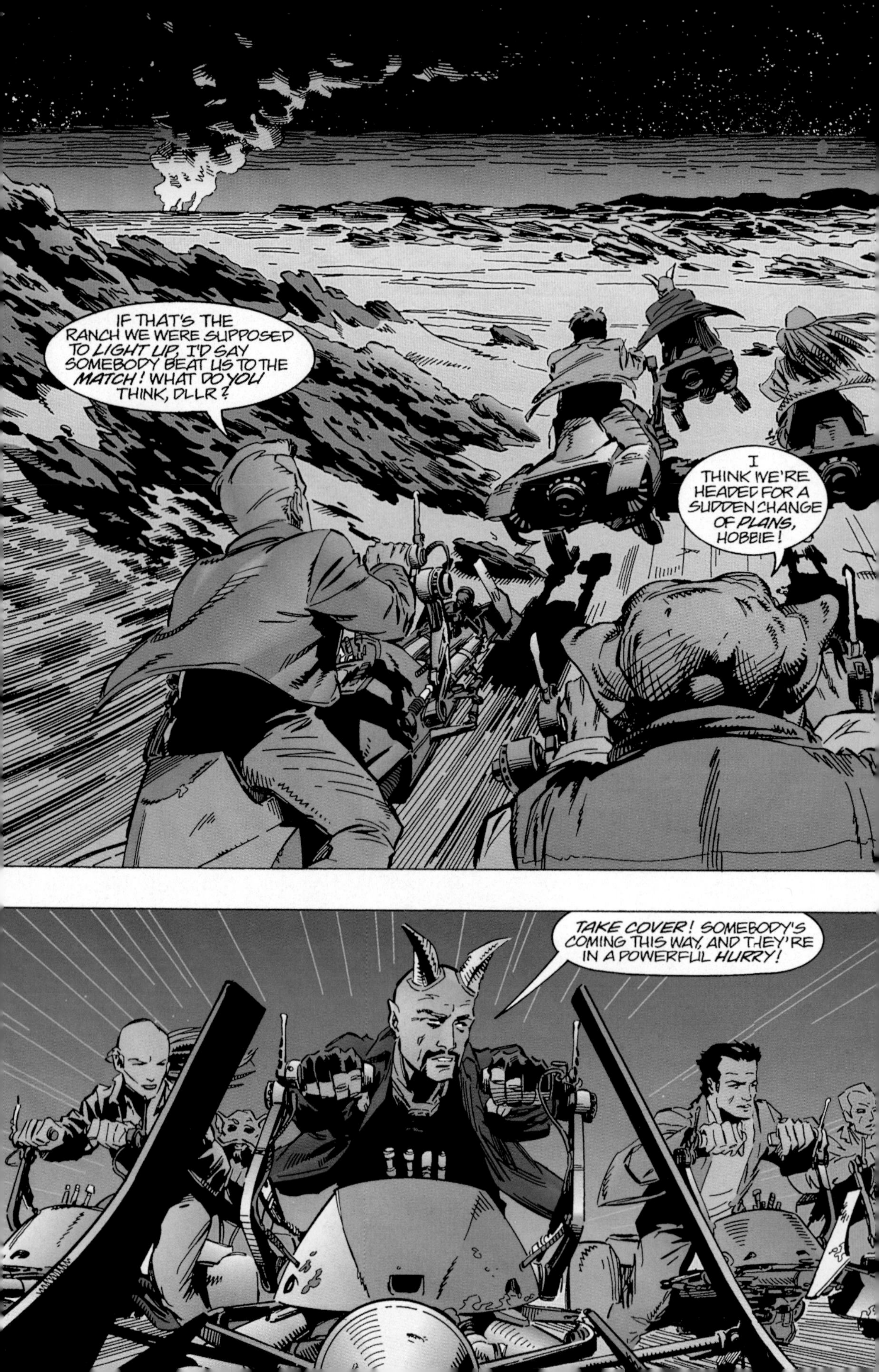
IF THAT'S THE RANCH WE WERE SUPPOSED TO LIGHT UP, I'D SAY SOMEBODY BEAT US TO THE MATCH! WHAT DO YOU THINK, DLLR?
I THINK WE'RE HEADED FOR A SUDDEN CHANGE OF PLANS, HOBBIE!
TAKE COVER! SOMEBODY'S COMING THIS WAY, AND THEY'RE IN A POWERFUL HURRY!

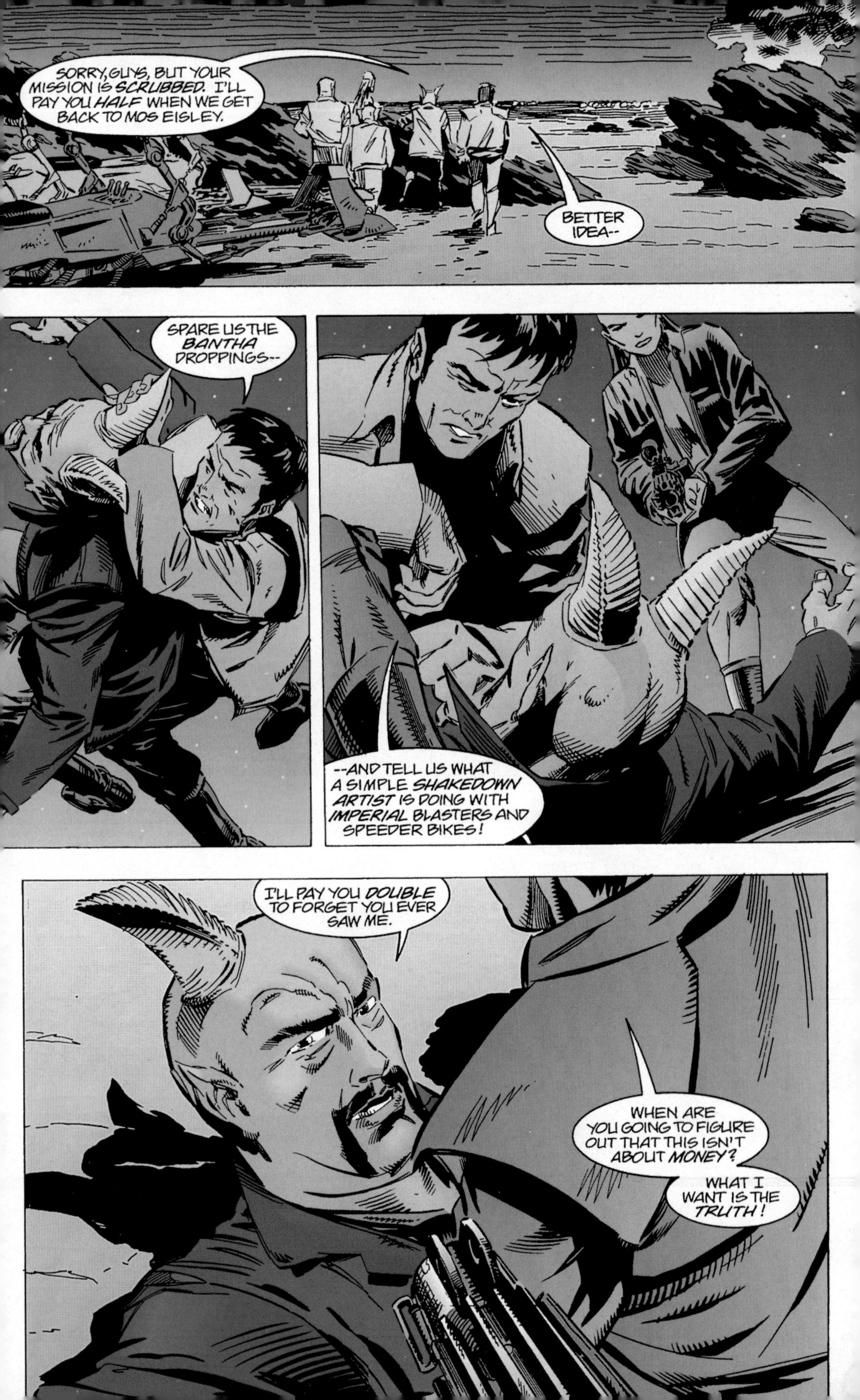
SORRY, GUYS, BUT YOUR MISSION IS SCRUBBED. I'LL PAY YOU HALF WHEN WE GET BACK TO MOS EISLEY.
BETTER IDEA--
SPARE US THE BANTHA DROPPINGS--
--AND TELL US WHAT A SIMPLE SHAKEDOWN ARTIST IS DOING WITH IMPERIAL BLASTERS AND SPEEDER BIKES!
I'LL PAY YOU DOUBLE TO FORGET YOU EVER SAW ME.
WHEN ARE YOU GOING TO FIGURE OUT THAT THIS ISN'T ABOUT MONEY?
WHAT I WANT IS THE TRUTH!

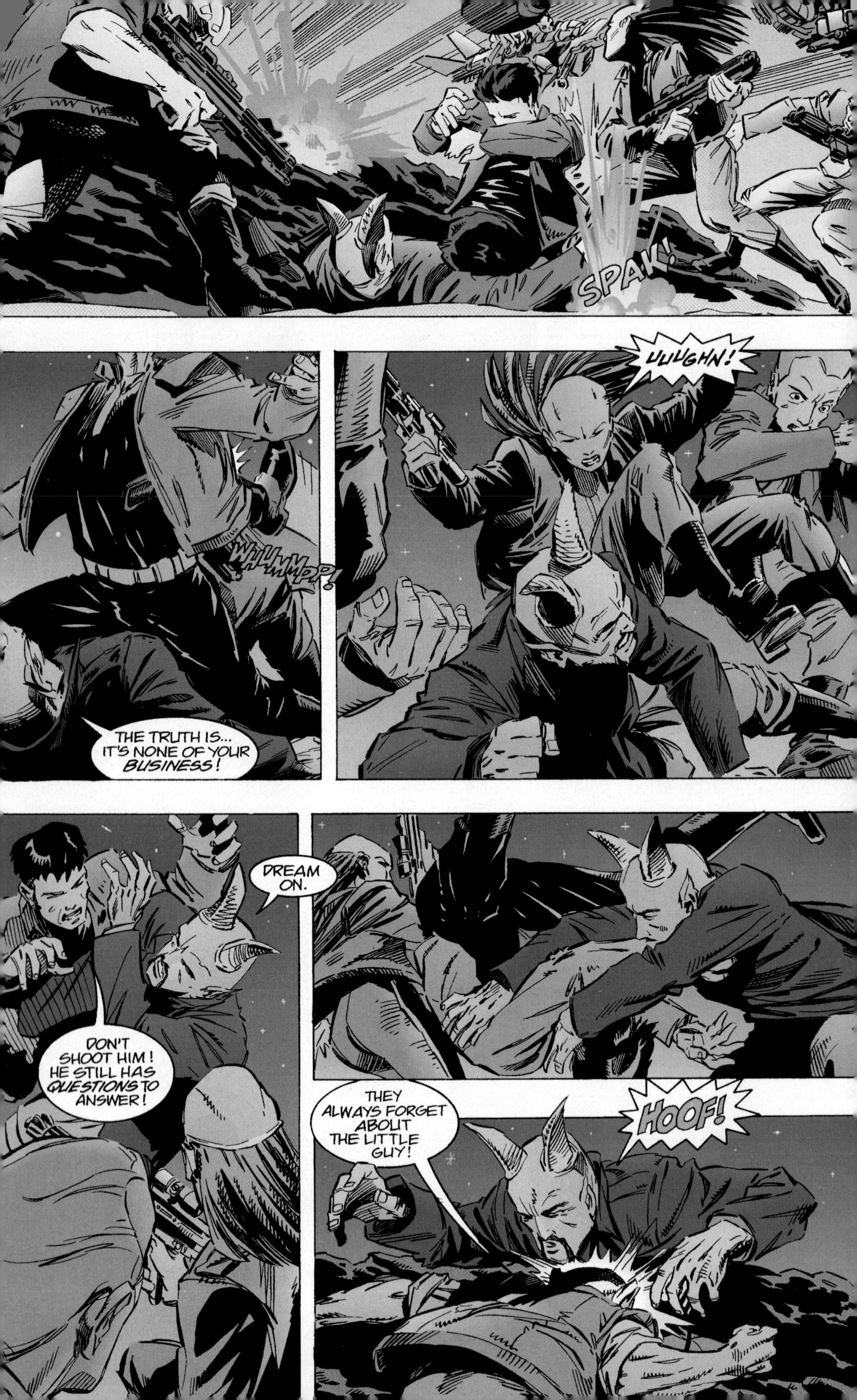
SPAK!
WHUMMPP!
THE TRUTH IS... IT'S NONE OF YOUR BUSINESS!
UUUGHN!
DREAM ON.
DON'T SHOOT HIM! HE STILL HAS QUESTIONS TO ANSWER!
THEY ALWAYS FORGET ABOUT THE LITTLE GUY!
HOOF!

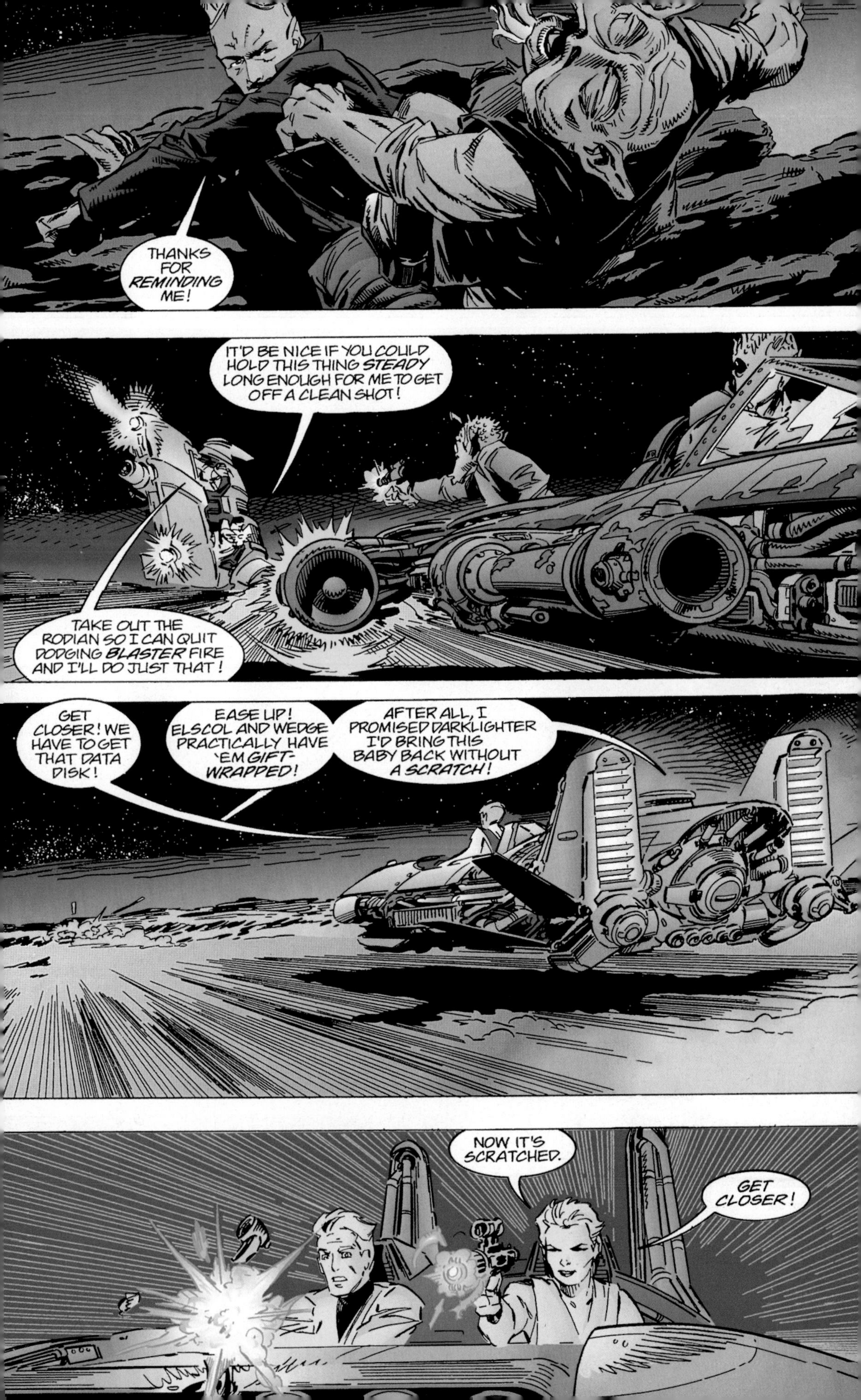
THANKS FOR *REMINDING* ME!
IT'D BE NICE IF YOU COULD HOLD THIS THING *STEADY* LONG ENOUGH FOR ME TO GET OFF A CLEAN SHOT!
TAKE OUT THE RODIAN SO I CAN QUIT DODGING *BLASTER* FIRE AND I'LL DO JUST THAT!
GET CLOSER! WE HAVE TO GET THAT DATA DISK!
EASE UP! ELSCOL AND WEDGE PRACTICALLY HAVE 'EM *GIFT-WRAPPED*!
AFTER ALL, I PROMISED DARKLIGHTER I'D BRING THIS BABY BACK WITHOUT A *SCRATCH*!
NOW IT'S SCRATCHED.
GET CLOSER!

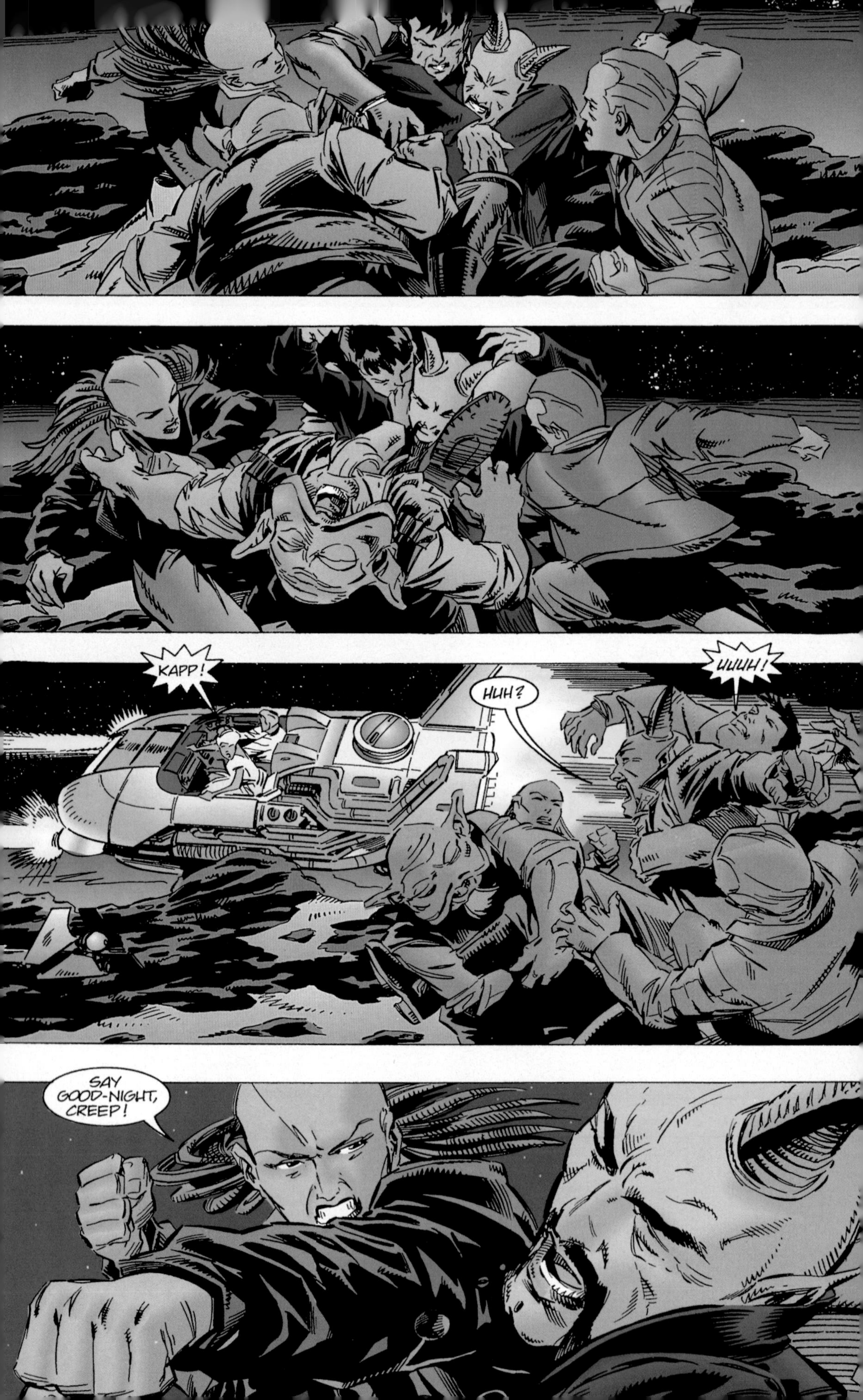
KAPP!
HUH?
UUUH!
SAY GOOD-NIGHT, CREEP!

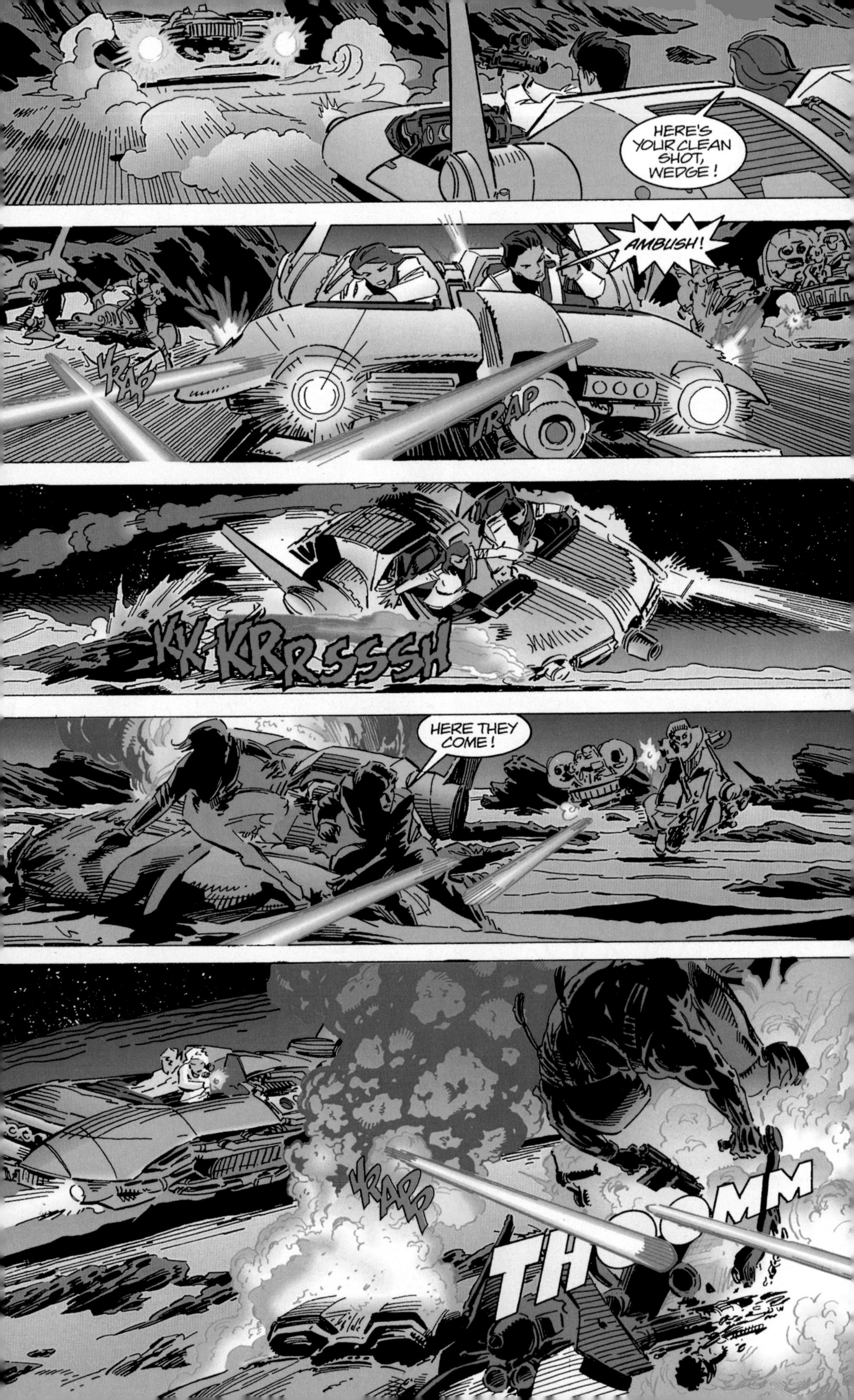
HERE'S YOUR CLEAN SHOT, WEDGE!
AMBUSH!
VRAP
VRAP
KKKRRSSSSH
HERE THEY COME!
VRAPP
THOOMMM

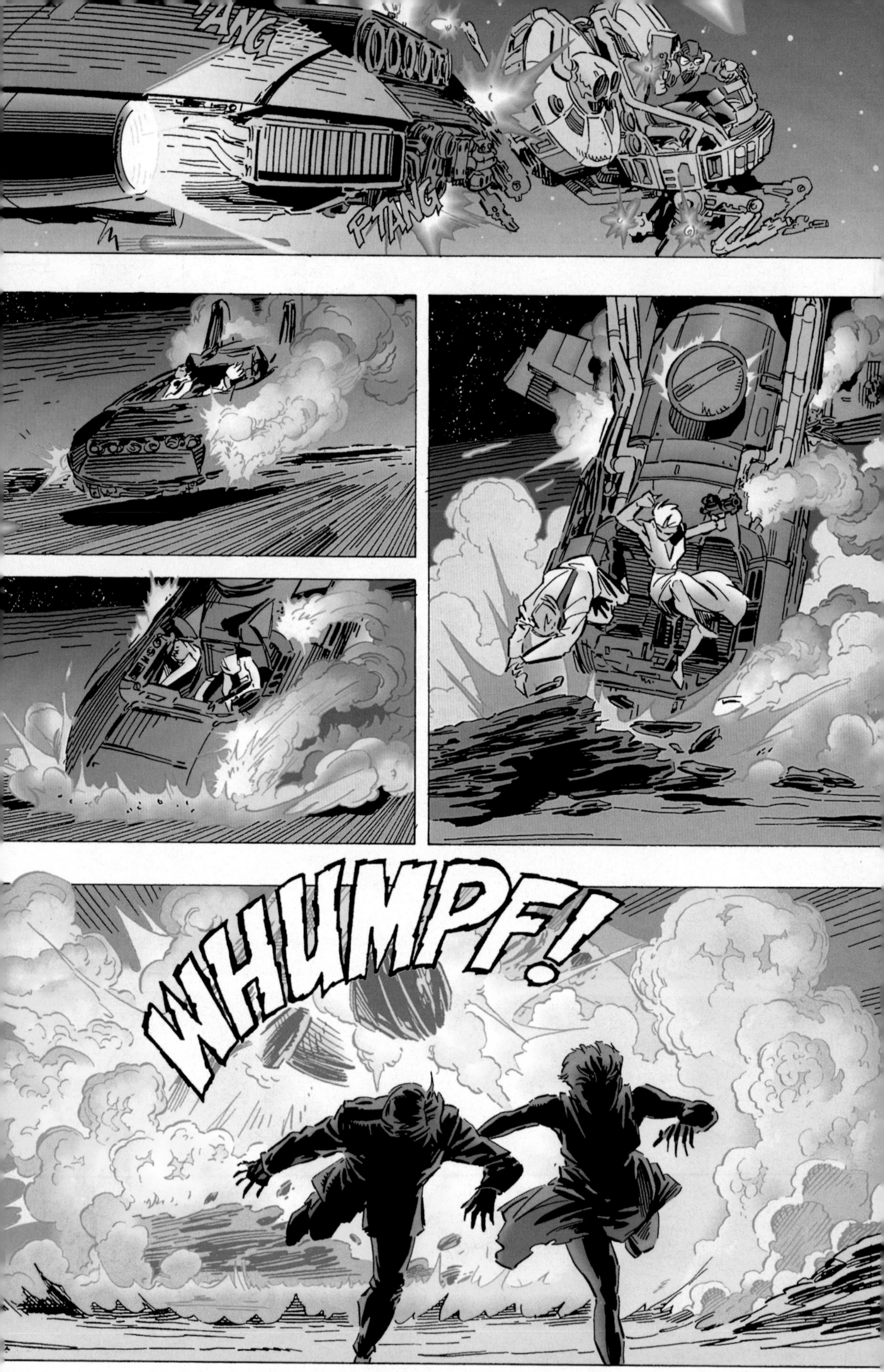
ANG
PTANG
WHUMPF!

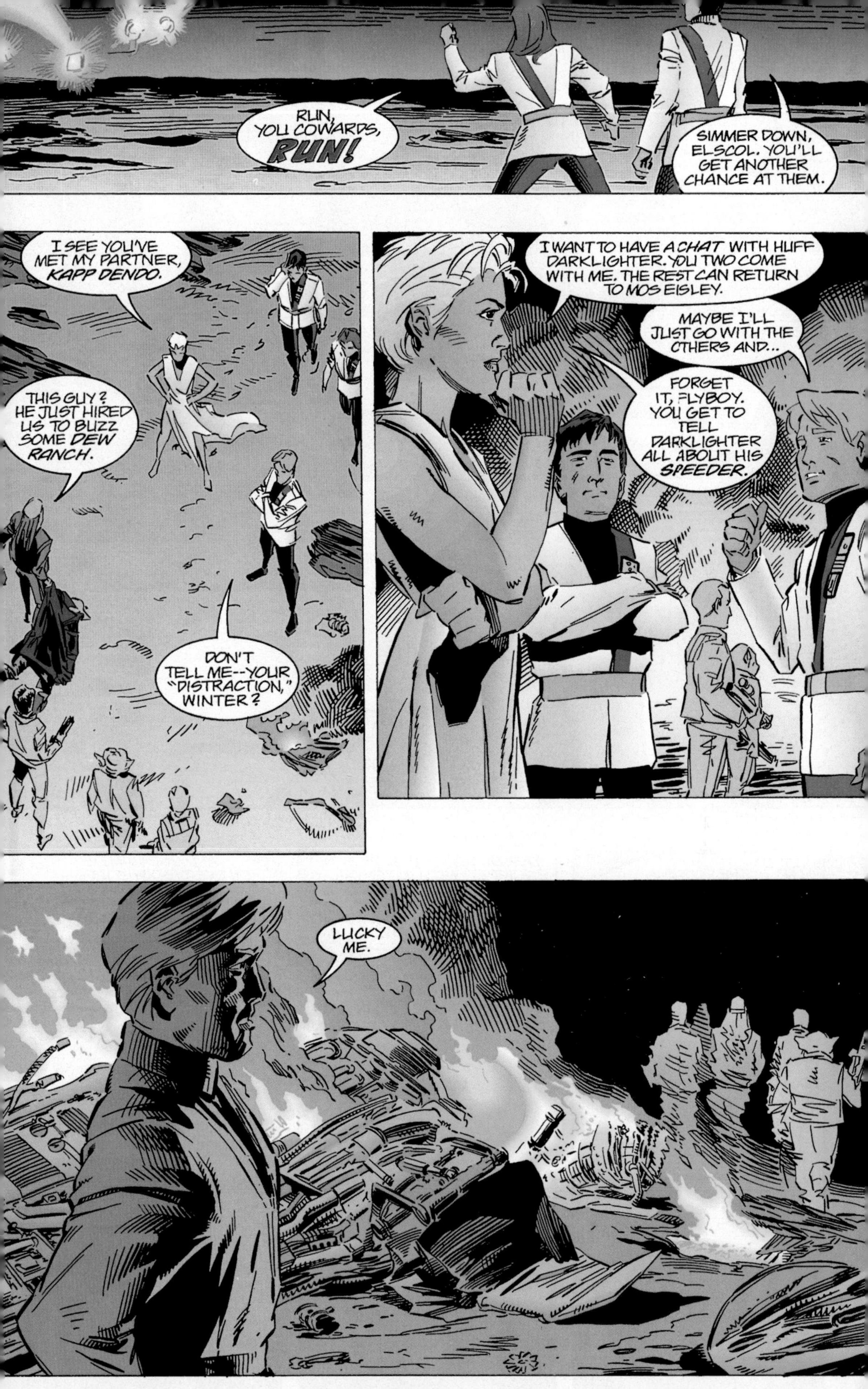
RUN, YOU COWARDS, RUN!
SIMMER DOWN, ELSCOL. YOU'LL GET ANOTHER CHANCE AT THEM.
I SEE YOU'VE MET MY PARTNER, KAPP DENDO.
THIS GUY? HE JUST HIRED US TO BUZZ SOME DEW RANCH.
DON'T TELL ME--YOUR "DISTRACTION," WINTER?
I WANT TO HAVE A CHAT WITH HUFF DARKLIGHTER. YOU TWO COME WITH ME. THE REST CAN RETURN TO MOS EISLEY.
MAYBE I'LL JUST GO WITH THE OTHERS AND...
FORGET IT, FLYBOY. YOU GET TO TELL DARKLIGHTER ALL ABOUT HIS SPEEDER.
LUCKY ME.

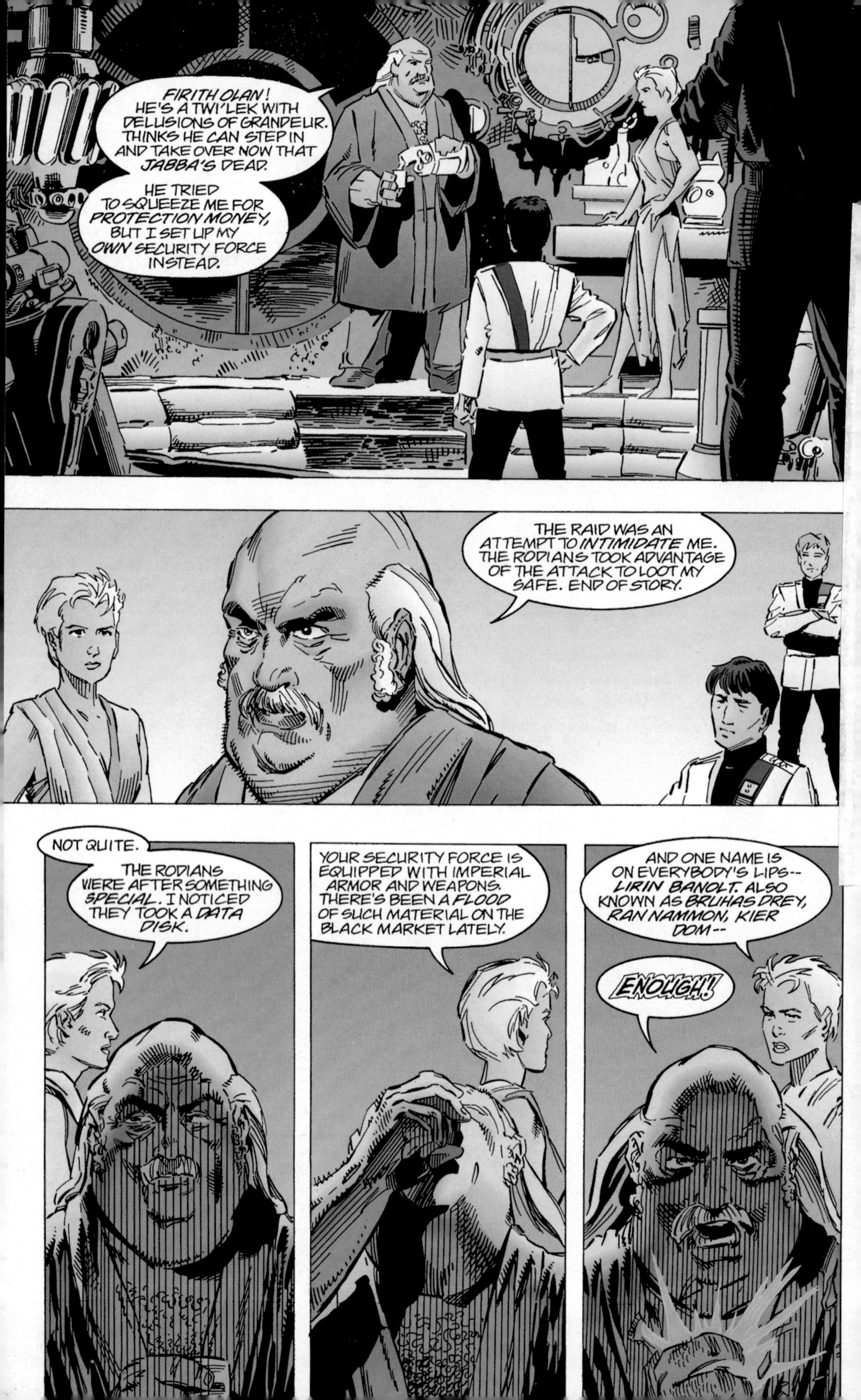
FIRITH OLAN! HE'S A TWI'LEK WITH DELUSIONS OF GRANDEUR. THINKS HE CAN STEP IN AND TAKE OVER NOW THAT JABBA'S DEAD.
HE TRIED TO SQUEEZE ME FOR PROTECTION MONEY, BUT I SET UP MY OWN SECURITY FORCE INSTEAD.
THE RAID WAS AN ATTEMPT TO INTIMIDATE ME. THE RODIANS TOOK ADVANTAGE OF THE ATTACK TO LOOT MY SAFE. END OF STORY.
NOT QUITE.
THE RODIANS WERE AFTER SOMETHING SPECIAL. I NOTICED THEY TOOK A DATA DISK.
YOUR SECURITY FORCE IS EQUIPPED WITH IMPERIAL ARMOR AND WEAPONS. THERE'S BEEN A FLOOD OF SUCH MATERIAL ON THE BLACK MARKET LATELY.
AND ONE NAME IS ON EVERYBODY'S LIPS-- LIRIN BANOLT. ALSO KNOWN AS BRUHAS DREY, RAN NAMMON, KIER DOM--
ENOUGH!!

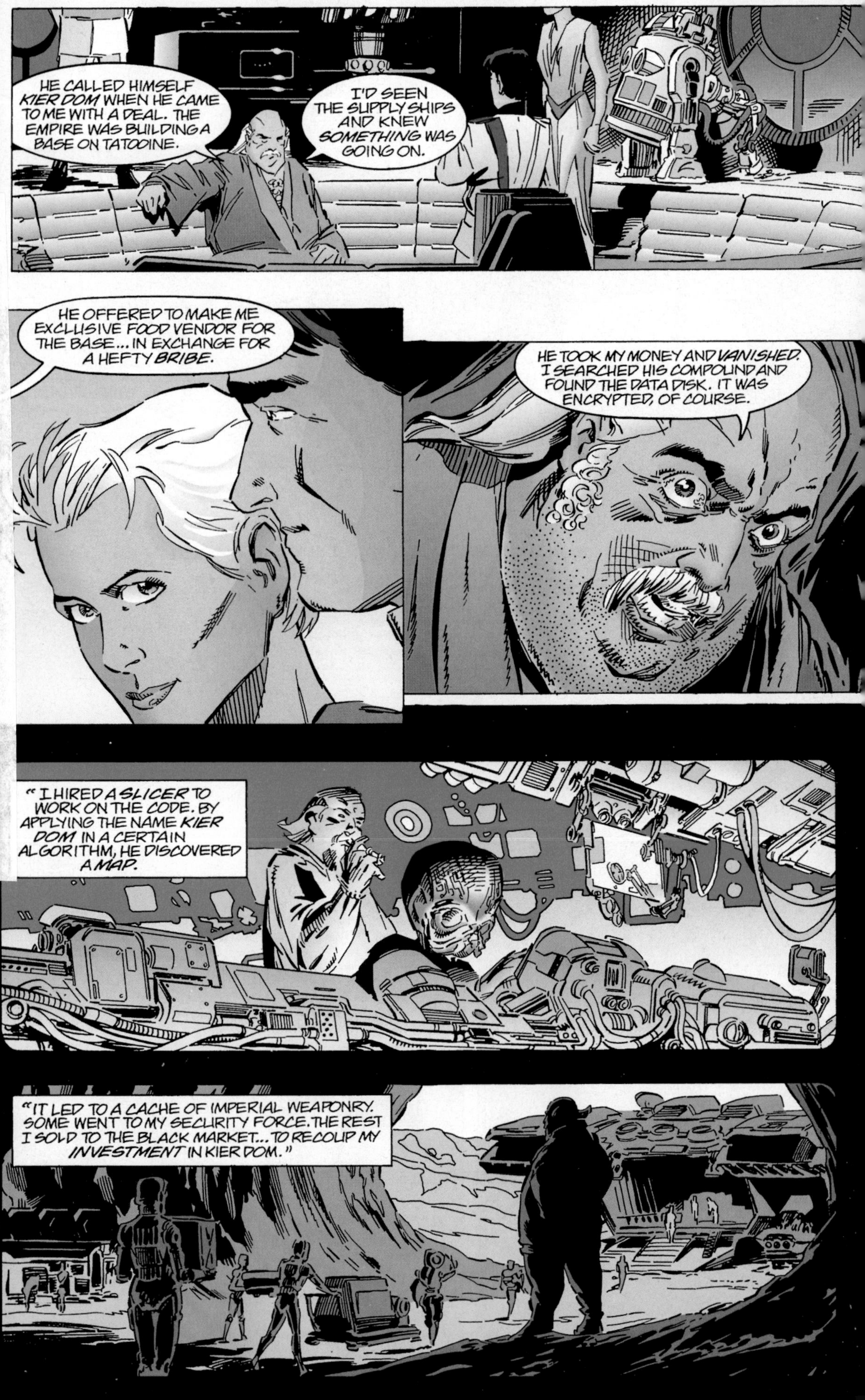
HE CALLED HIMSELF KIER DOM WHEN HE CAME TO ME WITH A DEAL. THE EMPIRE WAS BUILDING A BASE ON TATOOINE.
I'D SEEN THE SUPPLY SHIPS AND KNEW SOMETHING WAS GOING ON.
HE OFFERED TO MAKE ME EXCLUSIVE FOOD VENDOR FOR THE BASE... IN EXCHANGE FOR A HEFTY BRIBE.
HE TOOK MY MONEY AND VANISHED. I SEARCHED HIS COMPOUND AND FOUND THE DATA DISK. IT WAS ENCRYPTED, OF COURSE.
"I HIRED A SLICER TO WORK ON THE CODE. BY APPLYING THE NAME KIER DOM IN A CERTAIN ALGORITHM, HE DISCOVERED A MAP.
"IT LED TO A CACHE OF IMPERIAL WEAPONRY. SOME WENT TO MY SECURITY FORCE. THE REST I SOLD TO THE BLACK MARKET... TO RECOUP MY INVESTMENT IN KIER DOM."

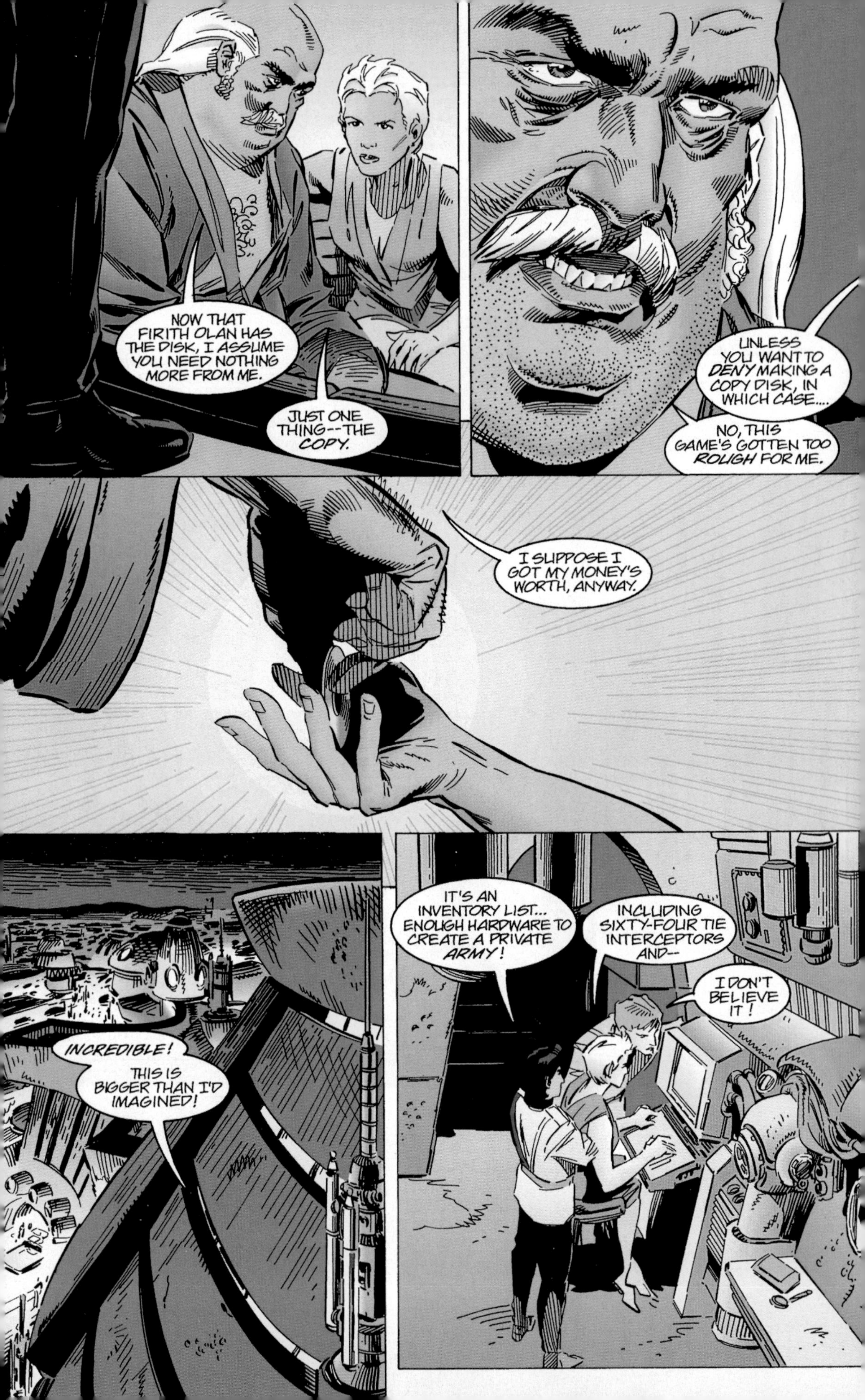
NOW THAT FIRITH OLAN HAS THE DISK, I ASSUME YOU NEED NOTHING MORE FROM ME.
JUST ONE THING--THE COPY.
UNLESS YOU WANT TO DENY MAKING A COPY DISK, IN WHICH CASE....
NO, THIS GAME'S GOTTEN TOO ROUGH FOR ME.
I SUPPOSE I GOT MY MONEY'S WORTH, ANYWAY.
INCREDIBLE!
THIS IS BIGGER THAN I'D IMAGINED!
IT'S AN INVENTORY LIST... ENOUGH HARDWARE TO CREATE A PRIVATE ARMY!
INCLUDING SIXTY-FOUR TIE INTERCEPTORS AND--
I DON'T BELIEVE IT!

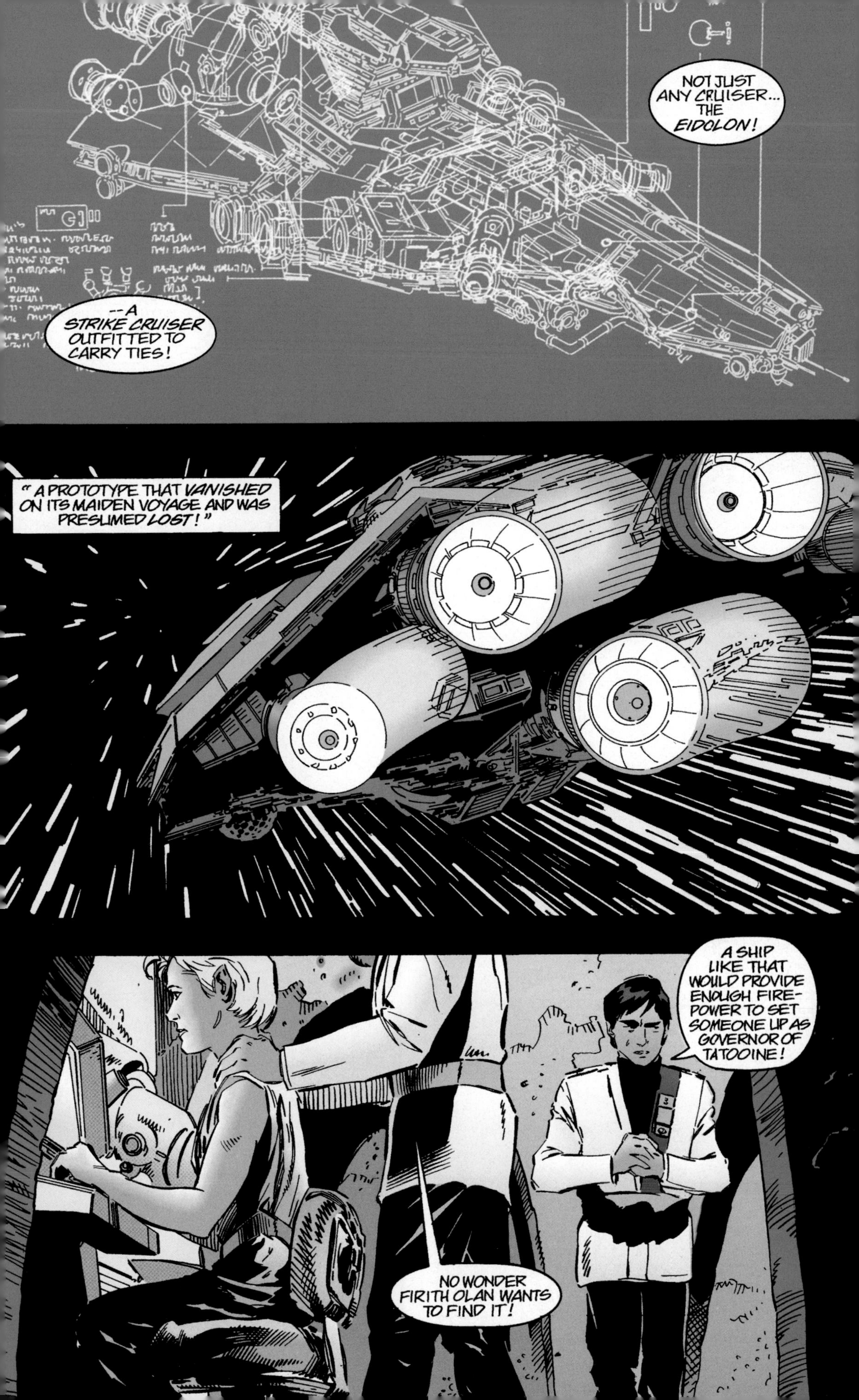
--A STRIKE CRUISER OUTFITTED TO CARRY TIES!
NOT JUST ANY CRUISER... THE EIDOLON!
"A PROTOTYPE THAT VANISHED ON ITS MAIDEN VOYAGE AND WAS PRESUMED LOST!"
A SHIP LIKE THAT WOULD PROVIDE ENOUGH FIRE-POWER TO SET SOMEONE UP AS GOVERNOR OF TATOOINE!
NO WONDER FIRITH OLAN WANTS TO FIND IT!

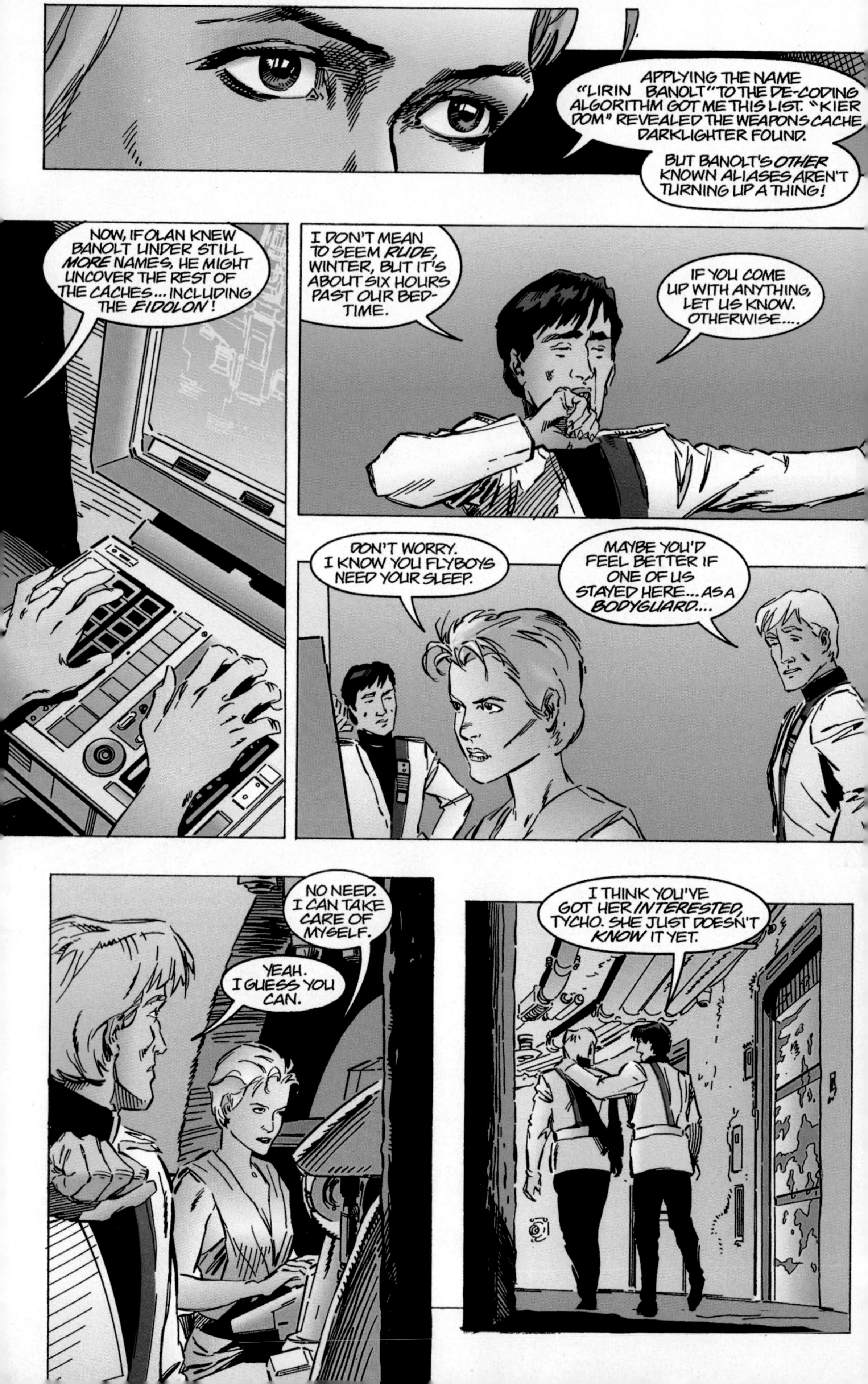
APPLYING THE NAME "LIRIN BANOLT" TO THE DE-CODING ALGORITHM GOT ME THIS LIST. "KIER DOM" REVEALED THE WEAPONS CACHE DARKLIGHTER FOUND.
BUT BANOLT'S OTHER KNOWN ALIASES AREN'T TURNING UP A THING!
NOW, IF OLAN KNEW BANOLT UNDER STILL MORE NAMES, HE MIGHT UNCOVER THE REST OF THE CACHES... INCLUDING THE EIDOLON!
I DON'T MEAN TO SEEM RUDE, WINTER, BUT IT'S ABOUT SIX HOURS PAST OUR BED-TIME.
IF YOU COME UP WITH ANYTHING, LET US KNOW. OTHERWISE....
DON'T WORRY. I KNOW YOU FLYBOYS NEED YOUR SLEEP.
MAYBE YOU'D FEEL BETTER IF ONE OF US STAYED HERE... AS A BODYGUARD....
NO NEED. I CAN TAKE CARE OF MYSELF.
YEAH. I GUESS YOU CAN.
I THINK YOU'VE GOT HER INTERESTED, TYCHO. SHE JUST DOESN'T KNOW IT YET.

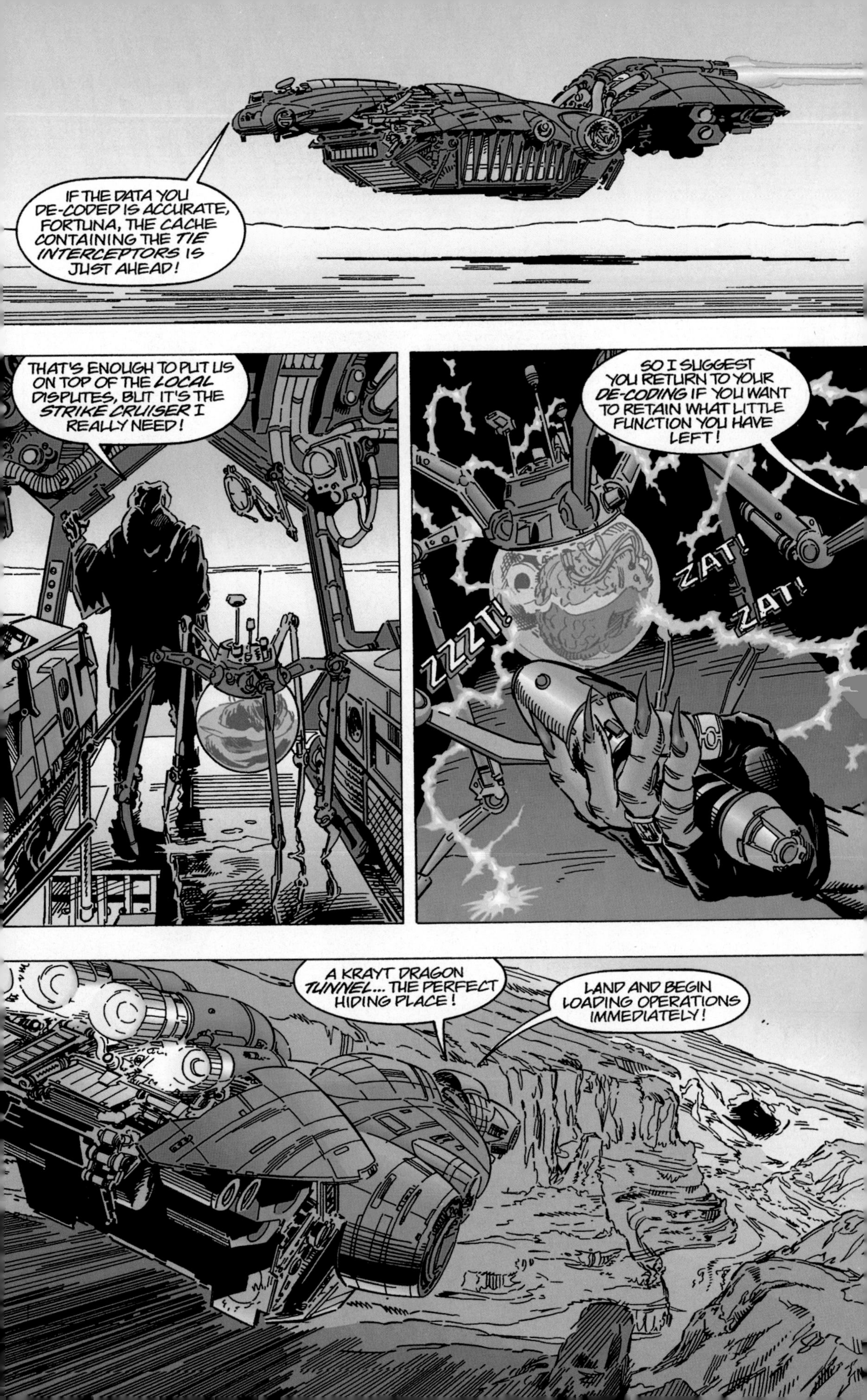
IF THE DATA YOU DE-CODED IS ACCURATE, FORTUNA, THE CACHE CONTAINING THE *TIE INTERCEPTORS* IS JUST AHEAD!
THAT'S ENOUGH TO PUT US ON TOP OF THE *LOCAL* DISPUTES, BUT IT'S THE *STRIKE CRUISER* I REALLY NEED!
SO I SUGGEST YOU RETURN TO YOUR *DE-CODING* IF YOU WANT TO RETAIN WHAT LITTLE FUNCTION YOU HAVE LEFT!
ZZZT!
ZAT!
ZAT!
A KRAYT DRAGON *TUNNEL*... THE PERFECT HIDING PLACE!
LAND AND BEGIN LOADING OPERATIONS IMMEDIATELY!

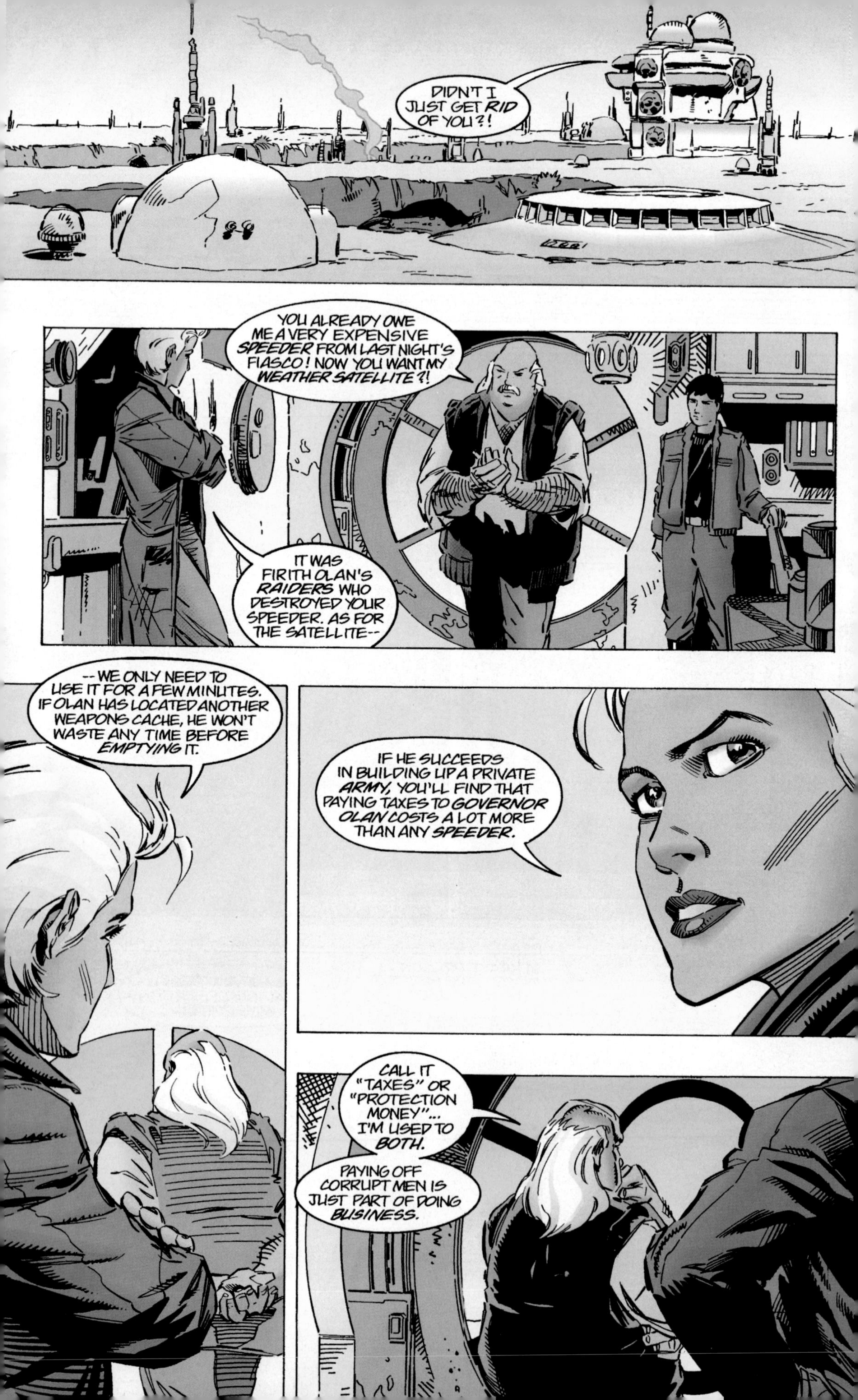
DIDN'T I JUST GET RID OF YOU?!
YOU ALREADY OWE ME A VERY EXPENSIVE SPEEDER FROM LAST NIGHT'S FIASCO! NOW YOU WANT MY WEATHER SATELLITE?!
IT WAS FIRITH OLAN'S RAIDERS WHO DESTROYED YOUR SPEEDER. AS FOR THE SATELLITE--
--WE ONLY NEED TO USE IT FOR A FEW MINUTES. IF OLAN HAS LOCATED ANOTHER WEAPONS CACHE, HE WON'T WASTE ANY TIME BEFORE EMPTYING IT.
IF HE SUCCEEDS IN BUILDING UP A PRIVATE ARMY, YOU'LL FIND THAT PAYING TAXES TO GOVERNOR OLAN COSTS A LOT MORE THAN ANY SPEEDER.
CALL IT "TAXES" OR "PROTECTION MONEY"... I'M USED TO BOTH.
PAYING OFF CORRUPT MEN IS JUST PART OF DOING BUSINESS.

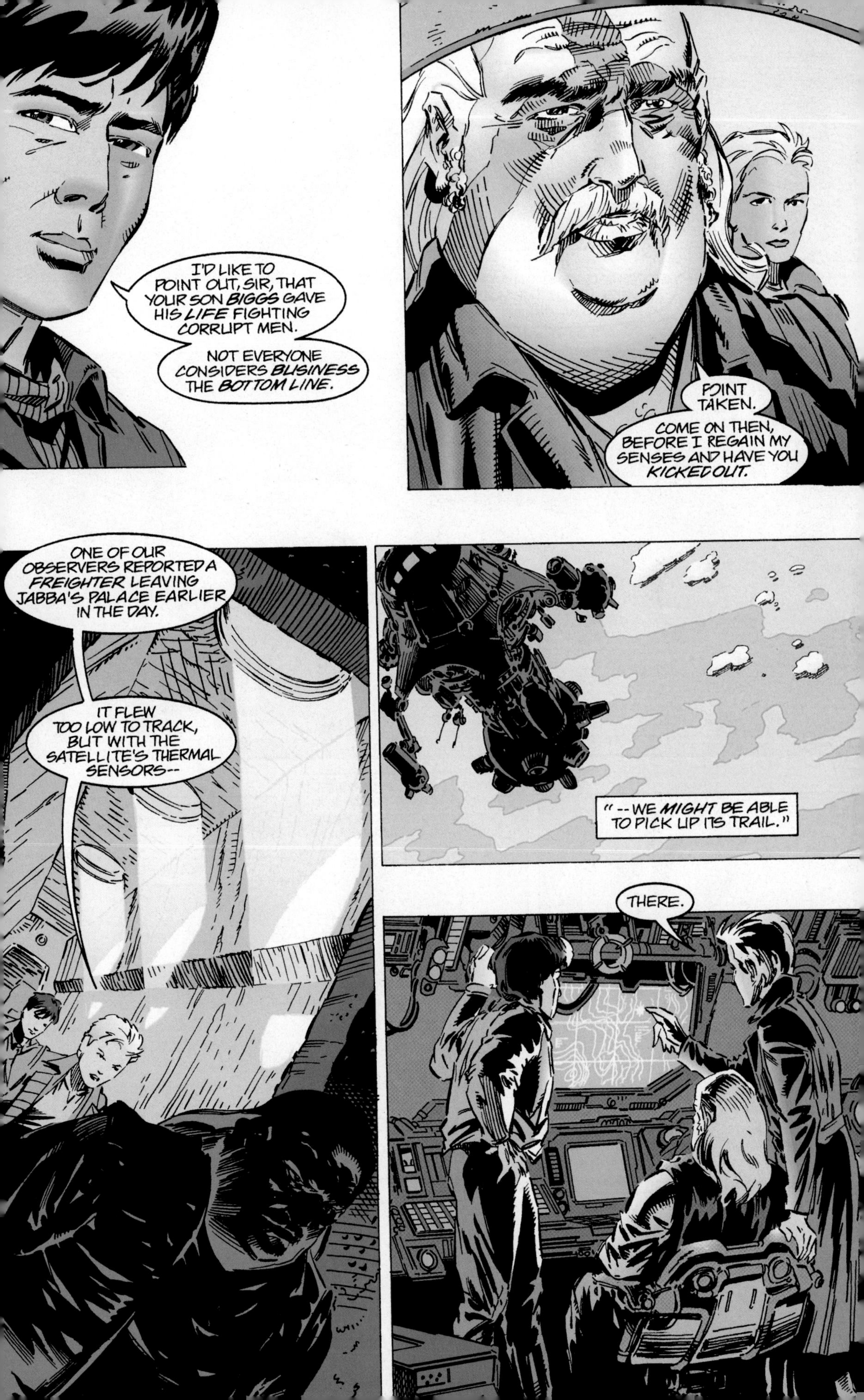
I'D LIKE TO POINT OUT, SIR, THAT YOUR SON BIGGS GAVE HIS LIFE FIGHTING CORRUPT MEN.
NOT EVERYONE CONSIDERS BUSINESS THE BOTTOM LINE.
POINT TAKEN.
COME ON THEN, BEFORE I REGAIN MY SENSES AND HAVE YOU KICKED OUT.
ONE OF OUR OBSERVERS REPORTED A FREIGHTER LEAVING JABBA'S PALACE EARLIER IN THE DAY.
IT FLEW TOO LOW TO TRACK, BUT WITH THE SATELLITE'S THERMAL SENSORS--
"--WE MIGHT BE ABLE TO PICK UP ITS TRAIL."
THERE.

MORE TIES, MORE TARGETS, CAPTAIN!

WHAT'RE THE CHANCES THAT OLAN HAS THOSE TIES OPERATIONAL, WEDGE?

EXCELLENT. I JUST HOPE HE DOESN'T HAVE THE *PILOTS* TO PUT THEM ALL IN THE AIR!

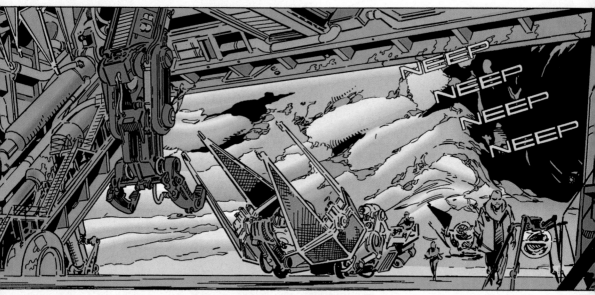

NEEP
NEEP
NEEP
NEEP

I KNEW ROGUE SQUADRON WOULD FIND US! LUCKILY--

NEEP
NEEP
NEEP

"--I'M WELL PREPARED TO *GREET* THEM!"

THERE ARE YOUR TARGETS, TYCHO! TAKE YOUR PICK!

LOOKS LIKE THERE'S PLENTY FOR EVERYBODY!

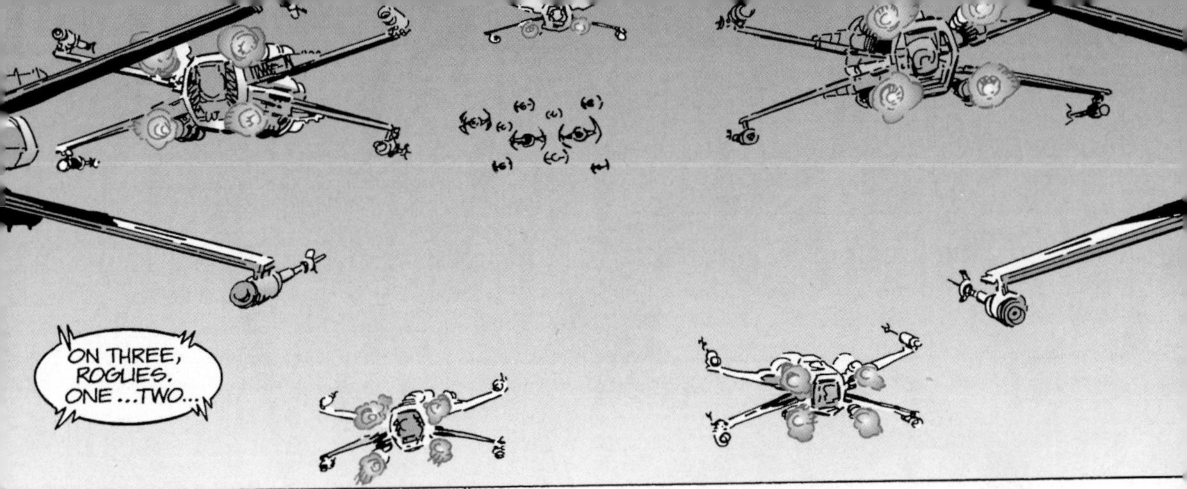
ON THREE, ROGUES. ONE ...TWO...

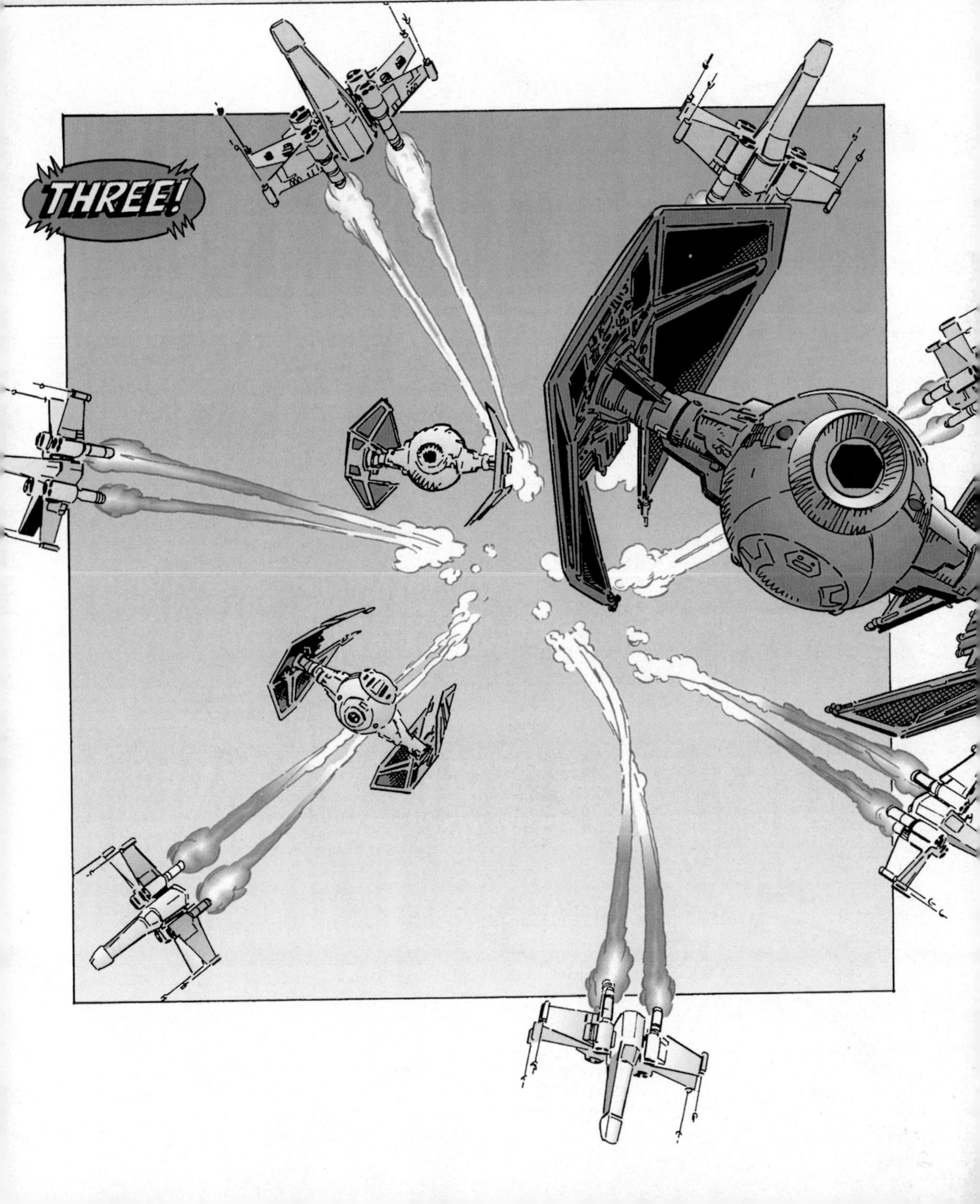
THREE!

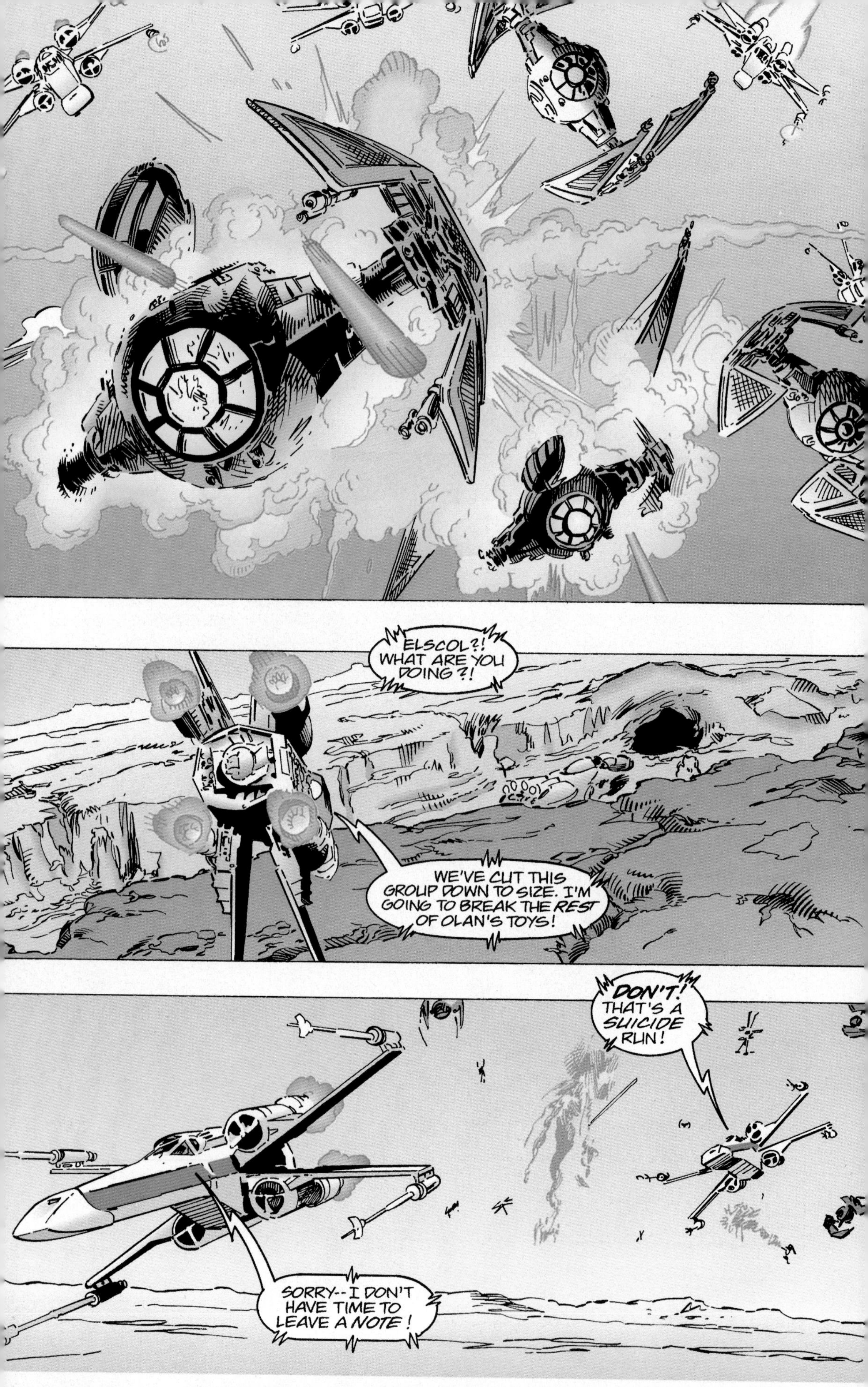
ELSCOL?! WHAT ARE YOU DOING?!
WE'VE CUT THIS GROUP DOWN TO SIZE. I'M GOING TO BREAK THE REST OF OLAN'S TOYS!
DON'T! THAT'S A SUICIDE RUN!
SORRY-- I DON'T HAVE TIME TO LEAVE A NOTE!

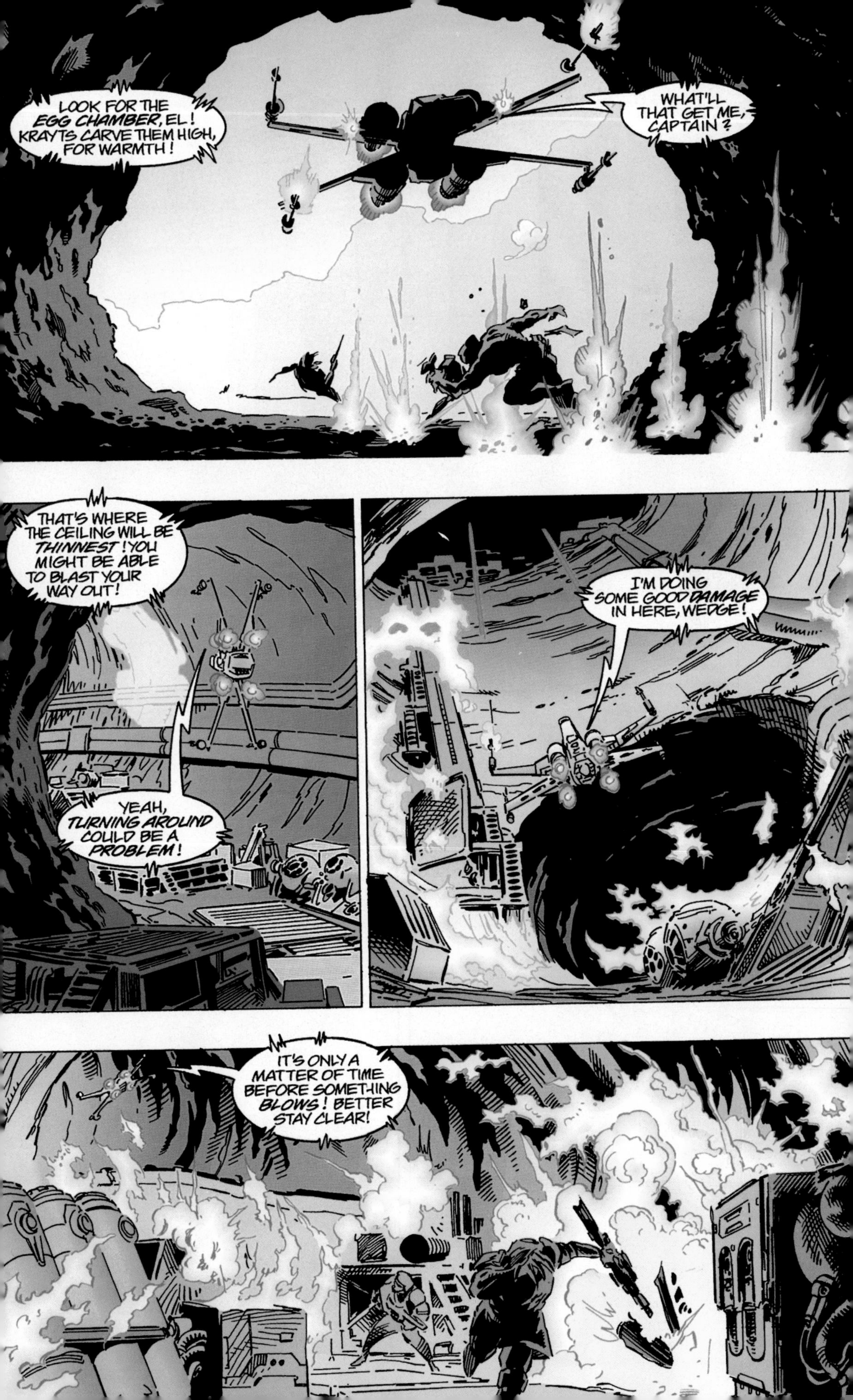
LOOK FOR THE EGG CHAMBER, EL! KRAYTS CARVE THEM HIGH, FOR WARMTH!
WHAT'LL THAT GET ME, CAPTAIN?
THAT'S WHERE THE CEILING WILL BE THINNEST! YOU MIGHT BE ABLE TO BLAST YOUR WAY OUT!
YEAH, TURNING AROUND COULD BE A PROBLEM!
I'M DOING SOME GOOD DAMAGE IN HERE, WEDGE!
IT'S ONLY A MATTER OF TIME BEFORE SOMETHING BLOWS! BETTER STAY CLEAR!

THIS IS IT, CAPTAIN!
IF THIS WORKS, LUNCH IS ON ME!

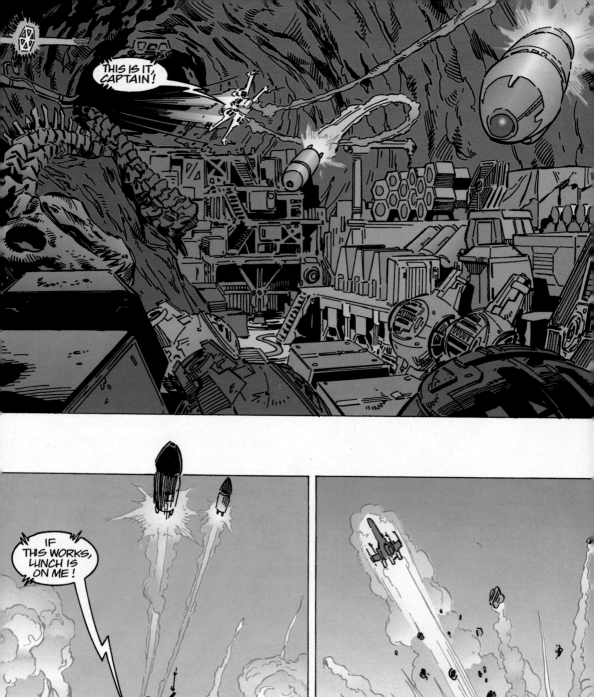

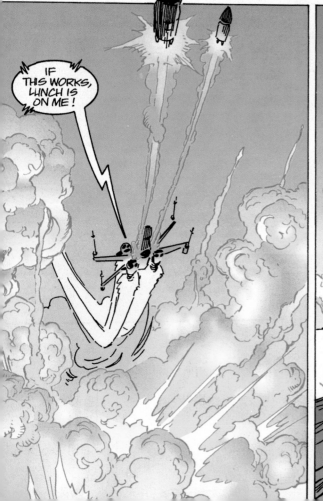

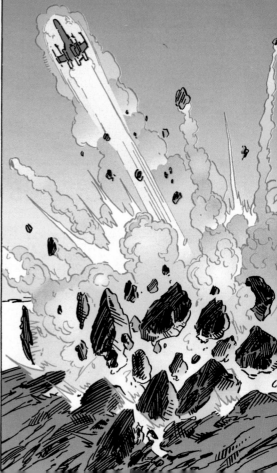

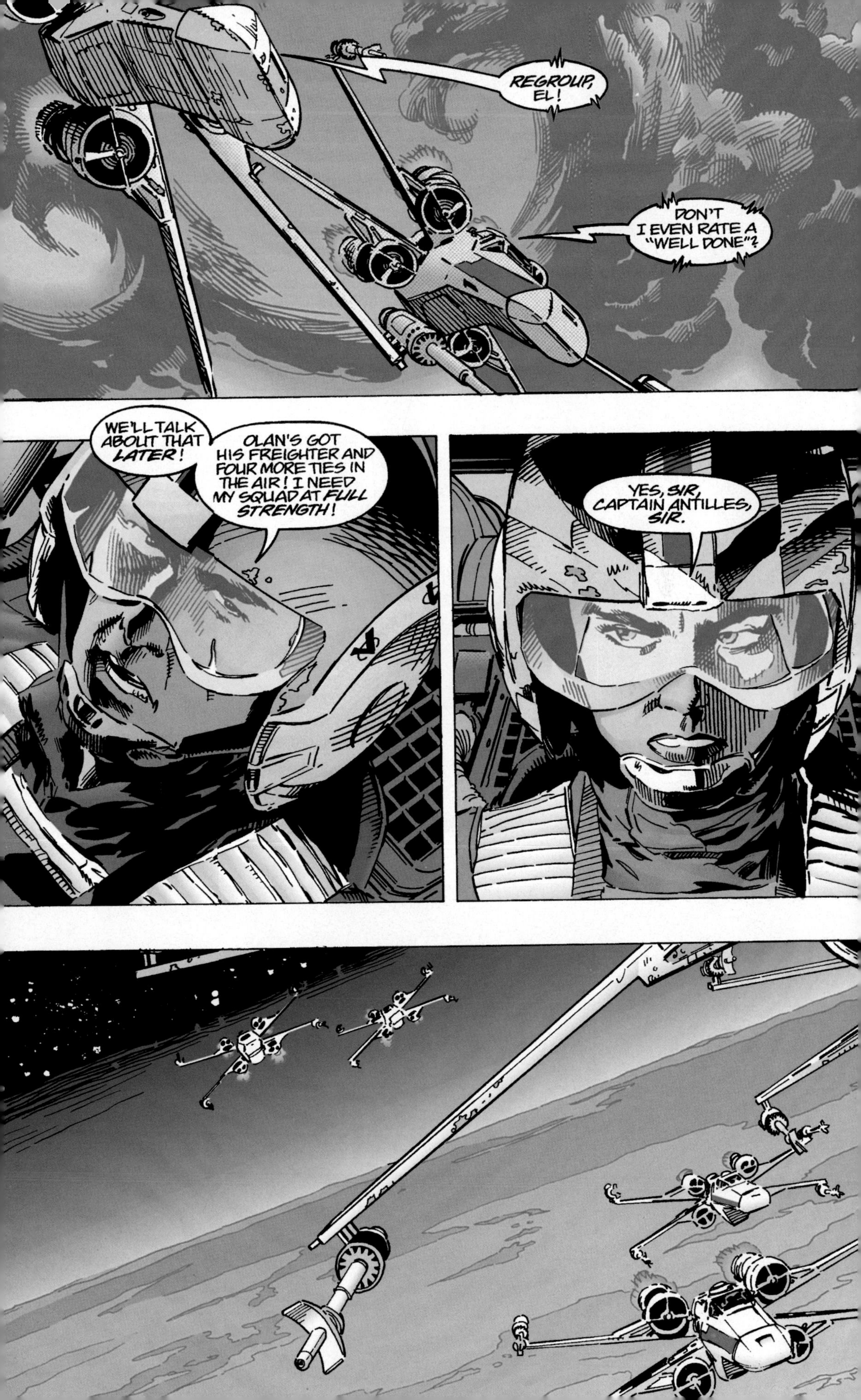
REGROUP, EL!
DON'T I EVEN RATE A "WELL DONE"?
WE'LL TALK ABOUT THAT LATER!
OLAN'S GOT HIS FREIGHTER AND FOUR MORE TIES IN THE AIR! I NEED MY SQUAD AT FULL STRENGTH!
YES, SIR, CAPTAIN ANTILLES, SIR.

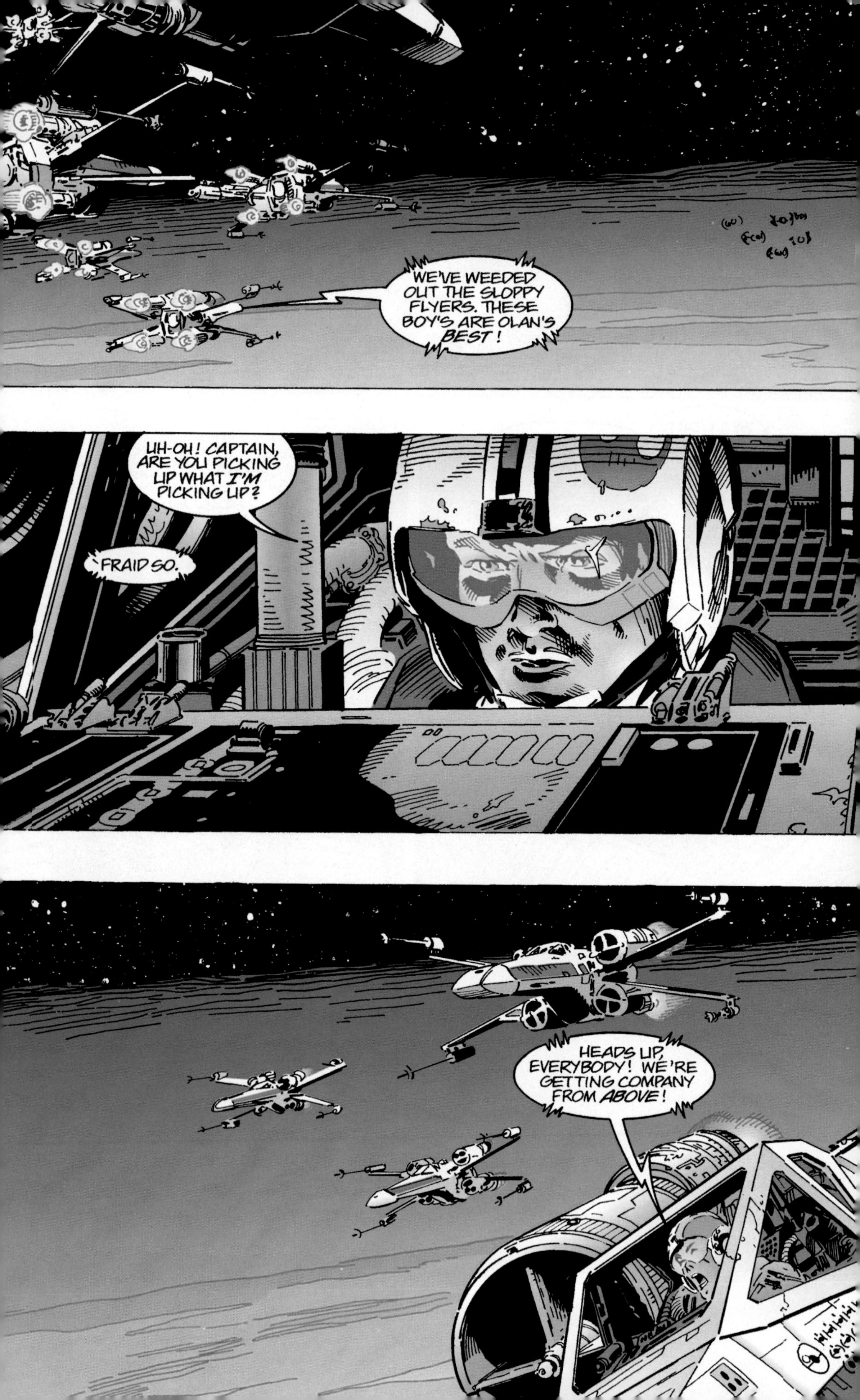
WE'VE WEEDED OUT THE SLOPPY FLYERS. THESE BOY'S ARE OLAN'S BEST!
UH-OH! CAPTAIN, ARE YOU PICKING UP WHAT I'M PICKING UP?
'FRAID SO.
HEADS UP, EVERYBODY! WE'RE GETTING COMPANY FROM ABOVE!

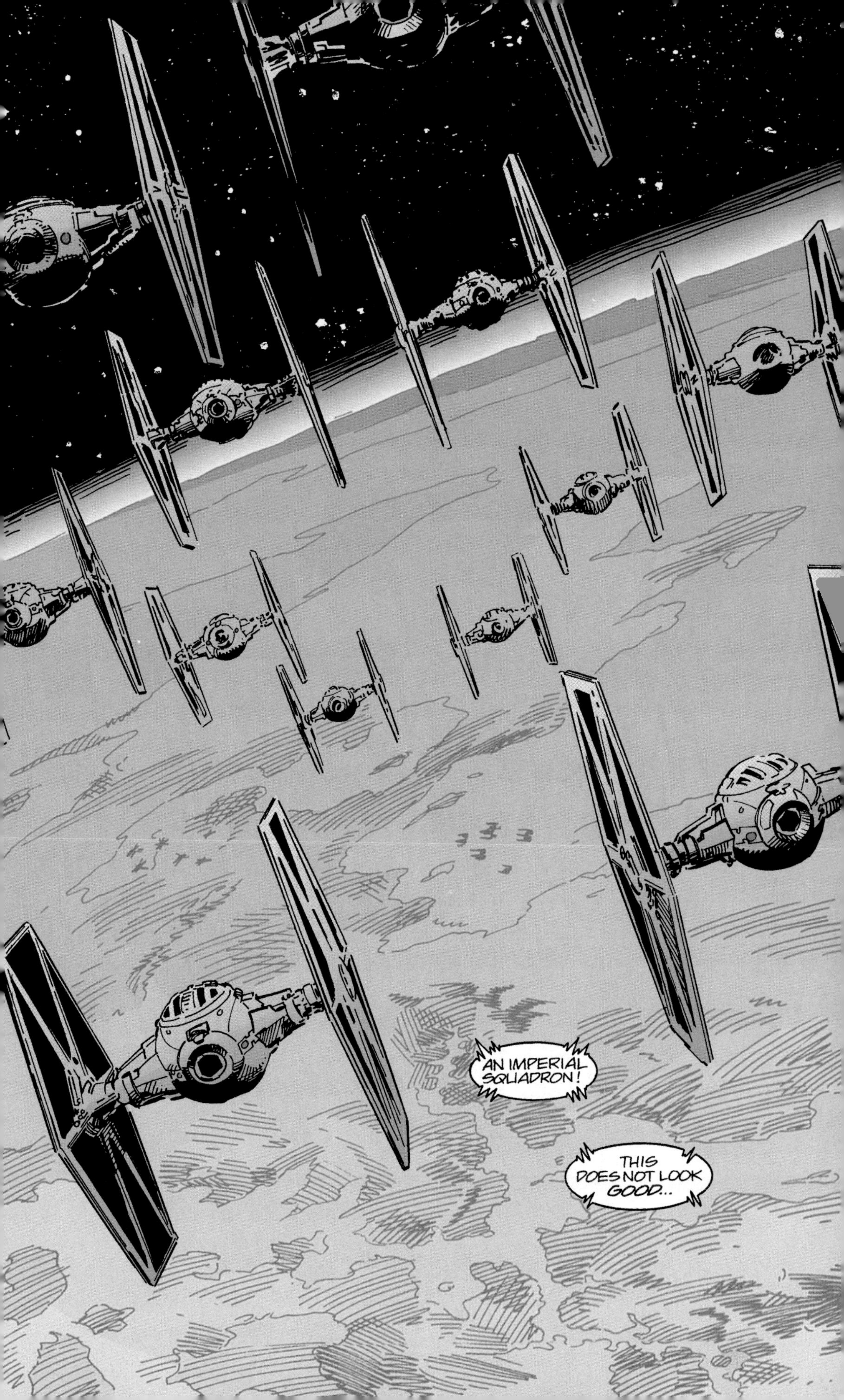
AN IMPERIAL SQUADRON!
THIS DOES NOT LOOK GOOD...

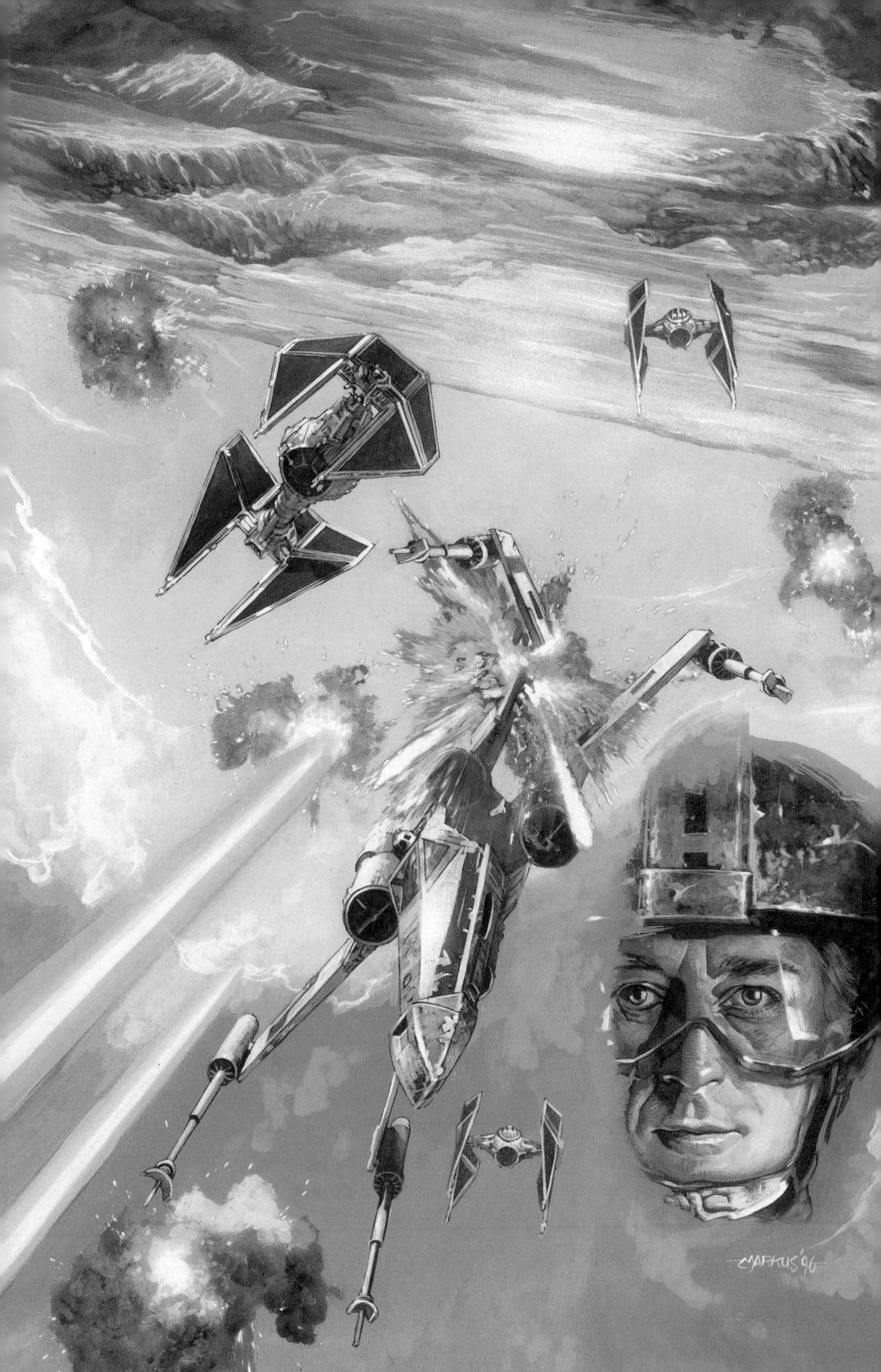

***STAR WARS: X-WING ROGUE SQUADRON #11* — "BATTLEGROUND: TATOOINE, CHAPTER 3"**

PLOTTER: MICHAEL A. STACKPOLE • SCRIPTER: JAN STRNAD • PENCILER: JOHN NADEAU • INKER: JORDI ENSIGN
COLORIST: DAVE NESTELLE • LETTERER: VICKIE WILLIAMS • EDITOR: PEET JANES • COVER ARTIST: MARK HARRISON

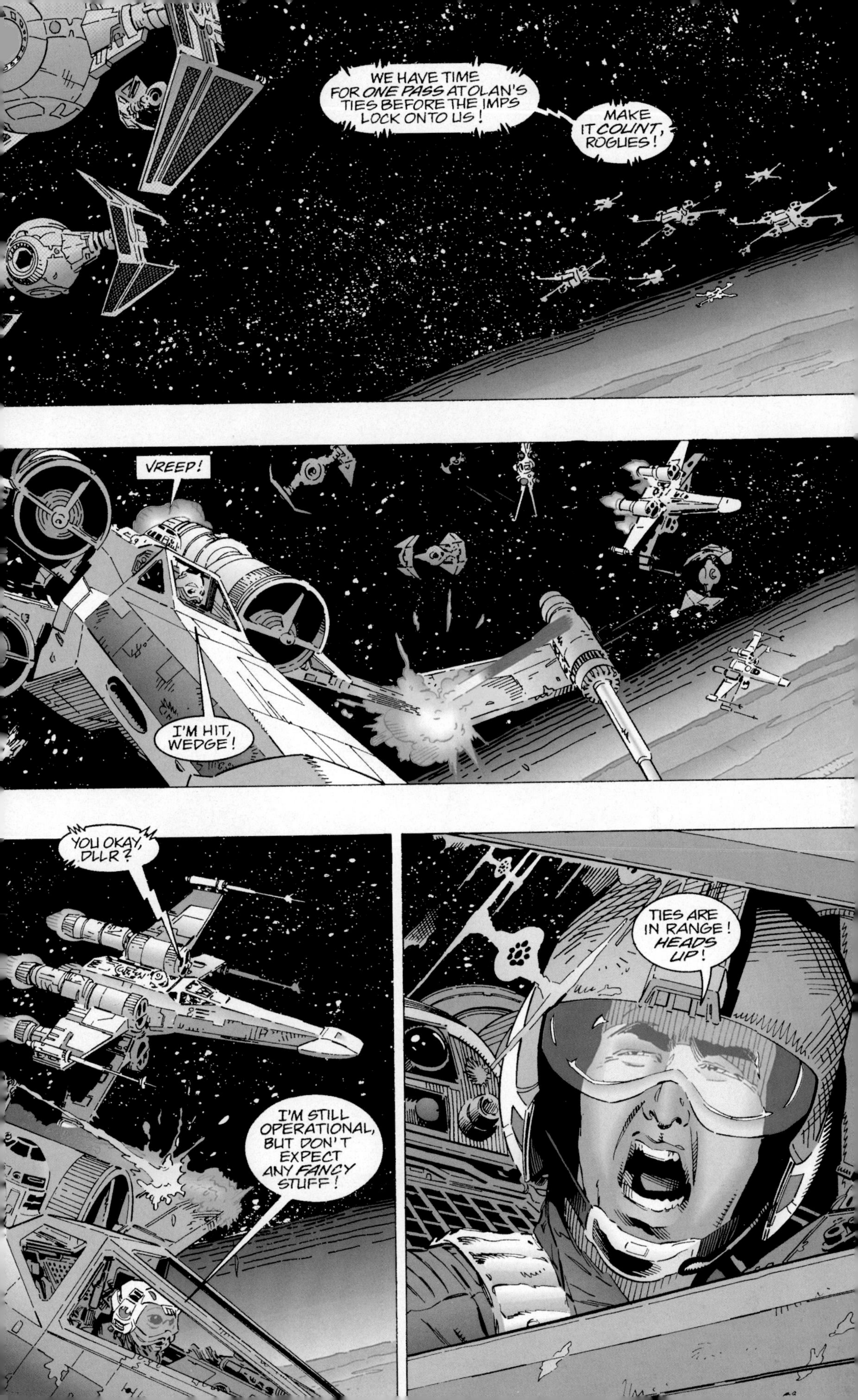
WE HAVE TIME FOR ONE PASS AT OLAN'S TIES BEFORE THE IMPS LOCK ONTO US!
MAKE IT COUNT, ROGUES!
VREEP!
I'M HIT, WEDGE!
YOU OKAY, DLLR?
I'M STILL OPERATIONAL, BUT DON'T EXPECT ANY FANCY STUFF!
TIES ARE IN RANGE! HEADS UP!

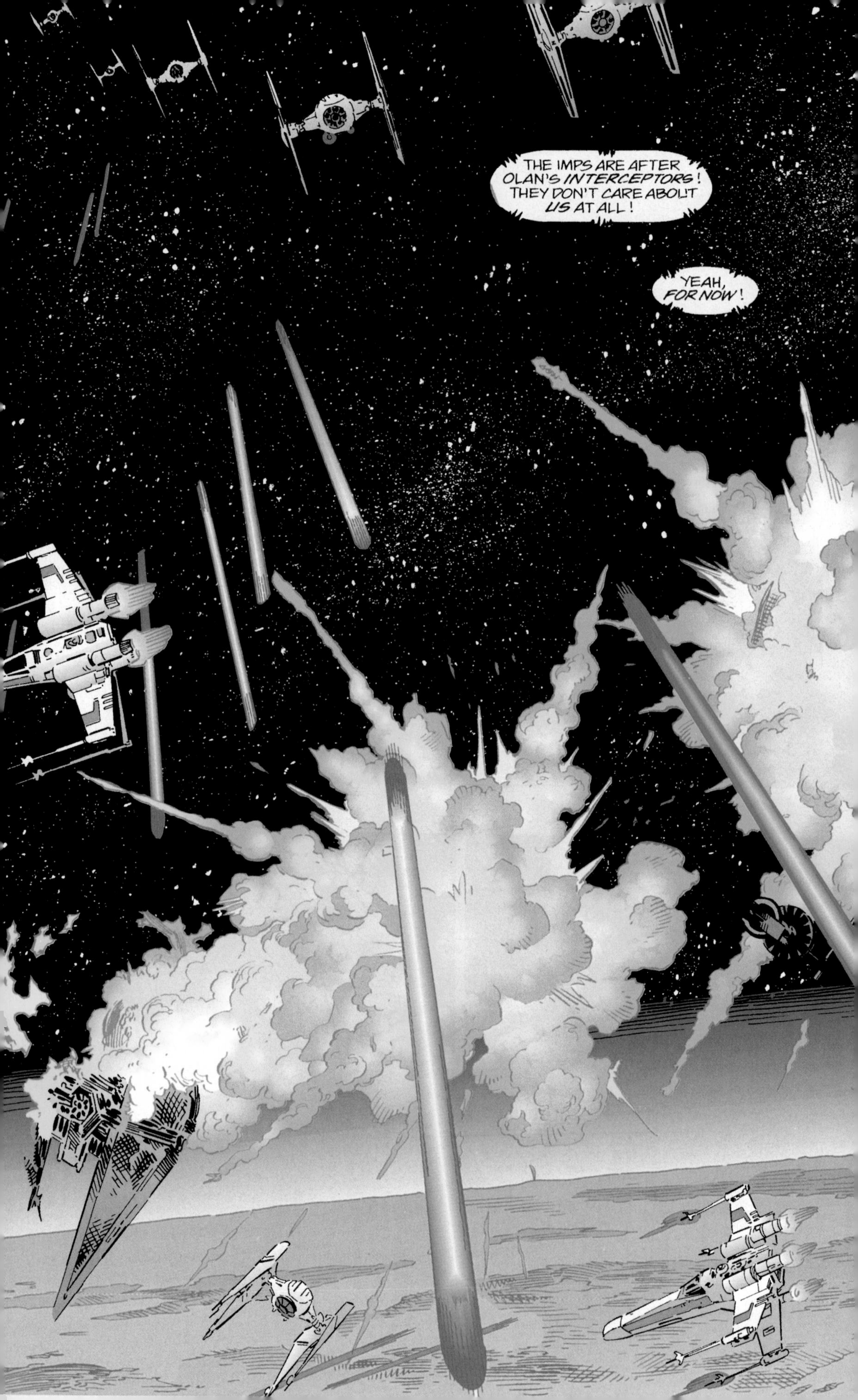
THE IMPS ARE AFTER OLAN'S INTERCEPTORS! THEY DON'T CARE ABOUT US AT ALL!
YEAH, FOR NOW!

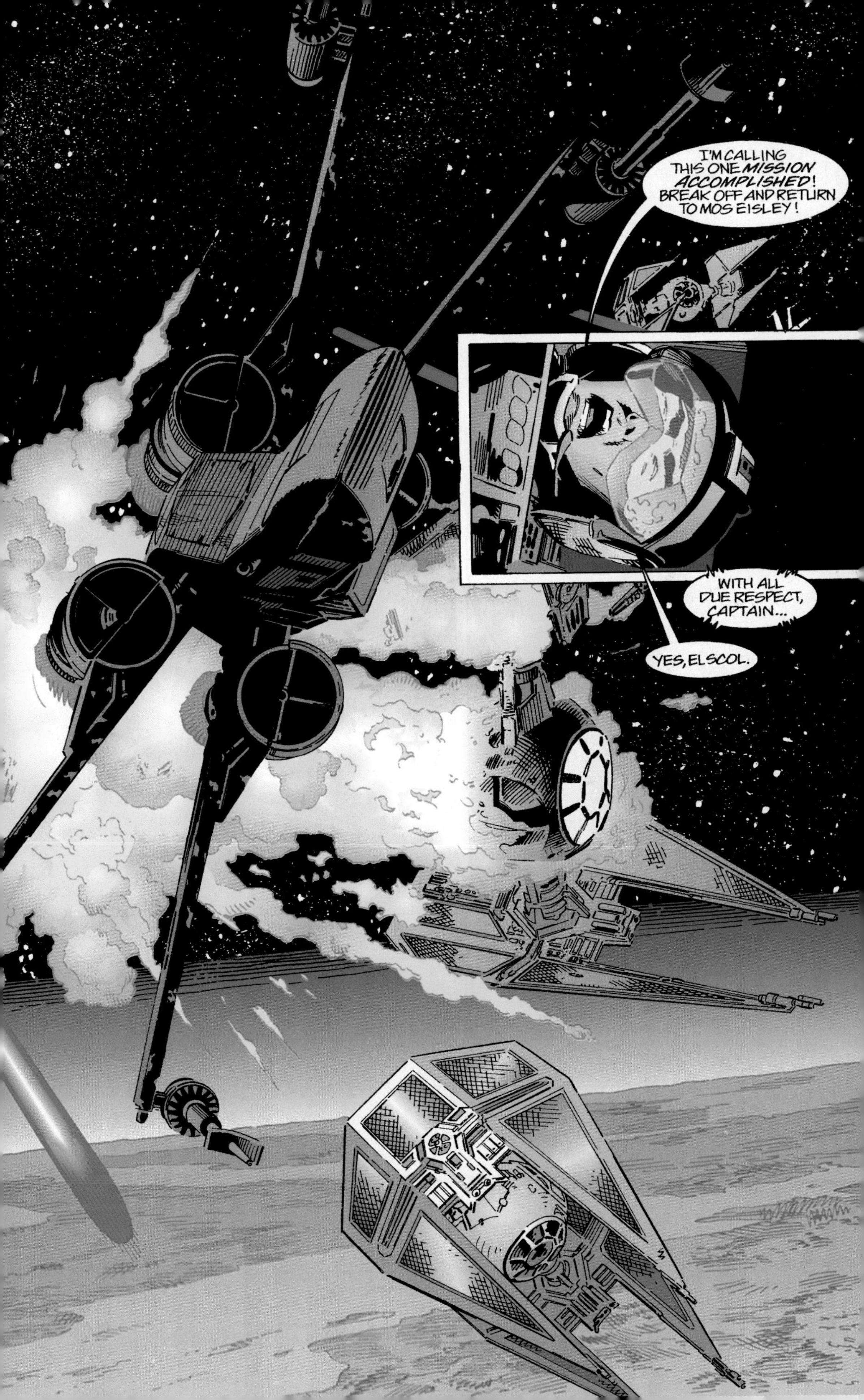
I'M CALLING THIS ONE MISSION ACCOMPLISHED! BREAK OFF AND RETURN TO MOS EISLEY!
WITH ALL DUE RESPECT, CAPTAIN...
YES, ELSCOL.

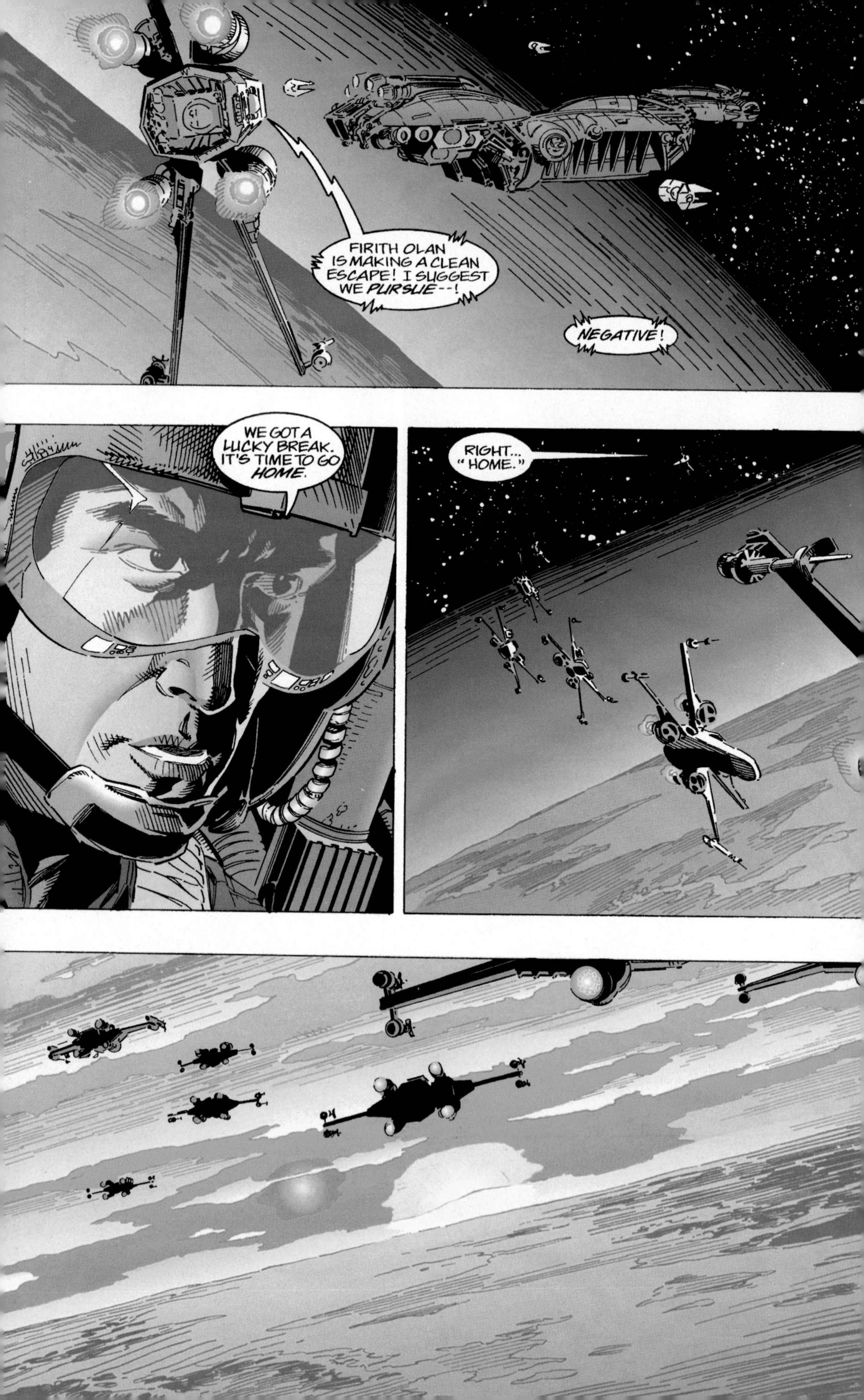
FIRITH OLAN IS MAKING A CLEAN ESCAPE! I SUGGEST WE PURSUE--!
NEGATIVE!
WE GOT A LUCKY BREAK. IT'S TIME TO GO HOME.
RIGHT... "HOME."

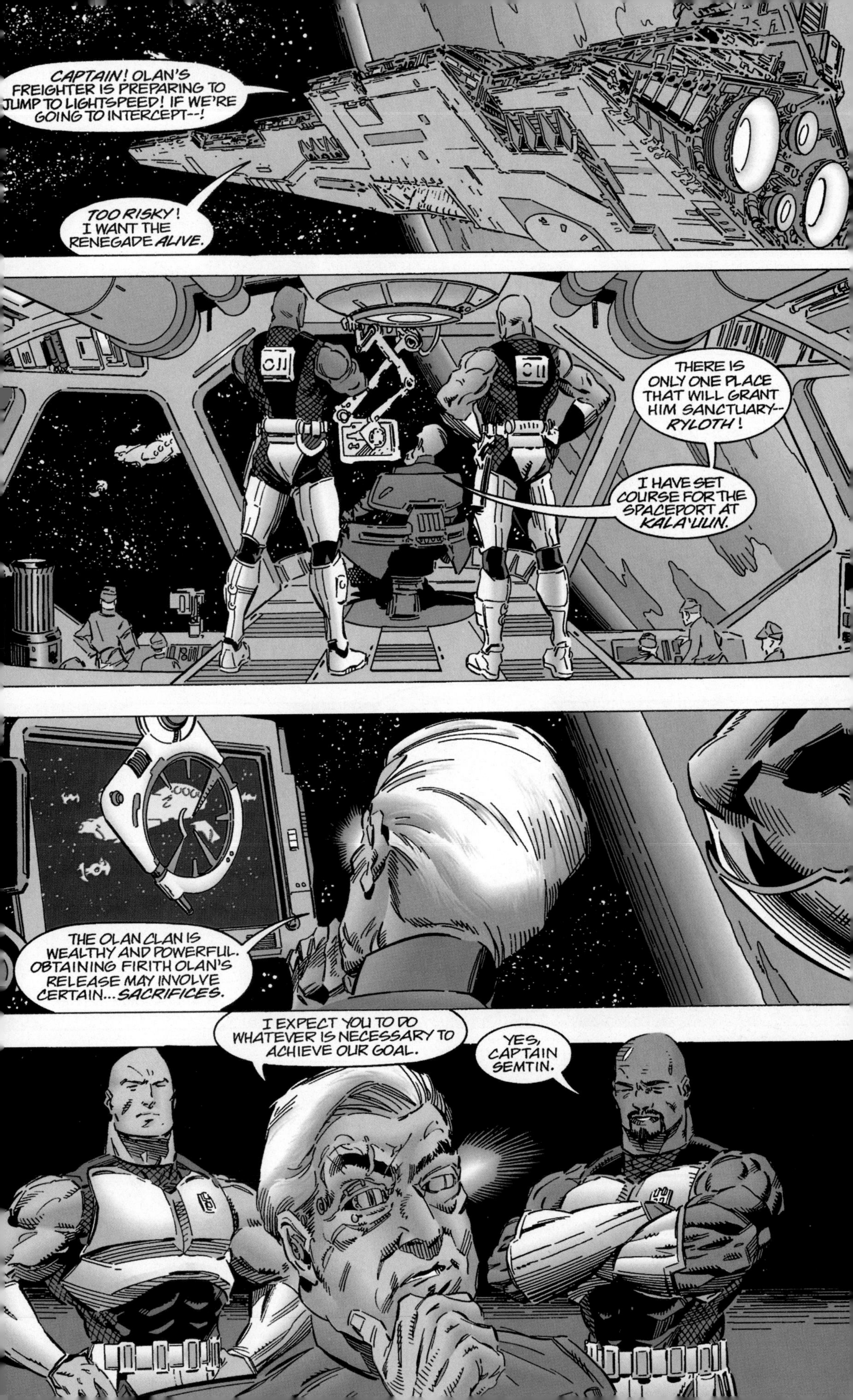
CAPTAIN! OLAN'S FREIGHTER IS PREPARING TO JUMP TO LIGHTSPEED! IF WE'RE GOING TO INTERCEPT--!
TOO RISKY! I WANT THE RENEGADE *ALIVE*.
THERE IS ONLY ONE PLACE THAT WILL GRANT HIM SANCTUARY-- *RYLOTH*!
I HAVE SET COURSE FOR THE SPACEPORT AT *KALA'UUN*.
THE OLAN CLAN IS WEALTHY AND POWERFUL. OBTAINING FIRITH OLAN'S RELEASE MAY INVOLVE CERTAIN... *SACRIFICES*.
I EXPECT YOU TO DO WHATEVER IS NECESSARY TO ACHIEVE OUR GOAL.
YES, CAPTAIN SEMTIN.

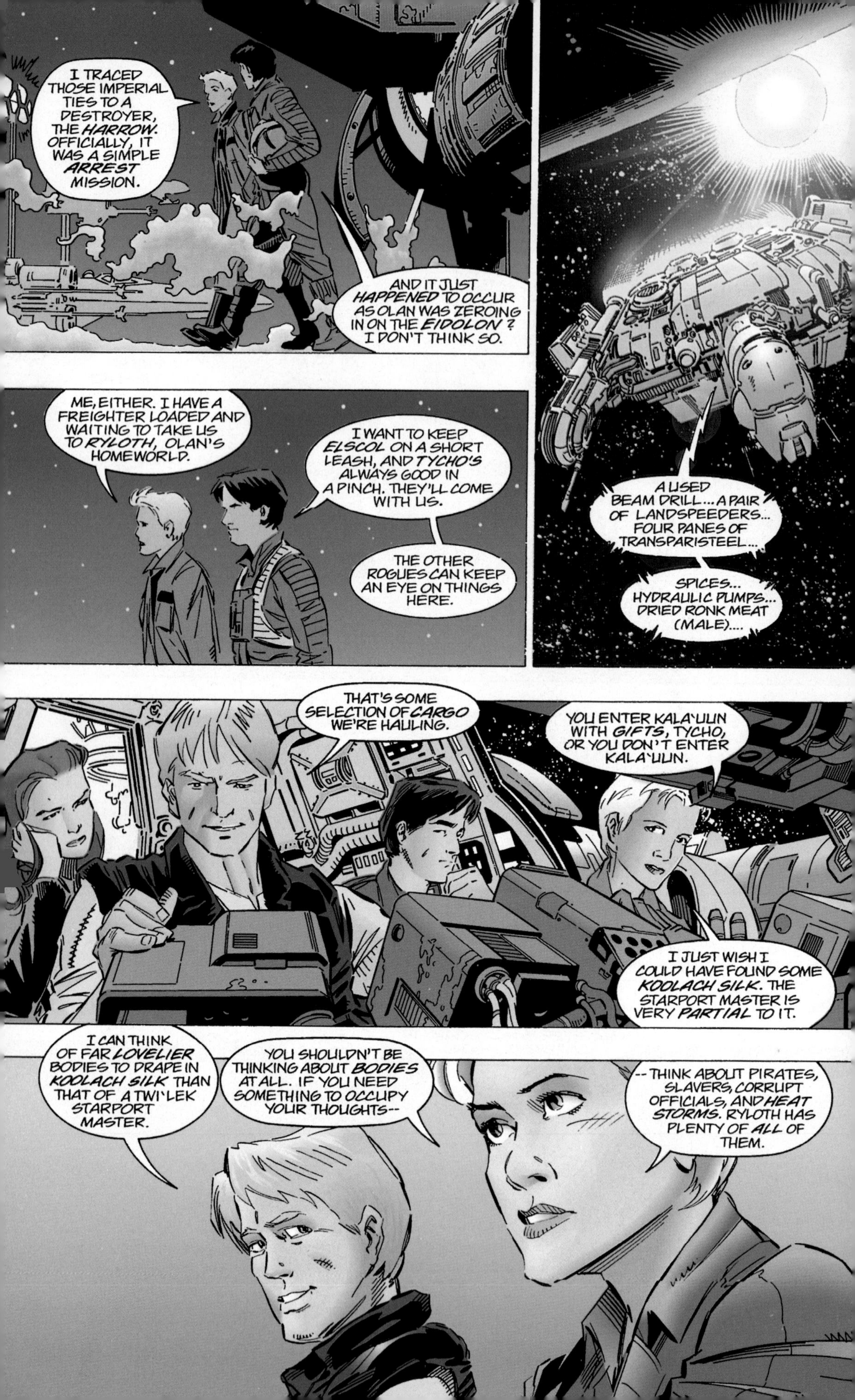
I TRACED THOSE IMPERIAL TIES TO A DESTROYER, THE HARROW. OFFICIALLY, IT WAS A SIMPLE ARREST MISSION.
AND IT JUST HAPPENED TO OCCUR AS OLAN WAS ZEROING IN ON THE EIDOLON? I DON'T THINK SO.
ME, EITHER. I HAVE A FREIGHTER LOADED AND WAITING TO TAKE US TO RYLOTH, OLAN'S HOMEWORLD.
I WANT TO KEEP ELSCOL ON A SHORT LEASH, AND TYCHO'S ALWAYS GOOD IN A PINCH. THEY'LL COME WITH US.
THE OTHER ROGUES CAN KEEP AN EYE ON THINGS HERE.
A USED BEAM DRILL... A PAIR OF LANDSPEEDERS... FOUR PANES OF TRANSPARISTEEL...
SPICES... HYDRAULIC PUMPS... DRIED RONK MEAT (MALE)....
THAT'S SOME SELECTION OF CARGO WE'RE HAULING.
YOU ENTER KALA'UUN WITH GIFTS, TYCHO, OR YOU DON'T ENTER KALA'UUN.
I JUST WISH I COULD HAVE FOUND SOME KOOLACH SILK. THE STARPORT MASTER IS VERY PARTIAL TO IT.
I CAN THINK OF FAR LOVELIER BODIES TO DRAPE IN KOOLACH SILK THAN THAT OF A TWI'LEK STARPORT MASTER.
YOU SHOULDN'T BE THINKING ABOUT BODIES AT ALL. IF YOU NEED SOMETHING TO OCCUPY YOUR THOUGHTS--
--THINK ABOUT PIRATES, SLAVERS, CORRUPT OFFICIALS, AND HEAT STORMS. RYLOTH HAS PLENTY OF ALL OF THEM.

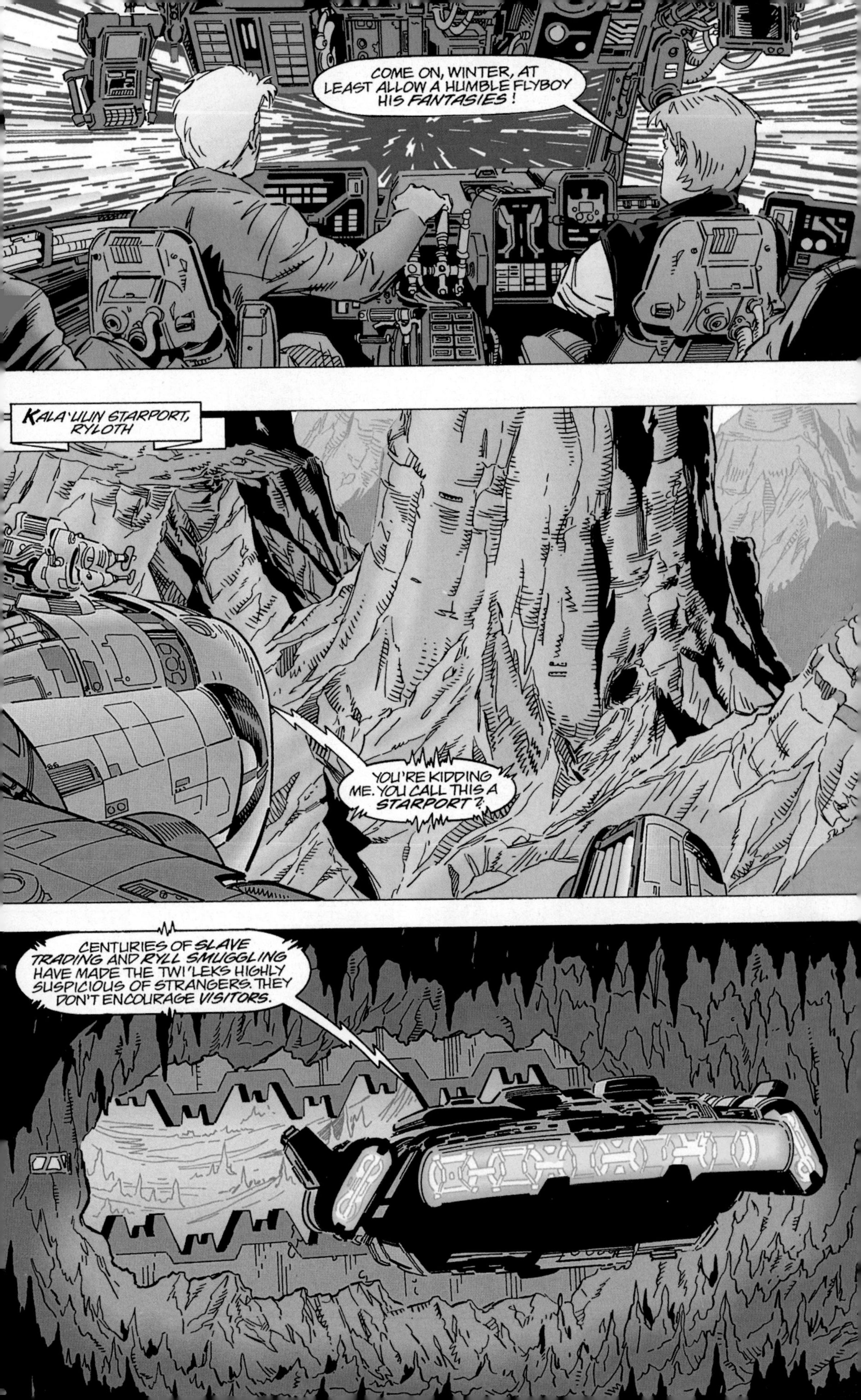
COME ON, WINTER, AT LEAST ALLOW A HUMBLE FLYBOY HIS FANTASIES!
KALA'ULIN STARPORT, RYLOTH
YOU'RE KIDDING ME. YOU CALL THIS A STARPORT?!
CENTURIES OF SLAVE TRADING AND RYLL SMUGGLING HAVE MADE THE TWI'LEKS HIGHLY SUSPICIOUS OF STRANGERS. THEY DON'T ENCOURAGE VISITORS.

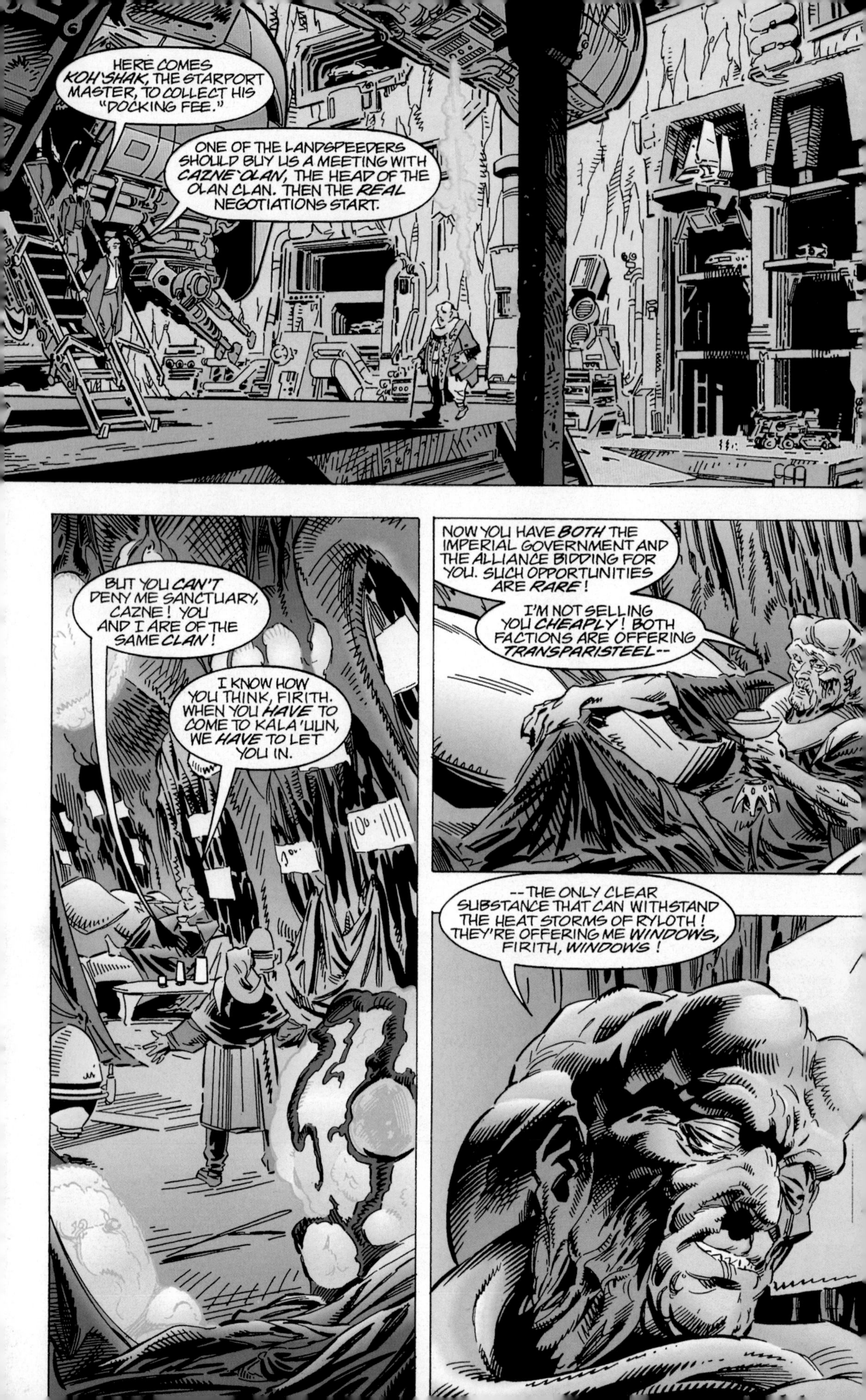
HERE COMES KOH'SHAK, THE STARPORT MASTER, TO COLLECT HIS "DOCKING FEE."
ONE OF THE LANDSPEEDERS SHOULD BUY US A MEETING WITH CAZNE'OLAN, THE HEAD OF THE OLAN CLAN. THEN THE REAL NEGOTIATIONS START.
BUT YOU CAN'T DENY ME SANCTUARY, CAZNE! YOU AND I ARE OF THE SAME CLAN!
I KNOW HOW YOU THINK, FIRITH. WHEN YOU HAVE TO COME TO KALA'UUN, WE HAVE TO LET YOU IN.
NOW YOU HAVE BOTH THE IMPERIAL GOVERNMENT AND THE ALLIANCE BIDDING FOR YOU. SUCH OPPORTUNITIES ARE RARE!
I'M NOT SELLING YOU CHEAPLY! BOTH FACTIONS ARE OFFERING TRANSPARISTEEL--
--THE ONLY CLEAR SUBSTANCE THAT CAN WITHSTAND THE HEAT STORMS OF RYLOTH! THEY'RE OFFERING ME WINDOWS, FIRITH, WINDOWS!

REFUSE THEM, AND I'LL SEND YOU ENOUGH TRANSPARISTEEL TO BUILD A *PALACE*!

AN EMPTY PROMISE, AND WE BOTH KNOW IT. *"A GIFT IN HAND"* AND ALL THAT.

NO, YOU'LL BE TURNED OVER TO ONE OR THE OTHER. IF IT'S ANY CONSOLATION, THERE WILL BE SOME *AMUSEMENT* INVOLVED.

" I'VE ORDERED A *CONTEST* WITH *YOU* AS THE PRIZE. TWO MEMBERS OF THE ALLIANCE AGAINST TWO IMPERIAL WARRIORS.

"THE STARPORT MASTER IS PREPARING THE COMBATANTS EVEN AS WE SPEAK."

DID YOU GET A LOOK AT OUR COMPETITION, WEDGE? THOSE GUYS HAVE *SPECIAL FORCES* WRITTEN ALL OVER THEM!

"THEY'RE *BIGGER* THAN US, *STRONGER* THAN US, AND *MEANER* THAN US."

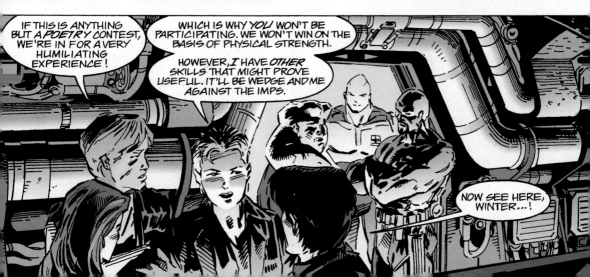

IF THIS IS ANYTHING BUT *A POETRY* CONTEST, WE'RE IN FOR A VERY HUMILIATING EXPERIENCE!

WHICH IS WHY *YOU* WON'T BE PARTICIPATING. WE WON'T WIN ON THE BASIS OF PHYSICAL STRENGTH.

HOWEVER, I HAVE *OTHER* SKILLS THAT MIGHT PROVE USEFUL. IT'LL BE WEDGE AND ME AGAINST THE IMPS.

NOW SEE HERE, WINTER...!

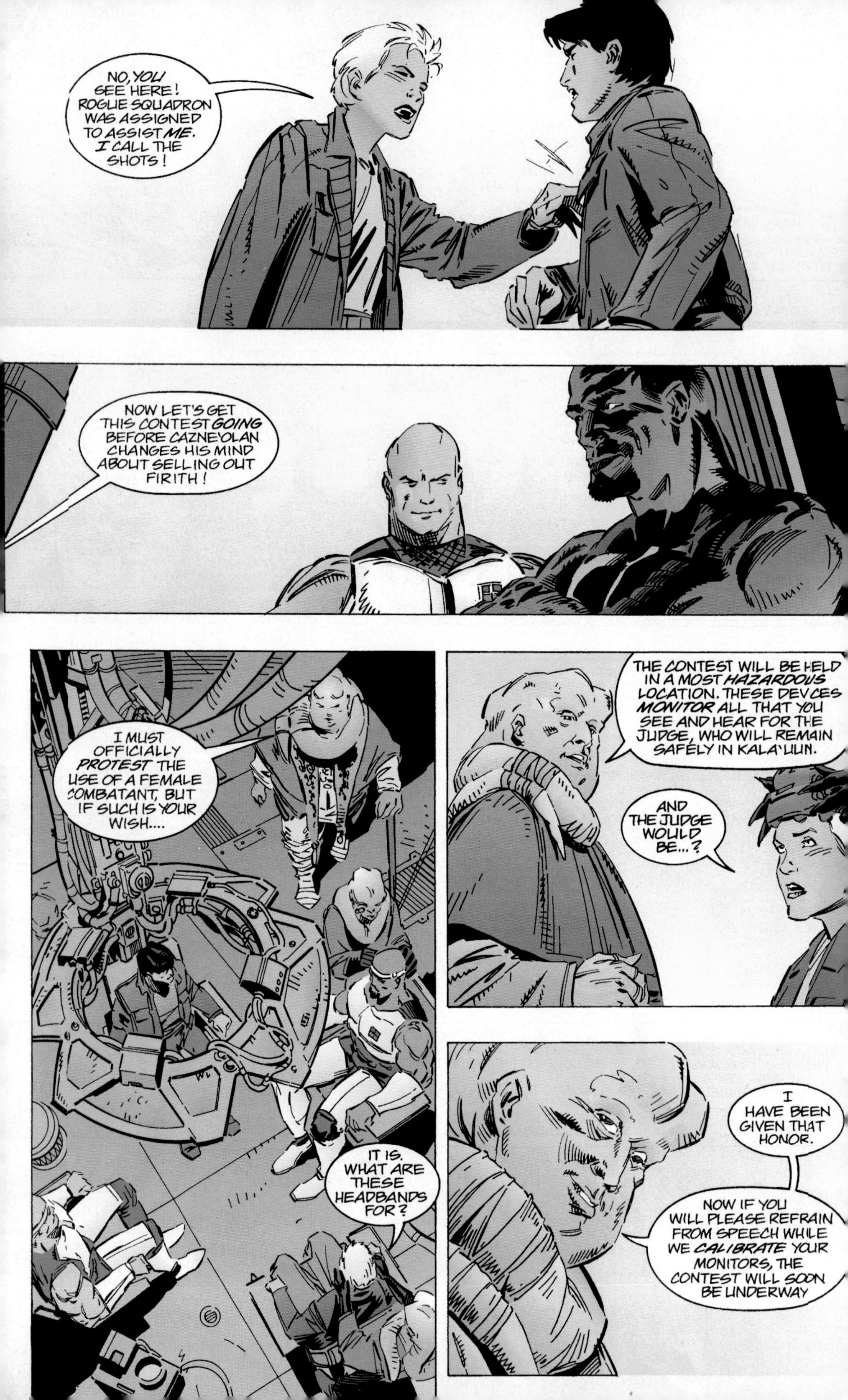
NO, *YOU* SEE HERE! ROGUE SQUADRON WAS ASSIGNED TO ASSIST *ME*. *I* CALL THE SHOTS!
NOW LET'S GET THIS CONTEST *GOING* BEFORE CAZNE'OLAN CHANGES HIS MIND ABOUT SELLING OUT FIRITH!
I MUST OFFICIALLY *PROTEST* THE USE OF A FEMALE COMBATANT, BUT IF SUCH IS YOUR WISH....
IT IS. WHAT ARE THESE HEADBANDS FOR?
THE CONTEST WILL BE HELD IN A MOST *HAZARDOUS* LOCATION. THESE DEVCES *MONITOR* ALL THAT YOU SEE AND HEAR FOR THE JUDGE, WHO WILL REMAIN SAFELY IN KALA'UUN.
AND THE JUDGE WOULD BE...?
I HAVE BEEN GIVEN THAT HONOR.
NOW IF YOU WILL PLEASE REFRAIN FROM SPEECH WHILE WE *CALIBRATE* YOUR MONITORS, THE CONTEST WILL SOON BE UNDERWAY

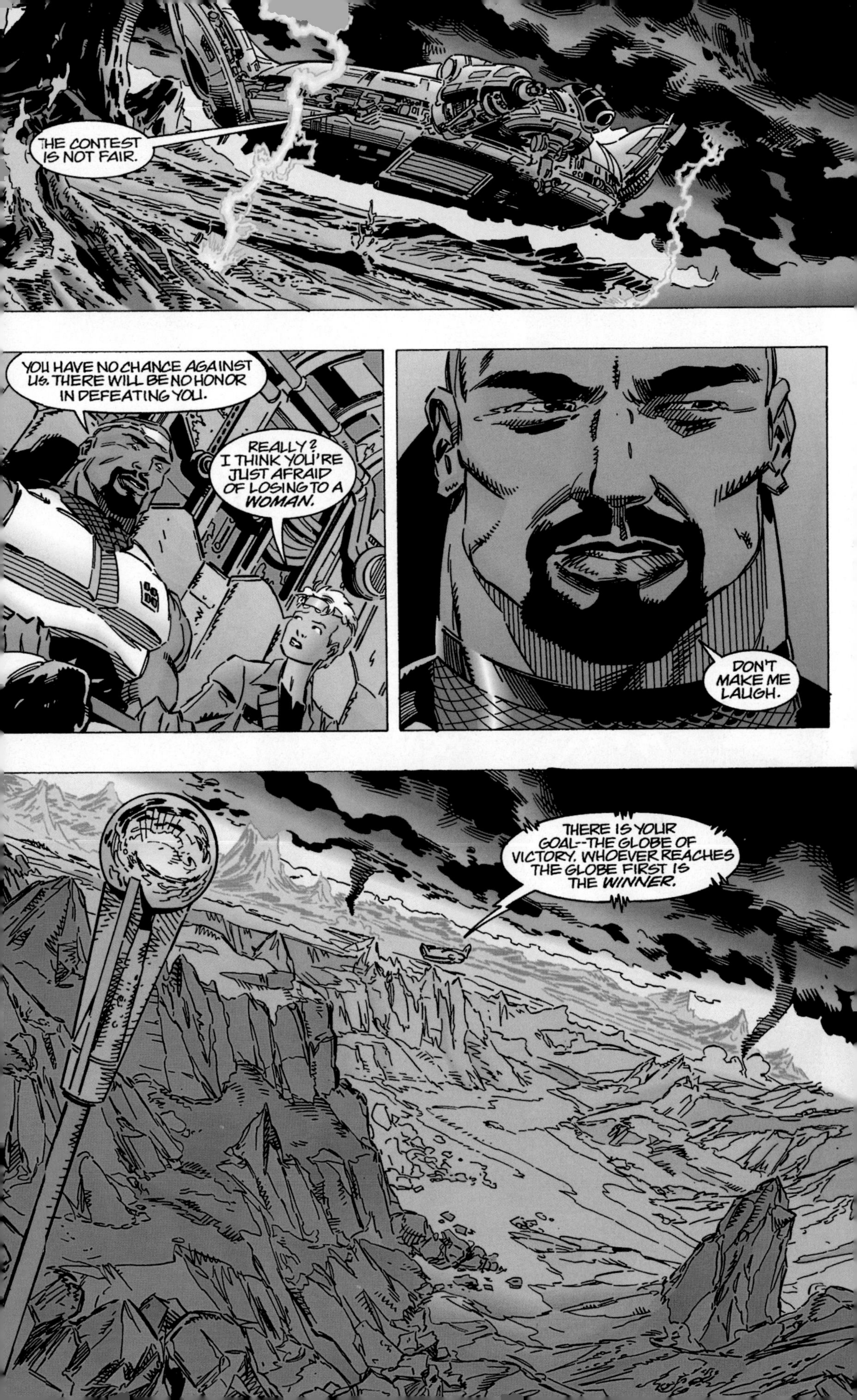
THE CONTEST IS NOT FAIR.
YOU HAVE NO CHANCE AGAINST US. THERE WILL BE NO HONOR IN DEFEATING YOU.
REALLY? I THINK YOU'RE JUST AFRAID OF LOSING TO A *WOMAN.*
DON'T MAKE ME LAUGH.
THERE IS YOUR GOAL--THE GLOBE OF VICTORY. WHOEVER REACHES THE GLOBE FIRST IS THE *WINNER.*

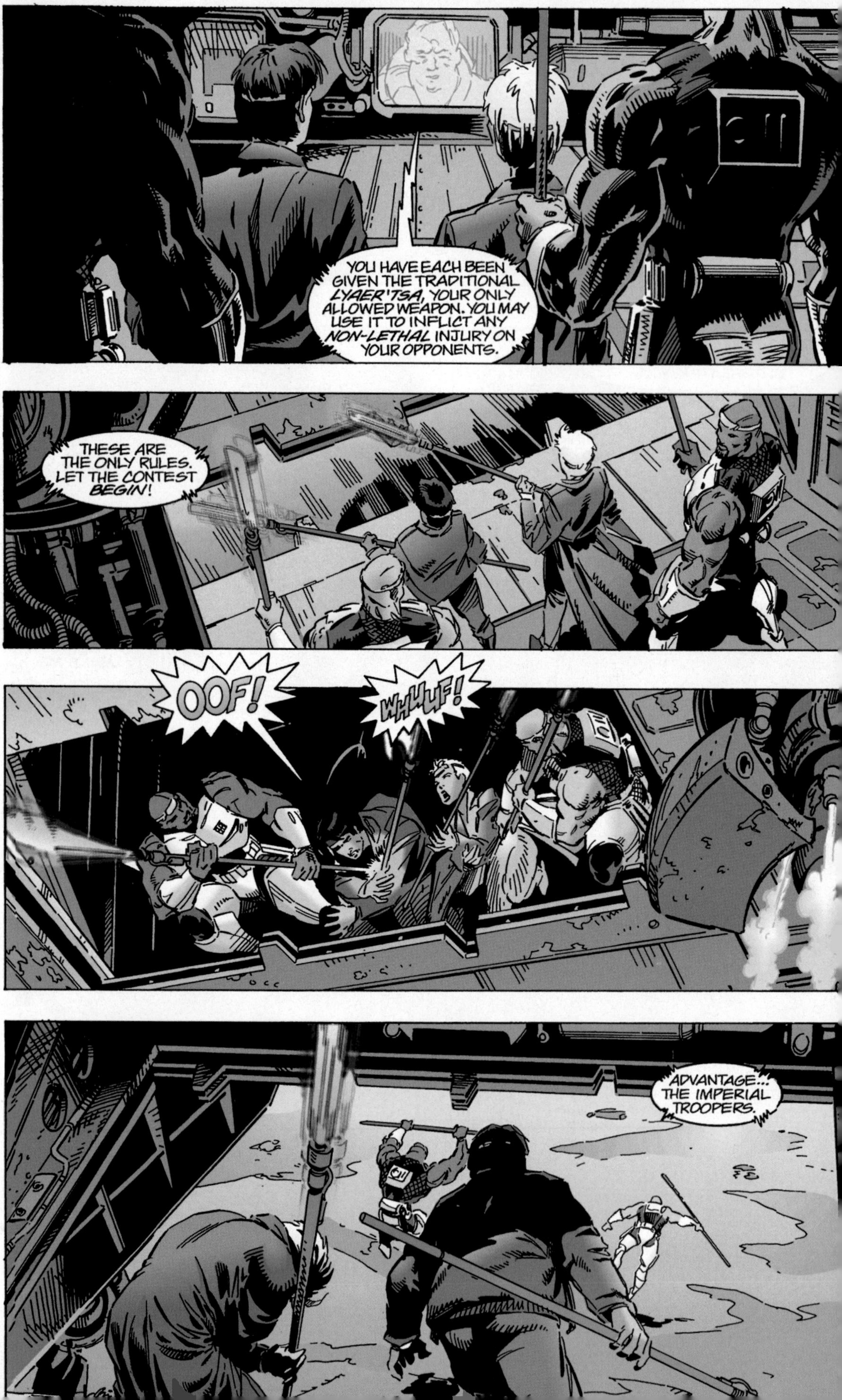
YOU HAVE EACH BEEN GIVEN THE TRADITIONAL *LYAER'TSA*, YOUR ONLY ALLOWED WEAPON. YOU MAY USE IT TO INFLICT ANY *NON-LETHAL* INJURY ON YOUR OPPONENTS.
THESE ARE THE ONLY RULES. LET THE CONTEST *BEGIN*!
OOF!
WHHUF!
ADVANTAGE... THE IMPERIAL TROOPERS.

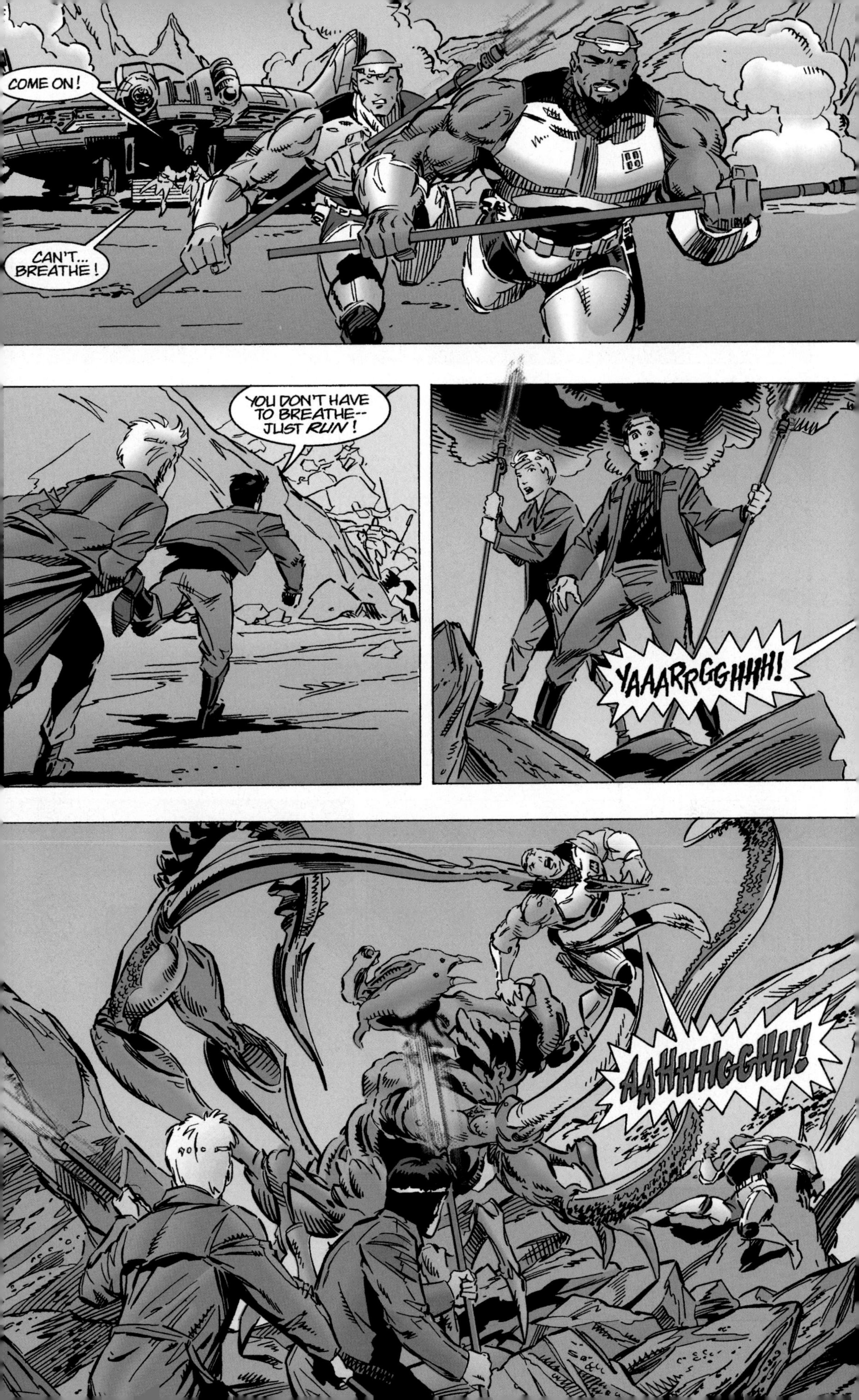
COME ON!
CAN'T... BREATHE!
YOU DON'T HAVE TO BREATHE-- JUST RUN!
YAAARRGGHHH!
AAHHHGGHH!

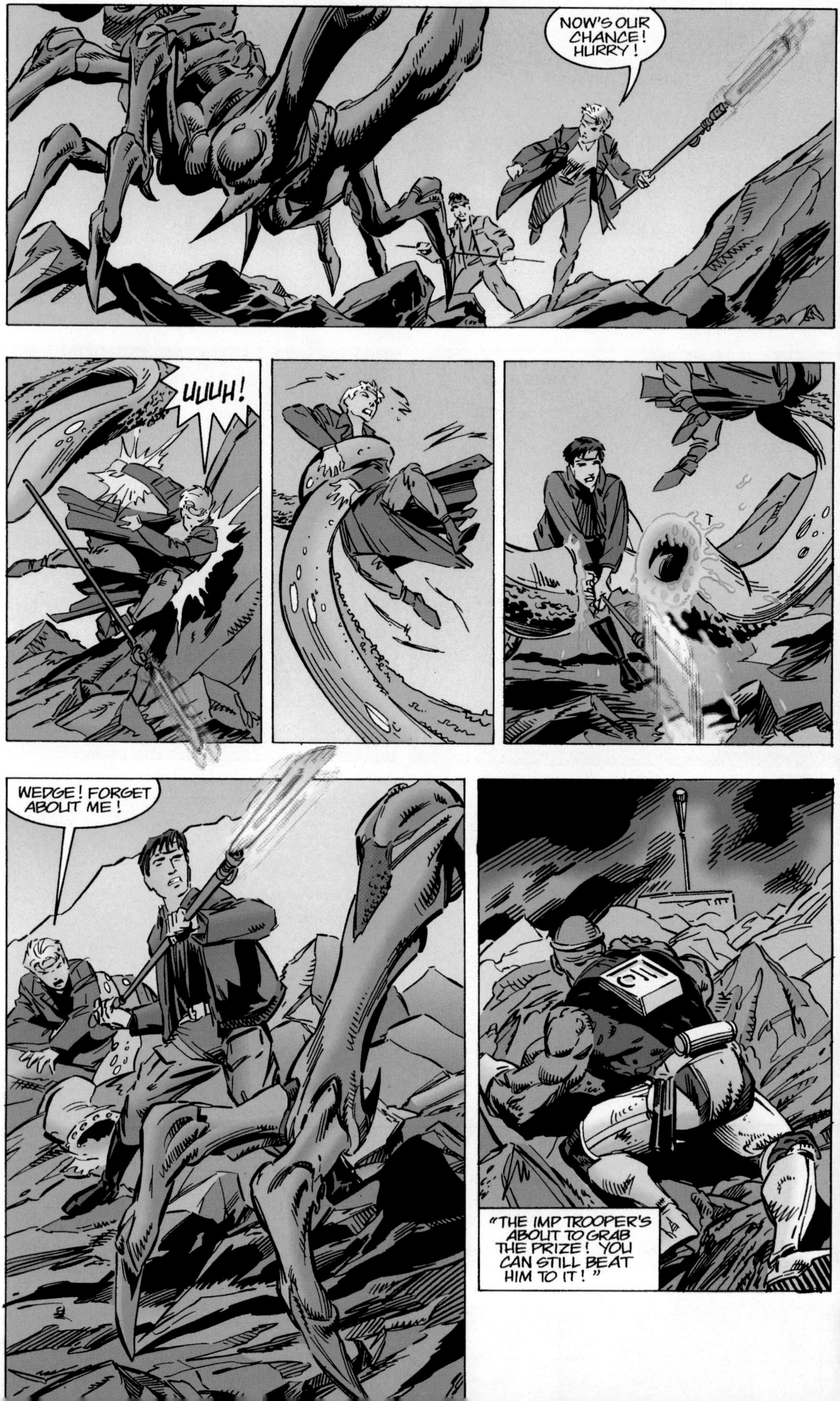
NOW'S OUR CHANCE! HURRY!
UUUH!
WEDGE! FORGET ABOUT ME!
"THE IMP TROOPER'S ABOUT TO GRAB THE PRIZE! YOU CAN STILL BEAT HIM TO IT!"

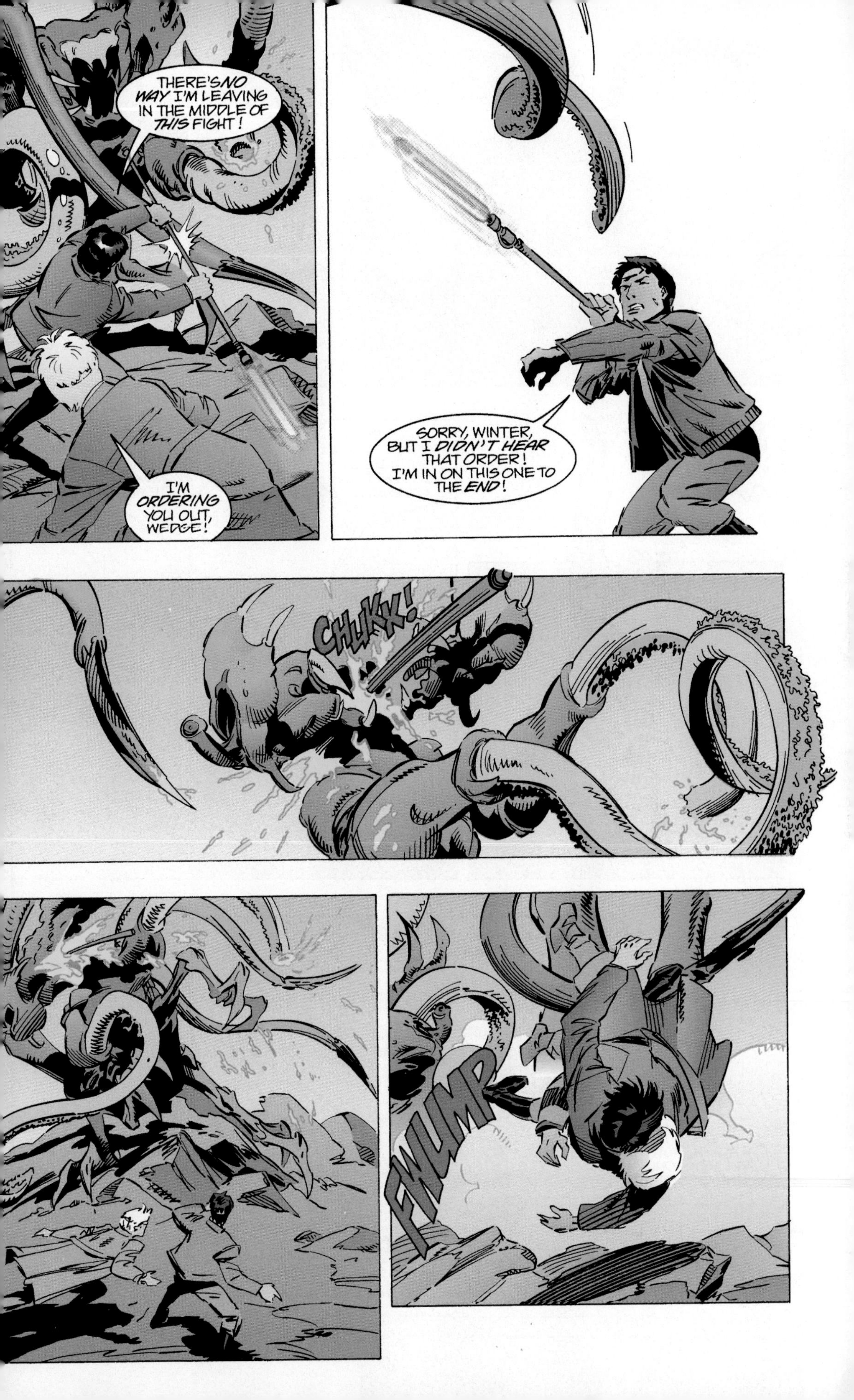
THERE'S NO WAY I'M LEAVING IN THE MIDDLE OF THIS FIGHT!
I'M ORDERING YOU OUT, WEDGE!
SORRY, WINTER, BUT I DIDN'T HEAR THAT ORDER! I'M IN ON THIS ONE TO THE END!
CHUKK!
CHUMP

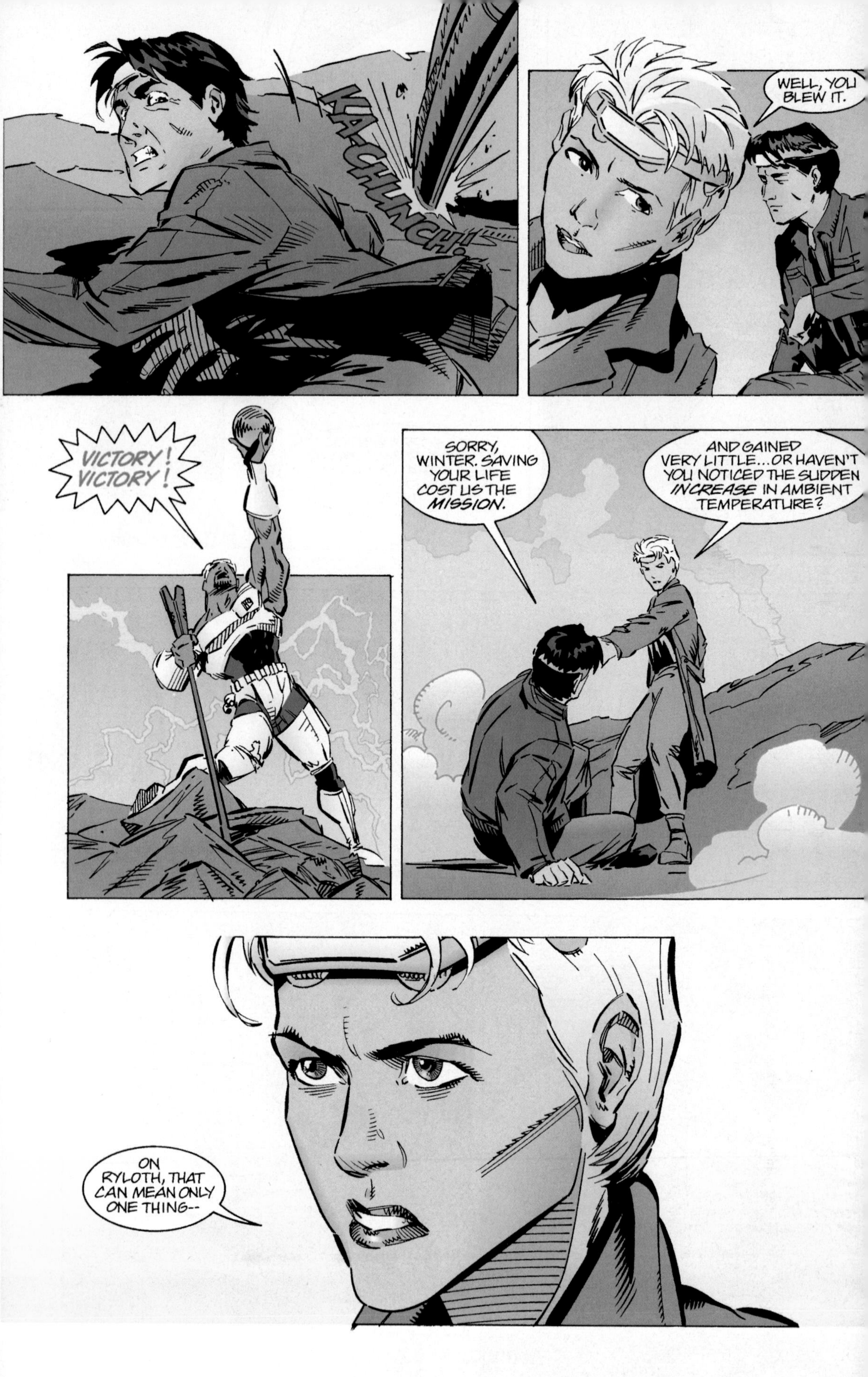
KA-CHUNCH!
WELL, YOU BLEW IT.
VICTORY! VICTORY!
SORRY, WINTER. SAVING YOUR LIFE COST US THE MISSION.
AND GAINED VERY LITTLE... OR HAVEN'T YOU NOTICED THE SUDDEN INCREASE IN AMBIENT TEMPERATURE?
ON RYLOTH, THAT CAN MEAN ONLY ONE THING--

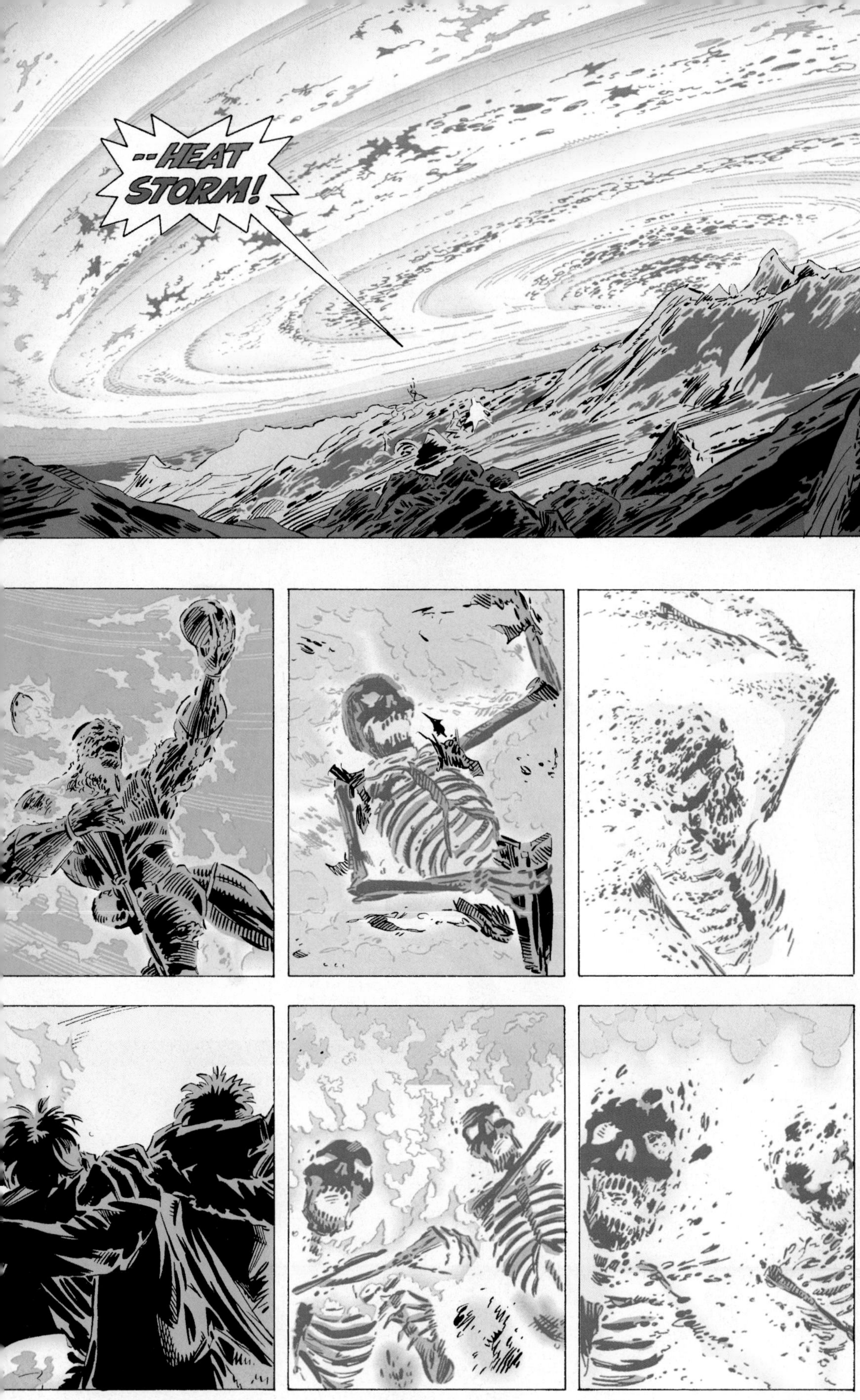
--HEAT STORM!

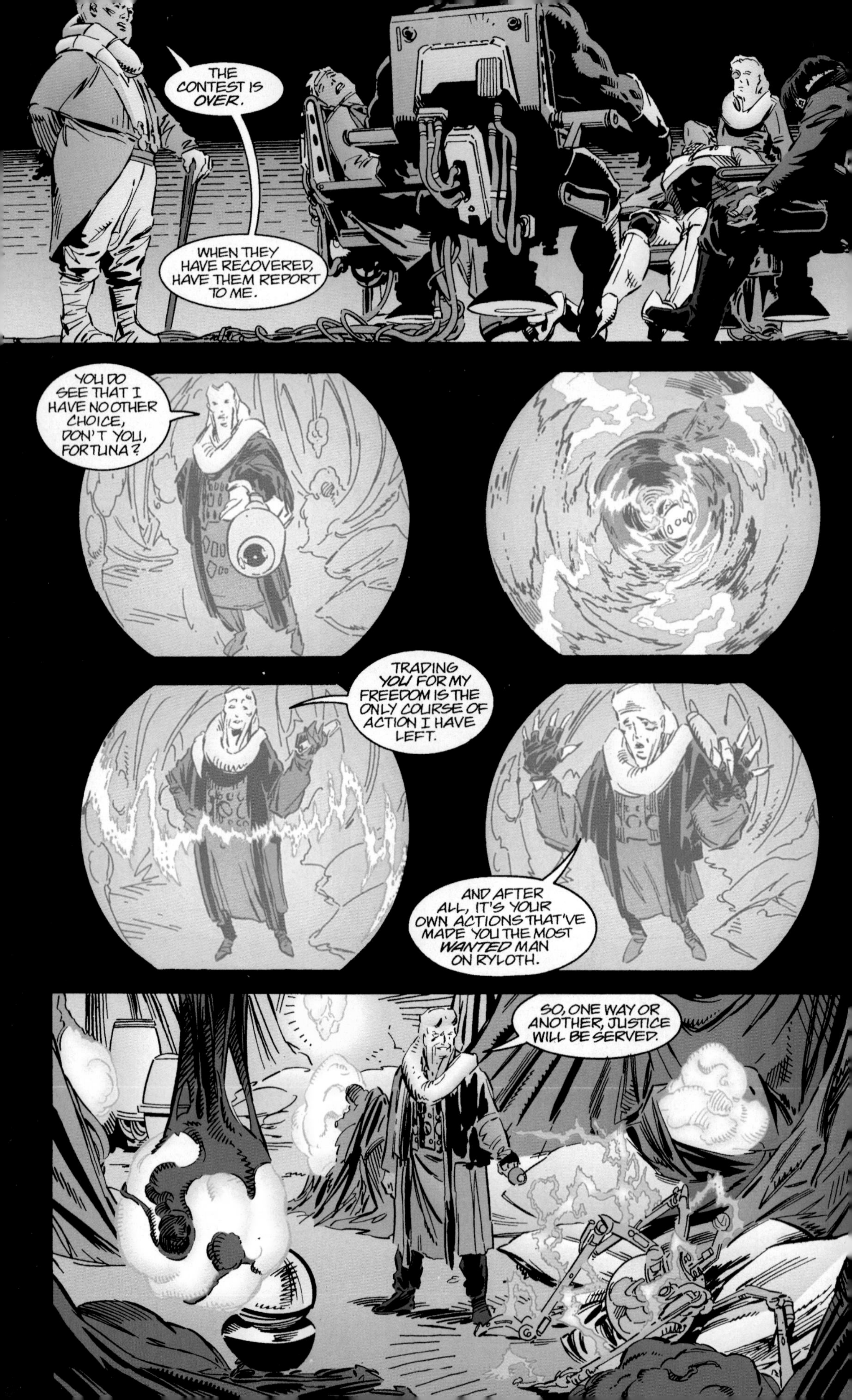
THE CONTEST IS OVER.
WHEN THEY HAVE RECOVERED, HAVE THEM REPORT TO ME.
YOU DO SEE THAT I HAVE NO OTHER CHOICE, DON'T YOU, FORTUNA?
TRADING YOU FOR MY FREEDOM IS THE ONLY COURSE OF ACTION I HAVE LEFT.
AND AFTER ALL, IT'S YOUR OWN ACTIONS THAT'VE MADE YOU THE MOST WANTED MAN ON RYLOTH.
SO, ONE WAY OR ANOTHER, JUSTICE WILL BE SERVED.

PERHAPS SUCH DRASTIC MEASURES DO NOT NEED TO BE TAKEN, FIRITH OLAN.

WHAT...?!

I SUGGEST THAT YOU LISTEN VERY CAREFULLY TO THE OFFER I AM ABOUT TO MAKE. YOUR LIFE DEPENDS ON IT.

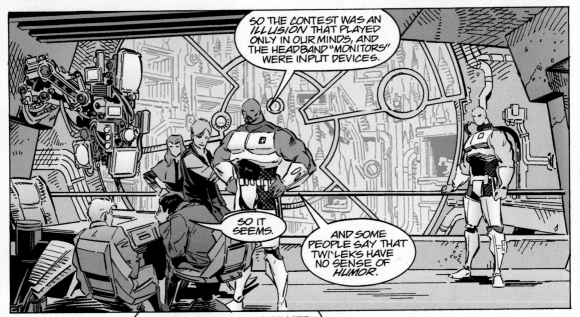

SO THE CONTEST WAS AN *ILLUSION* THAT PLAYED ONLY IN OUR MINDS, AND THE HEADBAND "MONITORS" WERE INPUT DEVICES.

SO IT SEEMS.

AND SOME PEOPLE SAY THAT TWI'LEKS HAVE NO SENSE OF *HUMOR.*

NONETHELESS, YOU CONDUCTED YOURSELF WELL, REBEL. MY NAME IS *SIXTUS QUIN,* AND I SALUTE YOU--

--EVEN THOUGH YOUR DEVOTION TO YOUR COMRADE DID COST YOU THE *CONTEST.*

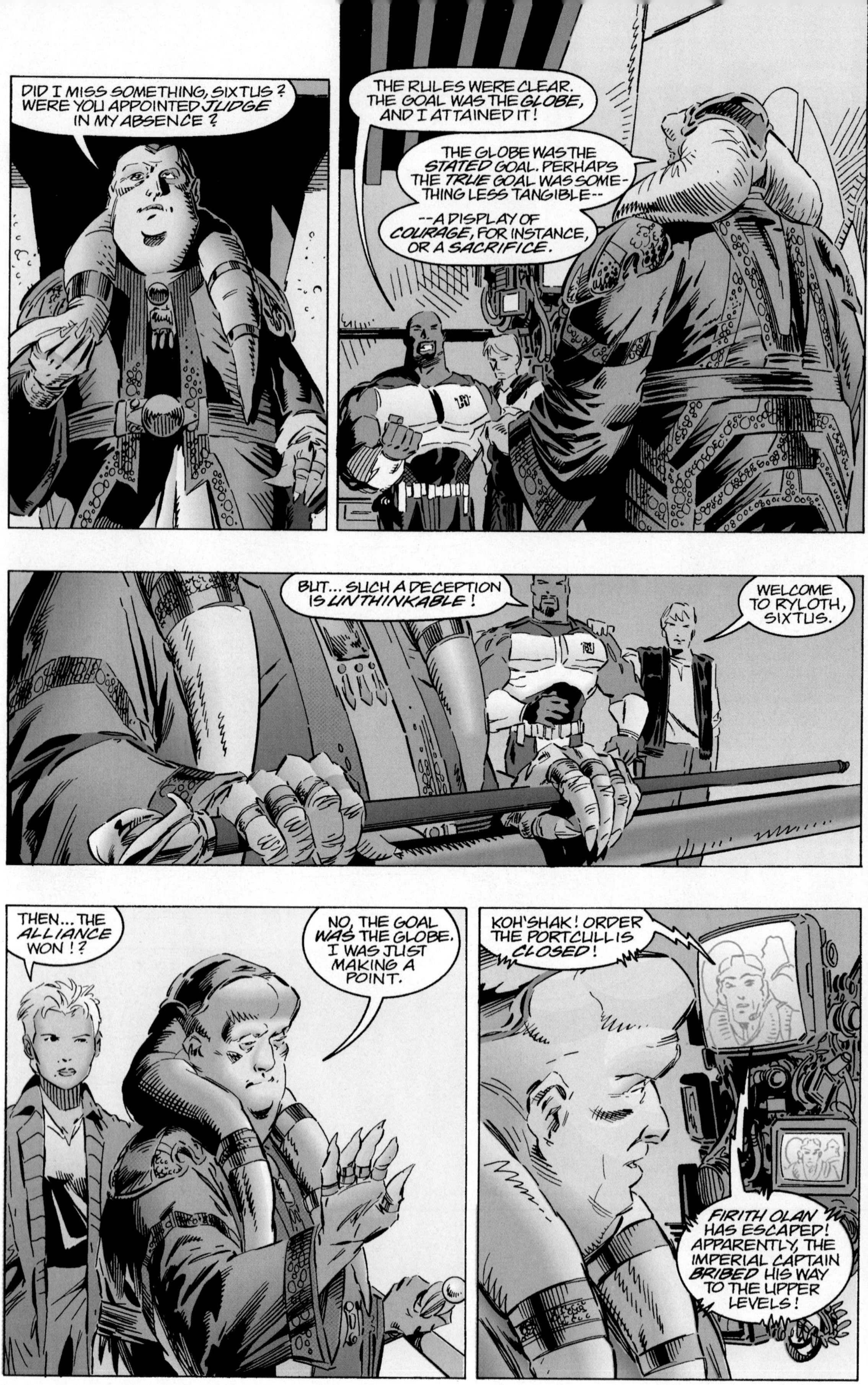
DID I MISS SOMETHING, SIXTUS? WERE YOU APPOINTED JUDGE IN MY ABSENCE?
THE RULES WERE CLEAR. THE GOAL WAS THE GLOBE, AND I ATTAINED IT!
THE GLOBE WAS THE STATED GOAL. PERHAPS THE TRUE GOAL WAS SOMETHING LESS TANGIBLE--
--A DISPLAY OF COURAGE, FOR INSTANCE, OR A SACRIFICE.
BUT... SUCH A DECEPTION IS UNTHINKABLE!
WELCOME TO RYLOTH, SIXTUS.
THEN... THE ALLIANCE WON!?
NO, THE GOAL WAS THE GLOBE. I WAS JUST MAKING A POINT.
KOH'SHAK! ORDER THE PORTCULLIS CLOSED!
FIRITH OLAN HAS ESCAPED! APPARENTLY, THE IMPERIAL CAPTAIN BRIBED HIS WAY TO THE UPPER LEVELS!

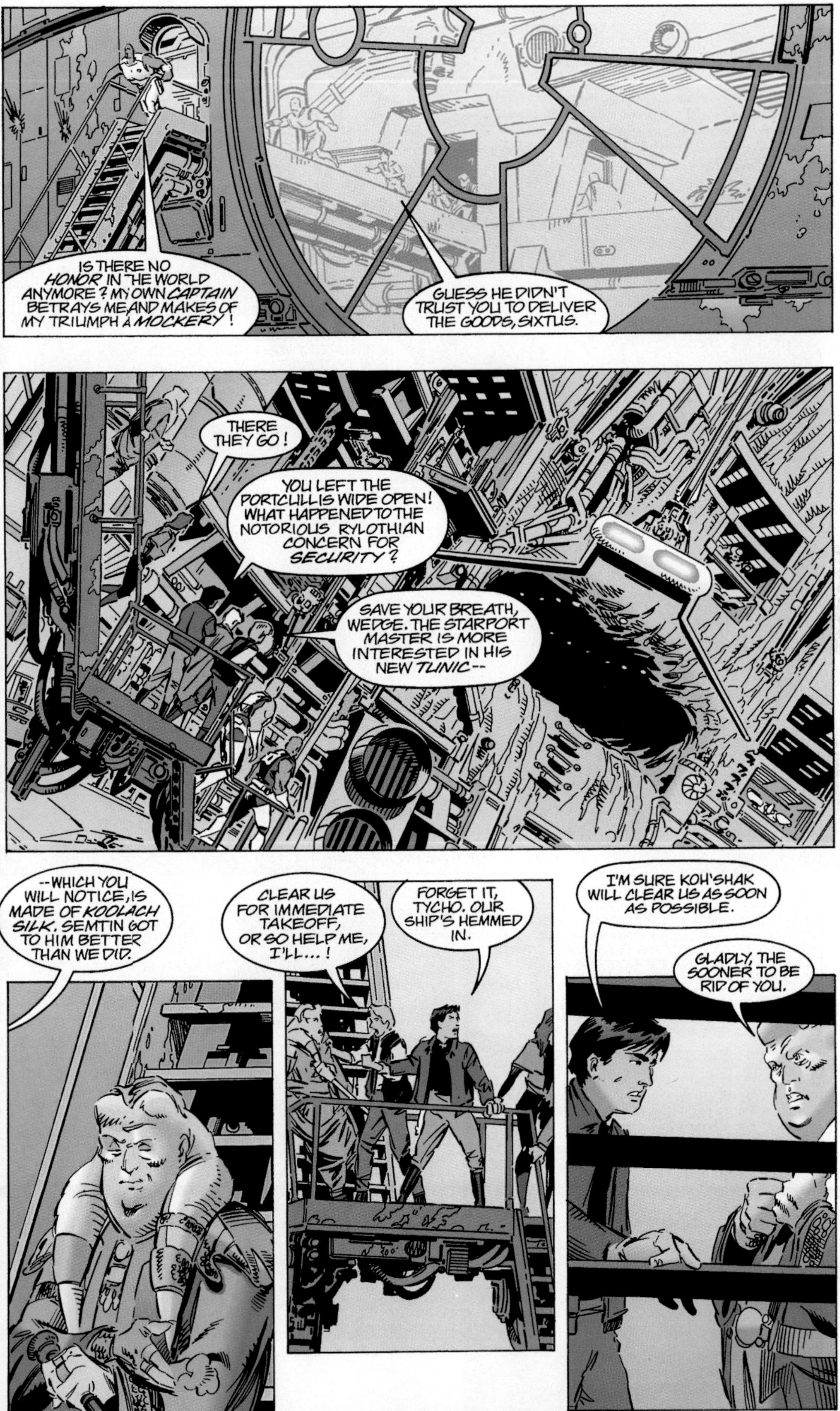

IS THERE NO HONOR IN THE WORLD ANYMORE? MY OWN CAPTAIN BETRAYS ME, AND MAKES OF MY TRIUMPH A MOCKERY!
GUESS HE DIDN'T TRUST YOU TO DELIVER THE GOODS, SIXTUS.
THERE THEY GO!
YOU LEFT THE PORTCULLIS WIDE OPEN! WHAT HAPPENED TO THE NOTORIOUS RYLOTHIAN CONCERN FOR SECURITY?
SAVE YOUR BREATH, WEDGE. THE STARPORT MASTER IS MORE INTERESTED IN HIS NEW TUNIC--
--WHICH YOU WILL NOTICE, IS MADE OF KOOLACH SILK. SEMTIN GOT TO HIM BETTER THAN WE DID.
CLEAR US FOR IMMEDIATE TAKEOFF, OR SO HELP ME, I'LL...!
FORGET IT, TYCHO. OUR SHIP'S HEMMED IN.
I'M SURE KOH'SHAK WILL CLEAR US AS SOON AS POSSIBLE.
GLADLY, THE SOONER TO BE RID OF YOU.

PRETTY ODD, SHARING A DRINK WITH AN IMPERIAL TROOPER.

I AM A TROOPER *NO MORE* ! MY CAPTAIN HAS SHOWN HIMSELF TO BE WITHOUT HONOR.

NO OFFENSE, SIXTUS, BUT SURELY YOU KNEW BEFORE NOW THAT MARL SEMTIN WAS A *DEVIOUS, SELF-SERVING* OPPORTUNIST... OR SOMETHING *LIKE* ONE !

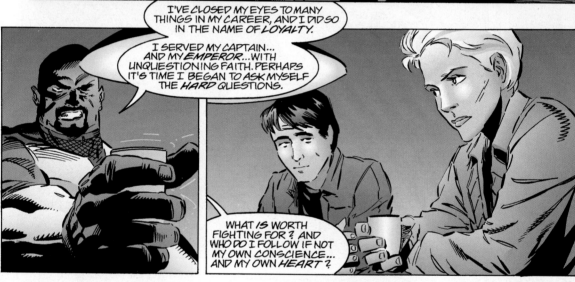

I'VE *CLOSED MY EYES* TO MANY THINGS IN MY CAREER, AND I DID SO IN THE NAME OF *LOYALTY.*

I SERVED MY CAPTAIN... AND MY *EMPEROR*...WITH UNQUESTIONING FAITH. PERHAPS IT'S TIME I BEGAN TO ASK MYSELF THE *HARD* QUESTIONS.

WHAT *IS* WORTH FIGHTING FOR ? AND WHO DO I FOLLOW IF NOT MY OWN CONSCIENCE... AND MY OWN *HEART* ?

MARL SEMTIN HAS *ABANDONED* SEPTAAS AND MYSELF HERE, ALONG WITH A DOZEN SEASONED TROOPERS. UNDER RYLOTHIAN LAW, IF WE CANNOT FIND PASSAGE, WE CAN BE SOLD INTO *SLAVERY.*

SEMTIN AND OLAN ARE SURELY BOUND FOR TATOOINE. TAKE US THERE, AND LET US DEAL WITH THE *TRAITOR.*

YOU THINK I SHOULD HELP YOU AND YOUR TROOPERS CONTINUE TO FIGHT FOR THE *EMPIRE* ?

NO ! NOT FOR THE EMPIRE, BUT FOR *HONOR* !

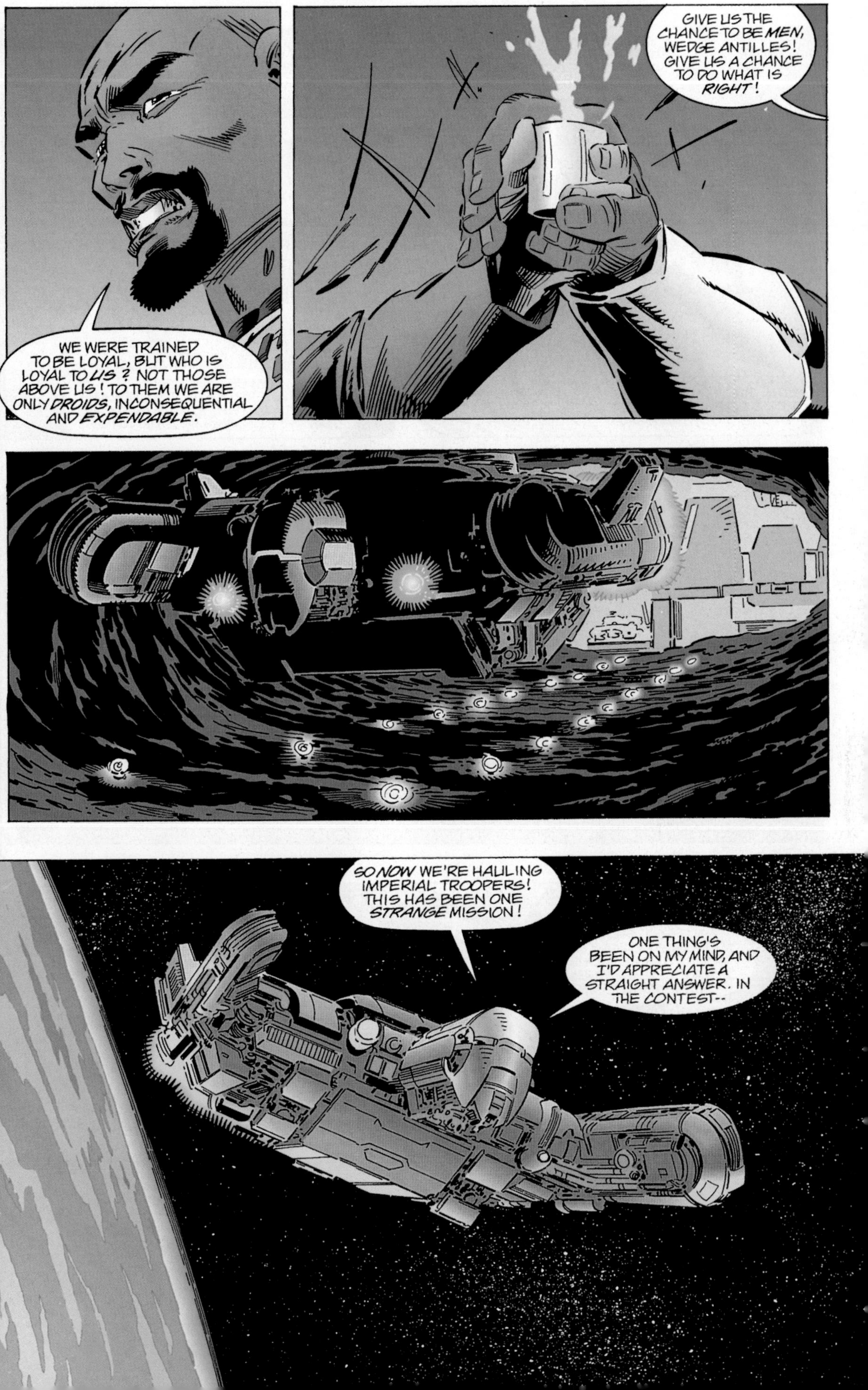
WE WERE TRAINED TO BE LOYAL, BUT WHO IS LOYAL TO US? NOT THOSE ABOVE US! TO THEM WE ARE ONLY DROIDS, INCONSEQUENTIAL AND EXPENDABLE.
GIVE US THE CHANCE TO BE MEN, WEDGE ANTILLES! GIVE US A CHANCE TO DO WHAT IS RIGHT!
SO NOW WE'RE HAULING IMPERIAL TROOPERS! THIS HAS BEEN ONE STRANGE MISSION!
ONE THING'S BEEN ON MY MIND, AND I'D APPRECIATE A STRAIGHT ANSWER. IN THE CONTEST--

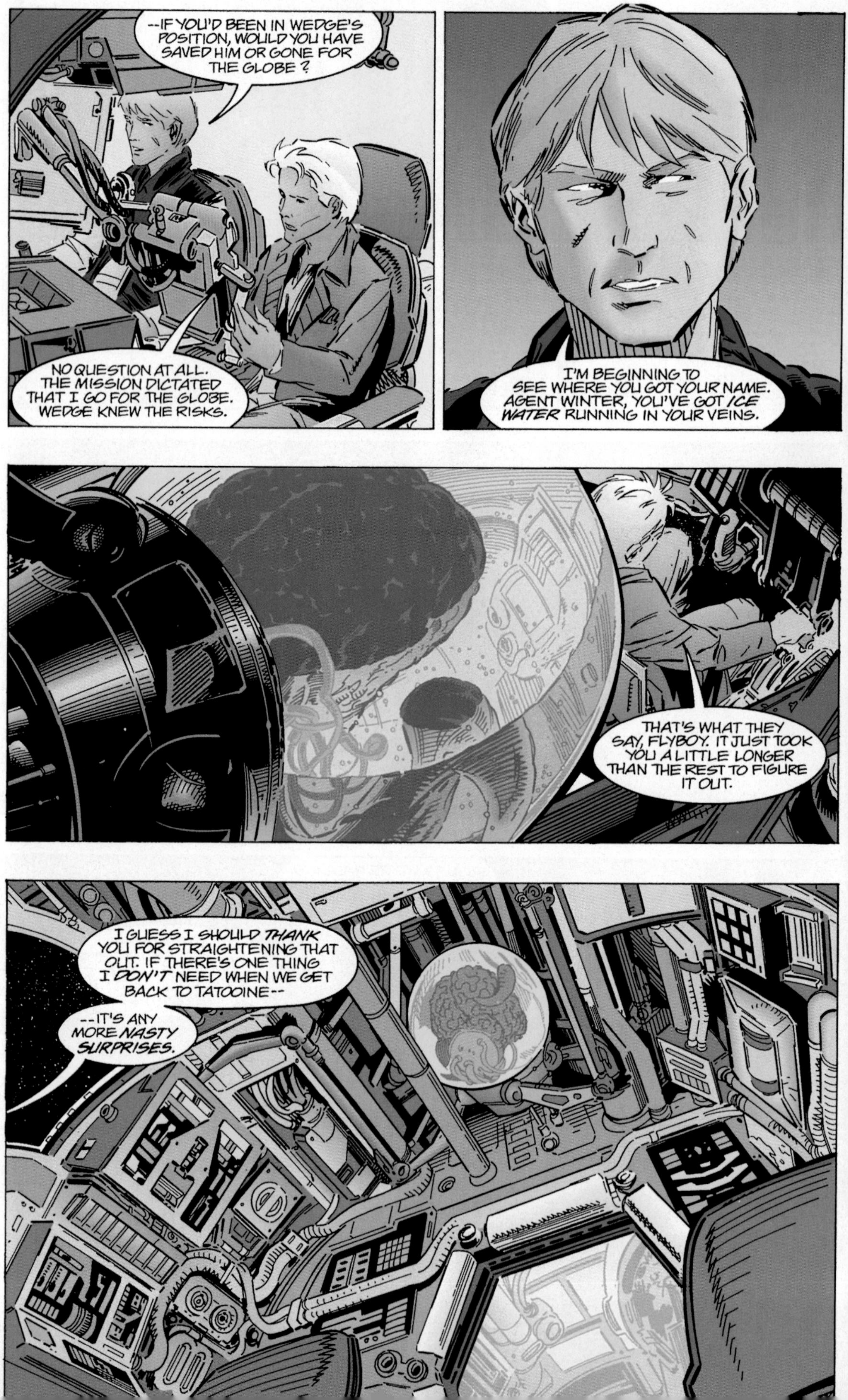
--IF YOU'D BEEN IN WEDGE'S POSITION, WOULD YOU HAVE SAVED HIM OR GONE FOR THE GLOBE?
NO QUESTION AT ALL. THE MISSION DICTATED THAT I GO FOR THE GLOBE. WEDGE KNEW THE RISKS.
I'M BEGINNING TO SEE WHERE YOU GOT YOUR NAME. AGENT WINTER, YOU'VE GOT *ICE WATER* RUNNING IN YOUR VEINS.
THAT'S WHAT THEY SAY, FLYBOY. IT JUST TOOK YOU A LITTLE LONGER THAN THE REST TO FIGURE IT OUT.
I GUESS I SHOULD *THANK* YOU FOR STRAIGHTENING THAT OUT. IF THERE'S ONE THING I *DON'T* NEED WHEN WE GET BACK TO TATOOINE--
--IT'S ANY MORE *NASTY SURPRISES*.

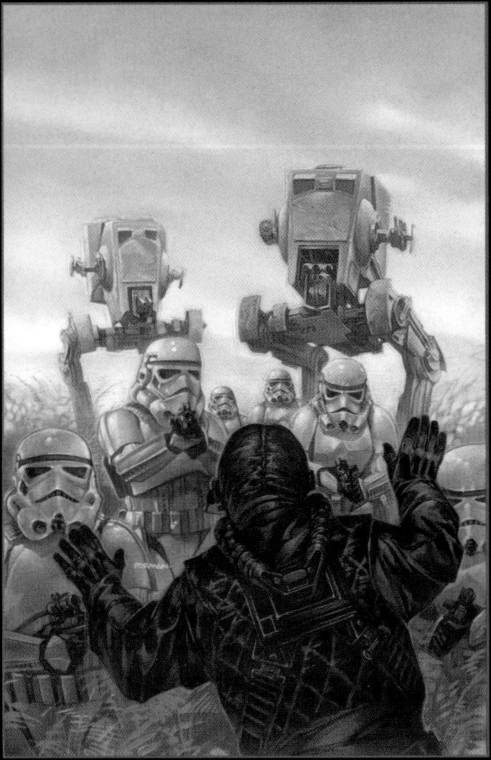

ORIGINAL VERSION OF *STAR WARS: X-WING ROGUE SQUADRON #4*'S COVER ART. DAVE DORMAN WAS ACCIDENTALLY INSTRUCTED TO PAINT THE FOREGROUND CHARACTER AS A TIE FIGHTER PILOT INSTEAD OF AN IMPERIAL OFFICER. THE ERROR WAS CAUGHT AND CORRECTED BEFORE THE ISSUE WAS PUBLISHED.

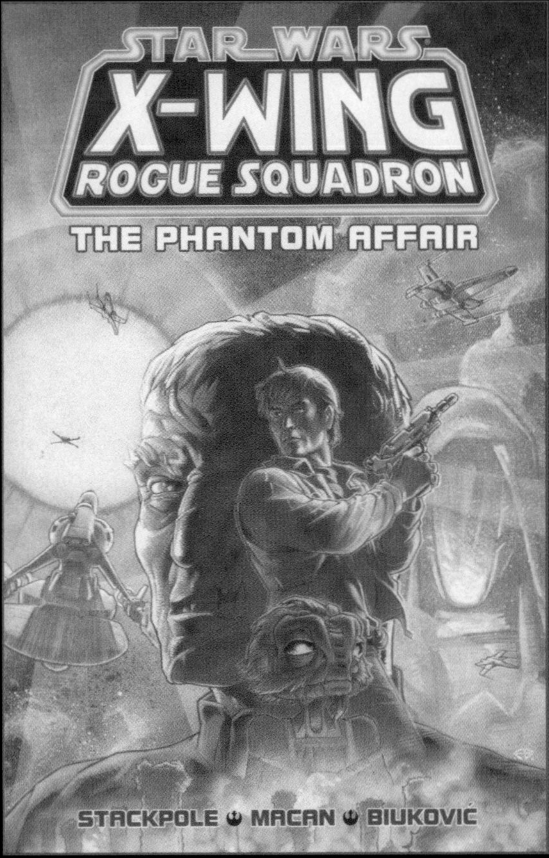
STAR WARS
X-WING
ROGUE SQUADRON
THE PHANTOM AFFAIR
STACKPOLE MACAN BIUKOVIĆ

*STAR WARS: X-WING ROGUE SQUADRON — THE PHANTOM AFFAIR TPB* COVER ART BY EDVIN BIUKOVIĆ

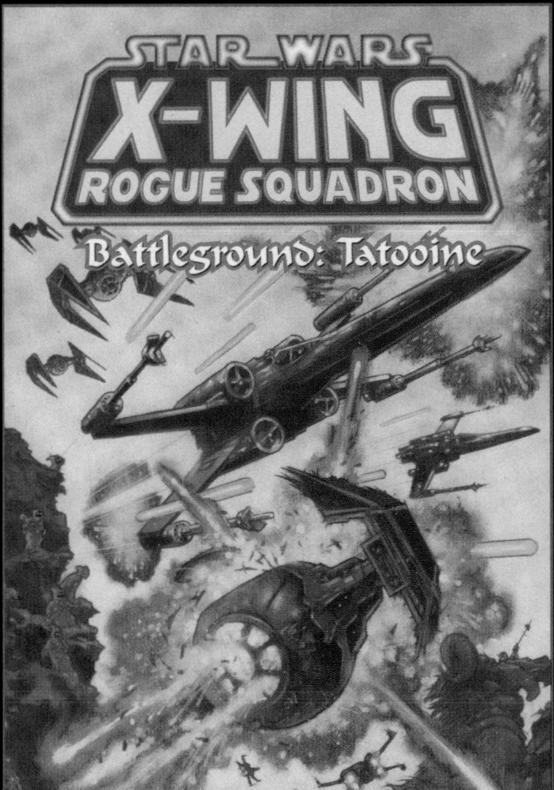
STAR WARS
X-WING
ROGUE SQUADRON
Battleground: Tatooine
STACKPOLE STRNAD NADEAU ENSIGN
Introduction by TIMOTHY ZAHN

*STAR WARS: X-WING ROGUE SQUADRON — BATTLEGROUND: TATOOINE TPB* COVER ART BY JOHN K. SNYDER III

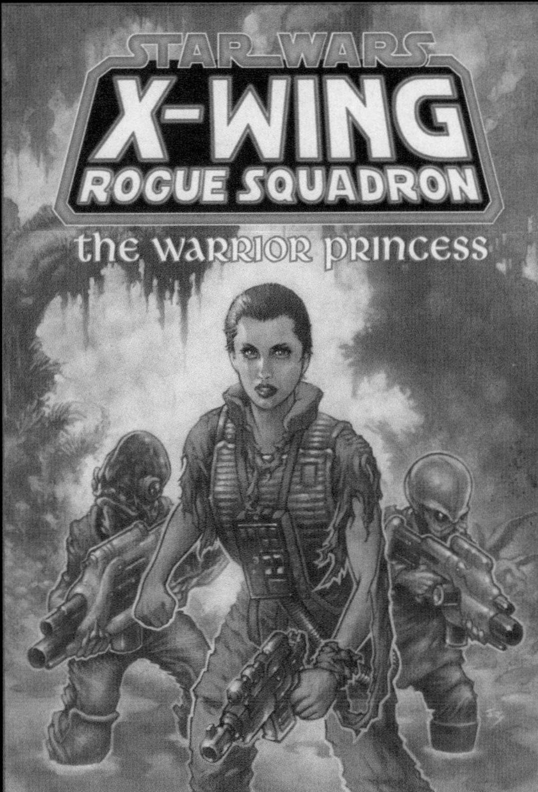
STAR WARS
X-WING
ROGUE SQUADRON
the warrior princess
STACKPOLE TOLSON NADEAU ENSIGN

*STAR WARS: X-WING ROGUE SQUADRON — THE WARRIOR PRINCESS TPB* COVER ART BY JOHN K. SNYDER III

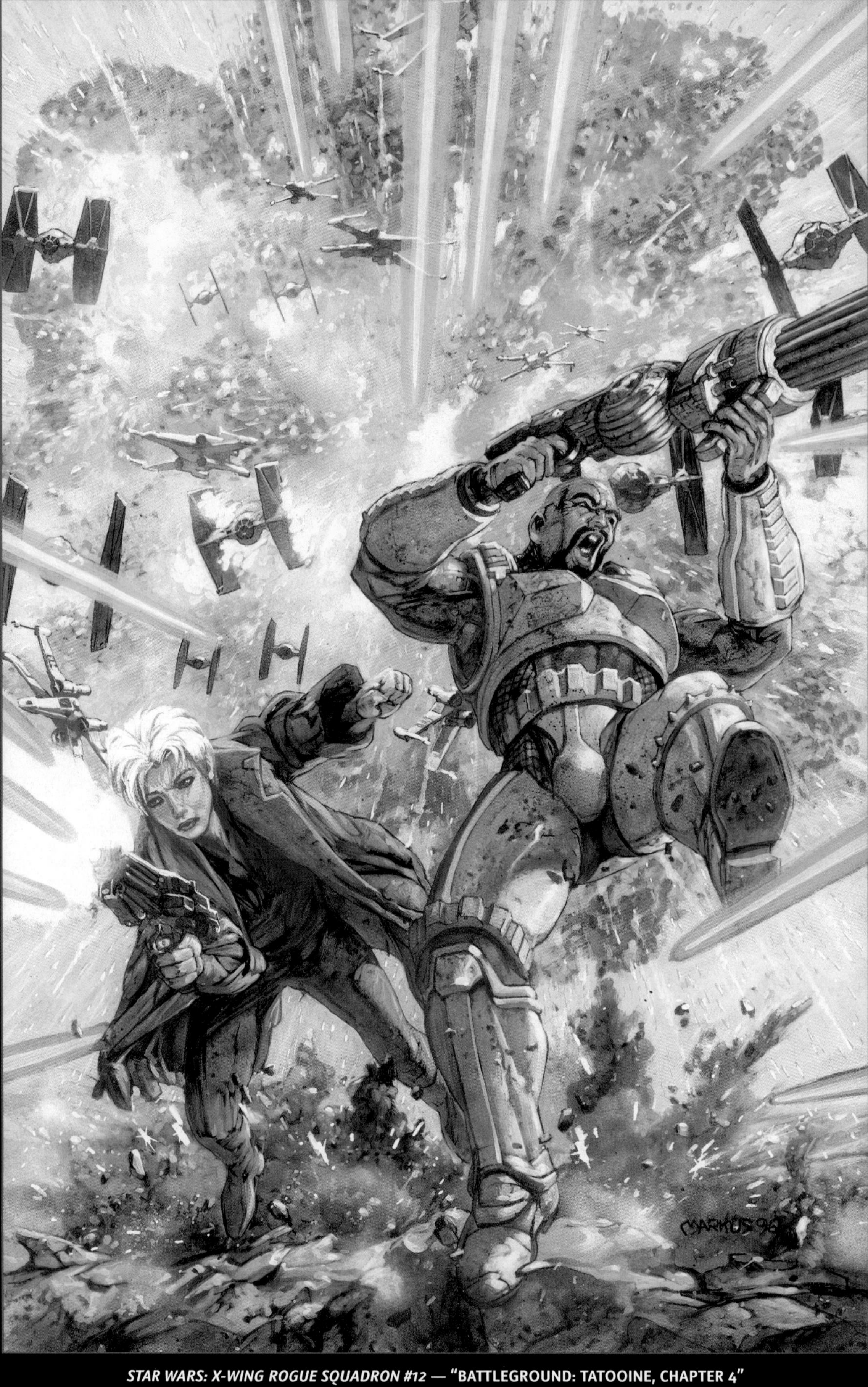

***STAR WARS: X-WING ROGUE SQUADRON #12*** **— "BATTLEGROUND: TATOOINE, CHAPTER 4"**

PLOTTER: MICHAEL A. STACKPOLE • SCRIPTER: JAN STRNAD • PENCILER: JOHN NADEAU • INKER: JORDI ENSIGN
COLORIST: DAVE NESTELLE • LETTERER: VICKIE WILLIAMS • EDITOR: PEET JANES • COVER ARTIST: MARK HARRISON

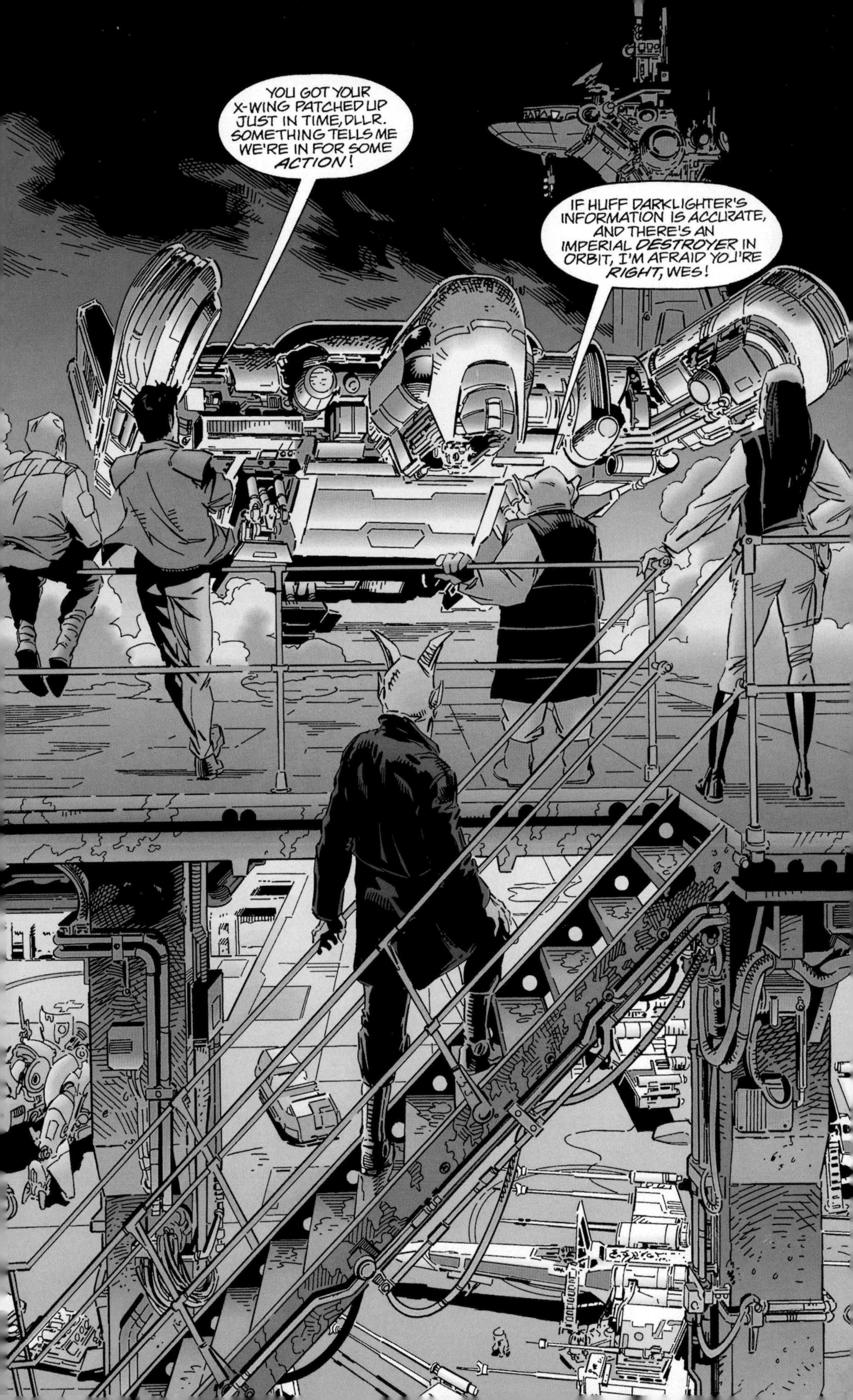
YOU GOT YOUR X-WING PATCHED UP JUST IN TIME, DLLR. SOMETHING TELLS ME WE'RE IN FOR SOME ACTION!
IF HUFF DARKLIGHTER'S INFORMATION IS ACCURATE, AND THERE'S AN IMPERIAL DESTROYER IN ORBIT, I'M AFRAID YOU'RE RIGHT, WES!

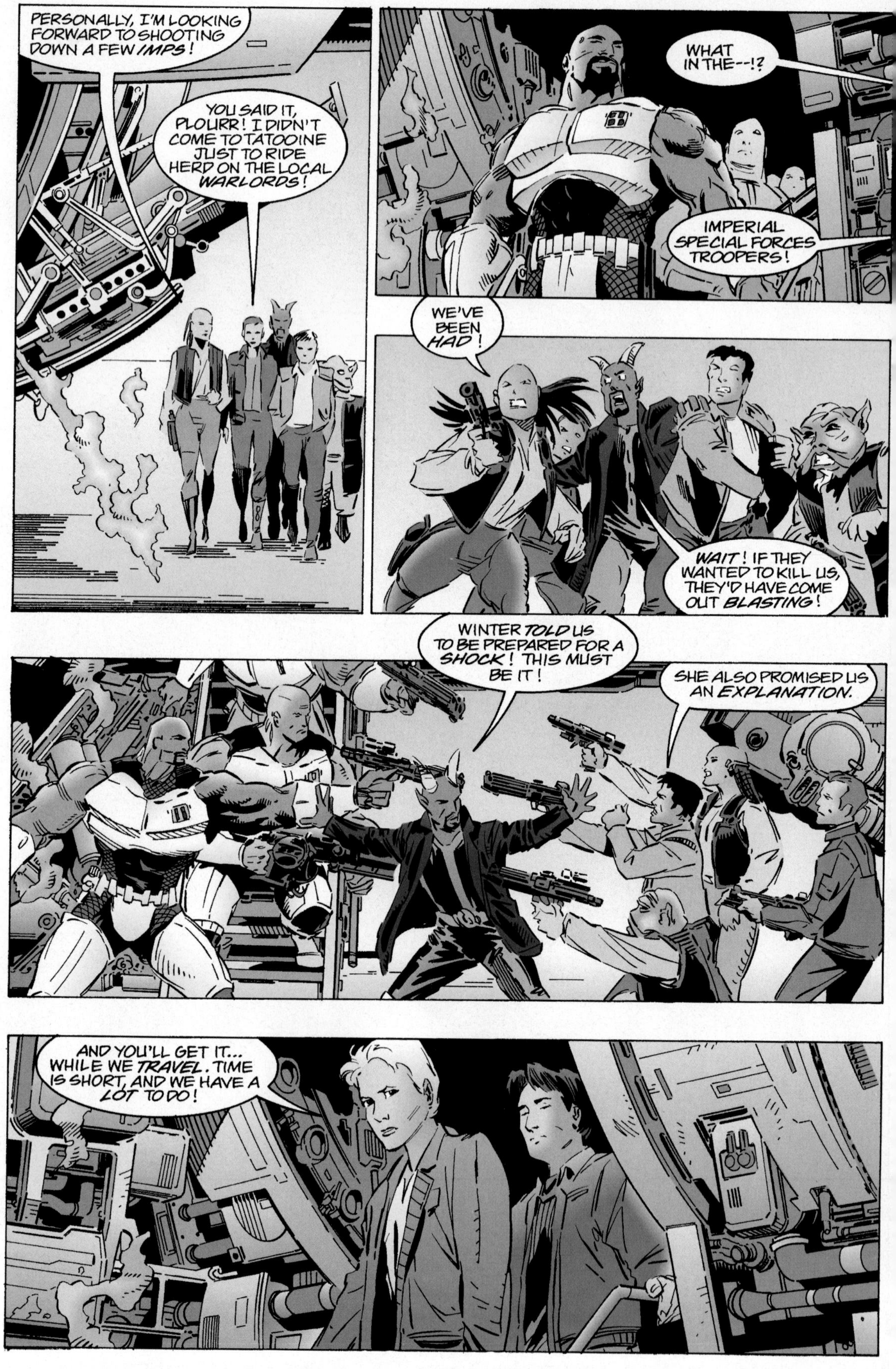
PERSONALLY, I'M LOOKING FORWARD TO SHOOTING DOWN A FEW *IMPS*!
YOU SAID IT, PLOURR! I DIDN'T COME TO TATOOINE JUST TO RIDE HERD ON THE LOCAL *WARLORDS*!
WHAT IN THE--!?
IMPERIAL SPECIAL FORCES TROOPERS!
WE'VE BEEN *HAD*!
*WAIT*! IF THEY WANTED TO KILL US, THEY'D HAVE COME OUT *BLASTING*!
WINTER *TOLD* US TO BE PREPARED FOR A *SHOCK*! THIS MUST BE IT!
SHE ALSO PROMISED US AN *EXPLANATION*.
AND YOU'LL GET IT... WHILE WE *TRAVEL*. TIME IS SHORT, AND WE HAVE A *LOT* TO DO!

THE EMPIRE IS *UNSTABLE*, OLAN. *PURGES* OF HIGH-RANKING OFFICIALS ARE ALL TOO COMMON.

ONE SUCH OFFICIAL, *SATE PESTAGE*, WISELY *DIVERTED* FUNDS FROM A CERTAIN MILITARY PROJECT TO BUILD A PRIVATE *RETREAT* ON TATOOINE.

YOU MEAN, THE *EIDOLON...!*

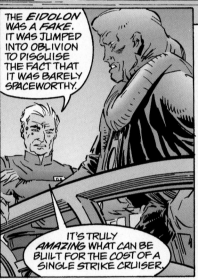

THE *EIDOLON* WAS A *FAKE*. IT WAS JUMPED INTO OBLIVION TO DISGUISE THE FACT THAT IT WAS BARELY SPACEWORTHY.

IT'S TRULY *AMAZING* WHAT CAN BE BUILT FOR THE COST OF A SINGLE STRIKE CRUISER.

*SEMTIN*! YOUR DROID'S STEERING US STRAIGHT INTO THE MOUNTAINSIDE!

YES. HE'S FOLLOWING HIS PROGRAMMED INSTRUCTIONS. IF ONLY *ORGANIC* FOLLOWERS WERE SO UNQUESTIONING, EH?

WHAT ARE YOU DOING?! TELL HIM TO *TURN*! IF THIS IS SOME KIND OF SICK *JOKE...?!*

IF IT WERE A *JOKE*, SOMEONE WOULD BE LAUGHING, WOULDN'T THEY?

DO YOU HEAR ANYONE LAUGHING?

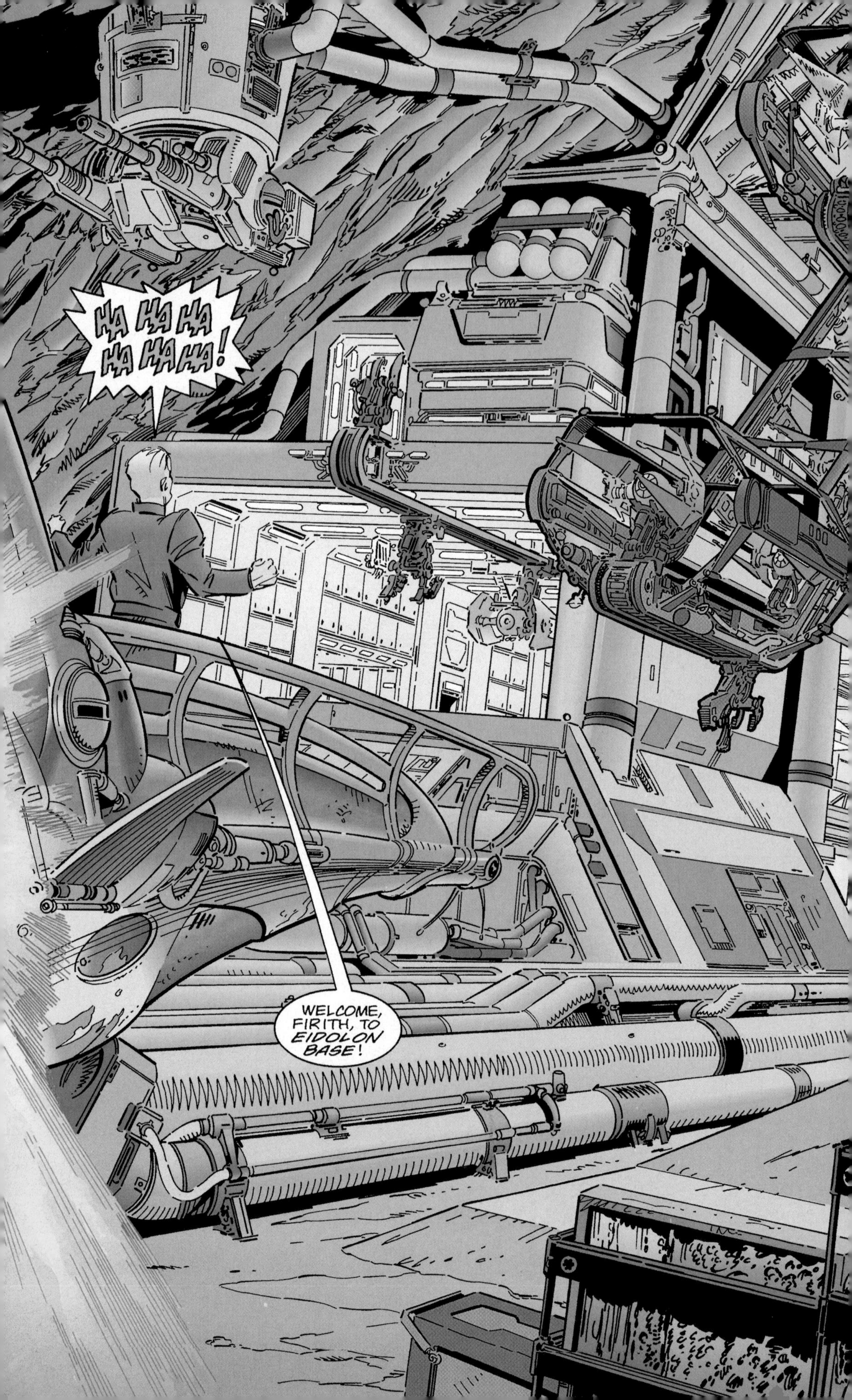
HA HA HA
HA HA HA!
WELCOME, FIRITH, TO *EIDOLON BASE*!

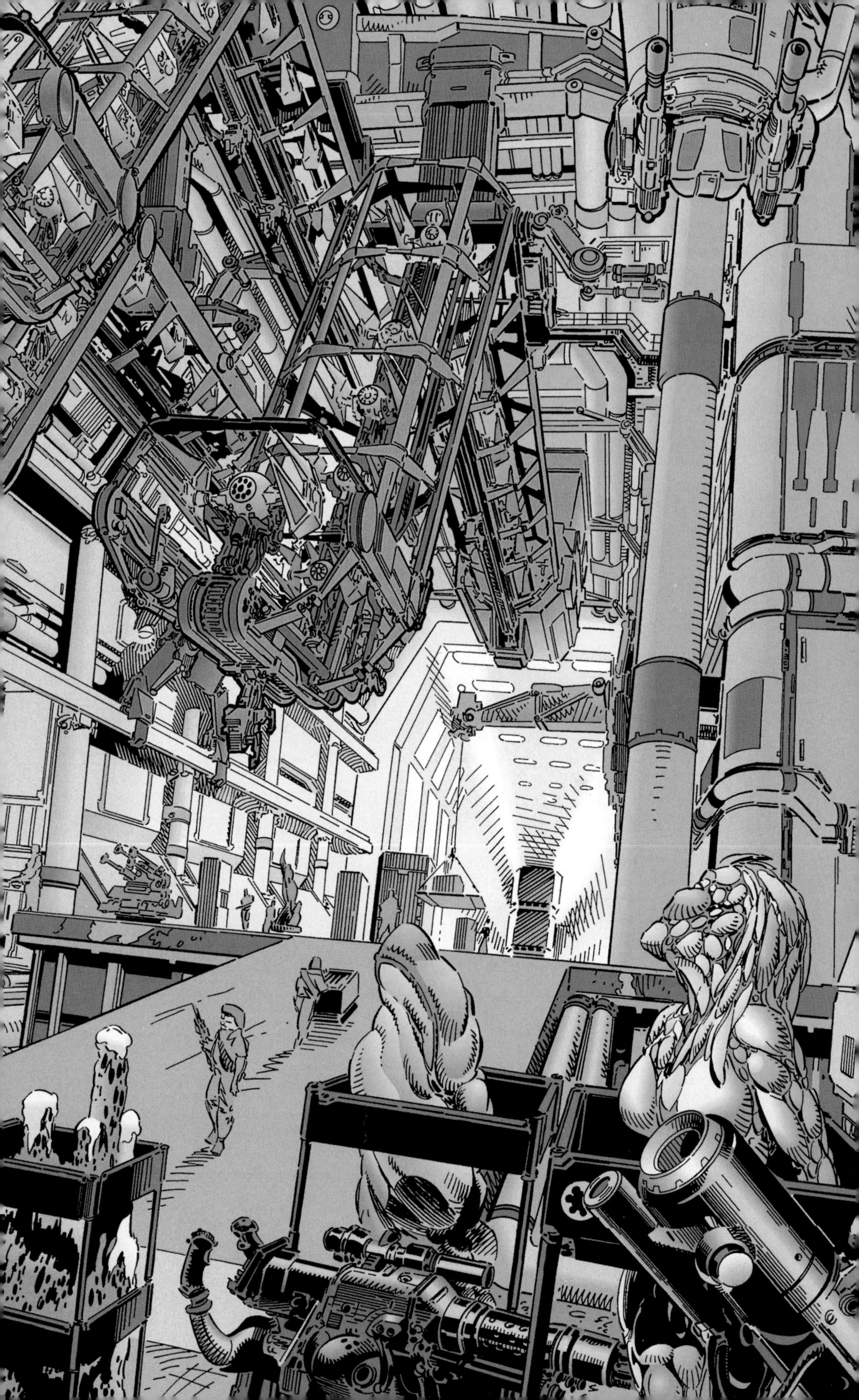

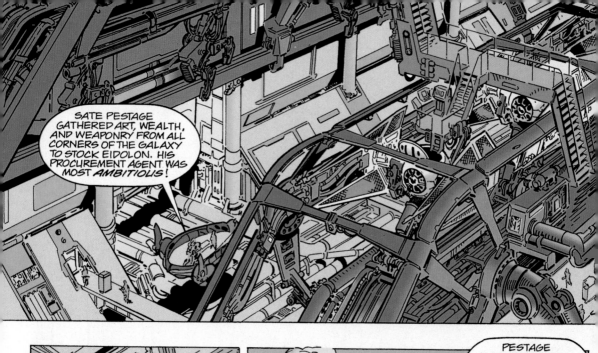

SATE PESTAGE GATHERED ART, WEALTH, AND WEAPONRY FROM ALL CORNERS OF THE GALAXY TO STOCK EIDOLON. HIS PROCUREMENT AGENT WAS MOST *AMBITIOUS!*

*TOO* AMBITIOUS, ACTUALLY. WHEN BANOLT THREATENED TO *EXPOSE* THE BASE IF PESTAGE REFUSED TO PAY HIS PRICE, HE WAS... *REMOVED.*

PESTAGE NEEDS SOMEONE TO *MANAGE* EIDOLON UNTIL HE NEEDS IT. WITH SUCH RESOURCES AT HIS DISPOSAL, SUCH A MANAGER WOULD *NATURALLY* BECOME GOVERNOR OF TATOOINE.

I'M OFFERING THE JOB TO *YOU*, FIRITH OLAN, IF YOU *WANT* IT.

YOU'RE FREE TO *REFUSE,* OF COURSE.

ONE WOULD BE A *FOOL* TO REFUSE SUCH A GENEROUS OFFER! I *ACCEPT!*

GOOD! NOW WE SHOULD READY OURSELVES FOR *ATTACK!*

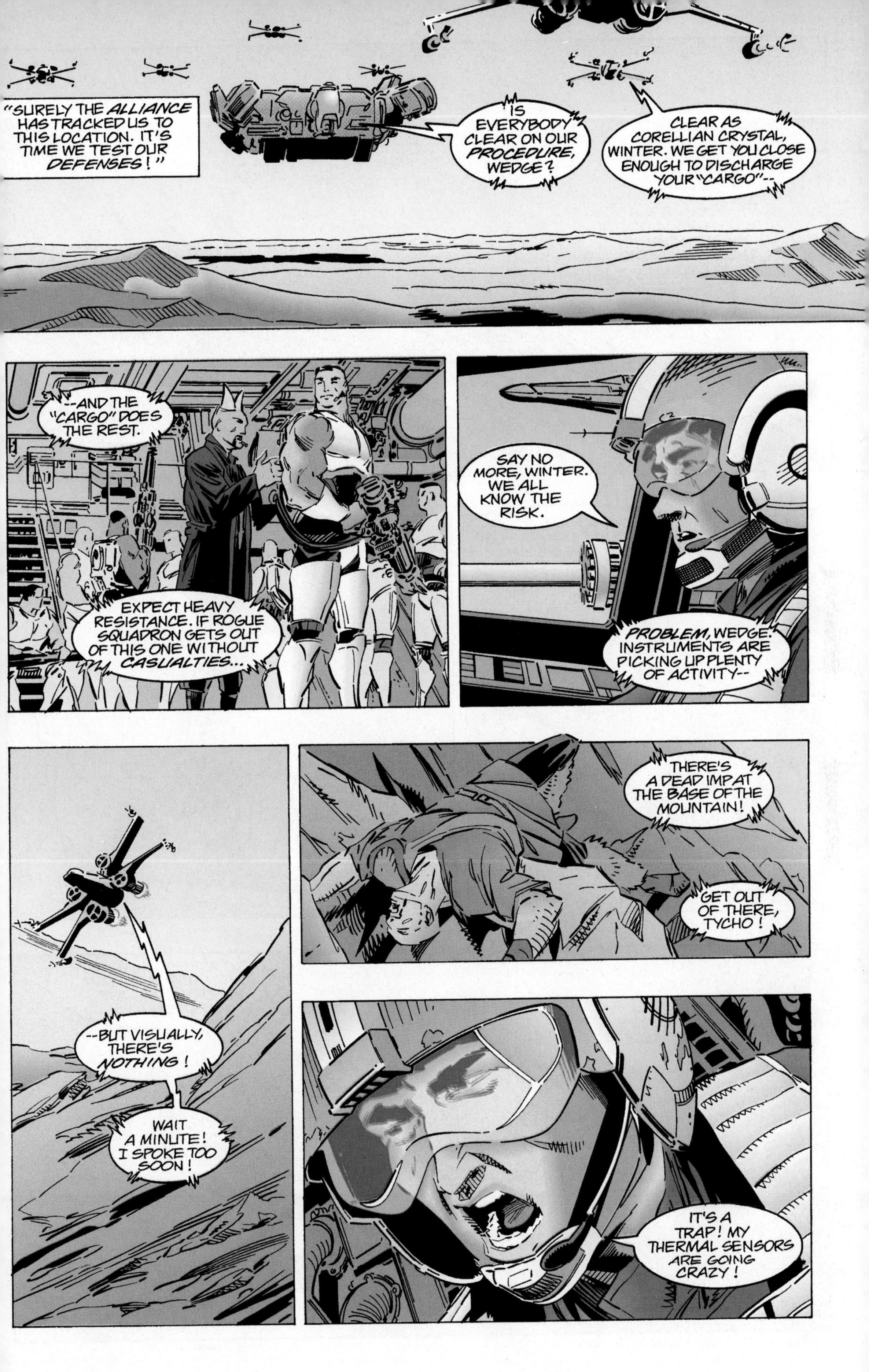
"SURELY THE ALLIANCE HAS TRACKED US TO THIS LOCATION. IT'S TIME WE TEST OUR DEFENSES!"
IS EVERYBODY CLEAR ON OUR PROCEDURE, WEDGE?
CLEAR AS CORELLIAN CRYSTAL, WINTER. WE GET YOU CLOSE ENOUGH TO DISCHARGE YOUR "CARGO"--
--AND THE "CARGO" DOES THE REST.
EXPECT HEAVY RESISTANCE. IF ROGUE SQUADRON GETS OUT OF THIS ONE WITHOUT CASUALTIES...
SAY NO MORE, WINTER. WE ALL KNOW THE RISK.
PROBLEM, WEDGE. INSTRUMENTS ARE PICKING UP PLENTY OF ACTIVITY--
--BUT VISUALLY, THERE'S NOTHING!
WAIT A MINUTE! I SPOKE TOO SOON!
THERE'S A DEAD IMP AT THE BASE OF THE MOUNTAIN!
GET OUT OF THERE, TYCHO!
IT'S A TRAP! MY THERMAL SENSORS ARE GOING CRAZY!

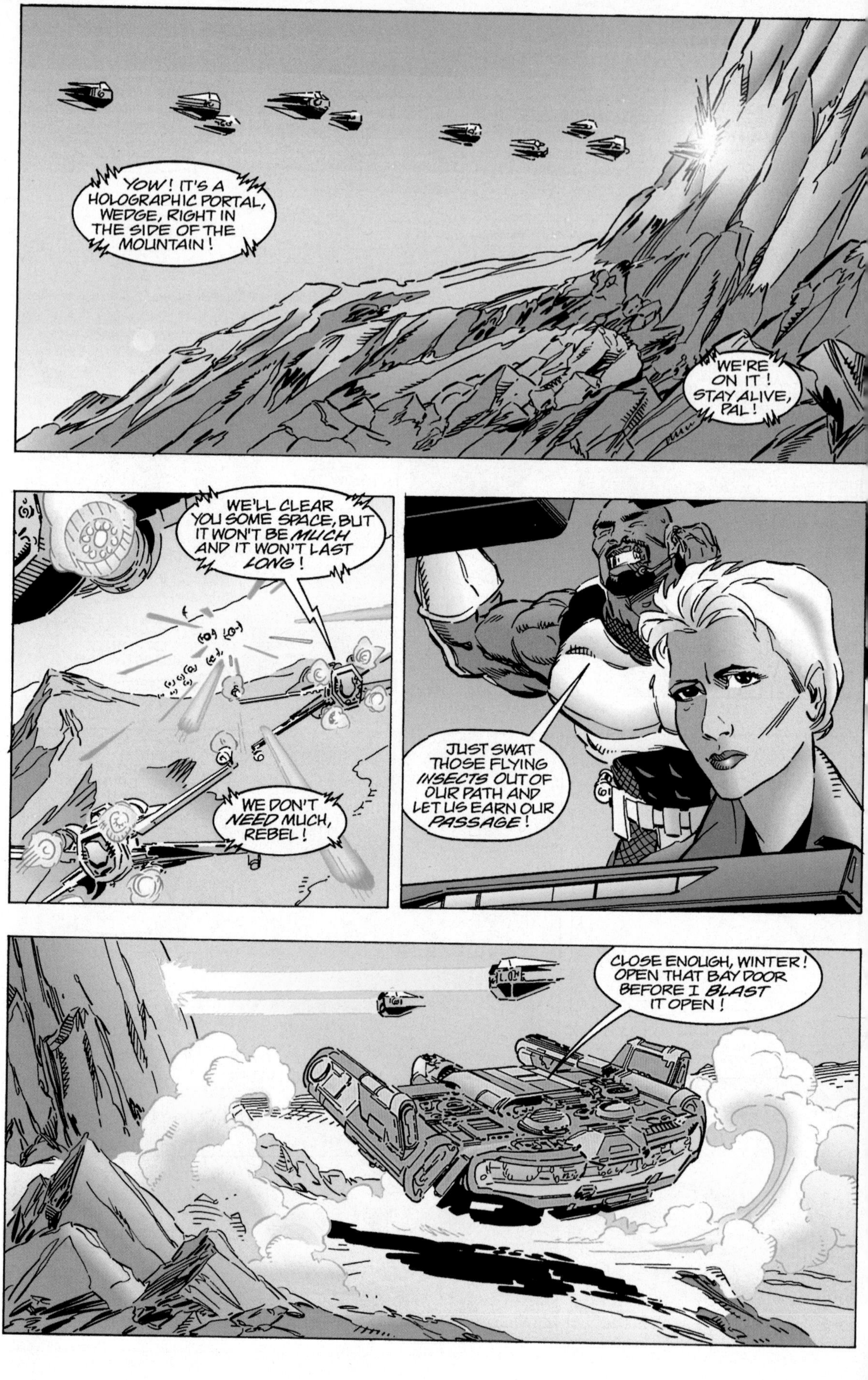
YOW! IT'S A HOLOGRAPHIC PORTAL, WEDGE, RIGHT IN THE SIDE OF THE MOUNTAIN!
WE'RE ON IT! STAY ALIVE, PAL!
WE'LL CLEAR YOU SOME SPACE, BUT IT WON'T BE MUCH AND IT WON'T LAST LONG!
WE DON'T NEED MUCH, REBEL!
JUST SWAT THOSE FLYING INSECTS OUT OF OUR PATH AND LET US EARN OUR PASSAGE!
CLOSE ENOUGH, WINTER! OPEN THAT BAY DOOR BEFORE I BLAST IT OPEN!

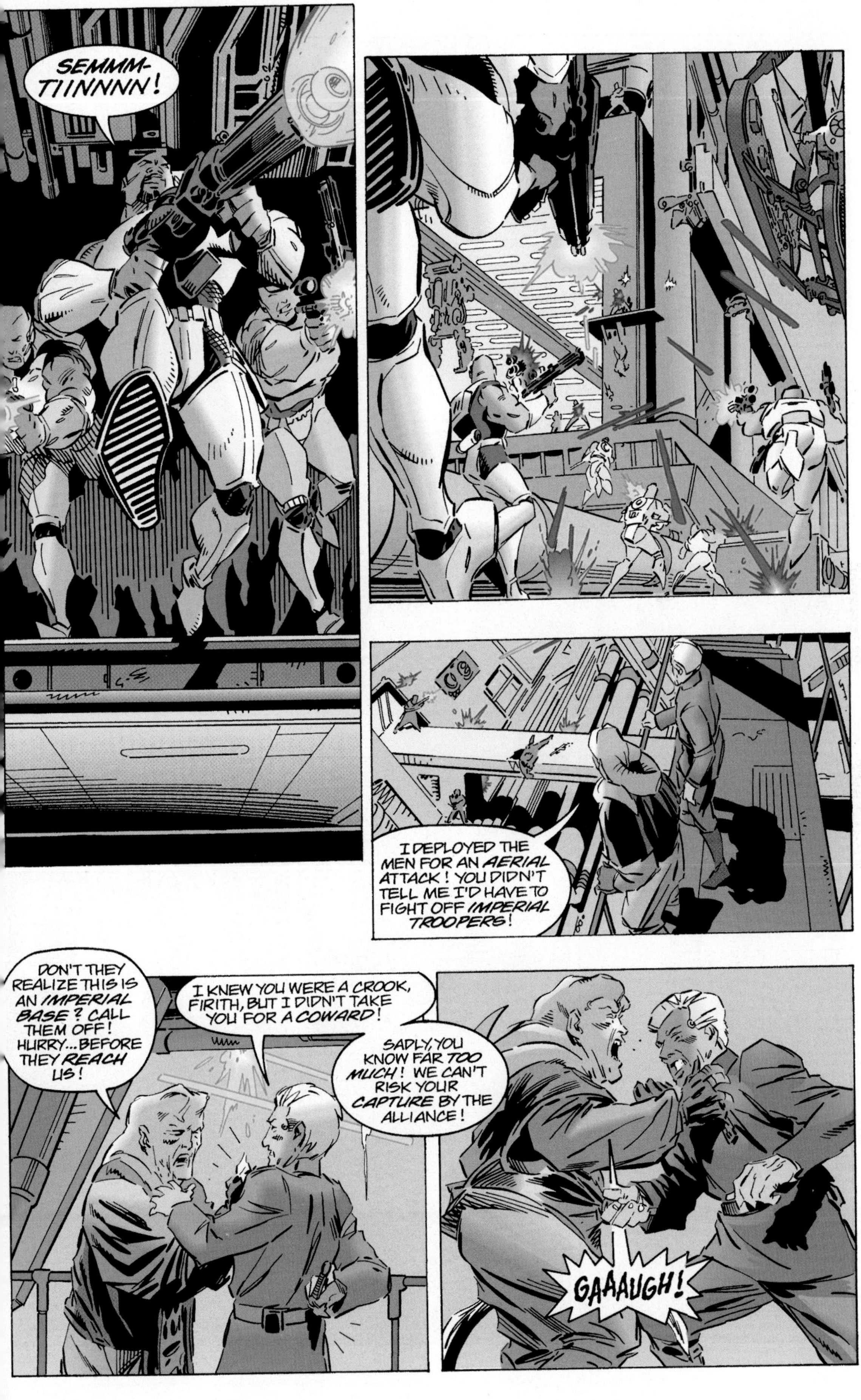
SEMMM-TIINNNN!
I DEPLOYED THE MEN FOR AN AERIAL ATTACK! YOU DIDN'T TELL ME I'D HAVE TO FIGHT OFF IMPERIAL TROOPERS!
DON'T THEY REALIZE THIS IS AN IMPERIAL BASE? CALL THEM OFF! HURRY... BEFORE THEY REACH US!
I KNEW YOU WERE A CROOK, FIRITH, BUT I DIDN'T TAKE YOU FOR A COWARD!
SADLY, YOU KNOW FAR TOO MUCH! WE CAN'T RISK YOUR CAPTURE BY THE ALLIANCE!
GAAAUGH!

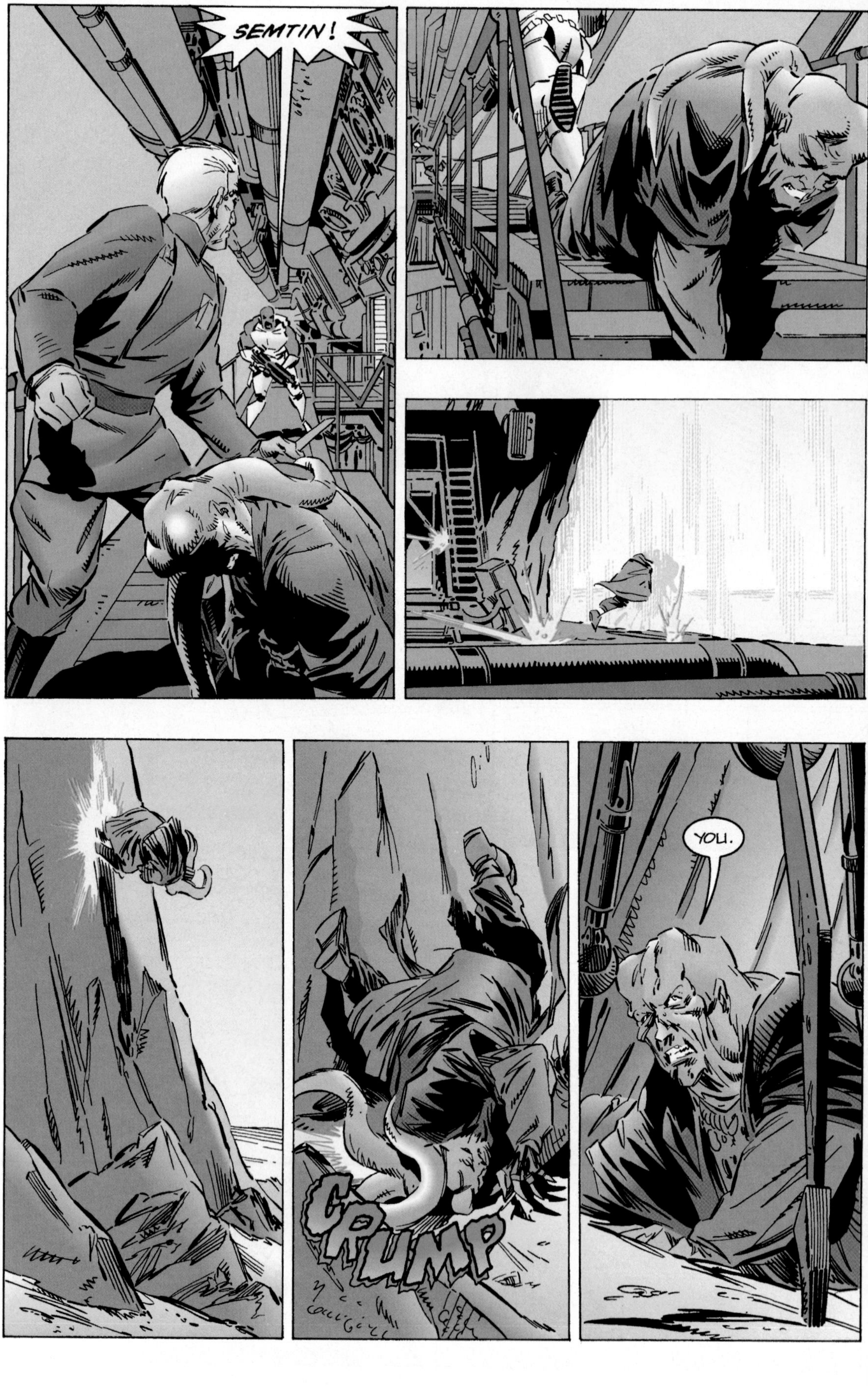
SEMTIN!
YOU.
CRUMP

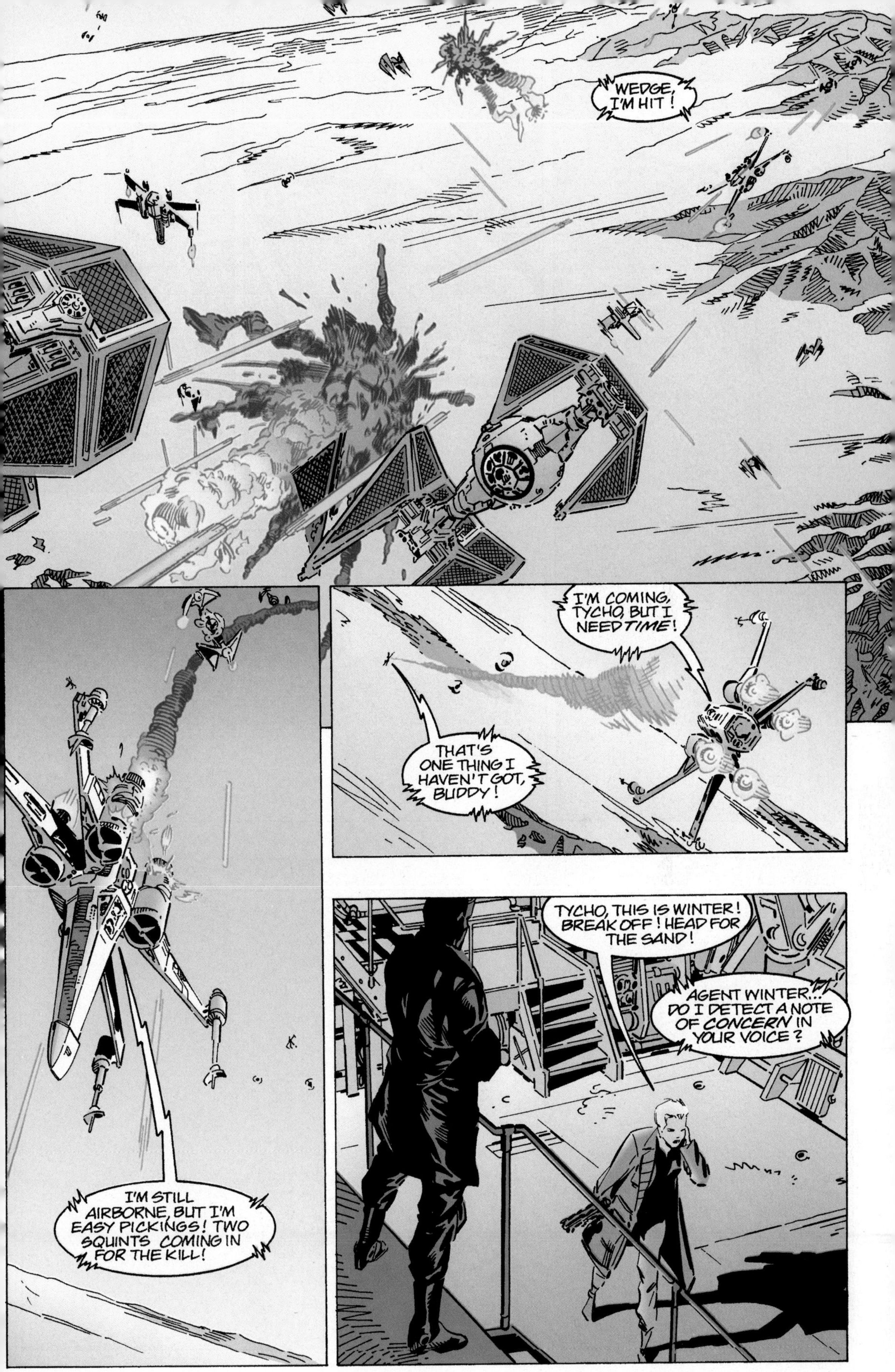
WEDGE, I'M HIT!
I'M COMING, TYCHO, BUT I NEED TIME!
THAT'S ONE THING I HAVEN'T GOT, BUDDY!
I'M STILL AIRBORNE, BUT I'M EASY PICKINGS! TWO SQUINTS COMING IN FOR THE KILL!
TYCHO, THIS IS WINTER! BREAK OFF! HEAD FOR THE SAND!
AGENT WINTER... DO I DETECT A NOTE OF CONCERN IN YOUR VOICE?

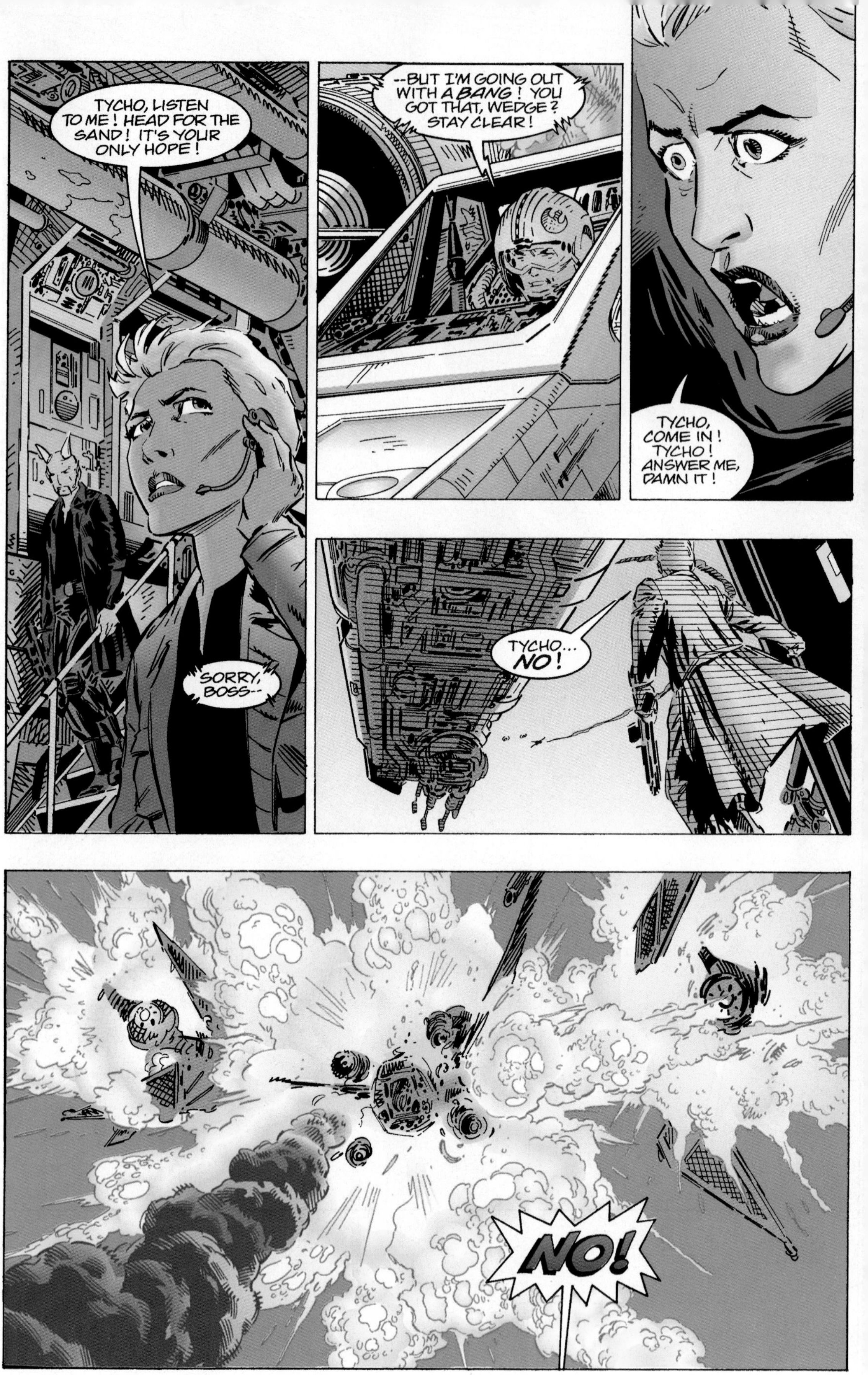
TYCHO, LISTEN TO ME! HEAD FOR THE SAND! IT'S YOUR ONLY HOPE!
SORRY, BOSS--
--BUT I'M GOING OUT WITH A BANG! YOU GOT THAT, WEDGE? STAY CLEAR!
TYCHO, COME IN! TYCHO! ANSWER ME, DAMN IT!
TYCHO... NO!
NO!

NO...

WEDGE, COME IN... THIS IS ELSCOL. I HAVE TO POINT OUT, CAPTAIN--

--THAT WE STILL HAVE AN IMPERIAL *DESTROYER* IN ORBIT. IT CAN RAIN A *PLANETARY BOMBARDMENT* ON THIS ENTIRE REGION!

SUGGEST THAT I TRY--

*NEGATIVE, ELSCOL!*

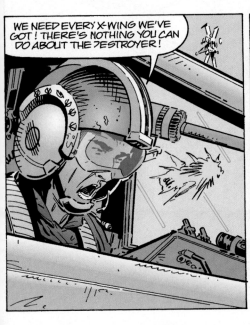

WE NEED EVERY X-WING WE'VE GOT! THERE'S NOTHING YOU CAN DO ABOUT THE *DESTROYER!*

WE'LL SEE ABOUT THAT.

THIS ISN'T *HEROISM*, ELSCOL... IT'S *DESERTION!*

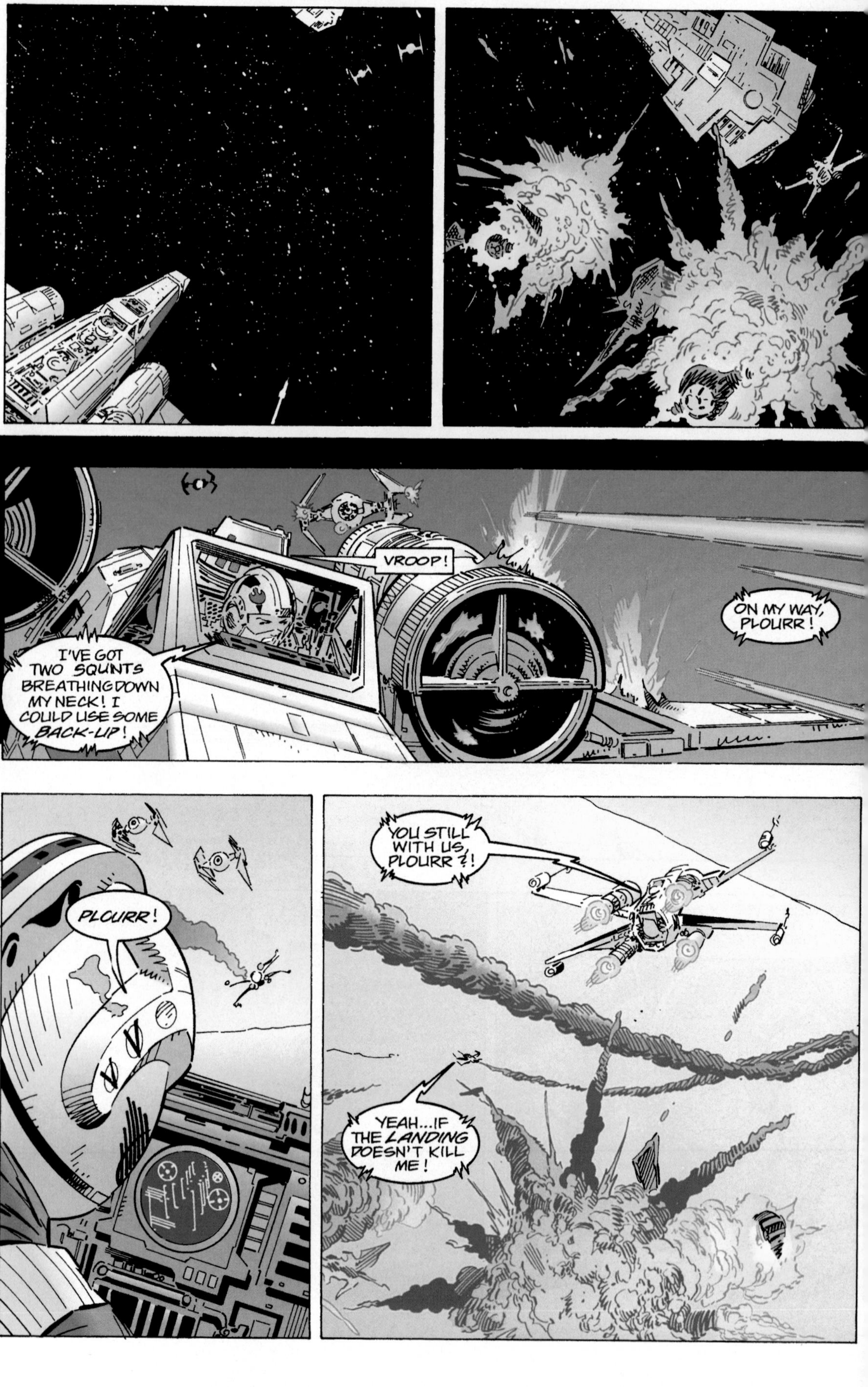
VROOP!
ON MY WAY, PLOURR!
I'VE GOT TWO SQUINTS BREATHING DOWN MY NECK! I COULD USE SOME BACK-UP!
PLOURR!
YOU STILL WITH US, PLOURR?!
YEAH...IF THE LANDING DOESN'T KILL ME!

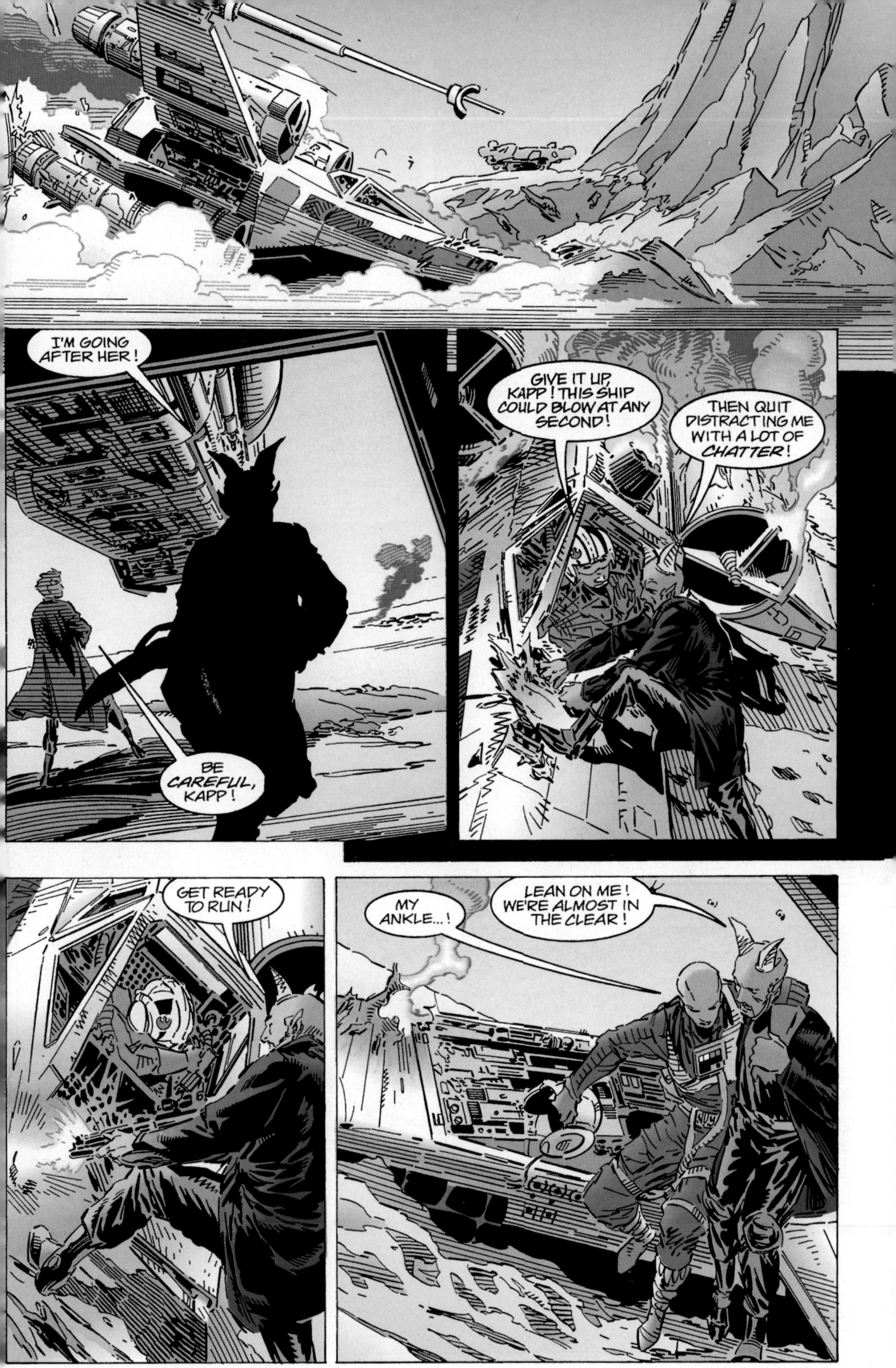
I'M GOING AFTER HER!
BE CAREFUL, KAPP!
GIVE IT UP, KAPP! THIS SHIP COULD BLOW AT ANY SECOND!
THEN QUIT DISTRACTING ME WITH A LOT OF CHATTER!
GET READY TO RUN!
MY ANKLE...!
LEAN ON ME! WE'RE ALMOST IN THE CLEAR!

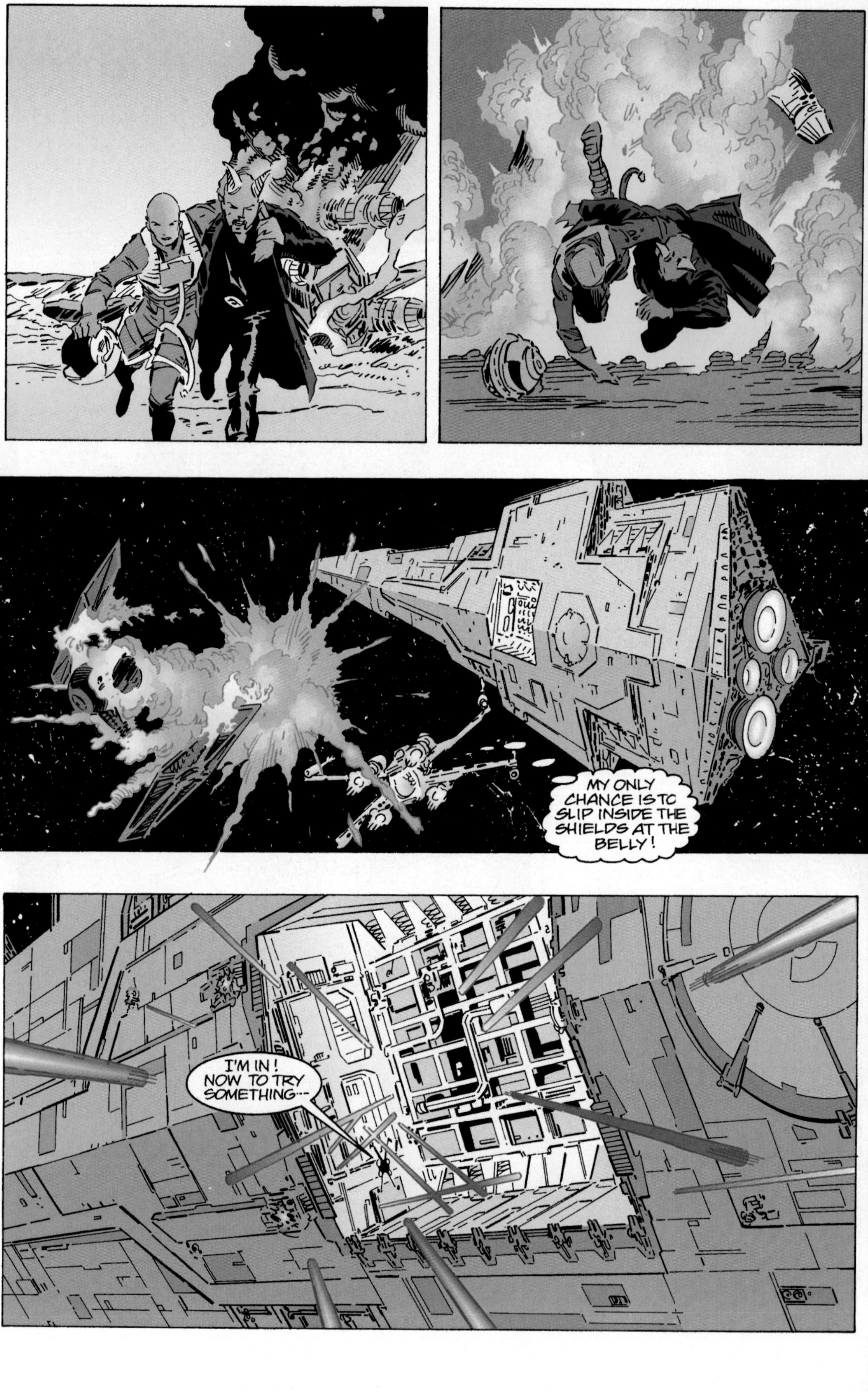
MY ONLY CHANCE IS TO SLIP INSIDE THE SHIELDS AT THE BELLY!
I'M IN! NOW TO TRY SOMETHING--

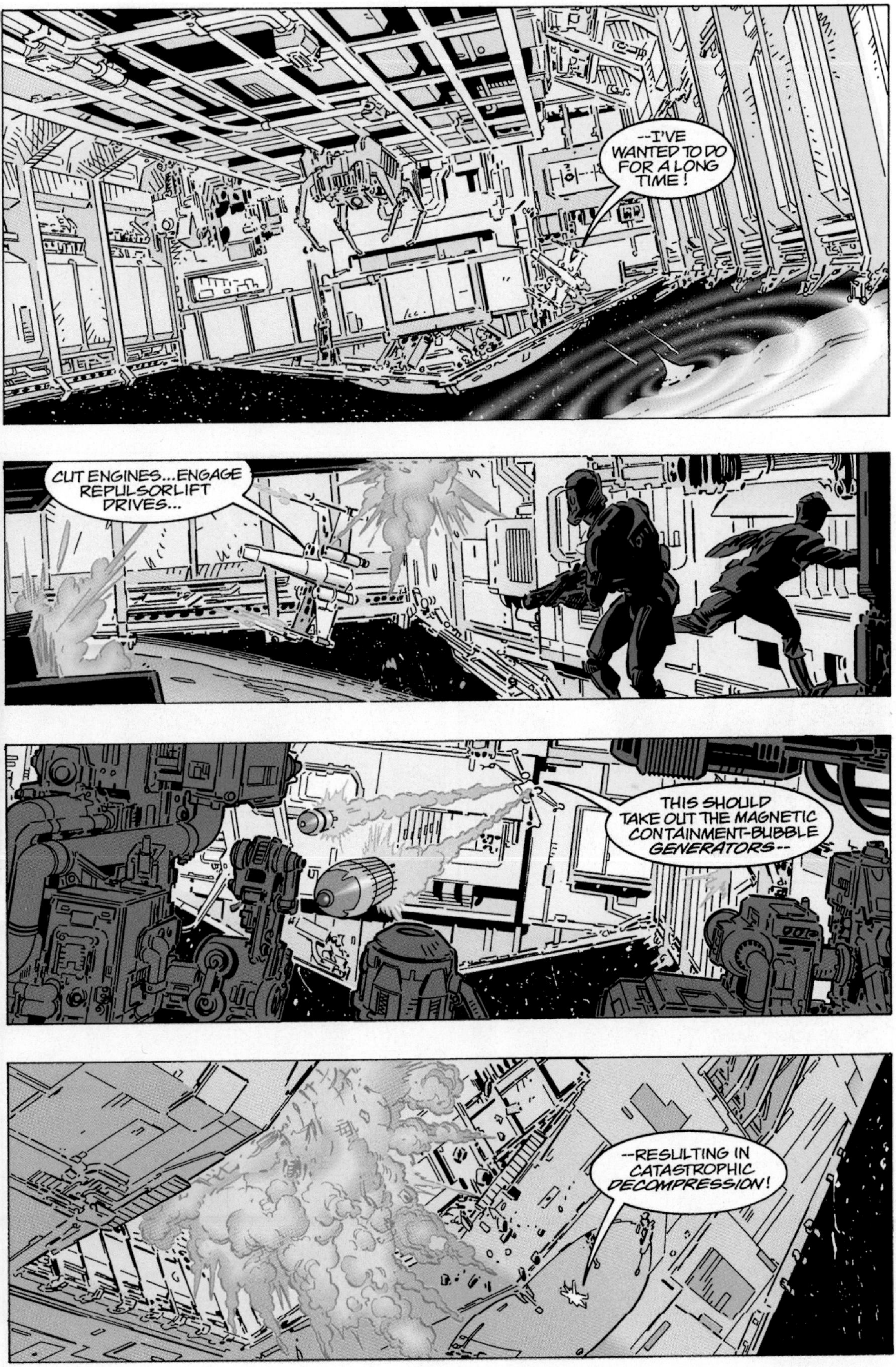
--I'VE WANTED TO DO FOR A LONG TIME!
CUT ENGINES...ENGAGE REPULSORLIFT DRIVES...
THIS SHOULD TAKE OUT THE MAGNETIC CONTAINMENT-BUBBLE GENERATORS--
--RESULTING IN CATASTROPHIC DECOMPRESSION!

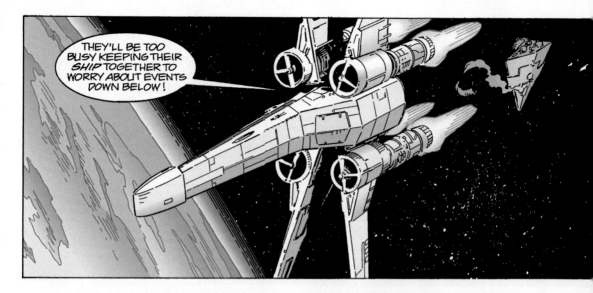

THEY'LL BE TOO BUSY KEEPING THEIR *SHIP* TOGETHER TO WORRY ABOUT EVENTS DOWN BELOW!

CAPTURING FIRITH WAS NO *IMPERIAL* MISSION! AND THIS BASE, I'LL WAGER, WAS BUILT ENTIRELY FROM *EMBEZZLED FUNDS!*

IT'S A CHANGING WORLD, SIXTUS! ONE MUST ADAPT OR DIE!

EVEN IF IT MEANS ABANDONING YOUR OWN MEN TO *SLAVERY!?*

I TOLD YOU THE MISSION WOULD INVOLVE SACRIFICES! YOU SHOULD BE WILLING TO GIVE UP YOUR VERY *LIFE* FOR YOUR EMPEROR!

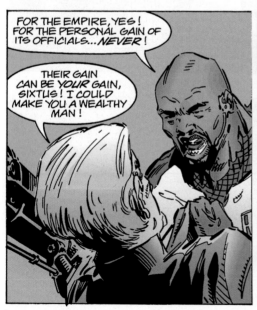

FOR THE EMPIRE, YES! FOR THE PERSONAL GAIN OF ITS OFFICIALS... *NEVER!*

THEIR GAIN CAN BE *YOUR* GAIN, SIXTUS! I COULD MAKE YOU A WEALTHY MAN!

I CARE ONLY ABOUT *HONOR,* AND YOU, SEMTIN, HAVE *NONE!*

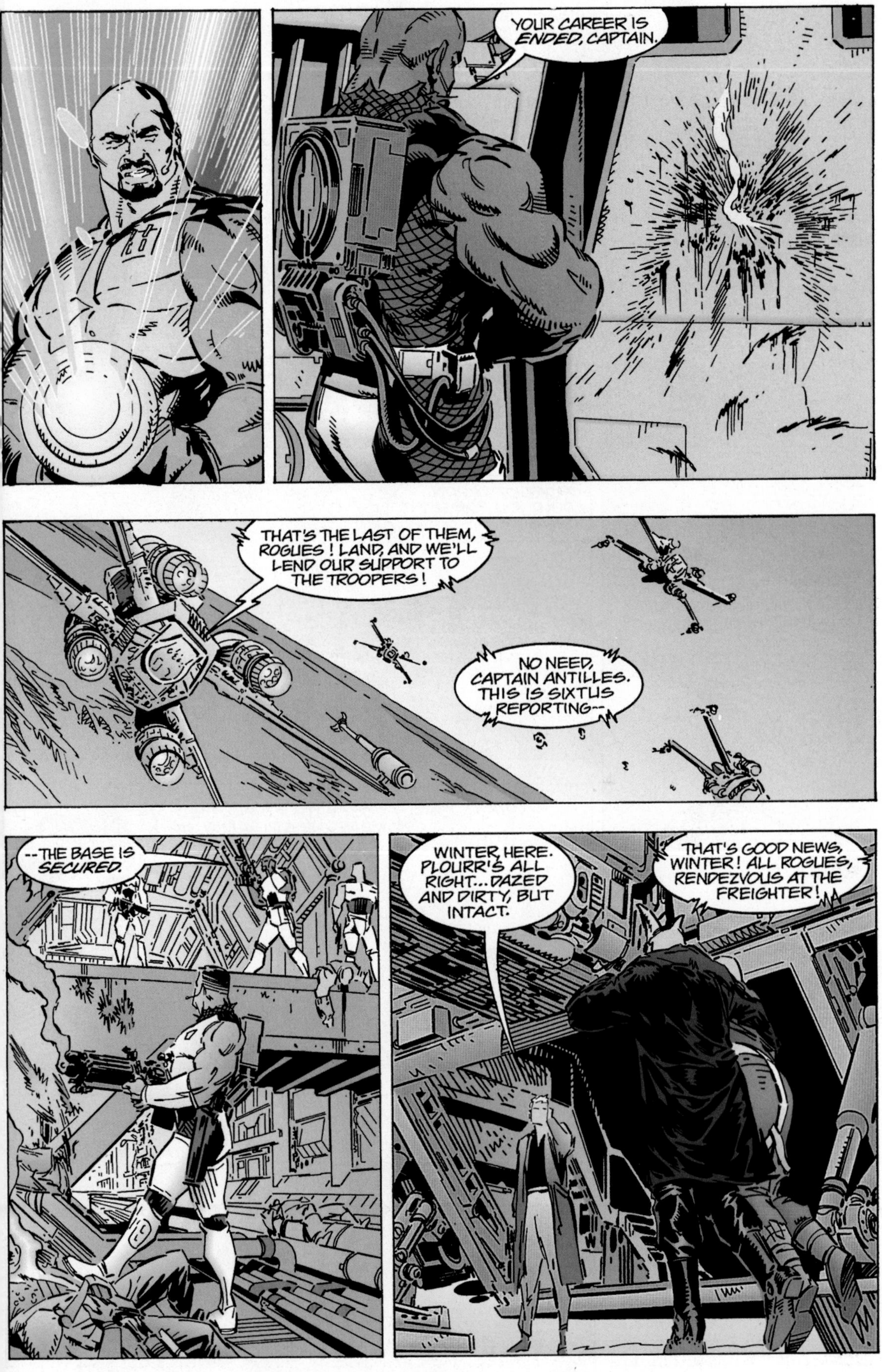
YOUR CAREER IS ENDED, CAPTAIN.
THAT'S THE LAST OF THEM, ROGUES! LAND, AND WE'LL LEND OUR SUPPORT TO THE TROOPERS!
NO NEED, CAPTAIN ANTILLES. THIS IS SIXTUS REPORTING--
--THE BASE IS SECURED.
WINTER, HERE. PLOURR'S ALL RIGHT... DAZED AND DIRTY, BUT INTACT.
THAT'S GOOD NEWS, WINTER! ALL ROGUES, RENDEZVOUS AT THE FREIGHTER!

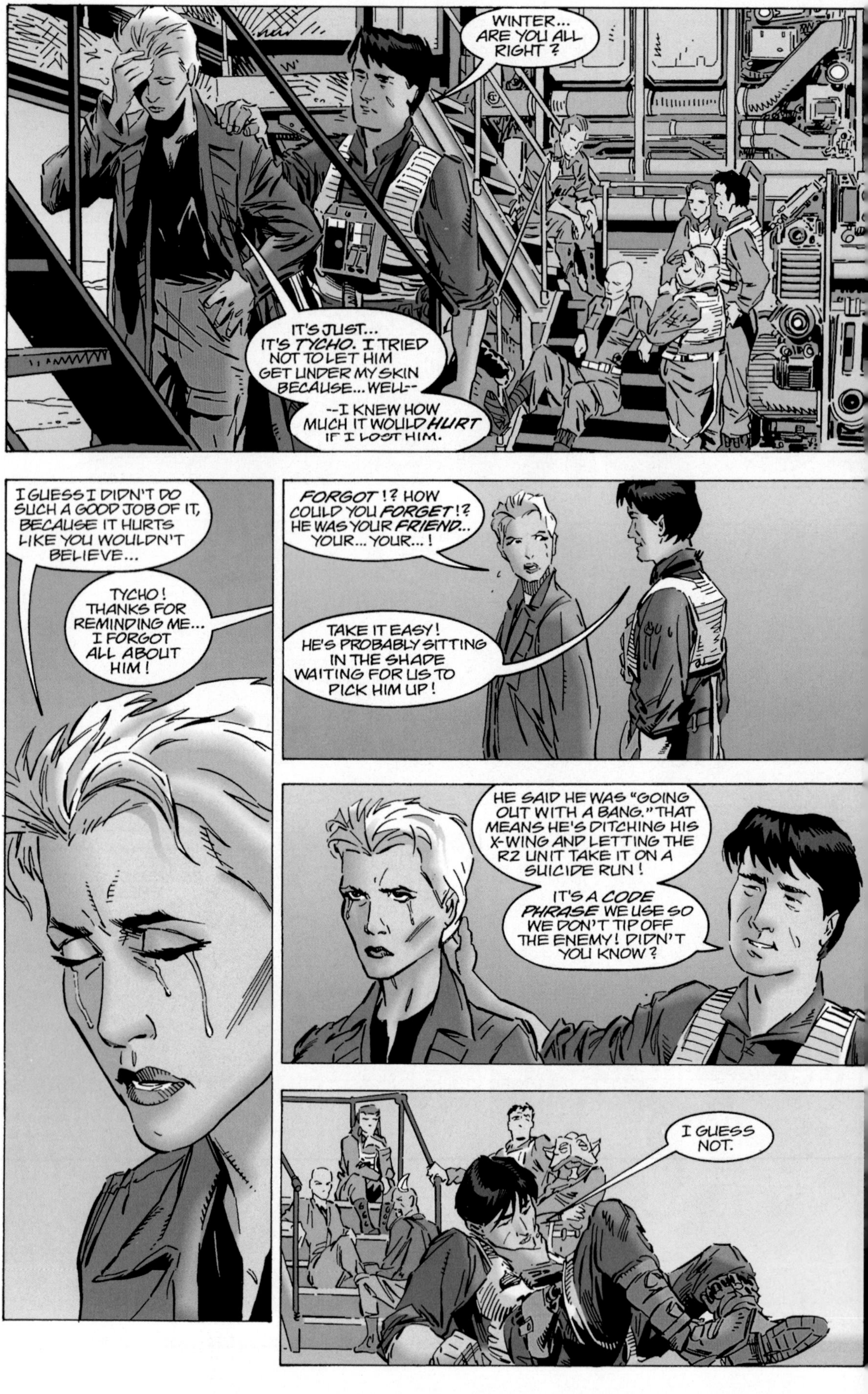
WINTER... ARE YOU ALL RIGHT?
IT'S JUST... IT'S TYCHO. I TRIED NOT TO LET HIM GET UNDER MY SKIN BECAUSE... WELL--
--I KNEW HOW MUCH IT WOULD HURT IF I LOST HIM.
I GUESS I DIDN'T DO SUCH A GOOD JOB OF IT, BECAUSE IT HURTS LIKE YOU WOULDN'T BELIEVE...
TYCHO! THANKS FOR REMINDING ME... I FORGOT ALL ABOUT HIM!
FORGOT!? HOW COULD YOU FORGET!? HE WAS YOUR FRIEND... YOUR... YOUR...!
TAKE IT EASY! HE'S PROBABLY SITTING IN THE SHADE WAITING FOR US TO PICK HIM UP!
HE SAID HE WAS "GOING OUT WITH A BANG." THAT MEANS HE'S DITCHING HIS X-WING AND LETTING THE R2 UNIT TAKE IT ON A SUICIDE RUN!
IT'S A CODE PHRASE WE USE SO WE DON'T TIP OFF THE ENEMY! DIDN'T YOU KNOW?
I GUESS NOT.

YOU SHOULD SEE *SOME* BENEFIT FROM YOUR HELP—THE WEAPONRY FROM EIDOLON BASE WILL GO A LONG WAY TOWARD ARMING THE *LEGITIMATE* GOVERNMENT OF TATOOINE AND CONTROLLING THE *WARLORDS*.

*HMPH!* EITHER WAY, I'M STILL PAYING MONEY TO *SCOUNDRELS.*

AT LEAST YOU'LL BE PAYING IT TO SCOUNDRELS YOU *VOTED* FOR.

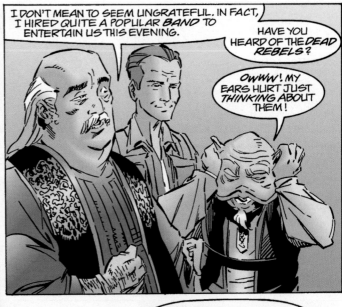

I DON'T MEAN TO SEEM UNGRATEFUL. IN FACT, I HIRED QUITE A POPULAR *BAND* TO ENTERTAIN US THIS EVENING.

HAVE YOU HEARD OF THE *DEAD REBELS?*

*OWWW!* MY EARS HURT JUST *THINKING* ABOUT THEM!

I HAVE TO APOLOGIZE AGAIN FOR THE MIX-UP, WINTER. I DIDN'T REALLY MEAN TO *WORRY* YOU THAT WAY.

I WAS ONLY WORRIED ABOUT ONE THING, TYCHO—

—THAT I WOULDN'T BE ABLE TO GIVE YOU THAT *KISS* I PROMISED YOU WHEN YOU FIRST ARRIVED.

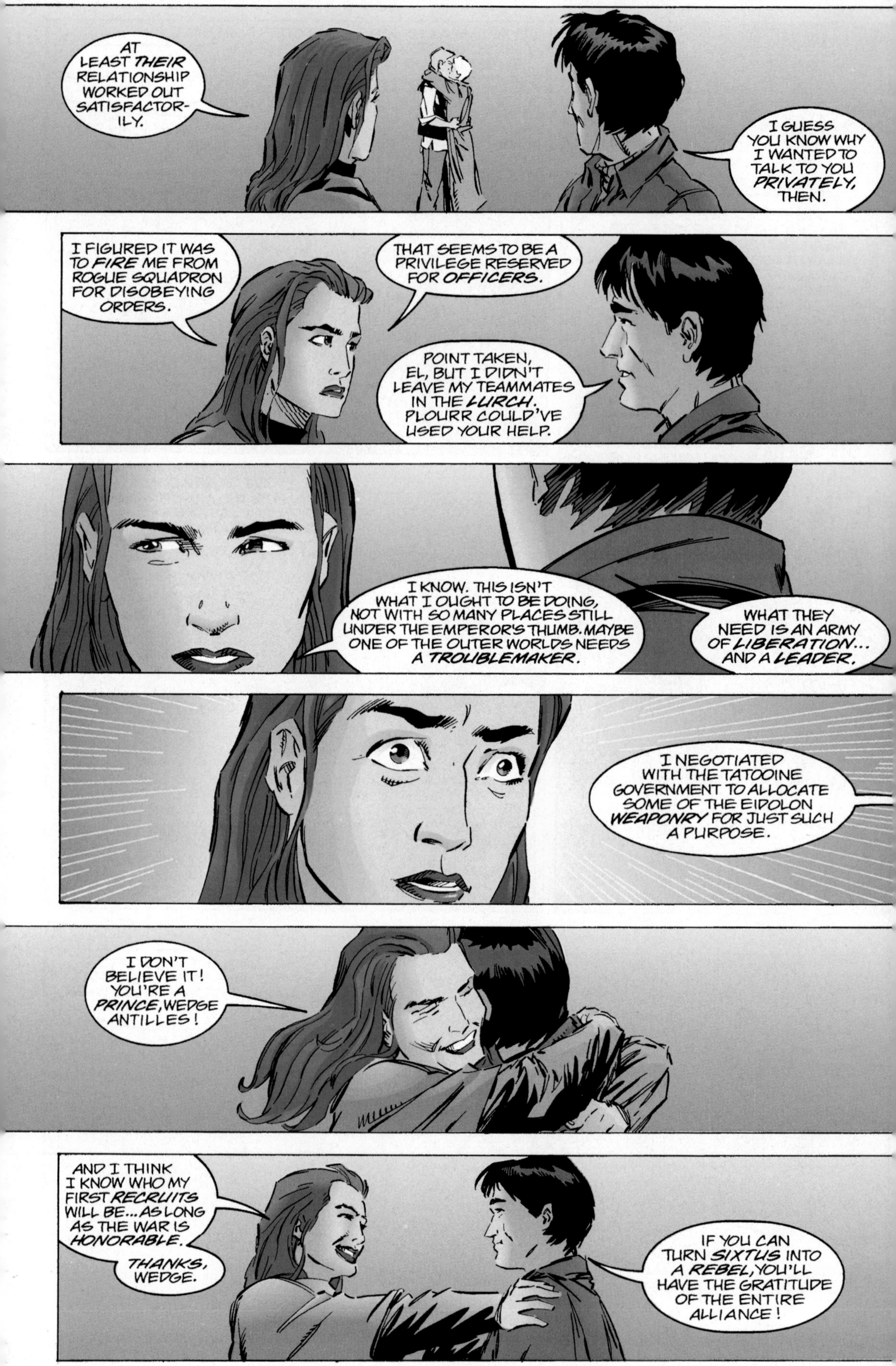
AT LEAST THEIR RELATIONSHIP WORKED OUT SATISFACTOR-ILY.
I GUESS YOU KNOW WHY I WANTED TO TALK TO YOU PRIVATELY, THEN.
I FIGURED IT WAS TO FIRE ME FROM ROGUE SQUADRON FOR DISOBEYING ORDERS.
THAT SEEMS TO BE A PRIVILEGE RESERVED FOR OFFICERS.
POINT TAKEN, EL, BUT I DIDN'T LEAVE MY TEAMMATES IN THE LURCH. PLOURR COULD'VE USED YOUR HELP.
I KNOW. THIS ISN'T WHAT I OUGHT TO BE DOING, NOT WITH SO MANY PLACES STILL UNDER THE EMPEROR'S THUMB. MAYBE ONE OF THE OUTER WORLDS NEEDS A TROUBLEMAKER.
WHAT THEY NEED IS AN ARMY OF LIBERATION... AND A LEADER.
I NEGOTIATED WITH THE TATOOINE GOVERNMENT TO ALLOCATE SOME OF THE EIDOLON WEAPONRY FOR JUST SUCH A PURPOSE.
I DON'T BELIEVE IT! YOU'RE A PRINCE, WEDGE ANTILLES!
AND I THINK I KNOW WHO MY FIRST RECRUITS WILL BE... AS LONG AS THE WAR IS HONORABLE.
THANKS, WEDGE.
IF YOU CAN TURN SIXTUS INTO A REBEL, YOU'LL HAVE THE GRATITUDE OF THE ENTIRE ALLIANCE!

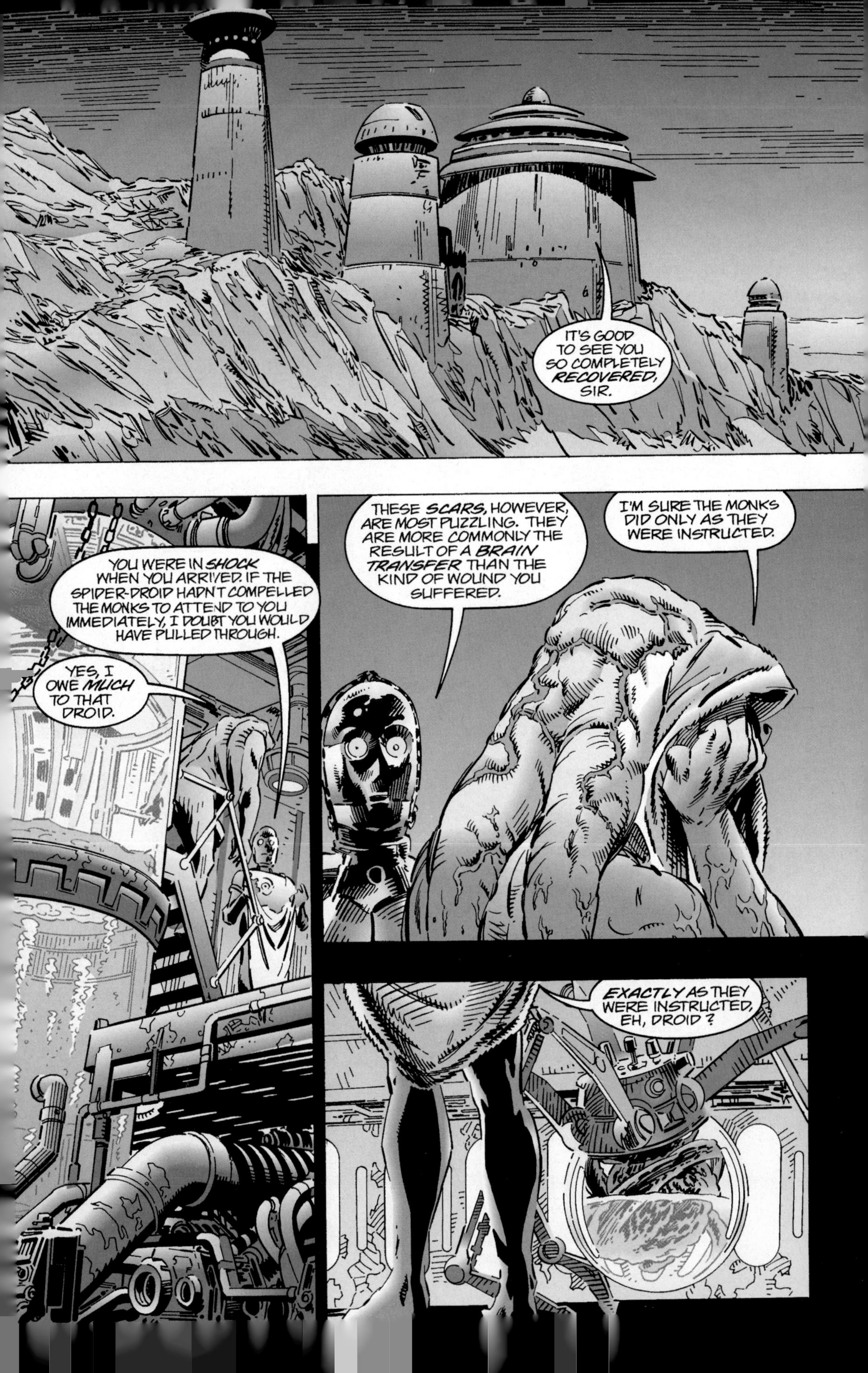
IT'S GOOD TO SEE YOU SO COMPLETELY RECOVERED, SIR.
YOU WERE IN SHOCK WHEN YOU ARRIVED. IF THE SPIDER-DROID HADN'T COMPELLED THE MONKS TO ATTEND TO YOU IMMEDIATELY, I DOUBT YOU WOULD HAVE PULLED THROUGH.
YES, I OWE MUCH TO THAT DROID.
THESE SCARS, HOWEVER, ARE MOST PUZZLING. THEY ARE MORE COMMONLY THE RESULT OF A BRAIN TRANSFER THAN THE KIND OF WOUND YOU SUFFERED.
I'M SURE THE MONKS DID ONLY AS THEY WERE INSTRUCTED.
EXACTLY AS THEY WERE INSTRUCTED, EH, DROID?

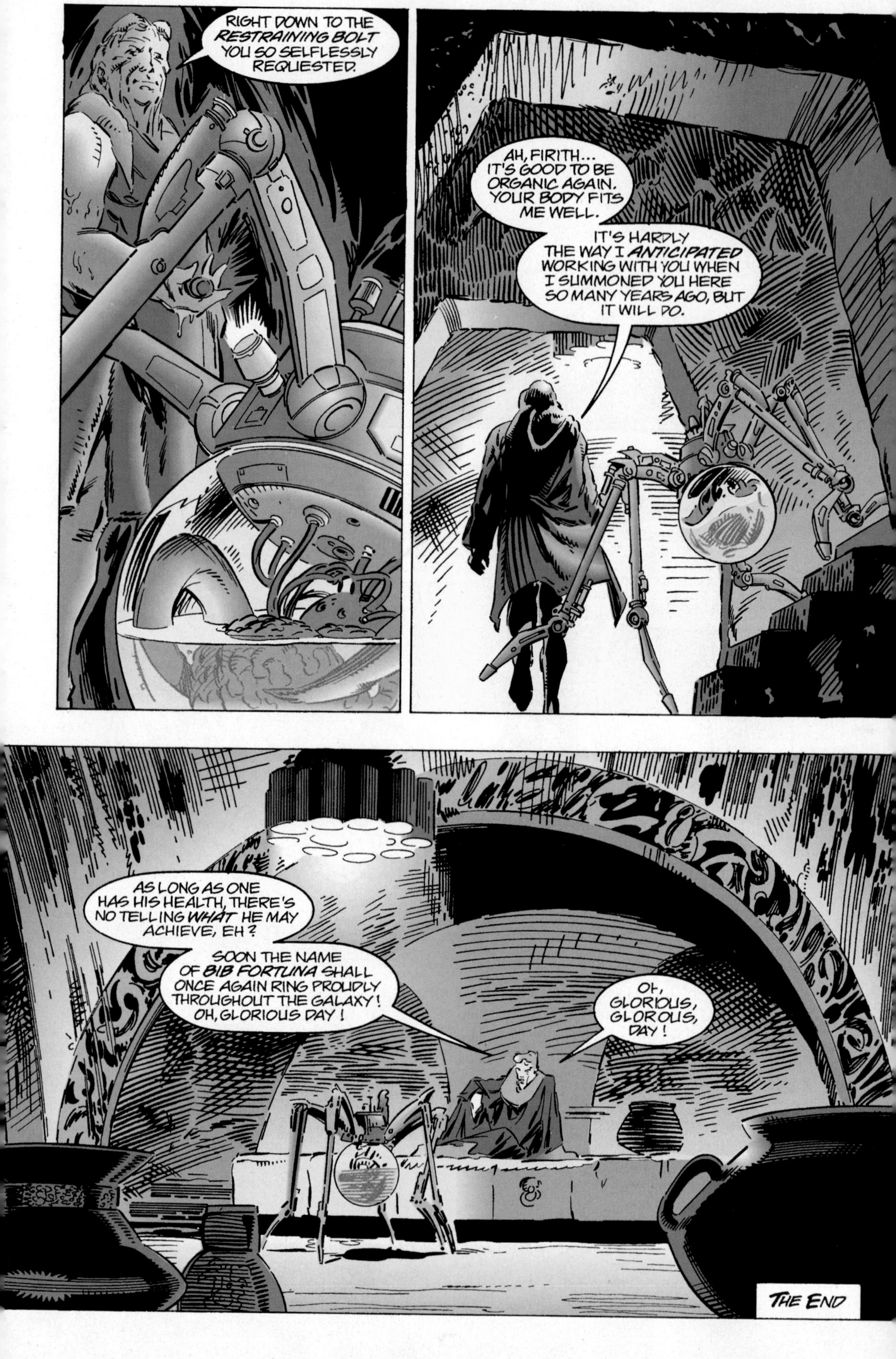
RIGHT DOWN TO THE RESTRAINING BOLT YOU SO SELFLESSLY REQUESTED.
AH, FIRITH... IT'S GOOD TO BE ORGANIC AGAIN. YOUR BODY FITS ME WELL.
IT'S HARDLY THE WAY I ANTICIPATED WORKING WITH YOU WHEN I SUMMONED YOU HERE SO MANY YEARS AGO, BUT IT WILL DO.
AS LONG AS ONE HAS HIS HEALTH, THERE'S NO TELLING WHAT HE MAY ACHIEVE, EH?
SOON THE NAME OF BIB FORTUNA SHALL ONCE AGAIN RING PROUDLY THROUGHOUT THE GALAXY! OH, GLORIOUS DAY!
OH, GLORIOUS, GLOROUS, DAY!
THE END

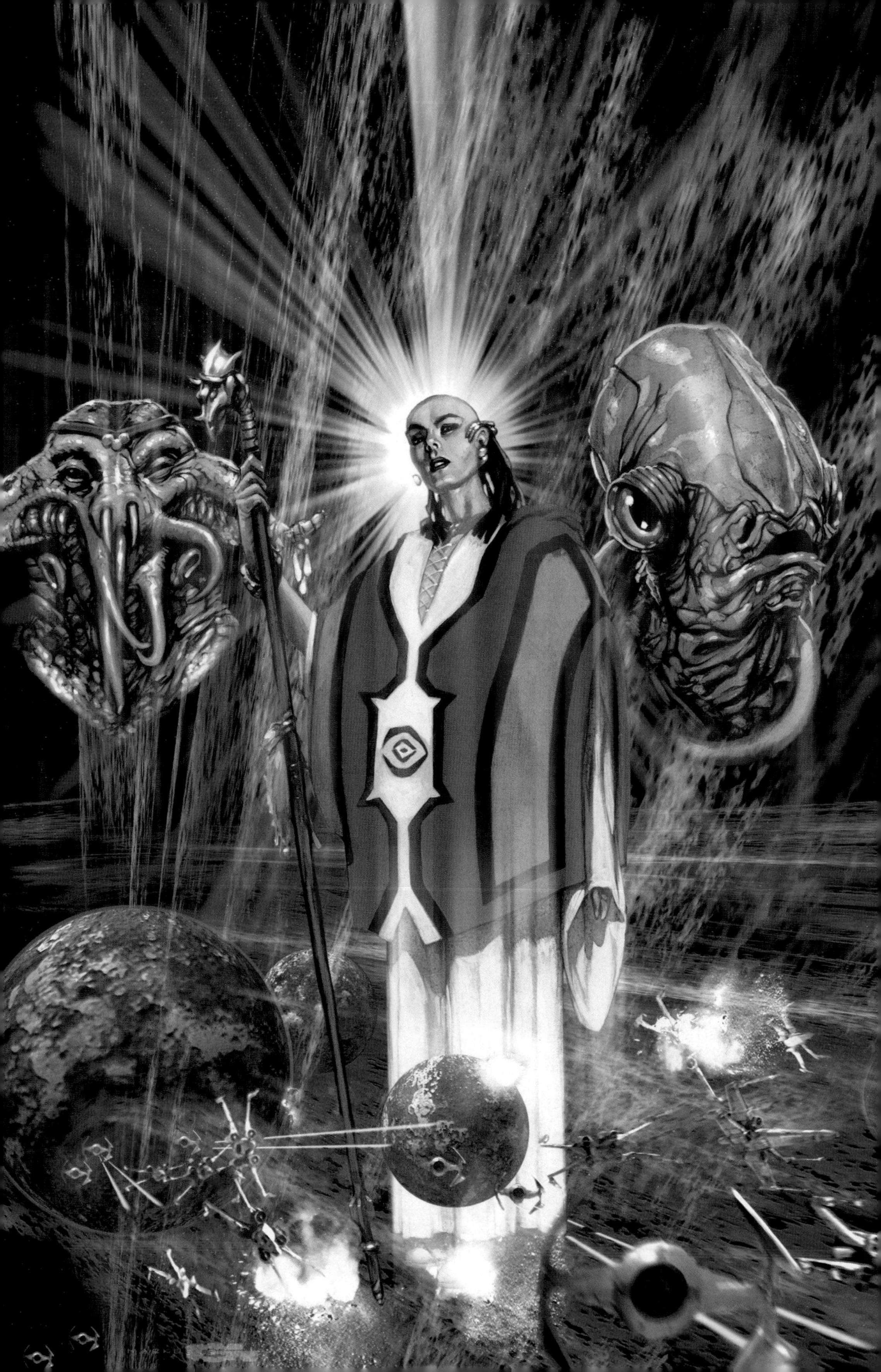

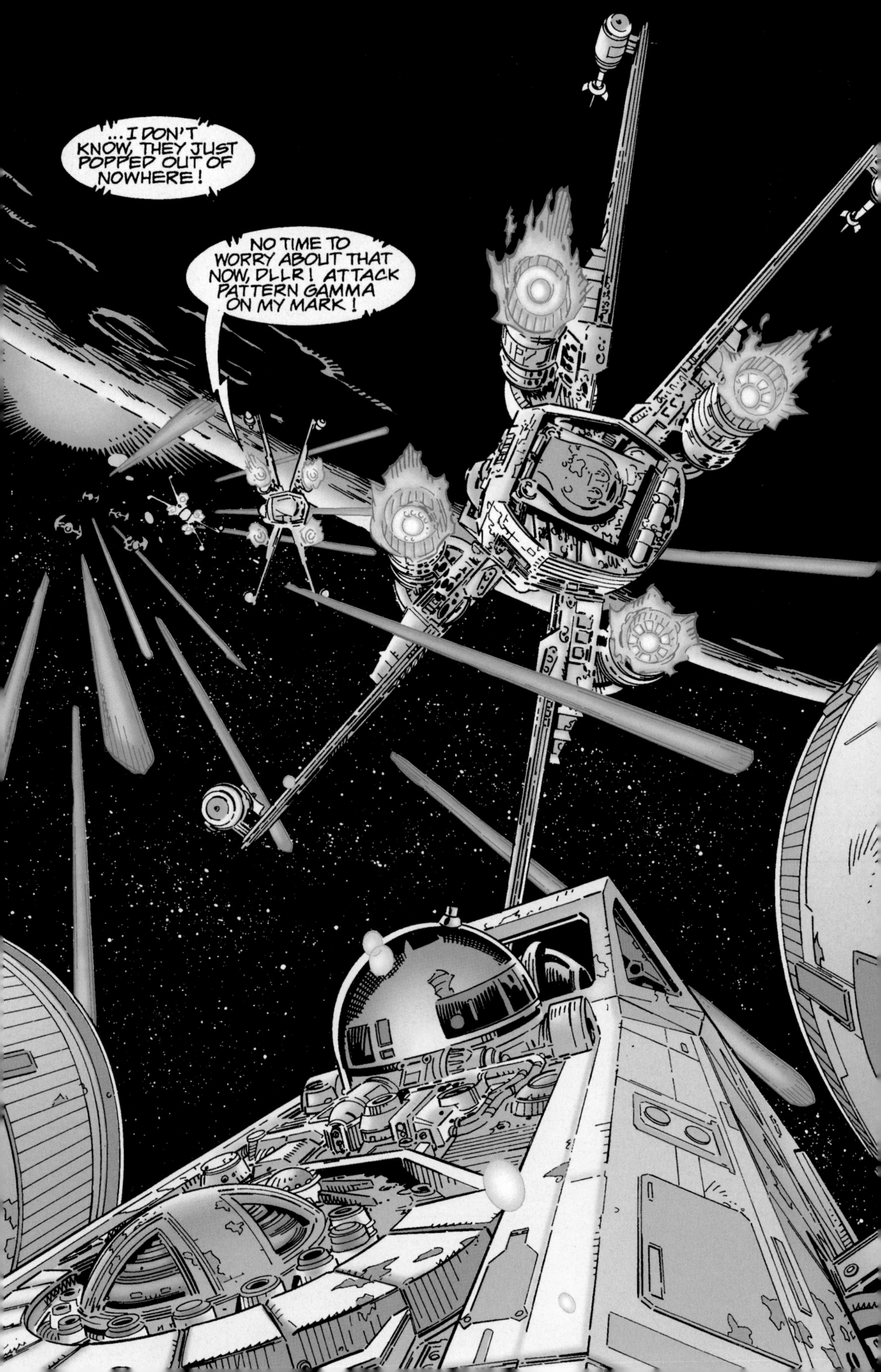
...I DON'T KNOW, THEY JUST POPPED OUT OF NOWHERE!
NO TIME TO WORRY ABOUT THAT NOW, DLLR! ATTACK PATTERN GAMMA ON MY MARK!

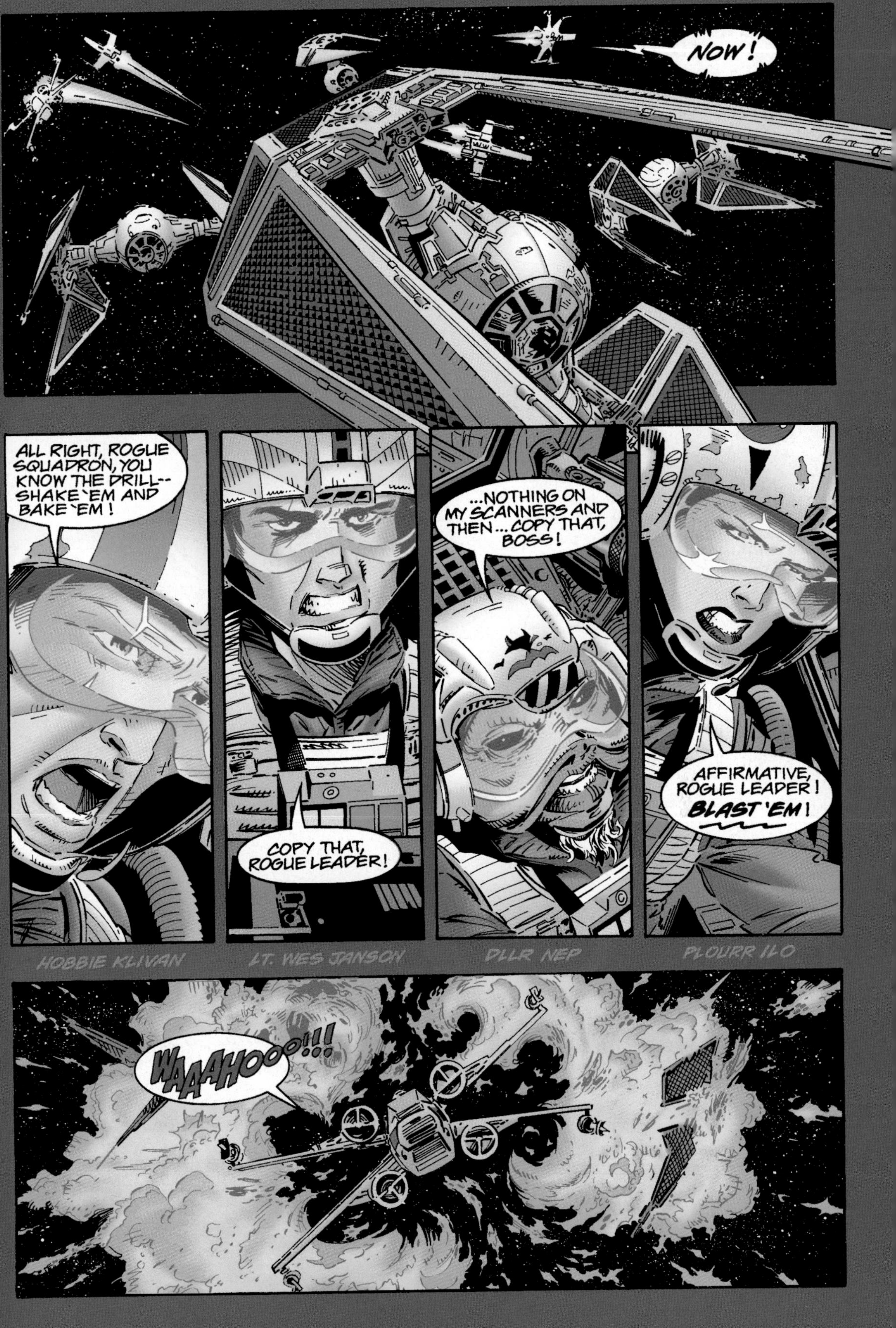
NOW!
ALL RIGHT, ROGUE SQUADRON, YOU KNOW THE DRILL-- SHAKE 'EM AND BAKE 'EM!
COPY THAT, ROGUE LEADER!
...NOTHING ON MY SCANNERS AND THEN... COPY THAT, BOSS!
AFFIRMATIVE, ROGUE LEADER! BLAST 'EM!
HOBBIE KLIVAN
LT. WES JANSON
DLLR NEP
PLOURR ILO
WAAAHOOO!!!

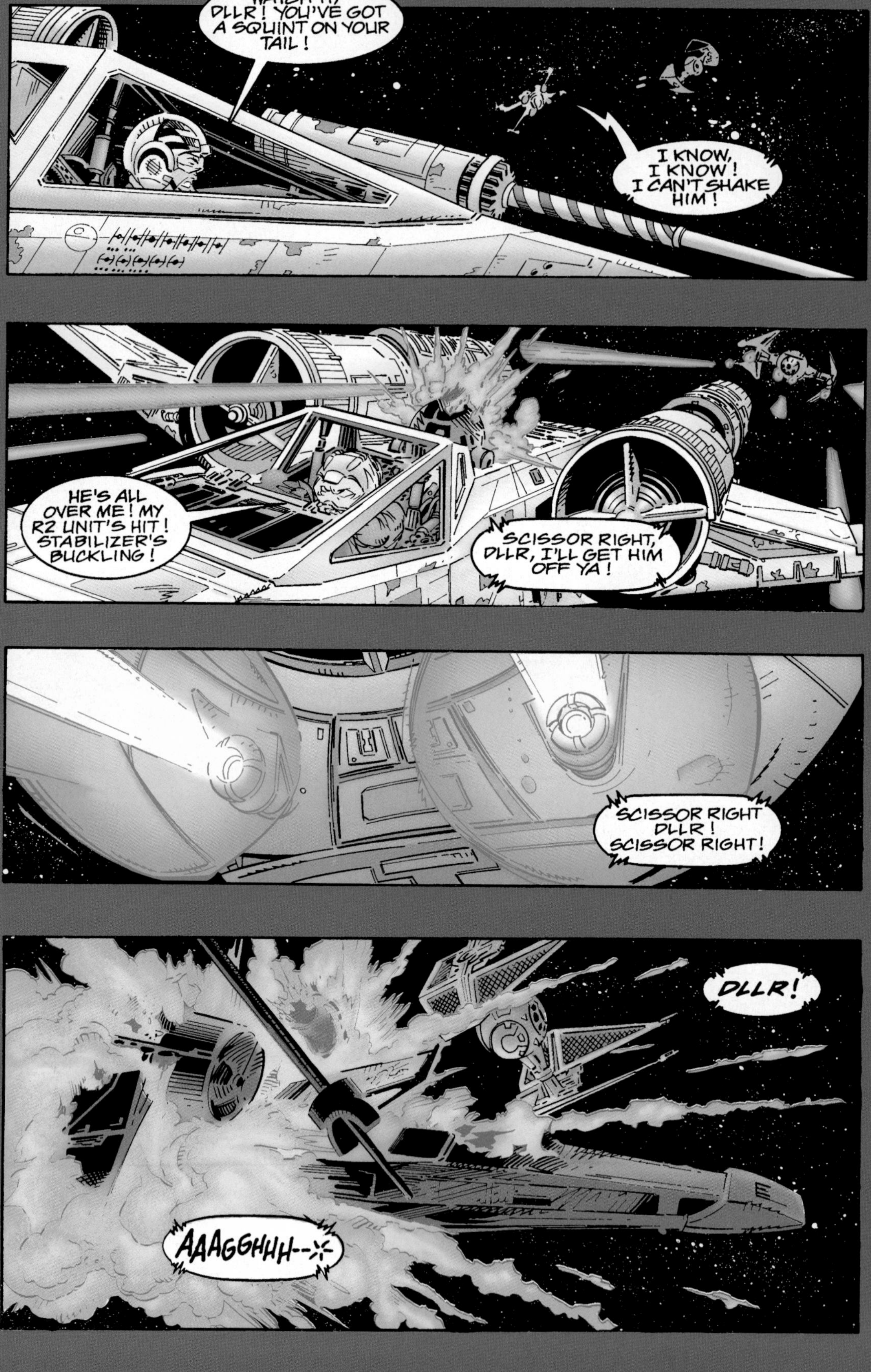
WATCH IT, DLLR! YOU'VE GOT A SQUINT ON YOUR TAIL!
I KNOW, I KNOW! I CAN'T SHAKE HIM!
HE'S ALL OVER ME! MY R2 UNIT'S HIT! STABILIZER'S BUCKLING!
SCISSOR RIGHT, DLLR, I'LL GET HIM OFF YA!
SCISSOR RIGHT DLLR! SCISSOR RIGHT!
DLLR!
AAAGGHHH--

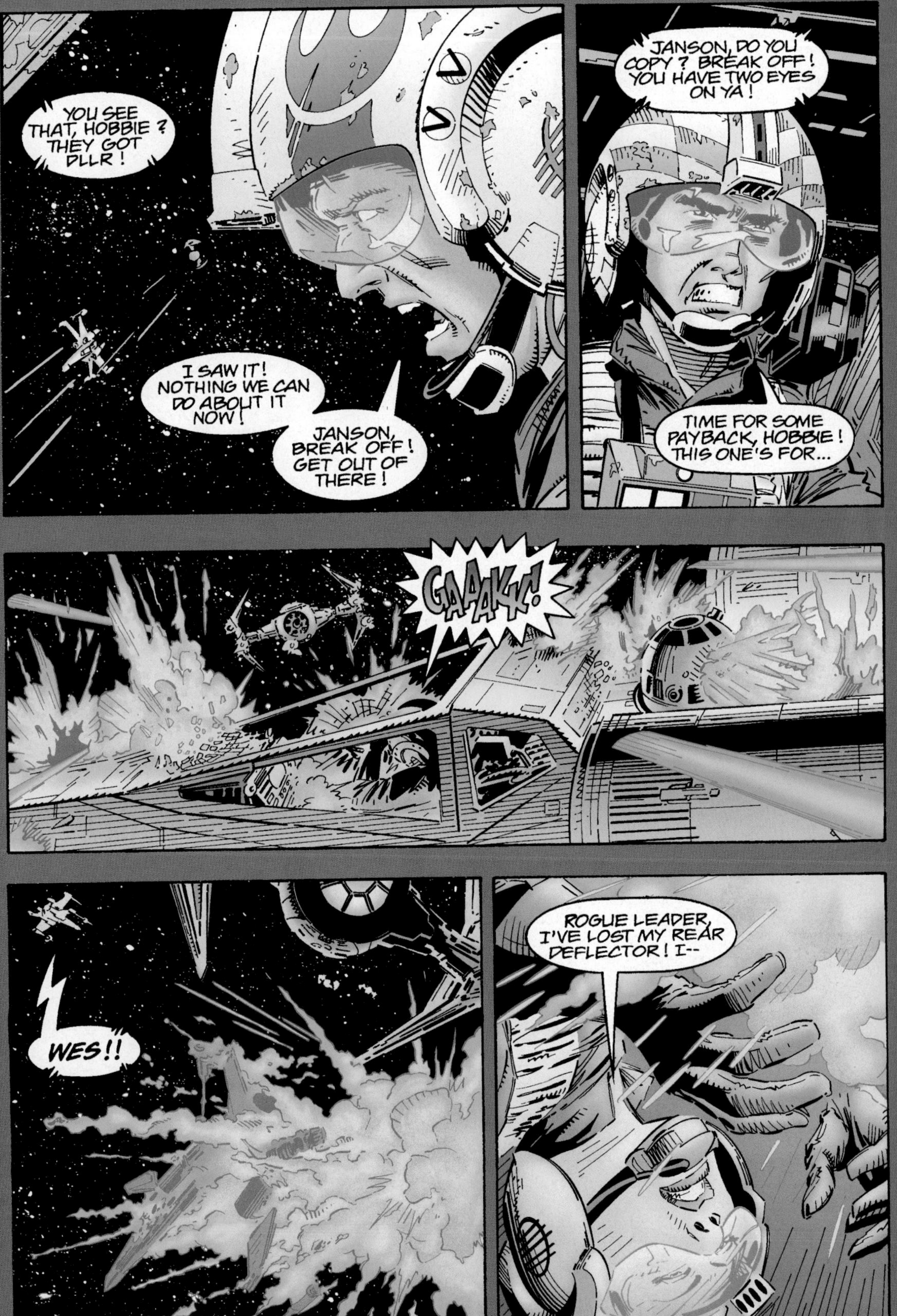
YOU SEE THAT, HOBBIE? THEY GOT DLLR!
I SAW IT! NOTHING WE CAN DO ABOUT IT NOW!
JANSON, BREAK OFF! GET OUT OF THERE!
JANSON, DO YOU COPY? BREAK OFF! YOU HAVE TWO EYES ON YA!
TIME FOR SOME PAYBACK, HOBBIE! THIS ONE'S FOR...
GAAAKK!
WES!!
ROGUE LEADER, I'VE LOST MY REAR DEFLECTOR! I--

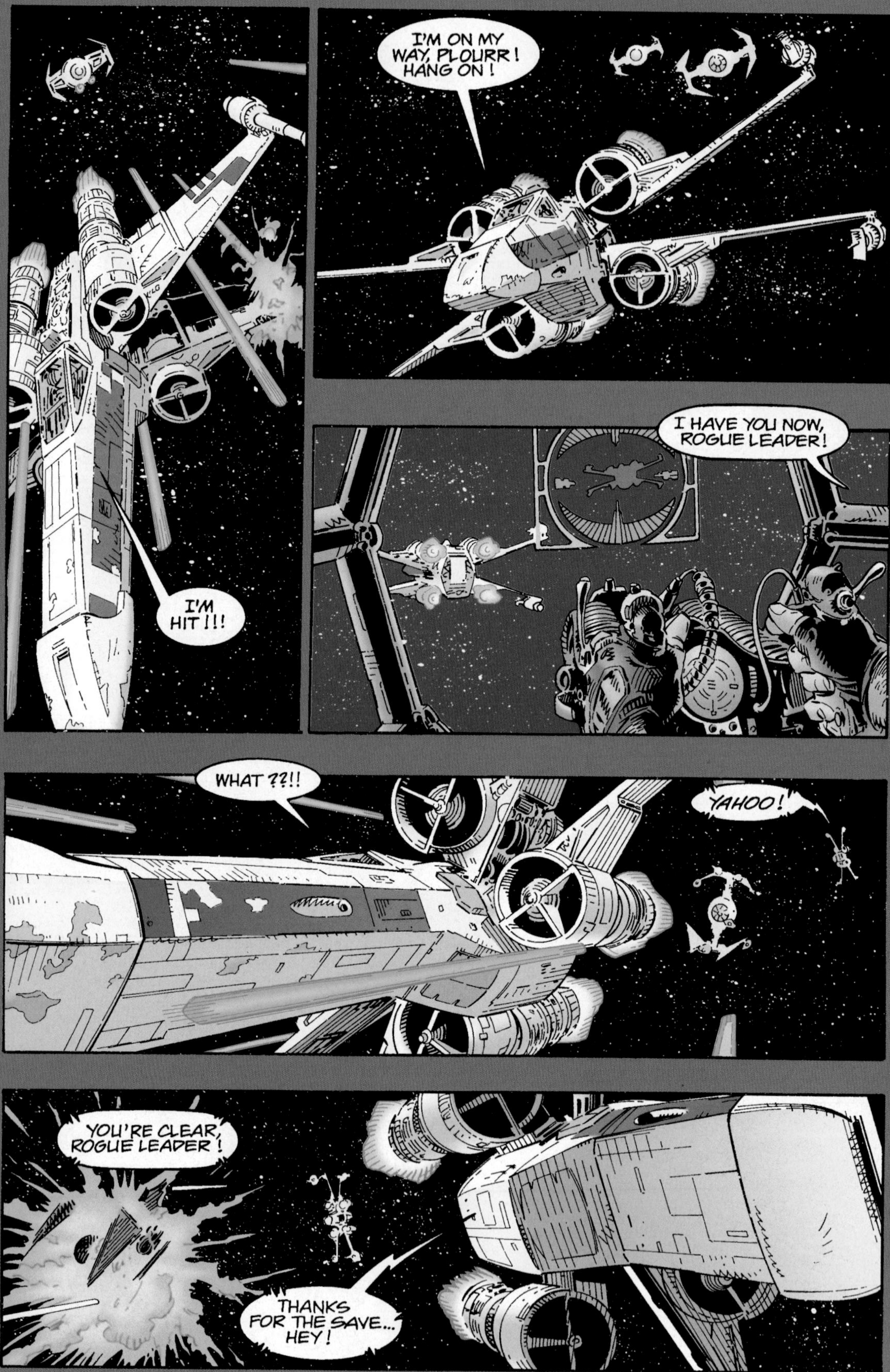
I'M ON MY WAY, PLOURR! HANG ON!
I'M HIT!!!
I HAVE YOU NOW, ROGUE LEADER!
WHAT ??!!
YAHOO!
YOU'RE CLEAR, ROGUE LEADER!
THANKS FOR THE SAVE... HEY!

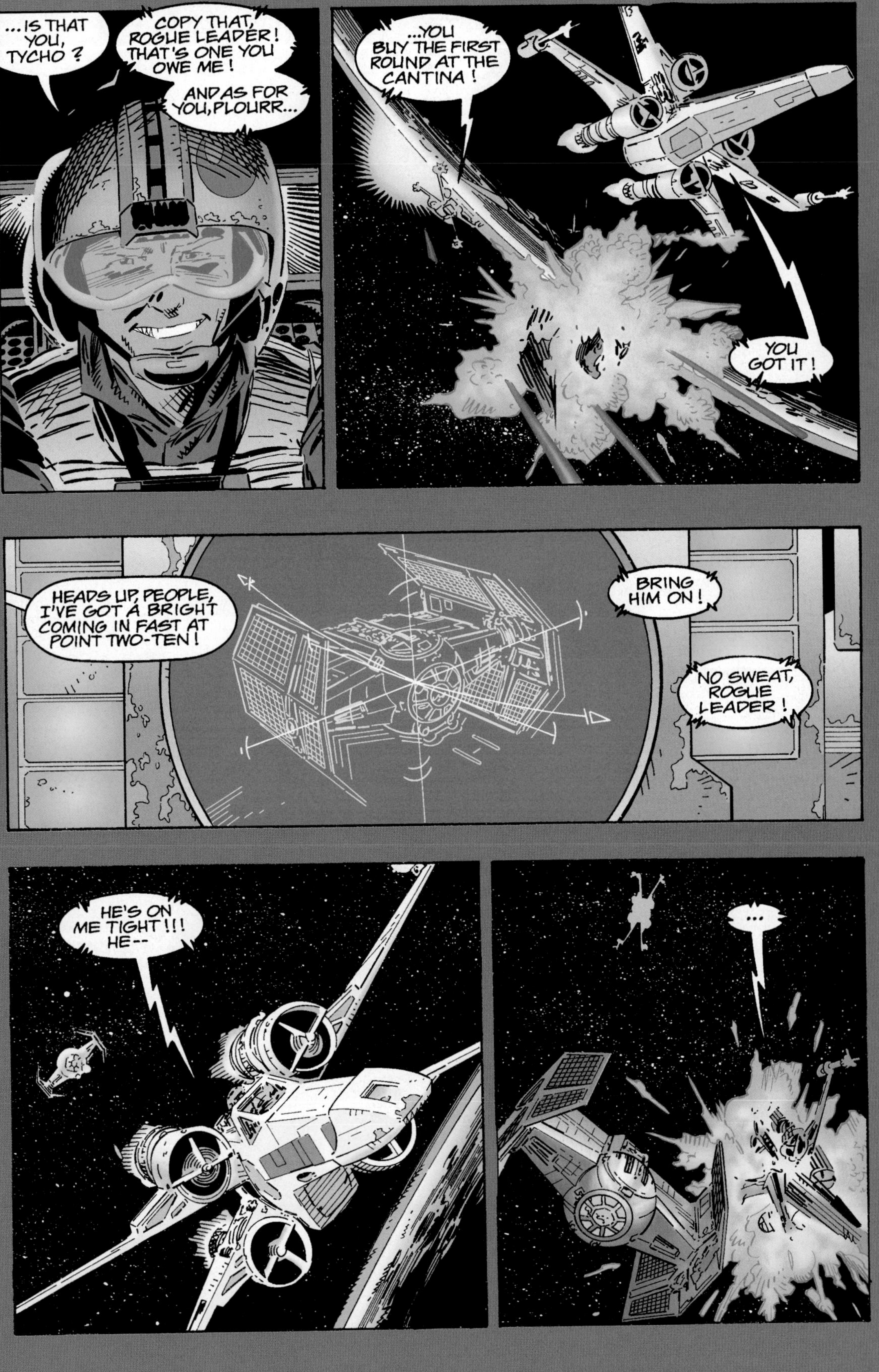
...IS THAT YOU, TYCHO ?
COPY THAT, ROGUE LEADER! THAT'S ONE YOU OWE ME!
AND AS FOR YOU, PLOURR...
...YOU BUY THE FIRST ROUND AT THE CANTINA!
YOU GOT IT!
HEADS UP, PEOPLE, I'VE GOT A BRIGHT COMING IN FAST AT POINT TWO-TEN!
BRING HIM ON!
NO SWEAT, ROGUE LEADER!
HE'S ON ME TIGHT!!! HE--
...

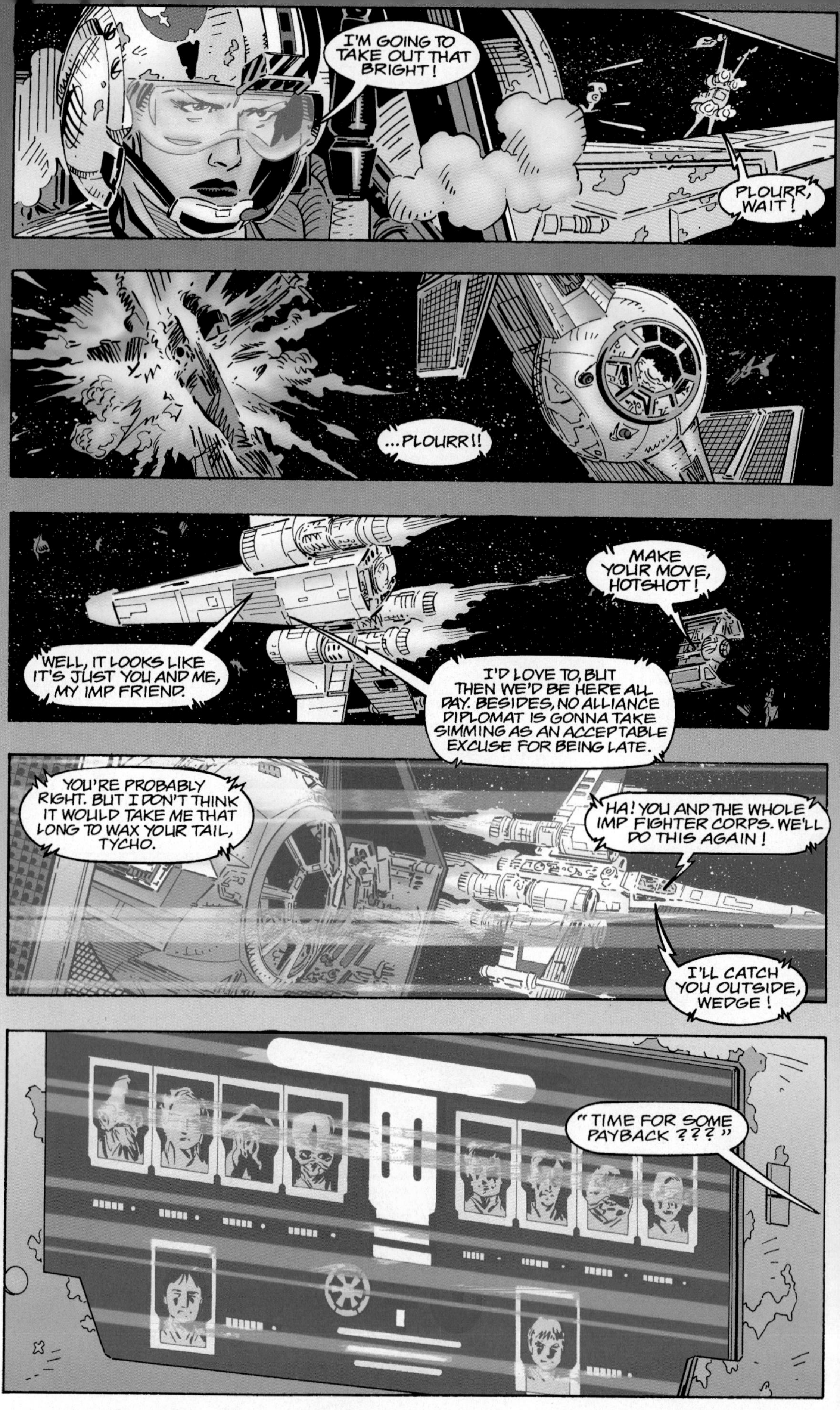
I'M GOING TO TAKE OUT THAT BRIGHT!
PLOURR, WAIT!
...PLOURR!!
MAKE YOUR MOVE, HOTSHOT!
WELL, IT LOOKS LIKE IT'S JUST YOU AND ME, MY IMP FRIEND.
I'D LOVE TO, BUT THEN WE'D BE HERE ALL DAY. BESIDES, NO ALLIANCE DIPLOMAT IS GONNA TAKE SIMMING AS AN ACCEPTABLE EXCUSE FOR BEING LATE.
YOU'RE PROBABLY RIGHT. BUT I DON'T THINK IT WOULD TAKE ME THAT LONG TO WAX YOUR TAIL, TYCHO.
HA! YOU AND THE WHOLE IMP FIGHTER CORPS. WE'LL DO THIS AGAIN!
I'LL CATCH YOU OUTSIDE, WEDGE!
"TIME FOR SOME PAYBACK???"

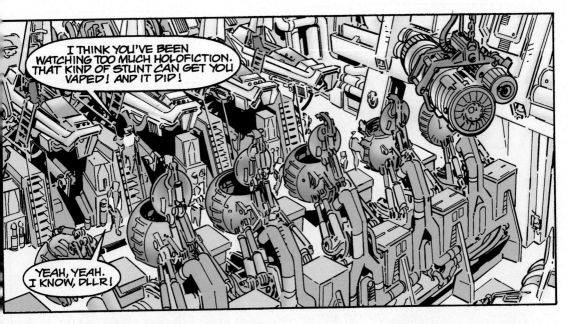

I THINK YOU'VE BEEN WATCHING TOO MUCH HOLOFICTION. THAT KIND OF STUNT CAN GET YOU VAPED! AND IT DID!

YEAH, YEAH. I KNOW, DLLR!

YEAH! WHO RIGGED THE SIMULATOR SEATS WITH AN ELECTRICAL CHARGE, ANYWAY? THAT WAS SOME ZAP!

I FELT THE SENSATION TO BE... EXHILARATING!

IT'S JUST WHEN I HEARD YOU SCREAM, SIMILATOR OR NOT, YOU SOUNDED LIKE YOU WERE REALLY HURT. NOW I KNOW WHAT MADE YOU DO THAT.

I'VE GOT AN IDEA!

YEAH, YOU WOULD, NRIN!

UM...WELL... IT WAS ME.

ACTING ON WEDGE'S ORDERS, OF COURSE.

YOU!!??

HA! I KNEW IT!

YOU SEE, WEDGE BELIEVED THAT THE SIMULATOR LACKED THE PROPER AMOUNT OF REALISM FOR SUCH BATTLE-HARDENED VETERANS AS OURSELVES.

HE FELT THAT A BIT OF EXTRA SIMULATION WAS REQUIRED TO BRING ABOUT THE PROPER RESPONSE.

AND I CONCURRED.

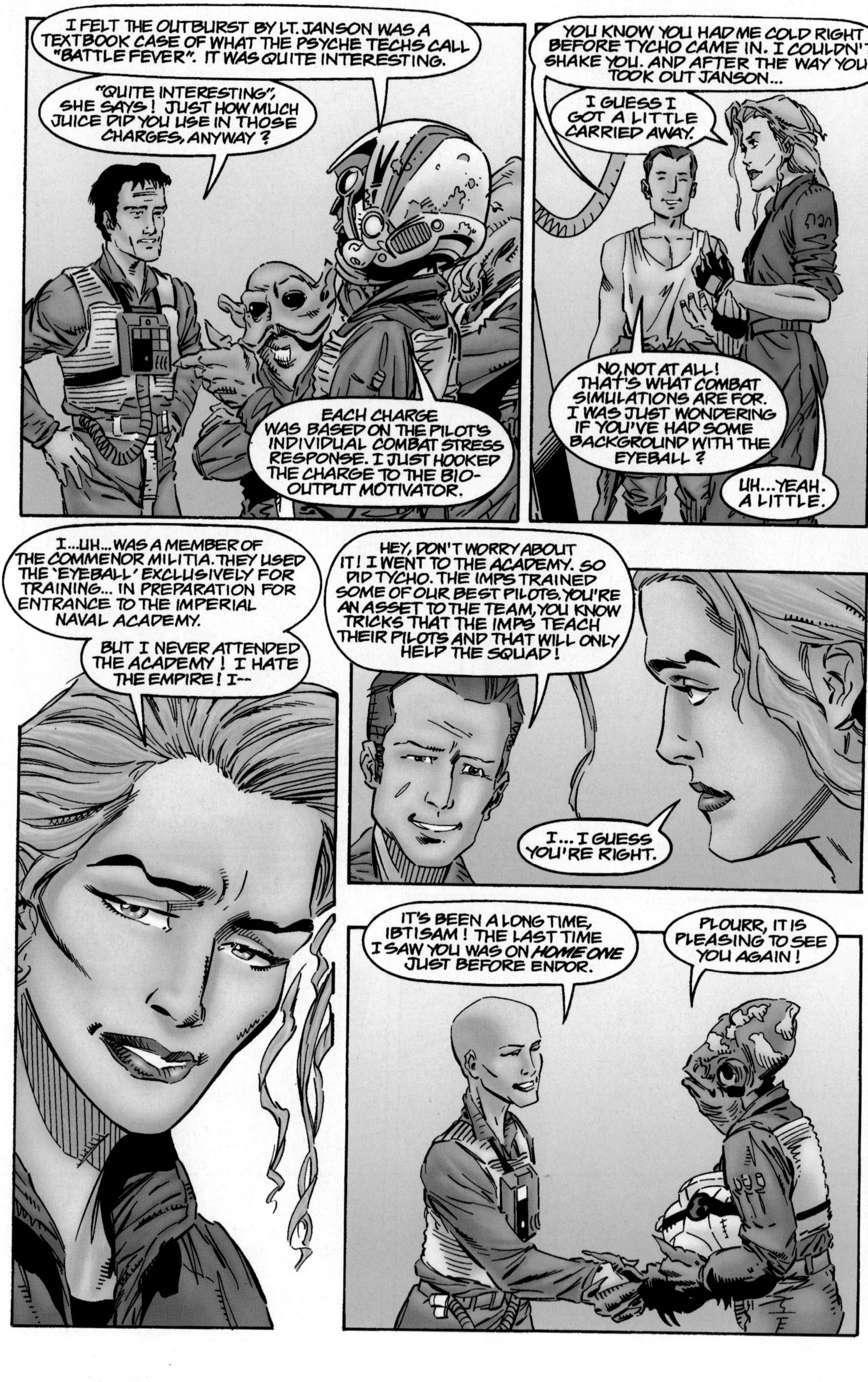
I FELT THE OUTBURST BY LT. JANSON WAS A TEXTBOOK CASE OF WHAT THE PSYCHE TECHS CALL "BATTLE FEVER". IT WAS QUITE INTERESTING.
"QUITE INTERESTING", SHE SAYS! JUST HOW MUCH JUICE DID YOU USE IN THOSE CHARGES, ANYWAY?
EACH CHARGE WAS BASED ON THE PILOT'S INDIVIDUAL COMBAT STRESS RESPONSE. I JUST HOOKED THE CHARGE TO THE BIO-OUTPUT MOTIVATOR.
YOU KNOW YOU HAD ME COLD RIGHT BEFORE TYCHO CAME IN. I COULDN'T SHAKE YOU. AND AFTER THE WAY YOU TOOK OUT JANSON...
I GUESS I GOT A LITTLE CARRIED AWAY.
NO, NOT AT ALL! THAT'S WHAT COMBAT SIMULATIONS ARE FOR. I WAS JUST WONDERING IF YOU'VE HAD SOME BACKGROUND WITH THE EYEBALL?
UH...YEAH. A LITTLE.
I...UH...WAS A MEMBER OF THE COMMENOR MILITIA. THEY USED THE 'EYEBALL' EXCLUSIVELY FOR TRAINING... IN PREPARATION FOR ENTRANCE TO THE IMPERIAL NAVAL ACADEMY.
BUT I NEVER ATTENDED THE ACADEMY! I HATE THE EMPIRE! I--
HEY, DON'T WORRY ABOUT IT! I WENT TO THE ACADEMY. SO DID TYCHO. THE IMPS TRAINED SOME OF OUR BEST PILOTS. YOU'RE AN ASSET TO THE TEAM, YOU KNOW TRICKS THAT THE IMPS TEACH THEIR PILOTS AND THAT WILL ONLY HELP THE SQUAD!
I... I GUESS YOU'RE RIGHT.
IT'S BEEN A LONG TIME, IBTISAM! THE LAST TIME I SAW YOU WAS ON *HOME ONE* JUST BEFORE ENDOR.
PLOURR, IT IS PLEASING TO SEE YOU AGAIN!

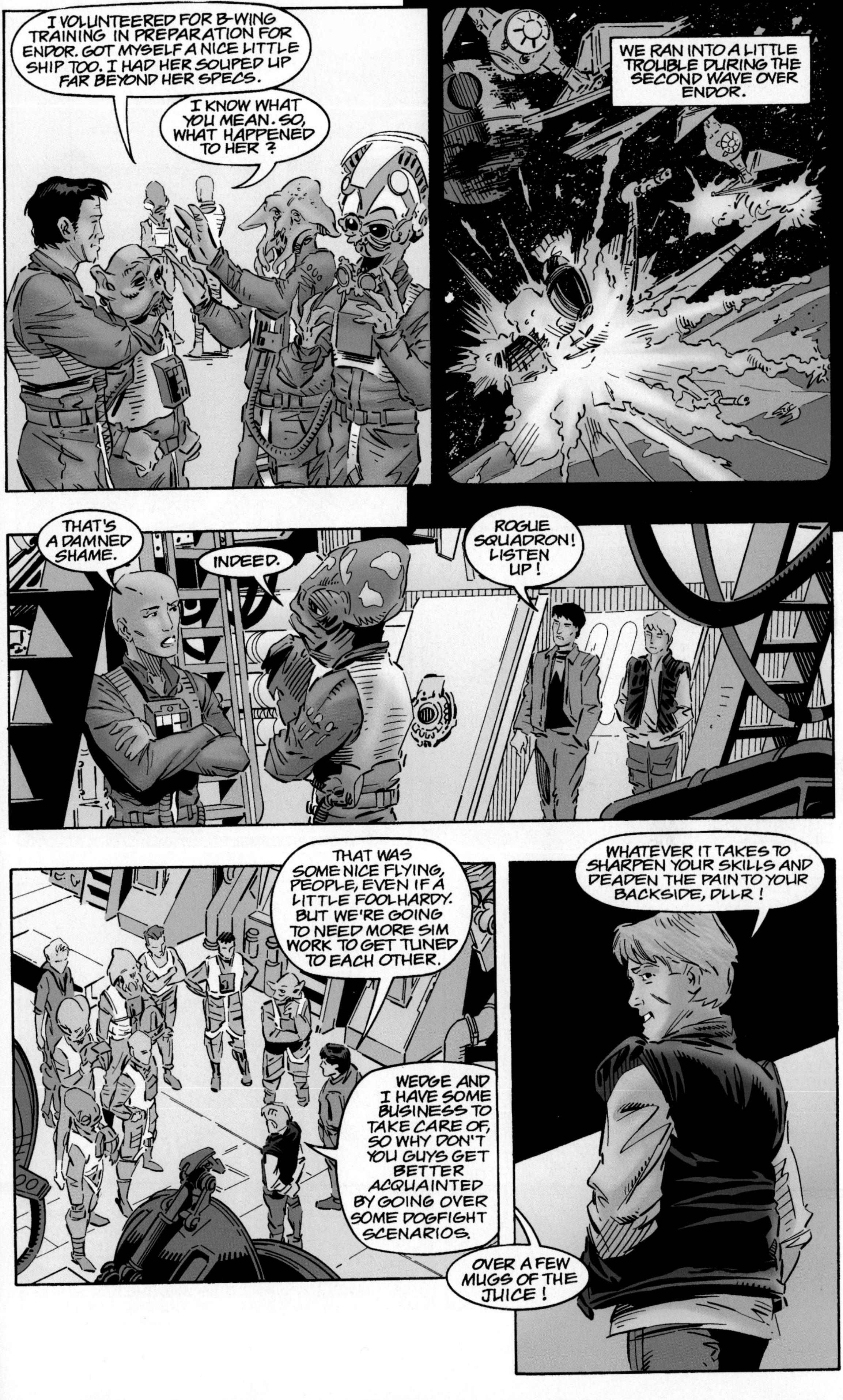
I VOLUNTEERED FOR B-WING TRAINING IN PREPARATION FOR ENDOR. GOT MYSELF A NICE LITTLE SHIP TOO. I HAD HER SOUPED UP FAR BEYOND HER SPECS.
I KNOW WHAT YOU MEAN. SO, WHAT HAPPENED TO HER ?
WE RAN INTO A LITTLE TROUBLE DURING THE SECOND WAVE OVER ENDOR.
THAT'S A DAMNED SHAME.
INDEED.
ROGUE SQUADRON! LISTEN UP !
THAT WAS SOME NICE FLYING, PEOPLE, EVEN IF A LITTLE FOOLHARDY. BUT WE'RE GOING TO NEED MORE SIM WORK TO GET TUNED TO EACH OTHER.
WEDGE AND I HAVE SOME BUSINESS TO TAKE CARE OF, SO WHY DON'T YOU GUYS GET BETTER ACQUAINTED BY GOING OVER SOME DOGFIGHT SCENARIOS.
WHATEVER IT TAKES TO SHARPEN YOUR SKILLS AND DEADEN THE PAIN TO YOUR BACKSIDE, DLLR !
OVER A FEW MUGS OF THE JUICE !

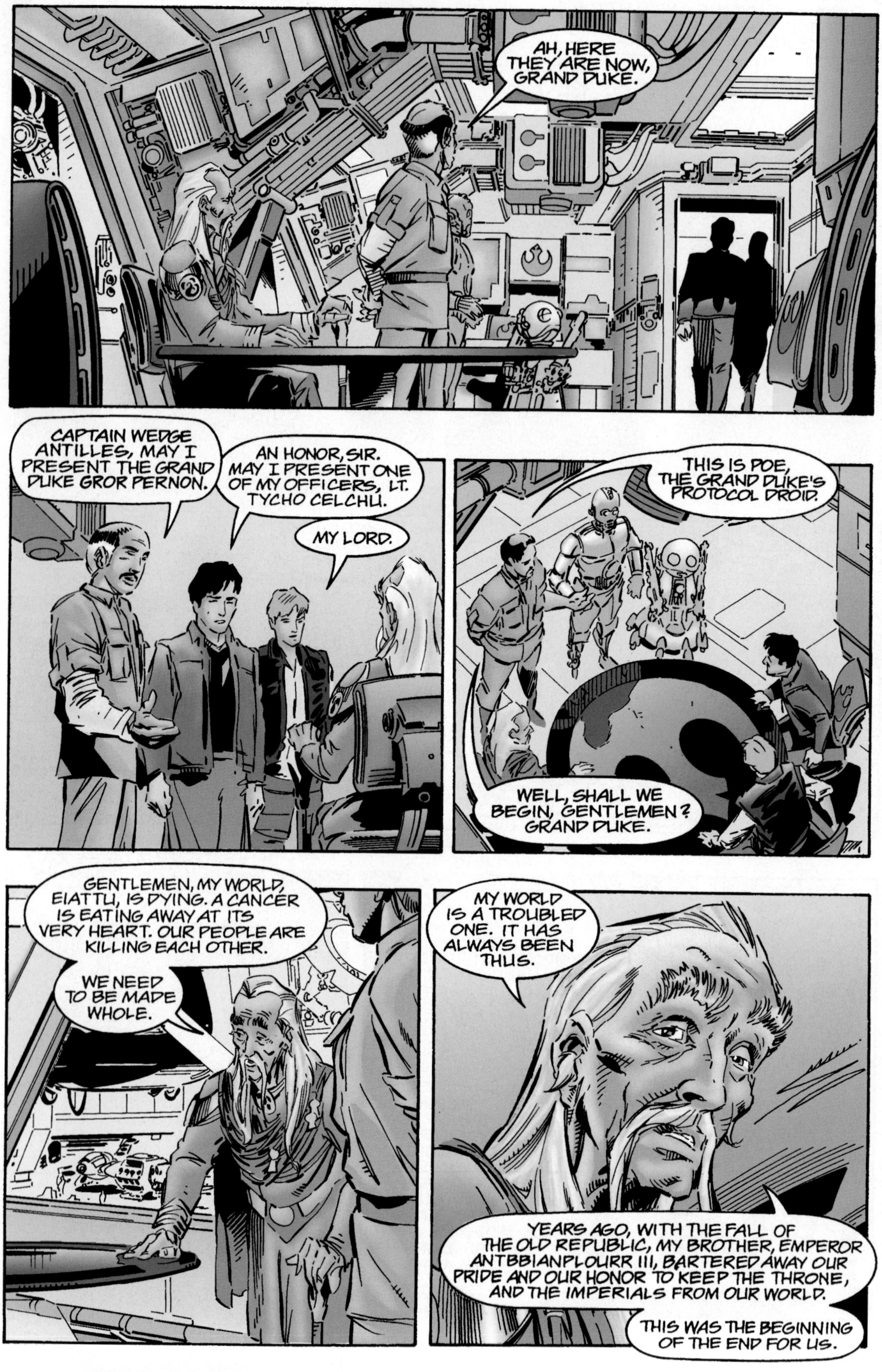
AH, HERE THEY ARE NOW, GRAND DUKE.
CAPTAIN WEDGE ANTILLES, MAY I PRESENT THE GRAND DUKE GROR PERNON.
AN HONOR, SIR. MAY I PRESENT ONE OF MY OFFICERS, LT. TYCHO CELCHU.
MY LORD.
THIS IS POE, THE GRAND DUKE'S PROTOCOL DROID.
WELL, SHALL WE BEGIN, GENTLEMEN? GRAND DUKE.
GENTLEMEN, MY WORLD, EIATTU, IS DYING. A CANCER IS EATING AWAY AT ITS VERY HEART. OUR PEOPLE ARE KILLING EACH OTHER.
WE NEED TO BE MADE WHOLE.
MY WORLD IS A TROUBLED ONE. IT HAS ALWAYS BEEN THUS.
YEARS AGO, WITH THE FALL OF THE OLD REPUBLIC, MY BROTHER, EMPEROR ANTBBIANPLOURR III, BARTERED AWAY OUR PRIDE AND OUR HONOR TO KEEP THE THRONE, AND THE IMPERIALS FROM OUR WORLD.
THIS WAS THE BEGINNING OF THE END FOR US.

AFTER MY BROTHER'S DEATH, HIS ONLY SON, UTHORR FERRELL CARTHA ASCENDED THE THRONE. HE FAIRED NO BETTER. THE EMPIRE CONTINUED TO PRESS ITS HEELS TO OUR NECKS.

FIVE YEARS UNDER HIS IMPOTENT RULE AND THE EMPIRE DISPATCHED THE GRAND MOFF THARIL TAVIRA AND A GARRISON OF STORMTROOPERS TO TAKE CONTROL.

AND THAT WAS WHEN THE NOBLES REBELLED.

...YES, THE REVOLUTION. A PROUD PEOPLE THAT COULD NO LONGER WATCH ITS OWN DEATH. THE NOBLES OVERTHREW THE ROYAL FAMILY, EXILING THEM TO A REMOTE AREA OF THE PLANET.

AND THEN, CALAMITY.

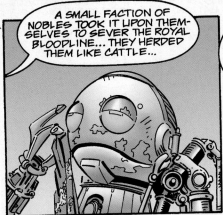

A SMALL FACTION OF NOBLES TOOK IT UPON THEMSELVES TO SEVER THE ROYAL BLOODLINE... THEY HERDED THEM LIKE CATTLE...

...AND SLAUGHTERED THE ROYAL FAMILY. MY NEPHEW AND HIS CHILDREN. ALL DEAD.

OR SO WE THOUGHT.

IMPERIAL INVESTIGATORS CONFIRMED THE DEATHS, IDENTIFYING ALL THE BODIES SAVE THAT OF THE YOUNGEST PRINCESS AND THE PRINCE.

WHEN WE HEARD THIS, WE THOUGHT IT A CRUEL TRICK PLAYED BY THE IMPERIALS.

THAT IS UNTIL LAST MONTH, WHEN PRINCE HARRANDATHA RETURNED.

WHAT?

YES, IT IS TRUE. THE PRINCE HAS RETURNED TO BRING ABOUT A NEW GOVERNMENT TO EIATTU. THE NOBLES, NOW KNOWN AS THE PRIAMSTA, FIGHT THE IMPERIALS AS WELL AS THE PRINCE AND HIS MISGUIDED PEOPLE'S LIBERATION BATTALION.

WHAT IS IT YOU WANT FROM US, LORD DUKE? I'M SURE THE ALLIANCE CAN HELP YOU WITH PEACEFUL NEGOTIATIONS, BUT--

WE HAVE RECEIVED A CODED MESSAGE FROM MRLSST, SENT BY ONE OF OUR CITIZENS LIVING THERE.

THE MESSAGE STATES THAT THE PRINCESS IS ALIVE AND ON THIS WORLD. WE'VE MADE INQUIRIES THROUGH THE ALLIANCE NETWORK AND HAVE IDENTIFIED THE LOST PRINCESS.

YOUR MISSION, CAPTAIN ANTILLES, IS TO ESCORT THE PRINCESS BACK TO EIATTU.

WITH THE RETURN OF THE PRINCESS, PERHAPS THE BICKERING BETWEEN THE PRIMS AND THE PLB CAN BE PUT TO AN END.

THE ALLIANCE AND THE GRAND DUKE HAVE COME TO AN UNDERSTANDING ON THIS MATTER. THE ALLIANCE WOULD BENEFIT GREATLY WITH EIATTU UNITED. ALL WE ASK OF YOU AND YOUR TEAM IS TO HELP BRING IT ABOUT.

WE SERVE THE ALLIANCE, BUT WHY US? SURELY, ALLIANCE NEGOTIATORS WOULD BE BETTER SUITED TO THIS.

POE WILL BE YOUR DIPLOMATIC LIAISON TO THE PEOPLE OF EIATTU.

I AM YOUR HUMBLE SERVANT.

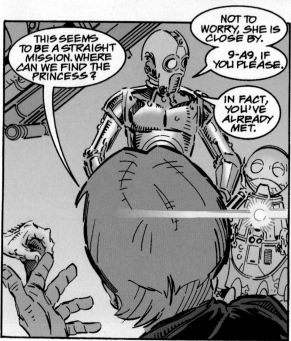

THIS SEEMS TO BE A STRAIGHT MISSION. WHERE CAN WE FIND THE PRINCESS?

NOT TO WORRY, SHE IS CLOSE BY.

9-A9, IF YOU PLEASE.

IN FACT, YOU'VE ALREADY MET.

SITHSPAWN! I'D NEVER HAVE GUESSED.

NOR I. IF YOU'LL FOLLOW ME, GENTLEMEN.

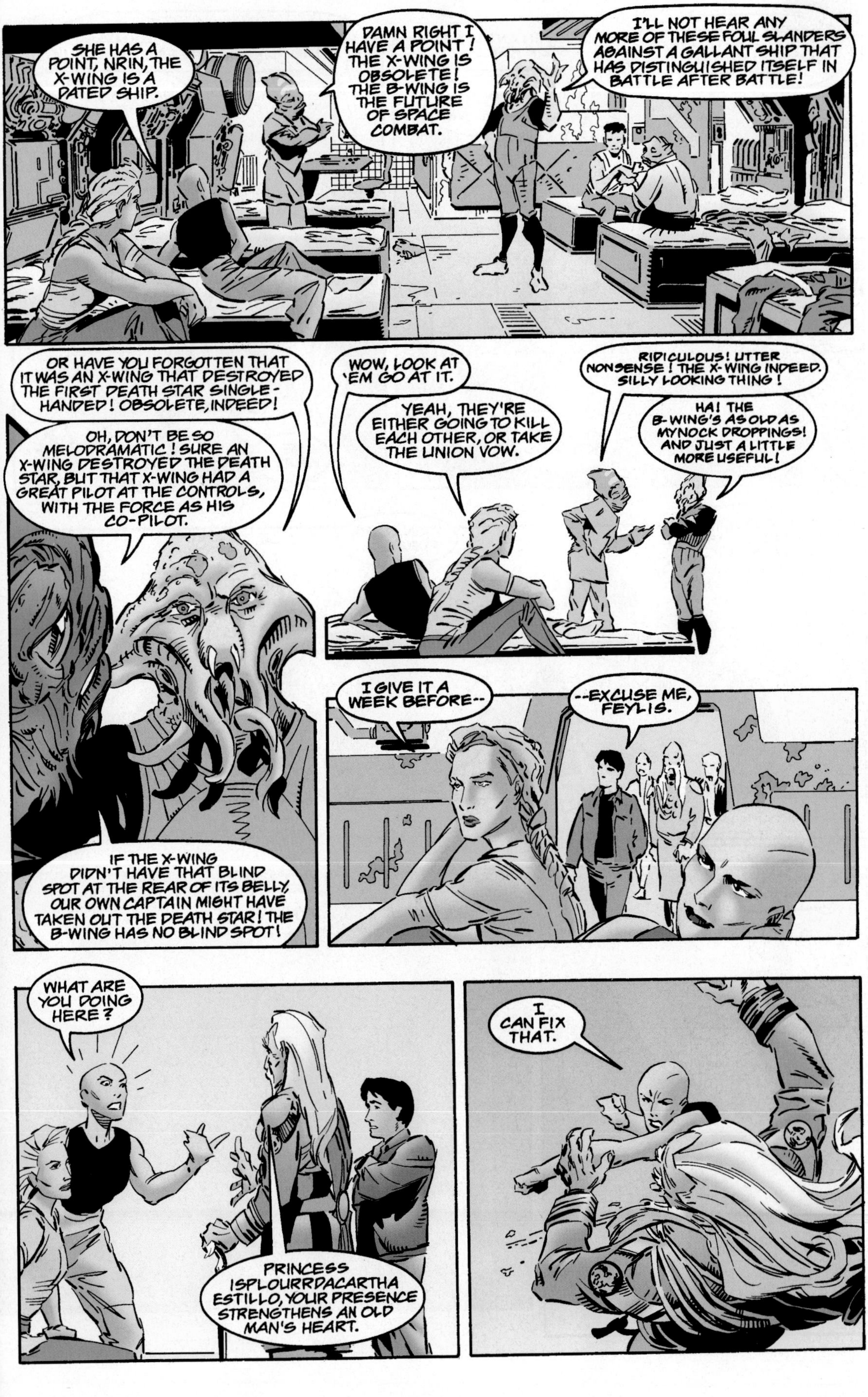
SHE HAS A POINT, NRIN, THE X-WING IS A DATED SHIP.
DAMN RIGHT I HAVE A POINT! THE X-WING IS OBSOLETE! THE B-WING IS THE FUTURE OF SPACE COMBAT.
I'LL NOT HEAR ANY MORE OF THESE FOUL SLANDERS AGAINST A GALLANT SHIP THAT HAS DISTINGUISHED ITSELF IN BATTLE AFTER BATTLE!
OR HAVE YOU FORGOTTEN THAT IT WAS AN X-WING THAT DESTROYED THE FIRST DEATH STAR SINGLE-HANDED! OBSOLETE, INDEED!
OH, DON'T BE SO MELODRAMATIC! SURE AN X-WING DESTROYED THE DEATH STAR, BUT THAT X-WING HAD A GREAT PILOT AT THE CONTROLS, WITH THE FORCE AS HIS CO-PILOT.
IF THE X-WING DIDN'T HAVE THAT BLIND SPOT AT THE REAR OF ITS BELLY, OUR OWN CAPTAIN MIGHT HAVE TAKEN OUT THE DEATH STAR! THE B-WING HAS NO BLIND SPOT!
WOW, LOOK AT 'EM GO AT IT.
YEAH, THEY'RE EITHER GOING TO KILL EACH OTHER, OR TAKE THE UNION VOW.
RIDICULOUS! UTTER NONSENSE! THE X-WING INDEED. SILLY LOOKING THING!
HA! THE B-WING'S AS OLD AS MYNOCK DROPPINGS! AND JUST A LITTLE MORE USEFUL!
I GIVE IT A WEEK BEFORE--
--EXCUSE ME, FEYLIS.
WHAT ARE YOU DOING HERE?
PRINCESS ISPLOURRDACARTHA ESTILLO, YOUR PRESENCE STRENGTHENS AN OLD MAN'S HEART.
I CAN FIX THAT.

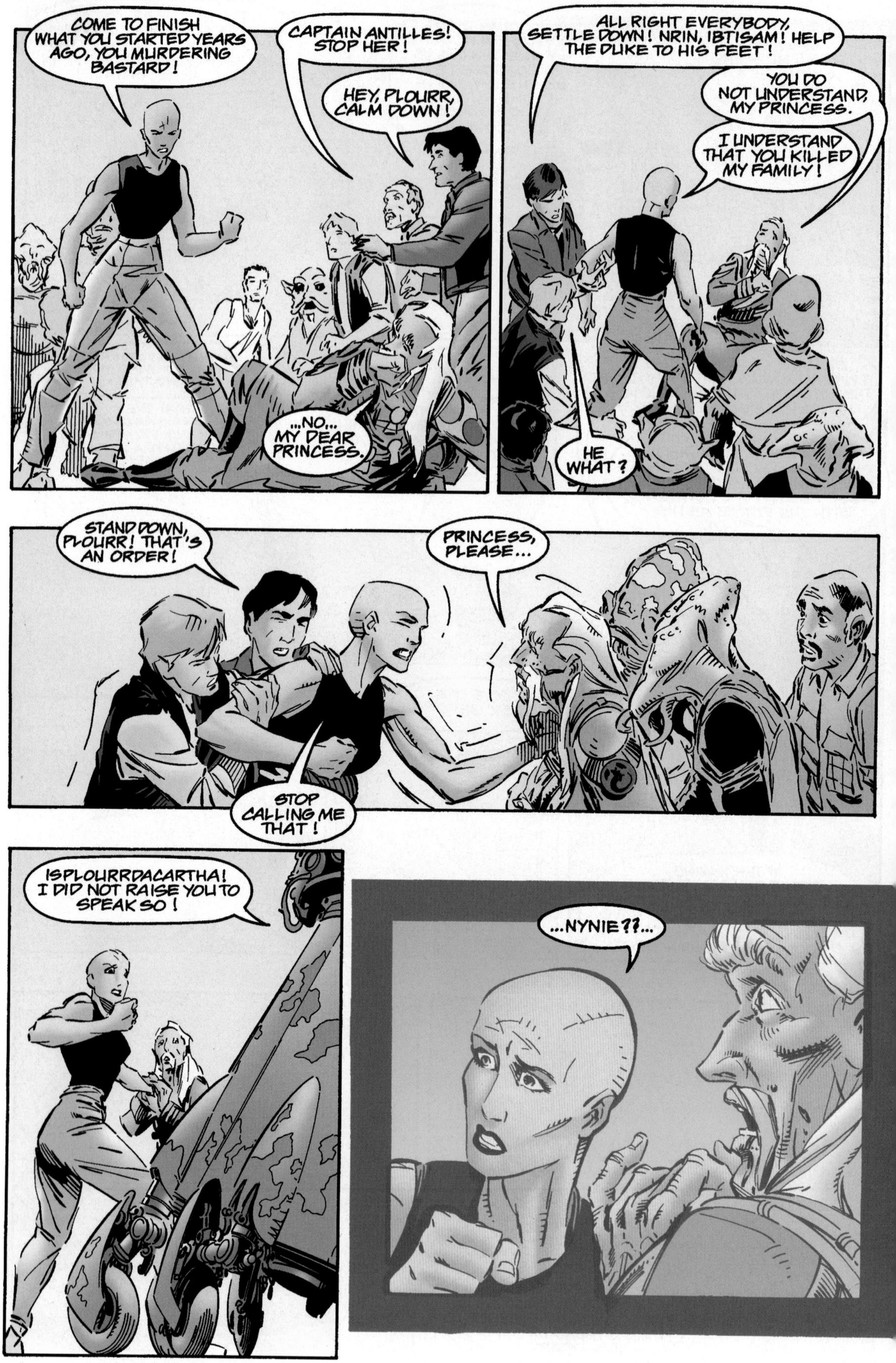
COME TO FINISH WHAT YOU STARTED YEARS AGO, YOU MURDERING BASTARD!
CAPTAIN ANTILLES! STOP HER!
HEY, PLOURR, CALM DOWN!
...NO... MY DEAR PRINCESS.
ALL RIGHT EVERYBODY, SETTLE DOWN! NRIN, IBTISAM! HELP THE DUKE TO HIS FEET!
YOU DO NOT UNDERSTAND, MY PRINCESS.
I UNDERSTAND THAT YOU KILLED MY FAMILY!
HE WHAT?
STAND DOWN, PLOURR! THAT'S AN ORDER!
PRINCESS, PLEASE...
STOP CALLING ME THAT!
ISPLOURRDACARTHA! I DID NOT RAISE YOU TO SPEAK SO!
...NYNIE??...

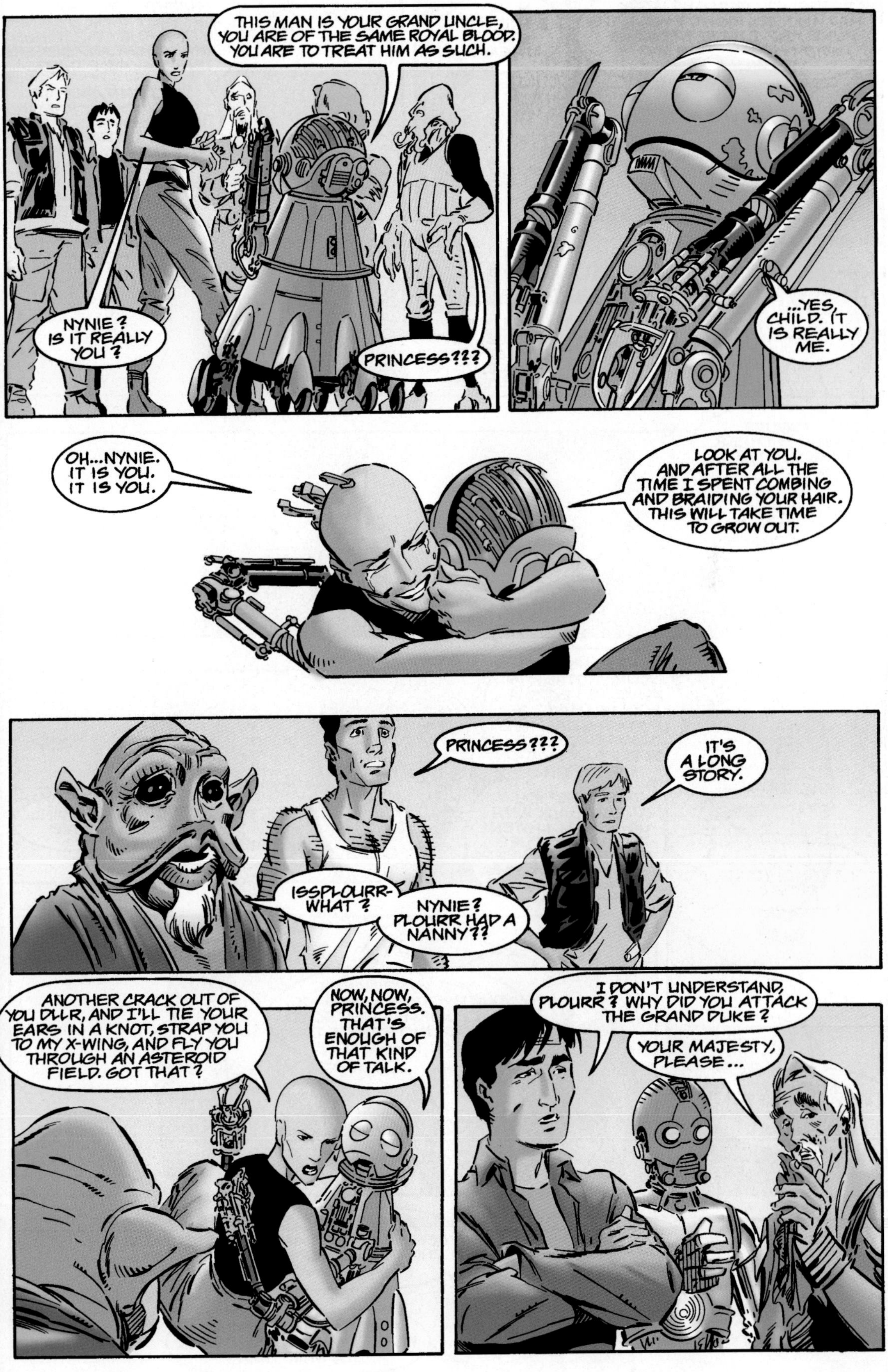
THIS MAN IS YOUR GRAND UNCLE, YOU ARE OF THE SAME ROYAL BLOOD. YOU ARE TO TREAT HIM AS SUCH.
NYNIE? IS IT REALLY YOU?
PRINCESS???
...YES, CHILD. IT IS REALLY ME.
OH...NYNIE. IT IS YOU. IT IS YOU.
LOOK AT YOU. AND AFTER ALL THE TIME I SPENT COMBING AND BRAIDING YOUR HAIR. THIS WILL TAKE TIME TO GROW OUT.
PRINCESS???
IT'S A LONG STORY.
ISSPLOURR-WHAT?
NYNIE? PLOURR HAD A NANNY??
ANOTHER CRACK OUT OF YOU DLLR, AND I'LL TIE YOUR EARS IN A KNOT, STRAP YOU TO MY X-WING, AND FLY YOU THROUGH AN ASTEROID FIELD. GOT THAT?
NOW, NOW, PRINCESS. THAT'S ENOUGH OF THAT KIND OF TALK.
I DON'T UNDERSTAND, PLOURR? WHY DID YOU ATTACK THE GRAND DUKE?
YOUR MAJESTY, PLEASE...

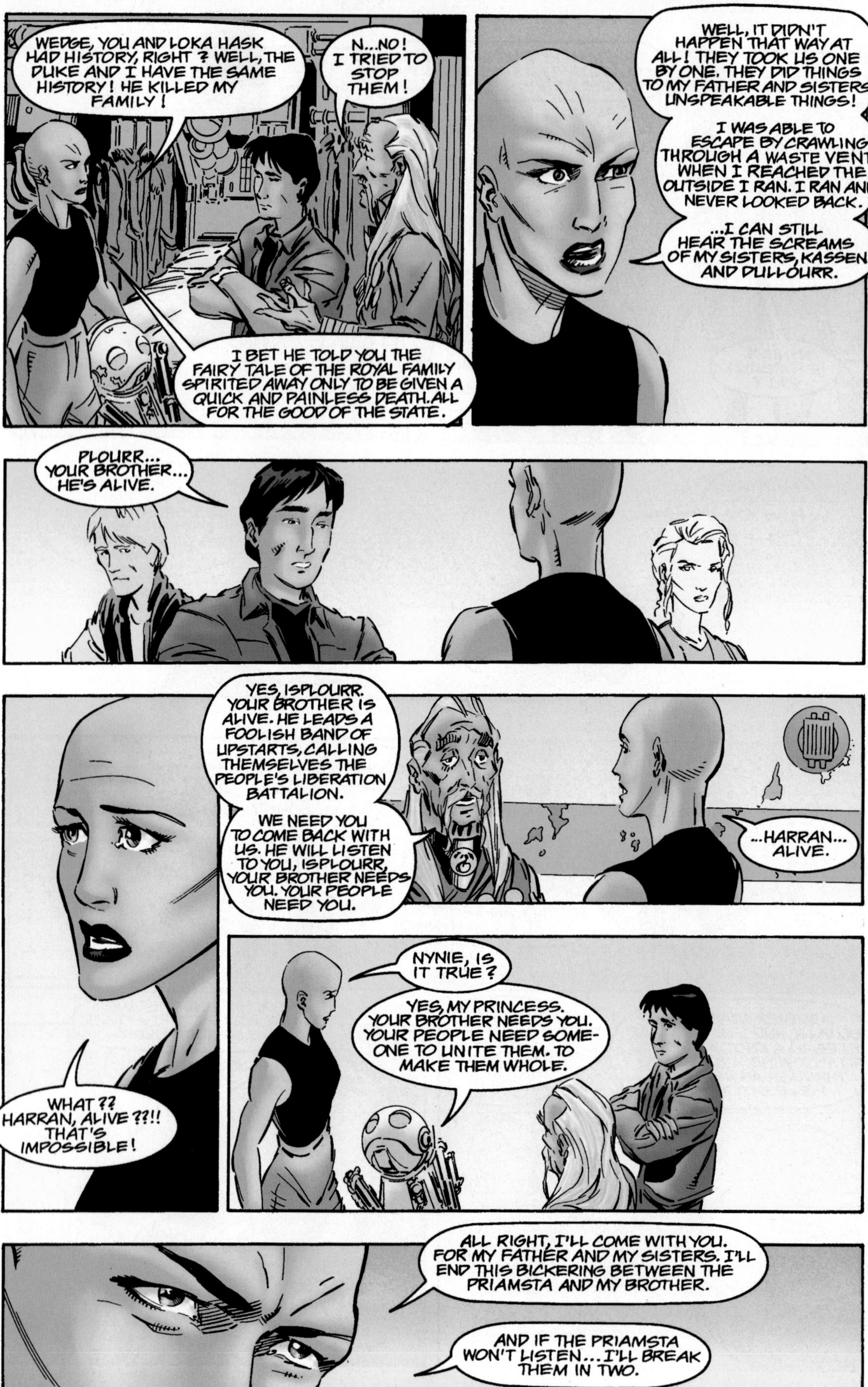
WEDGE, YOU AND LOKA HASK HAD HISTORY, RIGHT ? WELL, THE DUKE AND I HAVE THE SAME HISTORY ! HE KILLED MY FAMILY !
N...NO! I TRIED TO STOP THEM !
I BET HE TOLD YOU THE FAIRY TALE OF THE ROYAL FAMILY SPIRITED AWAY ONLY TO BE GIVEN A QUICK AND PAINLESS DEATH. ALL FOR THE GOOD OF THE STATE.
WELL, IT DIDN'T HAPPEN THAT WAY AT ALL! THEY TOOK US ONE BY ONE. THEY DID THINGS TO MY FATHER AND SISTERS, UNSPEAKABLE THINGS!
I WAS ABLE TO ESCAPE BY CRAWLING THROUGH A WASTE VENT. WHEN I REACHED THE OUTSIDE I RAN. I RAN AND NEVER LOOKED BACK.
...I CAN STILL HEAR THE SCREAMS OF MY SISTERS, KASSEN AND DULL-OURR.
PLOURR... YOUR BROTHER... HE'S ALIVE.
YES, ISPLOURR. YOUR BROTHER IS ALIVE. HE LEADS A FOOLISH BAND OF UPSTARTS, CALLING THEMSELVES THE PEOPLE'S LIBERATION BATTALION.
WE NEED YOU TO COME BACK WITH US. HE WILL LISTEN TO YOU, ISPLOURR, YOUR BROTHER NEEDS YOU. YOUR PEOPLE NEED YOU.
...HARRAN... ALIVE.
WHAT ?? HARRAN, ALIVE ??!! THAT'S IMPOSSIBLE!
NYNIE, IS IT TRUE ?
YES, MY PRINCESS. YOUR BROTHER NEEDS YOU. YOUR PEOPLE NEED SOME-ONE TO UNITE THEM. TO MAKE THEM WHOLE.
ALL RIGHT, I'LL COME WITH YOU. FOR MY FATHER AND MY SISTERS. I'LL END THIS BICKERING BETWEEN THE PRIAMSTA AND MY BROTHER.
AND IF THE PRIAMSTA WON'T LISTEN... I'LL BREAK THEM IN TWO.

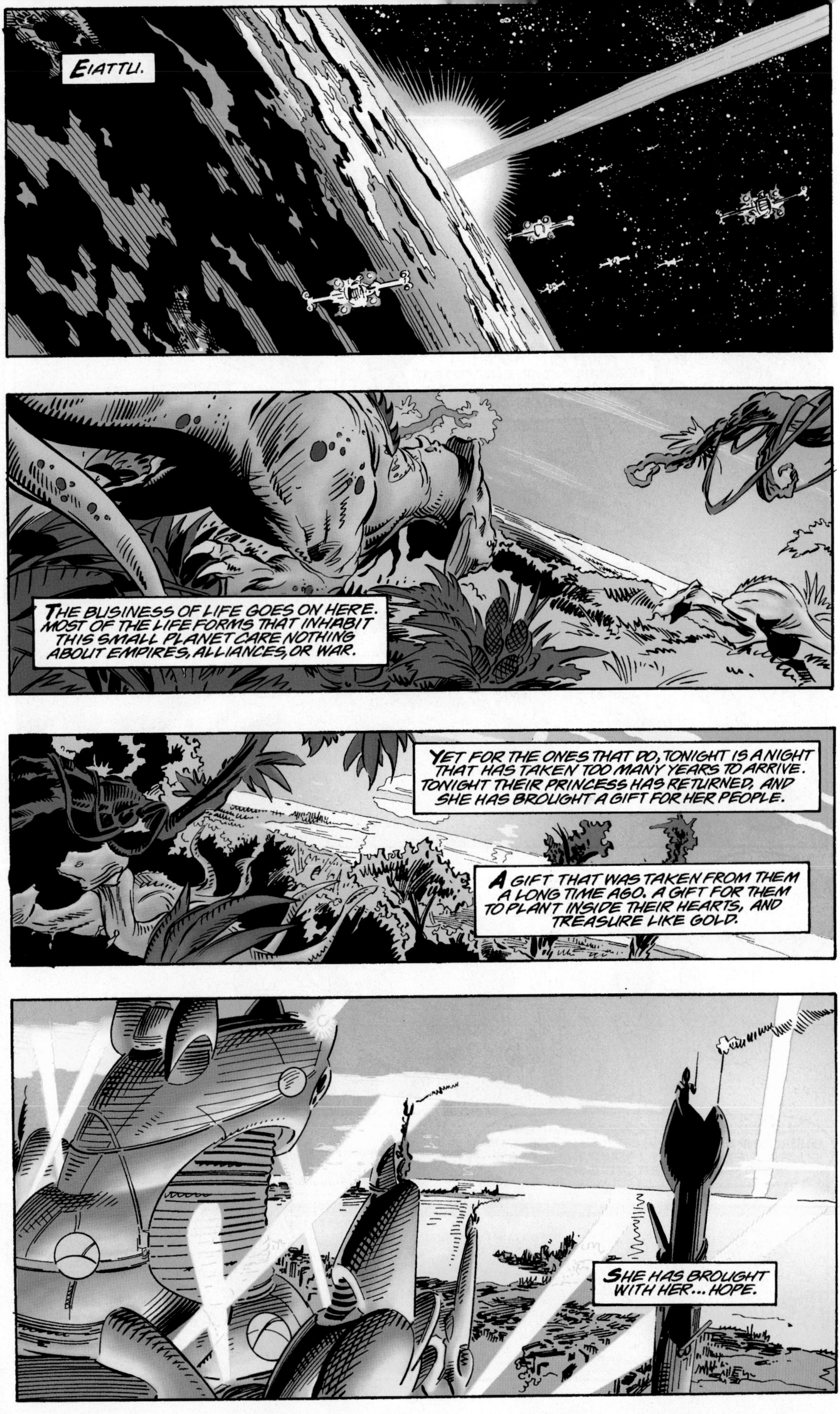
EIATTU.
THE BUSINESS OF LIFE GOES ON HERE. MOST OF THE LIFE FORMS THAT INHABIT THIS SMALL PLANET CARE NOTHING ABOUT EMPIRES, ALLIANCES, OR WAR.
YET FOR THE ONES THAT DO, TONIGHT IS A NIGHT THAT HAS TAKEN TOO MANY YEARS TO ARRIVE. TONIGHT THEIR PRINCESS HAS RETURNED, AND SHE HAS BROUGHT A GIFT FOR HER PEOPLE.
A GIFT THAT WAS TAKEN FROM THEM A LONG TIME AGO. A GIFT FOR THEM TO PLANT INSIDE THEIR HEARTS, AND TREASURE LIKE GOLD.
SHE HAS BROUGHT WITH HER... HOPE.

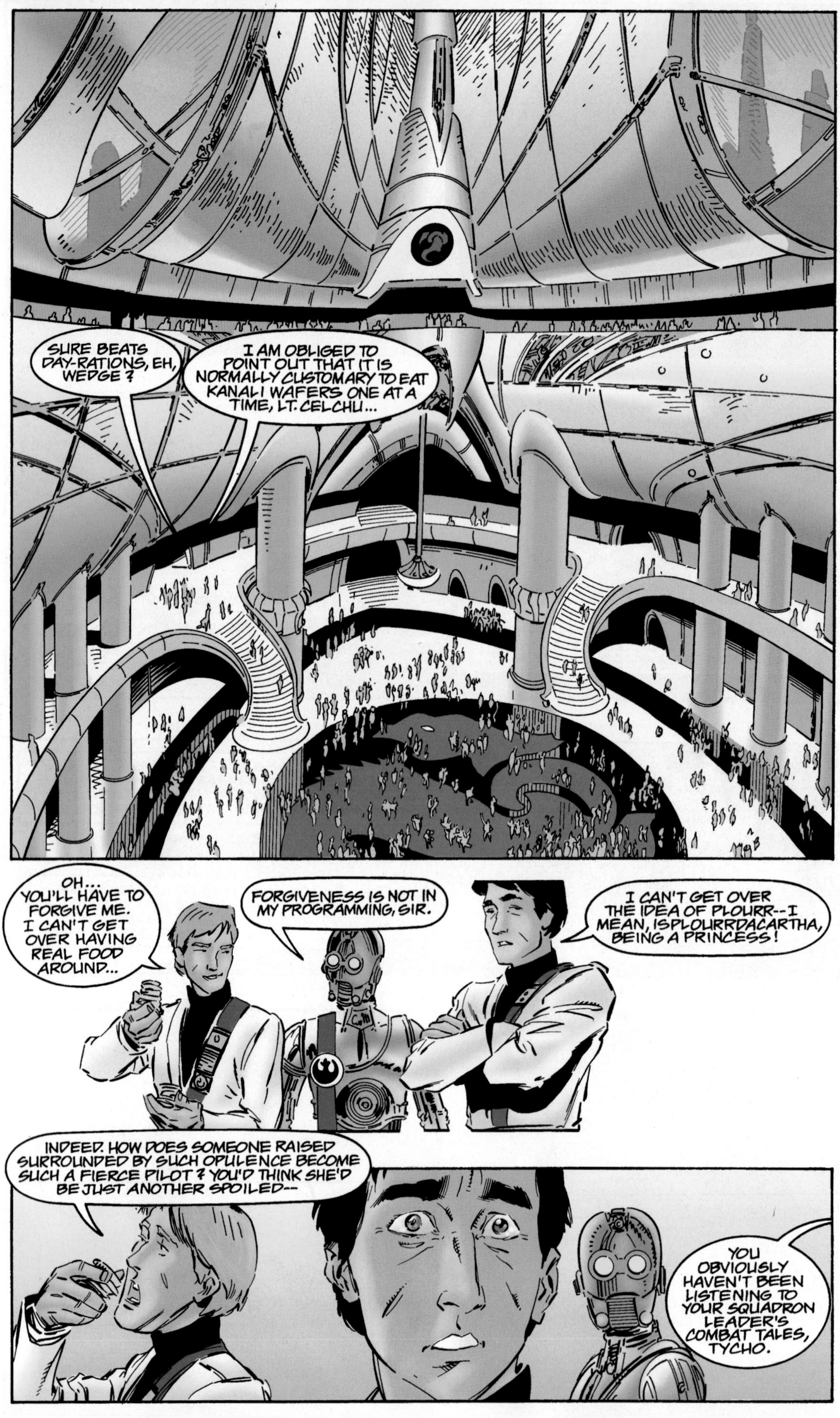
SURE BEATS DAY-RATIONS, EH, WEDGE?
I AM OBLIGED TO POINT OUT THAT IT IS NORMALLY CUSTOMARY TO EAT KANALI WAFERS ONE AT A TIME, LT. CELCHU...
OH... YOU'LL HAVE TO FORGIVE ME. I CAN'T GET OVER HAVING REAL FOOD AROUND...
FORGIVENESS IS NOT IN MY PROGRAMMING, SIR.
I CAN'T GET OVER THE IDEA OF PLOURR--I MEAN, ISPLOURRDACARTHA, BEING A PRINCESS!
INDEED. HOW DOES SOMEONE RAISED SURROUNDED BY SUCH OPULENCE BECOME SUCH A FIERCE PILOT? YOU'D THINK SHE'D BE JUST ANOTHER SPOILED--
YOU OBVIOUSLY HAVEN'T BEEN LISTENING TO YOUR SQUADRON LEADER'S COMBAT TALES, TYCHO.

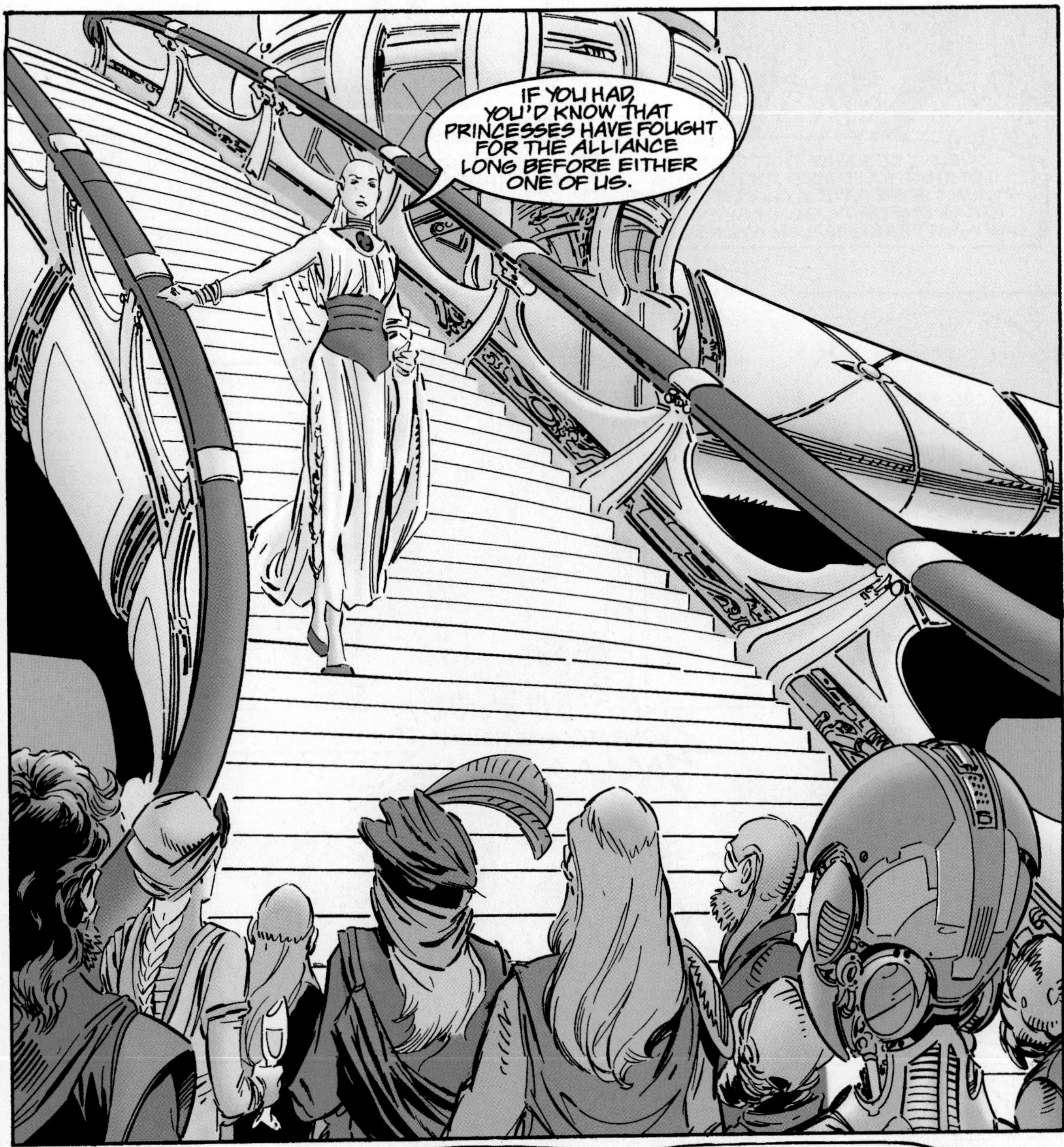
IF YOU HAD, YOU'D KNOW THAT PRINCESSES HAVE FOUGHT FOR THE ALLIANCE LONG BEFORE EITHER ONE OF US.

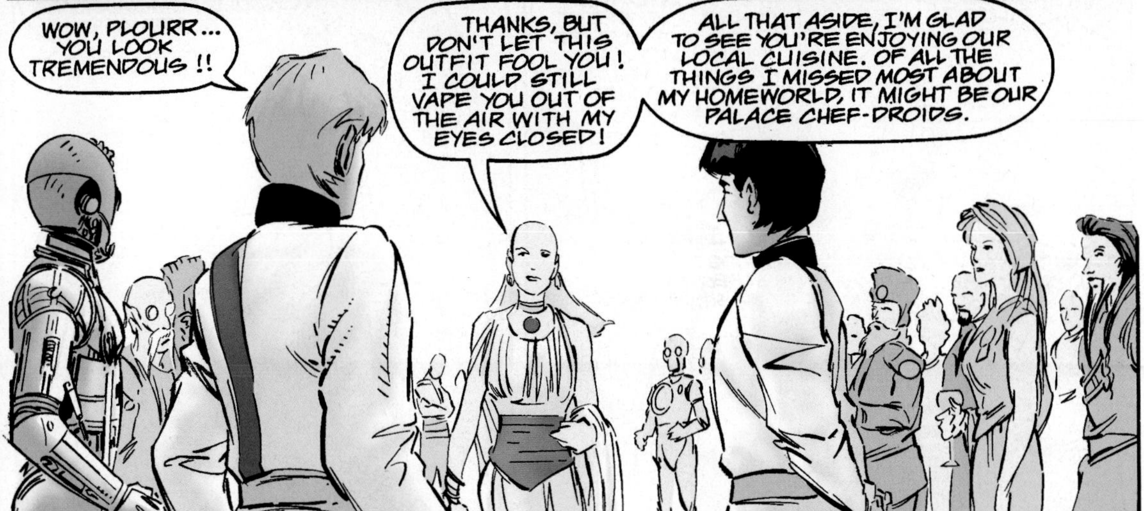
WOW, PLOURR... YOU LOOK TREMENDOUS !!
THANKS, BUT DON'T LET THIS OUTFIT FOOL YOU ! I COULD STILL VAPE YOU OUT OF THE AIR WITH MY EYES CLOSED!
ALL THAT ASIDE, I'M GLAD TO SEE YOU'RE ENJOYING OUR LOCAL CUISINE. OF ALL THE THINGS I MISSED MOST ABOUT MY HOMEWORLD, IT MIGHT BE OUR PALACE CHEF-DROIDS.

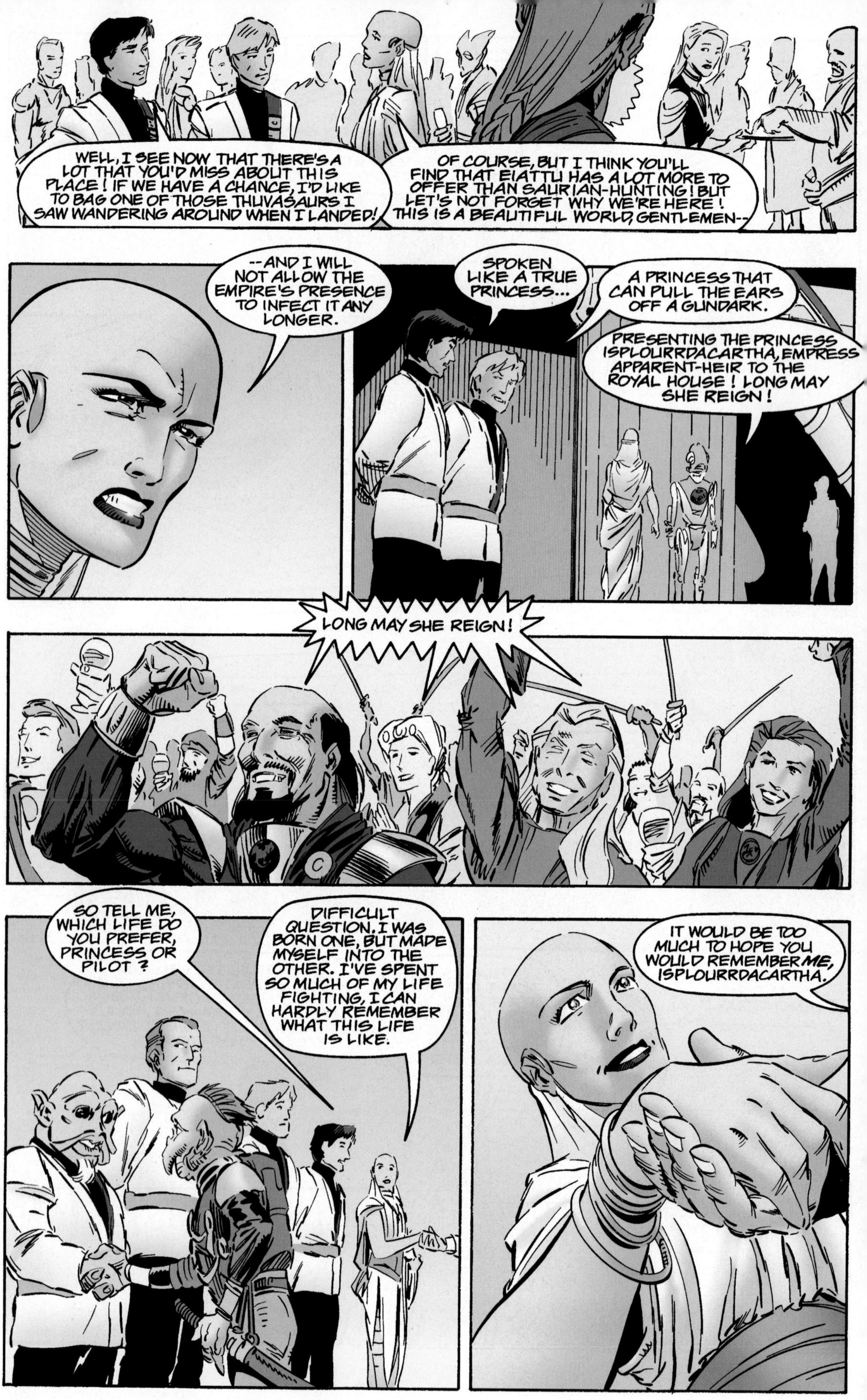
WELL, I SEE NOW THAT THERE'S A LOT THAT YOU'D MISS ABOUT THIS PLACE! IF WE HAVE A CHANCE, I'D LIKE TO BAG ONE OF THOSE THUVASAURS I SAW WANDERING AROUND WHEN I LANDED!
OF COURSE, BUT I THINK YOU'LL FIND THAT EIATTU HAS A LOT MORE TO OFFER THAN SAURIAN-HUNTING! BUT LET'S NOT FORGET WHY WE'RE HERE! THIS IS A BEAUTIFUL WORLD, GENTLEMEN--
--AND I WILL NOT ALLOW THE EMPIRE'S PRESENCE TO INFECT IT ANY LONGER.
SPOKEN LIKE A TRUE PRINCESS...
A PRINCESS THAT CAN PULL THE EARS OFF A GUNDARK.
PRESENTING THE PRINCESS ISPLOURRDACARTHA, EMPRESS APPARENT-HEIR TO THE ROYAL HOUSE! LONG MAY SHE REIGN!
LONG MAY SHE REIGN!
SO TELL ME, WHICH LIFE DO YOU PREFER, PRINCESS OR PILOT?
DIFFICULT QUESTION. I WAS BORN ONE, BUT MADE MYSELF INTO THE OTHER. I'VE SPENT SO MUCH OF MY LIFE FIGHTING, I CAN HARDLY REMEMBER WHAT THIS LIFE IS LIKE.
IT WOULD BE TOO MUCH TO HOPE YOU WOULD REMEMBER *ME*, ISPLOURRDACARTHA.

COUNT RIAL PERNON.

WHY NO, I'M AFRAID I DON'T. YOU ARE?

RIAL...AH, YES, I DO RECALL...IF YOU WILL EXCUSE ME.

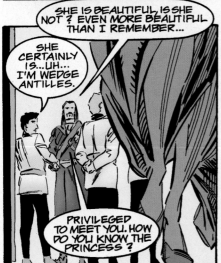

SHE IS BEAUTIFUL, IS SHE NOT? EVEN MORE BEAUTIFUL THAN I REMEMBER...

SHE CERTAINLY IS...UH... I'M WEDGE ANTILLES.

PRIVILEGED TO MEET YOU. HOW DO YOU KNOW THE PRINCESS?

I'M HER COMMANDING OFFICER. HOW DO YOU KNOW HER?

I AM HER SECOND COUSIN. WE GREW UP TOGETHER.

I DO ADMIT, I AM A LITTLE DISAPPOINTED IN HER REACTION. YOU WOULD THINK SHE WOULD BE HAPPIER TO SEE HER FUTURE HUSBAND...

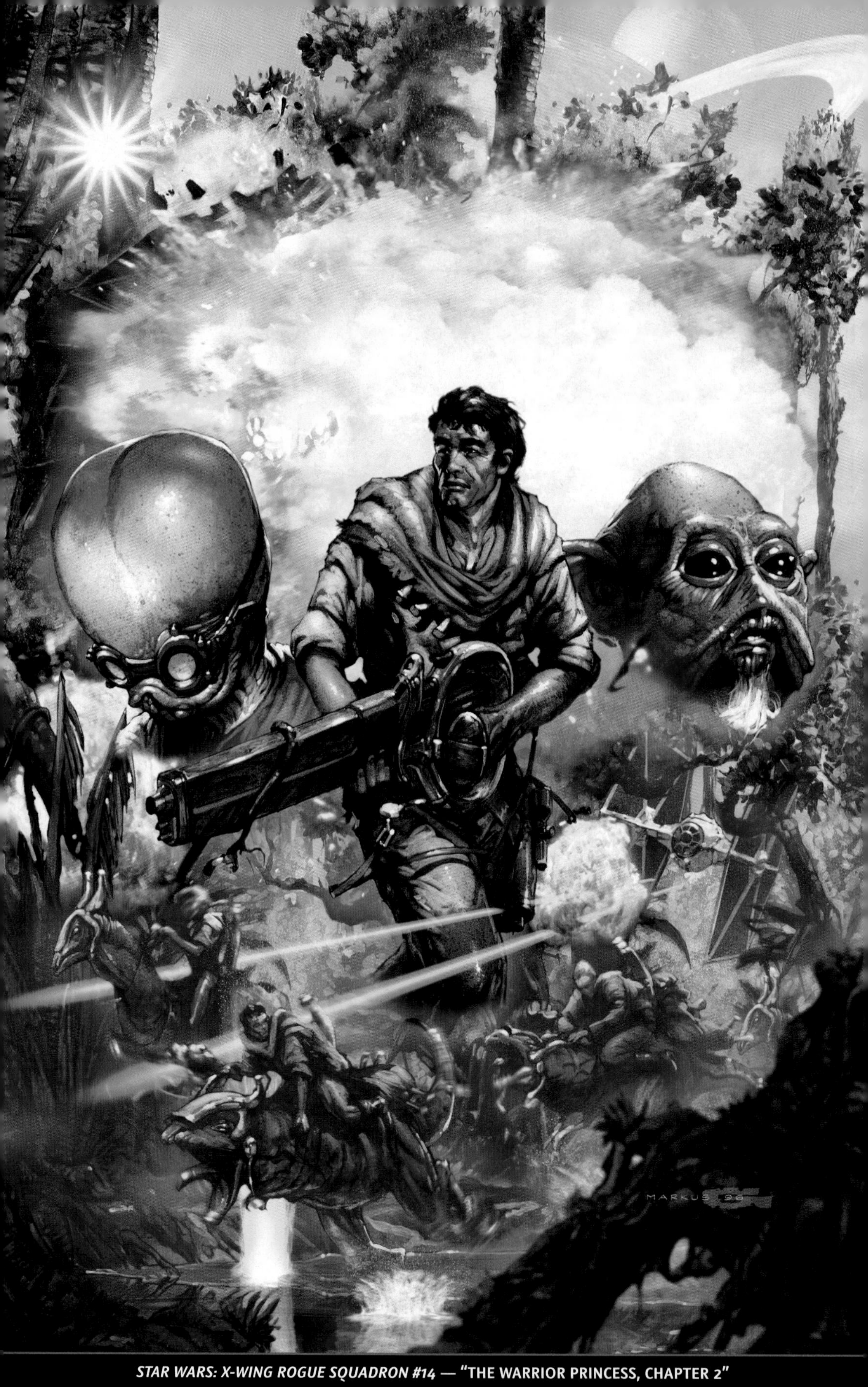
MARKUS 96

***STAR WARS: X-WING ROGUE SQUADRON* #14 — "THE WARRIOR PRINCESS, CHAPTER 2"**

PLOTTER: MICHAEL A. STACKPOLE • SCRIPTER: SCOTT TOLSON • PENCILER: JOHN NADEAU • INKER: JORDI ENSIGN
COLORIST: DAVE NESTELLE • LETTERER: VICKIE WILLIAMS • EDITOR: PEET JANES • COVER ARTIST: MARK HARRISON

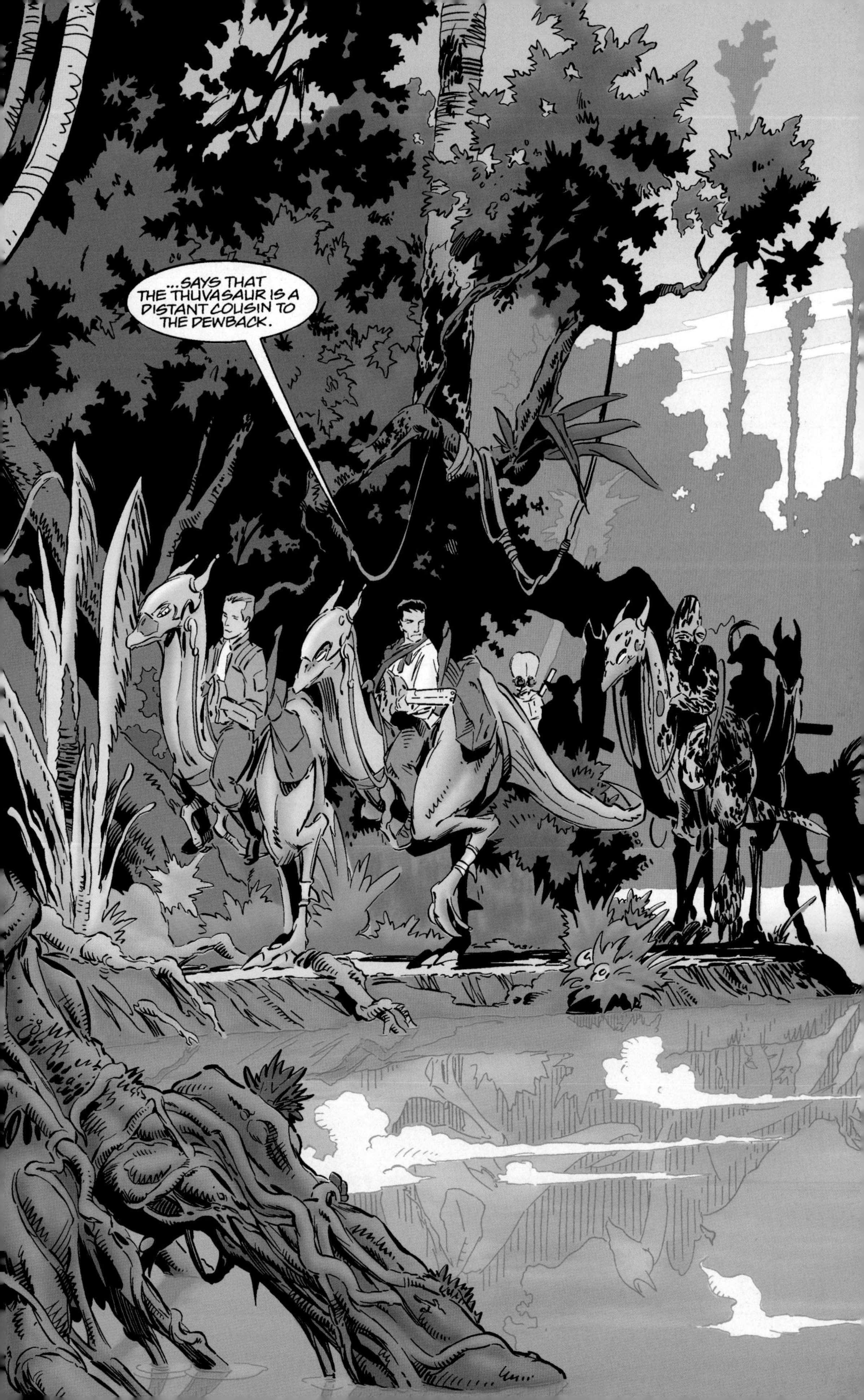
...SAYS THAT THE THUVASAUR IS A DISTANT COUSIN TO THE DEWBACK.

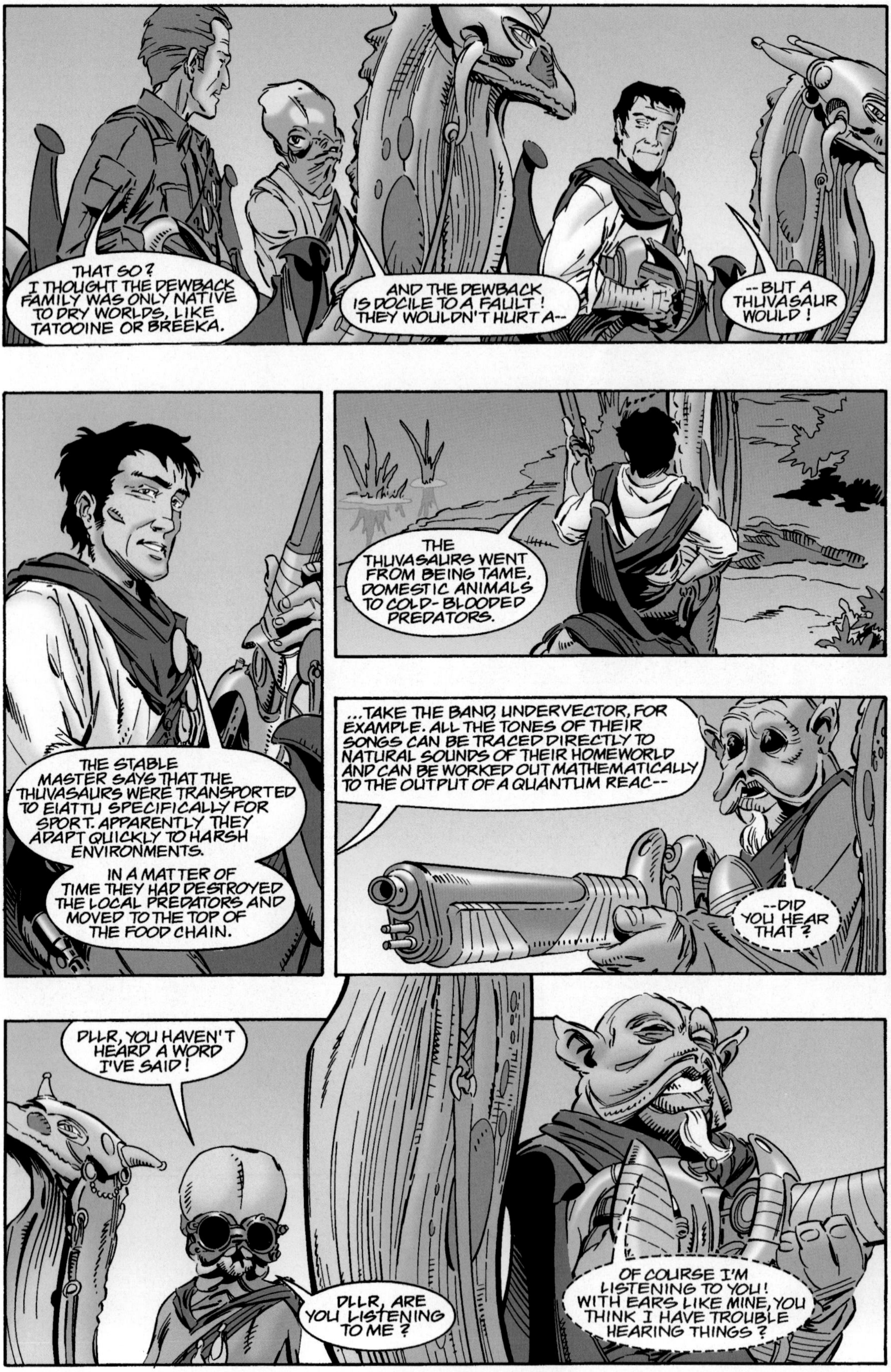
THAT SO? I THOUGHT THE DEWBACK FAMILY WAS ONLY NATIVE TO DRY WORLDS, LIKE TATOOINE OR BREEKA.
AND THE DEWBACK IS DOCILE TO A FAULT! THEY WOULDN'T HURT A--
--BUT A THUVASAUR WOULD!
THE STABLE MASTER SAYS THAT THE THUVASAURS WERE TRANSPORTED TO EIATTU SPECIFICALLY FOR SPORT. APPARENTLY THEY ADAPT QUICKLY TO HARSH ENVIRONMENTS.
IN A MATTER OF TIME THEY HAD DESTROYED THE LOCAL PREDATORS AND MOVED TO THE TOP OF THE FOOD CHAIN.
THE THUVASAURS WENT FROM BEING TAME, DOMESTIC ANIMALS TO COLD-BLOODED PREDATORS.
...TAKE THE BAND, UNDERVECTOR, FOR EXAMPLE. ALL THE TONES OF THEIR SONGS CAN BE TRACED DIRECTLY TO NATURAL SOUNDS OF THEIR HOMEWORLD AND CAN BE WORKED OUT MATHEMATICALLY TO THE OUTPUT OF A QUANTUM REAC--
--DID YOU HEAR THAT?
DLLR, YOU HAVEN'T HEARD A WORD I'VE SAID!
DLLR, ARE YOU LISTENING TO ME?
OF COURSE I'M LISTENING TO YOU! WITH EARS LIKE MINE, YOU THINK I HAVE TROUBLE HEARING THINGS?

DLLR, WHAT'S THE MATTER? WHY ARE YOU SO JUMPY?

DO YOU KNOW WHAT THOSE THUVASAURS CAN DO? WE WALK INTO THIS FORCE-FORSAKEN SWAMP WITH NO GUIDE AND NO TRACKING DEVICES, AND YOU ASK ME WHY I'M SO JUMPY?

BESIDES, I KEEP HEARING SOMETHING JUST OUT OF EARSHOT AND I CAN'T MAKE IT OUT.

AND AS FOR UNDERVECTOR'S MUSIC, THEY STINK LIKE TAUN TAUN DROPPINGS!

CAN YOU BELIEVE IT? PLOURR A PRINCESS, AND NOT ONE OF HER CREWMATES SUSPECTED!

I SAW THE NOBILITY IN HER EYES FROM THE MOMENT I MET HER.

SUCH TRAGEDY IN PLOURR'S LIFE. HER FAMILY KILLED, A LIFE ON THE RUN IN FEAR OF SOMEONE DISCOVERING HER TRUE IDENTITY. AND NOW--

UMM, NRIN? WHY ARE YOU WEARING THAT HAT?

IT'S PART OF THE TRADITIONAL HUNTING UNIFORM OF THE EIATTU NOBLES. THEY'VE WORN IT FOR GENERATIONS...

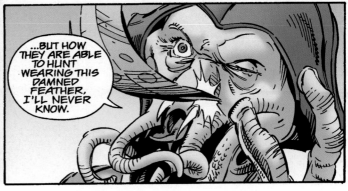

...BUT HOW THEY ARE ABLE TO HUNT WEARING THIS DAMNED FEATHER, I'LL NEVER KNOW.

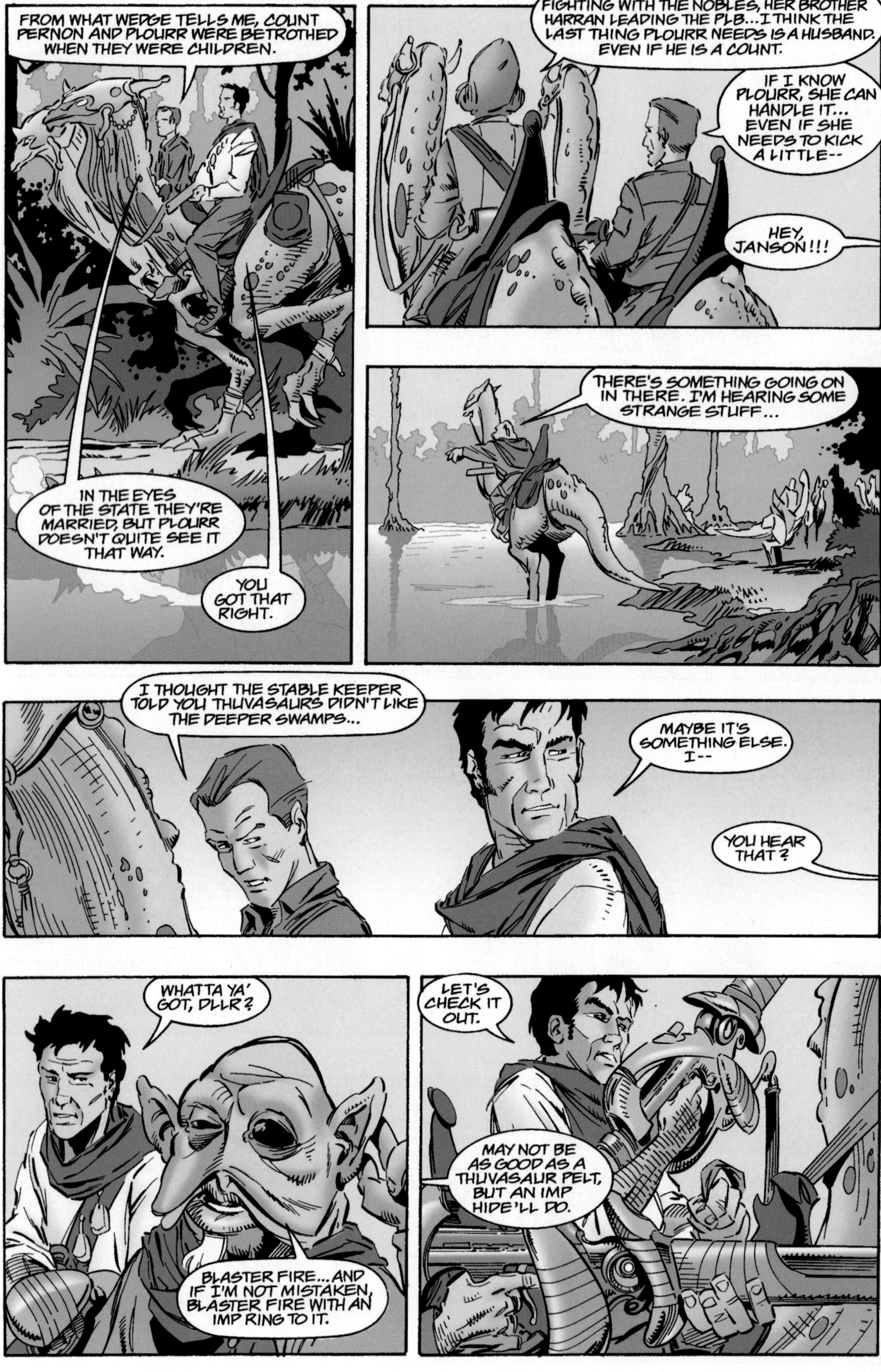
FROM WHAT WEDGE TELLS ME, COUNT PERNON AND PLOURR WERE BETROTHED WHEN THEY WERE CHILDREN.
IN THE EYES OF THE STATE THEY'RE MARRIED, BUT PLOURR DOESN'T QUITE SEE IT THAT WAY.
YOU GOT THAT RIGHT.
WITH ALL THAT'S HAPPENED, THE FIGHTING WITH THE NOBLES, HER BROTHER HARRAN LEADING THE PLB... I THINK THE LAST THING PLOURR NEEDS IS A HUSBAND. EVEN IF HE IS A COUNT.
IF I KNOW PLOURR, SHE CAN HANDLE IT... EVEN IF SHE NEEDS TO KICK A LITTLE--
HEY, JANSON!!!
THERE'S SOMETHING GOING ON IN THERE. I'M HEARING SOME STRANGE STUFF...
I THOUGHT THE STABLE KEEPER TOLD YOU THUVASAURS DIDN'T LIKE THE DEEPER SWAMPS...
MAYBE IT'S SOMETHING ELSE. I--
YOU HEAR THAT?
WHATTA YA' GOT, DLLR?
BLASTER FIRE... AND IF I'M NOT MISTAKEN, BLASTER FIRE WITH AN IMP RING TO IT.
LET'S CHECK IT OUT.
MAY NOT BE AS GOOD AS A THUVASAUR PELT, BUT AN IMP HIDE'LL DO.

SON OF A JUMPING--

THIS IS THE SITE OF THE LAST PEOPLE'S LIBERATION BATTALION ATTACK.

HOW MANY WERE INJURED, COUNT PERNON?

FIFTEEN GUARDS AND AN IMPERIAL BANKER. THE ATTACK HAPPENED DURING THE TRANSPORT OF THE IMPERIAL PAYROLL, SO THERE WERE NO CIVILIANS IN THE AREA.

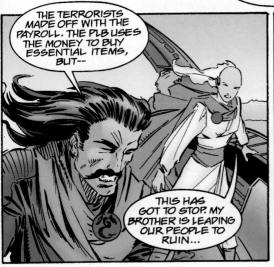

THE TERRORISTS MADE OFF WITH THE PAYROLL. THE PLB USES THE MONEY TO BUY ESSENTIAL ITEMS, BUT--

THIS HAS GOT TO STOP. MY BROTHER IS LEADING OUR PEOPLE TO RUIN...

WEDGE HERE.

≷SQUAWK≷ WE'VE STEPPED INTO SOMETHING AWFUL DEEP HERE! A BUZZZER'S NEST OF IMPS HAVE US PINNED DOWN!!

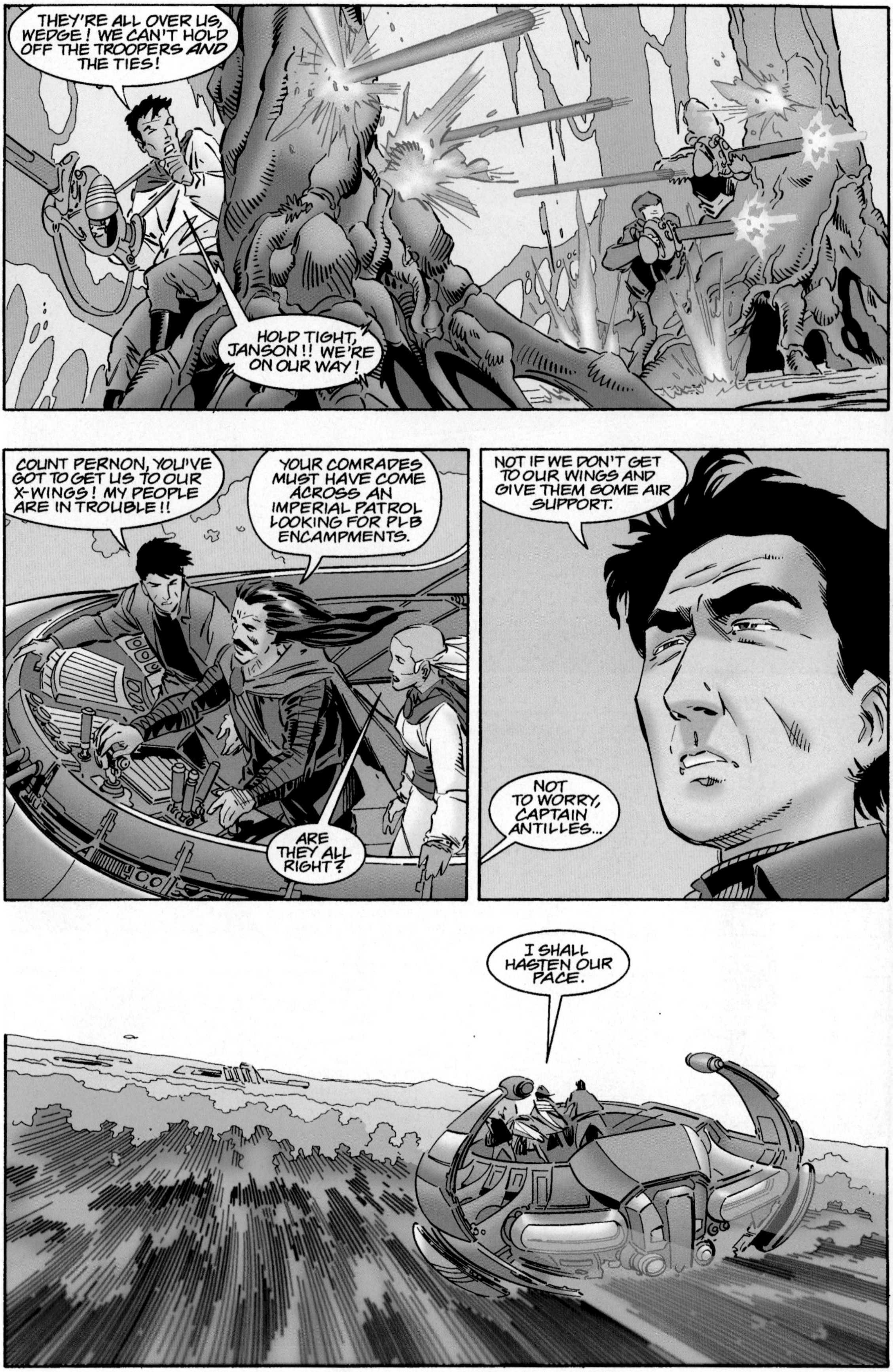
THEY'RE ALL OVER US, WEDGE! WE CAN'T HOLD OFF THE TROOPERS AND THE TIES!
HOLD TIGHT, JANSON!! WE'RE ON OUR WAY!
COUNT PERNON, YOU'VE GOT TO GET US TO OUR X-WINGS! MY PEOPLE ARE IN TROUBLE!!
YOUR COMRADES MUST HAVE COME ACROSS AN IMPERIAL PATROL LOOKING FOR PL-B ENCAMPMENTS.
ARE THEY ALL RIGHT?
NOT IF WE DON'T GET TO OUR WINGS AND GIVE THEM SOME AIR SUPPORT.
NOT TO WORRY, CAPTAIN ANTILLES...
I SHALL HASTEN OUR PACE.

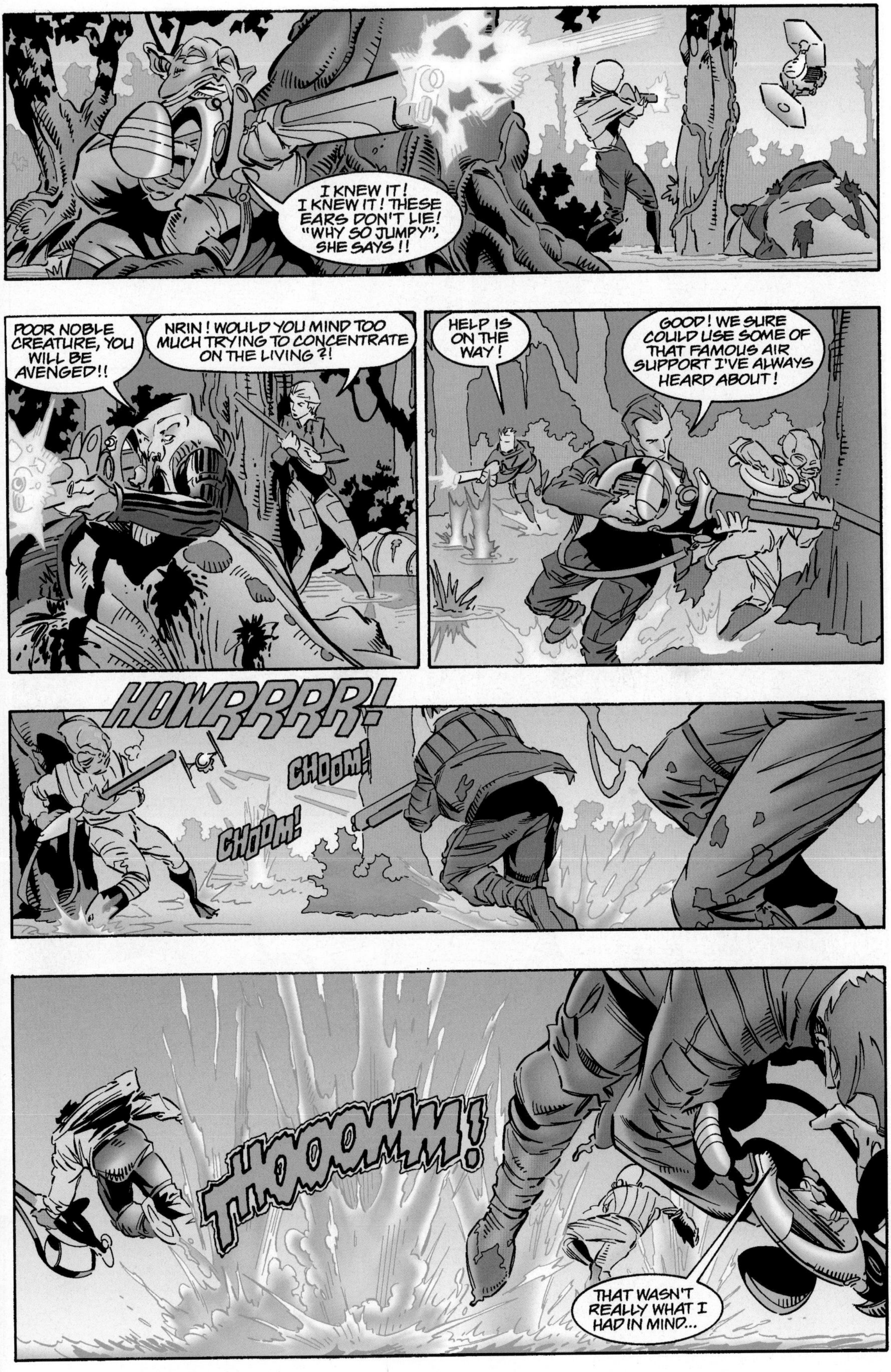
I KNEW IT! I KNEW IT! THESE EARS DON'T LIE! "WHY SO JUMPY", SHE SAYS!!
POOR NOBLE CREATURE, YOU WILL BE AVENGED!!
NRIN! WOULD YOU MIND TOO MUCH TRYING TO CONCENTRATE ON THE LIVING?!
HELP IS ON THE WAY!
GOOD! WE SURE COULD USE SOME OF THAT FAMOUS AIR SUPPORT I'VE ALWAYS HEARD ABOUT!
HOWRRRR!
CHOOM!
CHOOM!
THOOOMM!
THAT WASN'T REALLY WHAT I HAD IN MIND...

MY PRINCESS, I MUST PROTEST--

STOW IT, RIAL! I MAY BE THE PRINCESS OF THE REALM, BUT I'M ALSO A MEMBER OF ROGUE SQUADRON, AND I INTEND TO BLAST SOME IMPS!!

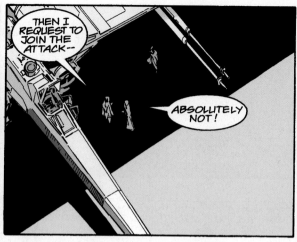

THEN I REQUEST TO JOIN THE ATTACK--

ABSOLUTELY NOT!

SORRY, PLOURR! RIAL FLIES WITH US. YOU MAY BE HIS PRINCESS, BUT I *LEAD* ROGUE SQUADRON.

WHAT ARE YOU FLYING?

A Z-95 HEADHUNTER.

A Z-95? THOSE THINGS CAN'T KEEP UP WITH AN X-WING! YOU'LL BE A SITTING MYNOCK!!

THEN I GUESS YOU'LL HAVE TO PROTECT ME.

THE Z-95'S A GOOD FIGHTER, COMPARABLE TO ANYTHING WE HAVE. WELCOME ABOARD!

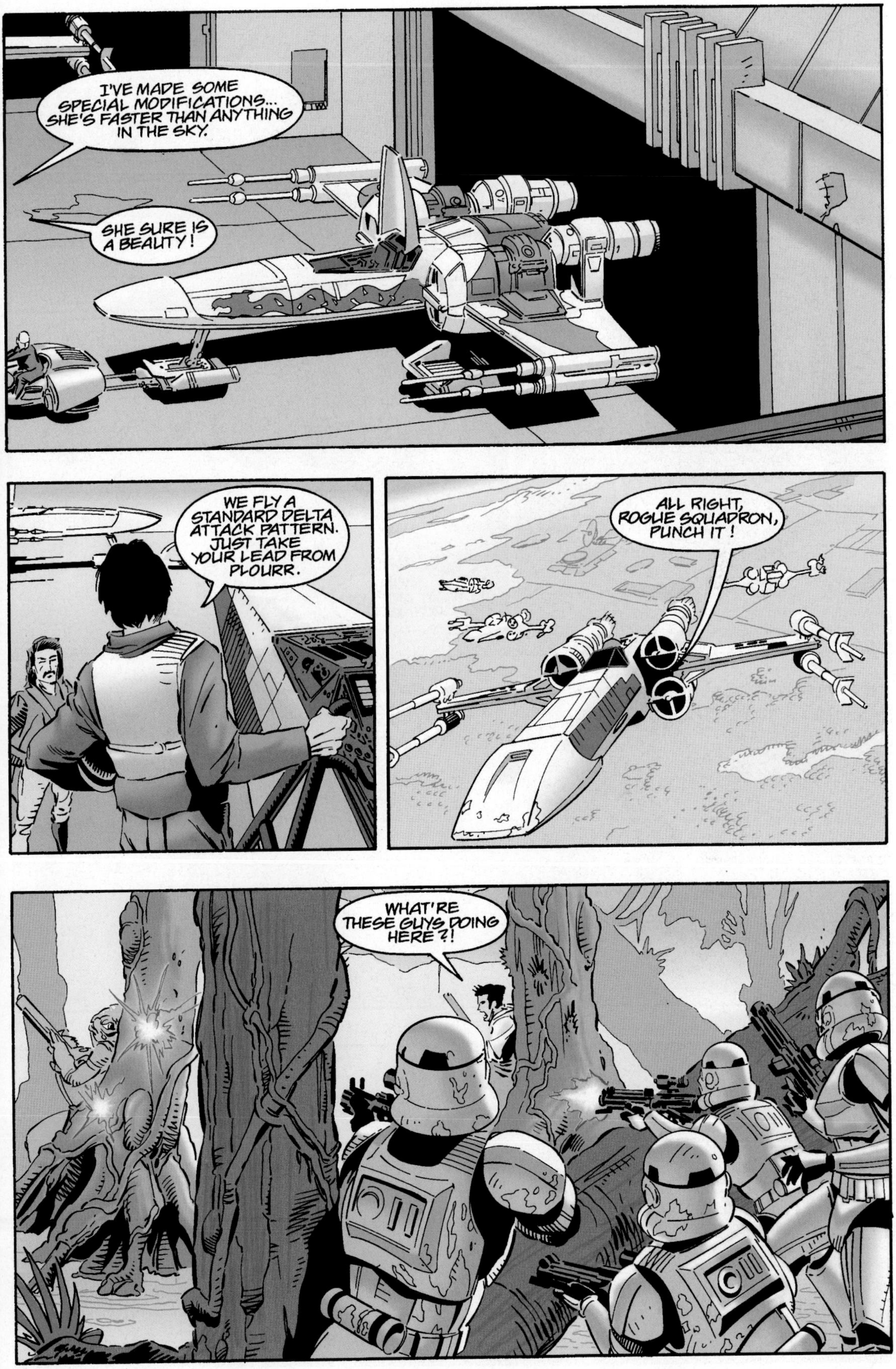
I'VE MADE SOME SPECIAL MODIFICATIONS... SHE'S FASTER THAN ANYTHING IN THE SKY.
SHE SURE IS A BEAUTY!
WE FLY A STANDARD DELTA ATTACK PATTERN. JUST TAKE YOUR LEAD FROM PLOURR.
ALL RIGHT, ROGUE SQUADRON, PUNCH IT!
WHAT'RE THESE GUYS DOING HERE?!

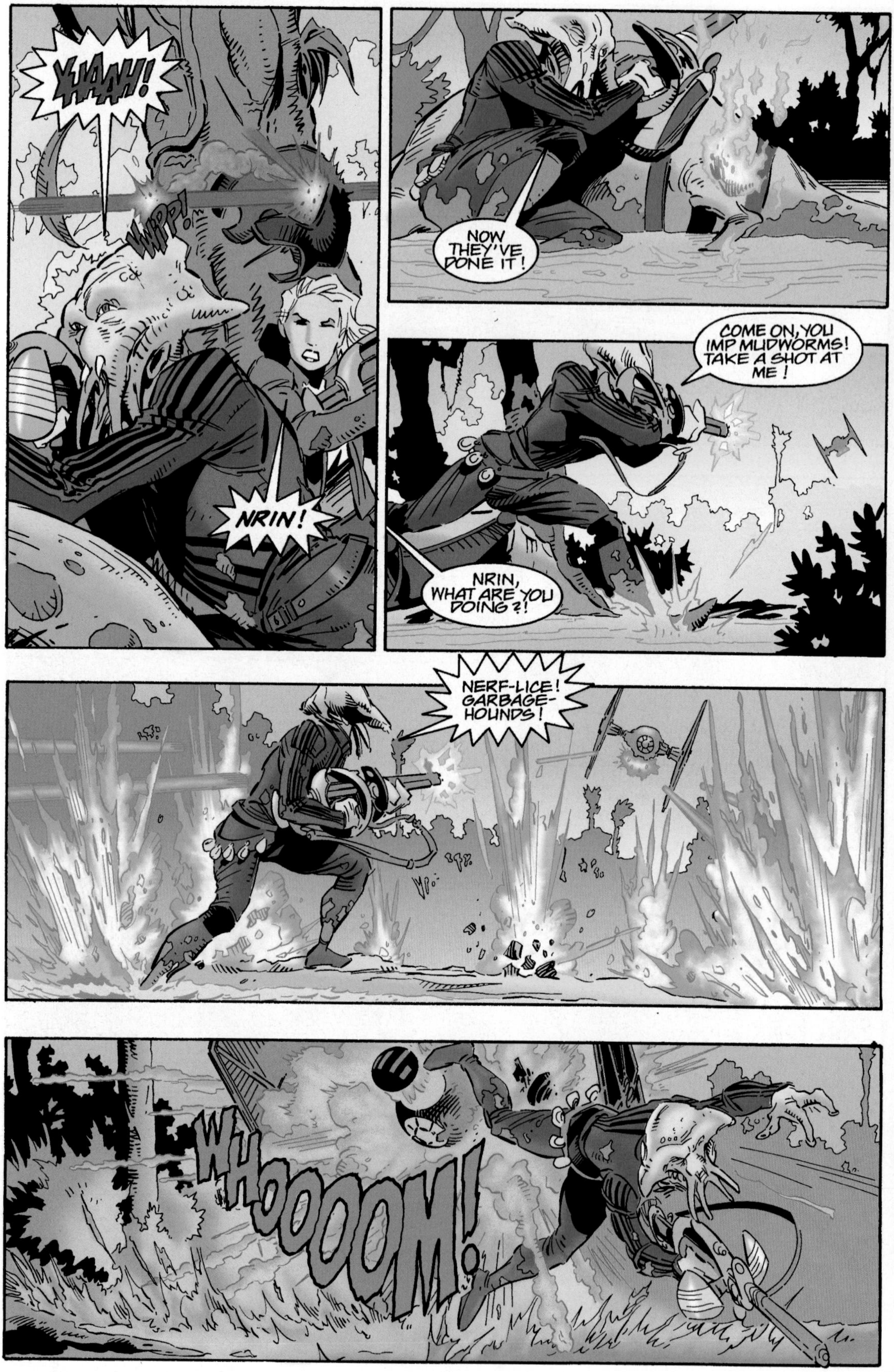
YAAAH!
WHIPP!
NRIN!
NOW THEY'VE DONE IT!
COME ON, YOU IMP MUDWORMS! TAKE A SHOT AT ME!
NRIN, WHAT ARE YOU DOING?!
NERF-LICE! GARBAGE-HOUNDS!
WHOOOOOM!

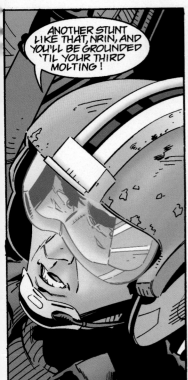

ANOTHER STUNT LIKE THAT, NRIN, AND YOU'LL BE GROUNDED 'TIL YOUR THIRD MOLTING!

NOW, GET SOME COVER!

YES SIR, CAPTAIN ANTILLES, SIR!!

RIAL, GET OUT OF THERE! YOU'VE GOT TWO ON YOUR TAIL!

NOT TO WORRY, MY PRINCESS. I HAVE THEM RIGHT WHERE I WANT THEM.

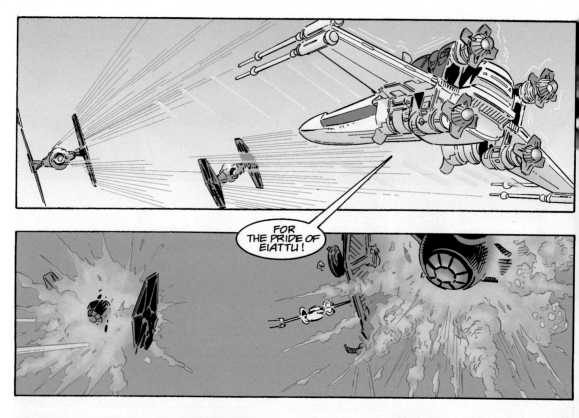

FOR THE PRIDE OF EIATTU!

WOW, WHOEVER'S IN THAT Z-95 SURE HAS GUTS TO PULL A SILERIAN STALL IN THAT CRATE.

WE GOTTA GET SOMEBODY ON THEIR FLANK, JANSON! WE'RE GETTING POUNDED--

LOOKS LIKE YOU GOT YOUR WISH, HOBBIE!!

LIBERATION!!!

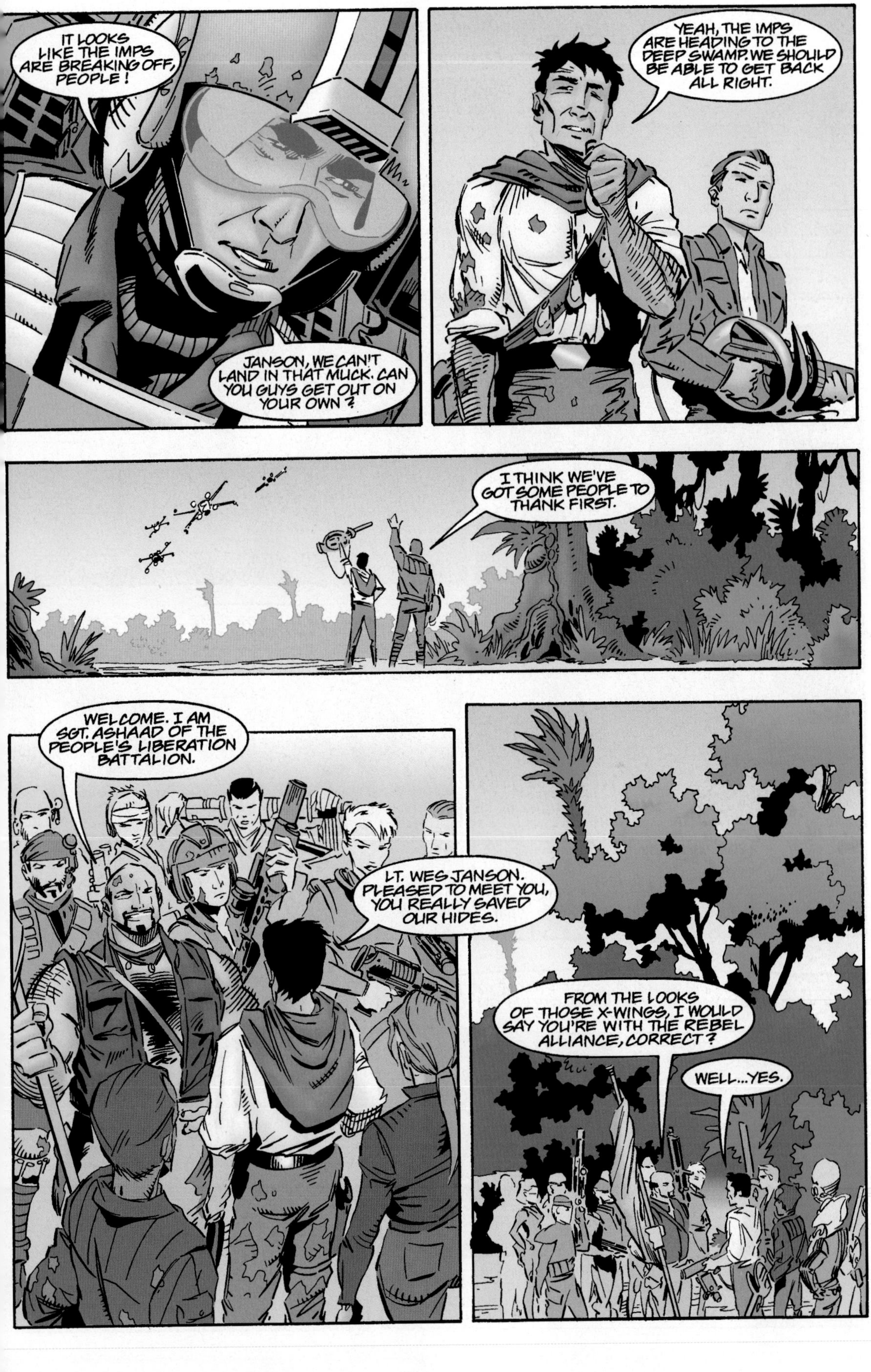
IT LOOKS LIKE THE IMPS ARE BREAKING OFF, PEOPLE!
JANSON, WE CAN'T LAND IN THAT MUCK. CAN YOU GUYS GET OUT ON YOUR OWN?
YEAH, THE IMPS ARE HEADING TO THE DEEP SWAMP. WE SHOULD BE ABLE TO GET BACK ALL RIGHT.
I THINK WE'VE GOT SOME PEOPLE TO THANK FIRST.
WELCOME. I AM SGT. ASHAAD OF THE PEOPLE'S LIBERATION BATTALION.
LT. WES JANSON. PLEASED TO MEET YOU, YOU REALLY SAVED OUR HIDES.
FROM THE LOOKS OF THOSE X-WINGS, I WOULD SAY YOU'RE WITH THE REBEL ALLIANCE, CORRECT?
WELL...YES.

WONDERFUL, AN ENEMY OF THE EMPIRE IS AN ALLY OF OURS. COME, OUR CAMP IS NEARBY, MY COMMANDER WILL WISH TO HAVE A WORD WITH YOU.

THAT WAS *SOME* FLYING, COUNT PERNON! I THOUGHT THOSE EYEBALLS HAD YOU COLD.

I THINK HE'D EVEN GIVE YOU A RUN, PLOURR... I MEAN, PRINCESS ISPLOURRDACARTHA...

I WAS ONLY PERFORMING MY DUTY TO MY WORLD AND PRINCESS.

COME NOW, COUNT PERNON. YOUR SKILL IN FLIGHT DOES THE THRONE PROUD.

YOU HONOR ME, MY PRINCESS.

OH, COME ON! STOP IT, RIAL!

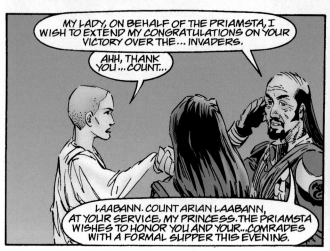

MY LADY, ON BEHALF OF THE PRIAMSTA, I WISH TO EXTEND MY CONGRATULATIONS ON YOUR VICTORY OVER THE... INVADERS.

AHH, THANK YOU... COUNT...

LAABANN. COUNT ARIAN LAABANN, AT YOUR SERVICE, MY PRINCESS. THE PRIAMSTA WISHES TO HONOR YOU AND YOUR... COMRADES WITH A FORMAL SUPPER THIS EVENING.

WE WOULD BE HONORED!

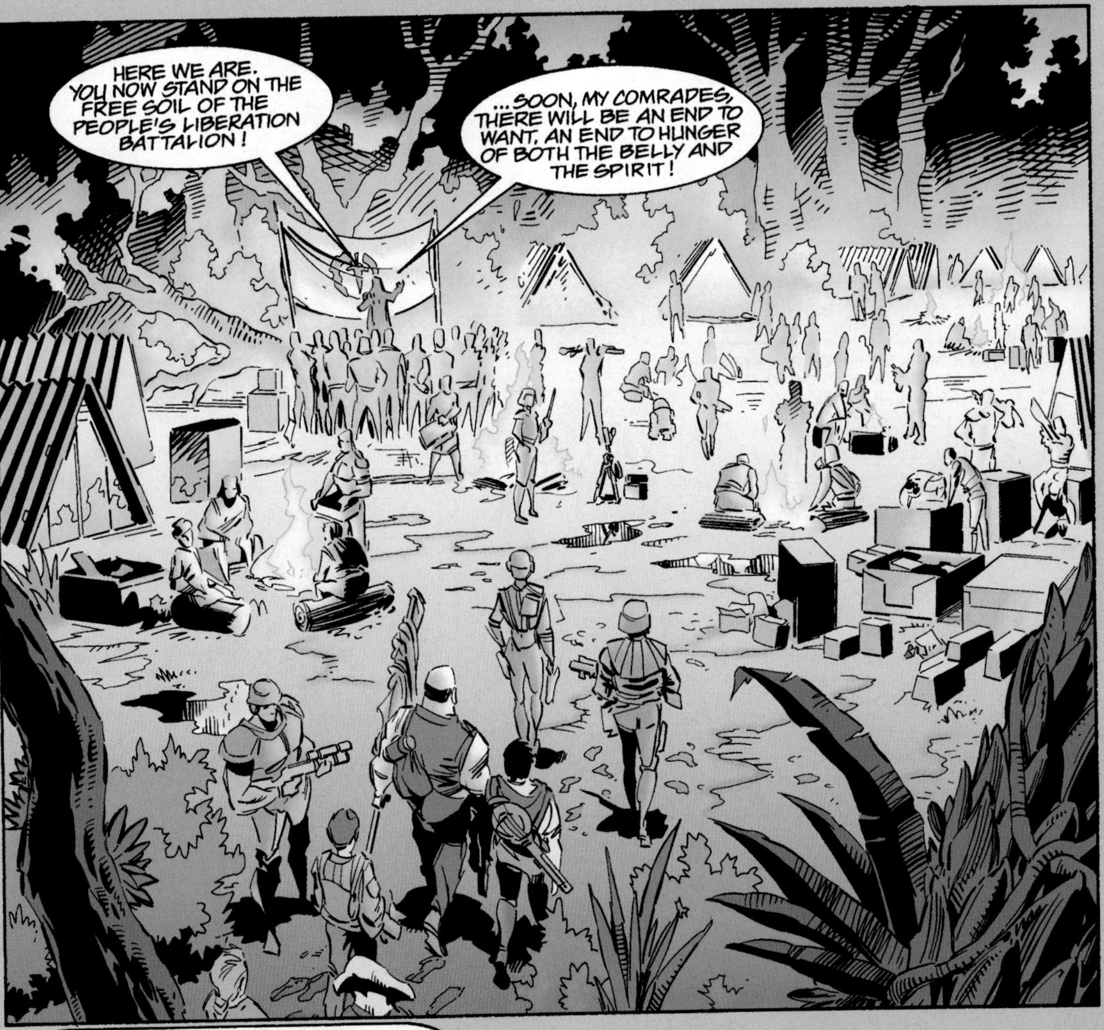
HERE WE ARE. YOU NOW STAND ON THE FREE SOIL OF THE PEOPLE'S LIBERATION BATTALION!
...SOON, MY COMRADES, THERE WILL BE AN END TO WANT, AN END TO HUNGER OF BOTH THE BELLY AND THE SPIRIT!

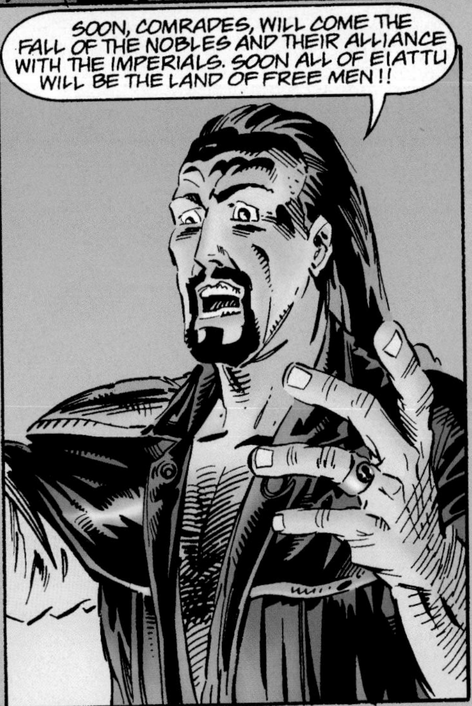
SOON, COMRADES, WILL COME THE FALL OF THE NOBLES AND THEIR ALLIANCE WITH THE IMPERIALS. SOON ALL OF EIATTU WILL BE THE LAND OF FREE MEN!!

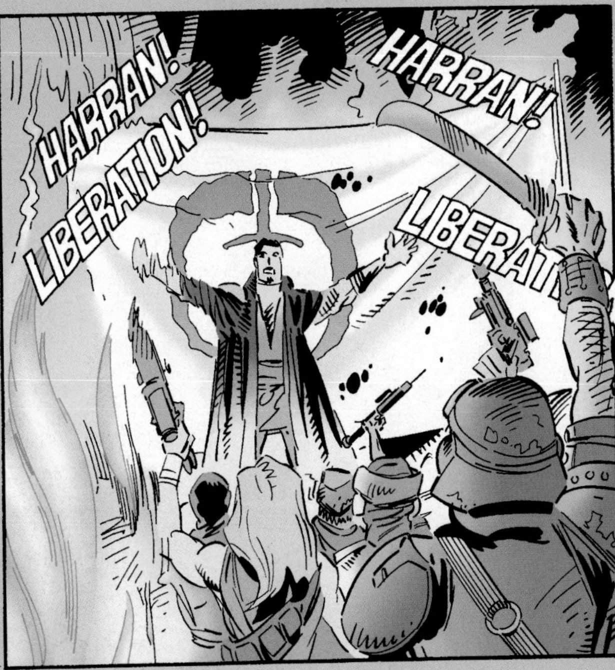
HARRAN! LIBERATION!
HARRAN!
LIBERATION!

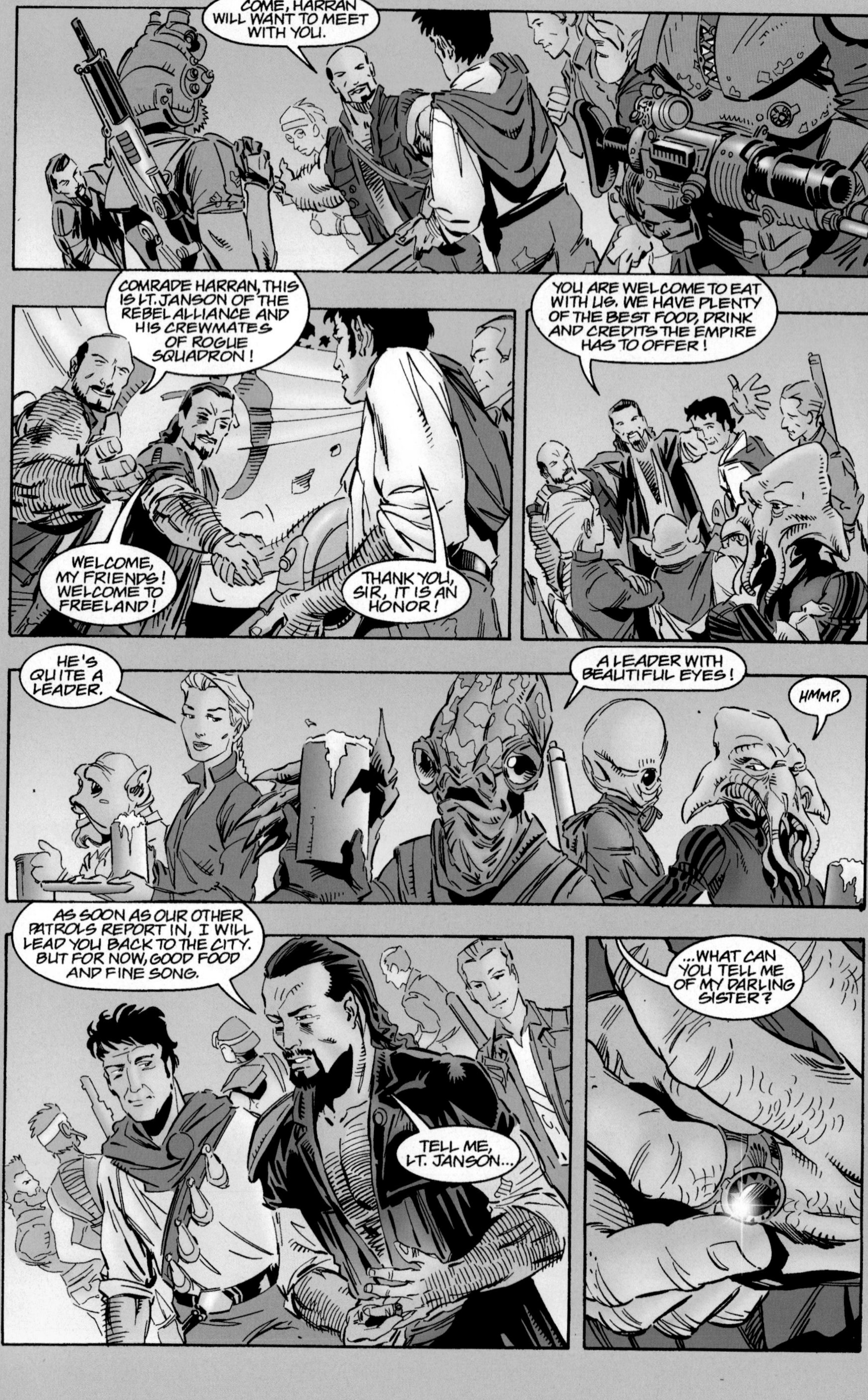
COME, HARRAN WILL WANT TO MEET WITH YOU.
COMRADE HARRAN, THIS IS LT. JANSON OF THE REBEL ALLIANCE AND HIS CREWMATES OF ROGUE SQUADRON!
WELCOME, MY FRIENDS! WELCOME TO FREELAND!
THANK YOU, SIR, IT IS AN HONOR!
YOU ARE WELCOME TO EAT WITH US. WE HAVE PLENTY OF THE BEST FOOD, DRINK AND CREDITS THE EMPIRE HAS TO OFFER!
HE'S QUITE A LEADER.
A LEADER WITH BEAUTIFUL EYES!
HMMP.
AS SOON AS OUR OTHER PATROLS REPORT IN, I WILL LEAD YOU BACK TO THE CITY. BUT FOR NOW, GOOD FOOD AND FINE SONG.
TELL ME, LT. JANSON...
...WHAT CAN YOU TELL ME OF MY DARLING SISTER?

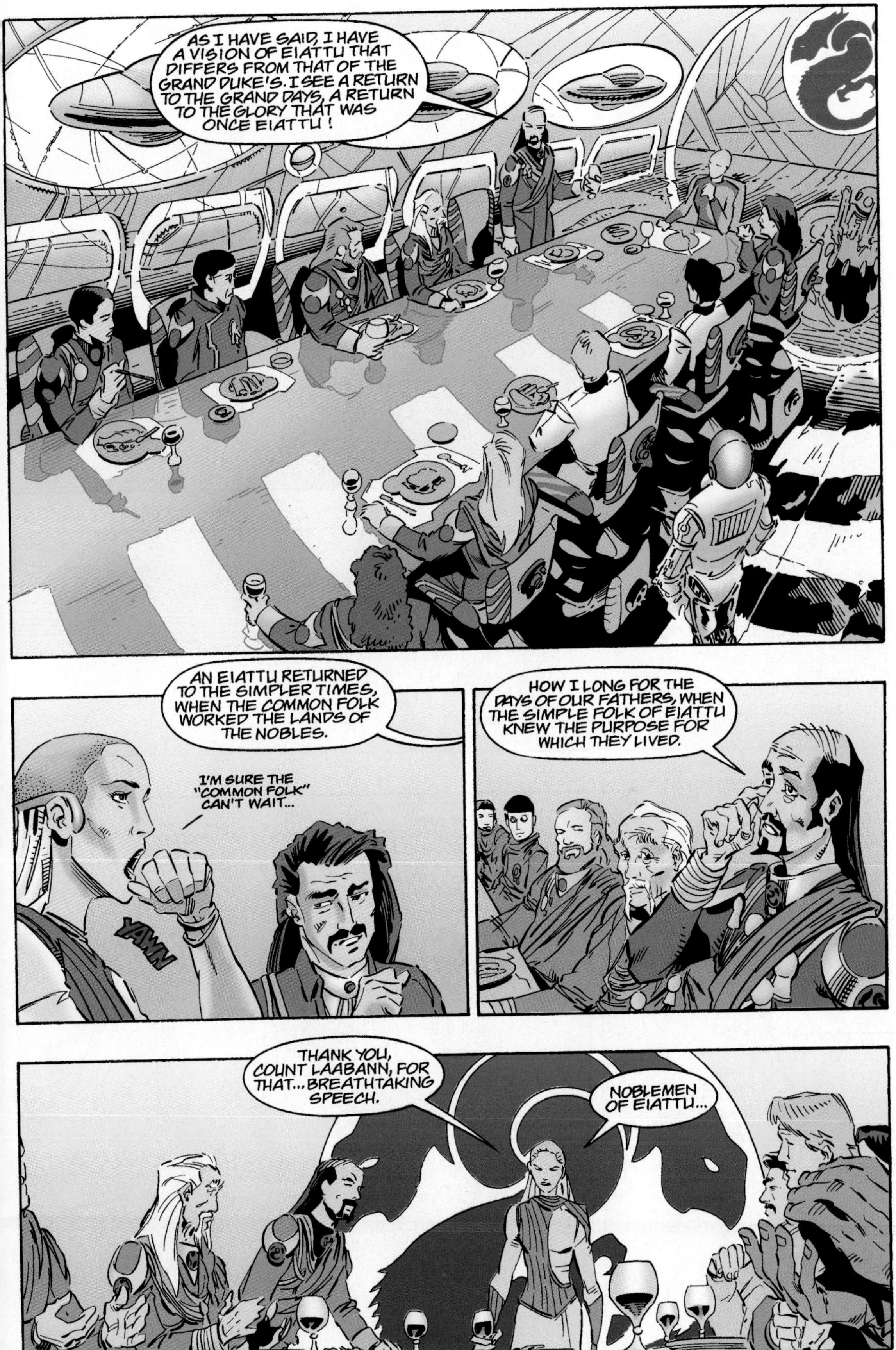
AS I HAVE SAID, I HAVE A VISION OF EIATTU THAT DIFFERS FROM THAT OF THE GRAND DUKE'S. I SEE A RETURN TO THE GRAND DAYS, A RETURN TO THE GLORY THAT WAS ONCE EIATTU!
AN EIATTU RETURNED TO THE SIMPLER TIMES, WHEN THE COMMON FOLK WORKED THE LANDS OF THE NOBLES.
I'M SURE THE "COMMON FOLK" CAN'T WAIT...
YAWN
HOW I LONG FOR THE DAYS OF OUR FATHERS, WHEN THE SIMPLE FOLK OF EIATTU KNEW THE PURPOSE FOR WHICH THEY LIVED.
THANK YOU, COUNT LAABANN, FOR THAT... BREATHTAKING SPEECH.
NOBLEMEN OF EIATTU...

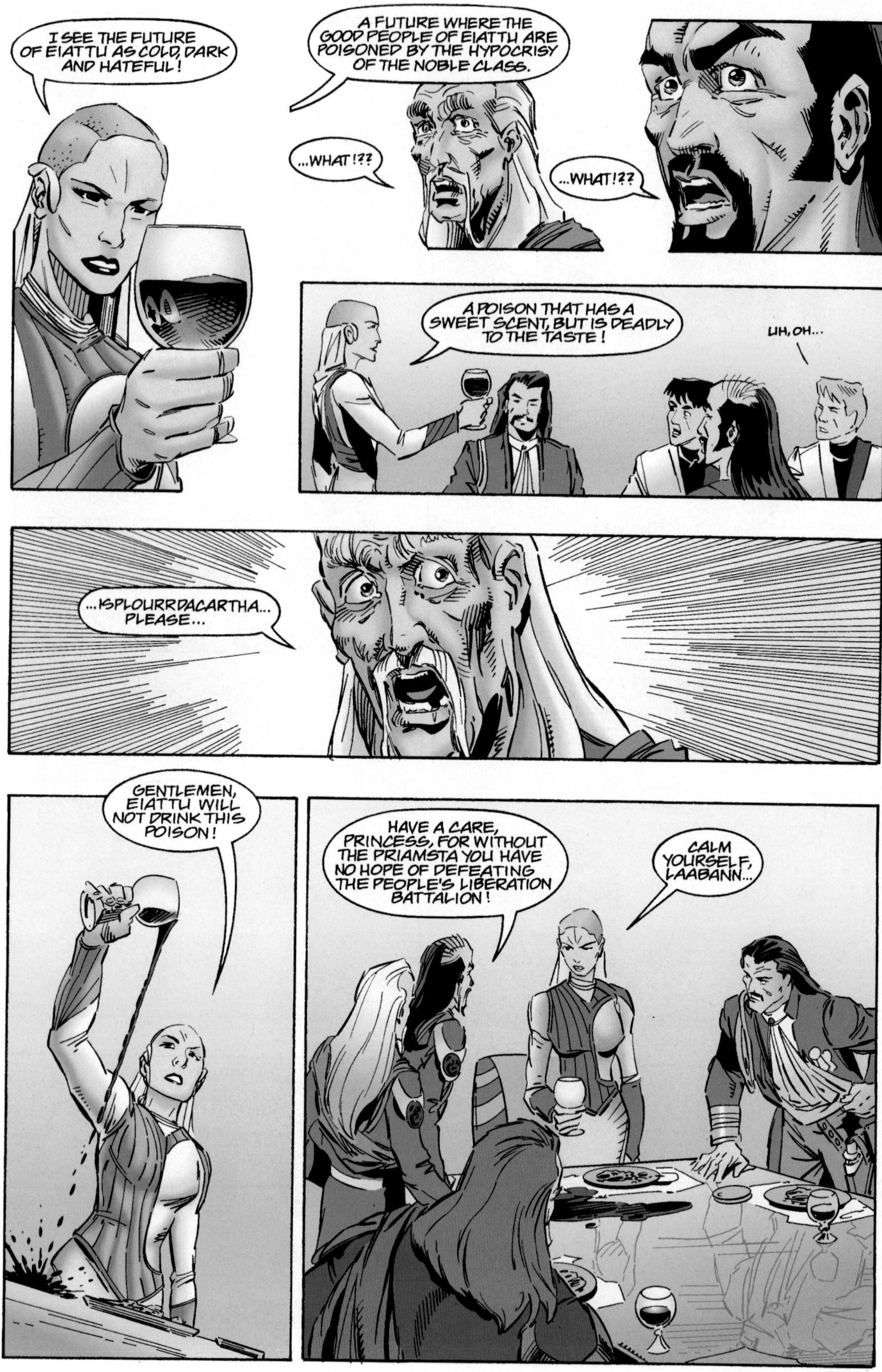
I SEE THE FUTURE OF EIATTU AS COLD, DARK AND HATEFUL!
A FUTURE WHERE THE GOOD PEOPLE OF EIATTU ARE POISONED BY THE HYPOCRISY OF THE NOBLE CLASS.
...WHAT!??
...WHAT!??
A POISON THAT HAS A SWEET SCENT, BUT IS DEADLY TO THE TASTE!
UH, OH...
...ISPLOURRDACARTHA... PLEASE...
GENTLEMEN, EIATTU WILL NOT DRINK THIS POISON!
HAVE A CARE, PRINCESS, FOR WITHOUT THE PRIAMSTA YOU HAVE NO HOPE OF DEFEATING THE PEOPLE'S LIBERATION BATTALION!
CALM YOURSELF, LAABANN...

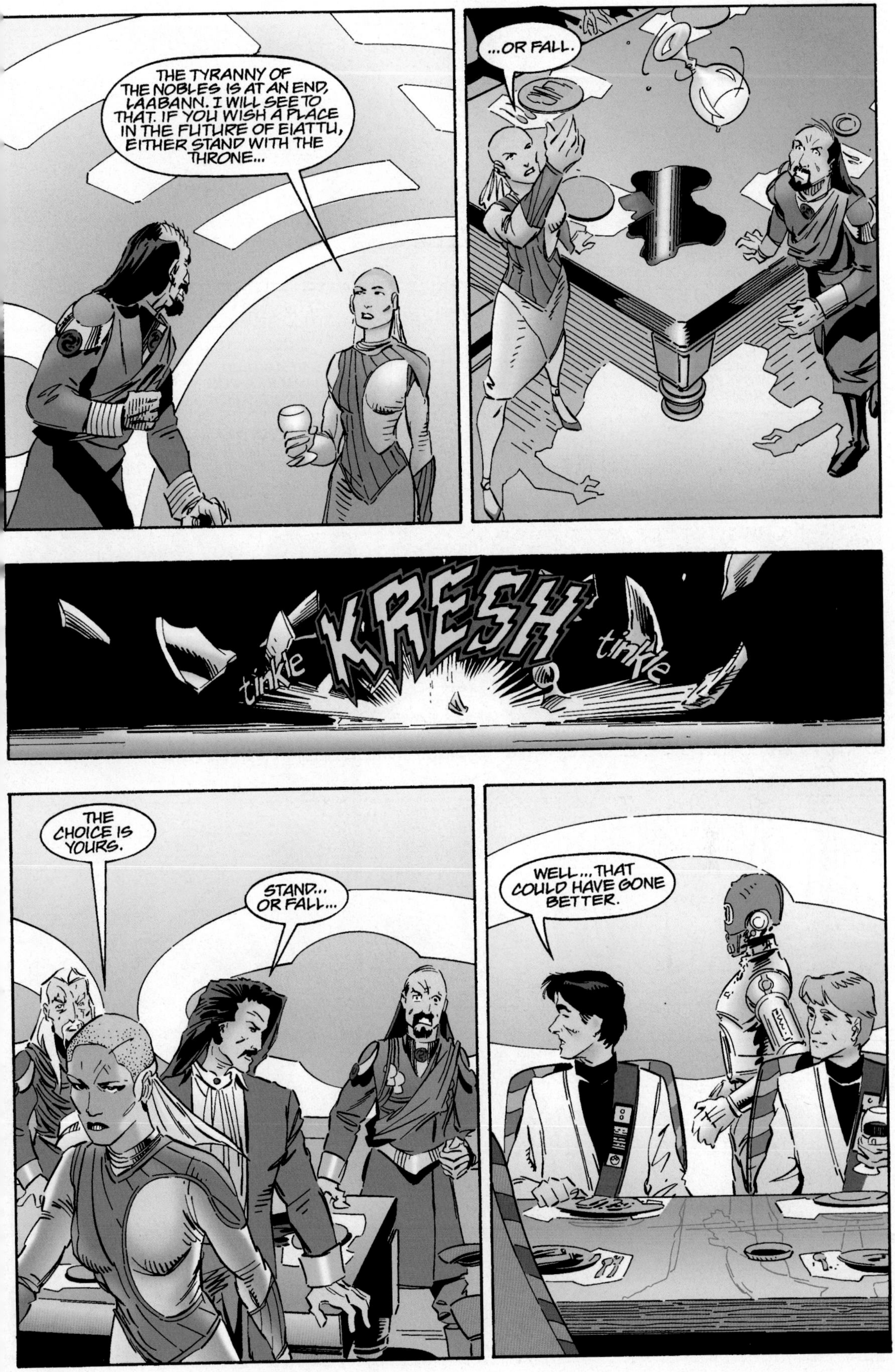
THE TYRANNY OF THE NOBLES IS AT AN END, LAABANN. I WILL SEE TO THAT. IF YOU WISH A PLACE IN THE FUTURE OF EIATTU, EITHER STAND WITH THE THRONE...
...OR FALL.
tinkle
KRESH
tinkle
THE CHOICE IS YOURS.
STAND... OR FALL...
WELL... THAT COULD HAVE GONE BETTER.

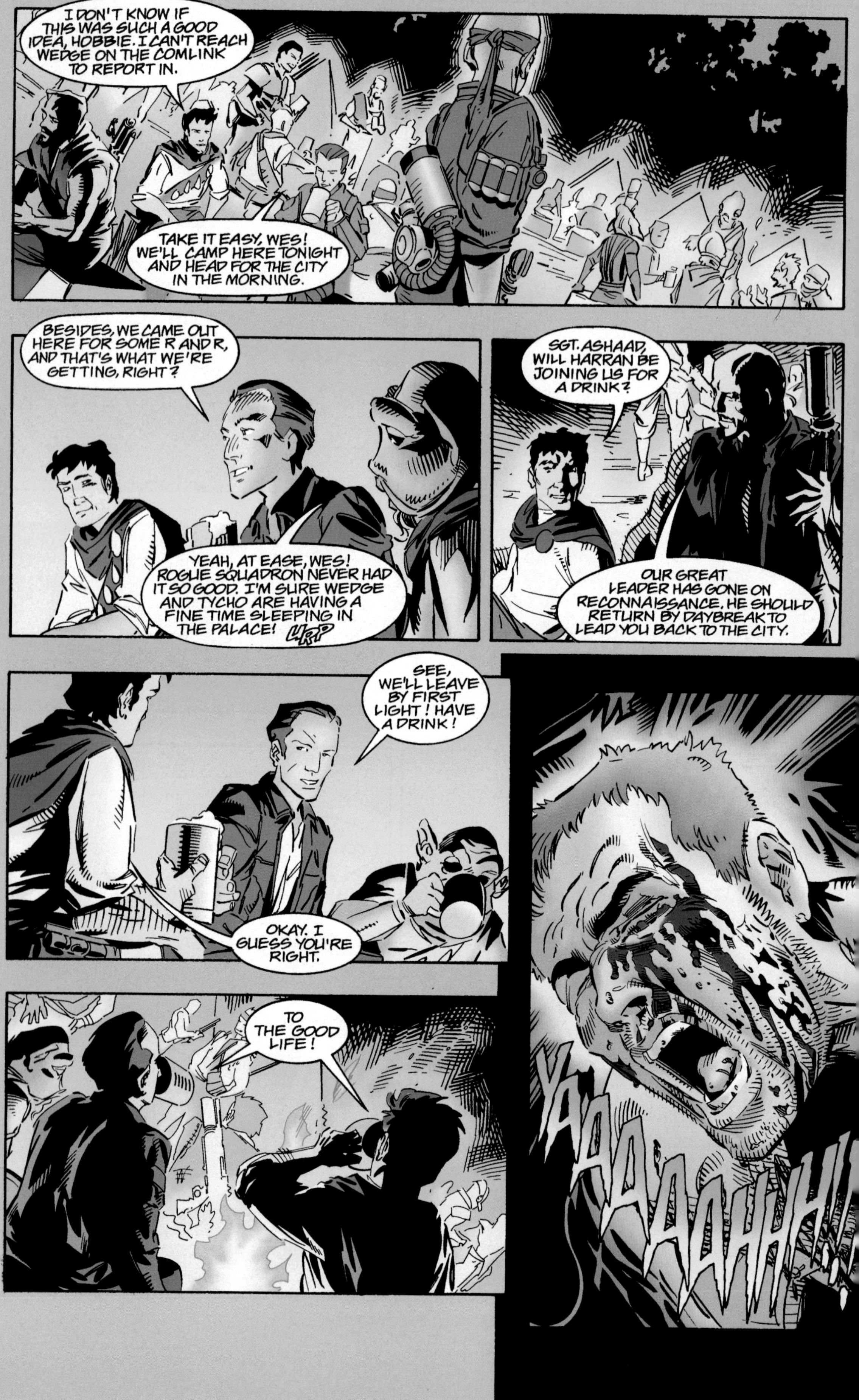
I DON'T KNOW IF THIS WAS SUCH A GOOD IDEA, HOBBIE. I CAN'T REACH WEDGE ON THE COMLINK TO REPORT IN.
TAKE IT EASY, WES! WE'LL CAMP HERE TONIGHT AND HEAD FOR THE CITY IN THE MORNING.
BESIDES, WE CAME OUT HERE FOR SOME R AND R, AND THAT'S WHAT WE'RE GETTING, RIGHT?
YEAH, AT EASE, WES! ROGUE SQUADRON NEVER HAD IT SO GOOD. I'M SURE WEDGE AND TYCHO ARE HAVING A FINE TIME SLEEPING IN THE PALACE!
URP
SGT. ASHAAD, WILL HARRAN BE JOINING US FOR A DRINK?
OUR GREAT LEADER HAS GONE ON RECONNAISSANCE. HE SHOULD RETURN BY DAYBREAK TO LEAD YOU BACK TO THE CITY.
SEE, WE'LL LEAVE BY FIRST LIGHT! HAVE A DRINK!
OKAY. I GUESS YOU'RE RIGHT.
TO THE GOOD LIFE!
YAAAAHH!!

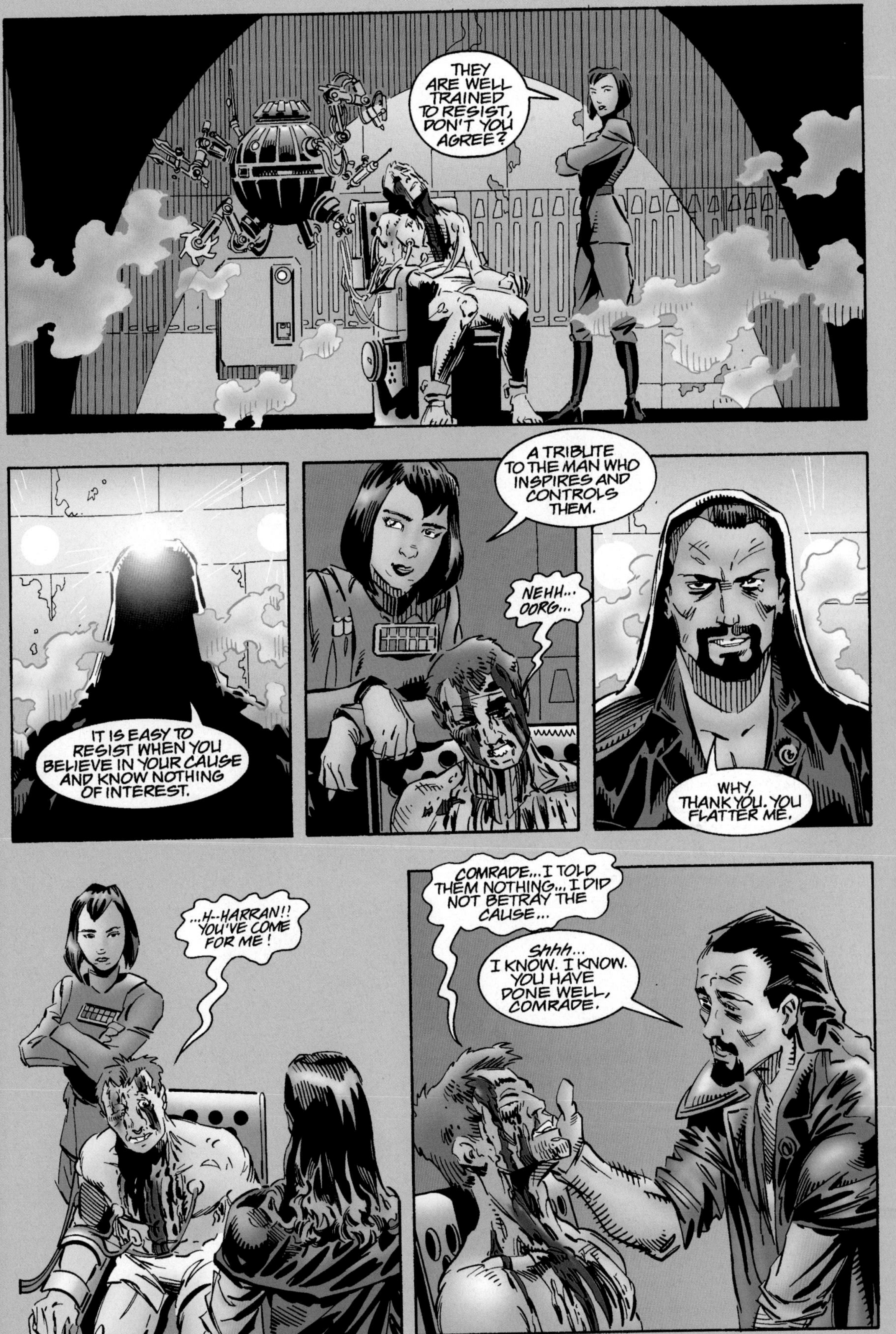
THEY ARE WELL TRAINED TO RESIST, DON'T YOU AGREE?
IT IS EASY TO RESIST WHEN YOU BELIEVE IN YOUR CAUSE AND KNOW NOTHING OF INTEREST.
A TRIBUTE TO THE MAN WHO INSPIRES AND CONTROLS THEM.
NEHH... OORG...
WHY, THANK YOU. YOU FLATTER ME.
...H--HARRAN!! YOU'VE COME FOR ME!
COMRADE... I TOLD THEM NOTHING... I DID NOT BETRAY THE CAUSE...
Shhh... I KNOW. I KNOW. YOU HAVE DONE WELL, COMRADE.

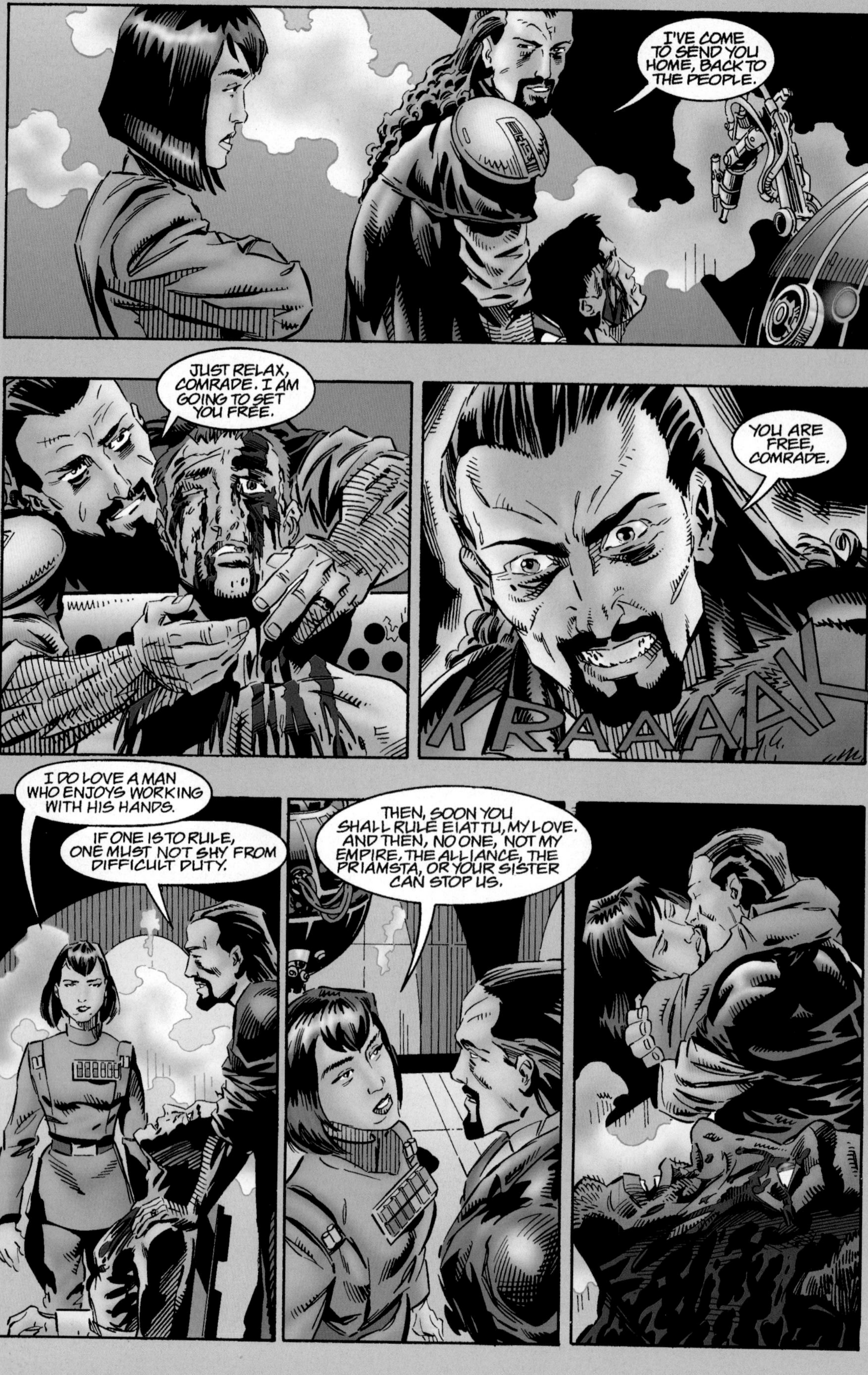
I'VE COME TO SEND YOU HOME, BACK TO THE PEOPLE.
JUST RELAX, COMRADE. I AM GOING TO SET YOU FREE.
YOU ARE FREE, COMRADE.
KRAAAAK
I DO LOVE A MAN WHO ENJOYS WORKING WITH HIS HANDS.
IF ONE IS TO RULE, ONE MUST NOT SHY FROM DIFFICULT DUTY.
THEN, SOON YOU SHALL RULE EIATTU, MY LOVE. AND THEN, NO ONE, NOT MY EMPIRE, THE ALLIANCE, THE PRIAMSTA, OR YOUR SISTER CAN STOP US.

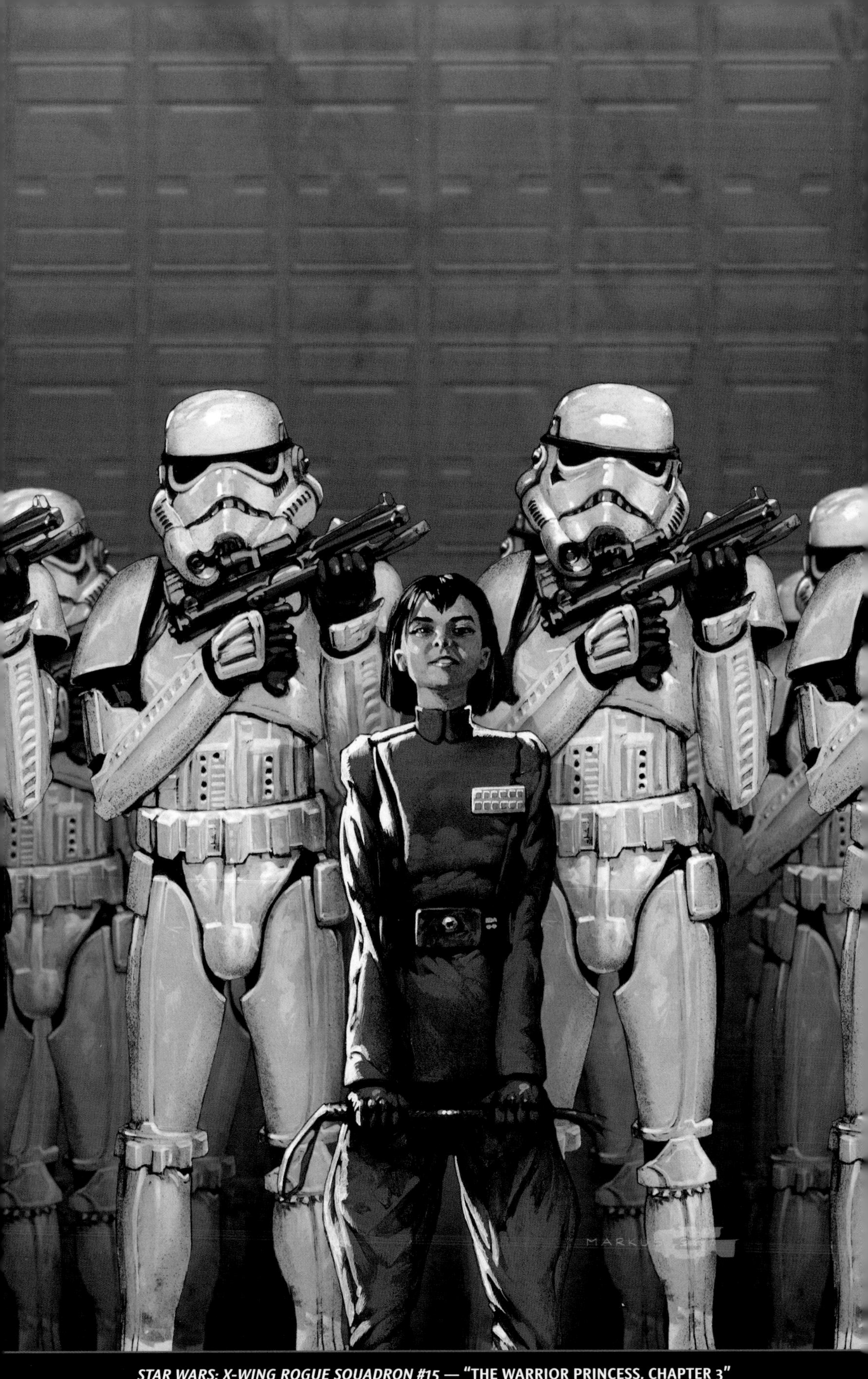

*STAR WARS: X-WING ROGUE SQUADRON #15* — "THE WARRIOR PRINCESS, CHAPTER 3"

PLOTTER: MICHAEL A. STACKPOLE • SCRIPTER: SCOTT TOLSON • PENCILER: JOHN NADEAU • INKER: JORDI ENSIGN
COLORIST: DAVE NESTELLE • LETTERER: VICKIE WILLIAMS • EDITOR: PEET JANES • COVER ARTIST: MARK HARRISON

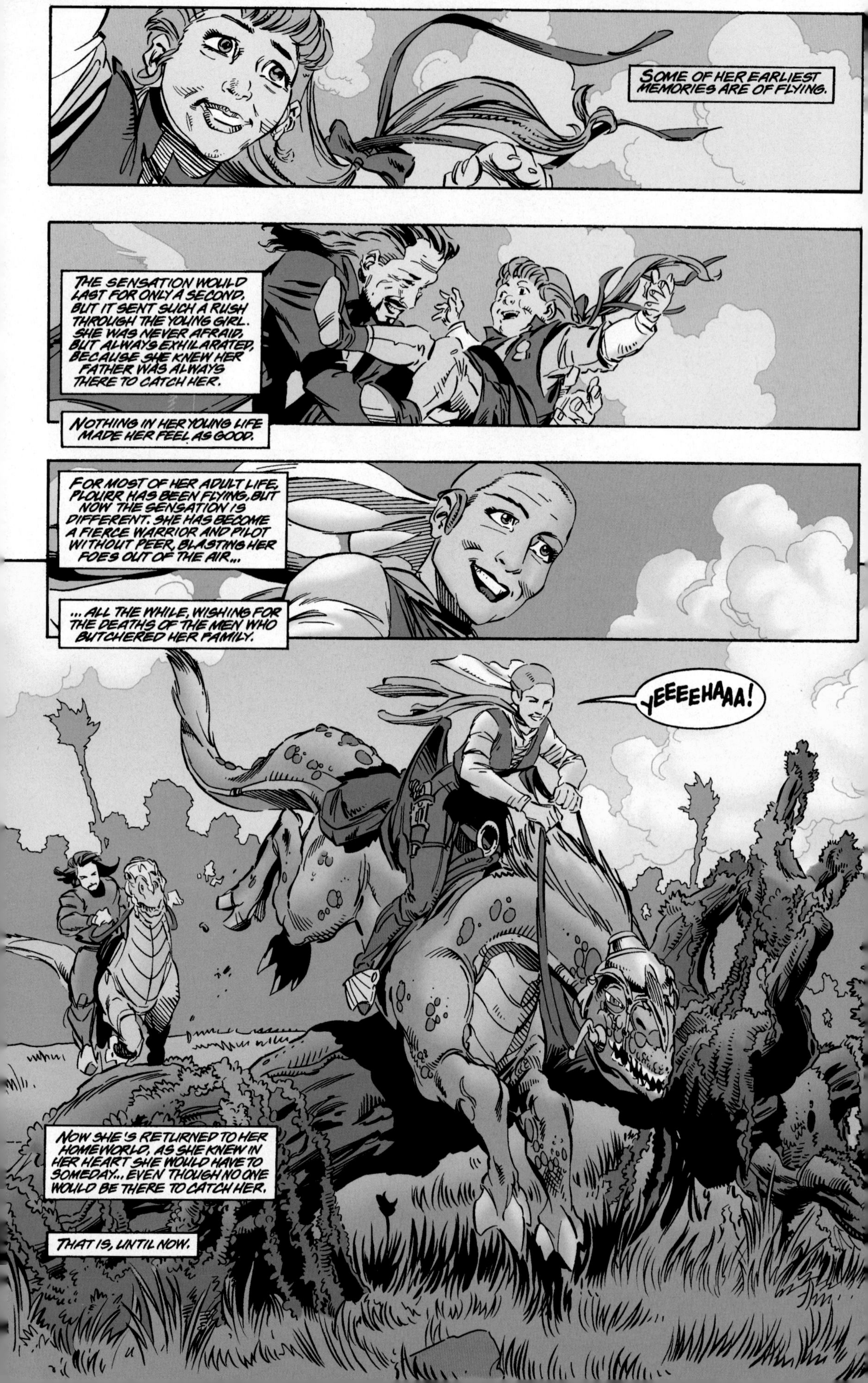
SOME OF HER EARLIEST MEMORIES ARE OF FLYING.
THE SENSATION WOULD LAST FOR ONLY A SECOND, BUT IT SENT SUCH A RUSH THROUGH THE YOUNG GIRL. SHE WAS NEVER AFRAID, BUT ALWAYS EXHILARATED, BECAUSE SHE KNEW HER FATHER WAS ALWAYS THERE TO CATCH HER.
NOTHING IN HER YOUNG LIFE MADE HER FEEL AS GOOD.
FOR MOST OF HER ADULT LIFE, PLOURR HAS BEEN FLYING, BUT NOW THE SENSATION IS DIFFERENT. SHE HAS BECOME A FIERCE WARRIOR AND PILOT WITHOUT PEER, BLASTING HER FOES OUT OF THE AIR...
...ALL THE WHILE, WISHING FOR THE DEATHS OF THE MEN WHO BUTCHERED HER FAMILY.
YEEEEHAAA!
NOW SHE'S RETURNED TO HER HOMEWORLD, AS SHE KNEW IN HER HEART SHE WOULD HAVE TO SOMEDAY... EVEN THOUGH NO ONE WOULD BE THERE TO CATCH HER.
THAT IS, UNTIL NOW.

YOU RIDE WELL, MY COUNT! NOT MANY CAN KEEP UP WITH ME WHEN I GET GOING!!

SO I SEE! I WOULD NOT HAVE THOUGHT THAK-RIDING TO BE A REQUIREMENT OF ALLIANCE FLIGHT TRAINING!

IT'S NOT. IN FACT, I HAVEN'T EVEN SEEN A THAK SINCE I WAS A CHILD.

BUT... I GUESS SOME THINGS YOU JUST DON'T FORGET...

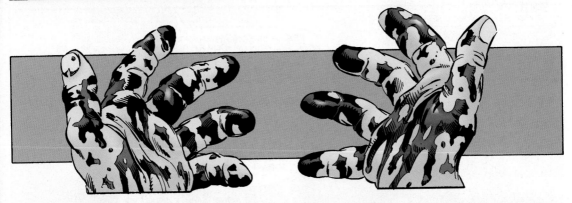

...NO MATTER HOW HARD YOU TRY.

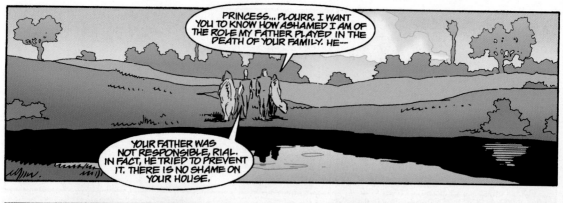

PRINCESS... PLOURR. I WANT YOU TO KNOW HOW ASHAMED I AM OF THE ROLE MY FATHER PLAYED IN THE DEATH OF YOUR FAMILY. HE--

YOUR FATHER WAS NOT RESPONSIBLE, RIAL. IN FACT, HE TRIED TO PREVENT IT. THERE IS NO SHAME ON YOUR HOUSE.

NOR ON YOU, MY COUNT.

PERHAPS. I ONLY WISHED TO EASE THE PAIN OF YOUR RETURN IN SOME SMALL WAY. IT MUST BE DIFFICULT FOR YOU BEING HERE, ALL MEMORIES OF THIS PLACE, AFTER SEEING THEM DIE...

THANKFULLY, I NEVER SAW IT... BUT HEARING THEIR SCREAMS WAS ENOUGH. I REALIZED WHAT WAS HAPPENING AND RAN. I GUESS I DIDN'T REALIZE THAT I WAS LEAVING THEM.

MAYBE IF I HAD GONE BACK, I COULD'VE DONE SOMETHING--

STOP. THERE IS NOTHING YOU COULD HAVE DONE, YOU ARE ALIVE NOW, AND NOT ONLY CAN YOU AVENGE THEM, BUT SAVE THEIR WORLD AS WELL.

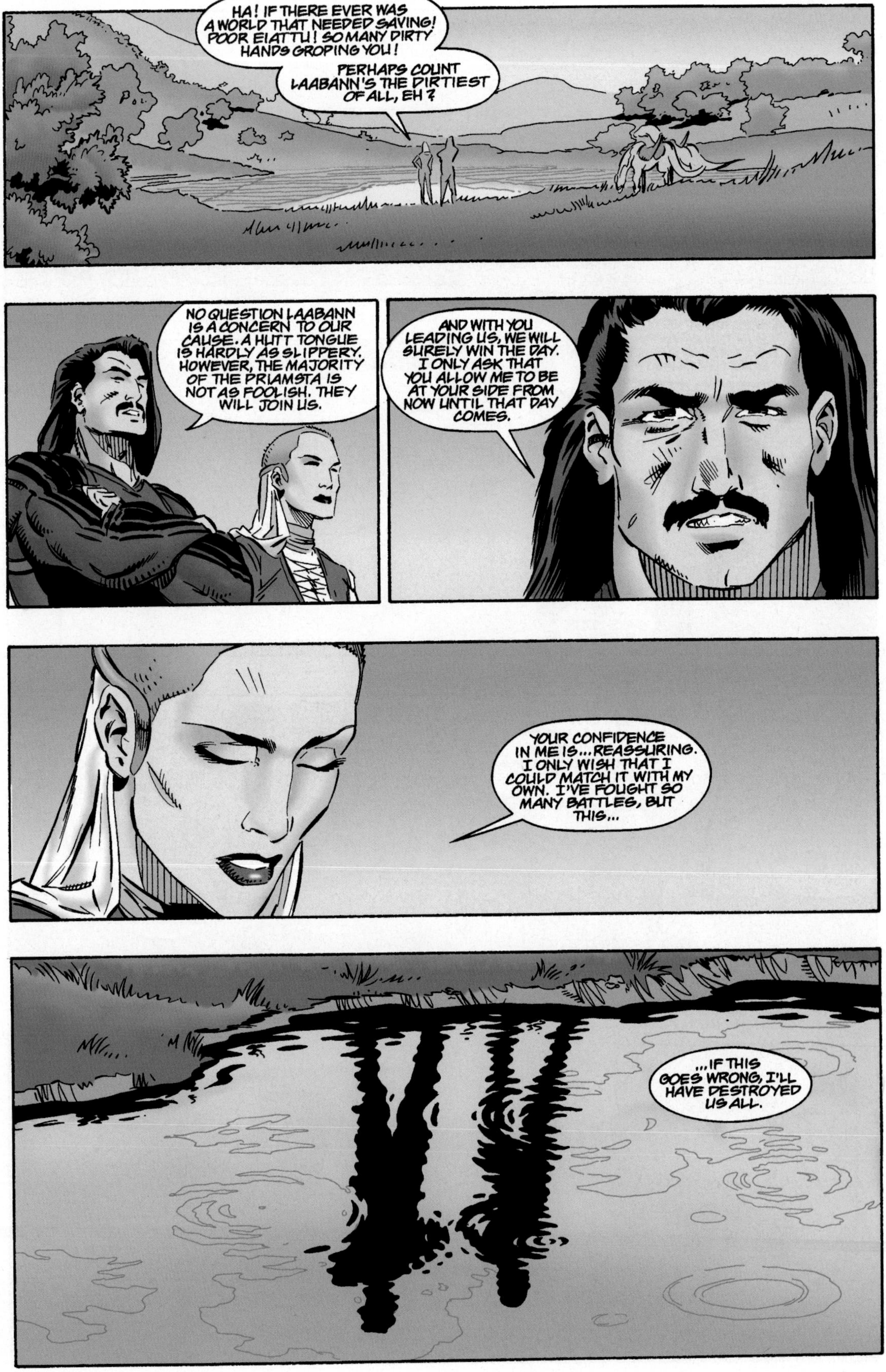
HA! IF THERE EVER WAS A WORLD THAT NEEDED SAVING! POOR EIATTU! SO MANY DIRTY HANDS GROPING YOU!
PERHAPS COUNT LAABANN'S THE DIRTIEST OF ALL, EH?
NO QUESTION LAABANN IS A CONCERN TO OUR CAUSE. A HUTT TONGUE IS HARDLY AS SLIPPERY. HOWEVER, THE MAJORITY OF THE PRIAMSTA IS NOT AS FOOLISH. THEY WILL JOIN US.
AND WITH YOU LEADING US, WE WILL SURELY WIN THE DAY. I ONLY ASK THAT YOU ALLOW ME TO BE AT YOUR SIDE FROM NOW UNTIL THAT DAY COMES.
YOUR CONFIDENCE IN ME IS... REASSURING. I ONLY WISH THAT I COULD MATCH IT WITH MY OWN. I'VE FOUGHT SO MANY BATTLES, BUT THIS...
...IF THIS GOES WRONG, I'LL HAVE DESTROYED US ALL.

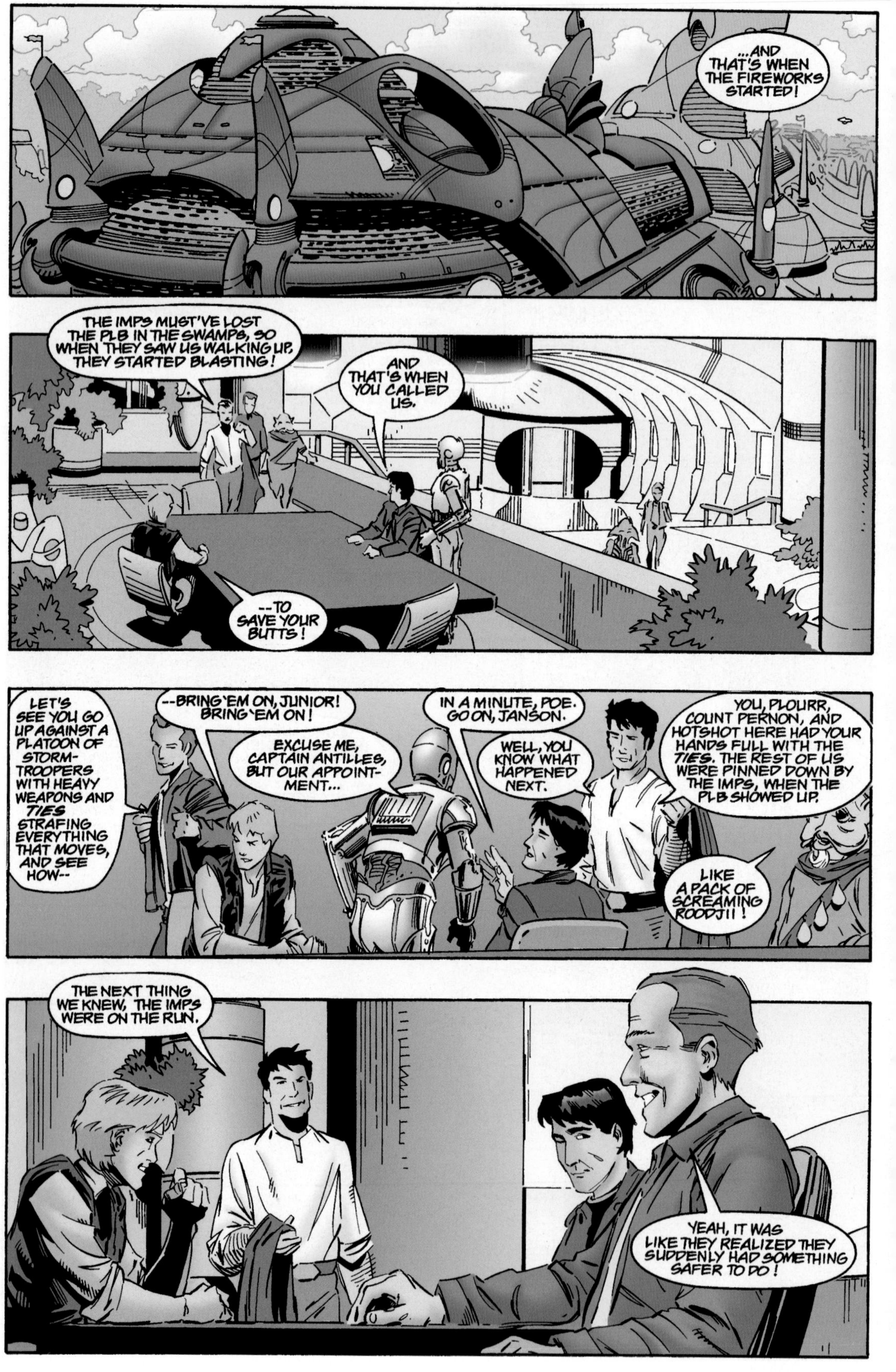
...AND THAT'S WHEN THE FIREWORKS STARTED!
THE IMPS MUST'VE LOST THE PLB IN THE SWAMPS, SO WHEN THEY SAW US WALKING UP, THEY STARTED BLASTING!
AND THAT'S WHEN YOU CALLED US.
--TO SAVE YOUR BUTTS!
LET'S SEE YOU GO UP AGAINST A PLATOON OF STORM-TROOPERS WITH HEAVY WEAPONS AND *TIES* STRAFING EVERYTHING THAT MOVES, AND SEE HOW--
--BRING 'EM ON, JUNIOR! BRING 'EM ON!
EXCUSE ME, CAPTAIN ANTILLES, BUT OUR APPOINT-MENT...
IN A MINUTE, POE. GO ON, JANSON.
WELL, YOU KNOW WHAT HAPPENED NEXT.
YOU, PLOURR, COUNT PERNON, AND HOTSHOT HERE HAD YOUR HANDS FULL WITH THE *TIES*. THE REST OF US WERE PINNED DOWN BY THE IMPS, WHEN THE PLB SHOWED UP.
LIKE A PACK OF SCREAMING ROODJII!
THE NEXT THING WE KNEW, THE IMPS WERE ON THE RUN.
YEAH, IT WAS LIKE THEY REALIZED THEY SUDDENLY HAD SOMETHING SAFER TO DO!

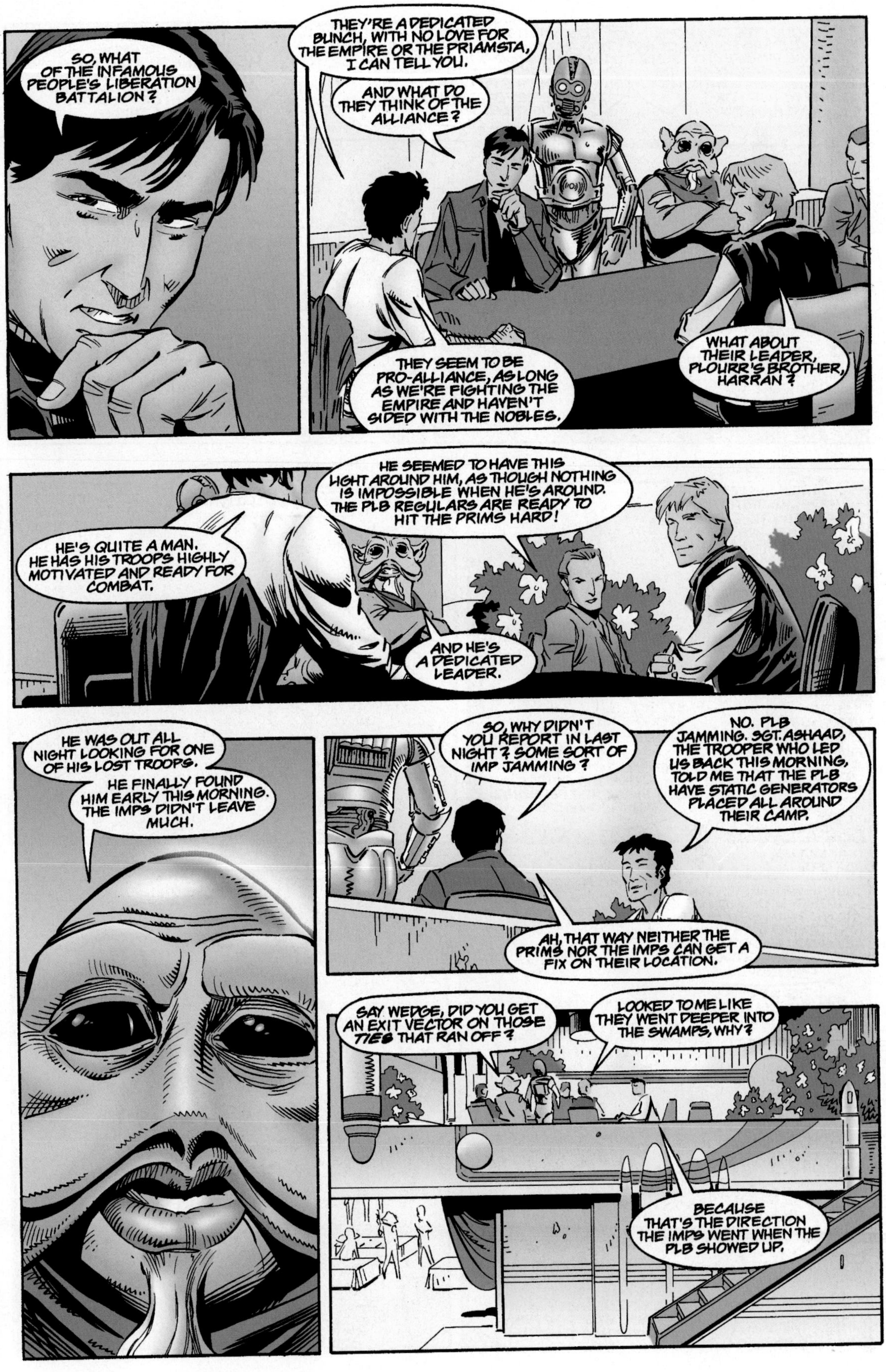
SO, WHAT OF THE INFAMOUS PEOPLE'S LIBERATION BATTALION?
THEY'RE A DEDICATED BUNCH, WITH NO LOVE FOR THE EMPIRE OR THE PRIAMSTA, I CAN TELL YOU.
AND WHAT DO THEY THINK OF THE ALLIANCE?
THEY SEEM TO BE PRO-ALLIANCE, AS LONG AS WE'RE FIGHTING THE EMPIRE AND HAVEN'T SIDED WITH THE NOBLES.
WHAT ABOUT THEIR LEADER, PLOURR'S BROTHER, HARRAN?
HE'S QUITE A MAN. HE HAS HIS TROOPS HIGHLY MOTIVATED AND READY FOR COMBAT.
HE SEEMED TO HAVE THIS LIGHT AROUND HIM, AS THOUGH NOTHING IS IMPOSSIBLE WHEN HE'S AROUND. THE PLB REGULARS ARE READY TO HIT THE PRIMS HARD!
AND HE'S A DEDICATED LEADER.
HE WAS OUT ALL NIGHT LOOKING FOR ONE OF HIS LOST TROOPS.
HE FINALLY FOUND HIM EARLY THIS MORNING. THE IMPS DIDN'T LEAVE MUCH.
SO, WHY DIDN'T YOU REPORT IN LAST NIGHT? SOME SORT OF IMP JAMMING?
NO. PLB JAMMING. SGT. ASHAAD, THE TROOPER WHO LED US BACK THIS MORNING, TOLD ME THAT THE PLB HAVE STATIC GENERATORS PLACED ALL AROUND THEIR CAMP.
AH, THAT WAY NEITHER THE PRIMS NOR THE IMPS CAN GET A FIX ON THEIR LOCATION.
SAY WEDGE, DID YOU GET AN EXIT VECTOR ON THOSE TIES THAT RAN OFF?
LOOKED TO ME LIKE THEY WENT DEEPER INTO THE SWAMPS, WHY?
BECAUSE THAT'S THE DIRECTION THE IMPS WENT WHEN THE PLB SHOWED UP.

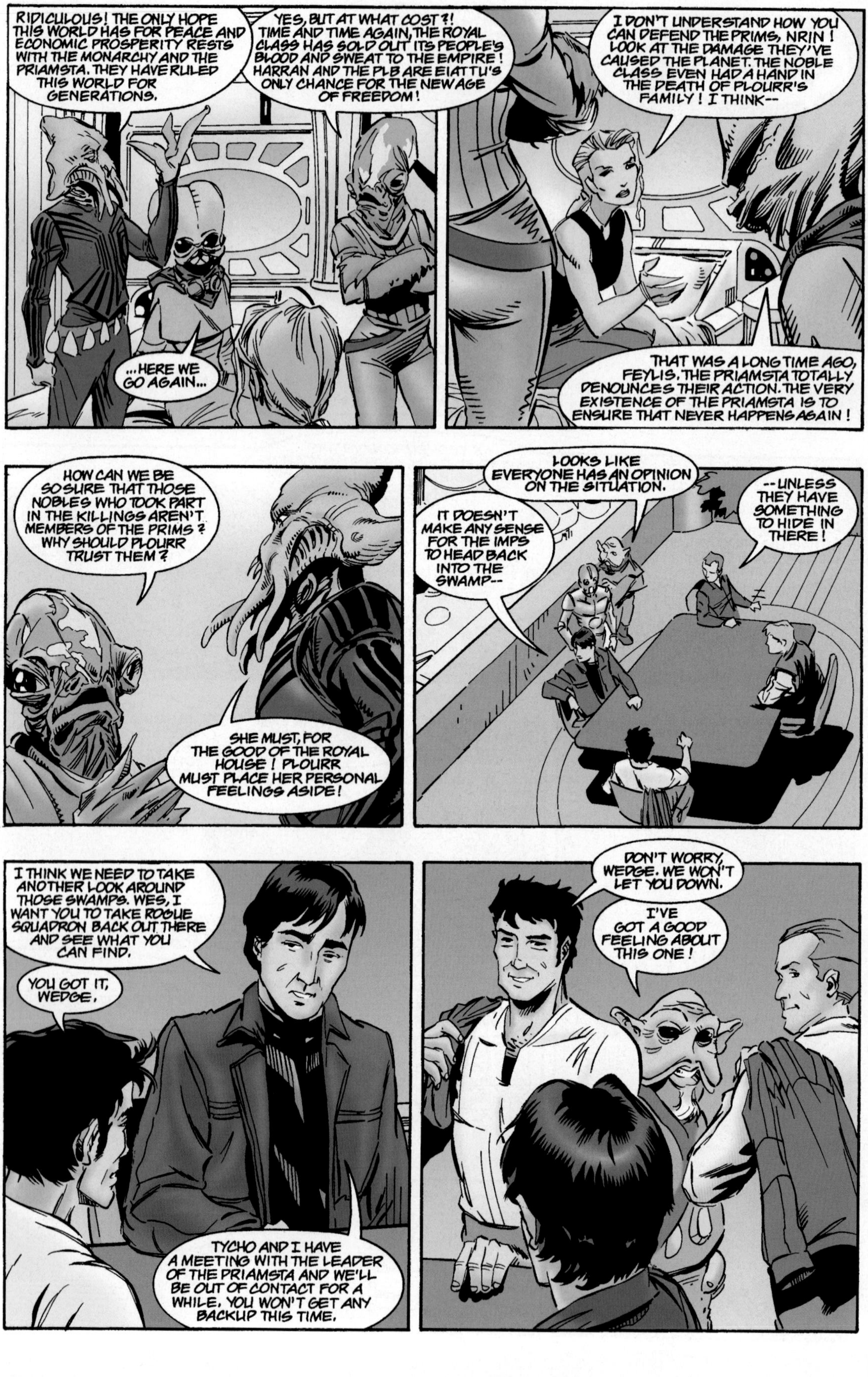
RIDICULOUS! THE ONLY HOPE THIS WORLD HAS FOR PEACE AND ECONOMIC PROSPERITY RESTS WITH THE MONARCHY AND THE PRIAMSTA. THEY HAVE RULED THIS WORLD FOR GENERATIONS.
YES, BUT AT WHAT COST?! TIME AND TIME AGAIN, THE ROYAL CLASS HAS SOLD OUT ITS PEOPLE'S BLOOD AND SWEAT TO THE EMPIRE! HARRAN AND THE PLB ARE EIATTU'S ONLY CHANCE FOR THE NEW AGE OF FREEDOM!
...HERE WE GO AGAIN...
I DON'T UNDERSTAND HOW YOU CAN DEFEND THE PRIMS, NRIN! LOOK AT THE DAMAGE THEY'VE CAUSED THE PLANET. THE NOBLE CLASS EVEN HAD A HAND IN THE DEATH OF PLOURR'S FAMILY! I THINK--
THAT WAS A LONG TIME AGO, FEYLIS. THE PRIAMSTA TOTALLY DENOUNCES THEIR ACTION. THE VERY EXISTENCE OF THE PRIAMSTA IS TO ENSURE THAT NEVER HAPPENS AGAIN!
HOW CAN WE BE SO SURE THAT THOSE NOBLES WHO TOOK PART IN THE KILLINGS AREN'T MEMBERS OF THE PRIMS? WHY SHOULD PLOURR TRUST THEM?
SHE MUST, FOR THE GOOD OF THE ROYAL HOUSE! PLOURR MUST PLACE HER PERSONAL FEELINGS ASIDE!
LOOKS LIKE EVERYONE HAS AN OPINION ON THE SITUATION.
IT DOESN'T MAKE ANY SENSE FOR THE IMPS TO HEAD BACK INTO THE SWAMP--
--UNLESS THEY HAVE SOMETHING TO HIDE IN THERE!
I THINK WE NEED TO TAKE ANOTHER LOOK AROUND THOSE SWAMPS. WES, I WANT YOU TO TAKE ROGUE SQUADRON BACK OUT THERE AND SEE WHAT YOU CAN FIND.
YOU GOT IT, WEDGE.
TYCHO AND I HAVE A MEETING WITH THE LEADER OF THE PRIAMSTA AND WE'LL BE OUT OF CONTACT FOR A WHILE. YOU WON'T GET ANY BACKUP THIS TIME.
DON'T WORRY, WEDGE. WE WON'T LET YOU DOWN.
I'VE GOT A GOOD FEELING ABOUT THIS ONE!

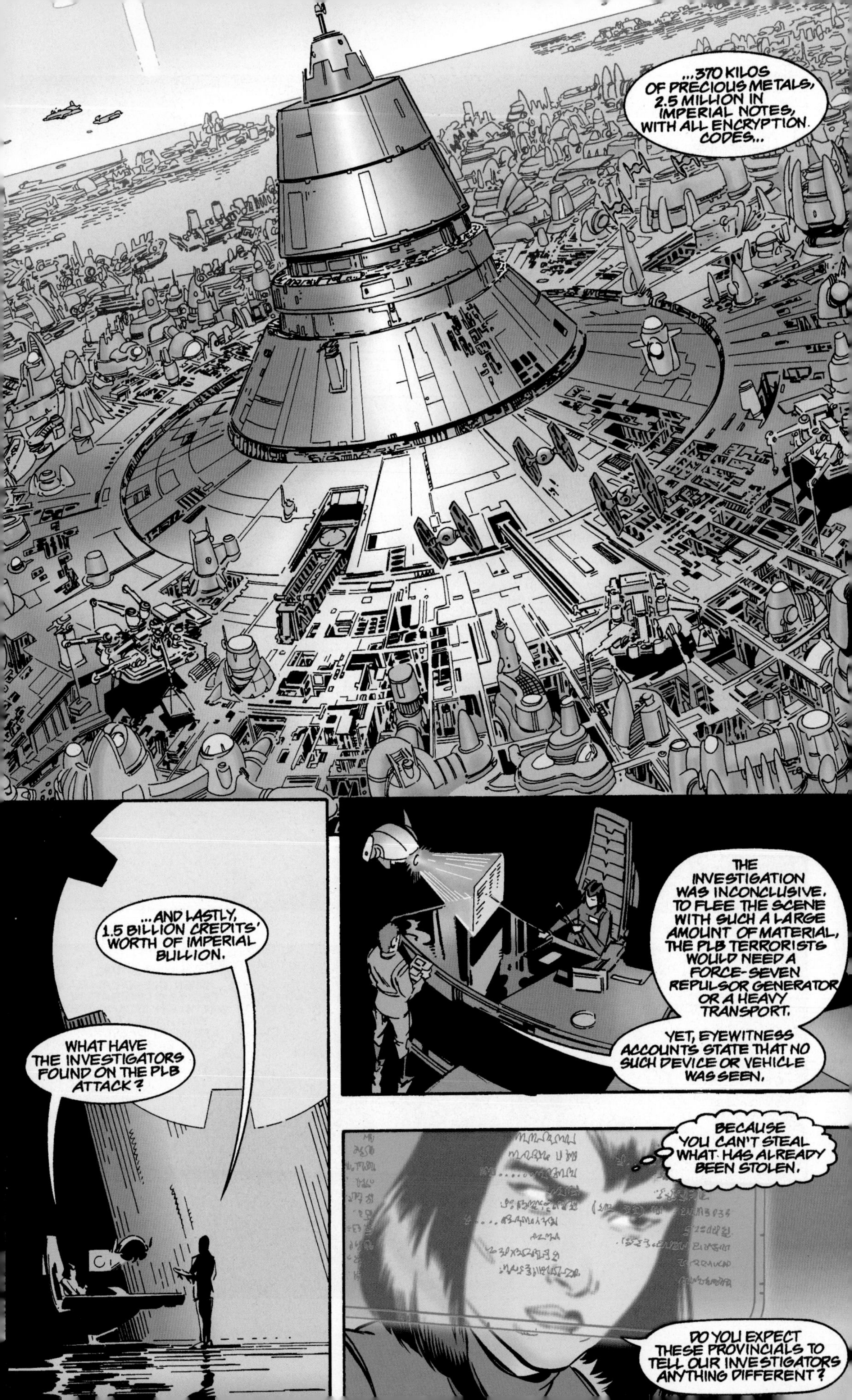
...370 KILOS OF PRECIOUS METALS, 2.5 MILLION IN IMPERIAL NOTES, WITH ALL ENCRYPTION CODES...
...AND LASTLY, 1.5 BILLION CREDITS' WORTH OF IMPERIAL BULLION.
WHAT HAVE THE INVESTIGATORS FOUND ON THE PLB ATTACK?
THE INVESTIGATION WAS INCONCLUSIVE. TO FLEE THE SCENE WITH SUCH A LARGE AMOUNT OF MATERIAL, THE PLB TERRORISTS WOULD NEED A FORCE-SEVEN REPULSOR GENERATOR OR A HEAVY TRANSPORT.
YET, EYEWITNESS ACCOUNTS STATE THAT NO SUCH DEVICE OR VEHICLE WAS SEEN.
BECAUSE YOU CAN'T STEAL WHAT HAS ALREADY BEEN STOLEN.
DO YOU EXPECT THESE PROVINCIALS TO TELL OUR INVESTIGATORS ANYTHING DIFFERENT?

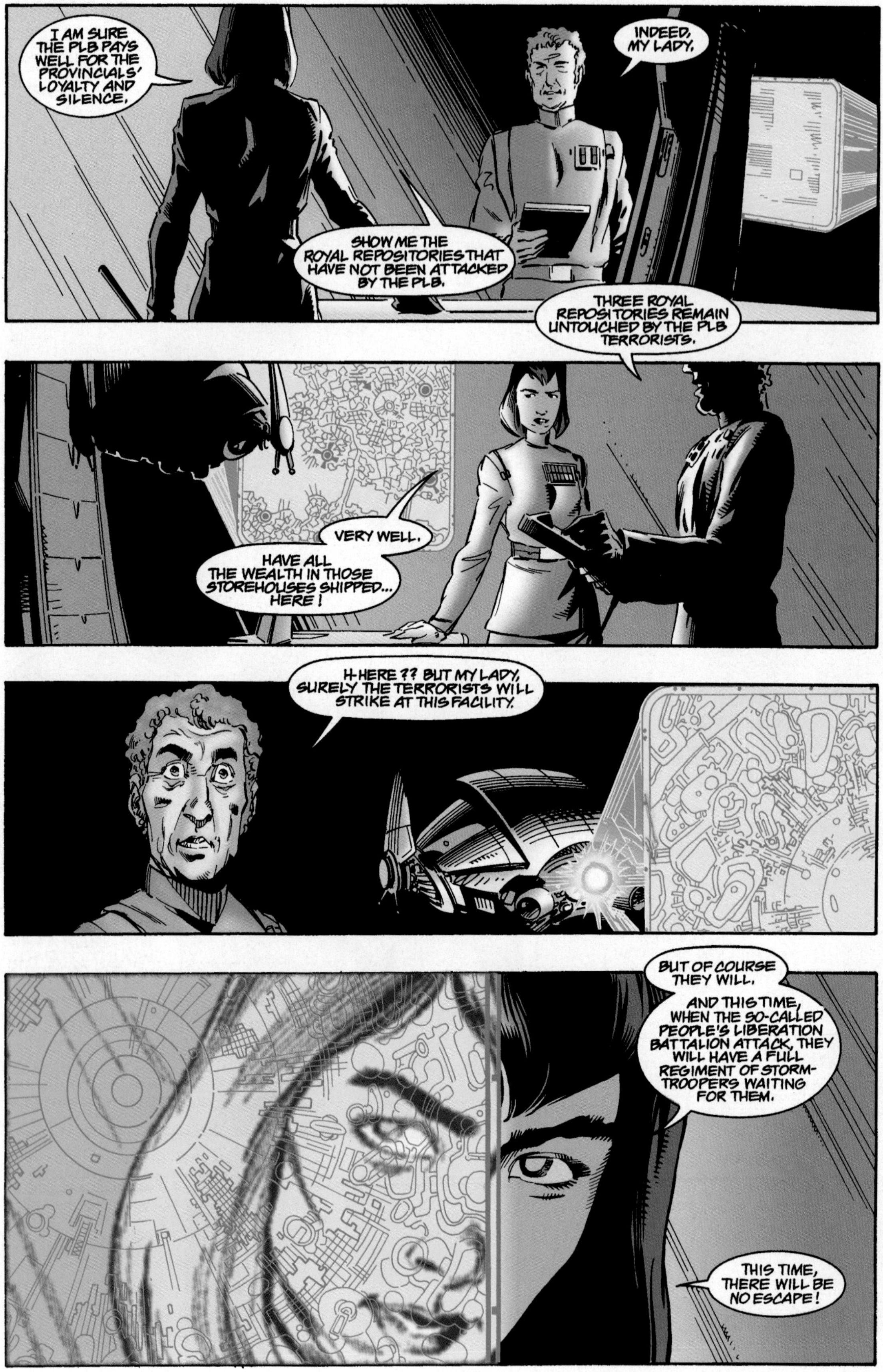
I AM SURE THE PLB PAYS WELL FOR THE PROVINCIALS' LOYALTY AND SILENCE.
INDEED, MY LADY.
SHOW ME THE ROYAL REPOSITORIES THAT HAVE NOT BEEN ATTACKED BY THE PLB.
THREE ROYAL REPOSITORIES REMAIN UNTOUCHED BY THE PLB TERRORISTS.
VERY WELL.
HAVE ALL THE WEALTH IN THOSE STOREHOUSES SHIPPED... HERE!
H-HERE?? BUT MY LADY, SURELY THE TERRORISTS WILL STRIKE AT THIS FACILITY.
BUT OF COURSE THEY WILL.
AND THIS TIME, WHEN THE SO-CALLED PEOPLE'S LIBERATION BATTALION ATTACK, THEY WILL HAVE A FULL REGIMENT OF STORM-TROOPERS WAITING FOR THEM.
THIS TIME, THERE WILL BE NO ESCAPE!

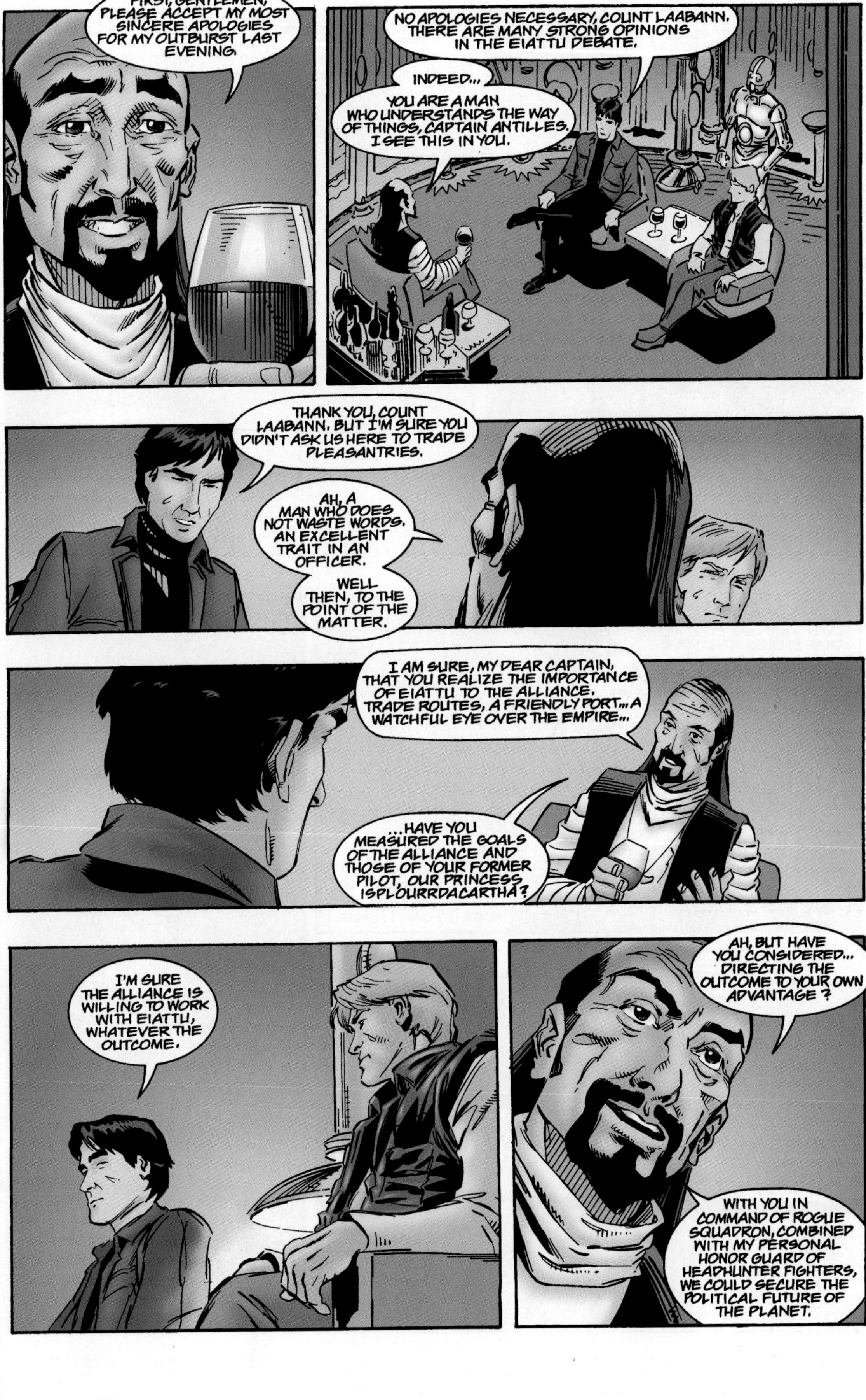
FIRST, GENTLEMEN, PLEASE ACCEPT MY MOST SINCERE APOLOGIES FOR MY OUTBURST LAST EVENING.
NO APOLOGIES NECESSARY, COUNT LAABANN. THERE ARE MANY STRONG OPINIONS IN THE EIATTU DEBATE.
INDEED...
YOU ARE A MAN WHO UNDERSTANDS THE WAY OF THINGS, CAPTAIN ANTILLES. I SEE THIS IN YOU.
THANK YOU, COUNT LAABANN. BUT I'M SURE YOU DIDN'T ASK US HERE TO TRADE PLEASANTRIES.
AH, A MAN WHO DOES NOT WASTE WORDS. AN EXCELLENT TRAIT IN AN OFFICER.
WELL THEN, TO THE POINT OF THE MATTER.
I AM SURE, MY DEAR CAPTAIN, THAT YOU REALIZE THE IMPORTANCE OF EIATTU TO THE ALLIANCE. TRADE ROUTES, A FRIENDLY PORT... A WATCHFUL EYE OVER THE EMPIRE...
...HAVE YOU MEASURED THE GOALS OF THE ALLIANCE AND THOSE OF YOUR FORMER PILOT, OUR PRINCESS ISPLOURRDACARTHA?
I'M SURE THE ALLIANCE IS WILLING TO WORK WITH EIATTU, WHATEVER THE OUTCOME.
AH, BUT HAVE YOU CONSIDERED... DIRECTING THE OUTCOME TO YOUR OWN ADVANTAGE?
WITH YOU IN COMMAND OF ROGUE SQUADRON, COMBINED WITH MY PERSONAL HONOR GUARD OF HEADHUNTER FIGHTERS, WE COULD SECURE THE POLITICAL FUTURE OF THE PLANET.

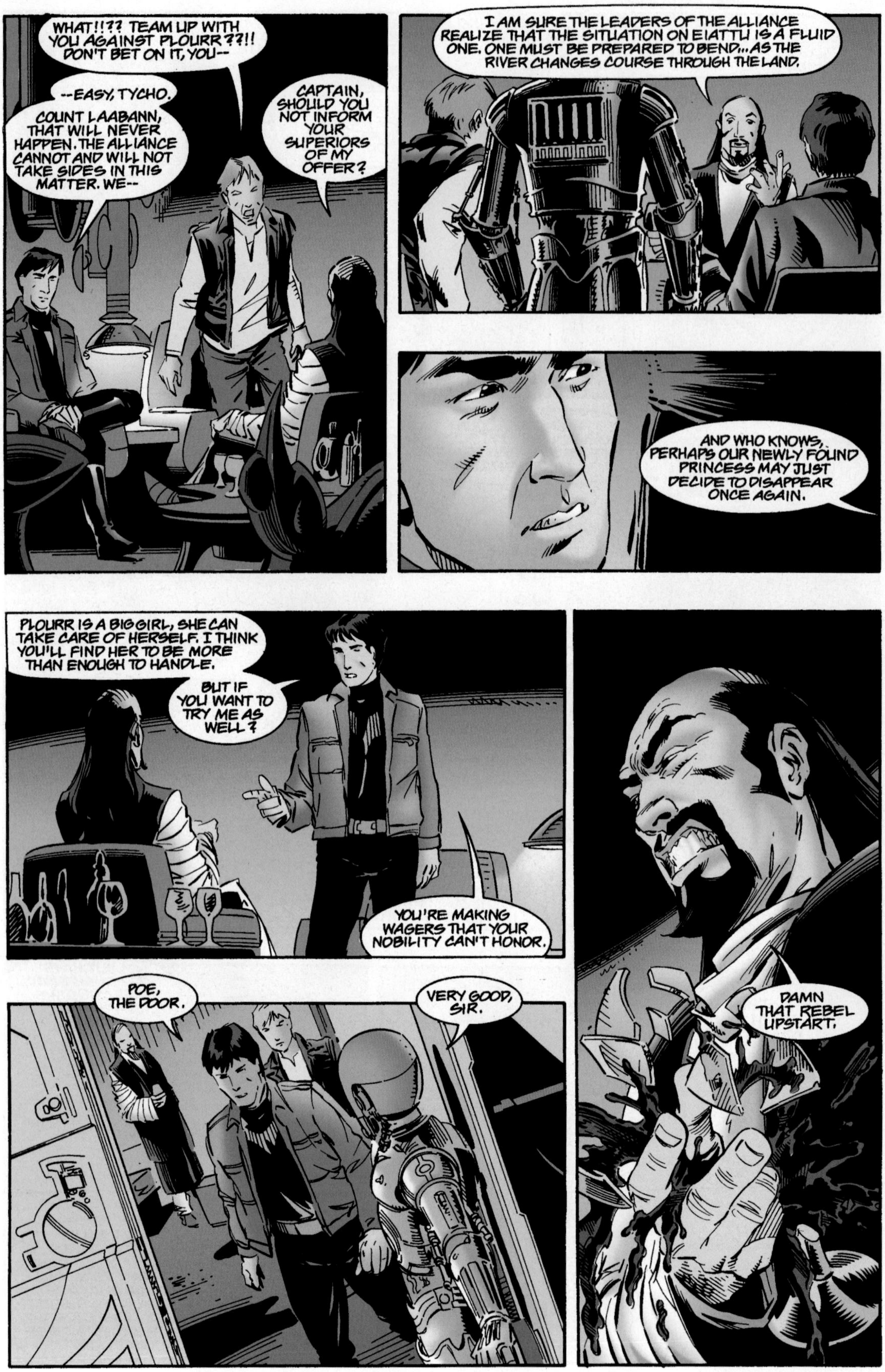
WHAT!!?? TEAM UP WITH YOU AGAINST PLOURR??!! DON'T BET ON IT, YOU--
--EASY, TYCHO.
COUNT LAABANN, THAT WILL NEVER HAPPEN. THE ALLIANCE CANNOT AND WILL NOT TAKE SIDES IN THIS MATTER. WE--
CAPTAIN, SHOULD YOU NOT INFORM YOUR SUPERIORS OF MY OFFER?
I AM SURE THE LEADERS OF THE ALLIANCE REALIZE THAT THE SITUATION ON EIATTU IS A FLUID ONE. ONE MUST BE PREPARED TO BEND... AS THE RIVER CHANGES COURSE THROUGH THE LAND.
AND WHO KNOWS, PERHAPS OUR NEWLY FOUND PRINCESS MAY JUST DECIDE TO DISAPPEAR ONCE AGAIN.
PLOURR IS A BIG GIRL, SHE CAN TAKE CARE OF HERSELF. I THINK YOU'LL FIND HER TO BE MORE THAN ENOUGH TO HANDLE.
BUT IF YOU WANT TO TRY ME AS WELL?
YOU'RE MAKING WAGERS THAT YOUR NOBILITY CAN'T HONOR.
POE, THE DOOR.
VERY GOOD, SIR.
DAMN THAT REBEL UPSTART.

THE PLB OR THE PRIAMSTA, THESE ARE THE ALLIES I HAVE TO CHOOSE FROM? AT LEAST I KNOW WHERE THE EMPIRE STANDS!

I KNOW YOU WILL MAKE THE RIGHT CHOICE.

OH? AND JUST HOW DO YOU KNOW?

BECAUSE I KNOW YOU...JUST AS EVERY HUSBAND SHOULD KNOW HIS WIFE.

I'M NOT YOUR WIFE!!!

YAAAAA!!!

I'M SORRY. BUT HOW CAN YOU CONTINUE TO HOLD ON TO THESE RIDICULOUS, ARCHAIC TRADITIONS?

WHAT IF I HAD BEEN DEAD ALL THESE YEARS, KILLED WITH MY FAMILY? WHO WOULD YOU LOVE THEN?

NO ONE. I WOULD HAVE DIED WITH YOU.

YES, I AM BOUND BY THESE "RIDICULOUS, ARCHAIC TRADITIONS." BECAUSE THEY ARE MY DESTINY. AS THEY ARE YOURS.

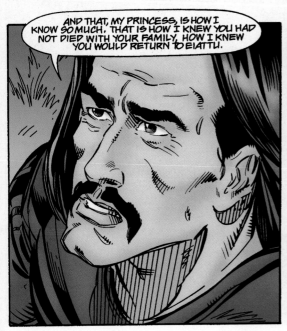

AND THAT, MY PRINCESS, IS HOW I KNOW SO MUCH, THAT IS HOW I KNEW YOU HAD NOT DIED WITH YOUR FAMILY, HOW I KNEW YOU WOULD RETURN TO EIATTU.

BECAUSE IT IS YOUR DESTINY TO RECLAIM THE THRONE...AND IT IS MY DESTINY TO BE AT YOUR SIDE WHEN YOU DO SO.

I DO LOVE YOU... AND I WILL MARRY YOU. AND I CAN SEE IN YOUR EYES THAT TRUTH IS DAWNING ON YOU.

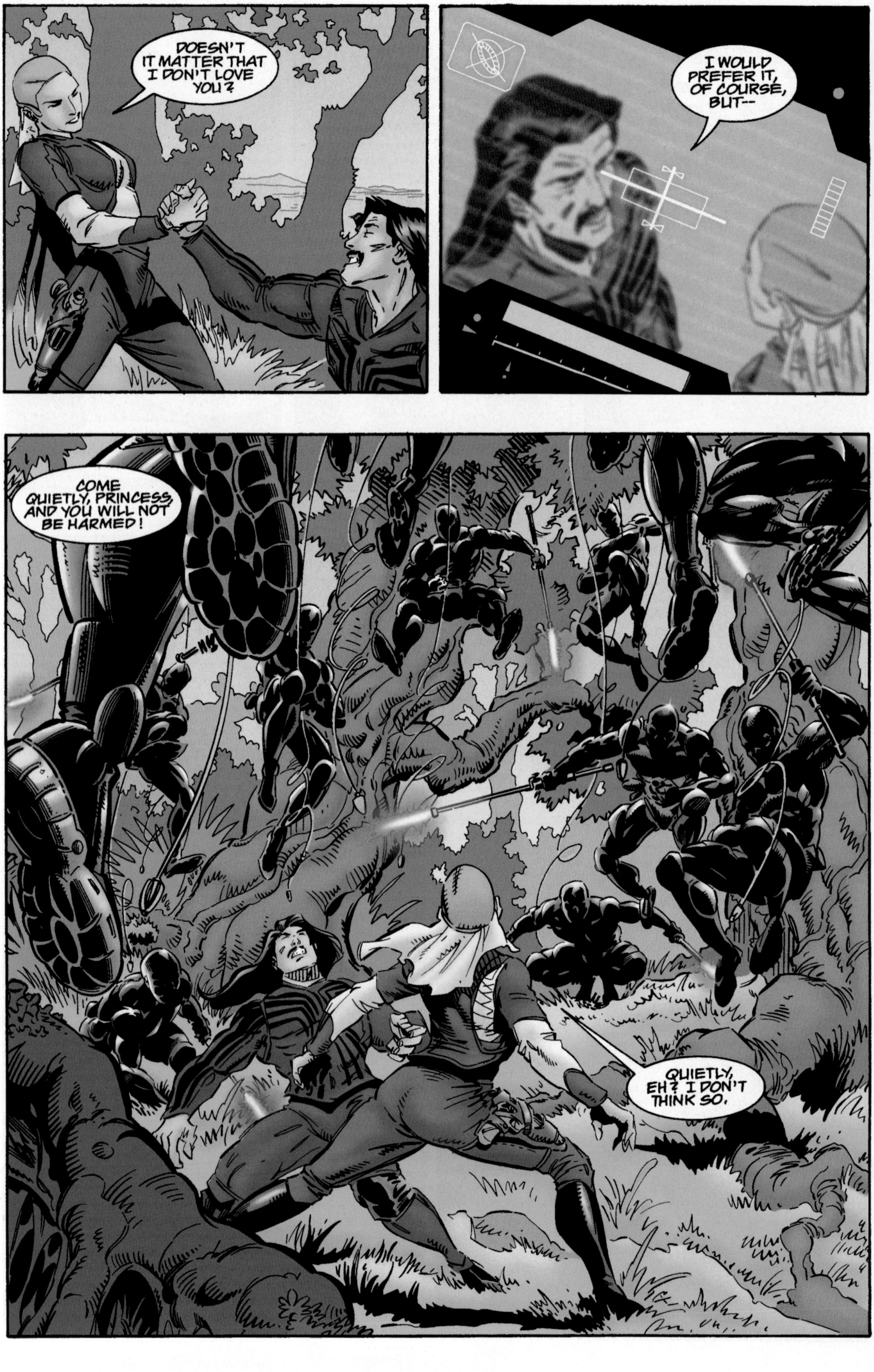
DOESN'T IT MATTER THAT I DON'T LOVE YOU?
I WOULD PREFER IT, OF COURSE, BUT--
COME QUIETLY, PRINCESS, AND YOU WILL NOT BE HARMED!
QUIETLY, EH? I DON'T THINK SO.

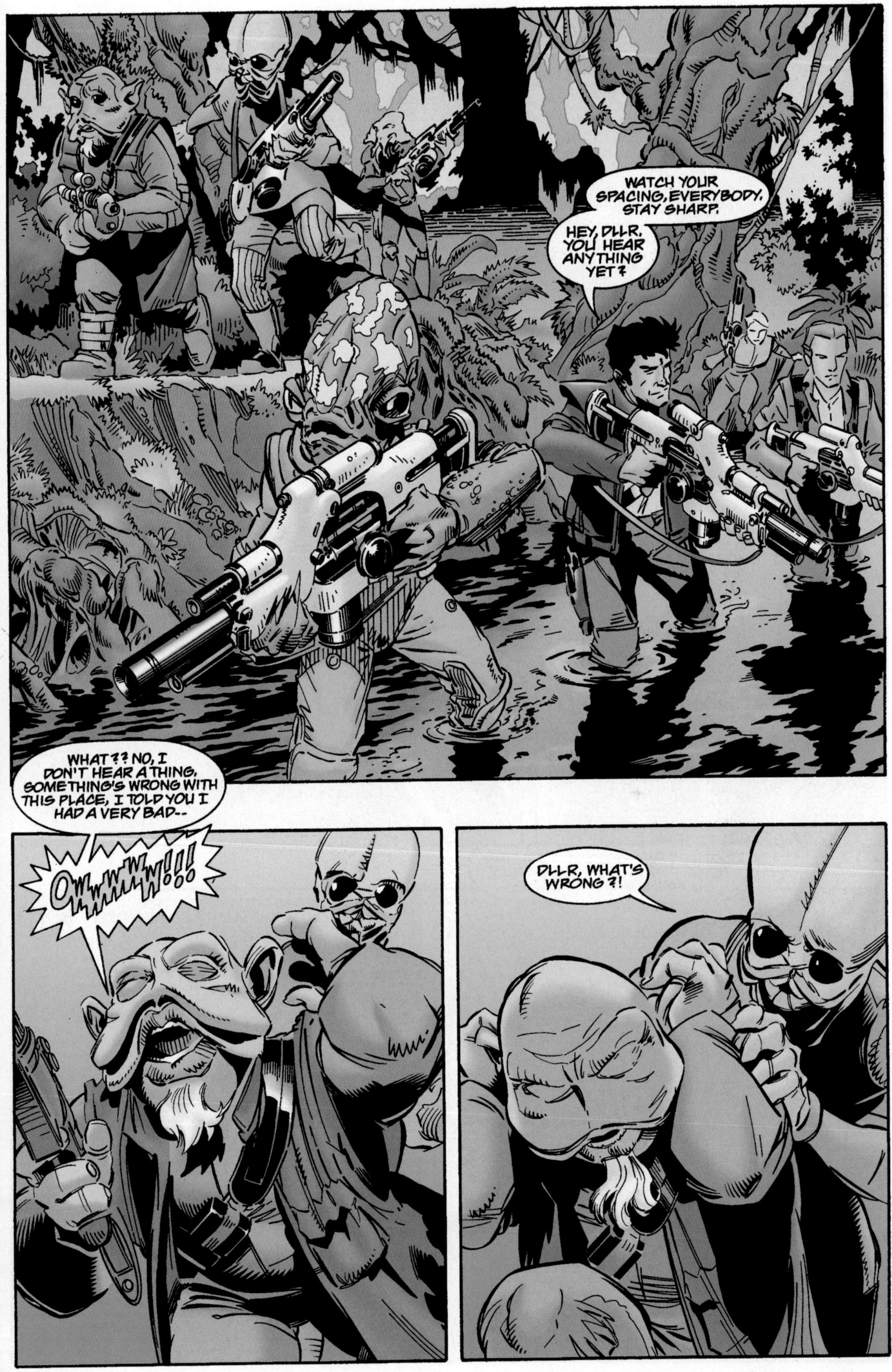
WATCH YOUR SPACING, EVERYBODY. STAY SHARP.
HEY, DLLR, YOU HEAR ANYTHING YET?
WHAT?? NO, I DON'T HEAR A THING. SOMETHING'S WRONG WITH THIS PLACE, I TOLD YOU I HAD A VERY BAD--
OWWWWW!!!
DLLR, WHAT'S WRONG?!

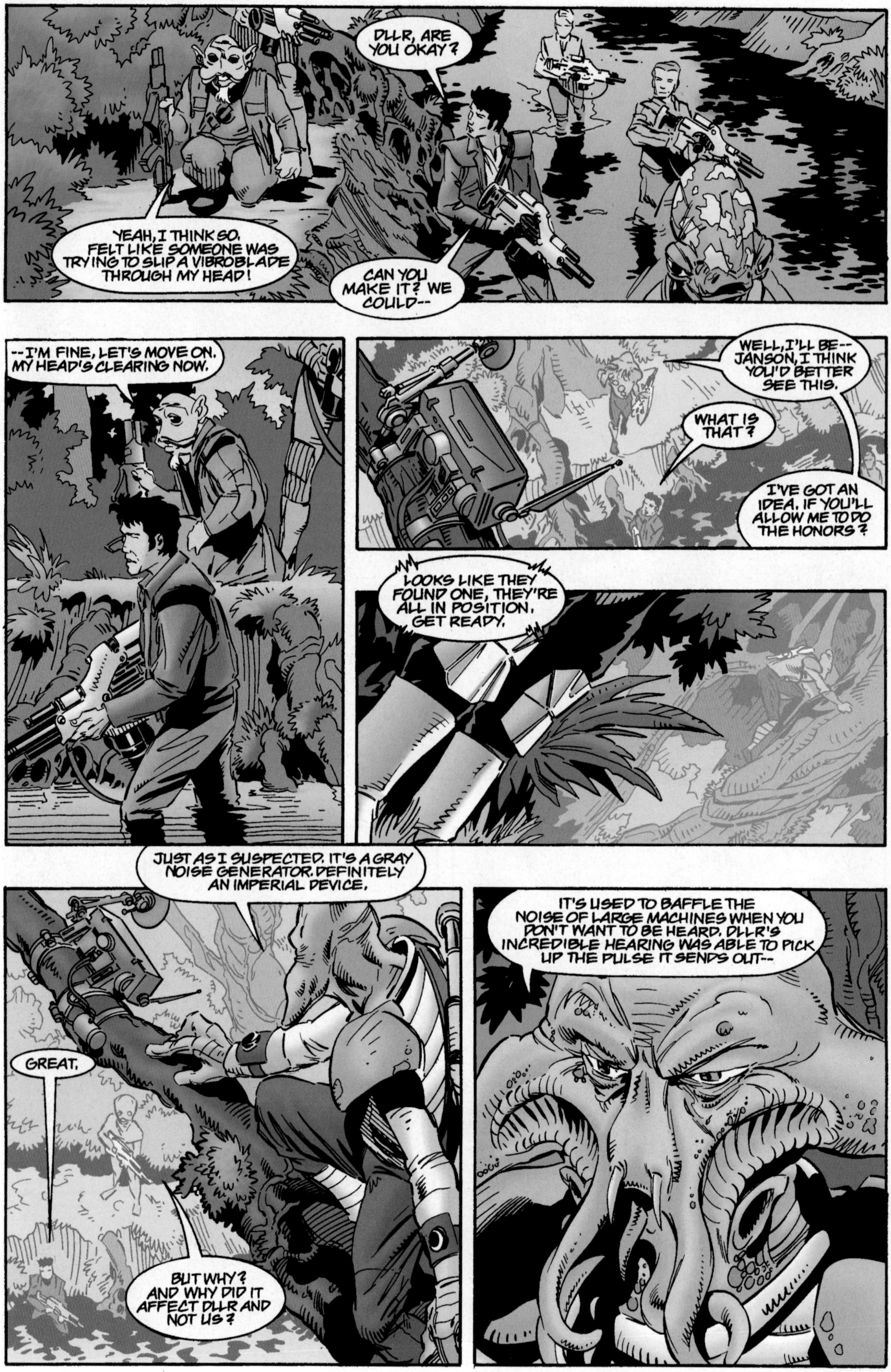
DLLR, ARE YOU OKAY?
YEAH, I THINK SO. FELT LIKE SOMEONE WAS TRYING TO SLIP A VIBROBLADE THROUGH MY HEAD!
CAN YOU MAKE IT? WE COULD--
--I'M FINE, LET'S MOVE ON. MY HEAD'S CLEARING NOW.
WELL, I'LL BE-- JANSON, I THINK YOU'D BETTER SEE THIS.
WHAT IS THAT?
I'VE GOT AN IDEA. IF YOU'LL ALLOW ME TO DO THE HONORS?
LOOKS LIKE THEY FOUND ONE, THEY'RE ALL IN POSITION. GET READY.
JUST AS I SUSPECTED. IT'S A GRAY NOISE GENERATOR. DEFINITELY AN IMPERIAL DEVICE.
GREAT.
BUT WHY? AND WHY DID IT AFFECT DLLR AND NOT US?
IT'S USED TO BAFFLE THE NOISE OF LARGE MACHINES WHEN YOU DON'T WANT TO BE HEARD. DLLR'S INCREDIBLE HEARING WAS ABLE TO PICK UP THE PULSE IT SENDS OUT--

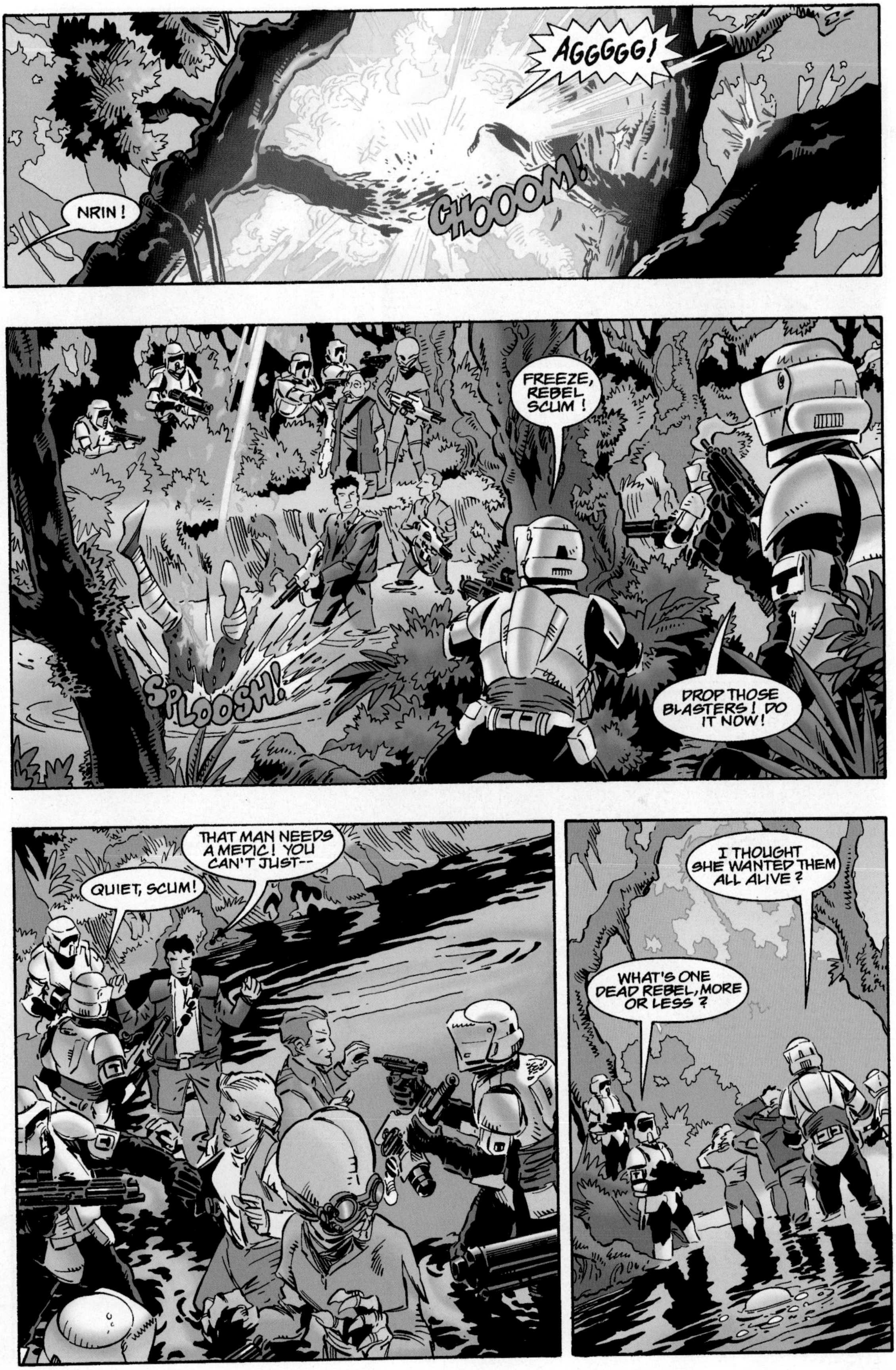
AGGGGG!
NRIN!
CHOOOM!
FREEZE, REBEL SCUM!
SPLOOSH!
DROP THOSE BLASTERS! DO IT NOW!
THAT MAN NEEDS A MEDIC! YOU CAN'T JUST--
QUIET, SCUM!
I THOUGHT SHE WANTED THEM ALL ALIVE?
WHAT'S ONE DEAD REBEL, MORE OR LESS?

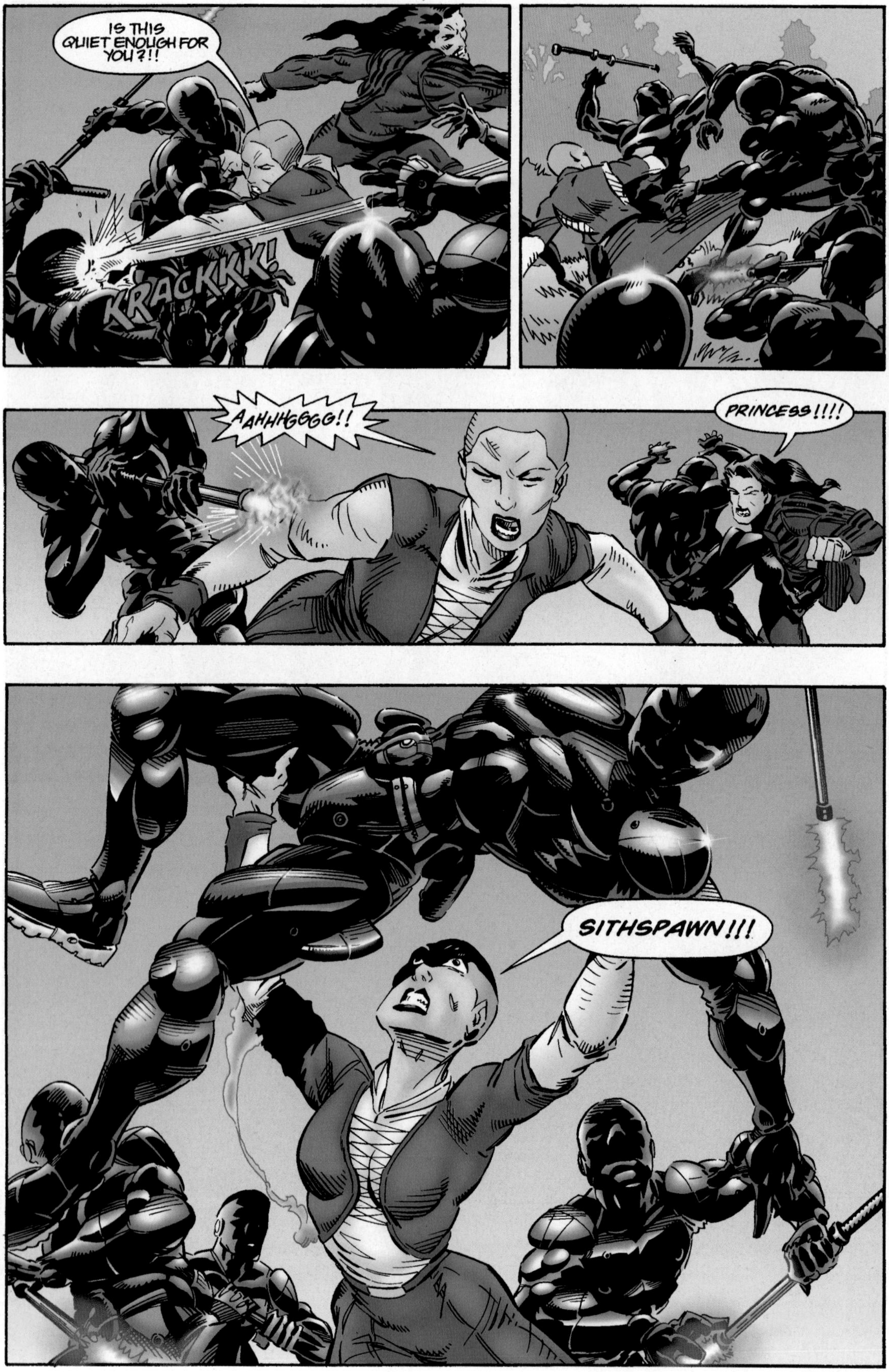
IS THIS QUIET ENOUGH FOR YOU?!!
KRACKKK!
AAHHHGGGG!!
PRINCESS!!!!
SITHSPAWN!!!

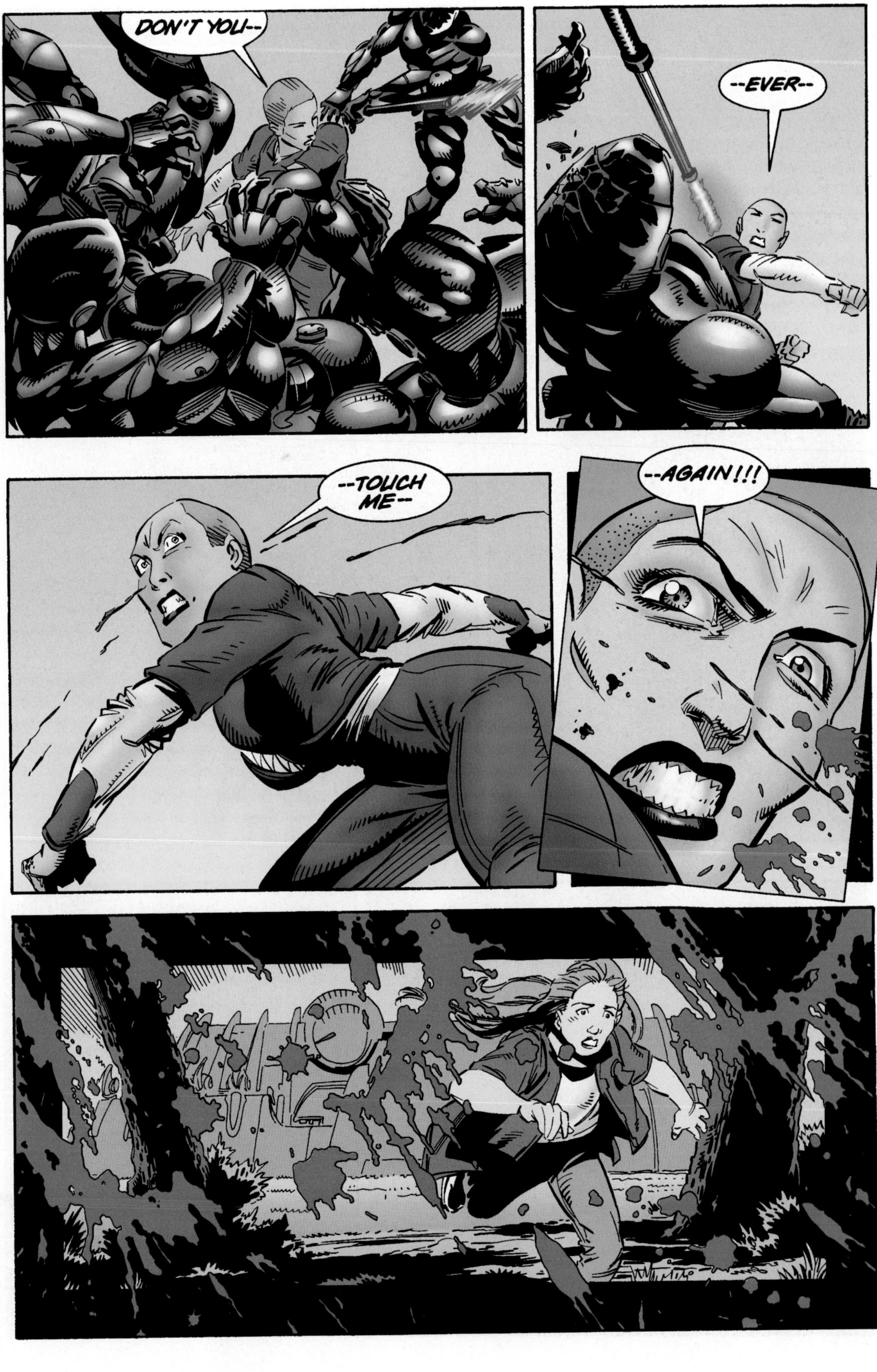
DON'T YOU--
--EVER--
--TOUCH ME--
--AGAIN!!!

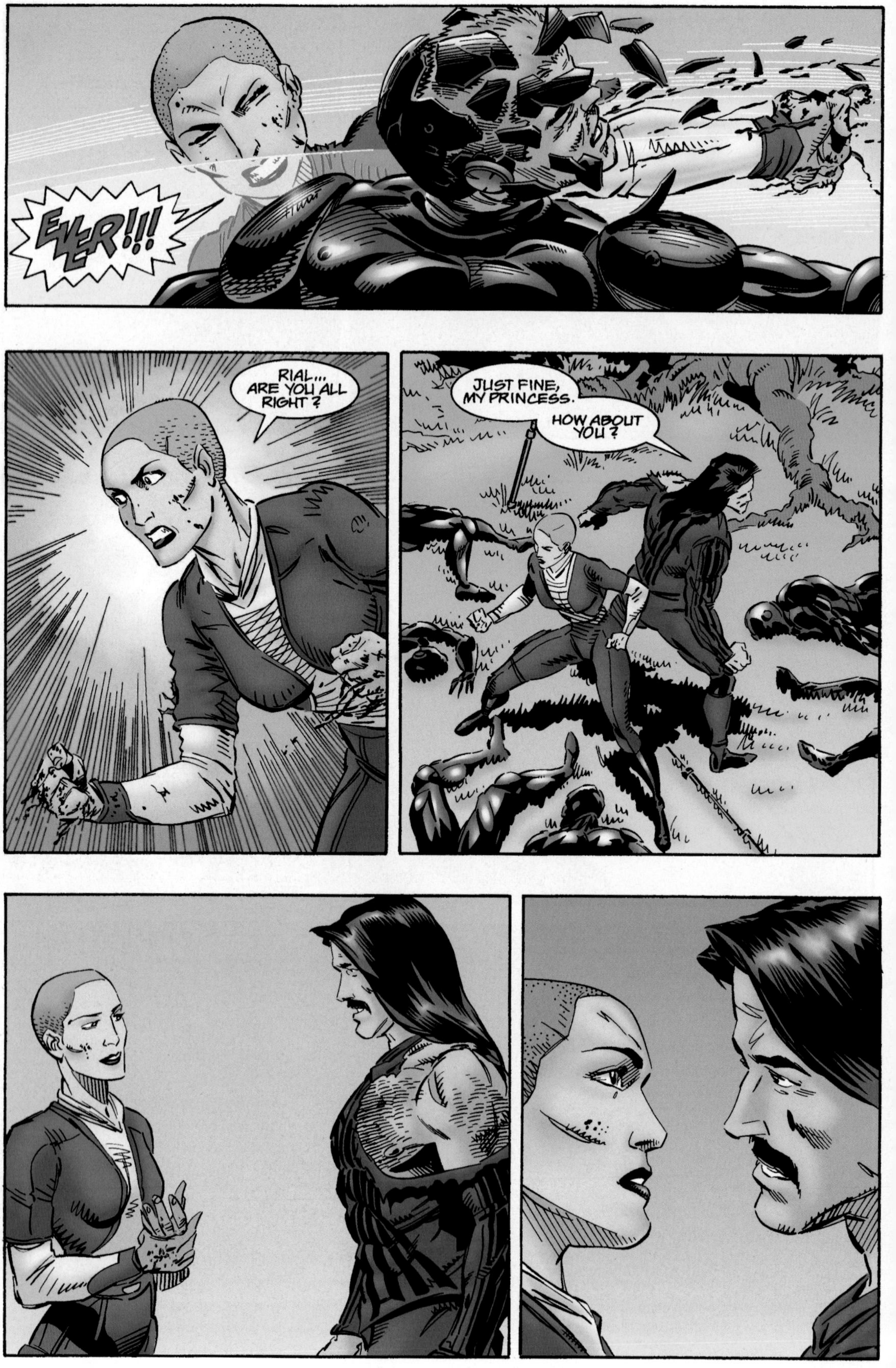
EVER!!!
RIAL... ARE YOU ALL RIGHT?
JUST FINE, MY PRINCESS.
HOW ABOUT YOU?

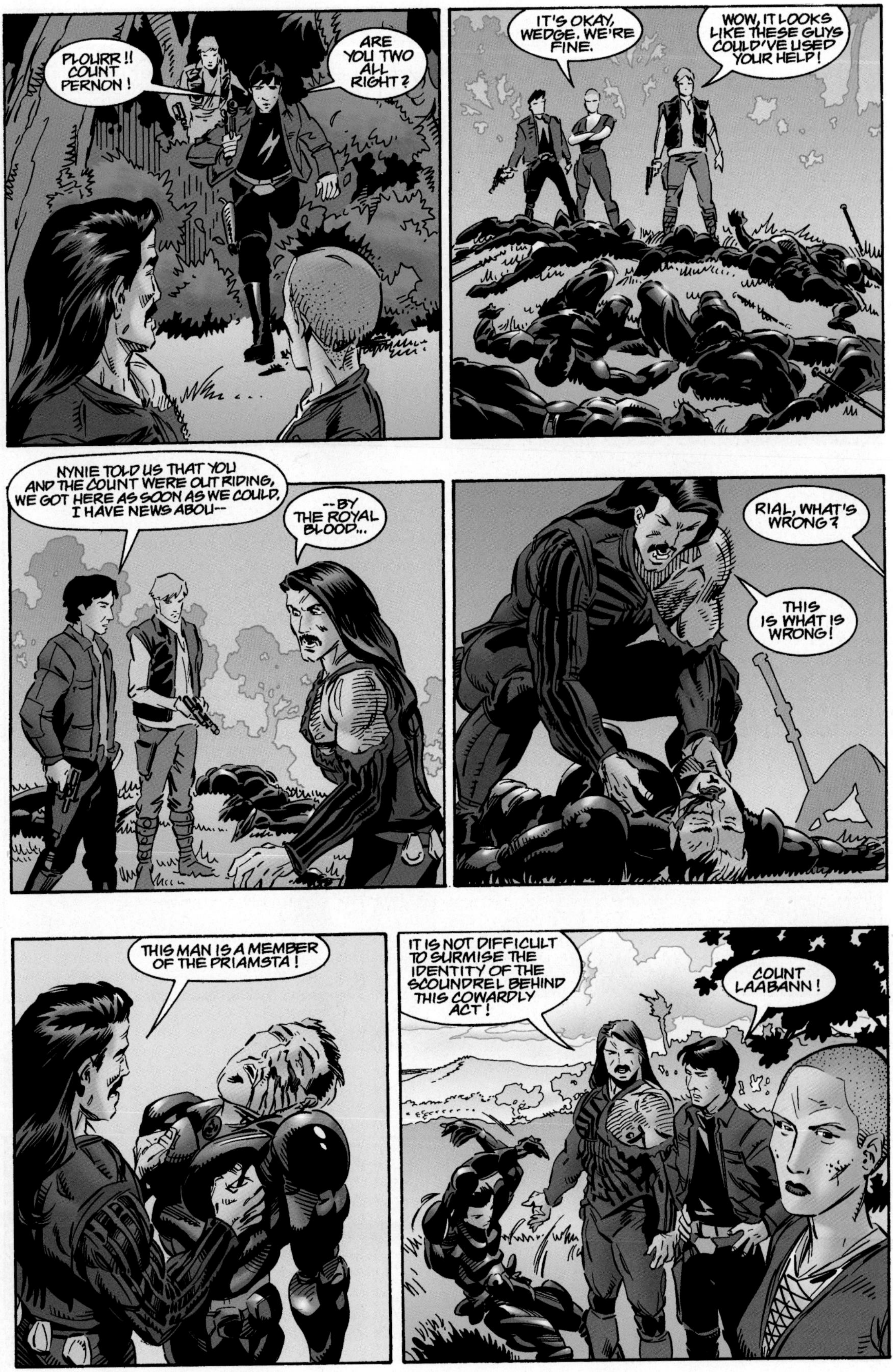
PLOURR!! COUNT PERNON!
ARE YOU TWO ALL RIGHT?
IT'S OKAY, WEDGE. WE'RE FINE.
WOW, IT LOOKS LIKE THESE GUYS COULD'VE USED YOUR HELP!
NYNIE TOLD US THAT YOU AND THE COUNT WERE OUT RIDING, WE GOT HERE AS SOON AS WE COULD, I HAVE NEWS ABOU--
--BY THE ROYAL BLOOD...
RIAL, WHAT'S WRONG?
THIS IS WHAT IS WRONG!
THIS MAN IS A MEMBER OF THE PRIAMSTA!
IT IS NOT DIFFICULT TO SURMISE THE IDENTITY OF THE SCOUNDREL BEHIND THIS COWARDLY ACT!
COUNT LAABANN!

HOW CAN YOU BE SO SURE, WEDGE?

BECAUSE TYCHO AND I MET WITH HIM THIS MORNING, WHERE HE PROPOSED THAT ROGUE SQUADRON JOIN HIM IN THE FIGHT AGAINST YOU.

SUCH TREACHERY! I WILL SURELY SEND HIM THE WAY OF HIS GRANDFATHERS FOR THIS!

THIS WAS AN ATTEMPT TO KIDNAP YOU, PLOURR. LAABANN KNEW HE COULDN'T KILL YOU WITHOUT HAVING THE ALLIANCE SIDE AGAINST HIM. BUT WITH YOU IN HIS HANDS HE COULD USE YOU AS A BARGAINING CHIP.

DO YOU SEE, PRINCESS?! YOUR CHOICE IS CLEAR! YOU MUST SIDE WITH PLB AND YOUR BROTHER, HARRAN!

YOU'RE RIGHT, RIAL. I KNOW NOW THAT I CAN'T TRUST THE PRIMS, AND COUNT LAABANN MUST BE DEALT WITH.

IT WOULD SEEM THAT MY ONLY CHOICE IS TO ALLY MYSELF WITH MY BROTHER. BUT--

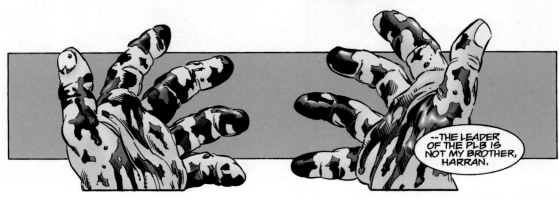

--THE LEADER OF THE PLB IS NOT MY BROTHER, HARRAN.

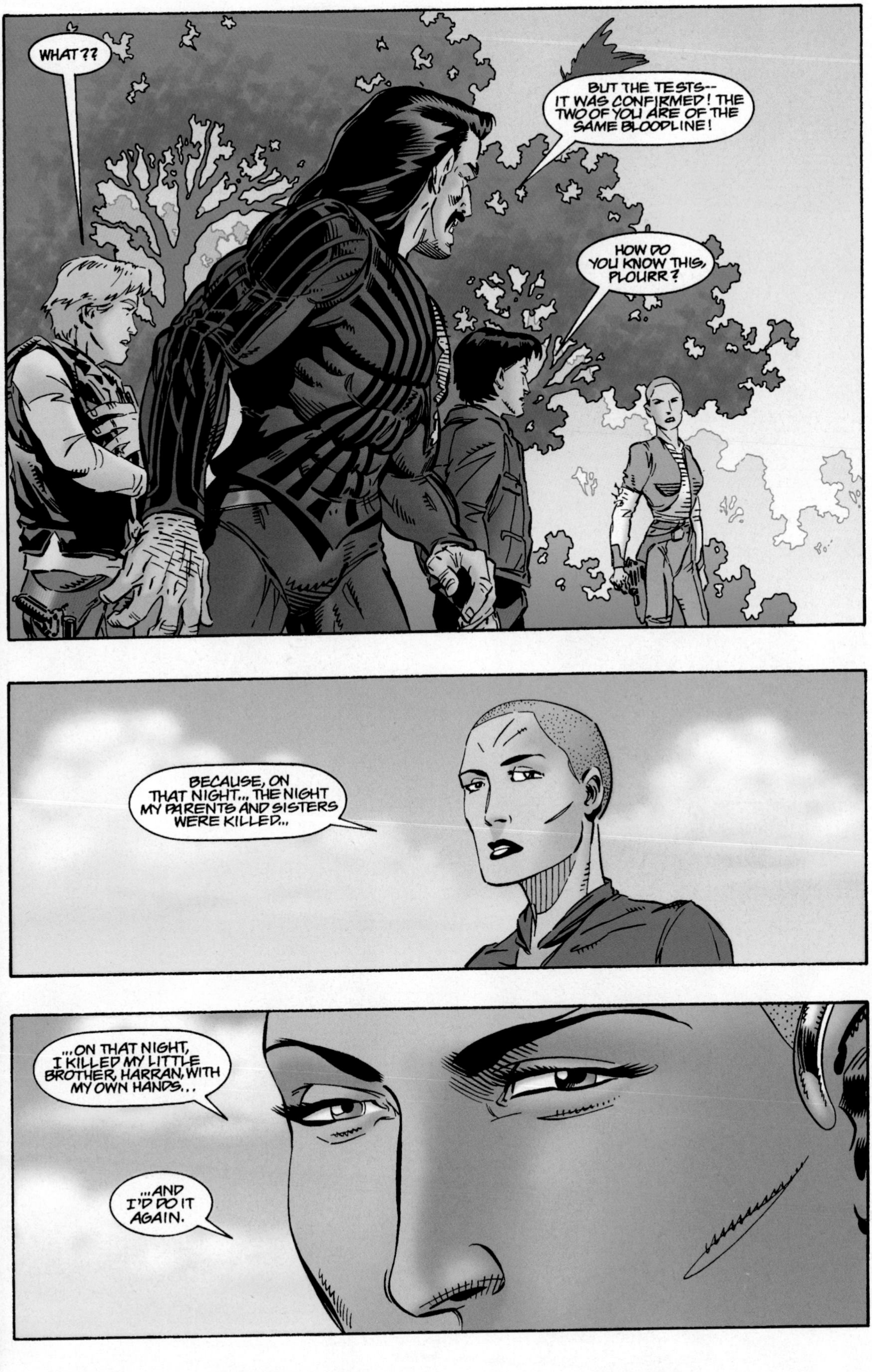
WHAT??
BUT THE TESTS-- IT WAS CONFIRMED! THE TWO OF YOU ARE OF THE SAME BLOODLINE!
HOW DO YOU KNOW THIS, PLOURR?
BECAUSE, ON THAT NIGHT... THE NIGHT MY PARENTS AND SISTERS WERE KILLED...
...ON THAT NIGHT, I KILLED MY LITTLE BROTHER, HARRAN, WITH MY OWN HANDS...
...AND I'D DO IT AGAIN.

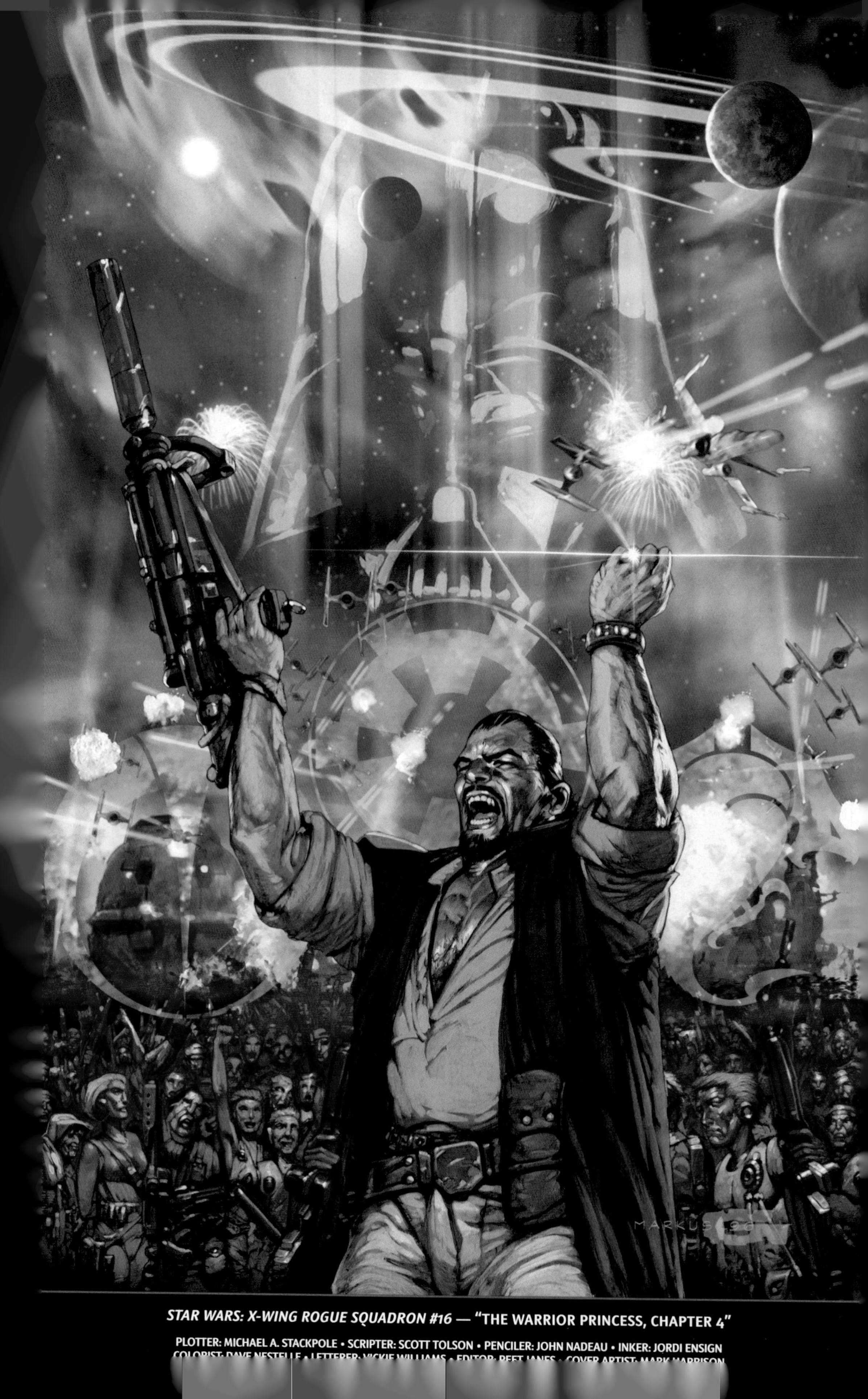
MARKUS

***STAR WARS: X-WING ROGUE SQUADRON #16*** **— "THE WARRIOR PRINCESS, CHAPTER 4"**

PLOTTER: MICHAEL A. STACKPOLE • SCRIPTER: SCOTT TOLSON • PENCILER: JOHN NADEAU • INKER: JORDI ENSIGN
COLORIST: DAVE NESTELLE • LETTERER: VICKIE WILLIAMS • EDITOR: PEET JANES • COVER ARTIST: MARK HARRISON

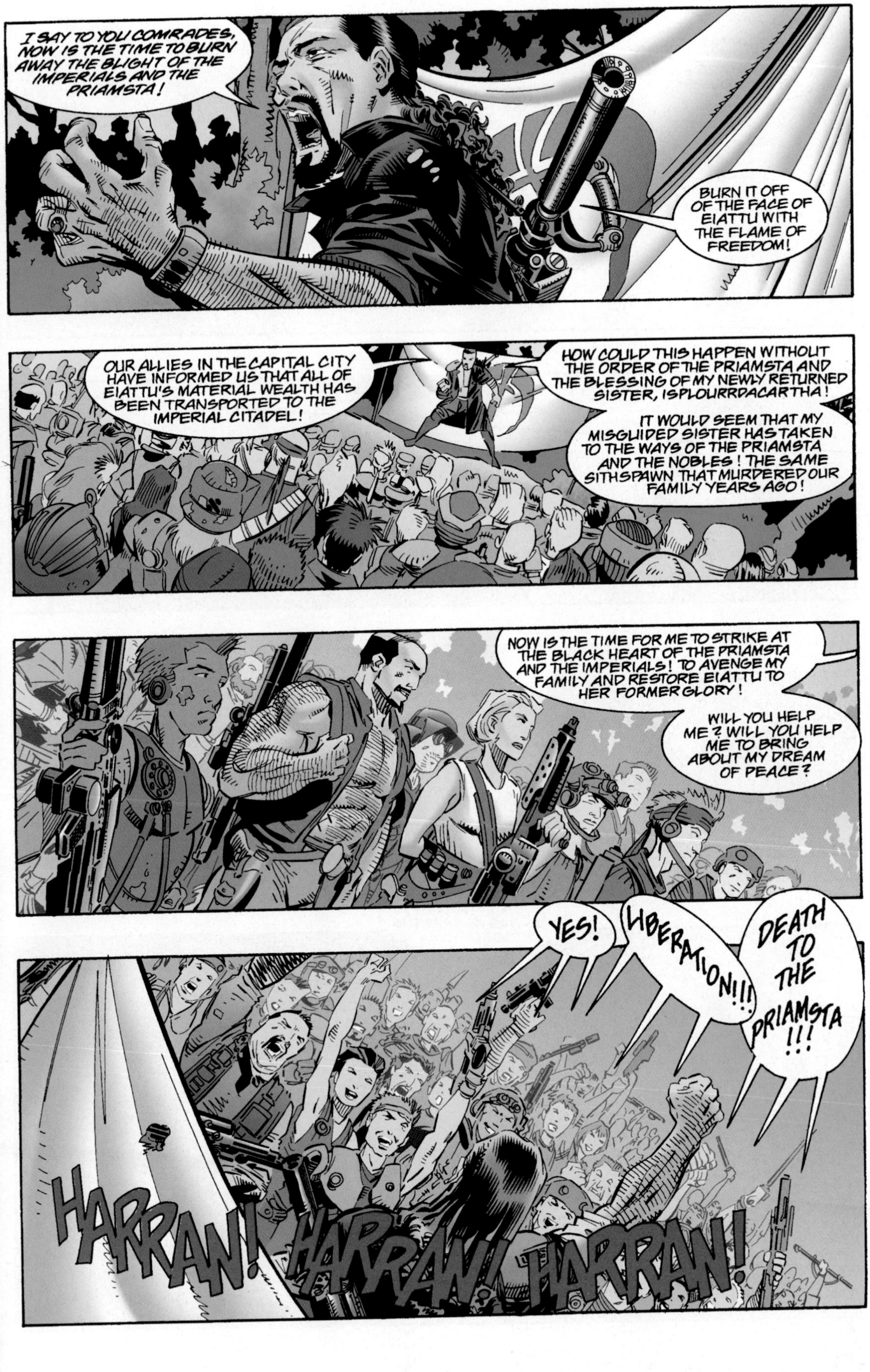
I SAY TO YOU COMRADES, NOW IS THE TIME TO BURN AWAY THE BLIGHT OF THE IMPERIALS AND THE PRIAMSTA!
BURN IT OFF OF THE FACE OF EIATTU WITH THE FLAME OF FREEDOM!
OUR ALLIES IN THE CAPITAL CITY HAVE INFORMED US THAT ALL OF EIATTU'S MATERIAL WEALTH HAS BEEN TRANSPORTED TO THE IMPERIAL CITADEL!
HOW COULD THIS HAPPEN WITHOUT THE ORDER OF THE PRIAMSTA AND THE BLESSING OF MY NEWLY RETURNED SISTER, ISPLOURRDACARTHA!
IT WOULD SEEM THAT MY MISGUIDED SISTER HAS TAKEN TO THE WAYS OF THE PRIAMSTA AND THE NOBLES! THE SAME SITHSPAWN THAT MURDERED OUR FAMILY YEARS AGO!
NOW IS THE TIME FOR ME TO STRIKE AT THE BLACK HEART OF THE PRIAMSTA AND THE IMPERIALS! TO AVENGE MY FAMILY AND RESTORE EIATTU TO HER FORMER GLORY!
WILL YOU HELP ME? WILL YOU HELP ME TO BRING ABOUT MY DREAM OF PEACE?
YES!
LIBERATION!!!
DEATH TO THE PRIAMSTA!!!
HARRAN! HARRAN! HARRAN!

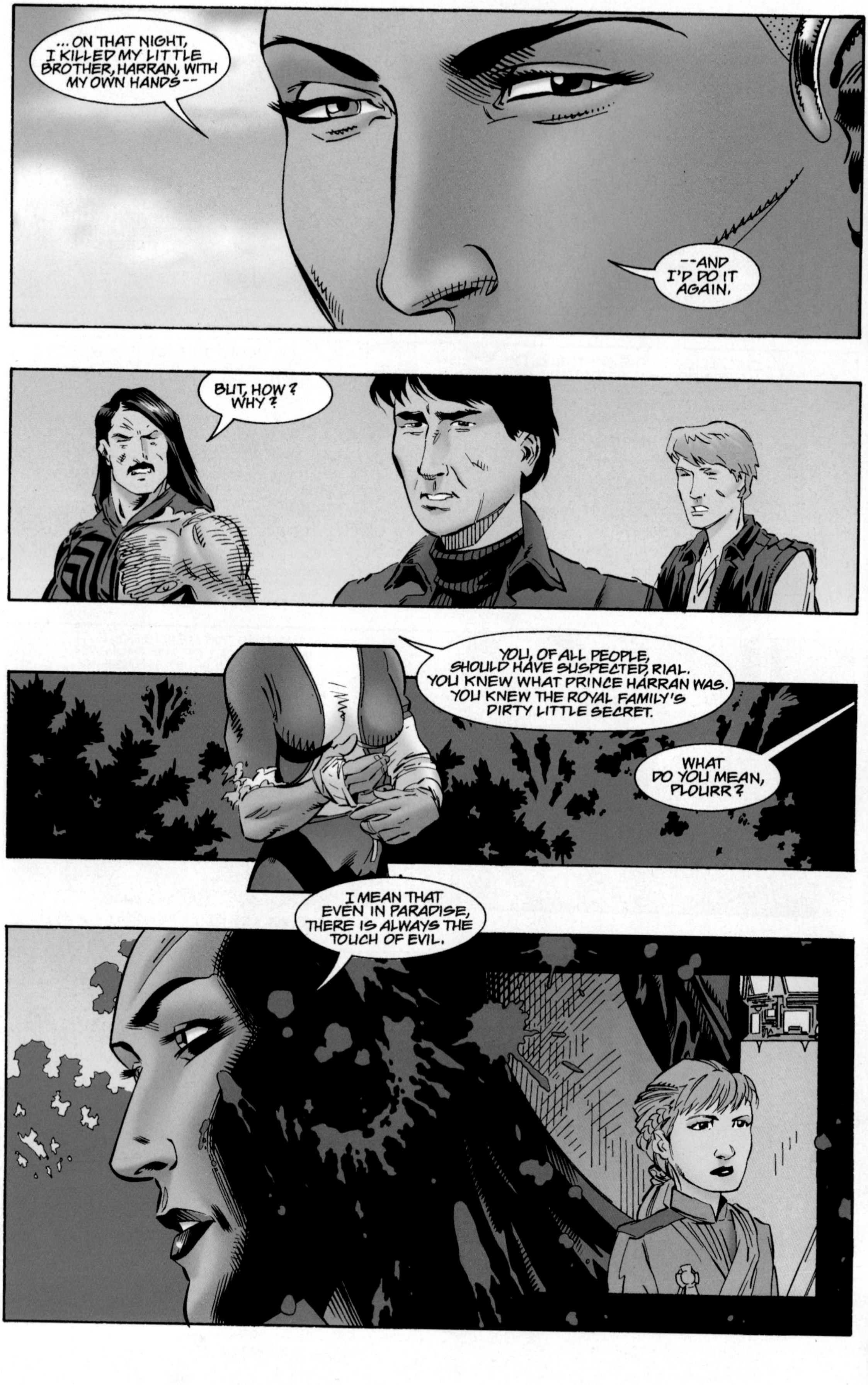
...ON THAT NIGHT, I KILLED MY LITTLE BROTHER, HARRAN, WITH MY OWN HANDS--
--AND I'D DO IT AGAIN.
BUT, HOW? WHY?
YOU, OF ALL PEOPLE, SHOULD HAVE SUSPECTED, RIAL. YOU KNEW WHAT PRINCE HARRAN WAS. YOU KNEW THE ROYAL FAMILY'S DIRTY LITTLE SECRET.
WHAT DO YOU MEAN, PLOURR?
I MEAN THAT EVEN IN PARADISE, THERE IS ALWAYS THE TOUCH OF EVIL.

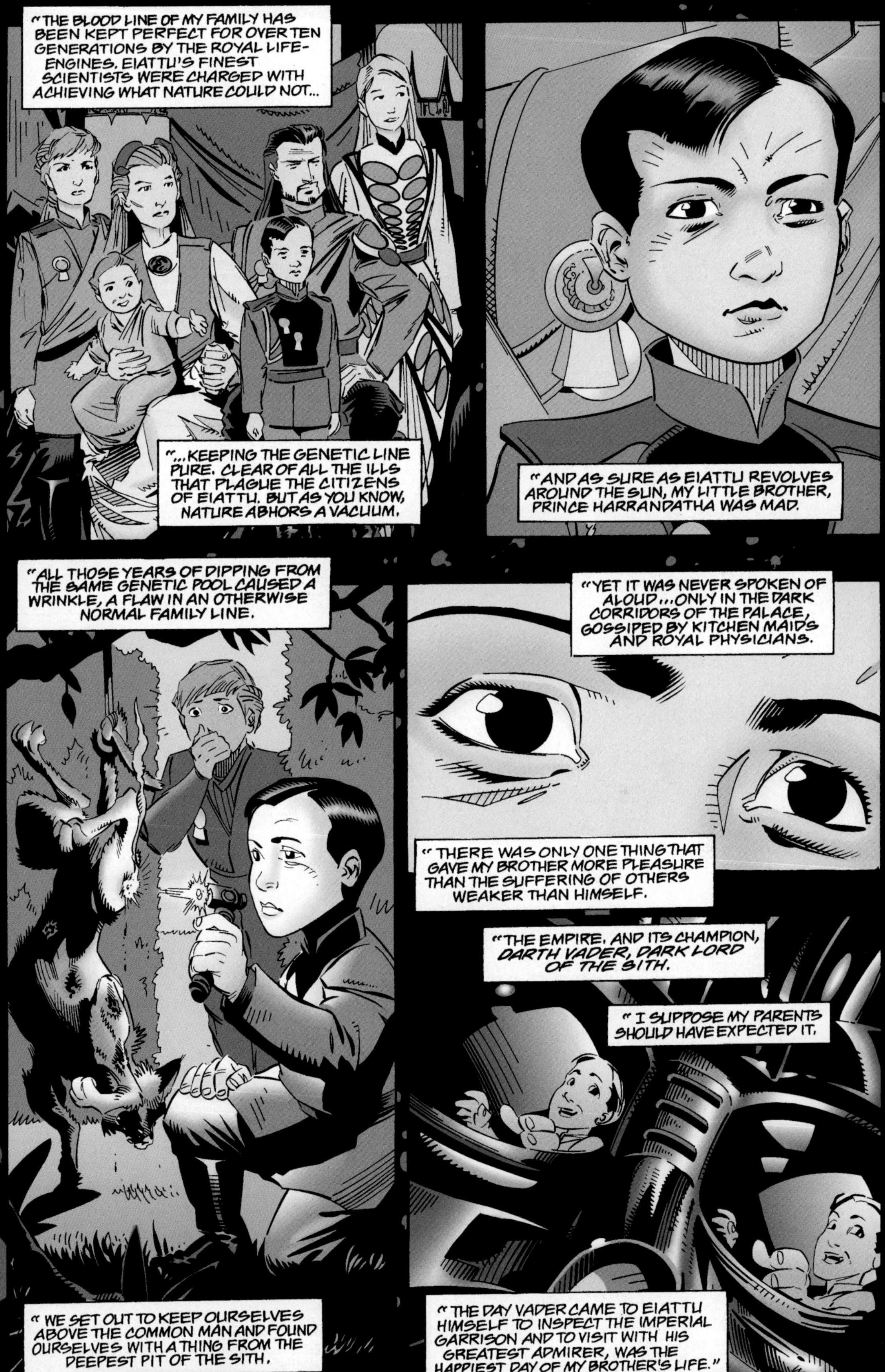
"THE BLOOD LINE OF MY FAMILY HAS BEEN KEPT PERFECT FOR OVER TEN GENERATIONS BY THE ROYAL LIFE-ENGINES. EIATTU'S FINEST SCIENTISTS WERE CHARGED WITH ACHIEVING WHAT NATURE COULD NOT...
"...KEEPING THE GENETIC LINE PURE. CLEAR OF ALL THE ILLS THAT PLAGUE THE CITIZENS OF EIATTU. BUT AS YOU KNOW, NATURE ABHORS A VACUUM.
"AND AS SURE AS EIATTU REVOLVES AROUND THE SUN, MY LITTLE BROTHER, PRINCE HARRANDATHA WAS MAD.
"ALL THOSE YEARS OF DIPPING FROM THE SAME GENETIC POOL CAUSED A WRINKLE, A FLAW IN AN OTHERWISE NORMAL FAMILY LINE.
"WE SET OUT TO KEEP OURSELVES ABOVE THE COMMON MAN AND FOUND OURSELVES WITH A THING FROM THE DEEPEST PIT OF THE SITH.
"YET IT WAS NEVER SPOKEN OF ALOUD...ONLY IN THE DARK CORRIDORS OF THE PALACE, GOSSIPED BY KITCHEN MAIDS AND ROYAL PHYSICIANS.
"THERE WAS ONLY ONE THING THAT GAVE MY BROTHER MORE PLEASURE THAN THE SUFFERING OF OTHERS WEAKER THAN HIMSELF.
"THE EMPIRE. AND ITS CHAMPION, DARTH VADER, DARK LORD OF THE SITH.
"I SUPPOSE MY PARENTS SHOULD HAVE EXPECTED IT.
"THE DAY VADER CAME TO EIATTU HIMSELF TO INSPECT THE IMPERIAL GARRISON AND TO VISIT WITH HIS GREATEST ADMIRER, WAS THE HAPPIEST DAY OF MY BROTHER'S LIFE."

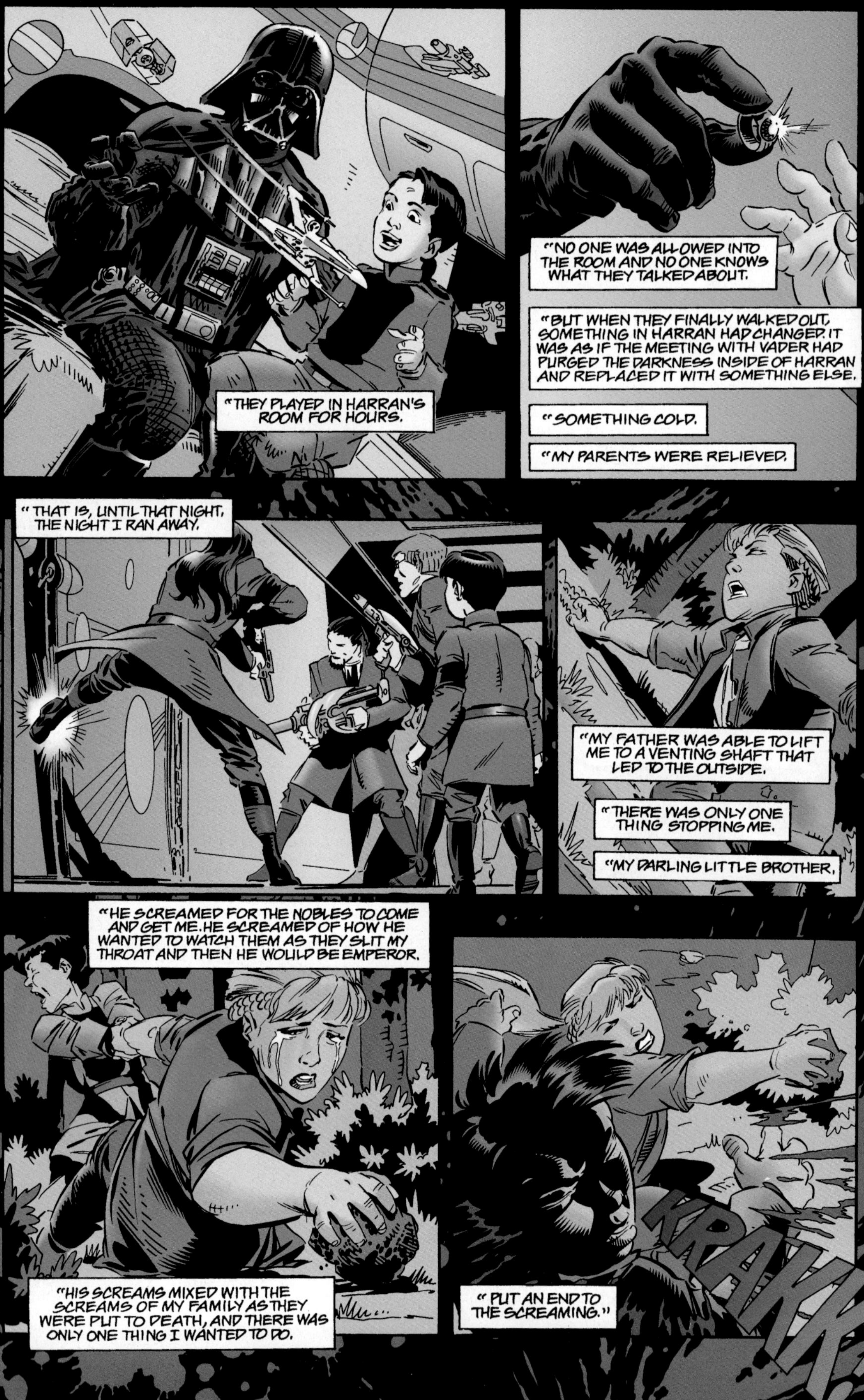
"THEY PLAYED IN HARRAN'S ROOM FOR HOURS.
"NO ONE WAS ALLOWED INTO THE ROOM AND NO ONE KNOWS WHAT THEY TALKED ABOUT.
"BUT WHEN THEY FINALLY WALKED OUT, SOMETHING IN HARRAN HAD CHANGED. IT WAS AS IF THE MEETING WITH VADER HAD PURGED THE DARKNESS INSIDE OF HARRAN AND REPLACED IT WITH SOMETHING ELSE.
"SOMETHING COLD.
"MY PARENTS WERE RELIEVED.
"THAT IS, UNTIL THAT NIGHT, THE NIGHT I RAN AWAY.
"MY FATHER WAS ABLE TO LIFT ME TO A VENTING SHAFT THAT LED TO THE OUTSIDE.
"THERE WAS ONLY ONE THING STOPPING ME.
"MY DARLING LITTLE BROTHER.
"HE SCREAMED FOR THE NOBLES TO COME AND GET ME. HE SCREAMED OF HOW HE WANTED TO WATCH THEM AS THEY SLIT MY THROAT AND THEN HE WOULD BE EMPEROR.
"HIS SCREAMS MIXED WITH THE SCREAMS OF MY FAMILY AS THEY WERE PUT TO DEATH, AND THERE WAS ONLY ONE THING I WANTED TO DO.
"PUT AN END TO THE SCREAMING."
KRAKK!

"I DRAGGED HIS BODY INTO THE BRUSH. IT DIDN'T TAKE LONG FOR A PACK OF THUVASAURS TO PICK UP THE SCENT."

PRINCESS...

PLOURR...IF THE LEADER OF THE PLB IS NOT YOUR BROTHER, THEN WHO IS HE?

YOU CAN BET HE'S AN IMPERIAL SPY.

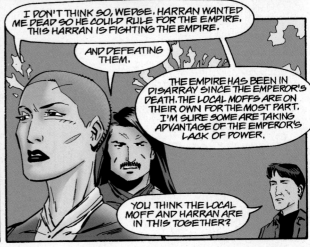

I DON'T THINK SO, WEDGE. HARRAN WANTED ME DEAD SO HE COULD RULE FOR THE EMPIRE. THIS HARRAN IS FIGHTING THE EMPIRE.

AND DEFEATING THEM.

THE EMPIRE HAS BEEN IN DISARRAY SINCE THE EMPEROR'S DEATH. THE LOCAL MOFFS ARE ON THEIR OWN FOR THE MOST PART. I'M SURE SOME ARE TAKING ADVANTAGE OF THE EMPEROR'S LACK OF POWER.

YOU THINK THE LOCAL MOFF AND HARRAN ARE IN THIS TOGETHER?

IF I KNOW MOFF TAVIRA, SHE IS BEHIND THIS ENTIRE CHARADE, I--

WHAT THE--!?

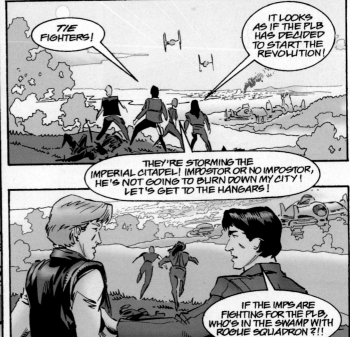

TIE FIGHTERS!

IT LOOKS AS IF THE PLB HAS DECIDED TO START THE REVOLUTION!

THEY'RE STORMING THE IMPERIAL CITADEL! IMPOSTOR OR NO IMPOSTOR, HE'S NOT GOING TO BURN DOWN MY CITY! LET'S GET TO THE HANGARS!

IF THE IMPS ARE FIGHTING FOR THE PLB, WHO'S IN THE SWAMP WITH ROGUE SQUADRON?!!

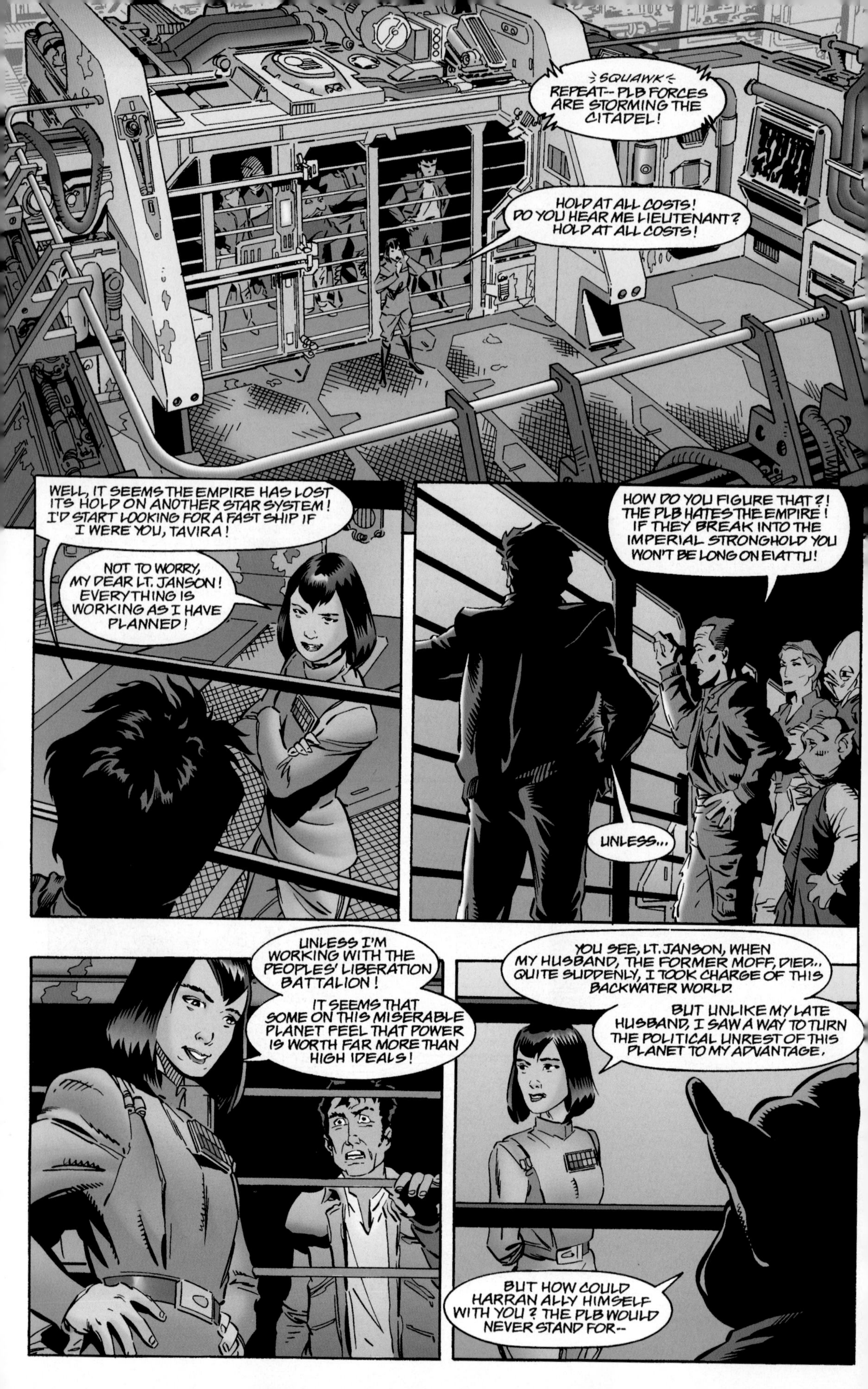
≈SQUAWK≈
REPEAT-- PLB FORCES ARE STORMING THE CITADEL!
HOLD AT ALL COSTS! DO YOU HEAR ME LIEUTENANT? HOLD AT ALL COSTS!
WELL, IT SEEMS THE EMPIRE HAS LOST ITS HOLD ON ANOTHER STAR SYSTEM! I'D START LOOKING FOR A FAST SHIP IF I WERE YOU, TAVIRA!
NOT TO WORRY, MY DEAR LT. JANSON! EVERYTHING IS WORKING AS I HAVE PLANNED!
HOW DO YOU FIGURE THAT?! THE PLB HATES THE EMPIRE! IF THEY BREAK INTO THE IMPERIAL STRONGHOLD YOU WON'T BE LONG ON EIATTU!
UNLESS...
UNLESS I'M WORKING WITH THE PEOPLES' LIBERATION BATTALION!
IT SEEMS THAT SOME ON THIS MISERABLE PLANET FEEL THAT POWER IS WORTH FAR MORE THAN HIGH IDEALS!
YOU SEE, LT. JANSON, WHEN MY HUSBAND, THE FORMER MOFF, DIED.. QUITE SUDDENLY, I TOOK CHARGE OF THIS BACKWATER WORLD.
BUT UNLIKE MY LATE HUSBAND, I SAW A WAY TO TURN THE POLITICAL UNREST OF THIS PLANET TO MY ADVANTAGE.
BUT HOW COULD HARRAN ALLY HIMSELF WITH YOU? THE PLB WOULD NEVER STAND FOR--

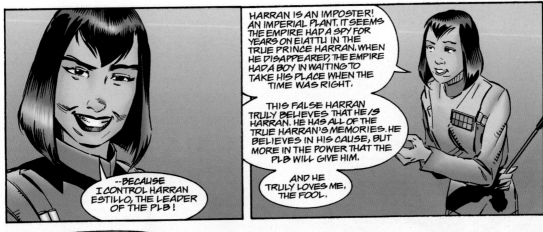

HARRAN IS AN IMPOSTER! AN IMPERIAL PLANT. IT SEEMS THE EMPIRE HAD A SPY FOR YEARS ON EIATTU IN THE TRUE PRINCE HARRAN. WHEN HE DISAPPEARED, THE EMPIRE HAD A BOY IN WAITING TO TAKE HIS PLACE WHEN THE TIME WAS RIGHT.

THIS FALSE HARRAN TRULY BELIEVES THAT HE IS HARRAN. HE HAS ALL OF THE TRUE HARRAN'S MEMORIES. HE BELIEVES IN HIS CAUSE, BUT MORE IN THE POWER THAT THE PLB WILL GIVE HIM.

AND HE TRULY LOVES ME, THE FOOL.

--BECAUSE I CONTROL HARRAN ESTILLO, THE LEADER OF THE PLB!

YOU SEE, I FEEL THE EMPIRE IS NOT LONG FOR THIS SYSTEM. I INTEND TO GET WHAT I CAN, WHILE I CAN.

IF HARRAN SUCCEEDS, I CAN LEAVE THIS BACKWARD PLANET TO THE PLB. I HAVE RAIDED ENOUGH CREDITS TO DO ANYTHING, GO ANYWHERE.

OR, I CAN MARRY HARRAN, KILL HIM, AND RULE POOR EIATTU AS HIS WIDOW.

EITHER WAY, I'LL HAVE WHAT I WANT.

THEN WHY DO YOU NEED US?

I DON'T. HOSTAGES, PERHAPS, IF PLANS SHOULD GO AWRY.

BUT THEY WON'T.

AS SOON AS I KNOW THE OUTCOME OF THE BATTLE...

...I'LL KILL YOU ALL.

THIS IS NOT GOOD.

WE'VE GOT TO GET OUT OF HERE.

NOW THAT'S A GOOD PLAN!

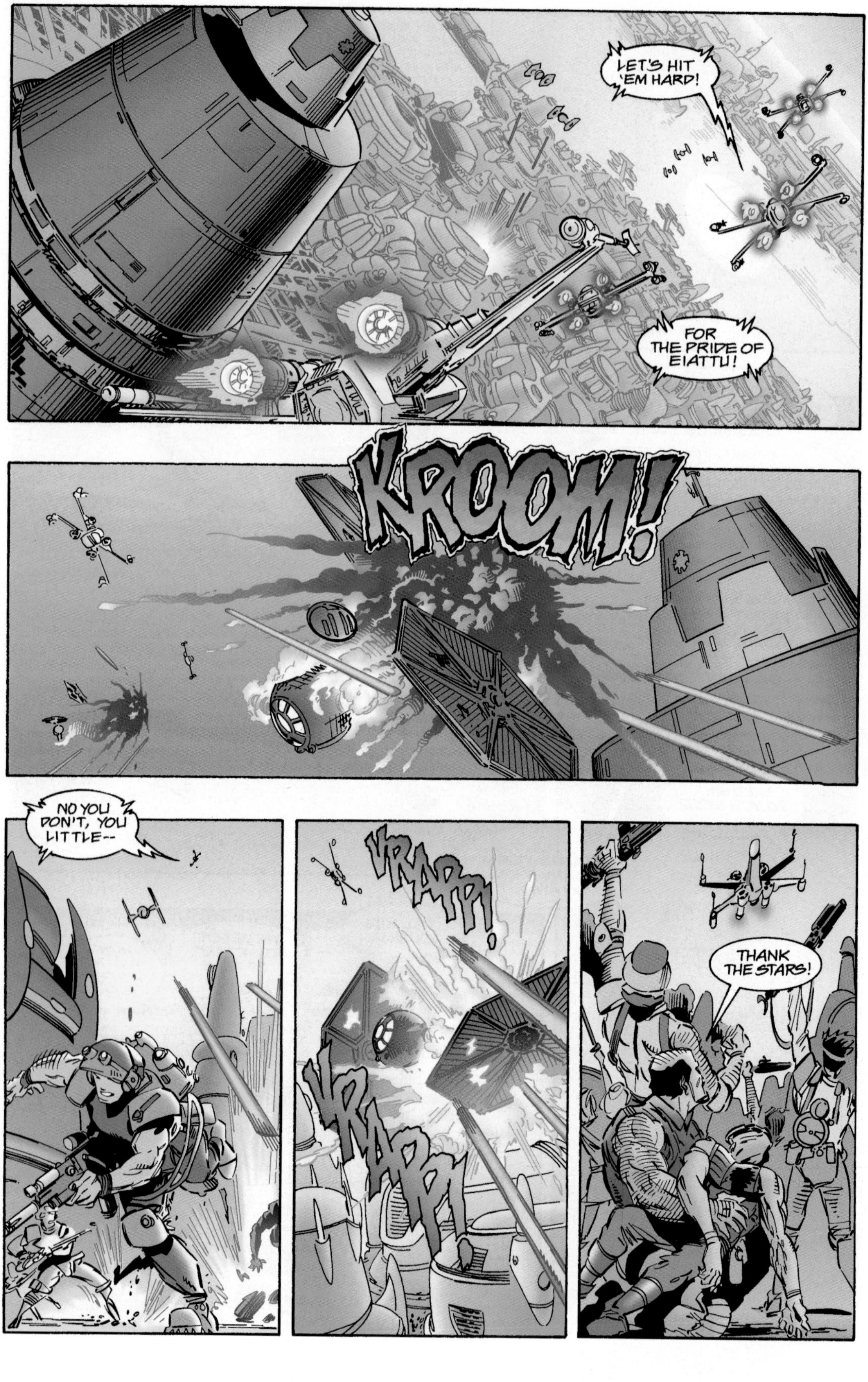
LET'S HIT 'EM HARD!
FOR THE PRIDE OF EIATTU!
KROOM!
NO YOU DON'T, YOU LITTLE--
VRAPP!
VRAPP!
THANK THE STARS!

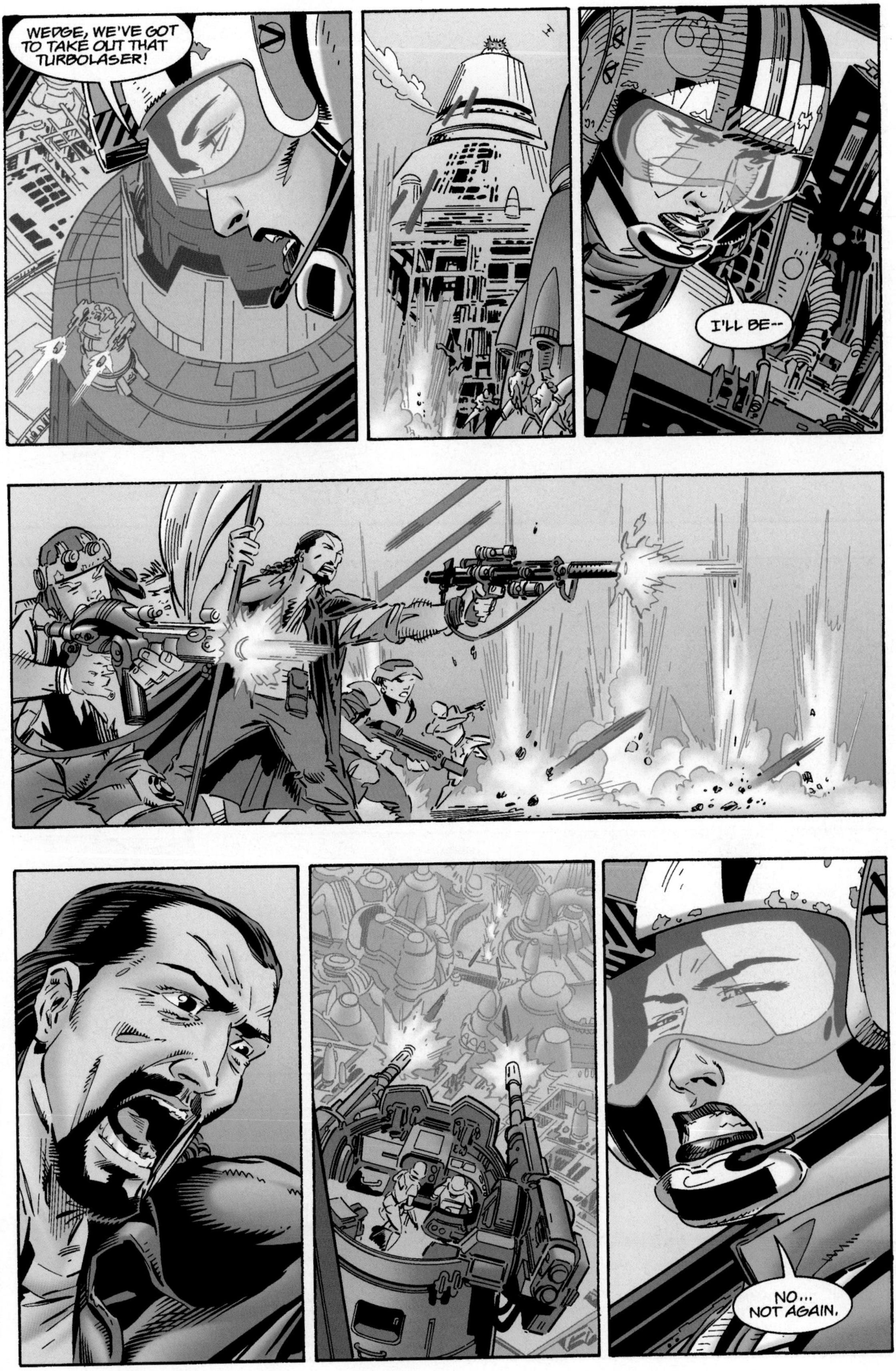
WEDGE, WE'VE GOT TO TAKE OUT THAT TURBOLASER!
I'LL BE--
NO... NOT AGAIN.

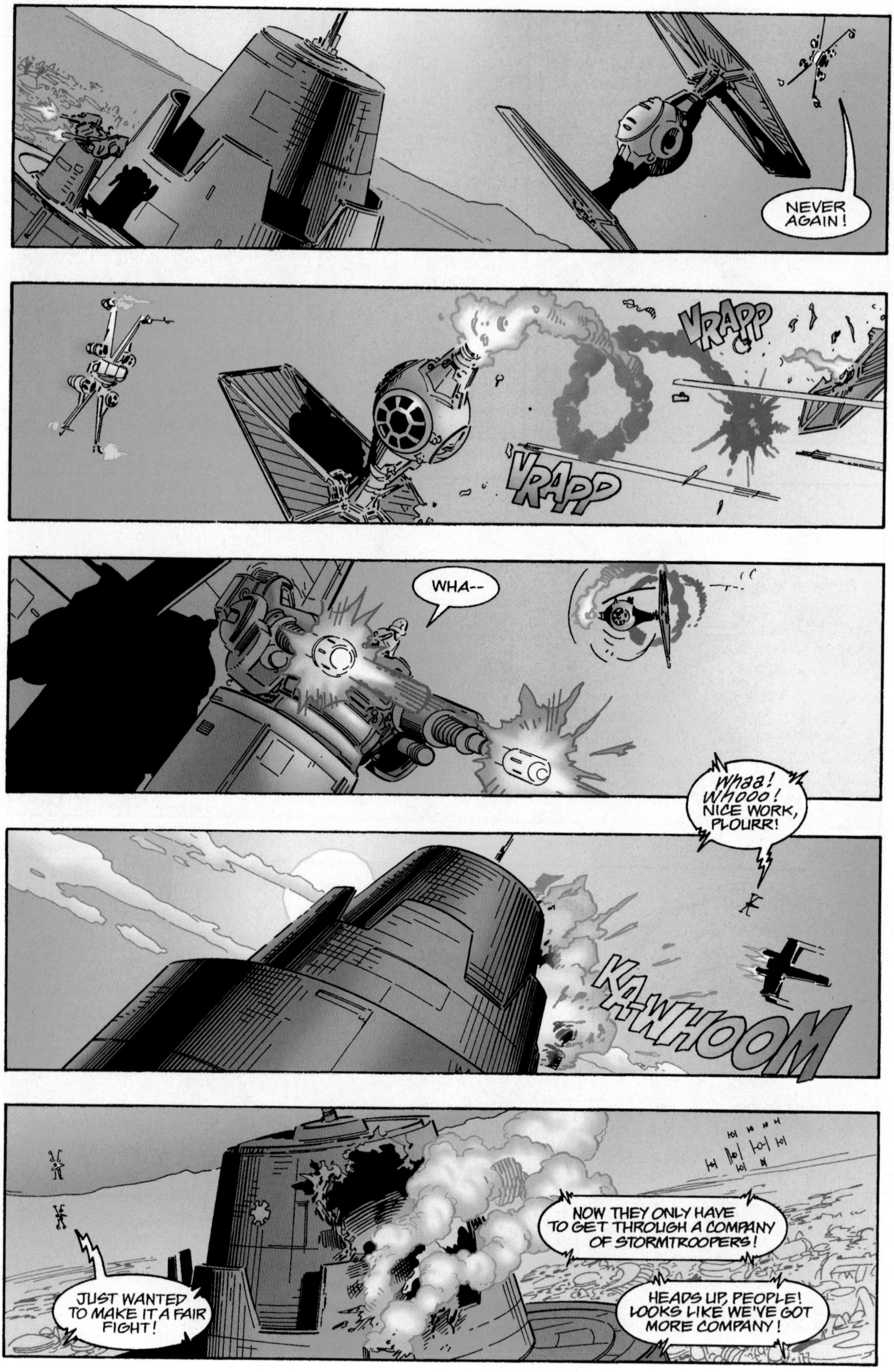
NEVER AGAIN!
VRAPP
VRAPP
WHA--
Whaa! Whooo! NICE WORK, PLOURR!
KA-WHOOM
NOW THEY ONLY HAVE TO GET THROUGH A COMPANY OF STORMTROOPERS!
JUST WANTED TO MAKE IT A FAIR FIGHT!
HEADS UP, PEOPLE! LOOKS LIKE WE'VE GOT MORE COMPANY!

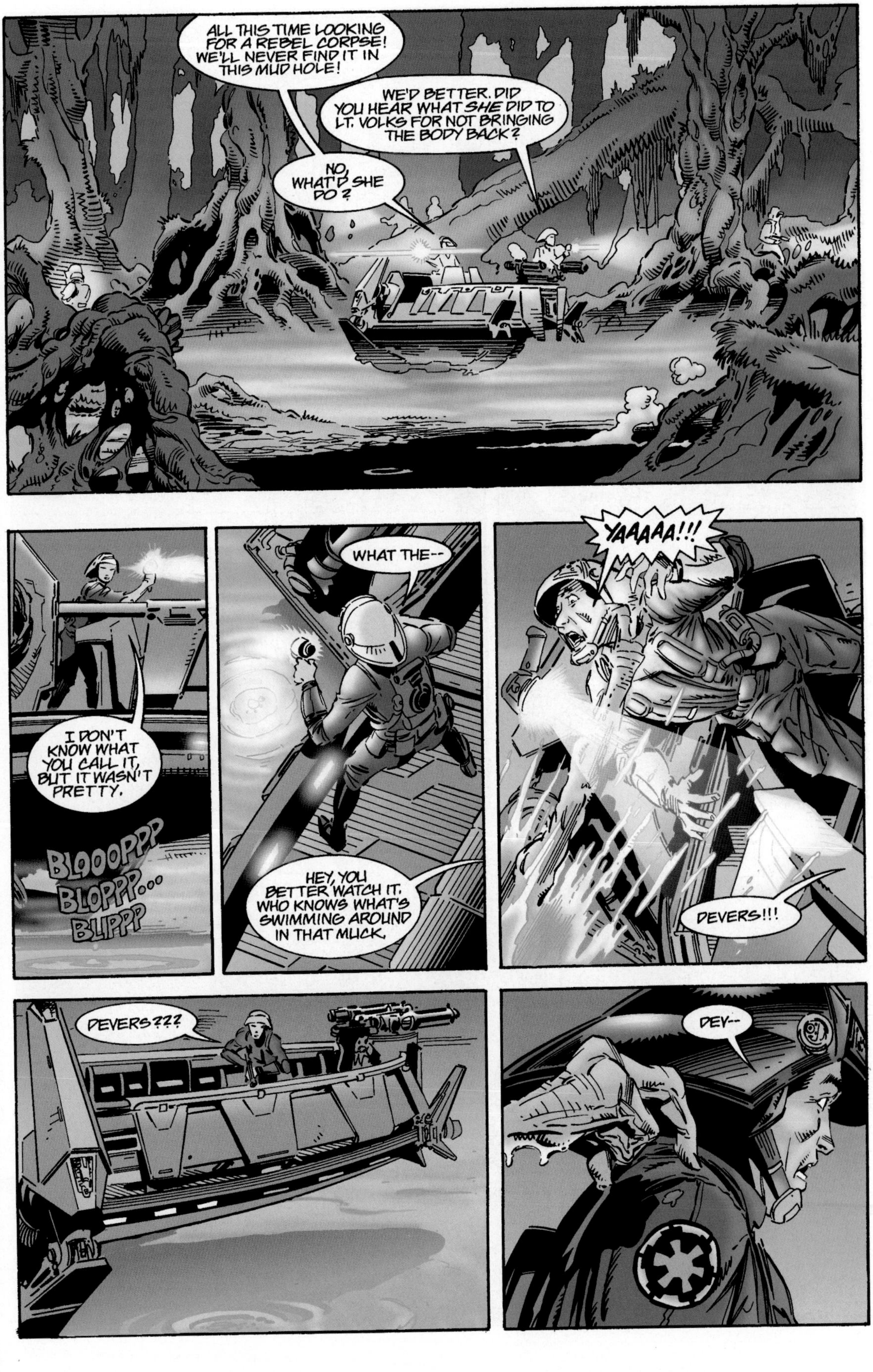
ALL THIS TIME LOOKING FOR A REBEL CORPSE! WE'LL NEVER FIND IT IN THIS MUD HOLE!
WE'D BETTER. DID YOU HEAR WHAT SHE DID TO LT. VOLKS FOR NOT BRINGING THE BODY BACK?
NO, WHAT'D SHE DO?
I DON'T KNOW WHAT YOU CALL IT, BUT IT WASN'T PRETTY.
BLOOOPPP
BLOPPP...
BLIPPP
WHAT THE--
HEY, YOU BETTER WATCH IT. WHO KNOWS WHAT'S SWIMMING AROUND IN THAT MUCK.
YAAAAA!!!
DEVERS!!!
DEVERS???
DEV--

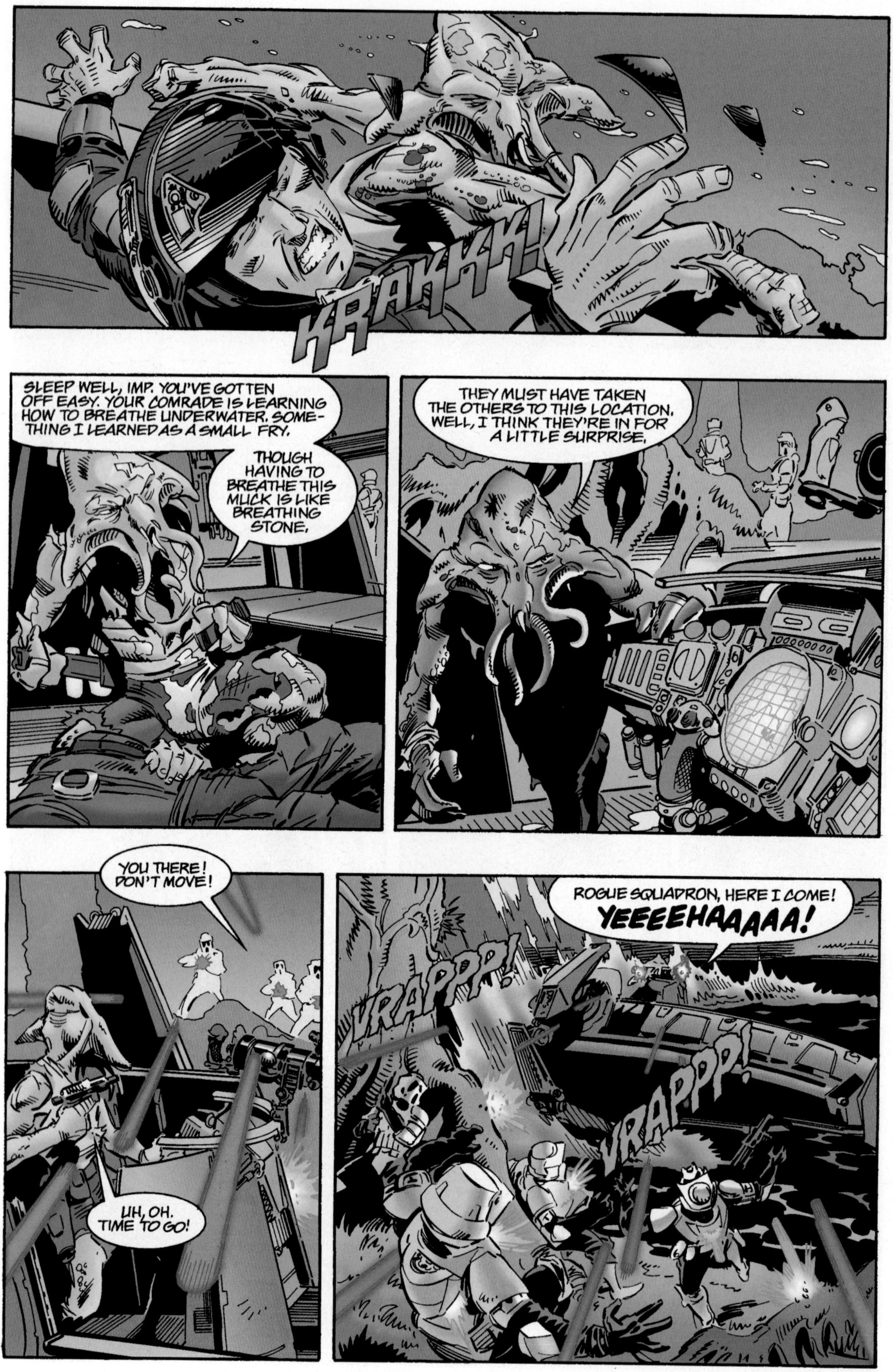
KRAKKK!
SLEEP WELL, IMP. YOU'VE GOTTEN OFF EASY. YOUR COMRADE IS LEARNING HOW TO BREATHE UNDERWATER. SOMETHING I LEARNED AS A SMALL FRY.
THOUGH HAVING TO BREATHE THIS MUCK IS LIKE BREATHING STONE.
THEY MUST HAVE TAKEN THE OTHERS TO THIS LOCATION. WELL, I THINK THEY'RE IN FOR A LITTLE SURPRISE.
YOU THERE! DON'T MOVE!
UH, OH. TIME TO GO!
ROGUE SQUADRON, HERE I COME!
YEEEEHAAAAAA!
VRAPPP!
VRAPPP!
VRAPPP!

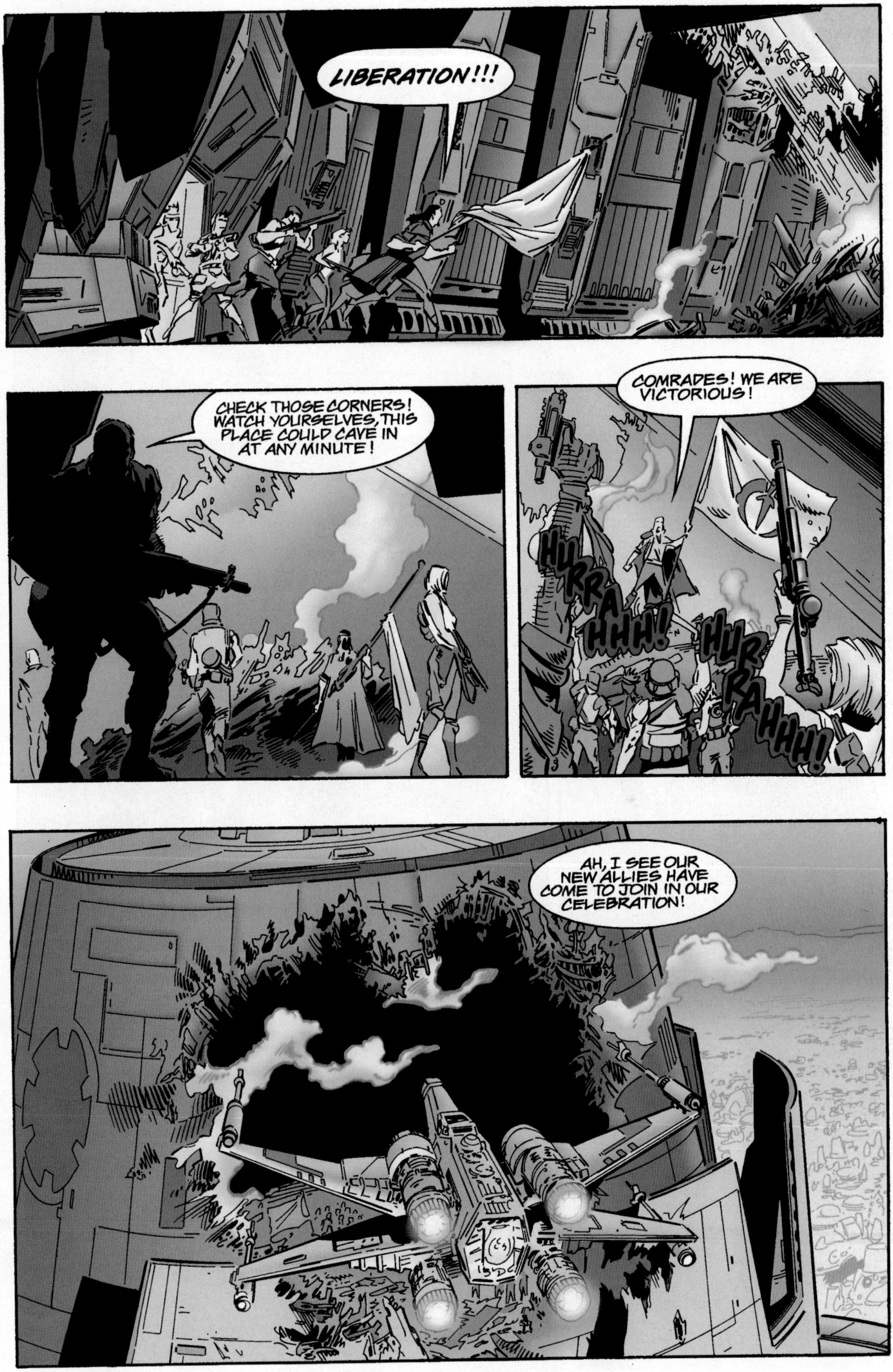
LIBERATION!!!
CHECK THOSE CORNERS! WATCH YOURSELVES, THIS PLACE COULD CAVE IN AT ANY MINUTE!
COMRADES! WE ARE VICTORIOUS!
HURRAHHH!
HURRAHHH!
AH, I SEE OUR NEW ALLIES HAVE COME TO JOIN IN OUR CELEBRATION!

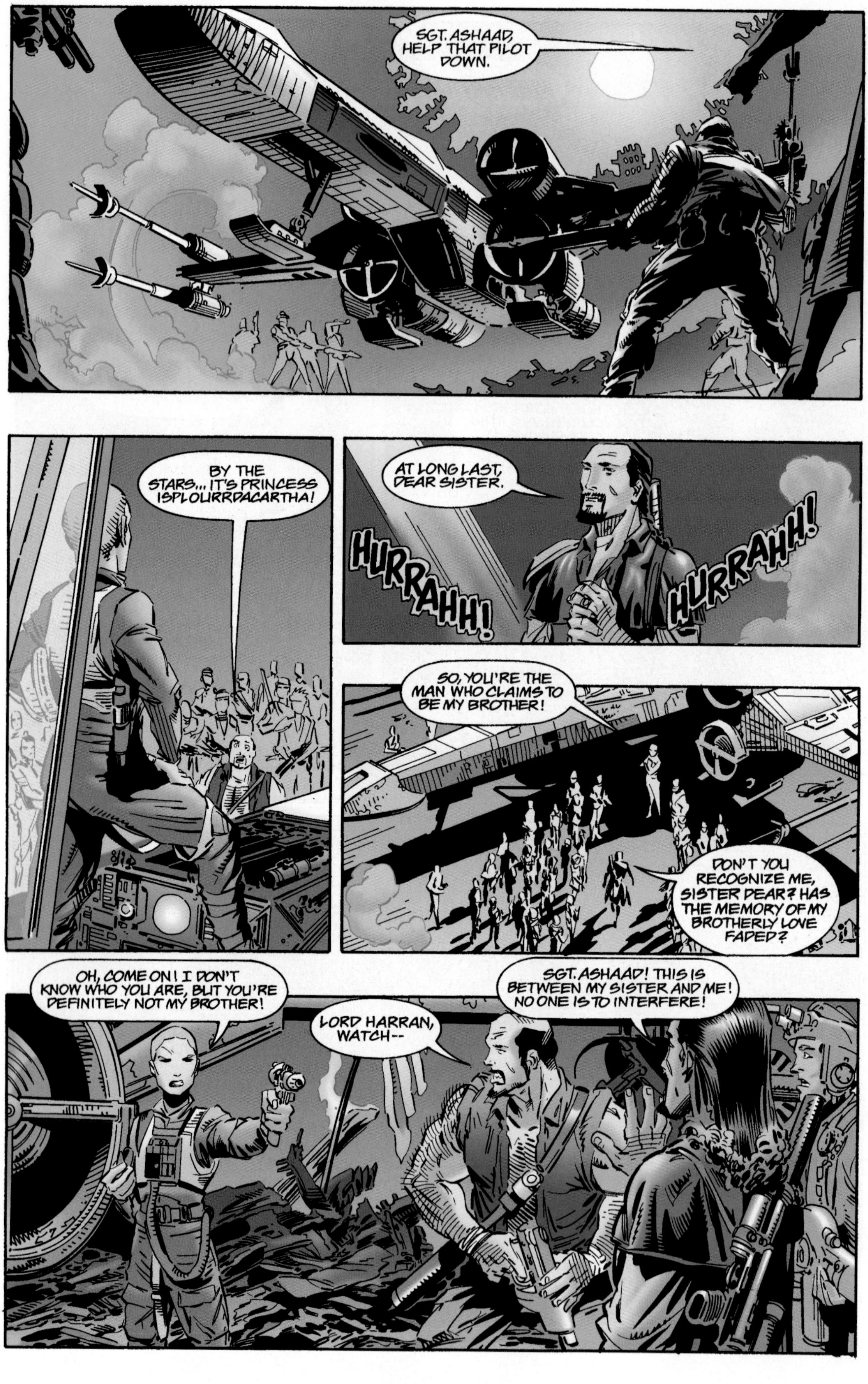

SGT. ASHAAD, HELP THAT PILOT DOWN.
BY THE STARS... IT'S PRINCESS ISPLOURRDACARTHA!
AT LONG LAST, DEAR SISTER.
HURRAHH!
HURRAHH!
SO, YOU'RE THE MAN WHO CLAIMS TO BE MY BROTHER!
DON'T YOU RECOGNIZE ME, SISTER DEAR? HAS THE MEMORY OF MY BROTHERLY LOVE FADED?
OH, COME ON! I DON'T KNOW WHO YOU ARE, BUT YOU'RE DEFINITELY NOT MY BROTHER!
LORD HARRAN, WATCH--
SGT. ASHAAD! THIS IS BETWEEN MY SISTER AND ME! NO ONE IS TO INTERFERE!

THIS MAN IS AN IMPOSTOR! A PLANT TO CREATE UNREST BETWEEN THE NOBLES AND THE CITIZENS OF EIATTU!

THE TRUE HARRAN DIED YEARS AGO ON THE NIGHT MY FAMILY WAS MURDERED!

HOW DO YOU KNOW THIS, SISTER DEAR? HOW DO YOU KNOW THAT I WAS KILLED THAT HORRIBLE NIGHT?

BECAUSE *I* KILLED YOU!

PRINCE HARRAN WAS MAD! AN ABOMINATION, CREATED FROM YEARS OF GENETIC TAMPERING!

PRINCE HARRAN WAS ALSO AN IMPERIAL SPY, CORRUPTED BY DARTH VADER HIMSELF!

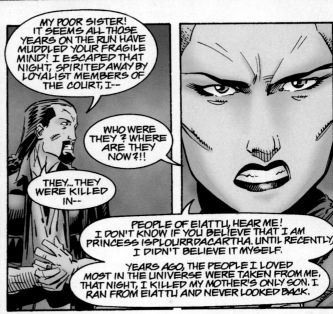

MY POOR SISTER! IT SEEMS ALL THOSE YEARS ON THE RUN HAVE MUDDLED YOUR FRAGILE MIND! I ESCAPED THAT NIGHT, SPIRITED AWAY BY LOYALIST MEMBERS OF THE COURT, I--

WHO WERE THEY? WHERE ARE THEY NOW?!!

THEY... THEY WERE KILLED IN--

PEOPLE OF EIATTU, HEAR ME! I DON'T KNOW IF YOU BELIEVE THAT I AM PRINCESS ISPLOURRDACARTHA. UNTIL RECENTLY, I DIDN'T BELIEVE IT MYSELF.

YEARS AGO, THE PEOPLE I LOVED MOST IN THE UNIVERSE WERE TAKEN FROM ME. THAT NIGHT, I KILLED MY MOTHER'S ONLY SON. I RAN FROM EIATTU AND NEVER LOOKED BACK.

NOW I KNOW THAT YOU CAN NEVER RUN FROM YOUR HOME. EIATTU IS THE BIRTHWORLD OF MY FATHER AND MOTHER, OF MY ENTIRE FAMILY. EIATTU TOOK EVERYTHING I HAD AWAY FROM ME, YES.

BUT IT GAVE EVERYTHING TO ME, AS WELL, AND ALL THOSE THINGS, MY FAMILY AND THEIR LOVE ARE HERE, IN EVERY BLADE OF GRASS, IN ALL THE ROLLING HILLS....

...AND IN YOU GOOD PEOPLE.

THIS MAN HAS LEAD YOU TO VICTORY OVER THE IMPERIAL INVADERS, SOMETHING THAT NO LEADER OF EIATTU WAS ABLE TO ACCOMPLISH. BUT HE IS BUT A PAWN OF THE MOFF LEONIA TAVIRA.

LIES....

**LIES!! I CAME BACK TO THIS PLANET TO SAVE MY PEOPLE FROM THE OPPRESSION OF THE NOBLES! TO BRING ABOUT A NEW AGE TO OUR WORLD.**

**WHAT HAS *SHE* DONE BUT CODDLE THE PRIAMSTA AND THE IMPERIALS!**

**I LED YOU PEOPLE TO VICTORY! I--**

**--I ALMOST WISH THAT YOU WERE MY BROTHER, AT LEAST THEN I WOULD NOT HAVE TO LIVE WITH THE GUILT I'VE CARRIED ALL THESE YEARS.**

**BUT YOU'RE NOT MY BROTHER, YOU'RE A LIE, A FALSE HOPE TO A HELPLESS PEOPLE.**

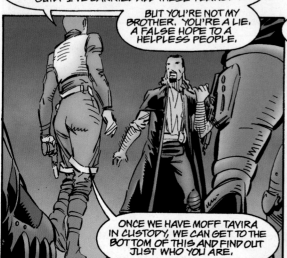

**GET BACK! SGT. ASHAAD, STOP HER!**

**B-BUT, MY LORD...**

**ONCE WE HAVE MOFF TAVIRA IN CUSTODY, WE CAN GET TO THE BOTTOM OF THIS AND FIND OUT JUST WHO YOU ARE.**

**YOU SEE, THESE PEOPLE DON'T NEED US.**

**THIS IS THE STRENGTH OF EIATTU, NOT ITS LEADERS, ITS STRENGTH LIES IN ITS PEOPLE.**

**AND THAT RING, "BROTHER DEAR," JUST ISN'T YOU!**

**I SAID STAY BACK!!! STOP HER!!!**

**I--I AM PRINCE HARRAN ESTILLO! L-L-LEADER OF THE PEOPLE'S LIBERATION BATTALION!!! I-I--**

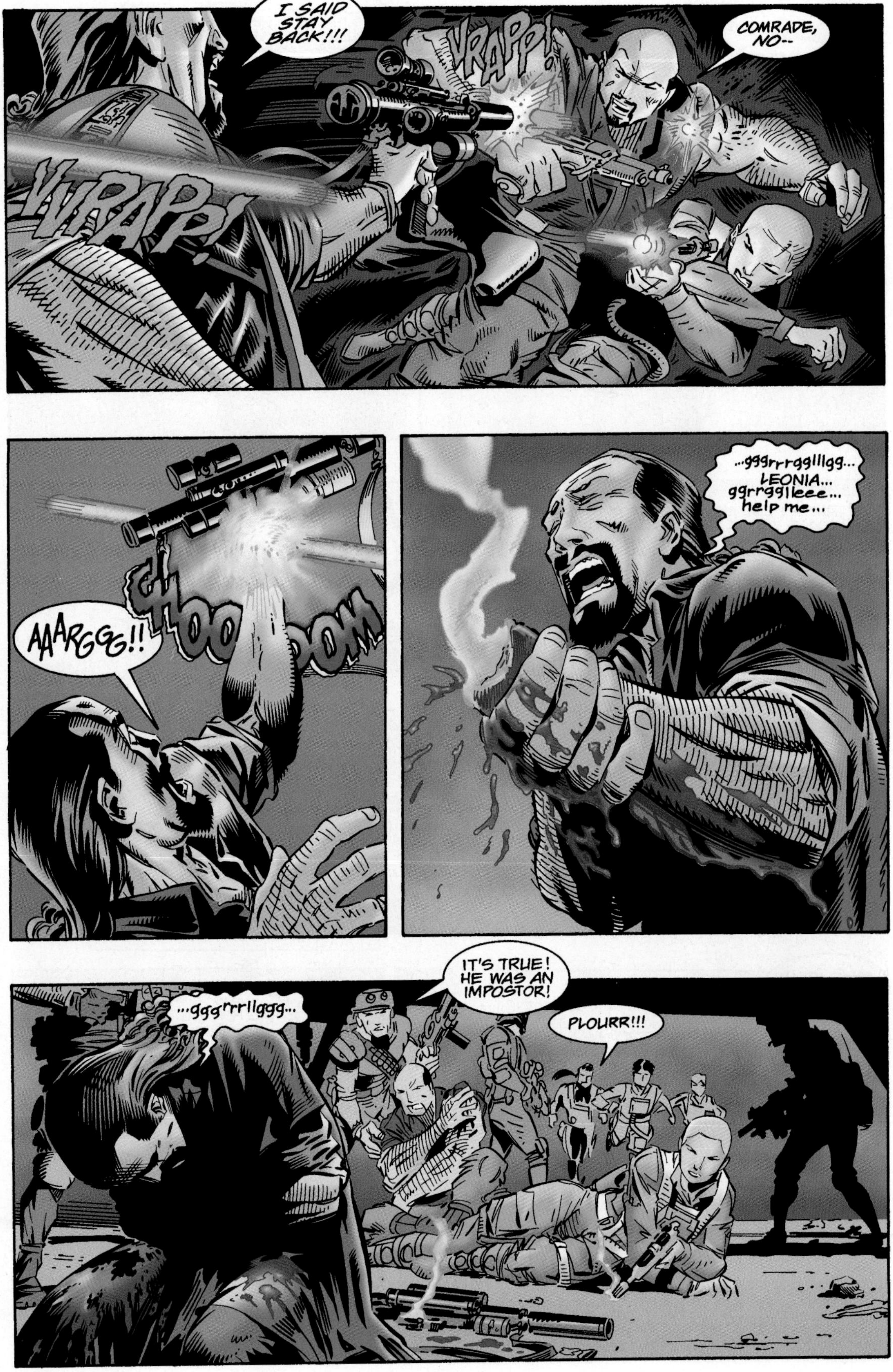
I SAID STAY BACK!!!
VRAPP!
COMRADE, NO--
VVRAPP!
AAARGGG!!
CHOOOOOM!
...gggrrrgglllgg... LEONIA... ggrrggilleee... help me...
...gggrrrllggg...
IT'S TRUE! HE WAS AN IMPOSTOR!
PLOURR!!!

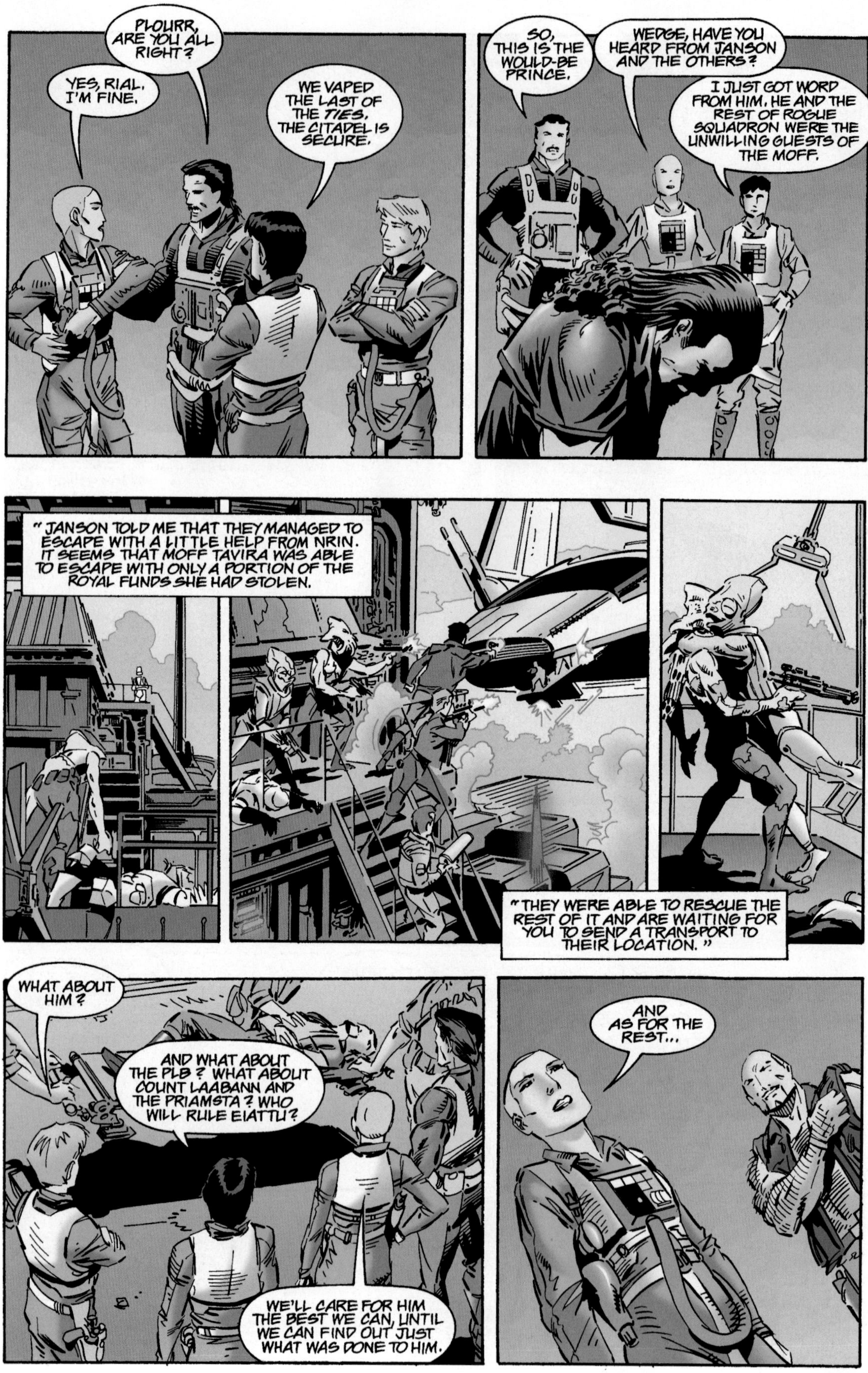
PLOURR, ARE YOU ALL RIGHT?
YES, RIAL, I'M FINE.
WE VAPED THE LAST OF THE TIES. THE CITADEL IS SECURE.
SO, THIS IS THE WOULD-BE PRINCE.
WEDGE, HAVE YOU HEARD FROM JANSON AND THE OTHERS?
I JUST GOT WORD FROM HIM. HE AND THE REST OF ROGUE SQUADRON WERE THE UNWILLING GUESTS OF THE MOFF.
"JANSON TOLD ME THAT THEY MANAGED TO ESCAPE WITH A LITTLE HELP FROM NRIN. IT SEEMS THAT MOFF TAVIRA WAS ABLE TO ESCAPE WITH ONLY A PORTION OF THE ROYAL FUNDS SHE HAD STOLEN.
"THEY WERE ABLE TO RESCUE THE REST OF IT AND ARE WAITING FOR YOU TO SEND A TRANSPORT TO THEIR LOCATION."
WHAT ABOUT HIM?
AND WHAT ABOUT THE PLB? WHAT ABOUT COUNT LAABANN AND THE PRIAMSTA? WHO WILL RULE EIATTU?
WE'LL CARE FOR HIM THE BEST WE CAN, UNTIL WE CAN FIND OUT JUST WHAT WAS DONE TO HIM.
AND AS FOR THE REST...

ARE YOU SURE YOU WON'T JOIN US, PLOURR? THERE'S STILL TIME, YOU KNOW.

I APPRECIATE THAT, BUT MY DUTY IS... MY LIFE IS HERE.

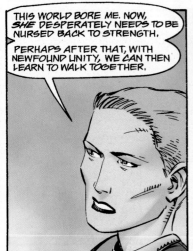

THIS WORLD BORE ME. NOW, *SHE* DESPERATELY NEEDS TO BE NURSED BACK TO STRENGTH.

PERHAPS AFTER THAT, WITH NEWFOUND UNITY, WE CAN THEN LEARN TO WALK TOGETHER.

"REGARDLESS OF WHERE THOSE STEPS MAY TAKE US, THE ACTIONS OF CERTAIN PARTIES WILL NOT BE FORGOTTEN."

EVEN THOUGH MOFF TAVIRA GOT AWAY WITH A FAIR AMOUNT OF IMPERIAL BULLION, WE'LL DO OUR BEST TO TRACK HER DOWN FOR YOU--

NO NEED TO CONCERN YOURSELF WITH THAT. THE MAJORITY OF THE FUNDS ARE STILL IN MY POSSESSION.

WHAT ABOUT THE IMPOSTOR? WHAT HAPPENS TO HIM NOW?

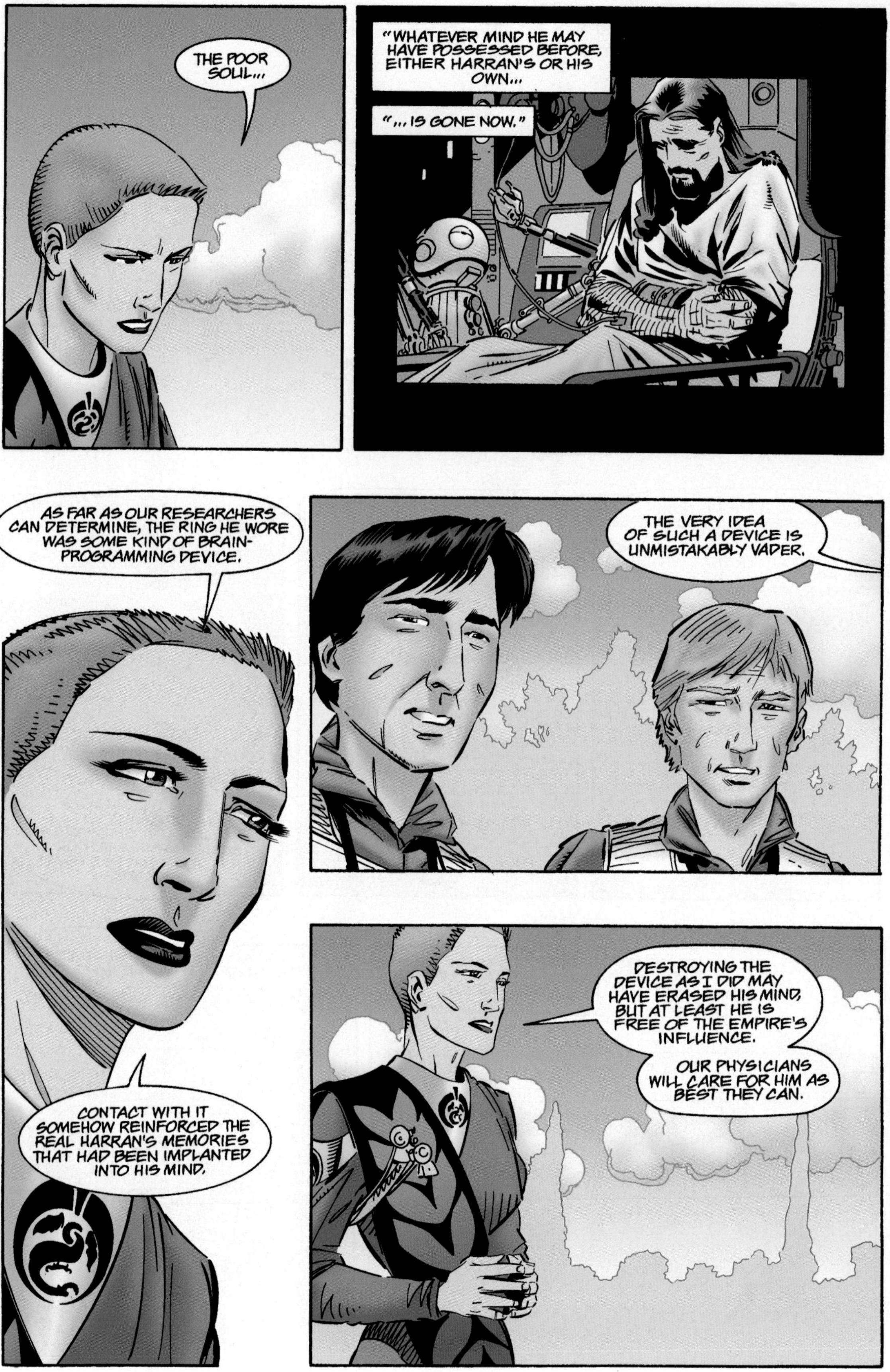
THE POOR SOUL...
"WHATEVER MIND HE MAY HAVE POSSESSED BEFORE, EITHER HARRAN'S OR HIS OWN...
"...IS GONE NOW."
AS FAR AS OUR RESEARCHERS CAN DETERMINE, THE RING HE WORE WAS SOME KIND OF BRAIN-PROGRAMMING DEVICE.
CONTACT WITH IT SOMEHOW REINFORCED THE REAL HARRAN'S MEMORIES THAT HAD BEEN IMPLANTED INTO HIS MIND.
THE VERY IDEA OF SUCH A DEVICE IS UNMISTAKABLY VADER.
DESTROYING THE DEVICE AS I DID MAY HAVE ERASED HIS MIND, BUT AT LEAST HE IS FREE OF THE EMPIRE'S INFLUENCE.
OUR PHYSICIANS WILL CARE FOR HIM AS BEST THEY CAN.

PERHAPS A JEDI'S HELP, ONCE WE'VE OFFICIALLY JOINED THE ALLIANCE.

YOU'LL BE MISSED, PLOURR. YOU'RE A GREAT LEADER AND A DAMN GOOD PILOT.

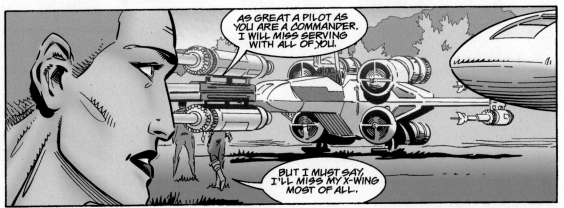

AS GREAT A PILOT AS YOU ARE A COMMANDER, I WILL MISS SERVING WITH ALL OF YOU.

BUT I MUST SAY, I'LL MISS MY X-WING MOST OF ALL.

I DON'T THINK YOU SHOULD MISS HER AT ALL. IF YOUR PLACE IS HERE, THEN SO IS HERS.

AFTER ALL, YOU MAY NEED HER.

DOES THAT MEAN YOU'LL KEEP A SPOT OPEN IN ROGUE SQUADRON FOR ME?

YOU'LL ALWAYS BE WELCOME, PLOURR.

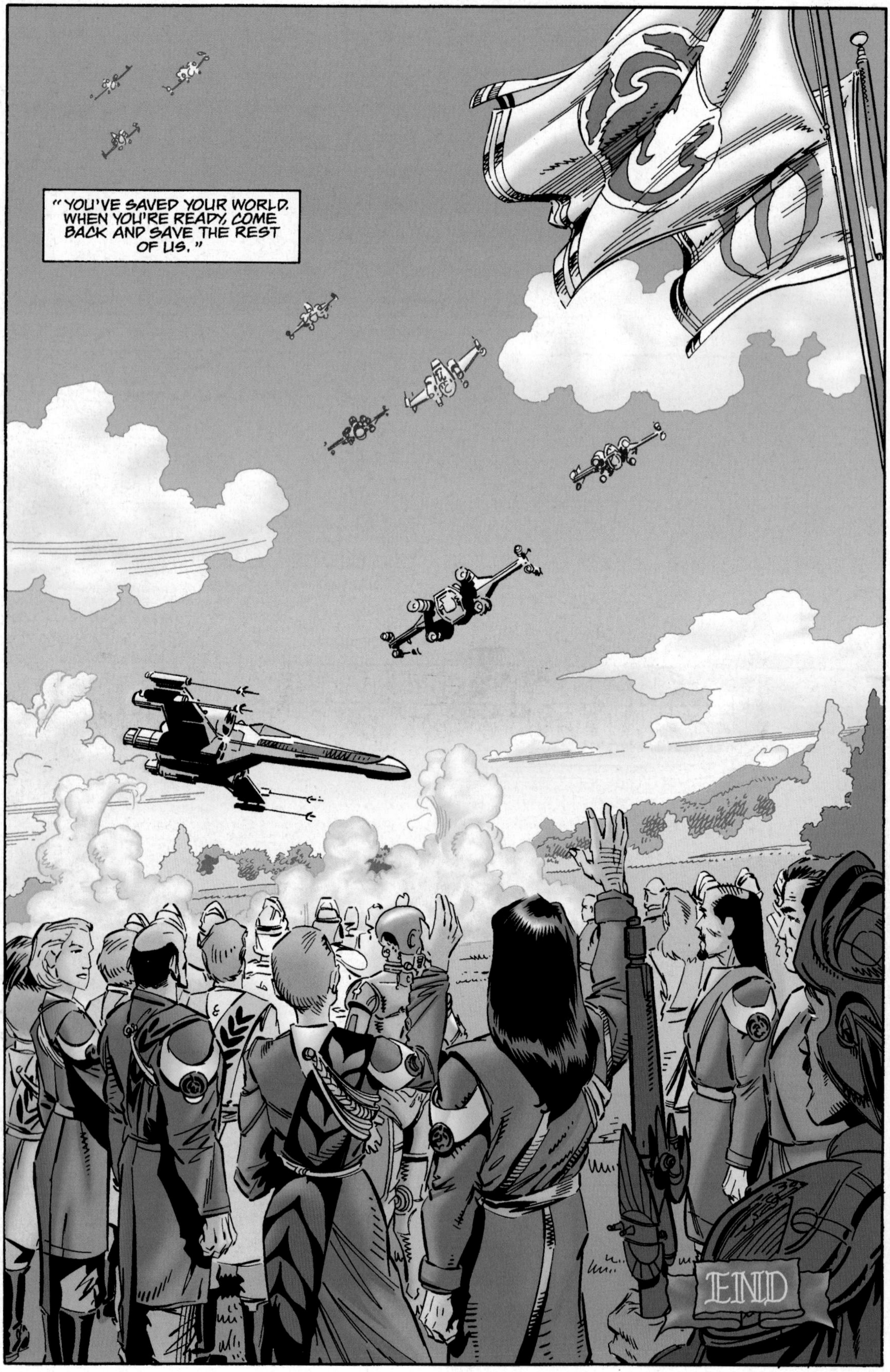
"YOU'VE SAVED YOUR WORLD. WHEN YOU'RE READY, COME BACK AND SAVE THE REST OF US."
END

*STAR WARS: X-WING ROGUE SQUADRON — THE PHANTOM AFFAIR TPB*
CREATOR DEDICATIONS AND INTRODUCTION BY STAN SAKAI

Dedicated to...

...the memory of Gladys MacIntyre, whose skill as a storyteller I have always sought to imitate and whose grace as a human being I can only hope to emulate.

—Michael A. Stackpole

...George Lucas, for getting me into all this trouble.

—Edvin Biuković

This one is for SFera, to dissect at will.

—Darko Macan

...my cousin John for help above and beyond. To Dark Horse and Lucasfilm for faith and George Lucas for the imagination. To Magz for her love.

—Gary Erskine

--------

Okay, I admit I'm not a *Star Wars* aficionado. I don't know or care to know the differences between the Z-95 Headhunter and the X-wing. For me, the story pretty much begins and ends with the movies.

However, I do know a good story when I read one, and *The Phantom Affair* is one terrific read.

Michael Stackpole has done an amazing thing. He has taken a tertiary character from the movies, fleshed him out, given him a history and motivations and made him real. And made his companions real. And made the struggle against the Empire much more epic than the exploits of Luke, Han, and Leia. He has written a very intelligent story involving hoaxes and plot twists that keep you on your toes. Things are not what they appear to be but are always more than what they seem.

The script by Darko Macan is superb. I have been a Macan fan since I first saw his series *Sergei* from a small publisher and followed him through two *Grendel* miniseries and eagerly await whatever new projects he is involved with. His forte has always been great characterizations. We can feel Elscol's pain and loneliness and then her shock to find that her beloved Throm, whose lifeless body she once held in her arms, is back from the dead. Or is he? As I said, nothing is what it appears. And the dialogue he gives each player is wonderful and never forced. Even such casual lines as Koyi stating that there are "twelve brands of ice" are true gems. The pacing is a study of balance: quiet introspection followed by breathtaking violence; grim determination mixed with dry humor all culminating in an explosive climax.

Ahh, now the artwork. The first word that comes to mind is "cinematic." This is truly as if you're reading a movie. The action sequences are handled expertly, always depicting the ideal instant never a frame too early or too late. Even more impressive are the subtle nuances of the art — Gade Yedan's arrogant posture; Wedge's jaw set in determination; even the way Mirax dusts off the stair before sitting herself down — all are beautiful touches in a medium too well known for its over-the-top action and heroic posturings. The artists at times weave their camera in and out of the action taking us on a roller-coasterlike ride and at other times slowing it down giving us a chance to catch our breath. Page and panel compositions are original, varied, and always clearly thought out. They are in command of their craft, telling the story with the skill of the best movie directors.

Dave Nestelle's choice of colors and handling of tones brings each panel to life and gives each scene the mood it deserves from fiery action to the desolation of despair. His use of bottom-lighting in the club scene is especially effective.

I commend the creators of this book for an outstanding job. They drew me into the story from the first page with the towering vegetation and the children viewing the wonder of the distant dogfight in the night sky and held me until those X-wings roared past in the last panel. This is storytelling at its very finest.

As I said, I'm not a *Star Wars* devotee, but I do know what I like. I'll be following the adventures of Wedge Antilles and the Rogue Squadron for some time to come not only in the comics but also in Stackpole's many excellent novels.

INTRODUCTION BY TIMOTHY ZAHN

I should have known the minute Mike Stackpole was invited into the *Star Wars* universe that there was going to be trouble.

I first met Mike briefly at Coastcon in 1993, but I didn't really start getting to know him until Hurricon a year later when we had dinner with a mutual acquaintance. (I think they let me buy, but I could be mistaken.) He seemed a pleasant enough fellow, though I freely admit to a slight resentment that his convention stories were so much better than mine.

Mike was no stranger to the world of science fiction, of course. He'd been writing in the sci-fi game field since 1978, turning out game modules, rule books, and the occasional short story. He had also begun to branch out into novels, defining for the world just what a proper Battletech book should be. He would continue on considerably in that direction, both in other shared universes as well as creating his own original work. But that's getting ahead of things.

I ran into him off and on after that at various conventions, with our interactions staying mostly on the hi-how-are-you-what-are-you-working-on-these-days sort of level. Sometimes we grabbed lunch together. Often — not always — I let him buy.

And then in 1995, out of the blue, I picked up the phone and there was Mike. It seemed he'd just been contracted to write a series of *Star Wars* X-Wing books for Bantam and wanted to discuss the Rogue Squadron group I'd created for my own *Star Wars* books. He explained the basic storyline and time frame he had in mind, and I provided what feedback I could about the squadron and the political/military situation that existed during that period. He thanked me, hung up, and settled down to write.

There is one view — I don't know how widely held — that the various *Star Wars* novelists are rather like an exclusive, genteel sort of private club. Following that analogy, you might say that Mike's arrival into the club was with a whooping cannonball into the pool. Here came the hotshot pilots of Rogue Squadron: brash, cocky, sometimes argumentative, often loud. (Yes, I know that Han and Chewie were also loud; but this was a *different* kind of loud.)

I suppose I assumed that my involvement with this project was now over. How little I knew. Barely had the first X-Wing book hit the stands when Mike was on the phone again, this time asking if he could use the character Talon Karrde in one of his upcoming books. We discussed the scene he had in mind and Karrde's likely behavior under the particular circumstances, and I gave him the okay.

Not that he needed my permission to use Karrde if he wanted to, you understand. Everything I or anyone else had contributed to the *Star Wars* saga was owned by Lucasfilm, and, as a new member of the club Mike automatically had full and open access to the complete grab bag. His call to me was simply a matter of professional courtesy, combined with the equally professional attitude of wanting to do the best job he could with every aspect of his books.

At any rate, he promised to send me a copy of the chapter when it was done, and in due course it arrived.

Frankly, I was surprised. Very *pleasantly* surprised. Out of the several pages he'd written Karrde into, I found maybe three words I thought should be changed. Three *words*. Clearly, Mike had a pretty good grasp of my characters.

I soon had a chance to try things the opposite direction. I was contracted to write one more *Star Wars* book for Bantam (which eventually grew into two books, but that's a different story), and as I finished the outline and started to work, I gave Mike a call to make sure our plots weren't going to step on each other's toes. Midway through the conversation, I suddenly realized that something he was planning to do with Booster Terrik would mesh perfectly with a plot point I already had written into my outline. I pointed this out and suggested the connection, got his enthusiastic approval to add Booster to my story, and sent him the chapter when it was done. He asked for changes in about — you guessed it — three words, and the process of throwing multiple links between our books had begun.

Eventually, it fell into an almost predictable routine. One of us would call the other with a five-minute question about something he was doing; and by the time we hung up the phone — usually an hour or so later — we had found another link or two we could set up. Eventually, Mike added Mara Jade and Winter to his roster of crossover characters; I returned the favor by working Corran Horn and Mirax into mine.

He finished his books, and, once again, I assumed my involvement with his project was over. Again, how little I knew. For here came Dark Horse Comics and a brand-new series of X-Wing *comics*. Before long, naturally, Mike was busy doing the stories for them.

And once again, we were back into the old routine. One of us would call the other to discuss conventions or signings or just basic news from the Outer Rim of the publishing world (we'd branched out beyond mere plot points by now), and he would tell me what he was planning to do and add it to my growing story development. Sometimes the link wasn't quite perfect, and we'd spend another half hour coming up with a way to tweak it so that it *would* work for both of our storylines.

Somewhere along the way, Mike was offered two more *Star Wars* books, one of them another X-Wing adventure and the other a so-called "mainstream" *Star Wars* book. More phone calls, more links. Some of them, in fact, we batted around so much that it's hard for me to remember which of us had the original idea in the first place.

But while you're waiting for those books, you have *Battleground: Tatooine* to keep you company. Originally in four parts, it brings Wedge Antilles and Rogue Squadron back to where the *Star Wars* saga first began: the hot, desert world of Tatooine, home of Luke Skywalker. Arriving for what was supposed to be essentially a courtesy call, they will instead find danger, intrigue, teamwork, snappy dialogue — in short, the kind of storytelling Mike does best. Along with Mike's story, you'll also find a great script by Jan Strnad and terrific artwork and lettering by the team of John Nadeau, Jordi Ensign, Perry McNamee, Dave Nestelle, Vickie Williams, and Mark Harrison. For a comic book, after all, is very definitely a collaborative creation.

Oh, and the trouble I mentioned at the beginning of this introduction, the trouble I should have known was coming? There'll be plenty of that, too. Trouble for Wedge, trouble for Rogue Squadron, trouble for the whole New Republic. Creating trouble, you see, is yet another of those things Mike does so well.

But don't take my word for it. Turn to where the story starts, prepare yourself for the frantic roller-coaster world of Rogue Squadron, and dive on in. And enjoy.

Oh, and, Mike — next time, lunch is on me.

—Timothy Zahn